Contents

There are details of well over 2,000 fascinating places to visit i ▮▮▮▮
England, Scotland, Wales, the Channel Islands, the Isle of Man, Northern ▮▮▮▮
Irish Republic – so wherever you are, you should find just the place for your day out.

About this book

The Directory

The directory is arranged in countries:

England, Northern Ireland and the Republic of Ireland are listed in alphabetical location order within each county. Scotland and Wales are listed in alphabetical location within regions - the countries that comprise each region are listed below the region heading. Towns or cities of outstanding interest have an entry giving a general description and mentioning features (such as landmarks or streets) not necessarily included in this guide.

Opening dates quoted in the guide are inclusive - for instance, where you see Apr-Oct, that place will be open from the beginning of April to the end of October.

Prices quoted are, as far as possible, those which are expected to be in force in 1998. However, some establishments have been unable to give us their projected prices and for those we have given 1997 prices prefixed by an asterisk. If no price is quoted, you should check with the establishment concerned before you visit. A number of the places which do not charge admission at all may ask for a voluntary donation.

SYMBOLS
In order to give you as much information as possible in the space available, we have used the following symbols in the guide:

	ENGLISH	FRANÇAIS	DEUTSCH	ITALIANO	ESPAÑOL
☎	Telephone number	Numéro de téléphone	Telefonnummer	Numero telefonico	Número telefónico
♿	Suitable for visitors in wheelchairs	Les invalidens fauteuils roulants pourrant y accéder	Für Rollstuhltahrer zugänglich	Accessibile agli handicappeti	Acondicionado para visitantes en silla de reudas
✳	Indicates 1997 price	Prix 1997	1997 Preise	Indica i prezzi del 1997	Indica los precios de 1997
🅿	Parking at Establishment	Stationnement à l'établissement	Parken an Ort und Stelle	Parcheggio in loco	Aparcamiento en el establecimiento
P	Parking nearby	Stationnement tout près	Parken in der Nähe	Parcheggio nelle vicinanze	Aparcamiento cerca del
☕	Refreshments	Rafraîchissements	Erfrischungen	Snack-bar	Refrescos
✗	Restaurant	Restaurant	Restaurant	Ristorante	Restaurante
🚫	No dogs	Chiens non permis	Hundeverbot	Cani non accettati	Se prohiben los perros
🚌	No coaches	Les groupes en cars pas admis	Keine Reisebusgesellschaften	Non si accettano comitive in pullman	Non se admiten los grupos de viajeros en autobús
	Cadw-(Welsh Historic Monuments)	Cadw-Monument ancien (Pays de Galles)	Cadw-Historiches Gebaude (Walisland)	Cadw-Monumento storico (Galles)	Cadw-Monumento histórico (Gales)
✪	English Heritage	English Heritage	English Heritage	English Heritage	English Heritage
✪	National Trust	National Trust	National Trust	National Trust	The National Trust
✪	National Trust for Scotland	National Trust en Ecosse	National Trust in Schottland	National Trust per la Scozia	The National Trust de Escocia
▮	Historic Scotland				

ABBREVIATIONS In the same way, we have abbreviated certain pieces of information:

	ENGLISH	FRANÇAIS	DEUTSCH	ITALIANO	ESPAÑOL
BH	Bank Holidays	Jours fériés	Bankfeiertage	Festività nazionale	Días festivos (bancos y comercio)
PH	Public Holidays	Jours fériés	Feiertage	Festività nazionale	Días festivos
Etr	Easter	Pâques	Ostern	Pasqua	Semana Santa
ex	except	sauf	ausser	eccetto	excepto
IR£	Irish punts	Punts irlandais	Punts Irisch	Punts irlandesi	Punts irlandeses
Free	Admission free	Entrée gratuit	Freier eintritt	Ingresso gratuito	Entrada gratuita
£1	Admission £1	Entrée £1	Eintritt £1	Ingresso £1	Entrada £1
ch 50p	Children 50p	Enfants 50p	Kinder 50p	Bambini 50p	Niños 50p
ch 15 50p	Children under 15 50p	Enfants de moins de 15 ans 50p	Kinder unter 15 Jahren 50p	Bambini sotto i 15 anni 50p	Los niños de menores de 15 años 50p
Pen	Senior Citizens	Retraites	Rentner	Pensionati	Jubilados
Party	Special or reduced rates for parties booked in advance	Tarifs spéciaux ou réduits pour groupes réservés d'advance	Sondertarife oder Ermässigungen für im voraus bestellte Gesellschaften	Tariffe speciali o ridotte per comitive che prenotano in anticipo	Tarifas especiales o reducidas para los grupos de viajeros que reserven de anternano
Party 30+	Special or reduced rates for parties of 30 or more booked in advance	Tarifs spéciaux ou réduits pour groupes de 30 ou plus réservés d'advance	Sondertarife oder Ermässigungen für im voraus bestellte Gesellschaften von wenigstens 30 Personen	Tariffe speciali o ridotte per comitive di 30 o più persone che prenotano in anticipo	Tarifas especiales o reducidas para grupos de 30 viajeros, o más, que reserven de anternano

Credit & Charge Cards are now taken by a number of establishments for admission charges. We have included them at the end of the establishment entry. The cards are represented by symbols as follows:

 Mastercard **American Express** **Visa** **Diners Club** **Connect** **Delta** **Switch**

Telephone Numbers have the STD code shown before the telephone number. (If dialling Northern Ireland from England use the STD code, but for the Republic you need to prefix the number with 00353).

Visitors with Disabilities should look for the wheelchair symbol showing where all or most of the establishment is accessible to wheelchair-bound visitors. We strongly recommend that you telephone in advance of your visit to check the exact details, particularly regarding access to toilet and refreshment facilities. **Guide dogs** are usually accepted where the establishments show the 'No Dogs' symbol – unless stated otherwise. For the **hard of hearing** induction loops are indicated.

Photography is restricted in some places and there are many where it is only allowed in specific areas. Visitors are advised to check with places of interest on the rules for taking photographs and the use of video cameras.

Each country is colour coded for ease of identification

Key to Colour Coding

England	▬▬▬▬▬
Channel Islands	▬▬▬▬▬
Scotland & Islands	▬▬▬▬▬
Isle of Man	▬▬▬▬▬
Wales	▬▬▬▬▬
Northern Ireland	▬▬▬▬▬
Republic of Ireland	▬▬▬▬▬

£4 off a main course meal for two!

Whilst you are out travelling, here's the ideal opportunity to sample the delights of quality home cooking with £4 off a main course meal when any two adult main course meals are purchased at a Brewers Fayre pub restaurant.

There really is nothing to rival the quality and value of a visit to Brewers Fayre - the friendliest of pub restaurants where the whole family are made very welcome - especially children. If you and your family call in for a lunch time snack or wish to sample the delicious home cooked food, from succulent

steaks to a hearty haddock, you can always experience good food, good service and great value at Brewers Fayre.

With over 360 restaurants throughout the UK there's bound to be a Brewers Fayre near you wherever you're travelling this year.

Call Brewers Fayre on 0345 023028 for a brochure to find out the nearest restaurant to you.

Your Favourites Just Get Better

The AA Hotel Booking Service

Now AA Members have a free, simple way to find a place to stay for a week, weekend, business trip or a one-night stopover.

Telephone

0990 050505

to make a booking. Please have your AA Membership number ready. Office hours 8.30am - 7.30pm Monday - Saturday.

Are you looking for somewhere in the Lake District that will take pets; a city-centre hotel in Glasgow with parking facilities, or do you need a B & B near Dover which is handy for the Eurotunnel?

The AA Booking Service can not only take the hassle out of finding the right place for you, but could even

get you a discount on a leisure break or business booking. And if you are touring round the UK or Ireland, simply give the AA Hotel Booking Service your list of overnight stops, and from one phone call all your accommodation can be booked for you.

AA Hotel Booking Service

Full listings of the 7,920 hotels and B & Bs available through the Hotel Booking Service can be found and booked at the AA's Internet Site:
http://www.theaa.co.uk/hotels

New Entries in the 1998 Guide

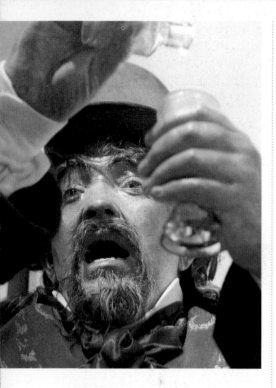

ENGLAND

CAMBRIDGESHIRE
Oliver Cromwell's House, ELY

CUMBRIA
The Armitt, AMBLESIDE
Aquarium of the Lakes, LAKESIDE

HAMPSHIRE
Moors Valley Country Park and Forest, RINGWOOD

KENT
Druidstone Wildlife Park, BLEAN
Russian Submarine, FOLKESTONE
LONDON

**BBC Experience,
Broadcasting House,** W1A
The Golden Hinde, SE1
London Aquarium, SE1
**Shakespeare's Globe
Exhibition,** SE1

NORTHAMPTONSHIRE
Shire Falconry Centre,
DESBOROUGH

OXFORDSHIRE
The River and Rowing Museum,
HENLEY-ON-THAMES

SUFFOLK
Abbey Visitor Centre, BURY ST
EDMUNDS

WEST MIDLANDS
**Jewellery Quarter Discovery
Centre,** BIRMINGHAM

YORKSHIRE WEST
Thackray Medical Museum,
LEEDS

ISLE OF MAN
House of Manannan, PEEL
Old Grammar School, CASTLETOWN

SCOTLAND

ABERDEENSHIRE
Dunnottar Castle, STONEHAVEN

ARGYLL & BUTE
Barcaldine Castle, Barcaldine,
NR OBAN
CLACKMANNANSHIRE

Alloa Tower, ALLOA
Mill Trail Visitor Centre, ALVA

SCOTTISH BORDERS
Harmony Garden, MELROSE

STIRLING
Breadalbane Folklore Centre,
KILLIN
**Royal Burgh of Stirling Visitor
Centre,** STIRLING

WALES

CARMARTHENSHIRE
Dinefwr Park, LLANDEILO

CEREDIGION
Llanerchaeron, NR ABERAERON

CONWY
Conwy Suspension Bridge, CONWY
Ty Mawr, PENMACHNO

POWYS
The Judge's Lodging, PRESTEIGNE

REPUBLIC OF IRELAND

CO ARMAGH
**Lough Neagh Discovery Centre -
Oxford Island National Nature
Reserve,** CRAIGAVON

CO CORK
The Queentown Story, COBH

CO DUBLIN
James Joyce Centre, DUBLIN

WHERE THE FUN IS ALWAYS BUILDING.

LEGOLAND® Windsor is a different kind of family theme park. A land where children are in control and where adventure, excitement and fun are the order of the day.

Come and visit Britain's most popular new attraction, for a full day's entertainment for all the family.

Children will have more fun than they can imagine as they learn to drive a car and earn a LEGOLAND licence.

They can pan for pirate gold, ride The Dragon through the heights and depths of the new Dragon Knight's Castle, or explore Miniland, a kingdom made entirely of LEGO® bricks.

In fact there are more than 40 rides, attractions and live shows to enjoy.

LEGOLAND® Windsor is open every day from 14th March to 1st November. The park is open from 10am to 6pm and until 8pm during school holidays.

To book in advance, or for more information phone 0990 04 04 04. Or call for our exciting Special Events programme. Our website address is www.legoland.co.uk

Rail inclusive tickets are available from most stations. And great value short breaks at local hotels. See your travel agent for further details.

0990 04 04 04

Discover our
eventful
days

Stokesay Castle, Shropshire

From magnificent castles, abbeys and stately homes to hidden gems in beautiful countryside settings, English Heritage properties offer you the real history of England. Taste the excitement of the past as many of our properties come alive with an action packed programme of historic re-enactments, living history, music and drama. With over 400 properties across the country we guarantee an eventful day out.

Brodsworth Hall and Gardens, Yorkshire

Rievaulx Abbey, Yorkshire

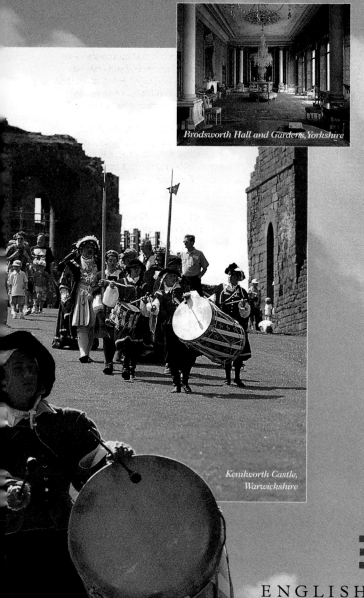

Kenilworth Castle, Warwickshire

For a free brochure on what to do and see call us now on 0171 973 3434

ENGLISH HERITAGE

What's On – Selected Events

CECIL HIGGINS GALLERY,
Bedford, Bedfordshire
- 17 Mar-7 June - Out From Under - Australian Art in English Collections. Featuring contemporary Aboriginal art from the Central and Western Desert regions.
- 16 June-6 September - Regency - highlighting design, art, and decorative arts of the period 1800-1830.
- 15 September-6 December - Dolls, Dolls' Houses and Dollmaking (Teddy Bears, too).

CHATSWORTH, Derbyshire
- 9-10 May - Angling Fair
- 20-21 June - Chatsworth Flower and Garden Show
- 5-6 September - Country Fair - with massed pipe and military bands, hot-air balloons, trade stalls, etc

NATIONAL TRAMWAY MUSEUM,
Crich, Derbyshire
- 25 May - A 'Yesterday' Mayday - the Edwardian way, with old-fashioned games and a Maypole
- 7 June - Tram-jam-boree - busy, bustling streets and plenty of vintage trams
- 14 June - 'Mane' Event - a chance to ride in a horse-tram
- 12 July - Funtasia - Children get in free with a full-fee paying adult, and enjoy bouncy castles, clowns, competitions etc
- 30-31 August - National Festival of Transport - many vintage vehicles, most of which can be ridden in, jostling for space with the trams.
- 6 September - 'Mane Event - the final chance this year to ride in a horse-drawn tram
- 13 September - 'In Living Memory' - free admission for those who arrive in Victorian or Edwardian costume.
- 25 October - 'Starlight Special' - The Red House Carriage Museum lend their horse-drawn omnibus to help give the feel of the past, with old-fashioned street lights and cobbles underfoot.
- 26 October-1 November - Treasure Trail - children's event, different clues for different ages and the chance to win prizes.

CITY MUSEUM,
Plymouth, Devon

TANK MUSEUM,
Bovington, Dorset
- Firepower & Mobility Displays - see tanks in action - every Thursday at noon throughout July, August and September, plus every Friday at noon during August.
- 25 May - Dorset Children's Show
- 26 July - Battle Day Spectacular (please telephone to confirm)
- 20 September - Wessex Classic Car Show

TUTANKHAMON EXHIBITION,
Dorchester, Dorset
A special exhibition to celebrate the 75th Anniversary of the discovery of the Tomb

PRIEST'S HOUSE,
Wimborne, Dorset
- 1 April-30 May and 7 September-31 October - 'The Swinging 60s' - life during the decade of The Beatles, 'Ban the Bomb' and the Moon Landings
- 10 June-31 August - 'Football Crazy - focussing on the nation's favourite sport in the year of the World Cup

HEVER CASTLE, Hever, Kent
- 10-13 April - Easter Weekend - Easter Egg Trail and local brass bands
- 2-4 May - May Day Music and Dance - traditional dancing with Morris Dancers
- 23-25 May - Merrie England Weekend - Archery and foot combat demonstrations, medieval music and dance, medieval stalls
- June-August - Summer Music Season - local bands will perform on the castle forecourt every Sunday afternoon
- 26-28 June - Gardners' Weekend - including Gardners' Question Time with BBC Radio Kent
- 25 July, 1,8,15,22,30,31 - August Jousting - The Knights of Royal England will present traditional jousting contests
- 26 July, 2,9,16,23,30,31 - August Longbow Achery - The Company of 1415 will demonstrate the use of the Longbow as a military weapon
- 11-13 September - Patchwork and Quilting Exhibition
- 24 October-1 November - Medieval Half-Term Fun - indoor activities for children on certain days - please telephone for details.

STANFORD HALL,
Swinford, Leicestershire
- 19 April - Lancia Giorno della Montecarlo (provisional)
- 26 April - Riders Association of Triumph Rally
- 3 May - VW Owners Club Rally - (Warks & Leics Branch)
- 10 May - Suzuki Motorcycle Owners Club Rally (provisional)
- 16 May - Wartburg/IFA Owners Club UK Rally (provisional)
- 17 May - Leicestershire Ford RS Owners Club Rally (provisional)
- 24 May - Capri Club International National Rally
- 7 June - Lea-Francis Owners Club Rally
- 14 June - Alfa-Romeo Owners Club National Rally
- 21 June - Ford AVO Owners Club Rally
- 28 June - American Civil War Society (Battle 3pm)
- 5 July - Velocette Motorcycle Owners Club Rally
- AC Owners Club Rally (provisional)
- 12 July - Sporting Escort Owners Club National Rally
- Norton Rotary Enthusiasts' Club Rally
- 19 July - Honda Motorcycle Owners Club Rally
- 26 July - Vintage Motorcycle Club Founders Day Rally
- 2 August - Monkey Bike Rally (provisional)
- 8 August - The 1998 Music and Fireworks Spectacular
- 9 August - Francis Barnett Motorcyle Owners Club Rally
- Triumph Sports 6 Owners Club Rally
- 23 August - Midlands Austin 7 Car Club Rally
- Salmons Tickford Enthusiasts Club Rally
- 6 September - Scott Motorcycle Owners Club Rally
- 3-4 October - Crafts at Stanford Hall (Lady Fayre)

CHURCH FARM MUSEUM,
Skegness, Lincolnshire
- June - Woolly Days - traditional sheepshearing with demonstrations of spinning, dyeing, and general woolcraft
- July - Victorian Times - a week of traditional rural and domestic craft demonstrations
- August - Garden Party
- August - Teddy Bears' Picnic
- September - Classic and vintage car and motorcycle rally
- October - Steam threshing - four days of threshing and other demonstrations
- October - Model Engines Day - model steam traction engines on display
- October - Apple Day - celebrating the many varieties of British apples

NATIONAL GALLERY, WC2
- 3 April-31 May - Henry Moore and the National Gallery - to celebrate the centenary of Moore's birth, this exhibition explores his association with the Gallery, and includes works which he admired and maquettes which show the influence of paintings in the Gallery (Room 1)
- 6 May-2 August - Masters of Light: Dutch Painting from Utrecht during the Golden Age
- 15 July-11 October - Through Canaletto's Eyes - Based on five of the Gallery's paintings of Venice by Canaletto, the exhibition will examine how the artist set about making his paintings, with the help of drawings, prints and photographs of the sites. (Sunley Room)
- 16 September-13 December - Jonathan Miller...On Reflection - paintings selected by Dr Jonathan Miller, examining reflections and mirrors, and showing how painters of different periods represent reflective surfaces.
- 11 November-31 January - Signorelli in British Collections - London has the largest collection of works by the Renaissance artist Luca Signorelli, but he remains less well known and understood than his major contemporaries. This exhibition surveys his whole career. (Sunley Room)

MAPLEDURHAM ESTATE,
Mapledurham, Oxfordshire
- 24-26 April - Craft Fair
- 9-10 May - Civil War Battle Re-enactment
- 10 May - National Mills Day

SHUGBOROUGH HALL,
Shugborough, Staffordshire
- 18-19 April - Gamekeepers Fair - stalls, falconry, demonstrations, clay shoots
- 25-26 April - Staffordshire Spring Flower Show
- 3-4 May - Classic Car Event
- 17 May - Dressage Festival - Staffordshire's national dressage competition
- 23-25 May - Spring Craft Show
- 6 June - Magic of the Movies - open air concert
- 7 June - Donkey Day - at Shugborough Park Farm
- 13 June - Afternoon of Scottish Country Dance
- 21 June - All About Pigs - Shugborough Park Farm
- 4-5 July - Gardeners' Weekend
- 18 July - Fireworks and Lazer Symphony Concert
- 19 July - Goose Fair - the characters, entertainers and market stalls of the 1820 village fair at Shugborough Park Farm

- 2 August - Victorian Street Market - costumed merchants and street entertainers
- 22 August - Last Night of the Proms - with fireworks
- 29-31 August - Summer Craft Festival
- 13 September - Wedding and Home Show
- 10-11 October - Christmas Craft Show
- 30-31 October - Hallowe'en - spooky fun
- 7 November - Bonfire Night - fireworks
- 8-11 December - Christmas at Shugborough - Victorian evenings with festive decorations, Christmas market etc

ICKWORTH HOUSE,
Horringer, Suffolk
- 18-19 April - Wood Fair
- 10 May - Bury Festival Garden Tour
- 14 May - Bury Festival Chandelier Tour
- 16 May - Bury Festival Archaeological Tour
- 18 May - Bury Festival Chandelier Tour
- 24 May - RAC Rally
- 9-10 July - Ickworth Proms
- 8-9 August - Bury St Edmunds Amateur Radio Society Event
- 13 August - Ickworth's Great Eccentrics Day
- 22 August - Classic Car Rally
- 20 September - Plant Fair
- 7-8, 14-15,21-22,28-29 November - Pudding Weekend
- 28-29 November - Advent Lunch
- 6, 13,19 December -Christmas Lunch

GOODWOOD HOUSE,
Goodwood, Sussex (West)
12-14 June Festival of Speed

LEONARDSLEE,
Lower Beeding, Sussex (West)
- 2-4 May - Bonsai Weekend - demonstrations and advice
- 27-28 June - Country Craft Fair

WEST DEAN GARDENS,
West Dean, Sussex (West)
- 27-28 June - The Garden Event
- 5-18 July - Pergola Open Air Theatre
- 15-16 August - Chilli Fiesta
- 18 October - Apple Day

WARWICK CASTLE,
Warwickshire
- 10-14 April - The King's Progress - the Earl and his household prepare for the visit of Richard III, join in their celebrations, watch the knights and falconry displays
- 23 April - St George's Day
- 2-4 May - May Day Mummers - listen to medieval storytellers and see the 13th century

knights in combat
- 23-25 May - Jousting Weekend
- Every weekday in June, July and August - medieval craftsmen at work, including Fletcher, Potter, Smith
- 6-7 June - Tudor Mercenaries
- 13-14 June, 4-5 July, 22-23 - August - Knights in Combat
- 20-21 June - A Royal Victorian Weekend
- 27-28 June, 11-12 July, 8-9 August - Large Birds of Prey
- 18-19 July, 1-2 August - Jousting Weekend
- 24 October-1 November - Puritans, Daggers and Witchcraft - learn about witch trials and the ghosts of Warwick Castle
- December - Christmas at the Castle - Victorian decorations, special Christmas Lunches

BIRMINGHAM BOTANIC GARDENS,
Birmingham, West Midlands
- 26 April - Orchid Show
- 10 May - Plant Market
- 14 June - Bonsai Show
- 13 August - Alpine Lecture
- 29-31 August - Bonsai Exhibition
- 20 September - Dahlia Show
- 25 October - Christmas Market
- 29 November - Craft Fair

WILTON HOUSE,
Wilton, Wiltshire
- 12 April - Easter Egg Treasure Hunt
- 18-19 April - Celebration of Shakespeare
- 5-7 June - Wessex Craft Fayre
- 27-28 June - Wilton Horse Trials
- 18 July - Open Air Concert and Fireworks
- 2 August - 'Have a Go' at Archery
- 16 August - Teddy Bears' Picnic
- 12-13 September - Flowers in the Cloisters

SEVERN VALLEY RAILWAY,
Kidderminster, Worcester
- 18-19 April - Model Engineering Weekend
- 25-26 April - Spring Steam Gala
- 16-17 May - Heavy Horse Weekend
- 30-31 May, 6-7 June, 5-6 September - Friends Thomas the Tank Engine Weekends
- 4-5 July - 1940s Weekend
- 18-20 September - Autumn Steam Gala
- 9-10 October - Diesal Gala
- 11 October - Classic Vehicle Day
- 29 November, 5-6, 12-13, 19-20, 24 December - Santa Specials
- 26 December-3 January - Mince Pie Specials

HAREWOOD HOUSE,
Harewood, Yorkshire (West)
During 1998 Harewood House will celebrate the Year of Photography through a programme of exhibitions
- March-April - Seeing is Believing - interactive exhibition featuring historical photographic equipment to the latest digital imaging techniques

WALES

MUSEUM OF WELSH LIFE,
St Fagans, Cardiff
- 18-19 April - Historic Car Rally
- 2-4 May - Battle of St Fagans (300th Anniversary) and May Fair Festival
- 21 June - Midsummer Concert
- 1 August - Everyman Open Air Theatre
- 26-27 September - Harvest Festival
- 31 October - Hallowe'en Event
- 2-6 December - 1940s Christmas Celebration

COSMESTON VILLAGE,
Penarth, Vale of Glamorgan
- 12-13 April - Living History and 'Have a Go' Archery - village staff will be baking, cooking, gardening, etc, whilst a longbow group gives displays
- 3-4 May - Living History and 'Have a Go' Archery - staff will be baking etc whilst a longbow group gives displays.
- 24-25 May - Medieval Court and Trial Sessions - Judges, trials, punishments, trial by ordeal, combat etc
- 27-28 June - Call to Arms 1346 - Preparations for the Battle of Crecy - bowyers, fletchers, armourers etc
- 25-26 July - Medieval Battle and Jousting 1316 - the theme is the Welsh uprising led by Llewellyn Bren, Lord of Senghenydd. Jousting and combat displays culminating in a battle as the village is attacked by the Welsh
- 30-31 August - Grand Medieval Fair
- 26-27 September - Civil War Weekend
- 31 October - Hallowe'en - Cosmeston by night, spooky goings-on etc
- 20 December - Medieval Christmas Celebrations

SCOTLAND

ARCHAEOLINK,
Oyne, Aberdeenshire
- 25-26 July - Roman Weekend - battle re-enactment of Mons Grampius (AD83) Roman games, Celtic combat, crafts,

marching drills and chariot display

SANQUAR TOLBOOTH,
Sanquhar, D&G
- 15-18 August - 400th Anniversary of the Royal Burgh of Sanquhar - exhibition about the tradition of The Riding of the Marches

MUSEUM OF LEAD MINING,
Wanlockhead, D&G
- 23-24 May - British Gold Panning Championships
- 5 July - Mineral Road Show
- 23 August - Family Fun Day
- 13 September - Scottish Festival
- 31 October - Hallowe'en Event

BO'NESS & KINNEIL RAILWAY, Bo'ness, Falkirk

CALLANDER HOUSE, Falkirk
- 23 May-9 August - Battle of Falkirk 1298 - an exhibition commemorating the anniversary of this battle

CLAN DONALD CENTRE,
Armadale, Highland
- 16 May - Scottish Harp Competition
- 13 June - Sheepdog Trials
- 30 June-4 July - Archery Tournament
- 19 June - Piping Competition

MUSEUM OF FLIGHT,
East Fortune, East Lothian
- 18-19 July - Festival of Flight

NORTHERN IRELAND

US GRANT ANCESTRAL HOMESTEAD,
Dungannon, Co Tyrone
- April - Easter Bunny Day
- May - 'May Madness'
- 1-5 June - Teddy Bears Picnic
- 4 July - Yankee Doodle Day
- 29 July - Clogher Valley Agricultural Show
- 3 October - Vintage Bygones Display
- 31 October - Hallowe'en Event

ROWALLANE GARDEN,
Saintfield, Co Down
- 20 June - Midsummer Jazz Evening
- 21 June - Horse Drive
- 8-9 August - Wood Turning Event
- 12-13 December - Yuletide Market

REPUBLIC OF IRELAND

ARDGILLAN CASTLE,
Co Dublin
- 1-17 August - Craft Potter Society of Ireland Ceramics Exhibition

Strange tales

BRITAIN and Ireland have a great heritage of ancient monuments, historic sites and stately homes. They also have an invisible heritage of story: the gossip that passed for news before television and radio - what people thought had happened - and imaginative embroideries about the world they lived in.

Strange Tales

Many tales concerned the landscape and answered the questions how? and why? The Irish told of how the **Giant's Causeway** (212) was built as stepping stones across the Irish Sea by the giants of Scotland and Ireland so that they could visit one other. The Scottish giant Fir Ruadh (the Red Man) used it to visit Fionn Mac Cumhaill. People in the 12th century said that **Peak Cavern** (40) was the Mouth of Hell and because a perpetual wind blew from it those of the 16th called it "the Devil's Arse".

(Above): Peak Cavern in Castleton, Derbyshire.
(Right): The Giant's Causeway, Co Antrim.

Locals explained marks like horseshoes on boulders in the Sapey brook between Tedstone Delamere and Upper Sapey as the indelible hoofprints of the mare and colt that carried St Catherine Audley to **Ledbury** (72). They said that the "snakestones", fossil ammonites, found around **Whitby** (157) and once assumed originally to have had heads, were serpents which St Hilda turned to stone in AD 651 while clearing the site for the monastery she founded there. (Three snakestones are now the arms of Whitby Urban District Council.) Curious stones attracted customs as well as folktales. Children used to run twelve times round the Druid's Stone - an erratic - outside St Mary's Church, **Bungay** (128), calling on the Devil to appear. Until recently, people laid flowers and fruit at the feet of La Gran'mère du Chimquière, a standing stone at the churchyard gate of **St Martin** (164), on May Day for good luck.

Fishermen paced seven times singing round Granny Kempoch, a monolith on Kempoch Point across Gourock Bay from **Greenock** (191), in the hope of securing favourable winds. **A**ncient monuments, whose origin could only be guessed at, were fantastically accounted for. The stone circle of **Callanish** (172) is called in Gaelic *Fir Chreig*, "the False Men". Local tradition said that the stones were giants who refused baptism by St Kieran and so were turned to stone. Sixteenth-century visitors to the ruined walls of **Silchester** (69), Roman *Calleva*, were shown a gateway half blocked with rubble which locals called "Onion's Hole". They claimed that Onion had been a giant who lived in the old city. Silbury Hill, near **Avebury** (147), was said to be the burial mound of King Sil, hence its name, though excavations from 1776 onwards have not found him. **C**astles and abbeys, especially ruined ones, inspired rumours of subterranean passages. **Stokesay Castle** (121) has one, as does the abbey of **Culross** (177) and the ruined Gisborough Priory, **Guisborough** (154). Before its reconstruction in 1875, the ruins of **Castell Coch**, "the Red Castle" (210), were supposed

The stone circle of Callanish is called in Gaelic *Fir Chreig*, "the False Men"

(Above): Callanish Stone Circle, Isle of Lewis.
(Below): Stokesay Castle, Shropshire.

to be linked by a tunnel with Cardiff Castle. In it was a treasure-chest, and chained to it to guard against treasure-seekers was a pair of huge eagles that not even silver bullets could kill. **I**n a primeval deep under **Castle Rushen** (166) giants lie spellbound until the end of the world. King Arthur, too, lies in enchanted sleep in a cavernous hall with his court and hounds around him. On a table lies a bugle, a sword and a garter, and his sleep will last until someone blows the bugle, and cuts the garter with the sword. Rival candidates for this sleeping place include Sewingshields Castle, now levelled, north-east of **Housesteads** (112), **Brinkburn Priory** (112), **Richmond Castle** (156), **Dunstanburgh Castle** (112), Freebrough Hill, south of **Peak Cavern** (40) and the Eildon Hills overlooking **Melrose Abbey** (194). **T**he houses of the great are breeding grounds of romance. The little manor house of **Trerice** (35) is where in the reign of Edward IV Sir John Arundell came to avoid fulfilment of a prophecy:

When upon the yellow sand,
Thou shalt die by human hand.

(Above): Minster Lovell Hall.
(Below): Salisbury Cathedral.

To safeguard against this, he moved here from Efford, on the north Cornish coast. But some years later, the Earl of Oxford seized St Michael's Mount and Sir John got his death wound in the attempt to retake it, on **Marazion** (33) sands. **Marwell Hall** (66) is haunted by a White Lady, who presages misfortune. She may be the "lost bride" who, on her wedding-night, challenged the wedding guests to a game of hide-and-seek. She hid in an oak chest with a heavy lid in a remote part of the house, and was trapped there. Only years later did someone lift the lid and find a skeleton wearing a bridal wreath. **Minster Lovell** (117), too, claims this story. At Combe Sydenham Hall, **Monksilver** (124), is preserved "Drake's cannon-ball". Hearing in the Antipodes that his wife was about to re-marry, he fired a cannon into the sea and the ball passed clean through the globe and fell between bride and groom at the altar. Drake's wife realized that he was alive and called off the wedding. "Drake's cannon-ball" was supposed to roll in times of national danger, probably from confusion with Drake's Drum at **Buckland Abbey** (43). If taken away, it returned of its own accord. The same was said of a "Screaming Skull" in **Smailholm Tower** (194), but another "Screaming Skull", at **Burton Agnes** Hall (153), simply made a racket until someone returned it. To avoid future trouble it was bricked up in a niche in

The choirboys tickled him to "make him merry", but overdid it and tickled him to death.

the wall. In churches, curious tombs gave rise to endless speculation. Trees have split the tomb in Tewin churchyard of Lady Anne Grimston of **Gorhambury** (74), who died in 1713. Tradition says that, as she laying dying, she wished that, if the resurrection of the body were true, trees would grow from her grave to prove it. In **Salisbury Cathedral** (149), the miniature effigy of a bishop on the north side of the nave was long said to represent a Boy Bishop. The choirboys tickled him to "make him merry", but overdid it and tickled him to death. Because he died in office, he was buried in his mitre and cope. Legend and history often intertwined. The difficulty of identifying King Harold's body after the Battle of Hastings in 1066, coupled with confusion over his burial place - possibly **Waltham Abbey** (57) - led to a belief that he had not died. There were rumours of a hermit, scarred and blinded in his left eye, living many years at **Chester** (28) in a cell near the now ruined church of St John, later anachronistically identified with The Hermitage. King Henry I visited him and on his deathbed confirmed that it was Harold. **Jedburgh Abbey** (192) was where on 14 October 1285 King Alexander III married Jolande, daughter of the Count de Dreux. The wedding festivities in Jedburgh Castle that night were shockingly interrupted when the glittering assembly of French and Scottish nobility became aware that a spectre had joined their dance. This inspired Edgar Allan Poe's "The Masque of the Red Death", best known from Roger Corman's chilling 1964 film starring Vincent Price. But perhaps what people most loved to talk about was the supernatural. In St Mary's Church, **Kington** (72), is the tomb of Sir Thomas Vaughan, killed in battle in 1469. Locals identified him with "Black Vaughan" of Hergest Court. He was so wicked that after death he could not rest, but came back "stronger and stronger" until twelve parsons "read him down" into a silver snuff-box and laid him for a thousand years at the bottom of Hergest Pool. **Dunvegan** Castle (174) on Skye displays the Fairy Flag, given to a Macleod by his

(Top): Jedburgh Abbey.
(Left): Culzean Castle.

The Mermaid of Zennor with her human husband and children.

fairy wife. A fairy boy saved the life of a "Laird o' Co'" **Culzean Castle**, (188). **Stowmarket** (131) was well-known for its sandy-haired fairies, and when a **Blasket** (221) islander was asked of the lonely island of Inisicíleáin, south-west of Great Blasket, "Are there any fairies in the Inis?" the reply was, "Why, it is black with them!" In **Dryburgh Abbey** (188) lived a spirit called Fatlips, a little man wearing heavy iron shoes. These were worn also by Redcaps, who haunted Border castles, murdering benighted travellers and catching the blood in their caps. **Hermitage Castle** (191) had one. **Ogmore Castle** (209) had a White Lady who guarded a treasure under the tower floor. Southown Road, **Great Yarmouth** (105)

was the haunt of Old Scarf, a shape-shifter sometimes taking the form of a dog. If you laid a straw on the ground in front of him, he would rattle his chain and howl. A bogey called the galley-beggar used to toboggan down the hill between Over and **Nether Stowey** (124) on dark winter nights sitting on a hurdle and hooting with laughter. Under the waters of Pendour Cove lived the Mermaid of **Zennor** (35) with her human husband and children - or so said Zennor people accounting to strangers for the mermaid on a bench-end in their parish church.

Many of the places mentioned in the article appear in the book, and the page number is given in brackets. If they do not appear, the page number listed is given to indicate the general area.

YORK

BEDFORDSHIRE

AMPTHILL
Houghton House
(1m NE off A421)
Now a ruin, the mansion was built for Mary Countess of Pembroke, the sister of Sir Philip Sidney. Inigo Jones is thought to have been involved in work on the house, which is said to be the 'House Beautiful' in Bunyan's 'Pilgrim's Progress'.
Open all reasonable times.
Free.
🅿 ᕦ ⌗

BEDFORD
Bedford Museum
Castle Ln MK40 3XD (in town centre, close to town bridge and Embankment)
☎*01234 353323 Fax 01234 273401*
The museum is devoted to local history and natural history, with 19th-century room sets and displays of birds and mammals, agriculture, archaeology, fossils and minerals. There is a changing programme of children's activities, temporary exhibitions and special events. Please telephone for details.
Open all year, Tue-Sat 11-5, Sun 2-5. (Closed Mon ex BH Mon afternoon, Good Fri & Xmas).
Free, except charge is made for some special events which are advertised locally.
P *(50 mtrs)* ᕦ *(lift available on request, subject to staff availability) toilets for disabled shop* ⌗

Cecil Higgins Art Gallery & Museum
Castle Ln MK40 3RP
☎*01234 211222 Fax 01234 327149*
The rooms in this award-winning recreated Victorian mansion are arranged in the manner of a house still lived in, to authenticate the atmosphere. The adjoining modern gallery has an outstanding collection of ceramics, glass, prints and watercolours, and is set in gardens leading down to the river embankment. A regular programme of thematic exhibitions is taken from the gallery's own collection of watercolours, prints and drawings. Exhibitions for 1998 include: Out from Under (until 7 June) - Australian art in English collections, Regency Art (16 June-6 Sept) & Dolls and Teddies (15 September-6 December). Please ring for details.
Open all year, Tue-Sat 11-5, Sun 2-5, BH Mon 2-5. (Closed Mon, Good Fri & 25-26 Dec).
Free.
P *(50 yds)* ᕦ *toilets for disabled shop* ⌗ *(ex guide dogs)*

ELSTOW
Moot Hall
(signposted off Elstow Road)
☎*01234 266889 & 228330*
Fax 01234 228921
The restored medieval timber-framed market hall has a collection of 17th-century furniture and items relating to the life and times of John Bunyan, who was born nearby. These include a fine collection of his works, notably *Pilgrim's Progress*.
Open 2 Apr-Oct, Tue-Thu, Sat & BH's 2-5; Sun 2-5.30. (Closed Mon ex BH's & Fri). Phone to confirm,
P ᕦ *shop* ⌗
Details not confirmed for 1998

LEIGHTON BUZZARD
Leighton Buzzard Railway
Pages Park Station, Billington Rd LU7 8TN (0.75m SE on A4146 signposted in and around Leighton Buzzard)
☎*01525 373888*
Fax 01525 377814
The original light railway was built to carry sand in 1919, and after its redundancy in 1967 the railway society took over its three and a half mile length. It is now a 2ft gauge passenger-carrying line through varied scenery with over 50 locomotives, including 11 resident steam engines from West Africa, India, Spain and Britain. The line is now one of England's foremost narrow gauge preservation centres. A programme of industrial train displays will take place throughout the year. Special events planned for 1998 include: Easter Steam Weekend (10-13 April) Heritage Weekend (4-5 July), Autumn steam-up (5-6 September). Ring for leaflet with other events and heritage display information.
Open, operating dates Suns & BH Mons 15 Mar-11 Oct; Good Fri; Wed 27 May-26 Aug; Tue & Thu in Aug; Sat 11 Apr, 2 & 23 May, 4 Jul, 1-29 Aug & 5 Sep. Trains run to Stonehenge Works. Return journey lasts 65 mins. Trains run from 11.15pm. Xmas trains run Sat & Sun 5-20 Dec, advanced booking advised.
Return ticket £4.50 (ch 2-15 £1, pen £3.50 & ch under 2 free). Party 10+.
P 🖵 ᕦ *(platform & train access for wheelchairs) toilets for disabled shop*
Cards: 🅰 ▭ ▨

LUTON
John Dony Field Centre
Hancock Dr, Bushmead LU2 7SF (signposted off A6, Old Bedford Rd)
☎*01582 486983 & 422818*
Fax 01582 422805
The John Dony Field Centre is a purpose built study centre for exploring the rich landscapes and fascinating plants and animals of the Luton area. Featuring permanent displays of local archaeology, natural history and the management of the local nature reserve. It explains how ancient grasslands and hedgerows are conserved and follows 4000 years of history from Bronze Age to modern times. There are temporary displays on topics of environmental interest, and various special events including the Bushmead Festival (July). Please telephone for details.
Open all year, Mon-Fri 9.30-4.45, Sun 9.30-1. Closed BHs.
Free.
P ᕦ *toilets for disabled* ⌗ *(ex guide dogs)*

Luton Museum & Art Gallery
Wardown Park, Old Bedford Rd LU2 7HA
☎*01582 546722 & 546739*
Fax 01582 546763
A Victorian mansion standing in Wardown Park contains displays illustrating the natural and cultural history, archaeology and industries of the area. Follow the development of Luton's hat industry in the 19th and 20th centuries and admire the extensive hat and lace collections. Also on view are costumes, dolls, straw marquetry, decorative and fine arts, several Victorian settings and the Bedfordshire and Hertfordshire Regimental Collections.
Open all year, Mon-Sat 10-5, Sun 1-5 (Closed Xmas & 1 Jan).
Free.
P 🖵 ᕦ *(parking adjacent to entrance, lift to 1st floor) toilets for disabled shop* ⌗

Stockwood Craft Museum & Gardens
Stockwood Country Park, Farley Hill LU1 4BH (signposted from M1 junct 10)
☎*01582 738714 & 546739*
Fax 01582 546739
The Museum is set in period gardens which incorporate the Ian Hamilton Finlay Sculpture Gardens. The Mossman collection of horse drawn vehicles traces the history of transport from Roman times to the 1940's. The complex also includes working stables and craft demonstrations are held at weekends in the summer. Easter Craft Festival, Easter Monday. Please telephone for details of special events.
Open all year; Mar-Oct, Tue-Sat 10-5, Sun & BH Mons 10-6; Nov-Mar, weekends 10-4. (closed Xmas & 1 Jan)
Free.
P 🖵 ✕ *licensed* ᕦ *(chair lift in Transport gallery, dedicated parking) toilets for disabled shop* ⌗

The narrow gauge railway at Leighton Buzzard dates back to 1919.

SAFEWAY STATESMAN

OLD WARDEN
The Shuttleworth Collection
Old Warden Aerodrome SG18 9EP (2m W from rdbt on A1, Biggleswade by-pass)
☎01767 627288
Fax 01767 627745
Housed in seven hangars on a classic grass aerodrome, 40 working historic aeroplanes span the progress of aviation with exhibits ranging from a 1909 Bleriot to a 1941 Spitfire. A garage of roadworthy motor vehicles explores the eras of the 1898 Panhard Levassor to the Railton sports car of 1937. The 19th-century coach house displays horsedrawn vehicles from 1880 to 1914. 1998 Flying Displays: 3 & 16 May, 7 & 20 June, 5 & 18 July, 2 & 16 August, 6 September, 4 October.
Please ring 0891 323310 for details.
Open all year, daily 10-4 (3pm Nov-Mar). Closed 10 days at Xmas, up to and including 1 Jan.
£6 (ch 5-16, students & pen £4). Flying Display Days, per car £9 to £22 (depends on no in car). Others £6 (ch, pen £4). Group 20+. Family tickets.
🅿 ✗ licensed & (passageways between hangars are ramped) toilets for disabled shop ✿

SANDY
RSPB Nature Reserve
The·Lodge SG19 2DL (1m E, on B1042 Potton Rd)
☎01767 680541
A number of waymarked paths and formal gardens make this, the headquarters of the Royal Society for the Protection of Birds, popular with visitors. (The house and buildings are not open to the public.) Two species of woodpecker, nuthatches and common woodland birds may often be seen, as may muntjac deer.
Open daily 9am-9pm or sunset.
£2 (ch 50p, concessions £1) Family £4.
🅿 & toilets for disabled shop ✿
Cards: 🆇 🖃 🆇 🖃 🕢

SILSOE
Wrest Park House & Gardens
MK45 4HR (three quarters of a mile E off A6)
☎01525 860152
The formal gardens designed over 150 years ago include alterations by 'Capability' Brown, and form a serene and beguiling setting for this elegant 19th century mansion.
Open Apr-1 Nov, daily 10-6 (or dusk if earlier).
£2.95 (ch £1.50, concessions £2.20). Personal stereo tour included in price.
🅿 🖵 ✿ (in certain areas) ⚎

WHIPSNADE
Whipsnade Wild Animal Park
LU6 2LF (M1 junct 9/12, signposted or M25 junct 21, signposted)
☎01582 872171
Fax 01582 872649
Whipsnade is set in 600 acres of beautiful parkland and is home to over 2,500 animals, many of which are endangered. It is one of Europe's largest conservation centres. Wallabies, peacocks, tamarinds and Chinese water deer roam freely in the Park. Things to do and see include free-flying Birds of the World demonstration, sealions, Elephant Encounter, Discovery Centre, Squirrel Monkey Island, Passage through Asia, Children's Farm, Runwild Playarea, Tiger Falls, the Great Whipsnade Railway, and new for 1998 - Lemurs, and Hippo Pools. You can explore the Park on foot (among the free roaming animals), by car, or on the free Safari Tour Bus and be eye to eye with a giraffe! Ring for details of special events.
Open Easter-Sept Mon-Sat 10-6, Sun 10-7. Sept-Oct daily 10-4, Feb-Easter daily 10-4.
❊Prices under review.
🅿 (charged) 🖵 ✗ licensed & (free entry for disabled cars) toilets for disabled shop ✿ (no exceptions)
Cards: 🆇 🖃 🆇 🖃 🕢

TIME FLIES AT OLD WARDEN!

Europe's largest collection of pre-World War II aircraft

The Shuttleworth Collection brings to life the pioneering days of transport history; seven floodlit hangars display unique aeroplanes, including a 1909 Bleriot, a classic 1930s Gloster Gladiator and victorious machines from two world wars, as well as remarkable road vehicles like the 1898 Panhard Levassor. Our flying displays take place from May to October, and during the winter months there is always much to see. Call our Hotline for full information.

Information Hotline
0891 323310
(45p per minute cheap rate, 50p per minute at all other times)

Open daily from 10am.
Last admission 4pm (3pm Nov-Mar).

• FREE PARKING
• RESTAURANT
• SHOP

THE Shuttleworth COLLECTION

OLD WARDEN AERODROME, OFF THE A1, BIGGLESWADE, BEDS.

WOBURN
Woburn Abbey
MK43 0TP
☎01525 290666
Fax 01525 290271
This palatial 18th-century mansion is the home of the Duke of Bedford. The house dates from 1744 but was remodelled in 1802 by Henry Holland. Originally a Cistercian Abbey, the Dukes of Bedford have lived at Woburn since 1547. There is a valuable art collection in the house with paintings by Canaletto, Rembrandt, Van Dyck, Gainsborough and many others. There is also an extensive collection of 18th-century furniture, both French and English. Fourteen state apartments are on view and the private apartments are shown when not in use by the family. The house stands in 3000 acres of parkland, famous for its collection of varieties of deer. Many special events are held during the year, including Craft Fairs, a De-Havilland Tiger Moth Fly-In (Aug), Lilliput Lane Collectors Show (June) and a Commercial Vehicles Road Run.
Open 1 Jan-21 Mar; Abbey Sat & Sun only 11-4, Deer park 10.30-3.45; 22 Mar-27 Sept; Abbey weekdays 11-4, Sun & BH 11-5; 3 Oct-1 Nov Sat & Sun only; Deer Park weekdays 10-4.30, Sun & BH 10-4.45.
Abbey & Deer Park £7.50 (ch over 12yrs £3.00, pen £6.50). Family ticket £19-£21.50. Deer Park only car & passengers £5. Motorcycles & passengers £2.
🅿 🖵 & (wheelchairs accommodated by prior arrangement) toilets for disabled shop ✿
Cards: 🆇 🖃 🆇 🖃 🕢

Woburn Safari Park
Woburn Park MK17 9QN (from M1, junc 13)
☎01525 290407 Fax 01525 290489
Within the 3000 acres of parkland belonging to Woburn Abbey, is an area of over 300 acres set aside as a Safari Park. A collection of many species of animal has made Woburn justifiably famous among Safari Parks. Woburn's own safari road passes through an African plains area stocked with eland, zebra, hippos and rhinos. Then through the well-keepered tiger and lion enclosures and on past bears and monkeys. The pets' corner, sea lion·and parrot shows, and elephant displays, are all popular attractions. Special events are held on all Bank Holidays and during summer school holidays. The large new leisure complex also offers a boating lake and adventure playgrounds.
Open daily, 7 Mar to 1 Nov, 10am-5pm. £10.50 (ch3-17 £7. pen £7.50). Ch under 3 free.
🅿 ✗ licensed & toilets for disabled shop ✿
Cards: 🆇 🖃 🆇 🖃 🕢

BERKSHIRE

BASILDON
Basildon Park
Lower Basildon RG8 9NR (7m NW of Reading on W side of A329)
☎0118 984 3040
Fax 0118 984 1267
This lovely 18th-century house, built of golden Bath stone, fell into decay in the 20th century, but was rescued and beautifully restored by Lord and Lady Iliffe. The first feature to impress the visitor is the classical front with its splendid central portico and pavilions. Inside there are delicate plasterwork decorations on the walls and ceilings and an elegant staircase. The most impressive room is the Octagon drawing room, with its fine pictures and furniture, and three big windows overlooking the River Thames. The Shell Room and Bamboo Room are also notable for their decorations. There is a small formal garden, and a pretty terrace garden overlooks the grounds.
House open 1 Apr-1 Nov, Wed-Fri 1-5.30;

Sat, Sun & BH Mon 1-5.30 (Closed Good Fri). Park & garden 1-27 Mar, wknds 12-5, otherwise as house (ex wknds & BH Mon 12-5).1 Apr-1 Nov 11.30-5.30.
House & grounds £2.80, family ticket £10; Grounds only £1.60, family ticket £4.
🅿 🖵 & (driven buggy) toilets for disabled shop ✿ (ex in grounds) 🎗

Beale Park
Lower Basildon RG8 9NH (signposted from M4 junc 12)
☎0118 984 5172 Fax 0118 984 5171
Ornamental pheasants, peacocks, parrots, owls, cranes and wildfowl can be seen here in a pleasant riverside setting (a designated area of Outstanding Natural Beauty), together with Highland cattle and rare breeds of sheep, a pets' corner and a tropical house. There is a craft centre, and a children's playground with paddling pools and sandpits. There is also excellent fishing in season. The park has an information/education facility, and numerous events and exhibitions are held during the year.
River trips are another attraction, and a narrow gauge railway runs around the park every day. Amidst all this is the unusual focal point of the mausoleum, built by Mr Child Beale in memory of his parents, surrounded by a large and varied collection of statues, fountains and walks. Special events for 1998 include: Medieval craft fair, flower show, Christmas craft show, two model boat shows, fireworks, three horse shows. Please ring for details.
Open daily, Mar-Sep 10-6. Last admission 5pm. Oct-Dec 10-5. Last admission 4pm. £4 (ch under 3 free, 3-16 £2.50, students £2 pen £3). Disabled £2 (disabled ch free). Unemployed half price for up to 2 adults plus 2 ch. Party. Family.
🅿 🖵 & (wheelchair available, parking) toilets for disabled shop ✿

ETON
Dorney Court
Dorney SL4 6QP (signposted from M4 exit 7, via B3026)
☎01628 604638 Fax 01628 665772
This enchanting brick and timber manor house (c1440) stands in a tranquil setting. It has tall Tudor chimneys and a splendid great hall and has been the home of the present family since 1510.
Open 3-4 & 24-25 May & Mon-Thu Jul-Aug, 1-4.30 (last admission 4pm).
£4.50 (ch under 9 £2.50, pen & NT members £4)
🅿 🖵 shop garden centre ✿
Cards: 🆇

MAIDENHEAD
Courage Shire Horse Centre
Cherry Garden Ln, Maidenhead Thicket SL6 3QD (off A4 0.5m W of A4/A423/A423M jct)
☎01628 824848 Fax 01628 828472
Visitors are free to wander around and meet the horses, or take a free tour with an experienced guide who will introduce you to the horses and explain the care and history of the 'gentle giants' of the equestrian world. See the harness maker at work, and certain days will find the farrier or cooper in attendance. Dray rides are also available.
Open Mar-Oct, daily 10.30-5. Last admission 4pm.
🅿 🖵 ✗ licensed & (wheelchair available) toilets for disabled shop
Details not confirmed for 1998
Cards: 🆇 🖃 🖃

NEWBURY
Newbury District Museum
The Wharf RG14 5AS (from London take M4 junct 13, then Southbound on A34 for 3miles, follow signs for town centre.)
☎01635 30511 Fax 01635 519562
The museum is situated in two picturesque and historic buildings in the centre of Newbury, the Cloth Hall built in 1627, and the Granary built in 1720. Apart from local history and archaeology, birds and fossils, the museum displays costume and other decorative art. Special features are the two Civil War battles of

Newbury (1643 and 1644) and the history of ballooning.
Open all year, Apr-Sep Mon-Sat (ex Wed) 10-5, Sun & BH's 1-5; Oct-Mar Mon-Sat (ex Wed) 10-4. Open Wed during school holidays.
Free.
P (15yds) & shop ※ (ex guide dogs)

READING

Blake's Lock Museum
Gasworks Rd, off Kenavon Dr RG1 3DH
☎ 0118 939 0918 Fax 0118 959 0630
Reading's museum of industrial heritage on the banks of the River Kennet houses a wealth of displays including a Victorian printer's workshop, bakery, barber's shop and a fully restored gypsy caravan. The Turbine House, with turbines dating from the 1920s, and the Screen House, containing an occasional series of temporary exhibitions, are now open. The Reading Waterfest, a celebration of Reading's waterways, takes place in June.
Open all year, Tue-Fri 10-5, Sat, Sun & BH Mon 2-5. Parties by arrangement. Telephone to check Christmas opening times.
Free.
P (0.5m) & toilets for disabled shop ※

Museum of English Rural Life
University of Reading, Whiteknights Park RG6 6AG (2m SE on A327)
☎ 0118 931 8660 Fax 0118 975 1264
This museum houses a fascinating national collection of agricultural, domestic and crafts exhibits, including wagons, tools and a wide range of other equipment used in the English countryside over the last 150 years. Family groups will find the exhibitions especially attractive, and special facilities such as videos and teaching packs are available for school parties, on request. The museum also contains very extensive documentary and photographic archives, which can be studied by appointment.

Open all year, Tue-Sat, 10-1 & 2-4.30. (Closed BH's & Xmas-New Year).
£1 (ch free & pen 75p).
P & shop ※
Cards: ▨ ▥ ⑤

The Museum of Reading
The Town Hall, Blagrave St RG1 1QH
☎ 0118 939 9800
Fax 0118 939 9881
Discover the development of Reading through the ages from a Saxon settlement on the banks of the River Kennet to the commercial heart of today's Thames Valley. Experience the crowning of a medieval king, the sounds of singing in the Abbey, the smells of Victorian Reading - biscuits baking and beer brewing. Also on show is a full-size Victorian replica of the Bayeux Tapestry. The Silchester Gallery, featuring a permanent display of artefacts found at the Roman site of Calleva Atrebatum, and the Exhibitions Gallery, which features changing displays, are now open.
Open all year, Tue-Sat 10-5, Sun & BH 2-5.
Free.
P (200m) ▨ ✗ licensed & (lifts parking space) toilets for disabled shop ※ (ex guide dogs)
Cards: ▨ ▥ ▧ ▨ ⑤

RISELEY

Wellington Country Park & National Dairy Museum
RG7 1SP (signposted off A33)
☎ 0118 932 6444
Fax 0118 932 6445
The country park consists of 350 acres of woodland and meadows, set around a lake in the countryside between Reading and Basingstoke. The National Dairy Museum in the grounds outlines the history of the dairy industry in Britain. There is also a Thames Valley Time Trail, which traces the development of earth and mineral resources in the area. Other attractions are the collection of farm

There is an opportunity to take a dray ride after meeting the horses and learning their history at the Courage Shire Horse Centre.

animals, a deer park and a miniature steam railway. Five nature trails are marked out, in addition to a fitness course and adventure playground. It is also possible to fish, sail, windsurf and row here.
Open all year, Mar-Oct, daily 10-5.30.
£3.70 (ch £1.90)
P ▨ & (fishing platform & nature trail for disabled) toilets for disabled shop
Cards: ▨ ▥

WINDSOR
The town of Windsor owes its existence to the famous castle which has been a home of British monarchs for almost 900 years. The castle, on its outcrop above the River Thames, stands above the townand has been magnificently restored after the fire in 1992. It is the largest inhabited castle in the world and through the ages has been much altered. Most of the present structure was due to work done by George IV and many of the buildings in the town are from this period. Windsor also flourished during the Victorian period and the town's station was built to celebrate Queen Victoria's Jubilee. The south and east of the town are bounded by 5000 acres of Windsor Great Park. Across the river is Eton, England's most famous school, founded by Henry VI in 1440 and educator of no less than 20 British Prime Ministers.

Crown Jewels of the World Museum
47-50 Peascod St SL4 1DE
☎ 01753 833773 Fax 01753 833722
A short walk from Windsor Castle, this unique museum displays replica crown and court jewels of some 12 countries including Austria, Britain, France, Germany, Russia and Iran. Voted a 'Treasure House' of Britain by BBC TV and valued at many millions of pounds by

world-famous jewellers, this collection authentically recreated by master jewellers has been assembled over the past 100 years. As most of the originals no longer exist, here visitors can enjoy a rare heritage experience of breath-taking splendour and thrilling history of Crown Jewels of the World all under one roof
Open Apr-Oct, daily 11-5. Other times by arrangement.
£3.50 (ch £2, pen & student £2.50). Family ticket £10. Party 10+.
P (300yds) shop ※

Frogmore House
Home Park SL4 1NJ (entrance from B3021)
☎ 01753 831118 (recorded info)
Fax 01753 832290
The long and distinguished history of Frogmore House dates back even further than the present building of 1618, being previously owned by Henry VIII. Subsequent residents have included Charles II's architect, Hugh May, who built the present house, a Duke of Northumberland, Queen Charlotte, Queen Victoria and Queen Mary. It has 19 rooms, and an original mural, discovered only six years ago during redecoration, can be seen on the stairway.
Open: 6-7 & 20 May 10am-7pm (last admission 6pm), 27 May (mausoleum only) 11am-4pm (last admission 3.30pm), 11 Aug-1 Oct Tues-Thurs: prebooked groups only. 29-31 Aug 10am-5.30pm (last admission 4pm).
May openings: house: £3.20 (ch 8-16 £1.10,no children under 8 in house, pen £2.20), gardens & mausoleum: £3.50 (ch Free if accompanied, pen £2.50). 29-31 Aug £4.70 (ch 8-16 £2.70, pen £3.70).
P shop ※
Cards: ▨ ▥ ▧ ▨ ⑤

Household Cavalry Museum
Combermere Barracks, St Leonards Rd SL4 3DN
☎ 01753 755203
This is one of the finest military museums in Britain. There are comprehensive displays of the uniforms, weapons, horse furniture (tack, regalia,

➤

etc) and armour used by the Household Cavalry from 1600 to the present day.
Open all year Mon-Fri (ex BH) 9-12.30 & 2-4.30.
Free.
& shop ✸

Legoland Windsor
Winkfield Rd SL4 4AY (2m from town centre on B3022 Windsor to Ascot road)
☎ 0990 040404
Fax 01753 626300
Set in 150 acres of Windsor Great Park, Legoland Windsor offers visitors over 40 hands-on activities, rides, themed playscapes and more Lego bricks that you would ever dream possible. There are are quiet areas and restaurants and facilities around the park to ensure the day out is enjoyable for everyone. Visitors can get fully involved in the world of Lego at the Driving School, the Boating School, in the Imagination Centre and the Wild Woods Pirate Area. There are a number of shows including a Circus Show and a spectacular Stunt Show. Marvel at the world in minature in Miniland where many well-known cities have been recreated out of Lego bricks. New for 1998: Ride the Dragon in the Dragon Knight's Castle. Tickets can be booked in advance.
Open 14 Mar-27 Sept, plus weekends and half term in Oct.
✲£15.50(ch £12.50, pen £11.5) Groups 25+.
🅿 🕭 ✗ *licensed* & *toilets for disabled shop* ✸ *(ex guide dogs)*
Cards: 🄰 🄱🄲🄳 🄾 🄵🄶 🄷 🄸

St George's Chapel
SL4 1NJ
☎ 01753 865538
Fax 01753 620165
The chapel is an impressive feature of Windsor Castle. Begun in 1475 by Edward IV, and completed in the reign of Henry VIII, it is a fine example of Perpendicular architecture which, with its large windows, gives a light and spacious effect. The magnificent fan vaulting on the ceiling, the chantries, the ironwork and intricate carving on the choir stalls, all add to this superb building. The choir stalls are dedicated to the Order of Knights of the Garter founded by Edward III. Each stall displays the arms of every knight who has sat there and above it are the banner and crested helm of the present holder.
Open weekdays 10-4, Sun 2-4. (Closed 26 & 27 Apr, 16-19 Jun, 24-25 Dec & occasionally at short notice).
& shop ✸
Details not confirmed for 1998

Savill Garden (Windsor Great Park)
SL4 2HT (via Wick Ln, Englefield Green, near Egham. nearest M-way junct is no 13 off M25)
☎ 01753 860222 Fax 01753 859617
The world famous Savill Garden covers some 35 acres of woodland and includes hundreds of different varieties of plants. It is at its peak in spring but, with its range of shrubs such as magnolias and rhododendrons, dry garden, herbaceous borders and formal rose gardens, there is a wealth of colour and interest throughout the year. Queen Elizabeth Temperate House is a recent addition. Special events for 1998 include plant fairs (9 May, 29 August).
Open all year, daily 10-6 (10-4 Nov -Feb). (Closed 25-26 Dec).
£3.80 (ch 16 free, pen £3.30). Party 20+.
🅿 ✗ *licensed* & *toilets for disabled shop (& plant centre)* ✸
Cards: 🄰 🄳🄲 🄵 🄷 🄸

Valley Gardens (Windsor Great Park)
SL4 2HT (off A30, approached via Wick Road, Englefield Green, Egham)
☎ 01753 860222 Fax 01753 859617
These gardens are near Virginia Water, a lake created in the 18th century. The gardens cover some 400 acres of woodland and are noted especially for their outstanding range of

rhododendrons, camellias, magnolias and other trees and shrubs. It is worth visiting at any time of the year as there are plants for each season.
Open all year, daily sunrise-sunset. (Car park 8am-7pm or sunset if earlier)
Free to pedestrians. Car park charge £3.
🅿 *(charged)* & *toilets for disabled* ♿

Windsor Castle
SL4 1NJ
☎ 01753 831118 Fax 01753 832290
The castle, which covers 13 acres is the official residence of HM The Queen and the largest inhabited castle in the world. It was begun as a wooden fort by William the Conqueror, but has been added to by almost every other monarch. Henry II erected the first stone building, including the famous Round Tower. Many alterations have been made since then. In the 14th century Edward III enlarged the royal apartments and also founded the Order of Knights of the Garter, based at Windsor. During the 17th century the Castle began to be altered from a fortress to a palace and substantial rebuilding was done during the reign of Charles II. Sir Jeffrey Wyattville (1766-1840) was the architect for alterations made by George IV. The castle is in three parts - the Upper Ward which includes the State Apartments, now magnificently restored following the fire of 1992, the Middle Ward, with its Round Tower, and the Lower Ward where St George's Chapel is situated.
Queen Mary's Dolls House which is the exquisite dolls' house, designed for Queen Mary in the 1920s by Lutyens, is also displayed at Windsor Castle. Every piece of furniture, decoration, tableware and equipment in the miniature house has been carried out in perfect detail on a scale of 1:12.
Open all year, daily except 10 April, 15 June & 25-26 Dec. Nov-Feb 10am-4pm (last admission 3pm), Mar-Oct 10am-5.30pm (last admission 4pm).
£9.50 (ch 16 £5, pen £7) Family ticket £21.50
🅿 *(400yds)* & *(except The Gallery) toilets for disabled shop* ✸
Cards: 🄰 🄳🄲 🄵 🄷 🄸

BRISTOL

Bristol City Museum & Art Gallery
Queen's Rd BS8 1RL
☎ 0117 922 3571 Fax 0117 922 2047
The museum has regional and international collections representing ancient history, natural sciences, and fine and applied arts. Displays include dinosaurs, Bristol ceramics, silver, Chinese and Japanese ceramics. A full programme of Special Exhibitions take place throughout the year. Ring for details.
Open all year, daily 10-5.
Prices under review.
P *(NCP 400 yds)* 🕭 & *(lift) toilets for disabled shop* ✸

Bristol Industrial Museum
Prince's Wharf, Prince St BS1 4RN
☎ 0117 925 1470 Fax 0117 729 7318
The museum is housed in a converted dockside transit shed. Motor and horse-drawn vehicles from the Bristol area are shown, with locally built aircraft and aero-engines. Railway exhibits include the

industrial locomotive 'Henbury', steamed about once a month. There are also machines used in local industry, and displays on the history of the port. The steam tug "Mayflower" also takes trips around the harbour most weekends in the summer.
Open Apr-Oct, Sat-Wed 10-5; Jan-Mar & Nov-Dec, Sat & Sun 10-5.
Prices under review.
🅿 *(charged)* & *toilets for disabled shop* ✸

Bristol Zoo Gardens
Clifton BS8 3HA
☎ 0117 973 8951
Fax 0117 973 6814
Enjoy an exciting real life experience and see over 300 species of wildlife in beautiful gardens. Recent additions include a large moated outdoor gorilla exhibit, a huge walk through aviary and an extensive new children's play area. These join favourites such as the Aquarium, Reptile House and the recently opened

BRISTOL
Bristol has been a crossroads of world exploration and trade since long before John Cabot left its quay for the New World in 1496. It was the main port for exporting the wool that made the West Country wealthy and during the 18th century Bristol flourished on the slave trade. Many of her fine terraces and grand buildings were built on the enormous riches this created. Clifton, once a village on the steep cliffs above the docks is the most attractive part and is where the University is to be found. Brunel's famous supension bridge was built to provide access from Clifton across the deep Avon Gorge. Nowadays Bristol is no longer a major trading port and many of the dock areas have been restored to provide leisure facilities.

Blaise Castle House Museum
Henbury Rd, Henbury BS10 7QS (4m NW of city, off B4057)
☎ 0117 950 6789 Fax 0117 959 3475
The mansion was built in the 18th century for a Quaker banker, and is now Bristol's Museum of Social History. It stands in extensive grounds which were planned by Humphry Repton. Nearby Blaise Hamlet is a picturesque little estate village designed by John Nash.
Open 1 Apr-31 Oct, Sat-Wed, 10-5.
Free.
🅿 & *shop* ✸

Discover the wonders of science at the exciting 'Hands-On' Exploratory Centre in Bristol.

Bug World and Twilight World. The popular 'hands-on' Activity Centre, the interactive Zoolympics trail, bird displays, special events and feeding time talks, make it an educational as well as enjoyable day out. Special events run throughout the school holidays. There's also a summer evening events programme which includes theatre productions and picnics. Each year there's a Christmas grotto and carol concerts.
Open all year, daily (ex 25 Dec) from 9am. Closing times approx 5.30pm (summer) 4.30pm (winter).
P *(charged)* ☕ ✗ *licensed* ♿ *toilets for disabled shop* ⊗
Details not confirmed for 1998
Cards: 🔲 ▦ 🔲 ⑤

Cabot Tower & Brandon Hill Nature Reserve
Brandon Hill, Great George St BS1
☎0117 926 0767
Fax 0117 929 7703
The tower stands over 100ft high, giving superb views for photography, and was built in 1897-8 to commemorate Cabot's arrival in North America on 24 June 1497. It stands on Brandon Hill, a municipal park since 1924, and is surrounded by a rock garden and ornamental ponds. There is also a nature reserve which was created as one of the first urban reserves in Britain. It features ponds, a hay meadow, butterfly garden, mini forest and heathland plot. The Wildlife Trust have a centre on the hill.
Open all year. Tower normally 9.30-dusk; Nature Reserve & Park open all times; Nature Reserve HQ open weekdays, 9-5 (for further details tel 0117 929 5490).
Free.
P *(0.25 mile) (pay & display meter)* ♿

Exploratory Hands-on-Science Centre
Bristol Old Station, Temple Meads BS1 6QU (Follow signs to Temple Meads train station, Centre is next to station)
☎0117 907 9000 & 907 5000 info line
Fax 0117 907 8000
As its name suggests, this is a science centre which invites the visitor to try things out. Bubbles and bridges, lights and lasers, magnets and mirrors - they are all here to discover and enjoy. Come to the Exploratory and find out for yourself! Visit the Stardome for a trip round the Galaxy or the hands-on music and sound gallery with the world's largest acoustic guitar. Special for 1998: A new permanent body gallery opening in March, and Fantastic Fireworks (Oct 31). Ring for details of these and other special events.
Open all year, daily 10-5 (Closed 23-26 Dec).
£5 (ch 5-17 £3.50, ch under 5 free). Family ticket £15.

P *(MSCP 50 yds)* ☕ ♿ *(lift to first floor) toilets for disabled shop* ⊗
Cards: 🔲 ▦

Georgian House
7 Great George St BS1 5RR
☎0117 921 1362
Fax 0117 922 2047
A carefully preserved example of a late-18th-century merchant's town house, with many original features and furnished to illustrate life both above and below stairs. New bedroom now open, with four-poster bed. Small display recounting Bristol's involvement in the slave trade.
Open Apr-Oct, Sat-Wed, 10am-5pm.
Prices under review.
P ⊗

Harveys Wine Museum
12 Denmark St BS1 5DQ
☎0117 927 5036
Fax 0117 927 5002
Founded in 1796 by a Bristol merchant, Harveys of Bristol is one of the oldest and most famous wine firms, and has been based here since the company started. The wine cellars date back to the 1220s and Bristol cream sherry was first blended in the cellars in the 1880s. Now the cellars house a collection devoted to wine including 18th-century drinking glasses, bottles, decanters, and corkscrews. There are guided tours with tutored tastings for groups (minimum 30). It is often possible for other visitors to join groups but please telephone in advance to check. The museum has just been refurbished to celebrate Harvey's bicentenary, and includes scenes depicting Bristol's wine trading history. Please telephone for details.
Open all year, Mon-Sat 10-5. Closed Sun & BH.
P *(5 mins walk) (parking meters)* ✗ *licensed shop* ⊗
Details not confirmed for 1998
Cards: 🔲 ▦ 🔲 🔲 ⑤

John Wesley's Chapel(The New Room)
36 The Horsefair, Broadmead BS1 3JE
☎0117 926 4740
This is the oldest Methodist chapel in the world. It was built in 1739 and extended in 1748, both times by John Wesley. Both chapel and living rooms above are preserved in their original form. John Wesley Day is 24 May, special events are held, please telephone for details.
Open all year, daily 10-4. (Closed Sun, Weds in winter & BH). Upstairs rooms closed 1-2pm.
Donation requested. £2.50 for guided tour.
P *(250yds)* ♿ *shop* ⊗ *(ex guide dogs)*

Maritime Heritage Centre
Gas Ferry Rd BS1 6UN
☎0117 926 0680
The centre explores 200 years of Bristol shipbuilding, with special reference to Charles Hill & Son, and their predecessor, James Hillhouse.
Open all year, daily 10-5.30, 4.30pm in winter. (Closed 24 & 25 Dec).
Free.
P *(charged)* ♿ *toilets for disabled* ⊗

Red Lodge
Park Row BS1 5LJ
☎0117 921 1360
Fax 0117 922 2047
The house was built in 1590 and then altered in 1730. It has fine oak panelling and carved stone chimneypieces and is furnished in the style of both periods. The garden has recently been laid out in Elizabethan style.
Open Apr-Oct, Sat-Wed 10am-5pm.
❋£1 (ch 16 & full time students free, concessions 50p).
P *(NCP, adjacent)* ⊗

SS Great Britain
Great Western Dock, Gas Ferry Rd BS1 6TY (off Cumberland Rd)
☎0117 926 0680 Fax 0117 925 5788
The SS Great Britain was built and launched in Bristol on 19 July 1843. She was the first ocean-going propeller-driven, iron ship in history. Designed by Isambard Kingdom Brunel, she had a varied active life for 43 years, both as a liner and a cargo vessel. Her first voyages were to America, then for some 25 years she carried thousands of emigrants to Australia: the voyages to Australia were interrupted twice when she became a troop ship for the Crimean War and the Indian Mutiny. Abandoned in the Falkland Islands in 1886, her wreck provided storage facilities in Port Stanley for 50 years. In 1970 what remained of her rusting carcass was towed back to Bristol and she is now being restored to her original 1843 appearance at the Great Western Dock in which she was built.
Open all year daily 10-5.30, 4.30pm in winter. (Closed 24 & 25 Dec).
£4.50 (ch £3, pen £3.50). Family ticket £12.50.
P *(charged)* ☕ ♿ *shop* ⊗
Cards: 🔲 ▦ 🔲 🔲 🔲 🔲 🔲 ⑤

BUCKINGHAMSHIRE

AYLESBURY ▦
Buckinghamshire County Museum
St Mary's Square, Church St HP20 2QP
☎01296 331441
Fax 01296 334884
Recently refurbished, Buckinghamshire's largest museum consists of a range of period buildings. Innovative, 'touchable' displays are based on eight county-linked themes, including lacemaking, villages, wildlife, Romans and Celts, jewellery and fossils. There are interpretive galleries, featuring a 16th century wall painting in a medieval dwelling and a 'hands on' 19th century dining room, and a large regional Art Gallery showing several exhibitions throughout the year. Various special exhibitions will also take place, please telephone for details. Also on site is the Roald Dahl Children's Gallery, a magical world where Roald Dahl's stories come to life through hands-on exhibits in this lively, unique 2-storey gallery, which includes the Giant Peach, Fantastic Mr Fox's tunnel, and the Great Glass Elevator.
Open all year, Mon-Sat 10-5, Sun & BHs 2-5. (Closed 25-26 Dec). Roald Dahl Children's Gallery as above in school holidays, Mon-Fri 3-5 term time.
Free to general museum, occasional charge for special exhibitions. Dahl Gallery £2.50 (ch 3 £2, under 3 free), term time £1.50 (ch £1.25), pre-booking advisable.
P *(200 yds)* ☕ ♿ *(purpose built restrooms for disabled chair lifts) toilets for disabled shop* ⊗
Cards: 🔲 ▦ 🔲 ⑤

BEACONSFIELD ▦
Bekonscot Model Village
Warwick Rd HP9 2PL (2.7m junc 2 M40, 4m junc 16 M25).
☎01494 672919
Fax 01494 675284
Bekonscot is a miniature wonderland, depicting rural England in the 1930s. Be a giant in this magical patch of nostalgia, with a Gauge 1 model railway meandering through six little villages, each with their own miniature population going about daily routines.   ➤

Open 14 Feb-1 Nov, daily 10-5.
£3.60 (ch £1.80, pen & students £2.50).
Party 13+.
🅿 💺 ♿ *(wheelchair loan) toilets for disabled shop ❀ (ex guide dogs)*

CHALFONT ST GILES
Chiltern Open Air Museum
Newland Park, Gorelands Ln HP8 4AD
(off B4442)
☎ *01494 871117 & 875542*
Fax 01494 872163
The museum aims to preserve traditional
Chilterns buildings by rebuilding them
here. Among the buildings dismantled
and brought to the site are a toll house,
cart sheds, stables, granaries, a forge,
barns, an Iron Age house, a pair of 18th-
century cottages and a 1947 prefab.
There is a nature trail through the 45
acres of parkland and there is also an
adventure playground. Special events
planned for 1998 include Rare Breeds
Show (24/25 May), Live Crafts (2-4 May),
Childrens's Days (1/2 Aug), Transport Day
(13 Sep) - ring to confirm dates.
Open Apr-Sep, Tue-Fri 2-6, wknds
& BH's 10-6; Aug, daily 10-6; Oct-1
Nov 10-5.
£4 (ch 16 £2.50 over 60's £3.50, ch 4
free). Family ticket £12.
🅿 💺 ♿ *(Braille guide books & taped*
guides available, wheelchairs) toilets for
disabled shop

Milton's Cottage
Dean Way HP8 4JH (5m from M40
junct 2)
☎ *01494 872313*
This timber-framed, 16th-century cottage
with its charming garden, is the only
surviving home in which John Milton
lived and worked. He completed Paradise
Lost and started Paradise Regained here.
First editions of these works are among
the many rare books and artefacts on
display. Ring for details of an arts festival
which should take place mid-June.
Open Mar-Oct, Wed-Sun 10-1 & 2-6. Also
open Spring & Summer BH.

£2 (ch 15 60p). Party 20+.
🅿 ✗ *licensed ♿ (special parking area*
closer to cottage) shop ❀

CHICHELEY
Chicheley Hall
MK16 9JJ (A422 between Newport
Pagnell and Bedford)
☎ *01234 391252 Fax 01234 391388*
Built for Sir John Chester between 1719
and 1723, this is one of the finest and
least-altered 18th-century houses in
England, with wonderful Georgian
craftsmanship in its brickwork, carving,
joinery and plasterwork. It has a naval
museum, English sea pictures and
furniture, and an 18th-century dovecote.
Open Apr-May & Aug. Easter Sun/Mon,
May B/H, Aug BH & BH Mon 2.30-6.
Last entry 5pm. Booked parties at most
times.
£5 (ch £1.50). Parties 20+.
🅿 💺 *shop ❀*

CLIVEDEN
Cliveden
SL6 0JA (2m N of Taplow)
☎ *01628 605069 Fax 01628 669461*
The 375 acres of garden and woodland
overlook the River Thames, and include a
magnificent parterre, topiary, lawns with
box hedges, and rose and water gardens.
The palatial house, home of the Astors, is
now a hotel, 3 rooms only of the house
can be visited on certain afternoons.
Open Grounds Mar-2 Nov daily 11-6,
Nov-Dec daily 11-4 (Woodlands only 1
Mar-1 Nov). House Apr-Oct, Thu & Sun 3-
6 by timed ticket. (Last admission 5.30)
Grounds: £4.80. House: £1 extra. Family
ticket £12.
🅿 ✗ *licensed ♿ (powered vehicle &*
wheelchairs available) toilets for disabled
shop ❀ (ex in woodland)

HIGH WYCOMBE
Wycombe Local History & Chair Museum
Castle Hill House, Priory Av HP13 6PX
☎ *01494 421895 Fax 01494 421897*

The museum is situated in an 18th-
century house set in attractive and
historic grounds. The displays explore the
history of the Wycombe area focusing on
the chair making industry, with
interactive displays, changing exhibitions
and more.
Open all year, Mon-Sat 10-5, Sun
(seasonal-please telephone for details).
Closed on BHs except special events -
ring for details.
Free.
🅿 ♿ *shop ❀*

HUGHENDEN
Hughenden Manor
HP14 4LA (1.5m N of High Wycombe, on
W side of A4128)
☎ *01494 532580*
Benjamin Disraeli, later Earl of
Beaconsfield and twice Prime Minister,
bought the house in 1847 and lived there
until his death in 1881. It still has many of
his books and other possessions.
House open 1-30 Mar, Sat & Sun only.
Apr-Oct, Wed-Sun & BH Mon 1-5. Last
admission 4.30. Gardens same dates as
house 12-5. Park open all year. (closed on
Good Friday)
£4. Family ticket £10. Garden only £1 (ch
50p). Park free.
🅿 💺 ♿ *(braille leaflet and taped guide)*
toilets for disabled shop ❀ (ex in park &
car park only)

LONG CRENDON
Courthouse
HP18 9AN (2m N of Thame, via B4011)
Probably built as a wool store in the early
1400s, but also used as a manorial
courthouse until the late 19th century,
the timber-framed building stands out,
even in a picturesque village of 16th-and
17th-century cottages. Although the
windows and doors have been altered
and the chimney stack is Tudor, the
magnificent timber roof is original.
Open, Upper storey Apr-Sep, Wed 2-6,
Sat, Sun & BH Mons 11-6.
£1
P *(street) ❀*

MIDDLE CLAYDON
Claydon House
MK18 2EY (off A413, entrance by North
drive only).
☎ *01296 730349 Fax 01296 738511*
The rather sober exterior of this 18th-
century house gives no clue to the
extravagances that lie inside, in the form
of fantastic rococo carvings. Ceilings,
cornices, walls and overmantels are
adorned with delicately carved fruits,
birds, beasts and flowers by Luke
Lightfoot, and his Chinese room is
particularly splendid. The second Earl of
Verney commissioned Lightfoot to

decorate the rooms and built many other
additions to the house besides; but his
ambition eventually bankrupted him and
by 1783 he had to sell up. His successor
proceeded to demolish two-thirds of the
house. Florence Nightingale was a
frequent visitor and relics of her Crimean
experiences are displayed here.
Open 4 Apr-1 Nov: Sat-Wed 1-5pm,
Closed Good Friday. Last admission
4.30pm.
£4. Family ticket £10.
🅿 💺 ♿ *(Braille guide) toilets for disabled*
❀ (ex car park)

QUAINTON
Buckinghamshire Railway Centre
Quainton Rd Station HP22 4BY (Off A41
Aylesbury to Bicester Road. 7miles NW
of Aylesbury)
☎ *01296 655720 & 655450 (info) Fax*
01296 655720
The Centre houses an interesting and
varied collection of about 20 locomotives
with 40 carriages and wagons from
places as far afield as South Africa, Egypt
and America. Many items date from the
last century, while others were built as
recently as the 1960s. Visitors can take a
ride on full-size and miniature steam
trains and stroll around the 20-acre site to
see locomotives and rolling stock. Other
memorabilia is displayed in a small
museum. The Centre regularly runs
steam locomotive driving courses for
visitors including 2 hours on the footplate
actually driving and firing a steam engine.
Special events for 1998 include: Easter
Circus Days (12-13 April), Annual Bus
Rally (25 May), Thomas the Tank Engine
(13-14 June & 12-13 September), Vintage
Vehicle Rally (31 August).
Open with engines in steam Etr-Oct, Sun
& BH Mon; Jul-Aug, Wed; 11am-5pm.
Dec Sat & Sun Santa's Magical
Steamings-advanced booking
recommended. Also open for static
viewing Sun Jan-Mar 11-4 & Sat Jan-Oct
11-4.
Steaming Days; £3.50 (ch & pen £2.50).
Family ticket £10. BH wknds £4.50 (ch &
pen £3). Family ticket £14. Static viewing;
£2 (ch & pen £1).
🅿 💺 *shop*
Cards: 💳

STOWE
Stowe House
MK18 5EH
☎ *01280 813164 ext 282 Fax 01280*
822769
Set within the National Trust's
landscaped gardens, Stowe is one of the
most majestic houses of the 18th
century. Stowe owes its pre-eminence to
the vision and wealth of two owners.
Viscount Cobham called in the leading

Not evidence of poltergeist activity, but an exhibit at the Wycombe Local History
and Chair Museum!

The elegant grounds of West Wycombe Park sweep down from the Palladian mansion to a curving artificial lake.

designers of the day to lay out the gardens and commissioned several leading architects - Vanbrugh, Gibbs, Kent and Leoni - to decorate them with garden temples. From 1750 to 1779 Earl Temple, his nephew and successor, continued to expand and embellish both gardens and house. The house has now become a major public school.
Open 23 Mar-12 Apr & 6 Jul-6 Sep. Daily 2-5pm, 12-5pm Sun. May occasionally be closed if booked for private functions. Please ring for confirmation.
£2 (ch £1).
🅿 ♿ *shop* ✖ *(ex guide dogs)*
Cards: 🔳 💳

Stowe Landscape Gardens
HP18 5EH (3m NW of Buckingham)
☎01280 822850 Fax 01280 822437
One of the supreme creations of the Georgian era, the first formal layout was adorned with many buildings by Vanbrugh, Kent and Gibbs; in the 1730s Kent designed the Elysian Fields in a more naturalistic style, one of the earliest examples of the reaction against formality, leading to the evolution of the landscape garden; miraculously, this beautiful garden survives; its sheer scale must make it Britain's largest work of art. Special events for 1998 include: Music and Fireworks, Kite festival and Open Air Theatre. Please ring for details.
Open 20 Mar-12 Apr, daily; 13 Apr-5 Jul, Mon, Wed, Fri & Sun; 6 Jul-6 Sep daily; 7 Sep-1 Nov, Mon, Wed, Fri & Sun; 27 Dec-5 Jan, daily. 10-5 (or dusk if earlier). Last admission 1hr before closing. (Closed 24-26 Dec).
£4.40(ch £2.10). Family ticket £11.00
🅿 ♿ *(unsuitable manual wheelchairs,powered batricars available) toilets for disabled shop* ✖

WADDESDON
Waddesdon Manor
HP18 OJH (gates off A41)
☎01296 651211 Fax 01296 651293
Waddesdon Manor was designed by the French architect Destaileur in the 1870s for Baron Ferdinand de Rothschild. The Renaissance style château was conceived as a showcase for the Baron's prodigious collection of works of art, which includes French Royal furniture, Savonnerie carpets and Sèvres porcelain as well as important portraits by Gainsborough and Reynolds and works by Dutch and Flemish masters of the 17th century. The wine cellars, which house more than 15,000 bottles of Rothschild wine, are also open to the public. The garden includes a fine example of a Victorian parterre, a Rococo-style aviary, shrubberies and woodland. Many events are organised

throughout the year including floodlit openings, wine tastings, garden workshops and collection study days. Please ring 01296 651226 for details.
Open, Grounds & Aviary only, Mar-20 Dec, Wed-Sun & BH Mon 10-5. House 2 Apr-1 Nov, Thu-Sun & BH Mon 11-4, also open Wed in Jul & Aug. Entrance by timed ticket.
Grounds & Aviary £3 (ch £1.50). Family ticket £7.50. House - Adult & ch £6. Tickets bookable in advance at booking charge of £2.50 per transaction (tel 01296 651226).
🅿 ✖ *licensed* ♿ *(wheelchairs available braille guide) toilets for disabled shop* ✖ *(ex guide dogs in grounds)* ✖
Cards: 🔳 💳 📇 🔳 ⑤

WEST WYCOMBE
West Wycombe Caves
HP14 3AJ (on A40)
☎01494 524411 (office) & 533739 (caves) Fax 01494 471617
The entrance to West Wycombe caves is halfway up the hill that dominates the village. On the summit stands the parish church and the mausoleum of the Dashwood family. The caves are not natural but were dug on the orders of Sir Francis Dashwood between 1748 and 1752. Sir Francis, the Chancellor of the Exchequer, was also the founder of the Hell Fire Club, whose members were reputed to have held outrageous and blasphemous parties in the caves, which extend to approximately one-third of a mile underground. The entrance consists of a large forecourt with flint walls, from which a brick tunnel leads into the caves, where tableaux and curiosities are exhibited in various chambers, including the Great Hall of Statues.
Open all year, Mar-Oct, daily 11-6; Nov-Feb, Sat & Sun 1-5.
£3 (ch & pen £1.50). Party 20+.
🅿 ♿ ♿ *toilets for disabled shop garden centre* ✖ *(ex guide dogs)*

West Wycombe Park
HP14 3AJ (S of A40)
☎01628 488675
Set in 300 acres of beautiful parkland, the house was rebuilt in the Palladian style, between 1745 and 1771, for Sir Francis Dashwood. Inside there is a good collection of tapestries, furniture and paintings. Of particular note are the painted ceilings by Borgnis. The park was laid out in the 18th century and given an artificial lake and classical temples, some of which were designed by Nicholas Revett. The Temple of Venus has recently been reconstructed. The park was later rearranged by a follower of 'Capability' Brown.
Open, House & grounds Jun-Aug, Sun-

Thu 2-6. Grounds only 1 Apr-end May, Sun & Wed 2-6 & Etr, May Day & Spring BH Sun & Mon 2-6. Last admission 5.15. Entry by timed tickets on wkdays. Parties must book in advance.
House & grounds £4.40. Grounds only £2.60. Family ticket £11.
🅿 ♿ *(partial access to ground floor & gardens)* ✖ ✖

WING
Ascott
LU7 OPS (.50m E, on S side of A418)
☎01296 688242
Fax 01296 681904
The house, once the property of the de Rothschilds, was given to the National Trust in 1950. The bequest included a collection of French and Chippendale furniture, pictures by such notable painters as Hogarth, Gainsborough and Rubens. There is also a collection of paintings by Hobbema, Cuyp and other Dutch painters. The collection of Oriental porcelain has some outstanding pieces of K'ang Hsi and of the Ming and Sung dynasties. Outside there are 260 acres of land of which 12 are gardens. There are many unusual trees, with thousands of naturalised bulbs, and also a formal garden.
Open: Apr-7 May daily ex Mon 2-6: 13 May-30 Aug Wed & Sun 2-6.
House & Garden £5.40.
🅿 ♿ *(wheelchairs available) toilets for disabled* ✖ ✖

CAMBRIDGESHIRE

CAMBRIDGE
The heart of the ancient university city is the row of colleges which lines the River Cam and overlooks the Backs on the other side of the river. This area of lawns and trees was reclaimed from rough marshland by Richard Bently, Master of Trinity College from 1669 to 1734, and it makes a lovely place to walk. In medieval times, this would have been a very different scene: the Cam was a busy commercial river, and the town was a centre for trade. The university is considered to have begun in 1209, when a group of students arrived after fleeing from riots in Oxford. The colleges are open to the public on most days during daylight, though there are certain restrictions during term time. A good place to start is King's College Chapel, with its glorious fan vaulting. There is a permanent exhibition, 'Kings: The Building of a Chapel', which brings together the chapel's history, architecture, art, heraldry and music. From here, the colleges of Trinity, St John's, Clare and others can easily be reached on foot - or hire a bicycle to see the city in the authentic way.

Cambridge & County Folk Museum
2/3 Castle St CB3 0AQ
☎01223 355159
The timber-framed White Horse Inn is an appealing setting for the Folk Museum. It houses items covering the everyday life of the people of Cambridgeshire from the 17th century to the present day. There are also temporary exhibitions. Special exhibitions and children's activity days take place throughout the year. Please telephone for details.
Open all year, Apr-Sep, Mon-Sat 10.30-5, Sun 2-5. Oct-Mar, Tue-Sat 10.30-5, Sun 2-5. (Last admissions 30 mins before closing) Closed Jan 1, Good Friday, Dec 24-31.
£1 (ch 5-16, disabled, students, UB40s & pen 50p)
🅿 *(300 yds) (pay and display on street parking)* ♿ *(braille & tape guides) shop* ✖

Fitzwilliam Museum
Trumpington St CB2 1RB
☎01223 332900 Fax 01223 332923
The Fitzwilliam is one of the oldest museums in Britain, and is housed in an imposing building designed for the purpose in 1834. It is the fine art museum of the University of Cambridge and, in the early days, it was only open to 'properly dressed' members of the public, and then only three days a week. The museum has particularly good English and Continental ceramics and English glass, with some outstanding Oriental work, and paintings by Titian, Veronese, Canaletto and many other famous names, including leading French Impressionists. There are Egyptian, Greek and Roman antiquities, and other treasures include medieval illuminated manuscripts, ivories, miniatures, carvings and armour. There are special exhibitions throughout the year. Regular guided tours for which a small charge is made are conducted on Sundays at 2.30pm. Other times by prior arrangment.
Open all year Tue-Sat 10-5, Sun 2.15-5 plus Etr Mon, Spring & Summer BH. (Closed Good Fri, May Day & 24 Dec-1 Jan).
🅿 *(400 yds) (2hr max, metered)* ♿ ♿ *(preferably pre-arranged) toilets for disabled shop* ✖
Details not confirmed for 1998
Cards: 🔳 💳

Scott Polar Research Institute Museum
Lensfield Rd CB2 1ER
☎01223 336540 Fax 01223 336549
The institute is an international centre for polar studies, and has a museum with displays of Arctic and Antarctic expeditions, with special emphasis on those of Captain Scott. Other exhibits include Eskimo work and other arts of the polar regions. Also shown are displays on current scientific exploration. A special exhibition is shown every summer.
Open all year, Mon-Sat 2.30-4. Closed for some public & university hols. The museum will be closed completely until July 1998 for construction work.
Free.
🅿 *(400mtrs)* ♿ *shop* ✖

University Botanic Garden
Cory Lodge, Bateman St CB2 1JF (1.5m S of city centre)
☎01223 336265 Fax 01223 336278
The garden was founded in 1762, mainly for the study of medicinal plants, and was transferred to its present site in 1846. It now covers 40 acres and has interesting collections of trees and shrubs; botanical groups of herbaceous perennials; along with a lake, woodland and rock garden. The glasshouses contain sub-tropical and tropical plants. Features include a Winter Garden, Chronological Bed, Scented Garden and collection of native British plants. The Gardens hold nine National Collections including Geranium, Tulip and Alchemilla.
Open all year daily 10-6 (summer), 10-5 (autumn & spring), (10-4) winter. Glasshouses 10-12.30 & 2-3.45. Closed 25-26 Dec. Entry by Bateman St and Hills Rd gates on weekdays & by Bateman Street gate on weekends & BH.
£1.50 (ch & pen £1).
🅿 *(on street parking bays-pay & display)* ♿ ♿ *(scented garden for the visually impaired) toilets for disabled shop* ✖ *(ex guide dogs)*

University Museum of Archaeology & Anthropology
Downing St CB2 3DZ
☎01223 337733 Fax 01223 333503
The museum covers humanity's development from the earliest times throughout the world, with anthropolgy displays and extensive sections on British archaeology and local archaeology in particular. The Torres Strait exhibition opens summer 1998.
Open all year Tues-Sat 2-4.30.(Closed 1 wk Etr, Aug BH & 24 Dec-2 Jan)
Free.
🅿 *(100yds) (short-term parking)* ♿ *(lift available) shop* ✖

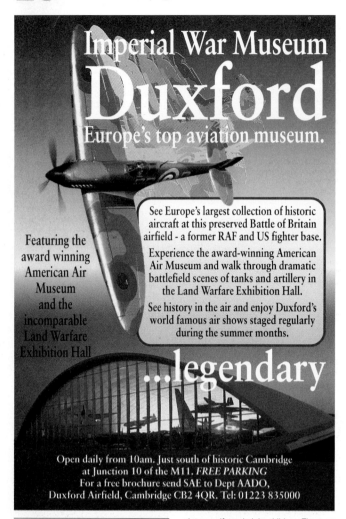

DUXFORD

Duxford Airfield
CB2 4QR (off junc 10 of M11 on A505)
☎ *01223 835000 Fax 01223 837267*
This former Battle of Britain fighter station has hangars dating from World War I. It is now home to most of the Imperial War Museum's collection of military aircraft, armoured fighting vehicles, midget submarines and other large exhibits. There are over 140 historic aircraft on the airfield, and also on display is the Duxford Aviation Society's collection of civil aircraft, including the prototype Concorde 01. Major flying displays are held in summer, and pleasure flights can be taken during summer weekends. Those with aircraft may apply to land them at the airfield; those without can try the popular flight simulator. View Europe's finest collection of historic American combat aircraft, while children will also enjoy two adventure playgrounds and a hands-on exhibition which explains how aircraft fly. Special events for 1998 include: Spitfire Anniversary Air Show (2-3 May), other air shows (7 June, 6 September, 11 October) and a Military Vehicle & Large-Scale Flying Model Display (1-2 August).
Open all year, mid Mar-mid Oct daily 10-6; mid Oct-mid Mar daily 10-4. (Closed 24-26 Dec)
£6.40 (ch, students, UB40 £3.20 pen £4.20). Family ticket £18.00. Under 5's free, Disabled visitors and carers charged at half appropriate full rate. Parties.
🅿 🍴 ♿ *(wheelchair available-phone in advance) toilets for disabled shop* ✖
Cards: ▭ ▭ ▭ ▭

ELY

Oliver Cromwell's House
29 St Mary's St CB7 4HF (adjacent to St Mary's church)
☎ *01353 662062 Fax 01353 668518*
Cromwell inherited the house and local estates from a maternal uncle and moved here in 1636, along with his mother,

sisters, wife and eight children. There are displays and period rooms dealing with Cromwell's life, the Civil War and domestic life in the 17th century, as well as the history of The Fens and the house itself, from its medieval origins to its role as an inn in the 19th century.
Open all year: Apr-Sep, daily 10-6; Oct-Mar, Mon-Sat 10-5.15.
❊*£2.30 (concessions £1.80). Family ticket £5.*
🅿 *(100yds)* ♿ *shop*

Ely Cathedral
CB7 4DL
☎ *01353 667735 Fax 01353 665658*
The Octagon Tower of Ely Cathedral can be seen for miles as it rises above the surrounding flat fenland. A monastery was founded on the site by St Etheldreda in 673, but the present cathedral church dates from 1083 and is a magnificent example of Romanesque architecture.
Open daily, summer 7am-7pm, winter 7.30-6 (5pm Sun).
£3 (concessions £2.20). Ch 12 free in family group.
🅿 🍴 ✗ *licensed* ♿ *toilets for disabled shop* ✖ *(ex guide dogs)*

The Stained Glass Museum
The Cathedral CB7 4DN
☎ *01353 660347 Fax 01223 327367*
The museum is situated in the cathedral and was established in 1972 to rescue and preserve fine stained glass, which might otherwise be lost and is the only one of its kind in the country. One exhibit shows how stained-glass windows are designed and made. There is an exhibition of approximately 100 panels dating from the 13th century to the present day, they are displayed at eye level in back-lit cases. A large panel, from the Royal Collection at Windsor, is on loan to the museum for twenty-five years and depicts George III from a portrait by Sir Joshua Reynolds executed by James Pearson in 1793. An audio tour lasts 25 minutes, and there are activities for

children, as well as a souvenir and book shop. The museum is undergoing refurbishment during 1998 and may be closed for one or two months. Please ring to avoid disappointment.
Open daily, Mon-Fri 10.30-4.30, Sat & BH 10.30-5 & Sun 12-6.
£2.50 (ch, students & pen £1.50). Party 10+.
🅿 *400yds* 🍴 *shop* ✖ *(ex guide dogs)*

HAMERTON

Hamerton Wildlife Park
PE17 5RE (off A14 at junct with B660 signed Old Weston/Kimbolton)
☎ *01832 293362 Fax 01832 293677*
A wildlife breeding centre, dedicated to the practical conservation of endangered species including gibbons, marmosets, lemurs, wildcats, meerkats, Britain's only

group of breeding sloths and many more. There is also a large and varied bird collection, with several species unique to Hamerton. Over 120 species in all. Other attractions include a children's play area, and undercover viewing of many mammals.
Open Summer daily 10.30-6; winter daily 10.30-4. (Closed Xmas)
🅿 🍴 ♿ *toilets for disabled shop* ✖
Details not confirmed for 1998

LINTON

Chilford Hundred Vineyard
Chilford Hall CB1 6LE (signposted from A1307 and A11)
☎ *01223 892641 Fax 01223 894056*
Taste and buy award-winning wines from the largest vineyard in Cambridgeshire. See the grapes growing in the 18-acre

One of Linton Zoo's famous Sumatran tigers.

vineyard and take a winery tour to learn how English wine is made and appreciate the subtle difference between each of the Chilford quality wines. Special Events include: Antique Fair (1-4 May), East Midlands Doll Fair (24 May, 6 Sep), Eastern Events Craft Fair (To be confirmed), Farm Bygones Auction (11 Apr & 24 Oct), National Patchwork Exhibition (27-29 Mar & 13-15 Nov).
Open 1 Apr-30 Oct 11-5.30.
Guided tours £4.50 (ch free). Party 15+.
P ⬤ & toilets for disabled shop
Cards: 🔲 🔲 🔲 🔲 🔲 🔲

Linton Zoological Gardens
Hadstock Rd CB1 6NT (exit M11 at junct 9/10, situated on B1052 off A604/A1307, signposted)
☎01223 891308 Fax 01223 891077
Conservation and education are the main concerns of this zoo which was established in 1972. The many species of animals and birds are housed in 16 acres of landscaped enclosures as like their natural habitats as possible. There is a herd of 12 Aldabra giant tortoises, Grevy's zebra, Brazilian tapir, Golden Lion tamarins, snow leopards, Toco toucans, Sumatran tigers and many others. A special education programme enhances and complements the conservation work and will include days when you can meet and touch boa constrictors, as well as other reptiles, bats, parrots and owls. 24 hour recorded information line 0891 424201.
Open daily 10-6 or dusk (ex 25 Dec). Last admission 45 minutes before closing time.
❊£4 (ch 2-13 £3, pen £3.75).
P ⬤ & toilets for disabled shop ✖

LODE
Anglesey Abbey
CB5 9EJ (6m NE of Cambridge on B1102 (signposted from A14).)
☎01223 811200 Fax 01223 811200
A medieval undercroft has survived from the priory founded here in 1135, but the

house dates mainly from 1600. Thomas Hobson of 'Hobson's choice' was one of the owners. A later owner was Lord Fairhaven, who amassed the huge collection of pictures, including hundreds of views of Windsor Castle. He also laid out the beautiful gardens, with a great collection of garden statuary.
Open House: 21 Mar-11 Oct, Wed-Sun & BH Mon 1-5; closed Good Fri. Garden: 21 Mar-1 Nov, Wed-Sun & BH Mon 11-5.30; 6 Jul-13 Sep, daily 11-5.30; Lode Mill: 21 Mar-1 Nov, Wed-Sun & BH Mons 1pm-5pm. Last admission 4.30pm.
'Snowdrop' weekends 7/8, 14/15, 21/22 Feb 11am-4pm.
£5.80 (ch £2.90). Sun & BH Mon £6.80. Garden only £3.40. Party rates available.
P ⬤ ✖ licensed & (electric buggy, braille guide) toilets for disabled shop garden centre ✖ (ex guide dogs) ✖
Cards: 🔲 🔲 🔲

PETERBOROUGH
Longthorpe Tower
☎01733 268482
Rare wall paintings of religious and educational subjects are on show in this 13th to 14th century fortified house, which formerly belonged to the de Thorpe family. The house is unique in having the finest surviving medieval domestic wall paintings in Northern Europe.
Open Apr-1 Nov, daily 10-6 (or dusk if earlier). Wknds & BH's 12-5.
£1.30 (ch 70p, students, pen & UB40 £1).
✖ ⬤

Peterborough Cathedral
PE1 1XS (access from A1 juncts with A605 or A47)
☎01733 343342 Fax 01733 52465
Behind the huge Early English arches and Perpendicular porch of the West Front, is one of the finest examples of Norman architecture in the country with superb examples of early rib-vaulting in the aisles and a truly magnificent Norman apse. The painted wooden ceiling dates from

1220. East of the apse is the New Building (1496-1508) with exquisite fan vaulting. The former grave of Mary Queen of Scots is in the South Presbytery aisle. American music festival - 26 Jun-4 Jul.
Open all year, daily 8.30-5.15 (8pm summer) Free - donations towards the cost of upkeep are requested.
P (300yds) (no parking within cathedral precincts) ⬤ & (touch & hearing centre, braille guide, ramps to grnd floor) shop ✖ (ex guide dogs or in grounds)
Cards: 🔲

RAMSEY
Abbey Gatehouse
Abbey School
The ruins of this 15th-century gatehouse, together with the 13th-century Lady Chapel, are all that remain of the abbey. Half of the gatehouse was taken away after the Dissolution. Built in ornate late-Gothic style, it has panelled buttresses, and friezes around both the doorway and the oriel window above it.
Open Apr-Oct, daily 10-5 (or dusk).
Free.
✖ ✖

WANSFORD
Nene Valley Railway
Wansford Station, Stibbington PE8 6LR (A1 west of Peterborough)
☎01780 784444 Fax 01780 784440
A preserved steam railway with seven-and-a-half miles of track through the picturesque Nene Valley, and locomotives and rolling stock from Europe and the UK. Passengers can enjoy a leisurely train ride along the River Nene. There is a museum, engine shed, cafe and souvenir shop. There are facilities for the disabled at Wansford and a specially adapted carriage on each train.
Open end Feb-Etr, Sun; Apr, Sep & Oct, wknds; May-Aug, daily ex Mondays, (but inc BH Mondays). Some midweek days at other times.
£7.50 (ch £3.50, other concessions £5.50). Family ticket £17.50. Prices under review.
P ⬤ & (disabled access to trains) toilets for disabled shop
Cards: 🔲 🔲 🔲 🔲 🔲

WIMPOLE
Wimpole Hall
SG8 0BW (M11 junct 12, 8miles SW of Cambridge off A603)
☎01223 207257 Fax 01223 207838
Although Wimpole Hall is one of the grandest mansions in East Anglia, it is perhaps the 360 acres of parkland that make it unusual. The parkland was devised and planted by no less than four of the country's celebrated landscape designers, Charles Bridgeman, 'Capability' Brown, Sanderson Miller and Humphrey Repton. Under the pastures lie the remains of a medieval village with evidence of tracks and ridge-and-furrow farming. The house, which was given to the National Trust in 1976, dates back to 1640, but was altered into a large 18th-century mansion with a Georgian façade. The inside is the work of a number of important architects. Lord Harley's library and the gallery are the work of James Gibbs, and the Yellow Drawing Room was designed by Sir John Soane in about 1793. The chapel has a wonderful painted trompe l'oeil ceiling by Sir James Thornhill. The Garden has two recently restored colourful parterres. Special events for 1998 include: Swing concert with fireworks (18 July), The Blues Band with fireworks (19 July), The Cotton Club with fireworks (22 August), Alan Price (23 August), Christmas Craft Fair (21-22 November).
Open 14-Mar-1 Nov, Tue-Thu, Sat & Sun & Good Fri 1-5, BH Sun & Mon 11-5. Also open Fri in Aug 1-5.
£5.50 (ch £2.25). Party. Joint ticket with Home Farm £7.50. Garden only £2.
P ⬤ ✖ licensed & (braille guide, battery operated vehicle, stairlift) toilets for disabled shop ✖ (ex park only) ✖
Cards: 🔲 🔲 🔲 🔲 🔲

Wimpole Home Farm
SG8 0BW (M11 junct 12 8m SW of Cambridge off A603)
☎01223 207257
Fax 01223 207838
When built in 1794, the Home Farm was one of the most advanced agricultural enterprises in the country. The group of thatched and timbered buildings was designed by Sir John Soane for the 3rd Earl of Hardwicke. The Great Barn, now restored, holds a display of farm machinery and implements of the kind used at Wimpole over the past two centuries. On the farm there is a wide selection of rare breeds of domestic animals, including the black-and-white Bagot goat which was rescued from extinction. In the stables, there are once more the rare breed of Suffolk Punch horses. A special children's corner and a woodland play area are additional attractions. Special events planned for 1998 include: Lambing Weekends (14-15, 21-22, 28-29 March), Children's Fun Days (13 April, 4 & 25 May), Heavy Horse Show & Craft Fair (5-6 September).
Open 14 Mar-1 Nov, Tue-Thu & Sat-Sun; daily Aug; Good Fri & Mon 10.30-5; 3 Nov-6 Mar Sat & Sun 11-4. (Closed Xmas & New Year).
NT members £2.20 (ch £1.10). Non members £4.20 (ch £2.50, under 3 free). Party. Joint ticket with Hall £7.50
P ⬤ ✖ licensed & (braille guide) toilets for disabled shop
Cards: 🔲 🔲 🔲 🔲 🔲 🔲

WISBECH
Peckover House & Garden
North Bank PE13 1JR
☎01945 583463 Fax 01945 583463
In a town with many elegant Georgian merchant's houses, Peckover House is one of the finest. It is named after a banker who purchased the house in 1777. His bank was part of the group which formed Barclays Bank in 1896. The house dates from 1722 and the interior has Rococo decoration in plaster and wood. The two-acre garden is a delightful and colourful example of Victorian planting, still with its 19th-century design. In the kitchen garden there are greenhouses with orange trees still bearing fruit after 250 years.
Open, House, Garden & Tearoom 28 Mar-1 Nov, wknds, Wed & BH Mon 12.30-5.30pm. Garden only: Apr-Oct, Mon & Tue & Thur 12.30-5.30.
House & garden £3.20 (ch £1.60). Party. Garden only £2 on days when only garden is open.
P (400yds) ⬤ & toilets for disabled ✖ ✖

Wisbech & Fenland Museum
Museum Square PE13 1ES (on A17)
☎01945 583817
Fax 01945 589050
The museum, which was purpose-built in 1847 and retains almost all of its original cases and fittings, contains a fine collection of ceramics and *objets d'art* and has a new gallery of geology. There are exhibits on the archaeology and natural history of Wisbech and the surrounding Fenland. Many items relate to Fenland life. Also of interest are the pictures; oils, water colours and photographs; the European and Oriental art; and exhibitions: Thomas Clarkson - Slavery and the Slave Trade, History from Coins, and The Middle Ages. Parish Registers, and a collection of over 14,000 books including early manuscripts, originally forming the library of the literary society, are in the town library. There is a programme of special exhibitions and evening lectures. Special events for 1998 include: Townshend 200th Anniversary Exhibition (Townshend was a major benefactor of this museum and the V&A) - 7 Mar-25 Apr, Peckover Exhibition (important local family and museum benefactors) - July-August.
Open all year, Tue-Sat 10-5 (4pm Oct-Mar). Closed Xmas.
Free. (Museum libraries & archives available by appointment only).
P (100 yds) shop ✖

CHESHIRE

BEESTON
Beeston Castle
CW6 9TX (on minor road off A49 or A41)
☎01829 260464
This ruined stronghold dates back to around 1220 and was built by the Earl Ranuf of Chester in an almost inaccessible position. Set on a steep hill, the ruins include the remains of the inner and outer wards, and give spectacular views of the surrounding countryside. An exhibition explains the history of the castle.
Open all year, Apr-1 Nov, daily 10-6 (or dusk if earlier); 2 Nov-31 Mar daily 10-4. £2.70 (ch £1.40, concessions £2.00).
🅿 shop ⌀ *(in certain areas)* ♿

CAPESTHORNE
Capesthorne Hall
SK11 9JY (On A34 between Congleton and Wilmslow)
☎01625 861221 & 861779
Fax 01625 861619
Capesthorne has been the home of the Bromley-Davenport family and their ancestors, the Capesthornes and the Wards, since Domesday times. The present house, replacing an earlier timber-framed structure dates from 1719 and was designed by the Smiths of Warwick. It was subsequently altered by Edward Blore in 1837 and after a disastrous fire in 1861 the whole of the centre portion was rebuilt by Anthony Salvin. Capesthorne contains a great variety of sculptures, paintings and other contents including a collection of American Colonial furnishings. There are gardens, lakes, a nature trail and woodland walks.
Open Mar-Oct, Wed-Sun & BH's (Closed Xmas & New Year). Park & Garden 12-6, Hall 1.30-3.30.
🅿 ♨ ✗ *licensed* ♿ *toilets for disabled shop*
Details not confirmed for 1998

CHESTER
Chester is one of Britain's most appealing cities. It is famed for its picturesque black and white buildings, but it is also a lively town that does not simply live on its past. The best way to start a visit is to walk around the medieval walls; there are small museums in some of the towers. The star attraction within the walls is the group of double-decker streets called the Rows, where stairs lead up to first-floor shops. The town is filled with timber-framed buildings, many of which are more Victorian than medieval, but are nonetheless attractive. There is also a Norman cathedral, extensively restored by Sir George Gilbert Scott. Roman Chester should not be forgotten. The city began as an important Roman military base, and the remains of a Roman amphitheatre lie outside the walls. To get a feel of Roman times, visit the Grosvenor Museum, which has evocative items such as memorial stones to Roman soldiers and their families.

Cheshire Military Museum
The Castle CH1 2DN
☎01244 327617 Fax 01244 327617
Exhibits from the history of the Cheshire Regiment, Cheshire Yeomanry, 5th Royal Inniskilling Dragoon Guards, and 3rd Carabiniers. Display of the work of George Jones, Victorian battle artist, and an exhibition of life in barracks in the 1950's. New for 1998 - Tableau of Malaya 1958.
Open all year, daily 10-5. (Closed 22 Dec-2 Jan).
£1 (ch & pen 50p).
🅿 *(within 400yds)* ♿ *shop*

Chester Cathedral
St Werburgh St CH1 2HU (opposite the town hall)
☎01244 324756 Fax 01244 341110
Founded as a Benedictine monastery in 1092 on the sites of earlier churches. The monastery was dissolved by Henry VIII and in 1541 it became the cathedral church of newly created Diocese of Chester. Consequently, the building is an unusually well preserved example of a medieval monastic complex, displaying all the main periods of Gothic architecture. The Quire stalls of 1380 are some of the finest medieval woodwork in the country. The building was restored in the 19th century and contains work by Gilbert Scott, Clayton, Pugin and Kempe. There are daily services and visitors are welcome to join in.
Open daily 7.30-6.30 (subject to alteration).
Donation of £2 per person requested.
P *(multi-storey)* ♨ ✗ *licensed* ♿ *(induction loop, tactile model) toilets for disabled shop* ⌀

Chester Heritage Centre
St Michael's Church, Bridge St Row CH1 2HJ
☎01244 402008 Fax 01244 347587
The centre aims to introduce visitors to the history of Chester's buildings and encourage them to explore the city. There are displays and an audio visual show.
Open Mon-Sat 11-5, Sun 2-5. Telephone for further details. Closed Nov-Feb & Good Friday.
✳*Admission fee payable.*
P *(440yds) shop* ⌀
Cards: 🖃 🖃

Chester Visitor Centre
Vicars Ln CH1 1QX (opposite Roman Amphitheatre)
☎01244 319019 Fax 01244 322221
Over 2000 years of Chester's history are illustrated by a video and a life-size reconstruction of a scene in the Chester Rows during Victorian times. There is a tourist information desk and guided tours depart regularly from the Centre. Working craft shops offer a large variety of gifts. Craft fairs take place on Bank Holiday weekends.
Open all year daily 9am-6pm.
P *(200yds)* ♨ ♿ *shop*
Details not confirmed for 1998

Chester Zoo
Upton-By-Chester CH2 1LH (2m N of city centre off A41)
☎01244 380280 Fax 01244 371273
Chester Zoo is the largest zoological gardens in the UK with 5000 animals in 500 species and is widely acclaimed for its conservation work, and award winning gardens. Features include large outdoor islands for chimps, orang-utans and monkeys; Tropical Realm aquarium; children's farm; penguin pool; elephant island; birds of prey. Spring 1998 sees the opening of the Bat Cave, the largest enclosure in the world for endangered bat species.
Open all year, daily from 10. Closing times vary with season from 7am high summer to 4.30 winter. (Closed 25 Dec).
✳*£8.50 (ch 3-15 £6 & pen £6.50). Party 15+*
🅿 ♨ ✗ *licensed* ♿ *(electric scooters-prebooked audio guide for blind) toilets for disabled shop* ⌀
Cards: 🖃 🖃 🖃 🖃 🖃 🖃

Deva Roman Experience
Pierpoint Ln, (off Bridge St) CH1 1NL
☎01244 343407 Fax 01244 343407
Stroll along reconstructed streets experiencing the sights, sounds and smells of Roman Chester. From the 'streets' of Deva (the Roman name for Chester) you return to the present day on an extensive archeological 'dig', where you can discover the substantial Roman, Saxon and medieval remains beneath modern Chester. The museum has a 'hands-on' area displaying both local and national finds.

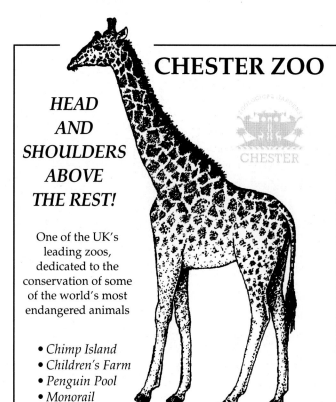

Open daily 9-5. Closed 25-26 Dec. £3.80 (ch16 1.90, under 5's free, pen £3). Family ticket £10. Prices under review.
P *(200yds)* ♿ *shop* ⌀ *(ex guide dogs)*

Grosvenor Museum
27 Grosvenor St CH1 2DD
☎01244 402008 Fax 01244 347587
This award-winning museum tells the story of the Roman army in Chester, and has a reconstructed Roman graveyard full of original tombstones. Other attractions include the Chester Race Cups which are part of a dazzling display of silver; period rooms which date from the 1680s to the 1920s; and the Natural History Gallery where visitors can learn of the past and present wildlife of Chester. Major exhibition: "Two Faces of Rome" - features computer-created, 3D buildings of Roman Chester, and artefacts from Chester's twin city of Sens in Northern France.
Open all year, Mon-Sat 10.30-5, Sun 2-5. (Closed Good Fri, 24-26 Dec & 1 Jan). Free.
P *(440yds)* ♨ ♿ *shop* ⌀
Cards: 🖃 🖃

"On the Air" The Broadcasting Museum
42 Bridge St Row CH1 1NN (next to Owen Owen department store)
☎01244 348468 Fax 01244 348468
'On the Air' tells the story of British radio and TV broadcasting from the 'Cat's Whisker' to digital TV. Visitors have the opportunity to find out for themselves, using many hands-on exhibits and audio-visual displays how broadcasting has changed our lives. The exhibition is built around a fascinating collection of radio and TV bygones, with period settings from the 1920s to the 1950s.
Open Jan-Etr, Tue-Sat 10-5; Etr-Xmas Mon-Sat 10-5, Sun 11-4.30.
£1.95 (ch £1, pen £1.50). Family ticket £5.50.
P *(100yds)* ♿ *shop* ⌀ *(ex guide dogs)*
Cards: 🖃 🖃 🖃 🖃 🖃

CHOLMONDELEY
Cholmondeley Castle Gardens
SY14 8AH (off A49/A41)
☎01829 720383
Fax 01829 720383
The extensive pleasure gardens are dominated by a romantic Gothic Castle built in 1801 of local sandstone. The gardens are imaginatively laid out with fine trees and water gardens, and have been extensively replanted from the 1960s with rhododendrons, azaleas, cornus, acer and many other acid loving plants. There are also herbaceous borders, a rose and lavender garden, lovely lakeside and woodland walks, rare breeds of farm animals, inlcuding llamas, and an ancient private chapel. Special events are held throughout the year, please telephone for details.
Open Apr-Sep, Wed & Thu 12-5, Sun & BH 12-5.30.
£2.50 (ch 75p, pen £2).
🅿 ♨ ♿ *(disabled car park near tearoom) toilets for disabled shop garden centre*

CREWE
The Railway Age
Vernon Way CW1 2DB (signposted on entry to Crewe)
☎01270 212130
Located in Crewe town centre this superb railway entertainment is suitable for the whole family. Attractions include miniature and standard gauge railways, three working signal boxes, restored diesel and steam engines, a children's corner and play area. Mainline steam locomotives also visit. Please ring for details of special events.
Open daily, mid Feb-mid Dec 10-4
🅿 ♨ ♿ *toilets for disabled shop*
Details not confirmed for 1998

DISLEY
Lyme Park
SK12 2NX (off A6, 6.5m SE of Stockport)
☎01663 762023 Fax 01663 765035
Home of the Legh family for 600 years

and the largest house in Cheshire. Part of the original Elizabethan house remains with 18th and 19th century additions by Giacomo Leoni and Lewis Wyatt. Four centuries of period interiors include Mortlake tapestries, Grinling Gibbons carvings, and a unique collection of English clocks. Set in extensive historic gardens with a conservatory by Wyatt, a lake, and the 'Dutch' garden. There is a 1,400 acre park, home to red and fallow deer, with magnificent views of the Pennine Hills and Cheshire Plain. Lyme Park featured as Pemberley in the BBC's production of Pride and Predjudice.
Open - Hall, 29 Mar-29 Oct, 1.30-5. (Closed Thur & Fri).Telephone for details (01663) 766492. Park all year, Gardens Apr-Oct daily 11-5. For winter opening ring for details.
P ⬛ & *(by arrangement) toilets for disabled shop ⬓ (ex park on lead)* ⬕
Details not confirmed for 1998

ELLESMERE PORT ▬▬▬
Boat Museum
South Pier Rd L65 4FW
☎0151 355 5017 Fax 0151 355 4079

Set in over 1300 acres of country park, with 15 acres of formal and informal Victorian gardens, Lyme Park boasts an imposing Palladian front and courtyard.

The museum occupies a historic dock complex at the junction of the Shropshire Union and Manchester Ship Canals. These docks were one of the most important points for transferring goods between sea-going vessels and the smaller craft of the inland waterways. There are over 60 floating craft, ranging from a small weedcutter to a 300-ton coaster, many of which visitors can climb aboard and explore. Boat trips are also available. There are eight indoor exhibitions on canal life and local history which are housed in the restored warehouses of the dock, together with period worker's cottages, blacksmith's forge and working engines. The original restored steam engines can be seen 'in steam' on the first Sunday of each month. Many special events and craft courses take place throughout the year.
Open Summer daily 10-5. Winter daily (ex Thu & Fri) 11-4. (Closed 25 & 26 Dec).
P ⬛ & *(resources pack for blind & deaf) toilets for disabled shop*
Details not confirmed for 1998
Cards: ▨ ▨

GAWSWORTH ▬▬▬
Gawsworth Hall
SK11 9RN (2.5m S of Macclesfield on A536)
☎01260 223456
Fax 01260 223469
This fine Tudor black-and-white manor house was the birthplace of Mary Fitton, thought by some to be the 'Dark Lady' of Shakespeare's sonnets. Pictures and armour can be seen in the house, which also has a tilting ground - now thought to be a rare example of an Elizabethan pleasure garden. Special events throughout the season, including: Open air theatre festival (Jun-Aug), Cheshire Area Nafas Flower Festival (29-31 May).
Open daily, 9 Apr-4 Oct, 2-5pm. £3.80 (ch £1.90). Party 20+.
P ⬛ & *(disabled parking in front of house) shop ⬓ (guide dogs in garden only)*
Cards: ▨

JODRELL BANK SCIENCE CENTRE & ARBORETUM ▬▬▬
Jodrell Bank Science Centre, Planetarium & Ar boretum
SK11 9DL (A535 Holmes Chapel to Chelford rd)
☎01477 571339
Fax 01477 571695
The Science Centre stands at the feet of one of the largest, fully-steerable radio telescopes in the world, the Lovell telescope, a landmark both in Cheshire and in the world of astronomy. There are exhibitions on space, energy, astronomy and satellites. Interactive exhibits enable visitors to 'get to grips' with science. There are shows every three quarters of an hour in the Planetarium. Outside, visitors may walk through 35 acres of tree-lined walkways in the Arboretum, beautiful in every season, and visit the Environmental Discovery Centre. Star Tracking exhibition June-October. Ring for details of other activities and temporary exhibitions.

Open daily 3rd weekend in Mar-last weekend in Oct, 10.30-5.30. Xmas & school holidays (ex 23-25 Dec) 11-4.30. £4 (ch £2, pen £2.80) includes Exhibition, Planetarium, Arboretum & Environmental Discovery Centre. Family ticket £11.50. Children under 5 not admitted to the Planetarium.
P ⬛ & *(Audio loop) toilets for disabled shop ⬓ (ex guide dogs)*

KNUTSFORD ▬▬▬
Tabley House
WA16 0HB (leave M6 junct19 onto A5033 follow brown signs)
☎01565 750151
Fax 01565 653230
Home of the Leicester family since 1272, the present magnificent 18th-century Grade I mansion, was designed by John Carr of York for the Leicester family. Tabley has the first great collection of English pictures, furniture by Chippendale, Gillow and Bullock, and other fascinating family memorabilia. Friendly stewards are available to talk about the Leicester's 700 years at Tabley. The chapel built in 1678 was moved in 1927 to save it from salt mine subsidence. Please call administrator for events planned for 1998.
Open Thu-Sun & BH, 2 Apr-31 Oct, 2-5 (last entry 4.30).
£3.50 (ch & students £1)
P ⬛ & *(Phone administrator in advance for help) toilets for disabled shop ⬓*

Tatton Park
WA16 6QN (5m from M6, junc 19, or M56 junc 7)
☎01565 654822 Fax 01565 650179
One of England's most complete historic estates, Tatton Park is one of the great playgrounds of the north-west, with gardens and a 1000-acre country park offering fishing, sailing and walking, as well as various events throughout the year. The centrepiece is the great Georgian mansion, whose gardens were first laid out by Humphry Repton, ➤

followed in the 19th century by Sir Joseph Paxton, who designed the Italian-style terraces in front of the house. Later, in the 20th century, Japanese gardeners created a Japanese garden with a Shinto temple beside one of the lakes, and also to be seen are a newly restored orangery and a fern house, as well as colourful expanses of flowers. The park is big enough to absorb its visitors and still provide room for wildlife, and the mere is especially interesting for its wildfowl in winter. A variety of signposted walks includes an historic landscape trail. The house itself has sumptuous furnishings and pictures including two Canalettos. Also of interest are the kitchens and cellars. The Home Farm is stocked with animals and working as it was fifty years ago. Old Hall is the original medieval manor house and a guided tour transports you through five hundred years of Tatton history. There is also an adventure playground. There is a regular programme of special events, including craft and antique fairs, flower shows, carriage driving trials, classic and sportscar shows and concerts. Please telephone for details.
Open Apr-Sep, Park 10.30-6, Gardens, 10.30-5 Mansion, Farm & Old Hall (guided tours only), 12-4, (all ex Park closed Mon ex BH Mon); 1-24 Oct Mansion, Farm & Old Hall wknds only; 25 Oct-Mar, Park 11-5, Gardens 11-4. (Closed Mon & 24-25 Dec), Farm Sun only & Shop 11.30-4. (Last admission 1hr before closure).
All-in ticket £8.50 (ch 15 £5.50) Family £25; Mansion £2.80 (ch 15 £1.80) Family £8; Gardens £2.80 (ch 15 £1.80) Family £8; Old Hall £2.50 (ch 15 £1.50) Family £8; Farm & stables £2.50 (ch 15 £1.50) Family £8. Any two attractions £4 (ch 15 £2.50) Family £12.
P *(charged)* ☕ ♿ *(Old Hall & areas of Farm not accessible) toilets for disabled shop garden centre* ✿ *(ex in Park)* 🐾
Cards: ▪ ▪

MACCLESFIELD
Hare Hill
SK10 4QB (4m N off B5087)
☎ 01625 828981
The beautiful parkland at Hare Hill also features a pretty walled garden and pergola. A brilliant display of rhododendrons and azaleas can be seen in late spring. There are also woodland paths and ponds.
Open 28 Mar-30 Oct Wed, Thu, Sat, Sun & BH Mons 10-5.30. Parties by written appointment with the Head Gardener. Special openings (to see rhododendrons & azaleas) 11 May-1 Jun daily 10-5.30; (Closed Nov-Mar).
❄️*£2.50 (ch £1.25). £1.50 per car (refundable on entry to garden).*
P *(charged)* ♿ *(wheelchair available braille guides)* ✿ *(ex guide dogs)* 🐾

Macclesfield Silk Museum
Heritage Centre, Roe St SK11 6UT
☎ 01625 613210 Fax 01625 617880
The silk museum presents the story of silk in Macclesfield through a colourful audio-visual programme, exhibitions, textiles, garments, models and room settings. It is situated in the Heritage Centre, formerly a Sunday school for child labourers. A full programme of musical and artistic events is available throughout the year at the Heritage Centre.
Open all year, Mon-Sat 11-5, Sun & BH Mon 1-5. (Closed Good Fri, 24-26 Dec & 1 Jan)
£2.50 (concessions £1.75). Family ticket £6.75. Joint ticket with Macclesfield Silk Museum £4.40 (concessions £2.50). Family ticket £9.90
P 🍴 ✗ *licensed* ♿ *(ramps & chairlift) toilets for disabled shop* ✿
Cards: ▪ ▪

Paradise Mill
Park Ln SK11 6TJ
☎ 01625 618228
An award-winning museum where knowledgeable guides, many of them former silk mill workers, illustrate the silk production process with the help of demonstrations from weavers. The museum was a working silk mill until 1981 when the last handloom weaver retired, and 26 handlooms have been fully restored in their original setting. Exhibitions and room settings give an impression of working conditions at the mill during the 1930s.
Open all year, BH Mon & Tue-Sun 1-5 (1-4 in winter). (Closed Good Fri, 24-26 Dec & 1 Jan).
❄️*£2.50 (concessions £1.75). Family ticket £6.75. Joint ticket with Macclesfield Silk Museum £4.40 (concessions £2.50). Family ticket £9.90*
P *(400 yds)* ♿ *shop* ✿
Cards: ▪ ▪

MOULDSWORTH
Mouldsworth Motor Museum
Smithy Ln CH3 8AR (6m E of Chester, off B5393, close to Delamere Forest & Oulton Park Racing Circuit, signposted)
☎ 01928 731781
Housed in an amazing 1937 large Art Deco building close to Delamere Forest, this is a superb collection of over 60 motor cars, motorcycles and bicycles. There is also a massive collection of automobilia - old signs, pumps, tools, mascots and badges, as well as old motoring toys, Dinky cars and pedal cars all complimented by a motoring art gallery. The gallery has posters and advertising material and is always expanding. The owner is motoring cartoonist James Peacop and he is also a lecturer and school parties are encouraged for a guided tour and structured talk. There are plenty of 'hands on' activities for children such as brass rubbing and a children's quiz. Motoring clubs visit on Sundays, bringing interesting vehicles with them. The surrounding countryside is ideal for picnics. Please phone for events arranged for 1998.
Open Etr weekend, early May holiday Mon, Spring Bank Hol Sun-Mon & Aug BH weekend; Sun, Feb-Nov; also Wed, Jul-Aug, noon-5.
£2.50 (ch £1, reductions for pensioners Wed only Jul-Aug £2)
P ♿ *(hands on items) shop*

NANTWICH
Stapeley Water Gardens
London Rd, Stapeley CW5 7LH (off junc 16 M6, 1m S of Nantwich on A51)
☎ 01270 623868 & 628628
Fax 01270 624919
Stapeley Water Gardens consists of three main areas. The Palms Tropical Oasis is a glass pavilion which is home to Koi carp, Giant Amazon water-lilies, sharks, piranhas, parrots and exotic flowers, whilst the two-acre Water Garden Centre houses, amongst other things, the National Collection of water-lilies. The site is also the home of a large angling centre.
Open Mon-Fri 9-6, wknds & BHs 10-6/7pm. (Winter 9-5, wknds & BHs 10-5). The Palms Tropical Oasis open from 10am, closing times as Garden Centre. Water Garden Centre only, open Sun 11-5 (winter 10-4).
The Palms Tropical Oasis £3.35 (ch £1.75, pen £2.65).
P 🍴 ✗ *licensed* ♿ *(free wheelchair loan service) toilets for disabled shop garden centre* ✿
Cards: ▪ ▪ ▪ ▪ ▪

NESTON
Liverpool University Botanic Gardens (Ness Gardens)
Ness Gardens L64 4AY (off A540 near Ness-on-Wirral)
☎ 0151 353 0123 Fax 0151 353 1004
The University of Liverpool's Botanic Garden is one of the most beautiful learning gardens in the country. Its long association with plant collectors continues to this day, and ensures a wide range of plant material attractively displayed to provide interest for academics, horticulturists and amateurs alike. Open throughout the year, visitors can admire tree and shrub collections, a notable heather garden, water and rock gardens and well stocked herbaceous borders and glasshouses. Gift shop, plant sales area and cosy coffee shops combine to provide a pleasant day out. There is also a regular programme of lectures, courses and special events throughout the year for which tickets must be obtained in advance.
Open all year, Nov-Feb, daily 9.30-4; Mar-Oct, daily 9.30-dusk. Closed 25 Dec.
£4 (ch free with adult, concessions £3.50)
P 🍴 ✗ *licensed* ♿ *(wheelchair route) toilets for disabled shop garden centre* ✿ *(ex guide dogs)*
Cards: ▪ ▪ ▪ ▪ ▪

NETHER ALDERLEY
Nether Alderley Mill
Congleton Rd SK10 4TW (1.5m S of Alderley Edge on E side of A34)
☎ 01625 523012
This fascinating water-mill was originally built in the 15th century, and is much larger inside than its outward appearance would suggest. Inside there are tandem overshot water-wheels, original Elizabethan timber work, and Victorian machinery which was restored to full working order in the 1960s after being derelict for 30 years. The original atmosphere of a working mill has been preserved as far as possible, and wheat is ground occasionally for demonstration purposes, water permitting.
Open Apr-May & Oct & 1 Nov, Wed, Sun & BH Mon 1-4.30; Jun-Sep, Tue-Sun & BH Mon 1-5. Parties by arrangement. £2 (ch £1)
P *shop* ✿ 🐾

NORTHWICH
Arley Hall & Gardens
Great Budworth CW9 6NA (5m N)
☎ 01565 777353 & 777284
Fax 01565 777465
Owned by the same family since medieval times, the present Arley Hall is a good example of the early Victorian Jacobean

style and contains fine furniture, plasterwork, panelling and family portraits. There is also a private family chapel designed by Anthony Salvin. The gardens rank amongst the finest in the country and extend over 12 acres. They include a magnificent double herbaceous border, shrub rose collection, walled garden, unique clipped Ilex avenue, yew hedges, herb garden, scented garden and a woodland garden with rhododendrons, azaleas and exotic trees. Various events held throughout the year. Contact the hall for a full programme.

Open Etr to end Sept, Tue to Sun & BH 11-5. Hall times vary.
Gardens, Grounds & Chapel £3.60 (ch 6-16 £1.80, pen £3). Family ticket £9. Hall £2.50 (ch 6-16 £1.20). Party 15+.
🅿 🍴 ✗ *licensed* ♿ *(ramps parking by entrance) toilets for disabled shop garden centre*

Salt Museum
162 London Rd CW9 8AB (signposted from A556)
☎ *01606 41331 Fax 01606 350420*
Britain's only Salt Museum tells the fascinating story of Cheshire's oldest industry. Models, reconstructions, original artefacts and audio-visual programmes throw new light on something we all take for granted.
Open Tue-Fri 10-5, wknds 2-5. Open BH Mons.
£1.75 (ch 85p).
🅿 🍴 ♿ *(inductory video with induction loop facilities) toilets for disabled shop* 🚫

PECKFORTON
Peckforton Castle
Stone House Ln CW6 9TN (off A49 towards Taporley)
☎ *01829 260930 Fax 01829 261230*
This 19th-century castle was described by Sir Gilbert Scott as 'the largest and most carefully and learnedly executed Gothic mansion of the present day ... not only a Castle in name but it is a real ... medieval fortress, capable of standing a siege from an Edwardian army'. The silhouette of this impressive castle can be seen for many miles across the Cheshire Plain with its castellated ramparts and round hexagonal towers.

The black and white façade of Little Moreton Hall is one of the best examples of half-timbered architecture in England.

The Great Hall is stone vaulted with a minstrels' gallery and fine staircase around a central pentagonal well contributing to the Grade I listed status of Peckforton. Special events include family entertainment every Sunday and Bank Holidays, and medieval re-enactments.
Open Etr-mid Sept, daily 10-6.
£2.50 (concessions £1.50). Party 20+
🅿 ♿ *toilets for disabled shop* 🚫
Cards: 💳 💳

RUNCORN
Norton Priory
Tudor Rd, Manor Park WA7 1SX (from M56 junct 11 in direction of Warrington, signposted)
☎ *01928 569895*
Displays tell the fascinating story of the transformation of the medieval priory into a Tudor manor house and then into an elegant Georgian mansion amid fine gardens. Special events for 1998: Eggstra Activities (10 Apr), Incredible Insects (25 May), Heritage Weekend (12-13 Sep), Horticultural Show (20 Sep), Fruit for the Future (18 Oct), Plant Sale (31 Oct), plus major outdoor exhibition of fibre art in the autumn.
Open all year, Apr-Oct, Mon-Fri 12-5; Sat, Sun & BHs 12-6; Nov-Mar daily 12-4. (Closed 24-26 Dec & 1 Jan). Walled Garden open Mar-Oct.
£3 (ch 5-16, students, UB40's & pen £1.70).
🅿 ♿ *(wheelchairs available, Braille guide, audio tapes, parking) toilets for disabled shop garden centre* 🚫 *(ex woodland garden)*

SCHOLAR GREEN
Little Moreton Hall
CW12 4SD (4m SW of Congleton on A34)
☎ *01260 272018*
Perhaps one of the best examples of half-timbered architecture in England, Little Moreton Hall stands with moat and gatehouse in all its original and ornate glory. Although building began about 100 years earlier, by 1580 the house was much as it is today. Inside, the long gallery, the chapel and the great hall are its most splendid features and notable too are some of the pieces of oak furniture. Little Moreton was used as a location for Granada TV's 1996 adaptation

of Moll Flanders. An exhibition of costumes from the series is planned for Apr-Oct. Please ring for details of this and other special events.
Open 22 Mar-2 Nov, Wed-Sun 12-5.30, BH Mon 11-5.30; 8 Nov-21 Dec, weekends 12-4.
🅿 *(charged)* ✗ *licensed* ♿ *(wheelchair & electric vehicle available, Braille guide) toilets for disabled shop* 🚫 🐕
Cards: 💳 💳

STYAL
Quarry Bank Mill & Styal Country Park
Quarry Bank Mill SK9 4LA (M56 junct 5, signposted)
☎ *01625 527468 Fax 01625 539267*
Quarry Bank Mill is a Georgian cotton mill now restored as a working museum of the cotton industry and powered by a waterwheel. There are galleries illustrating all aspects of the textile process, spinning, weaving, dyeing etc and the role of the founders (the Gregs), pioneers of the factory system. Other attractions include the factory 'colony' nearby with its shop, cottages and chapels. The original 1790 apprentice house, which was the home of young pauper apprentices, is fully restored and open to visitors as a 'living exhibit'. The garden is laid out in Victorian 'utilitarian' style, growing fruits, vegetables and herbs using the same methods as 150 years ago. The museum is still developing, therefore displays and facilities will be changed from time to time. The mill is set in a lovely valley and there are pleasant walks through woodland or by the deep ravine of the River Bollin. New for 1998: Three new galleries and an audio-visual theatre centred on a working 1840s beam engine.
Mill open all year, Apr-Sep daily 11-6 (last admission 4.30); Oct-Mar Tue-Sun 11-5 (last admission 3.30). Apprentice House & Garden, as Mill opening times during school hols, Tue-Fri 2pm-Mill closing time during school term. Sat & Sun as for Mill. (Closed Mon all year ex BH Mon and

school hols). Country Park open daily dawn-dusk.
Mill and Apprentice House £5.50 (ch £3.50). Mill £4.20 (ch £3). Family ticket £15. Apprentice House & Garden £3.50 (ch £2.50). Styal Country Park £1.50 per car.
🅿 *(charged)* 🍴 ✗ *licensed* ♿ *toilets for disabled shop* 🚫 *(ex in Park)* 🐕
Cards: 💳 💳

WIDNES
Catalyst: The Museum of the Chemical Industry
Mersey Rd WA8 0DF (signed from jnct 7 of M62 and jnct 12 of M56)
☎ *0151 420 1121 Fax 0151 495 2030*
Discover a world where science and technology come alive, with over 100 interactive exhibits and hands-on displays guaranteeing a fun-filled day out for all the family. Discover the past in our exhibition 'Birth of an Industry'. Take a trip to the spectacular glass-walled Observatory 100 feet above the River Mersey. A range of special events is planned throughout the year. Please ring for details.
Open all year, BH Mon, Tue-Fri daily 10-5, wknds 11-5. (Closed Mon ex BH's, 24-26 Dec & 1 Jan).
£4.35 (ch £3.10, concessions £3.65). Family ticket £12.95.
🅿 🍴 ♿ *toilets for disabled shop* 🚫
Cards: 💳 💳 💳 💳

CORNWALL & ISLES OF SCILLY

BODMIN
Duke of Cornwall's Light Infantry Museum
The Keep, Victoria Barracks PL31 1EG (on B3268 beside steam railway)
☎ *01208 72810 Fax 01208 72810*
The museum was started at the Depot in ➤

1925 and contains Armoury and Medals displays, a Uniforms room, and the Main Historical Gallery which traces the history of the Regiment from its formation in 1702 to its amalgamation with the Somerset Light Infantry in 1959, with pictures and relics devoted to the major campaigns of the Regiment from 1702 to 1945.
Open all year Mon-Fri, Sun during Jul & Aug 9-5. Closed Etr & Xmas.
£2 (ch 50p). Parties 10+.
🅿 *shop*

Pencarrow
Washaway PL30 3AG (3m W on unclass road off A389 & B3266)
☎ ***01208 841369***
This Georgian house is still a family home, and has a superb collection of pictures, furniture and porcelain. The 50 acres of formal and woodland gardens include a Victorian rockery, Italian and American gardens, a lake, an ice house and an ancient British encampment. There are 700 different rhododendrons and an internationally acclaimed conifer collection. There is also a craft centre and a children's play area. Charity Day in aid of Cornwall Gardens Trust will be held on 16th May.
Open Etr-15 Oct, Sun-Thu, 1.30-5; BH Mon & 1 Jun-10 Sep 11-5. (Last tour of the House 5pm).
House & Garden £4 (ch £2). Gardens only £2 (ch free). Party.
🅿 ☕ ♿ *toilets for disabled shop & plant shop* 🐕 *(ex gardens)*

CALSTOCK

Cotehele
St Dominick PL12 6TA (2m E of St Dominick)
☎ ***01579 351346***
Fax 01579 351222
The granite and slate house dates from the 15th century and was built for the Edgcumbe family. They moved south to Mount Edgcumbe in the 16th century, and left Cotehele virtually untouched, apart from some building work up to 1627 and in the mid 19th century. Inside there are tapestries, embroideries, furniture and armour; and outside there is a beautiful garden on different levels, including a formal Italian style garden, terraces, a Cornish Valley garden, medieval stewpond, dovecote, and an 18th-century tower with lovely views of the surrounding countryside. There is a restored water mill in the valley below, and an outstation of the National Maritime Museum. The restored sailing barge 'Shamrock' can be seen from the quay. Woodland and riverside walks available all year round. Please phone for details of events.
Open 1 Apr-1 Nov, House, daily (ex Fri) 11-5; (11-4.30 Oct). Mill, daily (ex Fri) 1.30-5.30 (4.30 Oct) - open Fri in Jul & Aug (4.30 Oct). Garden & Shop daily 11-5 (4.30 Oct). Last admission 30 mins before closing. Nov-Mar garden & woodland open daylight hours.
House, Gardens & Mill £5.60. Grounds £2.80. Family ticket £14. Party.
☕ ✕ *licensed* ♿ *(limited access in garden, braille guide) toilets for disabled shop* 🐕 *(ex guide dogs)*
Cards:

CHYSAUSTER ANCIENT VILLAGE

Chysauster Ancient Village
(2.5m NW of Gulval, off B3311)
☎ ***01736 61889***
This ancient Celtic village, 2000 years old, includes 9 drystone houses arranged mostly in pairs along the oldest known village street in England. A fascinating site conveying a strong sense of living history in a spectacular setting.
Open Apr-1 Nov, daily 10-6 (or dusk if earlier in Oct).
£1.60 (ch 80p, pen, students & UB40 £1.20).
🅿 🐕 #

DOBWALLS

Dobwalls Family Adventure Park
PL14 6HD (0.5 N of A38)
☎ ***01579 320325 & 321129 Fax 01579 21345***
Dobwalls invites visitors to ride on its two-mile-long stretches of miniature American railroads. There are steam and diesel locos, and visitors can take the Rio Grande ride through the forests or the Union Pacific route over the prairies. Ten scaled-down locomotives include the Union Pacific Big Boy, and there are tunnels, embankments, lakes and canyons. Also at Dobwalls is Adventureland - eight action-packed areas filled with adventure play equipment including aerial cableways and three totally enclosed slides. There are also remote-controlled model boats and American-style trucks and trailers, a shooting gallery, Aquablasters and an Edwardian 'penny' amusement arcade.
Open Etr-Sep, daily 10-6 (last admission 4.30pm). Oct, Sat & Sun only & school half term (check as dates may differ).
🅿 ☕ ♿ *(motorised & manual wheelchairs available) toilets for disabled shop*
Details not confirmed for 1998

FALMOUTH

Pendennis Castle
TR11 4LP (1m SE)
☎ ***01326 316594***
This castle is a testament to the quality of the coastal defences erected by Henry VIII. The well preserved granite gun fort and outer ramparts with great angled bastions defended against invasion from the sea, but it was captured from the land after a long siege during the Civil War.
Open all year, Apr-Jun & Sep-1 Nov, daily 10-6 (or dusk if earlier); Jul-Aug, daily 9-6; 2 Nov-31 Mar, daily 10-4. Closed 24-26 Dec & 1 Jan.
£3.00 (ch £1.50, concessions £2.30).
🅿 ♿ *shop* 🐕 *(in certain areas)* #

FOWEY

St Catherine's Castle
(three quarters of a mile along footpath off A3082)
The ruined stronghold was one of the many castles built by Henry VIII to defend the coast. It was restored in 1855.
Open all year, any reasonable time.
Free.
#

GODOLPHIN CROSS

Godolphin House
TR13 9RE (situated off the A303 between Townshend and Godolphin)
☎ ***01736 762409***
The former home of the Earls of Godolphin dates from the 15th century, but is most notable for the colonnade added in 1635. Inside is Wootton's painting, Godolphin Arabian, one of the three Arab stallion ancestors of all British bloodstock. The original stables house old farm wagons.
Open May & Jun, Thu 2-5; Jul-Sep, Tue & Thu 2-5; Aug, Tue 2-5, Thu 10-1 & 2-5. Open BH Mons. Parties by arrangement at anytime throughout the year including Sun.
🅿 ☕ ♿ *shop (plants)* 🐕
Details not confirmed for 1998
Cards:

GOONHAVERN

World in Miniature
Bodmin Rd TR4 9QE (on B3285)
☎ ***01872 572828 Fax 01872 572829***
There are four major attractions for the price of one at this enchanting theme park. Visitors can stroll amongst the world's most famous landmarks such as the Taj Mahal and the Statue of Liberty, all in miniature scale, set in spectacular gardens. Then there is Tombstone, a wild-west town complete with saloon, bank, shops, livery stable and jail. The Adventure Dome is the original super cinema 180 direct from the USA where you experience the thrills and spills of two great films without leaving your seat. Finally, there are the gardens, twelve acres of beautifully landscaped grounds with over 70,000 plants and shrubs.
Open 5 Apr-2 Nov, daily 10-4 (5pm Jul-Aug).
✻*£3.99 (ch under 5 free,ch5-13 £1.75, pen £3.50).*
🅿 ☕ ♿ *toilets for disabled shop garden centre*
Cards:

GWEEK

National Seal Sanctuary
TR12 6UG (pass RNAS Culdrose & take A3293 & then B3291 to Gweek, the sanctuary is signposted from village)
☎ ***01326 221361 & 221874 Fax 01326 221210***
The National Seal Sanctuary at Gweek in Cornwall is Britain's largest seal rescue facility and offers a unique opportunity to learn more about these beautiful creatures. Every year it rescues, rehabilitates and releases around 30 sick or abandoned seal pups. Follow the pups on their journey from the hospital, into our outdoor nursery and convalescence pools before, fit and healthy once again, they are released back into the sea. Set on the upper reaches of the beautiful Helford River the Sanctuary also provides a comfortable and secure home for resident adult seals and sea lions whose injuries have prevented them from returning to the wild.
Open all year, daily from 9am. (Closed 25 Dec).
✻*Please call for admission prices.*
🅿 ☕ ♿ *(wheelchair available) toilets for disabled shop*
Cards:

HELSTON

Flambards Village Theme Park
Culdrose Manor TR13 0GA (0.5m S on A3083)
☎ ***01326 573404 Fax 01326 573344***
Three award-winning, all-weather attractions can be visited on one site here. Flambards Victorian Village is an evocative recreation of streets, shops and house interiors from the turn of the century, including a 'time capsule' chemist's shop. Britain in the Blitz is a life-size wartime street featuring shops, a pub and a living room with Morrison shelter; and Cornwall Aero Park covers the history of aviation from 'those magnificent men in their flying machines' to Concorde. Cornwall's Exploratorium, is a 'hands-on' science playground for the whole family. There are many rides from the gentle to the daring, including the Hornet Rollercoaster, Flambards Family Log Flume, Cyclopter Monorail, Balloon Race and new play areas for very young children. Other attractions include a maze, the Hall of Miscellany, a huge children's playground and picnic area. Various events in 1998 may include: Easter Egg Extravaganza (13 Apr), Kernow Old Vehicle Club Rally (17 May), Flambards in Bloom (18 Jul-2 Aug), Music & Fireworks (10, 17, 24, 31 Aug). Ring for further details and to confirm these provisional dates.
Open 8 Apr-1 Nov 10-5. Extended opening 27 Jun-30 Aug to 6pm. Closed some Fri/Mons in low season.
Prices under review.
🅿 ☕ ♿ *(free loan of wheelchairs) toilets for disabled shop garden centre* 🐕 *(ex guide dogs)*
Cards:

LAND'S END

Land's End
TR19 7AA (on A30 from Penzance)
☎ ***01736 871501 & 871844***
Fax 01736 871812
The most westerly point of mainland England draws countless visitors to its dramatic cliff scenery. On a clear day the Isles of Scilly, 28 miles away, can be seen together with the Wolf Rock Lighthouse and the Seven Stones Reef, where the Torrey Canyon met its end in 1967. The 200-acre site is the setting for wild coastal walks and amazing natural rock formations; and innovative exhibitions have been set up to trace the geology, wildlife and maritime history of the area. The attractions include The Last Labyrinth, Relentless Sea, and Deep Sea Quest - an exciting new simulated submarine experience. During the main season (mid-July-August) fireworks every Thursday (weather permitting).
Open all year, site & exhibitions from 10am daily. Times adjustable during winter. Closed 24-25 Dec.
✻*£2 parking charge plus 'pay as you go' for attractions.*
🅿 *(charged)* ☕ ✕ *licensed* ♿ *(free admission for disabled & helper) toilets for disabled shop (some restricted areas)*
Cards:

LANHYDROCK

Lanhydrock
PL30 5AD (2.5m SE of Bodmin, signposted from A30, A38 & B3268)
☎ ***01208 73320 Fax 01208 74084***
Lanhydrock is approached along an avenue of beeches through a wooded park. It looks Tudor, but only the charming gatehouse, entrance porch and north wing date from the 16th century. The rest was rebuilt after a fire in 1881, and the house now gives a vivid picture of life in Victorian times. The 'below stairs' sections are particularly interesting and include a mighty kitchen, larders, dairy, bakehouse, cellars, and servants' quarters. Notable among the grander rooms is the long gallery, which has a moulded ceiling showing Old Testament scenes. The windows overlook the formal gardens with their clipped yews and bronze urns; the higher garden famed for its magnolias and rhododendrons, climbs the hillside behind the house. Open Air Concert: The London Ragtime Orchestra and Chris Barber Jazz & Blues Band plus fireworks (11 Jul).
Open 1 Apr-1 Nov: House daily (ex Mon), but open BH Mon 11-5.30 (11-5 in Oct). Gardens daily from 1st Mar, last admission half hour before closing. Winter Gardens Nov-Feb during daylight hours.
House & Grounds £6.20 (ch £3). Grounds £3.10 (ch £1.50). Family ticket £15.50. Party.
🅿 ☕ ✕ *licensed* ♿ *(house accessible ex 2nd floor) toilets for disabled shop garden centre* 🐕 *(ex on lead in park)*
Cards:

LANREATH

Lanreath Farm & Folk Museum
Churchtown PL13 2NX (A390 from Liskeard, then B3359 for Looe/Polperro, signposted)
☎ ***01503 220321***
A hands on Countryside Museum reflecting bygone times in Cornwall. Implements and equipment from the farmhouse, dairy and farmyard are displayed, together with mill workings rescued from a derelict mill house. Demonstrations of local crafts are given on weekday afternoons from 2-4pm. Play phones, pets, and models to operate make it a fun place as well as educational.
Open Etr-May & Oct, daily 11-5; Jun-Sep, daily 10-6.
£2.50 (ch £1, under 5 free). Party.
🅿 ☕ ♿ *shop*

LAUNCESTON

Launceston Castle
☎ ***01566 772365***
Dominating this old market town is the ruin of the 12th-and 13th-century castle. Built in the early years of the Norman Conquest, the castle soon became a symbol of the status and authority of the Earls of Cornwall and the centre from which they administered their great estates.
Open Apr-1 Nov, daily 10-6 (or dusk if earlier). Closed 24-26 Dec & 1 Jan.
£1.60 (ch 80p, students, pen & UB40 £1.20)
♿ *(outer bailey only)* 🐕 #

Launceston Steam Railway
St Thomas Rd, Newport PL15 8DA (from A30 well signposted)
☎ 01566 775665
The Launceston Steam Railway links the historic town of Launceston with the hamlet of New Mills. Travelling through the pretty countryside of the Kensey Valley, the trains are hauled by locomotives built in Victoria's reign. Tickets are valid for unlimited travel on the day of issue and you can break your journey at various points along the track. At New Mills there are a range of waymarked footpaths, a riverside picnic area and a water mill. Launceston Station houses railway workshops, a transport museum, gift shop and book shop. There are sometimes two engines in steam with double-headed trains on Wednesdays in July and August.
Open Good Fri-Etr Mon, then Tue & Sun until Whitsun. Daily Jun-Sep (Closed Sat). Tue & Sun in Oct. 10.30-4.30.
✳£5.20 (ch £3.50, pen £4.70). Family ticket £16.80. Dogs 50p. Prices under review.
🅿 🍴 ♿ shop

Lawrence House
9 Castle St PL15 8BA
☎ 01566 773277 & 774518
The local history museum of this proud Cornish town is housed in one of several well-preserved red brick Georgian houses, and was once a rendezvous for French officer prisoners during the Napoleonic wars. The displays and artefacts all relate to the history and social history of Launceston.
Open Apr-early Oct, Mon-Fri 10.30-4.30. Other times by appointment. Closed BH's.
Free but donations requested.
P (50yds) (public parking) 🐾 (ex guide dogs) 🥤

LOOE
Monkey Sanctuary
St Martins PL13 1NZ (4m E off B3253)
☎ 01503 262532 Fax 01503 262532
A protected breeding colony of rare Amazon woolly monkeys enjoy life here in the wooded grounds of Murrayton monkey sanctuary. Visitors may see monkeys in their extensive territory and sometimes out in the grounds. Talks are given throughout the day and display rooms give information about life for the monkeys both in Cornwall and in their natural habitat.
Open 5 Apr-Sep, Sun-Thu 10.30-5.
✳£4 (ch £1.50 & pen £3).
🅿 🍴 ♿ (disabled toilets in car park) toilets for disabled shop 🐾

MADRON
Trengwainton Garden
Penzance TR20 8RZ
☎ 01736 363021
Fax 01736 368142
Rhododendrons and magnolias grow in profusion at Trengwainton, along with many plants that won't usually grow outdoors in Britain. The mild climate

means that seed collected on expeditions to the Far East and southern hemisphere have flourished to produce a magnificent display in this 20th-century garden.
Open 1 Mar-29 Oct, Sun-Thu also Good Fri 10-5.30. (Mar & Oct 11-5). Last admission 30 mins before closing.
£3. Family ticket £7.50.
🅿 ♿ (braille guide) toilets for disabled shop garden centre 🥤
Cards: 🔲 🔲

MARAZION
St Michael's Mount
TR17 0HT (0.5m S of A394)
☎ 01736 710507 & 710265
Fax 01736 711544
Rising like a fairytale castle from the sea, St Michael's Mount can be reached on foot by a causeway at low tide, or by ferry at high tide in the summer only. It has been a church, priory, fortress and a private home in its time, and is still the home of Lord St Levan, whose ancestor St John Aubyn acquired it in 1660. The house is a medieval castle to which a magnificent east wing was added in the 1870s. There are splendid plaster reliefs of hunting scenes, Chippendale furniture in the elegant Blue Drawing Room, and collections of armour and pictures.
Open Apr-30 Oct, Mon-Fri 10.30-5.30. Last admission 4.45. Mar-May special educational visits by prior arrangement, Tue only. The Castle and grounds are open most weekends during the summer season. These are special charity open days and NT members are also asked to pay.
£3.90 Family ticket £10. Party 20+.
P (on mainland) 🍴 ✗ licensed shop (Apr-Oct) 🐾 🥤

MAWNAN SMITH
Glendurgan
TR11 5JZ (1m W on road to Port Navas, signposted))
☎ 01208 74281
This delightful garden, set in a valley above the River Helford, was started by Alfred Fox in 1820. The informal landscape contains beautiful trees and shrubs from all over the world, including the Japanese loquat, Mexican cypress and tree ferns from New Zealand. There is a maze, and a Giant's Stride which is popular with children. The house is not open.
Open 3 Mar-Oct, Tue-Sat & BH Mon 10.30-5.30 (last admission 4.30). (Closed Good Fri).
£3.20 (ch £1.60). Family ticket £8.
🅿 ♿ (braille guide) toilets for disabled shop garden centre 🐾 (ex guide dogs) 🥤
Cards: 🔲 🔲

Trebah Garden
TR11 5JZ (signposted at Treliever Cross roundabout on A39)
☎ 01326 250448
Fax 01326 250781
A 25-acre wooded ravine garden descending 200 feet from the 18th-century house down to a private cove on the Helford River. The cascading Water

Garden has pools of giant Koi carp and exotic water plants winding through two acres of blue and white hydrangeas and on to the beach. Glades of huge subtropical tree ferns and palms, giant gunnera, furcraea and echium, as well as rhododendrons and many other trees and shrubs. The beach is open to visitors and Tarzan's Camp provides an exciting play area for children. There are children's trails and activities all year and the Trebah Paraglide for the over fives. Special events for 1998 include: Easter Egg Hunt (9-26 Apr), D-Day Commemoration (7 Jun), Annual Plant Sale (19-20 Sep), Children's Activities (26-30 Oct), Christmas Santa Trail (13, 20-21 Dec).
Open daily 10.30-5 (last admission).
Mar-Oct £3.20 (pen £3, ch & disabled £1, ch under 5 free); Nov-Feb £1 (concessions 50p). Party 12+.
🅿 🍴 ♿ shop garden centre
Cards: 🔲 🔲 🔲 🔲 🔲

NEWQUAY
Dairy Land Farm World
Summercourt TR8 5AA (Signposted from A30 at exit for Mitchell/Summercourt)
☎ 01872 510246
Fax 01872 510349
Dairy Land Farm World was the first farm tourism diversification of its kind in the UK. Here, visitors can watch while the cows are milked to music on a spectacular merry-go-round milking machine. The life of a Victorian farmer and his neighbours is explored in the Heritage Centre, and a Farm Nature Trail demonstrates farming and nature in harmony with informative displays along pleasant peaceful walks. Children will have fun getting to know the farm animals in the safety of the Farm Park. They will also enjoy the playground, assault course and indoor play areas. Special events include an Easter Egg Hunt, a Father's Day Special and a Hallowe'en celebration. Ring for details.
Open daily, late Mar-Oct 10.30-5. Xmas opening telephone for details.
✳£4.95 (ch 3-15 £3.95, pen £4.35). Family £14.95. Party.
🅿 🍴 ✗ licensed ♿ (wheelchairs for loan; disabled viewing gallery - milking) toilets for disabled shop 🐾
Cards: 🔲 🔲

Newquay Zoo
Trenance Park TR7 2LZ (off A3075)
☎ 01637 873342
Fax 01637 851318
Education and conservation are the key issues at this exciting Zoological Centre. Apart from attractions such as the Monkey enclosures, penguin pool, tropical house and lion house all of which have been designed for maximum 'creature comfort' the park also boasts a Maze, an Oriental Garden, an activity Play Park, a Tarzan Trail Assault Course, and a tortoise enclosure which houses the tortoises that the Zoo is given each year. There are regular feeding times with talks, and animal encounter sessions.
Open daily, Etr-Oct, daily 9.30-6; Nov-Etr 10-4. Closed Christmas Day.
£4.50 (ch £3, pen £3.50 & disabled £3).Family ticket £14. Prices under review.
🅿 🍴 ♿ toilets for disabled shop 🐾
Cards: 🔲 🔲 🔲 🔲

PENTEWAN
The Lost Gardens of Heligan
PL26 6EN (signposted from A390 & B3273)
☎ 01726 844157 & 843566
Fax 01726 843023
Covering an area of 80 acres, this is the largest garden reclamation project in Britain. Four walled gardens are being restored to their former glory including the re-planting of Victorian varieties of fruit and vegetables. A feature of the garden is 'The Jungle' - a collection of palms, tree ferns and bamboo. The visitor will find plenty to see here including a New Zealand and an Italian garden, a grotto, wishing well and rockeries. Various events are held throughout the year including walks, horticultural events, theatre workshops and educational courses. Cornwall's Theatre of Flowers (Cornwall Garden Society Spring Flower Show) is held 24-26 Apr.
Open all year, daily 10-6 (last admission 4.30pm). Closed 25 Dec.
£4.50 (ch 5-15 £2, pen £4.00, ch under 5 free).
🅿 🍴 ♿ (free loan of wheelchairs) toilets for disabled shop garden centre
Cards: 🔲 🔲 🔲 🔲 🔲

The 25 wooded acres of Trebah Gardens descend 200 feet to the sea.

POOL
Cornish Engines
East Pool TR14 7AW
☎01209 216657 Fax 01209 612142
Impressive relics of the tin mining industry, these great beam engines were used for pumping water from 2000ft below and for lifting men and ore from the workings below ground. The mine at East Pool is being converted into Cornwall Industrial Heritage Centre, the first phase of which is open providing information on many other sites in Cornwall.
Open 28 Mar-2 Nov, daily 11-5.
£3.(concessions £2.50, students £1.50)
Family ticket £8. Party.
🅿 & shop ✗ (ex guide dogs) 😾
Cards: 🖃 ▭

PROBUS
Trewithen
Grampound Rd TR2 4DD (on A390)
☎01726 882763 & 883647
Fax 01726 882301
The Hawkins family has lived in this charming, intimate country house since it was built in 1720. The internationally renowned landscaped garden covers some 30 acres and grows camellias, magnolias and rhododendrons as well as many rare trees and shrubs seldom seen elsewhere. The nurseries are open all year.
Open, House Apr-Jul & Aug BH, Mon & Tue 2-4. Gardens open Mar-Sep, Mon-Sat 10-4.30, also Sun in Apr & May.
🅿 🍷 & toilets for disabled garden centre
Details not confirmed for 1998
Cards: 🖃 ▭ ▭ ◉ 🖃 🖃

RESTORMEL
Restormel Castle
PL22 ODB (one and a half miles N of Lostwithiel off A390)
☎01208 872687
With a commanding view over the Fowey Valley, the castle perched on a high mound is surrounded by a deep moat. The huge circular keep of this splendid Norman castle survives in remarkably good condition.
Open Apr-1 Nov, daily 10-6(or dusk if earlier).
£1.630 (ch 80p, concessions £1.20).
🅿 & ✗ ⚹

ST AUSTELL
Charlestown Shipwreck & Heritage Centre
Quay Rd, Charlestown PL25 3NJ (1.25m SE A3061)
☎01726 69897 Fax 01726 68025
Charlestown is a small and unspoilt village with a unique sea-lock china-clay port. It was purpose built in the 18th century by Charles Rashleigh. The Shipwreck and Heritage Centre houses the largest display of shipwreck artefacts in the UK, along with a series of lifesize tableaux and photographs depicting village life, an audio-visual describing the local heritage, a Scarborough Lifeboat and a lifeboat display. There is also an important 'History of Diving' display.
Open Mar-Oct, daily 10-5 (later in high season). Last admission 1 hour before closing. Bookings taken out of season.
🅿 (charged) 🍷 ✗ licensed & (ramps) toilets for disabled shop
Details not confirmed for 1998
Cards: 🖃 ▭ ▭ 🖃 🖃

Wheal Martyn China Clay Heritage Centre
Carthew PL26 8XG (2m N on B3274)
☎01726 850362 Fax 01726 850362
The Wheal Martyn Museum tells the story of Cornwall's most important present-day industry: china clay production. The open-air site includes a complete 19th-century clayworks, restored for this purpose. There are huge granite-walled settling tanks, working water-wheels and a wooden slurry pump. Other exhibits include a 220ft pan kiln, horse-drawn wagons and two steam locomotives used in the industry, and a restored 1914 Peerless lorry. The story of china clay in Cornwall over two centuries is shown using indoor displays. There is also a short audio-visual programme, and a working pottery. Outside again there are nature trails, a children's adventure trail and the spectacular viewing area of a modern china-clay pit.
Open Apr-Oct, 10-6 (last admission 5pm).
£4.25 (ch £2.25, pen/student £3.50)
🅿 & shop
Cards: 🖃 ▭

ST IVES
(Park your car at Lelant Station and take advantage of the park and ride service. The fee includes parking and journeys on the train between Lelant and St Ives during the day).

Barbara Hepworth Museum & Sculpture Garden
Barnoon Hill TR26 1AD (M5 to Exeter, A30 onto Penzance & St Ives)
☎01736 796226 Fax 01736 794480
Turner visited St Ives in 1811. Then, after the railway was established in 1880, the town became a popular haunt for artists; what was once a busy fishing port took on a distinctly Bohemian atmosphere as the net-lofts and fish-cellars were converted into studios. The house and garden that Dame Barbara Hepworth called home from 1949 until her death in 1975 is now a museum displaying 47 sculptures and drawings covering the period 1928-74, photographs, documents and other memorabilia. Visitors can also visit her workshops, which house a selection of tools and some unfinished carvings. Administered jointly with the Tate Gallery St Ives. Please phone for details of special events.
Open all year, Apr-Sep, Mon-Sat 11-7, Sun & BHs 11-5; Oct-Mar, Tue-Sun 11-5. (Closed 24-26 Dec).
£3 (concessions £1.50)
🅿 (880 yds) & (accessible with assistance) shop ✗

Tate Gallery St Ives
Porthmeor Beach TR26 1TG (M5 to Exeter, then A30 onto Penzance & St Ives)
☎01736 796226 Fax 01736 794480
Tate Gallery St Ives opened in June 1993 and offers a unique introduction to modern art, where over 200 works can be seen at any one time in the surroundings and atmosphere which inspired them. The gallery presents changing displays from the Tate Gallery's Collections, focusing on the post-war modern movement St Ives is so famous for. The displays are complemented by a series of exhibitions and artists' projects, which explore the diversity of contemporary arts practice. Events Programme. Guided Tours. Friends of Gallery Scheme. Education Studio. Lecture programme. 1998 exhibitions include: until April 26 - Roger Hilton, Marlow Moss Reconstructed, & Ralph Freeman. Apr-Nov - John Wells & John Beard. Ring for further details.
Open all year, Apr-Sept, Mon-Sat 11-7, Sun & BHs 11-5; Oct-Mar, Tue-Sun 11-5, (Closed 24-25 Dec).
£3.50 (includes one child under 16), concessions £2.
🅿 (800yds) 🍷 ✗ licensed & toilets for disabled shop ✗

ST MAWES
St Mawes Castle
TR2 3AA (on A3078)
☎01326 270526
The castle at St Mawes was built by Henry VIII in the 1540s, roughly the same time as Pendennis Castle in Falmouth. Together they were to guard the mouth of the Fal estuary; their present state of excellent preservation is largely due to their comparatively trouble-free history. Smaller but built in the same 'clover leaf' design as Pendennis, St Mawes particularly is renowned as a fine example of military architecture. The dungeons, barrack rooms and cannon lined walls provide great interest for both adults and children. Today the castle stands in delightful sub-tropical gardens featuring plants from around the world.
Open Apr-1 Nov, daily 10-6 (or dusk if earlier); 2 Nov-Mar, Fri-Tues 10-4 (closed 1-2pm). Closed 24-26 Dec & 1 Jan.
£2.50 (ch £1.30, concessions £1.90)
🅿 & shop ✗ ⚹

SANCREED
Carn Euny Ancient Village
(1.25m SW, off A30)
Four courtyard houses and a number of round houses dating from the 1st century BC can be seen at Carn Euny. There is also a 66ft long 'fogou': a subterranean passage leading to a circular chamber and used as a hiding place by the ancient inhabitants of this site.
Open any reasonable time.
🅿 ⚹
Details not confirmed for 1998

TINTAGEL
Old Post Office
PL34 0DB
☎01840 770024
A small, 14th-century manor house, tumble-roofed with thick uneven slates, it served as a receiving office for letters from 1844 to 1892, hence its name.
Open 1 Apr-1 Nov, daily 11-5.30, (Oct 11-5). Last admission 30 mins before closing.
£2.20 Party. Family ticket £5.
P (opposite) & (braille guide) shop ✗ (ex guide dogs) 😾

Tintagel Castle
(on Tintagel Head, half a mile along uneven track from Tintagel, no vehicles)
☎01840 770328
The romantic castle ruins have been divided by the erosion of the sea and make a dramatic sight. Is it the place the Romans called Durocornovium? Was it a Celtic monastery? Or was it the stronghold of the kings of Cornwall in the Dark Ages? Whatever the secrets of this place and its associations with Merlin the magician and King Arthur, it remains one of the most spectacular spots in Britain. New site interpretation panels and the exhibition help explain the mystery and wonder of this majestic site.
Open all year, Apr-1 Nov, daily 10-6 (or dusk if earlier); 2 Nov-Mar, daily 10-4. Closed 24-26 Dec & 1 Jan. (Please note there is a steep climb up steps to reach the castle)
P (in village) shop ✗ ⚹

TORPOINT
Antony House
PL11 2QA (2m NW, off A374)
☎01752 812191
A fine, largely unaltered mansion, built in brick and Pentewan stone for Sir William Carew between 1711 and 1721. The stable block and outhouses remain from an earlier 17th-century building. Most of the rooms in the house are panelled and contain contemporary furniture and family portraits. The grounds, which overlook the River Lynher, were redesigned by Humphry Repton. They include an 18th-century dovecote and, near the river estuary, the Bath Pond House, with plunge bath and a panelled changing room (may be seen only after previous written application to the adminstrator).
Open Apr-29 Oct, Tue-Thu & BH Mons (also Sun Jun-Aug), 1.30-5.30. Last admission 4.45.
£4. Woodland Garden £2.50. Combined Gardens only £3. Party.
🅿 🍷 (braille guide) shop ✗ 😾
Cards: 🖃 ▭

TREDINNICK
Shires Family Adventure Park
Trelow Farm PL27 7RA (off A39)
☎01841 540276
This 120-acre park specialises in Shire Horses, and visitors can see mares with foals. There are two horse shows a day which take place under cover and are

Tintagel Castle, perched highh above the Cornish cliffs, is famous as the legendary home of King Arthur

fully seated, and cart and train rides are also available. The work of the blacksmith is also on display and there is a museum of carriages, a video room and the largest display of show harnesses in the country. The unique owl sanctuary enable owls to fly freely in a twilight atmosphere. There is a 30 acre children's world of adventure playground, and small animals and special rare breeds can be seen. A train service enables visitors to get around the park. Ring for details of special events.
Open Good Fri-Oct daily 10-5. (Closed Sat in Oct)
£5.50 (ch £3.50, pen £4)
🅿 🍴 ✕ *licensed* ♿ *(most areas are ramped) toilets for disabled shop*

TRELISSICK GARDEN
Trelissick Garden
TR3 6QL
☎*01872 862090 Fax 01872 865808*
Trelissick is both a garden and an estate of tranquil beauty. Set amidst more than 500 acres of sweeping park and farmland, there are glorious panoramic views down the Carrick Roads to Falmouth and the sea. The garden is a plantsman's delight, famed particularly for its large collection of hydrangeas, camellias, rhododendrons and exotic and tender plants which thrive in the mild climate. The Cornish Apple Orchard opened in 1996 and contains the definitive collection of Cornish apple varieties and is particularly lovely in spring. The estate is surrounded by miles of old oak and beech woodland. There is a restaurant, shop, and art and craft gallery. Telephone for details of events.
Open 1 Mar-1 Nov, Mon-Sat 10.30-5.30, Sun 12.30-5.30. Woodland walks open all year.
£4. Family ticket £10.Party rate. Car park charge £1.50 (is refundable).
🅿 *(charged)* ✕ *licensed* ♿ *(Braille guide, batricar & manual wheelchairs) toilets for disabled shop* ♻ *(ex in woodland walk & park)* 🐕
Cards: 🔲 ▬ ▭

TRERICE
Trerice
TR8 4PG (3m SE of Newquay off A3058 at Kestle Mill)
☎*01637 875404 Fax 01637 879300*
Built in 1571 for Sir John Arundell, the picturesque Elizabethan house has unusual curved and scrolled gables, which may have been influenced by Sir John's stay in the Netherlands. The hall has an imposing window of 576 panes of glass, and throughout the house are fine plasterwork ceilings, fine furniture and a large clock collection. A museum of lawnmowers is housed in the barn. The garden includes an orchard of Cornish apple trees. Ring for details of special events.
Open 1 Apr-1 Nov, Wed-Fri, Sun & Mon 11-5.30; daily 27 Jul-6 Sep (Oct 11-5).

Last admission 30 mins before closing. House £4. Family ticket £10. Party.
🅿 🍴 ♿ *(braille guide) toilets for disabled shop* ♻ *(ex guide dogs)* 🐕
Cards: 🔲 ▬ ▭ ▱

TRURO
Royal Cornwall Museum
River St TR1 2SJ (follow A390 towards town centre)
☎*01872 272205 Fax 01872 240514*
The museum has interesting and well-laid out displays on the history of the county, and a world-famous collection of minerals. There are paintings and drawings, including a number of Old Masters, and some excellent exhibits of pottery, pewter, Japanese ivories, lacquerwork and toys. An extension houses two temporary exhibition galleries and a cafe. Other galleries house displays of mining and minerals, archaeology, Cornish history, and Egyptian artefacts. New Gallerys of the Natural History of Cornwall & Costume and Textiles open in 1998. Contact the museum for a full programme of temporary exhibitions.
Open all year, Mon-Sat 10-5. Library closes 1-2. (Closed BHs).
£2.50 (unaccompanied ch 50p, pen & students £1.50)
P *(200 yds)* 🍴 ♿ *(lift, ramps to main entrances) toilets for disabled shop* ♻
Cards: 🔲 ▭ ▬ 🔳 ▱

WENDRON
Poldark Mine and Heritage Complex
TR13 0ER (on B3297)
☎*01326 573173 Fax 01326 563166*
This Cornish tin mine has three levels open to the public; an 18th-century village, museums and a cinema showing a film on the history of Cornish mining. On the surface there are restaurants, shops, gardens and children's amusements. The area around the mine has been laid to lawn and shows the West Country's largest collection of antiquities, including a 40ft beam engine.
Open Etr-Oct, daily 10-5.30 (last admission 4).
🅿 🍴 ✕ *licensed* ♿ *shop (ex grounds)*
Details not confirmed for 1998
Cards: 🔲 ▬ ▭ 🔳

ZENNOR
Wayside Folk Museum
TR26 3DA (4m W of St Ives, on B3306)
☎*01736 796945*
This is the oldest private museum in Cornwall, founded in 1937, and covers every aspect of life in Zennor and District from 3000BC to the 1930s. Over 5000 items are displayed in fourteen workshops and rooms covering wheelwrights, blacksmiths, agriculture, fishing, wrecks, mining, domestic and archaeological artefacts. A photographic exhibition entitled People of Past Zennor

tells the story of the village and its people. The Miller's Cottage has a kitchen, parlour, mill and three working waterwheels. The delightful gardens are bounded on one side by a river. The majority of displays are under cover. New displays include: Childhood Memories, Mermaids, Dairy and History of the Wayside.
Open daily, Apr 11-5, May-1st wk Oct 10-6, Oct half term 11-5.
£2 (ch £1.50, over 60's £1.75). Party rates 10+.
P *(50 yds)* 🍴 ♿ *shop* ♻
Cards: 🔲 ▬

CUMBRIA

ALSTON
South Tynedale Railway
The Railway Station, Hexham Rd CA9 3JB (0.25m N, on A686)
☎*01434 381696 & 382828 (timetable)*
Running along the beautiful South Tyne valley, this narrow-gauge railway follows the route of the former Alston to Haltwhistle branch. At present the line runs between Alston and Gilderdale, but an extension of the lines to Kirkhaugh in Northumberland opened in 1997,

Open Mar 28-31; Apr 1-6, 12, 13, 19, 20, 26, 27; May 3-5, 10, 11, 17, 18, 24-31; Jun & Sep, Thu & wknds; Jul & Aug daily; Oct, wknds; Dec Santa & Mince Pie Specials. Please enquire for times of trains.
🅿 🍴 ♿ *(railway carriage for wheelchairs-pre-booking required) toilets for disabled shop*
Details not confirmed for 1998

AMBLESIDE
The Armitt
Rydal Rd LA22 9BL (beyond Bridge House opposite main car park)
☎*015394 31212 Fax 015394 31313*
A Lakeland Heritage experience... a chronicle of the Lakes from Roman times to the 20th century. Talk to John Ruskin, watch your own lantern slide show, explore Lakeland scenery with photographer Herbert Bell. Talk to Oscar Gnospelius the early seaplane pioneer and admire the treasury of Beatrix Potter's original natural history watercolours, never before permanently displayed to the public. All this and much more in a fascinating state of the art setting.
Open all year, daily 10-5 (last entrance 4.30pm). Closed 25 Dec.
£2.80 (ch £1.80). Party.
🅿 ♿ *(chairlift to upstairs library) toilets for disabled shop* ♻

APPLEBY-IN-WESTMORLAND
Appleby Castle
CA16 6XH (on A66, castle is top of the main street)
☎*017683 51402 Fax 017683 51082*
The grounds of this beautifully preserved Castle provide a natural setting for a Farm Park featuring rare breeds of British farm animals and also a large collection of ornamental waterfowl and unusual birds. The fine Norman Keep and the Great Hall of the house are open to the public. Clifford family portraits and part of the Nanking Cargo are on display in the Hall. The view from the top of the ancient Keep is spectacular and well worth a visit. An added attraction is the introduction of a Nursery Garden in the old walled kitchen garden. The buildings in the Old Stable Courtyard, provide a display area for the Made in Cumbria Exhibition, featuring the work of the highly skilled craftspeople of the area.
Open 22 Mar-Oct, daily 10-5 (last admission); Oct, daily 10-4.
🅿 🍴 ✕ ♿ *(assistance available) shop garden centre*
Details not confirmed for 1998

Birdoswald Roman Fort is the only point along Hadrian's Wall where all the components of the Roman frontier system are found

BORDER REGIMENT AND KING'S OWN ROYAL BORDER REGIMENT MUSEUM

34th & 55th | **4th, 34th & 55th**

Carlisle Castle, Cumbria CA3 8UR
Telephone 01228 32774

Displays on two floors relate the 300 year history of Cumbria's County Infantry Regiment and include uniforms, weapons, equipment, medals, silver, pictures, memorabilia, dioramas, video presentations, armoured car, field and anti-tank guns.
The Castle, the Regiment's home since 1873, houses the barracks of the former Regimental Depot.

Extensive archives · Enquiries welcome · Museum shop

For admission and other details see gazetteer entry

Brantwood
CONISTON CUMBRIA LA21 8AD
Home of John Ruskin 1872 - 1900
Tel: (015394) 41396

Ruskin Watercolours and memorabilia, glorious woodland walks, restaurant, craft gallery and bookshop

---

BARROW-IN-FURNESS
Furness Abbey
LA13 0PJ (1.5m NE on unclass road)
☎01229 823420
Built in 1147, Furness Abbey is impressive even as a ruin. The extensive red sandstone remains of the church and other buildings are a reminder that this was a very wealthy Cistercian establishment, and the setting is the beautiful 'Glen of Deadly Nightshade' near Barrow. There is also a museum with fine examples of stone carving and a fascinating exhibition.
Open all year, Apr-1 Nov, daily 10-6 (or dusk if earlier); 2 Nov-Mar, Wed-Sun 10-4 (closed 1-2). Closed 24-26 Dec & 1 Jan.
£2.50 (ch £1.30, concessions £1.90).
Personal stereo tour included in admission.
🅿 ♿ ❀ (in certain areas) ⚏

BIRDOSWALD
Roman Fort
CA6 7DD (signposted off A69 from Brampton)
☎016977 47602 / 4
Fax 016977 47605
This unique section of Hadrian's Wall enjoys a most picturesque setting overlooking the Irthing Gorge. There is no other point along the Wall where all the components of the Roman frontier system can be found together. But Birdoswald isn't just about the Romans, it's also about border raids in the Middle Ages, about the Victorians, and about recent archaeological discoveries. The Visitor Centre brings its fascinating history to life. Please telephone for details of August Bank Holiday events.
Open Etr-Oct, daily 10-5.30. Winter opening by prior arrangement only.
£1.95 (ch £1, pen £1.45). Party 10+
🅿 ♥ ♿ (ramp) toilets for disabled shop (not in tea room)
Cards: 🅱 ▭

BRAMPTON
Lanercost Priory
CA8 2HQ (2.5m NE)
☎016977 3030
The Augustinian priory was founded in around 1166. The nave of the church has survived and in use as the local parish church, providing a striking contrast with the ruined chancel, transepts and priory buildings.
Open Apr-1 Nov, daily 10-6 (or dusk if earlier).
£1.90 (ch £1, concessions £1.40).
🅿 ♿ ❀ ⚏

BROUGH
Brough Castle
(S of A66)
☎0191 261 1585
Standing on the site of the Roman Verterae, the castle was built in the 12th and 13th centuries to replace a stronghold destroyed by the Scots. The later castle also fell into ruin, but was restored in the 17th century by Lady Anne Clifford. The keep and curtain walls can be seen.
Open any reasonable time.
Free.
🅿 ❀ ⚏

BROUGHAM
Brougham Castle
CA10 2AA (1.5m SE of Penrith on minor road off A66)
☎01768 62488
On the quiet banks of the River Eden lie the ruins of one of the strongest castles in the region, founded in the 13th century and restored in the 17th by the strong minded Lady Anne Clifford. There is an exhibition of Roman tombstones from the nearby fort.
Open Apr-1 Nov, daily 10-6 (or dusk if earlier in Oct).
£1.90 (ch £1, pen, student & UB40 £1.40)
🅿 ♿ (ex keep) ⚏

CARLISLE
Carlisle Castle & Border Regiments Museum
CA3 8UR (north side of Carlisle city centre, close to station)
☎01228 591880 & 32774 (museum)
Fax 01228 21275
This medieval castle, where Mary Queen of Scots was once imprisoned, has a long history of warfare and feuding. An exhibition marks the Jacobite Rising in 1745 when Prince Charlie took the castle. In the gatehouse is a suite of rooms furnished in medieval style. The castle is also the home of the Museum of the King's Own Border Regiment (included in the admission price).
Open all year, daily Apr-Sep 9.30-6; Oct-Nov 10-dusk. Winter months 10-4.
£2.90 (ch £1.50 concessions £2.20).
Includes admission to museum.
🅿 (400 yds) ♿ (parking for disabled at Castle) shop ❀ ⚏

Carlisle Cathedral
CA3 8TZ
☎01228 35169 & 48151
Fax 01228 48151
Founded in 1122 as a Norman Priory for Augustinian canons. The chancel roof is magnificently decorated and the cathedral features an exquisite east window. Special events include: Art Exhibition (23 July-3 August), Book Fair (13 June) and Border Cathedrals Music Festival (10-11 October). Ring the cathedral office to confirm these provisional dates.
Open daily throughout the year, Mon-Sat 7.30-6.15, Sun 7.30-5, summer BHs 9.45-6.15, winter BHs, Xmas & New Year 9.45-4.
Suggested donation of £2 per adult.
🅿 ✗ licensed ♿ (disabled parking Radar key for toilet from vestry) toilets for disabled shop ❀ (ex guide dogs)

Guildhall Museum
Green Market CA3 8JE
☎01228 819925
Fax 01228 810249
The Guildhall was once the meeting place of Carlisle's eight trade guilds, and it still has an atmosphere of medieval times. It is an early 15th-century building with exposed timber work and wattle and daub walls. The displays include items relating to the guilds, and other reminders of life in medieval Carlisle.
Open Good Fri-Sep, Tue-Sun 1-4. Winter by arrangment.
50p (concessions 25p).
🅿 (500yds) shop ❀

Tullie House Museum & Art Gallery
Castle St CA3 8TP
☎01228 34781 Fax 01228 810249
Travel back into the mists of time and let the real stories of historic Carlisle and Border history unfold before you. Curiosity entices you to begin a journey of discovery as you stroll through Luguvalium (Roman Carlisle), climb part of Hadrian's turf Wall and experience a land inhabited by eagles and peregrines. Peep into Isaac Tullie's study as it might have been when he sat down to record in his diary how the Roundheads laid siege to his Royalist city in 1644, or sit in the 1st-class compartment of a railway carriage and recall the days of steam locomotion.
Open all year, Mon-Sat 10-5, Sun, 26 Dec & 1 Jan noon-5. Closed 25 Dec.
Ground floor (including Art Gallery & Old Tullie House) - Free. Upper floors - £3.50 (concessions £2.50)
🅿 (5mins walk) ♥ ✗ licensed ♿ (chair lift, sound guide) toilets for disabled shop ❀
Cards: 🅱 ▭ ▭ ▭ ▭ 🅖

COCKERMOUTH
Jennings Brewery Tour
The Castle Brewery CA13 9NE
☎01900 823214 Fax 01900 827462
Jennings Brothers have been brewing traditional beers for 160 years and still use today the methods used by the founder in 1828. Situated in the shadow of Cockermouth Castle, the water for the brewing process is still drawn from the well which supplied the Castle with pure water.
Tours: 17-21 Feb & 24 Mar-31 Oct, Mon-Fri 11am & 2pm; 14 Jul-29 Aug, extra tour at 12.30pm; 5 Apr-12 Jul, Sats at 11am; Etr & 19 Jul-31 Aug, wknds at 11am & 2pm,
🅿 shop ❀
Details not confirmed for 1998
Cards: 🅱 ▭

Lakeland Sheep & Wool Centre
Egremont Rd CA13 0QX (M6 junct 40, W on A66 to rdbt at Cockermouth on A66/A586 junction)
☎01900 822673 Fax 01900 822673
Come face to face with 19 different breeds of live sheep. Stage show with 'One Man and his Dog' demonstration and sheep-shearing. Shows four times daily, mid Feb-mid Nov
Open daily 9-6 (ex 25 Dec).
£3 (ch £2).
🅿 ♥ ✗ licensed ♿ (hearing loop system) toilets for disabled shop ❀
Cards: 🅱 ▭ ▭ ▭ ▭ 🅖

Lanercost Priory was founded in 1166 by the Augustinians

The Steam Yacht Gondola returned to active service on Lake Coniston in 1980.

Wordsworth House
Main St CA13 9RX
☎01900 824805 Fax 019468 61235
William Wordsworth was born here on 7th April 1770, and happy memories of the house had a great effect on his work. He played on the garden terrace with his sister Dorothy, and the inside staircase, panelling and other features are original. Portraits and other items connected with the poet are displayed. Please ring for details of concerts and other events during the season.
Open Apr-30 Oct, Mon-Fri 11-5. Also Sats 11 Apr,2 & 23 May, and all Sats 27 Jun-5 Sep & 24 Oct. (Last admission 4.30pm). £2.80 (ch £1.40). Family ticket £7.50. Party. Ask for details of discount with Dove Cottage,the Wordsworth Museum and Rydal Mount.
P ✗ shop

CONISTON
Brantwood
LA21 8AD (2.5m SE off B5285, unclass rd. Regular ferry services from Coniston Pier)
☎015394 41396 Fax 015394 41263
Brantwood, former home of John Ruskin, is one of the most beautifully situated houses in the Lake District with fine views across Coniston Water. Inside there is a large collection of Ruskin paintings and other memorabilia, while outside visitors can enjoy delightful nature walks through the Brantwood Estate. Ring for a full season programme of exhibitions, and musical and theatrical events.
Open mid Mar-mid Nov, daily 11-5.30. Rest of year, Wed-Sun 11-4. (closed 25-26 Dec).
House & Estate £3.90 (ch £1, student £2.10). Family ticket £9.50. Estate only £1.75. Party.
P ✗ licensed toilets for disabled shop (& plant sales)
Cards:

Ruskin Museum
The Institute LA21 8DU
☎015394 41164
The Victorian writer John Ruskin lived nearby, and the museum displays photocopies of letters and sketchbooks and other relics, with portraits of the writer and his circle. There are also minerals and examples of Ruskin Lace, based on a design which he brought back from Italy and which became popular with local lace makers. Other material relates to the Campbells and their Coniston water speed record bids, and to Coniston itself. Major rebuilding work is underway so prospective visitors should telephone and check on the current situation.
Open Etr-Oct, daily 10-1 & 2-4.
P (50 yds)
Details not confirmed for 1998

Steam Yacht Gondola
Pier Cottage LA21 8AJ
☎015394 41288
Launched in 1859, the graceful Gondola worked on Coniston Water until 1937, and came back into service in 1980. Now visitors can once again enjoy her silent progress and old-fashioned comfort.
Open Apr-1 Nov to scheduled daily timetable. Trips commence 11 at Coniston Pier; on Sat 12.05. Piers at Coniston, Park-a-Moor at SE end of lake & Brantwood. (Not NT).
Ticket prices on application.
P

DALEMAIN
Dalemain
CA11 0HB (between Penrith & Ullswater on the A592)
☎017684 86450 Fax 017684 86223
The stately home of Dalemain was originally a medieval pele tower, which was added to in Tudor times and later, with the imposing Georgian façade completed in 1745. It has splendid oak panelling, Chinese wallpaper, Tudor plasterwork and fine Queen Anne and Georgian furniture. The rooms include a Victorian nursery and a housekeeper's room. The tower contains the Westmorland and Cumberland Yeomanry Museum, and there is a countryside museum in the 16th-century cobbled courtyard. The grounds include a deerpark and gardens that have very rare plants and a collection of over 100 old fashioned roses. 1998 special events: 18-19 July - Dalemain Craft Fair.
Open 5 Apr-4 Oct, Sun-Thu. 10.30-5, Gardens, tearoom, shop and agricultural & countryside museums. 11.15-5, House. House £5 (ch £3) Family £13. Gardens £3. (ch free when accompanied) Party rates.
P ✗ licensed (ramp access at entrance, setting down & collection point) toilets for disabled shop garden centre

GRASMERE
Dove Cottage & The Wordsworth Museum
LA22 9SH (S, off A591, immediately before Grasmere village)
☎015394 35544 & 35547
Fax 015394 35748
Wordsworth called Grasmere 'the loveliest spot that man hath ever found.' He lived at Dove Cottage from 1799 to 1808, and during that time wrote much of his best-known poetry. The house is kept in its original condition, as described in the journals of his sister Dorothy, and the award-winning museum displays manuscripts, paintings and various items associated with the poet. Near the cottage is the former schoolroom where he taught, and Wordsworth, his wife and sister, and other members of the family, are buried in the churchyard. 1998 events include an exhibition commemorating the bicentenary of the first publication of the Lyrical Ballads. Ring for dates.
Open daily 9.30-5.30, last admission 5pm. (Closed 12 Jan-8 Feb & 24-26 Dec). £4.40 (ch £2.20). Family ticket available. Party. Reciprocal discount with Rydal Mt & Wordsworth House.
P ✗ licensed toilets for disabled shop
Cards:

HARDKNOTT CASTLE ROMAN FORT
Hardknott Castle Roman Fort
(at W end of Hardknott Pass)
The fort is at the western end of the hair-pinned (and hair-raising) Hardknott Pass, which has gradients of 1 in 3. On this astonishing site above Eskdale, the Romans built a walled and ramparted fort covering nearly three acres, with a bath house and parade ground outside. The remains of the building can be seen.
Open any reasonable time. Access may be hazardous in winter.
Free.
P

HAWKSHEAD
Beatrix Potter Gallery
Main St LA22 0NS
☎015394 36355 Fax 015394 36118
An annually changing exhibition of Beatrix Potter's original illustrations from her children's storybooks. Housed in the former office of her husband, solicitor William Heelis. Also a display of her life as an author, artist, farmer and determined preserver of her beloved Lake District.
Open Apr-1 Nov & Good Friday Sun-Thu 10.30-4.30 (last admission 4). Admission is by timed ticket including NT members. £2.80 (ch £1.40).
P (300metres) (braille guide) shop

HOLKER
Holker Hall & Gardens
Cark in Cartmel, Grange over Sands LA11 7PL (from M6 junct 36, on A590, signposted)
☎015395 58328
Fax 015395 58776
Dating from the 16th century, the new wing of the Hall was rebuilt in 1871 after a disastrous fire. It has notable woodcarving and many fine pieces of furniture which mix happily with family photographs from the present day. Magnificent 25-acre award-winning gardens, both formal and woodland, are adjacent to the Hall; here you will find a fantastic limestone cascade and other water features. The Lakeland Motor Museum, exhibitions, deer park and adventure playground are further attractions. An MG rally will be held here on 30 August, and this is also the venue for the Great Garden and Countryside Festival, (29-31 May). This will feature horticultural displays, festival gardens, floral art, countryside displays, traditional and modern crafts, W.I. Marquee, society displays etc. Please ring for full details.
Open Apr-30 Oct Sun-Fri 10-6. Last entry to grounds, hall & motor museum 4.30pm.
£3.35 (ch over 6 £1.90, ch under 6 free). Family ticket £9.85.
P (ramps, handrails) toilets for disabled shop

KENDAL
Abbot Hall Art Gallery
Kirkland LA9 5AL
☎01539 722464
Fax 01539 722494
The ground floor rooms of this splendid house, reputedly designed in 1759 by John Carr of York, have been restored to their period decor, including the original carvings and fine panelling. The rooms make a perfect setting for the Gillow furniture and *objets d'art* displayed here, while the walls are hung with paintings by Romney, Gardner, Turner and Ruskin. The gallery has a fine collection of 18th- and 19th-century watercolours of the Lake District and exceptionally good 20th-century British art, including works by Barbara Hepworth, Frink, Ben Nicholson, Sutherland, Piper and Hitchens. Please telephone for details of exhibitions.
Open 11 Feb-22 Dec, Mon-Sun 10.30-5 (reduced hours in winter, Feb, Mar, Nov & Dec) please telephone for details.
P (chair lifts in split level galleries) toilets for disabled shop
Details not confirmed for 1998

Abbot Hall Museum of Lakeland Life & Industry

Kirkland LA9 5AL
☎01539 722464 Fax 01539 722494
The life and history of the Lake District has a uniqueness which is captured by the displays in this museum, housed in Abbot Hall's stable block. The working and social life of the area, its people and places are well illustrated by a variety of exhibits including period rooms, a Victorian Cumbrian street scene and a farming display. One of the rooms is devoted to the memory of Arthur Ransome, another to John Cunliffe's Postman Pat.
Open 11 Feb-22 Dec, daily 10.30-5. Reduced hours Feb, Mar, Nov & Dec, please telephone for details.
🅿 ♨ *shop* ✿
Details not confirmed for 1998

Kendal Museum

Station Rd LA9 6BT
☎01539 721374 Fax 01539 722494
The archaeology and natural history of the Lakes is dealt with in this popular museum which also features a world wildlife exhibition and a gallery devoted to Alfred Wainwright - the author who was honorary clerk to the museum.
Open Mar-Dec, daily 10.30-5. Reduced hours Feb, Mar. Nov & Dec, please telephone for details.
🅿 ♿ *(chair lift) toilets for disabled shop* ✿
Details not confirmed for 1998

KESWICK
Keswick Museum & Gallery

Fitz Park, Station Rd CA12 4NF
☎017687 73263
A mecca for writers, poets and artists, Keswick's attractions are well illustrated in this museum and gallery. Names such as Coleridge, Wordsworth, Southey, Lamb and Walpole can be found among the exhibits which include letters, manuscripts and other relics from the time these literary luminaries spent in the Lake District. One of Ruskin's paintings is among the collections in the art gallery and there is a fine scale model of the Lakes dating from 1834. The comprehensive geology collection is of national importance and contains magnificent mineral examples from the Caldbeck Fells. The natural history displays cover animal and bird life of the region, including a golden eagle. Fitz Park contains formal gardens and a children's adventure playground. There are monthly exhibitions by local artists and craft workers. Ring for details of special events celebrating the museum's centenary.
Open Etr(Good Fri)-31 Oct, daily 10-4. £1 (ch, pen, students, UB40's & disabled 50p). Party 10+, 10% disc.
P (5 mins) ♿ *(ramp at front entrance) shop* ✿

Mirehouse

CA12 4QE (3m N of Keswick on A591)
☎017687 72287
Fax 017687 72287
Undoubtedly a great place for children - there are four adventure playgrounds - but Mirehouse has its fair share of cultural interest, and a walk along the beautiful lake shore will take you past the place where Tennyson wrote much of *Morte d'Arthur.* Inside the 17th-century house there is much original furniture adorning the graceful rooms. Portraits and manuscripts of Francis Bacon, Carlyle and, of course, Tennyson are on display. Classical piano music is played on regular opening days. Children are welcome inside as well as ouside, with plenty of things to find and do including riding a large Victorian rocking horse. Outside, the flowers in the walled garden attract the bees and butterflies, and make this sheltered spot perfect for picnics. There is also a wildflower meadow and access to the 10th century Lakeside church. Mirehouse is also the venue for concerts attached to Keswick Jazz Festival at the end of May, and bobbin lace demonstrations are held each Wednesday in June, July and September. Also by the rose garden, behind the house, is a Victorian cloister, another good place for picnics.
Open Apr-Oct. House: Wed, Sun, (also Fri in Aug) 2-last entry 4.30. Grounds: daily 10.30-5.30. Parties by arrangement Mar-Nov.
House & grounds £3.50 (ch £1.75). Grounds only £1.50 (ch 80p). Family ticket £9.50 (2 adults & up to 4 children)
🅿 ♨ ♿ *(notes available listing facilities) toilets for disabled* ✿ *(ex in grounds on lead)*

LAKESIDE
Aquarium of the Lakes

LA12 8AS (M6 junct36, signposted Barrow/Southern Lakes, take A590 to Newby Bridge. Turn right over bridge)
☎015395 30153 Fax 015395 30152
New award-winning freshwater aquarium. Discover the country's largest collection of freshwater fish, including the predatory pike. Walk underwater along a recreated lakebed and marvel at the antics of the resident ducks as they dive for food.
Open all year, daily from 10am. Closed 25 Dec.
❋*£4.50 (ch £2.95). Family ticket £14.50.*
🅿 *(charged)* ♨ ♿ *(lift to first floor) toilets for disabled shop*
Cards: 🅰 🆖 📇 📇 📇

LEVENS
Levens Hall

LA8 (M6 junct 36. 5m S of Kendal, on A6)
☎015395 60321 Fax 015395 60669
The most remarkable feature is the

topiary garden, laid out in 1694 and little changed. The Elizabethan mansion was built onto a 13th-century pele tower and has fine plasterwork and panelling. A steam engine collection adds further interest.
Open - House & gardens Apr-15 Oct, Sun-Thur. Gardens 10-5. House 12-5. Last admission 4.30. Steam collection 2-5.
House & garden £5.20 (ch £2.80), garden only £3.80 (ch £2.10).
🅿 ♨ ♿ *(ramps within garden) toilets for disabled shop (plants on sale)* ✿
Cards: 📇

MUNCASTER
Muncaster Castle, Gardens & Owl Centre

CA18 1RQ (1m E on A595)
☎01229 717614 & 717393 (owl centre)
Fax 01229 717010
Diverse attractions are offered at this castle, the seat of the Pennington family since the 13th century. Inside is a fine collection of 16th-and 17th-century furnishings, embroideries and portraits, whilst the grounds have a nature trail, a children's play area, and a profusion of rhododendrons, camellias, magnolias and azaleas. There is also an extensive collection of owls, as this is the headquarters of the World Owl Trust. Closed circuit television on some nests allows an intimate look, and there are continuous owl videos throughout the day in the Old Dairy Theatre. 'Meet the Birds' daily. Please ring for details.
Open Castle; 29 Mar-1 Nov, Sun-Fri 12.30-4 (last entry). Garden & Owl Centre, all year, daily 11-5. Parties by arrangement.
Castle, Gardens & Owl Centre £5.20 (ch £3.10) Family £14.50. Gardens & Owl Centre only £3.50 (ch £2) Family 39.50. Party.
🅿 ♨ ✕ *licensed* ♿ *(wheelchair loan,induction loop,tape for partially sighted) toilets for disabled shop garden centre*
Cards: 🅰 🆖 📇 📇 📇

Muncaster Water Mill

CA18 1ST (1m NW on A595 by railway bridge)
☎01229 717232
There has been a mill on this site since the 15th century, and flour and oatmeal are still ground on the premises. The water is brought three-quarters of a mile from the River Mite to the 13ft overshot water wheel, and all the milling equipment is water driven. This old manorial mill is served by the Ravenglass and Eskdale Railway.
Open Apr-Oct, daily, Jun-Aug 10.30-5.30, Apr-May & Sep-Oct 11-5.
🅿 ♿ *shop* ✿ *(ex grounds)*
Details not confirmed for 1998

NEAR SAWREY
Hill Top

LA22 0LF (2m S of Hawkshead)
☎015394 36269 Fax 015394 36118
Beatrix Potter wrote many Peter Rabbit books in this little 17th-century house which contains her furniture and china.
Open 1 Apr-1 Nov, Sat-Wed & Good Friday 11-5. Last admission 4.30pm. £3.80 (ch.£1.70)
🅿 *(braille guide, handling items) shop* ✿
✿

PENRITH
See Dalemain

Wetheriggs Country Pottery

Clifton Dykes CA10 2DH (approx 2miles off A6 S from Penrith, signposted)
☎01768 892733 Fax 01768 892722
Wetheriggs is the UK's only remaining steam-powered pottery. Working pottery and Crafts, 'Have a Go!' workshop - throw your own pot, modelling in clay, paint your own pot or animal. Old Workings and Museum, Tearooms, large pottery and crafts shops, rare breeds, newt pond and nature area. Special events - Steam Events with Fred Dibnah 5 Apr, & 3/4 Oct.
Open all year daily 10am-5.30pm, closed Xmas/New Year.
Free.
🅿 ♨ ♿ *toilets for disabled shop garden centre*
Cards: 🅰 🆖 📇 📇 📇

RAVENGLASS
Ravenglass & Eskdale Railway

CA18 1SW (close to the A595)
☎01229 717171 Fax 01229 717011
This narrow gauge steam railway was laid in the 19th century to carry iron ore from the mines at Boot. It began to carry passengers and then other freight, including quarried stone, once the mines were closed. The railway was given the nickname 'Owd Ratty' after its contractor, a man called Ratcliffe. It is now a passenger line, where both steam and diesel locomotives are used during the summer months to pull the open and saloon coaches. The railway runs through beautiful countryside for the seven mile journey from Ravenglass, on the coast, up to the terminus at Dalegarth. Purpose-built toilets for wheelchair users at Ravenglass, Eskdale and intermediate stations. Please ring for details of special events for 1998.
Open: trains operate all year. Mar-Nov & between Xmas & New Year, daily; some winter weekends, please enquire . Limited service Jan & Feb except school hols.
Return fare £6.30 (ch 5-15 £3.10). Family ticket £14.90
🅿 *(charged)* ♨ ✕ *licensed* ♿ *(special coaches - prior notice advisable) toilets for disabled shop*
Cards: 🅰 🆖 📇 📇 📇

RYDAL
Rydal Mount

LA22 9LU (1.5m, from Ambleside on A591 to Grasmere)
☎015394 33002 Fax 015394 31738
The family home of William Wordsworth from 1813 until his death in 1850, Rydal Mount incorporates a pre-1574 farmer's cottage. Now owned by descendants of Wordsworth, the house contains important family portraits, furniture, and many of the poet's personal possessions, together with first editions of his work. Placed in a lovely setting overlooking Windermere and Rydal Water, the house is surrounded by what has been described as one of the most interesting small gardens in England. They were designed by Wordsworth himself. Evening visits for groups can be organised on request, including a tour of the house and gardens, with poetry readings, wine and gingerbread at a small charge. Please telephone for details of the Daffodil Tour (March-May), and the Coffin Trail (November-March). The Lake District Summer Festival takes place during August.

A stop on the picturesque 7-mile route of the Ravenglass and Eskdale narrow-gauge railway is tthe restored, working Muncaster Mill – on a site occupied by a mill since 1470.

Most of Sizergh Castle was built between the 15th and the 18th centuries but its origins lie in a 13th century pele tower.

Open Mar-Oct daily 9.30-5; Nov-Feb daily (ex Tue) 10-4 (Closed 10 Jan-1 Feb). Free.
🅿 🅱 *shop* ✖

SEDBERGH
National Park Centre
72 Main St LA10 5HL
☎ 015396 20125
At the north-western corner of the Yorkshire Dales National Park, Sedbergh is set below the hills of the Howgill Fells. The rich natural history of the area and the beautiful scenery created a need for this Visitor Centre; maps, walks, guides, local information and interpretative displays are all found here. There is a full tourist information service.
Open Apr-Nov, daily 10-5.
🅿 *(charged)* 🅱 *(accessible with help Radar key scheme) toilets for disabled shop*
Details not confirmed for 1998

SELLAFIELD
The Sellafield Visitors Centre
CA20 1PG (off A595, signposted)
☎ 019467 27027 Fax 019467 27021
Enter the Sellafield Visitors Centre, and computerised technology takes you into the 21st century. Designed to inform and entertain the whole family, it features 'hands-on' interactive scientific experiments, intriguing shows and fascinating displays of technology.
Open all year, Apr-Oct daily 10-6, Nov-Mar daily 10-4. (Closed 25 Dec). Free.
🅿 🍽 🅱 *(induction loop) toilets for disabled shop* ✖

SHAP
Shap Abbey
(1.5m W on bank of River Lowther)
Shap Abbey was founded by the Premonstratensian order in 1199, and dedicated to St Mary Magdalene. The abbey was dissolved in 1540 and most of the ruins date from the 13th century, some of which are standing to first floor height. The most impressive feature is the 16th-century west tower of the church.
Open any reasonable time.
Free.
🅿 🅱 ⌗

SIZERGH
Sizergh Castle
LA8 8AE (3.5m S of Kendal)
☎ 015395 60070 Fax 015395 60070
The castle has a 60-foot high pele tower, built in the 14th century, but most of the castle dates from the 15th to the 18th centuries. There is a Great Hall and some panelled rooms with fine carved overmantles and adze-hewn floors. The gardens were laid out in the 18th century and contain the Trust's largest limestone rock garden.
Open 1 Apr-24 Oct, Sun-Thu 1.30-5.30; Garden open 12.30. Last admission 5pm.
£4 (ch £2). Family ticket £11. Garden £2. Party 15+.
🅿 🍽 🅱 *(wheelchair and powered buggy for use, braille guide etc) toilets for disabled shop* ✖ 🐾

SKELTON
Hutton-in-the-Forest
CA11 9TH (on B5305)
☎ 017684 84449 Fax 017684 84571
Hutton-in-the-Forest is a beautiful historic house set in magnificent woods which were once part of the medieval forest of Inglewood. The house consists of a 14th-century pele tower with 17th, 18th, and 19th century additions. Inside is a fine collection of furniture, portraits, tapestries and china, a 17th-century gallery and cupid staircase. The lovely 1730s walled garden is a wonderful setting for the large collection of herbaceous plants. There are also 19th-century topiary terraces, a 17th century dovecote and a woodland walk with impressive specimen trees.
Open, House; 1-4 & 10,12,13 Apr; 1 May-4 Oct Thu, Fri & Sun, also BH Mons. Grounds daily (ex Sat) 11-5. Groups any day booked in advance from Apr-Oct.
£3.50 (accompanied ch 7 free, ch £1.50, students £2.50). Family ticket £9. Grounds £2 (ch free & students £1).
🅿 🍽 *shop*

TEMPLE SOWERBY
Acorn Bank Garden
CA10 1SP (6m E of Penrith on A66)
☎ 017683 61893 Fax 017684 82067
The small but delightful garden of some two and a half acres has a particularly interesting walled kitchen garden. It has been turned into a herb garden with an extensive collection of over 180 varieties of medicinal and culinary herbs. Scented plants are grown in the small greenhouse. A circular walk runs beside the Crowdundle Beck. The mill is being restored and will be open to visitors during 1998. Special events include: Newtwatching (28 May) & Apple Day (18 October).

Open 28 Mar-1 Nov, daily 10-5.30 (last admission 5pm).
£2.20 (ch £1.10). Family ticket £5.80. Party.
🅿 🅱 *toilets for disabled shop* ✖ 🐾

TROUTBECK
Townend
LA23 1LB (on S outskirts of village)
☎ 015394 32628
The house is one of the finest examples of a 'statesman' (wealthy yeoman) farmer's house in Cumbria. It was built in 1626 for George Browne, and the Browne family lived there until 1943. Inside is the original home-made carved furniture, with domestic utensils, letters and papers of the farm.
Open 1 Apr-1 Nov, Tue-Fri, Sun & BH Mon 1-5 or dusk if earlier. Last admission 4.30pm.
£2.80 (ch £1). Family ticket £7.50.
🅿 🍽 🐾

ULVERSTON
Laurel & Hardy Museum
4c Upper Brook St LA12 7BH
☎ 01229 582292 & 861614
Ulverston was the birthplace of Stan Laurel, so perhaps it is not then so surprising that the town should boast the world's only Laurel and Hardy museum, now extended to more than double the original floor area. Exhibits include a display of Oliver Hardy memorabilia obtained from Harlem, Georgia (Ollie's birthplace), and waxwork figures of Laurel and Hardy from the House of Wax at Great Yarmouth. Newsreels and documentary films are shown continuously and hourly talks given on Laurel and Hardy. Special children's show at weekends and during school holidays.
Open all year, daily 10-4.30. (Closed 25 Dec).
🅿 *(100 yds)* 🅱 *toilets for disabled shop*
Details not confirmed for 1998
Cards: 🌀 🔤

WINDERMERE
Lake District National Park Visitor Centre
Brockhole LA23 1LJ (on A591, between Windermere and Ambleside)
☎ 015394 46601 & 01539 73126(minicom) Fax 015394 45555
Brockhole, built in 1899 for a wealthy businessman, is a large house, set in 32 acres of landscaped gardens and grounds, standing on the eastern shore of Lake Windermere. It became England's first National Park Visitor Centre in 1969. Operated by the Lake District National Park Authority its purpose is to help vistors to enjoy and appreciate England's largest National Park. The Centre offers exhibitions, audio-visual programmes, lake cruises, an exciting adventure playground and an extensive events programme. After major refurbishment the Visitor Centre reopens in April '98 with new interactive exhibitions about the Lake District - A must for anyone wishing to know more about the area. Edwardian gardens designed by Thomas Mawson provide year-round interest. Contact the park for 1998 events programme.
Open 4 Apr-1 Nov, daily 10-5pm. Grounds and gardens only open all year. Free.
🅿 *(charged)* 🍽 ✖ *licensed* 🅱 *toilets for disabled shop*
Cards: 🌀 🔤 💳 🔤 🔟

Windermere Steamboat Museum
Rayrigg Rd LA23 1BN (0.25m N Bowness Bay)
☎ 015394 45565 Fax 015394 48769
A unique and historic collection of Victorian and Edwardian steamboats and vintage motorboats which reflects the enormous part boating has played over many years in the history of Lake Windermere - a popular lake for both motorboat and sailboat enthusiasts. Many of the exhibits in this extensive collection are still afloat and in working order, including the oldest steamboat in the world - the S L Dolly of 1850. There are special displays telling the social and commercial history of England's largest lake. Steamboat trips daily, weather permitting. Special events planned for 1998 include: monthly art exhibitions, Model Boat Rally (9 May), Classic Motor Boat Rally (1 August), Steam Boat Association Rally (July).
Open 23 Mar-1 Nov daily, 10-5. Steamboat trips subject to availability & weather.
❋*£2.90 (ch £1.50, pen & students £2.60). Family ticket £7.60. Party 12+. Prices under review.*
🅿 🍽 🅱 *toilets for disabled shop*
Cards: 🌀 🔤 🔤

DERBYSHIRE

BAKEWELL
See advertisement

BOLSOVER
Bolsover Castle
S44 6PR (on A632)
☎ 01246 823349
The castle is an enchanting and romantic spectacle, situated high on a wooded hilltop dominating the surrounding landscape. Built on the site of a Norman castle, this is largely an early 17th century mansion. Explore the 'Little Castle' or 'keep', a unique celebration of Jacobean romanticism with its elaborate fireplaces, panelling and wall-paintings. There is also an impressive 17th century indoor Riding School, built by the Duke of Newcastle, which is still occasionally used, and an exhibition of the Duke of Newcastle's horsemanship.
Open all year, Apr-1 Nov, daily 10-6 (or dusk if earlier in Oct); 2 Nov-Mar, Wed-Sun 10-4. Closed 24-26 Dec & 1 Jan.
£2.90 (ch £1.50, pen, students & UB40 £2.20). Personal stereo tour included in admission.
🅿 🅱 *(keep not accessible) shop* ✖ ⌗

BUXTON
Poole's Cavern (Buxton Country Park)
Green Ln SK17 9DH (from A6 or A515 follow Tourist signs)
☎ 01298 26978 Fax 01298 26978
Limestone rock, water and millions of years created this magnificent natural cavern containing thousands of spectacular crystal formations including the longest stalactite in the Peak District. A guided journey lasting 45 minutes leads the visitor through chambers used as a shelter by Bronze-Age cave dwellers, Roman metal workers and as a hideout by the infamous robber Poole. Attractions include the underground source of the River Wye, the 'Poached Egg Chamber', Mary Queen of Scots Pillar, the Grand Cascade and underground sculpture formations. The cave has a level path with only 16 steps and a constant temperature of 7c (44f). Above ground is a woodland country park with trails to the panoramic view from Solomon's Temple.
Open Mar-Oct, daily 10-5. (Open in winter for groups only)
❋*£3.80 (ch £2, pen & student £3). Party 15+. Family tickets.*
🅿 🍽 🅱 *toilets for disabled shop* ✖ *(ex in woodland)*

CALKE
Calke Abbey
DE73 1LE (9m S of Derby, on A514)
☎ 01332 863822
Fax 01332 865272
This fine baroque mansion dating from the early 18th century was built for Sir John Harpur and remained the family home until its acquisition by the National Trust who describe it as the 'house that time forgot'. Among its treasures are an extensive natural history collection, a magnificent Chinese silk state bed (its hangings in mint condition), and a spectacular red and white drawing room. The house stands in extensive wooded parkland and also has walled flower gardens. Guided tours available but no photography allowed in the house. ➤

Open 1 Apr-1 Nov Sat-Wed (incl BH Mon); House & church 12.45-5.30 Gardens from 11am. Last admission 5pm. Park open all year, Apr-Oct closes 9pm or dusk if earlier, Nov-Mar closes at dusk. House, church & garden closed Sat 15 Aug. Admission to house for all is by timed ticket, obtained on arrival. £4.90 (ch £2.45). Family ticket £12.25.
P X licensed & (braille guide, hearing system, buggy/wheelchair available) toilets for disabled shop

CASTLETON
Blue-John Cavern & Mine
Buxton Rd S33 8WP
☎01433 620638 & 620642 Fax 01433 621586
The cavern is a remarkable example of a water-worn cave, and measures over a third of a mile long, with chambers 200ft high. It contains 8 of the 14 veins of Blue John stone, and has been the major source of this unique form of fluorspar for nearly 300 years.
Open all year daily 9.30-6 (or dusk) (telephone for Jan & Feb opening times). Conducted tours every 10-15 mins, tour takes 50min-1 hour. Closed 24-26 Dec & 1 Jan.
✱£4.50 (ch £2.50 pen £3, student £3.50) Family ticket £13. Party.
P (100yds) shop
Cards: ■ ■ ■ ■ ■ ■

Peak Cavern
S33 8WS (on A625)
☎01433 620285
This is one of the most spectacular natural limestone caves in the Peak District, and has an electrically-lit underground walk of about half a mile. Ropes have been made for over 500 years in the 'Grand Entrance Hall', and traces of a row of cottages can be seen.
Open Etr-end Oct, daily 10-5.(last tour 4pm). Nov-Easter weekends only 10-4 (last tour 3pm).
✱£4 (ch £2, other concessions £3). Prices under review.
P (charged) shop
Cards: ■ ■

Peveril Castle
Market Place S30 2WX (on S side of Castleton)
☎01433 620613
William Peveril, one of William the Conqueror's most trusted Knights, guarded the King's manors in the peak from this natural vantage point. Today's visitor is greeted with spectacular views across the Hope valley and beyond, and the area is a Site of Special Scientific Interest.
Open all year, Apr-1 Nov, daily 10-6 (or dusk if earlier in Oct); 2 Nov-Mar, Wed-Sun 10-4. Closed 24-26 Dec & 1 Jan.
£1.75 (ch 90p, concession £1.30)
shop

Speedwell Cavern
Winnats Pass S33 8WA (off A625, 0.5m W of Castleton Village).
☎01433 620512 Fax 01433 621888
Visitors descend 105 steps to a boat which takes them on a one-mile underground exploration of the floodlit cavern with its 'bottomless pit'.
Open all year, daily 9.30-5. (Closed 25 Dec).
£5 (ch £3) at all times.
P (charged) shop
Cards: ■ ■ ■ ■ ■ ■

Treak Cliff Cavern
S33 8WP (0.75m W of Castleton on A625)
☎01433 620571 Fax 01433 620519
Discover the rich deposits of the rare and beautiful Blue John Stone and fine stalactites and stalagmites on a guided tour of the Caverns, which are illuminated by electric lighting and have safe, clean footpaths. The Dream Cave, Aladdin's Cave, Fairyland Grotto, the Seven Dwarfs, the Fossil Cave, the Dome of St Paul's, the Witches Cave and the 'Pillar' - the largest piece of Blue John ever found are all seen in the quarter of a

mile tour which lasts about 40 minutes. Open all year, Mar-Oct daily 9.30-5.30, Nov-Feb daily 10-4. (Closed 25 Dec). All tours are guided & last about 40 mins. Last tour starts 40 mins before closing. Adults £4.95 (ch5-15 £2.25). Family ticket £13.
P shop
Cards: ■ ■ ■ ■

CHATSWORTH
Chatsworth
DE45 1PP (8m N of Matlock on B6012)
☎01246 582204 Fax 01246 583536
Chatsworth is the palatial home of the Duke and Duchess of Devonshire, and has one of the richest collections of fine and decorative arts in private hands. Inside there is a splendid painted hall, and a great staircase leads to the even finer chapel, which is decorated with marble, paintings, statues and paintings on walls and ceiling. There are magnificent pictures, furniture and porcelain, and a memorable trompe l'oeil painting of a violin on the music room door. The park is one of the finest in Britain. It was laid out by 'Capability' Brown, but is most famous as the work of Joseph Paxton (later Sir Joseph), who became head gardener in the 19th century. Notable features include the Cascade and the Emperor Fountain, which sends up a jet of water to 290ft. Other attractions are the farmyard and adventure playground. Guided tours are available at extra cost. Numerous events planned for 1998 include: Chatsworth Angling Fair (9-10 May), Country Fair (5-6 September).
Open 18 Mar-1 Nov. House & garden 11-4.30, Farmyard 10.30-4.30
House & Garden £6.25 (ch £3, students & pen £5). Family ticket £16. Garden only £3.60 (ch £1.75, students & pen £3). Family ticket £9. Farmyard & Adventure Playground £3.00. Car park £1.
P (charged) X licensed & (3 electric wheelchairs available for garden) toilets for disabled shop garden centre (ex park & gardens)
Cards: ■ ■ ■ ■ ■

CRESWELL
Creswell Crags Visitor Centre
off Crags Rd S80 3LH (1m E off B6042)
☎01909 720378
The deep narrow gorge of Creswell Crags is pitted with 24 caves and rock shelters which were used for seasonal camps by Stone Age hunter-gatherers. Unusual finds from within the caves include pieces of decorated animal bone and the remains of animals which have long since become extinct, such as the woolly mammoth and hyena. A visitor centre at one end of the gorge explains the importance of the site, with an exhibition and an audio-visual showing what life was like in prehistoric times. From there, a trail leads through the gorge, where visitors can look into some of the caves through grills; guided cave tours are organised throughout the year. There is a picnic site at the centre, and various events are held.
Open all year, Feb-Oct, daily, 10.30-4.30; Nov-Jan, Sun only 10.30-4.30.
✱Free (under review). Cave/site tour £1.95 (ch £1.45).
P & (wheelchair loan) toilets for disabled shop

CRICH
National Tramway Museum
DE4 5DP (off B5035)
☎01773 852565 Fax 01773 852326
This unique 'action stop' offers a mile-long scenic journey through a Period Street to open countryside with panoramic views. Visitors can enjoy unlimited vintage tram rides. The exhibition hall houses the largest national collection of vintage electric trams from home and abroad. Other attractions include a video theatre, shops, cafe, a playground and picnic areas. There is plenty to see and do, both indoors and outdoors. Events planned for 1998 include Tram Jamboree, Horse Tram Day,

Children's Day 'Funtasia', Festival of Transport, Treasure Hunt, Starlight Special. Please telephone for dates.
Open daily, Apr-Oct (ex Apr 24 & Fridays in May), Sept & Oct (Special Fri openings on May 29, Sep 4, Oct 23 & 30, & Nov 1) 10-5.30 (6.30 Wknd & BH).
£5.90 (ch £3, pen £5.10). Family ticket £16.20
P & Braille guidebooks, ramps, converted tram, talktype facility toilets for disabled shop Specialist books, model kits
Cards: ■ ■ ■ ■

CROMFORD
Cromford Mill
Mill Ln DE4 3RQ
☎01629 824297 Fax 01629 823256
Sir Richard Arkwright established the world's first successful water-powered cotton spinning mill at Cromford in 1771. The Arkwright Society are involved in a major restoration to create a lasting monument to an extraordinary genius. Guided tours available.
Open all year, daily 9-5 (Closed 25 Dec). Guided tours 10-4.
P X & toilets for disabled shop
Details not confirmed for 1998

DENBY
Denby Pottery Visitors Centre
Derby Rd DE5 8NX (8m N of Derby, on B6179)
☎01773 740799 Fax 01773 570211
Guided factory tours show the intricate skills of the potters craft, including throwing, turning, glazing and decorating. The museum illustrates the history of Denby Pottery. There is a large factory shop selling Denby products. Within the courtyard area are the self service restaurant, a Dartington Crystal Factory Shop, a florist and children's play area. Please check tour times and availabilty prior to arriving at the visitor centre.
Open all year. Full factory tours, Mon-Thu 10.30 & 1. Craftroom only, daily 10-3.15. Factory shop, Mon-Sat 9.30-5, Sun 11-5. Visitors Centre Mon-Sat 9.30-5, Sun 10-5. Factory tours £3.75 (ch & pen £2.25). Craftroom only £2.75 (ch & pen £1.75).
P X licensed & (lift) toilets for disabled shop garden centre (ex guide dogs)
Cards: ■ ■ ■ ■ ■

DERBY
Derby Museum & Art Gallery
The Strand DE1 1BS
☎01332 716659 & 716669 Fax 01332 716670
The museum has a wide range of displays, notably of Derby porcelain and of paintings by the local artist Joseph Wright (1734-97). Also antiquities, natural history and militaria, as well as many temporary exhibitions.
Open all year, Mon 11-5, Tue-Sat 10-5, Sun & BHs 2-5. (Closed Xmas telephone for details).
Free.
P (50yds) & (lift to all floors) toilets for disabled shop (ex guide dogs)

Industrial Museum
The Silk Mill, Silk Mill Ln, off Full St DE1 3AR
☎01332 255308 Fax 01332 255804
The museum is set in an early 18th-century silk mill and adjacent flour mill. Displays cover local mining, quarrying and industries, and include a major collection of Rolls Royce aero-engines from 1915 to the present. There is also a new railway section. Temporary exhibitions are held.
Open all year, Mon 11-5, Tue-Sat 10-5, Sun & BHs 2-5. (Closed Xmas telephone for details).
Free.
P & (lift to all floors) toilets for disabled shop (ex guide dogs)

Pickford's House Social History Museum
41 Friar Gate DE1 1DA
☎01332 255363 Fax 01332 255804
The house was built in 1770 by the architect Joseph Pickford as a combined workplace and family home, and stands in Derby's most handsome street. Pickford's house now shows domestic life at different periods, with Georgian reception rooms and service areas and a 1930s bathroom. Other galleries are devoted to temporary exhibitions, especially on social history, textiles and costume themes. There is also a display on the growth of Georgian Derby, and on Pickford's contribution to Midlands architecture. The garden has been reconstructed in the Georgian style.
Open all year, Mon 11-5, Tue-Sat 10-5, Sun & BHs 2-5. Closed Xmas, telephone for details.
Free.
P & shop (ex guide dogs)

ELVASTON
Elvaston Castle Country Park
Borrowash Rd DE72 3EP (signposted from A6 & A52)
☎01332 571342 Fax 01332 758751
The 200-acre park was landscaped in the early 19th century, and became one of Britain's first country parks in 1968. Restored after 30 years of neglect, it includes elaborate topiary gardens from the 19th-century scheme, and a walled kitchen garden now planted out as an Old English Garden with herbaceous borders, roses and scented herbs. The old estate workshops have been restored as an Estate Museum, with exhibitions of blacksmithing, saddlery and other traditional crafts associated with country houses at the turn of the century. There are also nature trails and numerous walks, exhibitions and displays, and a caravan and campsite. Events include craft fairs in March, May, June, and October, antique fairs in April, May, August and November, and much more. A full list of events is available on request.
Open all year, daily dawn-dusk. Museum, Apr-Oct, Wed-Sat 1-4.30, Sun & BH's 10-4.30.

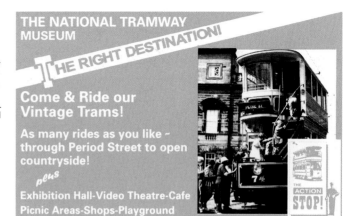

Museum: £1.20 (ch & pen 60p). Family ticket £3.
🅿 *(charged)* 🍴 ✕ *licensed* ♿ *toilets for disabled shop*

EYAM
Eyam Hall
EYAM S32 5QW (in village centre)
☎ *01433 631976 Fax 01433 631603*
Built for and still occupied by the Wright family, Eyam Hall is an intimate 17th-century manor house situated in the heart of the famous "plague village". The Hall offers a glimpse of three centuries of domestic history through the eyes of one family in portraits, furniture, tapestries, costumes and family memorabilia. Converted farm buildings house the Eyam Hall Craft Centre where there are many diverse local products for sale.
Open: House: 15 Apr-1 Nov, Wed,Thur,Sun & BH: first tour 11am, last tour 4.30pm. Craft centre open Tue-Sun 28 Feb-24 Dec 10.30-5.30.
£3.50 (ch £2.50, pen & concessions £3.00). Family ticket £10.50. Party.
🅿 🍴 ✕ *licensed* ♿ *(disabled may enter by special gate, avoiding steps) toilets for disabled shop* 🐾 *(ex guide dogs)*
Cards: 🌑 ▭ ▭ ▭

HADDON HALL
Haddon Hall
DE45 1LA (1.5 S of Bakewell off A6)
☎ *01629 812855 Fax 01629 814379*
Originally held by the illegitimate son of William the Conqueror, Haddon has been owned by the Dukes of Rutland since the 16th century. Little has been added since the reign of Henry VIII, whose elder brother was a frequent guest. Despite its time-worn steps, no other medieval house has so successfully withstood the ravages of time. There is also a world renowned rose garden. Special events include a Flower Festival from 15-24 June.
Open 1 April-30 Sept, 11am-5pm.
£5.50 (ch £3 & pen £4.75). Family ticket £14.75. Party 20+.
🅿 *(charged)* ✕ *licensed* ♿ *shop* 🐾
Cards: 🌑 ▭

HARDWICK HALL
Hardwick Hall
S44 5QJ (2m S M1 Junc 29)
☎ *01246 850430 Fax 01246 854200*
The splendid Elizabethan mansion is celebrated as the creation of Bess of Hardwick, a redoubtable character, who was married and widowed four times and became immensely rich in the process. She began the magnificent building at 70 after the death of her fourth husband, the Earl of Shrewsbury. They quarrelled and separated, but he left her even richer than before.
The house is remarkable for its vast area of windows, which become taller from the ground floor up. The six towers are topped by Bess's monogram, ES. Inside, the house and contents, such as Bess's great jewel chest, have escaped change because her descendants lived mainly at Chatsworth instead. The High Great Chamber and the long gallery were probably designed to display the tapestries which line them. The latter room is also hung with Cavendish portraits. There are numerous other tapestries, with some fine needlework by Bess and her ladies, and by Mary, Queen of Scots, who was the Earl of Shrewsbury's prisoner for 15 years. In the kitchen are hundreds of 18th-and 19th-century pots, pans and plates, all marked with a ducal coronet. The gardens are laid out in walled courtyards, and there is a large park.
Open 1 Apr-1 Nov Wed, Thu, Sat, Sun & BH Mon 12.30-5. (Closed Good Fri). Last admission 4.30pm. Garden 1 Apr-1 Nov daily 12-5.30. Park all year daily dawn-dusk. Car park closes 6pm.
House & garden £6 (ch £3). Family ticket £15. Garden only £2.70 (ch £1, family £6.50)
🍴 ✕ *licensed* ♿ *(hearing scheme wheelchair if prebooked) toilets for disabled shop* 🐾 *(ex in park on leads)* 🐾
Cards: 🌑 ▭

ILKESTON
American Adventure Theme Park
DE7 5SX (off M1 junct 26, signposted)
☎ *01773 531521 Fax 01773 716140*
This is one of Britain's few fully themed parks, based on the legend of a whole continent. The experiences of a day out here are widely varied, from the heartpounding action of the Missile Rollercoaster in Spaceport USA, to the wet and wild excitement of the Rocky Mountain Rapids ride and the Nightmare Niagara log flume. Take a gentle excursion across Lake Reflection aboard a Mississippi paddle steamer, watch a shoot-out in Silver City, see the glamorous Lazy Lil's Saloon Show, or experience the carnival atmosphere of Mexicoland.
Open Easter-end Oct daily from 10am.
❋*£11.99 (ch under 0.9m free, otherwise £9.99, pen £1.99). Party.*
🅿 🍴 ✕ *licensed* ♿ *(free wheelchair hire) toilets for disabled shop* 🐾 *(ex guide dogs)*
Cards: 🌑 ▭ ▭ ▭ 🅂 🅹

KEDLESTON HALL
Kedleston Hall
DE22 5JH (5m NW of Derby)
☎ *01332 842191 Fax 01332 841972*
Thought by many to be the finest Robert Adam house in the country, Kedleston has been the Derbyshire home of the Curzon family for over eight centuries. The original house was demolished at the end of the 17th century when the rather muddled start to the building of the present mansion began. The architect Matthew Brettingham gave Kedleston its present day plan of a main block and two wings linked by corridors; James Paine is responsible for the imposing north front. It wasn't until 1760 that Adam appeared on the scene. He built the south front and designed most of the interior including the awe-inspiring marble hall, regarded as one of the most splendid rooms in Europe. There are some notable pictures, furniture and china displayed in the house together with an Indian Museum containing the collection accumulated by Lord Curzon, Viceroy of India from 1898 to 1905. The charming boathouse and bridge in the gardens were also designed by Adam.
Open - House; 28 Mar-1 Nov, Sat-Wed 1-5.30, last admission 5pm, (closed Good Fri). Garden; same as house but open 11-6. Park; 28 Mar-1 Nov daily 11-6, 2 Nov-20 Dec, Sat & Sun 12-4 (entry charge £2 on Thu/Fri for park only).
£4.70 (ch £2.40). Family ticket £11.50.
🅿 ✕ *licensed* ♿ *(braille guide, wheelchair, self-drive vehicle) toilets for disabled shop* 🐾 *(ex in park, must be on leads)* 🐾
Cards: 🌑 ▭

MATLOCK
Riber Castle Wildlife Park
DE4 5JU (A614 to Tanley, via Alders Lane and Carr Lane to Riber)
☎ *01629 582070 Fax 01629 582073*
The wildlife park is set in the grounds of ruined 19th-century Riber Castle on 853ft-high Riber Hill and enjoys magnificent views over the Derwent Valley and towards Crich Stand. The park houses a unique collection of animals and birds - rare and endangered species such as lynx, otters, wild boar and owls live happily alongside marmots, Shetland ponies, goats, tortoises, wallabies, rabbits and many more. Ornamental pheasants, peafowl and emus can also be seen. Many breeding programmes are in progress. There are daily animal and bird feeding sessions.
Open all year, daily from 10am. (Summer last admission 5pm, winter 3-4.30pm). Closed 25 Dec.
🅿 🍴 ♿ *(ramp to cafe and bar. Wide mainly flat paths) toilets for disabled shop* 🐾 *(in animal section)*

MATLOCK BATH
Heights of Abraham
DE4 3PD (on A6 next to railway station)
☎ *01629 582365 Fax 01629 580279*
High on a hill above the village of Matlock Bath are the Grounds of the Heights of

➤

Abraham. Until recently the climb to the summit was only for the very energetic, but now alpine-style cable cars provide a leisurely and spectacular way of reaching the top from their starting point near Matlock Bath Railway Station. Once inside the Grounds there is plenty to do for the whole family. Two famous show caverns provide fascinating tours, one is introduced by a multivision programme and the other tells the story of a 17th-century lead miner. A coffee shop, licensed restaurant and picnic sites take advantage of the superb views. There is also a nature trail, the Victoria Prospect Tower and play area, the Owl Maze, the Explorers Challenge and landscaped water gardens. Your cable car ticket includes all the attractions in the grounds and both cavern tours.
Open daily Etr-Oct 10-5 (later in high season) for Autumn & Winter opening telephone for details.
❋£5.95 (ch £3.90 & pen £4.95).
P (300m) 🍽 ✗ licensed & toilets for disabled shop
Cards: 🄰 🄱 🄲

Peak District Mining Museum
The Pavilion DE4 3NR (off A6)
☎ 01629 583834
A large and rewarding display, ideal for families, explains the history of the Derbyshire lead industry from Roman times to the present day. The geology of the area, mining and smelting processes, the quarrying and the people who worked in the industry, are all illustrated by a series of static and moving exhibits. The museum also features an early 19th-century water pressure pumping engine - the only one of its kind in Britain. A new exhibit is the interactive 'Hazards of Mining' display.
Open all year, daily 11-4 (later in summer season). (Closed 25 Dec).
Museum & Mine: £3 (ch, students, disabled & pen £2.25). Family £7. Museum only or mine only £2 (ch, students, disabled £1.50). Family £4. Party rates.
🅿 (charged) 🍽 & shop

Temple Mine
Temple Rd DE4 3NR (off A6)
☎ 01629 583834
In the process of being restored to how it was in the 1920s and 1930s, this old lead and fluorspar workings makes interesting viewing. A self-guided tour illustrates the geology, mineralisation and mining techniques.
Open all year, Summer 12-4, Winter timed visits during afternoon.
Museum & Mine: £3 (ch, pen, disabled £2.25). Family ticket £7. Museum only or mine only: £2 (ch, pen, disabled £1.50), Family £4. Party rates.
P shop ⌘ guide dogs

MELBOURNE
Melbourne Hall
DE73 1EN (9m S of Derby on A514)
☎ 01332 862502 Fax 01332 862263
In 1133 Henry I gave his royal manor of Melbourne to the first Bishop of Carlisle; hence the surprisingly large parish church of St Michael and St Mary. The lease was then sold to Sir John Coke (Charles I's Secretary of State) in 1628 and the house is still owned by his descendants. Through the centuries the hall has been converted from manor house to a much grander residence which has been the home of two of Britain's most famous Prime Ministers: Lord Melbourne and Lord Palmerston. It features fine collections of pictures and antique furniture, but its chief appeal is its intimate and 'lived in' atmosphere. The glorious formal gardens are among the finest in Britain, and were laid out in about 1720 by royal gardeners London and Wise, who followed the style of the great French garden designer, Le Nôtre. Special events are usually held each Sunday afternoon in August.
Open, house daily throughout Aug only (ex first three Mons) 2-5. Prebooked parties by appointment in Aug. Gardens Apr-Sep, Wed, Sat, Sun & BH Mon 2-6. House Tue-Sat (guided tour) £2.50 (ch £1, pen £2), Sun & BH Mon (no guided tour) £2 (ch 75p, pen £1.50). House & Garden (Aug only) £4.50 (ch £2.50, pen £3.50). Garden only £3 (pen £2). Family £8.
P (200 yds) 🍽 & (ramp at garden entrance) shop ⌘

MIDDLETON BY WIRKSWORTH
Middleton Top Engine House
Middleton Top Visitor Centre DE4 4LS (0.5m S from B5036 Cromford/Wirksworth road)
☎ 01629 823204
Fax 01629 825336
Set above the village of Middleton, site of one of Britain's very few limestone mines, a beam engine built in 1829 for the Cromford and High Peak Railway can be seen in its octagonal engine house. The engine's job was to haul wagons up the Middleton Incline, and its last trip was in 1963 after 134 years' work. The visitor centre tells the story of this historic railway, and there is also a picnic area alongside the High Peak Trail, popular with cyclists, walkers and riders.
Open: High Peak Trail all year; Information Centre, wknds all year, wkdays in summer; Bicycle hire, summer season daily (Etr-Dec wknds only). Engine House Etr-Oct first wknd in month (engine in motion). Static Engine 50p (ch 25p). Working Engine £1 (ch 50p).
🅿 (charged) & (ex Engine house) toilets for disabled shop

OLD WHITTINGTON
Revolution House
High St S41 9LA (on B6052 off A61, signposted)
☎ 01246 453554 & 345727
Fax 01246 345720
Originally the Cock and Pynot alehouse, this 17th century cottage was the scene of a meeting between local noblemen to plan their part in the Revolution of 1688. The house is now furnished in 17th-century style. A video relates the story of the Revolution and there is a small exhibition room.
Open 10 Apr-11 Nov, daily 10-4. Xmas opening 16 -24 Dec & 27 Dec-3 Jan, daily 10-4.
Free.
P (100yds) & shop ⌘ (ex guide dogs)

RIPLEY
Midland Railway Centre
Butterley Station DE5 3QZ (1m N of Ripley on B6179)
☎ 01773 747674 & 749788
Fax 01773 570721
This centre not only operates a regular steam-train passenger service, but also provides the focal point for a fascinating industrial museum project. Its aim is to depict every aspect of the golden days of the Midland Railway and its successors. The working section of the railway line extends for some three and a half miles between Butterley Station and Riddings. Exhibits range from the steam locomotives of 1866 to an electric locomotive. There is also a large section of rolling stock spanning the last 100 years. 'Specials' run from the centre include Wine and Dine trains and Santa Specials. Also of interest is the narrow-gauge railway, an award-winning country park, a demonstration signal box, Victorian railwayman's cottage, and a farm park. The many special events throughout 1998 include Friends of Thomas the Tank Engine Days, vintage weekends, and Santa Specials. Please telephone for a complete list.
Open: every Sunday from 25th Jan, every Saturday from 24th Jan-7th Nov & 28th Nov-27th Dec, every Wednesday from 1st Apr-29th Oct(ex 11th June). Daily 21 Feb-1 Mar, 7-19 Apr, 23-31 May, 22-25 June, 14 July-7 Sept, 24 Oct-1 Nov. £7.95 (pen £6.50, ch £1) Two children free with each adult. Party 15+.
🅿 🍽 & (special accommodation on trains) toilets for disabled shop
Cards: 🄰 🄱 🄲 🄳 🄴

SUDBURY
Sudbury Hall
DE6 5HT (6m E of Uttoxeter)
☎ 01283 585305
Fax 01283 585139
This fine country house was started in 1664 by Lord George Vernon. It has unusual diapered brickwork, a carved two-storey stone frontispiece, a cupola and a large number of tall chimneys. The interior is particularly interesting, with work by some of the best craftsmen of the day: there are plasterwork ceilings by Bradbury and Pettifer, ceiling paintings by Laguerre, a fine carved staircase by Edward Pierce and an overmantel by Grinling Gibbons. The Museum of Childhood, also run by the National Trust, contains a Victorian schoolroom, collections of toys since the Victorian era, and displays depicting the working lives of children in the early 19th century.
Open 1 Apr-1 Nov, Wed-Sun + BH Mon (closed Good Fri) 1-5.30pm or sunset if earlier. Wknds throughout season and all open days in July/Aug 12.30-5. Last admissions 30 mins before closing. Gardens open 12.30-6pm.
House £3.50 (ch £1.60). Family ticket £8.60. Museum of Childhood £3.50. Joint ticket £5.50. Joint Family ticket £13.70. Party.
🅿 🍽 & (wheelchair available. braille guide. hearing system) toilets for disabled shop ⌘ (ex in grounds) 🐾

WIRKSWORTH
Wirksworth Heritage Centre
Crown Yard DE4 4ET (on B5023 off A6)
☎ 01629 825225
The Centre has been created in an old silk and velvet mill. The three floors of the mill have interpretative displays of the town's past history as the hub of a prosperous lead-mining industry. Each floor offers many features of interest including a computer game called 'Rescue the injured lead-miner' and a mock-up of a natural cavern. The lifestyle of a quarryman in the early 1900's is recreated in the Quarryman's House Place. Some unusual local customs such as tap dressing and 'clypping the church' are explained. There are also workshops showing the skills of cabinetmakers and a silversmiths. If you visit Wirksworth during Spring Bank Holiday, you can also see the famous Well Dressings.*Open mid Feb-Etr & Nov Wed-Sat 11-4, Sun 1-*

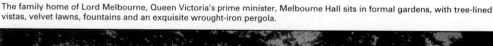
The family home of Lord Melbourne, Queen Victoria's prime minister, Melbourne Hall sits in formal gardens, with tree-lined vistas, velvet lawns, fountains and an exquisite wrought-iron pergola.

4. Etr-mid Jul & mid Sep-Oct Tue-Sat 10.30-4.30, Sun 1-4.30. mid Jul-mid Sep daily 10-5. Also BH Sun & Mon. Last admission 40 mins before closing.
❈£1 (ch & pen 80p) Family ticket £2.80. Party 20+.
P (80 yds) (pay & display) ⬛ ✖ licensed shop ◈ (ex guide dogs)

DEVON

APPLEDORE
North Devon Maritime Museum
Odun House, Odun Rd EX39 1PT
☎01237 422064
Appledore's traditional activities of boat-building and fishing make the village a suitable home for the museum. Each room shows a different aspect of North Devon's maritime history, including steam and motor coasters. There is also a full-size reconstruction of an Appledore kitchen of around 1900. A Victorian schoolroom, recreating an Appledore schoolroom c1890-1900, is available (with costumes) for school parties. There are also video showings, a research room with record office service point for parish records, and a large collection of photographs and documents (by appointment only).
Open Etr-Oct, daily 2-5, May-Sep, Mon-Fri 11-1pm.
£1 (ch 30p & pen 70p).
P (opposite) & (hands-on items for visually impaired) toilets for disabled shop ◈ (ex guide dogs)

ARLINGTON
Arlington Court
EX31 4LP (7m NE of Barnstaple, on A39)
☎01271 850296 Fax 01271 850711
Built in 1822, Arlington Court is filled with a fascinating collection of *objets d'art*: pewter, shells and model ships as well as furniture and costumes from the 19th century. The biggest attraction, however, is the collection of carriages and horsedrawn vehicles, and rides are available. Around the house is a landscaped park grazed by Shetland ponies and sheep. There is a Victorian garden and a conservatory, and nature trails may be followed through the woods and by the lake. Family Fun Run (18 Apr), North Devon Dressage Competition (13 September), & Carriage Driving Trials (18-19 July). Ring for further details.
Open Apr-Oct, Sun-Fri 11-5.30; also Sat of BH wknds. Footpaths through park and woods open Nov-Mar during daylight hours.
House & grounds £5.10. Grounds only £2.80.
P ⬛ ✖ licensed & (wheelchairs available - ramped steps at house) toilets for disabled shop ◈ (ex in park) ♨
Cards: 🅰 ▭ ▭

BARNSTAPLE
Marwood Hill Gardens
EX31 4EB (signposted off A361)
☎01271 42528
The gardens with their three small lakes cover 18 acres and have many rare trees and shrubs. There is a large bog garden and a walled garden, collections of clematis, camellias and eucalyptus. Alpine plants are also a feature, and there are plants for sale.
Open daily dawn to dusk.
£2 (ch 12 free if accompanied).
P ⬛ & garden centre

BEER
Pecorama Pleasure Gardens
Underleys EX12 3NA (from A3052 take B3174, Beer road, signed)
☎01297 21542 Fax 01297 20229
The gardens are high on a hillside, overlooking the delightful fishing village of Beer. A miniature steam and diesel passenger line offers visitors a stunning view of Lyme Bay as it runs through the Pleasure Gardens. These feature 'Melody Close' and the 'Top Spot' where entertainment is staged during high season. Other attractions include an aviary, crazy golf and children's activity area. The main building houses an exhibition of railway modelling in various small gauges, displayed in settings around the house and gardens. There are souvenir and railway model shops, plus full catering facilities. The annual Pecorama Steam and Model Festival will take place on 13-14 June. Live steam exhibits including full-size traction engines and scale model locomotives will be on display.
Open Etr-Oct (including Autumn Half Term) , Mon-Fri 10-5.30, Sat 10-1. Also Sun at Etr & Whitsun-Aug.
❈£3.20 (ch 4-14 £1.75, under 4 free, pen £2.90, over 80's & disabled helpers free).
P ⬛ ✖ licensed & (wheelchair available, some areas of garden steep) toilets for disabled shop souvenirs, Dartington glass ◈ ex guide dogs
Cards: 🅰 ▭ ⑩ ▭ ▭ 🅂

BICKINGTON
Gorse Blossom Miniature Railway and Woodland Park
TQ12 6JD (off A38, W of Newton Abbot at Drumbridges if westbound or Goodstone if eastbound)
☎01626 821361
Unlimited rides are allowed on the three-quarters of a mile, seven and a quarter-inch gauge steam railway line, set amid 35 acres of woodland, about half of which is open to the public. Other attractions include a remarkable outdoor model railway in a mountain setting, based on a line through the Swiss Alps; woodland walks, a nature trail, woodland assault course and giant slide, toytown village and children's play area. For a small extra charge children and adults may drive a ride-on miniature train.
Open Apr-30 Oct, daily 10.30am (last admission 3.45).
£3.90 (ch 3-15 £2.90 & pen £3.50)
P ⬛ & toilets for disabled shop

BICKLEIGH
Bickleigh Castle
EX16 8RP (off A396 follow signs from Bickleigh Bridge)
☎01884 855363
The 'castle' is really a moated and fortified manor house, and was formerly the romantic home of the heirs of the Earls of Devon and later the Carew family. The small detached thatched chapel is said to be the oldest complete building in Devon. It dates from the early Norman period and, like the medieval Gatehouse, survived the destruction which followed the Civil War. The Carew family acquired the house in the 16th century, and it was Admiral Sir George Carew who commanded the Mary Rose on her first and last voyage. He drowned with his men when the ship capsized and sank. There is an exhibition on the ship and on Tudor maritime history, with features on the Titanic, model ships of bygone days, domestic objects and toys from the 18th century onwards. More traditional features of interest include the Great Hall, armoury (including fine Civil War armour), guardroom, Elizabethan bedroom and the 17th-century farmhouse. The garden is moated and the tower can be climbed for views of the Exe Valley and of the castle complex.
Open Etr wk (Good Fri-Fri), then Wed, Sun & BH to late May BH, then daily (ex Sat) to 1st Sun Oct.
£4 (ch 5-15 £2). Family ticket £11. Party 20+.
P ⬛ & (specially arranged tours with experienced guide) shop garden centre ◈ (ex guide dogs)

BICTON
Bicton Park
East Budleigh EX9 7DP (2m N of Budleigh Salterton on B3178)
☎01395 568465 Fax 01395 568889
Bicton Park offers many attractions, but the central one is over 50 acres of colourful gardens, shrubs, woodlands, lakes, ponds and fountains, with an Italian garden and a wonderful restored palm house. This has tropical and sub-

This complete thatched Norman chapel stands among the later buildings of Bickleigh Castle, really a moated and fortified manor house.

tropical areas, where bananas and other exotica flourish. There are also fuchsia, geranium and temperate houses. A modern building houses the James Countryside Museum, which has farm tools, wagons and a cider press among its fascinating displays. Not to be forgotten either are the fun world and adventure playground, the Phibbers Family Tree indoor children's play area, Gotchaland, Bicton Woodland Railway, crazy golf, bird garden and tropical house.
Open all year Apr-Sep 10-6, Oct-Mar 10-4.
P ⬛ ✖ licensed & (adapted carriage on woodland railway, wheelchairs) toilets for disabled shop garden centre
Details not confirmed for 1998
Cards: 🅰 ▭ ▭

BLACKMOOR GATE
Exmoor Zoological Park
South Stowford EX31 4SG (off A399)
☎01598 763352 Fax 01598 763352
These natural and landscaped gardens cover an area of 12.5 acres with a waterfall, streams and a lake with penguins, swans and other water birds, all roaming at liberty. There are aviaries with tropical and exotic birds, and many animal enclosures containing lemurs, marmosets, capybara, rabbits, pigs, tamarins and many more. Set aside from the gardens is Tarzanland for the children. The zoo specializes in close encounters, handling sessions, and keepers' talks.
Open daily, Apr-Oct 10-6; Nov-Mar 10-4. Closed 25-26 Dec.
£4.25 (ch 3-16 £2.75, under 3 free, pen £3.75), Family £12.
P ⬛ & toilets for disabled shop ◈

BUCKFASTLEIGH
Buckfast Abbey
TQ11 0EE (off A38 on A384 Dartbridge turnoff, follow tourist signs for 0.5m)
☎01364 642519 Fax 01364 643891
The story of Buckfast Abbey is a remarkable one. The monastery was originally founded in 1018, but the monks left during the Dissolution in the 16th century. Monks returned to the site in 1882 and considered restoring it; in 1907 four (mostly inexperienced) monks began rebuilding the church; and now Buckfast Abbey is once again a religious community. The church was built on the old foundations, using local blue limestone and Ham Hill stone. One of the most beautiful features is the great modern east window, which was the work of Father Charles, a craftsman in stained glass. Other monks have other skills: in beekeeping, farming, and the making of Buckfast tonic wine. In recent years restoration work has continued in the precinct, where several medieval monastic buildings survive including the 14th century guest hall which is open to the public and contains an exhibition of the history of the Abbey. Monthly concerts are held at the Abbey, please telephone for details.
Open all year daily 5.30am-9.30pm. (visitor facilities 9-5.30 (summer) 10-4.30 (winter))
Free. (Exhibition 75p, child 30p).
P ⬛ & (level site, braille plan, wheelchair available) toilets for disabled shop ◈
Cards: 🅰 ▭ ▭ ▭ 🅂

Buckfast Butterfly Farm & Dartmoor Otter Sanctuary
TQ11 0DZ (off A38, at Dart Bridge junct, follow tourist signs)
☎01364 642916 Fax 01803 762769
Visitors can wander around a specially designed, undercover tropical garden, where free-flying butterflies and moths from around the world can be seen. The otter sanctuary has large enclosures with underwater viewing areas. There are special observation holts where sleeping otters can be seen. Feeding times are 11.30, 2.00, and 4.30, when there are also talks from the keeper.
Open Good Fri-end Oct, daily 10-5.30 or dusk (if earlier).
£4.45 (ch £2.95, pen £3.95), Family £11.95
P ⬛ & (wheelchair ramps) shop ◈ ex guide dogs
Cards: 🅰 ▭ ▭ 🅂

BUCKLAND ABBEY
Buckland Abbey
PL20 6EY (off A386 0.25m S of Yelverton, signed)
☎01822 853607 Fax 01822 855448
Originally a prosperous 13th-century Cistercian Abbey, and then home of the Grenville family, Buckland Abbey was sold to Sir Francis Drake in 1581. By then the abbey church had been converted ➤

into a handsome house with oak panelling and fine plasterwork, and it was his home until he died at sea in 1596. It belonged to the Drake family until 1946. Several restored buildings house a fascinating exhibition about the abbey's history. Among the exhibits is Drake's drum, which is wreathed in legend and is said to give warning of danger to England. There are also craft workshops, which are open at various times, and some lovely walks. Events for 1998: Summer Craft Fair (27-28 June), Family Fun Day (August 21), Buckland Country Days (12-13 September), A Tudor Experience (10-11 October), Holiday activities for families (August & December), Traditional Abbey Christmas Decorations (December, up to Xmas).
Open Apr-1 Nov, daily (ex Thurs) 10.30am-5.30pm. 7 Nov-end Mar, Sat & Sun 2pm-5pm. Last admissions 45mins before closing.
Abbey & grounds £4.30 (ch £2.10). Grounds only £2.20 (ch £1). Party 15+. (Car park charge refundable against purchase of admission ticket).
🅿 *(charged)* ✗ *licensed* ♿ *(wheelchairs & motorised buggy available) toilets for disabled shop* ❀ 🐕

CHITTLEHAMPTON
Cobbaton Combat Collection
Cobbaton EX37 9RZ (signed from A361 & A377)
☎ *01769 540740 & 540414 Fax 01769 540740*
World War II British and Canadian military vehicles, war documents and military equipment can be seen in this private collection. There are over fifty vehicles including tanks, one a Gulf War Centurian, and a recent Warsaw Pact section. There is also a section on 'Mum's War' and the home front. The children's play area includes a Sherman tank.
Open Apr-Oct, daily 10-6. Winter, most weekdays, phone for details.
£4 (ch £2, pen £3.50)
🅿 🍴 ♿ *shop* ❀ *ex guide dogs*
Cards: 🆓 💳 💳

CHUDLEIGH
Canonteign Falls
EX6 7NT (off A38 at Chudleigh/Teign Valley juntion onto B3193 and follow tourist signs for 3m)
☎ *01647 252434 Fax 01647 52617*
A magical combination of waterfalls, woodlands and lakes. Devon at its best, wild and beautiful. A must for all visitors to Devon.
Open all year, Mar-Oct, daily 10-6; Nov-Apr, Sun only 10-5.
£3.50 (ch £2.25 & pen £3). Party 12+.
🅿 🍴 ✗ *licensed shop*
Cards: 🆓 💳 💳 💳 💳

CLOVELLY
The Milky Way Adventure Park
EX39 5RY (on the A39, 2m from Clovelly)
☎ *01237 431255 Fax 01237 431735*
One of the West Country's leading attractions offers you a day in the country that's simply out of this world. Attractions include Time Warp - the South West's largest indoor adventure zone; the North Devon Bird of Prey Centre with twice daily displays; laser target shooting; archery; Cuddling Corner with bottle feeding show time and much much more.
Open 21 Mar-Oct, daily 10.30-6.
🅿 🍴 ♿ *toilets for disabled shop*
Details not confirmed for 1998
Cards: 🆓 💳 💳 💳

CLYST ST MARY
Crealy Adventure Park
Sidmouth Rd EX5 1DR (leave M5 junct 30 onto A3052 Exeter to Sidmouth road)
☎ *01395 233200 Fax 01395 233111*
Crealy Adventure Park, the biggest park in the West Country offers a complete, one-stop day out for all the family where excellent value combined with first rate care equals an unforgettable experience. The West Country's leading animal park - animals to feed, hold, ride, milk and

cuddle! Plus wet & wild bumper boats; peaceful riverside meadow, lake and trails; huge indoor and outdoor playgrounds; rip-roaring racetracks. Our vast Big Barns complex ensure that rain or shine you'll be fine. There are exciting events every weekend - ring for further details.
Open daily, Apr-Oct, 10-6; Nov-Mar 10.30-5.(closed 25-26 Dec).
✻*£4.50 (ch, pen & students £3.75). Family ticket £15.25.*
🅿 🍴 ✗ *licensed* ♿ *(Carers admitted free) toilets for disabled shop*
Cards: 🆓 💳 💳 💳 💳

COMBE MARTIN
Bodstone Barton Farmworld & Playland
Berrydown EX34 0NT (2m S, off A3123)
☎ *01271 883654 Fax 01271 883654*
Set in an area of outstanding natural beauty, Bodstone Barton is a 17th-century farm covering 160 acres. The farm is run by both traditional and modern methods, and visitors can see goats being milked by hand. Attractions include an adventure playground, and rides by tractor, trailer and horse-drawn cart. There is a nature trail to follow, with an abundance of wildlife to be seen. A collection of agricultural and domestic items are on show, with 20,000 square feet under cover. Visitors can watch heavy horses being groomed and harnessed. There are lots of rides, and a large undercover children's area - 'Playland'.
Open all year, daily 10-5 Jun-Aug, 10.30-5 May & Sep, 11-5 Apr & Oct.
🅿 🍴 ✗ *licensed* ♿ *(ramps) toilets for disabled shop* ♿
Details not confirmed for 1998

The Combe Martin Motorcycle Collection
Cross St EX34 0DH (adjacent to the main car park, behind beach)
☎ *01271 882346*
The collection was formed in 1979 and contains British motorcycles displayed against a background of old petrol pumps, signs and garage equipment, exhibiting motoring nostalgia in an old world atmosphere.
Open Etr then 16 May-30 Oct, daily 10-5. £2.50 (ch & pen £1.50, ch 10 and under accompanied free).
P *(adjacent to site)* ♿ *toilets for disabled shop*

Combe Martin Wildlife Park & Dinosaur Park
EX34 0NG (M5 jct 7 then A361 towards Barnstaple and turn rt onto A399)
☎ *01271 882486 Fax 01271 882486*
Twenty acres of woodland complete with streams, cascading waterfalls, ornamental gardens, tropical plants and rare trees make this the most natural wildlife park in Britain. Visitors can see otters, and Meerkats 'on guard', living in the largest enclosure in Europe - a man-made desert. There is also a large selection of primates, mammals and birds. The Domain of the Dinosaurs has partially animated life-size dinosaurs set in prehistoric woodland. A new attraction is the Earthquake Canyon Ride, which features earthquakes, torrents of water, and animated characters.
Open Etr-Oct, daily 10-4 (last admission)
✻*£5.95 (ch & disabled £3.50, ch under 3 free, pen £4.50). Party 10+.*
🅿 🍴 ♿ *(car service) toilets for disabled shop* ❀ *inc guide dogs*

COMPTON
Compton Castle
TQ3 1TA (off A381 near Marldon)
☎ *01803 872112*
A fortified house of the 14th to 16th centuries, Compton has been the home of the Gilbert family (related to Sir Walter Raleigh) for 600 years. Much of the appeal of Compton is due to its completeness. The Great Kitchen still has its bread ovens and knife-sharpening marks, and the withdrawing room has squints through which occupants could watch services in the chapel. The original

14th-century hall was restored in the 20th century, complete with the solar, or living room, above. The towers, portcullis entrances and curtain walls were added in the 16th century, when there were French raids in the area. A look-out squint in the wall allows a watch to be kept from the hall door. There is a rose garden outside.
Open Apr-Oct Mon, Wed & Thu 10-12.15 & 2-5.
Castle & garden £2.80
🅿 ❀ 🐕
Cards: 🆓 💳

DARTMOUTH
Bayard's Cove Fort
TQ6 9AT (on riverfront)
The low, circular ruined stronghold was built by the townspeople to protect the harbour. It stands at the southern end of the cove, where the cobbled quay was used as a location for *The Onedin Line*.
Open at all reasonable times.
Free.
🅿 ❀ *(in certain areas)* ♿

Dartmouth Castle
TQ6 0JN (1m SE off B3205, narrow approach road)
☎ *01803 833588*
The castle dates from 1481 and was one of the first to be designed for artillery. It faces Kingswear Castle on the other side of the Dart estuary, and a chain could be drawn between the two in times of war. The timber-framed opening for the chain can still be seen.
Open all year, Apr-1 Nov, daily 10-6 (or dusk if earlier); 2 Nov-Mar, Wed-Sun 10-4. Closed 24-26 Dec & 1 Jan.
£2.50 (ch £1.30, concessions £1.90).
🅿 *shop* ❀ ♿

Woodland Leisure Park
Blackawton TQ9 7DQ (W, off A3122)
☎ *01803 712598 Fax 01803 712680*
A beautiful 60-acre park with indoor and outdoor attractions for all the family. There are 12 playzones including a

commando course, three Watercoasters, 500m Tornado Toboggan Run, action tracks, amazing matrix and a special toddlers' play village, also 34,000sq ft of under cover play area including two triple-level venture areas. The Circus Playdrome has bouncy castles, dressing up in circus costumes, ball pools and a circus ring. The large animal complex and wildlife walkabout has hundreds of animals and birds, and there is an international wildfowl collection and Bee Observatory. Live entertainment days all through the school holidays, including an Easter Extravaganza.
Open 12 Feb-Nov daily.
✻*£4.50 (ch £4.25). Family ticket £16.50.*
🅿 🍴 ♿ *(ramps) toilets for disabled shop* ❀
Cards: 🆓 💳 💳

DREWSTEIGNTON
Castle Drogo
EX6 6PB (4m S of A30)
☎ *01647 433306 Fax 01647 433186*
The granite castle is one of the most remarkable designs of Sir Edwin Lutyens, and was built between 1910 and 1930 for Julius Drewe, who retired at 33 after founding the Home and Colonial Stores. It is a fascinating combination of medieval might and 20th-century luxury, with its own telephone and hydro-electric systems, and craftsmanship of a high order. The castle stands at 900ft, on a rocky crag overlooking the gorge of the River Teign. There are wonderful views from the gardens and extensive walks into the Teign gorge and surrounding countryside.
Open Apr-Oct, daily (ex Fri but open Good Fri) 11-5.30. Garden open daily, 10.30-5.30.
Castle & grounds £5.20. Grounds only £2.40
🅿 🍴 ✗ *licensed* ♿ *(wheelchairs available, lift to lower ground floor) toilets for disabled shop garden centre* ❀ 🐕
Cards: 🆓 💳

EXETER

Exeter's history goes back to before the Romans, when the line of the present High Street was already established as an ancient ridgeway. The city prospered under the Romans, who built the wall and a bath house, and in the Middle Ages when the cathedral was built. This is where most visits begin, and it is well worth seeing for its magnificent nave, where clusters of pillars soar up into the web of fan vaulting in the roof. Other notable features are the intricately decorated bishop's throne, and the misericord carvings under the choir seats, including a crocodile and an elephant. Outside the cathedral is the Close, surrounded by charming buildings, and near by there are a number of interesting small churches. Highlights of the city include Rougemont House and its gardens, the Guildhall and the Maritime Museum. A more unusual attraction is the network of underground passages which brought water to the medieval city and can now be explored: the entrance is in the Princesshay shopping precinct.

Guildhall
High St EX4 3EB
☎01392 265500
This is one of the oldest municipal buildings still in use. It was built in 1330 and then altered in 1446, and the arches and façade were added in 1592-5. The roof timbers rest on bosses of bears holding staves, and there are portraits of Exeter dignitaries, guild crests, civic silver and regalia.
Open when there are no mayoral functions. Times are posted outside weekly. Special opening by arrangement. Free.
P (200yds) & toilets for disabled ❀

Maritime Museum
The Haven EX2 8DP (0.25m from Exe Bridges)
☎01392 58075
Afloat, ashore and under cover, there are over 170 boats at the museum, which is at the heart of the lively quay and canal area. The boats come from all over the world and are very varied, ranging from the oldest working steam dredger, Bertha, believed to have been built by Brunel, to dhows and coracles, a junk and a sampan, and a Venetian gondola. There are African dug-out canoes and frail-looking craft from the Pacific, and there is a large Danish harbour tug. One section

is occupied by the fascinating Ellerman collection of Portugese craft, and elsewhere is the Ocean Rowers' collection, featuring boats which have been rowed across the Atlantic. Another display shows the 1993/94 Trans-Pacific solo row of Peter Bird. The museum started with 23 vessels in 1969. It aims to rescue types of boats which are going out of use, and now has the world's largest collection of different boats. Visitors can look at, touch and also climb aboard some of the exhibits. Pleasant river and canal walks can be taken nearby. The Adventure play ship is a replica of the Mary Rose sister ship, Great Harry, and is complete with boarding nets and hammocks.
Open Apr-Sep, daily 10-5. Oct-Mar daily 10-4. Closed 25 Dec.
P (100yds) ⬛ & toilets for disabled shop
Details not confirmed for 1998

St Nicholas' Priory
Mint Ln, off Fore St EX4 3AT
☎01392 265858
Fax 01392 421252
The Benedictine priory was founded in 1087, and its remains include unusual survivals such as the Norman undercroft, a Tudor room and a 15th-century kitchen. Some fine plaster decoration can be seen, and there are displays of furniture and wood carving.
Open Etr-Oct, Mon, Wed & Sat 3-4.30pm Free.
P (200yds) shop ❀

Underground Passages
Boots Arcade, High St EX4 3RX
☎01392 265858 & 265887
Fax 01392 421252
A remarkable medieval water system with an introductory exhibition. Definitely not suitable for those inclined to claustrophobia. Britain's only ancient city passageways open to the public. Flat shoes are essential. All tours are guided, and there is an introductory 10-minute video plus exhibition.
Open Jul-Sep and school holidays Mon-Sat 10-5; rest of year Tue-Fri 2-5, Sat 10-5.
Sept-June £2.25 (ch, students, pen & UB40 £1.25). July-Aug £3.50 (ch, students, pen & UB40 £2.25). Family ticket £5.
P shop ❀

EXMOUTH
The World of Country Life
Sandy Bay EX8 5BU (M5 junct 30, take A376 to Exmouth, 1.5m off B3178 Exmouth to Budleigh Salterton road nr Littleham)
☎01392 873230 Fax 01392 873533
All weather family attraction - falconry, deer parks, adventure playgrounds, Pets Centre, animal nursery, steam and

vintage vehicles, Victorian 'street', working models, craft demonstrations, thousands of exhibits.
Open daily 24 Mar-Oct, 10-6.
£5.25 (ch 2-18 £4, pen £4.75). Family ticket £17.50. Wheelchair plus escort £3.50. Half price Sat (ex Jul/Aug) & 24-31 Oct.
P ⬛ & ✗ & (all parts accessible ex 'safari train') toilets for disabled shop ❀
Cards: 🅰 ══ 🅂 🄳

GREAT TORRINGTON
Dartington Crystal
Linden Close EX38 7AN (follow brown tourist signs)
☎01805 626262 Fax 01805 626263
Tours of the factory are conducted from the safety of viewing galleries that overlook the craftsmen. They can be seen carrying out the age-old techniques of glass manufacture and processing, and there are also studio glass-making demonstrations. The Visitor Centre has a permanent exhibition tracing the history of glass and crystal over the past 2000 years, and a video theatre adds a further dimension. The factory shop sells slightly imperfect crystal.
Open all year. Factory & Visitor centre: Mon-Fri 9.30-3.30. (Closed 16 Dec-2 Jan) Shop & Restaurant: Mon-Sat 9.30-5. Sun 10.30-4.30 (Closed 24-26 Dec & 1 Jan) ❉Full tour (inc Glass Centre) £2.75 (ch 6-16 free, pen £2.25). Party.
P & licensed & (special tours available, book in advance) toilets for disabled shop ❀
Cards: 🅰 ══ ══ 🄳

RHS Garden Rosemoor
EX38 8PH (1m SE of town on B3220)
☎01805 624067
Fax 01805 624717
Given to the RHS by Lady Anne Berry, who created the original 8-acre plantsman's garden, Rosemoor is the Royal Horticultural Society's first Regional Garden and Centre, second only to Wisley. An extra thirty-two acres have been added. The new Formal Garden includes 2000 roses in 200 varieties, colour theme gardens, herb garden, potager, cottage garden, foliage, winter garden, alpine terrace and extensive herbaceous borders. Elsewhere are stream and bog gardens, and a large walled fruit and vegetable garden. Lady Anne's Garden contains a collection of over 3500 plants from Europe, N & S America, Asia and New Zealand. "The Rosemoor Explorer" and "Senior Explorer" are free guides to the garden for children aged 6-10 & 11-15. Contact the Gardens for details of lectures, demonstrations and garden walks.
Open: Gardens all year; Visitor Centre Apr-Sep 10-6, Oct-Mar 10-5.
£4 (ch 6-16 £1). Party 10+.

P ✗ licensed & (Herb garden for disabled) toilets for disabled shop garden centre ❀ ex guide dogs
Cards: 🅰 ══ ══ 🅂

HONITON
Allhallows Museum
High St EX14 8PE (next to parish church of St Paul)
☎01404 44966 & 42996
The museum has a wonderful display of Honiton lace, and there are lace demonstrations from June to August. The town's history is also illustrated, and the museum is interesting for its setting in a chapel built in about 1200.
Open Mon before Easter to end of Sep, Mon-Sat 10-5; Oct, Mon-Sat 10-4. Winter opening by special arrangement.
£1 (ch 30p, pen 80p)
P (400 yds) & shop ❀

ILFRACOMBE
Ilfracombe Museum
Runnymede Gardens, Wilder Rd EX34 8AF
☎01271 863541
Ilfracombe was an important trading port from the 14th to the 16th centuries and during the Napoleonic Wars became a popular resort. The history, archaeology, geology, natural history and maritime tradition of the area are illustrated here, along with Victoriana, costumes, photographs and china. There is also a brass-rubbing centre.
Open all year, Etr-Oct 10-5.30 (Jul-Aug 7.30-10), Nov-Etr Mon-Sat 10-1.
£1 (ch & students 30p, under 5 free, pen 50p). Disabled free.
P (10yds) & (ramp) toilets for disabled shop ❀

Watermouth Castle
EX34 9SL (3m NE off A399)
☎01271 863879
Fax 01271 865864
Overlooking a beautiful bay, this 19th-century castle is one of North Devon's finest. It caters enthusiastically for the public, offering such unique experiences as a mechanical musical demonstration and the Watermouth Water Fountains. Other attractions include a tube slide, carousel and Gnomeland.
Open 5-9 Apr, Sun-Thu 1pm; 10-17 Apr Sun-Fri 11am; 19 Apr-14 May, Sun-Thu 1pm; 17 May-17 Jul, Sun-Fri 11am; 19 Jul-31 Aug, Sun-Fri 10am; 1-25 Sep, Sun-Fri 11am; 27 Sep-1 Nov, Sun-Thu 1pm. Closed on Sats. Last admission 4pm.
❉£5.25 (ch £4.25 & pen £4.25).
P ⬛ & (special wheelchair route) toilets for disabled shop ❀ (ex guide dogs)
Cards: 🅰 ══ 🅂

KILLERTON HOUSE & GARDEN
Killerton House & Garden
EX5 3LE (off B3181)
☎01392 881345
Elegant 18th-century house set in 18 acre garden with sloping lawns, shrub borders and herbaceous borders. A majestic avenue of beech trees runs from 18th and 19th century gardens up the hillside, past an arboretum of rhododendrums and conifers. The garden has an ice house and rustic summer house where the family pet bear was once kept. The main house is furnished with family portraits and period furniture. The Killerton Dress Collection is on display and there are also special costume displays in 1998. These include: 'Dressed to Kill' - glamorous costume from 1910 onwards. Open air concerts 18-19 July, Horse Trials 14 June.
Open: House, 14 Mar-1 Nov, Wed-Mon 11-5.30. Gardens all year, daily from 10.30am.
House & grounds £5. Grounds only £3.50.
P ⬛ ✗ licensed & (wheelchairs & motorised buggy available) toilets for disabled shop garden centre ❀ (ex in park) ⬛

Exeter Maritime Museum is in a canal basin crammed with craft from all over the world. In stone warehouses on the quayside of the River Exe, reached by ferry, are hundreds of sailing exhibits.

Visitors to Morwelham Quay may meet the Assayer in his office.

KINGSBRIDGE
Cookworthy Museum of Rural Life
The Old Grammar School, 108 Fore St
TQ7 1AW
☎01548 853235
The 17th-century schoolrooms of this former grammar school are now the setting for another kind of education. Reconstructed room-sets of a Victorian kitchen, an Edwardian pharmacy, a costume room and extensive collection of local historical items are gathered to illustrate South Devon life. A walled garden and farm gallery are also features of this museum, founded to commemorate William Cookworthy, 'father' of the English china clay industry. Please ring for details of special events.
Open all year, Apr-Sep Mon-Sat 10-5; Oct Mon-Fri 10.30-4. Nov-Mar groups by arrangement. Local history room Tue-Thu 10-12 & Wed also 2-4, other times by appointment.
P (100yds) & (Braille labels on selected exhibits) shop
Details not confirmed for 1998

KINGSWEAR
Coleton Fishacre Garden
Brownstone Rd, Coleton TQ6 0EQ (3m from village. Take Ferry Road and turn off at Toll House)
☎01803 752466 Fax 01803 752466
A beautiful stream fed valley garden set amid the spectacular South Devon coastline, created between 1925 and 1947 by Rupert and Lady Dorothy D'Oyly Carte. They experimented with a wide range of uncommon trees and rare exotic shrubs from around the world, a tradition the Trust has made Coleton rather special and a garden of interest throughout the year. From the formal wall garden and terraces surrounding the Lutyens inspired house the paths descend the wooded valley weaving along the contours, through quiet glades and past tranquil pools and towards Pudcombe Cove.
Open Mar, Sun only 2-5; Apr-Oct, Wed-Fri, Sun & BH Mon 10.30-5.30.
£3.50 (ch £1.70). Party 15+
P 🍴 (wheelchair available) shop garden centre ❀ (ex guide dogs) 🐾

KNIGHTSHAYES COURT
Knightshayes Court
EX16 7RQ (2m N of Tiverton off A396)
☎01884 254665 & 257381 Fax 01884 243050
This fine Victorian mansion, a rare example of William Burges' work, offers much of interest to all ages. The garden is one of the most beautiful in Devon, with formal terraces, amusing topiary. Pool garden and woodland walks. Plant Fair (17 May)
House open Apr-1 Nov, Sat-Thu & Good Fri 11-5.30. Nov-Dec, Sun 2-4 for pre-booked parties only. Garden Apr-1 Nov daily.
House & garden £5.10 (ch £2.50). Garden only £3.50 (ch £1.70).
P 🍴 & (wheelchairs available, braille & aidio guide) toilets for disabled shop garden centre ❀ (in park) 🐾
Cards: 🅰 🖃 ⓓ 💳 🖅 🅖

LYDFORD
Lydford Castle
EX20 4BH (off A386)
The great square stone keep dates from 1195. It is not built on a mound, as it seems to be, but had earth piled against the walls. The upper floor was a Stannary Court, which administered local tin mines, and the lower floor was used to imprison those who broke the forest and stannary laws.
Open all reasonable times.
Free.
P ✿

Lydford Gorge
EX20 4BH (off A386, between Okehampton & Tavistock)
☎01822 820441 & 820320 Fax 01822 820320
The spectacular gorge has been formed by the River Lyd, which has cut into the rock and caused swirling boulders to scoop out potholes in the stream bed. This has created some dramatic features, notably the Devil's Cauldron close to Lydford Bridge. At the end of the gorge is the 90ft-high White Lady Waterfall.
Open Apr-Oct, daily 10-5.30. (Nov-Mar, waterfall entrance only, daily 10.30-3).
P 🍴 shop 🐾
Details not confirmed for 1998
Cards: 🅰 🖃

MORWELLHAM
Morwellham Quay
PL19 8JL (4m W of Tavistock, off A390. signed)
☎01822 832766 & 833808
Fax 01822 833808
When copper was discovered in the hills near Tavistock the town reached new heights of prosperity. Morwellham was the nearest point to which sea-going ships could navigate and became the greatest copper port in Queen Victoria's empire. Once the mines were exhausted the port area disintegrated into unsightly wasteland, until 1970 when a charitable trust was set up for its restoration. It is now a thriving and delightful open-air museum. Visitors can ride by electric tramway (3 1/2 ton BEV battery electric locomation) underground into a copper mine, last worked in 1869. Visible copper ore seam, displays of mining techniques through history. Working 5.5m diameter underground water wheel. Stables at Morwellham house the shire horses which pull wagonettes for visitor rides along a section of the Duke of Bedford's old carriageway. A ship - the merchant sailing ketch 'Garlandstone' - is under restoration in Devon Consols Dock and can usually be boarded by visitors. The last but one wooden merchant vessel to be built in southern England, she was launched from Calstock, Cornwall, in 1908. Staff at Morwellham wear costume copied from the mid 19th century. Visitors (including children and dogs!) can try on replica costumes in the Limeburners Cottage. Plus: museums, video shows, demonstrations and activities (some especially for children). Unspoilt countryside, riverside and woodland trails surround the museum. New wildlife nature reserve sited in marshland, valley and woodland, with bird watching hides and nature trails. Separate restricted entry.
Open all year (ex Xmas wk) 10-5.30 (4.30 Nov-Etr). Last admission 3.30 (2.30 Nov-Etr).
❊£7.90 (ch 5-16 £5.50, pen & students £6). Family ticket £21. Party.
P 🍴 ✗ licensed shop ❀ (ex on lead)
Cards: 🅰 🖃
See advertisement on page 48.

NEWTON ABBOT
Bradley Manor
TQ12 6BN (on A381)
☎01626 54513
A National Trust property of 70 acres, the 15th-century house and chapel are surrounded by woodland. The River Lemon and a millstream flow through the estate.
Open Apr-Sep, Wed only 2-5; also Thu, 2 & 9 Apr, 17 & 24 Sep.
£2.60
P ❀ 🐕 🐾
Cards: 🅰 🖃

Hedgehog Hospital at Prickly Ball Farm
Denbury Rd, East Ogwell TQ12 6BZ (1.5m from Newton Abbot on A381 towards Totnes)
☎01626 62319 & 330685
Fax 01626 62319
See, touch and learn about this wild animal. In mid-season see baby hogs bottle feeding. Find out how to encourage hedgehogs into your garden and how they are put back into the wild. Talks on hedgehogs throughout the day, short basic video information about hedgehogs available. Busy, educational 'hands-on' farm.
Open 5 Apr-Oct, 10-5 (Oct 11-4). Last admission 1hr before closing.
£4.50 (ch 4-14 £2.95, pen £4.20, ch under 4 free). Family ticket £14.50. Disabled & helpers free.
P 🍴 ✗& (sensory garden, use of wheelchair, Braille menu) toilets for disabled shop ❀ ex guide dogs
Cards: 🅰 🖃 💳 🖅 🅖

Tuckers Maltings
Teign Rd TQ12 4AA (follow brown tourist signs from Newton Abbott rly station)
☎01626 334734 Fax 01626 330153
Tuckers Maltings is England's only working malthouse open to the public, producing malt from barley for over 30 West Country breweries. Vistors can learn all about the process of malting - watch a video programme, visit the hands-on discovery centre and taste the end product at the new in-house brewery. Guided tours last over an hour. Special events for 1997 include: Maltings Beer Festival (17-20 April).
Open Etr-Oct, daily 10am-4pm (Jul-Aug open to 5pm).
£4.20 (ch 5-15 £2.65, 16-17 £3.50, pen £3.90).
P (charged) 🍴 ✗ licensed & toilets for disabled shop
Cards: 🅰 🖃 💳 🖅 🅖

OKEHAMPTON
Museum of Dartmoor Life
3 West St EX20 1HQ
☎01837 52295
An attractive three-storey agricultural mill houses this museum, and the Dartmoor Tourist Information Centre and working craft studios are to be found in an adjoining courtyard. There is a cradle-to-grave display of Victorian life, and descriptive reconstructions of local tin and copper mines are complemented by a geological display of the moor. Local history, prehistory, domestic life, industry and environmental issues are explored, and a 1922 Bullnose Morris farm pickup with a wooden back shares pride of place with an ancient David Brown tractor in the agricultural section. An award-winning display depicts everyday life in Dartmoor. A shop sells crafts and books and an exhibition gallery changes its displays regularly. Exhibition galleries feature a reconstructed blacksmith's forge and wheelwright's shop, a cider press and railway relics. Various changing exhibitions, craft events and demonstrations are held throughout the year.
Open Etr-Oct, Mon-Sat 10-5 (also Sun, Jun-Sep). Nov-Mar weekdays only 10-4 (closed Xmas/New Year).
❊£1.60 (ch 5-16 & students 80p, pen £1.30). Family ticket £4.50. Party 10+. Prices under review.
P 🍴 & toilets for disabled shop

Okehampton Castle
(1m SW of town centre)
☎01837 52844
The chapel, keep and hall date from the 11th to 14th centuries and stand on the northern fringe of Dartmoor National Park.
Open all year, Apr-1 Nov, daily 10-6 (or dusk if earlier in Oct). (Closed 24-26 Dec & 1 Jan).
P ✿

OTTERTON
Otterton Mill Centre
EX9 7HG (between North Poppleford & Budleigh Salterton)
☎01395 568521 Fax 01395 568521
Mentioned in the Domesday Book, this water-powered mill grinds wholemeal flour used in the baking of bread and cakes sold on the premises. A gallery houses a series of exhibitions through the summer and autumn, and there are studio workshops for sculpture, pottery, woodturning, painting and printing. There is a co-operative craft shop. There are long and short riverside walks, and an annual exhibition of furniture design from West Country workshops. The Lower Otter Valley River Festival in July is co-ordinated from the Centre.
Open all year, daily, summer 10.30-5.30; winter 11-4.
£1.75 (ch 90p). Party.
P 🍴 & (free entry to ground floor) toilets for disabled shop garden centre
Cards: 🅰 🖃 🅖

OTTERY ST MARY

Cadhay
EX11 1QT (near jct of A30 & B3167)
☎01404 812432
A mile north-west of Ottery, over Cadhay Bridge, this beautiful Tudor and Georgian house is well worth a visit. It was begun in 1550 and stands around a courtyard.
Open Jul-Aug Tue, Wed & Thu. Also Sun & Mon of late spring & late summer BH's. 2-5.30.
£3 (ch £1.50). Party 20+ by appointment.
🅿 ♿ 🚫 *(ex in garden)*

Escot Aquatic Centre & Gardens
Fairmile EX11 1LU (0.5m off the A30 Exeter to Honiton road at Fairmile, signposted)
☎01404 822188 Fax 01404 822903
Escot House was built in 1837 after the original house was destroyed in a fire. The 220 acres of landscaped parkland were designed and built, possibly by Capability Brown, before the Kennaway family, the present owners, moved into the estate 200 years ago. Even in 1789 the gardens were renowned for their luxurious nature and were visited by King George III and Queen Charlotte. The gardens comprise a two-acre Victorian rose garden, extensive shrubbery with many fine specimen trees and in the gardens you will find a pair of otters, a troupe of wild boar, Pets Corner and Vietnamese pot-bellied pigs. Escot also house one of the finest Pet and Aquatic Centres in Devon. Set in the magnificent listed farm buildings, the extensive range of tropical and ornamental fish are a wonderful spectacle.
Open Etr-Oct 10-6; Oct-Etr 10-5.
🅿 ♨ ✗ *licensed* ♿ *toilets for disabled shop garden centre* 🚫 *(ex on lead)*
Details not confirmed for 1998
Cards: 🅰 💳 💲

PAIGNTON

Paignton & Dartmouth Steam Railway
Queens Park Station, Torbay Rd TQ4 6AF
☎01803 555872 Fax 01803 664313
Steam trains run for seven miles from Paignton to Kingswear on the former Great Western line, stopping at Goodrington Sands, Churston, and Kingswear, connecting with the ferry crossing to Dartmouth. Special events for 1998 include: Thomas the Tank Engine (8-9 August). Please ring for details of other special events.
Open Jun-Sep daily 9-5.30 & selected days Oct & Mar-May.
❋*Prices under review.*
P *(5mins walk)* ♨ ♿ *(wheelchair ramp for boarding train) toilets for disabled shop*

Paignton Zoo
Totnes Rd TQ4 7EU (1m, on A385)
☎01803 527936 Fax 01803 523457
See conservation in action at one of England's biggest zoos in the beautiful wooded setting of 75 acres gardens. With over 60 endangered species the zoo is working with good zoos around the world securing species survival. Meet the keepers who will explain how they care for the animals. Find out all about parrots as they show off their skills in Feathered Feats. Recent additions include a huge area for African lions and Sumatran tigers, a fascinating walk-through aviary and a wetland wildlife exhibit. Other favourites include the 'Jungle express' miniature railway, and the 'Jolly Jungle' children's play area and face painting. New attractions include the desert exhibit and ape centre. Special events: Easter Egg Safari (12-13 April), Mothers Day Carvery (22 March), British Wildlife Week (25-29 May). 1998 is the 75th Anniversary of Paignton Zoo so contact the zoo for information on special additional events.
Open all year, daily 10-6.30 (5pm in winter). Last admission 5pm (4pm in winter). (Closed 25 Dec).
£6.70 (ch 3-15 £4.60, pen £5.10). Family ticket £20.20. Party 15+. Prices under review.
🅿 ♨ ✗ *licensed* ♿ *(some steep hills wheelchair loan-booking advisable) toilets for disabled shop* 🚫 *(ex guide dogs)*
Cards: 🅰 💳 💳 🔲 💲

PLYMOUTH
To walk the narrow, cobbled streets of Plymouth's Barbican, to visit its ancient houses and to wander beside the quays of its historic Sutton Harbour is to tread in the wake of England's most intrepid seafarers. From here, in 1577, Drake sailed to circumnavigate the world, and 11 years later to defeat the Spanish Armada. In 1620 the Mayflower carried the Pilgrim Fathers to the New World, and in 1768 James Cook left in search of a southern continent. On Plymouth Hoe stands the Royal Citadel built, it is said, on the site where Drake played his game of bowls.

City Museum & Art Gallery
Drake Circus PL4 8AJ
☎01752 304774 Fax 01752 304775
The City Museum and Art Gallery is home to a Fine and Decorative Art Collection of paintings, prints and Reynolds family portraits, silver and Plymouth China, and the Cottonian Collection of Drawings, Sculpture and Books. There is a lively programme of art exhibitions, as well as archaeology, local and natural history displays, and the Discovery Centre with a 'hands-on' section for children. Lunchtime talks, childrens activities, and concerts are also on offer, please telephone for details. 1998 exhibitions will include: James Ravillious' photography (Feb-Mar), John Sibbeck's dinosaur illustrations (Feb-May), Modernism in Devon (June-July), Goya (June), and 'City and the Sea' - Plymouth's Maritime Heritage (all year). There will also be a free talk by Dame Janet Fookes on 12 March, as part of International Women's Week.
Open all year, Tue-Fri 10-5.30, Sat 10-5, BH Mon 10-5. (Closed Good Fri & 25-26 Dec).
Free.
P ♿ *(wheelchair available) toilets for disabled shop* 🚫 *ex guide dogs*

Merchant's House Museum
33 St Andrews St PL1 2AX
☎01752 304774 Fax 01752 304775
The largest and finest 16th-century house surviving in Plymouth. Inside visitors can discover various aspects of Plymouth's past, including a reconstructed Victorian pharmacy, life during World War II, and a Victorian schoolroom which is available for group bookings.
Open Apr-Sep, Tue-Fri 10-5.30, Sat 10-5, BH Mon 10-5 (summer), (closed 1-2)
❋*90p (ch 30p), half price last hour of opening, children under 7 free*
P *(400 yds)* ♿ *shop* 🚫

Plymouth Dome
The Hoe PL1 2NZ
☎01752 603300 & 600608 (recorded message) Fax 01752 256361
This high-tech visitor centre takes you on a journey through time, exploring the sounds and smells of an Elizabethan street, walking the gun-deck of a galleon, sailing with the epic voyages from Plymouth Sound, dodging the press gang, strolling with film stars on an ocean liner and witnessing the devastation of the blitz. Use high-resolution cameras to zoom in on ships and shoreline, or access computers to identify naval vessels. Examine satellite weather pictures as they arrive from space, keep up to date with shipping movements and monitor the busy harbour on radar. An excellent introduction to Plymouth and a colourful interpretation of the past. 1998 is the 300th Anniversary of the Eddystone Lighthouse. Ring for details of special events.
Open all year, daily, 4 Apr-24 May 9-6; 25 May-13 Sept 9-7.30; 14 Sep-1 Nov 9-6; 3 Nov-Mar 9-5.30. (Closed 25 Dec). Last admission one hour before closing.
❋*£3.95 (ch £2.50, ch under 7 free, pen £3.30). Family ticket £11.95. Party. Subject to review.*
P *(200 yds)* ♨ ♿ *(audio descriptions, induction loop, wheelchairs available) toilets for disabled shop* 🚫 *ex guide dogs*
Cards: 🅰 💳 🔲 💲

Prysten House
Finewell St PL1 2AD (immediately behind St Andrews Church, in city centre)
☎01752 661414 (Mon-Fri 9-1)
Thought to have been erected as a town house by Plymouth and London merchant Thomas Yogge, who bought the site in two lots in 1487 and 1498. It is also believed to have been used as a 'priest's house' by the Augustinian Order of preaching canons from Plympton Priory. After the dissolution of the monasteries in 1539 it fell into secular use for such purposes as a wine store and a bacon factory. Since 1923, it has been owned by St Andrew's Church and the people who give it life are in the main, ordinary Plymouthians, interested in preserving part of our national heritage. Embroiderers are working on a 253ft-long New World Tapestry - a section of it is now on show.
Open Apr-Oct, Mon-Sat 10-4 (last admission 3.30pm). Other times by appointment.
75p (ch & pen 30p). Party 15+.
P *(100 yds)* ♨ 🚫

Royal Citadel
(at the end of Plymouth Hoe)
☎01752 603300
Probably designed by Sir Thomas Fitz, this magnificent gateway was built in 1670 for the stronghold commenced by Charles II in 1666. The remaining buildings of the fort include the Guardhouse, Governor's House and Chapel.
Open for guided tours only May-Sep, daily. For security reasons tours may be suspended at short notice.
❋*£2.50 (ch£1.50, concessions £2). Tickets from Plymouth Dome below Smeaton Tower or Tourist Information Office, Civic Centre..*
🚫 ⚓

Restored after the Civil War, Powderham Castle is set in delightful gardens.

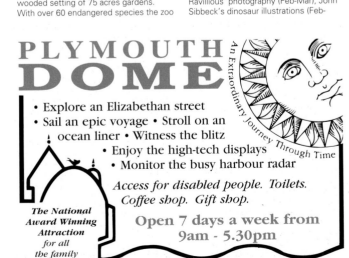

MORWELLHAM QUAY

Historic and Picturesque Riverside Village hidden in Tamar Valley Woodland in a Designated Area of Outstanding Beauty

Award winning visitor centre, established 1971.

Train ride into old Mine Workings - sound and light tableaux of mining history • Horse-drawn carriage ride • Staff wear reproduction costume - costume for visitors to try on themselves • Wooden ship under restoration • Way marked walks around section of Tavistock Canal • Farm buildings - Cottages - Docks - Quays - Lime kilns - Ore chutes • Reconstructed overhead railway • Blacksmith and Cooper's workshops • Video show • Museums • Activities and Demonstrations - some especially for children.

Average visit length 5-6 hours.

Family ticket. Concessions. Group rates. Open all week. All year (except Christmas) 10am-5.30pm in Summer. 10am-4.30pm in Winter - with Mine ride and Grounds only.

Last admission 2 hours before close.

Telephone 01822 832766 - Fax 01822 833808

off A390 - midway between Tavistock, Devon and Liskeard, Cornwall

---

Smeatons Tower
The Hoe PL1 2NZ
☎01752 603300 Fax 01752 256361
This famous lighthouse, a triumph of 18th-century engineering, was built on the treacherous Eddystone rocks fourteen miles out at sea to the south west of Plymouth. It was replaced by a larger lighthouse in 1882, and moved stone by stone to its present site on the Hoe. 1998 sees the 300th Anniversary of the Eddystone Lights. Ring for details of special events.
Open Good Fri-Sep, 10.30-4.30. Parties by appointment throughout the year.
75p (ch 40p, ch under 7 free, & pen 55p). Prices under review.
P *(500 yds)* ✿

PLYMPTON
Saltram House
PL7 1UH (2m W between A38 & A379)
☎01752 336546 Fax 01752 336474
Built on the site of a Tudor Mansion, this magnificent George II house still has its original contents. The collection of paintings was begun at the suggestion of Reynolds and includes many of his portraits. The saloon and dining room were designed by Robert Adam and have superb decorative plasterwork and period furniture. Set in beautiful surroundings with a shrub garden and 18th-century summer house, Saltram House has a lovely view of the Plym estuary. Special events include: Plant Fair (13 June); Family Days; Open Air Theatre; Saltram by Candlelight (last Saturday in October); Candlelight concerts during November and December.
Open Apr-1 Nov, Sun-Thu; House 12.30-5.30. Garden & Great Kitchen 10.30-5.30. Last admission 5pm.
£5.60 (ch £2.80). Gardens only £2.60 (ch £1.30). Family £14.
P *(charged)* ✿ ✗ *licensed* & *(wheelchairs available, lift, braille & audio guides) toilets for disabled shop* ✿ *(ex designated areas)* ✤
Cards: ▨ ▨ ▨ ⑤

POWDERHAM
Powderham Castle
EX6 8JQ (signposted off A379 Exeter/Dawlish road)
☎01626 890243
Fax 01626 890729
Built between 1390 and 1420, this ancestral home of the Earls of Devon was damaged in the Civil War. The house was restored and altered in later times and fine furnishings and portraits are displayed throughout. It is set in beautiful rose gardens with views over the deer park to the Exe Estuary. A new attraction for children is The Secret Garden, which is a delightful pets corner set in an old Victorian walled garden. Special events for 1998 include Powderham Horse Trials (4-5 July), 3 open air concerts (5 June, 1 & 8 August), Historic Vehicle Gathering (11-12 July).
Open 27 Mar-1 Nov, 10-5.30 (last admission 5pm). (Closed Sat).
❋*£4.95 (ch £2.85, pen £4.45). Family ticket £12.45. Party 10+*
P ✿ & *toilets for disabled shop* ✿ *(ex car park)*
Cards: ▨ ▨ ▨ ⑤

SALCOMBE
Overbecks Museum & Garden
Sharpitor TQ8 8LW (2.5m SW of Salcombe and 2m S of Malborough)
☎01548 842893
The garden at Overbecks is particularly stunning when the magnolias are in bloom; but its situation, on the most southerly tip of Devon, allows many tender and exotic plants to flourish; one of the most varied collections of trees, shrubs and flowering plants in the country is grown here. The Edwardian house displays toys, dolls and a natural history collection, and there is a 'secret room' for children in which they can search for "Fred" the friendly ghost. There is also a large collection of maritime history and local photographs.
Open Apr-Jul Sun-Fri 11am-5.30pm; Aug Daily 11am-5.30pm; Sept Sun-Fri 11am-

---

5.30pm; Oct Sun-Thurs 11am-5pm. Last admission 30 mins before closure. Museum & gardens £3.80. Gardens only £2.60.
P *(charged)* ✿ & *(ramp from garden, braille guide) shop* ✿ ✤ ✤
Cards: ▨ ▨ ▨

SOUTH MOLTON
Quince Honey Farm
EX36 3AZ (3.5m W of A361)
☎01769 572401 Fax 01769 574704
This is the largest bee farm in Britain. Visitors can view the honey-bees, without disturbing them, in a specially designed building with glass booths and tunnels. Observation hives enable visitors to see into the centre of the colony and view larvae and newly-hatched bees in the cells of the comb. Even the queen may be seen at the very heart of the hive. The farm shop sells a wide range of honey, including the local heather honey, as well as pure beeswax candles and polish.
Open daily, Apr-Sep 9-6; Oct 9-5; Shop only Nov-Etr 9-5. (Closed 25-26 Dec & 1 Jan).
P & *shop* ✿
Details not confirmed for 1998
Cards: ▨ ▨ ▨ ▨ ⑤

TAVISTOCK
See Morwellham

TIVERTON
Tiverton Castle
EX16 6RP (town centre)
☎01884 253200 & 255200
Fax 01884 254200
Dating from 1106, the castle dominates the River Exe. Only one circular Norman tower remains from the original four, and there is also a medieval gatehouse with walls 5ft thick. The castle was a Royalist stronghold during the Civil War but was taken by the Roundheads in 1645. It houses one of the finest collections of Civil War armour and arms in the country.
Open Etr-Jun & Sep, Sun,Thu & BH Mon's only 2.30-5.30; Jul & Aug, Sun-Thu 2.30-5.30.
£3.50 (ch 7-16 £2, disabled half price if accessing ground floor only)
P & *toilets for disabled shop* ✿ *(ex on leads in grounds)*

Tiverton Museum
Saint Andrew St EX16 6PH
☎01884 256295
This large and comprehensive museum consists of eight galleries and is housed in a restored 19th-century school. The numerous local exhibits include a Heathcote Lace Gallery featuring items from the local lacemaking industry (started by John Heathcote) in his house. There is also an agricultural section with a collection of farm wagons and implements. Other large exhibits include two waterwheels and a railway gallery that houses a GWR 0-4-2T Locomotive No.1442, other railway items, and a display on the Grand Western Canal.
Open Mon-Sat 10.30-4.30. (Closed 21 Dec-Jan).
£1 (ch 16 50p, accompanied ch free on Sat, pen & UB40 75p).
P *(100 yds)* & *shop* ✿

TORQUAY
Babbacombe Model Village
Hampton Av, Babbacombe TQ1 3LA (follow brown tourist signs from outskirts of town)
☎01803 328669 & 315315
Fax 01803 315173
Set in four acres of beautifully maintained, miniature landscaped garden, the village contains over 400 models and 1200ft of model railway. Authentic sound effects have been added, to create a whole new dimension. In summer, when the village is open until late, it is illuminated. City Lights, a new evening illuminations feature, depicts Piccadilly Circus in miniature. At the end of your visit, enjoy the new facility-'Tom's Tea House and Shop' – with breathtaking views over the model village. There are

---

also free trips on replica Edwardian open-top bus. Visit Father Christmas in his grotto during December plus a miniature wonderland of illuminations.
Open all year, Etr-Sep, daily 9am-10pm; Oct 9-9pm; Nov 9am-dusk. Dec please phone for details.
P *(charged)* ✿ & *(push button audio information) toilets for disabled shop garden centre*
Details not confirmed for 1998

'Bygones'
Fore St, St Marychurch TQ1 4PR (follow tourist signs into Torquay and St Marychurch)
☎01803 326108 Fax 01803 326108
Step back in time in this life-size Victorian exhibition street of over 20 shops including a forge, pub and period display rooms, housed in a former cinema. Exhibits include a large model railway layout, illuminated fantasyland, railwayana and military exhibits including a walk-through World War I trench. At Christmas the street is turned into a winter wonderland. A new set piece features Babbacombe John Lee ('the man they couldn't hang') in his cell. There is something here for all the family. Allow up to one hour.
Open all year, Jun-Aug 10am-10pm, (Fri & Sat 10-6); Sep, Oct, Mar, Apr & May 10-5; Nov-Feb 10-4, Sat & Sun 10-5. (Last admission 1 hour before closing). (Closed 25 Dec). Extended opening during school holidays.
£2.95 (ch 4-13 £1.95, pen £2.50). Family ticket £8.50.
P *(50 yds)* ✿ *shop* ✿

Kents Cavern Showcaves
The Caves, Wellswood TQ1 2JF (1.25m NE off B3199)
☎01803 294059 & 215136
Fax 01803 211034
Recognised as one of the most important archaeological sites in Britain, these showcaves provide a set of unique experiences. This is not only a world of spectacular natural beauty, but also a priceless record of past times, where a multitude of secrets of mankind, animals and nature have become trapped and preserved over the last 350,000 years. One hundred and seventy years after the first excavations and with over 70,000 remains already unearthed, modern research is still discovering new clues to our past. The showcaves are visited along well-lit paths and tours are accompanied by 'storytellers' who bring to life past scenes using props and the natural setting of the caves. A new exhibition re-creates scenes of the first explorers and excavators. Special events during 1998 include The Ghosts of Cavern Past tour, held on Monday to Thursday evenings (6-8.30, May 25-June 30) and Sunday to Friday evenings through July & August (6-9).
Open daily (ex 25 Dec). Oct-Mar 10-last tour 4pm; Apr-Jun & Sep 10-last tour 4.30pm; Jul-Aug 9.30-last tour 5pm. Evenings: May 25-Jun 30 (Mon-Thu) 6-8.30, Jul-Aug (Sun-Fri) 6-9. Daytime: £4 (ch 5-15 £2.60) Family £12 Ghost evening tour: £4.80, (ch £3.60) Family £15.80
P ✿ & *toilets for disabled shop* ✿
Cards: ▨ ▨ ▨ ⑤

Torre Abbey Historic House & Gallery
The Kings Dr TQ2 5JX (on sea front, next to Riviera Centre)
☎01803 293593 Fax 01803 215948
Torbay's most historic building was founded in 1196 as a monastery and later adapted as a country house. It contains historic rooms, the Cary family chapel, mementoes of crime writer Agatha Christie, and mainly 19th-century paintings, sculpture, antiques, and Torquay terracotta pottery. The medieval monastic remains, which include the great barn, guest hall, gatehouse and undercrofts, are the most complete in Devon and Cornwall. Special 'Quest' leaflet available for children. Rooms may

be hired. Special exhibitions throughout
the summer, including Flower Festival
11-14 September.
*Open daily Apr-1 Nov, 9.30-6. (Last
admission 5pm).*
*£2.75 (ch 15 £1.50, under 8 free, pen &
students £2.25). Family ticket £6.50.*
P *(100 yds)* 🍴 ♿ shop

TOTNES

Bowden House Ghostly Tales & The British Photographic Museum
TQ9 7PW
☎*01803 863664*
At Bowden House visitors are welcomed
by guides in 1740 Georgian dress. Parts
of the house date back as far as the 12th
century, but most of it was built in 1510
by John Giles, supposedly the wealthiest
man in Devon. In 1704 the Queen Anne
façade was added. The Grand Hall is
decorated in neo-Classical Baroque style,
and the Great Hall is adorned with 18th-
and 19th-century weaponry. The rooms
have been beautifully restored. The
museum has a large collection of vintage
cameras, a replica Victorian studio,
Edwardian darkroom, shops, and the Les
Allen movie pioneer display. There are
special Ghostly Tales Tours at 2, 3, and 4
o'clock. The house is set in twelve acres
of attractive grounds.

Once at the heart of a thriving wool region, Coldharbour Mill at Uffculme is now
a working museum. It shows every stage in producing woollen cloth and yarn.

*Open 3 Apr-26 Oct from noon. Bowden
House & Museum Mon-Thu & BH
Sun/Mon.*
*£4.50 (ch 10-13 £2.60, ch 6-9 £1.60, ch
under 6 free)*
P 🍴 ♿ *(museum only suitable) toilets
for disabled shop*

Guildhall
Rampart Walk, off High St TQ9 5QH
☎*01803 862147*
Fax 01803 862147
Originally the refectory, kitchens,
brewery and bakery for the Benedictine
Priory of Totnes (1088-1536), the building
was established as the Guildhall in 1553
during the reign of Edward VI. A
magistrates court and a prison opened in
1624, the same year of the
refurbishment of the council chamber
which is still used today. There are also
relics of the Civil War, and lists of the
mayors since 1359. Famous visitors to
the Guildhall have included past
monarchs such as Charles I and Charles
II as well as the present monarch Queen
Elizabeth II. Treasure Trail for children.
*Open Apr-Oct, Mon-Fri 10-1 & 2-5; Other
times by appointment.*
P *(50 yds) shop*
Details not confirmed for 1998

Totnes Castle
TQ9 5NU (on hill overlooking town)
☎*01803 864406*
A classic example of the Norman motte-
and-bailey castle, Totnes dates from the
11th century. The circular shell-keep is
protected by a curtain wall erected in the
13th century and reconstructed in the
14th. There are marvellous views from
the walls of the keep across the town to
the Dart valley.
*Open all year, Apr-1 Nov, daily 10-6 (or
dusk if earlier in Oct); 2 Nov-Mar, Wed-
Sun 10-4, (closed 1-2). Closed 24-26 Dec
& 1 Jan.*
£1.60 (ch 80p, concessions £1.20)
P *(70yds)* ⚧

Totnes Museum
70 Fore St TQ9 5RU (Totnes town
centre)
☎*01803 863821*
This four-storey, partly timbered house,
complete with connecting gallery to an
additional kitchen/buttery block, dates
from about 1575. It has a cobbled
courtyard and 16th-century fireplaces. It
is now a museum of furniture, domestic
objects, toys, dolls, costumes and
archaeology. One room is dedicated to
Charles Babbage who invented the
ancestor of modern computers. There is
a Tudor garden and Devon Record
Office (study centre), and constantly
changing displays of contemporary art
and craft from the Totnes area. Please
enquire about a range of events for
children.
*Open Etr-30 Oct, Mon-Fri & BHs 10.30-5,
Sat 2-5.*
❋*£1.50 (ch 5-16 50p).*
P *(440yds)* ♿ *Personal guided tours
available shop (ex small dogs)*

UFFCULME

Coldharbour Mill Working Wool Museum
Coldharbour Mill EX15 3EE (2m from
M5 J27, off B3181. Follow signs to
Willand)
☎*01884 840960*
Fax 01884 840858
Originally an important centre for the
wool trade, the Culm Valley now has
only one working woollen mill. This was
built as a grist mill in 1753, but was
converted to a wool mill in 1797 by a
Somerset woollen manufacturer,
Thomas Fox. He added a large red-brick
and stone factory in which serge, flannel
and worsted yarn was produced for
nearly 200 years. The mill closed in 1981
but was reopened as a Working Wool
Museum. Visitors can watch every stage
in the process of producing woollen
cloth and yarn on the two working levels
of the mill. There are also displays of
machinery and artefacts connected with
the wool trade, plus a weaver's cottage,
and dye and carpenters' workshops.
Visitors can see the 18ft diameter water
wheel awaiting restoration, and the 300-
horsepower Pollit and Wigzell steam

engine which powered the Mill until its
closure. An 1867 beam engine is being
erected. Knitting yarn and made-up
garments can be bought in the mill shop.
A new feature is the New World
Tapestry which tells the story of English
colonisation of the Americas in
humorous cartoon form.
*Open Apr-Oct, daily 10.30-5. Nov-Mar
Mon-Fri (please telephone for times).
Last tour 4pm.*
*£5 (ch 5-16 £2.50). Family ticket £13.50
Party 20+.*
P 🍴 ✕ *licensed* ♿ *shop*
Cards: 🅱 💳

YEALMPTON

National Shire Horse Centre
PL8 2EL (On A379, Plymouth to
Kingsbridge)
☎*01752 880268*
Fax 01752 881014
Some fine old farm buildings are at the
hub of this 60-acre farm with over 40
Shire horses. With the revival of interest
in the gentle giants, the farm has
become the National Shire Horse Centre.
Visitors are able to see not only the
heavy horses and their foals, but a
variety of other creatures as well. A
butterfly house permits a range of exotic
butterflies to be seen in their real habitat.
A craft centre, showing the skills of the
saddler and the falconer, among others,
is in the barns. Daily falconry flying
displays (at 1pm and 3.30pm), parades of
the Shire horses (at 11.30 and 2.30) and
a shire horse musical drive at 4.15pm
can be seen from April to the end of
October. Children are well catered for
with a pets' area, cart rides and an
adventure playground with free-fall
slide.
*Open all year, daily 10-5. (Closed 24-26
Dec).*
P 🍴 ✕ *licensed* ♿ *toilets for disabled
shop garden centre*
Details not confirmed for 1998
Cards: 🅱 💳

YELVERTON

Yelverton Paperweight Centre
4 Buckland Ter, Leg O'Mutton PL20 6AD
(off A386, Tavistock rd)
☎*01822 854250*
Fax 01822 854250
This unusual centre is the home of the
Broughton Collection - a glittering display
of paperweights of all sizes and designs.
The centre also has an extensive range of
modern glass paperweights for sale.
Prices range from a few pounds to over
£500. There is also a series of oil and
watercolour paintings by talented local
artists, a collection of which are scenes
of Dartmoor.
*Open 10-5, Apr-Oct: 7 days, Dec 1-24: 7
days. Nov, Jan-Mar weekends only.
Free.*
P *(100 yds)* ♿ *(ramp on request) shop*
Cards: 🅱 💳 💳 💳 💳

DORSET

ABBOTSBURY

Abbotsbury Swannery

New Barn Rd DT3 4JG (9m from Weymouth on the B3157 coastal road to Bridport)
☎ 01305 871684 & 871858
Fax 01305 871092

The colony was already in existence when, in the 14th century, the monks used the swans as a resource, and Abbotsbury is still a breeding ground for the only managed colonial herd of mute swans. The swans can be seen safely at close quarters, and the site is also home or stopping point for many wild birds. Reeds are harvested for thatching, and there is a 17th-century duck decoy. The highlight of the year is the cygnet season, end of May to the end of June, when there may be over 100 nests on site with an average of six eggs per nest. Hatching can take place before your very eyes.
Open Easter-Oct, daily 10-6, last admission 5pm
✻£4.80 (ch 5-16 £2 & pen £3.80). Family ticket £11.00.
🅿 ♨ ✗ & (wheelchair loan, herb garden for blind) toilets for disabled shop ⊗
Cards: 🅰 ══ British 🕿 🅖

ATHELHAMPTON

Athelhampton House & Gardens

DT2 7LG (on A35 1m E of Puddletown)
☎ 01305 848363
Fax 01305 848135

Athelhampton is one of the finest 15th-century houses in England, containing many magnificently furnished rooms including The Great Hall of 1485 and the newly opened library. The glorious Grade I gardens, dating from 1891, contain the world-famous topiary pyramids, fountains, the River Piddle and collections of tulips, magnolias, roses, clematis and lilies in season. Flower Show 28 May. MG Owners Club Car Rally - July.
Open Mar-Nov, daily 10.30-5. Also Sundays in Winter. (Closed Sat).
House & Garden £4.80 (ch £1.50, pen £4.50). Garden only £3 (ch free). Family £10. Party.
🅿 ♨ ✗ licensed & toilets for disabled shop ⊗ ex guide dogs
Cards: 🅰 ══ British 🕿 🅖

BEAMINSTER

Mapperton Gardens

DT8 3NR (2m SE off A356 & B3163)
☎ 01308 862645
Fax 01308 863348

Surrounding a manor house dating back to the 16th century are several acres of terraced valley gardens, with specimen trees and shrubs, and formal borders. There are also fountains, grottoes, stone fishponds and an orangery, and the garden offers good views and walks. The Mapperton Courtyard Fair is held annually (22 August 2-5pm) with craft demonstrations, stalls, house tours and local displays.
Open Mar-Oct, daily 2-6.
Gardens £3 (ch 5-18 £1.50, under 5 free).
🅿 & shop ⊗ (ex guide dogs)

Parnham

DT8 3NA (1m S on A3066)
☎ 01308 862204 Fax 01308 863494

The house is a fine Tudor mansion, but it is most famous as the home of John Makepeace and his furniture-making workshop. The workshop is open to visitors, and completed pieces are shown in the house. There are also continuous exhibitions by living designers and craftsmen. Surrounding the house are 14 acres of restored gardens, formal terraces and woodlands.
Open Apr-Oct: Sun, Tues-Thurs & BH's 10-5.
✻£5 (ch £2, under 5 free)
🅿 ✗ licensed & toilets for disabled shop
Cards: 🅰 ══ ══

BLANDFORD FORUM

Royal Signals Museum

Blandford Camp DT11 8RH (signposted off the B3082 Blandford/Wimborne road)
☎ 01258 482248 Fax 01258 482084

The history of army signalling from the Crimean War to the present day and the history of the Royal Corps of Signals is illustrated with displays of equipment, vehicles, paintings, uniforms, medals and badges.
Open Mon-Fri 10-5, Sat-Sun 10-4 (June-Sept). Closed 10 days over Xmas & New Year
£3 (ch £1.50, pen £2).
🅿 ♨ & (ramps & chair lift) toilets for disabled shop ⊗

BOURNEMOUTH

Bournemouth Bears

The ExpoCentre, Old Christchurch Ln BH1 1NE
☎ 01202 293544 Fax 01305 268885

Explore the wonderful world of the teddy and meet famous teddy-bear personalities. The Bournemouth Bears are a joy for young and old alike. There are old bears, new bears, gigantic bears, tiny bears, and bears of all kinds, including limited editions and special creations. A nostalgic journey for adults and a delight for the young.
Open all year, daily 9.30-5 (10-4 Oct-Mar).
✻£2.95 (ch £1.95, pen & students £2.50). Family ticket £8.50.
P (100mtrs) shop
Cards: 🅰 ══ British 🕿 🅖

Dinosaur Safari

The Expocentre, Old Christchurch Ln BH1 1NE (just off A338)
☎ 01202 293544 Fax 01305 268885

Everything you've ever wanted to know about dinosaurs at Bournemouth's great indoor hands-on adventure of discovery. Computers and interactive displays help you learn the answers to the mystery of the dinosaurs. Great fun for old and young alike. Compare yourself with the largest and the smallest dinosaurs. See actual-size reconstructions of dinosaurs, fossils and skeletal remains - both real and rare casts.
Open daily 10-5.30 (10-4 Oct & Mar). (Closed 24-26 Dec & Nov-Feb inclusive).
✻£2.95 (ch £1.95, pen/students £2.50). Family ticket £8.50
P (100mtrs) shop
Cards: 🅰 ══ British 🕿 🅖

Russell-Cotes Art Gallery & Museum

East Cliff BH1 3AA (follow signs from St Swithin's roundabout)
☎ 01202 451800 Fax 01202 451800

The museum was built in 1894 as East Cliff Hall. Together with a new extension called The Display Space, and the recently restored art galleries it houses collections of 17th-to 20th-century paintings, watercolours, sculpture, miniatures, ceramics, furniture and world wide collections. There is a lively year round events and educational programme.
Closed for major building and re-display work. Phase I opening Summer 1998 with new craft cafe and displays. Opening times will be Tues-Sun 10-5 (Closed 25 Dec)
Free.
P (200 yds) ♨ & (2 lifts, induction loop for some events) toilets for disabled shop ⊗

BOVINGTON CAMP

Clouds Hill

BH20 7NQ (4m SW of Bere Regis)
☎ 01929 405616

T E Lawrence ('Lawrence of Arabia') bought this cottage in 1925 when he was a private in the Tank Corps at Bovington. He would escape here to play records and entertain friends to feasts of baked beans and China tea. Lawrence's sleeping bag, marked 'Meum', can be seen, together with his furniture and other memorabilia. Three rooms only are on show.
Open 5 Apr-1 Nov, Wed-Fri, Sun & BH Mon 12-5 or dusk if earlier.
£2.30.
⊗ 🚗 ♨

The Tank Museum

BH20 6JG (off A352)
☎ 01929 405096 Fax 01929 405360

Situated in the heart of Hardy Country near Wool in Dorset, The Tank Museum is widely regarded as the finest of its kind in the world. Since its conception by Rudyard Kipling in 1923 the Museum has grown steadily from an initial 26 vehicles to the comprehensive and world-famous collection of today. An amibitious expansion prgramme has enlarged the Museum to a total of six halls, and the collection has increased to some 350 vehicles of every nationality, many of them unique and bizarre prototypes. The vehicles are displayed both chronologically and by area of conflict, allowing the visitor to "walk through" history. There are also interactive audio exhibits, period footage on video, and simulators. Special events include: Firepower and Mobility Displays, Battle Day Spectacular (26 July), a Classic Car Show (20 Sept), a Model Expo (21-22 March) and the Dorset Childrens Show (25 May). Telephone for more details.
Open all year, daily 10-5. (Closed 7 days over Xmas).
✻£5 (ch £3, ch 5 free, pen £4). Family ticket £13. Party 10+. Army free.
🅿 ✗ licensed & (wheelchairs available, Braille & audio tours) toilets for disabled shop ⊗
Cards: 🅰 ══ ══ British 🕿

BROWNSEA ISLAND

Brownsea Island

BH15 1EE (located in Poole Harbour)
☎ 01202 707744

Although it is popular and easy to reach from Poole, Brownsea still offers peace, seclusion and a sense of timelessness. Visitors can wander along woodland paths, lounge on beautiful beaches, admire the fine views of Corfe Castle and the Dorset coast, or join a guided tour of the 250-acre nature reserve managed by the Dorset Trust for Nature Conservation. The island is perhaps most famous, however, as the site of the first scout camp, held by Lord Baden-Powell in 1907. Scouts and Guides are still the only people allowed to stay here overnight. The lack of development on the island is due to its last private owner, Mrs Bonham Christie. She kept it as a kind of huge garden for animals, birds and flowers, and let peacocks roam free. Their descendants still thrive here, as do native red squirrels, and sika deer, introduced in 1896. A less welcome newcomer is the destructive mink. The island is also famous for its dragonflies, moths and butterflies, but most of all for its birds. The brackish lagoon supports a colony of Sandwich and common terns, with numerous waders in autumn and spring, and ducks in winter. There is also a heronry, one of Britain's largest.
Open 22 Mar-Sep, daily 10-5 (10-6 Jul-Aug); check for time of last boat.
♨ ✗ & toilets for disabled shop ⊗ ♨
Details not confirmed for 1998

CANFORD CLIFFS

Compton Acres Gardens

Canford Cliffs Rd BH13 7ES (on B3065)
☎ 01202 700778 Fax 01202 707537

The nine and a half acres of Compton Acres incorporate Japanese, Roman and Italian gardens, rock and water gardens, and heather gardens. There are fine views over Poole Harbour and the Purbeck Hills, and a fabulous collection of bronze and marble statuary.
Open Mar-Oct, daily 10-6 (last entry 5.15)
£4.75 (ch £1, student & pen £3.70). Party 20+
🅿 ♨ ✗ licensed & (level paths and ramps into shops and cafe) toilets for disabled shop garden centre ⊗

CHETTLE

Chettle House

DT11 8DB (6m NE of Blandford Forum off A354)
☎ 01258 830209 Fax 01258 830380

This small country house was designed by Thomas Archer, and is praised as a fine example of the English Baroque. Around the house there are beautifully laid-out gardens. There is an exhibition area and a vineyard. Plants for sale. Craft fayre on May 23-25.
Open Etr-5 Oct, daily 11-5. (Closed Tue & Sat).
✻£2 (ch free).
🅿 ♨ & ⊗

CHRISTCHURCH

Christchurch Castle & Norman House

(near Christchurch Priory)

All that remains of the castle buildings is a ruined keep and a Norman house, which was probably where the castle constable lived. The house is unusually well preserved, and still has its original windows and tall chimney. The keep is more dilapidated, but parts of the thick walls can be seen.
Open any reasonable time.
Free.
⌗

The splendid Italianate water gardens at Compton Acres are only one of a number of different styles of garden here. There are Japanese, Roman and rock gardens as well as woodland to explore

Red House Museum & Gardens
Quay Rd BH23 1BU
☎01202 482860 Fax 01202 481924
A museum with plenty of variety, featuring local history, archaeology, and natural history, displayed in this Georgian house. There is an outstanding costume collection, and there are gardens with a woodland walk and herb garden. Temporary exhibitions include contemporary art and change every few weeks.
Open all year, Tue-Sat 10-5, Sun 2-5. (Closed Mon ex BH).
£1 (ch & pen 60p). Family ticket £2.60.
P (200yds) 🍴 ♿ shop ⌀

CORFE CASTLE
Corfe Castle
BH20 5EZ (on A351)
☎01929 481294
The castle was first built in Norman times, and was added to by King John. It was defended during the Civil War by Lady Bankes, who surrendered after a stout resistance. Parliament ordered the demolition of the castle, and today it is one of the most impressive ruins in England. New for 1998: Castle View visitor centre with family exhibition. Special events for 1998 include Medieval and Civil War events, Archaeology Days, Evening opening and tours. Ring for details.
Open Mar-1 Nov, daily 10-5.30 (4.30pm early Mar & late Oct or dusk if earlier); 3 Nov-1 Mar daily 11-3.30. (Closed 25-26 Dec & 2 days end Jan)
£3.80 (ch £2). Family ticket £5.80-£9.60. Party 15+ by arrangement.
P (charged) 🍴 ✕ licensed shop 🐾

Corfe Castle Museum
West St BH20 5HE
☎01929 480415
The tiny, rectangular building was partly rebuilt in brick after a fire in 1780, and is the smallest town hall building in England. It has old village relics, and dinosaur footprints 130 million years old. A council chamber on the first floor is reached by a staircase at one end. The Ancient Order of Marblers meets here each Shrove Tuesday.
Open all year, Apr-Oct, daily 9.30-6; Nov-Mar, wknds and Xmas holidays 10-5. Free.
P 200 yards ♿ ⌀

CRANBORNE

DORCHESTER
Dinosaur Museum
Icen Way DT1 1EW (in centre of town, just off main High East St)
☎01305 269880
Fax 01305 268885
Britain's only museum devoted to dinosaurs has an appealing mixture of fossils, skeletons, life-size reconstructions and interactive displays such as the 'feelies'. There are audio-visual presentations, and the idea is to provide an all-round family attraction with new displays each year. Voted Dorset's Family Attraction of the Year in 1997.
Open all year, daily 9.30-5.30 (10-4.30 Nov-Mar). Closed 24-26 Dec.
£3.50 (ch £2.25, pen/student £2.75). Family ticket £9.95.
P (50 yds) ♿ shop
Cards: 🌑 ▦ 🌀 🌐 🔘

Dorset County Museum
High West St DT1 1XA
☎01305 262735 Fax 01305 257180
A visit to the museum is a must for anyone interested in the Dorset area and its fascinating archaeology. Displays cover prehistoric and Roman times, including sites such as Maiden Castle. There is a major new gallery on Dorset writers with sections on the Dorset poet William Barnes, the poet and novelist Thomas Hardy (with a reconstruction of his study), and twentieth century writers. Geology, natural history and rural crafts are also explored in the museum which has twice won the Museum of the Year Award.

Open daily 10-5. (Closed Sun Sep-Jun, Good Fri, 25 Dec).
❋£2.75 (ch, students, UB40 & pen £1.50). Family ticket £7.60. Party 15+.
P (150 yds) ♿ shop ⌀

Hardy's Cottage
Higher Bockhampton DT2 8QJ (3m E off A35)
☎01305 262366
Thomas Hardy was born in this thatched house in 1840. It was built by his great-grandfather and has not changed much in appearance since. The inside can only be seen by appointment with the tenant.
Open 5 Apr-1 Nov, Sun-Thu 11-5 or dusk if earlier. Open Good Fri.
£2.60. Interior by appointment.
P ♿ ⌀ ♿

Maiden Castle
DT1 9PR (2m S, access off A354, N of bypass)
The Iron Age fort of Maiden Castle ranks among the finest in Britain. It covers 47 acres, and has daunting earthworks which must once have been even bigger, with a complicated defensive system around the entrances. One of the main purposes of such castles may have been to protect grain from marauding bands, and the need for such protection seems to have grown during the Iron Age. The first fort was built in around 700BC on the site of an earlier Neolithic camp, and had just a single rampart. By the time it was completed, probably around 100BC, it embraced the whole plateau and had outer earthworks as well. It was excavated in the 1930s by Sir Mortimer Wheeler, who found a cemetery of defenders killed when the castle was attacked and then taken by Roman troops in AD43. There are good views.
Open any reasonable time. Free.
P ♿

The Military Museum of Devon & Dorset
The Keep, Bridport Rd DT1 1RN
☎01305 264066
Fax 01305 250373
Three hundred years of military history are covered, with displays on the Devon Regiment, Dorset Regiment, Dorset Militia and Volunteers, the Queen's Own Dorset Yeomanry, and Devonshire and Dorset Regiment (from 1958). The Museum uses modern technology and creative displays to tell the stories of the Infantry, Cavalry and Artillerymen of the Counties of Devon and Dorset showing the uniforms they wore, weapons they carried, and medals which were won plus the spectacular views of Dorchester from the battlements, also children's activities.
Open all year, Mon-Sat 9-5
£2.50, (ch, student & pen £1.50). Family ticket £7
P ♿ toilets for disabled shop ⌀

Teddy Bear House
Antelope Walk, Cornhill DT1 1BE (in the centre of Dorchester near Tourist Information Centre)
☎01305 263200 Fax 01305 268885
A visit to Teddy Bear House is in fact a visit to the home of Mr Edward Bear and his large family of human-sized teddy bears! Join the bears as they relax around the house or busy themselves making teddies in the amazing Old Dorset Teddy Bear Factory. It's where fantasy becomes reality! The shop contains hundreds of teddy bears of all kinds.
Open daily 9.30-5. (Closed Dec 25-26)
£2 (ch£1). Family £5.50
P (500 metres) shop ⌀
Cards: 🌑 ▦ 🌀 🌐 🔘

Tutankhamun Exhibition
High West St DT1 1UW
☎01305 269571 Fax 01305 268885
The exhibition recreates the excitement of one of the world's greatest discoveries of ancient treasure using sight, sound and smell. A reconstruction of the tomb and facsimiles of its contents are

displayed. The superbly preserved mummified body of the boy king can be seen, wonderfully recreated in every detail. See 'The Jewels of Tutankhamun', plus a special 75th Anniversary exhibition on the Discovery of the Tomb of Tutankhamun.
Open daily, 9.30-5.30, Nov-Mar 9.30-5. (Closed 24-26 Dec).
£3.50 (ch £2.25, pen/student £2.75). Family ticket £9.95.
P (200 yds) ♿ shop ⌀
Cards: 🌑 ▦ 🌀 🌐 🔘

MINTERNE MAGNA
Minterne Gardens
DT2 7AU (2m N of Cerne Abbas on A352)
☎01300 341370 Fax 01300 341747
Lakes, cascades, streams and many fine and rare trees will be found in these lovely landscaped gardens. The 18th-century design is a superb setting for the spring shows of rhododendrons, azaleas and spring bulbs, and the autumn colour.
Open 28 Mar-10 Nov, daily 10-7.
£3 (accompanied ch free).
P

POOLE
Poole Pottery
The Quay BH15 1RF
☎01202 666200 Fax 01202 682894
Founded in 1873, this well-known establishment has been producing its distinctive Poole Pottery since 1921. There is a display of past and present pottery manufacture. Self-guided factory tour. Other attractions include a factory shop, 'Have a Go' area, and a craft village.
Open all year, daily 10-4. (Closed 22 Dec-2 Jan).
P (500 yds) 🍴 ✕ licensed ♿ (wheelchairs available) toilets for disabled shop ⌀
Details not confirmed for 1998
Cards: 🌑 ▦ 🌀 🔘

ITALIAN GARDEN & PALM COURT 🌳 WOODLAND WALK & GLEN ✕
HEATHER GARDEN
GARDEN CENTRE
GIFT SHOP
ROCK & WATER GARDEN
RESTAURANT · TEA ROOM
JAPANESE GARDEN
BRASSERIE
ITALIAN GA...

The Relaxing way to spend a day!

Visit **Compton Acres** GARDENS OF THE WORLD

CANFORD CLIFFS · POOLE · DORSET · 01202 700778

Waterfront Museum & Scaplen's Court
4 High St BH15 1BW (off Poole quay)
☎01202 683138 Fax 01202 660896
Set in buildings dating from the medieval period, the Waterfront Museum tells the story of Poole's seafaring past. The visitor can learn of the Roman occupation, hear the smuggler tell his tale, see material raised from the Studland Bay wreck and visualise the first Scout Camp on Brownsea Island. The story is told using modern and audio visual techniques, hands-on and traditional museum displays. Scaplen's Court, just a few yards from the museum, is a beautifully restored domestic building dating from the medieval period. There is a Victorian school room, a kitchen and scullery in which cooking demonstrations take place from time to time, a children's room and other displays.
Waterfront Museum: open all year, daily from 10 (closes 3pm Dec-mid Feb, 4pm Nov & mid Feb-Mar, 5pm Apr-Jun & Sep-Oct, 8pm Jul-Aug). Scaplen's Court: Open Jul-Aug, daily 10-7.
❋Waterfront Museum: £1.50-£2.50 (ch 90p-£1.75, sen cit & student £1.30-£2.30). Scaplen's Court £1.45 (ch £1.10).
P 250meters 🍴 ♿ (ex Town Cellars & Scaplen's Court) toilets for disabled shop ⌀
Cards: 🌑 ▦

PORTLAND
Portland Castle
Castle Town DT5 1AZ (overlooking Portland harbour)
☎01305 820539
One of the best preserved of Henry VIII's coastal forts, built of white Portland stone. It was originally intended to thwart attack by the Spanish and French, and changed hands several times during the Civil War.
Open Apr-1 Nov, daily 10-6 (or dusk if earlier in Oct).
P ♿ shop ⌀ ♿

Portland Museum

217 Wakeham DT5 1HS (A354
Weymouth/Portland,through
Fortuneswell to Portland Heights
hotel,then English Heritage signs)
☎01305 821804 Fax 01305 761654
Avice's cottage in Thomas Hardy's book
'The Well-Beloved', this building is now a
museum of local and historical interest,
with varied displays. In the garden is the
casing of a German Second World War
bomb which was found in the centre of
the football pitch in 1995. Four thousand
people had to be evacuated whilst it was
defused. Regular temporary exhibitions
are held, including a shipwreck and
smuggling exhibition. The adjoining Marie
Stopes cottage houses domestic
bygones and a display of maritime
history. A new gallery displays Portland
history from the Stone Age to the 19th
century. Garden with picnic area. Phone
for details of special events
*Open: Summer(Etr-Oct) 10.30-5 (Closed
1-1.30 & all day Wed-Thu), Winter(Nov-
Etr). Groups by prior arrangement only
£1.60 (ch & students free, pen 80p).*
🅿 ♿ *(talking tapes for blind & partially
sighted) shop*

Built during the Restoration, the interior of Kingston Lacy House was later transformed into an Italian palazzo filled with countless works of art.

SHAFTESBURY
Abbey Ruins & Museum

Park Walk SP7 8JR
☎01747 852910
The abbey at Shaftesbury was part of a
nunnery founded by King Alfred in 888. It
became one of the wealthiest in the
country but was destroyed during the
Dissolution in 1539. The excavated ruins
show the foundations of the abbey. A
museum on the site displays carved
stones, decorated floor tiles and other
artefacts found during the excavations. A
guided trail around the ruins can be
followed using a numbered leaflet. An
attractive recent addition is the
Anglo/Saxon herb garden. Celebrations
for the Feast of St Edward (22-23 June).
*Open Apr-Sep daily, 10am-5pm.
£1 (ch 40p, pen & student 70p).*
P (250yds) ♿ *toilets for disabled shop*

SHERBORNE
Sherborne Castle

☎01935 813182 Fax 01935 816727
This 16th-century house, built by Sir
Walter Raleigh, is the 'new' castle and
has been the home of the Digby family
since 1617. The house was built beside
the ruins of the old castle, and in 1625
four wings were added to the original
1594 building. The house contains some
fine furniture, painting, porcelain and
many items of historical interest. The
grounds, with an artificial lake, were
designed by 'Capability' Brown in the
18th century. Tea and refreshments are
served in a Gothic dairy which is by the
lake. Ring for details of special events.
*Open Etr Sat-Sep, Thu, Sat, Sun & BH
Mons 1.30-4.30 (grounds 12.30-5).
❉£4.80 (ch £2.40, pen £4). Family ticket
£12. Grounds only £2.40 (ch £1.20). Party
25+.*
🅿 🍴 *shop ❄ (ex in grounds)*

Sherborne Museum

Abbey Gate House, Church Ln DT9 3BP
☎01935 812252
On show in this museum is a model of
Sherborne's original Norman castle, as
well as a fine Victorian doll's house and
other domestic and agricultural bygones.
There are also items of local geological,
natural history and archeological interest,
including Roman material. Photographs
of the Sherborne Missal of 1400 are on
display. The latest addition is a 15th-
century wall painting originally from a
house near the museum.
*Open Apr-Oct, Tue-Sat 10.30-4.30, Sun
2.30-4.30; BH Mon 2.30-4.30
£1 (ch & students free)*
P (400yds) ♿ *toilets for disabled shop ❄*

Sherborne Old Castle

D19 5NR (half a mile E off B31'45)
☎01935 812730
The castle was built between 1107 and
1135 by Roger, Bishop of Salisbury but
was captured and destroyed by
Cromwell's forces in the Civil War. The
ruins of the main buildings, the curtain
wall and the towers and gates date from
Norman times. The castle came into Sir
Walter Raleigh's possession in 1592.
*Open Apr-1 Nov, daily 10-6 (or dusk if
earlier in Oct); 2 Nov-Mar, Wed-Sun 10-4,
(closed 1-2pm). Grounds only open.
£1.60(ch 80p, concessions £1.20)*
🅿♿♿ 🚻

Worldlife & Lullingstone Silk Farm

Compton House, Over Compton DT9
4QN (entrance on A30, 2.5m W)
☎01935 474608 Fax 01935 429937
Worldlife has evolved from Worldwide
Butterflies. Visitors see what is being
done, and what can be done, for wildlife
and the environment. Set in the grounds
of lovely Compton House is the superb
collection of butterflies from all over the
world, flying free in reconstructions of
their natural habitats, including natural
jungle and a tropical palmhouse. The
collection has been built up over 30 years
and there are active breeding and
hatching areas on view as well as an
extensive specialist library for research.
Compton is also the home of the
Lullingstone Silk Farm which produced
unique English-reared silk for the last two
coronations and the Queen's and the
Princess of Wales' wedding dresses. At
the farm the complete process of silk
production is shown by exhibits and
film.
*Open Apr-Sep, daily 10-5.
Admission fee payable.*
🅿 🍴 ♿ *shop ❄*
Cards: 🔳 🔳 🔳 🔳 🔳

SWANAGE
Swanage Railway

Station House BH19 1HB (Park & ride
Station at Norden, signposted from A351)
☎01929 425800 & 424276 (timetable)
Fax 01929 426680
The railway from Swanage to Wareham
was closed in 1972. In 1976 the
Swanage Railway took possession and
over the past 20 years have gradually
restored the line, which now runs for 6
miles, passing the ruins of Corfe Castle.
*Open all year, wknds & BH; May-Oct,
daily 9.30-5.30; Santa Specials every
wknd in Dec.*
P (Park & Ride Norden) 🍴 ✗ licensed ♿
*(special disabled persons coach) toilets
for disabled shop
Details not confirmed for 1998*
Cards: 🔳 🔳 🔳 🔳 🔳

TOLPUDDLE
Tolpuddle Martyrs Museum

DT2 7EH (on A35, 7m E of Dorchester,
4.5m W of Bere Regis)
☎01305 848237
Fax 01305 848237
Tolpuddle is celebrated for the
agricultural workers from the village who
united to improve their wages and
conditions of employment. They were
arrested and transported in 1834 and
became known as the Tolpuddle Martyrs.
In the 1930s the TUC built a museum
and six cottages named after them. Also
in the village is the 'Martyrs Tree', an old
sycamore under which it is thought the
Martyrs met. The museum within the
cottages depicts the story of the martyrs.
The Tolpuddle Martyrs Rally is held on
the third Sunday of July each year,
12.30-4pm.

*Open all year, Apr-Oct, Tue-Sat 10-5.30,
Sun 11-5.30; Nov-Mar, Tue-Sat 10-4, Sun
11-4. Open BH Mon. (Closed 24 Dec-1 Jan).
Free.*
P (outside museum) ♿ *toilets for disabled
shop ❄*

VERWOOD
Dorset Heavy Horse Centre

Edmondsham Rd BH21 5RJ (1.25m NW,
signposted from Verwood).
☎01202 824040 Fax 01202 821407
Visitors can see the different breeds of
heavy horses and miniature and Shetland
ponies. There is an information area and
a display of farm implements and horse
harness. Trailer and pony rides (weather
permitting) are an additional attraction.
There are three 'live' commentaries daily
at 11.30am, 2pm and 4pm in the summer
season, and visitors are welcome to ask
staff about the horses and ponies, to
sponsor a horse or pony, and enquire
about any other aspect of the Centre.
*Open Good Fri-Oct, daily 10-5.
Commentaries at 11.15am, 2pm & 4pm.
£3.95 (ch 14 £2.25, pen £3.50). Family
ticket £11.*
🅿 🍴 ♿ *(free wheelchair loan) toilets for
disabled shop*
Cards: 🔳 🔳 🔳

WEST LULWORTH
Lulworth Castle

BH20 5QS (from Wareham, W on A352
for 1 mile, left onto B3070 to E Lulworth,
follow tourist signs)
☎01929 400352 Fax 01929 400563
Lulworth Castle, home of the Weld
Family since 1641, tragically burnt to the
ground in 1929, but is now restored and
open to the public. The exhibition
features the history of the building,
kitchen, wine cellar, activity room and a
chance to solve the Lulworth Riddle. In
the grounds visitors can enjoy the peace
of the chapel and visit the popular
summer farm. 1998 events include:
Country Gardening Festival (9-10 May),
Lulworth Castle House Open Days (10
May & 19 July), Open air concerts (13
June & 18 July), Horse Trials (1-2
August), Classic Car Event (23 August).
*Open daily, Nov-Mar 10-4; Apr-Oct 10-6
(closed 25 Dec).
Free.*
🅿 🍴 ♿ *(limited in castle due to grade
one listing) toilets for disabled shop*
Cards: 🔳 🔳 🔳 🔳 🔳 🔳

Lulworth Cove Heritage Centre

Lulworth Cove BH20 5RQ (From A352 go
to Wool, then onto B3071 and follow
brown signs)
☎01929 400587
The centre traces the history of Lulworth
from prehistoric through to modern

times. There is a comprehensive video display with breathtaking helicopter film of the coastline and surrounding countryside. Displays include coastal and other local wildlife, flora, geology and fossils of the area together with a global weather satellite station. The shop has local crafts as well as books and gifts. The centre is at Lulworth Cove with access to spectacular coastal walks including one to Lulworth Castle, 3 miles away.
Open daily Nov-Mar 10-4; Apr-Oct 10-6 (Closed 25 Dec)
Free.
🅿 *(charged)* & *toilets for disabled shop* ✍
Cards: ▨ ▨▨ ▨ ▨ ▨

WEYMOUTH
Deep Sea Adventure & Sharky's Play Area
9 Custom House Quay, Old Harbour DT4 8BG
☎ 01305 760690
Fax 01305 760690
A fascinating attraction telling the story of underwater exploration and marine exploits. This entertaining and educational exhibition fills the top three floors of an imposing Victorian grain warehouse. Discover the history of Weymouth's Old Harbour, compelling tales of shipwreck survival, explore the Black Hole and search for Ollie the Oyster. Also a unique display telling the gripping tale of the *Titanic* disaster. Sharkys Play Area is four floors of fun-packed adventure where children (5ft height limit) can jump, swing, slide and climb in a safe padded play area. Seperate toddler area for the under fives.
Open all year, daily 9.30-7 (high season 9.30-9). Closed 24-26 Dec.
Sharkys Play Area: Adults free (ch £2.75).
Deep Sea Adventure: £3 (ch 5-15 £2.50, pen/student £2.75). Family ticket £10. Party. Combined ticket for both attractions, ch £4.50, Family £14.
🅿 *(100yds)* ✗ *licensed* & *(lift & sign language for deaf) toilets for disabled shop* ✍

RSPB Nature Reserve Radipole Lake
The Swannery Car Park DT4 7TZ (within the town, close to seafront & railway station)
☎ 01305 778313
Fax 01305 773519
A popular reserve for families and birdwatchers alike, covering 222 acres, offers firm paths, hides and a visitor centre. Several types of warblers, mute swans, gadwalls, teals and great crested grebes are all based on the reserve. In the visitor centre there are viewing windows overlooking the lake. Phone for details of special events.
Open daily 9-5
£2 (ch 50p, concessions £1) Family ticket £4.
🅿 *(charged)* & *shop*
Cards: ▨ ▨▨ ▨ ▨

Sea Life Park
Lodmoor Country Park DT4 7SX (on A353)
☎ 01305 788255
Fax 01305 760165
The Sea Life Park is situated at the beautiful Lodmoor Country Park. Here you can marvel at the mysteries of the deep and discover amazing sea creatures from around our own shores in spectacular marine displays. Also includes the Tropical Jungle where exotic birds fly freely, the Blue Whale Splashpool, Cadbury's Sea Life Kingdom themed play area, and new 3-D interactive Shark Academy.
Open all year, daily from 10am. (Closed 25 Dec).
Prices under review.
🅿 *(charged)* ☕ & *toilets for disabled shop* ✍
Cards: ▨ ▨▨ ▨▨ ▨ ▨ ▨

WIMBORNE
Kingston Lacy House, Garden & Park
BH21 4EA (1.5m W on B3082)
☎ 01202 883402
One of the finest houses of its period in Dorset, Kingston Lacy House and 1500 of its 9000 acres were bequeathed to the National Trust in 1981 and opened to the public only in 1986. Until then, the house had been the home of the Bankes family for over 300 years. The original house was built between 1663 and 1665, but in the 1830s it was altered and given a stone façade by Sir Charles Barry for W J Bankes.
W J Bankes was a traveller and a collector and, not only did he add the grand Italian marble staircase and a superb Venetian ceiling, but treasures from Spain and an Egyptian obelisk. There is also a quite outstanding picture collection with works by Titian, Rubens, Velasquez, Reynolds and family portraits by Van Dyck and Lely. Please ring for details of special events. No photography is allowed in the house.
Open 8 Mar-1 Nov, daily ex Thu & Fri 12-5.30. Last admission 4.30pm; Park & Garden 8 Mar-1 Nov daily ex Thu & Fri 11.-6. Nov & Dec Fri-Sun 11-4. Last admission 5pm or dusk if earlier.
£6 (ch £3). Park & Gardens only: £2.50 (ch £1.25).Party 20+.
🅿 ✗ *licensed* & *(parking by arrangement) toilets for disabled shop* ✍ *(ex in north park)* ⛵

Knoll Gardens & Nursery
Stapehill Rd, Hampreston BH21 7ND (3m E between Wimborne and Ferndown off A31)
☎ 01202 873931 *Fax 01202 870842*
Over 4000 plant species from all over the world thrive here, all within a compact, mostly level six-acre site which is continually being expanded. There are water gardens with waterfalls, pools and a stream, a woodland walk, herbaceous borders, and many other features. It it also the home of the NCCPG collections of Phygelius and Ceanothus. A wide range of plants, mainly propagated in the Nursery, can be bought here, and there is a tearoom and spacious all-weather visitor centre with gift and book shops. Garden video presentations.
Open Mar Wed-Sun 10-4, Apr-Oct daily 10-5.30, Nov-Xmas Wed-Sat 10-4.
£3.40 (ch £1.70, student £2.40, pen £2.90). Party 20+.
🅿 ☕ ✗ *licensed* & *toilets for disabled shop garden centre* ✍
Cards: ▨ ▨▨ ▨ ▨ ▨ ▨ ▨

Priest's House Museum and Garden
23-27 High St BH21 1HR
☎ 01202 882533 *Fax 01202 882533*
Explore Wimborne's past through this award-winning local history museum set in an historic house with a working Victorian kitchen where regular cooking demonstrations are held, on the last Saturday of the month from 2pm-5pm. There are nine other rooms to see, along with regular special exhibitions covering aspects of the collections not normally on view, and a beautiful 300ft-long walled garden. The 'hands-on' archaeology gallery, an ironmonger's shop, Victorian stationer's shop, and toys and dolls are other attractions. Parties are welcome by arrangement.
Open Apr-Oct, Mon-Sat, 10.30-5. Also every Sun Jun-Sep. Special Christmas season.
✳*£2 (ch 90p, pen & students £1.60).*
Family ticket £5
🅿 *(200 yds)* & *(hands on archaeology gallery, audio tapes) shop* ✍

Stapehill Abbey
Wimborne Rd West BH21 2EB (2.5m E, off A31)
☎ 01202 861686
This early 19th-century abbey, home for nearly 200 years to Cistercian nuns, is now a busy working crafts centre with many attractions under cover. There are award-winning landscaped gardens,

parkland and picnic spots, and the Power to the Land exhibition. Special events for 1998 include: Spring Craft Fair (21-22 March), Flower & Garden Festival (19-22 June), Country World Weekend (25-26 July), Children's Weekend (22-23 August), Autumn Craft Fair (7-8 Nov), Christmas Weekends (Dec 5-6, 12-13, 19-20)
Open Etr-Sep, daily 10-5; Oct-Etr Wed-Sun 10-4. Closed 22 Dec-4 Feb.
£4.80 (ch 4-16 £3.30, students & pen £4.40). Family ticket £12.90. Party 20+.
🅿 & *toilets for disabled shop garden centre* ✍

CO DURHAM

BARNARD CASTLE
Barnard Castle
☎ 01833 38212
The town's name comes from Bernard Baliol, who built the castle in 1125. The castle clings to the steep banks of the Tees and is now a ruin, but it still has a 12th-century keep, and the remains of a 14th-century hall.
Open all year, Apr-1 Nov, daily 10-6 (or dusk if earlier); 2 Nov-Mar, Wed-Sun 10-4.
£2.20 (ch £1.10, concessions £1.70)
🅿 & *shop* ♿

The Bowes Museum
DL12 8NP (on A66)
☎ 01833 690606 *Fax 01833 637163*
This splendid French château-style mansion was built in 1869 by John Bowes, who made his fortune in Durham coal and married a French actress. They amassed an outstanding collection of works of art, and built the flamboyant château to house them. The museum is now run by Durham County Council, and its collections include paintings by El Greco, Goya and Canaletto among others; porcelain and silver, furniture, ceramics and tapestries. There is a local history section, and a formal garden. Temporary exhibitions are held.
Open May-Sep, Mon-Sat 10-5.30, Sun 2-5; Nov-Feb closes 4pm; Mar, Apr & Oct closes 5pm. (Closed 20-25 Dec & 1 Jan). Opening times under review.
✳*£3.50(concessions £2.50). Prices under review.*
🅿 ☕ & *(lift, ramped entrance, reserved parking) toilets for disabled shop* ✍
Cards: ▨ ▨▨

Egglestone Abbey
DL12 8QN (1m S on minor road off B6277)
The remains of this Premonstratensian abbey make a picturesque sight on the right bank of the River Tees. A large part of the church can be seen, as can remnants of monastic buildings.
Open any reasonable time.
Free.
🅿 & ♿

BEAMISH
North of England Open-Air Museum
DH9 0RG (off A693 & A6076 signposted off A1(M) junc 63)
☎ 01207 231811 *Fax 01207 290933*
Beamish, an open air museum, set in 200 acres of beautiful countryside, vividly recreates life in the north of England early this century. Visitors stroll down the cobbled streets of The Town to see fully stocked Co-operative shops, dentist's surgery, working pub, sweet shop and sweet factory. Guided tours are given underground at a real 'drift' mine in The Colliery Village, and a row of miner's cottages show how pitmen and their families lived. There is a Methodist chapel and a village school here too. Traditional breeds of animals and poultry fill the farmyard at Home Farm, and in the large farmhouse kitchen the farmer's wife goes about her daily chores. At The Railway Station, complete with goods yard, signal box and weighbridge house, locomotives and rolling stock are on display. Pockerley Manor and horse yard,

a fortified medieval manor house illustrating the life of a yeoman farming family almost 200 years ago. 1998 special events include: Dog Agility Festival (9-10 May), North Country Quilting (6-7 June & 15-16 August), Lace-Making Weekend (29-30 August).
Open all year: Summer, Apr-Oct, daily from 10am. Winter visits centred on The Town & tramway, other areas closed, Nov-Mar from 10am but closed Mon & Fri. Closing times vary according to season it is advisable to check.Also check for Christmas times.
✳*Summer £6.99-£7.99 (ch & pen £4.99). Winter £2.99 (ch & pen £1.99). Party 20+. Prices under review.*
🅿 ☕ & *toilets for disabled shop*
Cards: ▨ ▨▨ ▨▨ ▨ ▨

BISHOP AUCKLAND
Auckland Castle
Market Place DL14 7NP
☎ 01388 601627 *Fax 01388 605264*
The historic home of the Bishops of Durham with parts dating from the 12th century. The very fine private chapel was remodelled by Bishop Cosin in 1660 from the medieval banquet hall. Portraits of past Bishops line the throne room. There is a large public park and an unusual 18th-century deerhouse. New exhibition area showing the story of St Cuthbert and the role of the Prince Bishops in the North of England'. Various Special Events are planned - please telephone for details.
Open May-Jun, Fri & Sun: Jul, Thu,Fri & Sun; Aug Thu-Sun; also open BH Mon; hours 2-5.
🅿 & *shop* ✍
Details not confirmed for 1998

BOWES
Bowes Castle
DL12 9LD (on A66)
Built inside the earthworks of the Roman fort of 'Lavatrae', the castle is a ruin now, but the great Norman keep still stands three storeys high. It was built between 1171 and 1187.
Open any reasonable time.
Free.
♿ ♿

COWSHILL
Killhope Lead Mining Centre
DL13 1AR (3m W off A689 midway between Stanhope & Alston)
☎ 01388 537505 *Fax 01388 537617*
Visitors now have the opportunity to go into Park Level Mine at Killhope. Guided tours underground will explore the working conditions of lead miners. Equipped with hard hats and lamps, visitors will be led on tours lasting nearly an hour. The lead mine and 19th-century crushing mill have been restored to look as they would have done in the 1870s. Visitors are invited to get involved in activities such as separating lead ore from waste by working primitive machinery. A path leads to displays of lead mining through the ages. The 34ft water wheel is now restored and turning. There is a visitor centre and exhibition based on the life of miners and their families. Mineral Exhibition (5-6 September) & Workshops and activities during school holidays. Ring for details.
Open Apr-Oct, daily 10.30-5. Last entry 4.30pm. Nov, Sun 10.30-5.
£3.40 (ch, disabled, & UB40 £1.70, pen £2.40). Additional charge for mine visit £1.60(ch, disabled, UB40 80p)
🅿 & *toilets for disabled shop*
Cards: ▨ ▨▨ ▨ ▨

DARLINGTON
Darlington Railway Centre & Museum
North Rd Station DL3 6ST (0.75m N off A167)
☎ 01325 460532
The museum is housed in North Road Station, built 17 years after the world's first passenger train ran along the Stockton and Darlington line. The building has been carefully restored and part is still in use for train services. The prize exhibit is *Locomotion*, which pulled the first passenger train and was built by ➤

Robert Stephenson & Co in 1825. Several other steam locomotives are also shown, together with an early railway coach of about 1845 and a chaldron (coal) wagon. There are also models and other exhibits relating to the Stockton and Darlington and the North Eastern Railway companies. Locomotive restoration work takes place in the former goods shed nearby.
Open daily 9.30-5 (Closed Xmas & New Year); Last admission 4.30pm. May be subject to amendment.
🅿 ♿ *(guide tape for visually handicapped) toilets for disabled shop* ⊗
Details not confirmed for 1998

DURHAM
One of the most splendidly sited cities in Britain, Durham's rocky outcrop, washed on three sides by the River Wear, was from the earliest times a secure fortress against invading Scots and Danes. Towering majestically above a loop in the river, Durham Cathedral, with the castle close by makes an unforgettable picture of Norman splendour. During the Middle Ages the Prince-Bishops of Durham ruled the north of England and, such was their power, they ran Durham as a city state. The castle, now part of the university, was their palace from 1072 until 1836. The steep wooded banks of the river provide lovely walks and among Durham's other attractions is a celebrated Oriental Museum.

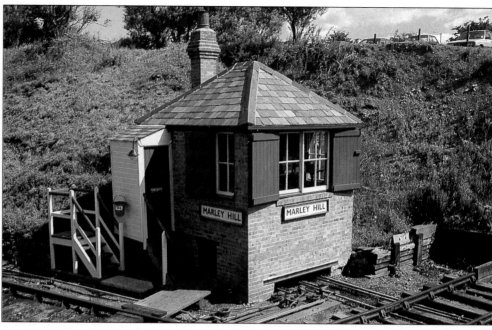
Home of 35 steam engines, Marley Hill Shed can be found at Tanfield Railway, the oldest existing railway in the world.

Durham Cathedral
DH1 3EH (A1(M) to Durham turn off at A690 into city take turning into the market place & follow signs)
☎ *0191 3864266 Fax 0191 3864267*
The cathedral was founded in 1093 as a shrine to St Cuthbert. His bones still rest in the Feretory. The cathedral is a remarkable example of Norman architecture set within an imposing site high above the River Wear. Together with the Castle, it is a World Heritage site. A full programme of concerts throughout the year. St Cuthbert's Day Procession (phone for details).
Open all year, daily, Sep-Apr 7.15-6, May-Aug 7.15-8.
Donations requested. Charge for ascent of Tower £2, Monk's Dormitory 80p, Treasury £1, Audio-Visual 50p
🅿 *(in city centre)* ♿ 🍴 *licensed* ♿ *(braille guide touch & hearing centre) toilets for disabled shop* ⊗

Durham Light Infantry Museum & Durham Art Gallery
Aykley Heads DH1 5TU (0.50m NW, turn right off A691)
☎ *0191 384 2214 Fax 0191 386 1770*
The history of the Regiment is told in displays of artefacts, medals, uniforms

and vehicles. The Art Gallery has a continuous programme of temporary exhibitions, and it holds regular lectures and concerts.
Open all year, Tue-Sat 10-4.30 & Sun 2-4.30 (Closed Mon, ex BHs).
£1.50 (concessions 75p)
🅿 🍴 ♿ *(wheelchair available, lift,ramp) toilets for disabled shop* ⊗
Cards: 💳

Finchale Priory
(3m NE)
☎ *0191 386 3828*
The lovely setting of the priory was chosen by St Godric in 1110 as a place for years of solitary meditation. The priory was begun in 1180, and was used by monks from Durham Cathedral. There are considerable remains of the 13th-century church.
Open Apr-Sep, daily noon-5.
£1.20 (ch 60p, concessions 90p)
🅿 *(charged)* ♿ ⊗ ♿

Oriental Museum
University of Durham, Elvet Hill DH1 3TH (signposted from A167 & A177)
☎ *0191 374 7911*
Fax 0191 374 3242
The museum has a remarkable collection of Oriental artefacts, ranging from Ancient Egypt to Japan.
Open Mon-Fri 9.30-1 & 2-5, Sat & Sun 2-5. (Closed Xmas-New Year).
£1.50 (ch, pen & students 50p)
🅿 ♿ *shop* ⊗
Cards: 💳 💳

HARTLEPOOL
Hartlepool Historic Quay
Maritime Av TS24 0XZ (from A19 take A179 and follow signs for marina then historic quay)
☎ *01429 860077 Fax 01429 867332*
Britain's maritime heritage brought to life! Step back in time to experience the sights, sounds and smells of an 1800's quayside. Enjoy the latest technology in 'Fighting Ships', a journey through a frigate of Nelson's navy, including a battle at sea! Watch George and Harry 'pressganged' into service. Learn about the birth of the Royal Navy in 'Seapower'. Visit the Quayside shops, gaol, admiral's house and the Hartness market. Play traditional games in 'Skittle Square'. A full programme of events and attractions are planned, including re-enactments by naval and military groups, craft fairs, musical events, Christmas and Easter themed events, phone for details.
Open daily 10-5 (10-7 in summer). Closed 25 Dec & 1 Jan.
£4.95 (concessions £2.50). Family ticket £13.
🅿 🍴 ✗ *licensed* ♿ *(all areas ramped or lift access) toilets for disabled shop* ⊗
Cards: 💳 💳 💳

HMS Trincomalee Trust
Jackson Dock TS24 0SQ (follow brown heritage signs)
☎ *01429 223193 Fax 01429 864385*
HMS Trincomalee launched in 1817 is the oldest British warship afloat today and is undergoing restoration. Locally-built small craft can also be seen. Guided tours.
Open all year, Mon-Fri 10.30-3.30, wknds & BH 10-4.30. (Closed Xmas & New Year inc Boxing day)).
£2.50 (concessions £1.50)
🅿 ♿ ⊗

Museum of Hartlepool
Marina Way, Jackson Dock TS24 0XZ
☎ *01429 222255*
Fax 01429 523477
The museum tells the story of Hartlepool from prehistory to the present day and includes many original artefacts, models, computer interactives and hands-on exhibits. See how iron and steel ships were built and climb aboard the fishing coble *The Three Brothers Grant.* The Humber ferry *Wingfield Castle*, a paddle steamer built in Hartlepool in 1934 is moored alongside the museum and houses further displays and a café. Traditional fishing and pilot cobles are moored in the dock. A traditional north craft event will be held in June 1998. Ring for details.

Open all year, daily (closed 25-26 Dec & 1 Jan).
Free.
🅿 🍴 ♿ *toilets for disabled shop* ⊗ *(ex guide dogs)*

STAINDROP
Raby Castle
P O Box 50 DL2 3AY (1m N, off A688)
☎ *01833 660 202 Fax 01833 660 169*
The stronghold of the powerful Nevill family until 1569, and the home of the Vane family since 1626. The fortress is built around a courtyard and surrounded by a moat (now dry). The castle was erected during Saxon times but is substantially 14th century, with parts added in nearly every century. It has an impressive gateway; nine towers of which the tallest is 80ft; a vast medieval hall; and a Victorian octagonal drawing-room. The 14th-century kitchen, with its collection of Victorian copper cooking utensils, was in use daily until 1954. The castle contains fine pictures from English, Dutch and Italian schools, interesting furniture and ceramics, and a good carriage collection. There are about five acres of gardens and an additional 200-acre park with both red and fallow deer. Ring for details of special events.
Open May-Jun, Wed & Sun; Jul-Sep, Sun-Fri; BH weekends, Sat-Wed (incl First). Castle open 1-5. Park & gardens 11-5.30, (last admission 4.30pm).
Castle, Gardens & Carriage Collection £4 (ch £1.50, pen £3). Family ticket £10. Park, Gardens & Carriage Collection £1.50 (ch & pen £1). Party25+.
🅿 🍴 ♿ *toilets for disabled shop* ⊗ *(ex in Park)*
Cards: 💳 💳 💳

TANFIELD
Tanfield Railway
Old Marley Hill NE16 5ET (on A6076 1m S of Sunniside)
☎ *0191 388 7545*
A 3-mile working steam railway and the oldest existing railway in the world. The Causey Arch, the first large railway bridge and the largest single span arch in Britain of its era, is the centrepiece of a woodland full of picturesque walks around a deep valley. The story of the early railway and collieries is told on a series of display boards, giving an interesting break in a return journey from Tanfield. You can ride in carriages that first saw use in Victorian times, and visit Marley Hill shed, which is the home of 35 engines; inside the shed you can see the stationary steam engine at work driving some of the vintage machine tools. The blacksmith is also often at work forging

new parts for the restoration work. A new station has opened at East Tanfield, the south end of the line. Throughout the year, the Tanfield Railway holds special days for both the family and those interested in railway heritage.
Open all year, summer daily 10-5; winter daily 10-4. Trains: Sun & Summer BH's weekends; also Thu & Sat mid Jul-Aug. Santa's Specials Sat & Sun in Dec (booking essential). Mince pie specials Boxing Day.
✳*Admission free. Train travel £3.50 (ch & pen £2)*
🅿 ☕ ♿ *(some trains can carry disabled visitors) toilets for disabled shop*

ESSEX

AUDLEY END
Audley End House
CB11 4JF (1m W of Saffron Walden on B1383(
☎*01799 522399*
Built by Thomas Howard, Earl of Suffolk, to entertain King James I, Audley End House was gradually demolished, and by the 1750's it was about the size seen today. There are still over 30 rooms to see, each with period furnishings and a stunning collection of art, including works by Canaletto and Van Goyen. Further highlights include the Great Hall with its Jacobean carved screen and the reception rooms designed by Robert Adam. The house and its gardens including a 19th-century parterre and rose garden, are surronded by an 18th-century landscape park.
Open Apr-Oct, Wed-Sun & BH's 11-6 (or dusk if earlier). Park and gardens open from 10am. Last admissions 5pm.
£5.90 (ch £3, concessions £4.50). Grounds £3 (ch £1.80, concessions £2.70)
🅿 *(charged)* ☕ ♿ *shop* 🚫 ♿

BRAINTREE
The Working Silk Mill
New Mills, South St CM7 3GB (follow brown tourist signs)
☎*01376 553393*
Fax 01376 330642
The Working Silk Museum is the country's last remaining company of handloom silk weavers. Fabric is woven on 150 year old handlooms for historic houses, the National Trust, English Heritage and royal palaces both here and abroad. Full production can be seen from processing the raw silk to weaving the fabric.
Open Mon-Fri, 10-12.30 & 1.30-5. Last admission to mill 12 noon and 4pm.
£3 (ch £1.70 pen/students £2). Family ticket £8.50Party.
🅿 ♿ *toilets for disabled shop* 🚫 *(ex guide dogs)*

CASTLE HEDINGHAM
Colne Valley Railway & Museum
Castle Hedingham Station CO9 3DZ (4m NW of Halstead on A604(being renumbered to A1017))
☎*01787 461174*
Fax 01787 462254
The old Colne Valley and Halstead railway buildings have been rebuilt here. Stock includes seven steam locomotives plus sixty other engines, carriages and wagons, in steam from Easter to December. There is also a five-acre riverside nature and picnic area. Visitors may also dine in style in restored Pullman carriages while travelling along the line. Please telephone for a free timetable and details of the many special events which include gala days, summer specials, Great Eastern Victorian Specials, photographic specials and Santa Specials. Thomas the Tank Engine (June 15-29, prebooking required).
Open all year, daily 10-dusk. Steam days, rides from 12-4. (Closed 23 Dec-1 Feb). Steam days every Sun and BH from Mothering Sunday to end Oct, Tue-Thu of

school summer holidays & special events.
Steam days £5 (ch £2.50 pen £4); Family ticket £12.50. Non-steam days (to view static exhibits only) £2 (ch £1); Family ticket £5.
🅿 ☕ ✕ *licensed* ♿ *(ramps for wheelchairs to get onto carriages) shop* 🚫

Hedingham Castle
CO9 3DJ (on B1058, 1m off A604)
☎*01787 460261 Fax 01787 461473*
This majestic Norman castle was built in 1140. It was besieged by King John, and visited by King Henry VII, King Henry VIII and Queen Elizabeth I and was the home of the de Veres, Earls of Oxford, for over 500 years. The Keep is one of the finest and best preserved in England and stands 100ft high. Children love to explore the castle with its splendid banqueting hall and minstrels' gallery. Visitors can enjoy the peaceful woodland

walks and perhaps have a picnic by the beautiful lake. Special events include: Medieval Entertainment (Easter Weekend & 25-26 May), Recreation of the visit of Henry VII in 1498 (25-26 July), Jousting Tournament (30-31 August). Please telephone for full details of this and other special events.
Open wk before Etr-Oct, daily 10-5. £3 (ch £2). Family ticket £9 (except for special events)
🅿 ☕ *shop*
Cards: 💳 💳 💳

COGGESHALL
Paycocke's
West St CO6 1NS
☎*01376 561305*
This timber-framed house is a fine example of a medieval merchant's home. It was completed in about 1505 and has interesting carvings on the outside timbers, including the Paycocke trade sign. Inside there are further elaborate ➤

Hedingham Castle has one of the best preserved and finest keeps in England.

carvings and linenfold panelling. Behind the house is a pretty garden.
Open 29 Mar-11 Oct Tue, Thu, Sun & BH Mon 2-5.30. (Closed Good Fri). Last admission 5pm.
£2 (ch £1).
P *(400yds)* & ✿ ⇔ ❧

COLCHESTER
Beth Chatto Gardens
Elmstead Market CO7 7DB
(7m E on A133)
☎01206 822007
Fax 01206 825933
The gardens were begun 36 years ago, when Beth Chatto and her husband began working on four acres of wasteland. Today the wasteland has become a garden of three areas, each with their own distinctive character and plants. First is the south-west facing dry garden, which is on gravel and has plants which can cope with drought, such as yucca and pineapple broom. It faces a group of oaks which shade the second area, with woodland and other shade-loving plants, including some chosen for their fine foliage. Lastly, there is the wetland garden, with five large pools filled with fish and surrounded by swathes of exotic and native bog plants. The former grass car park has been transformed into a new gravel garden for plants adapted to drought. A new larger car park is nearby. The nursery has over 2000 different plants.
Open all year, Mar-Oct, Mon-Sat 9-5; Nov-Feb, Mon-Fri 9-4. (Closed BHs).
P *garden centre* ❧
Details not confirmed for 1998
Cards: 🗠 ▰▱ 🗠

Colchester Castle Museum
Castle Park, High St CO1 1TJ
☎01206 282931 & 282932
Fax 01206 282925
This is the largest Norman Castle Keep in Europe. It was built over the remains of the magnificent Roman Temple of Claudius which was destroyed by Boudica in AD60.
Colchester was the first capital of Roman Britain, and the archaeological collections are among the finest in the country.

Displays include exciting 'hands-on' learning for all the family, an exhibition on medieval Colchester, and a new display on the Seige of Colchester 1648. Please telephone for details of the exciting range of associated holiday events.
Open all year, Mon-Sat 10-5, Sun (Mar-Nov) 2-5. Last admission 4.30pm. (Closed 24-26 Dec).
£3.50 (ch & concessions £2.20). Family ticket £9.
P *(town centre)* & *(ramps to all areas & lift) toilets for disabled shop* ❧
Cards: 🗠 ▰▱ 🗠
See advertisement on page 55.

Colchester Zoo
Stanway, Maldon Rd CO3 5SL (3m W of town B1022)
☎01206 330253
Fax 01206 331392
One of England's finest zoos, Colchester zoo has over one hundred and seventy five types of animals. Visitors can meet the elephants, handle a snake, and see parrots, seals, penguins and birds of prey all appearing in fun, informative daily displays. New enclosures include Penguin Shores, the Wilds of Asia for orangutans, and Chimp World. There is also an undercover soft play complex, road train, two adventure play areas, several eating places and gift shops, all set in forty acres of beautiful gardens. Telephone for details of special events.
Open all year, daily from 9.30. Last admission 5.30pm (1hr before dusk out of season). (Closed 25 Dec).
✱*£7 (ch 3-13 £5, pen £5, disabled £3.50). Family Super Saver ticket available. Prices under review.*
P ♨ ✕ *licensed* & *toilets for disabled shop* ❧
Cards: 🗠 ▰ 🗠

HADLEIGH
Hadleigh Castle
(three quarters of a mile S of A13)
☎01536 402840
A familiar sight from Constable's paintings, the castle was first built by Hubert de Burgh and has fine views of the Thames estuary. It is defended by

ditches on three sides, and the north-east and south-east towers are still impressive. The latter has a fireplace and three garderobe (latrine) shafts.
Open any reasonable time.
Free.
⌗

HARLOW
Harlow Museum
Passmores House, Third Av CM18 6YL
☎01279 454959
Harlow is best known as a new town, but the museum tells its story from Prehistoric and Roman to modern times, with a section on the Harlow Potters and the New Town. It is housed in an early Georgian building set in gardens. Part of the medieval moat from an earlier house can be seen.
Open all year, Thur-Sat 10-12.30 & 1.30-5. Last admission 4.15pm.
Free.
P & *shop* ❧

Mark Hall Cycle Museum & Gardens
Muskham Rd off First Av CM20 2LF (off A414, signposted)
☎01279 439680 Fax 01279 442786
The history of the bicycle is illustrated with over 80 examples, from an 1818 hobby horse to a plastic machine of 1982, and a wide range of accessories and memorabilia. There are also three walled gardens, a 17th-century herb garden and a cottage garden.
Open Tue/Wed 10am-4.30pm. Sun (1st & 3rd of each month) 11am-4pm.
£1.75 (ch & pen £1). Family ticket £4.50.
P & *toilets for disabled shop* ❧

HARWICH
Harwich Redoubt Fort
CO12 3TE (behind 29 Main rd)
☎01255 503429
The 180ft-diameter circular fort was built in 1808 in case of invasion by Napoleon. It has a dry moat and 8ft-thick walls, with 18 rooms for stores, ammunition and quarters for 300 men. The Redoubt is being restored by the Harwich Society, and contains three small museums. Ten guns can be seen on the battlements. Annual fete (25 May). Napoleonic Battle Re-Enactment (30 August).
Open May-Aug, daily 10-5; Sep-Apr, Sun only 10-5.
✱*£1 (accompanied ch free).*
P *(200yds) shop*

HEDINGHAM
See Castle Hedingham

LAYER MARNEY
Layer Marney Tower
CO5 9US (off B1022 Colchester to Maldon road, signposted)
☎01206 330784
Fax 01206 330784
Layer Marney Tower is the the tallest Tudor gatehouse in the country. Set within a range of buildings over 300 feet long, the gatehouse was intended to be the entrance to a courtyard which would have rivalled Hampton Court Palace. With the death of Henry, 1st Lord Marney in 1523, and of his son in 1525, the building work ceased before completion. What was built is remarkable, and is certainly one of the great buildings of the 16th century. The Tudor stableblock was converted onto the Long Gallery in 1910, and a large mid 15th century barn houses some of the rare breed farm animals. The parish church of St Mary the Virgin is set within the grounds, and contains some of the finest Italianate terracotta in the country, extensively used on the tombs of both Henry and John Marney. Terracotta is also used on the Tower itself and adjoining wings. The Tower may be climbed, and there are stunning views (weather permitting!) of the surrounding Essex countryside. Visitors may wander in the formal gardens and rare breeds farm, explore the barn, church and farm shop, and see the beautiful dolls' house in the Corsellis Room. Special events are planned,

including craft fairs, plays, and the church fete. Please telephone for details.
Open Apr-Sep, Mon-Fri 12-5, Sun 12-5 & BHs 11-5.
£3.25 (ch £1.75). Family ticket £9. Guided tour £4.50. Party 20+.
P ♨ & *(ramps in garden and farm) toilets for disabled shop* ❧ *(ex guide dogs)*

MISTLEY
Mistley Towers
CO11 1NJ (on B1352, 1.5m E of A137 at Lawford)
All that remains of the grand hall and church, commissioned by Richard Rigby and designed by Robert Adam, are the lodges built in 1782 for the hall, and two square, classic towers topped with drums and domes which Adam had added to an earlier church.
Open all reasonable times. Key available from Mistley Quay Workshops & Teashop.
Free.
& *(exterior only)* ❧ *(in certain areas)* ⌗

NEWPORT
Mole Hall Wildlife Park
Widdington CB11 3SS
☎01799 540400
The Park covers 20 acres and has been lovingly developed by the Johnstone family for over 40 years. The wide variety of animals range from South American Lama Guanaco to the mystical Kenyan Eagle Owls, the Leopard-like Serval Cat and the Formosan Sika Deer, which is extinct in the wild. Mole Hall is also home to 3 species of otter, being the first regular breeders in the UK of the North American Otter. Other residents include Chimpanzees, Muntjac, Vietnamese Pot-Bellied Pigs, and a complete range of more domestic animals such as ponies, rabbits, goats and sheep. An exciting addition to Mole Hall is the Tropical Butterfly Pavilion. An insect specialist will be on hand to answer your questions.
Open all year, daily 10.30-6 (or dusk). (Closed 25 Dec). Butterfly House open mid Mar-Oct.
P ♨ & *(Difficult in wet weather for wheelchairs) toilets for disabled shop garden centre* ❧
Details not confirmed for 1998

SAFFRON WALDEN
Saffron Walden Museum
Museum St CB10 1JL (take B184 & follow signs to Saffron Walden)
☎01799 510333
Fax 01799 510550
Built in 1834, this friendly museum lies near the castle ruins in the centre of town. Its collections include local archaeology, natural history, ceramics, glass, costume, furniture, toys, an ancient Egyptian room, a new natural history gallery and Discovery Centre.
Open all year, Mar-Oct, Mon-Sat 10-5, Sun & BHs 2.30-5; Nov-Feb, Mon-Sat, 10-4, Sun & BHs 2.30-4.30. (Closed 24 & 25 Dec).
£1 (concessions 50p & ch under 18 free).
P & *(ramp to entrance, spare wheelchairs, stairlift) toilets for disabled shop* ❧

SOUTHEND-ON-SEA
Central Museum & Planetarium
Victoria Av SS2 6EW (take A127 or A13 towards town centre museum is adjacent to Southend Victoria Railway Station)
☎01702 215640 & 215131
Fax 01702 215631
A fine Edwardian building housing displays of archaeology, natural history and local history, telling the story of man in the south-east Essex area. Also the only planetarium in the South East outside London. 1998 events include: History of Southend Exhibition (May-October), Star Tracking - Astronomy, time keeping and navigation through history (March-April), Photography (Nov-Dec). Ring for details.

In the Middle Ages, the buildings of the prosperous town of Saffron Walden were often decorated with elaborate plasterwork known as pargetting.

Open - Central Museum Mon-Sat 10-5 (Closed Sun & BH); Planetarium Wed-Sat, shows at 10, 11, noon, 2, 3 & 4. Central Museum free. Planetarium £2.15 (ch & pen £1.60). Family tickets £5.90. Party rates on request.
P (0.50m) (disabled only behind museum) & (planetarium not accessible) shop ⊗

STANSTED
House on the Hill Toy Museum
CM24 8SP (off B1383)
☎01279 813237
Fax 01279 816391
One of the largest toy museums in Europe, housed on two floors covering 7,000 sq. ft. A huge variety of toys, books and games from the late Victorian period up to the 1970s. There is a train room, space display, Teddy Bears' picnic, Action Men, Sindy, Barbie, military displays and much more. A puppet theatre provides lots of animation. Plus a Collector's Shop that buys and sells old toys.
Open daily, 10-5; (closed mid Dec to mid Jan.)
✤£3 (ch £2.20, pen & student £2.60). Party 15+.
P shop ⊗
Cards: ▨ ▥ ▩ ▧ ▨ ▨

Mountfitchet Castle & Norman Village
Mountfitchet CM24 8SP (off B1383, in centre of village)
☎01279 813237
Fax 01279 816391
Norman motte and bailey castle and village reconstructed as it was in Norman England of 1066, on its historic site. A vivid illustration of village life in Domesday England, complete with houses, church, seige tower, seige weapons, and many types of animals roaming freely. Animated wax figures in all the buildings give historical information to visitors. There are many special events planned throughout the year. Telephone for details and dates.
Open daily, 16 Mar-9 Nov, 10-5.
P ▦ & (laser commentaries) toilets for disabled shop ⊗
Cards: ▨ ▥ ▩ ▧ ▨ ▨

TILBURY
Tilbury Fort
RM18 7NR (half a mile E off A126)
☎01375 858489
The largest example of 17th century military engineering in England, the fort dates from the reign of Henry VIII, but is most famous for Queen Elizabeth I's review of the fleet and army gathered to fight the Spanish Armada. In about 1670

the fort was extensively altered for defence against the Dutch and the French - ironically, it was designed by a Dutchman in the French style. Visitors today can visit the militaria museum and enjoy extensive views of the River Thames. Children can explore the underground tunnels and may even fire an authentic 1943 anti-aircraft gun.
Open all year, Apr-Oct, daily 10-6 (or dusk if earlier); Nov-Mar, Wed-Sun 10-4. Closed 24-26 Dec & 1 Jan.
£2.30 (ch £1.20, pen, students & UB40 £1.70). Personal stereo tours included in admission price.
& shop ⊗ (in certain areas) ✿

WALTHAM ABBEY
Lee Valley Park Farms
Stubbings Hall Ln, Crooked Mile EN9 2EG (off B194)
☎01992 892781 & 892291
Fax 01992 893113
Lee Valley Park Farms offer the visitor two contrasting farms on one site. Hayes Hill Farm has a traditional style farmyard where visitors can see a range of farm animals, use the play area, picnic, and see machinery from earlier times. The centrepiece of the farm is a restored 16th-century barn. Your visit also includes a look around Holyfield Hall Farm, a working commercial dairy and arable farm of some 600 acres. There are 140 Friesian cows, and milking takes place at 2.45pm every day. Booked guided tours are available. Open Day - Whitsun Bank Holiday. Children's Theatre - Sundays in the summer holiday. Tractor and trailer rides - every weekend and during school holidays from April to October. 1998 also sees a Farm & Country Show (17 May), and Children's Entertainment every Sunday, June to September.
Open all year, Mon-Fri 10-4.30, wknds & BH 10-5.30pm.
✤£2.60 (ch & pen £1.70). Party 10+.
P ▦ & (graded concrete paths, signed routes) toilets for disabled shop

Waltham Abbey Gatehouse, Bridge & Entrance to Cloisters
Beside the great Norman church at Waltham are the ruins of the abbey buildings. Little remains but a 14th-century bridge and gatehouse, with both pedestrian and vehicle entrances, and part of the 12th-century north cloister. The bridge is named after King Harold, founder of the abbey. The church has an undercroft museum.
Open any reasonable time. Free.
✿

GLOUCESTERSHIRE

BARNSLEY
Barnsley House Garden
GL7 5EE (3m NE of Cirencester on B4425 Barnsley House is on right on entering village from Cirencester)
☎01285 740281 Fax 01285 740281
This lovely garden is the creation of Rosemary Verey, who since 1960 has transformed the older garden that was here. There are herbs and a knot garden, and best of all a vegetable garden planted as a French 'potager orné', with small paths forming a chequerboard around fruit trees trained as pyramids, ornamental brassicas and other decorative kitchen plants. They are planted for effect in groups rather than allotment-style rows, but not simply for show, being constantly cut, picked and used by the family. The garden is also interesting for its use of ground cover in the borders. Other features include a laburnum walk (good in early June) and a lime walk. Two 18th-century summerhouses, one Gothic, the other classical, complete the picture. The garden is open in aid of the National Garden Scheme 2 May and 6 June, and for the village festival which will be held May 9.
Open all year Mon, Wed, Thu & Sat 10-6; Parties & guided tours by appointment only. House not open.
£3 (ch free, pen £2).
P & shop garden centre ⊗

BERKELEY
Berkeley Castle
GL13 9BQ (on B4509 1.5m W of A38)
☎01453 810332
Home of the Berkeleys for almost 850 years, the castle is all one might expect - a great rambling place surrounded by 14ft thick walls, with a Norman keep, a great hall, medieval kitchens and some splendid apartments. It is most famous for the dungeon where Edward II was gruesomely murdered in 1327, at the instigation of his wife and the Earl of Mortimer. Outside there are Elizabethan terraced gardens and an extensive park. There is also a particularly good butterfly farm, with hundreds of exotic butterflies in free flight.
Open: Tue-Sun, 1-5 Apr-May. Tue-Sat 11-5, Sun 1-5, June & Sept. Mon-Sat 11-5, Sun 1-5 July & Aug. Sun only 1-5 Oct. BH Mon 11-5.
Castle & Gardens: £4.95 (ch £2.60, pen £3.95). Castle only: £1.75 (ch, pen 85p). Gardens only: £1.75 (ch 90p). Party 25+.
P ▦ shop ⊗
Cards: ▨ ▥

Jenner Museum
Church Ln, High St GL13 9BH (follow tourist signs from A38 to town centre, turn left into High St & left again into Church Ln)
☎01453 810631 Fax 01453 811690
This beautiful Georgian house was the home of Edward Jenner, the discoverer of vaccination against smallpox. The house and the garden, with its Temple of Vaccinia, are much as they were in Jenner's day. The displays record Jenner's life as an 18th-century country doctor, his work on vaccination and his interest in natural history. He is buried in the nearby church, which also has some fine monuments to the Berkeley family. To commemorate the bicentenary (1996) of Jenner's first vaccination experiment a permanent new exhibition on immunology (the medical science which he founded) was opened on the First Floor. This uses text, CD-ROMs and computer games to entertain and educate about this important branch of medicine.
Open Apr-Sep, Tue-Sat 12.30-5.30, Sun 1-5.30. Oct, Sun 1-5.30. (Closed Mon, ex BH Mon 12.30-5.30).
£2 (ch & students 75p, pen £1.50). Family ticket £5. Party20+
P & toilets for disabled shop ⊗

BOURTON-ON-THE-WATER
Birdland
Rissington Rd GL54 2BN (on A429)
☎01451 820480 Fax 01451 822398
Set in seven acres of natural woodland, landscaped gardens, lakes and waterways, Birdland is home to hundreds of birds from around the world. Attractions/Facilities include: Large colony of penguins; coffee shop; disabled access throughout; picnic areas; children's play area; gift shop. Dogs are admitted on leads.
Open all year, Apr-Oct, daily 10-6; Nov-Mar, daily 10-4. Last admission 1hr before closing. (Closed 25 Dec).
✤£3.75 (ch4-14 £2, pen £2.75). Party 10+.
P (adjacent) ▦ & toilets for disabled shop

Cotswolds Motor Museum & Toy Collection
GL54 2BY
☎01451 821255
Housed in a water mill on the River Windrush, the museum has cars and motorcycles from the vintage years up to the 1950s, with a collection of 800 advertising signs and some 8000 pieces of automobilia. Also here is the Childhood Toy Collection. Brum, the character from the children's BBC programme, lives at the museum.
Open Feb-Nov, daily 10-6.
£1.75 (ch 14 80p, ch 2 free). Family ticket £4.80. Party. Joint ticket available with Village Life Exhibition.
P (200 yds) parking for disabled available & shop

Folly Farm Waterfowl
GL54 3BY (2.5 W on A436)
☎01451 820285
Two miles from Bourton, this conservation centre in the Cotswolds has a series of pools and lakes with over 160 types of waterfowl, ducks, geese and poultry, including many rare and endangered species. Undercover pets' area where handreared animals and birds may be stroked. Also there are lavender fields in bloom in July and August, and the Cotswold Lavender shop is open all year.
Open all year, Apr-Sep daily 10-6; Oct-Mar 10-4.
P ▦ & (special car parking) toilets for disabled shop garden centre
Details not confirmed for 1998
Cards: ▨ ▥

Model Village
Old New Inn GL54 2AF
☎01451 820467 Fax 01451 810236
The model is built of Cotswold stone to a scale of one-ninth, and is a perfect replica

➤

of the village. It includes a miniature River Windrush, a working model waterwheel, churches and shops, with tiny trees, shrubs and alpine plants.
Open all year 9-6.30 (summer), 10-dusk (winter). (Closed 25 Dec).
£2 (ch £1.50, pen & students £1.80).
🅿 💷 ✕ *licensed shop*

Village Life Exhibition
The Old Mill GL54 2BY
☎ *01451 821255*
A complete Edwardian village shop is displayed with bathroom, kitchen and bedroom above. There is also a blacksmith's forge, a model of the old mill, photographs, toys and period advertising signs.
Open Feb-Nov, daily 10-6.
£1.75 (ch 80p, under 2 free). Joint ticket available with Costwolds Motor Museum. Family ticket £4.80.
P (200 yds) *(parking for disabled) shop*

CHEDWORTH
Chedworth Roman Villa
Yanworth GL54 3LJ (3m NW of Fossebridge on A429)
☎ *01242 890256 Fax 01242 890544*
The remains of a Romano-British villa, excavated 1864-66. Set in beautiful wooded combe, there are fine 4th century mosaics, two bath houses, and a temple with spring. The museum houses the smaller finds and there is a 9-minute video programme. Events include Archaeology Activity weekend (25-26 May), outdoor jazz concert (2 Aug), National Archaeology days (mid September). Please telephone for further details.
Open Mar-2 Nov, Tue-Sun & BH Mon 10-5; 4-30 Nov, Tue-Sun 10-4 also 6 & 7 Dec.
🅿 ♿ *(wheelchair available) toilets for disabled shop* ♿ ⛔
Details not confirmed for 1998

CHELTENHAM
Art Gallery & Museum
Clarence St GL50 3JT (close to town centre and bus station)
☎ *01242 237431 Fax 01242 262334*
The museum has an outstanding collection relating to the Arts and Crafts Movement, made famous by William Morris, including fine furniture and exquisite metalwork. The Art Gallery

contains Dutch and British paintings from the 17th-century to the present day. Of particular note is the Oriental Gallery which features pottery, costumes and treasures from the Ming Dynasty to the reign of the last Chinese Emperor.
An interesting addition to the section devoted to social history and archaeology is a true-to-life depiction of the exploits of Edward Wilson, one of Cheltenham's famous sons, who journeyed with Captain Scott on the ill-fated Antarctic Expedition of 1911-12. There is a continuous programme of special exhbitions throughout the year. Special exhibitions for 1998 include: Victorian Visions: Image and Reality in Victorian Britain (2 May-27 June), Earth & Fire: Winchcombe Pottery 1926-1998 (10 Oct-5 Dec). Ring for details of these and other events.
Open all year, Mon-Sat 10-5.20. (Closed BHs).
Free.
P 💷 ♿ *(handling tables for blind people with Braille labels) toilets for disabled shop* ♿
Cards: 🅰 💳

Holst Birthplace Museum
4 Clarence Rd, Pittville GL52 3JE (just off Evesham Rd)
☎ *01242 524846 & 237431 Fax 01242 262334*
The home and birthplace of Gustav Holst composer of *The Planets* who was born at this Regency house in 1874. The museum contains unique displays on the life of the distinguished musician, including his original piano. The rooms of the house have been carefully restored in the tradition of 'upstairs, downstairs' from the nursery at the top of the house to the working Victorian kitchen in the basement, each area evoking a slightly different period in the history of the house from Regency to Edwardian times.
Open all year, Tue-Sat 10-4.20 (Closed Mon & BHs)
£1.50 (concessions 50p)
P (100 yds) *shop* ♿

Pittville Pump Room & Museum
Pittville Park GL52 3JE (at N end of town, close to Cheltenham racecourse)
☎ *01242 523852 Fax 01242 262334*
The Pump Room is generally considered Cheltenham's finest building. It was built

in Greek Revival style in the 19th century, and has a colonnaded façade and a pillared and balconied hall. The first pump room was more humble, just a thatched shelter over a spring where pigeons had been noticed pecking at salt crystals.
The Pittville Pump Room was bought by the Borough in 1890 and has since been restored and the spa fountain was repositioned in 1960. Various functions are held and there is a museum showing the story of the town from the 18th century. Imaginative use of original costumes brings to life the history of Cheltenham from its Regency heyday to the Swinging Sixties. Special exhibitions are held throughout the year.
Open all year, May-Sep, daily 10-4.30; Oct-Apr, daily 10-4 (closed Tue) .
£1.50 (concessions 50p). Pump room free. Party.
🅿 *shop* ♿

CIRENCESTER
Corinium Museum
Park St GL7 2BX
☎ *01285 655611 Fax 01285 643286*
Cirencester was the second largest town in Roman Britain and the Corinium Museum displays use full-scale reconstructions to bring alive the way of life during this period in history. Special exhibitions are held throughout the year. There is a Cotswold Prehistory gallery, and a Medieval Cotswolds gallery. Recent additions are galleries on Roman military history, the Roman town of Corinium, and the Civil War in the Cotswolds. 'Building for the Disabled' award winner. Forthcoming exhibitions include: Gloucestershire Society of Botanical Illustrators (May-June), Brunel Brodeners Embroidery (June-July), Glevum Scribes Calligraphy (July-August), Tapestry Exhibition (Autumn)> Ring for further details.
Open all year, Apr-Oct, Mon-Sat 10-5, Sun 2-5; Nov-Mar, Tue-Sat 10-5, Sun 2-5. Also Jan-Feb. (Closed Xmas).
❋*£1.75 (ch 80p, students £1, pen £1.50). Family ticket £4.30. Party.*
P (440yds town centre) ♿ *(Braille guide for exhibits) toilets for disabled shop*

CLEARWELL
Clearwell Caves Ancient Iron Mines
GL16 8JR (1.5m S of Coleford town centre, off B4228)
☎ *01594 832535 Fax 01594 833362*
The mines were worked in Iron Age times, 2,500 years ago, and the industry grew under the Romans. Over half a million tons of ore were extracted in the 19th century, and mining continues today. Nine large caverns can now be explored, with deeper trips for the more adventurous. There are engine houses, blacksmith's shop and exhibits of local mining and geology from the Forest of Dean. Educational visits are a speciality and can be suited to particular projects or subjects. Christmas Fantasy will take place from 1st to 24th of December. Special 30th Anniversary Events include: Vintage machinery demonstrations, ochre painting courses, and Iron Age smelting demonstrations. Contact Caves for details.
Open Mar-Oct daily 10-5. Other times by arrangement. Christmas Fantasy 1-24 Dec, 10am-5pm daily.
£3 (ch £2, concessions £2.50)
🅿 💷 ♿ *("Hands-on" exhibits, contact in advance) toilets for disabled shop* ♿ *(ex guide dogs)*
Cards: 🅰 💳 💳 🅢

CRANHAM
Prinknash Abbey and Pottery
GL4 8EX (on A46)
☎ *01452 812066 Fax 01452 812529*
The abbey has become famous for its pottery in the 20th century, but its origins lie in the Middle Ages. Set in a large park, the old abbey building is a 12th-to 16th-century house which was used by Benedictine monks and guests of Gloucester Abbey until 1539. It became a priory and later an abbey for Benedictine monks from Caldey in 1928. Rich beds of

clay were discovered when foundations were being dug for a new building, and so the pottery was established. It has a distinctive style, and is sold in many parts of the world. The Pottery employs local craftspeople. The Monks are involved in other activities, including organ building, stained glass windows, printing and incense making.
Open all year. Abbey Church: daily 5am-8pm. Pottery: Mon-Sat 11-4.30 (Sun pm). Pottery shop & tearoom 9-5.30. (Closed Good Fri, 25 & 26 Dec).
Guided tour fee £1 (ch 50p).
🅿 💷 ♿ *toilets for disabled shop*
Cards: 🅰 💳 💳 💳 🅢

Prinknash Bird Park
Prinknash Abbey GL4 8EX
☎ *01452 812727*
Nine acres of parkland and lakes make a beautiful home for black swans, geese and other water birds. There are also exotic birds such as white and Indian blue peacocks and crown cranes, and the park supports fallow deer and pygmy goats, many of which are tame and can be hand fed. The Golden Wood is stocked with ornamental pheasants, and leads to the restored (and reputedly haunted) monks' fishpond, which contains trout. An 80-year old, free-standing, 16ft tall Wendy House in the style of a Tudor house has recently been erected near the picnic area.
Open all year, daily 10-5 (4pm in winter). Park closes at 6pm (5pm in winter). (Closed 25-26 Dec, 1 Jan & Good Fri).
❋*£3 (ch £1.60, pen £2). Party 10+. Prices under review.*
🅿 💷 *shop* ♿

DEERHURST
Odda's Chapel
(off B4213 near River Severn at Abbots Court SW of parish church)
The rare Saxon chapel was built by Earl Odda and dedicated in 1056. It was discovered as part of a farmhouse and has been restored.
Open any reasonable time.
Free.
⛭

DYRHAM
Dyrham Park
SN14 8ER (8m N of Bath)
☎ *0117 937 2501*
Dyrham Park is a splendid William and Mary house, with interiors which have hardly altered since the late 17th century. It has contemporary Dutch-style furnishings, Dutch pictures and blue-and-white Delft ware. Around the house is an ancient park with fallow deer. Jazz Festival 3-4 July 1998.
Open - House 3 Apr-1 Nov, daily ex Wed & Thu 12-5.30. (Last admission 5pm or dusk). Garden 3 Apr-1 Nov, daily ex Wed & Thu 11-5.30. Park open all year, daily 12-5.30 (open 11am on days that garden opens). Last admission 5pm or dusk. (Closed 25 Dec & 3-4 Jul for jazz concerts).
£5.40 (ch £2.70). Park & Garden only £2.80 (ch £1.40). Family £13.30.
🅿 💷 ✕ *licensed ♿ toilets for disabled shop* ♿ *(ex in dog walk area).* ⛔

GLOUCESTER
City Museum & Art Gallery
Brunswick Rd GL1 1HP
☎ *01452 524131 Fax 01452 410898*
Visit the City Museum, housed in an Elizabethan style building in the centre of historic Gloucester. Here you can see a range of exhibits showing the early life of the City, with dinosaur bones, unusual Roman remains and the amazing Birdlip mirror. You can also learn more about antique furniture and the decorative arts, with displays of Queen Anne furniture, ceramics, and paintings by well-known artists, like Turner and Gainsborough. The Museum also offers a programme of events and activities throughout the year. Phone for details.
Open all year, Mon-Sat 10-5. (Also Jul-Sep, Sun 10-4).
Free.

Cotswold Farm Park is devoted to rare breeds conservation and is home to nearly 50 flocks and herds of ancient British breeds of farm animals.

P *(adjacent)* & *(lift suitable only for manual wheelchairs) toilets for disabled shop*

Folk Museum
99-103 Westgate St GL1 2PG
☎01452 526467 Fax 01452 330495
A group of Tudor and Jacobean half-timbered houses illustrate the local history, domestic life and rural crafts of the city and county. Displays include Civil War armour, Victorian toys and games, farming, Severn fishing, kitchen equipment, model steam engines, shoemaker's workshop, and a school room c1900. There is a pin factory on the top floor with an 18th-century forge in situ. The new extensions house a reconstructed Double Gloucester Dairy, wheelwright and carpenter's workshops and ironmonger's corner shop. A new gallery of toys, games and childhood opened in 1997. A new gallery on cider-making in Gloucestershire is due to open in 1998. Special events include: Cotton motorcycle rally at rear of Folk Museum. Regular special exhibitions are held throughout the year - telephone for details.
Open all year, Mon-Sat 10-5. (Also Jul-Sep, Sun 10-4). Open BH Mon. Free.
P *(200yds)* & *(parking on request, ramps) shop*

National Waterways Museum
Llanthony Warehouse, The Docks GL1 2EH
☎01452 318054 Fax 01452 318066
For centuries goods were transferred at Gloucester Docks between inland craft bound for Wales and the Midlands, and larger vessels which could negotiate the Severn Estuary. The heyday of the docks came after the opening of the Gloucester and Berkeley Canal in 1827, and many of the warehouses built in the 19th century still stand. The museum is housed in the Victorian Llanthony warehouse, a seven-storey brick building with cast-iron columns, which now shows the role of inland waterways in Britain's fortunes. A traditional canal maintenance yard has been re-created alongside, with floating exhibits to investigate, including a steam dredger,and demonstrations are given of the crafts and skills needed to run the canals. During school holidays additional staffed activities take place between 11-4, for the whole family. Special events for 1998 include: Signwriting weekend (25-26 April), stationary engine rally (10 May), horses weekend (May 16-17), Modellers weekend (26-27 September).
Open all year, daily 10-6; (winter 10-5). (Closed 25 Dec).
£4.50 (ch & pen £3.50). Family tickets £10-£12.
P *(charged)* 🍴 & *(touch exhibits, wheelchair, lifts) toilets for disabled shop*
Cards: 🌐

Nature in Art
Wallsworth Hall, Tewkesbury Rd, Twigworth GL2 9PA (on A38, from village follow tourist signs)
☎01452 731422 Fax 01452 730937
An ever changing and ever growing collection portraying wildlife in any art medium, from any period and from all over the world, makes this the first museum of its kind. Dedicated to wildlife art of the highest international standards, there are many outstanding exhibits including sculpture (both indoor and outdoor), tapestries and ceramics. There is a comprehensive 'artist in residence' programme for ten months of the year. Events include regular monthly talks, film showings and a full programme of temporary exhibitions and art courses. A current collection includes the work by over 400 artists from nearly 50 countries, spanning 1500 years. More information about the events being held can be obtained by telephoning or sending for a programme. A purpose-built education/activity centre is used by schools and special interest groups and as a base for the museum's art courses. With work by artists as diverse as Picasso and David Shepherd, as well as ethnic art. Nature in Art has twice been commended in the National Heritage 'Museum of the Year' awards.
Open all year, Tue-Sun & BH's 10-5. Mon by arrangement. (Closed 24-26 Dec).
£3.10 (ch, pen & students £2.40, ch under 8 free). Family ticket £9.50. Party 10+
P & *(lift & ramps at entrance) toilets for disabled shop* *(ex guide dogs)*
Cards: 🌐

Robert Opie Collection-Museum of Advertising & Packaging
Albert Warehouse, Gloucester Docks GL1 2EH
☎01452 302309 Fax 01452 308507
While older members of the family can experience a nostalgic journey back through the memories of childhood, the younger ones can learn what life was like in Britain over the past 130 years, in this country's only Museum of Advertising & Packaging. Robert Opie has been collecting old and new advertisements, packs, comics, newspapers, games, toys and other artefacts of our everyday life for the past 35 years, and is still adding to this remarkable collection almost on a daily basis. All the items are placed in strict historical sequence so that visitors can see how dramatic the changes to our daily lives have been over the years.
Open all year, daily, 10-6; winter Tue-Fri 10-5, Sat & Sun 10-6. (Closed 25-26 Dec).
£3.50 (ch £1.25, pen & students £1.95). Family tickets £6.95. Party 10+.
P *(charged)* 🍴 & *shop* *(ex guide dogs)*

GREAT WITCOMBE
Witcombe Roman Villa
(off A417, half a mile S of reservoir in Witcombe Park)
The remains of a large Roman Villa, built around three sides of a courtyard. Several mosaic pavements have been preserved and there is also evidence of underfloor heating from a hypocaust.
Open any reasonable time. Guided tours may be available contact 0117 9750700 Free.
P ⚙

GUITING POWER
Cotswold Farm Park
GL54 5UG (signposted off B4077 from junc9 M5)
☎01451 850307 Fax 01451 850423
At the Cotswold Farm Park, the home of rare breeds conservation, there are nearly 50 breeding flocks and herds of the rarest and most fascinating British breeds of sheep, cattle, pigs, goats, horses, poultry and waterfowl. Set on the very top of the Cotswold Hills with magnificent views in all directions, this is the perfect opportunity to get to know a Bagot goat, cuddle a Cotswold lamb, stroke a mighty Longhorn ox, and admire generations of our living agricultural heritage. New born lambs and goat kids can be seen from 28 March to 4 May, spring calves in May, foals and sheep shearing in June and piglets throughout the year. New attractions include touch barn, woodland walk, farm nature trail, pets corner and adventure playground. Daily milking demonstrations July-Septmeber. See local press for details of special events including goat, pig and donkey shows and a vintage rally.
Open 28 Mar-4 Oct, daily 10.30-5. (10.30-6, Sun, BH & daily in Aug).
£3.50 (ch £1.80, pen £2.50). Party.
P 🍴 & *(ramps, wheelchair to let) toilets for disabled shop* *(only guide dogs inside)*
Cards: 🌐

HAILES
Hailes Abbey
(2m NE of Winchcombe off B4632)
☎01242 602398
In the Middle Ages the Cistercian abbey was one of the main centres of pilgrimages in Britain due to a phial possessed by the monks said to contain the blood of Christ. The museum displays include some fine high quality medieval sculpture and floor tiles.
Open Apr-Oct, daily 10-6 (or dusk if earlier in Oct); wknds in winter months 10-4, (closed 1-2). Closed 24-26 Dec & 1 Jan.
£2 (ch £1, concessions £1). Personal stereo tours included in admission, also available for the partially sighted and those with learning difficulties.
P & *shop*

LITTLEDEAN
Littledean Hall
GL14 3NR
☎01594 824213
Fax 01594 827337
The largest known Roman temple in rural Britain was unearthed here in 1984 and the manor itself was built in Norman times; its north front is on the site of a Saxon hall of the 11th century. The house has always been lived in, and remains relatively untouched since the 19th century. Inside there are interpretive displays illustrating the history of the English manor house, the Civil War, and the ghosts and legends of Littledean Hall. The grounds offer beautiful walks, some of the oldest trees in Dean, fish pools in the walled garden and, of course, the Roman excavations. The house features an unusual supernatural history. A balloon and airship museum opens in 1998, and packaging, toy & home front exhibitions will take place in the house. Ring for details of concerts, historical re-enactments and ghost tours.
Open - House, Grounds & Archaeological site, Apr-Oct, daily 11-5.
£3 (ch £1.50, pen £2.50)
P & *shop* *(ex in grounds)*

LYDNEY
Dean Forest Railway
Norchard Centre, New Mills, Forest Rd GL15 4ET (1m N at New Mills on B4234 well signposted from A48)
☎01594 845840 & 843423
recorded inf
Just north of Lydney lies the headquarters of the Dean Forest Railway where a number of steam locomotives, plus lots of coaches, wagons and railway equipment are on show and guided tours are available by arrangement. There is also a gift shop, museum, riverside walk and forest trail.
Open all year, daily for static displays. Steam days: Sun from Etr-Sep, Wed Jun-Aug. Santa special Dec. Additional days & school holidays telephone for details.
P 🍴 & *(boarded walkways, specially adapted coach for wheelchairs) toilets for disabled shop*
Details not confirmed for 1998
Cards: 🌐

MICKLETON
Hidcote Manor Garden
Chipping Campden GL55 6LR (1m E of B4632)
☎01386 438333
Fax 01386 438817
One of the most delightful gardens in England, created this century by the great horticulturist Major Laurence Johnston and comprising a series of small gardens within the whole, separated by walls and hedges of different species. The gardens are famous for rare shrubs, trees, herbaceous borders, 'old' roses and interesting plant species. Contact the Manor for details of an autumn series of lectures & Christmas meals.
Open, Gardens only 1 Apr-Sep, daily (ex Tue & Fri) 11-7; also open Tue in Jun & July only 11-7; Oct-1 Nov, daily (ex Tue & Fri) 11-6. Last admission 1hr before closing.
£5.50. Family ticket £13.80. Parties by prior written arrangement.
P 🍴 ✕ *licensed* & *(limited due to stone paths) toilets for disabled shop garden centre*

Kiftsgate Court Garden
Mickleton GL55 6LW (0.5m S off A46, adjacent Hidcote NT garden)
☎01386 438777 Fax 01386 438777
Kiftsgate Garden is spectacularly set on the edge of the Cotswold Escarpment, with views over the Vale of Evesham. It contains many rare plants collected by three generations of women gardeners, including the largest rose in England, the R. Filipes Kiftsgate.
Open Apr-May & Aug-Sep; Wed, Thu, Sun & BH Mon 2-6. Jun-Jul Wed, Thu, Sat & Sun 12-6.
£3.50 (ch £1)
🅿 ♨ *garden centre* ✤

MORETON-IN-MARSH
Batsford Arboretum
GL56 9QF (1.5m NW, off A44 from Moreton-in-Marsh)
☎01608 650722 Fax 01608 650290
This arboretum of some 50 acres overlooking the Vale of Evenlode boasts one of the largest private collections of woody plants in Great Britain. Of particular note are the oaks, maples, magnolias and cherries, with many conifers and other rare and unusual trees, shrubs and bamboos. Spring is a procession of colour with masses of naturalised bulbs, particularly daffodils and narcissi, followed by magnolias and cherries. Autumn is equally as attractive with the fiery oranges and reds of the Japanese maples.
Open Mar-5 Nov daily 10-5.
£3 (ch 11-16, pen £2.50. under 10's go free). Party 12+.
🅿 ♨ ⚹ *(some steep & slippery paths) toilets for disabled shop garden centre*

Cotswold Falconry Centre
Batsford Park GL56 9QB (1m E on A44)
☎01386 701043 Fax 01386 701043
Conveniently located by the Batsford Park Arboretum, the Cotswold Falconry gives daily demonstrations in the art of falconry. The emphasis here is on breeding and conservation, and eagles, hawks, owls and falcons may be seen flying.
Open Mar-Nov, 10.30-5.30. (Last admission 5pm).
£3 (ch 4-14 £1.50).
🅿 ⚹ *(no steps, wide doorways) toilets for disabled shop garden centre* ✤ *(none)*

Sezincote
GL56 9AW (1.5m on A44 Evesham rd)
The Indian-style house at Sezincote was the inspiration for Brighton Pavilion; its charming water garden adds to its exotic aura and features trees of unusual size.
Open: House, May-Jul & Sep, Thu & Fri 2.30-5.30. Garden only, all year (ex Dec) Thu, Fri & BH Mon 2-6 or dusk if earlier. House & garden £4.50. Garden only £3 (ch £1 under 5 free). Children not allowed in the House. Groups by appointment only.
🅿 ✤

NEWENT
The National Birds of Prey Centre
GL18 1JJ (1m SW on unclass Clifford's Mesne Road follow brown tourist signs)
☎01531 820286 Fax 01531 821389
Jemima Parry-Jones is becoming increasingly famous for her displays of falconry at shows and fairs all over the country. This is the 'home-base' for her exceptional collection of birds of prey. Trained birds can be seen at close quarters in the Hawk Walk and the Owl Courtyard and there are also breeding aviaries, a gift shop, bookshop, picnic areas, coffee shop and children's play area. Weather permitting, birds are flown four times daily in Summer and three times in Winter, giving an exciting and educational display. Major improvements mean that there are over 90 aviaries on view with 72 species. The centre leads the world in the field of captive breeding, and the best time to see young birds is May-July.
Open Feb-Nov, daily 10.30-5.30 or dusk if earlier.
🅿 ♨ ⚹ *toilets for disabled shop* ✤ *(no exceptions)*
Details not confirmed for 1998
Cards: 🄰 ▭ 🄹

The Shambles
Church St GL18 1PP (close to town centre near church)
☎01531 822144 Fax 01531 821120
A museum of cobbled streets, alleyways, cottages and houses set in over the an acre with exhibit shops and trades, even a tin chapel and cottage garden all helping to recreate the feel and atmosphere of Victorian life.
Open 15 Mar-Xmas, Tue-Sun & BH's 10-6 (or dusk).
£3.25 (ch £1.95, pen £2.85).
🅿 *(100 yds)* ♨ ⚹ *toilets for disabled shop*
Cards: 🄰 ▭ 🄼 🄹

NORTHLEACH
Cotswold Countryside Collection
Fosseway GL54 3JH (12m E of Cheltenham on A429)
☎01451 860715 Fax 01451 860091
The story of everyday rural life in the Cotswolds is told in this museum, housed in the remaining buildings of the Northleach House of Correction. It was one of a group of Gloucestershire's 'country prisons' built around 1789 by Sir Onesiphorus Paul. The Lloyd-Baker agricultural collection, one of the best in the country, exhibits a unique collection of Gloucestershire harvest-wagons. There is a 'below stairs' gallery showing a dairy, kitchen and laundry. There are also special exhibitions. Workshops on rag rug making, felt making, patchwork, natural dyeing and basket making are held. Special events for 1998 include: Caring for the Cotswolds (1-17 April), Underwear Exhibition (25 April-17 May), Gloucestershire Women's Institute Camera & Calligraphy Exhibition (12 Sept-4 Oct).
Open Apr-Oct, Mon-Sat 10-5, Sun 2-5 & BHs. Open at other times by prior arrangement.
✱*£1.60 (ch 80p, pen £1.40 & student £1). Family ticket £4. Party.*
🅿 ♨ ⚹ *(wheelchair available, parking at entrance) toilets for disabled shop*

Keith Harding's World of Mechanical Music
Oak House, High St GL54 3ET (at crossing of A40/A429)
☎01451 860181 Fax 01451 861133
A fascinating collection of antique clocks, musical boxes, automata and mechanical musical instruments, restored and maintained in the world-famous workshops, displayed in a period setting, and played during regular tours. There is an exhibition of coin operated instruments which visitors can play.
Open all year, daily 10-6.
£5 (ch 16 £2.50, under 3 free, pen & students £4). Family ticket £12.50. Disabled-helpers Free.
🅿 ⚹ *toilets for disabled shop* ✤ *(ex guide dogs)*
Cards: 🄰 ▭ 🄼 ⬚ 🄼 🄹

OWLPEN
Owlpen Manor
GL11 5BZ (3m E of Dursley off B4066, follow brown tourist signs)
☎01453 860261 Fax 01453 860819
This romantic Tudor manor house, dating from 1450 to 1616, contains unique 17th-century painted cloth wallhangings, furniture, pictures and textiles. There is an Arts and Crafts collection. The house is set in formal terraced gardens, and is part of a picturesque Cotswold manorial group including a Jacobean Court House, a watermill dating from 1728 (now holiday cottages), a Victorian church and medieval tithe barn.
Open Apr-Oct, Tue-Sun & BH Mon, 2-5.
£4.25 (ch £2). Party 30+
🅿 ♨ ✕ *licensed* ✤
Cards: 🄰 ▭ 🄼 🄼 🄹

PAINSWICK
Painswick Rococo Garden
The Stables, Painswick House GL6 6TH (on B4073 half a mile NW of Painswick)
☎01452 813204 Fax 01452 813204
This beautiful Rococo garden (a compromise between formality and informality) is the only one of its period to

survive completely. There are fascinating contemporary garden buildings with vistas, ponds, woodland walks, a kitchen garden and herbaceous borders, all set in a hidden Cotswold valley which is famous for snowdrops in the early spring. Ring for details of special events.
Open 2nd Wed in Jan-Nov, Wed-Sun, 11-5. (Daily in Jul & Aug)
£3 (ch £1.60, pen £2.70).
🅿 ♨ ✕ ⚹ *toilets for disabled shop*
Cards: 🄰 ▭

SLIMBRIDGE
WWT Slimbridge
GL2 7BT (off A38, signed from M5 junc 13 & 14)
☎01453 890333 & 890065
Fax 01453 890827
Founded in 1946 by the late Sir Peter Scott, Slimbridge is now the home of the world's largest collection of exotic wildfowl and the only place in Europe where all six types of flamingo can be seen. Up to 8,000 wild birds winter on the 800-acre reserve of flat fields, marsh and mudflats on the River Severn. First class viewing facilities are available and in winter, the towers and hides provide remarkable views of the migratory birds. Other features include a permanent indoor interactive exhibit, with videos, a computer game and large tanks with coral reef fish, freshwater fish, and peatland plants; and a Tropical House. There is a packed programme of events and activities throughout the year including evening talks and guided walks. New attractions include Pond Zone and a sustainable gardening exhibit which opens Summer 1998. Ring for details.
Open all year, daily from 9.30-5.30 (winter 4pm). (Closed 25 Dec).
✱*£5 (ch £3). Family ticket £13. Party 10+.*
🅿 ♨ ✕ *licensed* ⚹ *(wheelchairs, tapes for blind) toilets for disabled shop* ✤
Cards: 🄰 ▭ 🄼 🄼 🄹

SNOWSHILL
Snowshill Manor
WR12 7JU (3m SW of Broadway)
☎01386 852410
Fax 01386 852410
A Cotswold Tudor manor house, best known for Charles Paget Wade's collections of craftmanship and design, including musical instruments, clocks, toys, bicycles, weavers' and spinners' tools, and Japanese armour. His cottage, with its charming cottage garden, which is organically run, are also on view. Special Interest days include craft demonstrations, collector's days, and music in the garden. Please telephone for details.
Open Apr-Nov, daily (ex Tue & Good Friday) 1-5. Grounds & visitor facilities open May-Sep, noon-5.30. Last admission to manor 45 mins before closing.
£5.50 (ch £2.75). Family ticket £13.80. Grounds only £2.50.
🅿 ✕ *shop* ✤ ⚹
Cards: 🄰 ▭

SOUDLEY
Dean Heritage Centre
Camp Mill GL14 2UB (on B4227)
☎01594 822170
Located in the heart of the Forest of Dean, the Centre is set around a restored corn mill and its mill pond. It tells the fascinating story of this unique area with museum displays which include a reconstucted cottage, coal mine and waterwheel. There are also nature trails (one of which is level), picnic areas and barbecue hearths. Added attractions are an adventure playground, fowl and ducks, gift and craft shops and a cafe. New display for 1998: Voyce Clocks Collection - one of the largest collections of long case clocks made by a single family of clock makers in the country. Special events include: Victorian Day (31 May), Woodland Weekend (August Bank Holiday).

Open all year, daily, Feb, Mar & Oct 10-5, Apr-Sept 10-6, Nov-Jan weekends only 10-4. (Closed 24-26 Dec). Booked parties at other times by arrangement, ✱£2.95 (ch £1.60, students, pen & UB40 £2.50). Party 20+. Season tickets available. Prices under review.
🅿 🍽 ♿ toilets for disabled shop ⊘ (ex guide dogs)

STANWAY
Stanway House
GL54 5PQ (0.5m E of B4632 or B4077)
☎01386 584469 Fax 01386 584688
A thoroughly lived-in Jacobean manor house with unusual furniture, set in formal landscaped parkland. There is also a tithe barn and gatehouse.
Open Jun-Sep, Tue & Thu 2-5.
£3.50 (ch £1, pen £3). Party.
🅿 ♿

TETBURY
Chavenage House
GL8 8XP (2m NW of Tetbury signposted off B4014. 1m SE of Stroud off A46.)
☎01666 502329 & 01453 832700
Fax 01453 836778
Built in 1576, this unspoilt Elizabethan house contains some stained glass from the 16th-century and earlier, and some good furniture and tapestries. The owner during the Civil War was a Parliamentarian, and the house also contains Cromwellian relics. In more recent years, the house has been the location for 'Grace and Favour' the sequel to the television series 'Are You Being Served?', 'Poirot', 'The House of Elliot' and 'The Noel Edmunds Party'. There is a Shakespeare Week in July. Tours of the house, conducted by the owner or members of his family, are enlivened by many stories of ghosts etc.
Open May-Sep, Thu, Sun & BHs 2-5. Also Etr Sun & Mon. Other days by appointment only.
£3 (ch £1.50).
🅿 ♿ ⊘

ULEY
Uley Tumulus
(3.5m NE of Dursley on B4066)
This 180ft long barrow is known as Hetty Pegler's Tump. The Neolithic burial mound is about 85ft wide and is surrounded by a dry-built wall. It contains a central passage, built of stone, and three burial chambers.
Open any reasonable time.
Free.
⛺

WESTBURY-ON-SEVERN
Westbury Court Garden
GL14 1PD (9m SW of Gloucester on A48)
☎01452 760461
This formal water garden with canals and yew hedges was laid out between 1696 and 1705. It is the earliest of its kind remaining in England and was restored in 1971 and planted with species dated from pre 1700, including apple, pear and plum trees.
Open Apr-Nov, Wed-Sun & BH Mon 11-6. (Closed Good Fri). Other months by appointment only.
£2.70 (ch £1.35)
🅿 ♿ (braille guide, wheelchair available) toilets for disabled ⊘ ♨

WESTONBIRT
Westonbirt Arboretum
GL8 8QS (3m S Tetbury on A433)
☎01666 880220
Fax 01666 880559
This large arboretum was started in 1829 and contains one of the finest and most important collection of trees and shrubs in the world. There are 18,000 of them, planted from 1829 to the present day, covering 600 acres of landscaped Cotswold countryside. The visitor can follow 17 miles of waymarked trails or simply sit in a leafy glade and admire some of the great varieties of trees and shrubs which provide interest and colour throughout the year, even in winter, when the distinctive barks of the birches

Sudeley Castle was once the home of Catherine Parr, last wife of Henry VIII. The house features an impressive art collection and delightful gardens.

and maple are visible. Magnificent displays of Rhododendrons, Azaleas, Magnolias and the wild flowers of Silkwood can be seen in the Spring (March-June). There is a Visitor Centre with an exhibition, shop, and interesting video programme. The arboretum is managed by the Forestry Commission.
Open all year, daily 10-8 or sunset. Visitor centre & shop all year. (except Christmas & New Year)
£3.50 (ch £1, pen £2.50)
🅿 🍽 ♿ (electric & manual wheelchair for loan) toilets for disabled shop garden centre
Cards: 🌑 💳

WINCHCOMBE
Sudeley Castle & Gardens
GL54 5JD
☎01242 603197 & 602308
Fax 01242 602959
Set against the rolling Cotswold hills, Sudeley Castle, one of England's most delightful historic houses, has many royal connections. It was once the palace of Catherine Parr, who is buried in the Chapel; Henry VIII, Anne Boleyn, Lady Jane Grey and Elizabeth I stayed here; it was the residence of Charles I; and the headquarters of Prince Rupert during the Civil War. Today the Castle is the home of Lord and Lady Ashcombe. Surrounding the Castle are seven delightful gardens, which have gained recognition for their flower displays and topiary. The Queens Garden is famous for its rose collection, and a recent addition is a Tudor Knot Garden. Visitors can wander through avenues of majestic trees, shrubs, yew hedges and old fashioned roses. A wildfowl sanctuary, exhibition centre, plant centre, picnic area, children's adventure playground, shop and restaurant are other features of Sudeley. Special events will be held throughout 1998, please telephone for details.
Open daily: Mar, Gardens, plant centre & shop 11-4.30. Apr-Oct, Gardens, exhibition, shop & plant centre 10.20-5.30. Apr-Oct, Castle apartments & Church 11-5.

Castle & Gardens £5.50 (ch £3 & pen £4.80). Gardens only £4 (ch £1.80 & pen £3.20). Family ticket £14.
🅿 ✗ licensed shop garden centre ⊘

ALTRINCHAM
Dunham Massey Hall
WA14 4SJ (3m SW of Altrincham (off A56), junct 19 off M6 or junct 7 off M56)
☎0161 941 1025
Fax 0161 929 7508
A fine 18th-century house and park, home of the Earls of Stamford until 1976. It was remodelled in the early 1730s by the 2nd Earl of Warrington and altered again in the early 1900s. It contains fine 18th-century furniture and magnificent silverware made by Huguenot smiths. There are some thirty rooms to be seen including the library and the billiard room. Portraits of the Booth and Grey families (Earls of Warrington and Stamford) include one of Lady Jane Grey. A fully-equipped kitchen, butler's pantry and laundry are not to be missed. Fallow deer roam the park, which also has a working Elizabethan saw mill. The 30-acre garden is on an ancient site with moat, mount and orangery. There are mature trees and fine lawns with an extensive range of shrubs and water-loving plants. Special events for 1998 include Plantsman's Day (10 May), Walks with Head Gardener, and Drama in the Park. Telephone for details.
Open - House 4 Apr-1 Nov, Sat-Wed 12-5 (11-5 BH Sun & Mon), last admission 4.30. Garden 4 Apr-1 Nov, daily 11-5.30. House & Garden £5 (ch £2.50). House only £3 (ch £1.50). Garden only £3 (ch £1.50). Family ticket £12.50. Park only, £2.80 per car (NT members free), pre-booked coaches free.
➔

Dunham Massey Hall is a fine 18th-century house and park with a 30-acre garden and a working Elizabethan sawmill.

programme Return of the Antelope, where chairs loom overhead. See the spectacular Magic Show, then take part in a comedy debate in the House of Commons. Explore the history of cinema at Projections, experience Motion Master where the seats move with the action, see a spectacular 3-D and laser show, gasp as arms are severed in the squeamish make up show, and enjoy the All New Sooty Show. You should allow a possible five hours for your visit.
Open all year, daily summer 9.45-7 (last entry 4); winter 9.45-5.30 weekdays (last entry 3), 9.45-6.30 weekends & BH's (last entry 4). Closed Mon & Tue first half of Feb, Mar, Apr (except Etr), first half of Oct, Nov & Dec (except 28 & 29 Dec). Closed Mon May-Sep (except BH's). Closed 19-25 Dec. Open 1 & 2 Jan and weekends only.
P *(charged)* ♨ ✗ *licensed* & *(ramps & lift throughout) toilets for disabled shop* ✿
Details not confirmed for 1998

P *(charged)* ♨ ✗ *licensed* & *(braille guide, batricar & wheelchairs for loan) toilets for disabled shop* ✿ *(ex on lead in Park)* ♨
Cards: ▬ ▬ ▬

ASHTON-UNDER-LYNE
Museum of the Manchesters
Market Place OL6 6DL
☎ 0161 342 3078
Fax 0161 343 1732
The Museum of the Manchesters describes the social and regimental history of the Manchester Regiment. It traces the story back to its origins in the 18th century as the 63rd and 96th Foot to its amalgamation with the Kings Regiment in 1958. The Manchesters fought in both World Wars, the Boer War, and the Crimea. Features within the Museum include a major display on Women at War, a WWI trench, an Anderson shelter, and new for 1998, a computerised, interactive work-station designed especially for children. Live interpreters appear in the Museum at regular intervals throughout the year.
Open all year, Mon-Sat, 10-4. (Closed Sun). Free.
P *(50yds)* & *toilets for disabled shop* ✿ *(ex guide dogs)*

BRAMHALL
Bramall Hall & Park
SK7 3NX (from A6 turn right at Blossoms public house through Davenport village then turn right - signposted)
☎ 0161 485 3708
Fax 0161 486 6959
The large timber-framed hall dates from the 14th century, and is one of the finest black-and-white houses in Cheshire. It has rare 16th-century wall paintings and period furniture, and was the home of the Davenport family for 500 years before coming into the care of the Metropolitan Borough of Stockport. The house is set in 70 acres of beautiful parkland which has been landscaped in the style of Capability Brown. Newly opened Servants' Quarters, Victorian Kitchen and Boudoir. Available for weddings and corporate events. Special events for 1998 include: Bramall Arts Festival in June, which features Shakespeare, Opera, Jazz and Classical Concerts.
Open all year, Good Fri-Sep Mon-Sat 1-5, Sun 11-5; Oct-New Year's Day Tue-Sat 1-4, Sun 11-4; 2 Jan-Good Fri Sat & Sun 1-4. Closed 25-26 Dec.
£3.50 (concessions £2). Family ticket £8.50.
P ♨ & *(access for wheelchair users) toilets for disabled shop* ✿ *(ex guide dogs)*
Cards: ▬ ▬

MANCHESTER
Although the Romans established a fort near what is now Manchester's city centre, it was really cotton that created Manchester. In the 14th century Flemish weavers came to Britain and set up their trade. Four centuries later, in the Manchester area, their craft was revolutionised by men such as Samuel Crompton, who invented the spinning mule, Richard Arkwright inventor of the spinning frame and James Hargreaves creator of the spinning jenny who made the mass production of cloth possible. The 18th and 19th century progress brought prosperity to Manchester and there are a number of great houses nearby built from the wealth of cotton. Industrialisation also brought the need for transport, soon provided by a network of canals and railways which carried cotton and coal for the steam engines from the nearby pits. Manchester's history is celebrated in a heritage park of which Castlefield railway station forms a part and close by Salford Mining Museum gives a taste of life in the coal pits. Although the cotton trade died out and Manchester's canals are now used just for leisure, the city has remained a thriving commercial, cultural and business centre.

City Art Galleries
Mosley St/Princess St M2 3JL
☎ 0161 236 5244
Fax 0161 236 7369
The Mosley Street Galleries have permanent displays of European art, ceramics and silver which are displayed with furniture in an elaborate decorative scheme. The strength of this Gallery lies in the superb collection of Victorian art, especially the group of major Pre-Raphaelite paintings. Decorative and applied arts, including porcelain from early times to the 19th century, furniture and sculpture are also included in this magnificent collection.
Open Mon 11-5.30, Tue-Sat 10-5.30, Sun 2-5.30. The Princess St Gallery is closed from Spring 1998 for a major expansion programme.
Free.
P *(50m) (public area, spaces not guaranteed)* ♨ & *(stairclimber) toilets for disabled shop* ✿

Gallery of English Costume
Platt Hall, Rusholme M14 5LL
☎ 0161 224 5217
Fax 0161 256 3278
With one of the most comprehensive costume collections in Great Britain, this gallery makes captivating viewing. Housed in a fine Georgian mansion, the displays focus on the changing styles of everyday fashion and accessories, looking back over 400 years. Contemporary fashion is also illustrated and because of the vast amount of material in the collection, exhibitions are constantly changing and no one period is permanently illustrated. The costume library is available for research purposes, by appointment only. Displays for 1998 include: 17th-century dress and embroidery, women's dress 1740-1840, 19th-century printed cottons, women's fashion 1890s-1950s, mid-Victorian dress 1851-1887, Sixties Style, Modern fashion from 1970 on, menswear 1695-1995, textiles and embroideries from the Indian Sub-continent.
Open all year, Tue-Sat, 10-5.45; Nov-Feb closes at 4pm. Occasional closures on Sat at short notice, telephone to confirm opening.
Free.
P & *shop* ✿

Granada Studios Tour
Water St M60 9EA
☎ 0161 832 9090 & 0161 833 0880
Fax 0161 834 3684
Enter the world of television at Granada Studios Tour in the heart of the City Centre. Only here can you walk down Coronation Street, Downing Street and Baker Street in just one day. Visit the Giant Room, from the popular children's

John Rylands University Library of Manchester
150 Deansgate M3 3EH
☎ 0161 834 5343
Fax 0161 834 5574
Founded as a memorial to Manchester cotton-magnate and millionaire John Rylands (1801-88) this former private library now comprises the Special Collections Division of the John Rylands University Library of Manchester. It is a library of international renown, both for its manuscript and printed-book resources as well as its medieval-jewelled bindings. In total its holdings extend to five million books, manuscripts and archival items representing some fifty cultures and ranging in date from the third millennium BC to the present day. It is perhaps best known for its 2nd-century St John Fragment, the earliest known piece of New Testament writing in existence; its St Christopher Woodcut (1423), the earliest piece of western printing with an undisputed date; and its Gutenberg Bible (1455/6), the first book printed using moveable type. The Library's treasures are more than matched by the magnificent neo-Gothic surroundings designed by architect Basil Champneys at the instigation of Enriqueta Augustina Rylands, third wife and widow of John Rylands. Notable items from the collections are always displayed as part of the Library's varied exhibitions programme.
Open all year, Mon-Fri 10-5.30, Sat 10-1 (Closed BH & Xmas-New Year). Pre-booked groups only at other times.
P *(400yds) shop* ✿
Details not confirmed for 1998

Manchester Museum
The University, Oxford Rd M13 9PL (S of city centre on B5117)
☎0161 275 2634 Fax 0161 275 2676
The Manchester Museum is the only place in Manchester where you can cross the world's continents, explore 600 million years of life, and discover ancient civilizations - all in the space of one visit. Live reptiles and crocodilians in the vivarium, collections of mammals and fossils and 2,000 year old mummies from Egypt. Also coins, archery, minerals and dinosaur footprints.
Open all year, Mon-Sat 10-5. (Closed Sun, Good Fri, 25-26 Dec & 1 Jan). Please check times between Xmas & New Year.
P & (Provision for disabled telephone in advance) toilets for disabled shop ✻ (ex guide dogs)
Details not confirmed for 1998

Manchester Museum of Transport
Boyle St, Cheetham M8 8UW (1.5m N of Victoria Station)
☎0161 205 2122 & 0161 205 1082
Fax 0161 205 2122
The City's travel through the ages is illustrated here; among the many interesting exhibits are included over 70 buses and other vehicles from the area together with old photographs, tickets and other memorabilia. Please telephone for details of special events.
Open all year, Wed, Sat, Sun & BH 10-5. Parties at other times by arrangement.
✻£2.50 (ch accompanied £1.50). Family ticket £1.
P ▉ & toilets for disabled shop

Manchester United Museum & Tour Centre
Old Trafford M16 0RA (2m from city centre, off A56)
☎0161 877 4002 Fax 0161 876 5800
This Museum was opened in 1986 and is the first purpose-built British football museum. It covers the history of Manchester United in words, pictures, sound and vision, from its inception in 1878 to the present day. More than 400 exhibits are regularly on display.
The Museum reopens in spring 1998 with a new tour of the stadium, and special events will be taking place around this opening. Ring for details.
Open all year Tue-Sun & most BH Mons 9.30-4. (Closed 25 Dec). New opening times Spring 1998.
✻*Ground Tour, Museum & Trophy Room £5.50 (ch & pen £3.50). Museum & Trophy Room only £2.95 (ch & pen £1.95). Family ticket £14 & £6.95. Prices under review.*
P ▉ ✗ & toilets for disabled shop ✻
Cards: ▨ ▨

The Museum of Science and Industry in Manchester
Liverpool Rd, Castlefield M3 4FP (follow brown tourist signs from city centre)
☎0161 832 2244 0161 832 1830
Fax 0161 833 2184
The Museum of Science and Industry in Manchester offers endless fascination for adults and children. Located in the buildings of the world's oldest passenger railway station, the fun-filled galleries amaze, amuse and entertain. You can take off to the Air and Space Gallery which is packed with the planes that made flying history. Try the Super X Simulator and experience the thrills of flying without having to leave the ground. Visit Xperiment! the hands-on science centre where you can shake hands with yourself and walk away from your own shadow. Pit your wits at the puzzle desk and see if you've got what it takes to be a genius. Visit Underground Manchester and walk through a reconstructed Victorian sewer - complete with sounds and smells. See the wheels of industry turning in the Power Hall which houses the largest collection of working steam mill engines in the world. Fibres, Fabrics & Fashion is a new permanent textile gallery which follows the story of

Manchester. Ring for details of this and other exhibitions.
Open all year, daily 10-5. Last admission 4.30. (Closed 24-26 Dec).
£5 (concessions £3, ch under 5 free). Party 10+.
P (charged) ▉ & (lifts, hearing system) toilets for disabled shop ✻
Cards: ▨ ▨ ▨ ▨

Whitworth Art Gallery
University of Manchester, Oxford Rd M15 6ER (follow brown tourist signs)
☎0161 275 7450 Fax 0161 275 7451
The Whitworth Art Gallery is home to an impressive range of modern and historic drawings, prints, paintings and sculpture, the largest collection of textiles and wallpapers outside London and an internationally famous collection of British watercolours. Displays from these collections are changed regularly, providing a fresh new look to the Gallery. An ever-changing programme of temporary exhibitions also runs throughout the year, with the recently opened Mezzanine Court serving as an exciting new venue for sculpture display. Exhibitions for 1998 include: Turner (until 24 May), Richard Newton (until 17 May), and Common Threads (September-November).
Open Mon-Sat 10-5, Sun 2-5. (Closed Good Fri & Xmas-New Year). Free.
P ✗ licensed & (one wheelchair available, induction loop in lecture theatre) toilets for disabled shop ✻

PRESTWICH
Heaton Hall
Heaton Park M25 5SW
☎0161 773 1231 or 0161 236 5244 ext 123 Fax 0161 236 7369
Designed by James Wyatt for Sir Thomas Egerton in 1772, the house has magnificent period interiors decorated with fine plasterwork, paintings and furniture. Other attractions include a unique circular room with Pompeian-style paintings, and the original Samuel Green organ still in working order. Lively exhibitions and events programme, ring for details.
Open May to Sept, but phone for time details on 0161-236 5244.
✻*Free. Currently under review.*

P (charged) ✗ & (occasional 'touch tours'. Phone for details) toilets for disabled shop ✻

SALFORD
Lancashire Mining Museum
Buile Hill Park, Eccles Old Rd M6 8GL (signposted off A576)
☎0161 736 1832 Fax 0161 736 8581
Two reproduction coal mines, a gallery to illustrate the history and development of coal mining and exhibitions of mining art are housed in this listed Georgian building, designed by Sir Charles Barry, the architect of the Houses of Parliament. The reference library and archives are available for research purposes, by appointment only. Temporary exhibition 'Children in the Mines' 6 Sep-3 Jan, includes tunnel to crawl through and other activities.
Open all year, Mon-Fri 10-12.30 & 1.30-5, Sun 2-5. (Closed Sat, Good Fri, Etr Sun, 24-26 Dec & 1 Jan). Free.
P shop ✻
Cards: ▨ ▨ ▨

Salford Museum & Art Gallery
Peel Park, Crescent M5 4WU
☎0161 736 2649 Fax 0161 745 9490
The pride of this provincial gallery has to be its collection of L S Lowry's works which are displayed in the art gallery together with Victorian paintings and decorative arts. The small museum is equally revealing with its street scene reconstructed in the typical style of a northern industrial town at the turn of the century. Temporary exhibitions include 'Fantasy in Action: The Art of the Puppet Today' (3-31 May) (to coincide with this there will be a programme of puppet performances & family workshops with professional puppeteers), British cartoonists (8 Jun-19 July), African art, poetry, music & dance (22 Aug-27 Sept).
Open all year, Mon-Fri 10-4.45, Sat & Sun 1-5. (Closed Good Fri, Etr Sun, 25 & 26 Dec, 1 Jan). Free.
P ▉ & toilets for disabled shop ✻ (guide dogs)
Cards: ▨ ▨ ▨ ▨

Manchester's elaborate Town Hall was built during the Victorian era to display the city's wealth and importance from the Industrial Revolution.

UPPERMILL
Saddleworth Museum & Art Gallery
High St OL3 6HS (on A670)
☎01457 874093 & 870336
There really is something for everyone at Saddleworth Museum. Based in an old mill building next to the Huddersfield canal, the Museum brings to life the history of the Saddleworth area - a piece of Yorkshire stranded on the Lancashire side of the Pennines. Woollen weaving is the traditional industry, displayed in the 18th century Weaver's Cottage and the Victoria Mill Gallery. The textile machinery is run regularly by arrangement. The Victorian Rooms - Parlour, Bedroom, Kitchen, Scullery and Privy - show the life of one Saddleworth family in the 1890s. In the Art Gallery, exhibitions change monthly. Plus local history, farming, transport and vintage vehicles. Special for families - Family Boxes full of things to touch, do and discover, and 'Get Your Hands On This', our activity area for children of all ages. Special events: Vintage Vehicle Gala (14 June), Textile Working Days (March-October), Model Railway Weekend (18-19 April).
Open all year, Nov-late Mar, daily 1-4; late Mar-Oct, Mon-Sat 10-5, Sun 12-5.
✻*£1.20 (concessions 60p) Family ticket £3.*
🅿 ⅃ *(stairlift, ramps, braille & large print guides, wheelchair) toilets for disabled shop ⚘ (ex guide dogs)*

WIGAN
Wigan Pier
Wallgate WN3 4EU
☎01942 323666 Fax 01942 322031
Part museum, part theatre, Wigan Pier is a mixture of entertainment and education. Visit The Way We Were Heritage Centre with its seaside promenade, coalmine, workshops, market square and pub. Join in with the professional actors of the Wigan Pier Theatre Company as they bring the past to life with a packed programme of themed plays, Victorian music hall shows and the infamous schoolroom. Step aboard a canal boat to experience life in the Lancashire cotton mills across the canal at Trencherfield Mill. Here you will marvel at the world's largest working original mill steam engine, still in steam daily. Please telephone for details of special events.
Open all year, Mon-Thu 10-5; Sat & Sun 11-5. Closed 25-26 Dec & Fri (ex Good Fri).
🅿 ⅃ ✕ *licensed ⅃ toilets for disabled shop ⚘*
Details not confirmed for 1998
Cards: ▨ ▨

HAMPSHIRE

ALDERSHOT
Airborne Forces Museum
Browning Barracks, Queens Av GU11 2BU
☎01252 349619 Fax 01252 349203
Aldershot is the home of the 5th Airborne Brigade, and paratroopers can often be seen practising their drops above the town, so it is an appropriate home for the Airborne Forces Museum. It is easily identified by the World War II Dakota outside, and tells the story of the creation and operation of the parachute forces from 1940 onwards. There are aircraft models and briefing models for World War II operations, and a post-war display includes captured enemy arms, vehicles, dioramas of actions, parachutes, equipment and many scale models. There are Victoria and George Crosses among the medals on show. Telephone for details of special events.
Open all year, daily 10-4.30. (Closed Xmas).
✻*£2.50 (ch, students, pen and ex-servicemen £1)*
🅿 ⅃ *Wheelchair ramps shop ⚘*
Cards: ▨ ▨ ◐

Aldershot Military Museum
Evelyn Woods Rd, Queens Av GU11 2LG
☎01252 314598 Fax 01252 342942
A look behind the scenes at the daily life of both soldiers and civilians as Aldershot and Farnborough grew up around the military camps to become the home of the British Army. Displays include a Victorian barrack room and military tailor's shop, the birth of British aviation, the Canadian Army in Aldershot during World War II, and the Rushmoor Local History Gallery. Also military vehicle gallery and Field Marshal Montgomery's caravan shed. 19 July sees a day of re-enactments and marching bands.
Open Mar-Oct, daily 10-5; Nov-Feb, daily 10-4.30.
£2 (ch/pen/UB40 £1)
🅿 ⅃ *shop*

ALRESFORD
Watercress Line
The Railway Station SO24 9JG (stations at Alton & Alresford signposted off A31)
☎01962 733810
Fax 01962 735448
The Watercress Line, a preserved steam railway, runs through ten miles of rolling scenic countryside between Alton and Alresford. All four stations are authentically 'dressed' in period style, with attractive gardens and there are a locomotive yard and picnic area at Ropley. Please telephone for details of special events.
Open weekends throughout the year except for Nov & Jan, also some weekdays over Xmas, Easter school half term holidays and Jun-Aug. Alresford station shop & buffet open daily ex 25 Dec.
Unlimited travel for the day, £7.50 (ch £4.50, pen £5.50). Family ticket £22.
🅿 *(charged) ⅃ ✕ licensed ⅃ (ramps, access to trains) toilets for disabled shop*
Cards: ▨ ▨

AMPFIELD
Sir Harold Hillier Gardens & Arboretum
Jermyns Ln SO51 0QA (signposted off A3090 & B3057)
☎01794 368787
Fax 01794 368027
This is the largest collection of trees and shrubs of its kind in the British Isles. The plants come from different parts of the world, and include many rarities. The setting is 184 acres of attractive landscape, with something of interest at all times of the year. Superb colour is provided in particular during the spring and autumn seasons. Early opening - gates open at 5.30am, breakfast from 7am (18 Apr), Breakfast opening - tour at 8am, breakfast from 8.30 (31st May), Summer Celebration (21 Jun), Art Exhibition (1-31 Aug), Flower Festival (4-6 Sep).
Open all year, Apr-Oct daily 10.30-6, Nov-Mar daily 10.30-5 or dusk.
Apr-Oct: £4 (ch £1, pen £3.50). Nov-Mar: £3.50 (ch £1, pen £2.50). Party 10+.
🅿 ✕ *licensed ⅃ toilets for disabled garden centre ⚘*

ANDOVER
Finkley Down Farm Park
SP11 6NF (signposted from A303 & A343)
☎01264 352195
A wide range of farm animals and poultry can be seen here, including some rare breeds. The pets corner has tame, hand-reared baby animals that can be stroked and petted. There are also a Countryside Museum, housed in a barn, Romany caravans and rural bygones to see, an adventure playground and a large picnic area. Animal handling and feeding during the day as per timetable.
Open 15 March-Oct, daily 10-6. Last admission 5pm.
Prices under review.
🅿 ⅃ ⅃ *toilets for disabled shop ⚘*
Cards: ▨ ▨

One of the world's largest collections of vehicles and motoring memorabilia can be found at Beaulieu

ASHURST
Longdown Dairy Farm
Longdown SO40 4UH (off A35 between Lyndhurst & Southampton)
☎01703 293326 Fax 01703 293376
A wonderful opportunity to get close to lots of friendly farm animals - from piglets to ducklings, from goats to cows, and many, many more. Visitors can touch and feed many of the residents, watch the afternoon milking of our Jersey cows from the viewing gallery and learn about modern farming methods.
Open daily, 4 April-1 November, 10-5
✻*£3.80 (ch 3-14 £2.80, pen £3.50). Saver ticket £11.50 (2 adults + 2 children) £8 (1 adult + 2 children).*
🅿 ⅃ *toilets for disabled shop ⚘ (kennels provided)*
Cards: ▨ ▨ ⑤

New Forest Nature Quest
Longdown SO40 4UH (signposted, off A35)
☎01703 292166 Fax 01703 293376
Discover Britain's magnificent animal kingdom at the New Forest Nature Quest and help preserve its future as you explore the first such wildlife project in the UK. Surrounded by the sights and sounds of this ancient woodland, more than 20 carefully re-created natural settings bring you face to face with a variety of forest characters. See how the Nature Quest assists a range of important projects, helping to conserve our natural heritage for future generations. An opportunity to come face to face with an amazing variety of wildlife from foxes to black rats.
Open Apr-Oct from 10 daily, Nov-Mar weekends only (Closed Jan & Feb).
🅿 ✕ ⅃ *(ex woodland walk) toilets for disabled shop ⚘*
Details not confirmed for 1998
Cards: ▨ ▨ ⑤

BEAULIEU
Beaulieu : National Motor Museum
SO42 7ZN (M27 Westbound J2, A326, B3054, then follow tourist signs)
☎01590 612345 Fax 01590 612624
The venerable 16th-century house of Beaulieu is worth seeing just for its

lovely setting by the Beaulieu River, but it has become most famous as the home of the National Motor Museum. This is one of the world's largest collections of vehicles and motoring memorabilia, with the extra attraction of 'Wheels', a feature which takes visitors on an automated trip through a spectacular display of 100 years of motoring. Other attractions are a high-level monorail through the grounds, veteran bus rides and a replica of a 1930s country garage. The main house itself has a collection of fine paintings and furnishings. The house was once the gatehouse of the great abbey which once stood here, and ruins of other monastic buildings can be seen in the grounds. There is also an exhibition of monastic life. 1998 Special Events: (5 April) Boat Jumble; (9-10 May) Spring Autojumble; (July) Motorcycle World; (July) Palace House Prom; (5-6 September) Autojumble & Automart-the biggest in Europe; (31 October) Fireworks Fair. For further details of these events please ring the Museum.
Open all year - Palace House & Gardens, National Motor Museum, Beaulieu Abbey & Exhibition of Monastic Life, Etr-Sep 10-6; Oct-Etr 10-5. (Closed 25 Dec).
✻*£8.50 (ch £6, pen & students £7). Family £28 Party. Prices under review.*
🅿 ⅃ ⅃ *toilets for disabled shop*
Cards: ▨ ▨ ◐ ⑤

BISHOP'S WALTHAM
Bishop's Waltham Palace
SO3 1AH (on A333)
☎01489 892460
Bishop's Waltham Palace was among the greatest stately homes of the day. One of the most important residences of one of the wealthiest men in the land. Despite destruction by the Civil War, much still remains of the 12th and 14th century buildings, including the impressive three-storey tower and the soaring windows of the Great Hall.
Open Apr-Oct, daily 10-6 (or dusk if earlier).
£2 (ch £1, concessions £1.50).
🅿 ⅃ ⚘ *(in certain areas)* ✠

BOLDRE

Spinners

School Ln SO41 5QE (off A337, between Brockenhurst & Lymington)
☎01590 673347

The garden has been entirely created by the owners since 1960. It has azaleas, rhododendrons, camellias and magnolias, interspersed with primulas, blue poppies and other woodland and ground cover plants. The nursery (open all year) is famed for its rare and less common trees, shrubs and plants and attracts visitors from all over the world.

Open Apr-14 Sep daily 10-5. Other times on application. Nursery and part of garden open all year, but garden and nursery both closed on Sun & Mon.

£1.50 (accompanied ch under 6 free).

🅿 *garden centre* ✿

BREAMORE

Breamore House & Countryside

SP6 2DF (on A338, between Salisbury & Fordingbridge)
☎01725 512468
Fax 01725 512858

The handsome manor house was built in around 1583 and has a fine collection of paintings, china and tapestries. The museum has good examples of steam engines, and uses reconstructed workshops and other displays to show how people lived, worked and travelled a century or so ago. There is also a children's playground. Special events include: the Breamore Craft Shows 23-25 May, live steam model show 1-2 August, and 3 working weekends (9-10 May, 11-12 July & 12-13 September, 11-6)

Open Etr/Apr, Tue, Wed & Sun & Etr, May-Jul & Sep, Tue-Thu & Sat, Sun & all BH, Aug, daily 2-5.30 (Countryside Museum 1pm).

Combined tickets £5 (ch £3.50). Party.

🅿 💷 ⅋ *(ramps) toilets for disabled shop* ✿

BUCKLER'S HARD

Buckler's Hard Village & Maritime Museum

SO42 7XB (M27 Westbound J2, A326, B3054 then follow tourist signs)
☎01590 616203 Fax 01590 612624

This is a historic shipbuilding village, where wooden warships, including some of Nelson's fleet, were built from New Forest oak. In its busy days the wide main street would have been used for rolling great logs to the 'hard' where the ships were built, and the village would have been stacked high with timber. The 18th-century homes of a shipwright and labourer, and a master shipbuilder's office can be seen.

A typical inn scene has been reconstructed, complete with costumed figures, smells and conversation. The Maritime Museum tells the story of the local shipbuilding industry, and also has items from the voyages of Sir Francis Chichester, who moored his boats here. On the last Sunday in July The Bucklers Hard Village Festival is held with people in period costume to recapture all the atmosphere of the village fête. Special events: (13-14 June) Classic Boat Festival; (26 July) Buckler's Hard Village Festival.

Open all year, Etr-Spring BH 10-6; Spring BH-Aug 10-9; Sep-Etr 10-4.30. (Closed 25 Dec).

✳*£3 (ch £2, pen & student £2.50). Family ticket £8.50. Party. Prices under review.*

🅿 💷 ✗ *licensed* ⅋ *shop*
Cards: 🔲 📇 💳 💳 📅 🔳

BURGHCLERE

Sandham Memorial Chapel

RG15 9JT (4m S Newbury off A34)
☎01635 278394 Fax 01635 278394

Stanley Spencer was one of the most original talents of his generation of British painters, and his murals covering the walls of the Sandham Memorial Chapel at Burghclere are considered to be his greatest achievement. Painted during the years 1927 to 1932, the murals celebrate the daily routine of the common soldier during the Great War. They present a symbolic narrative which Spencer described as 'a mixture of real and spiritual fact'. Covering the entire East wall is the 'Resurrection of the Soldiers', an unforgettable image which dominates the Chapel. The Chapel takes everyone by surprise, no-one being prepared for the initial impact experienced on first seeing the interior. It leaves a lasting impression, and is unique among the properties of the National Trust.

Open Apr-Oct, Wed-Sun 11.30-5. Nov & Mar, Sat & Sun 11.30-4. Also open BH Mons, (but closed the Wed after) Dec-Feb by appointment only.

£2 (ch £1).

🅿 ⅋ ✿ 🐾

CHAWTON

Jane Austen's House

GU34 1SD
☎01420 83262

The house stands in the village street, and is where Jane Austen lived and wrote from 1809 to 1817. It has been restored to look as it would have done in the early 1800s, and items such as the author's donkey cart and writing table can be seen. Visitors are welcome to picnic in the garden in daylight hours. Refreshments are available in the village. Please telephone for details of special events.

Open daily Mar-1 Jan, also half term. Jan & Feb wknds only. (Closed 25 & 26 Dec).

🅿 *(300yds)* ⅋ *toilets for disabled shop* ✿
Details not confirmed for 1998

EXBURY

Exbury Gardens

Exbury Estate Office SO45 1AZ (3m from Beaulieu, off B3054)
☎01703 891203 Fax 01703 243380

Exbury Gardens is a 200-acre landscaped woodland garden on the East bank of the Beaulieu River and contains one of the finest collections of rhododendrons, azaleas, camellias and magnolias in the world - as well as many rare and beautiful shrubs and trees. A labyrinth of tracks and paths enable the visitor to explore and enjoy the countless intricate plantings, the cascades and ponds, a rose garden, rock garden, heather garden and iris garden, daffodil meadow and river walk. In July and August the 53 acre Summer Garden provides an ideal place for a peaceful picnic.The Autumn colours are spectacular. Special events include: Garden & Craft Show (3-6 May) and Arts & Crafts Festival (23-25 May).

Open daily Mar-2 Nov 10-5.30 or dusk if earlier. Summer garden open 7 Jul-12 Sep.

Mar-mid Jul: £3.30-£4.80 (ch 10-15 £2.20-£3.80, pen £2.80-£4.30 mid Sep-Oct: £2.80 (ch £1.70, pen £2.20). Summer 53 acres, mid Jul-mid Sep: £2.20 (ch & pen £1.70). Party 15+

🅿 💷 ⅋ *toilets for disabled shop garden centre*

GOSPORT

Royal Navy Submarine Museum & HMS Alliance

Haslar Jetty Rd PO12 2AS (M27 junc 11, follow signs for HMS Dolphin/RNH Haslar & Submarine Museum)
☎01705 529217 & 510354
Fax 01705 511349

The great attraction of this museum is the chance to see inside a submarine, and there are guided tours of *HMS Alliance*. The more conventional part of the museum covers the development of submarines from their earliest days. There is an emphasis on British boats, but an international view is also given, and there are models of practically every kind. Two periscopes from *HMS Conqueror* have now been installed in the museum, in the reconstruction of a nuclear submarine control room, giving panoramic views of Portsmouth Harbour. Outside, the dominant presence of the modern Royal Navy gives an exciting, topical flavour to a visit. A series of events are planned for the 50th anniversary of the launch of HMS Alliance.

Open all year, Apr-Oct 10-5.30; Nov-Mar 10-4.30. (Closed 24 Dec-1 Jan). Allow 3 hrs for visit. Last tour 1 hour before closing.

✳*£3.50 (ch & pen £2.50). Family ticket (2 adults & 4 ch) £9.50. Party 12+. Joint ticket with Fort Nelson & Royal Armouries now available. Discounted entry scheme "Follow the Drum", in association with Southern Military Museums.*

🅿 💷 ⅋ *(information in Braille) shop* ✿
Cards: 🔲 📇 💳 💳 🔳

HARTLEY WINTNEY

West Green House Gardens

West Green RG27 8JB (off A30, at Phoenix Green take sign to West Green Down, Thackhams Lane. House last left)
☎01252 844611
Fax 01252 844611

The gardens surrounding this Queen Anne house date back three hundred years and have been closed for the past three years for major repairs and replanting. When restoration is complete there will be ten acres of garden and pleasure grounds - four walled gardens, a lake, follies, green theatre, nymphaeum, mixed border and potager. Celebrated designers Oliver Hill and Quinlan Terry have contributed structures to the grounds.

Open 20 May-17 Aug, Wed-Sun 11am-4pm.

£3 (ch 7 free).

🅿 💷 ⅋ *(most areas accessible) toilets for disabled* ✿

HAVANT

Staunton Country Park

Middle Park Way PO9 5HB (off B2149)
☎01705 453405
Fax 01705 498156

This colourful Victorian park offers a wonderful range of attractions for all age ➤

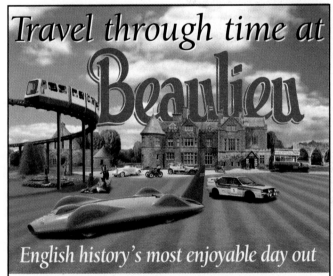

groups. Meet and feed the animals at the ornamental farm where there is a broad range of animals from llama and shirehorses to pot-bellied pigs and pigmy goats. Explore the Victorian tropical glasshouses with exotic flowers from around the world, including the giant Amazonian waterlily. Discover the history of the park in the visitor centre. Discover 1,000 acres of parkland with marked trails, picnic spots and an ornamental lake. Please telephone for details of special events. These include: Easter on the Farm (10-13 April), Countryside Skills (25-31 May), Tropicana (26 July), Summer Season (Aug School Hols), Heritage Days (12-13 Sept) & Hallowe'en (30-31 October)

Open 10-5 (4pm winter)
£3.40 (ch £2.50, pen £3).
Family £10.
🅿 ☕ ♿ *(wheelchair for visitors) toilets for disabled shop ✵ (dogs allowed in parkland)*
Cards: ▨ ▦ ▨

HIGHCLERE ▰▰▰▰▰
Highclere Castle
RG20 9RN (4.5m S of Newbury, off A34)
☎ 01635 253210
Fax 01635 225066
This splendid early Victorian mansion stands in beautiful parkland. It has sumptuous interiors and numerous Old Master pictures. Also shown are early finds by the 5th Earl of Carnarvon, one of the discoverers of Tutankhamun's tomb. Events planned for 1998 include: Southern Counties Country Show (24/25 May); Festival of Transport (2 August); Jaguar Car Rally (23 August): Craft Fair (29-31 August); Christmas Fair (4-6 December).
Open Tue-Sun 5 July-6 Sep. Last admission 4pm. Sat 11-3.30. Last admission 2.30pm.
🅿 ✗ *licensed ♿ (wheelchair available) toilets for disabled shop ✵*
Cards: ▨ ▦ ▨

Highclere Castle is really a sumptuous Victorian mansion. Within the house are many Egyptian relics brought back by the Earl of Carnarvon, who discovered the tomb of the pharaoh Tutankhamun.

HINTON AMPNER ▰▰▰▰▰
Hinton Ampner
So24 0LA (off A272, 1m W of Bramdean)
☎ 01962 771305 Fax 01962 771305
Set in superb Hampshire countryside, this is a delightful garden combining formality of design with informality of planting. It is full of scent and colour and offers walks with many unexpected vistas. After six years of restoration the garden is flourishing, with highlights including a dell and a sunken garden. The house, restored after a fire in 1960, displays a fine collection of Regency furniture and Italian paintings.
Open Garden: 15 & 22 Mar then 28 Mar-Sep, Sat, Sun, BH Mon, Tue & Wed 1.30-5.30. Last admission 5pm. House: 28 Mar-end Sept Tue & Wed only, Sat &

Sun in Aug 1.30-5.30.
House and Garden £4, garden only £3.
🅿 ☕ ♿ *(Braille guides, special parking) toilets for disabled ✵ ♨*

HURST CASTLE ▰▰▰▰▰
Hurst Castle
(on Pebble Spit S of Keyhaven)
☎ 01590 642344
Built by Henry VIII to guard against French and Spanish attack, Hurst Castle was the pride of England's coastal defences. Crouched low and menacing on its shingle spit, the castle has a fascinating history, including its involvement with smuggling in the 17th and 18th centuries. It was also garrisoned during both World Wars.
Open Apr-Jun & Sep-Oct, 10-5.30 (last admission 4.30) Jul-Aug, daily 10-6 (last admission 5.15pm).
£2 (ch £1, concessions £1.50).
☕ ✵ *(in certain areas)* ♿

LIPHOOK ▰▰▰▰▰
Bohunt Manor
GU30 7DL (on A3)
☎ 01428 722208
Bohunt includes woodland gardens with a lakeside walk, a water garden, roses and herbaceous borders, and a collection of ornamental ducks and geese. Several unusual trees and shrubs include a handkerchief tree and a Judas tree. The property has been given to the Worldwide Fund for Nature.
Open all year, daily.
£1.50 (ch free, pen £1).
🅿 ♿ *(flat access around lake) ✵*

Hollycombe Steam Collection
Iron Hill, Midhurst Rd GU30 7LP (1.5m SE on unclass rd)
☎ 01428 724900
This all-encompassing collection of steam-driven equipment includes a Bioscope showing old films, fairground organs, steam-driven roundabouts, big wheel, steam yacht, razzle dazzle, a steam farm and paddle steamer engine. There are demonstrations of threshing and steam rolling, and traction engine rides. Three steam-hauled trains run through a woodland setting with spectacular views of the South Downs. Please telephone for details of special events.
Open Good Friday, BH & Sun until 11 Oct, daily 20-24 Jul & 16-31 Aug
£5.50 (ch & pen £4.50). Saver ticket (2 adults & 2 ch) £17. Party 15+.
🅿 ☕ ♿ *shop ✵ (guide dogs on request)*
Cards: ▨ ▦ ▨ ▨

LYMINGTON ▰▰▰▰▰
Braxton Gardens
Braxton Courtyard, Lymore Ln SO41 0TX (leave A337 at Everton onto B3058 then turn left into Lymore Ln, Braxton Courtyard on left)
☎ 01590 642008

Beautiful gardens set around attractive Victorian farm buildings. A courtyard with raised lily pool leads into a walled garden which during the summer overflows with aromatic plants. Above the shop in a converted granary is the Tennyson Room, which is available for private hire. There are excellent walks in the surrounding countryside, coarse fishing during the season, and a variety of events take place throughout the year, including Spring, Autumn, and Goose Fayres. Ring for details.
Open daily,, 15 Mar-Oct 9-5, 10-5 wknds. Shorter opening hours in winter, please telephone for details.
Free, voluntary donations to National Gardens Scheme.
🅿 ♿ *shop ✵ (ex guide dogs)*
Cards: ▨ ▦ ▨ ▨

LYNDHURST ▰▰▰▰▰
New Forest Museum & Visitor Centre
Main Car Park, High St SO43 7NY
☎ 01703 283914 Fax 01703 284236
The story of the New Forest, including its history, traditions, character and wildlife, told through an audio-visual show and exhibition displays. The show features life-size models of Forest characters, and the famous New Forest embroidery.
Open all year, daily from 10am (Closed 25 Dec)
£2.50 (ch £1.50, pen £2). Family ticket £6.50.
🅿 ♿ *toilets for disabled shop*
Cards: ▨ ▦

MARWELL ▰▰▰▰▰
Marwell Zoological Park
Colden Common SO21 1JH (on B2177)
☎ 01962 777406 & 777407
Fax 01962 777511
Devoted to the conservation and breeding of rare wild animals, Marwell has a worldwide reputation. The animals are housed in spacious enclosures or can be seen grazing in paddocks, and there is an enclosure where animals can be approached and stroked by children. Covering 100 acres of parkland, the collection includes over 1000 animals, and some of the species here no longer exist in the wild. New animals are being added constantly. There is also a gift shop and many attractions for younger children, including a children's farmyard, Tropical World, Penguin World and road trains. Numerous events are held throughout the year, including a Christmas 'Winter Wonderland'.
Open all year, daily (ex 25 Dec), 10-6 (or dusk). Last admission 4.30pm or 1 hour before dusk (whichever is earliest).
❋ *£7 (ch 3-14 £5.50, pen £6.50). Cars entering zoo circuit £7. Free to orange badge holders. Party 20+.*
🅿 ☕ ✗ *licensed ♿ (special tours for visually impaired by arrangement) toilets for disabled shop ✵ (incl guide dogs)*
Cards: ▨ ▦ ▨ ◐ ▨ ▨

MIDDLE WALLOP
Museum of Army Flying
SO20 8DY (on A343, between Andover & Salisbury)
☎01980 674421 Fax 01264 781694
This award-winning museum's exhibits include Cody's Kite, World War I aircraft, military Austers of World War II and the largest collection of gliders in Europe. Photographs and dioramas tell the story of army aviation from the 19th century to the present day. Rotary and fixed wing aircraft operate during the week. There is a restaurant with a viewing gallery over the airfield. Special Events include Open Day (26 May), 'Music in the Air' (25 July), Wallop Challenge (27 July), and Festival of Free Flight (2,3 August). Please telephone for details.
Open all year, daily 10-4.30. Closed week prior to Xmas. Evening visits by special arrangement.
🅿 ✕ *licensed* & *(lifts to upper levels) toilets for disabled shop* ✿ *(ex in grounds)*
Details not confirmed for 1998
Cards: ▨ ▨ ▨ ▨

MINSTEAD
Furzey Gardens
SO43 7GL (1m S of junct A31/M3 Cadnam off A31 or A337 near Lyndhurst)
☎01703 812464 & 812297 Fax 01703 812297
The cottage which stands in Furzey Gardens dates from 1560 and with the gallery provides a charming venue for refreshments and displays of local arts and crafts. The eight acres of peaceful glades which surround the cottage include winter and summer heathers, rare flowering trees and shrubs and a mass of spring bulbs which produce a wonderful display after the winter months. There is a lake and adjacent nursery, which is run by the Minstead Training Project for Young People with Learning Disabilities, selling a wide range of produce at very reasonable prices.
Open daily 10-5 (or dusk if earlier). (Closed Xmas).
Gardens, cottage & gallery £3 (ch & disabled £1.50, student & pen £2.50). Nov-Feb reduced admission charge. Party 10+.
🅿 & *(gardens accessible for wheelchair visitors with assistance) shop garden centre* ✿

MOTTISFONT
Mottisfont Abbey Garden
SO51 0LP (4.5m NW Romsey, on the A3057)
☎01794 340757 Fax 01794 341492
Set picturesquely by the River Test, Mottisfont Abbey is an 18th-century house adapted from a 12th-century priory. The north front shows its medieval church origins quite clearly, and the monks' 'cellarium' is virtually complete. The garden has splendid old trees and a walled garden planted with the national collection of old-fashioned

roses. The estate includes Mottisfont village and surrounding farmland and woods. Details for open air events in summer can be obtained by ringing the Regional Box Office 01372 451596.
Open: Garden & Grounds 28 Mar-28 Oct, daily ex Thurs & Fri 12-6 (or dusk if earlier). Rose season 13-28 June daily 12-8.30. Whistler Room & Cellarium same days as garden 1-5. Derek Hill picture collection Sun & Mon 1-5.
£4,(ch £2) £5 when roses are at their best.
🅿 ✕ *licensed* & *(Braille guide, wheelchair available, volunteer driven buggy) toilets for disabled shop garden centre* ✿ ✿

NETLEY
Netley Abbey
(4m SE of Southampton, facing Southampton Water)
☎01703 453076
A romantic ruin, set among green lawns and trees, this was a 13th-century Cistercian abbey founded by Peter des Roches, tutor to Henry III. During the Dissolution part of the early English-style abbey was converted into a house; all that remains is an impressive shell. Nearby is the 19th-century Gothic-style Netley Castle.
Open Apr-Sep, daily, 10-6; Oct-Mar, daily, 10-4.
Free.
🅿 & ✿ ✿

NEW MILTON
Sammy Miller Motorcycle Museum
Bashley Cross Rd BH25 5SZ
☎01425 620777 Fax 01425 619696
This museum has machines dating back to 1900 and is accepted as the world's most interesting Motor Cycle Museum with many machines that are the only surviving ones in the world. The Racing collection is of exceptional interest with the opportunity to see these wonderful World Record Breaking Bikes and their history, including the first bike to lap a Grand Prix Course at over 100 miles per hour, the 4 cylinder supercharged 500cc AJS. There are also DKW, NSU, Motoguzzi MV, Norton, Rudge, Velocette, Sunbeam etc, and of course the three-wheel Morgan.
Open all year, daily 10-4.30.
🅿 ✿ & *toilets for disabled shop* ✿
Details not confirmed for 1998
Cards: ▨ ▨

OLD BASING
Basing House
Redbridge Ln RG24 7HB (signed from Basingstoke Ring Road)
☎01256 467294 Fax 01256 326283
A two-year siege culminated in 1645 with the destruction of the largest house of Tudor England. Built on the site of a Norman castle in 1530, the ruins of Basing House, including a 300ft long tunnel, are a fascinating study. There is a re-creation of a garden of 1600 and exhibitions showing the history of the house. A fine 16th-century tithe barn stands nearby.

The site of Porchester Castle was first fortified by the Romans. The Great Tower, built by Robert Assheton in 1367, is still an impressive sight.

Open Apr-Sep, Wed-Sun & BH 2-6.
£1.50 (ch & pen 70p). Registered disabled free.
🅿 & *(disabled parking by prior arrangement) toilets for disabled shop*

OWER
Paultons Park
SO51 6AL (exit junc 2 M27, near junc A31 & A36)
☎01703 814455 (rec info) & 814442 Fax 01703 813025
Paultons Park offers a great day out for all the family with over forty different attractions included in the admission price. Many fun activities include Rio Grande Railway, bumper boats, 6-lane astroglide, and exciting Runaway Train. Attractions for younger children include Kid's Kingdom, Spidernet, pet's corner, rabbit ride, pirate ship, flying saucer and the Magic Forest where nursery rhymes come to life. Glimpse the past in the Village Life Museum and Romany Experience. In a beautiful parkland setting with extensive 'Capability' Brown gardens landscaped with ponds and aviaries for exotic birds; lake and hedge maze. Recent additions are Tiny Tots Town for the under 6 year olds, the Wonderful World of Wind in the Willows,(an animated attraction) and a Family Teacup Ride. Christmas attraction opens end of November.
Open 21 Mar-1 Nov, daily 10-6.30. Earlier closing spring & autumn. Also open some dates in Nov & Dec.
❄*Admission fee payable. Range of Family Supersavers.*
🅿 ✿ ✕ *licensed* & *(wheelchair hire - some rides unsuitable) toilets for disabled shop* ✿
Cards: ▨ ▨ ▨ ▨ ▨ ▨

PETERSFIELD
Bear Museum
38 Dragon St GU31 4JJ (100yds from bottom of the High Street, signed)
☎01730 265108
This was the world's first Teddy Bear Museum, featured in the 'Ultimate Teddy Bear Book'. Children will love the museum because they are allowed to cuddle and play with some of the

exhibits. A variety of bears are displayed in the Victorian-style nursery while downstairs is the 'Teddy Bear's Picnic' where children are encouraged to sing along to the famous song and join in the fun of the large picnic scene. There is a shop selling high-quality limited editions.
Open Tue-Sat 10-5.
Free.
🅿 *shop* ✿
Cards: ▨ ▨ ▨ ▨ ▨ ▨

PORTCHESTER
Portchester Castle
PO16 9QW (off A27)
☎01705 378291
Evidence of the 3rd-century Roman fort can still be seen on this nine-acre site. A church built in 1133 still stands, showing its fine west front and carved font. Robert Assheton built the great tower in 1367, and buildings within the inner courtyard were converted to a palace by Richard II, and the remains of the kitchen, hall and great chamber are still apparent. This was the palace from which Henry V embarked for Agincourt, and Henry VIII stayed here with Anne Boleyn. In later times, although falling into disrepair, the castle was home to prisoners from the Napoleonic Wars.
Open all year, Apr-Oct, daily 10-6 (or dusk if earlier); Nov-Mar, daily 10-4. Closed 24-26 Dec & 1 Jan.
£2.50 (ch £1.30, concessions £1.90).
🅿 & *shop* ✿ *(in certain areas)* ✿

➤

of the great ships that once sailed from the port - HMS Victory, Mary Rose and HMS Warrior.
Portsmouth played a leading role in the World War II D-Day landings which are commemorated in the D-Day Museum at Southsea. Southsea and Portsmouth run into one, Portsmouth being home to the Navy and Southsea being a more traditional seaside town with a promenade, a fair, a leisure centre and a popular aquarium. Southsea also has a castle which formed part of Henry VIII's coastal defences.

Charles Dickens' Birthplace Museum
393 Old Commercial Rd PO1 4QL
☎01705 827261 Fax 01705 875276
Built in 1805, this is the birthplace and early home of the famous novelist. Now restored and furnished to illustrate the middle-class taste of the early 19th century, the museum displays items pertaining to Dickens' work, portraits of the family, and the couch on which he died. There are Dickens readings at 3pm on the first Sunday of each month, also at 11am during the Christmas opening period.
Open Mar-Oct, daily 10-5.30 (last admission 5pm). Also 30 Nov-20 Dec 10-4.30 (last admission 4pm).
£2 (ch & student £1.20, accompanied ch 13 free, pen £1.50p). Family ticket £5.20.
P (150mtrs) shop ✿
Cards: ▨ ▤

City Museum
Museum Rd PO1 2LJ (M27/M275 into Portsmouth, follow museum symbol on signposts)
☎01705 827261 Fax 01705 875276
Dedicated to local history and decorative and fine art. 'The Story of Portsmouth' displays room settings showing life in Portsmouth from the 17th century to the 1950s using modern audio-visual techniques. Newly added is the 'Portsmouth at Play' exhibition showing all aspects of leisure pursuits from the

Victorian period to the 1970's. The museum has a decorative and fine art gallery and temporary exhibition gallery.
Open all year, daily 10-5.30. Last admission 30 mins before closing. Closed 24-26 Dec and Record Office closed on public holidays.
Free.
P ♥ & (induction loops lift & wheelchair available) toilets for disabled shop ✿
Cards: ▨ ▤ ▨ ⑤

D-Day Museum & Overlord Embroidery
Clarence Esplanade PO5 3NT
(M27/M275 into Portsmouth follow D Day Museum signposts)
☎01705 827261 Fax 01705 875276
Portsmouth's D-Day Museum tells the dramatic story of the Allied landings in Normandy in 1944. The centrepiece is the magnificent 'Overlord Embroidery', 80 metres long with 34 individual panels. Experience the world's largest ever seaborne invasion and step back in time to scenes of wartime Britain. Military equipment, vehicles, genuine landing craft and personal memories complete this special story.
Open all year, Apr-Oct daily 10am-5.30pm. Nov-Mar Mon pm only 1-5pm. Tue-Sun 10am-5pm. Closed 24-26 Dec. Last admission 1 hour before closing.
£4.75 (ch £2.85, pen £3.60). Family ticket £12.35.
P (charged) ♥ & (induction loops sound aids for blind wheelchairs available) toilets for disabled shop ✿
Cards: ▨ ▤ ⑤

Eastney Beam Engine House
Henderson Rd, Eastney PO4 4QL
☎01705 827261 Fax 01705 875276
The engine house contains a pair of James Watt beam engines and reciprocal pumps built in 1887 and now restored to their original condition. One of the engines is steamed when the museum is open. Other marine engines, most in running order also in steam.
Open all year, last (whole) weekend of every month 1-5 (last admission 4.30pm).
£2 (ch & student £1.20, accompanied ch 13 free & pen £1.50). Family ticket £5.20.
P (adjacent or 300m) ✿

Now at Portsmouth's Naval Base, the flagship of Nelson's fleet at thee Battle of Trafalgar, HMS *Victory* is an outstanding example of naval restoration.

HMS Victory
HM Naval Base PO1 3PZ
☎01705 819604
Fax 01705 819604
Still in commission and manned by regular serving officers and men, Lord Nelson's famous flagship at the Battle of Trafalgar is, because of her age and historic significance, the world's most outstanding example of maritime restoration. A tour around her decks gives some idea of the sailors' way of life in Nelson's day, and visitors can see the spot where the Admiral received his fatal wound, and the surgery below decks where he eventually died.
Open Mar-Oct, daily 10-4.50; Nov-Feb, daily 10.30-3.50. (Closed 25 Dec).
P (charged) & (lower gun deck) toilets for disabled shop ✿
Details not confirmed for 1998
Cards: ▨ ▤ ▤ ⓞ ▨ ▨ ⑤

HMS Warrior 1860
Victory Gate, HM Naval Base PO1 3QX
☎01705 291379
Fax 01705 821283
Originally launched in 1860, *HMS Warrior* was the world's first iron-hulled armoured warship. Restored, with painstaking accuracy over a period of eight years in Hartlepool, she is now a permanent feature within Portsmouth Historic Dockyard. Visitors can wander at leisure throughout the four vast decks, showing the rich furnishings and excellent craftmanship. Everything except the sheer number of crew has been recreated. *HMS Warrior* is the only ship which spans the eras of wood, iron, sail and steam. Special Victorian Navy Days take place July 18-19. Please telephone for details.
Open all year, Mar-Oct 10-5.30; Nov-Feb 10-5. (Last admission 1 hr before closing). Closed 24-26 Dec.
✳£5.15 (ch £3.55 & pen £4.55). Family ticket £23.50.
P (200 yds) ♥ ✗ & (stairlift to main gun deck) toilets for disabled shop ✿

The Mary Rose Museum
HM Naval Base PO1 3LX (enter Portsmouth via M275 & follow signs for Portsmouth Historic Ships)
☎01705 750521 Fax 01705 870588
The spectacular raising of the *Mary Rose* in 1982 is remembered by millions. Remarkably preserved in the Solent silts for 437 years, Henry VIII's warship was a Tudor time-capsule, complete with the everyday possessions, clothing, food, tools and weapons of her 700 men. One of Britain's major tourist attractions, the *Mary Rose* provides a fascinating family day out. In her special dry-dock workshop in Portsmouth's historic dockyard, the great oak hull is being conserved.
In the Mary Rose Exhibition a twelve minute audio-visual presentation on the discovery, raising and conservation of the ship highlights the enormous endeavour which has gone into the world's most ambitious underwater archaeological project. The visitor will then enjoy all the more the fascinating exhibition of the treasures from the *Mary Rose*: a themed display of many of the 20,000 artefacts recovered, including longbows, cannon, gaming boards, clothing, combs, pewterware, lanterns, a shaving bowl - even the contents of the barber-surgeon's chest, with syringes and jars of ointment. Special evening openings can be arranged for pre-booked groups. Please telephone for details of special events.
Open all year, daily from 10am. (Closed 24 & 25 Dec).
✳£5.50 (ch & students £4, pen £4.75). All-in ticket for all ships on site £11 (ch & students £8, pen £9.50). Family ticket £26.
P (charged) ✗ licensed & (hands-on exhibits & audio guide for visually impaired) toilets for disabled shop ✿ (ex guide dogs)
Cards: ▨ ▤ ▤ ▨ ⑤

Natural History Museum & Butterfly House
Cumberland House, Eastern Pde PO1 3JN
☎01705 827261 Fax 01705 875276
The Natural History Museum contains wildlife dioramas and geology of the Portsmouth area, it has a full size reconstruction of an Iguanadon and other fossil remains. A riverbank scene with fresh water aquarium, Ice Age displays, woodland life and birds of Farlington Marshes can be seen. During the summer there are British and European butterflies flying free in the Butterfly House.
Open daily, Apr-Oct 10-5.30, Nov-Mar 10-4.30. Last admission 30 mins before closing. (Closed 24-26 Dec).
£2 (ch £1.40, accompanied ch 13 free & pen £1.60). Family ticket £5.40; Oct-Mar £1.50 (ch 90p & pen £1.10) Family ticket £3.90
P (200mtrs) shop ✿
Cards: ▨ ▤

The Royal Marines Museum
PO4 9PX (signposted from seafront)
☎01705 819385 Fax 01705 838420
The Royal Marines Museum tells the 330 year story of Britain's Sea Soldiers through dramatic displays, exciting films and videos, state of the art interactives and even a live snake and scorpion! But the museum is not just about war stories. Sumptuous rooms filled with priceless silver, sweeping stairways with splendid portraits and halls adorned with a world famous medal collection ensure there's something of interest to everyone. Ring for details of special events.
Open all year, Spring BH-Aug daily 10-5; Sep-May daily 10-4.30. (Closed 3 days Xmas)
£3.75 (ch £2, pen £2.75) Family ticket £10.
P ♥ ✗ licensed & (access for disabled and toilets from Etr 97) toilets for disabled shop ✿ (ex grounds)

Royal Naval Museum
HM Naval Base PO1 3NH (M275 into Portsmouth then follow signs)
☎01705 727562
Fax 01705 727575
This is the only museum exclusively devoted to the overall history of the Navy. A panorama of Trafalgar, with sound-effects, is complemented by relics of Lord Nelson, his officers and men. Uniforms, medals, figureheads and model ships are on show, and there is a wide range of displays, such as 'The Rise of the Royal Navy', 'Sailing Navy', 'The Victorian Navy', 'The Navy in the 20th Century', and to bring the picture right up to date, 'The Modern Navy'. The Pacific Fleet Exhibition commemorates the end of the Second World War in the Pacific. Please telephone for details of special events.
Open all year, daily 10-5. (Closed 25-26 Dec).
✳£3 (ch £2 & pen £2.50). Combined ticket available with HMS Victory.
P (200yds) ♥ & (exhibit for sight impaired groups by prior arrangement) toilets for disabled shop ✿ (ex small dogs if carried)

Southsea Castle
Clarence Esp PO5 3PA
☎01705 827261
Fax 01705 875276
Part of Henry VIII's national coastal defences, this fort was built in 1545 and contains displays illustrating. Portsmouth's development as a military fortress, including an audio-visual show and reconstructed scenes of 'Life in the Castle', underground tunnels, and panoramic views of the Solent and Isle of Wight. Home of Fort Cumberland Guard. Please telephone for details of special events, including Civil War, Tudor, and 19th Century Weekends.
Open all year, Apr-Oct, daily 10-5.30. Nov-Mar, Sat & Sun 10-4.30, and school holidays. (Closed 24-26 Dec).

Given to the first Duke of Wellington by the nation after the Battle of Waterloo, Stratfield Saye House is still home to his descendants.

£2 (ch & students £1.20, ch accompanied 13 free, pen £1.50). Family ticket £5.20.
P (charged) ⬛ & (wheelchair available) shop ⬛
Cards: ▨ ▨

Spitbank Fort
☎ 01329 664286 & 0831 608383
This massive granite and iron fortress was built in the 1860s as part of the coastal defences against the French. Standing one mile out to sea, it provides magnificent views across the Solent. The interior is a maze of passages connecting over 50 rooms on two levels. A Victorian cooking range is still in working order, as are the forge and a 402ft-deep well from which fresh water is obtained.
Open May-Sep, Tue-Sun. (Weather permitting).
⬤£5.75 (ch £4) includes ferry charge. Boat ride takes approx 20 mins, visitors should allow 2hr to view. Ferries depart HM Naval Base Portsmouth.
P ⬛

RINGWOOD
Moors Valley Country Park
Horton Rd, Ashley Heath BH24 2ET
(1.5m from Ashley Heath roundabout on A31 near Three Legged Cross)
☎ 01425 470721 Fax 01425 471656
With more than 700,000 visitors a year this is one of the most popular places to visit in the south of England. 15,00 acres of forest, woodland, heathland, lakes, river and meadows provide a home for a wide variety of plants and animals. There is a Visitor Centre, Play Area and Adventure Playground, picnic area, Moors Valley Railway, and Tree Top Trail.
Open all year (ex 25 Dec), 8-dusk. Visitor centre open 9.30-4.30 (later in summer). Prices under review - ring for details.
P (charged) ⬛ & (visitor centre & most of park accessible) toilets for disabled shop ⬛ (ex in park on lead)

ROCKBOURNE
Roman Villa
SP6 3PG (from Salisbury, take A354 to Blandford, follow signs from the side of Coombe Bissett.)
☎ 01725 518541
Discovered in 1942, about a mile outside the village of Rockbourne, the site features the remains of a 40 room Roman villa and is the largest in the area. Displays include mosaics and a very rare hypocaust system. The modern on-site museum displays the many artifacts found on the site during excavations. Special events for 1998 include: Roman Re-enactments (23-25 May & 29-31 August), Saxon/Viking re-enactments (8-9 August), and Heritage Days in September. Ring for further details.
Open Apr-Oct, Mon-Fri noon-5.30, Sat, Sun & BH 10.30-5.30; Jul & Aug daily 10.30-5.30.

⬤£2 (concessions £1).
P ⬛ & (ramps in/out of museum) toilets for disabled shop ⬛

ROMSEY
Broadlands
SO51 9ZD (main entrance on A31 Romsey by-pass)
☎ 01794 517888
Fax 01794 518884
Famous as the home of the late Lord Mountbatten, Broadlands is now lived in by his grandson Lord Romsey. An elegant Palladian mansion in a beautiful landscaped setting on the banks of the River Test, Broadlands was also the country residence of Lord Palmerston, the great Victorian statesman. Visitors may view the house with its fine furniture and pictures and mementoes of the famous, enjoy the superb views from the riverside lawns or relive Lord Mountbatten's life and times in the Mountbatten Exhibition and spectacular Mountbatten audio-visual presentation. Special events: 24-25 May - Country Fair. 11 July - BBC Big Band Concert. 14-15 July - Shakespeare Production. 17 July - Mozart with Fireworks. 25-26 Hampshire Flower Show. 7-9 August - Summer Craft Show. 12 September - Romsey Show. 6 November - Annual Broadlands Charity Firework Display. 14-15 November - Xmas Craft Show. Telephone for details.
Open daily, 13 Jun-6 Sep, 12-5.30. Last admission 4pm.
£5 (ch 12-16 £3.50, pen/stu/disabled £4.25). Party15+.
P ⬛ & toilets for disabled shop ⬛
Cards: ▨ ▨ ▨

SELBORNE
Gilbert White's House & The Oates Museum
The Wakes, High St GU34 3JH (on B3006)
☎ 01420 511275
Charming 18th-century house, home of famous naturalist, the Rev. Gilbert White, author of The Natural History and Antiquities of Selborne. Visitors can see furnished rooms, the original manuscript and wander round the glorious garden, which is being restored to its 18th century form. There are also exhibitions on two famous members of the Oates family, Captain Lawrence Oates, who accompanied Scott to the South Pole and Frank Oates, a Victorian explorer amd naturalist in South America and Africa. Special events include, Unusual Plants Fair (21,22 June); Jazz in June (21 June); Mulled Wine Day (23 November). Please telephone for details.
Open mid Mar-Xmas, daily 11-5, wknds only in winter. By appointment all year and evenings in summer.
P (200yds) ⬛ & shop ⬛
Details not confirmed for 1998
Cards: ▨ ▨ ▨ ▨ ▨

SHERBORNE ST JOHN
The Vyne
RG26 5DX (4m N of Basingstoke, off A340)
☎ 01256 881337 Fax 01256 881720
The Vyne was built at the beginning of the 16th century by William Sandys and later came into the Chute family, who owned the property until 1956 when it was bequeathed to the National Trust. Much of the exterior of the house is still 16th century but over the centuries there have been several major alterations, including the classical portico which was the earliest to be added to an English country house. Inside, the chapel with its original 16th-century stained glass, and the Oak Gallery, are both of note. The Gallery has superb linenfold panelling. There is also an 18th-century tomb chamber and a Palladian staircase. The house is set in a pleasant garden with a lake. Special events are held in the grounds; please telephone Regional Box Office 01372 451596 for details.
Open House 3 Jun-end Oct daily except Mon & Tue 1.30-5.30. Grounds 25 Mar-end Oct daily except Mon & Tue 12.30-5.30. Also open Good Fri & BH Mon. House & Grounds £4.50. Family ticket £11.25.Grounds only £2.50 (ch £1.25).
P ⬛ ✕ licensed & (Braille guide) shop ⬛ ⬛

SILCHESTER
Calleva Museum
Bramley Rd RG7 2LU
The museum deals with the Roman town of Calleva Atrebatum, the remains of which can be visited. Most of the 1.5 mile long city wall still stands, and is an impressive sight, and nearby are the remains of a large amphitheatre. Little else remains. Objects from the site, photos, maps and other material give a brief account of Calleva. Guides to the site are on sale at the Calleva Arms in the village. July & August should see an archaeological dig in progress. (See also Reading Museum).
Open daily 9am-sunset.
Free.
P

SOUTHAMPTON
God's House Tower
Winkle St SO1 1LX
☎ 01703 635904 & 832768
Fax 01703 339601
An early fortified building, dating from the 1400s and taking its name from the nearby medieval hospital, it now houses the city's Museum of Archaeology with exhibits on the Roman, Saxon and medieval towns of Southampton. There is also an exhibition of Egyptian objects collected in the Nineteenth Century.
Open Tue-Fri 10-12 & 1-5; Sat 10-12 & 1-4; Sun 2-5(closed BH's)
P (400 yds) shop ⬛
Details not confirmed for 1998

Southampton City Art Gallery
North Guild, Civic Centre, Commercial Rd SO14 7LP
☎ 01703 632601 Fax 01703 832153
This is the largest gallery in the south of England, with the finest collection of contemporary art in the country outside London. Housed in the beautifully refurbished 1930s NorthGuild complex, varied displays of landscapes, portrait paintings or recent British art are always available, as well as a special display, selected and hung by members of the public. Exhibitions for 1998 include: Chris Ofili - 9 Apr-31 May. Pre-Raphaelite Women Artists - 5 June-2 August.
Open all year, Tue, Wed & Fri 10-5, Thu 10-7, Sat 10-5, Sun 1-4. (Closed 25-27 & 31 Dec).
Free.
P (250yds) ⬛ & toilets for disabled shop ⬛

Southampton Hall of Aviation
Albert Rd South SO1 1FR
☎ 01703 635830
The Hall of Aviation was inspired by the development of the famous Spitfire aeroplane at the nearby Supermarine Aviation Works at Woolston. The Spitfire evolved from aircraft built for the Schneider Trophy air races, which the company won in 1931 with the Supermarine 6B. There is a Supermarine S6A on display as well as one of the last Spitfires produced, the Mark 24, and other aircraft of local interest.
The museum is built around a huge Sandringham flying-boat which visitors can board. It was operated out of Southampton Docks by Imperial Airways (BOAC) to all parts of the British Empire. There are also exhibits on aviation production and engineering in the south of England, 14 aircraft are on display here. ➤

Built at the end of the 15th century, Southampton's Tudor House Museum has a fine Hall and a fascinating Tudor garden.

Open all year, Tue-Sat 10-5, Sun 12-5. Also BH Mon & School Holidays. (Closed Xmas).
P *(150 yds)* & *(lift to all levels) toilets for disabled shop*
Details not confirmed for 1998

Southampton Maritime Museum
The Wool House, Town Quay SO1 1LX
☎01703 223941 & 635904
Fax 01703 339601
The Wool House was built in the 14th century. It was a warehouse for wool and has buttressed stone walls and chestnut roof timbering. It currently houses an interesting maritime museum with models and displays telling the history of the Victorian and modern port of Southampton. There are also exhibitions on the White Star Line, Titanic, and Queen Mary, Queen of the Seas. Late 1997 saw the launch of a new interactive Science room.
Open all year, Tue-Fri 10-12 & 1-5, Sat 10-12 & 1-4, Sun 2-5. (Closed BHs).
P *(400 yds) (metered parking adjacent)* & *shop*
Details not confirmed for 1998

Tudor House Museum
St Michael's Square SO1 0AD
☎01703 332513 & 635904
Fax 01703 339601
This fine half-timbered house, built at the end of the 15th century and therefore older than its name suggests, is now a museum. Exhibitions include a Tudor Hall and displays on Georgian and Victorian social and domestic life in Southampton as well as temporary exhibitions. The unique Tudor garden with knot garden, fountain and 16th-century herbs and flowers is not to be missed.
Continuing restoration and refurbishment work but open to the public.
P *(metered & disabled parking opposite)* & *(tape guide to garden) toilets for disabled shop*
Details not confirmed for 1998

STRATFIELD SAYE
Stratfield Saye House
RG7 2BT (off A33 between Reading & Basingstoke)
☎01256 882882

The house was built in 1630 and given by the nation to the first Duke of Wellington in 1817, after his victory over Napoleon at the Battle of Waterloo. Stratfield Saye remains the home of the Duke of Wellington and contains a unique collection of paintings, prints, and furniture as well as many mementoes of the Ist Duke, including his magnificent funeral carriage which weighs 18 tons and stands 17ft high. The Wellington Exhibition shows the life and times of the great statesman soldier, and in the grounds is the grave of Copenhagen, the Iron Duke's horse, who died in 1836. Please telephone for details of special events.
Open Sat & Sun in May and BH Mon; Daily ex Fri Jun-Aug; Sat & Sun in Sep. Groups by prior booking during week.
P ✗ *licensed* & *toilets for disabled shop* *(ex in grounds)*
Details not confirmed for 1998

Wellington Country Park & National Dairy Museum
RG7 1SP
☎0118 932 6444 Fax 0118 932 6445
(For full entry see Riseley, Berkshire)

TITCHFIELD
Titchfield Abbey
(half a mile N off A27)
☎01705 527667
Also known as 'Palace House', this used to be the seat of the Earl of Southampton. The abbey was founded in 1232 and closed during the Dissolution, allowing the Earl to build a fine Tudor mansion on the site in 1538. He incorporated the nave of the 13th-century church and the gatehouse into his new home.
Open Apr-Sep, daily, 10-6; Oct-Mar, daily, 10-4.
Free.
P & ♿ ⚏

TOTTON
Eling Tide Mill
Eling Toll Bridge SO40 9HF (2m W, signposted from A35)
☎01703 869575
Eling is the only remaining mill regularly

using tidal energy to grind wheat into flour. There has been a mill on this site for at least 900 years - a predecessor appeared in the Domesday Book. The present mill was extensively restored and reopened in 1980.
It has two sets of millstones, each separately driven, but only one set has been restored to working condition. The waterwheels were cast in iron and installed by Armfields of Ringwood at the beginning of the century. Flour ground at the mill is on sale.
Open all year, Wed-Sun, 10-4, also BH Mon in season.
P & *shop*
Details not confirmed for 1998

WEYHILL
The Hawk Conservancy
SP11 8DY (3m W of Andover, signposted from A303)
☎01264 772252
Fax 01264 773772
This is the largest centre in the south for birds of prey from all over the world including eagles, hawks, falcons, owls, vultures and kites. Exciting birds of prey demonstrations are held daily at noon, 2pm, and 3.30pm, including the 'Valley of the Eagles' at 2pm. Different birds are flown at these times and visitors may have the opportunity to hold a bird and adults can fly a Harris hawk. Wild heron and raptor feed at 4.30pm in Reg's meadow. Other facilities include: Toddlers play area, butterfly garden and study centre.
Open Mar-last Sun in Oct, daily from 10.30 (last admission 4pm).
✱*£5.50 (ch £3, pen £5).*
P ⚏ & *(Wheelchair area in flying grounds) toilets for disabled shop*
Cards: 🌑 ▨ ▭

WINCHESTER
Winchester was the royal capital of Saxon Wessex and of England until the late 12th century. To medieval and Tudor monarchs Winchester was traditionally the Camelot of King Arthur from whom they claimed descent. William the Conqueror built a great castle at Winchester but all that remains is the Great Hall. The castle was destroyed during the Civil War but in the 1680s Charles II commissioned Christopher Wren to build a new palace. Sadly it was never completed and became an army barracks. Winchester is dominated by its massive cathedral (one of the longest in Europe) which was also begun just after the Norman conquest. Around the cathedral there are ancient streets with buildings from many ages and an attractive walk along the banks of the River Itchen. Jane Austen spent her last years here and here memorial stone is in the cathedral.

Great Hall of Winchester Castle
Castle Av SO23 8PJ
☎01962 846476
The only remaining portion of William the Conqueror's first castle, it was completed in 1235 and is a fine example of 13th-century architecture. Purbeck marble columns support the roof and on the west wall hangs the Round Table purported to belong to King Arthur. A small medieval garden known as Queen Eleanor's Garden, leads off the Hall.
Open all year, Mar-Oct daily 10-5; Nov-Feb, daily 10-5, weekends 10-4. (Closed Good Fri & 25-26 Dec).
Donations welcome.
P *(200yds)* & *shop garden centre*
Cards: ▭▬

Guildhall Gallery
The Broadway SO23 9LJ
☎01962 848296 & 848289 Fax 01962 848299
Situated in the refurbished 19th-century Guildhall, the Gallery has a programme of changing contemporary exhibitions including fine art, paintings, prints, drawings, sculpture, ceramics, craft, and occasional displays of topographical works from the Winchester City Collection.
Open during exhibitions, Tue-Sat 10-5, Sun & Mon 2-5. (Closed Mon, Oct-Mar). Subject to alteration.
Free.
P *(100yds)* ⚏ ✗ *licensed* & *toilets for disabled shop*

Gurkha Museum
Peninsula Barracks, Romsey Rd SO23 8TS (off B3040)
☎01962 842832
Fax 01962 877597
This museum tells the fascinating story of the Gurkha's involvement with the British Army. Travel from Nepal to the North-West Frontier and beyond, with the help of life-sized dioramas, interactive exhibits and sound displays. Experience life in the Malayan jungle and the Falklands campaign. Special attractions are held at half term, Easter, summer and before Christmas. Telephone museum for details of special events.
Open all year, BH Mon, Tue-Sat 10-5. Telephone for opening times over Xmas. (Closed 25-26 Dec, 1 Jan and Tue following BH Mon)
£1.50 (pen 75p). Party 15+.
P & *(lift & stair lift) toilets for disabled shop*

Hospital of St Cross
SO23 9SD (1.5m S of city, on A3335)
☎01962 851375
Fax 01962 878221
The hospital was founded in 1132 for the benefit of 13 poor men and it is still functioning as an almshouse. Throughout the Middle Ages the hospital handed out the Dole - bread and beer - to travellers, and this is still done. The Church of St Cross (12th century); the Brethrens Hall and medieval kitchen, and the walled Master's Garden are all worthy of close inspection. It can be reached by footpath across the fields from Winchester, walking through beautiful watermeadows alongside the river.
Open all year, Apr-Oct, Mon-Sat 9.30-5; Nov-Mar 10.30-3.30. (Closed Sun, Good Fri & 25 Dec).
£2 (ch 50p, students & pen £1.25).
P *(200 yds)* ⚏ & *(A resident Brother can act as guide and assistant) toilets for disabled shop*

Royal Hampshire Regiment Museum & Memorial Gardens
Serle's House, Southgate St SO23 9EG
☎01962 863658
Fax 01962 888302
This fine, 18th-century, early Georgian house contains an excellent collection of militaria from the history of the Royal Hampshire Regiment. The gardens are a memorial to the Regimental dead.
Open all year, Mon-Fri 10-12.30 & 2-4; Apr-Oct wknds & BH noon-4.
Free.
P *(800mtrs)* & *shop*

Royal Hussars (PWO) Regimental Museum
Peninsula Barracks, Romsey Rd SO23 8TS
☎01962 828539
Fax 01962 828538
The Royal Hussars (Prince of Wales Own) were formed by the amalgamation of the 10th Royal Hussars (Prince of Wales Own) and the 11th Hussars (Prince Alberts Own) in 1969, both regiments having been raised at the time of the Jacobite Rebellion in 1715. Visitors to this museum will learn the story of the Royal Hussars (Prince of Wales Own) from its founding to the present day. The displays are laid out in chronological order

and the various themes are lavishly illustrated with paintings, prints, photographs and many artefacts, including, weapons, medals, uniforms and a collection of gold and silver. Another interesting exhibit is the cupboard in which a Private Fowler of the 11th Hussars spent three years and nine months whilst hiding from the Germans in World War II. The Royal Hussars (Prince of Wales Own) were amalgamated with the 14th/20th King's Hussars on 1 December 1992. The Regiment is now known as 'The King's Royal Hussars'.

Open 5 Jan-18 Dec, Tue-Fri 10-4, Sat, Sun & BH's 12-4.

P **&** *toilets for disabled shop* 🌮
Details not confirmed for 1998

Winchester Cathedral

SO23 9LS (in city centre - follow city heritage signs)
☎ *01962 853137 & 866854*
Fax 01962 841519

This magnificent cathedral, the longest medieval church in Europe, was founded in 1079 on the site where Christian worship had already been offered for over 400 years. Among its treasures are the 12th-century illuminated Winchester Bible, the font, medieval wall paintings and pavement, six chantry chapels and Triforium Gallery Museum.

Open all year, daily 8.30-6.30. Access may be restricted during services. Recommended donations requested £2.50 (ch 50p, pen & students £2). Family £5.

P 💷 ✕ *licensed* **&** *(chair lift to east end of Cathedral, touch & hearing model) toilets for disabled shop* 🌮

Winchester City Mill

Bridge St SO23 8EJ (by the city bridge between King Alfred's statue & Chesil St)
☎ *01962 870057*
Fax 01962 870057

The City Mill was built over the fastflowing River Itchen in 1744. The mill has a delightful small island garden and an impressive millrace. The waterwheel was restored in 1995.

Open Apr-Oct, Wed-Sun & BH Mons 11-4.45; Mar wknds only. Last admission 15 mins before closing.

Free.

P (200 yds) shop 🌮 🦽
Cards: ▨ ▨ ▨ ▨ ▨

Winchester City Museum

The Square SO23 9ES
☎ *01962 848269 Fax 01962 848299*

Located on the edge of the cathedral precinct, the museum has a well-laid-out display relating to the archaeology and history of the city and central Hampshire. An interesting exhibit is the interior of a 19th-century chemist's shop, which used to be in the High Street.

Open all year, Mon-Sat 10-5, Sun 2-5 (Closed Mon Oct-Mar, Good Fri, Xmas & 1 Jan).

Free.

& *shop* 🌮

Winchester College

77 Kingsgate St SO23 9PE (Central Winchester, S of Cathedral Close)
☎ *01962 621217 Fax 01962 621218*

Founded and built by Bishop William of Wykeham in 1382, Winchester College is one of the oldest schools in England. The college has greatly expanded over the years but the original buildings remain intact. The chapel and, during school term, the cloisters and Fromond's Chantry are open to the public. Also open is the War Cloister, which is reached by South Africa Gate. Dedicated in 1924, it contains memorials to Wykehamists who died in World War I and all battles since then.

Guided tours Mar-Sep daily (ex Sun am) 11, 2 & 3.15. Booked tour (parties of 10+) all year.

£2.50 (pen & students 18 £2)

P (250 yards) (Most streets have permit parking) **&** *toilets for disabled shop* 🌮

HEREFORDSHIRE

ASHTON
Berrington Hall

Berrington HR6 0DW (3m N off A49)
☎ *01568 615721*
Fax 01568 613263

An elegant neo-classical house of the late 18th century, designed by Henry Holland and set in a park landscape by 'Capability' Brown. The formal exterior belies the delicate interior with beautifully decorated ceilings and fine furniture, including the Digby collection and a recently restored bedroom suite, nursery, Victorian laundry and pretty tiled Georgian dairy. The attractive garden has interesting plants and a recently planted apple orchard in the walled garden. Special events throughout the year include Easter Egg Hunt and Horse Trials planned for August, please telephone for details.

Open Apr & Oct-1 Nov Fri, Sat, Sun & BH (closed Good Fri) 1.30-5.30. (4.30pm in Oct). May-Jun & Sept, BH Mon, Wed-Sun 1.30-5.30. Jul-Aug, daily 1.30-5.30. Last admission 30mins before closing. Garden open from 12.30-6 (Oct 5.30pm). Park Walk open Jul-Oct, same times as house.

£4. Family ticket £10. Grounds only £1.80.

P ✕ *licensed* **&** *(wheelchairs, stairclimber, braille guides) toilets for disabled shop* 🌮 🦽
Cards: ▨

BROCKHAMPTON
Lower Brockhampton

WR6 5UH (2m E of Bromyard on A44)
☎ *01885 488099*

A late 14th-century moated manor house, with an attractive detached half-timbered 15th century gatehouse, a rare example of this type of structure, and the ruins of a 12th century chapel. It lies north of the A44 and is part of a larger National Trust property covering over 1700 acres of Herefordshire countryside with various walks including a Sculpture Trail. Special events for 1998 include: 27 June - Concert with Bromyard Windband, 18 July - Renaissance concert with the Arden consort, 1 August - 'Toad of Toad Hall' Troubador Theatre. Ring for details.

Open: Medieval hall, Parlour, Minstrel gallery, Information room, gatehouse & chapel 29 Mar-Sept, Wed-Sun & BH Mon 10-5 (closed Good Fri). Oct, Wed-Sun 10-4.

£2. Family ticket £5.

P **&** *(special parking for disabled)* 🌮 🦽

CROFT
Croft Castle

HR6 9PW (off B4362)
☎ *01568 780246*

Home of the Croft family since Domesday (with a break of 170 years from 1750); walls and towers date from the 14th and 15th centuries; the interior is mainly 18th century, when the fine Georgian-Gothic staircase and plasterwork ceilings were added. There is a splendid avenue of 350-year-old Spanish chestnuts, and an Iron Age Fort (Croft Ambrey) may be reached by footpath. (An uphill walk of approximately 40 minutes.) Special events for 1998 include: Shakespeare & Sheridan in the garden, Jazz concert, Morris & Scottish dancers, Apple Fair, Teddy Bear Fashion Show. ring for details.

Open Etr Sat & Sun. Apr Sat, Sun & BH Mon 1.30-4.30. Oct-1 Nov Sat & Sun 1.30-4.30. May-Sep, Wed-Sun & BH Mon 1.30-5.30. Last admission to house half hour before closing. Parkland open all year. Closed Good Fri.

House & grounds £3.30. Family ticket £8.30. Grounds only, £1.50 per car.

P *(charged)* **&** *(parking available, braille guide)* 🌮 *(ex in parkland)* 🦽

DINMORE
Dinmore Manor

HR4 8EE (off A49, signposted)
☎ *01432 830322 Fax 01432 830503*

From its spectacular hillside location, the manor enjoys outstanding views of the surrounding countryside. The cloisters, South Room, Roof Walk, Chapel, Music Room (Great Hall), and Grotto are all open to the public. The chapel, dating back to the 12th century, is in a unique setting next to the rock garden, pools, the collection of old acers, and the 1200-year-old yew tree. Among the many attractions here are the remarkable collection of 1930s stained glass, an 18th-century chamber organ, a Victorian aeolian pipe organ, and two medieval sundials.

Open all year, daily 10-5.30.

£3 (accompanied ch 14 free).

P **&** *shop (plant centre)* 🌮 *(ex guide dogs)*

GOODRICH
Goodrich Castle

HR9 6HY (5m S of Ross-on-Wye, off A40)
☎ *01600 890538*

Goodrich Castle towers majestically over an ancient crossing of the River Wye commanding beautiful views of the surrounding countryside. The castle was built here in medieval times and saw much action during the Civil War, when a locally made cannon called 'Roaring Meg' was used to bombard the Royalist garrison ending a long siege. The cannon can still be seen at Hereford Cathedral. Goodrich has huge towers, graceful arches, chapel and an exciting maze of rooms and passages to be explored. There is also a gloomy dungeon in the Norman keep - a chilling reminder of its violent history.

Open all year, Apr-Oct, daily 10-6 (or dusk if earlier in Oct); Nov-Mar 10-4. Closed 24-26 Dec & 1 Jan.

£2.95 (ch £1.50, concessions £2.20)

P 🌮 ⚑

HEREFORD
Churchill House Museum & Hatton Art Gallery

3 Venn's Ln HR1 1DE
☎ *01432 267409 Fax 01432 342492*

The museum is laid out in a Regency house with fine grounds, and has 18th- and early 19th-century rooms, displays of costume, and a gallery devoted to works by the local artist Brian Hatton.

Open all year, 2-5, Apr-Sep, Tue-Sun; Oct-Mar, Tue-Sat, inc BH Mons.

P **&** *(access guide & tape, braille guides & plans) shop* 🌮
Details not confirmed for 1998

Cider Museum & King Offa Distillery

21 Ryelands St, Whitecross Rd HR4 0LW (off A438 to Brecon)
☎ *01432 354207*

In the heart of Herefordshire at the Cider Museum discover the fascinating history of cider making. The museum was the first to obtain a licence from Customs and Excise to distill cider for over 200 years. Special events for 1998 include: 16-24 May - Museums Week, 30-31 May - Beekeeping Weekend, 23 August - Ida Bennet demonstrates the craft of corn dollies, 19-28 Sept - Whiteways: The Story of a Devon Cider Maker, 17-31 October - Apple Day Celebrations. Ring for details of these and many other special events.

Open all year, Apr-Oct, daily 10-5.30; Nov-Mar, Tue-Sun 11-3. Pre-booked groups at any time.

£2.20 (ch, pen & students £1.70). Party 15+.

P **&** *shop* 🌮

Hereford Cathedral

Broad St HR1 2NG (signed from city inner ring roads)
☎ *01432 359880 Fax 01432 355929*

The See of Hereford is one of the oldest in England, the first bishop having been appointed in 676. THe cathedral is mainly ➤

Norman with a 13th-century Lady Chapel.
It also contains the Diocesan Treasure
and the St Thomas Becket Reliquary. The
Cathedral Guides provide tours at 11am,
1pm and 3pm from Easter til 1st October
and pre-booked tours 9.30-5 Mon-Sat.
Hereford's two unique treasures are
exhibited together in the new museum
building at the West front. The Mappa
Mundi - drawn in 1289, and the famous
Chained Library - containing over 1400
chained books and 227 manuscripts
dating from the 8th century.
*Cathedral open daily for visitors 9.30-5;
Mappa Mundi & Chained Library
Exhibition Mon-Sat 10-4.15 (last
admission), Sun 12-3.15.* ·
✱*Mappa Mundi & Chained Library
Exhibition £4 (concessions £3). Family
£10. Party 10+.*
P ♥ ✗ & *(touch facility for blind &
partially sighted) shop* ✤
Cards: 🄰 ▦ ▨ ▨ 🄶

Old House
High Town HR1 2AA
☎ 01432 364598
Fax 01432 342492
This good example of a Jacobean house
was built in around 1621, and was once
in a row of similar houses. The hall,
kitchens, and a bedroom with a four-
poster bed can be seen along with a
number of wall paintings. There are also
occasional special events so please ring
for details.
*Open Tue-Fri 10-1 & 2-5.30. (Sat, Apr-Sep
10-1 & 2-5.30; Oct-Mar 10-1). Mon 10-1.
Also open BH Mons 10-1 & 2-5.15. (Sun,
May-Sep 10-4).*
& *shop* ✤
Details not confirmed for 1998

KINGTON
Hergest Croft Gardens
HR5 3EG (0.25m W off A44)
☎ 01544 230160
From spring bulbs to autumn colour, this
is a garden for all seasons. One of the
finest collections of trees and shrubs
surround the Edwardian house; an old
fashioned kitchen garden has spring and
summer borders; and Park Wood, a
hidden valley, has rhododendrons up to
30ft tall. Flower Fair: Monday May 4th, in
aid of the Hereford Cathedral Perpetual
Trust.
*Open 10 Apr-1 Nov daily, 1.30-6.30.
£2.75 (ch 15 free). Party 20+*
P ♥ & *toilets for disabled shop garden
centre*
Cards: 🄰

LEDBURY
Eastnor Castle
Eastnor HR8 1RL (1.5m E, on A438)
☎ 01531 633160 & 632302
Fax 01531 631776
A magnificent Georgian castle in a
fairytale setting with a deer park,
arboretum and lake. Inside are tapestries,
fine art and armour. The Italianate and
Gothic interiors have been restored to a
superb standard. There is a children's

adventure playground and delightful
nature trails and lakeside walks.
Homemade teas are available. 1998
special events include: 3-4 May - Country
craft festival. 17 May - Steam Fair. 30-31
May - Flower & garden show. 11-14 June
- Art fair. 17-21 August - Children's Fun
Week. 30-31 August - Living History
(Wars of the Roses). 3-4 October -
Christmas craft fair.
*Open Etr-end Sep Sun & Bh Mon, Jul &
Aug Sun-Fri 11-5 last admission 4.30pm.
Castle & grounds £4.50 (ch £2). Grounds
£2.50 (ch £1).*
P ♥ ✗ & *shop garden centre*
Cards: 🄰 ▨ ⊙

SWAINSHILL
The Weir Gardens
HR4 7QF (5m W of Hereford, on A438)
☎ 01684 850051
A delightful riverside garden which is at
its best in spring when there are lovely
displays of naturalised bulbs set in
woodland and grassland walks. Cliff
garden walks can be taken here, with
fine views of the River Wye and the
Welsh hills.
*Open 14 Feb-1 Nov, Wed-Sun 11-6. Also
open Good Frand BH Mon.
£1.80*
P ✤ ⇢ 🂡

HERTFORDSHIRE

AYOT ST LAWRENCE
Shaw's Corner
AL6 9BX (at SW end of village)
☎ 01438 820307
George Bernard Shaw lived here from
1906 until his death in 1950. He gave the
house to the National Trust in 1946, and
the contents are much as they were in
his time. Among other items to be seen
are his hats, including a soft homburg he
wore for 60 years, his exercise machine,
fountain pen, spectacles and several
pictures.
*Open Apr-1 Nov. Wed-Sun & BH Mon 1-
5. Last admission 4.30pm. (Closed Good
Fri)
£3.20. Family ticket £8.*
P & ✤ 🂡

BERKHAMSTED
Berkhamsted Castle
HP4 1HF
☎ 01536 402840
Roads and a railway have cut into the
castle site, but its huge banks and
ditches remain impressive. The original
motte-and-bailey was probably built by
William the Conqueror's half brother, and
there is a later stone keep. The castle
was owned by the Black Prince, and King
John of France was imprisoned here.
*Open all year daily 10-4.
Free.*
P & ⌗

HATFIELD
Hatfield House
AL9 5NQ (2m from jct 4 A1(M) on A1000,
7m from M25 jct 23)
☎ 01707 262823 Fax 01707 275719
Robert Cecil built the great Jacobean
mansion in 1607-11. It replaced an older
palace where Elizabeth I had spent much
of her childhood, and is full of Elizabethan
associations, important portraits of the
queen, and historic possessions such as
her silk stockings, perhaps the first pair
worn in England. There are also other
celebrated pictures, tapestries and
armour, including some from the Spanish
Armada. Newer attractions include a
William IV kitchen (1833) and the National
Collection of Model Soldiers. Around the
house are the great park and gardens,
including a parterre planted with yews
and roses, a scented garden and knot
garden with typical plants of the 15th to
17th centuries. Hatfield is still the home
of the Cecils, who at one point had a
private waiting room at the nearby
railway station. There are nature trails,
and an adventure play area for small
children. Special events for 1998: Living
Crafts (7-10 May), Festival of Gardening
(20-21 June), Tudor Revels (18-19 July),
Hatfield Prom (1 Aug), National Pottery
and Ceramics Festival (7-9 August),
Opera in the Park (22 or 29 August),
Country Lifestyle Fair (11-13 September).
*Open 25 Mar-4 Oct. (Closed Good Fri).
House: weekdays 12-4, Sun 1-4.30.
(Closed Mon ex BH 11-4.30). Gardens:
daily 11-6.*
✱*House Park & Gardens £5.70 (ch £3.40,
pen £4.80). Park & Gardens £3.10 (ch
£2.30, pen £2.90). Party 20+.*
P ✗ *licensed* & *toilets for disabled shop
garden centre* ✤ *(ex park)*

KNEBWORTH
**Knebworth House, Gardens & Country
Park**
SG3 6PY (direct access from junct 7
A1(M) at Stevenage)
☎ 01438 812661 Fax 01438 811908

Home of the Lytton family since 1490,
the original Tudor manor was
transformed in 1843 by the spectacular
high Gothic decoration of Victorian
novelist Sir Edward Bulwer Lytton. The
interior includes a superb Jacobean Great
Hall with a splendid plaster ceiling and
magnificent panelling (the reredos, which
stretches across the width of the room,
is 17th century). Bulwer Lytton was a
well known statesman and author and
counted among his friends many famous
people, including Dickens and Disraeli,
who were all guests at Knebworth. There
is a fascinating exhibition on the British
Raj and some fine furniture and portraits.
Outside, the 20 acre formal gardens, laid
out by Lutyens in 1908, include a Jekyll
herb garden, a replanted maze, and
wilderness walks. The 250-acre park
includes many attractions for visitors.
There is a miniature railway, an extensive
adventure playground, and a deer park.
Knebworth is a popular venue for special
events and activities, including, in 1998,
Knebworth Country Show (3-4 May),
Hertfordshire Garden Show (16-17 May),
Antiques and Collectors Fair (13-14 June),
Fireworks and Laser Symphony Concert
(26 July), Hertfordshire Craft Fair (22-23
August).
*Open - Park, Playground & Gardens: 4 Apr-
20 Apr & 23 May-7 Sep. Weekends & BHs
25 Apr-17 May, also weekends only 12-27
Sep, 11-5.30. House: as Park (ex closed
Mon but open bank holidays), 12-5.*
✱*£5 (ch & pen £4.50); Park, Playground &
Gardens only: £4. Party 20+.*
P ♥ & *(with prior notice visitors can be
driven to front door) toilets for disabled
shop* ✤ *(ex in park)*

LETCHWORTH
**Letchworth Garden City Heritage
Foundation**
296 Norton Way South SG6 1SU
☎ 01462 482710 Fax 01462 486056
The Museum tells the history of the
world's first Garden City from its
foundation in 1903 up to the present. It is

Hatfield House has been the home of the Cecil family for 400 years. The present house has many memorabilia of Queen Elizabeth I who spent much of her childhood there.

housed in the original drawing offices of the Arts and Crafts architects Barry Parker and Raymond Unwin, who, in designing Letchworth, made Ebenezer Howard's concept of a Garden City a reality. The museum provides a valuble insight into this unique architectural and social concept which has set a precedent in town planning for the rest of the 20th century.
Open all year, Mon-Sat 10-5. (Closed 25-26 Dec).
Free.
P *(150 yds)* & *(parking by prior arrangement)* shop

Museum & Art Gallery
Broadway SG6 3PF
☎01462 685647
Fax 01462 481879
The museum is housed in an attractive building in the town centre. The main galleries feature local archaeology and natural history, with a regular programme of changing exhibitions being held in the Art Gallery. The Natural History Gallery includes examples of local wildlife in realistic settings representing habitats, such as hedgerows, woodland and farmland. Geology is also covered with a good selection of local fossils on display.

The Archaeology Gallery covers the history of man in North Hertfordshire from about 200,000BC to the 17th century. Important finds are included such as a collection of metalwork from a late Iron Age Chieftain's burial, and Roman material from local sites, including the Roman town of Baldock. Exhibitions in the Art Gallery are changed monthly and often feature work by local artists and craftspeople. 1998 exhibitions: Ancient Yesterdays (9 May-6 June) - Lino prints of animals in archaeology by Ben Venuto, The Haggo Family of Painters (13 June-12 July), Remember When (20 July-30 August) - early advertising and packaging, Sean Parfitt & Friends (7 September-3 October), and many more. Ring for further details.
Open all year Mon-Sat 10-5. (Closed most BHs).
Free.
P *(100 yd)* & *(special provisions on request)* shop

Since 1308 there has been a shrine to its patron saint in St Albans Cathedral. The cathedral was an important centre for pilgrims for hundreds of years.

Open Good Fri-mid Sep, Sat, Sun & BH 10.30-5.
✱*25p (ch 5-11 10p, accompanied ch under 5 free)*
P *(400yds) shop* ✤

Gardens of The Rose (Royal National Rose Society)
Chiswell Green AL2 3NR (2m S off B4630 Watford Rd in Chiswell Green Ln)
☎*01727 850461 Fax 01727 850360*
These are the gardens of the Royal National Rose Society, and include the International Trial Ground for new roses. The gardens contain over 30,000 plants in 1,650 different varieties. These include old-fashioned roses, modern roses and the roses of the future. The National Miniature Rose Show takes place on 8-9 August-entry free to visitors to the gardens. Special events for 1998 include: Rose & Garden Care (7-8 March & 10-11 October). A special season of musical concerts will be held from June to August. Phone for details.
Open 13 Jun-11 Oct, Mon-Sat 9-5, Sun & BH 10-6.
£4 (accompanied ch free, pen & UB40 £3.50, registered disabled £3). Party 20+.
P ♥ ♿ *(ramps where necessary) toilets for disabled shop*
Cards: ▧ ▨
See advertisement on page 73.

Gorhambury
AL3 6AH (entry via lodge gates on A414)
☎*01727 54051 Fax 01727 43675*
Pleasant house built by Sir Robert Taylor (1774-1784) to house an extensive picture collection of 17th-century portraits of the Grimston and Bacon families and their contemporaries. Also of note is the 16th-century enamelled glass collection and an early English pile carpet.
Open May-Sep, Thu 2-5.
P *shop* ✤
Details not confirmed for 1998

Museum of St Albans
Hatfield Rd AL1 3RR
☎*01727 819340 Fax 01727 837472*
Exhibits include the Salaman collection of craft tools, and reconstructed workshops.

The history of St Albans is traced from the departure of the Romans up to the present day. Special exhibitions this year will include a commemoration of the museum's centenary. Please ring for details.
Open all year, daily 10-5, Sun 2-5. Closed 25 & 26 Dec.
Free.
P ♿ *toilets for disabled shop* ✤
Cards: ▧ ▨

Roman Theatre of Verulamium
St Michaels AL3 6AH (off A4147)
☎*01727 835035*
Fax 01727 43675
The theatre was first discovered on the Gorhambury Estate in 1847 and was fully excavated by Dr Kathleen Kenyon in 1935. It is unique in England. First constructed around AD160, it is semi-circular in shape, 180ft across and could hold 1,600 spectators. Following modification over two centuries, the theatre was used for religious processions, ceremonies and plays.
Open all year, daily 10-5 (4 in winter).
P ♿ *shop*
Details not confirmed for 1998

St Albans Cathedral
Sumpter Yard AL1 1BY
☎*01727 860780*
Fax 01727 850944
An imposing Norman abbey church built on the site of the execution of St Alban, Britain's first martyr (c209AD). The cathedral is constructed from recycled Roman brick from nearby Verulamium. There is an ecumenical shrine to St Alban dated 1308, as well as many 13th-century wall paintings. There is a wide-screen audio visual presentation 'The Martyr's Cathedral' and a wide selection of guided tours by arrangement.
Open daily, 9-5.45
Suggested donation £2.50 per adult.
Audio-visual presentation 'The Martyr's Cathedral' £1.50 (ch £1). Group rates.
P *(200mtrs)* ✗ *licensed* ♿ *(touch & hearing centre, braille guides) toilets for disabled shop* ✤

Verulamium Museum
St Michaels AL3 4SW (follow signs for St Albans, museum signposted)
☎*01727 819339 Fax 01727 859919*
Verulamium was one of the largest and most important Roman towns in Britain. By the lst century it was declared a 'municipium', which gave its inhabitants the rights of Roman citizenship. No other British city was granted this honour. The town was attacked by Boudicca in AD61, but rebuilt after her defeat. The site is set within a 100-acre park. A mosaic and underfloor heating system can be seen in situ, and the museum shows finds, including mosaics, wall paintings, jewellery, pottery and other domestic items. There are recreated Roman rooms, excavation videos, 'hands-on' discovery areas and computer data bases which are accessible to visitors. Regular talks and demonstrations at weekends. On the second weekend of every month legionaries occupy the galleries and describe the tactics and equipment of the Roman Imperial Army and the life of a legionary.
Open all year weekdays 10-5.30, Sun 2-5.30.
✱*£2.80 (ch, pen & students £1.60).*
Family ticket £7.
P *(charged)* ♿ *toilets for disabled shop* ✤
Cards: ▧ ▨

TRING
The Walter Rothschild Zoological Museum
Akeman St HP23 6AP (signposted from A41)
☎*01442 824181 Fax 01442 890693*
This most unusual museum was founded in the 1890s by Lionel Walter, 2nd Baron Rothschild, scientist, eccentric and natural history enthusiast. It is famous for its magnificent collection of thousands of mammals and birds, and there are also displays of reptiles, fishes, insects and domestic dogs. There is even a well

known exhibition of dressed fleas. Extinct, rare, exotic and bizarre specimens in a unique Victorian setting. Exhibitions are organised throughout the year (details on request).
Open all year, Mon-Sat 10-5, Sun 2-5. (Closed 24-26 Dec).
£2.50 (ch5-17 £1.25, concessions £1.25, Ch under 5 free). Family ticket £6.
P ♿ *toilets for disabled shop* ✤

WARE
Scott's Grotto
Scott's Rd SG12 9JQ (off A119)
☎*01920 464131*
Scott's Grotto, built in the 1760s by the Quaker poet John Scott, has been described by English Heritage as 'one of the finest in England'. Recently restored by the Ware Society, it consists of underground passages and chambers decorated with flints, shells, minerals and stones, and extends 67ft into the side of the hill. Please wear flat shoes and bring a torch.
Open early Apr-end Sep, Sat & BH's 2-4.30. Other times by appointment only.
Donations
P *(on street)* ♿

KENT

AYLESFORD
Aylesford Priory
The Friars ME20 7BX (M20 J6 then signed)
☎*01622 717272 Fax 01622 715575*
Built in the 13th and 14th centuries and then closed down in the Reformation, the priory has been restored and is now a house of prayer, guesthouse, conference centre and a place of pilgrimage and retreat. It has fine cloisters, and displays sculpture and ceramics by modern artists and potters. A potter and an upholsterer are now at the Friars and visitors are welcome to watch them at work. Special

events for 1998: 25 May - Spring Fayre with family entertainments. 20 Jun - Salvation Army Spectacular with evening concert, 3 Jul - Kent County Youth Orchestra evening concert.
Open all year, daily 9-dusk. Gift & book shop May-Sep, 10-5; Oct-Apr, 10-4. Guided tours of the priory by arrangement.
Donations. £1.50 for annual fund-raising day.
P *(charged)* ☕ & *(wheelchairs available, ramps) toilets for disabled shop* ⊗

BEKESBOURNE
Howletts Wild Animal Park
CT4 5EL (off A2, 3m S of Canterbury)
☎01227 721286 Fax 01227 721853
Howletts is one of John Aspinall's wild animal parks and has the world's largest breeding gorilla colony in captivity. It also has tigers, small cats, free-running deer and antelope, snow leopards, bison, ratel, honey beadgers, African elephants, and many endangered species of monkeys. All are housed in natural enclosures with the aim of breeding offspring to be returned to safe wild areas. John Aspinall's other wild animal park is Port Lympne, at Lympne near Hythe.
Open all year, daily 10-5, (3.30pm in winter). Closed 25 Dec.
P ☕ ✗ *licensed* & *toilets for disabled shop* ⊗
Details not confirmed for 1998
Cards: ◼ ▦ ▤ ⑤

BELTRING
Whitbread Hop Farm
TN12 6PY (on A228)
☎01622 872068 Fax 01622 872630
The largest group of Victorian oast houses and galleried barns in the world stands at the centre of this stunning complex. Attractions include the Hop Story Exhibition, designed using modern audio-visual technology, Shire Horse Centre, birds of prey including daily owl-flying displays, Rural Museum, Animal Village, Pottery Workshop, restaurant, play area, nature trail and gift shop. Special events include Country Pursuits weekend, Military Vehicle Show, British Classic Sports Car Show. Please telephone for details.
Open all year, Summer 10-6 (last admission 5). Winter 10-4, (Closed 25-26 & 31 Dec)
✳*Summer: £4.50, ch (5-15) £3, Pen/disabled £3.50, Family £13. Winter: £1.50, ch 50p, Pen/disabled £1*
P ☕ ✗ *licensed* & *toilets for disabled shop*
Cards: ◼ ▦ ▤ ▨ ⑤

BIDDENDEN
Biddenden Vineyards
Little Whatmans TN27 8DH (0.5m S off A262)
☎01580 291726 Fax 01580 291933
The present vineyard was established in 1969 and now covers 22 acres. Visitors are welcome to stroll around the vineyard

and to taste wines, ciders and apple juice available at the shop. Bunny Hunt and Star Trek events held on Easter Sunday - please ring for details of forthcoming special events.
Open all year, Shop: Mon-Fri 10-5, Sat 10-5 (3pm Nov-Feb), Sun 11-5 (3pm Nov-Dec), BH 11-5 (Mar-Oct). Closed midday 24 Dec-2 Jan & Sun in Jan & Feb. Non-guided groups and individuals free. Pre-booked guided tours (minimum 12 adults) £2.50 (ch 10-18 £1, ch under 12 free).
P ☕ & *shop*
Cards: ◼ ▦ ▥ ▨ ⑤

BOROUGH GREEN
Great Comp Garden
TN15 8QS (2m E off B2016)
☎01732 882669 & 886154
A beautiful seven-acre garden created since 1957 by Mr and Mrs R Cameron for low maintenance and year-round interest. There is a plantsmans' collection of trees, shrubs, heathers and herbaceous plants in a setting of fine lawns and grass paths. Planting styles vary from woodland and informal walks to terraces and formal paths, with ruins, loved by children, and ornaments for additional interest. Unusual plants for sale. The 17th-century house is not open. Chamber music, classical concerts and other events are organised by the Great Comp Society, details from the Secretary, Great Comp Society at the above address.
Open Apr-Oct, daily 11-6.
P ☕ & *toilets for disabled garden centre* ⊗
Details not confirmed for 1998

BRASTED
Emmetts Garden
Ide Hill TN14 6AY (1m S of A25)
☎01732 868381 (Chartwell office) Fax 01732 868193
Emmetts is a charming hillside shrub garden, with bluebells in spring and fine autumn colours. It has magnificent views over Bough Beech Reservoir and the Weald. Emmetts Concert in August. Telephone 01892 891001 for details.
Open; Apr-1 Nov, wknds, Wed, BH Mon & Good Fri 11-5.30 (last admission 4.30pm). Special arrangement for pre-booked parties at other times.
✳*£3 (ch £1.50). Family ticket £7.50. Party.*
P ☕ & *(buggy service from car park to garden) toilets for disabled shop* ⊌

BROADSTAIRS
Bleak House Dickens Maritime & Smuggling Museum
Fort Rd CT10 1EY (off Eastern Esplanade, near Viking Bay)
☎01843 862224
The house was a favourite seaside residence of the novelist Charles Dickens. He wrote the greater part of David Copperfield and other works here, and drafted the idea for Bleak House. There are special exhibitions of relics

Charles Dickens' desk at Bleak House

salvaged from the Goodwin Sands, and of 'The Golden Age of Smuggling'.
Open Etr-Jun & Oct-Nov 10-6, Jul-mid Sep 10-9.
£2 (ch 12 £1.50, pen & students £2). Party 10+
P *(50 yds)* & *shop*

Dickens House Museum
Victoria Pde CT10 1QS
☎01843 862853
The house was immortalised by Charles Dickens in David Copperfield as the home of the hero's aunt, Betsy Trotwood. Dickens' letters and possessions are shown, with local and Dickensian prints, costumes and general Victoriana. The parlour is furnished as described in the novel.
Open Apr-mid Oct, daily 2-5.
£1 (ch 50p).
P *(400yds) shop* ⊗ *(ex guide dogs)*

CANTERBURY
A visit to Canterbury must naturally start at the cathedral. This is where Chaucer's pilgrims and countless others came to visit the shrine of Thomas à Becket, who was murdered near the steps to the north transept in the 12th century. The treasures of the shrine were carried off during the Dissolution, but its site is still marked, with the tomb of the Black Prince close by. The cathedral has an awe-inspiring high, narrow nave, and the cathedral's medieval stained glass is well worth studying for the stories it tells. Next to the cathedral are the ruins of the former monastery, and the medieval and later buildings of the King's School. An interesting walk can be taken from Christ Church Gate around streets with picturesque old buildings like Queen Elizabeth's Guest Chamber and the weavers' cottages beside the Stour. A short walk leads up the hill to St Martin's church, which was old in the time of the Venerable Bede and is probably the oldest church in England still in use. Older still is the prehistoric tumulus topped by a 19th-century obelisk in Dane John garden.

Canterbury Heritage Museum
Stour St
☎01227 452747
Fax 01227 455047
An award-winning museum in a breath-taking medieval building on the river bank close to the Cathedral, shops and other attractions. The tour starts in Roman times and continues up to the present day. Some of the most exciting of the city's treasures are shown: the Canterbury Cross, Anglo-Saxon gold, and Viking finds. The displays include (among many others) a reconstruction of Becket's tomb; a medieval street with a pilgrim badge shop; Christopher Marlowe (he was born in Canterbury); the city in the Civil War; and Stephenson's locomotive 'Invicta'. The latest feature is the Rupert Bear Gallery and a collection of Joseph Conrad memorabilia.
Open all year, Mon-Sat 10.30-5 & Sun (Jun-Oct) 1.30-5 (last admission 4pm). (Closed Good Fri & Xmas period).
✳*£1.90 (ch 95p, pen & students £1.25). Family ticket £4.35. Party 10+*
P & *shop* ⊗

Canterbury Roman Museum
Butchery Ln, Longmarket
☎01227 785575
Fax 01227 455047
Underground, at the level of the Roman town, you will find this famous Roman house with its mosaic floors. Following the discoveries of archaeologists, you walk through a fascinating reconstruction of Roman buildings, including a market place with stallholders' wares of the period. Displays reveal a wealth of objects rescued by excavations, including 2000-year-old swords and a silver spoon hoard. A computer-generated reconstruction video guides you on the tour, and there is a 'touch the past' area where you can handle artefacts.
Open all year, Mon-Sat 10-5; Sun (Jun-Oct) 1.30-5. Last admission 4pm. (Closed Good Fri & Xmas period).
£1.90 (ch 95p, pen & students £1.25). Family ticket £4.35. Party.
P & *(lift) toilets for disabled shop* ⊗

Canterbury Royal Museum, Art Gallery & Buffs Regimental Museum
High St CT1 2JE
☎01227 452747 Fax 01227 455047
The city's picture collection including the T S Cooper Gallery - England's leading Victorian animal painter; and the ➤

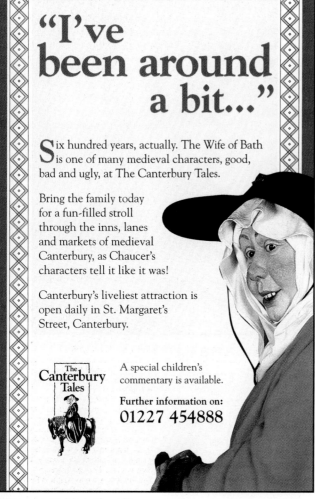
Canterbury and Europe Gallery which displays the fine archaeological objects and decorative arts resulting from close links over the centuries. Regular art events are held in the Special Exhibitions Gallery. Also housed here is the Buffs Regimental Museum, telling the story of one of England's oldest infantry regiments.
Open all year, Mon-Sat 10-5. (Closed Good Fri and Xmas period).
Free.
P shop

The Canterbury Tales
Saint Margaret's St CT1 2TG
☎01227 454888
Fax 01227 765584
Step back in time to join Chaucer's famous band of pilgrims on their journey to the shrine of St Thomas Becket in Canterbury Cathedral. Hear their tales of love, greed, chivalry and intrigue and experience life in the 14th century, complete with authentic sights, sounds and smells! Commentaries are available in English, Dutch, French, German, Italian, Japanese and Spanish. Special events include face painting in February and printing in October half-terms, a medieval food festival in August and Ghost tours of Canterbury throughout June, July and August. Please ring for more information.
Open all year, Mar-Jun & Sep-Oct daily 9.30-5.30; Jul-Aug daily 9-6; Nov-Feb Sun-Fri 10-4.30, Sat 9.30-5.30.
£4.85 (ch 5-16 £3.75, students & pen £3.95). Family ticket £14.
P (5 mins walk) ☕ & (notice required for wheelchairs) toilets for disabled shop
Cards:

Canterbury West Gate Museum
Saint Peter's St
☎01227 452747
Fax 01227 455047
The last of the city's fortified gatehouses sits astride the London road with the river as a moat. Rebuilt in around 1380 by

Archbishop Sudbury, it was used as a prison for many years. The battlements give a splendid panoramic view of the city and are a good vantage point for photographs. Arms and armour can be seen in the guardroom, and there are cells in the towers.
Open all year (ex Good Fri & Xmas period), Mon-Sat; 11-12.30 & 1.30-3.30.
✳80p (ch & disabled 40p, pen, students & UB40 50p). Family ticket £1.90. Party 10+.
P (100 yds) shop

Druidstone Wildlife Park
Honey Hill, Blean CT2 9JP (3m NW on A290)
☎01227 765168
Enjoy the company of the animals and birds in a relaxing country setting. Experience a taste of the South American plains with the rhea, mara and peccary. Make friends with the animals in the farmyard, meet the parrots, walk through the gardens which are home to the owls and wallaby, or along the woodland trail where you can see a surprising variety of wildlife.
Open 6 Apr-Oct, daily 10-5.30; Nov open wknds only.
£2.50 (ch £1.50 & pen £2).
P ☕ & toilets for disabled shop

St Augustine's Abbey
Longport CT1 1PF (off A28)
☎01227 767345
The abbey, founded by St Augustine in AD598, when he brought Christianity from Rome to England, is one of the oldest monastic sites in the country. It is fascinating to trace the signs of the various phases of the abbey's long history in its ruins.
Open all year, Apr-Oct, daily 10-6 (or dusk if earlier); Nov-Mar, daily 10-4. Closed 24-26 Dec & 1 Jan.
£2.50 (ch £1.30, concessions £1.90).
P & shop

Chartwell
TN16 1PS (2m S of Westerham, off B2026)
☎01732 866368 (info line) & 868381
Fax 01732 868193
The former home of Sir Winston Churchill is filled with reminders of the great statesman, from his hats and uniforms to gifts presented by Stalin and Roosevelt. There are paintings of Churchill and other works by notable artists, and also many paintings by Churchill himself. An exhibition gives visitors an insight into his life during his years at Chartwell, and his studio is arranged with easel and paintbox at the ready. The garden has walls and ponds that he laid out, and gives fine views. 1940s Concert (20 June). Ring 01892 891001
Open Apr-1 Nov, house, garden & studio, Wed-Sun & Bh Mon) 11-5.30. Open BH Mons & Tue in Jul/Aug. Last admission 4.30pm.
House, Garden & studio £5.20 (ch £2.60). Gardens only £2.60 (ch £1.30). Family ticket £13. Entrance by numbered ticket at times in summer to avoid congestion, waiting time can be spent in garden.
P ✗ licensed & toilets for disabled shop (ex garden)

Fort Amherst
Dock Rd ME4 4UB (adjacent to the A231 dock road)
☎01634 847747
Fax 01634 847747
Fort Amherst is reputed to be the finest Georgian fortress in Britain. Set in over 15 acres of attractive parkland the fortress sprawls across the hillside above the historic navel town of Chatham. A fascinating collection of caves, tunnels, gun-batteries and barracks gives visitors an awe-inspiring insight into the life of the Napoleonic soldier. Don't miss the magnificently re-activated 'Blitz Bunker' in the caves. Historic re-enactments take

place on most Sundays April - October. 27-28 Jun - Chatham Armed Forces Fundays - 5 hours of arena displays, bridgebuilding, shooting, unarmed combat, parachute displays etc. 17 Oct - Floodlit Trafalgar Night Tattoo.
Open daily 10.30-last entry 4pm.
✳£3.50 (ch, pen & students £2).
P ☕ & toilets for disabled shop
Cards:

Historic Dockyard
ME4 4TE (signposted from M25)
☎01634 812551
Fax 01634 826918
A Royal dockyard until 1984, now an 80-acre working museum with 47 Scheduled Ancient Monuments which form the most complete Georgian/early Victorian dockyard in the world. Eight museum galleries cover 400 years of shipbuilding history, and include the award-winning 'Wooden Walls' which shows through sights, sounds and smells, how 18th-century warships such as HMS Victory were built here. Visitors can see a working ropery, sail and flag-making, crafts workshops in action, and witness the restoration of the Victorian sloop Gannet in dry dock. Impressive buildings include huge covered slips, a Georgian Officers' Terrace, and the Commissioner's House (1704), Britain's oldest intact naval building whose pleasant garden is open to visitors. The Lifeboat Gallery tells the story of the lifeboat service. Horse-drawn wagon rides are available in the summer.
Open Apr-Oct, daily 10-5; Feb, Mar & Nov, Wed, Sat & Sun 10-4.
P ☕ ✗ licensed & (wheelchair available, Braille guides) toilets for disabled shop
Details not confirmed for 1998
Cards:

Chiddingstone Castle
TN8 7AD (off B2027, at Bough Beech)
☎01892 870347
The 'castle' is a 17th-century house,

almost completely rebuilt in the castle style c1800 by William Atkinson. It contains Stewart and Jacobite paintings and other relics, Egyptian and Oriental antiquities, and a fine collection of Japanese lacquer and swords. The interior has recently been refurbished with extra rooms open to visitors. The grounds are now undergoing restoration.
Open Apr-Oct. Apr-May & Oct, Sun; Jun-Sep, Wed-Fri & Sun. All BH's. Weekdays 2-5.30; Sun and BH 11.30-5.30. Other times for parties by arrangement. Castle may be closed at short notice for private functions.
£3.50 Sundays £4, (ch 5-15 £1.50). Party 20+ by prior arrangement.
🅿 💺 ♿ shop ⊗ (no exceptions)

DEAL

Deal Castle
Victoria Rd CT14 7BA (SW of Deal town centre)
☎01304 372762
This castle was part of a chain of coastal defences built by Henry VIII. It is a huge, austere structure built to carry 119 cannons and shaped like a Tudor rose, with every wall rounded to deflect shot. The dark passages and unrelenting walls are a grim reminder of what garrison life must have been like.
Open all year, Apr-Oct, daily 10-6 (or dusk if earlier); Nov-Mar, Wed-Sun 10-4. Closed 24-26 Dec & 1 Jan.
£3 (ch £1, concessions £2.30). Personal stereo tour included in admission price.
♿ shop ♯

Walmer Castle
Walmer, Kingsdown Rd CT14 7LJ (1m S on coast, off A258)
☎01304 364288
Like Deal Castle, Walmer was built by Henry VIII and has a similar design. It is the official residence of the Lord Warden of the Cinque Ports, a post once held by the Duke of Wellington who died here.

Dungeness Power Station looms large over the shingle beach and flat landscape of the spit on which it was built. There is a 'hi-tech' visitor centre and marked nature trails on the surrounding marshes.

His sparsely furnished bedroom can be seen. The castle is still used today by HM the Queen Mother. Rooms used by Her Majesty, including the dining room and drawing room, are open to visitors. The delightful castle gardens owe much of their appearance to two former Lords Warden, William Pitt and Earl Granville and are at their best in summer.
Open all year, Apr-Oct, daily 10-6 (or dusk if earlier in Oct); Nov-Mar, Wed-Sun 10-4, Jan-Feb wknds only. Closed 24-26 Dec, 1 Jan & when Lord Warden in residence.
£4 (ch £2, concessions £3). Personal stereo tour included in admission price, also available for the partially sighted, those with learning difficulties.
🅿 ♿ shop ⊗ (in certain areas) ♯

DOVER

Crabble Corn Mill
Lower Rd, River CT17 0UY (follow signs to River from A258)
☎01304 823292 Fax 01304 826040
Visit this beautifully restored working Kentish water mill dating from 1812. Regular demonstrations of waterwheel working and making stoneground wholemeal flour from Kentish organic wheat. Flour for sale, also home-baked produce in cafe. Exhibition space displays work of local artists and craftspeople. Easter Egg Hunt (Easter Sunday and Monday), National Mills Day (11 May), Country Fayre (Sunday of August Bank Holiday weekend).
Open all year, Etr-Jun & Sep, Sat & Sun 11-5; Jul-Aug, Wed-Sun 11-5; Winter Sun 11-5.
£2 (ch 15 £1, students & pen £1.50). Family ticket £5.
🅿 💺 ✕ licensed ♿ shop ⊗

Dover Castle and Hellfire Corner
CT16 1HU
☎01304 201628
Dover is a giant among castles. Perched high on the famous White Cliffs, it has protected the closest stretch of the English coast to Europe from the Iron Age to Second World War and beyond. Today much of the Castle's 2000 year history can be experienced by the visitor. The underground tunnel system, nicknamed Hellfire Corner, was originally built in medieval times. Only recently was the veil of official secrecy lifted to reveal that this was the command centre where some of the most important decisions of Second World War were made. The visitor can now explore this underground wartime nerve centre and, most recently, share the experience of the soldiers in the hospital and casualty dressing station also hidden here.
Open all year, Apr-Oct, daily 10-6 (or dusk if earlier); Nov-Mar, daily 10-4. Closed 24-26 Dec & 1 Jan.
£6.60 (ch £3.30, concessions £5).
🅿 ✕ ♿ shop ⊗ (in certain areas) ♯

Old Town Gaol
Dover Town Hall, Biggin St CT16 1DL (Follow brown tourist signs from Dover town centre)
☎01304 201200 Fax 01304 201200
High-tech animation, audio-visual techniques and 'talking heads' take visitors back to Victorian England to experience the horrors of life behind bars, listening, as they walk through the reconstructed courtroom, exercise yard, washroom and cells, to the stories of the felons and their jailers. You can even, if you so wish, try the prisoners' beds or find out what it is like to be locked in a 6ft x 4ft cell!
Open all year, Tue-Sat 10-4.30, Sun 2-

4.30. (Closed Mon & Tue, Oct-May). Telephone 01304 202723 for further information.
£3.20 (ch & pen £1.90).
🅿 (charged) ♿ shop ⊗

Roman Painted House
New St CT17 9AJ
☎01304 203279
Visit five rooms of a Roman hotel built 1,800 years ago, now famous for its unique, well-preserved Bacchic frescos. The Roman underfloor heating system and part of a late-Roman defensive wall are also on view. There are extensive displays on Roman Dover with video and commentary. Foreign language commentaries are available in French, German, and Dutch. Parties are welcome; tours by arrangement. Special events are held throughout the year.
Open Apr-Oct, Tue-Sun 10-6 (5pm in Apr, Sep & Oct), also BH Mon & Mon Jul & Aug. Last admission half hour before closing. Groups at other times by prior arrangement.
🅿 (touch table, glass panels on gallery for wheelchairs) shop ⊗
Details not confirmed for 1998

The White Cliffs Experience
Market Sq CT16 1PB (signposting on entering town centre from A2 and M20/A20, follow signs)
☎01304 214566 & 210101
Fax 01304 212057
This award-winning attraction located in the centre of Dover provides an entertaining and exciting encounter with life in Roman Britain and during the twentieth century. Visit the new 'Roman Encounters' and 'Our Finest Hours' and take two journeys into the past. Special events are staged during school holidays throughout the year, including a Holiday Fun Trail.
Open all year daily, Apr-Oct 10am-6pm (last admission 5pm), Nov-Mar 10am-5pm (last admission 4pm)
✳£5.50 (ch 4-14 £3.75, pen & students £4.25).
🅿 (150 yds) 💺 ♿ (lifts, ramped access, wheelchair & seat sticks) toilets for disabled shop ⊗
Cards: 🌐 🔲 💳 📧 📧 🔄

DUNGENESS

Dungeness Visitor Centre
TN29 9PP
☎01797 321815 Fax 01797 321844
The 'A' and 'B' power stations at Dungeness make an extraordinary sight in a landscape of shingle, fishing boats and owner-built houses. There is a high-tech information centre, with 'hands-on' interactive videos and many other displays and models including an environmental exhibition which depicts Dungeness from the Ice Age through to

➜

today. The nature trail clearly shows the rare shingle ridges, flora and fauna and completes an interesting day out. Prior bookings for tours is advisable.
Open: Information centre Etr-Oct, daily; Oct-Etr, Sun-Fri. Regular Tours of A & B power stations available. No children under 5 allowed on tour.
🅿 ♿ *(information centre only) toilets for disabled shop* 🐕
Details not confirmed for 1998

RSPB Nature Reserve
TN29 9PN (off Lydd to Dungeness rd, 1m SE of Lydd)
☎01797 320588 Fax 01797 321962
This coastal reserve comprises 2106 acres of shingle beach and flooded pits.It is a good place to watch breeding terns, gulls and other water birds. Wheatears, great crested and little grebes also nest. Outside the breeding season there are large flocks of teals, shovelers, mallards, and goldeneyes, goosanders, smews and both Slavonian and red-necked grebes. Dungeness is famous for migrants including many rarities. Phone for details of special events.
Open daily except Tue 9am-9pm (or sunset if earlier). Visitor Centre daily except Tue 9-4 summer, 9-4 winter. (Closed 25 & 26 Dec).
❄£2 (ch 50p, concessions £1.50). Family ticket £4.
🅿 ♿ *shop* 🐕
Cards: 🔲 🔲 🔲 🔲

DYMCHURCH
Martello Tower
(access from High St not seafront)
One of the many artillery towers which formed part of a chain of strongholds intended to resist an invasion by Napoleon. It is fully restored, with an original 24-pounder gun on the roof.
Open 10-13 Apr, 2-4 May, 9 May-11 Jul (wknds & BHs), 18 Jul-Aug, Sep (wknds), 2-5.30.
£1 (ch 50p, concessions 80p)
🐕 ♿

EDENBRIDGE
See Hever

EYNSFORD
Eynsford Castle
(off A225)
The walls of this castle, still 30ft high, come as a surprise in the pretty little village. The castle was begun in the 11th century by William de Eynsford, who later retired to become a monk. Also to be seen are the remains of the castle hall and ditch.
Open all year, Apr-Sep, daily 10-6; Oct-Mar, daily 10-4. (Closed 24-26 Dec & 1 Jan).
Free.
🅿 ♿ ♿

Lullingstone Castle
DA4 0JA (1m SW of Eynsford via A225)
☎01322 862114
Fax 01322 862115
The house was altered extensively in Queen Anne's time, and has fine state rooms and beautiful grounds. The 15th-century gate tower was one of the first gatehouses in England to be made entirely of bricks, and there is a church with family monuments. There are provisional arrangements to open under the National Gardens Scheme. 25-6 Jul - open air concerts. Please telephone for details.
Open, House Apr-June Sat, Sun & BH 2-6; July-Sept Sat/Sun 2-6; Parties by arrangement.
House & Gardens £3.75 (ch £1.50 & pen £3).
🅿 💺 ♿ *shop* 🐕

Lullingstone Roman Villa
(half mile SW off A225)
☎01322 863467
The excavation of this Roman villa in 1949 uncovered one of the most exciting archaeological finds of the century. Here you can see some of the most remarkable villa remains in Britain,

including wonderful mosaic tiled floors and wall paintings and the ruins of one of the earliest Christian chapels in Britain.
Open all year, Apr-Oct, daily 10-6 (or dusk if earlier); Nov-Mar, daily 10-4. Closed 24-26 Dec & 1 Jan.
£2.50 (ch £1.30, students, pen & UB40 £1.90). Personal stereo tour included in admission price.
🅿 🐕 ♿

FAVERSHAM
Fleur de Lis Heritage Centre
13 Preston St ME13 8NS
☎01795 534542
A thousand years of history and architecture in Faversham are shown in award-winning displays, an audio-visual programme, and a working vintage telephone exchange in this 16th-century building (a former coaching inn). There is a Tourist Information Centre and a bookshop. A special event held every year is the Faversham Open House Scheme (4,11,18 July) - over 20 historic properties in Faversham, usually not open to the public, can be visited on these dates. Admission to the properties is by programme only; for more details contact the Fleur de Lis Heritage Centre.
Open all year, Apr-Sep, daily 10-4; Oct-Mar, Mon-Sat 10-4.
£1.50, pen £1, ch 50p
P (200 yds) ♿ shop

FOLKESTONE
Russian Submarine
South Quay, Folkestone Harbour CT20 1QH (adjacent to Hoverspeed Seacat Terminal)
☎01303 240400
Fax 01303 240540
The fascinating history of U475 (known as The Black Widow) is shrouded in secrecy. Only the select few, the Chiefs of Staff of the former Soviet Navy, know the full history. Was it part of their plan for the U475 to patrol the waters off Cuba after the successful deployment of missiles on the island in 1963? We will probably never know how many times U475 came up to periscope depth to watch silently as the pride of our navy sailed by, comfortably within reach of the devestating power of the weapons on board...See for yourself what life was like for the captain and 74 crew.
Open all year, Mon-Fri 10-dusk, wknds 10-7. Closed 25 Dec.
£3.50 (ch £2, concessions £3). Family ticket £9. Party.
🅿 *(charged) shop* 🐕 *(inc guide dogs)*
Cards: 🔲 🔲 🔲 🔲

FORDWICH
Town Hall
The Square (off A28)
☎01227 710756
Fax 01227 710756
The timber-framed Tudor town hall and courtroom is thought to be the oldest and smallest in England. It overlooks the River Stour, peaceful now but hectic in the Middle Ages, because Fordwich was the port for Canterbury. The old town jail can also be visited.
Open Etr, Jun-Sep & Wed in Aug, Sun 2-4.
❄50p (ch 10p, students in group 25p).
🅿

GILLINGHAM
Royal Engineers Museum
Prince Arthur Rd, Brompton ME4 4UG (off B2004)
☎01634 406397
Fax 01634 822371
The museum is a treasure trove of the unexpected, covering the world-wide work of the Royal Engineers. Learn about the first military divers, photographers, aviators and surveyors; see exhibits as diverse as 24 Victoria Crosses, the regalia of 4 Field Marshals, memorabilia relating to General Gordon and Field Marshal Lord Kitchener, Wellington's battle map from Waterloo and a Harrier jump-jet. Conference and corporate facilities are also available. Please telephone for further details of special events.

Open all year, Mon-Thu 10-5, Sat-Sun & BH Mon 11.30-5. (Closed Good Fri, 25-26 Dec & 1 Jan). Friday by appointment only.
£3 (ch, pen & UB40s £1.50). Family ticket £6.50. Guided tour £4. Party 15+.
🅿 ♿ *(help available if required) toilets for disabled shop* 🐕

GOUDHURST
Finchcocks
TN17 1HH (off A262)
☎01580 211702
Fax 01580 211007
This fine early Georgian house stands in a spacious park with a beautiful garden, and contains an outstanding collection of keyboard instruments from the 17th century onwards. They have been restored to playing condition, and there are musical tours on all open days and private visits. Visually handicapped visitors may touch the instruments as well as hear them.
Open Etr-Sep, Sun & BH Mon 2-6; Aug, Wed, Wed, Thu & Sun only 2-6. Private groups on other days by appointment Apr-Oct.
🅿 💺 ✕ *licensed* ♿ *shop garden centre* 🐕
Details not confirmed for 1998

HAWKINGE
Kent Battle of Britain Museum
Aerodrome Rd CT18 7AG (on A260)
☎01303 893140
Once a Battle of Britain Station, today it houses the largest collection of authentic relics and related memorabilia of British and German aircraft involved in the fighting. Also shown are British and German uniforms and equipment, and full-size replicas of the Hurricane, Spitfire and Me 109 used in Battle of Britain films. Also the remains of nearly 600 crashed Battle of Britain aircraft.
Open Etr-Sep, daily 10-5; Oct, daily 11-4. Closed Nov-Etr. Last admission 1 hour before closing.
£3 (ch £1.50, pen £2.50). Group 10+.
🅿 ♿ *shop* 🐕

HERNE COMMON
"Brambles" Wildlife Park
Wealdon Forest Pk CT6 7LQ (on A291)
☎01227 712379
Fax 01227 712379
The 20-acre park has a nature trail leading through woodland where many birds and animals including sika deer, mara, guanaco, owls, Scottish wildcats and red foxes may be seen. Small rare breed farm animals, ponies and a miniature donkey may be fed with the food sold at the gate. There are also a walk-in rabbit enclosure and an indoor garden, an adventure playground and under-fives' playground.
Open Etr-end Sept 10-5, last entry 4.15
£3 (ch £1.50, pen £2).
🅿 💺 ♿ *(wheelchair ramps) toilets for disabled shop* 🐕

HEVER
Hever Castle & Gardens
TN8 7NG (M25 J5 or 6, 3m SE of Edenbridge, off B2026)
☎01732 865224 Fax 01732 866796
This enchanting, double-moated, 13th-century castle was the childhood home of Anne Boleyn. The estate was visited many times by Henry VIII during their long courtship. In 1903 it was bought and restored by the American millionaire William Waldorf Astor, and now shows superb Edwardian craftsmanship and an exhibition on scenes from the life and times of Anne Boleyn. Astor also transformed the grounds, creating a Tudor village (which is closed to the public but available for conferences and corporate hospitality), a lake, a spectacular Italian garden filled with antique sculptures; maze and a fine topiary. The miniature model houses exhibition contained in a purpose-built centre (no additional charge) illustrates life in English country houses from medieval to Victorian times. New additions to the gardens include a 110 metre herbaceous border and a 'splashing' water maze on the newly opened Sixteen Acre Island. Special events for 1998 include: May Day Music and Dance (2-4 May), Gardener's Weekend (26-28 June) and a Patchwork & Quilting Exhibition (11-13 September). Please ring for details of these and other events.
Open 1 Mar-Nov, daily. Castle 12-6; Gardens 11-6. Last admission 5pm. (Closes 4pm Mar & Nov).
❄Castle & Gardens £7 (ch 5-16 £3.80, pen £6). Family ticket £17.80. Gardens only £5.50 (ch 5-16 £3.60, pen £4.70). Family ticket £14.60. Party 15+.
🅿 💺 ✕ *licensed* ♿ *(wheelchairs available) toilets for disabled shop garden centre* 🐕 *(ex in grounds)*
Cards: 🔲 🔲 🔲 🔲

HYTHE
Romney Hythe & Dymchurch Railway- For details see gazetteer entry under **New Romney.**

IGHTHAM
Ightham Mote
TN15 0NT (2.5m S off A227, 6m E of Sevenoaks)
☎01732 810378 Fax 01732 811029
This beautiful medieval manor house, complete with moat and attractive garden, was given to the National Trust in 1985. It has been extensively remodelled through the centuries but is still a splendid example of medieval architecture: particularly the Great Hall, Old Chapel and crypt c1340. The house also features many important additions from great periods and notable features include the drawing room with its Jacobean fireplace and frieze, its Palladian window and the hand-painted Chinese wallpaper. During 1997, as part of the ongoing conservation and repair programme, work will continue on the house - restricting access to some parts of the house. The Robinson Library, not

normally open, will be shown, and a Conservation Exhibition explains the work in detail. Please note that the house is very busy on Sundays and Bank Holidays between 2pm and 4pm, so avoid these times if possible. There are open air concerts on in July. Ring (01892)891001 for details.

Open Apr-1 Nov, daily ex Tue & Sat, 11-5.30. Open Good Fri. Last admission 5pm. The house is very busy on Sun & BH between 2 and 4, a timed ticket system may be in operation.

£4.50 (ch £2.25). Family ticket £11.25.

P ⬛ & *(wheelchairs available,special parking ask at ticket office) toilets for disabled shop* ⌘ ✿

Cards: ▨ ▨ ▭ ◉

LAMBERHURST
Bayham Abbey
TN3 8BG (off B2169, 2m W in East Sussex)
☎01892 890381
Set in the wooded Teise valley, these ruins date back to the 13th century and include parts of the old church, cloisters and gatehouse.
Open Apr-Oct, daily 10-6 (or dusk if earlier). Winter wknds 10-4.
£2 (ch £1, concessions £1.50).
P & ✿

Owl House Gardens
TN3 8LY (1m NE off A21)
☎01892 890230 Fax 01892 891290
The Owl House is a small, timber-framed 16th-century house, a former haunt of wool smugglers. Surrounding it are 13 acres of gardens offering the visitor romantic walks with spring flowers, azaleas, rhododendrons, roses, shrubs and ornamental fruit trees. The sweeping lawns lead to lovely woodlands of oak and birch, and informal sunken water gardens.
Open all year, daily 11-6. (Closed 25-26 Dec & 1 Jan).
£4 (ch £1).
P & *shop (must be on lead)*

Although the romantic manor house of Ightham Mote is actually encircled by a moat, it is more likely that the name was derived from the Saxon word *moot* meaning 'place of assembly'.

Scotney Castle Garden
TN3 8JN (1m S, on A21)
☎01892 891081
Fax 01892 890110
The beautiful gardens at Scotney were carefully planned in the 19th century around the remains of the old, moated Scotney Castle. There is something to see at every time of year, with spring flowers followed by gorgeous rhododendrons, azaleas and a mass of roses, and then superb autumn colours. Open-air opera performances will be given 16-19 July. Ring 01892 891001 for details.
Open Garden - Apr-1 Nov. Old Castle open May-13 Sep Wed-Fri 11-6, Sat & Sun 2-6 or sunset if earlier. BH Sun & Mon 12-6 (Closed Good Fri) last admission 1hr before closing.
£3.80 (ch £1.90). Family ticket £9.50.
P & *(wheelchair available) shop* ⌘ ✿

LEEDS
For **Leeds Castle** see **Maidstone**

LYMPNE
Lympne Castle
CT21 4LQ (in village, 3.5m W of Hythe)
☎01303 267571
A small medieval castle built between the 12th and 15th centuries. Although it was largely remodelled and restored in 1905, it retains much of its former character. The view from the castle includes the military canal, dug as part of the coastal defences during the Napoleonic Wars, Romney Marsh and, in fine weather, the French coast across the Channel. There are exhibitions of toys and dolls, reproduction medieval memorial brasses and scale models of English cathedrals.

Open 25 May-13 Sep, Mon-Thu & occasional Sundays, 10.30-5.30. Other times by arrangement.
£2 (ch 50p).
P *shop*

Port Lympne Wild Animal Park,Mansion & Garden
CT21 4PD (off M20 junct 11)
☎01303 264647 Fax 01303 264944
John Aspinall's 300-acre wild animal park houses hundreds of rare animals: Indian elephants, wolves, bison, black and snow leopards, Siberian and Indian tigers, gorillas and monkeys. The mansion designed by Sir Herbert Baker is surrounded by 15 acres of spectacular gardens. Inside, the most notable features include the recently restored Rex Whistler Tent Room, Moroccan Patio and hexagonal library where the Treaty of Paris was signed after World War I. The ➤

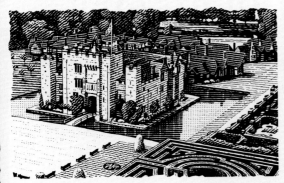

Arthur Spencer Roberts mural room depicts over 300 animals and birds from South East Asia. Safari trailers journey through some of the animal paddocks during peak times; please telephone to check availability.

Open all year, daily fr 10am, last admission 5pm summer, 3.30pm winter. (Closed 25 Dec).

🅿 🍴 ✗ *licensed* ♿ *(very limited access for disabled) toilets for disabled shop* ✖
Details not confirmed for 1998
Cards: 🟦 ▣ 🟦

MAIDSTONE

Leeds Castle

ME17 1PL (4m E, at junct 8 of M20/A20)
☎ *01622 765400 Fax 01622 735616*
The site of a manor of the Saxon royal family in the 9th century, Leeds was described by Lord Conway as 'the loveliest castle in the world'. Visitors may well agree with the sentiment. Built on two islands in the middle of a lake and set in 500 acres of landscaped parkland, it was converted into a royal palace by Henry VIII, and remained a royal residence for over three centuries. Today it has been beautifully restored and furnished; it has some beautiful pictures and other treasures, and, more unusual, a museum of medieval dog collars. Outside there are the Culpeper Flower Garden, the greenhouses, aviaries and vineyard, the 14th-century barbican and mill, the maze and grotto, and water and woodland gardens. Children especially love meeting the free-roaming waterfowl, which include peacocks as well as white and black swans. The Fairfax Hall, a 17th-century tithe barn, is the venue for 'Kentish Evenings' most Saturday nights (except during August). There are also many special events throughout the year, including a New Year's Day Treasure Trail, Festival of English Food (16-17 May), a Balloon and Vintage Car Fiesta (6-7 June), open-air concerts by the Royal Liverpool Philharmonic Orchestra (27 June and 4 July), Flower Festival (16-19 September), Grand Firework Spectacular (7 November).

Open all year daily, Mar-Oct 10-5 (Castle 11-5.30). Nov-Feb 10-3 (Castle from 10.15pm).

✳*Castle, Park & Gardens £8.80 (ch 5-15 £5.80, students & pen £6.80); Park & gardens £6.80 (ch 5-15 £4.30, students & pen £5.30). Family ticket £24, Park & gardens only £20. Party 20+.*

🅿 ✗ *licensed* ♿ *(Braille information, induction loops & wheelchair, lift) toilets for disabled shop garden centre* ✖
Cards: 🟦 ▣ 🟦 ▣

Maidstone Museum & Art Gallery

St Faith's St ME14 1LH (close to County Hall)
☎*01622 754497 Fax 01622 602193*
Set in an Elizabethan manor house which has been much extended over the years, this museum houses a surprising and outstanding collection of fine and applied arts, including oil paintings and watercolours, furniture, Roman, Anglo-Saxon and Medieval archeology, ceramics, costumes and a collection of Japanese art and artefacts. Natural history collections and displays relating to local industry are also featured, together with the museum of the Queen's Own Royal West Kent Regiment. Please apply for details of temporary exhibitions, workshops etc.

Open all year, Mon-Sat 10-5.15, Sun 11-4 & BH Mon 11-4. (Closed 25-26 Dec). Free.

🅿 *(100 yds)* 🍴 ♿ *shop* ✖

Museum of Kent Life

Lock Ln, Sandling ME14 3AU (From A229, follow signs for Aylesford. From M20 take junct 6 onto A229 Maidstone rd)
☎*01622 763936 Fax 01622 662024*
Kent's award-winning open air museum is home to an outstanding collection of historic buildings which house exhibitions on life in Kent 100 years ago. The UK's last traditionally working oast, plus barn granary and hoppers' huts along with the newly restored 18th century farmhouse are all open for visitors to explore. Also farm animals, venture playground, hop, herb and kitchen gardens, orchard, tearoom and shop. Picnic area available as well as riverboat trips in the summer. Special programme of events throughout the season includes Craft Weekend, Cider Festival, Bonfire Night Party. Please ring for details of these and other events.

Open Etr-Oct, daily 10-5.30.
£3.95 (concessions £2.45). Family ticket £11.

🅿 ✗ *licensed* ♿ *(wheelchairs available, ramps) toilets for disabled shop*

Tyrwhitt Drake Museum of Carriages

The Archbishop's Stables, Mill St ME15 6YE (close to River Medway & Archbishops Palace)
☎*01622 754497 Fax 01622 682451*
A wide array of horse-drawn carriages and vehicles is displayed in these late-medieval stables, which are interesting in themselves. The exhibits include state, official and private carriages, and some are on loan from royal collections.

Open all year, Apr-Oct daily 10.30-5.30; Nov-Mar noon-4.30. Last admission 4pm. (Closed 25-26 Dec).

✳*£1.50 (ch & pen £1).*
🅿 *(100 yds)* ♿ *shop* ✖

MATFIELD

Wildside, Badsell Park

Crittenden Rd TN12 7EW (on A228)
☎*01892 832549 & 832223 Fax 01892 837228*
A pleasant day in the country for all the family is offered at this attractive 180-acre fruit and arable farm. Children are able to handle young farm animals and pets in the Animal Park and Pet Area. There are nature trails to follow in beautiful countryside, a butterfly house with live tropical species and a new tropical ant house, picnic facilities and a play barn for toddlers and children up to eleven; outdoor play areas include wendy houses, a fort, fire engine and tractor. An Information Room gives details of farming and wildlife, including live insect displays. Strawberries, apples and other fruit and vegetables can be picked in season. Children's birthday and evening parties are a speciality and pony and tractor rides are available by arrangement.

Open all year, daily 10-5.30.
🅿 🍴 ♿ *toilets for disabled shop* ✖ *(ex on nature trail)*
Details not confirmed for 1998

MINSTER-IN-THANET

Minster Abbey

CT12 4HF
☎*01843 821254*
One of the first nunneries in England was built on this site in the 7th century. The house was rebuilt in later centuries, but is still a religious community and is run by Benedictine nuns. The ruins of the old abbey and the cloisters are open to the public and much of the Early English and Norman architecture can still be seen; there is one wing dating back to 1027, and a 12th century carving of Christ. Garden fete first Saturday in August.

Open all year, May-Sep, Mon-Fri 11-12 & 2-4.30, Sat 11-12; Oct-Apr, Mon-Sat 11-12.
Donations
🅿 ♿ *shop*

NEW ROMNEY

Romney, Hythe & Dymchurch Railway

New Romney Station TN28 8PL (off M20 junct 11, off A259 signed New Romney)
☎*01797 362353 & 363256 Fax 01797 363591*
The world's smallest public railway has its headquarters here. The concept of two enthusiasts coincided with Southern Railway's plans for expansion, and so the thirteen-and-a-half mile stretch of 15 inch gauge railway came into being, running from Hythe through New Romney and Dymchurch to Dungeness Lighthouse.

PENSHURST

A splendid 14th Century Manor House set in magnificent Tudor Gardens surrounded by gentle English parkland. **A** Venture Playground, a Toy Museum, a Family Exhibition, Fine food and Kentish cream teas. **I**t's a great day out for the whole family at Kent's award winning stately home.

PENSHURST PLACE AND GARDENS

Open 7 days from 28th Mar - 1st Nov 1998.
Gardens & Venture Playground 11.00 - 18.00.
House 12.00 - 17.30 (last entrance 17.00).
For details please call 01892 870307.
Penshurst, Tonbridge, Kent.
http://www.seetb.org.uk/penshurst/
E-mail: penshurst@pavilion.co.uk

THE HOUSE - THE GARDEN THE PLACE

Events planned for 1998 include a Steam and Diesel Gala (10 May), Friends of Thomas the Tank Engine (5 July & 5/6 September).
Open daily Etr-Sep, also wknds in Mar & Oct. For times apply to: The Manager, RH & DR., New Romney, Kent.
✻*Charged according to journey.*
🅿 *(charged)* ⬛ 🚻 *toilets for disabled shop*
Cards: ⬛ ⬛

PENSHURST
Penshurst Place & Gardens
TN11 8DG (from M25 junct 5 take A21 Hastings rd to Tonbridge North exit then follow signs)
☎01892 870307 Fax 01892 870866
The original manor house was built by Sir John de Pulteney between 1340 and 1345 and is perfectly preserved. Successive owners enlarged it during the 15th, 16th and 17th centuries, and the great variety of architectural styles creates an elaborate and dramatic backdrop for the extensive collections of English, French and Italian furniture, tapestries and paintings. The world-famous, chestnut-beamed Baron's Hall is the oldest and finest in the country, and the collection in the Toy Museum is much loved by children. The house is set in magnificent formal gardens first laid out in the 14th-century, and recently restored to their former glory. The leisure area includes an adventure playground and nature trail. The Weald of Kent Craft Show is held here on 2-4 May and 12-14 September. Other events planned for 1998 include Classic Motor Show (24-25 May), Tina May & Black Cat Jazz (5 June), Tudor Dancing (14 June), Alice in the Stage Garden (17 May & 28 June), Home Design & Interiors Exhibition (26-28 June), & Elizabethan Revelry (25-26 July & 1-2 Aug).
*Open: House 28 Mar-Sep daily. Gardens, Grounds & venture playground open 11-6 and also wknds from 28 Feb.
House & Grounds £5.70 pen,*
students & UB40 £5.30). Grounds, Toy Museum & Venture playground £4.20 (ch £2.80, pen, students & UB40 £3.70). Party 20+. Garden season ticket £20.
🅿 ✗ *licensed* ⬛ *(ramp into Barons Hall) shop* ✿
Cards: ⬛ ⬛ ⬛ ⬛ ⬛ ⬛ ⬛ ⬛

RAMSGATE
Maritime Museum
Clock House, Pier Yard, Royal Harbour CT11 8LS (follow Harbour signs)
☎01843 587765 Fax 01843 587765
The Maritime Museum Ramsgate is housed in the early 19th-century Clock House, a Grade II listed building, and contains four galleries depicting various aspects of the maritime heritage of the East Kent area. The adjacent restored dry dock and floating exhibits from the museum's historic ship collection include the steam tug Cervia and the Dunkirk little ship motor yacht Sundowner. Special events for 1998 include: Ships open day (4-5 July), Children's open day (30 July).
Open Mar-Sep daily 10am-5pm. Oct-Mar 5 days a week 9.30am-4.30pm. Combined ticket for museum & steam tug £1.50. (ch & pen 75p). Family £4.
🅿 *(charged)* ⬛ *(restricted) shop* ✿

RECULVER
Reculver Towers & Roman Fort
CT6 6SU (3m E of Herne Bay)
☎012273 66444
The Roman Regulbium was one of the forts built during the 3rd century to defend the Saxon Shore. The fort was in good condition until the 18th century, when erosion of the cliffs on which it stands caused part of the walls to collapse into the sea below. During the 7th century an Anglo-Saxon church was built on the site, and its floor plan can still be traced. The church was extended and, during the 12th century, the Normans built on a west front and two huge towers. These are still almost intact, providing a mariners' landmark.

*Open Apr-Sep, daily, 10-6; Oct-Mar, daily, 10-4.
Free.*
🅿 ⬛ ✿ 🚻

RICHBOROUGH
Richborough Castle
CT13 9JW (one and a half miles N of Sandwich off A257)
☎01304 612013
Now landlocked in the Kent countryside, Richborough Castle once stood on the coast, the bridgehead from which the Romans launched their invasion in AD43. The foundations of the great monumental archway built to mark the conquest of Britain, can still be seen. Today the remains of Richborough's massive fortified wall and defensive ditches convey a vivid impression of the power of the Roman empire, and the museum contains finds from the site.
*Open Apr-Oct, daily 10-6 (or dusk if earlier); Nov-Mar, 10-4 Wed-Sun. Wknds only Dec-Feb.
£2.50 (ch £1.30, concessions £1.90).*
🅿 ⬛ ✿ *(in certain areas)* 🚻

ROCHESTER
Charles Dickens Centre
Eastgate House, High St ME1 1EW
☎01634 844176
Fax 01634 827980
Eastgate House is a fine late Tudor building with an early 20th century extension. It houses a series of themed displays relating to the life and works of Charles Dickens. Many of the displays are brought dramatically to life using state-of-the-art special effects. There is an audio-visual theatre, which may be booked by groups in advance, in which a video presentation is shown relating to Dickens, his life, work, and connections with the Medway towns. In the garden is Dicken's Swiss chalet study from Gads Hill Place. Eastgate House appeared as Westgate House in Pickwick Papers and The Nun's House in Edwin Drood.
Open all year, daily 10-5.30. (Closed
Xmas). Last admission 4.45pm.
✻*£3 (ch, pen & students £2). Family ticket £8. Party 20+.*
🅿 *(250 yds) shop* ✿
Cards: ⬛ ⬛ ⬛ ⬛
See advertisement on page 82.

Guildhall Museum
High St ME1 1PY
☎01634 848717 Fax 01634 832919
The Guildhall Museum is contained in two adjacent buildings, one dating from 1687 and the other from 1909. The collections are arranged chronologically from Prehistory to the Victorian and Edwardian periods. They cover local history and archaeology, fine and decorative art. The collection of Victoriana is particularly fine. There is a special themed gallery on the subject of the prison hulks of the River Medway.
*Open all year, daily 10-5.30. (Closed Xmas).
Donations box.*
🅿 *(250 yds)* ⬛ ✿

Rochester Castle
ME1 1SX (by Rochester Bridge, A2, junc 1 M2, junc 2 M25)
☎01634 402276
This great Norman castle is one of the largest and best-preserved in England with walls 100 feet high and 12 feet thick. Inside, the splendid great hall with its gallery must be visited and a climb to the battlements is rewarded with superb views over the city of Rochester.
Open all year, Apr-Oct, daily 10-6; Nov-Mar, daily 10-4. Closed 24-27 Dec & 1 Jan.
✻*£2.70 (ch £1.30, concessions £2.10).*
shop 🚻

ROLVENDEN
C M Booth Collection of Historic Vehicles
Falstaff Antiques, 63 High St TN17 4LP (on A28)
☎01580 241234
The collection is made up of historic vehicles and other items of interest ➤

connected with transport. The main feature is the unique collection of three-wheel Morgan cars, dating from 1913. Also here is the only known Humber tri-car of 1904; and items include a 1929 Morris van, a 1936 Bampton caravan, motorcycles and bicycles. There is also a toy and model car display.
Open all year, Mon-Sat 10-6. Also some Sun & BHs. (Closed 25-26 Dec).
£1.50 (ch 75p)
P *roadside unrestricted shop*

SEVENOAKS
Knole
High St TN15 0RP (S end of Sevenoaks, E of A225)
☎01732 462100 & 450608 (info line) Fax 01732 465528
Thomas Bourchier, Archbishop of Canterbury, bought Knole in 1456 and set about transforming it from a simple medieval manor house into his palace; a century later the house was given to Henry VIII who extended it to even grander proportions. In the middle of the 16th century Knole was given to Thomas Sackville by Queen Elizabeth I; the Sackvilles kept the house for ten generations. Thomas lavished a fortune on the refurbishment and decoration of the house. Today, thanks to him, it is the largest house in England. He employed an army of builders, plasterers, upholsterers and glaziers including 300 specially imported Italians; where most Elizabethan houses had one Long Gallery, Knole has three. The State rooms are rich in architectural detail from the 17th and 18th centuries with fine portraits and outstanding furniture adding to their beauty. Outside, 26 acres of gardens contain formal walks among flower beds and fruit trees while beyond the encircling walls are further acres of undulating pasture and parkland open by courtesy of Lord Sackville. A series of recitals and plays are performed throughout the year. Ring 01892 891001 for details.
Open Apr-1 Nov, Wed-Sat 12-4 (last admission 3.30pm); Sun, BH Mon & Good Fri 11-5 (last admission 4pm), Garden 1st Wed in month, May-Sep.
£5 (ch £2.50). Garden £1. Deer Park free to pedestrians. Family ticket £12.50. Parking £2.50 per car.
P *(charged)* ☕ ✕ ♿ *toilets for disabled shop* ✗ *(ex in grounds)* ✿

SISSINGHURST
Sissinghurst Castle Garden
TN17 2AB (1m E of village)
☎01580 715330 Fax 01580 713911
The Tudor mansion of Sissinghurst Castle was bought in a neglected state in 1930 by Sir Harold Nicolson and his wife, the writer Vita Sackville-West. They set about restoring house and gardens and the gardens now rank among the most attractive and popular in England. Basing the design around the existing high Tudor walls and two stretches of water, axial walks, usually ending with a statue or archway, have been combined with small geometrical gardens. Each area is planted with a theme: either seasonal, such as the spring or summer garden; or colour, such as the White Garden or the Cottage Garden, planted mainly in orange or yellow. There is a rose garden with many old-fashioned varieties, a nuttery, a herb garden, a moat walk with a small lawn of thyme, woodland walks, an orchard and the beautiful Tower Lawn bordered with magnolias; there is also an oast house exhibition.
Open: Gardens Apr-15 Oct, Tue-Fri 1-6.30; Sat, Sun & Good Fri 10-5.30 (last admission 30mins before close. Closed Mon incl BH Mon). Due to limited capacity timed tickets are in operation so visitors may have to wait for admission, also the garden may be closed when its capacity has been reached.
£6 (ch £3).
P ✕ *licensed* ♿ *(Admission restricted to 2 wheelchairs at any one time) toilets for disabled shop* ✗ ✿

SITTINGBOURNE
Dolphin Sailing Barge Museum
Crown Quay Ln ME10 3SN (N on A2, signed)
☎01795 423215
The museum is dedicated to presenting the history of the Thames spritsail sailing barge, many of which were built along the banks of Milton Creek. Tools of the trade, photographs of many barges and associated artefacts can be seen at the barge yard along with the sailing barge Cambria. Privately owned barges are repaired - there are a forge, shipwright's shop and sail loft.
Open Etr-Oct, Sun & BHs 11-5. Other times by arrangement.
£1.50 (ch, pen & UB40 75p).
P ♿ *toilets for disabled shop*

SMALLHYTHE
Smallhythe Place
TN30 7NG (3m S of Tenterden on B2082)
☎01580 762334 Fax 01580 762334
Once a Tudor harbour master's house, this half-timbered, 16th-century building became Dame Ellen Terry's last home. It is now a museum of Ellen Terry memorabilia. The barn has been made into a theatre and is open most days courtesy of the Barn Theatre Company. Charming cottage garden, including Ellen Terry's rose garden.
Open Apr-28 Oct, Sat-Wed 1-5.30 or dusk if earlier, also Good Fri. Last admission 30 mins before closing. The Barn Theatre may be closed some days at short notice.
£3 (ch £1.50). Family ticket £7.50.
P ✗ ✿

SWINGFIELD MINNIS
The Butterfly Centre
McFarlanes Garden Centre CT15 7HX (on A260 by junction with Elham-Lydden road)
☎01303 844244
A tropical greenhouse garden with scores of colourful free-flying butterflies from all over the world among exotic plants such as bougainvillea, oleander and banana. The temperate section houses British butterflies, with many favourite species and some rarer varieties.
Open Apr-4 Oct, daily 10-5. Closed Easter Sunday.
£2 (ch £1.25 & pen £1.50). Family ticket £5.50-£6.
P ☕ ♿ *shop garden centre* ✗
Cards:

TUNBRIDGE WELLS
Tunbridge Wells Museum & Art Gallery
Civic Centre, Mount Pleasant TN1 1JN (adjacent to Town Hall)
☎01892 526121 & 547221 Fax 01892 534227
The museum displays local and natural history, archaeology, toys and dolls, and domestic and agricultural bygones. There is a fine display of Tunbridge ware. The art gallery has regularly changing exhibitions which include showings of the Ashton Bequest of Victorian oil paintings.
Open all year, daily 9.30-5. (Closed Sun, BH's & Etr Sat).
Free.
P *(200 yds)* ♿ *shop* ✗

UPNOR
Upnor Castle
ME2 4XG (on unclass road off A228)
☎01634 718742
This attractive turreted castle stands in a peaceful spot backed by wooded hills on the banks of the River Medway. It has seen a lot of action, particularly during the English Civil War in the 17th century, although more recently it has been used as a major gunpowder store.
Open Apr-Sep, daily 10-6.
P ♿ ✗ *(in certain areas)* #

WESTERHAM
Quebec House
TN16 1TD (on A25)
☎01892 890651 Fax 01892 890110
Westerham was the birthplace of General Wolfe who spent his childhood

in the multi-gabled, square brick house now renamed Quebec House. The house probably dates from the 16th century but was extended and altered in the 17th century. It contains a Wolfe museum and an exhibition on Wolfe and the Quebec campaign.
Open 5 Apr-27 Oct, Tue & Sun only 2-6 (last admission 5.30pm).
£2.50 (ch £1.25).
P *(adjacent)* ⊘ ♨

Squerryes Court
TN16 1SJ (.5m W of town centre, signed off A25) 10min from M25 J5 or 6)
☎ *01959 562345 & 563118*
Fax 01959 565949
This beautiful manor house, built in 1681, has been the home of the Wardes since 1731. It contains a fine collection of pictures, furniture, porcelain and tapestries, aquired by the family in the 18th century. Also on display are items relating to General James Wolfe of Quebec, a family friend, who received his first commission at Squerryes. The lovely garden was landscaped in the 18th century and has a lake, restored formal garden, and woodland walks. Homemade teas are served in the Old Library and on the tea lawn from 2-5pm. Picnics are welcome in front of the house by the lake. There is also a children's garden trail.
Open Apr-Sep, Wed, Sat & Sun, also BH Mon. Garden noon-5.30, House 1.30-5.30. (last entry 5pm).
House & grounds £3.90 (ch 14 £2.20 & pen £3.50). Grounds £2.40 (ch 14 £1.40 & pen £2.10)
P ▣ ᕬ *(part of grounds only)* toilets for disabled shop ⊘ *(ex in grounds)*

WEST MALLING
St Leonard's Tower
(on unclass road W of A228)
The fine early Norman tower is all that remains of a castle or fortified manor house built in about 1080 by Gundulf, Bishop of Rochester.
Open Apr-Sep, daily, 10-6; Oct-Mar, daily, 10-4.
Free.
ᕬ ♿

LANCASHIRE

BLACKPOOL
Blackpool is the British seaside town. Within easy access of the large industrial conurbations of Lancashire, its long sandy beaches became a major holiday destination in the 19th century. To add to its attractions the famous 518ft high Blackpool Tower was built, a smaller copy of the Eiffel Tower. At its base is the Circus and the Tower Ballroom, with its mighty Wurlitzer organ, which has been host to thousands of dancers. Today Blackpool has over 6.5 million visitors a year and the small pleasure beach has now become a vast complex of ferris wheels, roller coasters and other thrilling rides. In the evening from dusk till late, the Tower and the mile long Promenade are brightly lit with spectacular illuminations providing a focal point for the many tourists.

Blackpool Zoo Park
East Park Dr FY3 8PP (signed off M55 junct 4)
☎ *01253 765027 Fax 01253 798884*
This modern zoo, built in 1972, houses over four hundred animals within the 32 acres of landscaped gardens. There is a miniature railway and a children's play area, and also a mother and baby room.
Open all year daily, summer 10-6; winter 10-5 or dusk. (Closed 25 Dec).
✳*£5.50(ch £3, pen £3.30). Family £14.*
▣ ▦ ✗ *licensed* ᕬ *(limited number of wheelchairs available)* toilets for disabled shop ⊘
Cards: ▩ ▨ ▦ ▩ ⑤

Noted for its Gothic Revival Design, Lancaster's Shire Hall contains the coats of arms of all sovereigns from Richard I.

Sea Life Centre
Golden Mile Centre, Promenade FY1 5AA
☎ *01253 22445 Fax 01253 751647*
Here at the Sea Life Centre you can take a journey underwater without actually getting wet. Marine life can be viewed at close quarters, and visitors can walk through the largest shark display in Europe. Talks and feeding demonstrations throughout the day.
Open all year, daily 10-6 (peak season 9.30am-10pm). (Closed 25 Dec).
P *(100yds)* ▦ ✗ *licensed* ᕬ *(lift)* toilets for disabled shop ⊘
Details not confirmed for 1998
Cards: ▩ ▨ ▦ ▩ ⑤

CHARNOCK RICHARD
Camelot Theme Park
PR7 5LP (from M6 junct 27/28, or M61 junct 8)
☎ *01257 453044 Fax 01257 452320*
Camelot's variety of rides, shows and attractions ensures that there is something for everyone. From the adrenaline rush of the Tower of Terror and Pendragon's Plunge, to the rare breeds farm and the Sooty Show, Camelot is ideal for the whole family.
Open Apr-Oct. Telephone for further details.
£12.99 (ch over 1metre £12.99, under 1metre free, pen/disabled £6.50)
▣ ▦ ✗ ᕬ toilets for disabled shop ⊘ *(ex guide dogs)*
Cards: ▩ ▦ ▨ ▩ ⑤

CHORLEY
Astley Hall
Astley Park PR7 1NP (2m W off A581 Southport rd)
☎ *01257 515555*
Fax 01257 515556
A charming Tudor/Stuart building set in beautiful parkland, this lovely Hall retains a comfortable 'lived-in' atmosphere. There are pictures and pottery to see, as well as fine furniture and rare plasterwork ceilings. Special events: Archaeology weekend (12-13 September), Inspector Morse Exhibition (17 September-1 November).
Open Apr-Oct, Tue-Sun 12-5. Nov-Mar Fri-Sun 12-4.
£2.80 (concessions £1.80). Family ticket £6.50. Party.
P *(200 yds)* ᕬ shop ⊘

CLITHEROE
Clitheroe Castle Museum
BB7 2RA (in town centre)
☎ *01200 424635*
Fax 01200 426339
The museum in Castle House has a good collection of carboniferous fossils, and items of local interest. It is close to Clitheroe Castle, which ranks among Lancashire's oldest buildings and has one of the smallest Norman keeps in

England. Displays include local history and the industrial archaeology of the Ribble Valley, while special features include the restored Hacking ferry boat, Victorian kitchen with taped commentary, printer's and clogger's shops. There is a new 'Birds of the Ribble Valley' display. The grounds command magnificent views of the Ribble Valley.
Open from Feb 11-4.30. Mid Apr-Sep 11-5. Oct 11-4.30.
▣ ᕬ shop ⊘ *(ex guide dogs)*
Details not confirmed for 1998

LANCASTER
City Museum (also 15 Castle Hill)
Market Sq LA1 1HT
☎ *01524 64637*
Fax 01524 841692

The fine Georgian proportions of the old town hall are the setting for the City Museum, with its new gallery illustrating the history and archaeology of the city from prehistoric and Roman times onwards. Also housed here is the museum of the King's Own Royal Lancaster Regiment, which has a wealth of paintings, medals and documents relating to three centuries of this famous regiment's history. Changing exhibitions occupy the ground floor. The Cottage Museum, furnished in the style of an artisan's house of around 1820, faces Lancaster Castle. Reopening of King's Own Regimental Museum.
Open all year, Mon-Sat 10-5, (Closed Xmas-New Year). 15 Castle Hill, Etr-end Sep, daily 2-5. ➤

The log flume at Morecambe's Frontierland theme park provides a watery experience of the Wild West.

City Museum free. 15 Castle Hill 75p (concessions 25p)
P (5 mins walk) & (ramp to ground floor) shop ❀ (ex guide dogs)

Maritime Museum
St George's Quay LA1 1RB (from A6 follow signs to Lancaster town centre)
☎01524 64637
Fax 01524 841692
Graceful Ionic columns adorn the front of the Custom House, built in 1764 and home of the city's Maritime Museum since 1985. Inside, the histories of the maritime trade of Lancaster, the Lancaster Canal and the fishing industry of Morecambe Bay are well illustrated. An extension to the building houses preserved boats, audio-visual shows and reconstructions. Events for 1998 include an Easter Maritime Festival (Good Friday - Easter Monday) which will feature sea shanties, drama, talks and walks on maritime themes.
Open all year, daily, Etr-Oct 11am-5pm; Nov-Etr 12.30-4pm.
£2 (concessions £1).
P ❂ & toilets for disabled shop ❀ (ex guide dogs)

Shire Hall
Lancaster Castle, Castle Pde LA1 1YJ
☎01524 64998
Founded on the site of three Roman forts, Lancaster Castle dominates Castle Hill, above the River Lune. Its first fortifications date back to the 11th century. The Norman keep was built in about 1170 and King John added a curtain wall and Hadrian's Tower, restored in the 18th and 19th centuries. A turret named after John of Gaunt was used as a beacon to warn of the approach of the Armada. The Shire Hall, chiefly noted for its Gothic revival design, was built within the castle boundaries and contains a splendid display of heraldry, with the coats of arms of all the sovereigns from Richard I. The Crown Court (still sited here) was notorious as having handed out the greatest number of death sentences of any court in the land, while another exhibition displays the grim relics of early prison life.

Open Etr-1st wknd Nov, daily 10.30 (1st tour)-4 (last tour). Court sittings permitting -it is advisable to telephone before visiting except in August or at weekends.
✱£3 (ch, pen & students 1.75p). Part tour when Court in session £2 (ch & pen & students £1).
P (100m) (voucher system) & shop ❀ (ex guide dogs)
See advertisement on page 83.

LEIGHTON HALL
Leighton Hall
LA5 9ST (off M6 at junct 35A onto A6 & follow signs)
☎01524 734474 Fax 01524 720357
Early Gillow furniture is displayed among other treasures in the fine interior of this neo-Gothic mansiont. Outside a large collection of birds of prey can be seen, and flying displays are given at 3.30pm each afternoon (weather permitting). There are also fine gardens, a maze and a woodland walk. Special events for 1998 include: Concert and Fireworks (3 July), Shakespeare in the Garden (7-8 August), Rainbow Craft Fair (12-13 October), Dolls House and Miniatures Fair (18 October). Please telephone for details of these special events.
Open May-Sep, Sun, Tue-Fri & BH Mon from 2pm. For Aug only open from 11.30. (Last admission 4.30pm).
£3.60 (ch 5-16 £2.40, pen £3). Family ticket £11.
P ❂ & shop garden centre ❀ (ex in park)

LEYLAND
British Commercial Vehicle Museum
King St PR5 1LE (0.75m from junct 28 M6)
☎01772 451011 Fax 01772 623404
The largest commercial vehicle museum in Europe is located in a town long associated with the British motor industry. Over sixty restored British commercial vehicles are on display, ranging from horse-drawn examples to modern. Special exhibits include the oldest known preserved commercial vehicle, the 100 ton Scammell and the Popemobile.

Open Etr-end Oct, Sun, Tue, Wed only. Also BHs.
£4 (ch & pen £2). Family ticket £10.
P ❂ & (ramps to decked viewing area) toilets for disabled shop ❀

LYTHAM ST ANNES
Toy & Teddy Bear Museum
373 Clifton Dr North FY8 2PA (on A584, towards Blackpool)
☎01253 713705
The Tourism Award-Winning Toy and Teddy Bear Museum, set in one of St Annes famous period buildings, has a collection of old toys arranged in five large rooms and the Toytown Arcade. Charming displays include: Teddy's Wedding, Bears' Picnic and Bears at the Seaside. Other attractions include a Mini Motor Museum, a collection of more than 200 dolls, 35 dolls' houses, toy trains, working layouts, Dinky cars, aeroplanes, meccano, books and games.
Open Whitsun-Oct, daily 11-5 (closed Mon & Tue). Winter, Sun & school hols only 11-5.
£2.50 (ch & pen £1.75)
P & shop

MARTIN MERE
WWT Martin Mere
L40 0TA (6m from Ormskirk, off A59)
☎01704 895181 Fax 01704 892343
One of Britain's most important wetland sites where visitors can get really close to a variety of ducks, geese and swans from all over the world as well as two flocks of flamingos. Many of the birds are so friendly they will even feed from your hand! Thousands of wildfowl, including Pink-Footed geese, Bewick's and Whooper swans, winter here. Other features include a children's adventure playground, exhibition gallery, craft area and an educational centre. Facilities for disabled people include free wheelchair loan, purpose built toilets and braille notices around the grounds. There is a packed programme of events and activities throughout the year.
Open all year, daily 9.30-5.30 (4pm in winter). (Closed 25 Dec).
✱£4.50 (ch £2.50). Family ticket £11.50. Party 10+.
P ❂ & (wheelchair loan, Braille trail, heated hide) toilets for disabled shop ❀
Cards: ▨ ▨ ▨ ▨ 🏧

MORECAMBE
Frontierland - Western Theme Park
The Promenade LA4 4DG (from M6 take junct 34 northbound and junct 35 southbound)
☎01524 410024
Fax 01524 831399
One of the most popular tourist attractions in the North West, with over 1.3 million visitors a year. Situated directly on the Promenade, Frontierland is a western style theme park which offers over 40 rides and attractions, ranging from whiteknuckle rollercoasters to gentle rides fo younger children. There is also live entertainment during the summer season.
Open 12-26 Apr & 24 May-27 Sep, daily; 21 Mar-11 Apr & May Day-23 May, wknds only; Also school hol wk in Oct. Admission times under review.
✱Admission free. Rides Pass £8 (ch under 12 £6). Family ticket £24.
P (charged) ❂ & toilets for disabled shop ❀
Cards: ▨ ▨ ▨ ⊙ ▨ ▨ 🏧

PADIHAM
Gawthorpe Hall
BB12 8UA (off A671)
☎01282 771004
Fax 01282 770178
An early 17th-century manor house, Gawthorpe Hall was built around Britain's most southerly pele Tower, restored in 1850. The house contains fine panelling and moulded ceilings, a minstrels' gallery and Jacobean long gallery. A collection of portraits from the National Portrait Gallery and the Kay Shuttleworth Collections of costume, embroidery and lace are on show in the expanded exhibition areas.

Exhibitions during high season. Please ring for details.
Open all year, Garden: daily 10-6. Hall: Apr-Oct, Tue-Thu, Sat & Sun 1-5. Also open BH Mon & Good Friday. (Last admission 4.15pm).
House: £2.90 (ch £1.30). Family ticket £8. Garden free. Party 15+.
P ❂ & toilets for disabled ❀ ❦

PRESTON
Harris Museum & Art Gallery
Market Square PR1 2PP ((in town centre)
☎01772 258248 Fax 01772 866764
The Harris Museum and Art Gallery is an impressive Greek Revival building containing extensive collections of fine and decorative art including a Watercolour, Drawing and Prints gallery and gallery of Clothes and Fashion. The Story of Preston gallery covers the town's history and the lively exhibition programmes of contemporary art and social history are accompanied by events and activities throughout the year. 1998 exhibitions include: Dark Matter - Investigation into the links between art & science (March-May), Relative Values - Portraits (May-July), Moving Stories - Preston Culture (May-September), Lux - Work in Light (July-September).
Open all year, Mon-Sat 10-5. (Closed Sun & BHs).
Free.
P (5 mins walk) (orange badge disabled parking only) ❂ & (Wheelchair available. Chair lift mezzanine galleries) toilets for disabled shop ❀

ROSSENDALE
Helmshore Textile Museums
Holcombe Rd, Helmshore BB4 4NP (on B6325, approx 2m S of Haslingden town centre, singed off A56)
☎01706 226459
Fax 01706 218554
Two stone-built mills in a picturesque valley in the West Pennine Moors depicting the history of Lanchaire's textile industry. thorough working machinery, displays and exhibitions. Higher Mill is a woollen fulling mill with a recently restored waterwheel and next door is Whitaker's Mill which is complete with working carding and mule spinning machinery. Family groups and school visits are especially welcome.
Open Mon-Fri 2-5, Sun 1-5, Apr-Jun & Sep-Oct; Sun-Fri 1-5, Jul-Aug.Good Fri, Etr Sun & Mon 1-5, Etr Sat 2-5. Closed Sat ex Etr.
P ❂ & toilets for disabled shop ❀
Details not confirmed for 1998

Whitaker Park & Rossendale Museum
Whitaker Park, Rawtenstall BB4 6RE (off A681, quarter of a mile W of Rawtenstall centre)
☎01706 217777 & 226509
Former mill owner's house, built in 1840 and set in the delightful Whitaker Park. Displays include fine and decorative arts, a Victorian drawing room, natural history, costume, local and social history. Temporary exhibitions are held throughout the year, including Chris Speak's photography of the South Pennines (2-31 May).
Open Mon-Fri, 1-5; Sat 10-5 (Apr-Oct), 10-4 (Nov-Mar); Sun noon-5 (Apr-Oct), noon-4 (Nov-Mar). BH's 1-5. Closed 25-26 Dec, 1 Jan & afternoon 24 Dec)
Free.
P & ❀ (ex guide dogs)

RUFFORD
Rufford Old Hall
L40 1SG (off A59, 7m North of Ormskirk)
☎01704 821254
Fax 01704 821254
There is a story that William Shakespeare performed here for the owner Sir Thomas Hesketh in the Great Hall of this, one of the finest 16th century buildings in Lancashire. The playwright would have delighted in the magnificent Hall, with its intricately carved movable wooden screen. Built in 1530, it established the Hesketh family's seat for the next 250 years. The Carolean Wing, altered in

1821, features fine collections of 16th and 17th century oak furniture, arms, armour and tapestries.
Open Apr-Nov, Sat-Wed, Hall 1-5 (Last admission 4.30pm); Garden & shop 12-5.30.
£3.50 (ch £1.70). Family ticket £9.50. Garden only £1.80. (ch free during school hols)
P ✗ ⚹ *(braille guide, wheelchairs, adapted cutlery etc) shop ⚹ (ex in grounds)*

SAMLESBURY
Samlesbury Hall
Preston New Rd PR5 OUP (fr M6 Junct31 onto A677 for 3m)
☎01254 812010 & 812229
Fax 01254 812174
Samlesbury Hall is situated in 5 acres of beautiful grounds. A feature of this well restored half-timbered manor house, built during the 14th and 15th centuries, are the windows from nearby Whalley Abbey. Sales of antiques and collector's items, craft shows and temporary exhibitions are held all year round. Please ring for details.
Open all year ex last wk Dec & 1st 2 wks Jan, Tue-Sun 11-4.30.
£2.50 (ch 4-16 £1).
P ✗ *licensed* ⚹ *toilets for disabled ⚹ ⚹*

SILVERDALE
RSPB Nature Reserve
Mayers Farm LA5 0SW (close to Silverdale station)
☎01524 701601
A very popular nature reserve consisting of a large reed swamp with meres with willow and alder scrub in a valley with woodland on its limestone slopes. The reserve covers 321 acres. Britain's largest concentration of up to five pairs of bitterns breed here, together with bearded tits, reed, sedge and grasshopper warblers, shovelers, pochards, tufted ducks and marsh harriers. Black terns and ospreys regularly pass through in spring and greenshanks and various sandpipers in the autumn. Wintering wildfowl include large flocks of mallards, teals, wigeons, and shovelers. Thousands of starlings, swallows and wagtails roost seasonally in the reeds often attracting hunting sparrowhawks and hen harriers. Otters are resident and are sometimes to be seen from the hides as are roe and red deer. Phone for details of special events.
Open daily 9am-9pm (or sunset if earlier). Visitor Centre daily 10-5. (closed Xmas Day).
£3.50 (ch £1, concessions £2) Family £7.
P ⚹ ⚹ *(chair lift to 1st floor, ramp access to 4 hides) toilets for disabled shop ⚹*
Cards: 💳 💳 💳 💳

TURTON BOTTOMS
Turton Tower
BL7 0HG (on B6391, off A666 or A676)
☎01204 852203 Fax 01204 853759
This historic house incorporates a 15th-century tower house and Elizabethan half-timbered buildings. Restored in the 19th century, the house displays a major collection of carved wood furniture, mostly English, and period rooms depicting the Tudor, Stuart and Victorian eras. A product of the Renaissance, the house became associated with the Gothic revival and later typified the idealism of the Arts and Crafts movement. The gardens are being restored in late-Victorian style and include a tennis court constructed for the All England mixed doubles winner J C Kay. A varied programme of events in 1998 will include exhibitions and art activities relating to the restoration of the gardens.
Open May-Sep, Mon-Thu 10-12 & 1-5. Wknds 1-5; Mar, Apr & Oct Sat-Wed, 1-4; Nov & Feb, Sun 1-4. Other times by prior arrangement.
£2 (ch & pen £1). Family ticket £5. Guided tour with supper/lunch , prices vary.
P ⚹ ⚹ *toilets for disabled shop ⚹ (ex in grounds)*

WHALLEY
Whalley Abbey
BB7 9SS
☎01254 822268
Fax 01254 824227
These ruins of a 13th-century Cistercian abbey are set in the delightful gardens of the Blackburn Diocesan Retreat and Conference House, a 16th-century manor house with gardens reaching down to the River Calder. The remains include two gateways, a chapter house and the abbot's lodgings and kitchen.
Grounds open all year; coffee shop, shop & exhibition area, Jan-Dec daily 11-5.
£1.50 (ch 25p, pen £1).
P ⚹ ✗ *licensed* ⚹ *(chair lifts, ramps) shop ⚹ (ex guide dogs)*

LEICESTERSHIRE

ASHBY-DE-LA-ZOUCH
Ashby-de-la-Zouch Castle
☎01530 413343
The impressive ruins of a 14th century castle, its most striking feature is the splendid 15th-century Hastings Tower, named after Edward, Lord Hastings. He also built the chapel. His descendants entertained Henry VIII, Mary Queen of Scots, James I and Charles I. During the Civil War, the castle was held for over a year by royalists before being demolished. The remains include the tower, walls, underground passage and large kitchen. A torch is recommended for exploring the dark underground tunnel linking the tower to the kitchen.
Open Apr-Oct, daily 10-6 (or dusk if earlier); Nov-Mar, Wed-Sun 10-4.
£2.30 (ch £1.20, concessions £1.70).
P ⚹ ⚹ ⚹

BELVOIR
Belvoir Castle
NG32 1PD (between A52 & A607)
☎01476 870262
Fax 01476 870443
Although Belvoir Castle has been the home of the Dukes of Rutland for many centuries, the turrets, battlements, towers and pinnacles of the house are a 19th-century fantasy. Amongst the many treasures to be seen inside are paintings by Van Dyck, Murillo, Holbein and other famous artists. Also here is the museum of the Queens Royal Lancers. The castle's lovely terraced gardens are adorned with sculptures. Please ring for details of forthcoming events.
Open Apr-Sep, Tue-Thu, Sat-Sun & BH Mon 11-5.
P ⚹ ✗ *licensed* ⚹ *toilets for disabled shop ⚹*
Details not confirmed for 1998

COALVILLE
Snibston Discovery Park
Ashby Rd LE67 3LN (4.5m from M1 junct 22/2m from A42/M42 junct 13 on A50 on the West side of Coalville)
☎01530 510851 & 813256 Fax 01530 813301
This major science and industry museum is set on the 100-acre site of a former colliery. There are themed galleries: Science Alive, Light Fantastic, Virtual Reality, Textiles and Fashion, Engineering, Extractive Industries and Transport. An outdoor science play area, a fascinating guided tour of the colliery buildings by ex-miners, a country park with a nature trail, the Century Theatre, picnic areas, a golf course, fishing lakes and a special events arena are further attractions. Special events include: BBC Switch On/Tune In exhibition (until November),
Open all year, Oct-Mar daily 10-5; Apr-Oct daily 10-6. (Closed 25-26 Dec).
£4 (ch £2.75, concessions £2.95). Family ticket £10.
P ⚹ ⚹ *(Braille labels, touch tables, parking available) toilets for disabled shop ⚹*
Cards: 💳 💳

DONINGTON-LE-HEATH
Donington-le-Heath Manor House
Manor Rd LE67 2FW (S of Coalville)
☎01530 831259 Fax 01530 831259
This is a rare example of a medieval manor house, tracing its history back to about 1280. It has now been restored as a period house, with fine oak furnishings. The surrounding grounds include period gardens, and the adjoining stone barn houses a well stocked tea shop. Please telephone for details of special events.
Open Wed before Etr-Sep, Sun 2-6. Free.
P ⚹ ⚹ *shop ⚹*

KIRBY MUXLOE
Kirby Muxloe Castle
(off B5380)
☎01533 386886
When Lord Hastings drew up designs for his castle in the late 15th century, he first had to obtain 'licence to crenellate'. The moated, fortified, brick-built manor house was never completed: Hastings was executed a few years later and building work ceased. Kirby Muxloe Castle now stands as a ruin in his memory.
Open Apr-Nov, wknds & BH's 12-5.
£1.75 (ch 90p, concessions £1.30)
P ⚹ ⚹

LEICESTER
Abbey Pumping Station
Corporation Rd, Abbey Ln LE4 5PX (off A6, 1m from city centre)
☎0116 266 1330 Fax 0116 261 2851
Built as a Pumping Station in 1891. The Exhibition Hall hosts a public health exhibition entitled "Flushed with Pride" and looks at the science, ecology and history of toilets, water and hygiene. The site features a narrow gauge railway.
Open Apr-Dec, Mon-Sat 10-5.30, Sun 2-5.30. (Closed 24-26 Dec). Free.
P ⚹ *(loan of wheelchairs) toilets for disabled shop ⚹*

Belgrave Hall
(off Belgrave/ Coughborough road, 1 mile from Church Rd, off Thurcaston Rd, Belgrave LE4 5PE city centre)
☎0116 266 6590 Fax 0116 261 3063
A delightful three-storey Queen Anne house dating from 1709 with beautiful period and botanic gardens. Authentic room settings contrast Edwardian elegance with Victorian cosiness and include the kitchen, drawing room, music room and nursery. Ring for details of special events in 1998.
Open all year, Mon-Sat 10-5.30, Sun 2-5.30. (Closed 24-26 Dec). Free.
P ⚹ *(loan of wheelchair) toilets for disabled shop garden centre ⚹*

Jewry Wall Museum & Site
St Nicholas Circle LE1 4LB
☎0116 247 3021
Fax 0116 247 3011
Behind the massive fragment of the Roman Jewry wall and a Roman Baths site of the 2nd century AD is the Museum of Leicestershire Archaeology, which covers finds from the earliest times to the Middle Ages.
Open all year, Mon-Sat 10-5.30, Sun 2-5.30. (Closed Good Fri, 25/26 Dec & 1 Jan). Free.
P *(300yds) (limited on-street parking)* ⚹ *toilets for disabled shop ⚹*

Leicestershire Museum & Art Gallery
New Walk LE1 7EA
☎0116 255 4100
Fax 0116 247 3005
This major regional venue houses local and national collections. New galleries include 'Variety of Life' (natural history), 'Leicestershire's Rocks' (geology), 'Ancient Egyptians' and 'Discovering Art'. Decorative arts cover ceramics, silver and glass,
and an internationally famous collection of German Expressionism and other displays range from the Rutland Dinosaur, mummies, stunning collections of minerals, and thousands of butterflies. There are lots of 'hands on' exhibits and a changing programme of temporary exhibitions throughout the year. There are also lunchtime concerts and special events. ➤

See the evolution of the bell founders' craft at the Bell Foundry Museum

Battlefield Steam Railway also has a museum containing an extensive collection of fascinating railway artefacts.

Open all year, Mon-Sat 10-5.30, Sun 2-5.30. (Closed 24-26 Dec).
Free.
🅿 ♿ toilets for disabled shop ⊗ (ex guide dog)

Leicestershire Record Office
Long St, Wigston Magna LE18 2AH
☎ 0116 257 1080 Fax 0116 257 1120
Housed in a converted 19th-century school in Wigston, the Record Office is the centre for the history of Leicestershire. It holds photographs, electoral registers and archive film, files of local newspapers, history tapes and sound recordings, all of which can be studied. Records of the county's landed estates and families, borough archives dating back to 1103 and census returns for Leicestershire and Rutland going back to 1841. Please telephone for details of special events.
Open all year, Mon, Tue & Thu 9.15-5, Wed 9.15-7.30, Fri 9.15-4.45, Sat 9.15-12.15. (Closed Sun & BH wknds Sat-Tue).
Free.
🅿 ♿ toilets for disabled ⊗ 🚂

Newarke Houses
The Newarke LE2 7BY
☎ 0116 247 3222 Fax 0116 247 3011
This museum follows the story of Leicestershire's social history from the 16th century to the present day, showing everyday life and social change throughout the county. Clocks, toys, Victorian toilets, instruments and furniture are among the many collections. A reconstructed street scene gives glimpses of Victorian life and the fascinating life of Daniel Lambert, the famous 52-stone gaoler of the 18th century, is also told. Teddy Bear's Picnic - June 6.
Open all year, Mon-Sat 10-5.30, Sun 2-5.30. (Closed Good Fri, 25 & 26 Dec).
Free.
P (200 yds) shop ⊗

University of Leicester Botanic Gardens
Beaumont Hall, Stoughton Dr South, Oadby LE2 2NA (3m SE A6)
☎ 0116 271 7725
The grounds of four houses, now used as student residences and not open to the public, make up this 16-acre garden. A great variety of plants in different

settings provide a delightful place to walk, including rock, water and sunken gardens, trees, borders, heathers and glasshouses. 1998 special events: Open Day for National Gardens Scheme (26 July, adults £1.50), NCCPG 'Plant Fair' (6 September, adults £2).
Open all year, Mon-Fri 9-3.30. (Closed BHs).
Free.
🅿 ♿ ⊗

Wygston's House Museum of Costume
12 Applegate, St Nicholas Circle LE1 5LD
☎ 0116 247 3056 Fax 0116 2620964
Behind a Georgian street front hides a beautiful late medieval building which houses selections from the county's extensive collections of costumes and textiles. Re-displayed in 1993, the exhibits include a recreation of a 1920s draper's shop; fashionable outfits from 1805 to the present day; Victorian menswear, and a children's gallery. Themed temporary exhibitions take place throughout the year.
Open all year, Mon-Sat 10-5.30, Sun 2-5.30. (Closed Good Fri & 25-26 Dec)
Free.
P (150 yds) ♿ shop ⊗

LOUGHBOROUGH
Bell Foundry Museum
Freehold St LE11 1AR
☎ 01509 233414 Fax 01509 263305
Located in the former fettling shop of the John Taylor Bell Foundry, the museum is part of the largest working bell foundry in the world. Exhibits follow the evolution of the bell founder's craft, showing techniques of moulding, casting, turning and fitting, including modern craft practices.
Open all year, Tue-Sat 9.30-12.30 & 1.30-4.30. Evening tours by prior arrangement. Special tours of Bell Foundry on BH Mon 11-2.15.
🅿 ♿ toilets for disabled shop ⊗
Details not confirmed for 1998

Great Central Railway
Great Central Rd LE11 1RW (signposted from A6)
☎ 01509 230726 Fax 01509 239791
This private steam railway runs over eight miles from Loughborough Central to Leicester North, with all trains calling at

Quorn & Woodhouse and Rothley. The locomotive depot and museum are at Loughborough Central. A buffet car is run on most trains.
Open Sat, Sun & BH Mon & midweek May-Sep.
❋ Round trip £8. (ch & pen £5.25). Family ticket £17.25.

🅿 💷 ✗ licensed ♿ (Disabled coach available on most trains, check beforehand) toilets for disabled shop
Cards:

MARKET BOSWORTH
Battlefield Steam Railway Line
CV13 6NW (from A444/A447 take B585 to Market Bosworth and follow signs for Congerstone/Shackerstone.)
☎ 01827 880754
Together with a regular railway service (mainly steam) from Shackerstone to Shenton, there is an extensive railway museum featuring a collection of rolling stock and a multitude of other relics from the age of steam rail travel. With the opening of the extension in April 1992 of the line to Shenton (site of the Battle of Bosworth Field), the return passenger trip is nine miles. There is a dining train, the Tudor Rose, which offers Sunday lunches on certain dates. A number of special events are planned for 1998, ring for details.
Open all year, Station & Museum, Sat & Sun, 10.30-5.30. Passenger steam train service operates Etr-Oct, Sat, Sun & BH Mon. Diesel trains operate Jun-Sep, Wed & Sat only.
Shackerstone station: £1 (ch 5-15 free). Return train fare £5 (ch £2.50). Family ticket £14.
🅿 💷 ✗ ♿ shop
Cards:

Bosworth Battlefield Visitor Centre & Country Park
Ambion Hill, Sutton Cheney CV13 0AD (2.5m S off M69)
☎ 01455 290429
Fax 01455 292841
The Battle of Bosworth Field was fought in 1485 between the armies of Richard III and the future Henry VII. The visitor centre gives the viewer a comprehensive interpretation of the battle by means of exhibitions, models and a film theatre. There are also illustrated trails around the

battlefield, and special medieval attractions are held in the summer months. Full details of admission fees for special events and free leaflets are available on application.

Open all year - Country Park & Battle trails all year during daylight hours. Visitor Centre Apr-Oct, Mon-Fri 1-5, (from 11am Jul & Aug), wknds, BH Mon & Good Fri 11-6. Parties all year by arrangement.

🅿 *(charged)* 🍴 ♿ *toilets for disabled shop*
Details not confirmed for 1998

OADBY
Farmworld
Stoughton Farm Park, Gartree Rd LE2 2FB (signposted from A6 & A47)
☎ 0116 271 0355
Fax 0116 271 3211
Farmworld is a working farm that offers a feast of fun and surprises for all the family. Children will enjoy the Children's Farmyard and the playground, while their parents might appreciate the Edwardian Ale-house and the craft workshops and demonstrations. There are also Shire horses and cart rides, lakeside and woodland walks, nature trails and an interesting collection of rare farm animals.

Open all year, daily 10-5.30 (5pm in winter). (Closed 25 Dec - 3 Jan).
£4 (ch £2.50, pen £3.25). Family ticket £12. Party.

🅿 🍴 ♿ *(specifically designed viewing gallery) toilets for disabled shop* 🐕
Cards: 🏧 💳 💳 💳 🅂

SWINFORD
Stanford Hall
LE17 6DH (1.5m E of Swinford)
☎ 01788 860250
Fax 01788 860870
This beautiful William and Mary house on the River Avon was built in 1697 by Sir Roger Cave, ancestor of the present owner Lady Braye. The Ballroom is notable for its decoration and chimney-piece and the house contains antique furniture, paintings (including the Stuart Collection) and family costumes. There is a replica of Percy Pilcher's flying machine of 1898. In the grounds are a walled rose garden, an old forge, and a motorcycle museum. A craft centre based in the old stables can be seen on most Sundays. Outdoor pursuits include fishing and a nature trail, and the large number of events arranged for 1998 includes car and motorcycle owners club rallies, Music & Firework Spectacular on 8 August, and a craft fair in October. Please telephone for further details.

Open Etr Sat-end Sep, Sat, Sun, BH Mon & Tue following 2.30-5.30; noon on BH & Event Days (House 2.30). Last admission 5pm.
House & Grounds £3.80 (ch £1.90); Grounds only £2.10 (ch £1); Motorcycle Museum £1 (ch 35p). Party 20+.

🅿 🍴 ♿ *(museum also accessible) toilets for disabled shop* 🐕 *(ex guide dogs in park)*

TWYCROSS
Twycross Zoo Park
CV9 3PX (1.5m NW off A444)
☎ 01827 880250
Fax 01827 880700
Set up during the 1960s, Twycross Zoo Park specialises in primates, and also includes gibbons, gorillas, orang-utangs and chimpanzees. There is a huge range of monkeys from the tiny tamarins and spider monkeys to the large howler monkeys.

There are also various other animals such as lions, tigers, elephants and giraffes, and a pets' corner for younger children. Other attractions include a Sealion Pool with spectacular waterfall, Penguin Pool with underwater viewing and a Children's Adventure Playground.

Open all year, daily 10-6 (4pm in winter). (Closed 25 Dec).
£5.50 (ch £3.50, pen £4)

🅿 🍴 ♿ *toilets for disabled shop* 🐕

ALFORD
Manor House Museum
West St LN13 9DJ (on the A1104, in centre of town)
☎ 01507 463073
This thatched 17th-century manor house is now a folk museum with local history displays: a chemist's shop, shoemaker's shop, school room, wash house and garden, photographic display, veterinary display and a nursery and maid's bedroom. There are also displays of agricultural and craft tools, sweet making equipment, a kitchen and even a police cell. Please ring for details of special events.

Open Etr-first Fri in Oct daily, Mon-Sat 10-5, Sun 1-4.30.
£1.25(accompanied ch free)

🅿 🍴 *shop* 🐕

BELTON
Belton House Park & Gardens
NG32 2LS (3m NE Grantham on A607)
☎ 01476 566116 Fax 01476 579071
For many people Belton is the perfect country house, a handsome but not overwhelming grand mansion. It was the home of the Brownlow family for nearly three centuries before being given to the National Trust, and the family still has a flat in the house. The ground floor has a succession of state rooms, with the Marble Hall as its centrepiece. The name comes from the black and white marble floor, which is original. The walls are decorated with intricate wood carvings of birds, fruit, flowers and foliage, which have been attributed to Grinling Gibbons but are probably by Edmund Carpenter. There are more remarkable carvings in the formal saloon, which also has ornate plasterwork on the ceiling. Splendid furnishings and decorations throughout the house include tapestries and hangings, both old and modern, lovely garden scenes by Melchior d'Hondecoeter, family portraits, porcelain and fine furniture. Not to be forgotten are the rolling grounds and gardens, including an orangery and formal Italian garden, laid out in the 19th century. There are some attractive sculptures, and an adventure playground for children. Special events include Belton Horse Trials (18-19 April), summer concert (27 June), Family Fun Day (19 July). Please telephone for details.

Open 28 Mar-1 Nov, Wed-Sun & BH Mon (Closed Good Fri). House open 1-5.30 (last admission 5pm). Grounds open 11-5.30.
£5 (ch £2.50). Family ticket £12.50.

🅿 🍴 ✕ *licensed* ♿ *(braille guide, hearing scheme) toilets for disabled shop* 🐕 *(ex in grounds)* 🐕
Cards: 🏧 💳

CLEETHORPES
Pleasure Island Theme Park
Kings Rd DN35 0PL
☎ 01472 211511
Fax 01472 211087
Get ready for a sensational, fantastic value family fun day out. With over 50 international attractions, shows, and 55,000 square feet of undercover fun, visit the Old English village, Spain and Morocco and explore an African village.

Open from 23 Mar, please telephone for further opening times.
£8.50 (ch under 4 free, pen £4.50). Family ticket £28.

🅿 🍴 ✕ ♿ *toilets for disabled shop*
Cards: 🏧 💳 💳 🅂

CONINGSBY
Battle of Britain Memorial Flight Visitor Centre
LN4 4SY (on A153)
☎ 01526 344041
View the aircraft of the Battle of Britain Memorial Flight, comprising the only flying Lancaster in Europe, four Spitfires, one Hurricane, Dakota and a Chipmunk. Because of operational commitments,

specific aircraft may not be available. Ring the telephone number given for information before planning a visit.

Open all year, Mon-Fri, conducted tours 10-3.30. (Closed BH's & 2 wks Xmas). (phone prior to visiting to check security situation)

🅿 ♿ *(electric wheelchairs not allowed in hangers) shop* 🐕
Details not confirmed for 1998

ELSHAM
Elsham Hall Country & Wildlife Park
DN20 0QZ (on M180/A15 Humber Bridge junc 5)
☎ 01652 688698
Fax 01652 688240
Attractions include a children's animal farmyard, clocktower shop and art gallery, carp-feeding jetty, an arboretum and an adventure playground. There are nature trails and quizzes, a garden centre, craft centre with working craftsfolk, a tea room and restaurant and a theatre noted for its medieval banquets and jazz concerts. The Falconry Centre has an excellent selection of birds of prey, and there are flying displays most days, weather and birds permitting. The new Barn Theatre offers a wide variety of evening programmes, including Medieval Banquets and Viking Feasts. There are special events planned throughout the year, especially during the school holidays. For 1998 these include: hatching festival (Easter Sunday/Monday), Magical May Day (May Bank Holiday), children's festival (Whitsun Bank Holiday), and a children's folk festival (August Bank Holiday).

Open Etr Sat-mid Sep, daily 11-5. Mar & late Sep weekends only. (Closed Winter & Good Fri). Theatre/Craft Centre open by appointment only in winter and during season (with some workshops open at different times)
£3.95 (ch £2.50, pen £3.50 & ch under 3 free). Party 20+.

🅿 🍴 ✕ *licensed* ♿ *(fishing facilities for disabled) toilets for disabled shop garden centre* 🐕 *(ex guide dogs on leads)*
Cards: 💳

EPWORTH
Old Rectory
1 Rectory St DN9 1HX (on A161, 3m S of M180 junct 2)
☎ 01427 872268
John and Charles Wesley were brought up in the handsome rectory, which was built in 1709 and restored in 1957. This Grade I listed Queen Anne building is maintained by the World Methodist Council as 'The Home of the Wesleys' rather than as a museum. It displays items which belonged to John and Charles Wesley and their parents Samuel and Susanna. Some of the rooms are set out with period furniture much as the family would have known. Also in the house are paintings and prints concerning the lives and times of the Wesley family and commemorative china etc.

Open daily Mar-Oct, Mon-Sat 10-12 & 2-4, Sun 2-4 (only in Mar, Apr & Oct) May-Sept Mon-Sat 10am-4.30pm.Sun 2pm-4.30pm. Other times by prior arrangement.
£2 (ch £1).

🅿 🍴 ✕ ♿ *shop* 🐕
Cards: 🏧 💳

GAINSBOROUGH
Old Hall
Parnell St DN21 2NB
☎ 01427 612669 Fax 01427 612779
A complete medieval manor house dating back to 1460-80 and containing a remarkable Great Hall and original kitchen with room settings. Richard III, Henry VIII, the Mayflower Pilgrims and John Wesley all in their day visited the Old Hall. Special events during 1998 include craft fairs on 29 March and 28/29 November, Living History Weekend 24/25 May, and Town and Country Fair, 24/25 May.

Open all year, Mon-Sat 10-5; Etr-Oct, Sun 2-5.30. Closed 25-26 Dec, 1 Jan & Good Fri.
Admission charged.

🅿 *(100 yds)* 🍴 ♿ *(audio tour, induction loop) shop* 🐕

GRANTHAM
See Belvoir, Leicestershire

GRIMSBY
National Fishing Heritage Centre
Alexandra Dock DN31 1UZ (follow signs off M180)
☎ 01472 323345 Fax 01472 323555
The National Fishing Heritage Centre tells the story of the British Fishing Industry, arguably the nation's most gruelling and demanding occupation, as seen through the eyes of one of the world's greatest fishing ports - Grimsby. Visitors are given a rare opportunity to experience life at sea on a Grimsby trawler in the mid 1950's; they can see, hear, smell and touch a series of recreated environments which take them from the back streets of Grimsby to the distant fishing grounds of the Arctic Circle. Guided tours of the 'Ross Tiger' trawler are available.

Open all year, daily 10-6. (Closed 25-26 Dec & 1 Jan).

🅿 🍴 ♿ *(easy access route) toilets for disabled shop*
Details not confirmed for 1998
Cards: 🏧 💳

GRIMSTHORPE
Grimsthorpe Castle
PE10 0NB (on A151, 8m E of Colsterworth rbt on A1)
☎ 01778 591205 Fax 01778 591259
An historic home, the seat of the Willoughby de Eresby family since 1516. The architecture comprises a medieval tower and a Tudor quadrangular house with a Baroque north front by Vanbrugh. There are eight state rooms and two picture galleries with an important collection of furniture, pictures and tapestries. Formal gardens, parkland and lake. The Castle is now administered by ➤

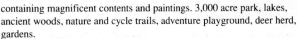

the Grimsthorpe and Drummond Castle Trust. Special events for 1998 include an open air concert (20 June), Summer Fair (5 Jul), Festival of Food, Drink, Folk and Dance (17-19 July), Antiques Festival (11-12 July), Rainbow Craft Fair (8-9 August), Heritage Weekend (12-13 September), and Christmas Gift Fair (November).
Open 12 Apr-27 Sep, Sun, Thu & BH's. Daily in Aug ex Fri & Sat. Park & Gardens 11-6, Castle 2-6 (last admission 5pm). Free.
P ⊕ ✗ *licensed* ⅆ *toilets for disabled shop*
Cards: ▨ ▨

HECKINGTON
The Pearoom
Station Yard NG34 9JJ (4m E of Sleaford, off A17)
☎ *01529 460765 Fax 01529 460948*
The Pearoom has a craft shop, galleries and workshops for ten resident craft workers. Their products include pottery, leather work, toys, and prints; and also there is a musical instrument restorer, a weaver-feltmaker, and a knitwear designer. An active programme of craft exhibitions runs throughout the year accompanied by a programme of weekend course activities. (For details telephone the Exhibition Officer). A commissioning centre was opened in 1993 showing the work of many local makers willing to work to commission. Members of the public are welcome to consult this register.
Open all year, Mon-Sat & BHs 10-5, Sun 12-5. Free.
P ⊕ ⅆ *toilets for disabled shop* ⊛

LINCOLN
Lincoln Castle
Castle Hill LN1 3AA
☎ *01522 511068*
Fax 01522 512150
Situated in the centre of Lincoln, the Castle, built in 1068 by William the Conqueror, dominates the Bailgate area alongside the great Cathedral. In addition to its many medieval features, Lincoln Castle has strong 19th-century connections and the unique Victorian prison chapel is perhaps the most awe-inspiring. The beautiful surroundings are ideal for historical adventures, picnics and special events which take place throughout the year. The Castle is now the home of the Magna Carta and there is a new exhibition interpreting and displaying this important document.
Open all year, British Summer Time Mon-Sat 9.30-5.30, Sun 11-5.30. Winter time Mon-Sat 9.30-4, Sun 11-4. Last admission 30 mins before closing. (Closed 25-26 Dec & 1 Jan).
£2.50 (ch £1, conssesions £1.50) family ticket £6.
P *(within 200yds)* ⊕ ⅆ *(video theatre also accessible) toilets for disabled shop* ⊛
Cards: ▨ ▨ ▨ ▨

Lincoln Cathedral
LN2 1PZ
☎ *01522 544544*
'The most precious piece of architecture in the British Isles' (John Ruskin)
Open all year, summer 7.15-8 (6pm winter).
P ⊕ ⅆ *toilets for disabled shop*
Details not confirmed for 1998

Museum of Lincolnshire Life
Burton Rd LN1 3LY (nr Castle)
☎ *01522 528448 Fax 01522 521264*
The region's largest and most varied social history museum where the past two centuries of Lincolnshire life are illustrated by displays of domestic implements, industrial machinery, agricultural tools and a collection of horse-drawn vehicles. The Royal Lincolnshire Regiment museum is also housed here. A full list of events and temporary exhibitions is available on request.
Open all year, May-Sep, daily 10-5.30; Oct-Apr, Mon-Sat 10-5.30, Sun 2-5.30.
✲ *£2 (ch 60p).*
P ⊕ ⅆ *(wheelchair available, parking space) toilets for disabled shop* ⊛

Usher Gallery
Lindum Rd LN2 1NN (in city centre, signed)
☎ *01522 527980 Fax 01522 560165*
Built as the result of a bequest by Lincoln jeweller, James Ward Usher, the Gallery houses his magnificent collection of watches, porcelain and miniatures, as well as topographical works, watercolours by Peter de Wint, Tennyson memorabilia and coins. As the Lincolnshire main visual arts venue, the Gallery also has an active exhibitions and 'outreach' programme; events for 1998 include: Medina Hammad - Regional Artist (3 May-5 July), Bartl, Brannan & Nadin (1 August-25 October), On Show 11 - Photography (5 September-15 November), Lincolnshire Artists Society (15 November-20 December), Lincolnshire Contemporary Crafts 10th Anniversary (28 November-31 December).
Open all year, Mon-Sat 10-5.30, Sun 2.30-5. (Closed Good Fri, Xmas & 1 Jan).
£2 (ch & students 50p).
P *(150yds)* ⊕ ⅆ *toilets for disabled shop* ⊛ *(ex guide dogs)*
Cards: ▨ ▨ ▨ ▨

LONG SUTTON
See Spalding

SCUNTHORPE
Normanby Hall Country Park
Normanby DN15 9HU (5m N off B1430)
☎ *01724 720588 Fax 01724 721248*
A whole host of activities and attractions are offered in the 350 acres of grounds that surround Normanby Hall including golf, riding, nature trails, gift shop and a farming museum. Deer herds can be spotted grazing in the parkland and many

species of wildfowl have their home here. Inside the Regency mansion there are fine rooms decorated and furnished in period style. In the grounds visitors will find the region's only fully restored and working walled Victorian kitchen garden, where original varieties of fruit and vegetables are grown using traditional methods. Ring for details of 1998's Special Events.
Open, Park all year, daily. Hall and family museum Apr, May & Sep 1-5pm (wknds) June-Aug 1-5pm daily. Oct-March by appointment only. Walled garden all year 11-5 daily, (4pm in winter)
✲ *Mon-Fri & winter season £1.50 per car. Summer Saturday £2.50 per car. Summer Sunday £3 per car.*
P *(charged)* ⊕ ✗ *licensed* ⅆ *(audio tour & sensory bed in walled garden) toilets for disabled shop garden centre*

SKEGNESS
Church Farm Museum
Church Rd South PE25 2HF
☎ *01754 766658 Fax 01754 766658*
A farmhouse and outbuildings that have been restored to show the way of life on a Lincolnshire farm at the end of the 19th century, with farm implements and machinery plus household equipment on display. A timber-framed cottage and a barn have been re-erected. In the barn there is a temporary exhibition and, at weekends during the summer, craftsmen give demonstrations and there are also school activity days. Livestock on show include Lincoln Longwool sheep. New for 1998 is the Boothby Barn, an 18th century threshing barn which has been reconstructed at Church Farm. Various special events include Woolly Days in June (sheepshearing, spinning and dyeing demonstrations), Victorian Times in July (a week of traditional rural and domestic craft demonstrations), Teddy Bears Picnic in August, Steam threshing demonstrations in September, and Apple Day in October. Please telephone for details of these and other events.
Open Apr-Oct, daily 10.30-5.30
£1 (ch 50p).
P ⊕ ⅆ *(wheelchair available) toilets for disabled shop* ⊛

Skegness Natureland Seal Sanctuary
North Pde PE25 1DB (north end of seafront)
☎ *01754 764345 Fax 01754 764345*
Natureland houses a specialised collection of animals including seals, penguins, tropical birds, aquarium, reptiles, pets' corner etc. Also free-flight tropical butterflies (May-Oct). Natureland is well known for its rescue of abandoned seal pups, and has successfully reared and returned to the wild a large number of these beautiful creatures. The hospital unit incorporates a public viewing area, and a large seascape seal pool (with underwater viewing). Additional attractions include the Sea Life Exhibition, floral displays and an animal brass rubbing house.
Open all year, daily at 10am. Closing times vary according to season. (Closed 25-26 Dec & 1 Jan).
✲ *£3.60 (ch £2.40, pen £2.90). Family ticket £11. Party rates.*
P *(100 yds)* ⊕ ⅆ *toilets for disabled shop*
Cards: ▨ ▨

SPALDING
Butterfly & Falconry Park
Long Sutton PE12 9LE (off A17 at Long Sutton)
☎ *01406 363833 & 363209*
Fax 01406 363182
The Park contains one of Britain's largest walk-through tropical houses, in which hundreds of butterflies and birds from all over the world fly freely. Outside are 15 acres of butterfly and bee gardens, wildflower meadows, wildfowl and conservation ponds, nature trail, farm animals, a pets' corner and a large adventure playground. At the Falconry Centre, falcons, hawks and owls can be seen, and there are daily falconry displays at 12 noon and 3pm. A farm museum opened in 1994, and 1995 saw the addition of an iguana den and an ant room where visitors can observe leaf-cutting ants in their natural working habitat. 'Reptile land' opened 1997, also 'Pheasants of the World'. New for 1998 Honey Farm. Special events: Barn Owl Sunday (19 July) - learn about owls and

Dating from 1068 and modified through the ages, Lincoln Castle stands in fine grounds beside Lincoln Cathedral. The grounds are a focal point for events in the city.

The Banqueting House is the only surviving part of Whitehall Palace

LONDON

LONDON
London is very much a city for exploring. It is rich in history, full of pageantry and culture to suit all tastes, with beautiful shops and parks, characterful pubs and cosmopolitan population. London is served by the largest underground network in the world, but to really see London, there are tours by double-decker bus, or by boat along the canals or the River Thames or, for the truly adventurous, by helicopter. The River Thames is at the heart of London's history from Henry VIII's magnificent Hampton Court Palace in the west, passing the centre of British Government, the Houses of Parliament, then past the City, St Paul's, the Tower and under Tower Bridge. On through London's famous docklands to the great palace at Greenwich in the east. Londoners love pageantry and there is some parade or spectacle almost daily, such as the Lord Mayor's Show, the State Opening of Parliament or the Changing of the Guard at Buckingham Palace. There are magnificent churches such as St Paul's Cathedral, the Byzantine-style Westminster Cathedral and Westminster Abbey, on a site occupied by a church for over 1300 years. In a city with 40 museums and nearly as many art gallleries, over 20 theatres and 30 street markets, a welcome break from the bustle can be found in the hundreds of acres of city parks that make London possibly the greenest capital city in the world.

see the 'Hawk & Owl Trust' stand & exhibition, Exotic Pets Day (17 May) - tarantulas, scorpions, pythons, hissing cockroaches and more!
Open 29 Mar-1 Nov, daily 10-6. (Sep & Oct 10-5).
£4.20 (ch 3-16 £2.90, pen £3.90). Family ticket £13-£15. Party.
P X licensed & (wheelchairs available) toilets for disabled shop (ex car park)
Cards:

Spalding Tropical Forest
Glenside North PE11 3SD
☎01775 710822 Fax 01775 710882
Spalding Tropical Forest is the largest of its kind in the British Isles. There are four zones: oriental, temperate, tropical and dry topics. Cascading waterfalls and lush, colourful tropical plants, including over a hundred species of orchid, create a wonderful atmosphere heavy with scents. There is also a Water Garden Centre and a Plant House where some unusual specimens are for sale.
Open daily summer 10-6, winter 10-dusk. Closed 25 Dec.
P & toilets for disabled shop garden centre
Details not confirmed for 1998
Cards:

Springfields Gardens
Camelgate PE12 6ET (1m E on A151, signposted from the Spalding by-pass)
☎01775 724843 713253 Fax 01755 711209
The 25-acre gardens provide an amazing spectacle in the spring when thousands of bulbs are blooming among the lawns and lakes. Special events for 1998 include: Springfields Horticultural Exhibition (5-8 February), Easter Craft Festival (12-13 March), Spalding Flower Festival and Country Fair (2,3,4 May). Please telephone for details of these and other events.
Open 21 Mar-11 May, daily 10-6 (last admission 5pm)
£3 (accompanied ch free, pen £2.70). Prices vary for special events.
P X licensed & (free wheelchair hire) toilets for disabled shop garden centre

STAMFORD
Burghley House Trust Limited
PE9 3JY (1.5m off A1 at Stamford)
☎01780 752451 Fax 01780 480125
This great Elizabethan palace was built by William Cecil, Queen Elizabeth I's first minister, and has all the hallmarks of that ostentatiously wealthy period. The vast

house is three storeys high and on the roof is a riot of pinnacles, cupolas and paired chimneys in classic Tudor style. However, inside there is very little of the Tudor period in evidence, as (apart from the kitchen) the house was restyled between 1680 and 1700. The state rooms are now Baroque, with silver fireplaces, elaborate plasterwork and painted ceilings. These were painted by Antonio Verrio, whose finest achievement here is the Heaven Room. The walls of the rooms are hung with superb tapestries and with pictures from the largest private collection of Italian Old Masters.
The grounds were landscaped during the 18th century by 'Capability' Brown and each year, in September, international horse trials are held.
Special events for 1998 include fireworks and laser concerts in the park on 24-25 July (booking office 01625 560000) and the Burghley Horse Trials (3-6 September).
Open Apr-4 Oct, daily, 11-4.30. (Closed 5 Sep).
❋Please telephone for admission charges.
P X licensed & (chairlift access to restaurant and staterooms) toilets for disabled shop
Cards:

Stamford Museum
Broad St PE9 1PJ (from A1 follow town centre signs from any Stamford exit)
☎01780 766317
Fax 01780 480363
The museum illustrates the history and archaeology of Stamford. Perhaps the most unusual exhibits are the clothes of Daniel Lambert (1770-1809), who died in Stamford, one of only three men in Britain recorded as weighing over 50 stone (317kg). These are displayed with the clothes of American midget, General Tom Thumb, who was 3ft 4in (102cm) when he died.
Open all year, Apr-Sep, Mon-Sat 10-5, Sun 2-5; Oct-Mar Mon-Sat 10-5.
Free.
P (200 yds) (on street parking is limited waiting) & shop (ex guide dogs)

Stamford Shakespeare Company
Rutland Open Air Theatre, Tolethorpe Hall, Little Casterton PE9 4BH (off A6121, follow heritage signs to Tolethorpe Hall)
☎01780 54381 Fax 01780 481954
Tolethorpe is an Elizabethan manor

house set in seven acres of grounds - an historic site listed in the Domesday Book. It was acquired by the nationally renowned amateur Shakespeare Company in a near derelict state in 1977 and since restored. Birthplace (c1550) of Robert Browne, the Elizabethan religious campaigner who founded a movement seeking independence from the established Church of England. Some of his followers sailed on the Mayflower in 1620 to become the Pilgrim Fathers of America, others later called themselves 'congregationalists'. A 600 seat open-air theatre with a covered auditorium in the grounds of Tolethorpe Hall is the venue for the Stamford Shakespeare Company's annual season, attracting more the 30,000 people. Phone or write for details.
Open daily 10-4, May-Sep. Rutland Open Air Theatre performances 1 Jun-29 Aug.
Hall & grounds £2 (ch 18 & pen £1)
P & toilets for disabled shop

TATTERSHALL
Tattershall Castle
LN4 4LR (S of A153)
☎01526 342543
This large fortified house was built in 1440 by Ralph Cromwell, Treasurer of England, and has a keep 100ft high. On each of the four storeys is a fine heraldic chimneypiece: these were sold at one point, but were rescued from export in 1911. There is also a museum in the guardhouse.
Open Apr-1 Nov, Sat-Wed & BH Mons (closed Good Fri) 10.30-5.30. Nov-20 Dec, Sat & Sun only 12-4pm.
£2.70 (ch £1.30). Family ticket £6.50.
P & toilets for disabled shop
Cards:

WOOLSTHORPE
Woolsthorpe Manor
23 Newton Way NG33 5NR (7m S of Grantham, 1m W of A1)
☎01476 860338
A fine stone-built, 17th-century farmhouse which was the birthplace of the scientist and philosopher Sir Isaac Newton, in 1642. He also lived at the house from 1665-66 during the Plague, after his time as an undergraduate at Cambridge. An early edition of his *Principia Mathematica* (1687) is in the house.
Open Apr-1 Nov, Wed-Sun & BH Mon 1-5.30. (closed Good Fri).
£2.60 (ch £1.30). Family ticket £6.50.
P

EC2
Bank of England Museum
Threadneedle St EC2R 8AH
☎0171 601 5545 Fax 0171 601 5808
The Museum is housed within the Bank of England itself, right at the heart of the City of London. It traces the history of the Bank from its foundation by Royal Charter in 1694 to its role today as the nation's central bank. There are gold bars from ancient times to the modern market bar, coins and a unique collection of banknotes, as well as pikes and muskets once used to defend the Bank. Documents relating to famous customers such as the Duchess of Marlborough, George Washington and Horatio Nelson, are displayed. The 18th-century Bank Stock Office, designed by Sir John Soane, has been reconstructed. Award-winning interactive systems allow visitors to look behind the doors of The Bank or observe the intricacies of banknote design, as well as new Foreign Exchange dealing games.
Open all year, Mon-Fri 10-5. (Closed wknds & BH's).
Free.
P (10 mins walk) & (advance notice helpful) toilets for disabled shop

SW1
Banqueting House at Whitehall Palace
Whitehall SW1A 2ER (Underground - Westminster)
☎0171 930 4179 Fax 0171 930 8268
Built between 1619 and 1622 during the reign of James I. Designed by Inigo Jones it is the only surviving building of the vast Whitehall Palace, destroyed by fire 300 years ago. The Palace has seen many significant royal events, including the execution of Charles I in 1649. The Banqueting House is a welcome retreat, away from the bustle of the city, and a hidden treasure for anyone interested in art and architecture: its Rubens ceiling paintings are stunning examples of the

➤

larger works of the Flemish Master and its classical Palladian style set the fashion for much of London's later architecture.
Open all year, Mon-Sat 10-5. (Closed Good Fri, 24-26 Dec, 1 Jan & BH's). Liable to close at short notice for Government functions.
£3.25 (ch 16 £2.15 (under 5 free) students & pen £2.50).
P & *toilets for disabled shop ✿ (ex guide dogs)*
Cards: ▨ ▨ ▨ ▨ ▨

SE1
Bramah Tea & Coffee Museum
The Clove Building, Butler's Wharf SE1 2NQ (Underground - London Bridge & Tower Hill)
☎ *0171 378 0222 Fax 0171 378 0219*
The museum tells the fascinating and informative story of the history of the tea and coffee trade carried on in this area for 350 years. A collection of over 1,000 teapots and coffee makers illustrate the many ways that tea and coffee have been made and served. Other displays include expresso machines from the 1950s, advertisements for instant coffee and information on the development of the filter machine. Also on display are 'tetsubin' tea kettles and a 'Raku' tea master bowl, used in the elaborate Japanese Tea Ceremony. Visitors can buy tea and coffee from the museum to take home as a souvenir of their visit.
Open all year, daily 10-6. (Closed 25 & 26 Dec).
P *(100yds)* ▨ & *toilets for disabled shop ✿*
Details not confirmed for 1998
Cards: ▨ ▨ ▨ ▨ ▨

WC1
British Museum
Great Russell St WC1B 3DG (Underground - Russell Sq,Tottenham Court Rd)
☎ *0171 580 1788 (recorded information) Fax 0171 323 8118*
The stern façade of the British Museum belies the rich and varied treasures within which make it one of the great museums of the world, showing the works of man from many civilisations, from prehistoric to comparatively recent times. Founded in 1753, the nucleus of the museum was the collections of Sir Hans Sloane and Sir Robert Cotton. The galleries are the responsibility of the following departments: Egyptian, Greek and Roman, Western Asiatic, Japanese, Prehistoric and Romano-British, Medieval and later, Coins and Medals, Oriental, Prints and Drawings, and Ethnography (based at the Museum of Mankind). The museum also displays famous books and manuscripts from the British Library collections. The original building, Montagu House was demolished, and Sir Robert Smirke commissioned to build a more suitable replacement on the site, which was completed in 1852; the famous domed Reading Room was added in 1857. Among the treasures not to be missed are the Egyptian mummies, the notorious and superb Elgin marbles, two of the four existing copies of the Magna Carta, Shakespeare's signature, Nelson's plan of the Battle of Trafalgar and the Sutton Hoo treasure. There is a regular programme of gallery talks, lectures and films, and young visitors can enjoy special children's trails.
Open all year, Mon-Sat 10-5, Sun 2.30-6. (Closed Good Fri, May Day, Xmas & 1 Jan).
▨ ✗ *licensed* & *(parking by arrangement; touch tour for visually impaired) toilets for disabled shop ✿*
Details not confirmed for 1998

W1
Broadcasting House Tour & Exhibition
Broadcasting House W1A 1AA (Underground - Oxford Circus, Great Portland St)
☎ *0870 6030304*
A day in the life of Broadcasting House - explore the corporation's heritage

through a series of interactive displays which allow visitors to try out a range of broadcasting activities including the chance to 'Present the Weather' 'Direct Eastenders', 'Commentate on a Sports Event' and 'Create a Radio Play'.
Open all year, daily 9.30-5.30 (last tour commences). Closed 25 Dec.
✳ *£5.75 (ch 15 £4, pen & student £4.35)*
P ▨ & *toilets for disabled shop*
Cards: ▨ ▨ ▨ ▨ ▨

SW1
Buckingham Palace
Buckingham Palace Rd (Underground - Victoria, Green Park)
☎ *0171 839 1377 Fax 0171 930 9625*
Buckingham Palace is the official London residence of Her Majesty The Queen, whose personal standard flies when Her Majesty is in residence. Each August and September the State Rooms are open to visitors. These principle rooms, which form the backdrop to the pageantry of court ceremonial and official entertaining, occupy the main west front overlooking the garden and are all opulently decorated with the finest pictures and works of art from the Royal Collection.
Open 10 August- 30 September 9.30am-4.30pm (provisional dates)
£9.50 (ch under 17 £5, pen £7) Family ticket £21.50.
P *(200yds)* & *(except gardens, pre booking essential) toilets for disabled shop ✿*
Cards: ▨ ▨ ▨ ▨ ▨

WC2
Cabaret Mechanical Theatre
33/34 The Market, Covent Garden WC2E 8RE (Underground - Covent Garden)
☎ *0171 379 7961 & 0171 240 3198 Fax 0181 693 7664*
The museum offers entertainment for the whole family here with an impressive collection of Automata. Buy a ticket in the foyer area, get it stamped by the mechanical stamping man and enter the magical world of Cabaret, where at the touch of a button or the insertion of a coin, machines are set in motion. The collection includes work by Paul Spooner, Ron Fuller and Tim Hunkin.
Open all year, Tue-Sat 10-6.30, Sun 11-6.30, Mon 10-6.30; school holidays daily 10-7. (Closed 25 & 26 Dec & 1 Jan).
£1.95 (ch, students, pen & UB40's £1.20). Family ticket £4.95.
P & *toilets for disabled ✿*
Cards: ▨ ▨ ▨ ⑤ ▨ ▨ ▨

SW1
Cabinet War Rooms
Clive Steps, King Charles St SW1A 2AQ (Underground - Westminster)
☎ *0171 930 6961 Fax 0171 839 5897*
The underground emergency accommodation used to protect the Prime Minister, Winston Churchill, his War Cabinet and the Chiefs of Staff during the Second World War provide a fascinating insight into those tense days and nights. Among the 21 rooms are the Cabinet Room, the Map Room (where information about operations on all fronts was collected) and the Prime Minister's room, which have been carefully preserved since the end of the war. Other rooms have been restored to their original appearance. New exhibition on Churchill & WWII opened in January. Audio-guides in 7 languages also available.
Open all year, daily 9.30-6. (10-6 Oct-Mar) last admission 5.15 (Closed 24-26 Dec).
✳ *£4.40 (ch £2.20, students £3.30, pen £3.30). Party 10+.*
P *(10 mins walk)* & *toilets for disabled shop ✿*
Cards: ▨ ▨ ▨ ▨ ▨

SW3
Carlyle's House
24 Cheyne Row SW3 5HL (Underground - Sloane Square)
☎ *0171 352 7087*
'The Sage of Chelsea' - distinguished essayist and writer of historical works,

Thomas Carlyle - lived in this 18th-century town house from 1834 until his death in 1881. His soundproofed study and the kitchen, where such literary notables as Tennyson, Thackeray and Browning were entertained have been preserved exactly as the Carlyles knew them.
Open Apr-1 Nov, Wed-Sun & BH Mons 11-5. Last admission 4.30. (Closed Good Fri)
£3.20 (ch £1.60).
P *(street metered)* ✿ 🚲 🚽

SW3
Chelsea Physic Garden
66 Royal Hospital Rd, (entrance in Swan Walk) SW3 4HS (Underground - Sloane Square)
☎ *0171 352 5646 Fax 0171 376 3910*
The second oldest botanic garden in England was begun in 1673 for the study of plants used in medicine by the Society of Apothecaries. By the late 18th century it was famous throughout Europe for its rare and unusual plants, and it is still used for botanical and medicinal research. For the visitor it offers displays of many fascinating plants, and is an oasis of peace and quiet amidst the hubbub of Chelsea. There will be exhibitions on Art and Healing in Ghana (third week July - first week September), and the Centenary of the London Sketch Club (Chelsea Flower Show Week). Also winter lectures, monthly from November to March.
Open Apr-Oct, Wed 12-5, Sun 2-6. Additional opening during Chelsea Flower Show week, 18-22 May & Chelsea Festival week Jun, 1-5. Groups at other times by appointment.
£3.50 (ch 5-15, students & unemployed £1.80).
P *(0.5m) (west end of Battersea Park)* ▨ & *(disabled parking) toilets for disabled shop garden centre ✿*
Cards: ▨

W8
Commonwealth Experience
Kensington High St W8 6NQ (Underground - High Street Kensington)
☎ *0171 371 3530 Fax 0171 610 5346*
The Commonwealth Experience is a world under one roof. Embark on a fun-packed adventure around the globe. Start with Heliride, a thrilling helicopter simulator ride over Malaysia, continue with Interactive World, a 'hands-on' activity centre that illuminates the fascinating world of natural phenomena. Then explore two floors of intriguing displays featuring the diverse landscapes, history and cultures of over 40 Commonwealth countries. All this is complemented by a regular programme of contemporary Commonwealth arts & crafts exhibitions together with special holiday workshops and activities for children.

Open, daily 10-5 (last admission 4.30pm). Closed 18-26 Dec.
£4.95 (ch £2.95, student & pen £3.95)
P *(500yds)* & *(lift from car park, intercom at Holland Park gate) toilets for disabled shop ✿*
Cards: ▨ ▨ ▨ ⑤

WC2
Courtauld Gallery
Somerset House, Strand WC2R 0RN (Underground - Temple, Embankment)
☎ *0171 873 2526 Fax 0171 873 2589*
The Galleries moved from the Woburn Square premises in March 1990 and opened at Somerset House on 15th June 1990. They contain the superb collection of paintings begun by Samuel Courtauld in the 1920s and 1930s and presented to the University of London in memory of his wife. This is the most important collection of Impressionist and post-Impressionist works in Britain and includes paintings by Monet, Renoir, Degas, Cézanne, Van Gogh and Gauguin. There are also works by Michelangelo, Rubens, Goya, and other notable Masters, as well as early Italian paintings. British and French 20th-century works given to the University by Roger Fry are also displayed here. Exhibitions are changed regularly.
Open Mon-Sat 10-6, Sun 2-6. The Gallery will be closed to visitors for refurbishment from 31 August 1997 to autumn 1998.
£4 (ch, pen & students £2).
P *(NCP Drury Lane)* ▨ & *(parking arranged, lift) toilets for disabled shop ✿*

SE17
Cuming Museum
155-157 Walworth Rd SE17 1RS (Underground - Elephant & Castle)
☎ *0171 701 1342 Fax 0171 703 7415*
The museum of Southwark's history. The worldwide collections of the Cuming family joined with the local history of Southwark, from Roman times through the days of Chaucer, Shakespeare and Dickens to the present day. Special exhibitions and lectures on local themes, please telephone for details.
Open all year, Tue-Sat 10-5. School & adult parties daily by appointment. (Closed BH's & Sat of BH wknd).
P *(20 yds) shop ✿*
Details not confirmed for 1998

SE1
Design Museum
Butler's Wharf, Shad Thames SE1 2YD (Underground - London Bridge)
☎ *0171 403 6933 Fax 0171 378 6540*
A museum of everyday objects situated in the Butler's Wharf conservation area. It is the first of its kind to show design in mass production and in the context of our lives.
Open all year (ex 25-26 Dec), Mon-Fri 11.30-6, Sat & Sun 12-6.
£5 (concessions £3.75)
P *(charged)* ▨ ✗ *licensed* & *(ramped entrance, wheelchair & lift) toilets for disabled shop ✿*
Cards: ▨ ▨ ▨ ⑤ ▨ ▨ ▨

WC1

Dickens House

48 Doughty St WC1N 2LF (Underground - Russell Square)
☎0171 405 2127 01493 701403 Fax 0171 831 5175
Charles Dickens lived in Doughty Street in his twenties and it was here he worked on his first full-length novel, *The Pickwick Papers* and later *Oliver Twist* and *Nicholas Nickelby*, celebrated for their acute observation of society on all levels, and their sympathy for the often unfortunate characters. Pages of the original manuscripts of Dickens's books are on view together with valuable first editions, his special marriage licence and many other personal mementoes. Dickens' drawing room has been reconstructed.
Open all year, Mon-Sat 10-5, last admission 4.30pm. (Closed Sun & some public hols).
✱£3.50 (ch under 16 £1.50, pen & students £2.50). Family ticket £7.
P (metered, 2 hrs max) ♿ shop ⊗
Cards: ◪ ▦ ▬ ▨

EC4

Dr Johnson's House

17 Gough Square EC4A 3DE (Underground - Temple, Blackfriars)
☎0171 353 3745
The celebrated literary figure, Dr Samuel Johnson, lived at 17 Gough Square between 1748 and 1759. It was here that he wrote his English Dictionary, and a facsimile first edition is on display at the house. The dictionary took eight and a half years to complete and contained 40,000 words. Johnson then undertook the formidable task of editing the complete works of Shakespeare.
The house in Gough Square, tucked away behind Fleet Street, is a handsome example of early 18th-century architecture. It was opened as a museum in 1912 and exhibits include a fine collection of prints, letters and other memorabilia from the life of a man who was to become the most quoted Englishman after Shakespeare.
Open all year, May-Sep, daily 11-5.30; Oct-Apr 11-5. (Closed Sun, BH's, Good Fri & 24 Dec).
✱£3 (ch £1, under 10 free, students & pen £2). Party.
shop ⊗

SE1

Florence Nightingale Museum

2 Lambeth Palace Rd SE1 7EW (Underground - Westminster, Waterloo . On the site of St Thomas' Hospital)
☎0171 620 0374 Fax 0171 620 0374
Florence Nightingale needs no introduction, but this museum shows clearly that she was more than 'The Lady with the Lamp'. Beautifully designed, the museum creates a personal setting in which are displayed Florence's prized possessions, a lamp from the Crimean War and nursing artefacts. The centrepiece is a recreated ward scene from the Crimea and audio-visual technology takes the museum beyond its four walls. Set on the site of the first School of Nursing, this museum is an interesting experience, showing the continued relevance of this remarkable woman.
Open all year, Tue-Sun 10-4 (last admission). (Closed Xmas, 1 Jan, Good Fri & Etr Sun).
£3.50 (concessions £2.50) Family ticket £7.
P (charged) ♿ toilets for disabled shop ⊗
Cards: ◪ ▦ ▬ ▨ ⑤

SE1

Golden Hinde Educational Museum

St Mary Overie Dock, Cathedral St SE1 9DG
☎0171 403 0123 Fax 0171 407 5908
A full size replica of Sir Francis Drake's famous 16th century galleon. Just like the original, this new Golden Hinde has circumnavigated the globe. Visitors may explore the five decks, and costumed

crew add to the atmosphere. Please telephone for details of special events, which include Living History re-enactments. There are holiday workshops for children and the ship is also available for private hire.
Open all year, Mon-Fri 10-4, Sun 10-4. Advisable to check as occasionally closed for functions.
£2.30 (ch 5 £1.50, under 5yrs free, concessions £1.90)
P (on street parking) shop
Cards: ◪ ▦ ▬ ▨ ⑤

SW1

Green Park

SW1 (Underground - Green Park)
The smallest of the central London parks, Green Park is aptly named, for the Tyburn stream runs just below the surface, maintaining its lush verdancy. It is situated in the triangle formed by Piccadilly, The Mall and Constitution Hill (where Charles II used to take his constitutional stroll) and was formerly meadowland. This informal character is still maintained today, for there are no flower borders here - just the springtime crocuses and daffodils which grow among the grass.

EC2

The Guildhall

Gresham St EC2V 5AE (Underground - Bank, St Paul's)
☎0171 606 3030 Fax 0171 260 1119
The Court of Common Council (presided over by the Lord Mayor) administers the City of London and meets in the Guildhall. Dating from 1411, when the Livery Companies raised money for its construction, the building was badly damaged in the Great Fire and again in the Blitz. The great hall, traditionally used for the Lord Mayor's Banquet and other important civic functions, is impressively decorated with the banners and shields of the livery companies, of which there are more than 90. Beneath it lies a 15th-century crypt, the largest of its kind in London. The Clock Museum, which has a collection of 700 exhibits, charts the history of 500 years of time-keeping. The Guildhall Library has an unrivalled collection of manuscripts, books and illustrations on all aspects of the capital city.
Open all year, May-Sep, daily 10-5; Oct-Apr, Mon-Sat 10-5. (Closed Xmas, New Year, Good Fri, Etr Mon & infrequently for Civic occasions).
♿ shop ⊗
Details not confirmed for 1998

SE1

HMS Belfast

Morgans Ln, Tooley St SE1 2JH (Underground - London Bridge)
☎0171 407 6434 Fax 0171 403 0719
Europe's last surviving big gun, armoured warship from World War II, *HMS Belfast* was launched in 1938 and served in the North Atlantic and Arctic with the Home Fleet. She led the Allied naval bombardment of German positions on D-Day, and was saved for the nation in 1971. A tour of the ship will take you from the Captain's bridge all the way down through nine decks to the massive boiler and engine rooms, well below the waterline. You can see inside the triple six-inch gun turrets; operate the light anti-aircraft guns; explore the shell rooms and experience what life was like for the crew by visiting the cramped messdecks, officers' cabins, galley, sick bay, dentist and laundry. There are special events for children over the summer holidays and the October half term which will this year include "Be A Sailor For The Day." Please telephone to confirm details.
Open all year, daily. Mar-Oct 10-6, last admission 5.15; Nov-28 Feb 10-5, last admission 4.15. (Closed 24-26 Dec).
✱£4.40 (ch £2.20, students & pen £3.30). Party 10+.
P (150yds) ☕ ♿ (wheelchair lift for access on board) toilets for disabled shop ⊗
Cards: ◪ ▦ ▬ ▨ ⑤

IMPERIAL WAR MUSEUM
The Museum of twentieth century conflict.
Lambeth Road, London SE1 6HZ

IMPERIAL WAR MUSEUM

DUXFORD AIRFIELD
A preserved wartime fighter base, now Europe's top aviation museum.
Duxford, Nr Cambridge, CB2 4QR

HMS BELFAST
The last of the Royal Navy's big gun armoured warships.
Morgan's Lane, Tooley Street, London SE1 2JH

OPEN DAILY
10.00AM-6.00PM
For information telephone
0171 416 5321

CABINET WAR ROOMS
Churchill's underground HQ in central London.
Clive Steps, King Charles Street, London SW1A 2AQ

SW1

Houses of Parliament

Westminster SW1A 0AA (Underground - Westminster)
☎0171 219 4272
From the time of Edward the Confessor to Henry VIII, the site of the present-day Houses of Parliament was the main residence of the monarch. Hence the often-used term the 'Palace of Westminster'. It was not until Henry VIII moved to Whitehall Palace in 1529 that the building was turned over to state institutions. A disastrous fire in 1834 destroyed most of the medieval palace and a competition was held for the design of a new Parliament building; Charles Barry was awarded the commission with his Gothic-style design (although Pugin was responsible for much of the decorative detail). Today the building stands at 940ft long, covers eight acres and includes 1100 apartments. There are over two miles of passages. To the south stands the lofty Victoria Tower where the Union Jack flies when Parliament is in session. At the north end of the building is the clock tower which contains Big Ben, the 13½-ton hour bell.
Telephone well in advance for information on how to go about arranging permits for a tour of the building, or to listen to debates from the Strangers Gallery. Tours must be arranged through a Member of Parliament.
P (250yds) ♿ (by arrangement) toilets for disabled shop ⊗ ⚐
Details not confirmed for 1998

W2

Hyde Park

W2 (Underground - Hyde Park Corner, Marble Arch)
Situated to the west of Park Lane, between Knightsbridge and Bayswater, and formerly a Royal hunting park, Hyde Park now consists of 340 acres of grass and trees, intersected by paths. The

Serpentine, at its centre, provides a habitat for wild creatures which cannot find sanctuary elsewhere in the city centre. It was the venue for the Great Exhibition in 1851, but is probably best known for Speakers' Corner, near Marble Arch, where, every Sunday, anyone can stand up and say just what they please.

SE1

Imperial War Museum

Lambeth Rd SE1 6HZ (Underground - Lambeth North)
☎0171 416 5000
Fax 0171 416 5374
Founded in 1917 and established in 1920 by an Act of Parliament, this museum illustrates and records all aspects of the two World Wars and other military operations involving Britain and the Commonwealth since 1914. It has recently undergone major renovations and although the vast collections are still housed within the imposing walls of the original building in Lambeth Road, it is now a thoroughly modern museum employing all the latest technology to make its exhibitions more vital and atmospheric for the visitor. Improvements include a new, large exhibition hall, art galleries and a shop and licensed restaurant. There are always special exhibitions and the programme of events includes film shows and lectures. The Imperial War Museum has a wealth of military reference material, although some reference departments are open to the public by appointment only. New permanent exhibitions include: Secret War - revealing for the first time the clandestine world of espionage, intelligence gathering and the work of Britain's Special Forces. Conflicts Since 1945 - concerning conflicts worldwide which British Commonwealth troops have been involved in. 1998 exhibitions include: ENIGMA and the Code Breakers (until 26 April) - hands-on interactive exploration of use of wartime technology in codebreaking; 1918 A Year of Decision

➤

(until 29 Nov) - exhibition marking the 80th Anniversary of the final year of WWI.
Open all year, daily 10-6. (Closed 24-26 Dec).
£4.70 (ch 5-16 £2.35, students, UB40 & pen £3.70).
P (metered) 🍴 &. *(disabled parking sometimes available at museum) toilets for disabled shop* ⚘
Cards: 🖦 ▭ ▭ ▭ 🖦 ⑤

W8
Kensington Gardens
W8 (Underground - Queensway, Lancaster Gate)
This was part of Hyde Park until William III enclosed his palace gardens and today, again, the two areas are not physically divided. A change of character is apparent, though, once you cross the invisible boundary which runs from north to south across the Serpentine Bridge. Kensington Gardens are noted for their tranquility and formality and include the Round Pond, Queen Anne's Orangery, the Sunken Garden and Flower Walk.

W8
Kensington Palace State Apartments & Royal Ceremonial Dress Collection
Kensington Gardens W8 4PX (Underground - High Street Kensington)
☎0171 937 9561 Fax 0171 376 0198
Acquired by William and Mary in 1689 when it was called Nottingham House, Kensington was altered extensively by Sir Christopher Wren and then later in the reign of George I, when William Kent painted the elaborate trompe l'oeil ceilings and staircases which can still be enjoyed at this more private Royal residence. Highlights of a visit to Kensington include the recently restored Kings Apartments with a fine collection of Old Masters; Tintoretto and Van Dyke amongst them. For 1998: (May) Re-Presentation of the Royal Ceremonial Dress Collection, (Summer) Jazz in the Orangery.
Open all year from May 1998 daily 10 am to 3.30 pm
Prices under review.
P (500yds) 🍴 &. *toilets for disabled shop* ⚘
Cards: 🖦 ▭ ▭ ▭ 🖦 ⑤

W14
Leighton House Museum & Art Gallery
12 Holland Park Rd W14 8LZ (Underground - High Street Kensington)
☎0171 602 3316 Fax 0171 371 2467
A uniquely opulent and exotic example of High Victorian taste, Leighton House was built for the President of the Royal Academy, Frederic Lord Leighton, by George Aitchison. The main body of the house was built in 1866 but the fabulous Arab Hall, an arresting 'Arabian Nights' creation, was not completed until 13 years later. The hall is decorated with gilt, ancient tiles from the Middle East and a fountain. Leighton was one of the great Victorian artists, and much of his work is displayed here, along with that of his contemporaries. Ring for details of a changing exhibition programme.
Open all year, daily 11-5.30. Garden open Apr-Sep 11-5. (Closed Sun & BH).
Donations.
⚘

W8
Linley Sambourne House
18 Stafford Ter W8 7BH (Underground - High Street Kensington)
☎0171 937 0663 Fax 0181 995 4895
The home of Linley Sambourne (1844-1910), chief political cartoonist at *Punch* magazine, has had its magnificent artistic interior preserved, almost unchanged, since the late 19th century. Also displayed are many of Sambourne's own drawings and photographs. Museums week 19-25 May, Dramatised performance in parts of the house. Numbers will be restricted.
Open Mar-Oct, Wed 10-4, Sun 2-5. At other times by appointment only.
£3. (ch 16 £1.50, pen £2.50).
P (metered parking) shop ⚘

SE1
London Aquarium
County Hall, Riverside Building, Westminster Bridge Rd SE1 7PB
☎0171 967 8000 Fax 0171 967 8029
One of Europe's newest, largest and most magnificent displays of global aquatic life. Immerse yourself in an unforgettable voyage of discovery through the waters of the world. Witness breathtakingly beautiful and dramatic underwater scenes, featuring thousands of living specimens from rivers, oceans and seas across our planet.
Open all year, daily 10-6. Last admission 1hr before closing. Closed 25 Dec.
✷*£6.50 (ch 3-14 £4.50, pen, students & unemployed £5.50, ch under 3yrs free). Family ticket £20.*
🍴 &. *(free entry for wheelchair users, wheelchairs available) toilets for disabled shop* ⚘
Cards: 🖦 ▭ ▭ 🖦 ⑤

SE1
London Dungeon
28-34 Tooley St SE1 2SZ (Underground - London Bridge)
☎0171 403 0606 Fax 0171 378 1529
The London Dungeon has won the British Tourist Authority's Award for Outstanding Tourist Enterprise. Its modest entrance off a street near London Bridge station will lead the visitor through to a series of slimy vaults where the seamy side of life in past centuries is convincingly re-created. Methods of torture and death, the tools of witchcraft and black magic and some of the more grisly medicinal practices are well represented. Viewing takes about 2 hours; this museum is not recommended for the faint-hearted.
Entry includes the 'Theatre of the Guillotine' show which uses the latest in interactive technology, and the 'Jack the Ripper' show, which presents a 20 minute tour through Jack's Victorian Whitechapel.
Open all year, daily, Apr-Sep 10-5.30; Oct-Mar 10-4.30.
£8.95 (ch 14 & pen £6.50, students £7.95).
P (NCP 200yds) 🍴 &. *toilets for disabled shop* ⚘
Cards: 🖦 ▭ ▭ 🖦 ⑤

NW1
London Planetarium
Marylebone Rd NW1 5LR (Underground - Baker Street)
☎0171 935 6861 Fax 0171 465 0923
A visit to the Planetarium consists of two interactive Space Zone areas plus a half hour star show under the famous green dome. The new star show "Planetary Quest" takes visitors on an intergalactic journey of discovery and is both educational and entertaining. Star shows every 40 minutes daily from 12:20pm. Shows start earlier at 10.20am during school holidays, on Bank Holidays and at weekends. Not recommended for under 5s.
Open daily (ex 25 Dec), star shows from 12.20, every 40 mins (10.20am wknds & holidays).
✷*£5.65 (ch 16 £3.70, pen £4.45).*
P (200 mtrs) &. *toilets for disabled shop* ⚘
Cards: 🖦 ▭ ▭ 🖦 ⑤

W2
London Toy & Model Museum
21-23 Craven Hill W2 3EN (Underground - Paddington)
☎0171 706 8000 Fax 0171 706 1993
Having been extensively redeveloped the London Toy and Model Museum reopened in April 1995. There are 21 themed galleries which include an Edwardian railway station with a full scale model of an engine where children can pretend to drive the train. The themed galleries even have sounds and smells to create the atmosphere. The mock-up of an Edwardian Nursery features replicas of Victorian games and toys which children can play with. The oldest toy is a Roman gladiator doll made 2000 years ago. A fascinating display of over 7000

Kensington Gardens were once the garden to Kensington Palace and are noted for their tranquility. This arch by sculptor Henry Moore provides a modern note.

exhibits including detailed working models, villages, railways and funfairs. There are vintage roundabout and train rides for the children in the delightful garden. There are hands-on workshops for schools. Special exhibition: April-September, 40 Years of Paddington Bear.
Open all year, daily 9-5.30.(Closed 24-26 & 31 Dec & 1 Jan).
£4.95 (ch 4-16 £2.95, concessions £3.95). Family ticket available.
P (metered on street) 🍴 &. *toilets for disabled shop* ⚘
Cards: 🖦 ▭ ▭ 🖦 ⑤

WC2
London Transport Museum
The Piazza, Covent Garden WC2E 7BB (Underground - Covent Garden, Leicester Sq)
☎0171 379 6344 & 0171 836 8557 Fax 0171 836 4118
Spectacular displays of buses, trams, tube trains, posters and more tell the story of travel, people and the growth London itself since 1800. 'Hands-on' fun with bus and train simulators, actors, working models and a lively programme of events and activities. Resource centre. Large shop. Cafe. New for 1998: Kid Zones (Children's Museum) opens.
Open all year, daily 10-6, Fridays 11-6. Last admission 5.15pm. (Closed 24-26 Dec).
£4.50 (concessions £2.50). Family ticket £11. Party.
P (5 mins walk) (parking meters) 🍴 &. *(lift & ramps) toilets for disabled shop* ⚘
Cards: 🖦 ▭ 🖦 ⑤

NW1
Madame Tussaud's
Marylebone Rd NW1 5LR (Underground - Baker Street)
☎0171 935 6861
Fax 0171 465 0923
Madame Tussaud's world-famous waxwork collection was founded in Paris in 1770. It moved to England in 1802 and found a permanent home in London's Marylebone Road in 1884. Over the last five years Madame Tussaud's has undergone a £21 million transformation. Visitors can mingle with the famous and infamous, meeting such diverse characters as Naomi Campbell, Eric Cantona, the Queen and Marilyn Monroe all in one afternoon. The Spirit of London is a fabulous new dark ride which takes visitors back in time through 400 years of London's history. And finally there's the newly revamped Chamber of Horrors which is more eerie and spinechilling than ever before.

Open all year 10-5.30 (9.30am wknds, 9am summer). (Closed 25 Dec).
✷*£8.95 (ch 16 £5.90, pen £6.75).*
P (200 mtrs) 🍴 &. *(except Spirit of London ride) toilets for disabled shop* ⚘
Cards: 🖦 ▭ ▭ 🖦 ⑤

SW1
Mall Galleries
The Mall SW1Y 5BD (Underground - Charing Cross)
☎0171 930 6844 Fax 0171 839 7830
These galleries are the exhibition venue for the Federation of British Artists. Eight art societies administered by the Federation hold their exhibitions here.
Open all year, daily 10-5.
£2 Depending on exhibition (ch & pen half price) Gallery Friends & Westminster Resident's card holders free.
P (50 yds) &. *(chairlft to galleries)* ⚘
Cards: 🖦 ▭ ▭ 🖦 ⑤

EC4
Middle Temple Hall
The Temple EC4Y 9AT (Underground - Temple, Blackfriars)
☎0171 427 4800 Fax 0171 427 4801
Between Fleet Street and the Thames are the Middle and Inner Temples, separate Inns of Court, so named because of the Knights Templar who occupied the site from about 1160. Middle Temple Hall is a fine example of Tudor architecture and was built during the reign of Elizabeth I (completed in about 1570). The hall has a double hammerbeam roof and beautiful stained glass showing the shields of past readers. The 29ft-long high table was made from a single oak tree from Windsor Forest; and portraits of George I, Elizabeth I, Anne, Charles I and Charles II, James, Duke of York and William III line the walls behind it. Sir Francis Drake was a visitor to and friend of the Middle Temple, and a table made from timbers from the *Golden Hind* - the ship in which he sailed around the world - is shown.
Open all year, Mon-Fri 10-12 & 3-4 (Closed BH & legal vacations).
Free.
&. ⚘ 🚐

EC3
The Monument
Monument St EC3R 8AH (Underground - Monument)
☎0171 626 2717 Fax 0171 796 2621
Designed by Wren and Hooke and erected in 1671-7, the Monument commemorates the Great Fire of 1666 which is reputed to have started in nearby Pudding Lane. The fire destroyed

This gruesome character is one of many artefacts in the Museum of the Moving Image which leads the visitor through cinematic history.

nearly 90 churches and about 13,000 houses. This fluted Doric column stands 202ft high (Pudding Lane is exactly 202ft from its base) and visitors can climb the 311 steps to a platform at its summit. The views over the City and beyond are splendid. Because of the steps, access is almost impossible for persons with severe disabilities: there is no lift or escalator.
Visitors are advised to check the opening dates before making a visit.
£1 (ch 16 50p).
⚘

SE1
Museum of Garden History
Lambeth Palace Rd SE1 7LB
(Underground - Waterloo)
☎0171 261 1891 *(between 11am-4pm)*
Fax 0171 401 8802
Adjacent to the south gateway of Lambeth Palace is the former church of St Mary-at-Lambeth, now the Museum of Garden History. There is a permanent exhibition on the history of gardens and a collection of ancient tools. Knowledgeable staff can advise visitors. The shop sells souvenirs, gifts and seeds from the plant collection. In a fine tomb in the replica 17th-century knot garden in the churchyard lie the two John Tradescants, pre-eminent 17th-century plantsmen and gardeners to Charles I and Charles II. Admiral Bligh of the *Bounty* is buried nearby.
Open 2 Mar-14 Dec, Mon-Fri 10.30-4, Sun 10.30-5.
P (100yds) ⚑ & (ramps) shop
Details not confirmed for 1998

EC2
Museum of London
150 London Wall EC2Y 5HN
(Underground - St Paul's, Barbican)
☎0171 600 3699 ext 240 or 280 Fax 0171 600 1058
Early December 1976 saw the official opening of the Museum of London. The collections of the former London and Guildhall museums were brought together in one specially designed building, located near the Barbican development. The site adjoins a stretch

of the original Roman wall which surrounded the city.
Devoted to and detailing all aspects of London life from pre-history to contemporary times, the museum offers a fascinating display presented in chronological order. The exhibits and tableaux are arranged to give the visitor a realistic view of life in the capital through the ages; archaeological levels are illustrated by a relief model of the Thames Valley which provides an apt starting point for the story. Features of special interest include the superb models of William the Conqueror's White Tower and old St Pauls; the audio-visual reconstruction of the Great Fire of London in 1666 (superbly atmospheric) and the exhibition of ceremonial London with the Lord Mayor's State Coach as its centrepiece. It is also worth looking out for the medieval hen's egg, a lift from Selfridges department store, and a 1930s Ford motor car. There is also a programme of temporary exhibitions, lectures and evening films throughout the year.
Open all year, Tue-Sat 10-5.50, Sun 12-5.50 (Closed 24-26 Dec, 1 Jan & every Mon ex BH's). Parties by arrangement.
P (NCP 600yds) & (wheelchairs available, lifts & induction loops, parking) toilets for disabled shop ⚘
Details not confirmed for 1998
Cards: ▨ ▧ ▨ ▨ ⑤

W1
Museum of Mankind
6 Burlington Gardens W1X 2EX
(Underground - Piccadilly Circus)
☎0171 323 8043 Fax 0171 323 8013
The ethnographical department of the British Museum was re-housed in 1970 at Burlington Gardens to form the Museum of Mankind. Its vast collections embrace the art and material culture of tribal, village and pre-industrial societies from most areas of the world other than Western Europe. It also houses archaeological collections from the Americas and Africa. The museum's policy is to mount a number of fascinating temporary exhibitions (usually lasting for at least a year) rather than have permanent displays on show,

although there are a number of outstanding exhibits on permanent display. The reserve collection is stored in Shoreditch and can be made available for serious study. Film shows and educational services are provided.
Open all year, Mon-Sat 10-5, Sun 2.30-6. (Closed Good Fri, May Day, Xmas & 1 Jan).
P (NCP 50yds) ⚑ & (parking available tel 0171-323 8047) toilets for disabled shop ⚘
Details not confirmed for 1998

SE1
Museum of the Moving Image
South Bank, Waterloo SE1 8XT
(Underground - Waterloo)
☎0171 401 2636 Fax 0171 815 1419
A ticket to the Museum of the Moving Image is a passport to the world of film and TV. Marvel at the unique collection of movie memorabilia, become a newsreader, make your own cartoon or fly like Superman - anything is possible. A cast of actors will guide you through over 40 display areas, which take you through the history of the moving image from the magic lanterns of the Victorians, through the dizzy heights of Hollywood and on to the high technology of today's video and TV.
Open all year, daily 10-6. Last admission 5pm. (Closed 24-26 Dec).
P ⚑ ✗ licensed & (for details ring 0171-815 1350) toilets for disabled shop ⚘
Details not confirmed for 1998
Cards: ▨ ▧ ▨ ▨ ▨ ⑤

EC1
Museum of The Order of St John
St John's Gate, St John's Ln EC1M 4DA
(Underground - Farringdon, Barbican)
☎0171 253 6644 Fax 0171 336 0587
One of the most obscure and fascinating museums in London, St John's Gate displays treasures that once belonged to the Knights Hospitaller. Maltese silver, Italian furniture, paintings, coins and pharmacy jars are among the objects on view. A new St John Ambulance Museum opened in Priory House, adjoining St John's Gate in 1997.
Open all year, Mon-Sat 10-5, Sat 10-4 (Closed Etr, Xmas wk & BH's). Guided tours 11 & 2.30 Tue, Fri & Sat.
P (meters/ NCP 300yds) & toilets for disabled shop ⚘
Details not confirmed for 1998

SW3
National Army Museum
Royal Hospital Rd, Chelsea SW3 4HT
(Underground - Sloane Square)
☎0171 730 0717 Fax 0171 823 6573
At the National Army Museum you can discover some of Britain's finest military treasures. It offers a unique insight into the lives of Britain's soldiers, from Privates to Field Marshals, from Tudor times to the present day. The displays include weapons, paintings, equipment, models, medals, and items from one of the world's largest collections of military uniforms. You can see life on the Western Front in a reconstruction of a World War I trench and also learn how soldiers coped with conditions as varied as the jungles of Burma, the mountains of Afghanistan, the plains of India, the snows of Canada, and the deserts of Kuwait. The fascinating exhibits on display include nine Victoria Crosses, a 400sq ft model of the Battle of Waterloo, Florence Nightingale's jewellery, and even the skeleton of Napoleon's horse. A new gallery, 'The Rise of the Redcoat' looks at the British Army from the bowmen of Henry V to the redcoats of George III. A special exhibition 'Soldiers of the Raj' opened in 1997 and will run until 1999. This tells the story of those men and women who served in the Indian Army from the 17th century to Independence in 1947.
Open all year, daily 10-5.30. (Closed Good Fri, May Day, 24-26 Dec & 1 Jan). Free.
🅿 ⚑ & (wheelchair lift to access lower ground floor) toilets for disabled shop ⚘

WC2
National Gallery
Trafalgar Square WC2N 5DN
(Underground - Charing Cross)
☎0171 747 2885 & 0171 839 3321
Fax 0171 930 4764
In 1824 the government bought the collection of pictures accumulated by John Julius Angerstein, a London underwriter, and exhibited them at his former residence in Pall Mall. These formed the major part of the collection of the National Gallery. Further bequests and purchases were made and by 1831 space had become limited, so plans were made for a special building to house the works of art. The present neo-classical building in Trafalgar Square was opened in 1838. All the great periods of Western European painting from 1260-1900 are represented here although only a limited selection of British works is displayed, as most of the national collection is housed at the Tate. The gallery's particular treasures include Van Eyck's *Arnolfini Marriage,* Velázquez's *Toilet of Venus,* Leonardo da Vinci's cartoon (the Virgin and Child with Saints Anne and John the Baptist), Rembrandt's *Belshazzar's Feast,* Van Gogh's *Sunflowers,* and Titian's *Bacchus and Ariadne.* The British paintings include Gainsborough's *Mr and Mrs Andrews* and Constable's *Haywain.* There are many more captivating masterpieces to be seen at the National Gallery which houses one of the finest and most extensive collections in the world. The Sainsbury Wing opened in 1991 and contains the early Renaissance works from 1260-1510. Lectures, guided tours and children's quizzes are available. Exhibitions for 1998 include: Henry Moore (3 April-31 May), Dutch 17th-Century painting from Utrecht (6 May-2 August), Canaletto (15 July-11 October), Jonathan Miller...on Reflection (16 September-13 December), Luca Signorelli (11 Nov-31 January 1999)
Open all year, Mon-Sat 10-6, Sun 12-6. (Wed until 8pm). Special major exhibitions open normal gallery times. (Closed Good Fri, 24-26 Dec & 1 Jan). Free. Admission charged for some major exhibitions.
P (100yds) ⚑ ✗ licensed & (wheelchairs available, induction loop in theatre, lifts) toilets for disabled shop ⚘
Cards: ▨ ▧ ▨ ▨ ▨ ⑤

WC2
National Portrait Gallery
2 St Martin's Place WC2H 0HE
(Underground - Charing Cross, Leicester Square)
☎0171 306 0055 Fax 0171 306 0056
With the aim of illustrating British history by means of a collection of portraits of famous, and infamous, men and women, the gallery's first home was established in George Street, Westminster. After several moves the collection was finally housed in its present accommodation in 1896. Located behind the National Gallery, the building was designed in the style of an Italian palazzo. A further wing was added in 1933. The portraits are arranged in chronological order from the top floor, starting with the medieval period and finishing with the present day. As well as paintings, there are sculptures, miniatures, engravings, photographs and cartoons among the displays. Special exhibitions for 1998 include Henri Cartier-Bresson: Portraits (until 7 June), Lewis Carroll (10 July-11 October) and Sporting Heroes (23 October-31 January 1999).
Open all year 10-6, Sat 10-6 & Sun 12-6. (Closed Good Fri, May Day, 24-26 Dec & 1 Jan).
Free (ex special exhibitions)
P (200yds) & (direct access, stair climber, touch tours) toilets for disabled shop ⚘

EC1
National Postal Museum
King Edward Building, King Edward St EC1A 1LP (Underground - St Paul's)
☎0171 776 3636 Fax 0171 776 3637
This museum is a philatelist's paradise; it

➜

contains the most comprehensive collection of postage stamps in the world. Established in 1965, the National Postage Museum has obtained a vast collection of material charting the history of the postal system since its inception. Exhibits include a display of numerous stamps issued worldwide since 1878; the R M Phillips collection of 19th-century British stamps, including the celebrated 'Penny Black', the Frank Staff collections of 'postal history' material, and Great Britain's reference display of stamps from King Edward VII to the present day. The museum also holds, on microfilm, the Thomas de la Rue correspondence archives, and a large amount of unique philatelic material, most of which is available for research by prior arrangement. Temporary displays are held throughout the year.
Open all year, Mon-Thu (ex BH) 9.30-4.30, Fri 9.30-4.30.
Free.
P (NCP car park) & *(main gallery accessible by prior arrangement) shop* ✍

SW7
The Natural History Museum
Cromwell Rd SW7 5BD (Underground - South Kensington)
☎ *0171 938 9123 Fax 0171 938 9066*
The Museum's collections were built up around the specimens collected by Sir Hans Sloane and formed a part of the nucleus of the British Museum. By 1860 the continued expansion of the collections meant that a separate natural history museum was required; it was not until 1881, though, that the new museum - The Natural History Museum - was opened. The vast and elaborate Romanesque-style building, with its terracotta facing showing relief mouldings of animals, birds and fishes, covers an area of four acres. In the Whale Hall a life-size model of the enormous Blue Whale can be seen, and in the Hall of Human Biology visitors can learn about the way their bodies work (including how it feels to be in the womb). Creepy Crawlies shows you how insects, spiders, crabs, and their relatives are important to humans, as both friends and foes. Ecology stresses your relationship with, and responsibility for, the natural world. A major permanent exhibition on dinosaurs includes new skeletons, recreated robotic models, and displays on how dinosaurs lived, why they became extinct, and how they were dug up and studied by scientists. A recent addition is the dynamic new Earth Galleries exhibitions, Visions of Earth, The Power Within and Restless Surface. These galleries invite visitors to look at the Earth in a new way, exploring the causes and effects of volcanoes, earthquakes, tidal waves and avalanches. New exhibitions for 1998 include: Myths & Monsters (Easter-September). There is a continuing programme of events workshops, lectures and videos

throughout the year, but especially at weekends and school holidays.
Open all year, Mon-Sat 10-5.50, Sun 11-5.50 (Closed 23-26 Dec).
❀ *£5.50 (ch 5-17 £2.80, concessions £3). Family ticket £15. Party. 1*
P (metered 180yds) ▼ ✗ *licensed* & *(ex top floor & one gallery, wheelchairs available) toilets for disabled shop* ✍
Cards: 🖃 ▭ ▭ ▭ ⑤

W1
Pollock's Toy Museum
1 Scala St W1P 1LT (Underground - Goodge Street)
☎ *0171 636 3452*
Teddy bears, wax and china dolls, dolls' houses, board games, toy theatres, tin toys, mechanical and optical toys, folk toys and nursery furniture, are among the attractions to be seen in this appealing museum. Items from all over the world and from all periods are displayed in two small, interconnecting houses with winding staircases and charming little rooms. Toy theatre performances available for groups.
Open all year, Mon-Sat 10-5. (Closed Sun & Xmas).
£2.50 (ch £1).
P (100 yds) & *shop*
Cards: 🖃 ▭ ▭ ▭

WC2
Public Record Office Museum
Chancery Ln WC2A 1LR (Underground - Temple, Blackfriars)
☎ *0181 876 3444 Fax 0171 404 7248*
The Public Record Office houses one of the finest, most complete archives in Europe, comprising the records of the central government and law courts from the Norman Conquest to the present century. It is a mine of information and some of the most interesting material is exhibited in its museum. Domesday Book is on permanent display.
Museum due to reopen Spring 1998. Please telephone for details.
& *shop* ✍ ♿
Details not confirmed for 1998

SW1
The Queen's Gallery
Buckingham Palace, Buckingham Palace Rd SW1A 1AA (Underground - Victoria)
☎ *0171 799 2331 (24hr info line)*
Fax 0171 930 9625
The Queen's Gallery at Buckingham Palace was first opened to the public in 1962 to display paintings, drawings, furniture and other works of art in the Royal Collection, one of the finest in the world. The Gallery is sited in a building originally designed as a conservatory by John Nash in 1831 and later converted into a chapel by Blore. The building suffered severe bomb damage in World War II and was not reconstructed until 1962; part of it still remains as the private chapel of Buckingham Palace. Exhibitions for 1998 include 'Monarchy and the Patronage of British Painting' (15 May-11 Oct) and Mark Catesby's 'Natural History of America' - water colours from the Royal Library (30 Oct-10 Jan 1999).
Open all year daily 9.30-4.30 (ex for short periods between exhibitions). Telephone 0171-799 2331 for detailed information. £4 (ch under 17 £2, pen £3) Family ticket £10. Combined ticket £6.50 (ch under 17 £3.50, pen £4.50) Family ticket £16. P (200yds) shop ✍ *(ex guide dogs)*
Cards: 🖃 ▭ ▭ ▭ ⑤

NW1
Regent's Park
NW1 (Underground - Baker Street)
The elegant charm of this park, north of Marylebone Road, can be attributed to John Nash, who laid it out, along with the imposing surrounding terraces, as part of a plan for a new palace which was never built. It now contains London Zoo (see separate entry), a boating lake, open-air theatre, Regent's Canal and the lovely Queen Mary's Rose Garden. There are a number of Victorian garden ornaments around the park and a group of fossil tree trunks are the only reminders that the Royal Botanic Gardens were once situated here.

W1
Rock Circus
London Pavilion, Piccadilly Circus W1V 9LA (Underground - Piccadilly Circus)
☎ *0171 734 7203 Fax 0171 734 8023*
Rock Circus is a unique and fun celebration of rock and pop music spanning forty years from the 1950s to the present day. Moving and static life-size figures, lasers, memorabilia, archive footage and personal stereo sound. Figures include: Bono, Jon Bon Jovi, Gloria Estefan and Mick Hucknall.
Open all year, daily 11-9, Tue 12-9, Fri & Sat 11-10pm, holiday periods in summer 10am-10pm, Tue 12-10. (Times vary during Xmas wk). Closed 25 Dec. P (200yds) & *(lift to all floors with member of staff) toilets for disabled shop* ✍
Details not confirmed for 1998
Cards: 🖃 ▭ ▭

W1
Royal Academy Of Arts
Burlington House, Piccadilly W1V 0DS (Underground - Piccadilly Circus)
☎ *0171 439 7438 & 0171 439 4996/7*
Fax 0171 434 0837
Known principally for its exhibitions, the Royal Academy of Arts was founded in 1768 and is Britain's oldest Fine Arts institution. Two of its founding principles were to provide a free school and to mount 'an annual exhibition open to all artists of distinguished merit', now known as the Summer Exhibition. Both continue today. The Royal Academy's most prized possession, Michelangelo's tondo, *The Virgin and Child with the Infant St John*, one of only four marble sculptures by the artist outside Italy, is on permanent display outside the Sackler Galleries.
Open all year, daily 10-6. (Closed 24-26 Dec & Good Fri.
▼ ✗ *licensed* & *toilets for disabled shop* ✍ ♿
Details not confirmed for 1998

SW1
The Royal Mews
Buckingham Palace, Buckingham Palace Rd SW1W 0QH (Underground - Victoria)
☎ *0171 799 2331 (info line)*
Fax 0171 930 9625
Designed by John Nash and completed in 1825, the Royal Mews houses the State Coaches. These include the Gold State Coach made in 1762, with panels painted by the Florentine artist Cipriani. It has been used for every coronation since that date. As one of the finest working stables in existence, the Royal Mews provides a unique opportunity for visitors to see a working department of the Royal Household. The Queen's State Carriages and Coaches are housed here together with their horses and State liveries.
Open 1 Jan-23 Mar & 2 Oct-31 Dec Wednesdays only, 24 Mar-2 Aug Tues-Thurs only 12-4pm (last admission 3.30pm). 3 Aug-1 Oct Mon-Thurs 10.30am-4.30pm (last admission 4pm). £4 (ch under 17 £2, pen £3) Family ticket £10. Combined ticket £6.50 (ch under 17 £3.50, pen 4.50) Family ticket £16. P (200yds) & *toilets for disabled shop* ✍ *(ex guide dogs)*
Cards: 🖃 ▭ ▭ ▭ ⑤

A large collection of dolls, teddy bears, board games and other toys are on display at Pollock's Toy Museum.

SW1
St James's Park
SW1 (Underground - St James's Park)
Situated between Buckingham Palace and Whitehall, this is the oldest of the Royal Parks in London, drained and converted into a deer park by Henry VIII in 1532. Charles II had the park redesigned in the style of Versailles, but the park as it exists today, with its lake, plantations and walks, was created by Nash for George IV. It remains one of the most delightful and popular places to relax, both for visitors and for workers, who frequently share their sandwiches with the large variety of waterfowl on the lake. There are also summer band concerts and refreshment facilities.

SW7
Science Museum
Exhibition Rd, South Kensington SW7 2DD (Underground - South Kensington)
☎0171 938 8000
Of all the Exhibition Road museums, the Science Museum is the most attractive to children (and often adults too). Among the displays are many working models with knobs to press, handles to turn and buttons to push to various different effects: exhibits are set in motion, light up, rotate and make noises. The collections cover the application of science to technology and illustrate the development of engineering and industry through the ages; there are galleries dealing with printing, chemistry, nuclear physics, navigation, photography, electricity, communications and medicine. A popular feature of the museum is the 'Launch Pad', an interactive children's gallery where children of all ages can carry out their own fun experiments. 'Food for Thought' is a permanent gallery which explains the impact of science and technology on today's food. The centrepiece of the Exploration of Space exhibition is the

Apollo 10. Britain's first 'jump jet' and an executive jet are just two of the exhibits in 'Flight', a fascinating aeronautics gallery. The Wellcome Museum of the History of Medicine features numerous reconstructions of important events in medical history. There is also a range of interactive areas for young people, including 'The Garden', the first interactive area in a UK museum for 3-6 year olds, 'Things' for 7-11's, 'The Network' for 8-12's and 'On Air' for 12-19 year olds. Please telephone for details of special events.
Open all year, daily 10-6. (Closed 24-26 Dec.)
🚻 & *toilets for disabled shop* 🐕
Details not confirmed for 1998
Cards: 🏧 ⬛ 🔵

SE1
Shakespeare's Globe Exhibition
New Globe Walk, Bankside SE1 9ED (Underground - London Bridge, walk along Bankside. Mansion House, walk across Southwark Bridge)
☎0171 928 6406 & 902 1500
Fax 0171 401 8261
Unparallel'd. Fantastical. The most astonishing site in London. Resolve to be amazed. Discover what an Elizabethan audience would have been like. Find out about the rivalry between the bankside theatres, the bear baiting and the stews. Hear about the penny stinkards and find out what a bodger is. Guides help to bring England's most important theatrical heritage to life.
Open all year; Sep-May, daily 10-5 (ex 24-25 Dec). May-Sep (theatre season), opening times restricted, phone for details.
❄£5 (ch £3, pen & students £4.50). *Family ticket £14.*
P (Upper Thames St) 🍴 ✗ *licensed* &
toilets for disabled shop 🐕
Cards: 🏧 ⬛ 🔵

NW1
Sherlock Holmes Museum
221b Baker St NW1 6XE (Underground - Baker Street)
☎0171 935 8866 Fax 0171 738 1269
221b Baker Street, that famous address of super-sleuth Sherlock Holmes, was opened as a museum in March 1990 to the great delight of admirers of the great detective. The first-floor rooms contain all the features familiar to the Holmes enthusiast, and an authentic Victorian atmosphere has been maintained throughout the house. The museum is of unique interest and visitors are encouraged to take photographs.
Open all year, daily 9.30-6. (Closed 25 Dec).
❄£5 (ch 8-16 £3).
P (250yds) ✗ *licensed shop* 🐕
Cards: 🏧 ⬛ 🔵

WC2
Sir John Soane's Museum
13 Lincoln's Inn Fields WC2A 3BP (Underground - Holborn)
☎0171 405 2107 & 0171 430 0175 (Info) Fax 0171 831 3957
Sir John Soane was responsible for some of the most splendid architecture in London, and his house, built in 1812, contains his collections of antiquities, sculpture, paintings, drawings and books. Included amongst his treasures are the *Rake's Progess* and *Election* series of paintings by William Hogarth, and the Sarcophagus of Seti I dating from 1290BC. Access to the architectural drawing collection (30,000 drawings from the Renaissance to the early 19th century) is by appointment only for researchers.
Open all year, Tue-Sat 10-5. Also first Tue of month 6-9pm. (Closed BH). Lecture tour Sat 2.30 (limited no of tickets sold from 2pm)
Free.
P (200yds) (metered parking) shop 🐕

SW1
Tate Gallery
Millbank SW1P 4RG (Underground - Pimlico)
☎0171 887 8000 & rec info 0171 887 8008 Fax 0171 887 8007
In 1892 Sir Henry Tate, the sugar magnate and prominent collector of contemporary British painting and sculpture, offered to finance the building of a new and permanent home for his growing collection of British Art. Sidney J R Smith was commissioned to design the new gallery on the site of the former Millbank Prison and the building was officially opened to the public in 1897. A number of extensions to the building have followed, the most recent being the Clore Gallery in 1987 which houses the Turner Bequest. In the early part of this century the gallery was able to expand its collection to include foreign 20th-century art. 1998 New Displays will include: Victorian painting (Rossetti, Dadd, Millais etc), Impressionism, Surrealism, Modern Art in Britain, and loaned works by Joseph Beuys, Andy Warhol etc. Contact the gallery for more details.
Open daily 10-5.50. (closed 24-26 Dec.) Free. Charge for major loan exhibitions.
P 🍴 ✗ *licensed* & (wheelchairs on request, parking by prior arrangement). *toilets for disabled shop* 🐕
Cards: 🏧 ⬛ 🔵

WC2
Theatre Museum
Russell St, Covent Garden WC2E 7PA (Underground - Covent Garden, Leicester Sq)
☎0171 836 7891 Fax 0171 836 5148
Major developments, events and personalities from the performing arts are illustrated in this appealing museum.. Stage models, costumes, prints, drawings, posters, puppets, props and a variety of other theatre memorabilia are displayed. Special exhibitions include 'Slap - the Art of Stage Make-up', and 'From Page to Stage' with the *Wind in the Willows*, based on the National

Theatre production. Daily guided tours, costume workshops, demonstrations on the art of stage make-up now available free with admission ticket. Also visitors can dress up in costumes from National Theatre companies and watch unique recordings of live performances from outstanding London and regional productions. Groups are advised to book in advance. Theatrical events are planned for 1998 include Dressing the Part - an exhibition on the art of the costumier including features on A Midsummer Night's Dream costumes and the different techniques used by stage and film.
Open all year, Tue-Sun 11-7. (closed Christmas Day and other public hols)
£3.50 (concessions £2). *Family ticket £8.*
P (meters, NCP 250yds) & *toilets for disabled shop* 🐕
Cards: 🏧 ⬛ 🔵

SE1
The Tower Bridge Experience
SE1 2UP (Underground - Tower Hill)
☎0171 378 1928 Fax 0171 357 7935
Tower Bridge is one of the capital's most popular landmarks. Its glass-covered walkways stand 142ft above the Thames, affording panoramic views of the river. Much of the original machinery for working the bridge is still in place and can be seen in the engine rooms. The bridge's exhibition, The Tower Bridge Experience, uses state-of-the-art effects to present the story of the bridge in a dramatic and exciting fashion. Ring for details of special events.
Open all year, Apr-Oct, 10-6.30; Nov-Mar 9.30-6 (last ticket sold 75 mins before closing). (Closed 24-26 Dec, 1 & 28 Jan).
£5.70 (ch 15, students & pen £3.90, ch 5 free). *Party 10+. Family £14.95.*
P (100yds) & (lifts to all levels, ramp for clear view from walkways) *toilets for disabled shop* 🐕
Cards: 🏧 ⬛ 🔵

EC3
Tower Hill Pageant
1 Tower Hill Ter EC3N 4EE (Underground - Tower Hill)
☎0171 709 0081 Fax 0171 702 3656
Tower Hill Pageant is the perfect introduction to 2000 years of London's history. Board a time-car to witness 26 tableaux including Viking raiders, the Great Fire, and the building of Tower Bridge. Continue your exploration in the Roman and Medieval museum galleries where there are over 1000 priceless artefacts discovered along the Thames. Telephone for details of special events.
Open all year daily from 9.30am. (Closed 25 Dec). Last admissions: Easter-Oct 5.30pm, (ex July & Aug: 6pm) Nov-Easter 4.30pm.
£6.95 (ch £4.95, pen & students £5.25). *Family ticket £16.95.*
P (50mtrs) 🍴 & (adapted time car for wheelchair users, ramps through museum toilets for disabled shop 🐕
Cards: 🏧 ⬛ 🔵

EC3
Tower of London
Tower Hill EC3N 4AB (Underground - Tower Hill)
☎0171 709 0765
Perhaps the most famous castle in the world, the Tower of London has played a central part in British history throughout the ages. The nucleus of the complex is the original White Tower, built by William the Conqueror as a show of strength to the people of London; it remains one of the most outstanding examples of Norman military architecture in Europe. Today it houses a selection from the Royal Armouries, the national collection of arms and armour based on the great arsenal of Henry VIII.
For a great part of its history, the Tower of London was used, among other things, as the State Prison. It was here that King Henry VIII had two of his wives executed, here that Lady Jane Grey died and here that Sir Walter Raleigh was imprisoned for 13 years. From the reign

➤

of Charles II its main use was as an arsenal, administrative centre and the headquarters of the Royal Mint (until 1812) but during both World Wars it reverted to a state prison and was used to incarcerate German spies.
The unique Yeoman Warders, or 'Beefeaters' play an important role in the protection of the Tower - home of the Crown Jewels - and are most informative and entertaining. Another feature of the Tower are the ravens whose continued residence is said to ensure that the Kingdom does not fail. The first new raven for 300 years was hatched in May 1989. Crowns and Diamonds, an exciting new exhibition on the evolution of Royal Crowns in Britain, opened in the Martin Tower in December 1996. The exhibition features a number of crowns never displayed to the public before and more than 12,000 rough and polished diamonds.
Open all year, Mar-Oct, Mon-Sat 9-6, Sun 10-6 (last admission 5pm); Nov-Feb, Tue-Sat 9-5, Sun 10-5 (last admssion 4pm). (Closed 24-26 Dec & 1 Jan).
❄£18.50 (ch £5.60, concessions £6.40).Family ticket £25.
P (100yds) (NCP Lower Thames St) ☕ ♿ toilets for disabled shop
Cards:

SW7
Victoria & Albert Museum
Cromwell Rd SW7 2RL (Underground - South Kensington)
☎0171 938 8500 Fax 0171 938 8341
The V&A is the world's finest museum of the decorative arts. Its collections span 2000 years and are housed in a magnificent Victorian and Edwardian complex of buildings, including Sir Aston Webb's Cromwell Road façade. The museum's collections comprise sculpture, furniture, fashion and textiles, paintings, silver, glass, ceramics, jewellery, books, prints, and photographs from Britain and all over the world. Highlights include the world's greatest collection of paintings by Constable and the national collection of watercolours; the famous 15th-century Devonshire Hunting Tapestries; the Dress Court showing fashion from 1500 to the present day; a superb Asian collection, including the much-loved Tippoo's Tiger; medieval treasures; magnificent collections of Renaissance and Victorian sculpture; the Jewellery Gallery including the Russian Crown Jewels; and the 20th Century Gallery, devoted to comtemporary art and design. There are also magnificent new galleries devoted to European art and design, glass and ceramics, ironwork, Chinese, European and Indian art, 20th-century design, and architect Frank Lloyd Wright. The most recent being the Raphael Gallery and the fully restored Silver Galleries. A Photography Gallery of 300,000 photographs spanning the entire history of the medium opens in May. Special exhibitions for 1998 include 'The Power of the Poster' (9 Apr-26 Jul) and 'Aubrey Beardsley' (8 Oct-4 Jan 1999).
Open all year, Tue-Sun 10-5.45, Mon 12-5.45. (Closed 24-26 Dec). Tel for BH openings. British Galleries closed for redevelopment.
£5 (concessions £3). UB40'S, disabled with carer, students & ch18 free.
P (500yds) ✕ licensed ♿ (braille guide, tour tape. for further info, please phone) toilets for disabled shop
Cards:

W1
Wallace Collection
Hertford House, Manchester Square W1M 6BN (Underground - Bond Street, Baker Street)
☎0171 935 0687 Fax 0171 224 2155
An elegant 18th-century town house makes an appropriate gallery for this outstanding collection of art. Founded by the 1st Marquis of Hertford and brought to England from Paris in the late 19th century by Richard Wallace (son of the 4th Marquis), it was bequeathed to the nation in 1897 and came on public display three years later. As well as an unrivalled representation of 18th-century French art with paintings by Boucher, Watteau and Fragonard, Hertford House displays a wealth of furniture, porcelain and beautiful works of art. It is the home of Frans Hals' ***Laughing Cavalier*** and of paintings by Gainsborough, Rubens, Delacroix and Titian. It also houses the largest collection of arms and armour outside the Tower of London.
Open all year, Mon-Sat 10-5, Sun 2-5. Apr-Sep, Sun 11-5 (Closed Good Fri, May Day, 24-26 Dec & 1 Jan).
Free.
P (NCP & meters) ♿ (ramp wheelchair available upon request) shop
Cards:

W1
Wellington Museum
Apsley House, 149 Piccadilly, (Hyde Park Corner) WIV 9FA (Underground - Hyde Park Corner)
☎0171 499 5676
Fax 0171 493 6576
Number One, London, is the popular name for one of the Capital's finest private residences, Apsley House, 19th-century home of the first Duke of Wellington. Originally designed by Robert Adam and built in the 1770's, its rich interiors have now been returned to their former glory as the private palace of the 'Iron Duke'. Once described as the 'most renowned mansion in the capital', it houses the Duke's magnificent collection of paintings, (including works by Velazquez, Goya, Rubens, Landseer, Lawrence, Wilkie, and Dutch and Flemish masters); silver, porcelain, sculpture and furniture. Today Apsley House on Hyde Park Corner is the last great London town house with its collections largely intact and family still in residence.
Open Tue-Sun 11-5. (Closed Mon ex BH Mon, Good Fri, May Day BH, 24-26 Dec & 1 Jan).
£4 (ch 12-17, pen, disabled, UB40 £2.50).
P (NCP Park Lane) ☕ ♿ (lift all parts accessible with help) shop
Cards:

EC1
Wesley's Chapel, House & Museum Of Methodism
49 City Rd EC1Y 1AU (Underground - Old Street)
☎0171 253 2262
Fax 0171 608 3825
Wesley's Chapel has been the Mother Church of World Methodism since its construction in 1778. The crypt houses a museum which traces the development of Methodism from the 18th century to the present day. Step back into 18th century London with a visit to Wesley's house - built by him in 1779, he lived here when not touring and preaching. Recently refurbished, you can discover the day to day running of a small Georgian townhouse. Special events for 1998 include: Conversion experience of John Wesley on 24 May 1738 (24 May), Anniversary of opening of Wesley's Chapel on All Saints Day 1778, (1 Nov).
Open all year, Mon-Sat & BH 10-4 (Closed 25 & 26 Dec). Main service 11am Sun followed by an opportunity to tour the museum and house.
House & museum £4 (ch, students, UB40's & pen £2)
♿ toilets for disabled shop

SW1
Westminster Abbey
SW1P 3PA
☎0171 222 5152
Fax 0172 233 2072
Westminster Abbey has been at the heart of English history for nearly a thousand years. It has been the setting for every coronation since 1066. The Abbey is a 'Royal Peculiar' and unlike other churches is under the jurisdiction of a Dean and Chapter subject only to the Sovereign. The Abbey was consecrated in 1065 but the present building is the result of great improvements by Henry III in the 13th century. The beautiful Gothic nave is the tallest in Britain and the Chapter House is one of the largest in England. The Norman Undercroft houses a museum with Coronation regalia and Royal effigies and the Pyx Chamber houses a display of plate. In the Abbey many famous people are buried including the Kings and Queens of England and in Poets' Corner are memorials to poets beginning with Chaucer to the present time.
Open all year. Abbey: Mon-Fri 9-4.45, Sat 9-2.45 & 3.45-5.45. Last admission 60 mins before closing. Cloister daily 8-6.
Royal Chapels £5 (ch 16 £2, pen & students £3). Family ticket £10.
P ☕ ♿ (areas accessible induction loop) shop

SW1
Westminster Cathedral
Victoria St SW1P 1QW (300 yards from Victoria Station)
☎0171 798 9055
Fax 0171 798 9090
Westminster Cathedral is a fascinating example of Victorian architecture. It was designed in the Early Christian Byzantine style by John Francis Bentley and its strongly oriental appearance makes it very distinctive. The foundation stone was laid in 1895 but the interior was never completed. The interior is awesome with fine marble work and mosaics. The fourteen Stations of the Cross are celebrated works by Eric Gill. The Campanile Bell Tower is 273ft high and has a four-sided viewing gallery with magnificent views over London. The lift is open daily 9am-5pm March-November but shut Mon-Wed from December-February.
Open all year, daily 7-7.
Free.
P (2hr metered parking) ♿ (ex side chapels) shop

SW1

Westminster Hall

Westminster SW1A 0AA (Underground - Westminster Hall)
☎ *0171 219 4272*
The great Westminster Hall, where Charles I was tried in 1649, has survived virtually intact since it was remodelled at the end of the 14th century. It even escaped the fire in 1834 which destroyed much of the medieval Palace of Westminster. The magnificent hammerbeam roof is the earliest surviving example of its kind.
Westminster Hall can only be viewed by those on a tour of the Houses of Parliament, which must be arranged by an MP or Peer.
& *toilets for disabled shop* ❀
Details not confirmed for 1998

SE1

Winston Churchill's Britain at War Experience

64/66 Tooley St SE1 2TF
☎ *0171 403 3171 Fax 0171 403 5104*
How did it feel to be a British citizen during World War II? Journey back in time for a stunning adventure that's exciting and educational. Take the lift to the London Underground and shelter from the air raids. Crouch in an Anderson Shelter and hear enemy aircraft overhead. The special effects recreate the sights, sounds and even the dust, smoke and smell of the London Blitz to enable you to feel and breathe the War years. Special activities for children in all school holidays, phone for details.
Open all year, Apr-Sep 10-5.30pm; Oct-Mar 10-4.30. (Closed 24-26 Dec) £5.95 (ch 16 £2.95, student, pen & UB40 £3.95). Family ticket £14.
P *(100mtrs)* & *shop* ❀
Cards: ▨▨▨

LONDON OUTER

BETHNAL GREEN (E2)

Bethnal Green Museum of Childhood

Cambridge Heath Rd E2 9PA (Underground - Bethnal Green)
☎ *0181 980 2415 Fax 0181 983 5225*
This Victorian hall, the original Victorian and Albert building, houses a multitude of childhood delights. Toys, dolls and dolls' houses, model soldiers, puppets, games, model theatres, children's costume and nursery antiques are all included in its well planned displays. There are Saturday workshops for children, and activities in the holidays.
Open all year, Mon-Thu & Sat 10-5.50, Sun 2.30-5.50. (Closed Fri, May Day, 24-26 Dec & 1 Jan).
P 🍴 *shop* ❀
Details not confirmed for 1998
Cards: ▨▨▨▨

Geffrye Museum

Kingsland Rd E2 8EA (Underground - Old Street)
☎ *0171 739 9893 Fax 0171 729 5647*
The Geffrye is one of London's most friendly and enjoyable museums, set in elegant 18th-century almshouses with delightful gardens, just north of the City. The museum presents the changing style of the domestic interior from 1600 to 1950. The displays lead the visitor on a walk through time, from the 17th century with oak furniture and panelling, past the refined elegance of the Georgian rooms and the ornate style of the Victorian parlour, to the 20th-century art deco and post war utility. The museum and garden are brought to life through drama, music, workshops and seminars, with special holiday activities for families and children. The award-winning herb garden is open from April to October. Every year Christmas is celebrated at the Geffrye in authentic historical style. The period rooms sparkle with festive decorations and 400 years of Christmas tradition

come to life. An 1800 sqm extension is scheduled to open in November 1998. This will provide new galleries for 20th-century furniture and interiors, a temporary exhibition gallery, design centre, new education facilities, a shop, and a restaurant.
Open all year, Tue-Sat 10-5, Sun & BH Mons 2-5 (Closed other PH & 24 Dec). Free.
P *(150yds) (on street parking)* 🍴 & *(wheelchair available) toilets for disabled shop* ❀

BEXLEY

Hall Place

Bourne Rd DA5 1PQ (near jct of A2 & A233)
☎ *01322 526574*
Fax 01322 522921
Hall Place is an attractive mansion of chequered flint and brick, but it is most interesting for its garden. This has topiary in the form of the 'Queen's Beasts'; rose, rock, peat and water gardens; and a herb garden with a fascinating range of plants (labelled in braille) for medicine and cooking. There is also a conservatory, a local studies centre and museum. Please telephone for details of the programme of temporary exhibitions, lectures and concerts in the museum and Great Hall.
Open all year, House: Mon-Sat 10-5, Sun & BHs 2-6 (summer); Mon-Sat 10-4.15 (winter). Gardens: Mon-Fri 7.30-dusk, Sat & Sun 9-dusk.
P 🍴 & *shop* ❀

BLACKHEATH (SE3)

Rangers House

Chesterfield Walk SE3
☎ *0181 853 0035*
This beautiful villa, built around 1700 on the edge of Greenwich Park, houses the important Suffolk collection of Jacobean and Stuart portraits. Also featured is the Dolmetsch collection of musical instruments and some fine furniture. There is a busy programme of chamber concerts, poetry readings, holiday projects and workshops. An Architectural Study Centre is open in the Coach House.
Open all year, Apr-Oct, daily 10-6 (or dusk if earlier); Nov-Mar, Wed-Sun 10-4. (Closed 24-25 Dec & 4-27 Jan). £2.50 (ch £1.30, concessions £1.90). Personal stereo tour included in admission.
P & *toilets for disabled* ❀ *(in certain areas)* ♿

BRENTFORD

Kew Bridge Steam Museum

Green Dragon Ln TW8 0EN (Underground - Gunnersbury district line then 237 or 267 bus)
☎ *0181 568 4757*
Fax 0181 569 9978
The Victorian pumping station has steam engines and six beam engines, of which

five are working and one is the largest in the world. A forge, diesel house, waterwheel and old workshops can also be seen along with London's only steam narrow-gauge railway which operates on the second and last weekend of each month from March to November. New permanent interactive exhibition - 'The Water for Life Gallery.' which tells the story of London's Water Supply from Pre-Roman times. 1998 Special Events include: Magic of Meccano show (April), Festival of Steam (October), Live steam model railway show (November), Historic fire engine rally (May), Tower open day (June & September).
Open all year, daily 11-5. In steam wknds & BHs. (Closed Good Fri & Xmas wk).
❉*Weekdays £2 (ch, students & pen £1). Family ticket £5; Sat & Sun £3.25 (ch, students & pen £1.80). Family ticket £8.50.*
P 🍴 & *(tours for partially sighted by arrangement) shop*
Cards: ▨▨ ❀

Musical Museum

368 High St TW8 0BD (Underground - Gunnersbury)
☎ *0181 560 8108*
This museum will take you back to a bygone age to hear and see a marvellous working collection of automatic musical instruments from small music boxes to a mighty Wurlitzer theatre organ. Working demonstrations. There will be a Street Organ Festival (end of June) and 14 concerts during the summer - please telephone for details.
Open Apr-Oct, Sat & Sun 2-5. Also Jul-Aug, Wed 2-4. (Tour 1hr 30mins).
P *(200 yds)* & *shop* ❀ *(guide dogs)*

CAMBERWELL (SE5)

South London Gallery

65 Peckham Rd SE5 8UH
☎ *0171 703 6120 Fax 0171 252 4730*
The gallery presents a programme of up to eight exhibitions a year of cutting-edge contemporary art, and has established itself as South East London's premier venue for contemporary visual arts. The Gallery also aims to bring contemporary art of the highest standards to audiences in South London and to assist in the regeneration of the area by attracting audiences from across Britain and abroad.
Open only when exhibitions are in progress, Tue-Fri 11-6, Thu 11-7, wknds 2-6 (Closed Mon).
P *(50yds)* ❀

CAMDEN TOWN (NW1)

The Jewish Museum

Raymond Burton House, 129-131 Albert St, Camden Town NW1 7NB (Underground - Camden Town)
☎ *0171 284 1997 Fax 0171 267 9008*
The Jewish Museum opens a window on to the history and religious life of the Jewish community in Britain and beyond. In 1995 it relocated to attractive new premises in an early Victorian house in Camden. Its stylish new galleries tell the story from the Norman Conquest to recent times, and illustrate Jewish religious life with outstanding examples of Jewish ceremonial art. Thre are changing exhibitions in the Gallery and audio visual programmes are available. Guided walks of Jewish London can be arranged.
Open Sun-Thu, 10-4. Closed Jewish Festivals & public holidays.
P & *toilets for disabled shop* ❀
Details not confirmed for 1998

The Victorian Room at the Geffrye Museum

CHESSINGTON

Chessington World of Adventures
KT9 2NE (M25 junc 9/10, on A243)
☎ 01372 727227 F
ax 01372 725050
At Chessington World of Adventures there's something different around every corner, from spine-tingling rides and fun-filled family attractions to crazy entertainers and rare and endangered animals all set in magnificently themed areas. From the awesomely terrifying Rameses Revenge with its three-way fear factor of height, speed and water in the ancient Forbidden Kingdom, to the Oriental delights of the Dragon River Water Ride in the Mystic East, there's something for everyone - even the smallest adventurers have their own themed land, Toytown, where everything is larger than life. There are now two new experiences: a new ride that... Bites! and a hair-raising close encounter with nature's nightmares. Special for 1998: Summer nights - late opening til 9pm (July & August), Fright Nights (end of season) late opening, enjoy spine-tingling rides in the dark, Special days for cubs, scouts, guides and youth groups take place throughout the year. Phone for details.
Open 23 Mar-1 Nov, daily. Late opening until 9pm during July & August.
✻*Admission fee payable. Phone for details.*
🅿 ⬛ ✗ *licensed* ♿ *(some rides not accessible disabled guide available) toilets for disabled shop* ⊘
Cards: ◨ ▤ ▦ ▥

CHISLEHURST

Chislehurst Caves
Old Hill BR7 5NB (off A222)
☎ 0181 467 3264
Fax 01883 742155
This labyrinth of caves has been called the enigma of Kent. Miles of mysterious caverns and passages hewn out of the chalk over some 8,000 years can be explored with experienced guides to tell the history and legends of the caves.
Open all year, daily during school hols (incl half terms). All other times Wed-Sun, 10-4. Closed 24-25 Dec.
£3 (ch & pen £1.50); longer tours: Sun & BH's only £5 (ch & pen £2.50).
🅿 ⬛ ♿ *(ramps) toilets for disabled shop* ⊘

CHISWICK (W4)

Chiswick House
Burlington Ln, Chiswick W4 2RP
(Underground - Gunnersbury)
☎ 0181 995 0508
Built by Lord Burlington in the 1720's, Chiswick House is internationally renowned as one of the finest English buildings inspired by the architecture of Ancient Rome. The rooms with their fine collection of art and the wonderful Italianate gardens complete with statues, temples, urns and obelisks, continue to delight visitors to this London villa. An introductory video and audio guide help to tell the story behind Chiswick House.
Open all year, Apr-Oct, daily 10-6 (or dusk if earlier); Nov-Mar, Wed-Sun 10-4. Closed 24-26 Dec & 4-17 Jan 1999.
£3.00 (ch £1.50, concessions £2.30). Personal stereo tour included in admission, also available for the partially sighted, those with learning difficulties, and in French & German.
🅿 ♿ *shop* ⊘ *(in certain areas)* ⊞

Hogarth House
Hogarth Ln, Great West Rd W4 2QN
(50yds W of Hogarth roundabout on Great West Road)
☎ 0181 994 6757
Fax 0181 862 7602
A small Georgian house once the home of William Hogarth, it is now a print gallery and has on view many of his famous engravings. It is near the Thames and other 18th-century houses along Chiswick Mall and also Chiswick House. It has a secluded garden and Hogarth's Mulberry Tree. The house has recently been restored and refurbished with money from the Heritage Lottery Fund and other organizations. There is an exhibition describing Hogarth and his life and work.
Open Apr-Oct, Tue-Fri 1-5, Sat-Sun 1-6; Nov-Mar, Tue-Fri 1-4, Sat-Sun 1-5. (Closed Mon, Jan, 25-26 Dec and Good Fri.
Free.
P *(25 & 50yds)* ♿ *toilets for disabled shop* ⊘

COLINDALE (NW9)

Royal Air Force Museum
Grahame Park Way NW9 5LL
(Underground - Colindale)
☎ 0181 205 2266 & 0181 200 1763
Fax 0181 205 8044
Seventy full-size original aeroplanes and other exhibits, all under cover, tell the fascinating story of flight through the ages. Extensive galleries show the political and historical impact of this means of transport and communication - including the incredible 'Battle of Britain Experience', the story of history's most famous air battle. Visitor facilities include a Tornado flight simulator, the Eurofighter 2000 three screen cinema, guided tours and the new 'touch and try' Jet Provost - climb in the cockpit and try out the controls for yourself. There is also a new walk-in TriStar cockpit and a walk-through Sunderland Flying Boat.
Open daily 10-6. (Closed 24-26 Dec & 1 Jan).
✻*£5.85 (pen £4.40, ch & concessions £2.95). Family ticket £15. Party 10+.*
🅿 ⬛ ✗ *licensed* ♿ *(lifts, ramps & wheelchairs available) toilets for disabled shop* ⊘
Cards: ◨ ▤ ▦ ▥ ▣

CRAYFORD

World of Silk
Bourne Rd DA1 4BP
☎ 01322 559401
Fax 01322 550476
Established in 1843 on the banks of the River Cray, David Evans are the last of the old London silk printers. You are invited to pre-book guided tours of the printshop and museum where you can learn about the traditional methods of printing silk and see today's craftsmen at work. There is a factory shop which sells gifts, fabric and fashion accessories at bargain prices. Special events for 1998: "Christening" exhibition (April-September), "Inspirational" Sewing Days (various Saturdays including 25 April, 7 Feb & 18 Sept), Block Printing demonstrations (3 Jan, 4 April, 4 July & 3 Oct), plus silk sales and Christmas sales. Please ring for details.
Open all year, Mon-Sat 9.30-5 (4.30 Sat). (Closed Sun & BH).
Museum only £1.50 (pen & student £1). Guided Tour of Craft Centre & Mill by appointment £2.50 (pen & student £2). Family ticket £8.
🅿 ⬛ ♿ *toilets for disabled shop* ⊘ *(ex guidedogs)*
Cards: ◨ ▤ ▦ ▥ ▣

DOWNE

Darwin Museum, Down House
Luxted Rd BR6 7JT (Off A233, signposted)
☎ 01689 859119
Down House was the home of Charles Darwin from 1842 until his death in 1882. The drawing room and Old Study are restored and furnished as they were when Darwin was working on his famous, and still controversial book *On the Origin of Species by means of Natural Selection*, first published in 1859. The Museum also includes collections and memorabilia from Darwin's voyage on HMS *Beagle*. There is one room dedicated to his illustrious grandfather Dr Erasmus Darwin. The garden is maintained as laid out by the Darwins, retaining the original landscaping, flint and brick walls and glass house, beyond which lies the famous Sand Walk or thinking path, along which Darwin took his daily walk. There are special displays at various times throughout the year; please telephone for recorded message.
Open all year, Wed-Sun 1-6 (last admission 5.30). Also BH Mon. (Closed 14 Dec-1 Jan & Feb).
🅿 ♿ *shop* ⊘
Details not confirmed for 1998

Built in 1869, the *Cutty Sark* was the fastest tea clipper in the world. She carried nearly 10 miles of rigging and an acres of sail.

DULWICH (SE21)

Dulwich Picture Gallery
College Rd SE21 7AD (N of South Circular A205 follow signs to Dulwich village)
☎*0181 693 5254 Fax 0181 693 0923*
The oldest public picture gallery in England, housing a magnificent collection of Old Masters, including works by Poussin, Claude, Rubens, Murillo, Van Dyck, Rembrandt, Watteau and Gainsborough. Originally assembled for the King of Poland by Noel Desenfans and Sir Francis Bourgeois in the 1790s. When Poland was partitioned, an alternative home was found for the paintings in 'the clean air of Dulwich'. The Gallery was designed by Sir John Soane, and the founders lie to this day in their mausoleum at the centre of the Gallery. Temporary exhibitions are held throughout the year. 1998 will include: Italy and British Art in the Age of Turner (4 March-24 May), Paula Rego (17 June-19 July), Pieter de Hooch (5 August-25 October).
Open all year, Tue-Fri 10-5, Sat 11-5, Sun 2-5. (Closed Mon). Guided tours Sat & Sun 3pm.
£3 (pen, students £1.50, UB40, disabled & ch free)
P ♿ *(wheelchair available) shop*
Cards:

EAST HAM (E6)

East Ham Nature Reserve
Visitor Centre, Norman Rd E6 4HN
☎*0181 470 4525*
This 10-acre nature reserve with grassland and woodland, has two nature trails with printed guides (braille version in preparation). One trail is suitable for all disabled visitors. There is a visitor centre with displays relating to natural history and the history of the churchyard nature reserve. New displays include a Victorian schoolroom, and an east-end war time kitchen.
Open Visitor Centre: wknds 2-5. Nature Reserve: summer, Mon-Fri 9-5, wknds 2-5; winter, Mon-Fri 9-4, wknds 2-4.
P (includes disabled bay) ♿ *(trails for wheelchairs & blind) toilets for disabled shop*
Details not confirmed for 1998

ELTHAM (SE9)

Eltham Palace House & Gardens
SE9
☎*0181 859 2112 ext 25*
Eltham Palace is noted for its great hall with a 15th-century hammerbeam roof and one of its most charming features is the old bridge, spanning the moat.
Closed for refurbishment. Due to reopen late 1998/early 1999.
£4 (ch £2 & concessions £3)

ENFIELD

Forty Hall Museum
Forty Hill EN2 9HA (M25 junct 25 onto A10, turn right into Bullsmoor Lane)
☎*0181 363 8196 & 0181 363 4046*
Fax 0181 367 9098
The mansion of Forty Hall was built in 1629 for Sir Nicholas Raynton, Lord Mayor of London, and then altered in the 18th century. It has fine plaster ceilings and collections of 17th-and 18th-century furniture, paintings, ceramics and glass. There are also local history displays and temporary exhibitions.
Open all year, Thu-Sun 11-5 & BH's.
Free.
P ♿ *(separate parking) toilets for disabled shop*

ESHER

Claremont Landscape Garden
Portsmouth Rd KT10 9JG (E of A307)
☎*01372 467806 & 469421*
Laid out by Vanbrugh and Bridgeman before 1720, extended and naturalised by Kent, this is the earliest surviving example of an English landscaped garden. Its 50 acres include a lake with an island pavilion, a grotto and a turf amphitheatre. There are also avenues and viewpoints. A Fête Champetre and jazz concert will be held on 15-19 July, telephone 01372 459950 for details. National Trust plant sale (18 May). The Belvedere Tower is open first weekend in the month February-November.
Open all year, Jan-Mar, Tue-Sun 10-5 or sunset if earlier, Apr-Oct Mon-Fri 10-6, Sat-Sun & BH Mon 10-7 (closed all day 14 Jul-19 Jul, closes 2pm); Nov-Mar Tue-Sun 10-5 or sunset if earlier. Closed 25 Dec and 1 Jan. Last admission 30 mins before closing.
£3 (ch £1.50). Family ticket £8.
P ♿ *(wheelchairs available, Braille guide) toilets for disabled shop (ex on leads Nov-Mar)*
Cards:

FINCHLEY (N3)

The Jewish Museum
The Sternberg Centre, 80 East End Rd, Finchley N3 2SY (Underground - Finchley Central)
☎*0181 349 1143*
Fax 0181 343 2162
The Jewish Museum traces the story of Jewish immigration and settlement in London, including a reconstruction of an East End tailoring workshop. It also has a Holocaust Education Gallery and provides educational programmes by arrangement. Linked with Jewish Museum at Camden as "London's Museum of Jewish Life."
Open all year, Sun 10.30-4.30, Mon-Thu 10.30-5. Closed Jewish festivals, public holidays & 24 Dec-4 Jan. Also closed Sun in Aug & BH wkends.
P (on street parking) ♿ *toilets for disabled shop*
Details not confirmed for 1998

FOREST HILL (SE23)

Horniman Museum & Garden
London Rd SE23 3PQ
☎*0181 699 2339 (rec info)*
0181 699 1872 Fax 0181 291 5506
Situated in 16 acres of gardens, the Horniman Museum has displays of world cultures, the 'Living Waters' Aquarium,natural history collections and an extensive exhibition of musical instruments from all over the world. Visitors can experience different instruments and the music they create through the use of interactive computers in the Music Room. There are regular concerts, special exhibitions and an education department.
Open all year, Mon-Sat 10.30-5.30, Sun 2-5.30 (Closed 24-26 Dec). Gardens close at sunset.
P (opposite museum) ♿ *(chair lift to parts of upper floor) toilets for disabled shop*
Details not confirmed for 1998

GREENWICH (SE10)

Cutty Sark Clipper Ship
King William Walk, Greenwich SE10 9HT
☎*0181 858 3445 & 0181 858 2698*
Fax 0181 853 3589
The fastest tea clipper to be built (in 1869) once sailed 363 miles in a single day. She has been preserved in dry dock since 1957 and her graceful lines dominate the riverside at Greenwich. Exhibitions and a video presentation on board tell the story of the ship and there is a magnificent collection of ships' figureheads. Restoration work can be seen while the ship is open to visitors, ie shipwrights, riggers etc. There is also a tea exhibition showing the story of tea, being displayed in the lower hold.
Open all year, daily 10-5, Sun 12-5; 6pm in summer. (Closed 24-26 Dec). Last ticket 30 mins before closing.
£3.50 (concessions £2.50). Family ticket £8.50. Party 10+.
P (100 yds metered) ♿ *shop*
Cards:

Gipsy Moth IV
Greenwich Pier, King William Walk SE10 9HT
☎*0181 858 3445 or 0181 858 2698*
Fax 0181 853 3589
Standing near the famous tea clipper is the yacht in which Sir Francis Chichester made the first single-handed sailing trip around the world, 'Racing against Time' in 1966-7.
Open Apr-Oct, most days 10-6. (Sun 12-6). Last ticket 30 mins before closing.
50p (ch 30p).
P (100 yds)

National Maritime Museum
Romney Rd SE10 9NF
☎*0181 858 4422 Fax 0181 312 6632*
The National Maritime Museum tells the story of Britain and the Sea. 20th-Century Sea Power uses videos of ships at sea, ship models and World War memories. The Nelson exhibition opens with a tableau on the war between England and France, followed by an amazing assemblage of paintings, cannon-balls, flags, trophies and souvenirs. Centrepiece is a shrine to Nelson with his bullet-holed coat and blood-stained breeches. Children will be delighted with the All Hands interactive gallery. NOTE: Several galleries are closed until 1999. Some items are now in the Queen's House next door.
Open all year, daily 10-5. (Closed 24-26 Dec).
P (50 yds) ✕ *licensed* ♿ *(wheelchair available stairlift advisory service) toilets for disabled shop*
Details not confirmed for 1998
Cards:

Old Royal Observatory
Greenwich Park SE10 9NF (off A2)
☎*0181 858 4422 Fax 0181 312 6632*
Charles II founded the Royal Observatory in 1675 'for perfecting navigation and astronomy'. It stands at zero meridian longitude and is the original home of Greenwich Mean Time. Set in the beautiful grounds of Greenwich Park, which were laid out to plans by the French gardener, Le Nôtre, who planned the grounds at Versailles, the Royal Observatory is part of the National Maritime Museum. Completely refurbished in 1993 it houses an extensive collection of historic timekeeping, astronomical and navigational instruments. Planetarium shows throughout the year. Events are planned for the school holidays.
Open all year, daily 10-5 (Closed 24-26 Dec).
P ♿ *toilets for disabled shop*
Details not confirmed for 1998
Cards:

The Queens House
Romney Rd SE10 9NF
☎*0181 858 4422 Fax 0181 312 6632*
The first Palladian-style villa in England, designed by Inigo Jones for Anne of Denmark and completed for Queen Henrietta Maria, wife of Charles I. The recent restoration has been carried out to show the house as it appeared when new, with bright silks and furnishings. The Great Hall, the State Rooms and a Loggia overlooking Greenwich Park are notable features. There is a fine collection of Dutch marine paintings, including some of the finest seascapes ever painted. Events reflecting the music and fashions of the Stuart period are held during the school holidays.
Open all year, daily 10-5. (Closed 24-26 Dec).
P (50 yds) ✕ *licensed* ♿ *(Blind kit/stairclimber/wheelchairs) toilets for disabled shop*
Details not confirmed for 1998
Cards:

Royal Naval College
King William Walk SE10 9NN
☎*0181 858 2154 Fax 0181 858 2652*
With the Queen's House as its focal point, the Royal Naval College occupies one of the masterpieces of English architecture; the grand sequence of buildings originally planned by Sir Christopher Wren towards the end of the 17th century as a hospital and refuge for disabled or veteran seamen of the Royal Navy. Additions were subsequently made by such notables as Vanbrugh, Hawksmoor and Ripley. The College was formerly used as a naval hospital (until 1873) and particularly splendid features include the chapel and the Painted Hall.
Open all year (Painted Hall and Chapel only), daily 2.30-5 (last admission 4.30). Visitors are advised to telephone to confirm opening days.
Free.
P (200m) (all local streets: yellow line roads) (can be given access if prior notice given) shop

HACKNEY WICK (E9)

Sutton House
2 & 4 Homerton High St E9 6JQ
☎*0181 9862264*
In London's East End, the building is a rare example of a Tudor red-brick house. Built in 1535 by Sir Rufe Sadleir, Principal Secretary of State for Henry VIII, the house has 18th century alterations and later additions.
Open 4 Feb-25 Nov, Wed, Sun & BH Mon 11.30-5.30. Sat 2-5.30pm. Last admission 5pm. (Closed Good Friday).
£1.90. Family ticket £4.50.
P (on street parking) ♿ *(induction loop braille guide) toilets for disabled shop*

HAM

Ham House
TW10 7RS (W of A307)
☎*0181 940 1950 Fax 0181 332 6903*
This lovely house was built in 1610 and redecorated by the Duke and Duchess of Lauderdale in the 1670s. The Duke was a member of Charles II's government, and followed the most fashionable style. There is a 17th-century garden which is currently being restored. There are secret servants' passages and stories that the house is haunted by a 17th-century Duchess. Special events include Spring Plant Fair, family picnic evenings, dairy demonstrations during school holidays, garden tours throughout the season. Ring for further details.
Open gardens: all year, Sat-Wed 10.30-6 or dusk if earlier. Closed 25-26 Dec & 1 Jan. House: 28 Mar-1 Nov, Sat-Wed 1-5. Last admission 4.30.
House £5 (ch £2.50). Family ticket £12.50. Garden only £1.50.
P (500 yds) ♿ *(Braille guide, wheelchairs available) toilets for disabled shop*

HAMPSTEAD (NW3)

Fenton House
Windmill Hill NW3 6SP (Underground - Hampstead)
☎*0171 435 3471*
Fax 0171 435 3471
A William and Mary mansion built about 1693 and set in a walled garden, Fenton House is now owned by the National Trust. It contains a display of furniture and some notable pieces of Oriental and European porcelain as well as the Benton Fletcher collection of early keyboard instruments, including a harpsichord once played by Handel. Summer concerts are arranged.
Open 1-22 Mar, Sat & Sun only 2-5; Apr-1 Nov, Sat-Sun & BH Mon 11-5pm, Wed-Fri 2-5pm. Last admission 30mins before closing.
£4. Family ticket £10.
♿

Freud Museum
20 Maresfield Gardens NW3 5SX (Underground - Finchley Road)
☎*0171 435 2002 & 0171 435 5167*
Fax 0171 431 5452
In 1938, Sigmund Freud left his home in Vienna as a refugee from the Nazi occupation and chose exile in England, transferring his entire domestic and working environment to the house at 20 Maresfield Gardens. He resumed work until his death here a year later. Freud's extraordinary collection of Egyptian, Greek, Roman and Oriental antiquities, his working library and papers, and his fine furniture including the famous desk and couch are all here. The house was bequeathed by his daughter Anna Freud ➔

Between 1839 and the 1970s many illustrious people were buried at Highgate Cemetery. Karl Marx, who lived in London from 1849 till his death in 1883, is one of its most well-known incumbents.

(1895-1982), whose pioneering development of her father's work is also represented. The museum has exhibitions on display and historic videos for viewing.
Open all year, Wed-Sun 12-5 (Closed BH's, telephone for Xmas Holiday times).
P & *(personal tours can be arranged if booked in advance) shop* ✿
Details not confirmed for 1998
Cards: ▨ ▥ ▥

Keats House
Keats Grove NW3 2RR (Underground - Hampstead)
☎*0171 435 2062 Fax 0171 431 9293*
The two Regency houses were occupied by John Keats and his fiancée Fanny Brawne. They have now been converted into one building and form a museum devoted to the life of this famous poet. Manuscripts, letters and personal mementoes are displayed.
Open all year, Apr-Oct Mon-Fri 10-1 & 2-6, Sat 10-1 & 2-5, Sun & BH 2-5; Nov-Mar Mon-Fri 1-5, Sat 10-1 & 2-5, Sun 2-5. (Closed Good Fri, Etr eve, May Day, 24-26 Dec & 1 Jan).
Free.
P (300yds) (residents parking in operation) shop ✿

Kenwood Iveagh Bequest
Hampstead Ln NW3 7JR (Underground - Hampstead)
☎*0181 348 1286 Fax 0181 348 7325*
Forming the most beautiful part of Hampstead Heath, the wooded grounds of Kenwood were laid out in the 18th century by the first Earl of Mansfield. He engaged Robert Adam to enlarge the house and transform it into a mansion, and the orangery and library are Adam's design. The library or 'Great Room' being considered one of his finest achievements. Edward Guinness, first Earl of Iveagh bought the estate in 1925 and bequeathed the grounds, house and its contents to the nation two years later. It contains a fine collection of paintings including Old Masters and 18th and 19th-century portraits by Gainsborough and Reynolds among others. Kenwood is a popular venue for outdoor summer events and musical evenings set beside the ornamental lake.
Open all year, Apr-Oct daily 10-6 (or dusk if earlier in Oct); Nov-Mar daily 10-4. (Closed 24-26 Dec & 1 Jan).
Free.
P ✗ *licensed* & *toilets for disabled shop* ✿ *(ex grounds)* ✠

HAMPTON COURT ▰▰▰▰▰
Hampton Court Palace
KT8 9AU (on A308)
☎*0181 781 9500 Fax 0181 781 5362*
The palace was started in the early 16th century by Cardinal Wolsey, Lord Chancellor to Henry VIII. When he fell out of favour he presented it to the king as a placatory gesture. Henry VIII expanded the palace by adding the hammerbeamed great hall, the immense kitchens and the Royal Tennis courts. Later monarchs (and Cromwell) left their own mark: Elizabeth I added plants from the New World to the garden, and William and Mary commissioned Wren to remodel part of the building. The result was the handsome King's Apartments, part of which were devastated by fire in recent years, but have now been gloriously restored after a six year programme. Today, pictures, furniture and tapestries can be seen, and there are handsome gardens and parkland close to the River Thames. Special attractions are the Tudor Kitchens, the orangery, the Great Vine, and the maze, laid out in the time of William III. Special events include Music Festival (June) Garden Festival (July), Grape Harvest (late August, early September). Please ring for details.
Open all year, mid Mar-26 Oct, Mon 10.15-6, Tue-Sun 9.30-6 (4.30pm 27 Oct-mid Mar). (Closed 24-26 Dec).
£8.50 (ch 5-16 £5.60, pen, students £6.40). Family £25.40
P *(charged)* ✆ ✗ *licensed* & *toilets for disabled shop 4 shops on site* ✿ *(ex in gardens)*
Cards: ▨ ▥ ▥ ▥ ▥ ▣

HIGHGATE (N6) ▰▰▰▰▰
Highgate Cemetery
Swains Ln N6 6PJ (Underground - Archway)
☎*0181 340 1834*
Highgate Cemetery is the most impressive of a series of large, formally arranged and landscaped cemeteries which were established around the perimeter of London during the first decades of Queen Victoria's reign. Visitors will discover a wealth of fine sculpture and architecture amongst the tombstones, monuments and mausoleums as well as the graves of such notables as the Rossetti family, George Eliot, Michael Faraday and Karl Marx.
Open all year. Eastern Cemetery: daily 10 (11 wknds)-5 (4 in winter). Western Cemetery by guided tour only: Sat & Sun 11-4 (3 in winter); midweek tours 12,2 & 4 (12, 2 & 3 in winter). No weekday tours in Dec, Jan & Feb. Special tours by arrangement. (Closed 25-26 Dec & during funerals).
East cemetery £1. Tour of West cemetery £3 (ch 8-16 £1, no ch under 8 on tours). Donations encouraged to assist restoration.
P *shop* ✿

ISLEWORTH ▰▰▰▰▰
Syon House
TW8 8JF (Approach via A310 Twickenham road into Park Rd)
☎*0181 560 0881 Fax 0181 568 0936*
Set in 200 acres of parkland, Syon House is the London home of the Duke of Northumberland whose family have lived here since the late 16th century. Originally an abbey, founded by Henry V, it became the property of the Duke of Somerset in 1547. It was here that Lady Jane Grey was offered the throne. During the second half of the 18th century the first Duke of Northumberland engaged Robert Adam to remodel the interior and 'Capability' Brown to landscape the grounds. Adam was also responsible for the furniture and decorations, and the result is particularly spectacular in the superbly coloured Ante-Room and Long Gallery. Ring for further details of special events.
Open Apr-Oct, Wed-Sun & BH 11-5 (last ticket 4.15pm). Fri-Sat closes 3.30pm.

Combined ticket for house and gardens £5.50 (concessions £4). Family ticket £13.
P ✆ & *toilets for disabled shop garden centre* ✿
Cards: ▨ ▥ ▥ ▥ ▣

Syon Park
TW8 8JF (A310 Twickenham road into Park Rd)
☎*0181 560 0881 Fax 0181 568 0936*
Contained within the 55 acres that make up Syon Park is one of the inspirations for the Crystal Palace at the Great Exhibition of 1851: a vast crescent of metal and glass, the first construction of its kind in the world and known as the Great Conservatory. It was designed by Fowler and built between 1820-27. The park also has a butterfly house and the largest garden centre in England. Although the horticultural reputation of Syon Park goes back to the 16th century - when the use of trees purely as ornaments was looked upon as unique - its beauty today is thanks to the master of landscape design, 'Capability' Brown. It is hardly believable that the peaceful haven he has created beside the River Thames is just nine miles from the centre of London. A miniature steam railway runs through the gardens (weekends April to October and Bank Holidays).
Open all year, daily 10-6 or dusk. (Closed 25 & 26 Dec).
P ✆ & *toilets for disabled shop garden centre* ✿
Details not confirmed for 1998
Cards: ▨ ▥

ISLINGTON (N1) ▰▰▰▰▰
The London Canal Museum
12/13 New Wharf Rd N1 9RT (Underground - Kings Cross)
☎*0171 713 0836*
The museum covers the development of London's canals (particularly Regent's Canal on which the museum is situated), canal vessels and trade, and the way of life of the canal people. It is housed in a

HAMPTON COURT PALACE

With its 500 years of royal history Hampton Court Palace has something to offer everyone. Set in sixty acres of world famous gardens the palace is a living tapestry of history from Henry VIII to George II. From the elegance of the recently restored Privy Garden to the domestic reality of the Tudor Kitchens, visitors are taken back through the centuries to experience the palace as it was when royalty was in residence.

Costumed guides and audio tours bring the palace to life and provide an insight into how life in the palace would have been in the time of Henry VIII and William III. Free family trails encourage a closer look at Hampton Court Palace, and there is even the chance to win a prize.

For information of seasonal activities, prices, opening hours, etc., ring
0181 781 9500.

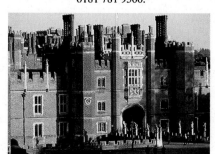

Getting There:
Car   The palace is on the A308 close to the A3, M3 and several Exits of the M25.
Train   32 minutes from Waterloo to Hampton Court Station via Clapham Junction.

former ice warehouse and stables and also illustrates horse transport and the unusual trade of importing ice from Norway; there are two large ice wells under the floor, one of which can be seen through a viewing hole. Facilities include an educational room, and temporary moorings for visitors who arrive by boat. There are occasional special exhibitions.
Open all year, Tue-Sun & BH Mon 10-4.30 (last admission 4). (Closed 24-26, 31 Dec, 1 Jan).
P (250yds) & shop
Details not confirmed for 1998

KEW

Kew Gardens (Royal Botanic Gardens)

TW9 3AB (Underground - Kew Gdns)
☎0181 940 1171 Fax 0181 332 5197
The world-famous gardens at Kew started as a mere nine-acre site, laid out by George III's mother, Princess Augusta in 1759 (she lived in the White House at Kew which has long since been demolished). In 1841 the gardens were given to the State and by 1904 the gardens covered 300 acres - their present size. The 19th-century botanist, Sir Joseph Banks, and head gardener, William Aiton (later curator), were largely responsible for laying the foundations of the great collection of plants, shrubs and trees which exist here today; a collection which not only gives great public enjoyment but also forms part of the world's foremost botanical research centre. The west of the gardens is largely woodland and arboretum, while the formal gardens, with their lawns and neatly manicured beds are in the eastern half. The site has inspired some notable architectural features, both old and very modern. The Palm House is perhaps the most elegant: an early example of glass and wrought iron, it was completed in 1848. But the most famous landmark at Kew is the Chinese Pagoda; it stands 163ft high in ten storeys. Plants that would not otherwise be seen in Britain are grown in houses which reproduce special climatic conditions and among many other features are art galleries, one showing the work of Victorian artist Marianne North. Wheelchairs are available (booking advisable) free of charge and there are purpose-built toilets for wheelchair users. Jazz Festival (third week July), Christmas events (December).
Open all year, Gardens daily 9.30-between 4 & 6.30pm on weekdays, between 4-8pm Suns & BH's, depending on the time of sunset.(Closed 25 Dec & 1 Jan)
✽£4.50 (ch 5-16 £2.50)

A curious landmark in south-west London is the 10-storey high Chinese Pagoda which is in the world-famous Kew Gardens.

P (charged) ▆ ✗ licensed & (16 seat bus tour: enquiries ring 0181-332 5623) toilets for disabled shop
Cards: ▨ ▨ ▨ ▨ ⑤

Kew Palace

Royal Botanic Gardens TW9 3AB (Underground - Kew Bridge)
☎0181 781 9540
A favourite country residence during the reign of the first three Hanoverian Kings, Kew was the site of several royal houses although only three of the buildings now remain. A fairly modest red-brick building, built in the Dutch style with gables, Kew Palace was built in 1631 and used for nearly a century until 1818 when Queen Charlotte died. It was opened to the public in 1899 and remains much as it was in George III's time, reflecting the quiet country life his family enjoyed here. Family paintings and personal relics, furniture and tapestries are on display, and a charming 17th-century garden has been recreated.
Closed for refurbishment.

Queen Charlotte's Cottage

Royal Botanic Gardens TW9 3AB (Underground - Kew Bridge)
☎0181 332 5189
The cottage is typical of the rustic-style edifices built by the gentry in the 18th century and was built for George III and Queen Charlotte as a home to their menagerie of exotic pets, as well as a picnic spot and summer house.
Open weekends only between May & Sept.
Free with entry to Botanical gardens.
shop

OSTERLEY

Osterley Park House

TW7 4RB (Underground - Osterley)
☎0181 560 3918
Fax 0181 758 2116
This Elizabethan mansion has been transformed into an 18th-century villa, its elegant interior decoration designed in neo-classical style by Robert Adam. The State Apartments include a Gobelin tapestry ante-room and a dressing-room decorated in the Etruscan style.
Open all year: Park & pleasure grounds, daily 9-7.30 or sunset if earlier. House: Apr-1 Nov, Wed-Sun 2-5, BH Sun & Mon 1-5. Last admission 4.30. (Closed Good Fri & 25-26 Dec).
£4. Family ticket £10.
P (charged) ▆ & toilets for disabled shop

POPLAR (E14)

London Docklands Visitor Centre

3 Limeharbour, Isle of Dogs E14 9TJ
☎0171 512 1111
Fax 0171 537 2549
Exhibition and video show tracing the area's fascinating history, illustrating London Docklands today and looking forward to the final fulfilment of the regeneration programme. A team of experienced information assistants is on hand to answer enquiries and guided tours of London Docklands can be arranged with prior notice.
Open all year, Mon-Fri 8.30-6, wknds & BH 9.30-5. (Closed Xmas).
Free.
P & (Ramp to entrance reserved parking induction loop for deaf) toilets for disabled
Cards: ▨ ⑩ ▨

REGENT'S PARK (NW1)

London Zoo

Regents Park NW1 4RY (Underground - Camden Town or Regents Park)
☎0171 722 3333
Fax 0171 586 5743
London Zoo is home to over 8000 animals, insects, reptiles and fish. Founded by Sir Stamford Raffles, the Zoo was opened to the public in 1828, and can claim the world's first aquarium, insect and reptile house. Visitors today can view rare and exotic animals, many of which are participating in captive breeding programmes. Daily events such as Animals in Action, feeding times and Animal Encounters, give visitors an insight into animal behaviour. There are reductions for groups, and free guided tours can be arranged. For youngsters there is a Children's Zoo and a whole range of educational programmes for schools. Exhibits include the Aquarium, Reptile House, the Moonlight World where day and night are reversed, and London's very own mountain range, Bear Mountain. Favourites at the Zoo include

black rhinos Rosie and Jos, and the very rare Asiatic Lions which are part of an endangered species breeding programme.
Open all year, daily from 10am. (Closed 25 Dec).
✽£8. (ch 4-14 £6, concessions £7). Saver ticket £24. Group 20+
P (charged) ▆ & (wheelchairs & booster scooter available) toilets for disabled shop
Cards: ▨ ▨ ▨ ⑩ ▨ ▨ ⑤

RICHMOND

Richmond Park

Holly Lodge, Richmond Park TW10 5HS (Underground - Richmond)
☎0181 948 3209
Fax 0181 332 2730
With its herds of deer, abundant wild life and centuries-old oaks, Richmond Park is a favourite haunt for visitors and naturalists. There is a formal garden at Pembroke Lodge, and the Isabella Plantation shows a wealth of exotic shrubs and wild flowers. Model sail boats are allowed on Adam's Pond, where the deer drink, and the 18-acre Pen Ponds have been specially made for angling (permit required).

ST JOHNS WOOD (NW8)

The M.C.C. Museum & Tour of Lord's

Lord's Ground NW8 8QN (Underground - St John's Wood)
☎0171 432 1033 Fax 0171 289 9100
Lord's was established in 1787 and it is the home of the MCC and cricket. When you tour this world-famous arena you follow in the footsteps of the 'greats' of the game, from W G Grace to Ian Botham. Daily guided tours take you behind the scenes at this historic venue. Highlights include the Long Room, a shrine for players and fans the world over, and the MCC Museum where the Ashes and a large collection of paintings and memorabilia are displayed. Other places of interest are the Real Tennis Court, the acclaimed Mound Stand with

➤

its magnificent views of the ground, and
the Indoor School. The MCC Museum is
also open on cricket days for spectators.
*Open all year, tours normally at noon &
2pm (times vary on certain cricket days).
There are no tours on major match days.
Telephone for details and booking).
Museum open match days Mon-Sat
10.30-5, Sun 1-5 to visitors who have
paid ground admission.
Guided tour £5.80 (ch, students & pen
£4.20) Museum £2 (concessions 50p).
Family ticket (2 adults & 2 ch) £18. Party
25+.*
🅿 ✗ *licensed* ♿ *(by arrangement) toilets
for disabled shop* ✸

Primrose Hill
NW8
Once part of the same hunting forest as
Regent's Park, Primrose Hill retains in its
name the rural character and charm that
it undoubtedly had in the past. The view
from the summit is panoramic and
encompasses virtually the whole of
central London. In 1842 its 62 acres
gained gaslights, a gymnasium and
respectability as a Royal Park.

TEDDINGTON
Bushy Park
Situated close to Hampton Court, this is
one of London's ten Royal Parks,
formerly hunting preserves, which were
opened to the public by Charles I and
Charles II. Bushy Park has a famous 3/4-
mile Chestnut Avenue which runs from
Hampton Court to the Teddington Gate.
This superb double row of enormous
trees, laid out by Wren, is best seen in
springtime.

TWICKENHAM
Marble Hill House
Richmond Rd TW1 2NL
☎ 0181 892 5115
An example of the English Palladian
school of architecture, Marble Hill House
was built between 1724 and 1729 for
Henrietta Howard, mistress of George II
and later Countess of Suffolk. Perfectly
proportioned in the Palladian style with
extensive grounds, the villa now contains
an important collection of paintings and
furniture including the Lazenby Bequest
Chinoiserie collection.
*Open all year, daily, Apr-Oct, 10-6 (or
dusk if earlier); Nov-Mar, Wed-Sun 10-4.
(Closed 24-25 Dec & 4-7 Jan).
£3 (ch £1.50, concessions 2.30)*
🅿 ⛴ ✗ *licensed* ♿ *toilets for disabled
shop* ✸ *(ex in grounds)* ⚍

Museum of Rugby & Twickenham Experience Tour
Rugby Football Union, Rugby Rd TW1
1DZ (M3 into London, A316 follow signs
to museum)
☎ 0181 892 2000 Fax 0181 892 2817
Located beneath the East Stand of the
Twickenham Stadium, home of the
England team and headquarters of the
Rugby Football Union. Bringing the
history of the game to life using
interactive displays, period set pieces and
video footage, there is also tour which
allows a glimpse behind the scenes,
including a visit to the England dressing
room, and magnificent views of the
stadium from the top of the stand. There
is a reference library available by
appointment. Please telephone for details
of special events.
*Museum: open Tue-Sat 10.30-5, Sun 2-5.
Last admission 4.30pm. Tours: 10.30am,
noon, 1.30pm, & 3pm; Sun 2pm &
2.30pm. No tours on match days or for
ch under 5yrs. Museum open on match
days for ticket holders only. Ground
closed Mon (ex BH), 24-26 Dec & Good
Friday.
Museum: £2.50 (ch/pen/student £1.50).
Twickenham Experience Tour: £2.50
(ch/pen/students £1.50). Joint ticket for
Museum and Tour £4 (ch/pen/students
£2.50). Family ticket £10.*
🅿 ⛴ ✗ *licensed* ♿ *(special tours and lifts
to all floors) toilets for disabled shop* ✸
Cards: ▨ ▨ ▨ ▨ ⑤

Orleans House Gallery
Riverside TW1 3DJ (off A305, along
Orleans Rd to Riverside)
☎ 0181 892 0221 Fax 0181 744 0501
The art gallery holds wide-ranging
temporary exhibitions throughout the year
and is adjacent to James Gibbs's baroque
Octagon Room. Built about 1720, the
surviving wings of Orleans House, where
Louis Philippe, Duc d'Orleans, King of
France 1830-48, lived during his exile. The
Octagon Room and Gallery are in a
woodland setting beside the River
Thames. Special Events include:
Collection of artefacts connected with Sir
Richard Burton & his wife Isabel (March-
April), Contemporary Art (May-June),
Contemporary Ceramics (July-August),
Osmund Caine (August), Museum of
Women's Art - exhibition of 20th century
female artists (yet to be decided) (Sept-
Oct), London Artists (Nov-Dec).
*Open all year, Tue-Sat 1-5.30 (4.30pm
Oct-Mar), Sun & BH 2-5.30 (Oct-Mar 2-
4.30). (Closed 24-25 Dec). Woodland
Gardens daily, 9-dusk.
Free.*
🅿 ♿ *(handling objects & large print labels
for some exhibitions) toilets for disabled
shop* ✸

WALTHAMSTOW (E17)
William Morris Gallery
Lloyd Park, Forest Rd E17 4PP
(Underground - Walthamstow Central)
☎ 0181 527 3782 Fax 0181 527 7070
William Morris was a great Victorian
artist, craftsman, poet and free thinker.
This house, his home from 1848 to 1856
and then known as Water House, has
been devoted to the life and work of
Morris, his followers, contemporaries and
the Morris Company. Recently
refurbished displays include fabrics,
stained glass, wallpaper and furniture,
much of which is still fashionable today.
To complete the picture of this innovative
period in the history of art and philosophy
there are also Pre-Raphaelite paintings,
sculpture by Rodin, ceramics and a
collection of pictures by Frank Brangwyn,
who worked briefly for Morris. A varied
programme of events is run by the
museum throughout the year, including a
centenary exhibition of works by Sir
Edward Burne-Jones (July-September).
*Open all year, Tue-Sat and 1st Sun in
each month 10-1 & 2-5. (Closed Mon &
BH's). Telephone for Xmas/New Year
opening times.
Free.*
🅿 ♿ *shop* ✸

WEMBLEY
Wembley Stadium Tours
Empire Way HA9 0DW (Underground -
Wembley Park)
☎ 0181 902 8833 Fax 0181 903 5733
Wembley is the world's most famous
stadium and is unique in the history of
sport and entertainment. From the FA
Cup Final in 1923, the 1948 Olympic
Games, the 1966 World Cup, Live Aid in
1985, to the 1992 European Cup Final,
Freddie Mercury Tribute Concert and Euro
96, many millions of people have
experienced the magic of Wembley
Stadium. It has also been the venue for
rugby league, greyhound racing, American
football, baseball, boxing and speedway.
On your stadium tour you will visit many
fascinating behind-the-scenes areas the
public do not normally see. Tour
highlights include the stadium's event
control rooms, television studio, cinema,
hospital, England changing room and the
player's tunnel. Take a trip around the
stadium on Wembley's own land train,
walk up the famous 39 steps to receive
the cup to the roar of the crowd and sit in
the Royal Box.
*Open all year, daily summer 10-4, winter
10-3 (Closed on major event days & 25 &
26 Dec).
£6.95 (ch & pen £4.95, students £5.75).
Party 20+.*
🅿 ⛴ *(limited tour by arrangement)
toilets for disabled shop* ✸ *(ex guide
dogs)*
Cards: ▨ ▨ ▨

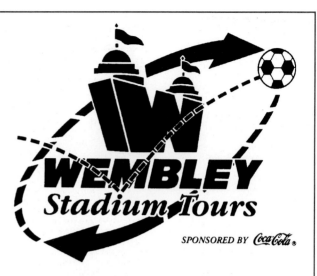
WIMBLEDON (SW19)
Wimbledon Lawn Tennis Museum
All England Club, Church Rd SW19 5AE
(Underground - Wimbledon Park)
☎ 0181 946 6131
Fax 0181 944 6497
Wimbledon is synonymous with lawn
tennis and the museum in the grounds of
the All England Lawn Tennis Club is the
only one of its kind in the world.
Trophies, pictures, displays and
memorabilia trace the development of
the game over the last century. There is a
Special Exhibitions Gallery.
*Open all year, Tue-Sat & summer BHs
10.30-5, Sun 2-5. (Closed Mon, winter
BHs & Fri-Sun before Championships &
middle Sun of Championships). Phone for
Xmas/New Year opening times.
£2.50 (concessions £1.50).*
🅿 ⛴ ♿ *(lift) toilets for disabled shop* ✸
Cards: ▨

WOOLWICH (SE18)
Museum of Artillery in the Rotunda
Repository Rd SE18 4BQ
☎ 0181 781 3127
Fax 0181 316 5402
The guns, muskets, rifles and edged
weapons that form the collections in this
museum are contained in the rotunda
designed by John Nash that once stood
in St James's Park. The collection tells
the story of the gun from its beginning in
the 13th-century to the present day, in an
unrivalled display of ordnance, including
ammunition.
*Open all year, Mon-Fri 1-4. (closed Sat,
Sun & all BH Mon's)
Free.*
🅿 ♿ *toilets for disabled shop* ✸

Thames Barrier Visitors Centre
Unity Way SE18 5NJ
☎ 0181 305 4188
Fax 0181 855 2146
Built to prevent the possibility of
disastrous flooding, the Thames Barrier
spans a third of a mile and is the world's

largest movable flood barrier. It is
sometimes described as the eighth
wonder of the world. The nearby visitors'
centre and exhibition on the South Bank
explains the flood threat and the
construction of this £480 million project,
now valued at £1 billion. Each month a
test closure of all ten gates, lasting over
2 hours, is carried out and the annual full
day closure of all ten gates takes place in
the autumn.
*Open all year, Mon-Fri 10-5, Sat & Sun
10.30-5.30. (Closed Xmas - telephone for
details). Evening openings by special
arrangements for groups - telephone for
details.*
🅿 *(charged)* ⛴ ✗ *licensed* ♿ *(lift from
river pier approach) toilets for disabled
shop* ✸
Details not confirmed for 1998
Cards: ▨ ▨ ▨ ⑤

MERSEYSIDE

BIRKENHEAD
Birkenhead Priory
Priory St L41 5JH
☎ 0151 666 1249
Founded in 1150, the Priory provided
accommodation for the Prior and 16
Benedictine monks. Most of the
buildings were neglected after the
Dissolution, but not all are ruined. An
interpretive centre traces the history and
development of the site. St Mary's, the
first parish church of Birkenhead, was
opened in 1821 adjacent to the Priory:
only the tower now stands. However, the
original clock mechanism and one bell
have been re-installed with new displays.
The tower offers superb views of the
River Mersey and the surrounding area.
*Open all year, Tue-Sat 10.30-1.30 & 2-5,
Sun 2-5 (Closed Xmas, New Year & some
BH's).*
🅿 ♿ *toilets for disabled shop* ✸ *(ex guide
dogs)*
Details not confirmed for 1998

HMS Plymouth & HMS Onyx
East Float, Dock Rd L41 1DJ (end of M53 all docks turn off follow tourist signs.)
☎0151 650 1573 Fax 0151 650 1473
HMS Onyx is the only submarine afloat in the UK that visitors can explore. She conducted a record-breaking 117 day patrol during the Falklands War. See how her men and members of the SBS and SAS lived in this unique attraction. Also visit the U534, the only WWII German U-Boat to be raised from the sea bed. Pre-booking advised.
Open all year, Sept-end Mar daily 10-4, Apr-end Aug daily 10-5. Closed 24-26 Dec.
£4.50 (ch £2.50, pen £3.50). Family ticket £11. Party 15+.
🅿 💺 *shop* 🚫

Williamson Art Gallery & Museum
Slatey Rd L43 4UE
☎0151 652 4177 Fax 0151 670 0253
English watercolours and works by the Liverpool school are an outstanding feature of the gallery, which was specially built for the purpose. There is a large collection of pictures by P Wilson Steer, and also on view are sculpture, ceramics (English, Continental and Oriental), glass, silver and furniture. Exhibitions are held throughout the year. The museum is linked to the gallery, and has displays on the history of the town and its port. Birkenhead was a hamlet before the 19th century, but grew large and rich through ship-building and the docks, so model ships are an important feature of this collection. Also on view are the Baxter Motor Collection, cars and motorbikes in a period garage setting. There is a full exhibition programme at the Gallery.
Open all year, Tue-Sat 10-5, Sun 2-5. (Closed BH's Xmas & Good Fri).
🅿 ♿ *shop* 🚫
Details not confirmed for 1998

LIVERPOOL
Liverpool was a small fishing village which grew to become one of the world's largest ports. Today the huge Liver Building, the last sight of home for millions of immigrants sailing for the New World, still dominates the now silent waterfront. The bustle of the shipping which used to enliven seven miles of waterfront is virtually stilled - but Liverpool's dockland has been reborn, with a superb maritime museum and a wide range of other exhibition centres forming a living village around the Albert Dock complex. This is a city with two cathedrals dominating the skyline, one Victorian Gothic on a splendid scale and one, ultra-modern. Many of the other public buildings are grand and stately, a sign of the wealth of earlier times. The imposing Walker Gallery houses the largest collections of paintings in Britain outside London. During the 1960s, after a period of decline, Liverpool again became famous as the home of the Beatles and the new music.

The Beatles Story
Britannia Pavilion, Albert Dock L3 4AA
☎0151 709 1963 Fax 0151 708 0039
The sights and sounds of the sixties can be relived at The Beatles Story. You can take a trip to Hamburg, 'feel' the cavern beat, 'tune in' to flower power, board the Yellow Submarine and battle with a Beatle brain computer. A magical history tour for all the family. There is an annual Beatles convention.
Open all year, daily 10-6 (last admission 1 hr before closing). (Closed 25 & 26 Dec).
🅿 ♿ *toilets for disabled shop* 🚫
Details not confirmed for 1998

Croxteth Hall & Country Park
L12 0HB (5m NE of city centre)
☎0151 228 5311 Fax 0151 228 2817
Visitors can step back in time and join an Edwardian house party when they visit the displays in Croxteth Hall - the Edwardian rooms are furnished with period pieces and character figures. The grounds of this former home of the Earls of Sefton contain a Victorian walled garden, a unique collection of rare breed animals, a miniature railway and an adventure playground. Croxteth Hall is a popular venue for special events; it also boasts an award-winning educational service.
Open, all facilities daily 11-5 in season (phone for details); Some facilities remain open through winter, hours on request.
🅿 💺 ♿ *toilets for disabled shop* 🚫 *(ex in park & grounds)*
Details not confirmed for 1998

HM Customs & Excise National Museum
Merseyside Maritime Museum, Albert Dock L3 4AQ
☎0151 478 4499 Fax 0151 478 4590
A chance to experience the activities of customs officers today through interactive, hands-on displays. You have the opportunity to detect concealed goods or spot the smugglers among a group of suspicious characters. There are a wide range of confiscated goods on display as well as sniffer dog demonstrations and a new exhibition on 18th-century smuggling.
Open all year, daily 10-5. Last admission 4. (Closed 23-26 Dec & 1 Jan)
£3 (concessions £1.50). Family ticket £7.50. Party 20+
🅿 *(charged)* 💺 ✗ *licensed* ♿ *(restricted wheelchair access to some areas) toilets for disabled shop* 🚫
Cards: 🅰 ▭ ▭ ▭ 🅢

Liverpool Football Club Visitors Centre Tour
Anfield Rd L4 0TH
☎0151 260 1433 Fax 0151 261 1695
This brand new football museum opened late 1997. The story of Liverpool FC is told through video, interactive exhibits, cups, trophies, flags, shirts and a specially commissioned film "This is Anfield". Try to score a penalty in Shankly's famous "sweat box", stand on the old Kop terraces, see the 1965 dressing room, and then take a guided tour around 'Fortress Anfield'.
Open: Museum daily 10am-5pm last admission 4pm. (closed 25-26 Dec) Closed on Thursdays (Oct-Mar) except to pre-booked educational visits. Match days 9am until last admission- 2hrs before kick off. Museum & Tour- tours are run subject to daily demand. Advance booking is essential to avoid disappointment.
Museum only £5 (ch 5-16 £3. pen £3) Family £13. Museum & Tour £8 (ch 5-16 £5, pen £5) Family £20.
🅿 ♿ *shop* 🚫
Cards: 🅰 ▭ ▭ ▭ ▭ 🅢

Liverpool Libraries & Information Services
William Brown St L3 8EW
☎0151 225 5429 Fax 0151 207 1342
The Picton, Hornby and Brown buildings, situated in the Victorian grandeur of William Brown Street, house Liverpool's collection of over one million books, forming one of Britain's largest and oldest public libraries. First editions, prints and fine bindings are permanently displayed at Hornby while the reference, international, scientific and technical collections are housed in the Picton and Brown buildings. The Liverpool Record Office is one of the country's largest and most significant County Record offices. Regular temporary exhibitions.
Open all year, Mon-Thu 9-7.30 (Fri & Sat 9-5). Closed PHs.
P *(300 yds)* 💺 ♿ *(lift) toilets for disabled* 🚫
Details not confirmed for 1998

Merseyside Maritime Museum
Albert Dock L3 4AA
☎0151 478 4499 Fax 0151 478 4590
A large award-winning museum in restored 19th-century docklands, which includes a Cooperage, and the Albert Dock Warehouse, containing varied displays about the Port of Liverpool. There are floating craft, outdoor exhibits of maritime crafts and demonstrations. Permanent displays include Emigrants to a New World, Art and the Sea, World of Models and Transatlantic Slavery Against Human Dignity. 'Anything to Declare?', HM Customs and Excise National Museum is located on the ground floor.
Open all year, daily 10-5 (Closed 23-26 Dec & 1 Jan).
£3 (ch, pen, students & UB40's £1.50). Family ticket £8. Party 20+.
🅿 *(charged)* 💺 ✗ *licensed* ♿ *((ex basement & pilot boat) lifts & free wheelchair) toilets for disabled shop* 🚫
Cards: 🅰 ▭ ▭ ▭ 🅢

Metropolitan Cathedral of Christ the King
Mount Pleasant L3 5TQ (clear signposting from Liverpool city centre)
☎0151 709 9222 Fax 0151 708 7274
A modern Roman Catholic cathedral which, situated on high ground as it is, provides a focal point on the Liverpool skyline. The imposing structure of curving concrete ribs and stained glass was designed by Sir Frederick Gibberd and consecrated in 1967. The glass was designed by John Piper and Patrick Reyntiens.
Open daily 8-6 (Sun 5pm in winter). Free.
🅿 💺 ♿ *(lift) toilets for disabled shop* 🚫
Cards: 🅰 ▭▭

Museum of Liverpool Life
Pier Head L3 4AA
☎0151 478 4080 Fax 0151 478 4590
This new museum explores the history of Liverpool, its people and their contribution to national life. Displays focus on three main themes: Mersey Culture, Making a Living and Demanding a Voice.
Open all year, daily 10-5. Closed 23-26 Dec & 1 Jan.
£3 (concessions £1.50) Family ticket £7.50. inc 12 months unlimited visits to museums of Liverpool life and other museums. Party 20+.
🅿 *(charged)* ♿ *(wheelchairs available) toilets for disabled shop* 🚫
Cards: 🅰 ▭ ▭ ▭ ▭ 🅢

Tate Gallery Liverpool
Albert Dock L3 4BB
☎0151 709 3223 & 0151 709 0507 (info)
Fax 0151 709 3122
A converted Vicorian warehouse with stunning views across the River Mersey, Tate Gallery, Liverpool offers visitors a unique opportunity to see the best of the national collection of 20th-century art. Complementing collection displays, the Gallery has a changing programme of exhibitions drawing upon works by internationally renowned artists from public and private collections across the world. Please contact the gallery for exhibition details.
Open Tue-Sun 10-6. (Closed Mon ex BH Mon & 1 Jan).
🅿 💺 ♿ *(wheelchairs available) toilets for disabled shop* 🚫
Details not confirmed for 1998

Walker Art Gallery
William Brown St L3 8EL
☎0151 478 4199 Fax 0151 478 4199
An outstanding collection of European paintings, and sculpture. Especially notable are the Italian, Netherlands, and Pre-Raphaelite and Victorian paintings. There is an award-winning sculpture gallery and temporary exhibitions are held throughout the year. 1998 exhibitions include: Bruce Weber (13 March-31 May), Drawings from the Weld-Blundell Collection (26 June-20 September), Irish 20th-Century Figurative Painting (October-January 1999). Please telephone for details. ➤

Open all year, Mon-Sat 10-5, Sun 12-5.
(Closed 23-26 Dec & 1 Jan).
🅿 (charged) ♨ ♿ (prior notice
appreciated, wheelchair on request)
toilets for disabled shop ✿

PORT SUNLIGHT
Port Sunlight Heritage Centre
95 Greendale Rd L62 4XE (junc 4 of M53
on B5137)
☎0151 644 6466 Fax 0151 645 8973
The picturesque garden village was built
by William Hesketh Lever for the workers
in his soap factory, the first sod for the
development being cut by Mrs Lever in
1888. The Heritage Centre tells the story
of the village, the factory and its workers
and a village trail incorporates the varied
architecture, beautiful open spaces and
the Lady Lever Art Gallery with its world-
famous collection of pre-Raphaelite
paintings and Wedgwood.
Open all year. Apr-Oct, daily 10-4. Nov-
Etr, Mon-Fri 10-4.
P (on road 1hr limit) ♿ shop ✿
Details not confirmed for 1998

PRESCOT
Knowsley Safari Park
L34 4AN (M62 exit 6 or M57 exit 2.
Follow 'safari park' signs)
☎0151 430 9009 Fax 0151 426 3677
A five-mile drive through the reserves
enables visitors to see lions, tigers,
elephants, rhinos, monkeys and many
other animals in spacious, natural
surroundings. Extra attractions include a
children's amusement park, reptile
house, pets' corner plus sealion shows
and a miniature railway.
Open, Game reserves Mar-Oct. Other
attractions Mar-Oct, daily 10-4.
£12 per car (incl all occupants). No soft-
topped cars (safari bus available). Coach
passengers £3.50 (ch 2-15 & pen £2.50).
🅿 ♨ ♿ toilets for disabled shop ✿
(kennels provided)
Cards: 🆇 ᕬ 🆇 🆇

Prescot Museum of Clock &
Watch Making
34 Church St L34 3LA
☎0151 430 7787 Fax 0151 430 7219
An attractive 18th-century town house
contains exhibits pertaining to the clock,
watch and tool-making industries of the
area. The display includes a
reconstruction of part of a traditional
watch-maker's workshop and examples
of hand tools and machinery used to
make the intricate parts of clock and
watch movements. There is a programme
of exhibitions, telephone for details.
Open all year, Tue-Sat & BH Mon 10-5,
Sun 2-5 (Closed 24-26 Dec, 1 Jan & Good
Fri).
Free.
P shop ✿

ST HELENS
Pilkington Glass Museum
Prescot Rd WA10 3TT (on A58, 1.5m
from town centre)
☎01744 692499 & 692014
Fax 01744 692727

Since the 18th century, St Helens has
gained a world-wide reputation for flat
glass production. The glass museum
traces the history of glassmaking from
the Egyptians to the present day, with
some of the finest examples of glass in
the world. Visitors can learn of the many
applications of glass in buildings,
transport, lighting, science and
technology. Other attractions are a
special mirrors display and the hands-on
interactive exhibits such as the working
periscope, and the night vision display.
Open all year, Mon-Fri 10-5; Sat, Sun &
BH 2-4.30 (Closed Xmas-New Year). Also
evenings for groups by appointment.
Free.
🅿 ♿ (stair lift not suitable for
wheelchairs) toilets for disabled shop ✿

SOUTHPORT
Atkinson Art Gallery
Lord St PR8 1DH
☎01704 533133 ext 2110
Fax 0151-934 2110
The gallery specialises in 19th-and 20th-
century oil paintings, watercolours,
drawings and prints, as well as 20th-
century sculpture. 1998 sees an
exhibition to co-incide with the British
Open Golf Championships held in
Southport (16-19 July), (subject to
confirmation).
Open all year, Mon, Tue, Wed & Fri 10-5,
Thu & Sat 10-1. (Closed 25-26 Dec & 1
Jan).
Free.
P (pay & display) ♿ shop ✿

The British Lawnmower Museum
106-114 Shakespeare St PR8 5AJ
☎01704 501336
Fax 01704 500564
The museum houses a private collection
of over 200 exhibits of garden machinery.
It was built up over a period of 30 years
and many of the machines were rescued
from scrap yards and restored to pristine
condition. In addition to grass cutting and
garden maintenance machinery dating
from 1830 and through the heyday of the
Industrial Revolution, there is also the
largest collection of vintage toy
lawnmowers and games in the world.
Plus a large range of safes and locks and
keys. Events for 1998 include: February -
a Museum Open Day, March -
Lawnmowers of the Rich and Famous
(inc Nicholas Parsons, Alan Titchmarsh &
Hilda Ogden!), September - Bring a Pet
Mower Day, October - Open Day. A
tribute to the Garden Machinery Industry
over the last 165 years. Please ring for
details of all special events.
Open daily except Sunday & BH
Mondays.
£1 (ch 50p)
P (50yds) shop ✿
Cards: 🆇 ᕬ 🆇 🆇 🆇 🆇 🆇

Southport Railway Centre
The Old Engine Shed, Derby Rd PR9 0TY
☎01704 530693
A thousand feet of standard gauge rail
connects the museum to the British Rail

system. Within the Railway Centre,
which is housed in the former Lancashire
and Yorkshire Engine Shed, are a large
collection of industrial steam and diesel
locomotives, as well as several industrial
locomotives, and also on display are local
buses, tramcars, traction engines and a
variety of other vehicles, making up what
is possibly the largest preservation centre
of its type in north-west England.
Open all year, Oct-May, Sat & Sun 1-5;
Jun-Sep, Sat & Sun 11-5; Jun & first wk
Sep wkdays (ex Fri) 1-4.30; Jul & Aug
wkdays (ex Fri) 10.30-4.30. Also BH
periods 11-5.
🅿 (charged) ♨ ♿ toilets for disabled
shop
Details not confirmed for 1998

Southport Zoo & Conservation
Trust
Princes Park PR8 1RX (from outskirts of
Southport follow brown tourist signs)
☎01704 538102
Fax 01704 548529
The zoo is situated in five acres of
landscaped gardens. Amongst the many
aninmals to be seen are lions, snow
leopards, lynx, chimpanzees, parrots,
penguins and llamas. An extension
houses a pets' corner barn, a giant
tortoise house, primate house,
porcupines and a baby chimpanzee
house. There is also a reptile house with
an aquarium. Gift shop. During the
summer there are snake handling
sessions with talks. A new mandrill
house and enclosure is due to be opened
this year, and there is an education
centre for schools etc who have booked
in advance. Special events: Mums free of
charge (if accompanying children 2-13) on
Mothers Day, ditto for Fathers Day,
Snake-handling sessions with talks
throughout the year. Easter trail
competition with prizes.
Open all year (ex 25 Dec) 10-6 in
summer, 10-4 in winter.
£3 (ch £2, pen £2.50). Party 20+
P (100 yds) (metered) ♨ ♿ (wide
pathways, wide doorways) toilets for
disabled shop

SPEKE
Speke Hall
The Walk L24 1XD (follow signs for
Liverpool Airport)
☎0151 427 7231 Fax 0151 427 9860
A remarkable timber-framed manor
house set in tranquil gardens and
grounds. The house has a Tudor Great
Hall, Stuart plasterwork, William Morris
wallpapers, Mortlake tapestries. Varied
gardens and estate, including rose
garden, stream garden, bluebell woods,
woodland walks, and stunning Mersey.
House open; Apr-29 Oct, daily (ex Mon
but open BH Mon) 1-5.30, 4 Nov-17 Dec,
Sat & Sun 12-4.30. Garden open daily (ex
Mon & Closed 24-26 Dec, 31 Dec, 1 Jan
& Good Fri).
🅿 ♨ ♿ toilets for disabled shop ✿ 🐾
Details not confirmed for 1998
Cards: 🆇 ᕬ

NORFOLK

BACONSTHORPE
Baconsthorpe Castle
NR25 6LN (three quarters of a mile N off
unclass road)
The castle was really a moated and semi-
fortified house, built by the Heydon
family in the 15th century. It is now a
ruin, but the gatehouses, curtain walls
and towers can still be seen.
Open all year daily 10-4.
Free.
🅿 ♨

BANHAM
Banham Zoo
The Grove NR16 2HE (on B1113)
☎01953 887771 & 887773
Fax 01953 887445
Enjoy a great day out among some of the
world's rare and endangered animals
including snow leopards, cheetahs,

Grevy's Zebra, jackass, penguins, many
exotic birds and a large collection of
primates. Daily animal feeding sessions
and keeper talks are not only fun but
educational too. Find out about penguins,
fur seals and squirrel monkeys. Wander
through the deer park, woodland walk,
and monkey jungle island. Other
attractions include an adventure
playground, road train, all weather activity
centre and soft play area. There are
activities and competitions throughout
the school half term holidays. Many
special events are planned throughout
the year. 1997 saw the arrival of tigers in
their new enclosures and the opening of
the Heritage Farm Barn with working
heavy horses.
Open all year, daily from 10am. (Closed
25-26 Dec).
✳£5.95 (ch under 4 free, ch 4-14 £3.95,
pen £4.95). Lower rates at other times.
Party.
🅿 ♨ ✕ licensed ♿ (3 wheelchairs for
hire) toilets for disabled shop ✿
Cards: 🆇 ᕬ 🆇 🆇 🆇

BLICKLING
Blickling Hall
NR11 6NF (on B1354, 1.5 miles NW of
Aylsham)
☎01263 733084
Fax 01263 734924
Flanked by dark yew hedges and topped
by pinnacles, the warm red brick front of
Blickling makes a memorable sight. The
house was built in the early 17th
century, but the hedges may be earlier.
They stand some 17ft tall and 10ft wide.
The centrepiece of the house is the
carved oak staircase which winds up in
double flights from the hall. It was
moved from another part of the house
and adapted to fit a new 18th-century
scheme. (There is also a lift.) On the first
floor is Blickling's most celebrated room,
the Long Gallery, where the 125ft-long
ceiling is covered in ornate Jacobean
plasterwork. The work was done by
Edward Stanyon, who charged £50.80
for the 'freat seeling'. Stanyon also
provided the intricate decorations for the
south drawing room, another of the
original state rooms, at 'fyve shillings
and six pence a yard square'. An equally
remarkable room is the Chinese
bedroom, which still has hand-painted
Chinese wallpaper from the 18th-
century. Amongst the house's fine
furnishing tapestries is a set of eight
17th-century Mortlake works, and the
many pictures include a Canaletto. The
grounds include woodland and a lake, a
formal parterre, and a dry moat filled
with roses, camellias and other plants. In
June, Blickling will be holding their
annual 'Last Night of the Proms' concert
at the back of the House overlooking the
acre. In July there will be the Lakeside
Jazz Festival in the park and in August
once again there will be the fireworks
and laser symphony concert.
Open 4 Apr-1 Nov, Tue-Sun & BH Mon 1-
4.30, Gardens open same as house also
daily in August.
£6 (ch £3) Family ticket.
🅿 ♨ ✕ licensed ♿ (wheelchairs &
batricars, Braille guide) toilets for disabled
shop garden centre ✿ 🐾
Cards: 🆇 ᕬ 🆇 🆇 🆇 🆇

BRESSINGHAM
Bressingham Steam Museum &
Gardens
IP22 2AB (on A1066 2.5 miles W of
Diss)
☎01379 687382 & 687386
Fax 01379 688085
Alan Bloom is an internationally
recognised nurseryman and a steam
enthusiast, and has combined his
interests to great effect at Bressingham.
There are three steam-hauled trains: a
10.25in gauge garden railway, a 15in
gauge running through two and a half
miles of the wooded Waveney Valley,
and a 2ft gauge running through two and
a quarter miles of Europe's largest hardy
plant nursery. There are standard gauge
engines on display. The Dell Garden has

The grounds of Felbrigg Hall have an orangery and a restored walled-garden which is overlooked by a dovecote for 2,000 birds.

5000 species of perennials and alpines, grouped in island beds; Foggy Bottom has wide vistas, pathways, trees, shrubs, conifers and winter colour (restricted opening). There is a collection of 50 road and rail engines, a number restored to working order. A steam roundabout is another attraction, and the Norfolk fire museum is housed here. Various events are held here during the year including Friends of Thomas the Tank Engine, please telephone for details.
Open - Steam Museum & Dell Garden - Apr-Oct, daily 10.30-5.30. Telephone to confirm details.
✻£3.90 (ch £2.40, pen £3.20).
🅿 ✗ licensed & (wheelchair can be taken onto Nursery Line Railway) toilets for disabled shop garden centre ✻
Cards: 🄰 🄳 🄽

BURGH CASTLE
Berney Arms Windmill
NR30 1SB
☎01493 700605
Access is by boat from Great Yarmouth or by rail to Berney Arms station: the road to the mill is unsuitable for cars. This lonely, seven-storey landmark dates back to the 19th century, and helped to drain the marshes. In earlier years it was also used to grind clinker for cement. The machinery for both functions can be seen.
Open Apr-Sep, daily 9-5.
£1.30 (ch 70p, concessions £1)
✻ ❖

The Castle
NR31 9PZ (off A143)
Burgh Castle was built in the third century AD by the Romans, as one of a chain of forts along the Saxon Shore - the coast where Saxon invaders landed. Sections of the massive walls still stand, (some parts faced with flint), and are protected by bastions where 'ballistae' or giant catapults may have been mounted.
Open any reasonable time.
Free.
❖

CAISTER-ON-SEA
Roman Town
The name Caister has Roman origins, and this was in fact a Roman naval base. The remains include the south gateway, a town wall built of flint with brick bonding courses, and part of what may have been a seamen's hostel.
Open any reasonable time.
Free.
❖

CASTLE ACRE
Castle Acre Priory
☎01760 755394
The priory was built for the Clunaic order by Earl Warren, son-in-law of William the Conqueror. Twenty-five monks once lived here in great state, but the priory fell into ruin after the Dissolution in 1536. Rising above the extensive remains is the glorious, arcaded west front of the priory church, a reminder of past splendour. The chapel can also be seen, and there is a 15th-century gatehouse.
Earl Warren also built a great castle, which was developed during the Middle Ages. Edward I was entertained there in 1297, at a time when the walls were 7ft thick. Today there are only ruins and earthworks, but even these are on an impressive scale.
Open all year, Apr-Oct, daily 10-6 (or dusk if earlier in Oct); Nov-Mar, Wed-Sun 10-4.
£2.95 (ch £1.50, concessions £2.20).
Personal stereo tour included in admission.
🅿 & shop ✻ (in certain areas) ❖

CASTLE RISING
Castle Rising Castle
PE31 6AH (off A149)
☎01553 631330
The fine Norman keep was built around 1140 by Henry Albini to celebrate his marriage to the widow of Henry I. The walls still stand to their full original height, towering above the 12 acres of impressive man-made earthworks, which form the castle grounds.
Open all year, Apr-Sep, daily 10-6; Oct, 10-4; Nov-Mar, Wed-Sun 10-4.
✻£2.30 (ch £1.20, concessions £1.70).
🅿 & (exterior only) toilets for disabled shop ✻ ❖

CROMER
Cromer Museum
East Cottages, Tucker St NR27 9HB
☎01263 513543 Fax 01263 511651
The museum is housed in five 19th-century fishermen's cottages, one of which has period furnishings. There are pictures and exhibits from Victorian Cromer, with collections illustrating local natural history, archaeology, social history and geology.
Open all year, Mon-Sat 10-5, Sun 2-5. Closed Mon 1-2. (Closed Good Fri, Xmas period & 1 Jan).
£1.10 (ch 50p, pen, students & UB40s 60p).
P (200yds) shop ✻

Lifeboat Museum
NR27 0HY
☎01263 512503 Fax 01263 512237
The museum in No 2 boat house at the bottom of The Gangway covers local lifeboat history and the RNLI in general. Also of interest is the Lifeboat Station on the pier, where a lifeboat has been stationed since 1804. The history of Cromer from 1804 to the present day is shown together with models of lifeboats. The museum will be housing the recently acquired lifeboat 'The H F Bailey' which served on the station from 1935 to 1945 and which saved 518 lives. Also at the museum are 'The Blogg medals'.
Lifeboat Day (6 August).
Open May-Oct, daily 10-4.
Free.
P & shop

FAKENHAM
See also Thursford Green

Pensthorpe Waterfowl Park & Nature Reserve
Pensthorpe NR21 0LN (signed off A1067 Norwich to Fakenham road)
☎01328 851465 Fax 01328 855905
Pensthorpe Waterfowl Park is situated in the valley of the River Wensum and covers 200 acres of beautiful Norfolk countryside. Based on old gravel workings, its five lakes are home to the largest collection of waterfowl and waders in Europe. With spacious walk-thorugh enclosures, a network of hardsurfaced pathways ensures close contact with birds at the water's edge. In the Courtyard Gallery year-round exhibitions of painting, wildlife photography and craftwork can be viewed. Leaflets and events information can be obtained by phoning.
Open all year, daily 11-5 mid Mar-end of year; weekends only 11-4 Jan-mid Mar.
✻£4.50 (ch £1.75, pen £4)
🅿 ✗ licensed & toilets for disabled shop
Cards: 🄰 🄳

FELBRIGG
Felbrigg Hall
NR11 8PR (off B1436)
☎01263 837444 Fax 01263 837032
Felbrigg is a 17th-century house built on the site of an existing medieval hall. In 1969 the last squire, Robert Wyndham Ketton-Cremer bequeathed the entire estate and its contents to the National Trust. The Hall contains a superb collection of 18th-century furniture, pictures and an outstanding library. There are 27 rooms to visit. The walled garden was first established in the 18th century, an octagonal dovecote containing 900 nesting niches was built in the 1750's and fully restored in 1937. A nursery was first established in 1676 with many varieties of trees, this later became the 550 acre wood which shelters the house from the North Sea. Special events for 1998 include: House Awakening Weekend (21-22 March), Lambing weekends (11-13 & 18-19 April), Agricultural Bygones Day (21 June), Woodland Open Day (28 October).
Open: House 28 Mar-1 Nov, Sat-Wed 1-5. BH Sun & Mon 11-5. Garden opens 11am. Park daily dawn-dusk.
House & garden £5.40 (ch £2.10). Garden £2.20 (ch £1).

 licensed & (battery operated vehicle for garden, braille guide) toilets for disabled shop ✻ (ex park) ❖
Cards: 🄰 🄳 🄽 🄾 🄿 🅂

FILBY
Thrigby Hall Wildlife Gardens
NR29 3DR (on unclass road off A1064)
☎01493 369477 Fax 01493 368256
The 250-year-old park of Thrigby Hall is now the home of animals and birds from Asia, and the lake has ornamental wildfowl. There are tropical bird houses, a unique blue willow pattern garden and tree walk and a summer house as old as the park. The enormous jungled swamp hall has special features such as underwater viewing of large crocodiles.
Open all year, daily from 10.
£5 (ch 4-14 £3.50, pen £4.50).
🅿 ⚑ & (wheelchairs available) toilets for disabled shop ✻
Cards: 🄰 🄳

FLEGGBURGH
The Village
Burgh St. Margaret NR29 3AF (on A1064 between Acle and Caister-on-Sea)
☎01493 369770 Fax 01493 369318
The Village is set in over 35 acres of Norfolk countryside. There is a working sawmill, a steam-hauled trailer ride and three live shows including the Compton-Christie organ. Other attractions include vintage vehicles, motorcycles, a 2ft narrow gauge railway, animals, fairground, adventure play area, Victorian gallopers and traditional crafts. Apple pressing in September.
Etr-Oct, daily 10-5. Other times not confirmed. Saturday is grounds only day (admission reduced accordingly)
£5.95 (ch £3.95 pen £5.45)
🅿 ⚑ ✗ licensed & toilets for disabled shop ✻
Cards: 🄰 🄳 🄽 🄾 🅂

GREAT BIRCHAM
Bircham Windmill
PE31 6SJ (0.5m W off unclassified Snettisham rd).
☎01485 578393
This windmill is one of the last remaining in Norfolk. Sails turn on windy days, and the adjacent tea room serves home-made cakes, light lunches and cream teas. There is also a bakery museum and cycle hire.
Open daily during school hols and bank holiday weekends. Wed-Sat at all other times between 5 Apr-26 Sept.
✻£2 (ch 50p, pen £1.75)
🅿 ⚑ shop

GREAT YARMOUTH
Elizabethan House Museum
4 South Quay NR30 2QH
☎01493 855746
A wealthy merchant built this house in 1596. It has been completely re-displayed to show a wealthy household through time from the 16th to 19th centuries. Visitors can see a Victorian kitchen, scullery and parlour, a Tudor bedroom and dining room, a Stuart (Civil War) 'conspiracy' room and a children's toy room.
Open 6-19 Apr, Mon-Fri 10-5, Sun 2-5 (closed Good Fri); 24 May-25 Sept, Sun-Fri 10-5.
£1.90 (ch 90p, concessions £1.40). Family ticket £4.70.
P (100yds) & shop ✻

Maritime Museum For East Anglia
Marine Pde NR30 2EN
☎01493 842267
The sea and the fishing industry have played an enormous part in East Anglia's history and this Maritime Museum has exhibits on each aspect. There are special displays on the herring fishery, the wherry, life-saving and the most recent industry - oil and gas in the North Sea.
Open Etr fortnight, Mon-Fri 10-5, Sun 2-5 (closed Good Fri); Sun before Whitsun-end Sep, Sun-Fri 10-5. Under review.
✻£1.10 (ch 50p, concessions 60p). Family ticket £2.70.
P shop ✻

Merrivale Model Village
Wellington Pier Gardens, Marine Pde NR30 3JG
☎ *01493 842097*
Set in attractive landscaped gardens, this comprehensive miniature village is built on a scale of 1:12. The layout includes a two and a half inch gauge model railway, radio-controlled boats, and over 200 models set in an acre of landscaped gardens. There are additional amusements and remote-controlled cars and boats. During the summer, from June to October, the gardens are illuminated after dusk.
Open Etr 9.30-6, Jun-Oct 9.30-10.
£2.80 (ch 3-14 £1.50, pen £2.30).
P (opposite) ☕ ♿ shop (ex on leads)

Old Merchant's House
Row 111 (follow signs to dock and south quay)
☎ *01493 857900*
Two 17th-century Row Houses, a type of building unique to Great Yarmouth, containing original fixtures and displays of local architectural fittings salvaged from bombing in 1942-43. Nearby are the remains of a Franciscan friary, with a rare vaulted cloister, accidentally discovered during bomb damage repairs.
Open Mar-Oct 10-6. Tours start from Row 111 houses at 10am, 11am, noon, 2pm, 3pm & 4pm.
£1.75 (ch 90p, concessions £1.30)

Ripley's Believe It or Not!
The Windmill, 9 Marine Pde NR30 3AH
☎ *01493 332217 Fax 01493 332295*
Collected from the four corners of the world, this fun museum contains the most odd and bizzare things you will ever see. Themed with special effects, you can see, touch and experience an assortment of oddities including videos of amazing human talents. Plenty for the whole family to enjoy - believe it or not!
Open Nov-Apr, wknds & school hols 10-4; Apr-Nov, daily - early season 10-5, main season 10-10.
P 500yds ♿ (free entry) shop
Details not confirmed for 1998
Cards:

Tolhouse Museum
Tolhouse St NR30 2SH
☎ *01493 858900 Fax 01493 745459*
This late 13th-century building was once the town's court house and gaol and has dungeons which can be visited. The rooms above contain exhibits on local history. The museum has become a brass rubbing centre and has a wide range of replica brasses from which rubbings can be made. Prices start at 50p and include materials and instructions.
Open 6-19 Apr, Mon-Fri 10-5, Sun 2-5 (closed Good Fri); 24 May-25 Sept, Sun-Fri 10-5. Under review.
£1.10 (ch 50p, concessions 60p). Family ticket £2.70. Tolhouse only 70p (ch 30p, concessions 40p).
P (100yds) (lift to ground & 2nd floor) shop

GRESSENHALL
Norfolk Rural Life Museum & Union Farm
Beech House NR20 4DR (A47, B1110 through East Dereham towards Holt, onto B1146 to Fakenham,museum is 1.5m on right)
☎ *01362 860563 Fax 01362 860385*
Housed in a former workhouse, the museum reflects the rural history of the county over the past 200 years. Displays on rural life include working on the land, agriculture, rural trades and crafts and village life and include Cherry Tree Cottage and garden, a typical farm labourer's home of the turn-of-the-century as well as reconstructed craftsmen's workshops. Union Farm is the museum's working farm which shows farming as it was before the age of the tractor. Worked with heavy horses and stocked with rare breeds of sheep, cattle, pigs and poultry. Farm trail, woodland and riverside walk, osier beds. Special events and demonstrations throughout the season, including National Museums Week (16-24 May), Workhouse Trails - guided tours giving an insight into the workhouse system (26-29 May, 1-4 Sep), Edwardian Extravaganza (25-26 Jul).
Open 5 Apr-1 Nov, Mon-Sat 10-5, Sun 12-5.30. Also BH Mons 10-5.

The rose-pink of Oxburgh Hall's brickwork creates a romantic image. It is approached through an iron gate and across the moat.

£3.80 (ch £1.70, concessions £2.80). Family ticket£9.30.
P ☕ ♿ (sound guide & wheelchair loan) toilets for disabled shop
Cards:

GRIMES GRAVES
Grimes Graves
(7m NW of Thetford off A134)
☎ *01842 810656*
Grimes Graves is a network of hundreds of pits, dug by Neolithic people who were mining for flint between about 3000BC and 1900BC. This is the largest known group of flint mines in Britain, and consisted of vertical shafts leading to galleries through the flint seams. Visitors today can go down a shaft to crouch in the gloom and imagine themselves prising out the flints with antler picks and wooden levers. Regular flint knapping demonstrations can be seen, while the on-site exhibition explains the full history of this fascinating site.
Open all year, Apr-Oct, daily 10-6 (or dusk if earlier); Nov-Mar, Wed-Sun 10-4. Last visit to pit 20 minutes before closing). £1.75 (ch 90p, concessions £1.30). A torch is useful.
P ♿ (exhibition area, grounds only; access track rough) shop (in certain areas)

HEACHAM
Norfolk Lavender
Caley Mill PE31 7JE (on A149 at junc with B1454)
☎ *01485 570384 Fax 01485 571176*
This is the largest lavender-growing and distilling operation in Britain. Different coloured lavenders are grown in strips and harvested in July and August. There are also rose and herb gardens and a fragrant Plant Centre. There are guided tours of the distillery and gardens; and minibus trips visit a large lavender field Guardians of the National Collection of Lavenders (Norfolk).
Open all year, daily 10-5. (Closed 25 Dec-4 Jan).
Admission to grounds Free. Guided tours £1.50. Trip to Lavender Field £3.95, mid Jun-mid Aug.
P ☕ ♿ (wheelchairs for loan) toilets for disabled shop garden centre
Cards:

HOLKHAM
Holkham Hall & Bygones Museum
NR23 1AB (off A149, 2m W of Wells-next-the-Sea
☎ *01328 710227 Fax 01328 711707*
This classic Palladian style mansion was built between 1734 and 1762 by Thomas Coke 1st Earl of Leicester, and is still home to his descendants. It has a magnificent alabaster entrance hall and the sumptuous state rooms house Greek and Roman statues, fine furniture and paintings by Rubens, Van Dyck, Claude, Poussin, Gainsborough and others. The park is equally fine, with deer, geese on the lake, and an impressive collection of trees, especially ilexes. The Bygones Museum, housed in the stable block adjoining the Hall, has over 5,000 items on display from gramophones to fire engines, coaches to cars, steam engines to motor cycles, and cameras to kitchens. Also of interest are the History of Farming exhibition, gift shop selling Holkham Pottery and the Holkham Nursery Gardens in the 18th century walled garden. Stately car boot sale in aid of Norfolk Churches Trust (23 May).
Open 24 May-Sep, Sun-Thu, 1-5. Etr, May, Spring & Summer BHs Sun & Mon 11.30-5.
Hall £4 (ch £2). Bygones £4 (ch £2). Combined ticket hall & Bygones: £6 (ch £3)
P ☕ ♿ toilets for disabled shop garden centre (guide dogs, in park on leads)

HORSEY
Horsey Windpump
NR29 4EF
☎ *01493 393904*
The windpump mill was built 200 years ago to drain the area, and then rebuilt in 1912 by Dan England, a noted Norfolk millwright. It has been restored since being struck by lightning in 1943, and overlooks Horsey Mere and marshes, noted for their wild birds and insects.
Open 28 Mar-Sep, daily 11-5. (Closed Good Fri).
£1.20
P (charged) ☕ shop
Cards:

HORSHAM ST FAITH
City of Norwich Aviation Museum
Old Norwich Rd NR10 3JF
☎ *01603 625309*
Administered by enthusiastic volunteers, the museum offers many displays relating to the aeronautical history of Norfolk. Several types of aircraft are on display, including a Vulcan bomber. Some aircraft are open to visitors allowing them to experience the conditions that air crew operate in. A new feature is the RAF 100 Group Memorial Museum Collection. A major addition to the history of a part of RAF Bomber Command that was unique to Norfolk in World War II.
Open all year, Etr, Apr-Oct daily 10-5, Tues-Sun. Nov-Mar Wed, Sat & Sun 10-4. £2.50 (ch, pen, & concessions £1.50)
P ☕ ♿ (assistance available) shop

HOUGHTON
Houghton Hall
PE31 6UE (1.25m off A148)
☎ *01485 528569 Fax 01485 528167*
This splendid Palladian house in beautiful parkland was built for Sir Robert Walpole. The staterooms have decorations and furniture by William Kent. There is a model soldier collection.
Open: House Etr Sun-last Sun Sep, Thu, Sun & BH's 2-5.30. Last admission 5pm. £5.50 (ch 5-16 £3, ch under 5 free). Excluding house £3 (ch 5-16 £2)
P ☕ ♿ toilets for disabled shop

KING'S LYNN
African Violet Centre
Terrington St Clement PE34 4PL (4m W of Kings Lynn, on A17)
☎ *01553 828374 Fax 01553 827520*

Elm Hill is a fine example of the narrow, winding, medieval streets that make Norwich such an attractive city.

Winner of 8 Chelsea Gold Medals the Centre is fascinating for plant lovers. Knowledgeable staff are on hand to offer advice for those interested in growing and caring for violets. There is a gift shop, tearoom and Orthodox Chapel which celebrates the Divine Liturgy on Sundays. Special weekend shows include: Orchids, Cactus and Bonsai. Ring for details.
Open daily 10-5. Closed Xmas/New Year. Free.
P ⚑ & *toilets for disabled shop garden centre* ⚘
Cards: 🂠 ⚏ ⚏ ⚏ ⚏ 🂠

Lynn Museum
Market St PE30 1NL
☎01553 775001 Fax 01553 775001
Once it was a walled city of considerable importance; its two great churches, two marketplaces and two Guildhalls testify to its size. King's Lynn was also a noted port and a stop on the Pilgrim's Way to Walsingham. The geology, archaeology and natural history of the area are the main collections in the local museum. Objects in the archaeology gallery include Bronze Age weapons and the skeleton of a Saxon warrior. Relics from the medieval town of Lynn include an important collection of pilgrim badges. Also see the Snarling Tiger, the Medieval Stonemason, the Victorian Ironmonger's Shop and the beautiful 19th century fairground roundabout horses of Frederick Savage.
Open all year, Tue-Sat, 10-5.
P *(500yds)* & *shop* ⚘
Details not confirmed for 1998

St George's Guildhall
27 Kings St
☎01553 773578 Fax 01553 770591
Although it has been used for many purposes, the theatrical associations of this 15th-century Guildhall are strongest: Shakespeare himself is said to have performed here. Its present use as the town's theatre was brought about in the 1950s after an 18th-century theatre, incorporated into the hall, was restored and enlarged. The annual King's Lynn Festival takes place towards the end of July. Ring for details.
When not in use as a theatre or cinema open Mon-Fri 10-4, Sat 10-1 & 2-3.30. (Closed Good Fri, Aug BH Mon, 25-26 Dec & 1 Jan).
Free.
P *(100yds) (pay & display)* ⚑ ✗ *licensed* ⚘ ♨

LITTLE WALSINGHAM
Walsingham Abbey Grounds
NR22 6BP (take B1105 from Fakenham)
☎01328 820259 Fax 01328 820098
In the grounds of the Abbey are the ruins of the original Augustinian priory built in the 1100s. The priory was built over the

shrine of Our Lady of Walsingham which had been established in 1061. The remains include the east wall of the church, and the south wall of the refectory still intact.
Open Apr-Jul Wed, Sat & Sun; Aug Mon, Wed, Fri, Sat & Sun; Sep Wed, Sat & Sun. Also BHs Etr-Sep. Other times through Estate office.
£1.50 (ch & pen 75p).
P *(100 yds)* & *toilets for disabled shop*

NORTH CREAKE
Creake Abbey
NR21 9LF (1m N off B1355)
Church ruin with crossing and eastern arm belonging to a house of Augustinian canons founded in 1206.
Open any reasonable time.
Free.
⚑

NORWICH
Norwich Cathedral's lofty spire - the highest Norman tower in Britain - is one among more than 20 towers and spires that thrust above the city's rooftops. The River Wensum winds round the city, enfolding the Norman castle and narrow streets and alleys that display many an old-world shop front. Famous for its mustard, printing and insurance today, in medieval times it was the centre of East Anglia's profitable wool trade and this part of England was among the most populous and prosperous.

Bridewell Museum
Bridewell Alley NR2 1AQ
☎01603 667228 Fax 01603 765651
Built in the late 14th century, this flint-faced merchant's house was used as a prison from 1583 to 1828. It now houses displays illustrating the trades and industries of Norwich during the past 200 years, including a large collection of locally made boots and shoes. There are also a reconstructed 1920s pharmacy, a 1930s pawnbrokers shop and a blacksmith's smithy. Special for children: "Hunt the Animals" quiz trail.
Open Apr-Sep, Tue-Sat, 10-5.
£1.30 (ch 60p, concessions 90p)
P *shop* ⚘

Guildhall
Guildhall Hill NR2 1NF
☎01603 666071 Fax 01603 765389
Visitors may visit the Council Chamber and view civic plate and insignia dating from 1549. The civic regalia is on view Monday to Friday 2-3.30pm, or at other times for parties by arrangement.

Open all year 6 days a week.
P *(200 yds)* & *toilets for disabled* ⚘
Details not confirmed for 1998

Norwich Castle Museum
Castle Meadow NR1 3JU
☎01603 223624 Fax 01603 765651
Norman Castle Keep built in the 12th century, and museum housing displays of art, archaeology, natural history, Lowestoft porcelain, Norwich silver, a large collection of paintings (with special emphasis on the Norwich School of Painters) and British ceramic teapots. There are also guided tours of the dungeons and battlements. A lively annual programme of exhibitions, children's events, trails and holiday activities, gallery and evening talks takes place throughout the year. Please ring for details.
Open all year, Mon-Sat 10-5, Sun 2-5. (Closed Good Fri, Xmas period & New Year).
Jul-Sep: £3.20 (ch £1.60, concessions £2.20). Family ticket £7.80. Oct-Jun: £2.40 (ch £1.10, concessions £1.60). Family ticket £5.70.
P *(200mtrs)* ⚑ & *(lift to first floor, special parking by prior arrangement) toilets for disabled shop* ⚘

Norwich Cathedral
The Close NR1 4DH (A47, A11 to city centre, inner ring rd to Barrack St rdbt, take rd towards city centre to Tombland)
☎01603 764385 & 767617 (weekends) Fax 01603 766032
Norwich is a beautiful Norman building set in the largest close in England. Originally a Benedictine foundation, it possesses the largest monastic cloisters in England and is of great architectural and artistic interest. The special features

include: the Saxon bishop's throne, nave bosses depicting scenes from the Bible from the Creation to the Resurrection; the 14th-century Despenser reredos. Services take place several times every day. A regular programme of concerts, recitals and exhibitions, details on request.
Open daily, 7.30-7 (6pm mid Sep-mid May).
Donations welcomed.
P *(440yds)* ⚑ & *(parking on site touch & hearing centre) toilets for disabled shop* ⚘

Royal Norfolk Regimental Museum
Shirehall, Market Av NR1 3JQ
☎01603 223649 Fax 01603 765651
Museum displays deal with the social as well as military history of the county regiment from 1685, including the daily life of a soldier. It is housed in an old courtroom of the historic Shirehall. It is linked to the Castle Museum by a tunnel through which prisoners were taken to court. This is followed by a reconstruction of a World War I communication trench. Audio-visual displays and graphics complement the collection. There is a programme of temporary exhibitions.
Open all year, Mon-Sat 10-5, Sun 2-5. Closed Good Fri, Xmas period & 1 Jan.
£1.30 (ch 60p, concessions 90p). Joint ticket with Castle Museum £5.
P *(400 yds)* & *(stair lift should be available, ring for details) shop* ⚘

Sainsbury Centre for Visual Arts
University of East Anglia NR4 7TJ
☎01603 456060 & 593199 Fax 01603 259401
The collection of Sir Robert and Lady Sainsbury was given to the University in 1973. European art of the 19th and 20th centuries is on display together with ethnographical art. You can see African tribal sculpture and Oceanic works along with North American and Pre-Colombian art. Egyptian, Asian and European antiquities are on show.
Open Tue-Sun 11-5. (Closed Mon & University closure at Xmas).
✱*Collection & exhibition £2 (concessions £1).*
P ⚑ ✗ *licensed* & *(parking, wheelchair available on loan) toilets for disabled shop* ⚘ *(guide dogs by arrangement)*
Cards: 🂠 ⚏ ⚏ ⚏ ⚏ 🂠

St Peter Hungate Church Museum
Princes St (near Elm Hill) NR3 1AE
☎01603 667231 Fax 01603 765651
Built in 1460, this fine church has a hammer-beam roof and good examples of Norwich painted glass. It is now a museum of church art and a brass rubbing centre with a wide selection of brasses to rub from; a charge is made which includes materials and instructions. New displays bring the social history of the parish to life.
Open Apr-Oct Mon-Sat 10-5.
Free. Brass rubbing materials from £1.50.
P & *shop* ⚘

OXBOROUGH
Oxburgh Hall
PE33 9PS
☎ 01366 328258
Fax 01366 328066
The outstanding feature of this 15th-century moated building is the 80ft high gatehouse which, unlike the rest of the hall, was spared from the alterations made in Victorian times. Two wings are built around a courtyard.
Henry VII lodged in the King's Room in 1487 and it is now furnished with a 17th-century bed, and wall hangings worked by Mary, Queen of Scots and Elizabeth Countess of Shrewsbury. A spiral staircase links the chambers to the room from which there are fine views across the countryside. A parterre garden of French design stands outside the moat, and there are woodland walks.
Open House, Garden & Estate Walks 29 Mar-2 Nov, Sat-Wed 1-5. (Garden 11-5.30); BH Mons 11-5. (Closed Good Fri).
🅿 ✗ *licensed* ♿ *(braille guide & wheelchairs available) toilets for disabled shop* ❀🚲
Details not confirmed for 1998
Cards: 🆑 🆑 🆑 🆑 🆑

REEDHAM
Pettitts Animal Adventure Park
NR13 3UA (off A47 at Acle)
☎ 01493 700094 01493 701403
Fax 01493 700933
Farmyard animals - rabbits, goats, ducks many of which have been hand raised, can be seen here along with more exotic creatures like wallabies, falabella horses, peacocks and chipmunks. The art of feather craft is demonstrated. Daily live entertainment is provided by children's entertainers and a country and western singing duo. Other attractions include the play area, train rides, and fun fare rides. Special events are planned throughout the season.
Open Etr Sun-Oct, daily 10-5.30. (Closed Sat).
£6.25 (ch £5.95 & pen £5.50). Disabled & helpers £5.50. Party.
🅿 ⚅ ✗ ♿ *(ramps to all areas) toilets for disabled shop*
Cards: 🆑 🆑 🆑 🆑

ST OLAVES
St Olaves Priory
(5.5m SW of Great Yarmouth on A143)
The fine brick undercroft seen in the cloister is one of the most notable features of the ruin of this small Augustinian priory: built in about 1216 it is an exceptionally early use of this material.
Open any reasonable time.
Free.
🏛

SANDRINGHAM
Sandringham House, Grounds, Museum & Country Park
PE35 6EN (off A148)
☎ 01553 772675
Fax 01485 541571
The private country retreat of Her Majesty The Queen, Sandringham House is at the heart of the beautiful estate which has been owned by four generations of monarchs.
The neo-Jacobean house was built in 1870 for Albert Edward, Prince of Wales and his wife Princess Alexandra, later King Edward VII and Queen Alexandra. The grand and imposing building, where all the main rooms used by the Royal Family when in residence are open to the public, Sandringham House has the warmth and charm of a well-loved family home. Visitors see portraits of the Royal Family, collections of porcelain, jade, quartz, enamelled Russian silver, gold and bronzes set amongst fine furniture. Sixty acres of glorious grounds surround the House and offer beauty and colour throughout the season with a rich variety of flowers, shrubs and magnificent trees, informally planted around lawns and lakes.
Sandringham Museum, situated within the grounds, contains fascinating displays of Royal memorabilia ranging from family photographs to vintage Daimlers, and an exhibition of the Sandringham Fire Brigade.
Open 9 Apr-4 Oct, daily (House closed 22 Jul-5 Aug inc; Museum & Grounds closed 27 Jul-5 Aug inc). House 11-4.45. Museum 11-5. Grounds 10.30-5. House, Museum & Grounds: £4.50 (ch £2.50, pen £3.50). Family ticket £11.50. Grounds & Museum £3.50 (ch £2, pen £3). Family ticket £9.
🅿 ⚅ ✗ *licensed* ♿ *(loan of wheelchairs, free transport in grounds) toilets for disabled shop* ❀
Cards: 🆑 🆑 🆑 🆑 🆑 🆑

Wolferton Station Museum
PE31 6HA
☎ 01485 540674
The museum is housed in the former Royal Retiring Rooms at Wolferton Station on the Sandringham Estate. They were built for King Edward VII and Queen Alexandra (when still Prince and Princess of Wales) in 1898, and have been used by all British monarchs from Queen Victoria to the present Royal Family, visiting foreign monarchs and heads of state and Royal guests on their journey to Sandringham. The displays include items and furniture from Royal Trains, Queen Victoria's Travelling Bed, railway relics and curios, Victorian and Edwardian fashions, jewellery, furniture and ephemera, Royal letters and photographs, a representation of a 1890's GER coach and much, much more.
Open Apr-Sep, Mon-Fri & Sun (pm only).
🅿 ♿ *shop* ❀ *(ex in grounds)*
Details not confirmed for 1998

Sandringham House, Museum and Gardens
01553 772675
Norfolk Country retreat of HM The Queen.
Open
Easter to mid-July and early August to October

Photograph by gracious permission of HM The Queen

SAXTHORPE
Mannington Gardens & Countryside
NR11 7BB (2.25m NE)
☎ 01263 584175 Fax 01263 761214
The moated manor house, built in 1460 and still a family home forms a centre-piece for the pretty gardens which surround it. Visitors can enjoy the roses - the chief feature of the gardens - and also lovely countryside walks. Special events take place throughout the season, including Nature Discovery Days for children. Also Countryside Day (24 May), Rose Week Events (June-July), Charity Day (6 September), Charity Garden Openings (26 April & 4 October).
Open: Gardens Jun-Aug, Wed-Fri 11-5; also Sun noon-5 May-Sep. Walks open every day from 9am. Hall open by prior appointment only.
Garden £3 (accompanied ch 16 free, students & pen £2.50). Walks free (car park for walkers £1).
🅿 ⚅ ♿ *(boardwalk across meadow) toilets for disabled shop garden centre* 🚲
See advertisement on page 107.

SHERINGHAM
North Norfolk Railway
Sheringham Station NR26 8RA
☎ 01263 822045 Fax 01263 823794
A steam railway with trains operating on most days from March to October, with extra days as the season progresses and a daily service in the summer. On Sundays, lunch is served on the train. At Weybourne station is a collection of steam locomotives and rolling stock, some of which are undergoing or awaiting restoration. These include several industrial tank engines and ex-Great Eastern mainline engines. The rolling stock includes suburban coaches, the Brighton Belle Pullmans and directors' private saloons and a vintage buffet saloon. There is also a museum of railway memorabilia and a souvenir and book shop.
Open Etr-Oct; daily during summer season; Dec (Santa special). Telephone 01263 825449 for timetable.
P *(adjacent)* ⚅ ♿ *(ramps to trains) shop*
Details not confirmed for 1998
Cards: 🆑 🆑

SNETTISHAM
Park Farm
PE31 7NQ (signposted on A149)
☎ 01485 542425 Fax 01485 543503
You can see farming in action here with lambing in the spring, sheep shearing in May and deer calving in June and July. Sheep, goats, lambs, rabbits, turkeys, ducks, chickens, ponies, piglets etc can be seen in the paddocks, and the sheep centre has over 40 different breeds. Take a safari ride around the estate to see the magnificent herd of red deer. Other attractions include a large adventure playground, horse and pony rides, 2.5 miles of farm trails, visitor centre and craft workshops, including pottery studio and leather worker. Sheep shearing demonstrations at Whitsun.
Open all year, Spring, Summer & Autumn, daily 10-5; Winter, Fri-Mon, 10-dusk. Closed Xmas day.
£3.95 (ch £2.75, pen £3.50). Family ticket £13.
🅿 ⚅ ♿ *(gravel paths, ramps where needed) toilets for disabled shop* ❀ *(ex on farm trails)*
Cards: 🆑 🆑 🆑 🆑 🆑 🆑 🆑

SOUTH WALSHAM
Fairhaven Garden Trust
2 The Woodlands, Wymers Ln NR13 6EA (9m NE of Norwich on B1140)
☎ 01603 270449 Fax 01603 270449
These delightful woodland and water gardens, with a private inner broad, offer peace and tranquility and a combination of cultivated and wild flowers. In spring there are masses of primroses and bluebells, with azaleas and rhododendrons in several areas. Candelabra primulas and some unusual plants grow near the waterways, which are spanned by small bridges. In summer the wild flowers come into their own, providing habitat for butterflies, bees and dragonflies. There is a separate bird sanctuary for bird watchers. Riverboats run from the gardens around the two South Walsham Broads, or to St Benets Abbey ruins. Primrose Week (19-26 April), Candelabra Primula Weeks (16-31 May), Autumn Colour Weeks (24-31 October).
Open 1 Apr-31 Oct, 11am-5.30pm. Tue-Sun. (open BH Mon)
£3 (ch £1, pen £2.70). Season tickets £10.
🅿 ⚅ ♿ *(ramp, grab rail) shop garden centre*
Cards: 🆑 🆑 🆑

THETFORD
Ancient House Museum
White Hart St IP24 1AA (in town centre)
☎ 01842 752599
An early Tudor timber-framed house with beautifully carved beamed ceilings, it now houses an exhibition on Thetford and Breckland life. This has been traced back to very early times, and there are examples from local Neolithic settlements. Brass rubbing facilities are available and there is a small period garden recreated in the rear courtyard.
Open all year, Mon-Sat, 10-5 (Closed Mon 12.30-1); Jun-Aug also Sun 2-5. (Closed Good Fri, Xmas period & New Year's Day).
80p (ch 30p, concessions 40p) in Jul & Aug. Rest of year free.
P *(20yds) shop* ❀

Thetford Priory
(on W side of Thetford near station)
The Cluniac monastery was founded in 1103, and its remains are extensive. The 14th-century gatehouse of the priory stands to its full height, and the complete ground plan of the cloisters can be seen.
Open any reasonable time.
Free.
❀ 🏛

Warren Lodge
(2m NW, on B1107)
The remains of a two-storey hunting lodge, built in the 15th century of flint with stone dressings.
Open any reasonable time.
Free.
🏛

THURSFORD GREEN
Thursford Collection
NR21 0AS (1m off A148)
☎ 01328 878477 Fax 01328 878415
This exciting collection specialises in organs, with a Wurlitzer cinema organ, fairground organs, barrel organs and street organs among its treasures. There are live musical shows every day, featuring all the material organs and the Wurtlizer show. The collection also includes showmen's engines, ploughing engines and farm machinery. There is a children's play area and a breathtaking 'Venetian gondola' switchback ride. Special evening musical events, details on request, and various shops with a Dickensian touch.
Open Apr-Oct, daily 12noon-5pm.
£4.40 (ch 4-14 £2, pen £4, ch under 4 free). Party 15+.
🅿 ⚅ ✗ ♿ *toilets for disabled shop* ❀
Cards: 🆑 🆑 🆑 🆑

TITCHWELL
RSPB Nature Reserve
PE31 8BB (6m E of Hunstanton on A149)
☎ 01485 210779
This is one of RSPB's most popular coastal reserves at all times of the year be it for summer avocets or wintering waders and wildfowl. A firm path takes you to three hides and on to the beach where a platform overlooking the sea is suitable for wheelchairs. A colony of avocets nest on the enclosed marsh with gadwalls, tufted ducks, shovelers and black-headed gulls. Bearded tits, water rails, bitterns and marsh harriers are found on the reedbeds. Common and little terns, ringed plovers and oystercatchers nest on the beach where large flocks of waders roost during the

Location: 9 miles N/E of Norwich on B1140 at South Walsham on the Norfolk Broads. Boat trips on the two South Walsham Broads.

Opening Times: April 1st to October 31st, Tuesday to Sunday 11am to 5.30pm. *Closed Mondays except Bank Holidays.*

Admission: Adults £3.00, OAPs £2.70, Child £1.00 (under 5s free). Group reductions. Morning coffee, light lunches, afternoon teas. Gift shop. Plant sales. Guided walks for pre-booked groups.

Owner: The Trustees of the Fairhaven Garden Trust

Contact: Mr G Debbage

Registered Charity No. 265686

FAIRHAVEN GARDEN TRUST

Woodland and water garden with private broad. Primroses, bluebells, candelabra primulas, rhododendrons in Spring. Shrubs and flowers, birds and butterflies.
Lovely colours in Autumn.

Enquiries: Tel/Fax 01603 270449

2 THE WOODLANDS, WYMERS LANE, SOUTH WALSHAM, NORWICH NR13 6EA

highest autumn tides. During the season many migrants visit the marsh including wigeon, black-tailed godwits, curlews, sandpipers and occasional rarities. In winter, brent geese and goldeneyes occur regularly with divers, grebes and seaducks offshore and snow bunting foraging on the beach. Phone for details of special events.
Open at all times. Visitor Centre daily 10-5 (4pm Nov-Mar)
Free.
P *(charged)* 🍴 & *toilets for disabled* ⚑
Cards: 🖃 🖃 🖃 🖃

WEETING
Weeting Castle
IP27 0RQ (2m N of Brandon off B1106)
This ruined 11th-century fortified manor house is situated in a rectangular moated enclosure. It is interesting also for its slight remains of a three-storeyed cross-wing.
Open any reasonable time.
Free.
⚑

WELLS-NEXT-THE-SEA
Wells & Walsingham Light Railway
NR23 1QB (A149 Cromer road)
☎01328 710631
(Wells Station Sheringham Rd (A149). Walsingham Station, Egmere Rd). The railway covers the four miles between Wells and Walsingham. It is unusual in that it uses ten and a quarter inch gauge track and is the longest track of this gauge in the world. The line passes through some very attractive countryside, particularly noted for its wild flowers and butterflies. This is the home of the unique Garratt Steam Locomotive specially built for this line.
Open daily Etr-Sep.
£5 return (ch £3.50 return).
P 🍴 & *shop*

WELNEY
WWT Welney
Pintail House, Hundred Foot Bank PE14 9TN (off A1101, N of Ely)
☎01353 860711 Fax 01353 860711
This internationally important wetland site on the beautiful Ouse Washes is famed for the breathtaking spectacle of wild ducks, geese and swans which spend the winter there. Impressive observation facilities, including hides, towers and an observatory, offer outstanding views of the huge numbers of wildfowl which include Bewick's and Whooper Swans, Wigeon, Teal and Shoveler. During summer, a nature walk across the reserve, through rich carpets of yellow, pink and purple wildflowers, looking for waders and warblers, is a delightful experience. Other features include floodlit evening swan feeds between November and February, an exhibition areas, gift shop and tea room. Facilities for disabled people include access to the main observatory, two hides for wheelchair users and access along one mile of the summer nature walk.

Open all year, daily 10-5. (Closed 25 Dec).
❄£3 (ch £1.80). Family ticket £7.80. Party 10+.
P 🍴 & *(wheelchair access to major parts of reserve) toilets for disabled shop* ⚑
Cards: 🖃 🖃 🖃 🖃 🖃

WEST RUNTON
Norfolk Shire Horse Centre
West Runton Stables NR27 9QH (on A149)
☎01263 837339 Fax 01263 837132
The Shire Horse Centre has a collection of draught horses and some breeds of mountain and moorland ponies. There are also exhibits of horse-drawn machinery, waggons and carts, and harnessing and working demonstrations are given twice every day. Other attractions include a children's farm, a photographic display of draught horses past and present, talks and a video show. There is a riding school on the premises as well.
Open 29 Mar-30 Oct. Closed Saturdays except June,July & Aug & BH.
£4.50 (ch £2.25, pen £3). Party.
P 🍴 ✗ *licensed* & *toilets for disabled shop* ⚑ *(ex on lead)*
Cards: 🖃 🖃 🖃 🖃 🖃 🖃

WEYBOURNE
The Muckleburgh Collection
Weybourne Military Camp NR25 7EG (on A149, coast road, 3miles W of Sheringham)
☎01263 588210 & 588608
Fax 01263 588425
The Muckleburgh Collection is the largest privately-owned military collection of its kind in the UK and incorporates the Museum of the Suffolk and Norfolk Yeomanry dating from the 18th century.

Its 3000 exhibits include restored and working tanks, armoured cars, trucks and artillery of World War II, and equipment including weapons from the Falklands and the Gulf War. Special model displays and diorama include military vehicles, aircraft and ships as well as radios and uniforms. Live tank demonstrations are run daily during summer high season. New exhibits include an extensive display of model ships, a Panzer 61 Swiss Tank and Chevrolet Portee. Also, two fully restored Boer War Field Cannons dated 1905. Royal British Legion Family Fun Day (26 July) featuring military bands, drum corps, motorcycle team displays, helicopter rides, tank displays, and much more. (Entrance £6 per car, admission free, coaches welcome).
Open 15 Feb-1 Nov.
£4 (ch £2 and pen £3). Family ticket £10.50.
P 🍴 ✗ *licensed* & *(ramped access, wheelchairs available) toilets for disabled shop* ⚑
Cards: 🖃

NORTHAMPTONSHIRE

CANONS ASHBY
Canons Ashby House
NN11 3SD
☎01327 860044 Fax 01327 860168
Home of the Dryden family since the 16th century, this is an exceptional small manor house, with Elizabethan wall paintings and Jacobean plasterwork. It has restored gardens, a small park and a church - part of the original 13th-century Augustinian priory.
Open 11 Apr-1 Nov, Sat-Wed & BH Mon (closed Good Fri) 1-5.30 or dusk if earlier. Last admission 5pm.
£3.60 (ch £1.80). Family ticket £8.90.
P 🍴 & *(hearing scheme taped guide wheelchair available) toilets for disabled shop* ⚑ *(ex on lead in home paddock)* 🐾
Cards: 🖃 🖃

DEENE
Deene Park
NN17 3EW (0.5m off A43, between Kettering & Stamford)
☎01780 450223 & 450278
Fax 01780 450282
Mainly 16th-century house of great architectural importance and historical interest. Home of the Brudenell family since 1514, including the 7th Earl of Cardigan who led the Charge of the Light Brigade. Large lake and park. Extensive gardens with old-fashioned roses, rare trees and shrubs.
Open BH's (Sun & Mon) Etr, May, Spring & Aug; Jun-Aug, Sun 2-5. Party 20+ by prior arrangement with House Keeper.
❄*Admission fee payable.*
P 🍴 & *(ramps to Old Kitchen and gardens) toilets for disabled shop* ⚑ *(ex guide dogs in garden only)*

Kirby Hall
NN17 3EN (on unclass road off A43, 4m NE of Corby)
☎01536 203230
A beautiful Elizabethan manor house boasting an unusual richness and variety of architectural detail in the Renaissance style. The extensive gardens were among the finest in England at their peak during the 17th century.
Open all year, Apr-Oct, daily 10-6 (or dusk if earlier); Nov-Mar, wknds 10-4. Closed 24-26 Dec & 1 Jan.
£2.30 (ch £1.20, concessions £1.70).
Personal stereo tours included in admission.
P & *shop* ⚑ *(in certain areas)* ⚑

DESBOROUGH
Shire Falconry Centre
West Lodge Rural Centre, West Lodge, Pipewell Rd NN14 2SH
☎01536 760666
Learn about birds of prey at the Centre, where their goals are education, conservation and preservation through a captive breeding programme, in order to safeguard the future of these beautiful creatures. Free-flying demonstrations are given throughout the day at regular intervals. Hawking Days, 'Hands-On Days' and courses are offered, giving you a chance to learn more about the birds. Please telephone for details.
Open all year, daily 10-5 (Nov-Feb weekends only)
❄£2.50 (ch £1, pen £1.50)
P 🍴 & *toilets for disabled shop* ⚑

HOLDENBY
Holdenby House Gardens & Falconry Centre
NN6 8DJ (7m NW of Northampton, off A50 or A428)
☎01604 770074
Fax 01604 770962
Once the largest house in England. Built to impress Elizabeth I. Subsequently the palace and prison of Charles I. Destroyed by a Parliamentarian. Restored in 1870 by the current owner's great-great-grandmother. Today the House, Garden, Falconry centre, Armoury, 17th century Farmstead and rare breeds of farm animal bring this unique and varied history alive. Homemade teas and shop (Sundays) Children's farm and play area. Ring for details of special events.
Open; Gardens & Falconry Centre Etr-end Sep, daily 2-6, Closed Sat. House open BH Mon 1-6 except May 5th.
❄*Gardens & Falconry Centre £2.75 (ch £1.75, pen £2.25). House, Gardens & Falconry Centre £3.75 (ch £2).*
P 🍴 & *(gravel paths with ramps) toilets for disabled shop*

Although Lyveden New Bield appears to be a ruin, it is actually the unfinished shell of a garden lodge dating from 1600.

KETTERING
Alfred East Gallery
Sheep St NN16 OAN
☎ 01536 534381 Fax 01536 534370
National, regional and local art, craft and photography are all displayed in around 20 exhibitions held each year at this well-run gallery. A collection of paintings by Sir Alfred East RA and Thomas Cooper Gotch on view by appointment, when not on display. There will also be a series of lunchtime concerts and talks on selected Fridays throughout the year. Exhibitions for 98 include: Pop Prints - 28 March-25 April, Picasso's Etchings - 29 August-26 September. Ring for brochure.
Open all year, Mon-Sat 9.30-5. (Closed BHs).
Free.
P *(300 yds)* ♿ shop ⌛

LYVEDEN NEW BIELD
Lyveden New Bield
PE8 5AT (4m SW Oundle via A427)
☎ 01832 205358
The 'New Bield', or 'new building', is an unfinished shell of a garden lodge dating from around 1600. It was designed by Sir Thomas Thresham to symbolise the Passion. The shape is a Greek cross, on which a frieze shows the cross, crown of thorns and other 'emblems of the Passion'. Even the building's dimensions are symbolic.
Open daily. Party by arrangement with the custodian.
£1.70 (ch 80p).
🚗 ⌛

NASSINGTON
Prebendal Manor House
PE8 6QG
☎ 01780 782575
Dating from the early 13th century and steeped in history, the house is the oldest manor in Northamptonshire. Included in the visit are the 15th-century dovecote and tithe barn museum. Unique to the region are the re-created 14th

century medieval garden. Home made teas are served in the Tithe Barn. Special events: Intoduction to Medieval Gardens and Herbs Day School (18 July), pre-booking essential.
Open May-June & Sept Sun & Wed 2-6pm. July & Aug Sun, Tue & Sat 1-6pm. BH Mon (closed Xmas)
£3.50 (ch £1). Party 20+.
P ⌛ ♿ *(ramps)* ⌛

NORTHAMPTON
Central Museum & Art Gallery
Guildhall Rd NN1 1DP
☎ 01604 39415 Fax 01604 238720
The Central Museum and Art Gallery reflects Northampton's proud standing as Britain's boot and shoe capital by housing a collection of boots and shoes which is considered one of the finest in the world. Fascinating footwear worn throughout the ages is just one of the attractions in the museum. Other displays include the History of Northampton, Decorative Arts , the Art Gallery, and special temporary exhibitions including: Natural Sciences (28 March-14 June), Justin Capp & Carry Akroyd (27 June-26 July), Philip Cox (8 Aug-13 Sept), 15th-18th century Italian Art (26 Sept-15 Nov), 85th Northampton Town & Country Art Society (28 Nov-3 Jan 1999).
Open all year, Mon-Sat 10-5, Sun 2-5. (Closed 25 & 26 Dec & 1 Jan). Please telephone to confirm times.
Free.
P *(200 yds)* ♿ *(wheelchairs available, large print catalogues) toilets for disabled shop* ⌛

ROCKINGHAM
Rockingham Castle
LE16 8TH (2m N of Corby, on A6003. Vehicle entrance S of junction A6003/A6116)
☎ 01536 770240
Set on a hill overlooking three counties, Rockingham Castle was built by William the Conqueror. The site of the original keep is now a rose garden, but the outline

The intriguing Triangular Lodge was built in Rushton by Sir Thomas Tresham as an expression of his Roman Catholicism.

of the Curtain Wall remains as do the foundations of the Norman Hall, and the twin towers of the gatehouse. The castle was a royal residence for 450 years. Then, in the 16th century Henry VIII granted it to Edward Watson, and the Watson family have lived there ever since.
The current building is basically Elizabethan, but every century since the 11th has had an influence somewhere, whether in architecture, furniture or works of art. James I was entertained here in 1603 and Charles Dickens, a frequent visitor, dedicated *David Copperfield* to the owners.
Open Etr Sun-18 Oct, Thu, Sun, BH Mon & following Tue (also Tues in Aug) 1-5. Grounds open at 11.30 am on Sun & BH Mon.
✲ *£4 (ch £2.60 & pen £3.60). Family ticket £11. Party. Grounds only £2.60.*
P ⌛ ♿ *(may alight at entrance, ramped) shop*

RUSHTON
Triangular Lodge
NN14 1RP
☎ 01536 710761
Almost every detail of the lodge built by Sir Thomas Tresham in 1593 has a meaning. Sir Thomas was a devout Roman Catholic, imprisoned for his beliefs, who built Rushton Triangular Lodge as an expression of his faith. The triangular shapes, inscriptions and emblems symbolise the Holy Trinity and the Mass, often through puns and word-play.
Open Apr-1 Nov, daily 10-6 (or dusk if earlier).
£1.30 (ch 70p, concessions £1).
♿ ⌛ ♿

STOKE BRUERNE
Canal Museum
NN12 7SE (4m S junc 15 M1)
☎ 01604 862229 Fax 01604 862229
The three storeys of a former corn mill have been converted to hold a marvellous collection of bygones from over two centuries of the canals. The museum is near a flight of locks on the Grand Union Canal. Among the hundreds of exhibits is the reconstructed interior of a traditional narrow boat, complete with furniture, crockery, brassware and traditional art. A display on local canals

includes a new large working model. There are genuine working narrowboats on show and the opportunity for a boat trip through the mile-long Blisworth Tunnel nearby.
Open Nov-Etr, Tue-Sun 10-4; Etr-Oct daily 10-6. (Closed Xmas).
P *(charged)* ♿ *(ramps radar key) toilets for disabled shop* ⌛
Details not confirmed for 1998

SULGRAVE
Sulgrave Manor
Manor Rd OX17 2SD (off B4525)
☎ 01295 760205 Fax 01295 760205
Sulgrave Manor was bought in 1539 by Lawrence Washington, wool merchant and twice Mayor of Northampton. It was here that George Washington's ancestors lived until 1656 when his great grandfather, John, emigrated to Virginia. The house that exists today is somewhat different from the one Lawrence Washington bought. His was larger, and much of the present house is a 20th-century restoration. Original parts include the porch, a screens passage, the great hall and the great Chamber. Over the porch is carved the original of the American flag, with three stars and two stripes plus Elizabeth I's arms. Inside there are many relics of George Washington, such as his velvet coat, a lock of hair, documents and portraits. Special events for 1998: (10-13 March) Easter Customs. (1-4 May) Georgian Living History. (23-31 May) Stars, Stripes & Stitches. (14 June) Dames Day. (27 June-5 July) Tudor Living History. (14-16 August) Outdoor Theatre Production. (29-31 August) The 55th Infantry American Civil War Re-enactment. (12-13 September) The Vikings. (26 September-4 October) Melford hys Companie Tudor Re-enactment. (17-18 October) Apple Day. (5-6, 12-13, 19-20 & 27-31 December) A Tudor Christmas.
Open Apr-Oct, Mon-Fri (ex Wed) 2-5.30, Sat, Sun & BH 10.30-1 & 2-5.30; Mar, Nov & Dec, Sat & Sun only 10.30-1 & 2-4.30; Other times by appointment. Closed 25-26 Dec & Jan.
£3.75 (ch £2). Party 12+. Special event days £4.50 (ch £2.25). Family ticket £12. Party 12+.
P ⌛ ♿ *shop garden centre* ⌛

WEEDON BEC
Old Dairy Farm Centre
Upper Stowe NN7 4SH (2m S of Weedon off A5)
☎01327 340525
Housed in a range of prize-winning converted 19th-century farm buildings and built around a working arable and sheep farm, the centre offers a wide range of shops, craft workshops and demonstration/conference room. There are many animals on view including some rare breed pigs, geese, donkeys, ducks, goats and various breeds of sheep.
Open 10 Jan-28 Feb, daily 10-4.30; Mar-24 Dec, daily 10-5.30.
🅿 ⬛ ✖ *licensed* ♿ *toilets for disabled shop* 🐾
Details not confirmed for 1998

NORTHUMBERLAND

ALNWICK
Alnwick Castle
NE66 1NQ
☎01665 510777 & 603942 wknds
Fax 01665 510876
Described by the Victorians as 'The Windsor of the North', Alnwick Castle is the main seat of the Duke of Northumberland whose family, the Percys, have lived here since 1309. This border stronghold has survived many battles, but now peacefully dominates the picturesque market town of Alnwick, overlooking landscape designed by Capability Brown. The stern, medieval exterior belies the treasure house within, furnished in palatial Renaissance style, with paintings by Titian, Van Dyck and Canaletto, fine furniture and an exquisite collection of Meissen china. The Regiment Museum of Royal Northumberland Fusiliers is housed in the Abbot's Tower of the Castle, while the Postern Tower contains a collection of early British and Roman relics. Other attractions include the Percy State Coach, the dungeon, the gun terrace and the grounds, which offer peaceful walks and superb views over the surrounding countryside. Events this year will include an Easter weekend craft, design and fashion show, a vintage car rally and Alnwick fair at the end of June, and an international music festival at the beginning of August; for a full programme of events and dates please telephone.
Open Etr-Sep, daily ex Fri, 11-5 (House noon-5). Last admission 4.15. Open BH's incl Good Fri.
Freedom ticket £5.75 (ch £3.50, pen £5.25). Family ticket £15. Grounds only £4 incl parking. Party 12+.
🅿 ⬛ ♿ *(Castle lift for those able to walk a little) toilets for disabled shop* 🐾
Cards: 🪙 💳

BAMBURGH
Bamburgh Castle
NE69 7DF (A1 Belford by-pass, East on B1342 to Bamburgh)
☎01668 214515 & 214208
Fax 01668 214060
Rising up dramatically on a rocky outcrop, Bamburgh Castle is a huge, square Norman castle. Restored in the 19th century by Lord Armstrong, it has an impressive hall and an armoury with a large collection of armour from HM Tower of London. Guide services are available.
Open daily, Apr-Oct, from 11-5. (last admission 4.30pm) Other times by prior arrangement.
✱£3.50 (ch £1.50 & pen £2.50). Party 15+.
🅿 *(charged)* ⬛ ♿ *shop* 🐾

Grace Darling Museum
Radcliffe Rd NE69 7AE
☎01668 214465
Pictures, documents and other reminders of the heroine are on display, including the boat in which Grace Darling and her father, keeper of Longstone Lighthouse, Farne Islands, rescued nine survivors from the wrecked 'SS Forfarshire' in 1838.
Open Etr-Sep, daily 10-5. Oct 12-4 or by appointment at other times.
🅿 *(400yds)* ♿ *(ramps on request) shop* 🐾
Details not confirmed for 1998

BARDON MILL
Vindolanda (Chesterholm)
Vindolanda Trust NE47 7JN (signposted from A69 or B6318)
☎01434 344277
Fax 01434 344060
Vindolanda was a Roman fort and frontier town, with remains dating back to the 3rd and 4th centuries. It was started well before Hadrian's Wall, and became a base for 500 soldiers. The headquarters building is well preserved, and a special feature is a full-scale reconstruction of Hadrian's turf and stone wall, complete with turret and gate tower. The civilian settlement lay just west of the fort and has been excavated. A vivid idea of life for both civilians and soldiers can be gained at the excellent museum in the country house of Chesterholm nearby. It has displays and reconstructions, and its exhibits include such homely finds as sandals, shoes and a soldier's sewing kit. There are also formal gardens. An open-air museum with Roman Temple, shop, house and Northumbrian croft opened recently.
Open daily from 10 am, all facilities mid Feb-mid Nov. closed mid Nov-early Feb.
£3.50 (ch £2.50, student & pen £2.90). Party.
🅿 ⬛ ♿ *toilets for disabled shop* 🐾
Cards: 🪙 💳

BELSAY
Belsay Hall, Castle and Gardens
NE20 0DX (on A696)
☎01661 881636
Belsay Castle, with its splendid turrets and battlements, dates from 1370 and was home for generations of the Middleton family, until they built the Jacobean manor house beside it, and then the magnificent Grecian-style Hall. Aside from the facinating buildings, Belsay has wonderful gardens and an excellent site exhibition.
Open all year, daily Apr-Oct 10-6 (or dusk if earlier), Nov-Mar, daily 10-4 (or dusk if earlier). Closed 24-26 Dec & 1 Jan.
£3.60 (ch £1.80, concessions £2.70).
🅿 ✖ ♿ *toilets for disabled shop* 🐾 *(in certain areas)* ⚏

BERWICK-UPON-TWEED
Berwick Barracks, Museum & Art Gallery
(on the Parade, off Church St, Berwick town centre)
☎01289 304493
Berwick is one of the outstanding fortified towns in Europe. The Elizabethan ramparts are some of the best artillery defences in England, and the barracks have changed little since 1721. The award-winning By Beat of Drum exhibition covers 200 years of the way soldiers lived and fought. The museum of the King's Own Scottish Borders uses audio-visual displays to bring the past vividly to life, and the Art Gallery houses the important Burrell collection.
Open all year, Apr-Oct daily 10-6 (or dusk if earlier); Nov-Mar Wed-Sun 10-4, closed 1-2pm.
£2.50 (ch £1.30, concessions £1.90).
🅿 ♿ *shop* 🐾 ⚏

Paxton House
TD15 1SZ (3m from A1 Berwick-upon-Tweed bypass on B6461 Kelso road)
☎01289 386291
Fax 01289 386660
Paxton House was built in 1758 for the Laird of Wedderburn in anticipation of his marriage to the natural daughter of Frederick the Great of Prussia. Unfortunately the marriage did not take place but the house still stands. It is a fine example of 18th-century neo-Palladian architecture having been designed by John and James Adam. Much of the house is furnished by Chippendale and the picture gallery is the largest private picture gallery in Scotland. The house is in 80 acres of gardens, parklands and woodlands beside the River Tweed, and the grounds include an exciting adventure playground. Special events include: Antiques Fair (March), Easter Egg Hunt (Easter Sunday), Paxton Craft & Country Fair (June 6-7).
Open daily from Good Fri-Oct. House & gallery noon-5, grounds 10-sunset. Last tour of house 4.15pm.
House & Grounds £4 (adult concessions £3.25). Family ticket £10.
🅿 ✖ *licensed* ♿ *(lifts to main areas of house, parking close to reception) toilets for disabled* 🐾
Cards: 💳 💳

CAMBO
Wallington House Walled Garden & Grounds
NE61 4AR
☎01670 774283
Dating from the 17th and 18th centuries, the house is set in a great moorland estate of over 12,000 acres. It is famed for its delicate plasterwork, including fine porcelain work and rare British pieces. There are also displays of dolls' houses and model soldiers, and the kitchen is filled with Victorian equipment. In the 19th century Ruskin and other writers and artists came here as guests of Sir William and Lady Trevelyan, who were renowned for their eccentricity and charm. One of the artists, William Bell Scott, painted the dramatic murals in the Central Hall. The gardens were partly laid out by Capability Brown, and include formal and woodland areas, and a conservatory with magnificent fuchsias. Please contact for details of special events, which will include open air concerts and theatre productions.
Open: House Apr-Sep, daily (ex Tue) 1-5.30, Oct-1 Nov, daily (ex Tue)1-4.30. Last admission half hour before closing. Walled garden Apr-Oct, daily 10-7 or dusk; Nov-Mar, 10-4 or dusk if earlier. Grounds open all year.
House, walled garden & grounds £4.30. Walled gardens & grounds only £2.30. Party.
🅿 ✖ ♿ *(Vessa Ventura scooter, braille guide) toilets for disabled shop garden centre* 🐾 *(ex on lead in grounds)* 🐕
Cards: 🪙 💳 💳 💳

CARRAWBROUGH
Roman Wall (Mithraic Temple)
(on B6318)
A farmer found the Mithraic Temple in 1949. It was excavated to reveal three altars to Mithras which date from the third century AD. They are now in the Museum of Antiquities in Newcastle, but there are copies on the site. The temple is on the line of the Roman wall near the fort of Brocolitia.
Open any reasonable time.
Free.
🅿 ⚏

CHILLINGHAM
Chillingham Castle
NE66 5NJ (signposted from A1 & A697)
☎01668 215359 & 215390
Fax 01668 215463
This remarkable castle fortress with its alarming dungeons and torture chamber, owned by Earl Grey and his descendants continuously since about 1200, is now undergoing restoration - and not only of stone and plasterwork, for state rooms are being brought back to life with tapestries, furniture, arms and armour. Romantic grounds laid out by Sir Jeffry Wyatville - fresh from his triumphs at Windsor Castle - command views over the Cheviots and include topiary gardens and woodland walks as well as parkland and a lake. Weddings, private functions and meals can be arranged, and fishing is available. Please ring for details of special events. ➜

Chillingham Castle

The home of Sir Humphry Wakefield Bt
Chillingham (Near Wooler)
Northumberland NE66 5NJ
Tel: 01668 215359

**ANCIENT CASTLE · CHILDREN MOSTLY FREE · LOTS TO SEE,
EVEN A TORTURE CHAMBER · LAKE · GARDENS ·
TEAROOMS · SHOP · MOUNTAIN VIEWS**

Open Good Friday-Easter Monday, May 1-September 30, 12noon-5pm
(Closed Tuesdays May and June). Or anytime by appointment for Groups.

Admission Adults £3.90, OAPs £3.75, Children FREE when accompanied,
Parties (over 10) £3.30 per head. Guided Tours available.

OCCASIONAL HOLIDAY LETS AVAILABLE WITHIN THE CASTLE

Open Etr wknd & May-Sep, daily (ex closed Tue in May, Jun & Sep) 12-5 (Last admission 5.30pm). Other times by prior arrangement.
❋*£3.75 (ch free with paying adult max 5, pen £3.50). Party 10+.*
P ⬛ ✗ *licensed & shop* ❀

Chillingham Wild Cattle Park
NE66 5NW (off B6348)
☎01668 215250
The park at Chillingham boasts an extraordinary survival: a herd of wild white cattle descended from animals trapped in the park when the wall was built in the 13th century; they are the sole surviving pure-bred examples of their breed in the world. Binoculars are recommended for a close view. Visitors are accompanied into the park by the Warden.
Open Apr-Oct, daily 10-12 & 2-5, Sun 2-5. (Closed Tue).
£3 (ch 50p & pen £2.50). Parties 20+
P ❀

CORBRIDGE
Corbridge Roman Site
(0.5m NW on minor road - signposted)
☎01434 632349
The remains of a Roman 'Corstopitum', built around AD210, include granaries, portico columns and the probable site of legionary headquarters. Finds from excavations at the site are displayed in a museum on the site.
Open all year, Apr-Oct, daily 10-6 (or dusk if earlier in Oct); Nov-Mar, Wed-Sun 10-4 (or dusk if earlier, closed 1-2pm). (Closed 24-26 Dec & 1 Jan).
£2.70 (ch £1.40, concessions £2.00).
P & ❀ *(in certain areas)* ♿

EMBLETON
Dunstanburgh Castle
NE66 3XF (1.5m E on footpaths from Craster or Embleton)
☎01665 576231
The skeletal ruins of the huge castle stand on cliffs 100ft above the North Sea. It was partly built by John of Gaunt, but was in ruins by Tudor times. Its setting has made it a favourite with artists, and Turner painted it three times.
Open all year, Apr-Oct, daily 10-6 (or dusk if earlier); 10-4; Nov-Mar, Wed-Sun 10-4 (or dusk if earlier). Closed 24-26 Dec & 1 Jan.
£1.70 (ch 90p, concessions £1.30)
P *(charged)* ♿

FORD
Heatherslaw Corn Mill
TD12 4TJ (signposted from A697 & A1 from Berwick-upon-Tweed)
☎01890 820338
Fax 01890 820384
This beautifully restored 19th-century water-powered double corn mill is in daily use, and you can see local wheat milled by traditional methods using the original machinery. Everything is visible, from the huge wooden water wheel to the slowly grinding burr stone, and you can taste the full flavour of the flour in delicious biscuits, bread and cakes produced by local bakers. There are also an exhibition area and gift shop. 10 May is National Mills Day.
Open Mar-Sep 10-6; Oct-Nov 10-5. Winter by arrangement.
£2 (ch & pen £1). Family ticket £5.50.
P ⬛ & *(Braille guide plus tactile facility) shop* ❀

Lady Waterford Hall
(signposted from A697, N of Wooler & A1 Berwick-upon-Tweed)
☎01890 820224
Fax 01890 820384
Commissioned as a school in 1860 by Louisa Anne, Marchioness of Waterford, this beautiful Victorian building was decorated with delightful murals of favourite Bible stories. Lady Waterford, a leading light among female artists, spent 21 years painting these outstanding murals, choosing the children of the village and their parents as models; many of her smaller works are also displayed in the gallery.
Open Mar-Nov, daily 10.30-12.30 & 1.30-5.30. Open by appointment in winter.
£1.25 (ch15 free, pen 75p).
P & *shop*

HOLY ISLAND (LINDISFARNE)
Lindisfarne Castle
TD15 2SH
☎01289 389244
The 16th-century castle was restored by Sir Edwin Lutyens in 1903 for the owner of *Country Life* magazine. The austere outside walls belie the Edwardian comfort within, and there is a little garden designed by Gertrude Jekyll.
Open Apr-29 Oct, daily (closed Fri ex Good Fri) 1-5.30. Last admission 5pm. Castle may open at the earlier time 11-5 in Jul & Aug. Island not accessible two hours before & four hours after high tide. Other times by arrangement with Administrator please phone for details.
£4. Family ticket £10.
P *(1m in village)* ❀ 🐾

Lindisfarne Priory
TD15 2RX (Can only be reached at low tide across a causeway. Tide tables posted at each end of the causeway)
☎01289 389200
St Aidan and monks from Iona founded a monastery here in the 7th century and from it spread Christianity to much of Northern England. They also produced the beautifully illuminated Lindisfarne Gospels (now in the British Library), but abandoned the monastery because of Viking raids in the 9th century. The beautiful priory ruins on Lindisfarne today date from the 11th century, and the award-winning exhibition in the museum tells the history of this magical site. The island is reached by a causeway at low tide: tide tables are posted at each end of the causeway, or telephone the custodian on the above number.
Open all year, Apr-Oct, daily 10-6 (or dusk if earlier); Nov-Mar, daily 10-4 (or dusk if earlier). Subject to tides. Closed 24-26 Dec & 1 Jan.
£2.70 (ch £1.40, concessions £2)
shop ❀ *(in certain areas)* ♿

HOUSESTEADS
Housesteads Roman Fort
Bardon Mills (2.5m NE of Bardon Mill on B6318)
☎01434 344363
Housesteads was the Roman fort of *Vercovicium*. It has a spectacular site on Hadrian's Wall, and is also one of the best preserved Roman forts. It covers five acres, including the only known Roman hospital in Britain, and a 24-seater latrine with a flushing tank. There is also a museum.
Open all year, Apr-Oct, daily 10-6; Nov-Mar, daily 10-4. (Closed 24-26 Dec & 1 Jan).
❋*£2.70 (ch 16 £1.40, concessions £2). Party reductions in winter.*
P *(0.25m from fort) shop* ❀ ♿

LONGFRAMLINGTON
Brinkburn Priory
NE65 8AS (off B6344)
☎01665 570628
The priory was founded in 1135 for the canons of the Augustinian order, and stands on a bend of the River Coquet. After the Dissolution of the Monasteries it fell into disrepair, but was restored in 1858; remaining medieval fittings include the font, double piscina and some grave slabs.
Open Apr-Oct, daily 10-6.
£1.50 (ch 80p, concessions £1.10).
P ❀ *(in certain areas)* ♿

NORHAM
Castle
TD15 2JY
☎01289 382329
One of the strongest border fortresses, this castle has one of the finest Norman keeps in the country and overlooks the River Tweed.
Open Apr-Oct, 10-6 (or dusk if earlier).
❋*£1.70 (ch 90p, concessions £1.30)*
P & ❀ ♿

PRUDHOE
Prudhoe Castle
NE42 6NA (on minor road off A695)
☎01661 833459
Standing on the River Tyne, this 12th-to 14th-century castle was the stronghold of the d'Umfravelles and Percys. The keep stands in the inner bailey and a notable gatehouse guards the outer bailey. Access is to the Pele Yard only.
Open Apr-Oct, daily 10-6 (or dusk if earlier).
£1.70 (ch 90p, concessions £1.30).
P *shop* ❀ *(in certain areas)* ♿

ROTHBURY
Cragside House, Garden & Grounds
(1m N of Rothbury, off A697 & B6341)
☎01669 620333 & 620150
This splendid Victorian masterpiece was built for Sir William (later the first Lord) Armstrong in stages, between 1864 and 1895. It was designed for him by the architect Richard Norman Shaw and the interior of the house reflects the taste and style of both its architect and its owner. The huge drawing room has a curved glass roof and 10-ton marble-lined inglenook. This was the first house in the world to be lit by electricity generated by water-power. The grounds, now 1000 acres of country park, were transformed by Lord Armstrong. He planted seven million trees, diverted streams and created lakes, a waterfall and winding paths. The formal garden includes greenhouses, Italian terraces, a rose loggia and an orchard house.
Open, Grounds: Apr-1 Nov, daily ex Mon 10.30-7; Weekends & selected days in Nov & Dec 10.30-4. House: daily (ex Mon, open BH Mon's) 1-5.30, last admission 4.45pm. Gardens Apr-1 Nov, daily ex Mon 10.30-6.30. Weekends & selected days in Nov & Dec.
House, Garden & Grounds & Visitor Centre £6. Garden, Grounds & Visitor Centre only £3.80. Family ticket for House, Garden & Grounds £15. Party.
P ⬛ ✗ *licensed & fishing pier braille guide toilets for disabled shop* ❀ *(ex in grounds on lead)* 🐾
Cards: 🟦 ◼ ▭ ▭

The huge mass of Dunstanburgh Castle is dwarfed by the rugged coastline. The castle has been in ruins ever since Tudor times.

WALWICK
Chesters Roman Fort & Museum
(0.5m W of Chollerford on B6318))
☎01434 681379
One of the Roman forts on Hadrian's Wall is now in the park of Chesters, an 18th-century mansion. The fort named *Cilurnum* housed 500 soldiers and covered nearly 6 acres. The excavations were started in the 19th century by the owner of Chesters, and have revealed a great deal about life in a Roman fort. A large wall and six gatehouses were built to defend the fort, but evidence revealed that it was destroyed and rebuilt three times. The standard of living appears to have been high: water was brought in by aqueduct, the commandant had underfloor heating in his house, and the soldiers' bath house had hot, cold, dry or steam baths, and latrines. The remains of the bath house are very substantial. There is a museum exhibiting artefacts from the site.
Open all year, Apr-Sep, daily 9.30-6; Oct, daily 10-dusk; Nov-Mar, daily 10-4 (or dusk if earlier). Closed 24-26 Dec & 1 Jan.
£2.70 (ch £1.40, concessions £2).
P ⬛ & shop ⌘ (in certain areas) ⇥

WARKWORTH
Warkworth Castle
NE66 OUJ
☎01665 711423
The castle is situated on a steep bank of the River Coquet, and dominates the town of Warkworth. It is a splendid ruin with its restored 15th-century keep and early 13th-century curtain wall. Once home of the turbulent Percy family, Sir Henry Percy (Harry Hotspur) was immortalised by Shakespeare in *Henry IV*. Nearby the castle is the 14th-century bridge over the river, with a rare bridge tower. This can now only be used by pedestrians.
Open all year, Apr-Oct, daily 10-6 (or dusk if earlier); Nov-Mar, daily 10-4 (or dusk if earlier, closed 1-2pm). Closed 24-26 Dec & 1 Jan.
£2.70 (ch £1.40, concessions £2)
P & ⌘ (in certain areas) ⇥

Warkworth Hermitage
☎01665 711423
Upstream from Warkworth Castle is the Hermitage, a refuge dug into the steep rockface of the riverbank by a 14th-century hermit. It consists of a chapel and two chambers to live in. The hermitage was occupied until the 16th century. Nearby is Coquet island, which was also the home of hermit monks.
Open Apr-Sep, Wed, Sun & BH's 11-5.
£1.50 (ch 80p, concessions £1.10)
P & ⌘ ⇥

NOTTINGHAMSHIRE

EASTWOOD
D H Lawrence Birthplace
8A Victoria St NG16 3AW (follow signs on A610)
☎01773 717353
Fax 01773 713509
D H Lawrence was born here on 11 September 1885, and the town and its surroundings influenced his writing throughout his life. The carefully restored house offers an insight into the author's early childhood and is also a good example of a Victorian working class home. Audio-visual presentations are held, and two new exhibition rooms show a model of *The Country of My Heart* and Lawrence's travels round the world. There are craft workshops adjacent.
Open all year, Apr-Oct, daily 10-5; Nov-Mar, daily 10-4. (Closed 24 Dec-1 Jan).
Evenings by arrangement only.
£1.75 (concessions £1)
P (100yds) (3 hour stay) shop ⌘
Cards: 🌑 🌑

EDWINSTOWE
Sherwood Forest Country Park & Visitor Centre
NG21 9HN (on B6034 N of village between A6075 and A616)
☎01623 823202 & 824490
Fax 01623 823202
At the heart of the Robin Hood legend is his original home Sherwood Forest, scene of many an outlaw tale. Today it is

There are over 300 acres of grounds at Newstead Abbey, once the home of Lord Byron. They include extensive water gardens.

a country park and visitor centre with 450 acres of ancient oaks and shimmering silver birches. Waymarked pathways guide visitors through the forest in whose midst stands the mighty 'Major Oak' - said to be Robin's favourite tree hideout. A colourful exhibition, 'Robin Hood's Sherwood Forest' can be seen in the Visitor Centre. A year round programme of events and activities, including the spectacular Robin Hood Festival, all bring the natural beauty and colourful history of the forest to life.
Country Park: open daily dawn to dusk.
Visitor Centre: open daily 10.30-5 (4.30pm Nov-Mar)
Admission free but car parking charges apply at weekends & BHs Easter-Oct, daily during summer school holidays.
P ⬛ & toilets for disabled shop

FARNSFIELD
White Post Modern Farm Centre
NG22 8HL (1m W)
☎01623 882977 & 882026 Fax 01623 883499
This National Award-winning working farm gives an introduction to a variety of modern farming methods. It explains how farms work, with exhibits such as llamas, deer, pigs, cows, snails, quails, snakes and fish. A kennel is provided for dogs. There is also lots to see indoors including the owl houses, incubator room, mousetown and a reptile house. There will be daily Nativity plays before Christmas. The Pet Centre introduces a brand new concept in pet education. Little Farmer Club pre-school group (autumn and winter term time), daily Farm Animal show, (summer).
Open all year, Mon-Fri 10-5. Wknds & BH's 10-6.
£3.95 (ch 4-16 £2.95, under 4 free, pen & people with special needs £2.95). Party 10+.
P ⬛ & (sign language, free hire wheelchairs, book if more than 6) toilets for disabled shop ⌘
Cards: 🌑 🌑 🌑 🌑 ⑤

HAUGHTON
World of Robin Hood
Haughton Farm DN22 8DZ (on B6387 just outside Walesby, signposted off A1)
☎01623 860210 Fax 01623 836003
Medieval history is brought to life in an adventure of sound and vision, taking the visitor back through time to the 12th century complete with sights, sounds and smells. Journey through the Crusades fought by King Richard I, to the life and times of Robin Hood, which includes a visit to a medieval market place - complete with waifs and wandering chickens. Venture into 'Robin Hood in Fairyland' where you will find Robin and the sheriff's men. Also visit the World of Owls and come face to face with our feathered friends.
Open 10.30-4, Aug 9-6. Telephone for winter opening times.
✳*£3.95 (ch & pen £2.95, under 5's free)*
P ⬛ ✗ licensed & toilets for disabled shop ⌘
Cards: 🌑 🌑

NEWARK-ON-TRENT
Millgate Museum of Social & Folk Life
48 Millgate NG24 4TS
☎01636 79403 Fax 01636 613279
Fascinating exhibitions - recreated streets, shops and houses in period settings. The museum displays illustrate the working and domestic life of local people, from Victorian times to 1950. The mezzanine gallery, home to a number of temporary exhibitions showing the work of local artists, designers and photographers.
Open all year, Mon-Fri 10-5, Sat & Sun & BH 1-5. Last admission 4.30.
Free.
P (250yds) & toilets for disabled shop ⌘

Newark Air Museum
The Airfield, Winthorpe NG24 2NY (easy access from A1, A46, A17 & Newark relief road, follow tourism signs)
☎01636 707170 Fax 01636 707170 ➡

The Nottingham and Beeston Canal

A diverse collection of transport, training and reconnaisance aircraft, jet fighters, bombers and helicopters, now numbering more than forty. An Undercover Aircraft Display Hall (twenty exhibits) and an Engine Hall make the museum an all-weather attraction. Everything is displayed around a WWII airfield dispersal. Various special events are planned (including an aviation car boot sale on 9th May) please ring for details.
Open all year, Mar-Sep, Mon-Fri 10-5, Sat & Sun 10-6; Oct-Feb, daily 10-4. (Closed 24-26 Dec). Other times by appointment.
✱*£3.50 (ch £2, pen £2.75). Family ticket £9. Party 10+.*
🅿 🅿 & *toilets for disabled shop*
Cards: 🔳 🔳 🔳 🔳 🔳 🔳

Vina Cooke Museum of Dolls & Bygone Childhood
The Old Rectory, Cromwell NG23 6JE (5m N of Newark off A1)
☎*01636 821364*
All kinds of childhood memorabilia are displayed in this 17th-century house: prams, toys, dolls' houses, costumes and a large collection of Victorian and Edwardian dolls including Vina Cooke hand-made character dolls. There will be an Easter Monday (13 April) extravaganza from 11am to 5pm including Morris dancing, puppet shows, craft stalls, displays etc.
Open all year, Tue-Thu 10.30-12 & 2-5. Sat, Sun & BH Mon 10.30-5. Mon, Fri & other times open by appointment.
£2.50 (ch £1, pen £2).
🅿 & *shop*

NEWSTEAD
Newstead Abbey
NG15 8GE (off A60)
☎*01623 793557 Fax 01623 797136*
This beautiful historic house, set in extensive parklands, is best known as the home of the poet, Lord Byron, who made the house and its ghostly legends famous. Visitors can see Byron's own rooms, mementoes of the poet and other splendidly decorated rooms which date from medieval to Victorian times. The grounds of over 300 acres include waterfalls, ponds, water gardens and Japanese gardens. Special events include

outdoor theatre and opera, Christmas events and Ghost Tours. Please telephone for details of Christmas Music and Storytelling Evening in December (not suitable for children under 10).
Open: Grounds all year, daily 9-dusk (ex last Fri in Nov); House Apr-Sep, daily 12-6. Last admission 5pm
✱*House & Grounds £3.50 (ch £1, pen & students £2). Grounds only £1.70 (concessions £1).*
🅿 🅿 ✗ *licensed & (audio tour for visually impaired, mobility car for loan) toilets for disabled shop*

Brewhouse Yard Museum
Castle Boulevard NG7 1FB
☎*0115 915 3600 Fax 0115 915 3601*
Housed in 17th-century cottages on a two-acre site with unusual local plants, the museum depicts everyday life in Nottingham over the past 300 years. Thousands of locally made or used objects are shown in a mixture of period rooms, re-created shops - including a 'between-the-wars' shopping street - and displays giving an insight into the everyday and special events that make up the lives of the people in Nottingham past and present. Rock Cottage houses a schoolroom and toyshop of the 1930s. Caves behind the houses, used in the past as air raid shelters as well as for

storage and cooking, are now part of the museum. Victorian May Day Celebrations on May Day Bank Holiday. Contact the museum for further details.
Open all year 10-5. (Nov-Feb 12-5). Last admission 4.45pm. (Closed 25-26 Dec). Free Mon-Fri but donations appreciated. Weekends & BH's £1.50 (concessions 80p). Family ticket £3.80. Joint ticket with Castle Museum £2 (ch £1). Family £5.
🅿 *(100yds)* & *(mobility car from Castle, wheelchairs available) toilets for disabled shop*
Cards: 🔳 🔳

Canal Museum
Canal St NG1 7ET
☎*0115 959 8835*
The history of the River Trent from the Ice Age to the present day is told in the ground and first floors and wharf of this 19th-century warehouse. Life size dioramas, models and an audio-visual presentation add impact to the displays which include local canal and river navigation, boats, bridges and archaeology.
Open all year, Wed-Sun 10-12 & 1-5.
🅿 *(400yds)* & *(wheelchairs available) toilets for disabled shop*
Details not confirmed for 1998

Castle Museum
NG1 6EL
☎*0115 915 3700 Fax 0115 915 3653*
This 17th-century building has a much restored 13th-century gateway. Now a museum and art gallery, a guided tour of the underground passages is conducted every afternoon except Sundays. A new, interactive 'Story of Nottingham' exhibition brings the history of the city alive for the visitor. Various special events are held throughout the year, with major temporary exhibitions, both historical and contemporary. There is an automated car in the grounds for disabled people. Various exhibitions are being held during the year.
Open all year, 10-5. (ex Fri Nov-Feb 12-5) Grounds 8-dusk. Closed 25 & 26 Dec. weekdays free, weekends & BH's £1.50 (ch & concessions 80p). Family ticket £3.80.
🅿 *(400 yds)* 🍴 ✗ *licensed & (chair lift, mobility car available) toilets for disabled shop*

The Caves of Nottingham
Drury Walk, Broadmarsh Centre NG1 7LS (within Broadmarsh Shopping Centre, on the first floor)
☎*0115 924 1424*
Step down into the past and explore 'Tigguo Cobac' - a city of caves. Listen to the unique audio tape as it guides you through 700-year-old man-made caves. See the medieval tannery, beer cellars, air raid shelters and the remains of Drury Hill, one of the most historic streets in Nottingham.
Open daily 10-5, Sun 11-5 (last admission 4.15pm, Sun 4pm). Closed 25 & 26 Dec. £2.95 (concessions £1.95). Family ticket £8.50.
🅿 *(charged) shop*
Cards: 🔳 🔳 🔳

The Galleries of Justice
The Shire Hall, High Pavement, Lace Market NG1 1HN
☎*0115 952 0555 Fax 0115 9520557*
Travel through more than 250 years of crime, punishment and law on this unique historic site. New for 1998 - Police Galleries - a truly arresting experience! Based in the original 1905 police station attatched to the Shire Hall complex, the Police Galleries offer a unique insight into policing through time, and includes objects from the museum's important police collection and criminal evidence from past infamous crimes . Visitors will attend a crime scene and be invited to assess the evidence through the use of forensic science, state of the art computers and eventually discover for themselves what is involved in an arrest. Be prepared for laundry duty when visiting the 1850s prison - just one of the interactive elements of the Crime and Punishment Galleries (opening late July, please telephone to confirm). See the original drying racks and copper and also the lead lined bath and changing cubicles in the bath house. Also see the transportation section and join the debate - what is prison for? Reform, punishment or rehabilitation?
Open Tues-Sun & BH Mon's Apr-Aug 10am-6pm. Sept-Mar 10am-5pm. Last admission one hour before closing. Closed 24-26 Dec.
Jan-Apr 5 £4.25 (concessions £2.95). Family ticket £11.95. Police galleries (6 Apr onwards) £3.95 (ch £3.50 concessions £3.75) Family £11.95. Police Galleries & Crime & Punishment galleries (20 July onwards) £7.95 (ch £4.95, concessions £6.95) Family £23.95.
🅿 🍴 & *(two lifts with braille control) toilets for disabled shop*
Cards: 🔳 🔳 🔳 🔳 🔳

The Lace Centre
Severns Building, Castle Rd NG1 6AA
☎*0115 941 3539*
The Lace Centre was opened in 1980 using financing from eight of Nottingham's leading lace manufacturers. Exquisite Nottingham lace fills this small building to capacity; there are even panels hanging from the beamed ceiling. There are demonstrations of lace-making on Thursdays from 2-4pm between Easter and the end of October. Situated below the Castle wall opposite the Robin Hood statue.
Open all year, Jan-Mar, daily 10-4; Apr-Dec, 10-5. Every Sun 11am-4pm. (Closed 25-26 Dec).
Free.
🅿 *(100 yds) (metered street parking)* & *shop*

The Lace Hall
High Pavement NG1 1HF
☎*0115 948 4221 Fax 0115 948 3102*
The invention and development of the world-famous Nottingham lace was explained at Lace Hall. Working machines, bobbin lace demonstrations,

Rufford Abbey
& COUNTRY PARK
Ollerton, Nottinghamshire NG22 9DF

CRAFTS SHOWCASE

Tour the restored 12th century Cistercian Abbey set in 170 acres of beautiful parklands.

EXPERIENCE:

- The New Restaurant • Gallery & Craft Centre •
- Plant & Herb Centre • Shops • and much more •

PLUS A YEAR ROUND EVENTS PROGRAMME
Centre Open From 10.30am

Easily accessible off the A1 (M)/A614 in North Nottinghamshire

Please ring (01623) 824153 for full details

Nottinghamshire **n** County Council
Leisure Services

---

period settings and talking figures created a lively and educational entertainment. The exhibition is temporarily closed for redevelopment until 1999 although the retail shop and coffee bar will remain open.
Exhibition closed for redevelopment in 1998.
No admission charges during redevelopment.
P (100yds) 🍴 ✗ licensed & (counters at lower level, lift to upper floor) toilets for disabled shop ✿

Museum of Costume & Textiles
43-51 Castle Gate NG1 6AF
☎0115 915 3500 Fax 0115 950 7182
Costume from 1730 to 1960 is displayed in appropriate room settings. Other rooms contain 17th-century costume and embroidery, dress accessories, the Lord Middleton collection and map tapestries. Knitted, woven and printed textiles are also on show, together with embroidery from Europe and Asia.
Open all year, daily 10-5. (ex Fri Nov-Feb 12-5). Closed 25-26 Dec. Under review.
Free.
P (200yds) & shop ✿

Natural History Museum
Wollaton Hall, Wollaton NG8 2AE (3m W, off A52 & A6514)
☎0115 915 3911 Fax 0115 915 3932
Standing in a large deer park, this imposing Elizabethan mansion by Robert Smythson dates back to 1580. A wide variety of displays include birds, mammals, fossils and minerals. The interactive World of Wildlife gallery is a recent addition, and the NatureQuest gallery opened in 1997. Ring for further details.
Open all year, Apr-Sep, Mon-Sat 10-4.30, Sun 1-4.30 (Fri 12-4.30 Nov-Feb) closed Christmas day & Boxing day; Park open Mon-Fri 8-dusk, Sat & Sun 9-dusk. Under review.
✱Weekdays free, weekends & BH £1.50 (concessions 80p) Family £3.80. Joint

ticket £2 (conssesions £1) Family £5. Grounds £1. Free for orange badge holders./
P (charged) & (special handling exhibition) toilets for disabled shop ✿
Cards: 🂠 ▨

Nottingham Industrial Museum
Courtyard Buildings, Wollaton Park NG8 2AE (3m W off A609 Ilkeston Rd)
☎0115 915 3910
Fax 0115 915 3941
Housed in the 18th-century stable block, displays illustrate Nottingham's industrial history, in particular those of lace and hosiery. Exhibits on the pharmaceutical industry, engineering, printing and the tobacco industry are also here. A beam (pumping) engine and heavy agricultural machinery are housed in a new extension. Victorian street furniture is displayed in a yard outside, along with a horse gin from a local coalmine. The beam engine and other engines are in steam regularly. Please contact the museum for dates and times.
Open all year, Apr-Sep, Mon-Sat 10-4.30, Sun 1-4.30; Oct-Mar, Thu-Sat 10-4.30, Sun 1.30-4.30.
Mon-Fri free. Sat, Sun & BH's £1.50 (ch 75p).
P (charged) & (hand & powered wheelchairs available) toilets for disabled shop ✿

Tales of Robin Hood
Maid Marian Way NG1 6GF
☎0115 948 3284
Fax 0115 950 1536
A marvel of special effects transporting the visitor to medieval Nottingham and the magical glades of the greenwood in search of Robin Hood. Travelling in the unique adventure cars the experience happens below, around and above you as the commentary (available in seven different languages) is piped into each car by portable compact disc players. Medieval banquets take place throughout the year and special events are held over

the summer and Bank Holiday weekends. An exclusive Christmas shop opens around November and children can experience the Medieval Christmas Grotto. Ring for further details.
Open all year, Apr-Oct 10-4.30; Nov-Mar 10-3.30.
✱£4.25 (ch £3.25, pen & students £3.75). Family ticket £12.95.
P (NCP) & (chairlift, specially adapted 'car') toilets for disabled shop ✿
Cards: 🂠 ▨ 💳 🂠 ▨ 🂠

OLLERTON
Rufford Abbey and Country Park
NG22 9DF (2m S of Ollerton, adjacent to A614)
☎01623 824153
Rufford Country Park is acres of woodland and parkland, at the heart of which stands the remains of a 12th century Cistercian Abbey. It houses an exhibition telling the story of the monastery and its later transformation into a grand country house. In the surrounding parkland, the lake is home to many species of wildlife and the formal gardens contain a variety of sculptures as well as roses and herbs. The restored Orangery was built as an open Bath House in 1730 and the stable block houses a Craft Shop and Gallery.
Open all year, Abbey and craft centre closed 25 Dec and 1 Jan.
Free.
P 🍴 ✗ licensed & (lift to craft centre) toilets for disabled shop garden centre ✿ (ex park)

RAMPTON
Sundown Kiddies Adventureland
(Sundown Pets Garden), Treswell Rd DN22 0HX (3m off A57 at Dunham crossroads)
☎01777 248274 Fax 01777 248967
The children's story book theme park: every child loves a story, and Sundown Adventureland is a land where those wonderful stories spring magically to life. The new village houses Santa's All Year Sleigh Ride, the Mouses' Tales Walkthrough, Musical Pet Shop, Witches' Cauldron and the Animated Market (bet you've never heard a goat yodel before!) Other attractions include; The Smugglers Cove with Boozey Barrel Boatride, Shotgun City, Rocky Mountain Railroad and Indoor Jungle (Height Restriction). The most recent attraction is the Fairy Tale Village where children can see, hear and join in the fun of the stories.
Open all year, daily 10-6, earlier in winter. (Closed 25-26 Dec & weekdays in Jan)
P 🍴 & toilets for disabled shop ✿
Details not confirmed for 1998

SUTTON-CUM-LOUND
Wetlands Waterfowl Reserve & Exotic Bird Park
Off Loundlow Rd DN22 8SB
☎01777 818099
Wetlands waterfowl reserve is a 32-acre site for both wild and exotic waterfowl. Visitors can see a collection of birds of prey, parrots, geese, ducks, and wigeon among others. There are also rabbits, chipmonks, deer, pigs, sheep, goats, ponies, donkeys, llama, and rheas.
Open all year, daily 10-5.30 (or dusk whichever is earlier). (Closed 25 Dec).
✱£1.50 (ch, pen & UB40 £1).
P 🍴 & (wheelchair available) shop ✿

WORKSOP
Clumber Park
The Estate Office, Clumber Park S80.3AZ (4.5m SE of Worksop, signposted from A1)
☎01909 476653 Fax 01909 500721
An impressive, landscaped park, laid out by Capability Brown. An outstanding feature is the lake running through the park, a haven for wildfowl, covering an area of 80 acres. Although the house itself has been demolished, there is still plenty for the visitor to see and enjoy. Other buildings that have survived include the stables, together with a restaurant, shop and information point, a classical bridge and Clumber Chapel, built in the Gothic Revival style. The park is a mixture of woodland, open grass and heathland. Please telephone for details of events.
Open all year, daily during daylight hours. Walled Garden, Victorian Apiary, Fig House, Vineries & Garden Tools exhibition Apr-Sep Sat, Sun & BH Mon 10-5. last admission 4.30pm. Conservation centre Apr-27 Sep Sat, Sun & BH Mon 1-5. Telephone for Chapel opening times)
Pedestrians free; cars, motorbikes & caravanettes £3, mini-coaches and cars with caravans £3.40, coaches: midweek: £7, weekends & BH £14.
P (charged) 🍴 ✗ licensed & (powered self-drive vehicle available if booked) toilets for disabled shop garden centre ♨

OXFORDSHIRE

BANBURY
Banbury Museum
8 Horsefair OX16 0AA
☎01295 259855 Fax 01295 270556
This museum, housed in the old boardroom of the Poor Law Guardians, overlooks Banbury Cross. There is an ➤

The gatehouse and gardens of Broughton Castle

exciting programme of temporary exhibitions. Holiday sessions and special events are regularly organised for children and there is a separate programme of exhibitions and displays by local artists. There is also a small herb garden. Events for 1998 include an exhibition to mark the 120th Anniversary of the Horton Hospital (until 28 April), British Gas Wildlife Photographer of the Year (11 Oct-15 Nov).
Open all year, Oct-Mar, Tue-Sat 10-4.30; Apr-Sep, Mon-Sat 10-5.
Free.
P *(behind museum)* ■ & *(induction loop) toilets for disabled shop* ✷

BROUGHTON
Broughton Castle
OX15 5EB (2m W of Banbury Cross on B4035 Shipston-on-Stour)
☎ *01295 262624 01869 337126 Fax 01869 337126*
Originally owned by William of Wykeham, and later by the first Lord Saye and Sele, the castle is an early 14th-and mid 16th-century house with a moat and gatehouse. Period furniture, paintings and Civil War relics are displayed.
Open Etr & 20 May-13 Sep, Wed & Sun (also Thu in Jul & Aug) & BH Sun & Mon 2-5.
£3.90 (ch 5-15 £2, pen & students £3.40). Party 20+.
P ■ & *toilets for disabled shop* ✷ *(ex in grounds on leads)*

BURFORD
Cotswold Wildlife Park
OX18 4JW (2m S of Burford on the A361)
☎ *01993 823006 Fax 01993 823807*
The 180-acre landscaped zoological park, surrounding a listed Gothic-style manor house, has a varied collection of animals from all over the world, from ants to rhinos, with tropical birds, a large reptile collection, aquarium and insect house. Other attractions include an adventure playground, a children's farmyard, animal brass-rubbing centre in the manor house and train rides during the summer months. Also during the summer there are Snake Days and bird of prey demonstrations by Geoff Dalton (weekends & BH Mondays). Penguin feeding times 11am and 4pm daily (except Fridays). Car Rallies & Snake Awareness Days, please phone for details.
Open all year, daily (ex 25 Dec) from 10am, last admission 5pm or dusk if earlier.
£5.50 (ch 3-16 & pen £3.50). Party 20+
P ■ ✗ *licensed* & *(parking, free hire of wheelchairs) toilets for disabled shop*
Cards: ▨ ▭ ▭ ▨

BUSCOT
Buscot Park
SN7 8BU (off A417)
☎ *01367 240786 Fax 01367 241794*
Much of the character of this 18th-century house is due to two relatively recent owners, the 1st Lord Faringdon, who bought the house in 1889, and his

son. They amassed most of the furniture, porcelain and other contents, as well as the many pictures forming the Faringdon Collection. It includes work by Reynolds, Gainsborough, Rembrandt, Murillo, several of the Pre-Raphaelites, and some 20th-century artists. Most memorable is the 'Legend of the Briar Rose', a deeply romantic series by Burne-Jones which fills the walls of the saloon.
The charming formal water gardens were laid out by Harold Peto in the early 20th century. There is also an attractively planted kitchen garden, with unusual concentric walls.
House & grounds Apr-Sep (incl Good Fri, Etr Sat & Sun) Wed-Fri 2-6. Also every 2nd & 4th wknd in each month 2-6 (last admission to house 5.30pm). Grounds as House but also Mon & Tue 2-6 (ex BH Mon)
House & Gardens £4.40 Grounds only £3.30.
P ■ ✷ ▨

DEDDINGTON
Deddington Castle
OX5 4TE (S of B4031 on E side of Deddington)
The large earthworks of the outer and inner baileys can be seen; the remains of 12th-century castle buildings have been excavated, but they are not now visible.
Open any reasonable time.
Free.
⌗

DIDCOT
Didcot Railway Centre
OX11 7NJ (on A4130 at Didcot Parkway Station)
☎ *01235 817200 Fax 01235 510621*
The biggest collection anywhere of Great Western Railway, including 20 steam locomotives, a diesel railcar, and a large amount of passenger and freight rolling stock. A typical GWR station has been re-created and original track has been relaid. Special events for 1998 include: Easter Steamings (10-13 April), Thomas the Tank Engine (2-4 October), Photographer's Evenings (30-31 October), Santa Steamings (11-13, 19-20 December)
Open all year, 4 Apr-27 Sep, daily 10-5, (11-4 Nov-Feb) Sat & Sun only rest of year. Steam days first & last Sun of each month from Mar, BH's, all Sun's Jun-Aug & Wed Jul-Aug & Sat in Aug.
£4-£8 (ch £3-£6.50, pen £3.50-£5.50).
P *(100 yds)* ■ & *(advance notice recommended) toilets for disabled shop*
Cards: ▨ ▭ ▭

GREAT COXWELL
Great Coxwell Barn
(2m SW of Faringdon between A420 & B4019)
☎ *01793 762209*
William Morris said that the barn was 'as noble as a cathedral'. It is a 13th-century stone-built tithe barn, 152ft long and 44ft wide, with a beautifully crafted framework of timbers supporting the

lofty stone roof. The barn was built for the Cistercians.
Open all reasonable times. For details please contact Estate Office.
✷*50p*
P ▨

HENLEY-ON-THAMES
Greys Court
Rotherfield Greys RG9 4PG (3m W)
☎ *01491 628529*
This appealing house has evolved over hundreds of years. The present gabled building has a pre-medieval kitchen but dates mainly from the 16th century. It stands in the courtyard of its medieval predecessor, facing the mid-14th-century Great Tower. Additions were made in the 18th century and there are some fine 18th-century decorations and furniture. The complex of gardens includes a white garden and a rose garden planted with old-fashioned varieties which leads into the walled area with ancient wisterias. Beyond this is the kitchen garden, and from here a bridge leads to a symbolic brick maze laid out in 1980. Also of great interest is the wheelhouse with its huge wheel, once turned by a donkey to bring water up from the well.
Open: House (part of ground floor only) Apr-Sep, Mon, Wed & Fri 2-6. (Closed Good Fri). Garden daily except Thu & Sun 2-6. Last admission 5.30pm. (Closed Good Fri).
House & Garden £4.40. Family ticket £11. Garden only £3.20 Family ticket £8.
P ■ ✷ ▨

River & Rowing Museum
Mill Meadows RG9 1BF (located between Hambleden and Marsh Locks)
☎ *01491 415600 Fax 01491 415601*
Your visit will take you on a spectacular journey through over 250,000 years of life on the river. Enjoy the quintessentially English town of Henley, whose livelihood has for centuries been shaped by the Thames. Discover the river's role in feeding the nation, its wildlife, nature, and transformation form a major trade route to a recreational paradise. Meet the people who shape Britain's oldest amateur sport, from innovative boatbuildres to athletes who strive for Olympic glory.
Opening summer 1998; Jun-Oct, Mon-Sat 10-5.30, Sun 11-5.30; Nov-Mar, Mon-Sat 10-4.30, Sun 11-4.30.
£4.95 (concessions £3.75). Family ticket £13.25. Party 10+.
P ■ ✗ *licensed* & *toilets for disabled shop* ✷
Cards: ▨ ▭ ▭

LONG WITTENHAM
Pendon Museum of Miniature Landscape & Transport
OX14 4QD
☎ *01865 407365*
This charming exhibition shows highly detailed and historically accurate model railway and village scenes transporting the visitor back into 1930s country landscapes. Skilled modellers can often be seen at work on the exhibits.
Open Sat & Sun 2-5, BH wknds 11-5 also Wed Jul & Aug 2-5. (Closed 1-26 Dec).
P ■ & *(phone in advance) toilets for disabled shop* ✷
Details not confirmed for 1998
Cards: ▨ ▭

MAPLEDURHAM
Mapledurham House
RG4 7TR (off A4074, follow tourist signs)
☎ *0118 972 3350 Fax 0118 972 4016*
The small community at Mapledurham includes the house, a watermill and a church, and is reached by travelling down a 'no through road', or by boat from the Caversham Promenade at Reading. The boat runs only when the house is open to the public but can be chartered by groups. The fine Elizabethan mansion, surrounded by quiet parkland which runs down to the River Thames, was built by the Blount family in the 16th century. Inside are paintings and family portraits collected over five centuries, great oak staircases and moulded Elizabethan ceilings. The estate has literary connections with the poet Alexander Pope, with Galsworthy's *Forsyte Saga* and Kenneth Graham's *Wind in the Willows*, and was the setting for the the film *The Eagle has Landed*, as well as featuring in various TV productions. Special events for 1998: Craft Fair (24-26 April), English Civil War Re-enactment (9-10 May).
Open Etr-Sep, Sat, Sun & BH's 2.30-5. Picnic area 12.30-6. Last admission 5pm. Group visits midweek by arrangement. Combined house, watermill & grounds £5 (ch £2.50). House & grounds £4 (ch £2). Watermill & grounds £3 (ch £1.50).
P ■ & *shop* ✷ *(ex park area)*

Mapledurham Watermill
RG4 7TR (off A4074)
☎ *0118 972 3350 Fax 0188 972 4016*
Close to Mapledurham House (above) stands the last working corn and grist mill on the Thames, still using traditional wooden machinery and producing flour for local bakers and shops. The

Greys Court was originally built in medieval times, but many additions and alterations, such as this elegant 18th-century sitting room, have made it a most appealing house.

watermill's products can be purchased in the shop. The mill can also be reached by river launch from Caversham Promenade at 2pm each day the house is open (details from the estate office). National Mills Day: 10th May.
Open Easter-Sep, Sat, Sun & BHs 1-5. Picnic area 12.30-6. Last admission 5. Groups midweek by arrangement. Watermill & grounds £3 (ch £1.50)
P 🍴 ♿ *shop* ✕ *(ex in country park)*

MINSTER LOVELL
Minster Lovell Hall & Dovecot
(adjacent to Minster Lovell church, 3m W of Witney off A40)
☎ 01993 775315
Home of the ill-fated Lovell family, the ruins of the 15th-century house are steeped in history and legend. One of the main features of the estate is the medieval dovecote which has survived intact through the centuries. The village of Minster Lovell is one of the prettiest in this outstanding area.
Open any reasonable time.
Free.
P *(ex Dovecot)* ✕ ⚏

NORTH LEIGH
North Leigh Roman Villa
(2m N)
Excavations have found this villa to have been occupied between the second and fourth centuries and reconstructed later in the period. A tessellated pavement and a 2-3 feet high wall span, are on show.
Open, grounds all year. No access to mosaic. Pedestrian access only from the main road - 600 yds.
Free.
✕ ⚏

Ashmolean Museum of Art & Archaeology
Beaumont St OX1 2PH (opposite The Randolph Hotel)
☎ 01865 278000 Fax 01865 278018
First opened in 1683 and the oldest museum in the country, the Ashmolean Museum was re-housed in C R Cockerell's building of 1845. Archaeological exhibits from Britain,

Europe, the Mediterranean, Egypt and the Near East are on show and the Heberden Coin Room contains coins and medals from all countries and periods. Italian, Dutch, Flemish, French and English oil paintings adorn the walls along with Old Masters and modern drawings, watercolours, prints and miniatures. Chinese and Japanese porcelain, paintings and laquer-work are gathered here as well as European ceramics, Tibetan art, Indian sculpture and paintings, metalwork and pottery from Islam and Chinese bronzes. Temporary exhibitions are held, including in 1998: Malchair and the Oxford School (until 12 April), The Forrest Reid Collection of Victorian Book Illustration (April-June), 17th-century French etchings (30 June-13 Sept), Drawings by Claude Lorrain (30 June-13 Sept).
Open all year, Tue-Sat 10-4, Sun 2-4. (Closed Etr & during St.Giles Fair in early Sep, Xmas & 1 Jan).
Free. Guided tours by arrangement.
P *(100-200metres)* 🍴 ♿ *(entry ramp from Beaumont St) toilets for disabled shop* ✕
Cards: ▨ 🎟 💳 🎫 🎴 ⑤

Carfax Tower
☎ 01865 792653
Excellent views of the city are to be seen from the top of this 14th-century tower which is all that remains of St Martin's Church. There is an historic display area on the first floor and an extensive souvenir area on the ground floor. Bellringings are organised by the Oxford Bell Ringers Society, to celebrate special events.
Open Mar-Oct, daily 10-6 (last entry 5.30).
P *(5 mins walk) shop* ✕
Details not confirmed for 1998

Harcourt Arboretum
Nuneham Courtenay OX44 9PX (400 yds S of Nuneham Courtenay on A4074)
☎ 01865 276920 Fax 01865 276920
The gardens consist of 55 acres of mixed woodland, meadow, pond, rhododendron walks and fine specimen trees.
Open May-Oct, daily 10-5; Nov-Apr, Mon-Fri 10-4.30. Closed 22 Dec-4 Jan & Good Fri-Etr Mon.
Free.
P ♿ ✕

Museum of Oxford
St Aldate's OX1 1DZ
☎ 01865 815559 Fax 01865 810187
Permanent displays depict the archaeology and history of the city from earliest times to the present day. There are temporary exhibitions, facilities for school parties and groups, an audio tour, and weekly free lectures and events Thursday lunchtime. Please telephone for details of special events.
Open all year, Tue-Fri 10-4, Sat 10-5. (Closed 25-26 Dec & Good Fri).
shop ✕
Details not confirmed for 1998
Cards: 💳

The Oxford Story
6 Broad St OX1 3AJ
☎ 01865 790055 Fax 01865 791716
The 800-year history of Oxford University is brought to life at this innovative exhibition. Sights, sounds - and smells - from the past are described by Magnus Magnusson as visitors take a seat and ride through the exhibition. Foreign language and child commentaries are available. For half-term (27-31 Oct) Face painting: Characters from Alice in Wonderland.
Open all year, Apr-Jun & Sep-Oct daily 9.30-5, Jul-Aug 9.30-5 & Nov-Mar daily 10-4.30 (weekends 5pm) (Closed 25 Dec) £4.95 (ch under 16 £3.95, pen & students £4.25). Family ticket £15.75.
P *(200yds) (pay & display)* ♿ *(ramped entrance & exit of exhibition) toilets for disabled shop* ✕
Cards: ▨ 🎟 💳 🎴 ⑤

St Edmund Hall
College of Oxford University OX1 4AR
☎ 01865 279000 Fax 01865 279090
This is the only surviving medieval academic hall and has a Norman crypt, 17th-century dining hall, chapel and quadrangle. Other buildings are of the 18th and 20th centuries.
Open all year. (Closed 23 Dec-3 Jan, 9-17 Apr & 28-31 Aug).
♿ *toilets for disabled shop* ✕
Details not confirmed for 1998

University of Oxford Botanic Garden
High St OX1 4AX
☎ 01865 276920 Fax 01865 276920
Founded in 1621, these botanic gardens are the oldest in the country and are of great interest. There is a collection of over 8000 species of plants from all over the world.
Open all year, daily 9-5 (9-4.30 Oct-Mar), Greenhouses, daily 2-4. (Closed Good Fri & 25 Dec).
Apr-Aug £2. otherwise free.
P *(0.5 mile)* ♿ *toilets for disabled* ✕

ROUSHAM
Rousham House
OX6 3QX (1m E of A4260. 0.5m S of B4030)
☎ 01869 347110
This attractive mansion was built by Sir Robert Dormer in 1635. During the Civil War it was a Royalist garrison, and had shooting holes cut into its doors. Sir Robert's successors, Masters of Ceremonies at Court during eight reigns, embellished Rousham by employing Court artists and architects. Rooms were also decorated by William Kent and Roberts of Oxford, during the 18th century. The house contains over 150 portraits and other pictures, and also much fine contemporary furniture. The gardens are a masterpiece by William Kent, and are his only work to survive unspoiled. Extending to over 30 acres, with the River Cherwell flowing through, they include classical buildings, cascades, statues, fine walled gardens with herbaceous borders, a small parterre and views over the river. There are longhorn cattle in the park.
Open all year, garden only, daily 10-4.30. House, Apr-Sep, Wed, Sun & BH Mon 2-4.30 (last entry).
House £2.50; Garden £3. Groups by arrangement. No children under 15.
P ♿ ✕

RYCOTE
Rycote Chapel
OX9 2PE (off B4013)
This small 15th-century private chapel was founded in 1449 by Richard Quatremayne. It has its original font, and a particularly fine 17th-century interior. The chapel was visited by both Elizabeth I and Charles I.
Open Apr-Sep, Fri-Sun & BH's 2-6. £1.60 (ch 80p, concessions £1.20)
P ♿ *(if assisted)* ✕ ⚏

The dovecot is a feature at Rousham House gardens which are one of the finest examples of William Kent's work as a landscape gardener and remain largely as he designed them.

STONOR

Stonor House & Park

RG9 6HF (on B480).

☎01491 638587 Fax 01491 638587

Home of Lord and Lady Camoys and occupied by the Stonor family for 800 years, the house dates back to 1190 but features a Tudor façade. It has a medieval Catholic chapel which is still in use today, and shows some of the earliest domestic architecture in Oxfordshire. Its treasures include rare furniture, paintings, sculptures and tapestries from Britain, Europe and America. The house is set in beautiful gardens with commanding views of the surrounding deer park. The Chiltern Craft Show will be held here on 28-31 August 1998, VW Car Rally (31 May), Classic Concert (27 June).

Open Apr-Sep, Sun 2-5.30; May-Sep, Wed 2-5.30; Jul-Aug, Thu 2-5.30; Aug, Sat 2-5.30; BH Mon 2-5.30. Parties by appointment Wed & Thu.

£4.50 (ch 14 accompanied free). Gardens only £2.50. Party 12+.

🅿 ⬛ & shop ✤ *(ex in grounds on lead)*

UFFINGTON

Castle, White Horse & Dragon Hill

(S of B4507)

The 'castle' is an Iron Age fort on the ancient Ridgeway Path over the Berkshire Downs. It covers about eight acres and has only one gateway. On the hill below the fort is the White Horse, a 375ft prehistoric figure carved in the chalky hillside. It was once thought to have been carved in 871 to celebrate King Alfred's victory over the Danes, but is now thought to be at least 2000 years old. It is best seen from the B4508.

Open - accessible any reasonable time. Free.

🅿 ⚏

WATERPERRY

Waterperry Gardens

OX33 1JZ (2.50m from A40, turn off at Wheatley)

☎01844 339226 & 339254 Fax 01844 339883

The manor of Waterperry is mentioned in the Domesday Book, and the little church next to the current house incorporates Saxon work, although it dates from early Norman times. It has some very old stained glass, brasses, and woodwork showing the crests of the FitzEly and Curson families who owned Waterperry from about 1250 to 1830.

The present house (not open) was rebuilt by Sir John Curson in 1713 and its elegant proportions reflect the classical tastes of the 18th century. The peaceful gardens and nurseries which surround the house were the home of a celebrated horticultural school between 1932 and 1971, and have fine herbaceous borders, a rock garden, riverside walk, shrub borders, lawns and trees. The horticultural centre now based at Waterperry maintains the earlier traditions with its extensive alpine, fruit, shrub and herbaceous nurseries, and the productive greenhouses. In 1998 there will be a major arts and crafts festival where artists and craftsmen from all over the world will demonstrate their talents (16-19 July). The 'Art in Action' gallery will be holding exhibitions throughout the year. National Apple Day-October. For details please telephone 01844 339254.

Open all year, Gardens (ex Xmas & New Year & during "Art in Action" 16-19 Jul). Apr-Oct 9-5.30, Nov-Mar 9-5 daily. Apr-Oct, £3 (ch 10-16 £1.50, ch under 10 free, pen £2.50). Nov-Mar £1.25 Party 20+

🅿 ⬛ ✗ & *(grounds partially accessible) shop garden centre* ✤ *(ex on leads)*
Cards: ▨ ▨ ▨ ▨ ▨ ▨ ▨

WITNEY

Cogges Manor Farm Museum

Church Ln, Cogges OX8 6LA (0.5m SE off A4022)

☎01993 772602

Fax 01993 703056

Farm museum with breeds of animals typical of the Victorian period, historic site and buildings including Manor House, dairy and walled garden. There is cooking on the kitchen range every afternoon, an historic trail, and riverside walk. The first floor of the Manor house has reopened following extensive restoration, and features 17th-19th century interiors and an explanation of the history of the building from 1250 to the present day. Special events for 1998 include: Easter lambs, shearing (24 May), steam threshing (19-20 September).

Open Apr-1 Nov, Tue-Fri & BH Mon 10.30-5.30, Sat & Sun 12-5.30. Early closing Oct. (Closed Good Fri). £3.25 (ch £1.75, pen, students & UB40 £2). Family ticket £9.

🅿 ⬛ & *(wheelchair available, staff able to assist) toilets for disabled shop*
Cards: ▨

WOODSTOCK

Blenheim Palace

OX20 1PX (M40 junct 9, follow signs to Blenheim, on A44 8m N of Oxford)

☎01993 811091 & 811325 (information line) Fax 01993 813527

The Royal Manor of Woodstock and the sum of £240,000 to build the Palace were given to the Duke of Marlborough by Queen Anne as a reward for his brilliant military victory over the French at the Battle of Blenheim in 1704. The Palace, begun in 1705, was designed by Sir John Vanbrugh. It was built on a very grand scale, covering seven acres including courtyards, and was completed

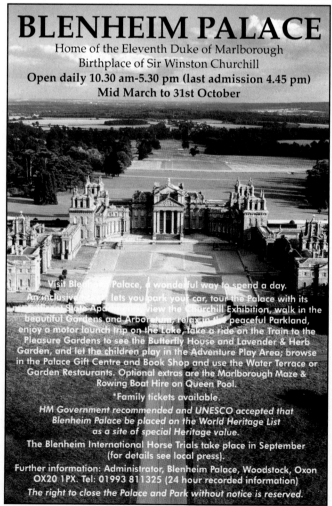

in 1722. The Palace has splendid State Rooms, a Long Library, magnificent tapestries and paintings as well as fine furniture. Of particular interest are carvings by Grinling Gibbons and the Hall ceiling painted to depict the 1st Duke presenting the plan of the Battle of Blenheim to Britannia by Sir James Thornhill.

The palace is set in a 2100-acre park landscaped by Capability Brown who created a lake spanned by a 390-ft bridge. There are also formal Italian and French gardens.

Sir Winston Churchill was born in the Palace in 1874 and he is buried nearby, at Bladon.

There is a pleasure garden, adventure playground and nature trail through the parkland, and other attractions include a motor launch, train and Butterfly House. Events held in the park during the year include a craft fair (May Bank Holiday) craft fair (August Bank Holiday) and the International Horse Trials (10-13 September); the Winston Churchill Memorial Concert (March) All events listed are provisional; please telephone for details.

Open: Palace & Gardens mid Mar-Oct, daily 10.30-5.30 (last admission 4.45pm). Park all year.
£7.80 (pen, 16-17 year olds & students £5.80). Family ticket £20. Group rates.
🅿 ♿ ✕ *licensed* ♿ *(ramps, disabled parking) toilets for disabled shop* ✖ *(ex in park on leads)*
Cards: 💳 💳 💳 💳 💳 💳

Oxfordshire County Museum
Fletcher's House OX20 1SN
☎ 01993 811456
Fax 01993 813239
Permanently displayed in Fletcher's House is an exhibition of the story of Oxfordshire and its people, from early times to the present day. The house, which is an elegant townhouse with pleasant gardens, also has temporary exhibitions.
Open all year, Jan-Apr & Oct-Dec, Tue-Fri 10-4, Sat 10-5, Sun 2-5; May-Sep Tue-Sat, 10-5, Sun 2-5. (Closed Good Fri & 25-26 Dec)
🅿 ♿ ♿ *shop* ✖
Details not confirmed for 1998
Cards: 💳 💳 💳

RUTLAND

LYDDINGTON
Bede House
☎ 01572 822438
The vast diocese of the Bishops of Lincoln, necessitated an episcopal residence in Lyddington. Bede House was built for the purpose in the late 15th century and it remains a good example of the period. It passed out of religious hands at the time of Henry VIII, and was later converted into an almshouse by the Earl of Exeter. The beautiful 16th-century wooden ceilings, 15th-century painted glass and grand fireplace are remnants of the building's former life as the palace of the Bishops of Lincoln.
Open Apr-1 Nov, daily 10-6 (or dusk if earlier).
£2.30 (ch £1.20, concessions £1.70).
♿ ✖ ✿

OAKHAM
Oakham Castle
off Market Place
☎ 01572 723654
Fax 01572 757576
An exceptionally fine Norman Great Hall of a 12th-century fortified manor house. Earthworks, walls and remains of an earlier motte can be seen along with medieval sculptures and unique presentation horseshoes forfeited by peers of the realm and royalty to the Lord of the Manor. Please enquire for details of any events in connection with Oakham Festival in June.
Open all year. Grounds daily 10-5.30 (4pm late Oct-late Mar). Great Hall Tue-

Sat & BH Mon 10-1 & 2-5.30, Sun 2-5.30 (4pm late Oct-late Mar).Closed Mon, Good Fri & Xmas.
Free.
🅿 *(400 yds) (disabled parking only by notification)* ♿ *shop* ✖

Rutland County Museum
Catmos St LE15 6HW (on A6003)
☎ 01572 723654
Fax 01572 757576
The Museum of Rutland Life has displays of farming equipment, machinery and wagons, rural tradesmen's tools, domestic collections and local archaeology, all housed in a splendid late 18th-century cavalry riding school. There is a special gallery on the Volunteer Soldier in Leicestershire and Rutland. A programme of temporary exhibitions takes place - please enquire for details.
Open all year, Mon-Sat 10-5. Sun 2-5 (Apr-Oct, 2-4 Nov-Mar). (Closed Good Fri & Xmas)
Free.
🅿 *(adjacent)* 🍴 ♿ *toilets for disabled shop* ✖

SHROPSHIRE

ACTON BURNELL
Acton Burnell Castle
SY5 7PE (on unclass road 8m S of Shrewsbury)
Now ruined, this fortified manor house was built in the late 13th century by Robert Burnell, the Chancellor of the time. It consisted of a central block with towers at the corners and a great hall and chapel on the upper floor. By 1420 the house was no longer being used, and part of it was converted into a barn in the 18th century.
Open at all reasonable times.
Free.
♿ ✿

ACTON SCOTT
Acton Scott Historic Working Farm
Wenlock Lodge SY6 6QN (follow tourist signs off A49)
☎ 01694 781306 & 781307
Fax 01694 781569
Acton Scott Historic Working Farm is a microcosm of an upland farm at the turn of the century. The heavy horses (there are no tractors here) work the Norfolk Four Course crop rotation as they have for a hundred years. Livestock here includes many rare breeds such as long and shorthorn cows, Shropshire sheep, Tamworth pigs and poultry. Throughout the farming season visitors can see ploughing, sowing, reaping and harvesting of both corn and root crops, and demonstrations by blacksmiths, farriers, wheelwrights, and woodland craftsman. Domestic life is recreated in the bailiff's cottage with butter-churning, cooking, baking and tending the garden. Special events for 1998 include: Goats & Kids (19 April), May Revels (4 May), Grand Spring Plant Sale (25 May), Sheep Shearing (31 May), Sheepdog Day (12 July), Donkeys & Mules (30 August), Steam Threshing Weekends (17-18 Oct & 31 Oct-1 Nov) and much more. Full programme available on request.
Open 31 Mar-1 Nov, Tue-Sun 10-5; BH Mon 10-5.
£3.25 (ch £1.50, under 5 free, pen £2.75).
🅿 ♿ *(Braille guide, wheelchairs available) toilets for disabled shop* ✖

ATCHAM
Attingham Park
SY4 4TP (4m SE of Shrewsbury on B4380)
☎ 01743 709203
Fax 01743 709352
An imposing entrance front with massive portico, colonnades and pavilions greets the visitor to Attingham. The house was constructed around an earlier building, but most of what one sees today dates from the 18th and early 19th centuries. This even applies to the garden, where the planting remains very much as

advised by Humphry Repton in 1797-8. The house was designed by George Steuart with the more 'masculine' rooms on the left of the entrance hall and the more 'feminine' rooms on the right. The entrance hall itself is elaborately decorated to imitate marble. Other notable decorations can be seen in the boudoir, which has intricate and delicate designs, the Italian-style drawing room, the oriental Sultana room and the red dining room. The picture gallery was designed by Nash, who made early use of curved cast iron and glass for the ceiling. The River Tern flows through the park, which has a herd of fallow deer. The estate of the house is on the site of the Roman town of Viroconium, and is also crossed by two Roman roads. It is also notable for two fine bridges carrying the old A5 over the Tern and Severn rivers.
House open 22 Mar-2 Nov, Sat-Wed (& Good Fri) 1.30-5, BH Mon 11-5. Pre-booked parties allowed daily ex Thu & Fri. Last admission 4.30pm. Grounds open all year, daily (ex 25 Dec), 8am-8pm.
🅿 🍴 ♿ *(2 electric self drive buggies) toilets for disabled shop* ✖ ♨
Details not confirmed for 1998

BENTHALL
Benthall Hall
TF12 5RX (on B4375)
☎ 01952 882159
The exact date of the house is not known, but it seems to have been started in the 1530s and then altered in the 1580s. It is an attractive sandstone building with mullioned windows, fine oak panelling and a splendid carved staircase.
Open Apr-Sep, Wed, Sun & BH Mon 1.30-5.30. Last admission 5pm. Other days by appointment only.
🅿 ♿ ✖ ♨
Details not confirmed for 1998
Cards: 💳 💳

BOSCOBEL
Boscobel House and The Royal Oak
(on unclass road between A41 and A5)
☎ 01902 850244
The house was built around 1600 by John Giffard, a Catholic, and the structure includes a number of hiding places. One of them was used by King Charles II after his defeat at the Battle of Worcester in 1651. A descendant of the oak tree where he also hid can be seen in the grounds. The site also features an exhibition about Charles' escape, as well as a Victorian farmyard with working smithy.
Open all year, Apr-Oct, daily 10-6 (or dusk if earlier); Nov-Mar, Wed-Sun 10-4, last admission 3.30pm. Entry to house by guided tour only. Closed 24-26 Dec & all Jan.
£3.95 (ch £2, concessions £3).
🅿 ♿ ♿ *shop* ✖ ♨

Whiteladies Priory (St Leonards Priory)
Only the ruins are left of this Augustinian nunnery, which dates from 1158 and was destroyed in the Civil War. After the Battle of Worcester Charles II hid here and in the nearby woods before going on to Boscobel House.
Open any reasonable time.
Free.
♨

BRIDGNORTH
Midland Motor Museum
Stanmore Hall, Stourbridge Rd WV15 6DT (2m on A458 Stourbridge Rd)
☎ 01746 762992
Fax 01746 768104
A notable collection of over 100 well-restored sports and sports racing cars, and racing motor cycles dating from 1920 to 1980. They are housed in the converted stables of Stanmore Hall and surrounded by beautiful grounds.
Open 11-5, Oct-Jun wknds only; 11-5 Jul-Sep daily.
🅿 ♿ *shop* ✖
Details not confirmed for 1998

BUILDWAS
Buildwas Abbey
TF8 7BW (on S bank of River Severn on B4378)
☎ 01743 701101
The beautiful, ruined, Cistercian abbey was founded in 1135, and stands in a picturesque setting. The church with its stout round pillars is roofless but otherwise almost complete.
Open Apr-Nov, daily 10-6. Please telephone for further details.
£1.75 (ch 90p, concessions £1.30)
♿ ✿

BURFORD
Burford House Gardens
WR15 8HQ (off A456)
☎ 01584 810777 Fax 01584 810673
The beauty of Burford House Gardens is a tribute to the late John Treasure who, since the early 1950's, transformed the setting of this early Georgian house into a garden of quiet serenity and fascination. Harmonising combinations of colour have been achieved, and especial use has been made of clematis - the garden, now boasting over 150 varieties, is home to the National Collection. The garden is famous for its range of unusual plants, many of which are sold in Treasures Plant Centre adjacent, who specialise in clematis, herbaceous, shrubs, trees and climbers. Also on site is the Burford House Gallery, Burford Buttery, Craft Shop and Craft Workshops. Special events this year: 4th Annual Botanical Exhibition and 2 contemporary art shows (April-October), Christmas Fair (early Nov-24 Dec). Ring for further details.
Open all year 10-5. dusk if earlier.
£2.50 (ch £1). Party 10+.
🅿 🍴 ✕ *licensed* ♿ *(ramp into gardens, sloping paths) toilets for disabled shop garden centre* ✖ *(ex in Plant Centre)*
Cards: 💳 💳 💳

COSFORD
Aerospace Museum
TF11 8UP (on A41, 1m S of Jct 3 on M54)
☎ 01902 374872 & 374112
Fax 01902 374813
This is one of the largest aviation collections in the UK. Exhibits include the Victor and Vulcan bombers, the Hastings, York and British Airways airliners, the Belfast freighter and the last airworthy Britannia. World War II Aircraft including the Spitfire, Mosquito and Hurricane. The research and development collection includes the notable TSR2, Fairey Delta, Bristol 188 and many more important aircraft. There is a British Airways exhibition hall and a comprehensive missile and aero engine display. The Large Model Association Aircraft Rally will be held on 18-19 July, and 14 June is Royal Air Force Cosford Open Day.
Open all year daily, 10-4 (last admission). (Closed 24-26 Dec & 1 Jan).
£5 (ch £3 & pen £3.50). Family ticket £12. Party 20+.
🅿 🍴 ♿ *(limited amount of wheelchairs on request) toilets for disabled shop* ✖
Cards: 💳 💳 💳 💳

HAUGHMOND ABBEY
Haughmond Abbey
(off B5062)
☎ 01743 709661
The ruined abbey was founded for Augustinian canons in around 1135, and partly converted into a house during the Dissolution. The chapter house has a fine Norman doorway, and the abbot's lodging and the kitchens are well preserved.
Open Apr-Oct, daily 10-6 (or dusk if earlier)
❋ *£1.75 (ch 90p, concessions £1.30).*
🅿 ♿ ✿

HODNET
Hodnet Hall Gardens
TF9 3NN
☎ 01630 685202 Fax 01630 685853
Sixty acres of landscaped gardens offer tranquillity among pools, lush plants and trees. Big game trophies adorn the 17th-

➤

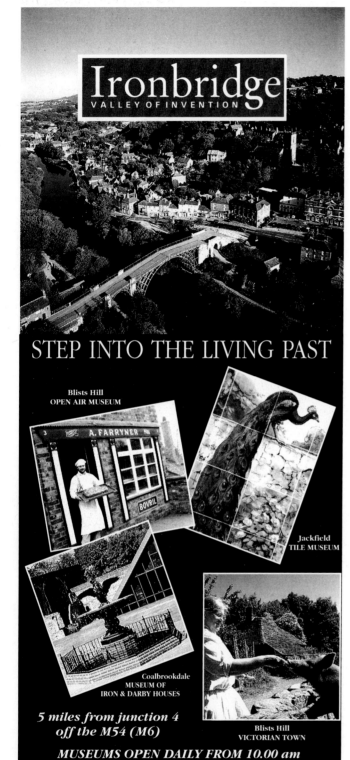

century tearooms, and plants are usually for sale in the kitchen gardens. The house, rebuilt in Victorian-Elizabethan style, is not open.
Open daily Apr-Sep, Tue-Sat 12-5, Sun & BH Mon 12 noon-5.30.
£3 (ch £1.20, pen £2.50). Party.
P ⬛ & *(2 wheelchairs available) toilets for disabled shop garden centre*

IRONBRIDGE
Ironbridge Gorge Museums
TF8 7AW (M54 junc 4, signposted)
☎*01952 433522 & 432166 (wknds)*
Fax 01952 432204
Ironbridge became famous when the world's first iron bridge was cast and built here in 1779, to span a narrow gorge over the River Severn. Now it is the site of a remarkable series of museums covering some six square miles. Perhaps the most appealing is the Blists Hill Victorian Town. Set in 42 acres of woodland, this recreated Victorian town offers the visitor a chance to step into the past and see how people lived and worked in the 1890s. The Coalbrookdale Furnace Site shows the technique of smelting iron ore, perfected here by Abraham Darby. Associated with the furnace is the Museum of Iron. Another of the museums is housed in the original buildings of the Coalport China Company, based here until 1926. It features ceramics, workshop and social history displays. There is also the Jackfield Tile Museum where there is tile manufacturing and a mining gallery. An introduction to the Ironbridge Gorge is given at the Ironbridge visitor centre. Special events include: Flower Festival (late June-early July), Bonfire Night (7 Nov), Hallowe'en (31 Oct).
Open all year, 10-5. Some small sites closed Nov-Mar. Telephone or write for exact winter details.
✳*£9 (ch £5.30, pen £8). Family £28). Passport to all sites, until all have been visited. It is therefore possible to return to Ironbridge on different days to ensure the whole atmosphere of this unique museum may be captured.*
P ⬛ ✗ *licensed & (wheelchairs loan, potters wheel at Coalport, braille guide) toilets for disabled shop ♻ (ex at Blists Hill)*
Cards: ▧ ▧ ▧ ▧ ▧ ▧

LILLESHALL
Lilleshall Abbey
TF10 9HW (1.5m SW off A518 on unclass road)
Some of the most impressive ruins in Shropshire stand in the beautiful grounds of Lilleshall Hall. Lilleshall Abbey was founded shortly before the middle of the 12th century and from the high west front visitors can look down the entire 228ft length of the abbey church.
Open Apr-Nov, wknds & BH's only, 12-5.
£1.30 (ch 70p, concessions £1)
P ♻ ⚜

LUDLOW
Ludlow Castle
Castle Square SY8 1AY
☎*01584 873355*
Ludlow Castle dates from about 1086 and was greatly extended as ownership passed through the de Lacy and Mortimer families to the Crown. In 1473, Edward IV sent the Prince of Wales and his brother - later to become the Princes in the Tower - to live in Ludlow, and Ludlow Castle became a seat of government with the establishment there of the Council for Wales and the Marches. Another royal resident was Prince Arthur, son of Henry Tudor and elder brother of Henry VIII. John Milton's *Comus* was first performed at Ludlow Castle in 1634; now contemporary performances of Shakespeare's plays, together with concerts, are put on in the castle grounds during the Ludlow Festival (2 weeks, end June-early July). In 1689 the Royal Welsh Fusiliers were formed at Ludlow by Lord Herbert of Chirbury, into whose family, the Earls of Powis, ownership of the castle later passed. The

Castle includes buildings ranging from the circular nave of the Norman chapel to an unusually complete range of medieval buildings and the Judges' Lodgings, built in the 16th century. Special events planned for 1998 include a Craft Fair (May Bank Holiday Weekend), Falconry Displays (Wednesdays, July-September), Ludlow Festival (End June-Early July). Contact castle office for details.
Open May-Sep daily 10.30-5; Rest of year 10.-4. Closed 25 Dec and week days in Jan.
£2.50 (ch £1.50, pen £2). Family ticket £7.50.
P *(100 yds)* & *toilets for disabled shop*
Cards: ▧ ▧

LYDBURY NORTH
Walcot Hall
SY7 8AZ
☎*0171 581 2782*
Fax 0171 589 0195
Built by Sir William Chambers for Lord Clive of India. The Georgian House possesses a free-standing and recently restored Ballroom, stableyard with matching clock towers and extensive walled garden, in addition to its ice house, meat-safe and dovecote. There is an Arboretum, noted for its rhododendrons and azaleas, specimen trees, pools and a lake.
Open BH Sun-Mon in May. Other times, by appointment.
£2.50 (ch under 15 free)
P & *(lift to 1st floor) toilets for disabled*

MORETON CORBET
Castle
A small 13th-century keep and the ruins of an impressive Elizabethan house are all that remain: the house was destroyed when Parliamentary forces captured it in 1644.
Open all reasonable times.
Free.
P & ⚜

MUCH WENLOCK
Much Wenlock Priory
☎*01952 727466*
The original priory was founded here as a convent in the 7th century. It was destroyed by the Danes but was rebuilt and grew over the years. The not inconsiderable remains of the 11th-century priory and subsequent additions are what the visitor will see today.
Open all year, Apr-Oct, daily 10-6; Nov-Mar, Wed-Sun 10-4. Closed 24-26 Dec & 1 Jan.
£2.30 (ch £1.20, concessions £1.70). Personal stereo tour included in price, also available for the partially sighted, those with learning difficulties and in French & German.
P ⚜

OSWESTRY
Old Oswestry Hill Fort
(1m N, accessible from unclass road off A483)
This Iron Age hill-fort covers 68 acres, has five ramparts and an elaborate western portal. It is abutted by part of the prehistoric Wat's Dyke.
Open any reasonable time.
Free.
⚜

Oswestry Transport Museum
Oswald Rd SY11 1RE
☎*01691 671749*
This Museum uses over 100 bicycles to display the history of cycling through the ages. Displays include bicycle parts, signs and Dunlop's development of the pneumatic tyre. There is also a large exhibition of the Cambrian Railways where visitors can see 12 railway engines and rolling stock. Train rides are also available. Ring for details.
Open all year, daily 10-4. (Closed 25-26 Dec).
P ⬛ & *shop*
Details not confirmed for 1998

QUATT

Dudmaston

WV15 6QN (4m SE of Bridgnorth on A442)

☎01746 780866 Fax 01746 780744

The 17th-century flower paintings which belonged to Francis Darby of Coalbrookdale are exhibited in this house of the same period, with modern works, botanical art and fine furniture. The house stands in an extensive parkland garden and there are dingle and lakeside walks; two estate walks (of 3.5 and 5 miles) start from Hampton Loade car park, six miles southeast of Bridgnorth on the A442. This year 'Illyria' will present *The Taming of the Shrew* and *Alice in Wonderland*.

Open Apr-Sep, Wed & Sun 2-5.30. House & Garden £3.50. Garden only £2.50. Family ticket £8.

P ▼ ✿ *(Braille guides, taped tours) toilets for disabled shop* ✿ *(ex in grounds)* ✿

Cards: ◪ ▦

SHREWSBURY

Clive House Museum

College Hill SY1 1LT

☎01743 354811 Fax 01743 358411

Town house with a long history, including a brief association in the 1760s with Robert, Lord Clive (Clive of India). Alongside social history and fine and decorative arts from the 18th and 19th centuries, displays on the history of natural history and Shropshire's natural historians are being developed. Temporary exhibition room, children's activities and walled garden.

Open all year, Tue-Sat 10-4, Sun end May-end Sep and Bank Hol Mon. (Closed mid Dec-mid Jan).

✱£2 (ch 50p, pen & student £1). Joint admission to Clive House, Rowley's House, Shrewsbury Castle & Regimental Museum £4 (ch £1, pen & students £2). P (in town centre) (on street parking by voucher only) ✿ shop ✿

Shrewsbury Castle and Shropshire Regimental Museum

The Castle, Castle St SY1 2AT

☎01743 358516 Fax 01743 354811

Re-opened in 1995 after a two year closure, the museum of The King's Shropshire Light Infantry and The Shropshire Yeomanry is housed within the main surviving building of Shrewsbury Castle. This was a Norman fortification commanding the historic town of Shrewsbury. Thomas Telford was responsible for alterations to the castle in the 18th century. The grounds incorporate the medieval 'motte' and the romantic 'Laura's Tower'. One room within the main building is licensed for civil marriages. Special events for 1998 include: Open Air Concert (12 June), International Music Festival Concert (late June), World Music Day (July), Open Air Theatre (July). Ring for further details.

Open Tue-Sat 10-4.30, also Sun from Etr-Sep & BH Mon. Castle grounds open Mon also. Closed Dec/Jan.

✱£2 (ch 50p, student & pen £1). Inclusive ticket to Rowley's House, Clive House & Regimental Museum £4 (ch £1, student & pen £2). Castle grounds free. P (3 mins NCP) (on street parking by voucher only) ✿ toilets for disabled shop ✿

Shrewsbury Quest

193 Abbey Foregate SY2 6AH (opposite Shrewsbury Abbey)

☎01743 243324 Fax 01743 244342

An opportunity to experience the sights, sounds and smells of medieval England. The Quest is based on 12th-century England in general and monastic life in particular, including a part dedicated to the world famous monk detective of fiction, Brother Cadfael. Recreated on Shrewsbury Abbey's original grounds, it makes use of Scheduled Monuments and Grade II listed buildings. There are two different levels of mysteries to be solved and their clues are to be found throughout The Quest which includes a Gatehouse, Cartshed, Cellarium, Guest Hall, Scriptorium, Brother Cadfael's workshop and a unique medieval herb garden. The Quest provides a full 'hands-on' experience for visitors, who are encouraged to create their own illuminated manuscript, try their hand at medieval cloister games and interact with the historical characters in this 12th-century world. Suitable for disabled and special needs visitors.

Open Apr-Oct 10-5 (last admission); Nov-Mar 10-4 (last admission).

£3.95 (ch £2.50, concessions £3.20).

P (charged) ✗ licensed ✿ (Braille maps, induction loop, lift) toilets for disabled shop ✿

Cards: ◪ ▦ ▭ ▦ ▦ ▣

STOKESAY

Stokesay Castle

SY7 9AH (1m S of Craven Arms off A49)

☎01588 672544

Well-preserved and little altered, this 13th-century manor house has a romantic setting. Special features are the timber-framed Jacobean gatehouse, the great hall and, reached by an outside staircase, a solar with 17th-century panelling.

Open all year, 22 Mar-Oct, daily 10-6 (or dusk if earlier in Oct); Nov-mid Mar, Wed-Sun 10-4 (closed 1-2pm Nov-Mar.

P ✿ (tape tour for visually handicapped, ramp for wheelchairs) toilets for disabled ✿

Details not confirmed for 1998

WESTON-UNDER-REDCASTLE

Hawkstone Historic Park & Follies

SY4 5UY (3m from Hodnet off A53)

☎01939 200300 Fax 01939 200311

Created in the 18th century by the Hill family, Hawkstone was once one of the greatest historic parklands in history. After almost one hundred years of neglect it has now been restored and designated a Grade I historic park. Visitors can once again experience this magical world of intricate pathways, arches and bridges, towering cliffs and follies, and an awesome grotto. The Grand Valley has wild flowers and tidy lawns, centuries-old oaks, wild rhododendrons and lofty monkey puzzles. The Park covers nearly 100 acres of hilly terrain and visitors are advised to wear sensible shoes and clothing. Allow 3-4 hours for the tour, which is well signposted. The setting for BBC TV series 'The Chronicles of Narnia' and 'One Foot in the Past', the park is believed by some to be the last hiding place of the Grail. New attractions: 'See & Hear King Arthur', and deer which have been reintroduced into the park after an absence of 150 years. There is generally a special event each month, and in 1998 these will include an Easter Egg Hunt (Easter weekend), Hallowe'en Ghost Hunts (30 October-2 November) and Father Christmas in the Grotto (29 Nov, 5-6, 12-13, 17-23 December)

Open 28 Mar-1 Nov, daily 10-6; Dec wknds only for Father Christmas visits.

£4.50 (ch £2.50, concessions £3.50) Family ticket £12. Group rates. Additional charge for special events & BH Mons.

P shop

Cards: ◪ ▦

WROXETER

Roman Town

(5m E of Shrewsbury, 1m S of A5)

☎01743 761330

These excavated remains of the Roman town of Virconium probably date from 140 - 150AD. There is a colonnade and a municipal bath. The museum has finds from both the Roman town and an earlier legionary fortress on the same site. It also offers educational facilities.

Open all year, Apr-Oct, daily 10-6 (or dusk if earlier); Nov-Mar, Wed-Sun 10-4 (closed 1-2pm). Closed 24-26 Dec & 1 Jan.

£2.95 (ch £1.50, concessions £2.20). Personal stereo tour included in admission.

P ✿ shop ✿ ✦

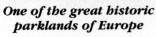
SOMERSET

AXBRIDGE

King John's Hunting Lodge

The Square BS26 2AP

☎01934 732012

Nothing to do with King John or with hunting, this jettied and timber-framed house was built around 1500. It gives a good indication of the wealth of the merchants of that time and is now a museum of local history, with old photographs, paintings and items such as the town stocks and constables' staves.

Open Etr-Sep, daily 2-5. Write for details of tours.

Free.

✿

BARRINGTON

Barrington Court Garden

TA19 0NQ (5m NE of Ilminster on B3168)

☎01460 241938

The house dates from the 17th century, but the gardens were created in the 1920s, with the help (through the post) of Gertrude Jekyll. They are laid out in 'rooms' and there is a large walled kitchen garden supplying fresh fruit and vegetables to the restaurant.

Open: Garden & Court House 1 Apr-31 Oct, daily ex Fri, 11-5.30, last admission 5pm.

£4.20 (ch £2.10). Party.

P ✗ licensed ✿ (batricars available, braille guides) ✿ ✿

BATH

Bath owes its fame and beauty to its hot water springs. The Celts had a shrine to the water goddess Sulis here, but Bath's story really begins with the Romans. They called it Aquae Sulis, and enjoyed the pleasures of soaking in the warm water over four centuries. The extensive remains of their baths are at the heart of the city, near the handsome medieval Abbey church. Most of Bath today, however, dates from Georgian times, when the fashionable world came to 'take the waters' in a social round led by Beau Nash, and described - not always kindly - by writers such as Jane Austen. The city is still filled with elegant Georgian terraces and other buildings of mellow Bath stone, notably the celebrated Pulteney Bridge, Circus and Royal Crescent. Highlights among the many places to visit include No 1 Royal Crescent, the Roman Baths and the neighbouring Pump Room. Nearly every street is attractive, with stylish shops to add to the pleasure of wandering. Should the hilly streets prove exhausting, the Kennet and Avon Canal has boating and a towpath walk. The city also has a rich cultural life, and an arts festival each May.

American Museum

Claverton Manor BA2 7BD (2.5m SE)

☎01225 460503 Fax 01225 480726

Claverton Manor is two miles south east of Bath, in a beautiful setting above the River Avon. The house was built in 1820 by Sir Jeffrey Wyatville, and is now a museum of American decorative arts. A series of rooms show American life from the 17th to 19th centuries, with special sections on American Indians and the Shakers, a distinctive collection of quilts, and miniature rooms. The gardens are also well worth seeing, and include an American arboretum and a replica of George Washington's garden at Mount Vernon. The Folk Art Gallery and the New Gallery are among the many exhibits in the grounds along with seasonal exhibitions. Winston Churchill made his

first political speech here in 1897. Exhibition of Shaker furniture (16 May-18 October). Please telephone for details of this and other special events.
Open 21 Mar-1 Nov, Tue-Sun 2-5. Gardens 1-6. BH Sun & Mon 11-5.
£5 (ch £3, pen £4.50).
P ☕ ♿ *toilets for disabled shop* 🐕 *(on leads only)*
Cards:

Bath Abbey
BA1 1LY
☎ ***01225 422462***
Fax 01225 429990
A 15th century Abbey church built on the site of the Saxon abbey where Edgar was crowned the first King of England in 973. The church is Perpendicular style with Norman arches and superb fan-vaulting. The famous West Front carvings represent the Founder-bishop's dream of angels ascending and descending from heaven.
Open all year, Mar-Oct 9-6, Oct-Mar 9-4. Closed for sightseeing Sun, Thu (am) and other times when services are taking place.
Visitors invited to give at least £1.50 each.
P ♿ *shop* 🐕

Bath Industrial Heritage Centre
Camden Works, Julian Rd BA1 2RH
☎ ***01225 318348***
Fax 01225 318348
The centre houses the Bowler collection, the entire stock-in-trade of a Victorian brass founder, general engineer and aerated water manufacturer, displayed so as to capture the atmosphere of the original premises. Also here is 'The Story of Bath Stone', with a replica of a mine face before mechanisation, and a Bath cabinet-maker's workshop, complete with tools and original drawings. A series of temporary exhibitions will include displays from the collection of travelling exhibitions, and there will be a series of lectures throughout the year.
Open all year, Etr-1 Nov, daily 10-5; Nov-Etr, wknds 10-5. (Closed 25-26 Dec).
£3 (ch, pen & students £2). Family ticket £7.50.
P ☕ *shop* 🐕

Bath Postal Museum
8 Broad St BA1 5LJ
☎ ***01225 460333***
Ralph Allen, 18th-century postal reformer and Postmaster of Bath, developed and expanded the mail routes throughout the country. John Palmer, another Bath citizen later the same century, was instrumental in introducing the first nationwide mail coach service. In May 1840 the world's first postage stamps, the famous Penny Black, were sold and sent from the building now occupied by the Bath Postal Museum. The museum has displays on written communications throughout history, exhibitions and films, and of course stamps.
Open all year, Mon-Sat 11-5; Sun 2-5. Mar-Dec Parties by appointment. (Closed Good Fri, 25-26 Dec & 1 Jan).
P *(200 yds)* ☕ ♿ *toilets for disabled shop* 🐕
Details not confirmed for 1998
Cards:

The Book Museum
Manvers St BA1 1JW
☎ ***01225 466000 Fax 01225 482122***
The Museum includes an exhibition of first and early editions of authors who lived in Bath, such as Jane Austen and Charles Dickens.
Open all year, Mon-Fri 9-1 & 2-5.30, Sat 9.30-1. (Closed 25 Dec & BH).
£2 (ch £1).
P *(NCP) shop* 🐕 🚌

The Building of Bath Museum
Countess of Huntingdons Chapel, The Vineyards, The Paragon BA1 5NA (M4 junct 18 down A46 towards Bath city centre. Take A4, 2nd exit at mini rdbt. Along road on right)
☎ ***01225 333895***
Fax 01225 445473
This new museum relates the fascinating story of how Georgian Bath was created. 17th Century Bath was a small medieval market town but in the space of 100 years it was transformed into one of the most beautiful, impressive, exciting and glamorous cities in Europe. The exhibition depicts elegant society life in "Beau" Nash's spa resort and explains how the splendid houses were constructed, from the laying of the first foundation stone to the last coat of paint. Exhibits include full-scale "hands-on" reconstructions, collections of original tools, architectural fragments and a series of spectacular models including the huge historic city model where famous buildings light up at the touch of a button. After a visit, the street scene outside seems like an extension of the exhibition: visitors stop and study doors and windows, peer down into basements or up at the chimney tops. The Building of Bath Museum provides an excellent and essential introduction for any visitor to Bath, which still remains one of the most elegant cities in Europe. Ring for details of special events such as concerts and lectures.
Open 11 Feb-1 Dec, Tue-Sun & BH's 10.30-5.
£3 (ch £1.50 & con £2). Party 10+.
P *(500 mtrs)* ♿ *shop* 🐕

Holburne Museum & Craft Study Centre
Great Pulteney St BA2 4DB
☎ ***01225 466669***
Fax 01225 333121
This elegant and historic building in a lovely garden setting, shows 17th-and 18th-century collections of fine and decorative art, notably silver, porcelain, glass, majolica, furniture and Old Masters, including Gainsborough. These are displayed together with work by 20th-century artists and crafts people, which embraces ceramics, woven and printed textiles, calligraphy and furniture. There is an annual programme of exhibitions, lectures, and events. Study facilities by appointment.
Open mid Feb-mid Dec, Mon-Sat & BHs 11-5, Sun 2.30-5.30 (Closed Mon Nov-Etr).
P ☕ ♿ *(lift to all floors) toilets for disabled shop* 🐕
Details not confirmed for 1998

Museum of Costume
Bennett St BA1 2QH
☎ ***01225 477789 477785***
Fax 01225 444793 & 477743
The Museum of Costume is one of the largest and most prestigious collections of fashionable dress for men, women and children covering the late 16th century to the present day. It is housed in Bath's famous 18th century Assembly Rooms designed by John Wood the Younger in 1771. Exhibition of modern fashion in 'Catwalk Classics' from 1st April. Connoisseur Period: August 1998. During the National Trust Connoisseur Period, the Assembly Rooms are fully open for viewing and a tea room is available in the formal garden. Entrance to the Assembly Rooms is free.
Open all year, Mon-Sat 10-5, Sun 11-5. (Closed 25 & 26 Dec).
£3.80 (ch £2.70). Family ticket £11. Combined ticket with Roman Baths, £8.40 (ch £5)
P *(park & ride recommended)* ♿ *(audio guides available) toilets for disabled shop* 🐕
Cards:

No 1 Royal Crescent
BA1 2LR
☎ ***01225 428126***
Fax 01225 481850
Bath is very much a Georgian city, but most of its houses have naturally altered over the years to suit changing tastes and lifestyles. Built in 1768 by John Wood the Elder, No 1 Royal Crescent has been restored to look as it would have done some 200 years ago. Two floors are furnished as they might have been in the 18th century, with pictures, china and furniture of the period, and there is also an interesting kitchen. Note the first-floor windows, which are the original length: all the others in the Royal Crescent were lengthened downwards in the 19th century.
Open 10 Feb-25 Oct, Tue-Sun 10.30-5; 27 Oct-29 Nov, Tue-Sun 10.30-4. Open BH Mon. (Closed Good Fri). Last admission 30 mins before closing.
£3.50 (ch, students & pen £2.50). Family ticket £8
P *shop* 🐕

Roman Baths & Pump Room
Abbey Church Yard BA1 1LZ
☎ ***01225 477785***
Fax 01225 444743
The descent to the Roman baths is a step back in time. The remains give a vivid impression of life nearly 2000 years ago. The baths, built next to Britain's only hot spring, served the sick and the pilgrims visiting the adjacent Temple of Sulis Minerva. The Spring was a sacred site lying within the courtyard of the Temple. Votive offerings and temple treasures discovered during the excavations of the Spring can be seen in the museum display. Today, the Temple Courtyard is beneath the Pump Room. This building became a popular meeting place in the 18th century when Bath became the leading resort for fashionable society. Inside the present Pump Room there is now a restaurant where morning coffee, lunches and teas can be taken to the accompaniment of music from the Pump Room Trio. The hot spa water can also be sampled.
Open all year, Apr-Jul & Sep, daily 9-6; Aug daily 9-6 & 8pm-10pm; Oct-Mar, Mon-Sat 9.30-5, Sun 10.30-5. Disabled visitors free admission to ground floor areas. Last admission 30 minutes before closing.
£6.30 (ch £3.80). Family ticket £16.50. Combined ticket with Museum of Costume £8.40 (ch £5)
P *(500yds) (park & ride recommended)* ✕ *licensed* ♿ *(sign language & audio tours) toilets for disabled shop* 🐕
Cards:

Royal Photographic Society
The Octagon, Milsom St BA1 1DN
☎ ***01225 462841***
Fax 01225 448688
The Octagon was built in 1796 as a chapel, but is now the headquarters of the world's oldest photographic society. A huge collection of cameras, the first photograph, and other classics are displayed. Temporary exhibitions often include top contemporary work. A variety of workshops, seminars and talks will be held throughout the year.
Open all year, daily 9.30-5.30, last admission 4.45pm. (Closed 25-26 Dec).
P *(5 mins walk)* ☕ ✕ *licensed* ♿ *(chair lift to all floors) toilets for disabled shop* 🐕
Details not confirmed for 1998

Sally Lunn's Refreshment House & Museum
4 North Pde Passage BA1 1NX
☎ ***01225 461634***
Fax 01225 447090
The history of this Tudor building can be traced back to Roman times. It is the oldest house in Bath, and became a popular meeting place in the 18th century. In the cellars, a fascinating museum reveals the findings of recent excavations. Here too is the original kitchen, with its faggot oven, Georgian cooking range and a collection of baking utensils. The traditional 'Sally Lunn' is still served in the restaurant: it is a bread like the French 'brioche', made with eggs and butter, popularly believed to have been named after its first maker, who came to Bath in 1680. Last week in October each year is the Bath 'Open Free Museum Week'.
Open all year, Museum - Mon-Fri 10-6, Sat 10-6, Sun 12-6; Refreshment rooms: Mon 10-6, Tue-Sat 10am-10.30pm & Sun 12-10.30pm. (Closed 25-26 Dec & 1 Jan). 30p (ch, students & pen free).
P ☕ ✕ *licensed (braille menu for the blind) shop* 🐕 🚌
Cards:

The Museum of Costume at Bath holds one of the largest collections of historical dress in the world.

Glastonbury Abbey is said to have been founded in AD61 by Joseph of Arimathea and is also claimed by some to be the last resting place of King Arthur.

CASTLE CARY
Hadspen Garden & Nursery
Hadspen House BA7 7NG (2m SE off A371)
☎01749 813707 Fax 01749 813707
Situated within a 17th-century curved wall, this 5-acre garden has borders planted with roses and herbaceous plants, many of which have been developed here. Plants grown in the garden are available in the adjoining nursery.
Open Mar-1 Oct, Thu-Sun & BHs 10-5. £2.50 (ch 50p). Free admission for wheelchair users.
🅿 ✕ ♿ *toilets for disabled garden centre*
⊘

CHARD
Forde Abbey
TA20 4LU (4m S of Chard)
☎01460 221290 Fax 01460 220296
This 12th-century Cistercian monastery was converted into a private dwelling in the mid-17th century by Cromwell's attorney general. In the house there are good pictures and furniture and an outstanding set of Mortlake tapestries. The large gardens are some of the finest in Dorset and include a kitchen garden, rock garden and bog garden as well as herbaceous borders and many outstanding trees.
Gardens, open all year, daily 10-4.30. Abbey & gardens Apr-Oct Sun, Wed & BH 1-4.30 (last admission). Prices under review.
🅿 ♿ *(wheelchair can be borrowed) toilets for disabled shop garden centre* ⊘ *(ex garden)*
Cards: ▨ ▭ ▭ ▨ 🅶

CHEDDAR
Cheddar Showcaves & Gorge
BS27 3QF (on B3135)
☎01934 742343 Fax 01934 744637
Britain's two most beautifully illuminated showcaves - spectacular Gough's Cave and the stunning colours of Cox's Cave - plus 'The Crystal Quest', a dark walk fantasy adventure underground. Visit 'Cheddar Man', Britain's oldest complete skeleton, and his world 9,000 years ago. Climb Jacob's Ladder to Pavey's Lookout Tower and Gorge Walk. The daring can pre-book an Adventure Caving Expedition (minimum age 12) - so much to do! All set in dramatic Cheddar Gorge. Scenic

Guided Tours of Cheddar Gorge by open-top double decker bus every 30 minutes from Easter to end of September. Please ring for details.
Open all year, Etr-Sep 10-5; rest of year 10.30-4.30. (Closed 24 & 25 Dec).
🅿 ✕ ♿ *(free entrance to Gough's cave, access limited) shop*
Details not confirmed for 1998
Cards: ▨ ▭

CLEVEDON
Clevedon Court
Tickenham Rd BS21 6QU (off B3130 1.5m E)
☎01275 872257
Clevedon Court is a remarkably complete manor house of around 1320. Additions have been made in each century, so it is now a pleasing variety of styles, with an 18th-century terraced garden. One owner, Sir Edmund Elton, was a celebrated potter, and there is a display of his work.
Open Apr-Sep, Wed, Thu, Sun & BH Mon 2-5. Last admission 4.30.
£4 (ch £2, ch under 17). Party 20+ by arrangement.
🅿 ✕ ⊘ ⚑

CRANMORE
East Somerset Railway
Cranmore Railway Station BA4 4QP (on A361 between Frome & Shepton Mallet)
☎01749 880417 Fax 01749 880764
Five steam locomotives and rolling stock can be seen at Cranmore station, which has an engine shed and workshops. The new art gallery displays David Shepherd's work. Steam train services (see timetable for Steam Days) include Santa Specials in December, and here also are a museum, wildlife information centre, restaurant and play area. Special events for 1998 include: Friends of Thomas weekends (May 23-25, August 15-16), Steam Dream (September 26-27), Teddy Bears Picnic (June 14), Steam Rally (August BH), Santa Special in December and a Jazz Night (July 25). Please telephone for details.
Open daily Mar-24 Dec from 10am. For days when steam trains are operating phone 01749 880417.
£5.50 (ch £3.50 & pen £4.50.) Non-steam days £2 (ch £1).
🅿 ✕ *licensed* ♿ *(ramp from road to platform) toilets for disabled shop*
Cards: ▨ ▭ ▭ ▨ 🅶

CRICKET ST THOMAS
Cricket St Thomas Wildlife Park
TA20 4DD (on A30)
☎01460 30755 Fax 01460 30668
The old and beautiful park of Cricket House still houses a wide variety of animals and birds, including elephants, camels, sealions, parrots and other exotic creatures. The wildlife enclosures have been designed to blend in with the surroundings as far as possible, and there have been successes with breeding, most notably of black swans. Shire horses can be seen at the Heavy Horse Centre, and there is a woodland railway. The house became well known as 'Grantleigh Manor' in the BBC television series *To The Manor Born*.
Open all year Apr-Oct, daily 10-6; Nov-Mar 10-5 or dusk (whichever is earlier).
🅿 ✕ *licensed* ♿ *toilets for disabled shop garden centre*
Details not confirmed for 1998

DUNSTER
Dunster Castle
TA24 6SL (3m SE of Minehead, approach from A39)
☎01643 821314
The setting of Dunster Castle is dramatic: it lies between Exmoor and the sea. Sub-tropical plants flourish in the 28-acre park and the terraced gardens are noted for exotica such as a giant lemon tree, yuccas, mimosa and palms. The castle's picturesque appearance is largely due to attractive 19th-century work, but handsome older features include intricately decorated ceilings, the superb 17th-century oak staircase and the gallery with its brightly painted wall hangings. The castle was the home of the Luttrell family for 600 years, and there is a dramatic 16th-century portrait of Sir John Luttrell. Other notable features include the elaborate 'thrown chair' and the leather-look wallpaper of the comfortable 19th-century library.
Open: Garden & park, daily 11-4 (10-5 Apr-Sep). Last admission 30 mins before closing. Castle, 30 Mar-Sept, Sat-Wed 11-5; 3 Oct-1 Nov, Sat-Wed 11-4. Closed 25 Dec. Castle, Garden & Park £5.20 (ch £2.70). Family ticket £13.40. Garden & park only £2.70 (ch £1.30). Family ticket to garden & park £6.70, includes exploration trail. Party 15+.
🅿 ♿ *(Braille guide, Batricar for grounds) toilets for disabled shop* ⚑

EAST HUNTSPILL
Secret World-Badger & Wildlife Reserve Centre
New Rd TA9 3PZ (Signposted from A38)
☎01278 783250 Fax 01278 783250
Discover the natural world that lives side by side with domestic animals at this Rescue Centre. Foxes, badgers, owls and much, much more can be seen in the surroundings of a traditional farm where the listed farmhouse, built in 1675, has been made into tearooms serving meals all through the day. Visit the nocturnal house where night creatures can be seen in their natural surroundings and an observation sett where you can watch badger life or discover the mysteries of the insect house. Farm demonstrations and talks are given half-hourly throughout the day. There is plenty to see or do for any age group rain or shine, at this all-weather, all-year-round facility. Tractor rides, shop, bicycle hire at Somerset's Level & Moors Visitors Centre. Dogs welcome on leads.
Open Mar-Nov, daily 10-6. Nov-Dec, daily 10-5. Feb- Mar, daily 10-5.
£4.75 (ch £3.50, pen £4.25). Family £15. Party.
🅿 ✕ ♿ *toilets for disabled shop garden centre*
Cards: ▨ ▭ ▭ ▨ ▨ 🅶

EAST LAMBROOK
East Lambrook Manor Garden
TA13 5HL (signed off A303, at South Petherton roundabout)
☎01460 240328 Fax 01460 242344
Walter and Margery Fish created the cottage-style garden after buying the 15th-century manor in 1937. Margery Fish's book *We Made a Garden* described the work, and aroused so much interest that she started a nursery to sell the types of plants she used. Plants are still sold. The garden is now Grade I listed and has been fully restored. NCCPG National Geranium Collection. Please ring for special events.
Open Mon-Sat 10-5, also 25 May for National Gardens Scheme. (Closed Nov-28 Feb).
🅿 *shop garden centre* ⊘
Details not confirmed for 1998

FARLEIGH HUNGERFORD
Farleigh Hungerford Castle
BA3 6RS (3.5m W of Trowbridge on A366)
☎01225 754026
The ruined 14th-century castle has a chapel containing wall paintings, stained glass and the fine tomb of Sir Thomas Hungerford who built the castle. His powerful family owned land from here to Salisbury. Family and castle are linked with various grim tales of hanging and murder.
Open all year, Apr-Oct, daily 10-6 (or dusk if earlier); Nov-Mar, Wed-Sun 10-4 (closed 1-2pm). Closed 24-26 Dec & 1 Jan.
£2.10 (ch £1.60, concessions £1.60).
🅿 ♿ ⊘ ♿

GLASTONBURY
Glastonbury Abbey
Magdalene St BA6 9EL (on A361 between Frome & Taunton)
☎01458 832267 Fax 01458 832267
Few places in Britain are as rich in myth and legend as Glastonbury. Tradition maintains that the impressive, medieval abbey ruins stand at the birth place of Christianity in Britain. This is where Joseph of Arimathea is said to have brought the Holy Grail (the chalice used by Christ at the Last Supper) and to have founded a chapel in AD61, planting his staff in the ground where it flowered both at Christmas and Easter. Later, it is said, King Arthur and Guinevere were buried at Glastonbury; and the abbey was a place of pilgrimage in the Middle Ages. The present abbey ruins date from after a fire in 1184, and are mostly of the 12th and 13th centuries. The Abbey fell into decay after the Dissolution. The modern display area contains artefacts and a model of the Abbey as it might have ➤

been in 1539, which together form a history of the Abbey. Special events for 1998 include: West of England Pilgrimage (4 July), Roman Catholic Pilgrimage (5 July), Miracle Play (24-27 June), Hearts on Fire Concert (18 July) and Royal Philharmonic Orchestra Concert (14-15 August). Please ring for details.
Open all year, daily, Jun-Aug 9-6; Sep-May 9.30-6pm or dusk, whichever is the earliest. Dec-Feb open at 10am. (Closed 25 Dec).
£2.50 (ch 5-16 £1, pen & students £2). Family ticket £5.50.
🅿 *(charged)* 🏆 ♿ *(all areas except Lady Chapel) toilets for disabled shop*

KINGSDON
Lytes Cary Manor
TA11 7HU (off A303)
☎ *01985 843600*
This charming manor, tucked away in the Somerset countryside, takes its name from the family who lived here for 500 years, the Lytes. Much of the present house was built by John Lyte in the 16th century although the oldest part, the chapel, dates from 1343. The Great Hall was a 15th-century addition and still boasts stained glass installed by John Lyte. His son, Henry, was a noted horticulturalist and he transformed the gardens at the manor; unfortunately these have not survived, but the present formal gardens are being restocked with plants that were commonly grown in his day.
Open Apr-Oct, Mon, Wed & Sat 2-6 or dusk if earlier. Last admission 5.30.
£4 (ch £2)
🅿 ♿ ♻ 🐾

MONKSILVER
Combe Sydenham Country Park
TA4 4JG
☎ *01984 656284 Fax 01984 656284*
The 16th-century house was the home of Sir Francis Drake's second wife, Elizabeth, and is currently being restored.

The only part of the house that visitors can see is the Court Room, which has been restored using, wherever possible, the materials of the period, and guides are on hand to answer questions from visitors. There are an Elizabethan-style garden, woodland walks, a medieval corn mill, picnic site, and a children's play area. There is also a fish farm with coarse fishing available.
Open Mar-Sep. Country Park: Sun-Fri 9-5. Other attractions open by guided tour, Spring BH-Sep, Mon, Thu & Fri at 2pm. Country Park: £2 per vehicle refunded when guided tour taken. Guided Tour: £4 (ch £2).
🅿 *(charged)* ♿ ♻ *(ex in park)*

MONTACUTE
Montacute House
TA15 6XP (off A3088)
☎ *01935 823289*
Set amidst formal gardens, Montacute House was built in honey-brown Ham stone by Sir Edward Phelips. He was a successful lawyer, and became Speaker of the House of Commons in 1604. The glittering expanse of windows and Flemish-style rounded gables date from his time, but the heraldic beasts and fluted columns were added in the 18th century. Inside there are decorated ceilings, ornate fireplaces, heraldic glass and fine wood panelling. A collection of tapestries, paintings, furniture and ceramics bequeathed by Sir Malcolm Stewart has enabled the house to be furnished in fitting style. Better still, the Long Gallery displays a permanent collection of Tudor and Jacobean portraits from the National Portrait Gallery in London.
Open, Garden & Park: Apr-1 Nov daily (ex Tue) 11.30-5.30 or dusk if earlier. 4 Nov-Mar Wed-Sun 11.30-4. House: Apr-1 Nov, daily (ex Tue) 12-5.30. Last admission 5pm.
House, Garden & Park £5.20 (ch £2.60); Garden & Park 1 Apr-3 Nov £2.90 (ch £1.30), 4 Nov-Mar £1.50. Party 15+.

🅿 ✗ *licensed* ♿ *(Braille guide) toilets for disabled shop garden centre* ♻ *(ex park)* 🐾

MUCHELNEY
Muchelney Abbey
TA10 0DQ
☎ *01458 250664*
Encircled by marshes, Muchelney seemed a suitably remote spot to found a Benedictine Abbey in the 8th century. All that is left are the 15th and 16th century ruins; the southern range of cloister buildings, containing the Abbot's lodging, is fairly well preserved. Nearby is a 14th-century priest's house, a rare example of domestic architecture from this period. There are also exhibitions of John Leach pottery and Stuart interior furnishings and tapestries.
Open Apr-Sep, daily 10-6.
£1.60 (ch 80p, concessions £1.20)
🅿 ♿ ♻ 🎏

NETHER STOWEY
Coleridge Cottage
TA5 1NQ (off A39)
☎ *01278 732662*
It was in this small cottage that Coleridge was most inspired as a poet and here that he wrote *The Ancient Mariner*. The Coleridge family moved to Nether Stowey in 1796 and became friendly with the Wordsworths who lived nearby, but the group were regarded with suspicion by the local population. The house was smaller and thatched, not tiled, in those days but otherwise little has changed.
Open Apr-1 Oct, Tue-Thu & Sun 2-5 (Parlour & Reading room only). In winter by written application to custodian.
£1.70. (ch 80p). Parties by arrangement with caretaker.
🅿 ♻ 🐾

NUNNEY
Nunney Castle
(3.5m SW of Frome, off A361)
Built by Sir John de la Mere in 1373, and supposedly modelled on France's Bastille, this crenellated manor house has one of the deepest moats in England. It was ruined by the Parliamentarian forces during the Civil War.
Open any reasonable time.
Free.
♿ 🎏

RODE
Rode Bird Gardens
BA3 6QW (off A36 between Bath & Warminster)
☎ *01373 830326 Fax 01373 831288*
Rode Bird Gardens consist of 17 acres of grounds, planted with trees, shrubs, and flower gardens, in a pretty and little-visited village. The bird collection consists of around 1200 birds of 200 different species, and there is also a clematis collection, an ornamental lake, a Pets' Corner, a children's play area, and an information centre. Plants are for sale. Children must be accompanied by an adult. A Woodland steam railway operates daily from Easter until the beginning of October, weather permitting. Events for 1998 include: a Railway Weekend (18-19 April), Selwood Steam (23-25 May), Crafts & Gardens Weekend (27-28 June), Parrot Weekend (4-5 July), a Steam in Miniature Weekend (11-12 July), 6th Steam & Vintage Meeting (19-20 Sept).
Open all year daily (ex 25 Dec); Summer 10-6 (last admission 5pm); Winter 10-dusk (last admission 1hr before closing time).
£4.50 (ch15 £2.50, pen £4) Family ticket £13.50). Train ticket £1.10 (ch & pen 90p).
🅿 🏆 ♿ *(special route, wheelchairs for hire) toilets for disabled shop* ♻
Cards: 🔲

SPARKFORD
Haynes Motor Museum
BA22 7LH (from A303 follow A359 road towards Castle Cary, the museum is clearly signposted)
☎ *01963 440804 Fax 01963 441004*

The museum contains a unique and extraordinary collection of over 300 veteran, vintage and classic cars, motorcycles, racing cars and bikes. Vehicles range from a 1903 Oldsmobile to sports cars of the 50s and 60s and modern day classics. American cars include a Model T Ford, Haynes V12, Cord, and Supercharged Auburn Speedster. Also at the museum is a 70 seater video cinema, picnic area, and the Pit Stop Cafe. When weather and staff availability permit, cars are shown on our own vehicle display track. The collection now features the only model J Durham bodied Deusenberg outside the US. New features for 1998 include the Hall of Motorsports with the Race Crash Display & Recreation of a Grand Prix start grid. There is also an extensive children's playground. Special events for 1998 include: Haynes Sporting Spring Classic (29 March), Haynes 2 1/2 Day Classic Tour (17-19 April), Haynes Veteran & Vintage Run (3 May), Haynes Falling Leaves Classic Tour (20 Sept). Ring for further details.
Open all year, Mar-Oct , daily 9.30-5.30; Nov-Feb, 10.30-5. Etr-summer hols open to 7.30pm. (Closed 25,26 Dec & 1 Jan).
£4.95 (ch 5 £2.95, concessions £4.25)
🅿 🏆 ♿ *(ramps & loan wheelchairs available) toilets for disabled shop* ♻ *(ex in grounds)*
Cards: 🔲

STOKE ST GREGORY
Willow & Wetlands Visitor Centre
Meare Green Court TA3 6HY (between North Curry & Stoke St Gregory)
☎ *01823 490249 Fax 01823 490814*
The levels and moors of Somerset are the most important areas of 'wetland' left in England. This centre shows how today's landscape has been created from marsh and swamp. The wetland wild flowers, insects and birds are all illustrated. There are sections on traditional industries based on locally found plants like withies and teasles. Models, drawings and photographs are used to give a fascinating insight into this unique area. There is a guided tour of this working industry, covering all aspects of withy growing and processing and a visit to the basket workshop to see basket making in progress. There is also a Basket Museum.
Open all year, Mon-Fri 9-5 (guided tours 10-4), Sat (no tours) 9-5. Closed Sun.
£1.95 (ch £1, pen £1.50). Party. Credit cards only accepted if total admission price exceeds £10.
🅿 ♿ *shop*
Cards: 🔲

STOKE-SUB-HAMDON
Stoke-Sub-Hamdon Priory
North St TA4 6QP (between A303 & A3088)
☎ *01985 843600*
This 15th-century house is built of Ham Hill stone and was once the home of the priests of the chantry belonging to the now vanished Beauchamp Manor. The 14th-and 15th-century farm buildings and the screens passage of the chantry remain, with part of the hall.
Open 1 Apr-31 Oct, daily 10-6. Great Hall only open to visitors.
Free.
🅿 🐾

STREET
The Shoe Museum
C & J Clark Ltd, High St BA16 0YA
☎ *01458 443131 Fax 01458 843110*
The museum is in the oldest part of the shoe factory set up by Cyrus and James Clark in 1825. It contains shoes from Roman times to the present, buckles, engravings, fashion plates, machinery, hand tools and advertising material. One section illustrates the early history of the shoe firm and its role in the town.
Open all year.
Free.
🅿 *(charged)* 🏆 ✗ ♿ *toilets for disabled shop* ♻

The Long Gallery of the Bishop's Palace at Wells

TAUNTON
Hestercombe Gardens
Hestercombe House, Cheddon Fitzpaine
TA2 8LQ (3m N, off A361 near Cheddon
Fitzpaine).
☎01823 413923 Fax 01823 413030
The late 19th-century house is now the
headquarters of the Somerset Fire
Brigade. The multi-level gardens and
orangery were originally planned in 1905
by Sir Edwin Lutyens and Gertrude
Jekyll, with raised walks, sunken lawns
and a water garden. To the north of the
house is an 18th century parkland with
ponds, cascades and follies all set in 35
acres of Arcadian landscape. Contact the
Gardens for details of special events.
Open all year, Apr-Sep, Mon-Fri 10-6 (10-
5 Oct-Mar). Closed 25-26 Dec.
🅿️ ♿
Details not confirmed for 1998

TINTINHULL
Tintinhull House Garden
BA22 9PZ (.5m S off A303)
☎01935 822545
An attractive, mainly 17th-century
farmhouse with a Queen Anne façade, it
stands in four acres of beautiful formal
gardens and orchard. The gardens were
largely created by Mrs Reiss, who gave
the property to the National Trust in 1953.
Open Apr-Sep, Wed-Sun & BH Mons 12-
6 (last admission 5.30pm).
£3.70 (ch £1.80)
🅿️ ❀ ♨

WASHFORD
Cleeve Abbey
TA23 0PS (0.25m S of A39)
☎01984 40377
The Cistercian abbey was founded at the
end of the 12th century and is now a
ruin. There is little left of the church, but
the gatehouse, dormitory and refectory
are in good condition, with traceried
windows, a fine timbered roof and wall
paintings to be seen.
Open all year, Apr-Oct, daily 10-6 (or dusk
if earlier); Nov-Mar, Wed-Sun 10-4
(closed 1-2pm). Closed 24-26 Dec & 1
Jan.
£2.50 (ch £1.30, concessions £1.90).
🅿️ ♿ shop ❀ (in certain areas) ✿

Tropiquaria
TA23 0JX (on A39)
☎01984 640688
Fax 01984 640688
Housed in a 1930s BBC transmitting
station, the main hall has been converted
into an indoor jungle with a 15-foot
waterfall, tropical plants and free-flying
birds. (Snakes, lizards, iguanas, spiders,
toads and terrapins are caged!)
Downstairs is the submarine crypt with
local and tropical marine life. Other
features include landscaped gardens,
outdoor aviaries, a children's playground,
the Shadowstring Puppet Theatre, and
'Wireless in the West' museum.
Open Apr-Sep, daily 10-5; Oct, daily 11-5,
Nov & Feb-Mar wknds & school hols 11-
5; 27-31 Dec, 11-5. (Closed 1-27 Dec).
✱£4.25 (ch £2.80, pen £3.50).
🅿️ 🍴 ♿ shop ❀
Cards: 🎴 ▰▱ 🎴 🎴

WELLS
The Bishop's Palace
Henderson Rooms BA5 2PD (next to
cathedral off the Market Sq)
☎01749 678691
Fax 01749 678691
Close to the cathedral is the moated
bishop's palace. The early part of the
palace, the bishop's chapel and the ruins
of the banqueting hall date from the 13th
century; The undercroft remains virtually
unchanged from this time. There are
several state rooms and a long gallery
which houses portraits of former
Bishops. The palace is ringed with
fortifications as well as the moat and
access can only be gained through the
14th-century gatehouse. The name of the
city is taken from the wells in the palace
grounds. Events include a Sealed Knot
battle re-enactment (1-2 August). Please
telephone for details.
Open Etr Sat-Oct, Tue-Fri & BH's; daily in
Aug 10.30-6 Sun 2-6. Gates close at
exactly 6pm.
£3 (ch 12 accompanied free, UB40's
£1.50, pen £2, disabled £1.50) . Party
10+.
P 🍴 ✗ licensed ♿ (free use of electric
wheelchair)

WESTON-SUPER-MARE
The Helicopter Museum
Weston Airport, Locking Moor Rd BS22
8PP (outskirts of town on A371)
☎01934 635227
Fax 01934 822400
A unique collection of more than 60
helicopters and autogyros is on display.
This is given a further dimension by
exhibits of models, photographs and
components to illustrate how the aircraft
work. From March to October on the
second Sunday in the month, 'Open
Cockpit Days' are held when visitors can
try out the pilot's seat of a real helicopter,
and receive instructions from museum
guides. Helicopters from this museum
are also featured in the Weston-super-
Helidays, which take place on the
seafront and include flying and static
displays of up to 50 helicopters. Recent
additions are a new display hangar and
several new exhibits, including G-Lynx,
the world's fastest helicopter, and a
Russian 'Hind' attack helicopter. Special
events include: Weston-Super-Helidays
(31 July-2 Aug), Engineering Weekends
(24-25 May-30-31 August).
Open all year, Nov-Mar Wed-Sun 10-4.
Apr-Oct daily 10-6. (closed 24-26 Dec & 1
Jan)
£3 (ch under 5 free, ch 5-16 £2, pen
£2.50). Family ticket £8. Party 15+.
🅿️ 🍴 ♿ toilets for disabled shop
Cards: 🎴 ▰▱ 🎴

Time Machine
Burlington St BS23 1PR
☎01934 621028
Fax 01934 612526
This museum, housed in the workshops
of the Edwardian Gaslight Company, is
set around a central courtyard with
displays on the seaside holiday, an old
chemist's shop, a dairy, and a fountain
with Victorian pavement mosaics.
Adjoining the museum is Clara's Cottage,
a Westonian home of the 1900s with
period kitchen, parlour, bedroom and
back yard. One of the rooms has an
additional display of Peggy Nisbet dolls.
Other displays in the museum include a
gallery of wildlife in the district, Mendip
minerals, mining and local archaeology.
There are also costume rooms, an
exhibition of early bicycles and a display
on the dentist in 1900. Changing
exhibitions are held in the art gallery, and
the "People's Collections" which
displays collections of people from the
North Somerset area. Contact museum
for further details.
Open all year: Mar-Sept daily 10-5, Nov-
Dec 10-4 & BH Mon. (Closed Xmas, New
Year)
£2 (ch £1, pen £1.75). Family ticket
£4.50. These tickets permit unlimited
free return visits for rest of financial year.
P (400 yds) (some disabled parking
outside museum) 🍴 ♿ toilets for
disabled shop ❀ (ex guide dogs)

WOOKEY HOLE
Wookey Hole Caves & Papermill
BA5 1BB
☎01749 672243
Fax 01749 677749
The Caves are the main feature of
Wookey Hole. Visitors enjoy a half mile
tour through the Chambers, accompanied
by a knowledgeable guide who points out
the amazing stalagmites and stalactites,
including the famous Witch of Wookey.
The guides use remote controlled lighting
to highlight geological features and
illustrate the history and myths
associated with the caves. Visitors also
take in the Victorian Papermill, at one
time amongst the largest handmade
papermills in Europe, which still sells
exquisite paper all over the world.
Visitors can watch paper being made in
the traditional way and have a go at
making paper. Also in the Mill is the
Magical Mirror Maze, an enclosed
passage of multiple image mirrors
creating an illusion of endless reflections.
After the fun of the maze, visitors move
on to a typical Old Penny Arcade where
they can purchase old pennies to operate
the original machines. The caves
museum and waterwheel complete the
tour.
Open all year, Mar-Oct 9.30-5.30; Nov-
Feb 10.30-4.30. (Closed 17-25 Dec).
✱£6.50 (ch £3.50, pen £5.50) Party 10+.
Various disabled concessions.
🅿️ ✗ licensed ♿ (Papermill only) toilets
for disabled shop ❀
Cards: 🎴 ▰▱ 🎴 🎴

YEOVILTON
Fleet Air Arm Museum
Royal Naval Air Station BA22 8HT
(on B3151)
☎01935 840077
Fax 01935 841524
Based at the Royal Naval Air Station, the
museum portrays the history and
achievements of the Royal Naval Air
Service, with examples from the early
days of kites and airships to the present
day. A collection of over 40 historic
aircraft, several unique, are on display as
well as a vast collection of costume,
medals and memorabilia. Special
exhibitions using modern audio visual
aids and displays put the exhibits in their
original context. These include World
War I, the Interwar Years, Battle of
Taranto, Skua Underwater Experience,
WRENS, recent conflicts and many more.
In addition, you can climb aboard and
walk through Concorde 002, the British
prototype. There are airfield viewing
galleries to watch aircraft taking off and
landing from the Naval Base. For children
there is a flight simulator and a Naval
Aviation Adventure playground. The
Ultimate Aircraft Carrier Experience
offers all the sights, sounds, smells and
action of a real aircraft carrier.
Open all year, daily (ex 24-26 Dec) 10-
5.30 (4.30pm Nov-Mar).
£5.80 (ch £3.30, pen £4.30). Family ticket
£15. Price revision due Apr.
🅿️ 🍴 ✗ licensed ♿ (wheelchairs
available) toilets for disabled shop ❀ (ex
guide dogs)
Cards: 🎴 ▰▱ ▱▰ 🎴 🎴 🎴

STAFFORDSHIRE

ALTON
Alton Towers
ST10 4DB
☎01538 702200
Fax 01538 702724
Alton Towers is the UK's most magical
experience.. with rides, shows and
attractions guaranteed to suit every
member of the family. Major new
attractions, include a new 'wild, wet and
white knuckle ride joining the awesome
Nemesis in Forbidden Valley. Family
favourites such as the Congo River
Rapids, Haunted House and Runaway
Mine Train are back to entice those who
prefer to sit out the frantic delights of the
bigger rides, or who simply want to enjoy
a ride experience with younger children
(or older parents!) The enchanting
children's areas of Storybook Land and
Old MacDonald's Farm, the Land of
Make Believe and Adventure Land, are
further enhanced with a new interactive
television attraction, and even Peter
Rabbit is ringing in the changes with a
new show. The Alton Towers Hotel
opened in March 1996, its weird and
wonderful array of artefacts and
memorabilia from a bygone age,
including a stunning 37 foot high flying
machine which dominates the glass
topped atrium. Add all this to 200 acres
of stunning landscaped gardens and the
majestic ruins of the Towers themselves,
and you have so much more than a single
day's entertainment.
Open mid Mar-early Nov 9am until 1 hr
after attractions close. Attractions 10-5,
6, 7 or 8 as shown daily at main entrance
gate.
🅿️ 🍴 ✗ licensed ♿ toilets for disabled
shop ❀
Details not confirmed for 1998
Cards: 🎴 ▰▱ ▱▰ 🎴 🎴 🎴

BIDDULPH
Biddulph Grange Garden
Grange Rd ST8 7SD (off A527, 0.5m N of Biddulph)
☎01782 517999
This exciting and rare survival of a high Victorian garden has undergone extensive restoration which will continue for a number of years. Conceived by James Bateman, the fifteen acres are divided into a number of smaller gardens which were designed to house specimens from his extensive and wide-ranging plant collection. An Egyptian Court, Chinese Pagoda, Willow Pattern Bridge and Pinetum, together with many other settings, all combine to make the garden a miniature tour of the world.
Open Apr-1 Nov, Wed-Fri 12-6. Sat-Sun & BH Mon 11-6 (last admission 5.30 or dusk if earlier); 7 Nov-20 Dec, Sat-Sun 12-4. Apr-Oct; £4 (ch £2). Family ticket £10. Nov-Dec; £2 (ch £1). Family ticket £5.
🅿 🍴 *shop* ⌀ ♣

BURTON-UPON-TRENT
The Bass Museum
Horninglow St DE14 1YQ (on A50)
☎01283 511000 Fax 01283 513509
The museum is housed in the Engineers' Department and Company's Joiner's Shop, built in 1866. Three floors of entertaining and interesting exhibits trace the history of the brewing industry from its earliest times to the present day. Outside there are larger exhibits, such as a 1917 steam lorry and a Daimler van in the shape of a bottle of IPA. Other attractions include a model of Burton as it was in 1921, stables with Shire horses, and a steam locomotive. There is a fine collection of drinking glasses – and there is also the beer. Special events for 1998 include: Easter Festival (April 11-13), Bretby Classic Car & Motorcycle Rally (May 4), Charolais Show (20 Sept), World Barrel Rolling Championships (27 Sept), Alvis Register Club Rally (21 Dec). Ring for further details.

Cheddleton Flint Mill

This unique water mill and museum specialises in the history and processes in the preparation of the materials used in the Pottery Industry.

Attractively located beside the Caldon Canal.
Three miles south of Leek on A520. Parking for 7 cars.
Interesting and valuable educational resource.
Open almost every day throughout the year.
Admission free but donations very welcome.

The Perfect Day – In Every Way

EYE-CATCHING DISPLAYS
If you want a great family day out, visit The Bass Museum. Based in Burton - at the heart of Britain's brewing capital - this fascinating experience brings brewing history right up to date.

**PERFECT –
COME RAIN OR SHINE**
With award-winning exhibitions, guided brewery tours, nostalgic working model brewery vehicles and the famous Bass Shire horses, this is the perfect day out for the family - whatever the weather! And don't forget the gifts you can buy from the Museum Shop.

MOUTH-WATERING FOOD
There's no better way to round off your trip than to sample the beers and enjoy a bite to eat in the restaurants. Cheers!

SOUNDS GREAT!
So why not treat yourself and your family soon!

THE BASS MUSEUM
PO Box 220, Horninglow Street,
Burton upon Trent, Staffordshire.
Tel: 01283 511000.
Open every day except
Christmas Day, Boxing Day
and New Year's Day.

Open all year, Mon-Fri 10-5, Sat & Sun 11-5. Last admission 4pm. (Closed 25-26 Dec & 1 Jan).
£3.75 (ch £2, pen £2.50). Family ticket £9.95. Party. Brewery tours by arrangement only, at extra charge (inc free glass of beer/lager/soft drink)
🅿 ✗ *licensed* ♿ *(lift to all floors) toilets for disabled shop* ⌀
Cards: ▨ ▨ ▨ ▨

CHEDDLETON
Cheddleton Flint Mill
Beside Caldon Canal, Leek Rd ST13 7HL
☎01782 502907
Two water mills complete with wheels are preserved here, and both are in running order. The 17th-century south mill was used to grind corn, but the 18th-century north mill was built to grind flint for the pottery industry. The restored buildings have displays on aspects of the pottery industry. Exhibits include examples of motive power, such as a Robey steam engine, and of transport, such as the restored 70ft horse-drawn narrow boat 'Vienna', which is moored on the Caldon Canal. There is also a haystack boiler of around 1770.
Open all year, Sat & Sun 2-5, Mon-Fri 10-5.
Donations.
🅿 ♿

HIMLEY
Himley Hall & Park
DY3 4DF (off A449, on B4176)
☎01902 324093 & 326665
Fax 01902 894163
The extensive parkland offers a range of attractions, including a nine-hole golf course and coarse fishing. The hall is only open to the public when exhibitions are taking place. Permanent orienteering course, a charge is made for the maps. Guided tours at the hall available by prior arrangement. Hall available for private hire. Ring for details of special events.
Open Mar-Sep, Tue-Sat 12-5, Sun 2-5. Closed Mon ex BH.
Free. Car park 70p
🅿 *(charged)* 🍴 ♿ *toilets for disabled*

LICHFIELD
Lichfield Cathedral
WS13 7LD
☎01543 306240
Fax 01543 306109
For 1300 years the Cathedral at Lichfield has been a major centre for prayer and for the worship of God. The first cathedral, built in 700AD to house the shrine of St Chad, was replaced by the Norman Cathedral begun in 1085 to house the growing number of pilgrims. The present Gothic building was built between 1195 and 1330. The shrine of St Chad was destroyed at the Reformation and during the sieges of the Civil War the fabric of the Cathedral was badly damaged. Restoration, begun in 1660, has continued ever since, notably under Gilbert Scott in the 19th century. The "Ladies of the Vale", the three spires of Lichfield Cathedral can be seen for many miles around. The Cathedral houses a number of treasures which include: the Lichfield Gospels, an 8th century illuminated manuscript; the medieval tiled floor of the Library; the 16th century Herkenrode windows in the Lady Chapel; sculptures by Sir Frances Chantry and Sir Jacob Epstein; and the Lang Lichfield collection of modern silver. The Cathedral is the venue for many musical events and the focus of the Lichfield Festival held each July. Ring for details of other special events.
Open daily 7.45-6.
Suggested donation of £3 for each adult visitor.
🅿 *(200mtrs)* 🍴 ♿ *(Touch & hearing centre for blind) toilets for disabled shop* ⌀

Lichfield Heritage Exhibition & Treasury
St Mary's Centre Market Square WS13 6LG
☎01543 256611
Fine silver in the Treasury and lively presentations on the Civil War and the siege of Lichfield Cathedral, including a video entitled 'Lichfield - A Walk Through History', are featured here. The displays, housed in the ancient Guild Church of St Mary's, tell the centuries-old story of the city. A viewing platform in the spire gives unique, panoramic views over the city. The City's ancient Charters and archives can be seen in the Muniment room and its social history studied through a collection of old photographs and memorabilia within the Heritage Collection Gallery.
Open all year, daily 10-5. Last admission 4.14pm. (Closed Xmas, New Year & Spring BH Mon).
🅿 *(200yds)* 🍴 ♿ *(lift) toilets for disabled shop* ⌀
Details not confirmed for 1998

Samuel Johnson Birthplace Museum
Breadmarket St WS13 6LG
☎01543 264972 Fax 01543 258441
A statue of Dr Johnson sits at one end of Market Square facing his birthplace on the corner of Breadmarket Street. The house, where Samuel's father had a bookshop, is now a museum containing many of Johnson's personal relics. His favourite armchair and walking stick are among the collection. Johnson Birthday celebrations 20 September.
Open daily 10.30-4.30. (Closed, Xmas, New Year & Sun Nov-Jan).
🅿 *(500 yds) shop* ⌀
Details not confirmed for 1998

MOSELEY
Moseley Old Hall
WV10 7HY
☎01902 782808 Fax 01902 782808
Charles II sheltered in Moseley Old Hall after the Battle of Worcester in 1651. He slept in the four-poster bed in the King's Room, and hid in a concealed space below a cupboard in the room. There are numerous pictures and other reminders of the king, and much of the furniture in the panelled rooms dates from around his time. The house itself is an Elizabethan timber-framed building which was encased in brick in the 19th century. The small garden has a nut walk, period herbs and plants, and a formal knot garden. For details of special events please send a 9" x 4" envelope.
Open 28 Mar-13 Dec; Mar-May Sat & Sun, BH Mon and Tues 1.30-5.30 (BH 11-5). June-Oct Wed-Sun, BH Mon and Tue; also Tue in July & Aug 1.30-5.30 (BH Mon 11-5); Nov & Dec: Sun 1.30-4.30 (guided tour only, last tour at 4pm). £3.60 (ch £1.80). Family ticket £9. Party 15+.
🅿 🍴 ✗ *licensed* ♿ *(toilets for disabled shop* ⌀ ♣
Cards: ▨ ▨

SHUGBOROUGH
Shugborough Estate
ST17 0XB (6m E of Stafford off A513, signposted from M6 junct 13)
☎01889 881388 Fax 01889 881323
Set on the edge of Cannock Chase, Shugborough is the magnificent 900-acre seat of the Earls of Lichfield. The 18th-century mansion house contains fine collections of ceramics, silver, paintings and French furniture. Part of the house is still lived in by the Lichfield family. Visitors can enjoy the Grade I listed historic garden and a unique collection of neo-classical monuments. Other attractions include the museum and the original servants quarters, the laundry, kitchens, brewhouse and coachhouses which have all been restored and are fully operational. Costumed guides show visitors how the servants lived and worked over 100 years ago. Shugborough Park Farm is a Georgian farmstead that has an agricultural

Shugborough

Ancestral Home of Lord Lichfield, Milford, Staffordshire
18th Century Mansion House • Servants'Quarters and Museum
• Georgian Farmstead and Rare Breeds Centre
Beautiful Gardens and Parkland • Neo-Classical Monuments
Tea rooms and National Trust Shop
OPEN 28th MARCH - 27th SEPT FROM 11.00 A.M. OCT - SUN ONLY
SITE OPEN ALL YEAR ROUND TO BOOKED PARTIES
Shugborough is 6 miles east of Stafford on the A513 Lichfield Road. 10 mins from junction 13, M6.
Further information: Telephone Little Haywood (01889) 881 388

museum, working corn mill and rare breeds centre. Special events include Gamekeepers' Fair (18-19 April), Victorian Street Market (2 Aug), Firework and Laser Symphony Concert (18 July), Gardeners Weekend (4-5 July), Hallowe'en (30-31 October), Christmas at Shugborough (8-11 December).Please telephone for details of these and other events.
Open 27 Mar-27 Sep, daily 11-5. Sun only Oct. Site open all year to pre-booked parties.
Entry to Estate £1.50. Mansion £3.50 (ch, pen & UB40's £2.50); County Museum £3.50 (ch, pen & UB40's £2.50); Combined ticket with Park Farm £8 (ch, pen & UB40's £6). Family ticket £18.
P *(charged)* X *licensed* & *(step climber for wheelchairs, 2 Batricars) toilets for disabled shop* *(ex in parkland)*
Cards:

STAFFORD
Shire Hall Gallery
Market Square ST16 2LD
☎01785 278345 Fax 01785 278327
A fine gallery housed in the 18th-century Shire Hall - one of Staffordshire's most magnificent buildings. Exhibitions of contemporary arts, historic courtrooms and a Crafts Council selected craft shop.
Open all year, Mon-Fri 10-5, Sat 10-5. Free.
P *(200 yds)* & *toilets for disabled shop*

STOKE-ON-TRENT
Stoke-on-Trent is at the heart of one of Britain's oldest industrial conurbations, known as The Potteries. From the 17th century the towns grew under a thick pall of smoke from the furnaces used to make millions of china articles for home use and export around the world. Perhaps the most famous of these were the exquisite Spode and Wedgwood china. Today the grimy face of the past is disappearing as factories are transformed into living and working museums of nearly 300 years of china production.

City Museum & Art Gallery
Bethesda St, Hanley ST1 3DE
☎01782 202173 Fax 01782 205033
The history of the Potteries under one roof, including a dazzling display of more than 5000 pieces of ceramics, predominantly from Staffordshire - the history of an industry as seen through its products. Other displays introduce the natural, social and archaeological history of the area, and a Mark 16 Spitfire commemorates its locally born designer - Reginald Mitchell.
Open all year, Mon-Sat 10-5, Sun 2-5. (Closed Xmas - New Year).

P *(500mtrs)* & *(lift, induction loop in theatre) toilets for disabled shop*
Details not confirmed for 1998

Etruria Industrial Museum
Lower Bedford St, Etruria ST4 7AF (M6 junct 11, A500 to city centre, signposted)
☎01782 287557 Fax 01782 260192
The Industrial Museum includes the Etruscan Bone and Flint Mill which was built in 1857 to grind materials for the agricultural and pottery industries. It is Britain's sole surviving, steam-powered potters' mill and contains an 1820's steam-driven beam engine, 1903 coal fired boiler and original grinding machinery. There is a working blacksmiths forge on site and there are regular demonstration of steam machinery from April to December (phone for details). Also for 1998 there are the 6th Etruria Canal Festival (6-7 June), and Christmas event (12-13 December). Also exhibitions in the Canal Warehouse on steaming weekends and a series of informal talks on industrial history on one Sunday afternoon per month (April-October).
Open all year, Wed-Sun 10-4. (Closed Xmas/New Year).
Free.
P & *shop*

Gladstone Pottery Museum
Uttoxeter Rd, Longton ST3 1PQ (on A50, signposted from A500 link with M6)
☎01782 319232 Fax 01782 598640
The last complete Victorian pottery factory from the days of bottle kilns. Tour the factory and see the pottery making skills of the craftsmen and craftswomen. You too can perhaps throw a pot or make a bone china flower. Excellent restaurant facilities offering a selection of hot and cold food. Homebaking a speciality. Our Museum shop stocks a wide range of gifts with craftspeople in mind. With its cobbled yard and giant bottle kilns, Gladstone perfectly captures the City's atmospheric past. Meet our head clerk of 1910 who will talk about life in the factory at that time. Discover the galleries of tiles and loos. New for 1998 is a new big screen cinema which has a multi-lingual feature for foreign visitors. There is also a new 'family-sized' potters' wheel where all the family can have a go at throwing a pot.
Open all year, daily 10-5 (last admission 4pm). Limited opening Xmas & New Year.
£3.75 (ch £2.25, students & pen £2.75). Family ticket £10.
P X *licensed* & *toilets for disabled shop*
Cards:

Royal Doulton Visitor Centre
Nile St, Burslem ST6 2AJ
☎01782 292434 Fax 01782 292424
The Royal Doulton Visitor Centre opened in May 1996 and has been officially named the home of the Royal Doulton figure. It houses over 1,500 Royal Doulton figures including many rare models in special themed displays. The Visitor Centre includes live demonstrations of skills such as figure painting and flower painting as well as a video theatre. The Sir Henry Doulton Gallery combines magnificent treasures from the varied Royal Doulton past with the opportunity to take tea from the finest Royal Doulton china. The Visitor Centre is open seven days a week whilst factory tours can be booked from Monday to Friday. A full promotional calendar is available on request.
Open all year, Mon-Sat 9.30-5, Sun 10-4. Factory tours by advance booking Mon-Fri 10.30-2.45. (Closed factory holidays & Xmas week).
Visitor Centre only £3 (concessions £2.25); Factory Tour & Visitor Centre £5.75 (concessions £4.75). Party 30+.
P X & *(ramps) toilets for disabled shop*
Cards:

Spode
Church St ST4 1BX (M6 junct 15. A500 into Stoke, follow one-way-system to Elenora St, entrance on right)
☎01782 744011 Fax 01782 747612
This is the oldest manufacturing ceramic factory on its original site (established in 1770) where Josiah Spode first perfected the formula of bone china. The centre conveys the history and heritage of the potteries, with the story of Spode in particular. Tours commence from the museum and visitors are shown production methods, under-glaze printing and processing to produce the finest tableware. Standard tours are one and a half hours and connoisseur tours two and a half hours. Prior booking is essential. Please telephone for details of special events.
Visitor Centre, Museum & Site factory shop. Mon-Sat 9-5, Sun 10-4. Factory Tours by prior appointment weekdays only, not available during factory closures – ring for details.

Visitor Centre & Museum £2.50 (ch over 5 & concessions £1.50). Standard factory tours £4 (ch over 12 & concessions £2.50). Connoisseur tour £6.50 & £4.50. Tours by appointment only.
P X & *(limited access for the disabled) toilets for disabled shop*
Cards:

Wedgwood Visitor Centre
Barlaston ST12 9ES (5m S)
☎01782 204141 & 204218 Fax 01782 204402
The complex includes an art gallery with works by Reynolds, Stubbs and Romney, and a reconstruction of Wedgwood's original 18th-century Etruria workshops. There are demonstrations of the traditional skills in the production of Wedgwood ware, and a museum containing a comprehensive collection of the works of Josiah Wedgwood from 1750. A video gives the history of Wedgwood wares and demonstrates the craft of Wedgwood production; there is a shop where products may be bought.
Open all year, Mon-Fri 9-5, Sat & Sun 10-5; (Closed Xmas & 1 Jan).
P X *licensed* & *toilets for disabled shop*
Details not confirmed for 1998

TAMWORTH
Drayton Manor Theme Park & Zoo
B78 3TW (on A4091)
☎01827 287979 Fax 01827 288916
A family theme park set in 250 acres of parkland and lakes with an open-plan zoo and zoo farm. There are over 50 rides and attractions for all age groups, including the ultimate white-knuckle ride, 7-Up Shockwave (the UK's first stand roller coaster), Splash Canyon Raft Ride, the amazing Pirate Adventure, Dinosaur Land, Jungle Cruise, Victorian Carousel, Looping Roller Coaster, Log Flume, children's corner and many more. Other features include The Haunting. Wristbands for unlimited rides or ride-as-you-go tickets. End of season firework ➤

displays, usually last weekend in Oct. Ring for details.
Park & Zoo open Etr-30 Oct, daily 10.30-6. Park (rides) 10.30-5, 6 or 7 (depending on season).
✻£3 (ch 4-15 & pen £2). Wristband for unlimited rides £9.50 (junior-under 1.2 metres tall £6.50). Wheelchair and helper £5 each.
P ✕ licensed ♿ toilets for disabled shop garden centre (ex in park)
Cards:

Tamworth Castle
The Holloway B79 7LR (from M42 junct 10 & M6 junct 12, access via A5)
☎01827 63563 Fax 01827 56567
The castle is a mixture of Norman, Gothic, Tudor, Jacobean and early 19th-century architecture, showing the tastes of its inhabitants over 800 years. It started as a Norman motte-and-bailey shell-keep, with the walls of its keep 10ft thick at the base; outer walls and a gatehouse were added in the 13th-century. The Tudor period brought additions of a more domestic sort with a splendid timber-roofed great hall and a warder's lodge. The Jacobean state apartments have fine woodwork, furniture and heraldic friezes, including 55 panels painted with the arms of the lords of the castle up to 1787. There is a Norman exhibition with 'speaking' knight, a haunted bedroom and Chapel, Annie Cooke's bedroom and a Victorian nursery. The Tamworth Story, an inter-active 'hands-on' exhibition of local history, a slide tape programme on local transport and illustrated signs on the Tower roof were introduced in April 1996. Outside are floral terraces and pleasure grounds with an adventure playground, ten pin bowling alley, Snow Dome and Peaks Leisure Centre. Contact the Castle for details of special events.
Open all year, Mon-Sat 10-5.30; Sun 2-5.30. Last admission 4.30.(Closed 24-26 Dec).
£3.40 (concessions £1.75). Family £8.55.
P (100yds & 400yds) ♿ (one wheelchair for use inside the castle) shop

WALL
Wall Roman Site
Watling St (off A5)
☎01543 480768
Wall was originally the Roman fort of Letocetum. It was situated at the crossroads of Watling Street and Rykneild Street, and was an important military base from about AD50. Excavations started in the 19th century revealed the most complete bath house ever found in Britain. There are three baths: cold, tepid and hot as well as a furnace room and an exercise hall. A small museum at the site exhibits finds from this and other nearby Roman sites.
Open Apr-Nov, daily 10-6 (or dusk if earlier)
✻£1.75 (ch 90p, concessions £1.30).
#

WESTON PARK
Weston Park
TF11 8LE (7m W of junc 12 of M6; 3m N of junc 3 on M54)
☎01952 850207 Fax 01952 850430
Built in 1671, this fine mansion stands in elegant gardens and a vast park designed by 'Capability' Brown. Three lakes, a miniature railway, and a woodland adventure playground are to be found in the grounds, and in the house itself there is a notable collection of pictures, furniture and tapestries.
Open Etr & 4 May-15 Jun, wknds & BH (all week 24 May-1 Jun; 16 Jun-27 Jul daily (ex Mon, Fri & 19 Jul); 28 Jul-Aug daily (ex 16-17 Aug); 1-21 Sep wknds only. Park 11-7 (last admission 5pm); House 1pm (last admission 4.30pm).
P ♿ (disabled route) toilets for disabled shop
Details not confirmed for 1998

WHITTINGTON
Staffordshire Regiment Museum, Whittington Barracks
WS14 9PY (on A51 between Lichfield/Tamworth)
☎0121 311 3240/3229 Fax 0121 311 3205
Situated adjacent to the barracks, the museum displays a collection of regimental militaria. The exhibits include the regiment's battle honours, captured trophies, a variety of weapons of different ages, medals, and uniforms past and present.
Open all year, Mon-Fri 9-4.30. Last admission 4pm. (Closed BH & Xmas-New Year). Parties at other times by arrangement.
Free.
P ♿ (ramps) toilets for disabled shop

WILLOUGHBRIDGE
The Dorothy Clive Garden
TF9 4EU (on A51 between Nantwich & Stone)
☎01630 647237 Fax 01630 647902
In the small village of Willoughbridge is a 200-year-old gravel quarry converted into a delightful woodland garden. The quarry is at the top of a small hill and the garden, which covers over 8 acres, has fine views of the countryside and adjoining counties. Among the tall oak trees are daffodils, rhododendrons and azaleas in profusion. There is also a variety of rare trees and shrubs, and water and rock gardens have been created among the steep banks. The garden provides colour and interest throughout the seasons from spring to glowing autumn tints.
Open 28 Mar-Oct daily 10-5.30.
£2.80 (ch up to 11 yrs free, ch 11-16: £1, pen £2.40). Party 20+.
P ♿ (wheelchairs for use, special route) toilets for disabled (ex on leads)

SUFFOLK

BUNGAY
Otter Trust
Earsham NR35 2AF (off A143)
☎01986 893470 Fax 01986 892461
Otters are a rare sight in the wild nowadays, but at the Otter Trust it is possible to see these beautiful creatures at close quarters. While they are entertaining to watch, one of the Trust's main aims is to breed this endangered species in captivity in sufficient numbers so that it can re-introduce young otters into the wild every year wherever suitable habitat remains to reinforce the vanishing wild population. This re-introduction programme has been running very successfully since 1983 and is carried out in conjunction with English Nature. The Trust has now introduced captive-bred otters into the wild in Norfolk, Suffolk, Dorset, Hampshire, Essex, Wiltshire and Hertfordshire and subsequent scientific monitoring has shown that all these animals are breeding successfully. This has resulted in the wild otter population of Norfolk increasing to almost what it was twenty years ago. The Otter Trust covers 23 acres on the banks of the River Waveney. As well as the otter pens there are three lakes with a large collection of European waterfowl, lovely riverside walks and picnic areas.
Open Apr (or Good Fri if earlier)-Sept, daily 10.30-6.
£4.50 (ch over 5 £2.50, pen £4). Disabled person & pusher free.
P ♿ toilets for disabled shop

BURY ST EDMUNDS
Abbey Visitor Centre
Abbey Precinct, Abbey Gardens IP33 1RS
☎01284 763110
Local history museum housed in 11th century Norman domestic building. Temporary exhibitions all year as well as resident collections which include 'Murder in the Red Barn' relics. Visitor centre with 'hands-on' activities and interpretation of Medieval life in Bury St Edmunds. Exhibitions for 1998 - History of Bury St Edmunds - May, World War One - September.
Open Etr Sat-Oct, daily 10-5.
Free.
P (200yds) ♿ shop

Otters are now a rare sight in the wild, but these delightful creatures are easy to view at the Otter Trust. They are bred here to introduce into the wild.

THE SUE RYDER FOUNDATION MUSEUM CAVENDISH SUFFOLK

This museum depicts the remarkable story of how the Foundation was established, its work today and its hopes for the future.

Open daily: 10am-5.30pm
Admission: Adults 80p,
Children 12 & under & OAPs 40p
Refreshments Rooms and delightful gardens adjoin the Museum. Lunches and light meals available. Lunch and Supper parties by arrangement. Menu on request. Gift Shop.

Advance bookings: Please write to:
The Sue Ryder Foundation, Cavendish, Suffolk CO10 8AY

Manor House Museum
Honey Hill IP33 1HF (in town centre)
☎01284 757072 Fax 01284 757079
The Georgian mansion specialises in costumes, textiles, horology and fine and decorative art from the 17th to the 20th centuries. There is a temporary exhibition gallery as well as workshops in textiles and horology. Events for 1998 include 'The Sparkling Twenties', 'Silversmith to Royalty - Wickes of Bury St Edmunds', 'Tudor Costumes', and 'Between Times - costumes and art of the 30s'. Workshops for schools - please ring for details.
Open all year Tues-Sun 10am-5pm. (closed Mon ex BHs. Closed Good Fri, 25/26 Dec)
£2.70 (concessions £1.75). Family £7.50. Group rates.
🅿 *(charged)* ⬛ ✗ *licensed* ♿ *(Special tours can be arranged for disabled groups) toilets for disabled shop* ⌀ ♨
Cards: 🆑 ▭ ▭

Moyse's Hall Museum
Cornhill IP33 1DX (in town centre)
☎01284 757488 Fax 01284 757079
Moyse's Hall is a rare 12th century Norman house built of flint and stone which has many original features still visible. Now a local history museum Moyse's Hall houses an eclectic collection which includes a display on the notorious William Corder "Murder in the Red Barn", the gibbet cage, medieval relics, and an important archaeology collection.
Temporary exhibitions: (until April) - Piecing together the Past, (May-Sept) - History of Bury St Edmunds, (Sept-Dec) - World War I. Summer activities for children during the holidays. Ring for details.
Open all year Mon-Sat 10-5, Sun 2-5. (Closed 25-26 Dec & Good Fri).
£1.25 (concessions 75p). Residents free.
P *(200yds)* ♿ *shop* ⌀
Cards: 🆑 ▭ ▭

CAVENDISH ▆▆▆▆▆
Cavendish Manor Vineyards & Nether Hall
CO10 8BX
☎01787 280221
The 15th-century manor house stands surrounded by its vineyards in the pretty Stour Valley village. Paintings and rural bygones are shown in the house and museum next to it. Tours of the vineyards and wine tasting are offered.
Open all year, daily 11-4.
£2.50 (ch 16 free)
🅿 ♿ *shop* ⌀

The Sue Ryder Foundation Museum
Sue Ryder Home & Headquarters CO10 8AY (on A1092 Long Melford to Clare road)
☎01787 280252
Fax 01787 280548
The museum shows the work and history of the small but effective international foundation which cares for the sick and disabled. The Home's garden and chapel are also open.
Open all year, daily 10-5.30. (Closed 25 Dec).
80p (ch 12 & pen 40p). Parties by appointment.
🅿 ✗ ♿ *toilets for disabled shop* ⌀

EASTON ▆▆▆▆▆
Easton Farm Park
IP13 0EQ (signed from A12 at Wickam Market, and from A1120)
☎01728 746475
Fax 01728 747861
A Victorian model farm setting situated in the picturesque Deben River Valley. There are lots of breeds of farm animals, some of which are rare and include Suffolk Punch horses, to be seen here. A purpose built dairy centre enables visitors to watch the cows being milked every afternoon, and, in complete contrast, there is the original Victorian Dairy which houses a collection of dairy bygones. Pets paddocks allow children to feed and touch the smaller animals whilst the Green Trail explores the natural habitats of plants and animals and provides grazing for the larger animals. 150 years of farming and food production are displayed in the 'foodchains' exhibition. Other attractions include: Adventure Playpit, picnic site and working Blacksmiths Forge. Special events are held throughout the season.
Open 22 Mar-Sep, daily 10.30-6. Closed Mon ex BHs and Jul-Aug.
❋*£4 (ch under 3 free, ch 3-16 £2.50, pen £3.50). Party 20+*
🅿 ⬛ ♿ *(special parking) toilets for disabled shop*
Cards: 🆑 ▭

EUSTON ▆▆▆▆▆
Euston Hall
IP24 2QP (on A1088, 3m S of Thetford)
☎01842 766366
Fax 01842 766764
Home of the Duke and Duchess of Grafton, this 18th-century house is notable for its fine collection of pictures, by Stubbs, Lely, Van Dyck and other Masters. The grounds were laid out by John Evelyn, William Kent and 'Capability' Brown, and include a 17th-century church in the style of Wren.
Open 4 Jun-24 Sep, Thu only & Suns 28 Jun & 6 Sep 2.30-5.
£3 (ch 50p, pen £2.50). Party 12+.
🅿 ⬛ ♿ *shop* ⌀ *(guide dogs by permission)*

FLIXTON ▆▆▆▆▆
Norfolk & Suffolk Aviation Museum
The Street NR35 1NZ (off A143, take B1062)
☎01986 896644
Situated in the picturesque Waveney Valley, the museum has over 24 historic aircraft including a Spitfire replica used in *The Battle of Britain* film; a Sea Vixen that flew in the Fleet Air Arm's aerobatic team 'Freds' Five', and a USAF Super Sabre in the colours of the Skyblazers aerobatic team. There is also a Bloodhound surface-to-air missile, a hangar with smaller buildings housing the museum's smaller exhibits, the 446th Bomb Group Museum, the Royal Observer Corps Museum and souvenir shop. New displays include: Decoy Sites and Wartime Deception, Fallen Eagles - Wartime Luftwaffe Crashes. Due for completion in 1998: The RAF Bomber Command Building. Special events:
Microlight Fly-In (6-7 June), Decoy Crews Reunion (7 June), WAAF/WRAF Reunion (12 July), Annual Fete (10 August), Royal Observer Corps Reunion (27 Sept), plus other events, please telephone for details.
Open Apr-Oct Sun & BH 10-5; Also school summer holiday period Tue-Thu 10-5. Parties at other times by arrangement.
Free.
🅿 ♿ *(ramp) toilets for disabled shop* ⌀

FRAMLINGHAM ▆▆▆▆▆
Framlingham Castle
IP13 9BP (on B1116)
☎01728 724189
Built by Hugh Bigod between 1177 and 1215, the castle has fine curtain walls, 13 towers and an array of Tudor chimneys. In the 17th century the castle was bequeathed to Pembroke College, which built almshouses inside the walls. It was here that Mary I waited through one anxious summer for news of whether she was to be queen.
Open all year, Apr-Oct, daily 10-6 (or dusk if earlier); Nov-Mar, daily 10-4. Closed 24-26 Dec & 1 Jan.
£2.95 (ch £1.50, concessions £2.20). Personal stereo tour included in admission.
🅿 ♿ *shop* ⌀ ⚲

HORRINGER ▆▆▆▆▆
Ickworth House, Park & Gardens
The Rotunda IP29 5QE (2.5m S of Bury St Edmunds)
☎01284 735270
Fax 01284 735175
The eccentric Earl of Bristol, also Bishop of Derry, created this equally eccentric house, begun in 1795, to display his European collection of art. There is much to interest general visitors and specialist parties with a wonderful collection of paintings including works by Titian, Gainsborough and Velasquez. The Georgian Silver Collection is considered the finest in private hands. Surrounding the house is an unusual Italianate garden created to compliment the architecture of the house. There are many Mediterranean species of plants, including olives and cypress. The visitor will travel through the Capability Brown designed parkland with many ancient oaks and beech trees. There is also a deer enclosure, waymarked walks and an adventure playground. Special events include: Bury Festival Tours (10, 14, 16 & 18 May), Ickworth Proms (9-10 July), Ickworth's Great Eccentrics Day (13 August), Pudding Weekend (14-15 & 21-22 November), Christmas Lunch (6, 13 & 19 December). Ring for details. ➤

Framlingham Castle has fine curtain walls, 13 towers and an array of Tudor chimneys.

in the very place that they were built. Soak up the atmosphere of the Long Shop, built in 1852 as one of the first production line engineering halls in the world. An award-winning museum with three exhibition halls full of items from the glorious age of steam. Special events - Open Day (4 April), Final Fling (18 October). Please telephone for details.
Open Apr-end of Autumn half term holiday, Mon-Sat 10-5, Sun 11-5.
£2.50 (ch 75p (under 5 free), concessions £1.50)
🅿 ♿ *toilets for disabled shop* ⊗

LINDSEY
St James's Chapel
Rose Green
Built mainly in the 13th century, this small thatched, flint-and-stone chapel incorporates some earlier work.
Open all year.
Free.
♿ ⊞

LONG MELFORD
Kentwell Hall
CO10 9BA (signposted off A134)
☎01787 310207
Fax 01787 379318
A mellow redbrick E-shaped Tudor mansion surrounded by a broad moat. Externally little altered, with many of the 16th-century service areas intact. Inside the House shows the changes wrought in a variety of styles by successive owners, including the present family. There is a unique brick-paved mosaic 'Tudor' rose maze. Fine gardens include Ancient Walled Garden with large Herb Garden and Potager. Clipped yews; woodland walks. Farm with Rare Breed Farm Animals based upon range of timber-framed buildings. Kentwell is best known for its unique Award-Winning Re-Creations of Tudor Life when up to 200 participants dress, speak and carry on daily activities in and around the hall as if in the 16th century. The biggest re-creation is the Great Annual Re-Creation which runs from 14 June to 5 July (open to pre-booked schools only on weekdays and general public on Saturdays, Sundays and Friday the 3rd). Re-creations also take place every Bank Holiday weekend and other selected weekends. Call Info-Line for current special events: 0891 517475 (50p per minute) Open Air Shakespeare: 24-25 July.
Open 8 Mar-7 June Sun only; 14 Jun-5 Jul, Sat & Sun for Re-Creation; 8 Jul-6 Sep, daily, 6 Sept-25 Oct Wed, Thur, Sun, 12-5 (11-5 Re-Creations, 11-6 for BH weekends). Open BH weekends from Etr-Aug, Sat-Mon.
Inclusive ticket £5.10 (ch £3.10, pen £4.30). Garden & Farm only £3 (ch £1.90, pen £2.60). Special prices apply for Re-Creations.
🅿 ✕ ♿ *toilets for disabled shop* ⊗
Cards: 🔳 ▭ ▭ ▭ 🔳 ☑

Melford Hall
CO10 9AA (off A134, 3miles N of Sudbury)
☎01787 880286
Queen Elizabeth I was a guest at this turreted, brick-built Tudor house in 1578, and it does not look very different on the outside today. It has its original panelled banqueting hall, and later features include an 18th-century drawing room, a Regency library and a Victorian bedroom. The house was owned for many years by the Parker family, which produced a number of admirals - hence the nautical flavour of the pictures. There is also a large collection of Chinese porcelain, and a display on Beatrix Potter, who was related to the Parkers and often stayed here. The garden has a Tudor pavilion, which may have been built as a guardhouse.
Open Apr, wknds & BH Mon 2-5.30; May-Sep, Wed-Sun & BH Mon 2-5.30; Oct, wknds 2-5.30. Last admission 5pm £4 (ch £2). Party.
🅿 ♿ *(stairlift) toilets for disabled* ⊗ *(ex in park)* ⧓

LOWESTOFT
East Anglia Transport Museum
Chapel Rd, Carlton Colville NR33 8BL (3m SW, on B1384)
☎01502 518459
A particular attraction of this museum is the reconstructed 1930s street scene which is used as a setting for working vehicles: visitors can ride by tram, trolley bus and narrow gauge railway. Other motor, steam and electrical vehicles are exhibited. There is also a woodland picnic area served by trams. Ring for details of special events.
Open Good Fri & Etr Sat 2-4, Etr Sun-Etr Mon 11-5. May-Sep, Sun & BH's 11-5; Jun-Sep, Wed & Sat 2-4.
£3 (ch 5-15 & pen £2). Party. Price includes rides.
🅿 🍴 ♿ *shop*

Maritime Museum
Sparrow Nest Gardens, Whapload Rd NR32 1XG (on A12)
☎01502 561963 511260
Models of ancient and modern fishing and commercial boats are exhibited, together with fishing gear and shipwrights' tools. There are an art gallery and a lifeboat display as well as a facsimile of a Drifter's Cabin complete with model fishermen.
Open May-Sep, daily 10-5. Etr, Fri-Mon. 50p (ch, students & pen 25p)
🅿 *(100 yds)* ♿ *shop*

Pleasurewood Hills Family Theme Park
Corton Rd NR32 5DZ (off A12 at Lowestoft)
☎01502 508200 Fax 01502 567393
After the initial admission fee there is nothing more to pay at this exciting family theme park which has over fifty rides, shows and attractions. After the

Open: House & Garden 23 Mar-3 Nov Tue, Wed, Fri, Sat & BH Mons 1-5; Garden all year daily 23 Mar-3 Nov 10-5. 4 Nov-Mar 10-4; Park daily 7am-7pm. House, Garden & Park £5.20 (ch £2.20); Garden & park £2 (ch 50p). Party 12+.
🅿 ✕ *licensed* ♿ *(braille guide batricars stairlift to shop & restaurant) toilets for disabled shop* ⊗ *(ex in park)* ⧓

IPSWICH
Christchurch Mansion
Soane St IP4 2BE (South side of Christchurch Park)
☎01473 253246 & 213761
Fax 01473 210328
The original house was built in 1548 on the site of an Augustinian priory. At the end of the 19th century the house and parkland were saved by the Cobbold family from redevelopment; today Christchurch Mansion, set in a beautiful park, shows off its period furnished rooms. There is also an art gallery with a lively temporary exhibition programme, a Suffolk artists' gallery, a good collection of Constables and Gainsboroughs, and furniture and ceramics.
Open all year, Tue-Sat 10-5 (dusk in winter), Sun 2.30-4.30 (dusk in winter). (Closed Good Fri & 24-26 Dec & 1-2 Jan). Open BH mon.
Free.
🅿 ♿ *(tape guide for partially sighted) shop* ⊗

Ipswich Museum
High St IP1 3QH
☎01473 213761 & 263550
Fax 01473 281274
The Museum has sections on Victorian Natural History, Suffolk wildlife, Suffolk geology, Roman Suffolk, and Peoples of the World. There is also one of the best bird collections in the country. Please ring for further information.

Open all year, Tue-Sat 10-5. (Closed Sun, BH's, 24-26 Dec & 1 Jan).
Free.
🅿 ♿ *shop* ⊗

LAVENHAM
Lavenham Guildhall
Market Place CO10 9QZ
☎01787 247646
Although it has been much restored, there are still many of the original Tudor features left in this picturesque timber-framed building. The hall and its small museum are a testament to the time when East Anglia had a flourishing woollen industry. There is a walled garden with a 19th-century lock-up and mortuary.
Open 28 Mar-1 Nov, daily 11-5. (Closed Good Fri).
£2.80 (accompanied ch free). Party.
🅿 *(adjacent)* 🍴 *shop* ⊗ ⧓

LEISTON
Leiston Abbey
(1m N off B1069)
For hundreds of years this 14th-century abbey was used as a farm and its church became a barn. A Georgian house was built into its fabric and this is now used as a retreat house for the local diocese. The rest of the abbey is in ruins, but remains of the choir and transepts of the church, and the ranges of cloisters still stand.
Open any reasonable time.
Free.
🅿 ♿ ⊞

Long Shop Museum
Main St IP16 4ES
☎01728 832189
Discover the Magic of Steam through a visit to the world famous traction engine manufacturers. Trace the history of the factory and Richard Garrett engineering. See the traction engines and road rollers

This reconstructed windmill at the Museum of East Anglian Life is just one of several buildings showing life as it used to be.

breathtaking rides such as the Wild Water Falls Log Flume Ride visitors can slow down the pace and enjoy the entertaining shows. Set in over 70 acres of landscaped gardens, offering all the fun you can handle with plenty of places to just relax. Train rides and chairlift make it easier to get around the park.
Open daily 23 Mar-6 Apr; weekends 12 Apr-15 May; daily 17 May-21 Sep. Selective opening end of Sep-2 Nov, phone for details.
Prices under review.
P ⬛ ✕ ♿ *toilets for disabled shop* ✆
Cards: 🆑 ▭ ▭ 🅶

NEWMARKET
National Horseracing Museum
99 High St CB8 8JL
☎ 01638 667333 Fax 01638 665600
Newmarket, set in beautiful countryside about 30 minutes' drive from Cambridge, is world-famous for its horseracing. Hidden behind the High Street are dozens of trainers' yards and studs, forming a magical world which can only be visited through the Museum's minibus tours. As well as meeting the horses and stable staff at close quarters, watch the horses on the historic gallops and see them in the equine swimming pool. At the Museum, find out about the history of racing from its Royal origins to Frankie Dettori - displays are updated every year. Retired jockeys will answer questions and let you ride the horse simulator at up to 40mph! New this year is 'Racing Karaoke' - record your own racing commentary. Ring for details of special tours.
Open 4 Mar-2 Nov, Tue-Sat (also BH Mons & Mon in Jul & Aug) 10-5.
✼£3.30 (ch £1, pen £2). Party 20+. Equine tours Tue-Sat when museum is open.
P (300yds) ⬛ ✕ licensed ♿ toilets for disabled shop ✆
Cards: 🆑 ▭ 🅶

ORFORD
Orford Castle
(on B1084)
☎ 01394 450472
Built by Henry II circa 1165, a magnificent keep survives almost intact with three

immense towers reaching to 90 feet. Inside there are many rooms to explore.
Open all year, Apr-Oct, daily 10-6; Nov-Mar, Wed-Sun, 10-4. Closed 24-26 Dec & 1 Jan.
£2.30 (ch £1.20, concessions £1.70).
P ✆ ♿

SAXMUNDHAM
Bruisyard Winery, Vineyard & Herb Centre
Church Rd, Bruisyard IP17 2EF (4m W of Saxmundham bypass (A12))
☎ 01728 638281 Fax 01728 638442
This picturesque, 10-acre vineyard produces the award-winning Bruisyard St Peter English wine. There are also a herb garden, water garden, a wooded picnic area, and a children's play area. English wine, herbs, crafts and souvenirs are for sale.
Open Feb-Xmas, daily 10.30-5.
£3.50 (ch £2, pen £3)
P ✕ licensed ♿ shop garden centre ✆ (ex in vineyard)
Cards: 🆑 ▭ ▭ ▭ 🅶

SAXTEAD GREEN
Saxtead Green Post Mill
(2.5m NW of Framlingham on A1120)
☎ 01728 685789
One of the finest examples of a traditional Suffolk post-mill can be seen at Saxtead Green. There has been a mill on the site at least since 1796 but the mill has been altered or rebuilt several times. The present structure dates from 1854; for those who climb the steep staircase into the body of the mill there is the reward of finding the now redundant millstones and other machinery in perfect order.
Open Apr-Oct, Mon-Sat 10-6 (or dusk if earlier). Closed 1-2pm.
£1.75 (ch 90p, concessions £1.30).
(exterior only) ✆ ♿

STOWMARKET
Museum of East Anglian Life
IP14 1DL (signposted from A14 and B1115)
☎ 01449 612229 Fax 01449 672307
The extensive, 70-acre, all-weather museum is set in an attractive river-valley

site. There are reconstructed buildings, including a water mill, a smithy and also a wind pump, and the Boby Building houses craft workshops. Also there are displays on Victorian domestic life, gypsies, farming and industry. These include working steam traction engines, the only surviving pair of Burrell ploughing engines of 1879, and a working Suffolk Punch horse. Other attractions include a charcoal burner at work and a new adventure playground. Various events are being held throughout the year, including the Napoleonic Battle Reconstruction (April), Beer Festival (June), Fire Services Extravaganza (August BH wknd), and Farming The Old Way (September). Please phone for details.
Open Apr-Oct.
✼Admission charged. Party. Telephone for details.
P (adjacent) ⬛ ♿ (wheelchairs available, special parking facilities) toilets for disabled shop
Cards: 🆑 ▭

SUDBURY
Gainsborough's House
46 Gainsborough St CO10 6EU
☎ 01787 372958 Fax 01787 376991
Gainsborough's House is the birthplace of Thomas Gainsborough RA (1727-88). The Georgian-fronted town house, with an attractive walled garden, displays more of the artist's work than any other gallery, together with 18th-century furniture and memorabilia. Commitment to contemporary art is reflected in a varied programme of exhibitions throughout the year. These include fine art, craft, photography, printmaking and sculpture.
Open all year - House Tue-Sat 10-5, Sun & BH Mons 2-5; (4pm Nov-Mar). (Closed Good Fri & Xmas-New Year).
P (300 yds) ♿ toilets for disabled shop ✆
Details not confirmed for 1998
Cards: 🆑 ▭

SUFFOLK WILDLIFE PARK
Suffolk Wildlife Park
Kessingland NR33 7SL (on A12)
☎ 01502 740291 Fax 01502 741104
Take a walk on the wildside at Suffolk's Premier Wildlife Attraction. Set in 100 acres of coastal parkland, you will see Giraffes, African Lions, Cheetahs, Chimpanzees, Zebra, African Antelope, colonies of Lemur monkeys living freely on their islands and the only Aardvarks in the country. Animal feeding times are both fun and informative, and you can find out more about Lions, Cheetahs, Aardvarks, Meerkats and Otters, Ring Tailed Lemurs and much more. Other attractions include the Safari Road Train, Explorer Trails, Crazy Golf, Bouncy Castles and large childrens play area.
Open all year, daily from 10am. (Closed 25-26 Dec).
Prices under review.
P ⬛ ♿ (wheelchairs available for hire) toilets for disabled shop ✆
Cards: 🆑 ▭ ▭ 🅶

WESTLETON
RSPB Nature Reserve Minsmere
IP17 3BY (signposted from A12 & Westleton)
☎ 01728 648281 Fax 01728 648770
One of the RSPB's most popular sites. It is famous for its nesting avocets, marsh harriers and bitterns. Ideal for families and birdwatchers alike, there are countryside walks of varying lengths and eight hides. A new Visitor Centre featuring interpretation, shop and tearoom is now open. Education programmes for school groups are also available. Full calender of events and actiities available from the reserve.
Open Wed-Mon 9am-9pm (or sunset if earlier). Visitor centre, shop & tearoom Apr-Oct 9-5, Nov-Mar 9-4.
£3.50 (ch 50p, concessions £2.50). Family ticket £7.
P ⬛ ♿ toilets for disabled shop ✆
Cards: 🆑 ▭ ▭ 🅶

WEST STOW
West Stow Anglo Saxon Village
West Stow Country Park IP28 6HG (off A1101)
☎ 01284 728718 Fax 01284 728277
The village is a reconstruction of a pagan Anglo-Saxon settlement dated 420-650 AD. Six buildings have been reconstructed on the site of the excavated settlement, using the same techniques, tools and building materials as were used in the original farming village (free audio guides available) and visitors can also see pigs and crops. The village is situated in the 125-acre West Stow Country Park. There are a Visitors' Centre and children's play area. Facilities for the disabled include purpose-built toilets for wheelchair users. Special events throughout the year include a Saxon Market on Easter Sunday and Monday.
Open all year, daily 10-5. Last entry 4.15pm.
✼£3.50 (ch £2.50). family ticket £10.
P ♿ (ramp, audio guides) toilets for disabled shop ✆
Cards: 🆑 ▭ 🅶

WOODBRIDGE
Woodbridge Tide Mill
Tide Mill Way
☎ 01473 626618
The machinery of this 18th-century mill has been completely restored. There are photographs and working models on display. Situated in a busy quayside, this unique building looks over towards the historic site of the Sutton Hoo Ship Burial. Every effort is made to run the machinery for a short time whenever the mill is open and the tides are suitable; details obtainable from tourist information offices or outside the mill.
Open Etr, then daily May-Sep. Oct wknds only. 11-5
✼£1 (ch 50p) .
P (400 yds) (no parking or turning in Tide Mill Way) ♿ shop ✆

SURREY

ASH VALE
RAMC Historical Museum
Keogh Barracks GU12 5RQ (off M3 junct 4 on A331 to Mytchett then follow tourist signs)
☎ 01252 340212
Fax 01252 340224
Some 2,500 items related to the work of the Royal Army Medical Corps are displayed, including a horsedrawn ambulance, a 1942 Austin K2 ambulance, items from the Gulf and Falklands Wars. Displays date from 1660 to the present day and the RAMC Memorial Chapel is now a wing of the museum. The external displays include an ambulance train coach.
Open all year, Mon-Fri 8.30-4. (Closed Xmas, New Year & BH). Wknds & BH by appointment only.
Free.
P ♿ toilets for disabled shop ✆

CHARLWOOD
Gatwick Zoo
Russ Hill RH6 0EG
☎ 01293 862312
Fax 01293 862550
The zoo covers almost 12 acres and has hundreds of birds and mammals. The monkey island has spider and squirrel monkeys, and other animals and birds can be seen in large, naturalised settings. Nearly all species breed each year. A play area for children up to 12 years old has been added.
Open all year, Mar-Oct, daily 10.30-6 (earlier by appointment for schools). Nov-Mar, 10.30-4 or dusk if earlier. (Closed 25-26 Dec). No butterflies during winter.
£3.95 (ch 3-14 £2.95, pen £3.45 ex Sun & BH). Admission price includes Butterfly House.
P ⬛ ♿ toilets for disabled shop ✆
Cards: 🆑 ▭ ▭ ▭ ▭ ▭ 🅶

A pair of Macaws at Birdworld bring a sudden flash of colour to the English countryside. They are among a wide range of fish and birds on display.

CHERTSEY
Thorpe Park
Staines Rd KT16 8PN (off M25 junct 11 or 13 then A320)
☎01932 562633 & 569393
Fax 01932 566367
The park offers 500 acres of family fun; over 100 attractions are included in the admission price. The attractions include No Way Out - the world's first "blackwards" ride, Loggers Leap - the highest log flume ride in the UK, Depth Charge water slide, Thunder River, Tea Cup ride, Thorpe Farm, Canada Creek Railway, Carousel Kingdom, lots of shows, and much more. There is free transport round the park by land train or water bus. The park is located one-and-three-quarter miles north of Chertsey on the A320. Recent additions include: DinoBoats - bumper boats for children, and 3 new waterslides leading into Fantasy Reef, from underneath Depth Charge.
Open Mar-Nov, daily 10-6 (or later). Last admission 1hr before closing.
Prices under review.
🅿 🍴 ✕ & toilets for disabled shop ⚓
Cards: 🅰 🔵 📇 ⊙ 📇 🔤 💳

CRAWLEY
See Charlwood

EAST CLANDON
Hatchlands
GU4 7RT (E off A246)
☎01483 222482 Fax 01483 223479
Robert Adam's first commission was to decorate the interior of this 18th-century house, and his work can be admired in the drawing room, library and other rooms. The attractive red brick house itself was probably designed by its first owner Admiral Boscawen, and is on seven different floor levels. It is given a regular appearance from the outside by the use of false windows. In 1988 the Cobbe Collection of keyboard instruments, paintings and furniture was installed here. This collection includes the largest number of composer-related keyboard instruments in the world, including instruments played by Chopin, Mahler and Elgar. The garden, by

Gertrude Jekyll, has been restored and new walks opened in the Repton park. Concerts are held in the house and gardens. Please contact Regional Box Office for details (01372) 451596.
Open 1 Apr-29 Oct, Tue-Thu, Sun & BH Mon 2-5.30. Last admission 5pm. (Closed Good Fri). Also open Fri in Aug. Gardens open as house. Park walks daily during open season 11.30-6.
£4.20 (ch £1.10). Joint ticket with Clandon Park £6. Grounds and Park walks £1.70. Family ticket £10.50.
🅿 ✕ licensed & (wheelchair available & special parking) toilets for disabled shop ⚓ 🌾
Cards: 🅰 📇 💳

FARNHAM
Birdworld & Underwaterworld
Holt Pound GU10 4LD (3m S on A325)
☎01420 22140
Fax 01420 23715
Eighteen acres of garden and parkland are home to a wide variety of birds, from the tiny tanager to the great ostrich, and many rare and unusual species. There are waterfowl as well as land birds; a Sea Shore Walk and Tropical Walk; and an aquarium with tropical, freshwater and marine fish. During the breeding season there are lots of rare baby birds to be seen in the Incubation Research Station. In the Heron Theatre vistiors can meet the keepers along with some of their favourite birds. The Owls Nest bookshop sells books on wildlife. Plant lovers will enjoy the extensive gardens. There is a picnic area with covered seating and a cafeteria for cream teas etc. Children's farm and play area. Facilities for the disabled include purpose-built toilets for wheelchair users. Wheelchairs are available on loan and there are good, solid paths around the grounds. There are animal handling sessions in the children's farm. Telephone for special events.
Open all year, daily from 9.30. (Closed 25 Dec).
🅿 🍴 & (wheelchairs available) toilets for disabled shop ⚓
Details not confirmed for 1998
Cards: 🅰 🔵 📇 🔤 🔤 💳

Farnham Castle Keep
(half mile N on A287)
☎01252 713393
The castle was started in the 11th century by Henry of Blois, Bishop of Winchester, at a convenient point on the way to London; his tower stood on the mound of the keep, which was later encased in high walls. Around the keep are a ditch and bank topped by a wall.
Open Apr-Oct, daily 10-6 (or dusk if earlier)
✳£2 (ch £1, concessions £1.50). Admission price includes a free Personal Stereo Guided Tour.
🅿 ⚓ 🏛

GREAT BOOKHAM
Polesden Lacey
RH5 6BD (2m S off A246)
☎01372 458203 & 452048
Fax 01372 452023
In Edwardian times, this attractive Regency house was owned by a celebrated society hostess, Mrs Ronald Greville. King George VI and Queen Elizabeth (the Queen Mother) spent part of their honeymoon here, and photographs of other notable guests can be seen. The house is handsomely furnished with the Greville collection of tapestries, porcelain, Old Master paintings and other works of art. With its mixed Edwardian and Regency flavour, the house is full of charm, and it is set in spacious grounds. The gardens include a walled rose garden and there are good views and wide lawns. There is also an open-air theatre, where plays are performed in summer; these will run from 20 June-5 July 1998. There will also be a Polesden Fair on July 5th. Please telephone for details of these special events.
Open all year. Grounds, Gardens & Landscaped walks: daily 11-6. House: Apr-1 Nov, Wed-Sun 1.30-5.30. Also BH Mon 11-5.30. (last admission 30mins before closing)
Grounds, Garden & Landscaped walks: £3 ; House: £3. Family &7.50. Party 15+.
🅿 🍴 ✕ licensed & (braille guide & disabled parking by arrangement) toilets for disabled shop ⚓ 🌾
Cards: 🅰 💳

GUILDFORD
Dapdune Wharf
Wharf Rd GU1 4RR (off Woodbridge Road)
☎01483 561389 & 455056
Fax 01483 31667
The Wey is one of the earliest historic waterways in Britain dating from 1653. The original barge building site, Dapdune Wharf opened to visitors for the first time in 1996. A series of exhibitions, models and displays tells the story of the Waterway, the people who lived and worked on it and the barges built there. A restored Wey barge, the 'Reliana', can be explored. The Navigations are 19.5 miles long from Godalming to Weybridge;they are fully accessible by a towpath and retain several old locks and weirs. They also support varied flora and fauna.
Open 29 Mar-2 Nov. Wed, wknds & BHs 11-5.
🅿 & toilets for disabled ⚓ (ex on lead) 🌾
Details not confirmed for 1998

Guildford Castle
GU1 3TU
☎01483 444702
Fax 01483 444444
The three-storey ruined castle keep dates from the 12th century and gives fine views; and the castle ditch has been transformed into a colourful garden which is attractive throughout the spring and summer. Band concerts are held occasionally during the summer months, and an open-air theatre is a feature of the gardens during July.
Open: Grounds daily 8-dusk (Closed 25 Dec); Keep Apr-Sep 10.30-6.
🅿 (50yds) &
Details not confirmed for 1998

Guildford House Gallery
155 High St GU1 3AJ (N side of High St, opposite Sainsbury's)
☎01483 444740 Fax 01483 444742
Important features of this fascinating building are the finely decorated plaster ceilings, panelled rooms, wrought iron balcony and window catches, together with the richly carved oak and elm staircase. Guildford House dates from 1660 and has been Guildford's art gallery since 1959. A changing selection from the Borough's Art Collection is on display, including pastel portraits by John Russell (1745-1806), topographical paintings and contemporary craftwork, as well as temporary exhibitions. Ring for details of 1998's special events.
Open Tue-Sat 10-4.45.
Free.
P (100yds) 🍴 & shop ⚓
Cards: 🅰 📇 🔤 🔤 💳

Loseley Park
GU3 1HS (2.5m SW, off A3 onto B3000)
☎01483 304440 Fax 01483 302036
Familiar to many from yoghurt pots, the Elizabethan house has notable panelling, decorated ceilings, a carved chalk chimneypiece and tapestries. There are trailer rides around the estate and a walled garden housing rose, herb, fruit and flower gardens. Telephone for details of special events.
Walled Garden open 4 May-26 Sep.
House and Trailer Rides open 25 May-29 Aug.
House & Gardens £4.50 (ch £2.75, ch under 3 free, pen/disabled £3.75).
Gardens only £2.25 (ch £1.25, pen/disabled £1.75). All-in-one ticket (inc trailer rides) Sat only £6.75 (ch £3.75, pen/disabled £5.75).
🅿 ✕ licensed & (wheelchair available, parking outside house) toilets for disabled shop ⚓

HASCOMBE
Winkworth Arboretum
Hascombe Rd GU8 4AD (1m NW on B2130)
☎01483 208477
This lovely woodland covers a hillside of nearly 100 acres, with fine views over the North Downs. The best times to visit are May, for the azaleas, bluebells and other flowers, and October for the autumn colours.
Open all year, daily during daylight hours. (could close when weather is bad)
£2.70 (ch £1.35). Family ticket £6.75.
🅿 🍴 shop (Apr-14 Nov, Wed-Sun 11-5.30) 🌾

OUTWOOD
Old Mill
Outwood Common RH1 5PW (off A25)
☎01342 843458 & 843644
This award-winning example of a post-mill dates from 1665 and is the oldest working windmill in England and one of the best preserved in existence. Standing 400ft above sea level, it is surrounded by common land and National Trust property. Ducks, goats and geese wander freely in the grounds, and there is a small museum of bygones.
Open Etr Sun-last Sun in Oct, Sun & BH Mons only 2-6. Other days & evening tours by arrangement.
£2 (ch £1).
🅿 & toilets for disabled shop

PAINSHILL PARK
Painshill Park
KT11 1JE (W of Cobham, on A245. entrance opposite Territorial Army offices)
☎01932 868113 Fax 01932 868001
Painshill Landscape Garden, a fascinating 18th-century landscape created by the Hon Charles Hamilton, was well-maintained until World War II. In 1981 a charitable trust was formed with the task of restoring this beautiful 158 acre garden. Visitors can take a circuit walk through a series of delightful scenes. The huge lake, filled by the power of a massive water wheel, meanders through the garden, giving a perfect setting for a

Gothic temple, ruined abbey, and a Turkish tent. The magical crystal grotto, hidden among the foliage on one of the islands, is approached across an elegant Chinese bridge. Beyond the lake, through an alpine valley, a castellated, Gothic tower can be seen through the trees. Hamilton was a knowledgeable plantsman and some of his unusual trees and shrubs have survived. A vineyard and many new shrub beds have been planted with appropriate plant material giving an unusual insight into 18th-century plantings. A series of lectures/workshops on 18-th century architecture and gardens are planned for 1998. Please telephone for details.
Open Apr-Oct, Tue-Sun & BH, 10.30-4.30. (gates close 6pm). Nov-Feb, Tue-Thu & Sat-Sun, 11-4 (or dusk if earlier). £3.80 (ch over 5 £1.50, concessions £3.30). Party 20+.
P 🍴 &. (2 wheelchairs available) toilets for disabled shop ✻
Cards: 💳 💳 💳 💳

REIGATE
Priory Museum
Bell St RH2 7RL (off A217)
☎ 01737 245065
The Priory Museum is housed in Reigate Priory which was originally founded before 1200, this Grade I listed building was converted to a mansion in Tudor times. Notable features include the magnificent Holbein fireplace, 17th century oak staircase and murals. The small museum has changing exhibitions on a wide range of subjects, designed to appeal to both adults and children. The collection includes domestic bygones, local history and costume.
Open Wed & Sat 2-4.30 in term time.
P &. ("Hands On" facilities) shop ✻
Details not confirmed for 1998

TILFORD
Rural Life Centre
Reeds Rd GU10 2DL (on A287, signed)
☎ 01252 792300 & 795571
Fax 01252 795571
The Old Kiln houses a collection of farm implements and machinery, and examples of the craft and trades allied to farming may be seen. The larger exhibits are displayed in the pleasant garden and woodland surroundings which cover

some ten acres. In the old farm buildings are a smithy and a wheelwright's shop, hand tools and other artefacts. There is also an arboretum and woodland walk. Special events for 1998 include 'Rustic Sunday' with craft demonstrations, sideshows and traditional events. (26 July).
Open Apr-Sep, Wed-Sun & BH 11-6. £3 (ch £1.50 & pen £2.50).
P 🍴 &. (3 wheelchairs for use) toilets for disabled shop

WEST CLANDON
Clandon Park
GU4 7RQ (on A247)
☎ 01483 222482
Fax 01483 223479
An 18th-century house, built by Leoni for the 2nd Lord Onslow, with stunning plasterwork and a fine collection of furniture and pictures. Also on display is a collection of Meissen Italian comedy figures and the Gubbay collection of porcelain, furniture and needlework. This is also home to The Queens Royal Surrey regimental museum. There is a garden with parterre, grotto and Maori House. Concerts are held in the Marble Hall, please contact Regional Box Office for details - 01372 451596.
Open Apr-29 Oct, Tue, Wed,Thu, Sun & Good Friday, Etr Sat & BH Mons, 11.30-4.30. Last admission 4pm. Garden open daily 9-dusk. Museum open as House, 12-5.
House & Garden £4.20 (ch £2.10). Family ticket £10.50. Combined ticket with Hatchlands £6.
P 🍴 ✕ licensed &. (wheelchairs, braille guide & disabled parking) toilets for disabled shop ✻ ✻
Cards: 💳

WEYBRIDGE
Brooklands Museum
Brooklands Rd KT13 7QN (exit M25 at junct 10/11, museum off B374)
☎ 01932 857381
Fax 01932 855465
Brooklands racing circuit was the birthplace of British motorsport and of British aviation. From 1907, when it opened, to 1987 when the British Aerospace factory closed, it was a world-renowned centre of engineering excellence. The Museum opened in 1991

on 30 acres of the original 1907 motor racing circuit. It features the most historic and steepest section of the old banked track and the 1-in-4 Test Hill. Many of the original buildings have been restored including the Clubhouse, the Shell and BP Petrol Pagodas and the Malcolm Campbell Sheds in the Motoring Village. Original Brooklands racing cars, motorcycles and bicycles, Vickers and Hawker aircraft including a Wellington bomber and a replica of A V Roe's 1908 bi-plane. Phone for details of special events which this year include: Cycle Festival (13 April), MG Day (19 April), British Sports Car Day (7 June), Italian Car Weekend (4-5 July).
Open Tue-Sun & BHs 10-5 (4pm in winter). Closed Good Friday & 23-31 Dec. £6 (ch 16 £4, pen & students £5). Family ticket £16.
P 🍴 &. toilets for disabled shop ✻

WISLEY
Wisley Garden
GU23 6QB (on A3, close to M25 junct 10)
☎ 01483 224234
Fax 01483 211750
These experimental gardens of the Royal Horticultural Society were established in 1904 near Wisley village. The property now covers over 240 acres, of which half is devoted to garden, and some to vegetables. The gardens have a wide variety of trees, shrubs and plants, many of which are unusual in Britain, and planted in their correct setting. There are also greenhouses and specialist gardens. The Royal Horticultural Society offer an advisory service at Wisley to members only. There is an information desk in the Plant Centre open to all. Special events in 1998 include: Orchids for all; Garden crafts; Family fortnight; Apple event; Natural art. Wisley runs an all-year-round programme of horticulturally-based interest courses. To obtain a full listing ring the Garden. Wisley Flower Show (28-30 July).
Open all year, Mon-Fri 10-7 or dusk (4.30pm Jan, Nov & Dec), opens 9am Sat. Sun members only 9-7 (4.30 Nov-Jan). (Closed 25 Dec). Glasshouses close at 4.15 or sunset Mon-Fri. £5 (ch 6-16 £1.75). Garden entry card £3.50. Party 10+.
P 🍴 ✕ licensed &. (free wheelchairs) toilets for disabled shop garden centre ✻
Cards: 💳 💳 💳

SUSSEX, EAST

ALFRISTON
Alfriston Clergy House
The Tye BN26 5TL (4m NE of Seaford, E of B2108, next to church in village)
☎ 01323 870001
The thatched and timber-framed parish priests' house was built in about 1350 and had not changed very much by 1896, when it was acquired by the National Trust. (It was the first building to be taken over by the Trust.) Now carefully and sensitively restored, it gives a vivid idea of medieval living conditions. Outside the house is a pretty cottage garden.
Open Apr-1 Nov, Sat-Mon, Wed & Thu 10-5 (or sunset if earlier). Last admission 30 mins before closing. £2.20.(ch £1.10). Family ticket £5.50.
P shop ✻ ✻

Drusillas Park
BN26 5QS (off A27)
☎ 01323 870234 & 870656
Fax 01323 870846
Drusilas is not only the most animal friendly zoo in the country, but also the most child friendly too. The enclosures are imaginative and creative, presenting the animals in an interesting and naturalistic setting. There is an excellent beaver compound and the penguin pool has good underwater viewing. The farmyard includes a full size artificial milking cow that children can actually 'milk'. 'Parrot Falls' is a spectacular exhibit featuring rare and beautiful

cockatoos. There is over an acre of adventure playland for children up to 12 years of age, a large red fire engine, tractors and all sorts of climbing, jumping and swinging fun. For rainy days there is a large indoor playbarn. Also there is a train ride through the llama paddocks, award winning toucans, a restaurant, 6 shops and famous gardens. Dates and times of special events to be advised.
Open all year, daily 10-5 or dusk if earlier, (ex 24-26 Dec).
P 🍴 ✕ licensed &. (sensory trail throughout park) toilets for disabled shop ✻ (ex gardens)
Details not confirmed for 1998
Cards: 💳 💳 💳

BATTLE
Battle Abbey
High St TN33 0AD (leave A21 onto A2100, abbey at end of Battle High St)
☎ 01424 773792
Built by William to atone for the terrible slaughter of the Battle of Hastings, the Abbey's high altar stood on the spot where Harold fell, and is still marked today by a memorial stone. An audio tour, exhibition and audiovisual displays tell you more of the history of this great site. The mile-long Battlefield Walk takes you round the full perimeter of the battlefield itself, where thousands of men once fought and died in this now peaceful English countryside.
Open all year, Apr-Oct, daily 10-6 (dusk if earlier in Oct); Nov-Mar, Wed-Sun 10-4 . Closed 24-26 Dec & 1 Jan. £4 (ch £2, concessions £3.60). (Personal stere tour available at an additional charge).
P (charged) &. shop ✻ (allowed in certain areas) ♿

Battle & District Historical Society Museum (opposite Abbey Green car park)
Memorial Hall TN33 0AQ
☎ 01424 775955
The focal point is a diorama of the Battle of Hastings and a reproduction of the Bayeux Tapestry. There are also local history exhibits. A Summer Arts Festival is held, and the Battle Festival takes place in June/July. Special displays of old photographs, toys etc are arranged throughout the season.
Open Etr-Sep, daily 10.30-4.30 (Sun 1.30-4.30). 80p (ch 20p, ch accompanied free).
P (20yds) shop ✻

Buckleys Yesterday's World
High St TN33 0AQ (next to Battle Abbey)
☎ 01424 775378
Fax 01424 775174
Refurbished for 1998: Experience a bygone age at one of the most unusual attractions in South east England. In a charming medieval house you'll see over 30 shop and room displays with thousands of authentic exhibits dating from Victorian times to the 1950s. To help you discover the past there are push button commentaries, moving figures and evocative smells. Delight in the nostalgia of the Victorian kitchen, grocers, chemists, 1930s country railway station, wireless shop, photographers or 1950s barbers shop and many more... Visitors can even come face to face with a moving and speaking life-size figure of Queen Victoria or visit the Penny Arcade, Miniature Golf Course, Childrens Play Village, Toddlers Activity Area, Nostalgic Video Show, or just relax on the lovely terrace with a chilled glass of locally grown wine, or a calorific cream tea from the Cafe. Due to the main buildings historic nature and location on top of a hill, disabled access is very limited.
Open all year, daily 10-6 (last admission 5pm) (Oct to Mar times subject to change). Closed 25-26 Dec & 1 Jan. £3.95 (ch £2.85, pen £3.65, disabled £2). Family ticket £11.95. Reduced admission Oct-Mar. Garden facilities only entry £1.25 per person. Group 15+.
P (100yds) 🍴 &. shop
Cards: 💳 💳

Although now well inland, Bodiam Castle was built as a coastal defence in 1385 – for the River Rother was then navigable by sea-going vessels.

Firle Place was remodelled in the 18th century from the original Tudor manor

BODIAM
Bodiam Castle
TN32 5UA (2m E of A21 Hurst Green)
☎01580 830436 Fax 01580 830398
Fairytale Bodiam is like the castles that children draw. Its tall curtain walls form a rectangular court with round drum towers at each corner, all reflected in the water of the moat. It was built in 1386-8 by Sir Edward Dalnygrigge, for comfort and defence. The walls measure some 6ft 6in thick, and the great gatehouse was defended by gun loops and three portcullises, of which one has survived. The castle walls have remained remarkably intact, and although the castle was gutted in the Civil War it still has over 30 fireplaces and 28 garderobes (latrines), each with a drain shaft to the moat. The remains of the chapel, halls, chambers and kitchens (with fireplaces) can be seen and the circular stairs to the battlements give access to some lovely views. Special events for 1998 include: Dragon Egg Hunt (10 Apr) and a new production of Alice in Wonderland. Tel: 01892 891001 for details.
Open 14 Feb-1 Nov, daily 10-6 or dusk if earlier; 3 Nov-3 Jan, Tue-Sun 10-4 or dusk. (Closed 24-26 Dec).
£3.30 (ch £1.65). Family ticket £8.25. Car £1.
P *(charged)* ✑ ✗ *licensed* ⅄ *(Braille guide, special parking on request) toilets for disabled shop* ✤ *(ex in grounds)* ✤
Cards: ▨ ▨ ▨ ▨

BRIGHTON
Booth Museum of Natural History
194 Dyke Rd BN1 5AA (from A27 Brighton by pass, 1.5m NW of town centre, opposite Dyke Rd Park)
☎01273 292777 Fax 01273 292778
The museum was built in 1874 to house the bird collection of Edward Thomas Booth (1840-1890). His collection is still on display, but the museum has expanded considerably since Booth's day and now includes thousands of butterfly and insect specimens, geology galleries with fossils, rocks and local dinosaur bones and a magnificent collection of animal skeletons, largely collected by F W Lucas (1842-1932), a Brighton solicitor. Conservation is also covered, with displays on the major habitats of Sussex showing how, over the ages, humans have managed and altered them. There is also a programme of exciting temporary exhibitions.

Open all year, Mon-Sat (ex Thu) 10-5, Sun 2-5. (Closed Good Fri, Xmas & 1 Jan). Free.
P *(two hour limit)* ⅄ *shop* ✤

Preston Manor
Preston Drove BN1 6SD (off A23)
☎01273 290900
Fax 01273 292871
This charming Edwardian manor house is beautifully furnished with notable collections of silver, furniture and paintings and presents a unique opportunity to see an Edwardian home both 'upstairs' and 'downstairs'. The servants' quarters can also be seen, featuring kitchen, butler's pantry and boot hall. The house is set in beautiful gardens, which include a pet's cemetery and the 13th century parish church of St Peter.
Open all year, Tue-Sat 10-5, Sun 2-5, Mon 1-5 (BH Mons 10-5). Closed Good Fri & 25-26 Dec.
✳*£2.95 (ch 5-15 £1.80, pen, students & UB40 £2.435). Family ticket £4.75-£7.70. Party 20+. Joint ticket with Royal Pavilion £6.25.*
P ✤

Royal Pavilion
BN1 1EE
☎01273 290900
Fax 01273 292871
Justifiably termed "The most extraordinary palace in Europe", this former seaside residence of King George IV with its myriad of domes and minarets and opulent interiors is a building no visitor to Brighton should miss. The £10 million structural restoration programme is now complete. Group tours by arrangement. Pavilion shop and tea room. Set in stunning, recently restored Regency gardens. Special events for 1998 include: Half term fun (February); Themed weekend of events/costumes guided tours etc (October); 'All That Glitters' - tours, lectures & displays by in-house conservation team (November). Ring for further details.
Open all year, Jun-Sep, daily 10-6; Oct-May, daily 10-5. (Closed 25-26 Dec).
✳*£4.10 (ch £2.50, concessions £3.) Family ticket £6.60-£10.70. Joint ticket with Preston Manor £6.25. Groups 20+.*
P *(NCP & on street)* ✑ ⅄ *(facilities for the blind by arrangement) toilets for disabled shop* ✤

Sea Life Centre
Marine Pde BN2 1TB
☎01273 604234 & 604233 (rec info)
Fax 01273 681840
The magnificent Brighton Sea Life Centre combines the timeless elegance of Victorian architecture with the most up-to-date marine life habitats. The underwater tunnel - the longest in Europe - winds its way through an enormous seabed, alive with sharks, rays, and conger eels. Newly-restored Victorian displays are now home to over 60 varieties of marine wildlife, including many unusual native and tropical species. Take a privileged peek into the Kingdom of the Seahorse, and find out more about these beautiful creatures and their complex behaviour.
Open all year, daily (ex 25 Dec), 10-6. Last admission 5.(Open later in summer & school holidays)
£5.50 (ch 4-14 £3.95, students & UB40 £3.95, under 4 free, free entry to the blind). Party 10+.
P *(200 yds)* ✑ ⅄ *toilets for disabled shop* ✤
Cards: ▨ ▨ ▨ ▨ ▨ ▨

BURWASH
Bateman's
TN19 7DS (0.5m SW off A265)
☎01435 882302 Fax 01435 882811
Rudyard Kipling lived at this lovely 17th-century ironmaster's house from 1902 to 1936. Kipling's study is kept much as it was then and among his many possessions to be seen around the property is his 1928 Rolls Royce. There are attractive gardens, with a restored watermill which grinds flour (Saturday afternoon only) for sale. Concerts with fireworks in August - 01892 891001.
Open 4 Apr-1 Nov, Sat-Wed 11-5.30, also open Good Fri, (last admission 4.30pm).
£4.70 (ch £2.35). Family ticket £11.75.
P ✑ ✗ *licensed* ⅄ *toilets for disabled shop* ✤ *(dog creche in car park)* ✤

EASTBOURNE
Eastbourne Redoubt Fortress
Royal Pde BN22 7AQ
☎01323 410300 Fax 01323 732240
This huge fortification was built in 1804 in case of invasion by Napoleon, and has places for 11 guns. It is now the home of the Sussex Combined Services Museum (The Royal Sussex Regiment and the Queen's Royal Irish Hussars) and the National Collection of the British Model Soldier Society. From July to September, '1812' Military Band Concerts with fireworks take place on Wed and Fri.
Open Etr-Oct, 9.30-5.30.
£2 (ch 16 & pen £1). Party.
P *(200 yds)* ✑ *shop*

"How We Lived Then" Museum of Shops & Social History
20 Cornfield Ter BN21 4NS
☎01323 737143
Over the last 40 years, Jan and Graham Upton have collected over 100,000 items which are now displayed on four floors of authentic old shops and room-settings, transporting visitors back to the age of their grandparents. Grocers, chemists, sweet shops, iron-mongers, tailors, cobblers, photographers, jewellers, music and toy shops are all represented in fascinating detail, as well as a Post Office, complete with dour postmistress. Other displays, such as seaside souvenirs, wartime rationing and Royal mementoes, help to capture 100 years of social history. The gift shop includes old fashioned sweets, reproduction tins, advertisements and tin-plate and Victorian-style greetings cards.
Open daily Feb-Dec, 10-5.30 (last entry 5pm).
£2.50 (ch 5-15 £1.50, pen £2). Party 10+.
P ⅄ *shop*

Tower 73 The Wish Tower
King Edward's Pde BN20 7XB
☎01323 410440
Fax 01323 63686
The Wish Tower exhibition is housed in Martello Tower 73, completed in 1806 and intended as a defence fortification against Napoleon. Today, an audio-visual show tells the story of Martello towers in south east England.
Open May-Sep, daily 9.30-5.30.
P *(100mtrs) shop* ✤ *(inc guide dogs)*
Details not confirmed for 1998

EXCEAT
The Living World
Seven Sisters Country Park BN25 4AD (on A259, 2m E of Seaford)
☎01323 870100
This is a living exhibition of small creatures: butterflies, bees, spiders, snails, moths, scorpions, marine life and others, in settings that are as near to nature as possible. The displays of this unique mini zoo are based in two old Sussex barns, situated in a 700-acre Country Park within the Heritage Coastline. A recent display includes the Bearded Dragon Lizards. Every Wednesday during school holidays, children can enjoy the 'mini beast' handling experience - visitors will be allowed to handle certain exhibits.
Open all year, mid Mar-1 Nov, daily; Nov-mid Mar, wknds & school holidays 10-5.
🅿 🍴 ✕ *licensed* � *toilets for disabled shop garden centre*
Details not confirmed for 1998

FIRLE
Firle Place
BN8 6LP (off A27, Eastbourne to Brighton road)
☎01273 858335 Fax 01273 858043
Home of the Gage family for over 500 years, the house has a Tudor core but was remodelled in the 18th century. Its treasures include important European and English Old Master paintings, fine English and French furniture, and porcelain, including notable examples from Sèvres and English factories. There are family monuments and brasses in the church at West Firle.
Open Jun-Sep, Sun, Wed & Thu; also Etr, Spring, May & Aug BH Sun & Mon 2-5. Party 25+.
🅿 ✕ *licensed* ⅙ *toilets for disabled shop* 🐾 *(ex in garden)*
Details not confirmed for 1998

FLIMWELL
Bedgebury National Pinetum
TN17 2SL (1.5m N off A21 onto B2079)
☎01580 211044
Fax 01580 212423
Bedgebury Pinetum is the national collection of conifers hardy in Britain. Some 320 species are currently on show, landscaped around three lakes and two streams. Rhododendron species and hybrids add to the collection's beauty and wildflowers are also plentiful. Visitors can walk in most areas, although two waymarked walks with information are included. There are areas of steep ground so it is advisable to wear stout shoes.
Visitor Centre open Mar-Xmas & wknds Jan/Feb. Pinetum daily all year.
£2.50 (ch £1.20, pen £2).
🅿 🍴 *shop*
Cards: 🅰 ➖ 🔵

GLYNDE
Glynde Place
Lewes BN8 6SX (off A27 between Lewes & Eastbourne)
☎01273 858224
Fax 01273 858224
A lovely Elizabethan manor with 18th-century additions, in a beautiful downland setting. It is still a family home, lived in by descendants of the original owner.
Open Jun-Sep, Wed & Sun 2-5, Also BH's & Suns in May. Garden open Suns in April.
£3.50 (ch £1.50).
🅿 🍴

GROOMBRIDGE
Groombridge Place Gardens & Enchanted Forest
TN3 9QG (off A264, on B2100)
☎01892 863999 & 861444
Fax 01892 863996
Surrounded by acres of breathtaking parkland, Groombridge Place has an intriguing history stretching back to medieval times. Flanked by a medieval moat, with a classical 17th-century manor as its backdrop, the beautiful formal gardens boast a rich variety of "rooms" together with extensive herbaceous borders. High above the walled gardens and estate vineyard, hidden from view, lies The Enchanted Forest, where magic and fantasy await discovery. Here are secret mysterious gardens to challenge and delight your imagination and reward your mind's ingenuity.
Open 10 Apr-25 Oct daily 10-6.
£5 (ch £3.50, pen & students £4.50).
🅿 🍴 ⅙ *toilets for disabled shop garden centre* 🐾
Cards: 🅰 ➖ 🔵 🔵

HAILSHAM
Michelham Priory
Upper Dicker BN27 3QS (2.5m W off A22)
☎01323 844224
Fax 01323 844030
Set on a tranquil moated island surrounded by spacious gardens, Michelham Priory is one of the most beautiful historic houses in Sussex. Founded in 1229 for Augustinian canons, the Priory is approached through a 14th-century gatehouse spanning the longest medieval moat in the country. Most of the original buildings were demolished during the Dissolution, but the remains were incorporated into a Tudor farm that became a splendid country house, now containing a fascinating array of exhibits. Outside, the picturesque gardens are enhanced by a working watermill, physic garden, smithy, rope museum and the dramatic Elizabethan Great Barn. Facilities include licensed restaurant and tearooms, picnic and play area and a Sussex crafts shop. Please telephone for details of special events.
Open 17 Mar-Oct, Wed-Sun (daily in Aug & BH Mons). Mar & Oct 11-4, Apr-Jul & Sep 11-5, Aug 10.30-5.30.
🅿 🍴 ✕ *licensed* ⅙ *(wheelchairs & braille guide available) toilets for disabled shop* 🐾 *(ex in car park)*
Details not confirmed for 1998
Cards: 🅰 ➖ 🔵 🔵 🔵

HALLAND
Bentley Wildfowl & Motor Museum
BN8 5AF (7m NE of Lewes, signposted on A22/A26/B2192)
☎01825 840573 Fax 01825 840573
Hundreds of swans, geese and ducks from all over the world can be seen on lakes and ponds along with flamingoes and peacocks. There is a fine array of Veteran, Edwardian and Vintage vehicles, and the house has splendid antiques and wildfowl paintings. The gardens specialise in old fashioned roses. Other attractions include woodland walks, a nature trail, audio-visual aids in the Education Centre, adventure playground, small animal section, and a miniature train which runs on summer Sundays, and Wednesdays in August. Quiz sheet available. Special events are planned for the summer.
Open 17 Mar-Oct, daily 10.30-4.30 (5pm Jul & Aug), House open from 12. Nov, Feb & part of Mar, wknds only. Estate closed Dec & Jan. House closed all winter.
🅿 🍴 ⅙ *(wheelchairs available) toilets for disabled shop* 🐾
Details not confirmed for 1998

HASTINGS
Hastings Embroidery
White Rock Theatre, White Rock TN34 1JX (situated on the A259 Seafront road opposite the pier)
☎01424 781010 Fax 01424 781170
The 80yd embroidery illustrates great events in British history from 1066 to modern times. It was sewn by the Royal School of Needlework, using threads, cords, metals, lace, jewels and appropriate cloths.
Open Tues-Sun 10am-5pm and BH Mondays.
£2 (ch, pen & student £1.50). Party.
🅿 *(charged)* ⅙ *toilets for disabled shop* 🐾
Cards: 🅰 ➖ 🔵 🔵

Old Town Hall Museum of Local History
Old Town Hall, High St TN34 3EW
☎01424 781166 Fax 01424 781165
Situated in the heart of Hastings Old Town, the museum was originally a Georgian Town Hall built in 1823. ➤

This magnificent silver candelabra showing the young Queen Victoria is just one of the many treasures at Glynde Place.

Great Dixter is a particularly notable half-timbered house set in grounds designed to display the English garden at its best.

Displays include the History of Hastings, the Battle of Hastings, the Cinque Ports and maritime history - smuggling, shipwrecks and fishing. Famous local personalities, including Logie Baird, inventor of television, are also featured.
Open Apr-Sep, Tue-Sun 10-1 & 2-5; Oct-Dec & Mar 2-4 (ex Wed). Dates may alter to allow for changes in displays.
P (150yds) ♿ shop
Details not confirmed for 1998

Smuggler's Adventure
St Clements Caves, West Hill TN34 3HY
☎*01424 422964*
Fax 01424 717747
A Smuggler's Adventure is a themed experience housed in a labyrinth of caverns and passages deep below the West Hill. Visitors first tour a comprehensive exhibition and museum, followed by a video theatre, before embarking on the Adventure Walk - a trip through several acres of caves with life-size tableaux, push-button automated models and dramatic scenic effects depicting life in the days of 18th-century smuggling.
Open all year daily, Etr-Sep 10-5.30; Oct-Etr 11-4.30. (Closed 25-26 Dec).
£4.40 (ch £2.70, pen & students £3.60). Family ticket £12.95.
P (500yds) shop
Cards:

1066 Story in Hastings Castle
Castle Hill Rd, West Hill TN34 3RG
☎*01424 781111*
Fax 01424 781133
The ruins of the Norman castle stand on the cliffs, close to the site of William the Conqueror's first motte-and-bailey castle in England. It was excavated in 1825 and 1968, and old dungeons were discovered in 1894. 'The Story of 1066', within the Castle grounds, is an exciting audio-visual experience covering the history of Hastings Castle and the famous battle of 1066. An unusual approach to the castle can be made via the West Hill Cliff Railway which is located in George Street precinct.
Open Apr-Sep 10-5 (5.30 school holidays). Oct onwards 11-3.30 (Closed Jan).
P ♿ *shop*
Details not confirmed for 1998

HERSTMONCEUX

The Truggery
Coopers Croft BN27 1QL (from A22 at Hailsham, Boship roundabout, take A271 in direction of Bexhill for 4m)
☎*01323 832314 Fax 01323 832314*
The art of Sussex trug making can be seen through all the work processes including preparing timber, use of the draw knife and assembly of trug.
Open May-Sept 10-5. Closed Sun & Mon ex BHs. Oct-Apr opening times may vary. Free.
P *shop*

HOVE

British Engineerium-Museum of Steam & Mechanical Antiquities
off Nevill Rd BN3 7QA
☎*01273 559583 Fax 01273 566403*
This restored Victorian water pumping station has an original working beam engine of 1876, and a French Corliss horizontal engine which won first prize at the Paris International Exhibition of 1889. There are also traction engines, fire engines, and many other full-size and model engines. Boilers are fired up and in steam the first Sunday of each month and Bank Holidays. Also open is an interactive exhibition for children, 'The Giant's Toolbox'.
Open all year, daily 10-4 (Closed wk prior to Xmas). In steam first Sun in month & BH's. £3.50 (ch, students & pen £2.50, ch under 5 free). Family ticket £10.
P ♿ *shop*

LEWES

Anne of Cleves House Museum
52 Southover High St BN7 1JA
☎*01273 474610 Fax 01273 486990*
This 16th-century town house was given to Anne of Cleves by her ex-husband, Henry VIII as part of her divorce settlement, though she never lived in the house. It is now devoted to Sussex arts and crafts, agricultural, industrial and domestic life, with a notable collection of Sussex ironwork including early gun-founding material. There is a medieval herb garden outside. In the summer guided tours take place to nearby Lewes Priory.
Open 25 Mar-10 Nov, daily 10-5.30 (Sun 12-5.30); 11 Nov-24 Mar, Tue & Thu 10-5.30.
P (25yds) (on street-2 hr restriction) shop
Details not confirmed for 1998

NEWHAVEN

Paradise Family Leisure Park
Avis Rd BN9 0DH (signposted off A26 & A259)
☎*01273 512123 Fax 01273 616000*
A unique Sussex attraction with 2 acres of delightful gardens and The Newhaven Botanic Garden, a spectacular collection of indoor botanical treasures set in 1/4 acre of landscaped gardens, all themed and under glass. Other attractions include Planet Earth and The Living Dinosaur Museum, Sussex in Miniature, Playland Park and a gift shop, garden centre and coffee shop. Ring the park for details of special events.
Open all year, daily. (Closed 25-26 Dec). £3.99 (ch £3.75, pen £3.85). Family ticket £14.99.Gardens only £2.99 (ch £2.85, pen £2.25).
P ✕ ♿ *(all areas level or ramped) toilets for disabled shop garden centre*
Cards:

NORTHIAM

Great Dixter
TN31 6PH (off A28)
☎*01797 252878 Fax 01797 252879*
Dating back to the 15th century, this half-timbered house has a notable great hall and fine gardens.
Open Apr-25 Oct, Tue-Sun & Bank Hol Mon, 2pm-5pm; Gardens open as house & also from 11am on 23-25 May & 31 Aug.
House & Gardens £4 (ch £1). Gardens only £3 (ch 50p). Party 25+.
P *shop garden centre*
Cards:

PEVENSEY

Pevensey Castle
BN24 5LG (off A259)
☎*01323 762604*
Witness to seventeen centuries of conflict, from its time as a Roman fortress to its use as a coastal base during the Second World War, this powerful castle has never been taken by force.
Open all year, Apr-Oct, daily 10-6 (or dusk if earlier in Oct); Nov-Mar, Wed-Sun 10-4 (closed 1-2pm). Closed 24-26 Dec & 1 Jan.
2.50 (ch £1.30, concessions £1.90).
P *(charged)* ♿ *(in certain areas)*

RYE

Lamb House
West St TN31 7ES
☎*01892 890651 Fax 01892 890110*
This 18th-century house was the home of novelist Henry James from 1898 until his death in 1916, and was later occupied by E F Benson, writer of the ***Lucia*** books, who was at one time Mayor of Rye. The house is surrounded by an attractive garden.
Apr-Oct, Wed & Sat 2-6 (last admission 5.30pm).
£2.50 (ch £1.25).
P

Rye Castle Museum
Rye Castle, Gun Garden TN31 7HH
☎*01797 226728*
The museum is housed in a stone tower built as a fortification in 1249. It was later used for 300 years as the town prison, and the cells remain. The display is of the Cinque Ports and local history, with sections on Rye's maritime interests, Rye pottery and life in Rye over the centuries. A topographical map of Romney Marsh with cliffline and changes in sea levels is part of the display. In 1998 the Museum will be open but with limited displays. Spring 1999 should see the grand re-opening of the Castle, and of a second site nearby which will more than double display area, and provide access to the disabled. Please ring for full details.
Open Jan-Mar weekends only 10.30-5.30; Apr-Oct daily 10.30-5.30 (last entry 5pm). Complete re-display and extension of collection during 1998. Full completion scheduled for Spring 1999. Limited displays while work is in progress
**£1.50 (ch 16 50p, ch 7 free, students & pen £1). Party 10 +.*
P (30yds) (street limited to 2hrs) *shop*

SHEFFIELD PARK

Sheffield Park Garden
TN22 3QX (5m E of Haywards Heath off A275)
☎*01825 790231 Fax 01825 791264*
Originally landscaped by 'Capability' Brown, in about 1775, to create a beautiful park with five lakes and a cascade, further extensive planting was done at the beginning of the 20th century. This has given Sheffield Park a superb collection of trees, with particular emphasis on those that give good autumn colour. In May and June masses of azaleas and rhododendrons give colour and later there are magnificent waterlilies on the lakes. The gardens and woodland cover nearly 200 acres. A 'Twenties Evening' is being held on June 27. Telephone 01892 891001 for details.
Open Mar: Sat & Sun 11-6. Apr-15 Nov, Tue-Sun & BH Mon 11-6 or sunset if earlier; 18 Nov-20 Dec: Wed-Sun 11-4. Last admission 1hr before closing. £4.20 (ch £2.10). Family ticket £10.50.
P ♿ *(powered self drive car & wheelchairs available) toilets for disabled shop*

SHEFFIELD PARK STATION

Bluebell Railway
Sheffield Park Station TN22 3QL (4.5m E of Haywards Heath, off A275)
☎*01825 723777 & 722370 (Train Information) Fax 01825 724139*
The Bluebell Railway runs historic steam trains through nine miles of pretty Sussex countryside. Trains run every weekend throughout the year and daily through the summer and school holidays. The headquarters of the Railway is Sheffield Park station, where visitors will find the locomotive sheds, gift shop, museum and restaurant. Trains operate between Sheffield Park, Horsted Keynes ad Kingscote. Please note that there is NO PARKING at Kingscote Station. If you wish to board the train here, catch the vintage bus (service 473) which connects Kingscote and East Grinstead. A luxurious Pullman dining train runs on Saturday evenings and Sunday lunchtimes and may be hired for private parties. Special events throughout the year include Vintage Bus Day (26 Apr), centenary of locomotive no 473 'Birch Grove' (13-14 Jun), Thomas the Tank Engine (provisional dates)(27-28 Jun), Collector's Fair (18-19 Jul), Steam Fair & Vintage Vehicle Rally (25-26 Jul), Starlight Special (24 Oct), Giants of Steam (25 Oct), plus Santa Specials in December, please ring for further details.
Open all year, Sat & Sun. Daily May-Sep. Santa Specials run Dec. For timetable and information regarding trains contact above.
**3rd class return fare £7.20 (ch £3.60). Museum & locomotive sheds only, £2 (ch £1). Supplementary available for 1st class travel. Pre-booked parties 20+.*
P ✕ *licensed* ♿ *toilets for disabled shop*
Cards:

SUSSEX, WEST

AMBERLEY

Amberley Museum
Houghton Bridge BN18 9LT (on B2139, between Arundel/Storrington, adjacent to Amberley Station)
☎*01798 831370 Fax 01798 831831*
This exciting working museum reflects the industrial history of the south east of England. Here you can visit the craftsmen - the blacksmith, potter, printer or boat-builder, and experience the sights, sounds and smells of their workshops. Take a ride on the workmen's train or on the narrow gauge railway, or enjoy the delights of the vintage motor buses. There are many other exhibits and displays to capture your interest and imagination within the magnificent 36-acre site including the Rural Telephone Exchange, Wheelwright's Shop, the Seeboard

The little town of Arundel nestling beside the River Arun, was protected by Arundel Castle, the ancient home of the Dukes of Norfolk.

Electricity Hall, and Paviors' Museum of Roads and Roadmaking. Allow at least three hours for a visit.
Open 20 Mar-3 Nov, Wed-Sun plus Bank Holiday Mon. Also open daily during local school holidays 27 Mar-14 Apr, 22 May-2 Jun, 17 Jul-1 Sep & 23 Oct-3 Nov.
🅿 💺 ⅃ *toilets for disabled shop*
Details not confirmed for 1998
Cards: 🖃 ⚏

ARDINGLY
Wakehurst Place Garden
RH17 6TN (1.5m NW, on B2028)
☎ *01444 894066*
Woodland and lakes linked by a pretty watercourse make this large garden a beautiful place to walk, and it also has an amazing variety of interesting trees and shrubs, a Winter Garden, and a Rock Walk. It is administered and maintained by the Royal Botanic Gardens at Kew.
Open all year, Nov-Jan 10-4; Feb & Oct 10-5; Mar 10-6; Apr-Sep 10-7. (Closed 25 Dec & 1 Jan). Last admission 30 mins before closing. Mansion closes one hour before garden.
✳*£4 (ch £1.50, students, UB40 & pen £2).*
🅿 ✗ ⅃ *(wheelchair available) toilets for disabled shop* ⚏ 🏛

ARUNDEL
Arundel Castle
BN18 9AB
☎ *01903 883136 Fax 01903 884581*
This great castle, home of the Dukes of Norfolk, dates from the Norman Conquest. Containing a very fine collection of furniture and paintings, it is still a family home reflecting the changes of nearly a thousand years.
Open Apr-last Fri in Oct, Sun-Fri 12-5. Last admission 4pm (Closed Sat & Good Fri).
£5.70 (ch 5-15 £4.20, pen £5.20). Party 20+
🅿 💺 *shop* ⚏
Cards: 🖃 ⚏ ⚏ 🗾

WWT Arundel
Mill Rd BN18 9PB (signposted from A27 & A29)
☎ *01903 883355 Fax 01903 884834*
More than a thousand ducks, geese and swans from all over the world can be

found here, many of which are so friendly that they will even feed from your hand. The wild reserve attracts a variety of wild birds and includes a reedbed habitat considered so vital to the wetland wildlife it shelters that it has been designated a Site of Special Scientific Interest. Visitors can walk on a specially designed boardwalk, right through this reedbed without getting their feet wet. Other features include four activity stations around the grounds where visitors of all ages can find out more about wetlands and their wildlife (opening times vary), a large viewing gallery and several comfortable hides from which to observe wild birds. Facilities for disabled people include free wheelchair loan, and purpose-built toilets. There is a packed programme of events and activities available throughout the year.
Open all year, daily. Summer 9.30-5.30; Winter 9.30-4.30. Last admission Summer 5pm; Winter 4pm. (Closed 25 Dec).
✳*£4.25 (ch £2.25). Family ticket £10.75. Party 10+.*
🅿 ✗ *licensed* ⅃ *(level paths, free wheelchair loan) toilets for disabled shop* ⚏
Cards: 🖃 ⚏ ⚏ 🗾

ASHINGTON
Holly Gate Cactus Garden
Billingshurst Rd RH20 3BB (B2133)
☎ *01903 892930*
A mecca for the cactus enthusiast, with more than 30,000 succulent and cactus plants, including many rare types. They come from both arid and tropical parts of the world, and are housed in over 10,000 sq ft of greenhouses.
Open all year daily, 9-5. (Closed 25-26 Dec).
£1.50 (ch & pen £1). Party 20+.
🅿 💺 ⅃ *shop garden centre*
Cards: 🖃 ⚏ ⚏

BIGNOR
Bignor Roman Villa & Museum
RH20 1PH (between A29 & A285)
☎ *01798 869259 Fax 01798 869478*
Rediscovered in 1811, this Roman house was built on a grand scale. It is one of the

largest known, and has spectacular mosaics. The heating system can also be seen, and various finds from excavations are on show. The longest mosaic in Britain (82ft) is on display here in its original position.
Open Mar-May & Oct 10-5 (Closed Mon ex BHs). Jun-Sep daily 10-6.
£3.25 (ch 16 £1.40, pen £2.25). Party 10+. Guided tours by arrangement.
🅿 💺 ⅃ *shop* ⚏

BRAMBER
Bramber Castle
BN4 3FB (on W side of village off A283)
A former home of the Dukes of Norfolk, this ruined Norman stronghold lies on a ridge of the South Downs and gives wonderful views.
Open any reasonable time.
Free.
🅿 🏛

CHICHESTER
Chichester Cathedral
West St PO19 1PX
☎ *01243 782595 Fax 01243 536190*
The beauty of the 900-year-old cathedral, site of the shrine of St Richard, is enhanced by many art treasures, ancient and modern. Events for 1998 include Festival of Flowers (28-30 May) and the Chichester Festivities (28 Jun-13 Jul).
Open daily, Etr-mid-Sep 7.30-7, mid Sep-Etr 7.30-5. Visiting restricted during services and concerts.
Donations invited.
🅿 *(within city walls)* 💺 ✗ ⅃ *toilets for disabled shop* ⚏

Mechanical Music & Doll Collection
Church Rd, Portfield PO19 4HN (1m E off A27)
☎ *01243 785421 & 372646*
Fax 01243 370299
A unique opportunity to see and hear barrel organs, polyphons, musical boxes, fair organs etc - all fully restored and playing for your pleasure. A magical musical tour to fascinate and entertain all ages. The doll collection contains fine examples of Victorian china and wax dolls, also felt and velvet dolls of the 1920s. A superb array of Victorian artefacts housed in a well-preserved Victorian church, this is a fascinating and very entertaining place for all the family.
Open Etr-Sep, Sun-Fri 1-5; Oct-Etr Sun only 1-5; Evening bookings by arrangement. Closed Dec.
✳*£2 (ch 75p).*
🅿 ⅃ *shop* ⚏

Pallant House
9 North Pallant PO19 1TJ
☎ *01243 774557 Fax 01243 536038*
The gallery is housed in a restored Queen Anne town house. The rooms contain fine furniture, and there is an Edwardian kitchen. Permanent collections on display include the Modern British Art of the Hussey and Kearley bequests; the Geoffrey Freeman collection of Bow

porcelain. There is a programme of temporary exhibitions, and the small garden is planted in 18th-century style. Ring for details of special events.
Open all year, Tue-Sat 10-5.15. (Closed Sun, Mon & BHs). (Last admission 4.45pm).
🅿 *(3 mins walk)* ⅃ *shop* ⚏ *(ex guide dogs)*
Details not confirmed for 1998

EAST GRINSTEAD
Standen
RH19 4NE (2m S of East Grinstead, signposted from B2110)
☎ *01342 323029 Fax 01342 316424*
Standen is a showpiece of the 19th-century Arts and Crafts movement. It was designed by Philip Webb for the Beale family, and was meant from the start to be decorated with William Morris wallpapers and fabrics. The interior has been carefully preserved, and the Morris designs to be seen here include Sunflower, Peacock, Trellis, and Larkspur, among others. The furniture is also in keeping, and includes contemporary brass beds from Heal's, furniture from the Morris firm, and ceramics by William de Morgan. Webb also designed some of the furniture and details such as the fire grates, finger plates for the doors, and the electric light fittings. There is a beautiful hillside garden. For events please contact the Regional Box Office 01372 451596.
Open 25 Mar-1 Nov, Wed-Sun (inc Good Fri) also BH Mon. House 12.30-4, Shop: 12.30-5, Garden: 12.30-6. 6 Nov-20 Dec,Garden & shop open, Fri-Sun, 1-4.Entry may be delayed at peak times. House & garden £5. Garden only £3(£2 in Nov-Dec). Children half price. Family ticket £12.50.Joint ticket which includes same day entry to Nymans garden £7, available Wed-Fri.
🅿 ✗ *licensed* ⅃ *shop* ⚏ *(ex part grounds)* 🏛
Cards: 🖃 ⚏ ⚏ ⚏ 🗾

FISHBOURNE
Fishborne Roman Palace
Salthill Rd PO19 3QR (N of A259 in Fishbourne)
☎ *01243 785859 Fax 01243 539266*
This is the largest known Roman residence in Britain, but the reason for building such a magnificent house here is not known. It was occupied from the 1st to the 3rd centuries AD, when its 100 or so rooms must have been a wonderful sight with their mosaic floors and painted walls; 25 of these mosaic floors can still be seen in varying states of completeness, including others rescued from elsewhere in the area. Outside, the northern part of the palace garden has been replanted to its original 1st-century plan. The museum gives an account of the history of the palace, and shows a full-size reconstruction of a Roman dining room. There are also an audio-visual theatre, mosaic-making area for children, a museum of Roman gardening and a reconstructed Roman garden. ➤

Denmans Garden has gradually developed over the last forty years and covers three and a half acres

Open all year, daily 11 Feb-13 Dec. Feb, Nov-Dec 10-4; Mar-Jul & Sep-Oct 10-5; Aug 10-6. Sun only 14 Dec-10 Feb 10-4.
🅿 🍴 ♿ *(self guiding tapes & tactile objects for the blind) toilets for disabled shop garden centre* ✸
Details not confirmed for 1998
Cards: 🖸 🖸 🖸 🖸 🖸

FONTWELL
Denmans Garden
BN18 0SU (5m E of Chichester on A27)
☎ 01243 542808 Fax 01243 544064
This garden has been created from land which was part of an estate owned by Lord Denman in the 19th century. The present three-and-a-half-acre garden was begun in the 1940s and has gradually developed over the last 50 years. There is a Walled Garden, bursting with masses of perennials, herbs and old-fashioned roses, and a Gravel Stream with grasses, bamboo and a pond. The South Garden has fine maples and cherry trees, and many mature, rare trees. A school of Garden Design is housed in the Clock House.
Open Mar-Oct daily 9-5.
£2.80 (ch £1.50, ch under 4 free, pen £2.50). Party 15+.
🅿 🍴 ♿ *garden centre* ✸
Cards: 🖸 🖸

GOODWOOD
Goodwood House
PO18 0PX (3m NE of Chichester)
☎ 01243 774107 Fax 01243 774313
Ancestral home of the Dukes of Richmond for 300 years, the 10th Duke's heir, The Earl of March and his Countess, now live in the house with their young family. Following refurbishment the State Apartments have taken on new life. The Egyptian Dining Room, unseen for 100 years, has been restored with its gilded cobras, vultures, scarabs and crocodiles. Unrivalled as an English ancestral collection, the paintings include works by Van Dyck, Reynolds, Stubbs and Canaletto. Goodwood, famous for historic motor racing, celebrates its Festival of Speed (12-14 Jun) in the park in June, and the re-opening of the Motor Circuit in September. Horse racing, high on the downs throughout the summer season, culminates in Glorious Goodwood at the end of July.
Open Etr Sun & Mon, then Sun & Mon until 28 Sep, also Tue-Thu in Aug. 1-5. (Closed 10 May, 14+15 June & 20 Sept) £5.50 (ch & disabled £2). Groups 25+.
🅿 🍴 ♿ *toilets for disabled shop* ✸

HANDCROSS
Nymans Garden
RH17 6EB (on B2114)
☎ 01444 400321 & 400777
Fax 01444 400253
Set in the Sussex Weald, Nymans has flowering shrubs and roses, a flower garden in the old walled orchard, and a secret sunken garden. There are some fine and rare trees. Summer events are held in the garden. Jazz Evenings (10-11 Jul), Teddy Bears' Picnic (21 Jul). For details please call regional box office (01372) 451596.
Open Mar-Oct, daily (ex Mon & Tue) but open BH Mon 11-6 or sunset if earlier. Last admission 1 hour before closing. June-July, garden open on Sun til 9pm. Winter wknds 12-4, restricted according to ground conditions. Phone for more information. £5. Family ticket £12.50, joint ticket which includes same day entry to Standen £7, available Wed-Fri.
🅿 🍴 ♿ *(wheelchair route, wheelchair available, braille guide) toilets for disabled shop* ✸ 🐾

HAYWARDS HEATH
Borde Hill Garden
Balcombe Rd RH16 1XP (1.5m N)
☎ 01444 450326 Fax 01444 440427
Borde Hill is Britain's best private collection of champion trees. Tranquil gardens with a rich variety of all season colour set in 200 acres of spectacular Sussex parkland and bluebell woods. Extensive new planting with a new rose and herbaceous garden designed in 1995 by Robin Williams for the summer. Planted from 1893 with trees and shrubs from China, Asia, Tasmania, the Andes and Europe, Borde Hill is known as an award-winning collection of azaleas, rhododendrons, and magnolias and for creating camellias Donation and Salutation. Attractions include coarse fishing, childrens' trout fishing, 'Pirates' adventure playground, tea room, restaurant, gift shop. New Bressingham plant centre. There are extensive woodland walks and lakes with picnic area. Wheelchairs can access most areas and dogs are welcome on leads. Garden Festival (18-19 April) Kids Animal Fair (26 April), Fuschia Show (11-12 August), Borde Hill Horse Trials (4-5 July),
Open all year, 10-6.
Garden & Parkland £3 (ch £1.50). Family ticket £8.
🅿 🍴 ✗ *licensed* ♿ *(wheelchairs available) toilets for disabled shop (on leads)*
Cards: 🖸 🖸

LITTLEHAMPTON
Littlehampton Museum
Manor House, Church St BN17 5EP
☎ 01903 715149
A small, friendly museum close to the High Street of this port and seaside resort. This is one of the few maritime museums in West Sussex, and there are also displays of local history, art, archaeology and a lively programme of temporary exhibitions. Please telephone for details of exhibitions.
Open all year Tue-Sat (incl Summer BH); 10.30-4.30.
Free.
P *(adjacent)* ♿ *(object handling sessions can be arranged for groups) shop* ✸

LOWER BEEDING
Leonardslee Gardens
RH13 6PP (4m SW from Handcross, at junct of B2110/A281)
☎ 01403 891212 Fax 01403 891305
This Grade I listed garden is set in a superb landscape in a peaceful 240 acre valley with walks around seven beautiful lakes, with delightful views. Open to the public since 1907, it is a paradise in spring, with banks of rhododendrons and azaleas along paths lined with bluebells. The Rock Garden is a kaleidoscope of colour in May. Peaceful in summer, and mellow with the autumn tints. There is a fascinating Bonsai exhibition, and an Alpine House with 400 plants in a rocky landscape. Wallabies (environmentally friendly mowing-machines!) live semi-wild in parts of the valley, and Axis, Fallow, and Sika Deer roam in the park. There is also a collection of Victorian Motor Cars. Special Events: Bonsai Weekend (2-4 May), Craft Fair (27-28 Jun).
Open Apr-31 Oct, daily 9.30-6 (May 9.30-8).
Apr & Jun-Oct £3.50, May £4.50, (ch £2).
🅿 🍴 ✗ *licensed shop garden centre* ✸

PETWORTH
Petworth House & Park
GU28 0AE (in centre of Petworth, A272/283)
☎ 01798 342207 & 343929
Fax 01798 342963
A 13-mile wall surrounds Petworth's acres. Rebuilt by the Duke of Somerset in the 17th century, all that remains of the 13th-century building is the chapel. The imposing 320ft west front faces the lake and great park, and was re-designed by Anthony Salvin between 1869 and 1872. The state rooms and galleries contain one of the finest art collections in England, including works by Gainsborough, Rembrandt and Van Dyck. Turner was a frequent visitor to Petworth, and a notable collection of his works is kept here. The carved room is said to be the most impressive in the house, with its lovely decoration by Grinling Gibbons. Over the last two years, six rooms in the servants' block have been opened, including the old

kitchen. Events include Spring Plant Fair (19 May), Craft Festival (23-25 May), Open Air Concerts (26-28 Jun), Kite Festival (4-5 July), please telephone for details.
Open 28 Mar-1 Nov, Sat-Wed (open Good Fri). House 1-5.30, last admission 4.30. Park open daily 8-sunset (ex 26-28 June). Extra rooms shown on weekdays but not BH)
£5 (ch £2.50). Family ticket £12.50. Party 15+.
🅿 🍴 ✗ *licensed* ♿ *(wheelchairs available, braille guide) toilets for disabled shop* ✸
Cards: 🖸 🖸 🖸

PULBOROUGH
Parham House & Gardens
Parham Park RH20 4HS (3m SE off A283, between Pulborough & Storrington)
☎ 01903 744888 (info line)
Fax 01903 746557
Surrounded by a deer park, fine gardens and 18th-century Pleasure Grounds in a beautiful downland setting, this Elizabethan family home contains an important collection of paintings, furniture, carpets and rare needlework. A brick and turf maze has been created in the grounds - designed with children in mind, it is called 'Veronica's Maze'. A special Garden Weekend is held on 18-19 July 1998. Steam Rally (13-14 Jun), Craft Show (21-23 Aug), Country Show (12-13 Sep).
Open 1 Apr-29 Oct, Wed, Thu, Sun & BH. Gardens 12-6; House 2-6 (last entry 5). Guided tours on Wed & Thu mornings and Mon, Tue & Fri afternoons by special arrangement.
❈ *House & Gardens £4.50 (ch 5-15 £1, pen £4). Family ticket £10. Gardens £3 (ch 50p). Party.*
🅿 🍴 ♿ *(wheelchairs available by arrangement/tape tour) shop garden centre* ✸ *(ex in grounds)*
Cards: 🖸 🖸 🖸 🖸 🖸

RSPB Nature Reserve
Uppertons Barns Visitor Centre, Wiggonholt RH20 2EL (on A283,1m S of Pulborough & 1m N of Storrington)
☎ 01798 875851
Fax 01798 873716
Set in the scenic Arun Valley and easily reached via the visitor centre on the A283 at Wigginholt, this is an excellent reserve for year-round family visits. A nature trail winds through hedgerow-lined lanes to viewing hides overlooking water-meadows. Breeding summer birds include nightingales and warblers, ducks and wading birds, and nightjars and hobbies on nearby heathland. In winter, thousands of colourful ducks, geese, swans and waders are joined by barn owl, peregrine falcon and occasional hen harrier. Unusual waders and hedgerow birds regularly pass through on spring and autumn migration. Other wildlife includes many butterfly and dragonfly species in the summer, with deer and smaller animals all year round. This years

events include: Seasonal guided walks/ activities for all ages, backgrounds and abilities. Contact Visitor Centre for an events leaflet.
Open daily, 9-9, (or sunset if earlier). Visitor centre daily, 10-5. Reserve closed 25 Dec, visitor centre closed 25-26 Dec. ✿£3 (ch 5-16 £1, concessions £2) Family £6. No group discounts at weekends or special events.
P ♥ ✗ *licensed* ₺ *(ramps at some hides/batricar bookable/easy gradient trail) toilets for disabled shop* ✿
Cards: ▣ ▦ ▨ ▢

SINGLETON
Weald & Downland Open Air Museum
PO18 0EU (6m N of Chichester on A286)
☎01243 811348
Fax 01243 811475
Situated in a beautiful downland setting, this museum displays more than 35 rescued historic buildings from south-east England. The buildings, ranging from early medieval houses to a 19th-century schoolhouse, have been re-erected to form a village and outlying farms and agricultural buildings. Among the exhibits there is a medieval farmstead working watermill, where corn is ground and flour is sold, a Tudor market hall, a blacksmith's forge, tollhouse and hands-on gallery. Longport House, a farmhouse from the Channel Tunnel site, forms a new reception centre.
There are displays of rural industries, including a charcoal burner's camp, and traditional building crafts.
Open all year, Mar-Oct, daily 10.30-5; Nov-Feb, Wed, Sat & Sun 10.30-5, also 26 Dec-2 Jan, 10.30-5.
P ♥ ₺ *toilets for disabled shop*
Details not confirmed for 1998
Cards: ▣ ▦ ▨ ▨ ▢
See advertisement on page 137.

SOUTH HARTING
Uppark
GU31 5QR (1.5m S on B2146)
☎01730 825415 or 01730 825857
Fax 01730 825873
On 30th August 1989 this late 17th-century house was partially destroyed by fire. The attic and the first floor were completely gutted, but many of the 18th-century contents were saved. Following the most ambitious restoration project ever undertaken by the National Trust, Uppark is re-open to the public. The garden, landscaped by Repton, and its magnificent views, can also be enjoyed.
Open Apr-29 Oct, Sun-Thu. House 1-5. Car park,woodland walk,garden & Exhibition 11.30-5.30. Last admission to house 4pm. Timed tickets will be in operation, so delays may occur or tickets may sell out on very busy days, pre-booking is possible.

House, garden & exhibition £5.50. Family ticket £13.75.
P ♥ ₺ *(ramps,lift,stair to exhibition) toilets for disabled shop* ✿ *(ex woodland walk & car park)* ≝

TANGMERE
Tangmere Military Aviation Museum Trust
PO20 6ES (off A27)
☎01243 775223
Fax 01243 775223
Based at an airfield which played an important role during the World Wars, this museum spans 70 years of military aviation and has a wide-ranging collection of relics relating to Tangmere and air warfare in the south-east of England. There are photographs, documents, models, uniforms, aircraft and aircraft parts on display along with a Spitfire cockpit simulator. A hangar houses the record-breaking aircraft Meteor and Hunter. The latest acquisition is a Supermarine Swift and there are also full-size replicas of a Spitfire and a Hurricane. Also a replica of the prototype Spitfire K504, on loan from the Spitfire society.
Open Mar-Oct, daily 10-5.30; Feb & Nov, daily 10-4.30.
£3 (ch £1.50 & pen £2.50).
P ♥ ₺ *(wheelchairs available) toilets for disabled shop*

WEST DEAN
West Dean Gardens
Estate Office PO18 0QZ (on A286,6m N of Chichester)
☎01243 818210 & 811301
Fax 01243 811342
An historic garden of 35 acres in a tranquil downland setting. Noted for its 300-ft long Harold Peto pergola, mixed and herbaceous borders, rustic summerhouses, water garden and specimen trees. The newly restored walled garden contains a fruit collection, Victorian glasshouses, an apple store, large working kitchen garden and a tool and mower collection. The Circuit Walk (two-and-a-quarter miles) climbs through parkland to the 45-acre St Roches Arboretum with its varied collection of trees and shrubs. The Visitors Centre provides a high level of facilities with a beautiful prospect of the River Lavant and West Dean Park. Events include: The Garden Event (27-28 Jun), Pergola Open Air Theatre (5-18 Jul), Chilli Fiesta (15-16 Aug), Apple Day (18 Oct).
Open 7 Mar-25 Oct, daily 11-5. Last ticket 4.30pm.
£3.50 (ch £1.50, pen £3). Party 20+.
P ✗ *licensed* ₺ *(reserved parking) toilets for disabled shop* ✿ *(ex guide dogs)*
Cards: ▣ ▦ ▨ ▢

TYNE & WEAR

JARROW
Bedes World & St Paul's Church
Church Bank NE32 3DY (off A185 nr South end of Tyne tunnel)
☎0191 489 2106 Fax 0191 428 2361
At Bede's World in Jarrow the fascinating world of the early Middle Ages has been brought to life in a remarkable way. A beautiful building complements the displays in Jarrow Hall with an exhibition area and finds from archaeological excavations in the North East, showing secular as well as religious life of the time. On the monastic site where Bede lived, and around the ancient church of St Paul (over 1300 years old), new signs have been installed to help visitors see the way in which successive phases of monastery buildings were constructed, from the first establishment around 681 (destroyed by Viking raids) to the rebuilding shortly after the Norman Conquest.
Outside the museum visitors can see Anglo-Saxon farming in action - with rare breeds of animals, authentic crops and Anglo-Saxon timber halls under construction. Special weekend events and living history re-enactments throughout the summer, including Anglo-Saxon cooking demonstrations (and tastings), bring the past vividly to life.
Open all year, Apr-Oct, Tue-Sat & BH Mons 10-5.30, Sun 2.30-5.30; Nov-Mar, Tue-Sat 10-4.30, Sun 2.30-5.30. Xmas-New Year opening times vary. Church open Apr-Oct 10-4.15; Nov-Mar 11-4.15 Mon-Sat & Sun 2.30-4.15. (May-Sept Sun 12-5.30). £3 (ch & concessions £1.50). Family ticket £7.20. UB40 family ticket £4. Party.
P ♥ ₺ *(electric wheelchair on request) toilets for disabled shop* ✿
Cards: ▣ ▦

NEWCASTLE UPON TYNE
Hancock Museum
Barras Bridge NE2 4PT
☎0191 222 7418 Fax 0191 222 6753
One of the finest museums of natural history in the country, the Hancock Museum houses geological exhibits and John Hancock's magnificent collection of birds. Travel back in time to Land of the Pharaohs and discover more about life and death in Ancient Eygpt. See the mummies; Irt-Irw, who was completely unwrapped in 1830. Her preserved remains give an intriguing insight into the effectiveness of the ancient art of embalming and mummification. The second mummy, Princess Bakh-Hor-Nekht is encased in her cartonnage but her face has been reconstructed using modern computer technology. The second part of the Earth galleries opened in 1997, exploring the cosmic and geological processes that have shaped the earth, and investigating the history of life on our planet.
Open all year, Mon-Sat, 10-5, Sun 2-5. Closed 25/26 Dec & 1 Jan.
✿£1.95 (concessions £1). Prices vary with special exhibitions.
P ♥ ₺ *(Lift,audio guides,braille guides) toilets for disabled shop* ✿
Cards: ▣ ▦ ▨ ▢

Laing Art Gallery
Higham PI NE1 8AG
☎0191 232 7734 & 0191 232 6989
Fax 0191 261 6191
British paintings and watercolours from the 18th-century to the present day are on display here, with works by Burne-Jones, Reynolds, Turner and others, including the Northumberland artist John Martin. A pioneering interactive display called Art on Tyneside shows paintings, costume, silver etc in period settings. There is also a programme of temporary exhibitions and a children's gallery designed specially for the under fives.
Open all year, Mon-Sat 10-5, Sun 2-5. (Closed 25 Dec).
♥ ₺ *toilets for disabled shop* ✿
Details not confirmed for 1998

Museum of Antiquities
The University NE1 7RU
☎0191 222 7849 Fax 0191 222 8561
Artefacts from north east England from prehistoric times to AD 1600 are on display here. The principal museum for Hadrian's Wall, this collection includes models of the wall, life-size Roman soldiers and a recently refurbished reconstruction of the Temple of Mithras. There is also a museum book shop.
Open all year, daily (ex Sun), 10-5 (Closed Good Fri, 24-26 Dec & 1 Jan). Free.
P (400yds) ₺ *(Large print guide) shop* ✿
Cards: ▣ ▦ ▨ ▢

ROWLANDS GILL
Gibside
NE16 6BG (6m SW of Gateshead, on B6314)
☎01207 542255
The important early 18th-century landscaped park contains a chapel, an outstanding example of Palladian architecture, built to a design by James Paine as the mausoleum for members of the Bowes family. It stands at one end of the Great Walk of Turkey oaks, looking towards the column of British Liberty. Walks have views to the ruined hall, orangery and other estate buildings. Open Air Concerts - Queen Tribute (17 Jul), Light Orchestral Classics and Fireworks (18 Jul). Other events - please ring for details.
Open Apr-1 Nov daily (ex Mon),11-5. Open BH Mon. Last admission 4.30. Grounds only 8 Nov-end Mar, Sun 10-4. £3. (Winter opening £2). Party.
P ♥ ₺ *(braille guide,wheelchair) shop* ✿ *(ex on leads)* ≝
Cards: ▣ ▦ ▨ ▢

SOUTH SHIELDS
Arbeia Roman Fort & Museum
Baring St NE33 2BB
☎0191 456 1369 454 4093
Fax 0191 427 6862
In South Shields town are the extensive remains of Arbeia, a 2nd-century Roman fort. It was the supply base for the Roman army's campaign against Scotland and was occupied for most of 300 years. The remains include fort defences, stone granaries, gateways, the headquarters, tile kilns and latrines. On the site of the west gate is a full-scale simulation of a Roman gateway with interior scenes of life at the fort. The museum exhibits site finds and gives background information. Archaeological excavations are in progress throughout the summer. Market Day in April - telephone for details.
Open all year, Apr-Sep, Mon-Sat 10-5.30, Sun 1-5; Oct-Mar, Mon-Sat 10-4. ✿Fort & Museum free of charge ex for 'Timequest'Archaeological Interpretation Gallery £1 (ch & concessions 50p).
P ₺ *(Minicom system) shop*

SUNDERLAND
Monkwearmouth Station Museum
North Bridge St SR5 1AP
☎0191 567 7075
Time stands still in this beautifully restored Victorian station. Travel and transport in the early 1900s are recorded with a look behind the scenes of the booking offices and guard's van. The brand new 'Play Station' activities area has been specifically designed for young visitors with regular organised events for children.
Open all year, Mon-Fri 10-5, Sat 10-4.30, Sun 2-5. Opening hours under review.
P ₺ *toilets for disabled shop* ✿
Details not confirmed for 1998

Museum & Art Gallery
Borough Rd SR1 1PP
☎0191 565 0723 Fax 0191 565 0713
Sunderland Museum is over 150 years old. Its age and reputation is reflected in the stunning collections of paintings, glass ware, pottery, fossils, minerals, birds and animals which illustrate the fascinating heritage of Wearside. Along with other industries, Sunderland is ➤

The ruins of Tynemouth Priory stand on a headland at the mouth of the River Tyne. This Benedictine foundation dates from the end of the eleventh century.

famous for shipbuilding, coal mining, glass making and pottery. Sunderland Museum records this important local history in the permanent displays: 'The Sunderland Story','Sunderland's Glorious Glass','...And Ships Were Born', and 'Coal'- a new and lasting tribute to mining in the region. The museum also has a varied and interesting series of temporary exhibitions with events for all the family.
Open all year, Mon-Fri 10-5, Sat 10-4.30, Sun 2-5.
P *(150 yds)* 🍴 & *toilets for disabled shop* ♿
Details not confirmed for 1998
Cards: 🆑 💳

TYNEMOUTH
Tynemouth Castle & Priory
NE30 4BZ (near North Pier)
☎0191 257 1090
The castle, fortifications and priory are a testament to the vital strategic importance of the site and its great religious significance. The soaring arches of the presbytery testify to a time when the priory was one of the richest in England and the Percy Chantry at the east end of the church is virtually complete. The restored gun battery and magazine can also be visited.
Open all year, Apr-Oct, daily 10-6 (or dusk if earlier); Nov-Mar, Wed-Sun 10-4 (or dusk if earlier, closed 1-2pm). Closed 24-26 Dec & 1 Jan.
£1.70 (ch 90p, concessions £1.30).
& *shop* ♿ ♿

WASHINGTON
Washington Old Hall
(follow signs for District 4 Washington New Town)
☎0191 416 6879
The home of George Washington's ancestors from 1183 to 1613, the Old Hall was originally an early medieval manor, but was rebuilt in the 17th century. The house has been restored and filled with period furniture. The property was given to the National Trust in 1956. There will be celebrations to mark American Independence Day.
Open Apr-1 Nov, Sun-Wed; open Good Fri,11-5. Last admission 4.30.
£2.50. Party.
P 🍴 *shop* ♿ ♿
Cards: 🆑 💳 💳

WWT Washington
NE38 8LE (signposted off A195 & A1231)
☎0191 416 5454
Fax 0191 416 5801
Set in a busy industrial area, on the north bank of the River Wear, WWT Washington is the home of a wonderful collection of exotic wildfowl from all over the world. There is also a heronry where visitors can watch a colony of wild Grey Herons on closed circuit television. The 100-acre site includes an area for wintering wildfowl which can be

observed from hides, and a flock of Chilean Flamingos. Other features include a discovery centre with activities for children, waterfowl nursery, large picture windows and a viewing gallery from which to observe the birds. Facilities for the disabled include free wheelchair loan, and purpose-built toilets. There is a packed programme of events and activities available throughout the year.
Open all year, daily 9.30-5 or dusk if earlier. (Closed 25 Dec).
✱*£4 (ch £2.40). Family ticket £10.40. Party 10+.*
P 🍴 & *(lowered windows in certain hides) toilets for disabled shop* ♿
Cards: 🆑 💳 💳 💳

WHITBURN
Souter Lighthouse
(coast road 2m S from South Shields)
☎0191 529 3161
This 150ft-high lighthouse was opened by Trinity House in 1871 and contains a bi-optic light, still in its original condition, which was the first reliable electrically powered lighthouse light. The Engine and Battery Rooms are all in working order and are included in the guided tour, along with the light tower, museum cottage and video. There is an education room and a restaurant. Ring for details of special events.
Open Apr-1 Nov daily ex Fri,(open Good Fri),11-5. Last admission 4.30.
£2.50. Party £2.
P 🍴 & *toilets for disabled shop* ♿
Cards: 🆑 💳 💳 💳

WARWICKSHIRE

ALCESTER
Ragley Hall
B49 5NJ (1.5m SW, off A435)
☎01789 762090
Fax 01789 764791
Ragley Hall is set in four hundred acres of parkland and gardens. The Great Hall contains some of England's finest Baroque plasterwork designed by James Gibbs. Graham Rust's mural The Temptation can be seen on the south staircase. Ample picnic areas beside the lake, as well as an adventure playground, maze and woodland walks. Events planned for 1998 include outdoor concerts (June, August, September), art exhibition (September), Transport Show (Jul) Gardeners shows (April and September).
Open 2 Apr-4 Oct, Thu-Sun & BH Mon; Jul-Aug park & garden open everyday. House 11-5, park & gardens 10-6. House (including garden & park) £5 (ch £3.50, pen £4.50).
P 🍴 & *(lift to first floor) toilets for disabled shop (ex in park & gardens)*

BADDESLEY CLINTON
Baddesley Clinton Hall
B93 0DQ (0.75m W off A4141)
☎01564 783294 Fax 01564 782706
A romantically-sited medieval moated house, dating from the 14th century, that has changed very little since 1634. With family portraits, priest holes, chapel, garden, ponds and lake walk. Midsummer opera on the lawn, 'Murder on the Menu' evening functions. An autumn lecture programme is planned, along with other events, please telephone for details.
Open 4 Mar-1 Nov, Wed-Sun & BH Mon,(closed Good Fri). Mar-Apr 1.30-5, May-Sept 1.30-5.30, Oct-1 Nov 1.30-5. (last admissions to house 30 mins before closing.)
£4.80. Family ticket £12. Grounds,restaurant & shop only £2.40.
P ✕ *licensed* & *(wheelchairs available,hearing scheme,braille guides) toilets for disabled shop* ♿ ♿
Cards: 🆑 💳

CHARLECOTE
Charlecote Park
CV35 9ER (5m E of Stratford, 1m W of Wellesbourne on B4086)
☎01789 470277 Fax 01789 470544
The home of the Lucy family since 1247, the present house was built in the 1550s and later visited by Queen Elizabeth I. The park was landscaped by 'Capability' Brown and has a herd of red and fallow deer, reputedly poached by Shakespeare and a flock of Jacob sheep first introduced in 1756. The principal rooms are decorated in Elizabethan Revival style. Medieval Craft Fayre (31 Jul-2 Aug).
Open 3 Apr-1 Nov; Fri-Tue 12-5. (closed Good Fri)
£4.80. Family ticket £12.
P ✕ *licensed* & *(Braille guides & hearing scheme available) toilets for disabled shop* ♿ ♿

COUGHTON
Coughton Court
B49 5JA (2m N,on E side of A435)
☎01789 762435
Fax 01789 765544
An impressive central gatehouse dating from 1530. During the Civil War this formerly moated and mainly Elizabethan house was attacked by both Parliamentary and Royalist forces, it suffered damage again in James II's reign. The contents of the Gatehouse south wing include some notable furniture, porcelain, portraits and relics of the Throckmorton family who have lived here since 1409. Two churches, tranquil lake, riverside walk and newly created formal gardens. Exhibitions on the Gunpowder Plot and Children's Clothes, also visitor centre with video. Outdoor concert with fireworks 25 Jul. Please telephone for details of concerts etc.

Open 14 Mar-end Apr, Sat-Sun 11.30-5; Etr Mon-Wed 11.30-5 (closed Good Fri); May-Sep, Sat-Wed 11.30-5. Also open Fri in July & Aug & 3-18 Oct, Sat-Sun 12-5. Grounds open 11-5.30, (days house open). Last admissions 30mins before closing time. On busy days entry to house by timed ticket.
£5.90 (ch 5-15 £2.95). Family ticket £18.50. Grounds £3.90. Family ticket £11.
P ✕ & *(Braille guide, wheelchair available) shop* ♿ ♿
Cards: 🆑 💳

FARNBOROUGH
Farnborough Hall
OX17 1DU (6m N of Banbury,0.5m W of A423)
☎01295 690202
A classical mid 18th-century stone house, still the home of the Holbech family, as it has been for 300 years; notable plasterwork, the entrance hall, staircase and two principal rooms are shown. The grounds contain charming 18th-century temples, a 1/4-mile terrace walk and an obelisk.
House, grounds & terrace walk open Apr-Sep, Wed & Sat, 3/4 May 2-6pm. Terrace walk Thu & Fri only, 2-6. Last admission 5.30pm.
House, Grounds & Terrace walk £2.90. Garden & Terrace walk £1.50. Terrace walk only (Thu & Fri) £1.
P & ♿ ♿

GAYDON
Heritage Motor Centre
Banbury Rd CV35 0BJ (Exit M40 at junc 12 and take B4100)
☎01926 641188
Fax 01926 641555
The largest purpose-designed road transport museum in the UK housing the largest collection of historic British cars anywhere in the world. Far more than a traditional car museum, the Centre has been specifically designed with family visitors in mind. Displays include Corgi and Lucas Museum collections, 1930s reconstruction garage, Engineering Gallery, Exhibition Gallery, and Fashion and Motoring. Other attractions on the 65-acre site include a children's playground, nature trail, unique Land Rover shuttle ride, spectacular four-wheel-drive demonstration circuit, Childrens' Hands-on Road Safety and a fantastic quad bike circuit for all the family (some activities at small additional cost). There are special activities for families and children at weekends and during school holidays. Special events for 1998 include: Spring Autotest (10 May), Triumph 75th Anniversary (31 May), BMC Marque Day (21 Jun), Centenary of the Riley Car (11-12 Jul), Supercar Sunday (19 Jul), Morris Minor 50th Anniversary (26 Jul), MG Marque Day (9 Aug). Please ring for further details.
Open all year, Apr-Oct, daily 10-6; Nov-Mar. daily 10-4.30. (check fo Christmas opening)
£5.50 (ch 5-16 £3.50, under 5 free, & senior £4.50). Family ticket £15.
P 🍴 ✕ *licensed* & *(lifts, wide doors, graded ramps & pathways) toilets for disabled shop* ♿
Cards: 🆑 💳 💳 💳 💳 💳 💳

KENILWORTH
Kenilworth Castle
☎01926 52078
Kenilworth is the largest castle ruin in England, the former stronghold of great lords and kings. Its massive walls tower over the peaceful Warwickshire landscape. The grim Norman keep with its twenty foot thick walls was already nearly 500 years old when Elizabeth I visited in 1575. The host, her favourite Robert Dudley, built a new wing for her to lodge in during her nineteen day stay. John of Gaunt's Great Hall was second only in width and grandeur to Westminster Hall and if you climb to the top of the tower beside the hall you will be rewarded by fine views over the countryside.

Open all year, Apr-Oct, daily 10-6 (or dusk if earlier); Nov-Mar, daily 10-4. Closed 24-26 Dec & 1 Jan.
£3.10 (ch £1.60, concessions £2.30).
🅿 ♿ shop ✲ ⊞

MIDDLETON
Ash End House Farm "The Childrens Farm"
Middleton Ln, Middleton B78 2BL
(signposted from A4091)
☎ 0121 329 3240
Fax 0121 329 3240
Ash End House is a children's farm, specifically set up with children in mind. They love to learn and experience new things, and what better way than when having fun. Children's guided tours give them a unique opportunity to get close to friendly farm animals. A host of animals from the gigantic shire horse, through to hatching tiny chicks and fluffy ducklings can be seen daily. There are also rare breeds such as Bagot goats, Saddleback pigs and Soay sheep. Special events are held during the year.
Open daily 10-5 or dusk in winter.
(Closed 25-27 Dec & 1 Jan).
£1.80 (ch £3.60 includes animal feed, badge, pony ride & fresh egg when available).
🅿 ♨ ♿ toilets for disabled shop ✲
See advertisement on page 128.

Middleton Hall
B78 2AE (on A4091)
☎ 01827 283095
Fax 01827 285717
Once the home of two great 17th-century naturalists, Francis Willoughby and John Ray, the Hall shows several architectural styles, from c.1300 to an 11-bay Georgian west wing. The grounds include a nature reserve, lake, meadow, orchard and woodland - all Sites of Special Scientific Interest - plus two walled gardens. This is also the home of the Middleton Hall Craft Centre, with craft studios and workshops in the former stable block. Events take place throughout the year including drama and vintage cars; a programme is available on

application to the Hon Secretary.
Open 30 Mar-28 Sep, Sun & BH's 2-5.
£1.50 (ch 14 & pen 70p)
🅿 ♨ ♿ (lightweight wheelchair available) toilets for disabled shop ⊛

NUNEATON
Arbury Hall
CV10 7PT (2m SW of Nuneaton, off B4102 Meriden road)
☎ 01203 382804 Fax 01203 641147
The 16th-century Elizabethan house, Gothicised in the 18th century, has been the home of the Newdegate family for over 450 years. It is the finest complete example of Gothic revival architecture in existance, and contains pictures, furniture, and beautiful plasterwork ceilings. The 17th-century stable block, with a central doorway by Wren, houses the tearooms and a large collection of veteran bicycles. There are landscaped gardens with woodland paths and lakes. There is a small gift shop. Special events for 1998 include a motor transport spectacular (7 Jun), craft fairs (13-14 Jun, 22-23 Aug).
Open Etr-Sep 2-5.30 (last admission 5pm). Hall & gardens: Sun & BH Mon. For other opening days & times, contact the Administrator.
£4.50 (ch £2.50) gardens only £3. (ch £2.)
🅿 ♨ ♿ shop ✲ (ex in grounds, on leads only)

PACKWOOD HOUSE
Packwood House
B94 6AT (on unclass road off A34)
☎ 01564 782024
Dating from the 16th century, Packwood House has been extended and much changed over the years. The house we see today is essentially the vision of one man - Graham Baron Ash. Sweeping aside changes made during the late 19th century, during the 1930's he recreated a typical Jacobean country home. An important collection of tapestries and textiles, including fine Bargello work assembled at this time awaits your discovery. The house, with its mainly 17th century furniture has warmth and

intimacy enhancing its unique character. Equally important are the stunning gardens, with renowned herbaceous borders, a riot of colour in the summer months, attracting many visitors, and the almost surreal topiary garden based on the Sermon on the Mount.
Open Etr-wknd-Sep, Wed-Sun, BH Mon, 1.30-6 (House 2-6); Oct, Wed-Sun, 12-4.30. Closed Good Fri. Last admission 30mins before closing time.
🅿 (charged) ♿ (wheelchairs available) toilets for disabled shop ✲ (ex guide dogs) ✸
Details not confirmed for 1998
Cards: ▨ ▨ ▨

RUGBY
The James Gilbert Rugby Football Museum
5 Saint Matthew's St CV21 3BY
☎ 01788 542426 Fax 01788 540795
An intriguing collection of Rugby football memorabilia is housed in the shop in which Gilbert's have made their world famous Rugby balls since 1842. From Monday-Friday 10am-5pm and Saturday 10am-2pm, watch a craftsman at work, hand-stitching the footballs. Situated near to Rugby School and its famous playing field.
Open all year, Mon-Fri 10-5, Sat 10-4.
Phone for holiday opening times.
Free.
P (500 yds) ♿ shop ✲
Cards: ▨ ▨ ▨

RYTON-ON-DUNSMORE
Ryton Organic Gardens
CV8 3LG (on B4029)
☎ 01203 303517
Fax 01203 639229
The gardens are the home of the Henry Doubleday Research Association, which researches organic gardening. The whole site is landscaped with thousands of young trees, and every plant is grown organically. Stroll around the herb garden, the bee garden, fruit beds, vegetable gardens, shrub borders and many other attractions, all showing how the organic gardener can use plants and planting schemes effectively. Displays on composting and safe pest control. There is a garden centre selling organically grown products, seeds and equipment, and also an Education Centre with exhibitions, courses and special events. For children there is a Swiss Chalet and play area and rare breeds of livestock during summer months. There is also an award-winning organic restaurant on site. Telephone for details of special events, including the anniversary of the founding of the Henry Doubleday Research Association (June).
Open all year 10-5.30. (Closed Xmas).
✱ £2.50 (ch £1, concessions £2)
🅿 ✗ licensed ♿ (wheelchairs available) toilets for disabled shop garden centre ✲
Cards: ▨ ▨ ▨ ▨ ▨

SHOTTERY
Anne Hathaway's Cottage
☎ 01789 292100
Before her marriage to William Shakespeare, Anne Hathaway lived in this substantial 12-roomed thatched Tudor farmhouse with her prosperous yeoman family. The house now shows many aspects of domestic life in 16th-century England, and has a lovely traditional cottage garden and Shakespeare tree garden.
Open all year, 20 Mar-19 Oct Mon-Sat 9-5, Sun 9.30-4; Jan-19 Mar & 20 Oct-Dec Mon-Sat 9.30-4, Sun 10-4. (Closed 23-26 Dec).
✱ £2.50 (ch £1.20).
🅿 (charged) ♨ ✗ licensed shop garden centre ✲

STRATFORD-UPON-AVON
At the very heart of England lies Stratford-upon-Avon, the birthplace of our most celebrated playwright, William Shakespeare. A charming market town, it

bustles with visitors, attracted by the lovely timbered houses, and the old-world gardens along the banks of the River Avon, and the famous Royal Shakespeare Theatre where some of the world's greatest actors regularly perform.

Butterfly Farm
Tramway Walk, Swan's Nest Ln CV37 7LS (south bank of River Avon opposite RSC)
☎ 01789 299288 Fax 01789 415878
Europe's largest live Butterfly and Insect Exhibit. Hundreds of the world's most spectacular and colourful butterflies, in the unique setting of a lush tropical landscape, with splashing waterfalls and fish-filled pools. See also the strange and fascinating Insect City, a bustling metropolis of ants, bees, stick insects, beetles and other remarkable insects. Get close to the world's largest spider, and see the dangerous and deadly in Arachnoland!
Open daily 10-6 (winter 10-5.30). Closed 25 Dec.
✱ £3.25 (ch £2.25, pen £2.75).
P (opposite entrance) ♿ toilets for disabled shop ✲
Cards: ▨ ▨ ▨ ▨

Hall's Croft
Old Town
☎ 01789 292107
A Tudor house with outstanding furniture and paintings where Shakespeare's daughter Susanna, and her husband, Dr John Hall, lived before moving to New Place on the dramatist's death. There is an exhibition on Tudor medicine, and fine walled gardens can also be seen.
Open all year, 20 Mar-19 Oct Mon-Sat 9.30-5; Sun 10-5; Jan-19 Mar & 20 Oct-Dec, Mon-Sat, 10-4; Sun 10.30-4. (Closed 23-26 Dec).
✱ £2.20 (ch £1).
P (100metres) (2hr limit on-street parking) ♨ ✗ ♿ (ramp access for garden & lawns) toilets for disabled shop ✲

New Place / Nash's House
Chapel St CV37 6EP
☎ 01789 292325
Only the foundations remain of the house where Shakespeare spent the last five years of his life and died in 1616. The house was destroyed in 1759, but the picturesque garden has been planted as an Elizabethan knot garden. There is a small museum of furniture and local history in the adjacent Nash's House.
Open all year, 20 Mar-19 Oct, Mon-Sat, 9.30-5, Sun 10-5; Jan-19 Mar & 20 Oct-Dec, Mon-Sat, 10-4, Sun 10.30-4. (Closed 23-26 Dec).
✱ £2.20 (ch £1).
P (250yds) ♿ toilets for disabled shop ✲

Royal Shakespeare Company Collection
Royal Shakespeare Theatre, Waterside CV37 6BB
☎ 01789 296655 Fax 01789 294810
The RSC gallery is housed in the original Victorian building which was part of Charles Flower's Shakespeare Memorial, opened in 1879, comprising Theatre, Paintings and Sculpture Gallery, Library and Reading Room, the latter were not destroyed when the Theatre was burnt down in 1926. Temporary exhibitions include work of artist(s) in residence.
Open all year, Mon-Sat 9.15-end evening interval, Sun 12-4.30 (Nov-Mar Sun 11-3.30).(Closed 24 & 25 Dec).Theatre tours usually Mon-Fri (ex matinee days), 1.30 & 5.30, Sun 12.30, 1.45, 2.45 & 3.45 (Nov-Mar, 11.30, 12.30, 1.45 & 2.45).
✱ Exhibition £2 (ch, pen & students £1.50). Family ticket £4. Theatre Tours £4 (ch, pen & students £3) - advisable to book in advance.
🅿 (charged) ♨ ✗ licensed ♿ toilets for disabled shop ✲
Cards: ▨

Coughton Court has been home for the Throckmorton family since 1409. The house contains notable furniture, porcelain and paintings.

Shakespeare's Birthplace
Henley St CV37 6QW
☎01789 204016 Fax 01789 296083
Shakespeare was born in the timber-framed house in 1564. It contains numerous exhibits of the Elizabethan period and Shakespeare memorabilia, and the acclaimed exhibition, Shakespeare; His Life and Background.
Open all year, 20 Mar-19 Oct Mon-Sat 9-5, Sun 9.30-5; 20 Oct-19 Mar Mon-Sat 9.30-4, Sun 10-4. (Closed 23-26 Dec). Last admission 1 hour before closing time.
£4.50 (ch £2). Three In-town Properties Ticket £7. (ch £3.50, concessions £5) Family £12 Five Properties Ticket £10(ch £5, concessions £9) Family £26.
P *(100 yds) (no parking outside Birthplace)* & *toilets for disabled shop* ❀
Cards: ▨ ▭ ▭ ▧ ⑤

The Teddy Bear Museum
19 Greenhill St CV37 6LF
☎01789 293160
Ten settings in a house which dates from Shakespeare's time, are devoted to bears of all shapes and sizes. Many very old bears are displayed and there are also mechanical and musical bears. Some of the bears belong to famous people, for example, Jeffrey Archer and Barbara Cartland, or are famous in their own right, such as the original Sooty and Fozzie bear.
Open all year, daily 9.30-6, Jan-Feb 9.30-5. Closed 25 & 26 Dec.
£2.25 (ch £1). Family ticket £5.95.Party 20+.
P *(30yds & 200yds) (access to ground floor shop only) shop* ❀
Cards: ▨ ▭ ▭ ▧ ▧ ⑤

UPTON HOUSE
Upton House
OX15 6HT (on A422, 7m NW of Banbury,12M SE of Stratford)
☎01295 670266
The house, built of mellow local stone, dates from 1695, but the outstanding collections it contains are the chief attraction. Assembled this century by the 2nd Lord Bearsted, they include paintings by English and Continental Old Masters, Brussels tapestries, Sèvres porcelain, Chelsea figures and 18th-century furniture. The garden is also of great interest, with terraces descending into a deep valley from the main lawn, herbaceous borders, the national collection of asters, kitchen garden, water gardens and lakes with ornamental fish. Please telephone for details of events.
Open 4 Apr-1 Nov, Sat-Wed & BH Mon 2-6; Closed Thu-Fri & Good Fri. Last admissions 5.30pm (Oct/Nov 5pm) £5 Family ticket £12.50. Garden only £2.50. Party.
P & *(Braille guide,parking nr house,buggy for lower garden) toilets for disabled shop* ❀
Cards: ▨ ▭ ▭

WARWICK
Lord Leycester Hospital
High St CV34 4BH
☎01926 492797
These lovely half-timbered buildings were built in the late 14th century and adapted into almshouses by the Earl of Leycester in 1571. The Hospital is still a home for ex-servicemen and their wives. Originally it was built as a Guildhouse and the old Guildhall, Great Hall, Chapel and courtyard remain. The buildings also house the Regimental Museum of the Queen's Own Hussars. The historic Master's Garden will open on Saturday afternoons from April to December.

Open all year, Tue-Sun & BH's 10-5 (4pm in winter). (Closed Good Fri & 25 Dec).
P ✗ & *shop*
Details not confirmed for 1998

Warwick Castle
CV34 4QU (2m from M40 exit 15)
☎01926 406600 Fax 01926 401692
Warwick Castle brings to life more than a thousand years of English history. In 1068 the first castle was built by orders of William the Conqueror. The castle has always been the central part of Warwick town and remains to this day the most noble of England's ancient fortresses. The Castle's medieval history comes alive in 'Kingmaker - A preparation for battle', where you'll experience the dramatic sights, smells and sounds of the household making ready. Set in 1471, these scenes recreate a time during the Wars of the Roses when Richard Neville, Earl of Warwick, known as 'Kingmaker', prepared his army within the safe walls of Warwick Castle. As time passed, the military importance of the Castle declined and the main living quarters were converted into a residence of the grandest style. The State Rooms, including the magnificent Great Hall, contain an outstanding collection of arms, armour, furniture and paintings. 'A Royal Weekend Party' recreates an actual Victorian house party in the summer of 1898 with a young Winston Churchill and the future King Edward VII in attendance. Peacocks roam the 60 acres of beautiful grounds and gardens, landscaped by 'Capability' Brown during the 1750s. Please telephone for details of special events.
Open daily 10-6 (5pm Nov-Mar). Closed 25 Dec.
✱*£8.95 (ch 4-16 £5.40 & pen £6.40). Family ticket £25. Party 20+.*
P *(charged)* ♥ ✗ *licensed* & *(free admission to wheelchair bound visitors) toilets for disabled shop* ❀
Cards: ▨ ▭ ▭ ▧ ⑤

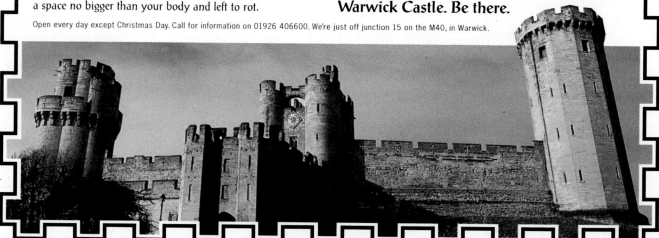

Warwickshire Yeomanry Museum
The Court House Vaults, Jury St CV34 4EW
☎01926 492212 Fax 01926 494837
After a great fire in 1694, the court house was rebuilt between 1725 and 1728 in a style that befitted the wealthy merchants of the town. In the vaults there is now a museum displaying militaria from the county Yeomanry, dating from 1794 to 1945. It includes regimental silver, some very fine paintings, uniforms and weapons. A small room in the cellars is devoted to Warwick Town Museum.
Open Good Fri-end Sep, Fri, Sat & Sun & BHs 10-1 & 2-4. Other times by prior arrangement.
P (300yds) shop ✍
Details not confirmed for 1998

WILMCOTE
Mary Arden's House and the Shakespeare Countryside Museum
(3m NW off A34)
☎01789 204016 Fax 01789 296083
Mary Arden was William Shakespeare's mother, and this picturesque, half-timbered Tudor house was her childhood home. The house is the main historic feature of an extensive complex of farm buildings which house displays of farming and country life, including a remarkable dovecote, kitchen circa 1900, a smithy and cooper's workshop. Daily demonstrations by The Heart of England Falconry. Rare breeds, duck pond and field walk.
Open all year, 20 Mar-19 Oct Mon-Sat 9.30-5, Sun 10-5; Jan-19 Mar & 20 Oct-Dec, Mon-Sat 10-4, Sun 10.30-4. (Closed 23-26 Dec).
£4 (ch £2) Family ticket £11. Five Properties Ticket £10 (ch £5 concessions £9) Family ticket £26.
P ☕ ♿ toilets for disabled shop ✍
Cards: 🅰 💳 💳 💳 🅢

WEST MIDLANDS

BIRMINGHAM
Birmingham is traditionally associated with the bustling energy of the Industrial Revolution, and its museums today commemorate the city's 19th-century role as one of the great workshops of the world. Most of the scars of industry have now healed, enabling today's visitors to appreciate Birmingham's many noble buildings and beautiful parks. The city has cherished its past, including a canal network which exceeds that of Venice. Today Birmingham's motorway links, modern airport and National Exhibition Centre assure that England's second city has a bright future.

Birmingham's Museum of Science and Industry has displays of engineering from the beginning of the Industrial Revolution to the present day. Exhibits included the earliest functioning steam engine.

Birmingham Botanical Gardens & Glasshouses
Westbourne Rd, Edgbaston B15 3TR (2m W of city centre,follow signs for Edgbaston,then brown tourist signs)
☎0121 454 1860 Fax 0121 454 7835
The gardens are a 15-acre 'oasis of delight' just 2 miles from the centre of Birmingham. Originally opened in 1832, they continue to be run by an independent educational charity. The Tropical House has a 24ft-wide lily pool and its lush tropical vegetation includes bromeliads, bananas, cocoa and other economic plants. Palm trees, ferns, orchids and insectivorous plants are displayed in the Palm House. The Orangery features a wide variety of citrus fruits and the Cactus House gives a desert scene with its giant agaves and opuntias. Outside there is colourful bedding on the Terrace and a tour of the gardens includes rhododendrons and azalea borders, Rose Garden, Rock Garden and a collection of over 200 trees. There are Domestic Theme Gardens, Herb and Cottage Gardens, the National Collection of Bonsai, a children's adventure playground and aviaries. Plant centre, gift shop, gallery, museum and refreshment pavilion. Bands play every Sunday afternoon throughout the summer. Please telephone for the diary of events and flower shows.
Open daily all year, wkdays 9-7 or dusk, Sun 10-8 or dusk whichever is earlier. (Closed 25 Dec).
£4 (£4.30 summer Sun, concessions £2.20)

P ☕ ✗ licensed ♿ (3 wheelchairs + 2 electric scooters available free) toilets for disabled shop garden centre ✍

Birmingham Railway Museum
670 Warwick Rd, Tyseley B11 2HL (3m S, A41 Warwick Rd)
☎0121 707 4696 Fax 0121 765 4645
This is a working railway museum with a fully equipped workshop. There are numerous steam locomotives and historic carriages, wagons and other vehicles. Steam-hauled train rides can be taken when available. Steam locomotive driving courses on an Express Passenger Steam and Tank Loco are also available. Various special events are planned, please telephone for details.
Open daily 10-5 or dusk if earlier. (Closed 25 & 26 Dec & 1 Jan).
P ☕ ✗♿ (ramps to platforms) shop ✍ (ex guide dogs)
Details not confirmed for 1998

City Museum & Art Gallery
Chamberlain Sq B3 3DH
☎0121 235 2834 Fax 0121 236 6227
One of the world's best collections of Pre-Raphaelite paintings can be seen here, including important works by Burne-Jones, a native of Birmingham. Older schools of art are represented by French, Dutch, Italian and other works from the 14th century to the present day, and also on display are costumes and fine silver, ceramics and textiles. The wide-ranging archaeology section has prehistoric, Greek and Roman antiquities, and also objects from the Near East, Mexico and Peru. This section includes the Pinto Collection of wooden artefacts. Another popular display is the excellent collection of coins. There is a natural history section in the museum, and objects related to local history are also shown. The Gas Hall, Birmingham's state-of-the-art exhibition gallery, has an excellent programme of touring exhibitions.
Open all year Mon-Sat 10-5, Sun 12.30-5. (Closed Xmas & 1 Jan). Free Guided tours Tue 1pm, Sat & Sun 2.30pm or by prior arrangement.
☕ ✗ licensed ♿ (lift) toilets for disabled shop ✍
Details not confirmed for 1998

The Jewellery Quarter Discovery Centre
75-79 Vyse St, Hockley B18 6HA
☎0121 554 3598 Fax 0121 554 9700
Discover the skill of the jeweller's craft and enjoy a unique tour of an original jewellry factory frozen in time. For over eighty years the family firm of Smith and Pepper produced jewellery from the factory where the Discovery Centre can now be found. This perfectly preserved 'time capsule' workshop has changed little since the beginning of the century.
Open all year, Mon-Fri 10-4, Sat 11-5. Closed Sun.
£2 (concessions £1.50). Family ticket £5. Party 10+ booked in advance.
P (pay & display) ☕ ♿ (tours for hearing/visually impaired booked in advance) toilets for disabled shop ✍
Cards: 🅰 💳 💳 🅢

Selly Manor Museum
Maple Rd, Bournville B30 2AE (off A38)
☎0121 472 0199 Fax 0121 414 1348
These two timber-framed manor houses date from the 13th and early 14th centuries, and have been re-erected in the 'garden suburb' of Bournville. There is a herb garden and regular exhibitions are held, with an annual craft fair on the first Saturday in November, and charity Christmas card fair in November and December.
Open mid Jan-mid Dec, Tue-Fri & BH 10-5. Open Sundays Apr-Sept, phone for details.
£1.50 (ch 50p)
P ♿ toilets for disabled shop ✍

BOURNVILLE
Cadbury World
Linden Rd B30 2LD (1m S of A38 Bristol Rd, on A4040 Ring Rd)
☎0121 451 4159 & 0121 451 4180 Fax 0121 451 1366
Visitors to Cadbury World are first of all transported to a tropical rainforest to see the Aztecs of the 16th century growing and trading cocoa beans, and even sample Emperor Montezuma's favourite drink - a mixture of cocoa, honey and spices. The introduction of chocolate to Europe follows, with a reconstruction of a cobbled square in Georgian England complete with White's Chocolate House. Here the story of the Cadbury family and their chocolate enterprise, including the creation of the Bournville factory and village, is related. There are further displays on packaging and marketing, early machinery, health and safety etc. A recent addition is Cadabra, which provides a gentle ride through a magical chocolate wonderland. Although there are no tours of the modern factory, the hand-processing units show all stages in the production of hand-made chocolates. The final part of the exhibition takes visitors through a children's fantasy factory where the production process for chocolate is illustrated in a lighthearted way. Please telephone for details of ➤

The late Victorian interior of a chairmaker's cottage has been carefully recreated as part of a whole village at the Black Country Museum.

special events and promotions.
Contact information line 0121 451 4180 for opening times.
£6.25 (ch 4-15 £4.50, concessions £5.25)
🅿 🍴 ✗ ♿ *(ex packaging plant) toilets for disabled shop* 🐾
Cards: ▨ ▩ ▧ ◑ ▨ ▨ 🅶

COVENTRY

Coventry Cathedral & Visitor Centre
7 Priory Row CV1 5ES
☎ 01203 227597 Fax 01203 631448
Coventry's old cathedral was bombed during an air raid of November 1940 which devastated the city. The remains have been carefully preserved. The new cathedral was designed by Sir Basil Spence and consecrated in May 1962. It contains outstanding modern works of art, including a huge tapestry designed by Graham Sutherland, the west screen (a wall of glass engraved by John Hutton with saints and angels), bronzes by Epstein, and the great baptistry window by John Piper. There is also an opportunity to enjoy an audio-visual display in the visitors' centre, which is open from Easter - October. International Church Music Festival (24-27 Jun).
Open all year, daily, Etr-Sep 9.30-6; Oct-Etr 9.30-4.30. Visitor centre open Oct-Apr 11am-3pm only.
Visitor centre £1.25 (ch 6 free, ch 6-16, students & pen 75p).Party 10+. Cathedral £2 donation. Camera charge £1. Video charge £3.
P (250 yds) 🍴 ✗ *licensed* ♿ *(lift, touch and hearing centre, paved wheelchair access) toilets for disabled shop* 🐾

Herbert Art Gallery & Museum
Jordan Well CV1 5QP
☎ 01203 832381 Fax 01203 832410
'Godiva City', tells Coventry's story over 1,000 years, through interactive exhibits, objects, pictures and words. Tape tour guide available. Changing displays of art, craft, social and industrial history. Sutherland's preparatory drawings for the famous Cathedral tapestry and many famous Godiva paintings. Excellent facilities for families and disabled people. Full activity programme throughout the year, please telephone for details.

Open all year, Mon-Sat 10-5.30, Sun 2-5. (Closed 24-31 Dec, 1 Jan)
Free.
P (500 yds) 🍴 ♿ *(parking for disabled,automatic doors,access to tea rooms) toilets for disabled shop* 🐾

Lunt Roman Fort
Coventry Rd, Baginton CV8 3AJ (S side of city, off Stonebridge highway, A45)
☎ 01203 832381
Fax 01203 832410
The turf and timber Roman fort from around the end of the 1st century has been faithfully reconstructed over many years. An Interpretation Centre is housed in the reconstructed granary. Other features include the main gateway, gyrus and ramparts. The audiotour brings the fort to life with a description of the experience of a soldier stationed at the Lunt, complete with sound effects! Please phone 01203 832381 for details. Regular visits from the XIV Geminae soldiers at weekends in the season.
Pre-booked parties 2 Feb-27 Nov, weekends/BH Mon. 4 Apr-25 Oct 10am-5pm, daily opening 18 July-6 Sept 10am-5pm.
❊£2.60 (ch £1.80), including audiotape guided tour. Party discounts if pre-booked.
🅿 ♿ *(ramp to Granary Interpretation Centre) toilets for disabled shop*

Museum of British Road Transport
St Agnes Ln, Hales St CV1 1PN
☎ 01203 832425
Fax 01203 832465
The museum illustrates the role of Coventry and the West Midlands in the development of transport throughout the world. There are over 400 exhibits, in displays of motor cars, commercial vehicles, motor cycles and associated items including die-cast models.
Open all year, daily 10-5. Closed 24-26 Dec.
£3.30 (ch & pen £2.30). Family ticket £8.90.
P (adjacent) 🍴 ♿ (audio tour) toilets for disabled shop 🐾
Cards: ▨ ▩ ▧

DUDLEY

Black Country Living Museum
Tipton Rd DY1 4SQ (on A4037, opposite Dudley Guest Hospital)
☎ 0121 557 9643 & 0121 520 8054
Fax 0121 557 4242
The museum is really a recreation of a Black Country village, complete with cottages, a chapel, chemist, baker and a pub serving real ale. One of the buildings is a chainmaker's house with a brewhouse, and demonstrations of chainmaking and glass cutting are given in traditional workshops. There is also a canal boat dock with a range of narrowboats, and boats set off daily for canal trips into the Dudley Tunnel, an eerie underground ride. Transport around the village is provided by an electric tramway. You can go underground in an 1850s mine, and see a replica of the world's first steam engine venture into a pit-pulled cottage (affected by subsidence due to mining). Costumed guides and demonstrations bring the buildings to life and regular 'Theme' weekends are held throughout the summer. Recent additions include a pair of unique cast iron houses, a fully working 1930s Fish and Chip shop, and a 1925 charabanc bus which transports visitors around the site. Please contact for details of special events
Open all year, Mar-Oct daily 10-5; Nov-Feb, Wed-Sun 10-4. (Closed 25 Dec).
❊£6.95 (ch 5-17 £4.50, pen £5.95). Family ticket £19.50. Party 20+(rates available on application)
🅿 🍴 ♿ (ramps available) toilets for disabled shop 🐾
Cards: ▩ ▧ 🅶

Dudley Zoo & Castle
2 The Broadway DY1 4QB (M5 junct 2 towards Wolverhampton/Dudley. Signposted)
☎ 01384 215300
The wooded grounds of Dudley Castle make a wonderful setting for the long-established, traditional zoo, which has animals from every continent. The castle ruins are impressive, and a chairlift and land train take you to the top of Castle Hill. An audio visual show of the castle's history and an interpretation of castle life in the medieval period are shown free of charge.
Open all year, Etr-mid Sep, daily 10-4.30; mid Sep-Etr, daily 10-3.30. (Closed 25 Dec).
£5.95 (ch & pen £3.90). Family ticket £19.70. Party 15+.
🅿 (charged) ✗ licensed ♿ (land train from gates to castle) toilets for disabled shop 🐾
Cards: ▨ ▩ ▧ ▨ 🅶

Museum & Art Gallery
St James's Rd DY1 1HU
☎ 01384 815575
Fax 01384 815576
The museum houses the Brooke Robinson collection of 17th, 18th and 19th century European painting, furniture, ceramics and enamels, also Japanese netsuke and inro, and Greek, Roman and Oriental ceramics. A fine geological gallery, 'The Time Trail' has spectacular displays of fossils from the local 'Wenlock' limestone and coal measures, and a wide variety of temporary exhibitions are staged throughout the year. For 1998, exhibitions include 'Art Attack', an interactive exhibition on art for all the family and 'Watch with Mother', a history of young children's television with a large selection of original puppets.
Open all year, Mon-Sat 10-5. (Closed some BHs).
Free.
P (25mtrs) ♿ shop 🐾
Cards: ▨ ▩ ▧

KINGSWINFORD

Broadfield House Glass Museum
Barnett Ln DY6 9QA
☎ 01384 273011
This magnificent collection of 19th-and 20th-century glass focuses on the cut, etched, engraved and coloured glass made

in nearby Stourbridge during the last century. Highlights include cameo glass by Alphonse Lechevrel and George Woodall, and rock crystal engraving by William Fritsche. Also on display are the Michael Parkington collection of 18th-, 19th-and 20th-century British glass, the Hulbert of Dudley collection, and the Notley/Lerpiniere collection of Carnival Glass.
Open all year, Tue-Fri & Sun 2-5, Sat 10-1 & 2-5. BH's 2-5.
🅿 ♿ shop ⊗
Details not confirmed for 1998

SOLIHULL
National Motorcycle Museum
Coventry Rd, Bickenhill B92 0EJ (nr junc 6, of M42, off A45 nr NEC)
☎01675 443311 Fax 0121-711 3153
Five exhibition halls showing British motorcycles built during the Golden Age of motorcycling. Spanning 90 years, the immaculately restored machines are the products of around 150 different factories. Over 650 machines are on show, most are owned by the museum, others are from collections or private owners. Restoration work is carried out by enthusiasts, and new motorcycles are acquired from all over the world. All the machines are made in Britain from the 1898 20mph Beeston 'Trike' to the 1992 TT winning 191mph Nortons, the museum is the legacy of almost a century of world-beating motorcycling and a glorious celebration of speed.
Open all year, daily 10-6. (Closed 24-26 Dec).
£4.50 (ch 12 & pen £3.50). Party 20+.
🅿 ✕ *licensed* ♿ *toilets for disabled shop*
⊗
Cards: 🖃 🖃 🖃 🖃 🖃 🖃

STOURBRIDGE
The Falconry Centre
Hurrans Garden Centre, Kidderminster Rd South, Hagley DY9 0JB (off A456)
☎01562 700014 Fax 01562 700014
The centre houses some 80 birds of prey including owls, hawks and falcons and is also a rehabilitation centre for sick and injured birds of prey. Spectacular flying displays are put on daily from midday. There are picnic areas. There are also outside cage bird aviaries and a cage bird shop.
Open all year, daily 10-5.30. (Closed 25 & 26 Dec).
£2.50 (ch & pen £1.50, disabled £1). Party 25+.
🅿 ✕ ♿ *shop garden centre* ⊗ *(ex guide dogs)*
Cards: 🖃 🖃

WALSALL
Walsall Leather Museum
Littleton St WS2 8EQ (On Walsall ring-road on North side of town)
☎01922 721153
Fax 01922 725827
Award winning working museum in the saddlery and leathergoods 'capital' of Britain. Watch skilled craftsmen and women at work in this beautifully restored Victorian leather factory. Displays tell the story of Walsall's leatherworkers past and present. Regular special exhibitions; collection of contemporary leather design. Large shop stocks range of Walsall-made leathergoods, many at bargain prices. Saddle Room Cafe serves delicious home-cooked cakes and light lunches. Attractive gardens with picnic seats. Groups very welcome, guided tours available. Special events leaflet on request. Leather Festival (1-2 Aug), Craft Fairs (4-5 Apr, 5-6 Dec).
Open all year, Tue-Sat 10-5 (Nov-Mar 4pm), Sun noon-5. Open BH Mon. Closed 24-26 Dec, 1 Jan & Etr Sun.
Free.
P (10metres) ✕ ♿ *toilets for disabled shop* ⊗
Cards: 🖃 🖃

WOLVERHAMPTON
Wightwick Manor
WV6 8EE (3m W, beside Mermaid Inn)
☎01902 761400 Fax 01902 764663
This house is unusual in that, although barely 100 years old, it is a gem of design

and architectural interest. It was begun in 1887 and in its style of decoration it is one of the finest examples of the achievements of the late 19th-century. The house was designed by Edward Ould, a follower of William Morris. All aspects of William Morris's talents are shown in this house - wallpapers, textiles, carpets, tiles, embroidery and even books. There are also paintings and drawings by Burne-Jones, D G Rosetti, Holman Hunt and others, glass by Kempe and tiles by de Morgan. The garden was laid out by Alfred Parsons and Thomas Manson, and reflects late Victorian and Edwardian design.
Open Mar-Dec, Thu, Sat & BH Sun & Mon 2.30-5.30.
£5.20 (accompanied ch & students £2.60). Gardens only £2.20.
🅿 ✕ ♿ shop ⊗

WORDSLEY
Stuart Crystal
Red House Glassworks DY8 4AA (on A491)
☎01384 828282
Fax 01384 70463
Fine glass has been made in the area since the beginning of the 17th century when French glass makers arrived in the area. The 200 year old Redhouse Glass Cone and associated building have recently been restored in the first stage of creating a museum. On the site there is also a factory shop, a chip repair service and glass sculpture. At the Red House factory the focal point is the Red House Cone. The tour of the factory shows the complete glassmaking process from glass-blowing to cutting and decorating.
Open all year, daily. (Closed 25-26 Dec & 1 Jan). Tours:Mon-Thu on the hour 10-4(not 12),Fri 10,11 & 1;Shop open 7 days,9-5.
🅿 ✕ ♿ *(Cone/Museum accesible-factory tours are not) shop* ⊗ *(ex guide dogs)*
Details not confirmed for 1998
Cards: 🖃 🖃 🖃 🖃 🖃

WIGHT, ISLE OF

ALUM BAY
The Needles Old Battery
West High Down PO39 0JH (0.75m SW)
☎01983 754772
This former Palmerston fort, built in 1862, has recently been restored. It sits 77m above sea level. A 65m tunnel leads to a look-out position with spectacular views of the Needles chalk stacks and lighthouse, and across the bay to Dorset. In the fort are two of the original 12-ton gun barrels: they were hauled up from the sea and now lie in the parade ground. The powder house has an exhibition of

the history of the Needles headland, from the establishment of the battery to the present day.
Open 22 Mar-29 Oct, Sun-Thu; also open Etr wknd & daily in Jul & Aug 10.30-5. (last admission 4.30).
£2.40 (ch £1.20). Family ticket £6.
♿ shop ⊗

The Needles Pleasure Park
PO39 0JD (signposted, on B3322)
☎01983 752401 & 408535
Fax 01983 755260
Overlooking the Needles on the heritage coastline at the western edge of the Island, the park has attractions for all the family. Super X provides thrills, whilst the Carousel conjures up memories of a bygone age. The chairlift to the beach enables visitors to enjoy the most famous view on the Island and the unique coloured sands. Entertainment is a regular feature of the pedestrianised Festival Street. New 'Children's World' fun park and amusements. Events for 1998 include a Motor Fair in August and several firework events. Please telephone for details.
Open Easter-early Nov, daily 10-5 (Aug Sun-Thu 10-6).
✱*No admission charged for entrance to Pleasure Park. Supersaver ticket £5 (ch £3.50). Chargeable attractions individually priced. Car parking charge.*
🅿 *(charged)* ✕ *licensed* ♿ *toilets for disabled shop*
Cards: 🖃 🖃 🖃

ARRETON
Haseley Manor
PO30 3AN (on Sandown to Newport rd)
☎01983 865420
Fax 01983 867547
This is the oldest and largest manor open to the public on the Island. Parts of the south wing have some of the original building, c1300, but the rest of the house is a mixture of styles including Georgian and Victorian. The manor fell into disuse and was derelict by the 1970s but has since been carefully restored and now 20 rooms can be viewed, furnished in period style. Tableaux of figures in costume appear in many of the rooms. Outside, there is a re-constructed 18th-century farm complete with animals, and a well-stocked herb garden. There is also a children's play area with a tree house, and a small lake with an island castle. Visitors can also see pottery demonstrations, and children can make and take away a mouse. Boxing Day Special - musicians etc, mulled wine and mince pies included in admission price.
Open Etr-Oct, daily 10-5.30.
£4.25 (ch £3.15, pen & party £3.50)
🅿 ✕ ♿ *toilets for disabled shop*
Cards: 🖃 🖃 🖃 🖃 🖃

BEMBRIDGE
Bembridge Windmill
PO30 4EB (0.5m S of Bembridge on B3395)
☎01983 873945
The only windmill on the island to survive, Bembridge mill was built about 1700 and was in use until 1913. The stone-built tower with its wooden cap and machinery have been restored since it was given to the National Trust in 1961.
Open Apr-30 Oct, daily (ex Sat) & Etr Sat & Jul-Aug, daily 10-5. Last admission 4.45.
£1.30 (ch 65p)
🅿 shop ⊗ ♿

Isle of Wight Shipwreck Centre & Maritime Museum
Providence House, Sherborne St PO35 5SB
☎01983 872223 & 873125 Fax 01983 873125
Situated at the centre of Bembridge village, this fine museum brings alive the maritime history of the Isle of Wight. There are six galleries displaying a unique collection of salvage and shipwreck items, early diving equipment, ship models, HMS *Swordfish*, and a model of the harbour.
Open late Mar-Oct, daily 10-5. (Other times by appointment-for parties only)
£2.35 (ch £1.35, pen & students £1.70).
🅿 ♿ *shop* ⊗
Cards: 🖃 🖃

BLACKGANG
Blackgang Chine Fantasy Park
PO38 2HN (off A3055)
☎01983 730330 Fax 01983 731267
Opened as scenic gardens in 1843 covering some 40 acres, the park has imaginative play areas, water gardens, maze and coastal gardens. Set on the steep wooded slopes of the chine are the themed areas Smugglerland (complete with pirate ship), Nurseryland, Dinosaurland, Fantasyland and Frontierland. Various special events are held throughout the year.
St Catherine's Quay has a maritime exhibition showing the history of local and maritime affairs, including engines in steam. It is in an attractive park that has been 'themed' into different areas, with a complete replica of a Victorian water-powered saw mill and a display of woodland skills and traditional crafts.
Open 30 Mar-1 Nov daily, 10-5.30.Whitsun & high season floodlit every evening (phone for details).
Combined ticket to chine, sawmill & quay £5.50 (ch 3-13 £4.50, pen £5). Family £18. Disabled £2.75. Return within 7 days - 50p per head.
🅿 *(charged)* ✕ ♿ *(some paths steep) toilets for disabled shop*
Cards: 🖃 🖃 🖃 🖃

A sturdy Pirate Ship is one of many attractions at the Fantasy Park on the cliffs of Blackgang Chine.

Osborne House was Queen Victoria's favourite residence and she died here in 1901

BRADING

Isle of Wight Waxworks
High St PO36 0DQ (on A3055)
☎01983 407286 Fax 01983 402112
Rub shoulders with famous and infamous characters through 2000 years of the island's colourful fantasies, legends and facts - brought to life in dramatic scenes with sound, light and animation. Visitors can also see the Ancient Rectory mansion (c1066 AD), the Chamber of Horrors, set in the castle dungeons, and adjacent Animal World of Natural History. Please ring for details of forthcoming special events.
Open all year, Summer 10-10pm; Winter 10-5.
P ☕ ✕ licensed ♿ (Disabled route planner,reduced rates) toilets for disabled shop
Details not confirmed for 1998
Cards:

Lilliput Antique Doll & Toy Museum
High St PO36 0DJ (A3055 Ryde/Sandown road, in Brading high street)
☎01983 407231
This private museum contains one of the finest collections of antique dolls and toys in Britain. There are over 2000 exhibits, ranging in age from 2000BC to 1945 with examples of almost every seriously collectable doll, many with royal connections. Also dolls' houses, teddy bears and rare and unusual toys.
Open daily, 10-5 (winter), 9.30-9.30pm (summer).
**£1.45 (ch & pen 95p, ch under 5 free). Party.*
P (200 yds) ♿ (ramps provided on request) shop

Morton Manor
PO36 0EP (off A3055 in Brading, well signposted)
☎01983 406168
The manor dates back to 1249, but was rebuilt in 1680 with further changes during the Georgian period. The house contains furniture of both the 18th and 19th centuries, but its main attraction lies in the beautiful gardens and the vineyard. The garden is landscaped into terraces, with ornamental ponds, a sunken garden and a traditional Elizabethan turf maze. In recent years vine-growing for wine has become popular on the island, and Morton Manor is one of the places to have an established vineyard and winery. A museum of winemaking relics has been set up, and has some unusual exhibits, including a modern working winery and video.
Open Apr-Oct, daily 10-5.30 (Closed Sat). £3.50,ch £1.50 & pen £3.25). Party 15+.
P ✕ licensed ♿ shop garden centre (ex house)

Nunwell House & Gardens
Coach Ln PO36 0JQ (Off Ryde-Sandown Rd, A3055)
☎01983 407240
Set in beautiful gardens, Nunwell is an impressive, lived-in and much loved house where King Charles I spent his last night of freedom. It has fine furniture and interesting collections of family militaria. In summer, concerts are occasionally held in the music room. Phone for details.
Open, House & Gardens, 13 Jul-23 Sept, Mon-Wed 1-5.Groups welcome when house open & at other times by appointment.
£4 inc guide book, (concessions)
P shop

CARISBROOKE

Carisbrooke Castle
PO30 1XY (one and quarter miles SW of Newport, off B3401)
☎01983 522107
A Norman castle adapted from a Saxon fort, Carisbrooke is the only medieval castle on the island. It is set on a hill 150ft high, and the 12th-century keep is built on an artificial mound of about 60ft. The keep overlooks the later Elizabethan and Jacobean additions and the strong castle walls. There are two medieval wells in the castle. The keep has a 160ft-deep well, reached by climbing 71 steps, and the other is housed in a 16th-century wellhouse in the courtyard. The winding gear was traditionally driven by a donkey, and a team of donkeys now gives displays of the machinery working. Charles I was a prisoner in the castle from 1647-48, and the castle was the home of the Governor of the island. His lodge is now the Isle of Wight Museum.
Open all year, Apr-Oct, daily 10-6 (or dusk if earlier in Oct); Nov-Mar, daily 10-4. Closed 24-26 Dec & 1 Jan.
£4 (ch £2, concessions £3).
P ☕ ♿ shop

FRESHWATER

Dimbola Lodge
Terrace Ln, Freshwater Bay PO40 9QE (off A3054)
☎01983 756814 Fax 01983 755578
Home of Julia Margaret Cameron, the pioneer Victorian portrait photographer who welcomed the cream of Victorian society to Dimbola and photographed them there. Currently being restored, the house offers the largest permanent collection of Cameron prints in the UK, as well as contemporary galleries exhibiting work by young, up and coming, and acclaimed photographers; and a large display of cameras and accessories. Special events include musical recitals, poetry readings, lectures etc. Please telephone for details.
Open all year 10-5 (closed Xmas).
**£1.75 (ch free).*
P ✕ ♿ shop

HAVENSTREET

Isle of Wight Steam Railway
The Railway Station PO33 4DS
☎01983 882204 Fax 01983 884515
When the Newport to Ryde railway was closed, Haven Street Station was taken over by a private company, the Isle of Wight Steam Railway. A number of volunteers restored the station, locomotives and rolling stock, and steam trains now run the five miles from Wootton, via Haven Street to Smallbrook Junction where there is a direct interchange with the BR Ryde-Shanklin line. Locomotives in operation include former LSWR tank engine ***Calbourne***, built in 1891, and LSBCR/Freshwater, Yarmouth & Newport Railway locomotive ***Freshwater,*** built in 1875. The rolling stock includes 70/80-year-old LBSCR/SECR carriages, plus vintage goods wagons. At Haven Street, the old gas works houses a display of Island railway memorabilia.
Open 9-19 Apr & 24 May-27 Sept: daily. 3-21 May: Sun, Wed & Thurs plus BH Mon. 26 Mar-30 Apr & 29 Oct Sun & Thurs.
**Return Fares £6 (ch 5-15 £4). Family ticket £19.*
P ☕ ♿ (with assistance) toilets for disabled shop

NEWPORT

Roman Villa
Cypress Rd PO30 1EX (S of Newport,signposted'Roman Villa')
☎01983 529720 Fax 01983 823841
Archaeologists have uncovered this 3rd-century Roman villa where visitors can now see the well-preserved baths and re-constructed rooms in which the family once lived. The site museum houses some of the finds from the excavation. Recent refurbishment has provided new displays in reconstructed rooms, a renewed artefact gallery and a Roman garden.
open Easter-Oct, daily 10-5. Other times by appointment.
**£1.75 (ch 90p. concessions £1.20)*
P (100 yds) ♿ shop

NEWTOWN

Old Town Hall
PO30 4AT (1m N of A3054 between Yarmouth & Newport))
☎01983 741052
The town hall is unusual in that it stands alone, surrounded by grass and a few houses, not in a crowded high street. Newtown was once the island's capital, returning two members to Parliament. It was badly burned in 1377 and never fully recovered. In 1699 the town hall was rebuilt and has been further restored recently. An exhibition depicts the exploits of the anonymous group of National Trust benefactors known as 'Ferguson's Gang'.
Open 29 Mar-28 Oct, Mon, Wed & Sun 2-5 (also open Good Fri, Etr Sat & Tue & Thu in Jul-Aug). Last admission 4.45pm. £1.20 (ch 60p)
P

OSBORNE HOUSE

Osborne House
PO32 6JY (1m SE of East Cowes)
☎01983 200022
Designed by Prince Albert and Thomas Cubitt and built between 1845 and 1848, Osborne was the Royal Family's private residence and Queen Victoria's favourite home. She lived at Osborne most of the time and died there in 1901. The house was designed to resemble an Italian villa, with terraced gardens overlooking Osborne Bay. The state and private apartments, which have been largely untouched since Victoria's death, are open to the public. The private apartments upstairs are cosy and comfortable and filled with all the paraphernalia of daily life. The large grounds are filled with every kind of English tree, a miniature fort and a Swiss cottage, where the Royal children learnt cooking and gardening. A horse-drawn carriage takes visitors to the Swiss cottage gardens and museum.
House open Apr-Nov, daily 10-5(last admission 4.30pm). Grounds 10-6 (last admission 5); Oct 10-5 or dusk if earlier.
House & grounds £6.50 (ch £.30, concessions £4.0). Grounds only £3.50 (ch £1.80, concessions £2.60)
P ☕ ♿ shop

ST LAWRENCE

Tropical Bird Park
Old Park PO38 1XR
☎01983 852583 & 853752
Fax 01983 854920
A bird park situated in the heart of the almost sub-tropical undercliff, in the grounds of Old Park. Enclosed by high stone walls are over 400 birds such as toucans, macaws and cockatoos. Woodland Trail is the home of eagles, storks, vultures and owls. On an ornamental lake are spoonbills, swans and ducks. An extra attraction is a showroom where Isle of Wight glass is blown and displayed.
Open Etr-Oct, 10-5; Oct-Etr, 10-4. (Closed 25 Dec).
**£3 (ch over 7 £2, pen £2.50), family ticket £7.25.*
P ☕ ♿ shop
Cards:

SHANKLIN

Shanklin Chine
PO37 6PF
☎01983 866432
Fax 01983 874215
Shanklin Chine is a natural gorge of great scenic beauty with a spectacular 45ft waterfall. A path winds down through the gorge, overhanging trees, ferns and other flora that cover its steep sides. The Heritage Centre features details of nature trails, rare flora and life in Victorian Shanklin. Features of historic interest include sections of PLUTO (pipeline under the ocean), which carried petrol to the Allied troops in Normandy. There is a

memorial to 40 Commando, Royal Marines. Pictorial History of Shanklin & Isle of Wight Exhibition, featuring "Poets and the Island - a celebration" in the Heritage Centre.
Open 9 Apr-21 May 10-5, 22 May-20 Sept 10-10 (illuminated at night) 21 Sept-18 Oct 10-5, (opening period may be extended depending on weather conditions)
£2 (ch 13 60p, pen & students £1.50). Party 10+.
P (400 yds) ♨ shop ❀ (ex on lead at all times)

SHORWELL
Yafford Water Mill Farm Park
PO30 3LH (on B3399)
☎ 01983 740610 & 741125
Fax 01983 740610
The mill is situated in attractive surroundings with a large mill pond. The great overshot wheel still turns and all the milling machinery is in working order. An unusual attraction is the millpond, which is home to a seal. The millstream has pools and falls with flowers and trees along its banks. There is a nature trail along the stream to the lakes - home to ducks, coots and moorhen. Old farm wagons, agricultural machinery and a narrow gauge railway can also be seen along with rare breeds of sheep, pigs and cattle. Across the lane is a picnic area and an adventure playground.
Open all year, daily 10-6 or dusk in winter. (Last admission 5pm).
P ♨ & toilets for disabled shop ❀ (ex guide dogs)
Details not confirmed for 1998

VENTNOR
Museum of the History of Smuggling
Botanic Gardens PO38 1UL (on A3055, 1m W of Ventnor)
☎ 01983 853677
Situated underground in extensive vaults, this unique museum shows methods of smuggling used over a 700-year period right up to the present day. There is an adventure playground in the Botanic Gardens.
Open Etr-Sep, daily 10-5.30.
£1.90 (ch & pen £1). Parties by arrangement.
P (charged) ♨ ✘ licensed shop garden centre

Ventnor Botanic Garden
Undercliff Dr PO38 1UL
☎ 01983 855397
Fax 01983 856154
Many rare and tender plants from all over the world can be found in the 22 acres of the Ventnor Botanic Garden, one of the Island's largest gardens. The temperate house features special displays which may be seen for a small charge. Facilities for the disabled include a garden of raised beds with highly scented plants. Guided tours by prior arrangement with the curator. There are two gift shops, a picnic area, and a children's playground which is suitable for children of all

abilities, including those in wheelchairs, pushchairs, and the visually impaired.
Open all year - Garden; Temperate House 8 Mar-1 Nov, daily 10-5.30 O8 Nov-Mar 1999, Sun 11-4.
Garden - free; Temperate House - 50p (ch 20p).
P (charged) ✘ licensed & toilets for disabled shop ❀ (ex in garden)
Cards: ▩ ▭

WROXALL
Appuldurcombe House
PO38 3EW (off B3327, half a mile W)
☎ 01983 852484
The manor house at Wroxall began as a priory in 1100. It later came into the hands of the Worsley family, who pulled down the original building and built Appuldurcombe in the Palladian style. Appuldurcombe has been a ruin since World War II, but the grounds, landscaped by Capability Brown, are still beautiful.
Open Apr-Nov, daily 10-6 (or dusk if earlier). Last admission 30 mins before closing.
❊£1.50 (ch 80p, concession £1.10)
P & ⊞

YARMOUTH
Yarmouth Castle
Quay St PO41 0PB (adjacent to car ferry terminal)
☎ 01983 760678
Now tucked away among newer buildings, this rather homely castle is in excellent repair. Visitors can see the Master Gunner's parlour and kitchen,

plus an unusually small great hall. Built during the reign of Henry VIII as a coastal defence, the open gun platform provides an excellent view of the harbour.
Open Apr-Oct, daily 10-6 (or dusk if earlier), closed 1-2pm.
£2 (ch £1, concessions £1.50)
P (200yds) & ❀ ⊞

WILTSHIRE

AVEBURY
Avebury Manor
SN8 1RF (6m W of Marlborough, from A4 take A4361/B4003)
☎ 01672 539250
Avebury Manor has a monastic origin, and has been much altered since then. The present buildings date from the early 16th century, with notable Queen Anne alterations and Edwardian renovation. The flower gardens contain medieval walls, and there are examples of topiary.
Open: Garden Apr-1 Nov, daily ex Mon & Thur, open BH Mon 11am-5.30pm.(last admission 5pm). House Apr-28 Oct Tue,Wed, Sun & BH Mon 2-5.30, (last admission 5pm).
❊Manor & garden £3 (ch £1.50). Garden £2.25 (ch £1). Museum £1.60 (ch 80p).
P & shop ❀ ♨

Avebury Museum
(Alexander Keiller Museum)
☎ 01672 539250
This is one of the most important prehistoric sites in Europe, and was built before Stonehenge. In the midst of it is the pretty village of Avebury, which is surrounded by circles of massive sarsen stones and an impressive circular embankment and ditch. An avenue of great stones leads to the site, which must have been a place of great religious significance. The small museum has recently been refurbished and contains many new exhibits. It is named after Alexander Keiller, the first archaeologist to analyse the site in a modern way. It shows finds from Avebury and from Windmill Hill, a Neolithic causewayed enclosure about 1.5 miles away, which is also part of the National Trust property. Educational facilities are provided.
Open all year, Apr-Oct, daily 10-6; Nov-Mar, 10-4. Closed 24-26 Dec & 1 Jan.
£1.60 (concessions 80p).
P & shop ❀ ⊞ ♨

BRADFORD-ON-AVON
Great Chalfield Manor
SN12 8NJ (3m SW of Melksham)
☎ 01985 843600
Built during the Wars of the Roses, the manor is a beautiful, mellow, moated house which still has its great hall. It was restored in the 1920s. There is a small 13th-century church next to the house.
Open Apr-29 Oct, Tue-Thu. Tours starting at 12.15, 2.15, 3, 3.45, 4.30.
£3.50.
P ❀ ♨

Tithe Barn
Over 160ft long by 30ft wide, the barn stands on Barton Farm, which belonged to Shaftesbury Abbey. It was probably used to store general farm produce as well as tithes of hay and corn. The roof is of stone slates, supported outside by buttresses and inside by an impressive network of great beams and rafters.
Open Apr-Oct, daily 10.30-5; Nov-Mar, daily 10.30-4.
Free.
P & ❀ ⊞

CALNE
Bowood House & Gardens
SN11 0LZ (off A4 in Derry Hill village)
☎ 01249 812102 Fax 01249 821757
Originally built in 1624, the house was unfinished when it was bought by the first Earl of Shelburne in 1754. He employed celebrated architects, notably Robert Adam, to complete the work, and what the visitor sees now is a handsome Georgian house. Adam's library is particularly admired, and also in the house is the laboratory where Dr Joseph Priestley discovered oxygen in 1774. There are fine paintings, sculptures, costumes and other displays. The chief glory of Bowood, however, is its 2000-acre expanse, 100 acres of which are pleasure gardens. They were laid out by 'Capability' Brown in the 1760s and are carpeted with daffodils, narcissi and bluebells in spring. The centrepiece is a lake, while terraces, roses, clipped yews and sculptures are a perfect complement to the house. There is also a hermit's cave, a temple and cascade; and for children there is a huge adventure playground. Please ring for details of special events.
Open Apr-1 Nov, daily 11-6, including BH. Rhododendron Gardens (separate entrance off A342) open 6 weeks during May & Jun 11-6.
House & Grounds £5.20 (ch £3 & pen £4.30). Party. Rhododendrons only £3.
P ♨ ✘ licensed & (parking by arrangement) toilets for disabled shop ❀
Cards: ▩ ▭ ▭ ▭ ▭ ▩ ▭

The fascinating and impressive sarsen stones at Avebury.

CORSHAM COURT
HOME OF THE METHUEN FAMILY

Corsham Court is one of England's finest Stately Homes. It was a Royal Manor in the days of the Saxon Kings, and the present building is based upon an Elizabethan Manor dating from 1582. Magnificent Georgian State Rooms were added in 1760.

It houses one of the oldest and most distinguished collections of Old Masters and Furniture in the country, and with its "Capability" Brown gardens and arboretum, and architecture by John Nash and Thomas Bellamy, Corsham Court provides the visitor with a wonderful opportunity to enjoy the many delights of the historic and beautiful Stately Home.

For opening times see gazetteer entry.

Tel/Fax: 01249 701610

CHIPPENHAM
Sheldon Manor

SN14 0RG (1.5m W, signposted from A420)

☎ 01249 653120 Fax 01249 461097

The Plantagenet manor house has a 13th-century porch and a 15th-century chapel. There are beautiful informal terraced gardens, with a water garden, ancient yews, a connoisseur collection of old-fashioned roses in profusion. In 1994 Sheldon Manor was awarded the Gold Award for the ASA/NPI Historic Houses Award as 'the house which best preserves its character, its authenticity and integrity in terms of architecture, furniture and contents but which, most importantly, remains a lived-in family home'.

Open Etr Sun & Mon, then every Sun, Thu & BH until 1 Oct, 12.30-6. House opens 2pm.
House & gardens £3.50 (pen £3.25). Garden only £2 (pen £1.75).
🅿 ♨ ✕ *licensed* ♿ *(wheelchair available) shop*

CORSHAM
Corsham Court

SN13 0BZ (4m W of Chippenham off the A4)

☎ 01249 701610 & 701611 Fax 01249 444556

The Elizabethan manor was built in 1582, and then bought by the Methuen family in the 18th century to house their collections of paintings and statues. 'Capability' Brown made additions to the house and laid out the park, and later John Nash made further changes. There is furniture by Chippendale, Adam, Cobb and Johnson inside, as well as the Methuen collection of Old Master paintings. The garden has flowering shrubs, herbaceous borders, a Georgian bath house, peacocks and a 15th-century gazebo.

Open Summer: Good Fri-Oct daily ex Mon but incl Bh's 11-5.30 last admission 5pm. Winter: Nov-Maundy Thu open weekends only 2-4.30pm last admission 4pm. (Closed December). Open throughout year by appointment for groups 15 +.
🅿 ♨ ♿ *shop* ✂
Details not confirmed for 1998

HOLT
The Courts

BA14 6RR (3m N of Trowbridge, on B3107)

☎ 01225 782340

Weavers came to The Courts to have their disputes settled until the end of the 18th century. The house is not open, but it makes an attractive backdrop to the gardens - a network of stone paths, yew hedges, pools and borders with a strange, almost magical atmosphere.

Open Apr-1 Nov, daily (ex Sat) 1.30-5.30. Out of season by appointment.
£3 (ch £1.50). Parties by arrangement.
♿ ✂ ✂

LACOCK
Lackham Country Attractions

SN15 2NY (3m S of Chippenham, on A350)

☎ 01249 443111
Fax 01249 444474

Various visitor attractions are situated within the 210-hectare estate of the Lackham College. Thatched and refurbished farm buildings accommodate the farm museum and the grounds feature a walled garden, glasshouses, rhododendron glades, riverside and woodland walks, a children's adventure playground and farm park. There is a major collection of historical roses in the Italian Garden. Also grown in this garden was the largest citron (large lemon) which earned a place in the Guinness Book of Records. The gardens have been extended to include a maze and gardens of the 17th, 18th and 19th centuries. For the children, Rupert Bear and his friends (models only) are in their new Nutwood.

Open Apr, May, Sept & Oct, weekends and Bank Hols. June, July & Aug, daily. 10am-5pm. Last entry 4pm.
£3 (ch £1, concessions £2). Family ticket £8. Season tickets. School/Student rates. Party 10+.
🅿 ♨ ✕ ♿ *(wheelchair available) toilets for disabled shop*

Lacock Abbey

SN15 2LG (3m S of Chippenham, E of A350)

☎ 01249 730227

Lacock Abbey is not only historic and beautiful, it was also the venue for a series of innovative photographic experiments by William Henry Fox Talbot, which led to the world's first photographic negative being made here in 1835. The abbey, set in a carefully preserved village of 14th-to 18th-century houses, was founded by Ela, Countess of Salisbury in the 13th century. At the Dissolution it was sold to William Sherrington, who destroyed the church and turned the nuns' quarters into a grand home. The cloisters from the original convent remain and other ancient features include an octagonal Tudor tower and half-timbered gables in the courtyard. In 1754 Sanderson Miller was commissioned to design a new entrance hall; this stands today as a superb example of the Gothic Revival style. A museum devoted to Fox Talbot (one of Sherrington's descendants) is housed in an old barn.

Museum,Cloisters & Grounds, Mar-1 Nov,daily 11-5.30. Closed Good Fri. Abbey, 1 Apr-1 Nov daily, ex Tue, 1-5.30. Last admissions 5pm..
Museum,Abbey,Grounds & Cloisters £5.50(ch £3) Grounds,Cloisters & Museum £3.50(ch £2).
🅿 ♿ *(taped guides) toilets for disabled shop* ✂ ✂

LONGLEAT
Longleat

The Estate Office BA12 7NW (Entrance on Warminster-Frome road A362).

☎ 01985 844400 Fax 01985 844885

The late Marquess of Bath was the first peer to open his house to the public on a regular basis, a trend which many would follow. The Longleat estate has now grown to offer the visitor a safari park (home to hundreds of wild animals, including Britain's only white tiger); an exciting Adventure Castle; a maze; safari boats; narrow-gauge railway and a multitude of exhibitions and other attractions. The centrepiece of all this tourist activity is the majestic Elizabethan house, built by Sir John Thynne in 1580 and decorated in the Italian Renaissance style in the late-19th century. It contains a mixture of furnishings and artefacts reflecting the tastes and interests of the Thynne family through the centuries, and the fully restored Victorian kitchens offer an interesting glimpse of life 'below stairs'. The magnificent grounds, laid out by 'Capability' Brown, offer many lovely walks. Heaven's Gate is particularly spectacular when the rhododendrons are flowering. Many special events are planned for 1998, including Needlecraft and Beading event (12-14 Jun), Pet Pig and Goat Show (7 Jun), Outdoor Concert (4 Jul), Dog Agility (11-13 Sep), telephone for details.

Open all year. House daily, 10-6 (Nov-Etr 10-4). Safari park, 21 Mar-1 Nov 10-6, last car admitted 5.30pm or sunset if earlier. House: £5 (ch £4, pen £4) Safari Park: £5.50 (ch £4.50 pen £4.50). Passport ticket for all attractions: £12 (ch & pen £10).
🅿 ♨ ✕ *licensed* ♿ *toilets for disabled shop* ✂ *(in Safari park-free kennels)*
Cards: 💳 💳 💳 💳 💳

LUDGERSHALL
Ludgershall Castle

SP11 9QR (7m NW of Andover on A342)

Although a ruin since the 16th century, this was once a royal castle and hunting palace. The visitor can see large earthworks of the Norman motte-and-bailey castle and the flint walling of the later hunting palace. The medieval cross stands in the main street of the village.
Open all reasonable times.
Free.
🅿 ♿ ✿

LYDIARD PARK
Lydiard Park

Lydiard Tregoze SN5 9PA (Nr M4 exit6. Follow brown Tourist Information signs)

☎ 01793 770401 Fax 01793 877909

Set in beautiful country parkland, this fine Georgian house belonged to the St John family for 500 years up until 1943 when the house and parkland were purchased by the Swindon Corporation. Since then the sadly dilapidated house has been gradually restored and refurbished with period furniture (in many cases original to the house) and a large St John family portrait collection (also original to the house). Exceptional plasterwork, early wallpaper, a rare painted glass window, and a room devoted to the talented 18th-century amateur artist, Lady Diana Spencer, can also be seen. Adjacent, the church of St Marys has many fine and unusual memorials to the St John family. The Park, now operating as a Country Park, offers a variety of pleasant woodland walks, spacious lawns, lakes and children's adventure playground.

Open all year, House: Mon-Sat 10-1 & 2-5.30, Sun 2-5.30. (Closed Good Fri & Xmas). Winter closing 4pm (Nov-Feb). Park: all year, daily closing at dusk each day.
🅿 *(charged)* ♨ ♿ *(Easiriders may be booked at visitors centre Tel:771419) toilets for disabled shop* ✂ *(ex park/guide dogs in house)*
Details not confirmed for 1998

MARLBOROUGH
Crofton Beam Engines

Crofton Pumping Station, Crofton SN8 3DW (6m SE of Marlborough, signposted from A338/A346/B3087 at Burbage)

☎ 01672 870300

The oldest working beam engine in the world still in its original building and still doing its original job, the Boulton and Watt 1812, is to be found in this rural spot. Its companion is a Harvey's of Hayle of 1845. Both are steam driven,

The Red Library at Longleat House contains 6,000 books and was decorated in Italian Renaissance style with tooled leather wall coverings.

from a hand-stoked, coal-fired boiler, and pump water into the summit level of the Kennet and Avon Canal with a lift of 40ft. Telephone Marlborough (01672) 870300 for information. The surrounding countryside is pleasant, and walks can be taken along the canal towpath and to a working windmill nearby.
Open daily 10 Apr-Oct. Steaming weekends 11-13 Apr, 2-4 May, 23-25 May, 27-28 Jun, 25-26 Jul, 29-31 Aug. Steaming weekend: £3 (ch £1, under 5 free & pen £2). Family ticket £7. Non-steaming weekends £1.50 (ch 50p, pen £1).
P 🍴 ♿ *(phone warden in advance for maximum access) shop ⚹ (no exceptions)*

MIDDLE WOODFORD
Heale Gardens, Plant Centre & Shop
SP4 6NT (4m N of Salisbury, between A360 & A345)
☎01722 782504
Heale House and its eight acres of beautiful garden lie beside the River Avon at Middle Woodford. Much of the house is unchanged since King Charles II sheltered here after the Battle of Worcester in 1651. The garden provides a wonderfully varied collection of plants, shrubs, and musk and other roses, growing in the formal setting of clipped hedges and mellow stonework, which are at their best in June and July. In January great drifts of snowdrops and aconites bring early colour and a promise of spring. Particularly lovely in spring and autumn is the water garden, planted with magnificent magnolia and acers, surrounding the authentic Japenese Tea House and Nikko Bridge which makes an exciting focus in this part of the garden. National Gardens Day 1st Sunday in August. Specialist plant centre.
Open all year, daily 10-5.
£2.75 (ch under 14 accompanied, free). Party 20+.
P ♿ *shop garden centre*
Cards: 💳 💳

SALISBURY
The Medieval Hall (Secrets of Salisbury)
Cathedral Close SP1 2EY
☎01722 412472 & 324731
Fax 01722 339983
Visit the historic 13th century Medieval Hall and watch the fascinating half-hour audio-visual guide to the city and region. A witty and informative soundtrack, specially composed music and some startling effects accompany hundreds of images to provide an insight into Salisbury's extraordinary past, the colourful city of today, and many of the attractions in the area. Enjoy refreshments 'while you watch'. Contact the Hall for full details of special events in 1998.
Open Apr-Oct, performances hourly 10-5 (last performance at 5pm). Doors open 20 mins prior to performance. Also open throughout year for prebooked groups.
£1.50 (ch 4 50p, ch 5-17 £1)
P (150m) 🍴 ♿ *shop*

Mompesson House
Chorister's Green, Cathedral Close SP1 2EL
☎01722 335659
With its high wrought-iron railings and perfect proportions this Queen Anne house makes an impressive addition to the elegant Cathedral Close in Salisbury. Inside there are no disappointments: the stucco ceilings, carved oak staircase and period furniture are more than matched by the important collection of 18th-century glasses, china and some outstanding paintings.
Open Apr-1 Nov, daily (ex Thu & Fri) 12-5.30. Last admission 5pm.
£3.40 (ch £1.70). Garden only 80p.
P 🍴 ♿ *shop ⚹ 🌳*

Old Sarum
(2m N on A345)
☎01722 335398
The story of Old Sarum began in pre-history: it was once the location for an Iron Age camp. What the visitor sees today, however, are the remains of a thriving community that grew up around a Norman cathedral and castle. When a new cathedral was built in nearby New Sarum, or Salisbury, the community was gradually abandoned, although until the Reform Bill of 1832 ten voters remained to return two members to parliament; at one time Pitt the Elder represented Old Sarum.
Open all year, Apr-Oct, daily 10-6 (or dusk if earlier); Nov-Mar, daily 10-4. Closed 24-26 Dec & 1 Jan.
£2 (ch £1, concessions £1.50).
P ♿ ⚹

Royal Gloucestershire, Berkshire & Wiltshire Regiment Museum
The Wardrobe, 58 The Close SP1 2EX
☎01722 414536
An interesting and historic building in Cathedral Close displaying mementoes, relics, uniforms and weapons. Riverside Garden also now open to the public.
Open Apr-Oct, daily 10-4.30; Feb, Mar & Nov, Mon-Fri 10-4.30. (Closed Dec & Jan).
£2.80 (ch 50p, students & pen £1.80).
P 🍴 ♿ *shop ⚹*

Salisbury Cathedral
SP1 2EF
☎01722 328726 Fax 01722 323569
Built between 1220 and 1258 Salisbury Cathedral is a masterpiece of medieval architecture. Its elegant spire at 123 metres (404 feet) is the tallest in England. Cathedral treasures include Europe's oldest working clock and an original Magna Carta. Please ring for deails of services and concerts.
Open all year, Sep-May 8-6.30, Jun-Aug 8-8.30. (6.30pm Sun).
£2.50 (ch 50p, pen & students £1.50). Family £5.
P *(charged)* 🍴 ♿ *(loop system, interpretive model for blind, wheelchairs) toilets for disabled shop*

Salisbury & South Wiltshire Museum
The King's House, 65 The Close SP1 2EN (in Cathedral Close)
☎01722 332151 Fax 01722 325611
One of the most outstanding of the many beautiful buildings in Cathedral Close also houses the local museum, winner of six awards. Covering an area that is so steeped in history - Stonehenge is not far away - there are many fascinating displays. Galleries include Stonehenge, Early Man, History of Salisbury, the Pitt Rivers collection, ceramics and pictures (Turner watercolours) and the Wedgwood room, a reconstruction of a pre-NHS surgery, a costume, lace and embroidery gallery. The newest exhibit is a fine, and very rare, bronze age gold torc. Exhibitions include 'the Green Mantle - English Landscape and Gardens in Embroidery' by Linda Chilton (16 May-4 Jul), 'A Brush with the Past', paintings by Fed Sinkinson (11 Jul-5 Sep). The summer exhibition features the history and enjoyment of sweets and chocolate (end Jun-end Sep). Also Museums Week (16-23 May) and Heritage Day (12 Sep).
Open all year Mon-Sat 10-5; also Suns Jul & Aug, 2-5. (Closed Xmas).
£3 (under 5's free, ch 75p, pen, students & UB40s £2). Party. Season tickets available.
P *(adjacent)* 🍴 ♿ *(parking by prior arrangement) toilets for disabled shop ⚹*
Cards: 💳 💳

STONEHENGE
Stonehenge
(2m W of Amesbury on junc A303 and A344/A360)
☎01980 624715
Stonehenge is one of the most famous prehistoric monuments in Europe and has been the source of endless speculation by archaeologists and others. The henge was started about 5,000 years ago, but was redesigned several times during the following 1,500 years. The earliest parts are an encircling ditch and bank which were made about 2,800BC. About 700 years later, huge Blue Stones, 80 in all and each weighing 2 tons, were brought from south-west Wales. However, before the work on these was finished, enormous sarsen stones weighing over 50 tons each were dragged from the Marlborough Downs and the whole thing was reorganised into the design we see today. This is made up of an outer ring with mortis-and-tenon-fitted lintels and an inner horseshoe of five pairs of uprights with lintels. Later on, the Blue Stones were re-erected. The axis of the horseshoe points towards the midsummer sunrise. The whole area was obviously a centre of great ceremonial activity and there are a number of monuments, massive earthworks, and over 300 burial mounds within a relatively small area. Little is known about the Bronze Age society that organised such a vast undertaking, but there was no connection with the Druids.
Open all year, daily, 16 Mar-May & Sep-10 Oct 9.30-6; Jun-Aug, 9-7; 16 Oct-15 Mar 9.30-4. Closed 24-26 Dec & 1 Jan. There is an audio tour available in six languages.
£3.90 (ch £2.00, concessions £2.90).
P 🍴 ♿ *shop ⚹ ⚹*

STOURHEAD
Stourhead House & Garden
BA12 6QH (off B3092)
☎01747 841152
The Palladian house was built in 1720 by Henry Hoare, a banker. It is not particularly outstanding, although it does contain some fine furniture. However, what makes Stourhead especially memorable are the superb gardens laid out by Henry Hoare II in 1741. He returned from his Grand Tour inspired by the gardens and landscapes he had seen in Italy, and was determined to create something similar in England. The result is one of the finest 18th-century landscape gardens in Europe. He built a grotto and a temple to Flora around two springs and then dammed the River Stour to create a large triangular lake. He also erected a Pantheon in 1754 and over the next few years built other temples.

Longleat's famous Safari Park is home to a large pride of magnificent lions as well as gorillas and the celebrated white tiger.

Much of the comprehensive tree-planting was done by his grandson who, in 1791, began a planting programme around the lake. There are many varieties of oak, elm, willow and exotic trees, and the rhododendrons, which, with the azaleas, make spring so spectacular at Stourhead, were first planted in 1791. Conifers were introduced in the 19th century, with further planting in the early 20th century. On the edge of the estate is King Alfred's Tower, a 160ft high, red-brick folly built in 1772 by Flitcroft. There are magnificent views across Somerset, Dorset and Wiltshire from the top. Events for 1998: Fête Champêtre 23-25 July. For other events telephone 0891 335203.
Open - House 28 Mar-1 Nov, Sat-Wed 12-5.30 or dusk if earlier. Last admission 5pm. Garden daily all year 9-7 or dusk if earlier (ex 23-25 Jul when garden closes at 5pm). King Alfreds Tower, 28 Mar-1 Nov, Good Fri & BH's Tue-Fri 2-5.30, wknds 11.30-5.30 or dusk if earlier. House £4.40 (ch £2.40). Garden £4.40 (ch £2.40), Nov-Feb £3.40 (ch 1.50). Family ticket £8. Combined House & Garden ticket £7.70 (ch £3.70) Family ticket £20.60. Parties 15+ (ex Nov-Feb). King Alfred's Tower £1.50 (ch 5-16 70p).
P 🍴 ✕ *licensed ♿ toilets for disabled shop ⚹ (ex in gardens Nov-Feb only) 🌳*

STOURTON
Stourton House Flower Garden
Stourton House BA12 6QF (3m NW of Mere, on A303)
☎01747 840417
Set in the attractive village of Stourton, the house has more than four acres of beautifully maintained flower gardens. Many grass paths lead through varied and colourful shrubs, trees and plants; and Stourton House also specialises in unusual plants, and dried flowers, many of which are for sale. It is also well-known for its collections of daffodils, delphiniums, and 270 different hydrangeas. Daffodil Day (19 Apr), Flower Gala (23-25 May), Delphinium Day (28 Jun), Hydrangea Day (23 Aug), Hydrangea Gala (13 Sep).
Open Apr-end Nov, Wed, Thu, Sun & BH Mon 11-6 (or dusk if earlier).Also open ➤

The Exhibition Hall at Wilton House tells the story of the Earls of Pembroke.

Dec-Mar for plant/dried flower sales.
£2.50 (ch 50p)
P ⚏ & *(wheelchairs available) toilets for disabled shop (plants for sale)* ❀ *(ex by arrangement)*

SWINDON
Great Western Railway Museum
Faringdon Rd SN1 5BJ (in Swindon town centre)
☎01793 466555
Fax 01793 484073
The museum is in the Great Western Railway Village in Swindon, once one of the busiest railway towns in Britain, and now has a fascinating collection of locomotives and other exhibits relating to the GWR. Among the locomotives are the historic **Dean Goods and King George V** and a replica of the broad gauge locomotive **North Star**. There is a comprehensive display of nameplates, models, posters and tickets and other railway paraphernalia, and a new exhibition 'Return to Swindon' celebrates Swindon's Railway Works and Village, complete with recreated Railway Workshop displays. Plans are underway for a new, enlarged Museum on the Swindon GWR Works Site. Funding for a new museum was granted in early 1997, and the existing site is likely to close early in 1999. The new museum will open at Easter 2000.
Open all year, Mon-Sat 10-5, Sun 2-5. (Closed Good Fri, 24-26 Dec & 1 Jan).
✳*£2.30 (ch £1.10, under 5 free). (Charge*

includes admission to the Railway Village museum).
P *(100 yds)* & *shop* ❀

TEFFONT
Farmer Giles Farmstead
SP3 5QY (off A303 at Teffont)
☎01722 716338 *Fax 01722 716993*
If you love the countryside you cannot fail to enjoy a visit to Farmer Giles Farmstead. Set in 175 rolling acres of glorious Wiltshire downland, it is a real working dairy farm which has opened its gates for you to explore. You can watch the cows being milked, bottle feed lambs and get to know a host of other animals and pets. There is an adventure playground with tractors to sap the energy of active youngsters and, for adults, a relaxing walk along the picturesque Beech belt, meeting Highland cattle and Shire horses along the way. Relax by the ponds and windpump, watch the fish feeding. Take a tractor and trailer ride to a high point on the farm and see panoramic views. Two large exhibition areas and a cosy restaurant offering tasty farmhouse meals make it a venue for all weathers with outdoor and indoor picnic. Special events include sheep shearing demonstrations, model aircraft flying, country craft festival, Father Christmas etc, please telephone for details.
Open 22Mar-9Nov, daily 10.30-6, wknds in winters. Party bookings all year. Closed 25-26 Dec

£3.95 (ch £2.85, pen £3.50) Family ticket £13.
P ✗ *licensed* & *(all facilities have access for the disabled) toilets for disabled shop*

TISBURY
Old Wardour Castle
SP3 6RP (2m SW)
☎01747 870487
The old castle was a hexagonal building, and there are substantial remains. The walls still stand to their original 60ft and it is possible to climb nearly to the top. It was built in 1392 by John Lord Lovel with later additions after 1570. It was twice besieged and badly damaged during the Civil War.
Open all year, Apr-Oct, daily 10-6 (or dusk if earlier); Nov-Mar Wed-Sun 10-4, (closed 1-2pm). Closed 24-26 Dec & 1 Jan.
£1.70 (ch 90p, concessions £1.30).
P & ✿

WESTBURY
Woodland Park & Heritage Centre
Brokerswood BA13 4EH (turn off A36 at Bell Inn, Standerwick. Follow brown Tourist Info signs)
☎01373 822238 & 823880
Fax 01373 858474
Woodland Heritage Centre & Woodland Park nature walks lead through 80 acres of woodlands, with a lake and wildfowl. Facilities include a woodland visitor centre (covering wildlife and forestry), two children's adventure playgrounds, indoor soft play area and guided walks and the Smokey Oak railway, over a third of a mile long. (Special catering facilities for parties of 10 or more.) Barbeque sites and fishing permits available.
Open all year; Park open daily 10-sunset. Museum open Mon-Fri 10-5 (summer), 12-3 (winter); Sat 2-6, Sun 10-6 (summer); Sun 2-4.30 (winter). Free admission for wheelchair users.
£2.50 (unaccompanied ch £1.50, accompanied ch 50p,pen £1.95)
P ⚏ & *shop*

WESTWOOD
Westwood Manor
BA15 2AF (1.5m SW of Bradford on Avon, off B3109)
☎01225 863374
The property of the National Trust, this late 15th-century stone manor house has some particularly fine Jacobean plasterwork. The house, which is situated by the parish church, was altered in 1610 but still retains its late Gothic and

Jacobean windows. Outside there is a superb modern topiary garden.
Open Apr-30 Sept, Sun, Tue & Wed 2-5
£3.50 (no reductions), house not suitable for children under 10.
P ❀ 🜂

WILTON (near Salisbury)
Wilton House
SP2 0BJ (3m W of Salisbury, on the A30)
☎01722 746720 746729(24 hr line)
Fax 01722 744447
A homicidal drunken Earl and Southern Command Headquarters during the Second World War - these are just some of the fascinating historical links introduced to visitors in the award-winning film, featuring Anna Massey, which provides a background to the Earls of Pembroke and the 450-year history of the Estate.
Built on the site of a 9th century nunnery founded by King Alfred, the Tudor origins of the house can still be seen in the tower which survived the 1647 fire and is now incorporated within the splendid 17th-century house, based on designs by Inigo Jones. Perhaps the most famous of the six State Rooms are the Double and Single Cube rooms with their fabulous painted ceilings. Gothic Cloisters were added in the early 19th century by James Wyatt. Wilton House boasts a world famous art collection with over 230 paintings on show.
Visitors can step back in time in the reconstructed Tudor Kitchen and the Estate's Victorian Laundry, relax in 21 acres of landscaped parkland, rose and water gardens, woodland and riverside walks. There is a massive children's adventure playground, quizzes, and 'The Wareham Bears', 200 costumed bears at their stately home. The featured exhibition for 1998 will examine the life of Florence Nightingale and her sponsor Lord Herbert, son of the 11th Earl of Pembroke. Events include Wessex Craft Fair (Jun 5-7), Wilton Horse Trials (Jun 27-28) Open Air Concert and Fireworks (18 July), Teddy Bear's Picnic (16 August). Please telephone for details.
Open 4 Apr-25 Oct daily 11-6. Last admission 5pm.
£6.75 (ch 5-15 £4, under 5 free, students & pen £5.75). Family ticket £17.50.
P ⚏ ✗ *licensed* & *toilets for disabled shop garden centre* ❀
Cards: 💳 💳

WOODHENGE
Woodhenge
(1.5m N of Amesbury, off A345 just S of Durrington)
Neolithic ceremonial monument of c.2300 BC, consisting of six concentric rings of timber posts, now marked by concrete piles. The long axis of the rings, which are oval, points to the rising sun on Midsummer Day.
Open all reasonable times.
Free.
P & ✿

WORCESTERSHIRE

BEWDLEY
Severn Valley Railway
Comberton Hill
☎01299 403816 & 01746 764361
Fax 01299 400839
(For full entry see Kidderminster)

West Midland Safari & Leisure Park
Spring Grove DY12 1LF (on A456)
☎01299 402114 *Fax 01299 404519*
A drive-around wild animal safari park with over 40 species of exotic animals to see. Pets' corner, Sealion show, Reptile House, Goat Walk and Deer Park. Other attractions include a variety of rides in the leisure area.

SEVERN VALLEY RAILWAY

Open Apr-Oct, daily 10-5 incl BH's.
✱£4.50 (ch 4 free). Book of ride tickets 5-£3.50, 10-£7 or 20-£12.50. Multi ride wristband £5.50.
P ♨ & *toilets for disabled shop*
Cards: ▨ ▨ ▨ ▨

BROADWAY
Broadway Tower Country Park
WR12 7LB (off A44)
☎01386 852390
Fax 01386 858829
The 65ft tower was designed by James Wyatt for the 6th Earl of Coventry, and built in 1799. The unique building now houses exhibitions on three floors, depicting its colourful past and various uses such as holiday retreat to the famous artist and designer William Morris. The viewing platform is equipped with a telescope, giving wonderful views over 13 counties. Around the Tower is a Country Park with adventure playground, BBQs, nature walks, giant chess and draughts, and animal enclosures. The park also specialises in breeding Red Deer, which can be seen in an environment very close to their natural habitat. Ring for details of special events.
Open Apr-Oct, daily 10-6. Nov-Mar (tower only) weekends weather permitting 11-4 or by prior booking.
£3 (ch £2.20, pen £2.50). Family ticket £9. Party.
P ♨ ✗ & *toilets for disabled shop*
Cards: ▨ ▨ ▨

BROMSGROVE
Avoncroft Museum of Historic Buildings
Stoke Heath B60 4JR (2m S, off A38)
☎01527 831886 & 831363
Fax 01527 876934
A visit to Avoncroft takes you through nearly 700 years of history. Here you can see 25 buildings rescued from destruction and authentically restored on a 15 acre rural site. The magnificent timbered roof of Worcester Cathedral's original Guest Hall dates from 1330.

There are 15th and 16th century timber framed buildings, 18th century agricultural buildings and a cockpit. There are industrial buildings and a working windmill from the 19th century, and from the 20th a fully furnished pre-fab. The National Telephone Kiosk Collection is also housed here, with 13 working kiosks dating from 1922. Most buildings are accessible to the disabled and there is a wheelchair available. Special events include Morris Minor Car Rally (27 April), Young Musicians Platform (2-4 May), Pole Lathe Turners Convention (11 May), Vintage and Classic Car Show (8 June), Volkswagon Rally (22 June), Children's Activity Weekend (5-6 July), MG Car Rally (27 July), Children's Activity Weekend (9-10 August).
Open Jul-Aug daily 10.30-5; Apr-Jun & Sep-Oct 10.30-4.30 (wknds 5.30). Closed Mon. Mar & Nov 10.30-4. Closed Mon & Fri. Open BHs.
£4.25 (ch £1.90, pen £3). Family ticket £10.50.
P ♨ & *(ramps, wheelchair available) toilets for disabled shop*
Cards: ▨ ▨ ▨

EVESHAM
The Almonry Museum
Abbey Gate WR11 4BG (on A4184, opposite Merstow Green, main North/South route through Evesham)
☎01386 446944
Fax 01386 442348
The 14th-century stone and timber building was the home of the Almoner of the Benedictine Abbey in Evesham. It now houses exhibitions relating to the history of Evesham Abbey, the Battle of Evesham, and the culture and trade of Evesham. Evesham Tourist Information Centre is also located here.
Open all year, Mon-Sat & BHs (ex Xmas) 10-5, Sun 2-5.
£1.50 (ch 16 free, pen 50p).
P (110 yds) shop ✸

HANBURY
Hanbury Hall
WR9 7EA (4.5m E of Droitwich, 1m N of B4090 and 1.5m W of B4091)
☎01527 821214 Fax 01527 821251
This William and Mary style red-brick house, completed in 1701, is a typical example of an English country house built by a prosperous local family. The house contains outstanding painted ceilings and staircase by Thornhill and the Watney collection of porcelain, while outside there are both a contemporary orangery and an ice house. The 18th century garden has recently been reopened. Please telephone for details of various events.
Open 29 Mar-28-Oct, Sun-Wed 2-6. Last admission 5.30 (dusk if earlier).
House & Garden £4.30 (ch £2). Family ticket £10.50. Garden only £2.50 (ch £1)
P ♨ & *(Braille guide) toilets for disabled shop ✸ (ex in park)* ⬤
Cards: ▨ ▨

KIDDERMINSTER
Hartlebury Castle State Rooms
Hartlebury DY11 7XX (5m S)
☎01299 250410
The elegant interior of this castle, the seat of the Bishops of Worcester since 850, reveals little of its long and sometimes troubled history. Its present Gothic appearance dates from the 18th century.
Open Etr Mon-7 Sep, 1st Sun in month plus BH Mon & Tue 2-5. Also Wed (Etr-Aug) 2-4.
P & shop ✸
Details not confirmed for 1998

Hereford & Worcester County Museum
Hartlebury Castle, Hartlebury DY11 7XZ (5m S of Kidderminster clearly signed from A449)
☎01299 250416 Fax 01905 766244
Housed in the north wing of Hartlebury Castle, the County Museum contains a delightful display of crafts and industries. There are unique collections of toys, costume, domestic life, room settings and horse-drawn vehicles as well as a reconstructed forge, schoolroom, wheelwright's and tailor's shop. A variety of special events are planned for 1998, please ring for details.
Open Mar-Nov, Mon-Thu 10-5, Bh's 11-5, Fri & Sun 2-5. (Closed Sat & Good Fri).
✱£1.90 (ch & pen 90p).
P ♨ & *(car parking close to main building) toilets for disabled shop ✸ (ex in grounds)*
Cards: ▨ ▨

Severn Valley Railway
Comberton Hill (on A448 (Comberton Hill), it is clearly signposted from all major roads)
☎01299 403816 & 01746 764361
Fax 01299 400839
The leading standard gauge steam railway, with one of the largest collections of locomotives and rolling stock in the country. Services operate from Kidderminster and Bewdley to Bridgnorth through 16 miles of picturesque scenery along the River Severn. Special steam galas and Friends of Thomas Weekends take place during the year along with Santa Specials. Saturday evening 'Wine and Dine' and 'Sunday Luncheon' trains are a speciality. There are footplate courses for those wishing to experience the thrill of driving and firing a steam locomotive. Special events - Spring Steam Gala (25-26 Apr), Heavy Horse Weekend (16-17 May), Friends of Thomas (30-31 May), 1940's Weekend (4-5 Jul), Friends of Thomas (5-6 Sep), Autumn Steam Gala (18-20 Sep), Classic Vehicle Day (11 Oct), Santa Specials (5-6, 12-13, 19-24 Dec), Mince Pie Specials (26 Dec-1 Jan).
Trains operate wknds throughout year, daily mid May to end Sep, plus school holidays & half terms, Santa Specials, phone for details.
Subject to Review.(Train fares vary according to journey. Main through ticket £9 return, Family ticket £20)
P ♨ & *(wc Kidderminster/Bridgnorth) toilets for disabled shop*
Cards: ▨ ▨ ▨ ▨ ▨

REDDITCH
Forge Mill Needle Museum & Bordesley Abbey Visitor Centre
Forge Mill, Needle Mill Ln, Riverside B98 8HY (N side of Redditch, off A441)
☎01527 62509
Fax 01527 584619
The museum is housed in the only remaining water-driven, needle-scouring mill, with machinery from the 18th century which is demonstrated regularly. Displays of finds from the nearby 12th-century Cistercian Abbey are shown in the Visitor Centre. Both the museum and the visitor centre are set in attractive surroundings within the Arrow Valley Park. Temporary exhibitions on local history and textile themes. Textile workshop programme. Events. Craft demonstrations 1st Sunday of the month Apr-Sep. Weekly concerts in June. Please telephone for details. ➤

Step into the past at the Avoncroft Museum of Historic Buildings

Open Easter-Sep, Mon-Fri 11-4.30, Sat & Sun 2-5; Feb-Easter & Oct-Nov, Mon-Thu 11-4 & Sun 2-5. Parties by arrangement. £1.80 (ch 55p, pen £1.30). Free admission for persons with disabilities, their carers, unemployed & students. Family ticket £4.20. Season tickets available for family (£10) and individual (£4) .
🅿 ✿ (wheelchairs with advance notice) toilets for disabled shop ⊗

SPETCHLEY
Spetchley Park Gardens
WR5 1RS (3m E of Worcester, off A422)
☎01905 345213 or 345224
The 110-acre deer park and the 30-acre gardens surround an early 19th-century mansion (not open), with sweeping lawns and herbaceous borders, a rose lawn and enclosed gardens with low box and yew hedges. There is a large collection of trees (including 17th-century Cedars of Lebanon), shrubs and plants, many of which are rare or unusual. A new garden within the old Kitchen Garden is now open. Specialist Plant Fair (26 Apr).
Open Apr-Sep, Mon-Fri 11-5, Sun 2-5; BH Mons 11-5. Other days by appointment. £2.90 (ch £1.40). Party 25+.
🅿 ⬤ & ⊗

STONE
Stone House Cottage Gardens
DY10 4BG (2m SE of Kidderminster, on A448)
☎01562 69902
A beautiful walled garden with towers provides a sheltered area of about one acre for rare shrubs, climbers and interesting herbaceous plants. Adjacent to the garden is a nursery with a large selection of unusual plants. There will be music from the towers in June. Send an SAE for details.
Open Gardens & nursery Mar-18 Oct, Wed-Sat 10-5.30.
£2, free for children.
🅿 & garden centre ⊗

WICHENFORD
Dovecote
(5.5m NW of Worcester, off B4204)
☎01684 850051
This large 17th-century dovecote has nearly 600 nesting boxes and is unusual in its timber-framed, wattle and daub construction, which was rarely used for dovecotes. The gabled roof appears to have a chimney, but it is actually an entrance for the birds.
Open Apr-1 Nov, daily 9-6 or sunset. (Closed Good Fri). Other times by prior appointment.
60p.
P (on street parking) ⊗ 🐾

WORCESTER
City Museum & Art Gallery
Foregate St WR1 1DT
☎01905 25371
Fax 01905 616979
The gallery has temporary art exhibitions from both local and national sources and the programme includes a wide range of supporting events; while the museum exhibits cover geology, local and natural history, including River Severn displays and activities. Of particular interest is a complete 19th-century chemists shop. There are collections relating to the Worcestershire Regiment and the Worcestershire Yeomanry Cavalry. Exhibitions planned for 1998 include: Truth to Materials - New Craft for the 90s (2 May-13 June), Field - an exhibition of work by 'The Paper Group' (20 Jun-1 Aug), Public Art Festival (26 Sep-7 Nov).
Open all year, Mon, Tue Wed & Fri 9.30-6, Sat 9.30-5.(Closed 25-26 Dec & 1 Jan also Good Fri)
Free.
🅿 ⬤ & (lift (Taylors Lane ent) induction loop Art Gallery) toilets for disabled shop ⊗

The Commandery
Sidbury WR1 2HU (M5 junct 7, A44, signposted)
☎01905 355071 Fax 01905 764586
This fine 15th-century, timber-framed building was the headquarters of Charles II's army during the Battle of Worcester in 1651. It has an impressive Great Hall with some good 15th-century stained glass, and the building is now England's only Civil War centre. There are spectacular audio-visual displays, including the trial of King Charles I - join the jury and decide the King's fate, and see the Scots' camp on the eve of the Battle of Worcester. Special events throughout the year, many based on the Civil War and Tudor periods. Living history by professional re-enactors a speciality. Please ring for details.
Open all year, Mon-Sat 10-5, Sun 1.30-5.30. (Closed 25 & 26 Dec and 1 Jan)
✱£3.40 (concessions £2.30). Family ticket £9.
🅿 (100 yds) ⬤ shop ⊗
Cards: 🟦 🟨

Elgar's Birthplace Museum
Crown East Ln, Lower Broadheath WR2 6RH (3m W, off A44 to Leominster).
☎01905 333224 Fax 01905 333224
The cottage where Sir Edward Elgar, the composer, was born in 1857 is now a museum. There is a comprehensive display of photographs, letters and personal effects.
Open daily ex Wed, May-Sep 10.30-6. Oct-15 Jan & 16 Feb-Apr 1.30-4.30.
✱£3 (ch 50p, students £1 & pen £2). Party.
P (50 yds) & shop ⊗ (ex in gardens)
Cards: 🟦 🟨

Hawford Dovecote
(3m N on A449)
☎01684 850051
An unusual square, half-timbered 16th-century dovecote. Access on foot only via the entrance drive to the adjoining house.
Open Apr-1 Nov, daily 9-6 or sunset. (Closed Good Fri). Other times by prior appointment only.
60p.
P (on street parking) ⊗ 🐾

Museum of Local Life
Friar St WR1 2NA
☎01905 722349
This interesting 500-year-old timber-framed house has a squint and an ornate plaster ceiling. It is now a museum of local life featuring a children's room, an Edwardian bathroom and displays of the Home Front of World War II. Displays show life in the town over the last 200 years. A variety of exhibitions and events are held throughout the year. Ring for details.
Open all year, Mon-Wed & Fri-Sat 10.30-5pm. Also Bank Hols. Closed 25-26 Dec and 1 Jan).
£1.50 (concesssions 75p, school's 60p)
P (200 yds) & shop ⊗

Museum of Worcester Porcelain
Severn St WR1 2NE (off A44, next to Worcester Cathedral)
☎01905 23221 Fax 01905 617807
Royal Worcester is Britain's oldest continuous producer of Porcelain and is world famous for its Fine Bone China. Tour the factory and discover the skills of the craftsmen and women at work. Appreciate over 240 years of England's finest heritage when you visit the Museum of Worcester Porcelain housing the world's largest collection of early Worcester pieces. Factory shops and family restaurant also on site. The newly refurbished 18th Century Gallery will reopen Easter 1998, and 19th and 20th Century Galleries will open later in the year.
Opening after refurbishment Etr 1998 when 1st of 4 galleries will open to public. Entire museum re-opened by late 1998. Telephone for details and times. Royal Worcester Factory tours continue Mon-Fri.
Prices under review.
🅿 (charged) ✗ licensed & (ex factory) toilets for disabled shop ⊗
Cards: 🟦 🟨 🟥 💳 🟩 🟪 🔵

Worcester Cathedral
WR1 2LH
☎01905 28854 & 21004 Fax 01905 611139
Worcester Cathedral with its 200 foot tower stands majestically beside the River Severn. The Crypt, built by St Wulstan in 1084, is a classic example of Norman architecture. The 12th century Chapter House and Cloisters are a reminder of the cathedral's monastic past. King John (who signed the Magna Carta) and Prince Arthur (elder brother of Henry VIII) are buried near the High Altar. There are exhibitions and guided tours. The cathedral choir sings during the school term at 5.30 evensong (not Thurs) and 11.00am and 4.00pm Sundays.
Open all year, daily 7.30-6.
Donations. (Suggested £2 per adult.)
P (500yds) ⬤ & (limited access due to nature of building) toilets for disabled shop ⊗ (ex guide dogs)

BEMPTON
RSPB Nature Reserve
YO15 1JF (take cliff road from B1229, Bempton Village)
☎01262 851179
Part of the spectacular chalk cliffs that stretch from Flamborough Head to Speeton. The reserve is approached up the cliff road from Bempton village. This is one of the sites in England to see thousands of nesting seabirds including gannets and puffins at close quarters.

Burton Agnes Hall & Gardens
NEAR DRIFFIELD EAST YORKS

A lovely Elizabethan house filled with treasures collected over four centuries including modern and Impressionist paintings. The old walled garden contains a large collection of plants, roses and clematis as well as a maze and giant games in coloured gardens.
There is a children's corner, cafe, ice cream parlour, gift shop and herb and dried flower shop.
A LOVELY DAY OUT FOR ALL THE FAMILY

Viewpoints overlook the cliffs which are best visited from April to July. Over two miles of chalk cliffs rising to 400ft with numerus cracks and ledges. Enormous numbers of seabirds nest on these cliffs including guilleots, razorbills, kittiwakes, fulmars, herring gulls and several pairs of shag. This is the only gannetry on the mainland of England and is growing annually. Many migrants pass off-shore including terns, skuas and shearwaters. Wheatears, ring ouzels, merlins and bluethroats frequent the clifftop on migration. Grey seal and porpoise are sometimes seen offshore. Please phone for details of events.
Open for visitor centre daily, Apr-Sep 10-5.
Free.
P *(charged)* ♥ & *toilets for disabled shop* ✿
Cards: ▨ ▧ ▨ ▨

BEVERLEY
Guildhall
Register Sq HU17 9AU
☎01482 867430 Fax 01482 872102
The Guildhall was established in 1500 and then rebuilt in handsome classical style in 1762. It is now used as a county court and Mayor's Parlour, but can be visited for its notable ceiling painting in the courtroom, its display of civic regalia, ancient charters and other treasures. A guide service is available.
Open Etr-Sep, Mon-Sat 9.30-5.30, Sun 10-2; Oct-Etr, Mon-Fri 9.30-5.30, Sat 10-4. For opening times of Mayor's Parlour please telephone for details.
P *(100yds)* & ✿
Details not confirmed for 1998

The Hall, Lairgate
HU17 8HN
☎01482 882255 Fax 01482 883913
Now used as council offices, the Hall is an 18th-century building with an interesting late 18th-century stucco ceiling, and a Chinese room with rare hand-painted wallpaper.
Open all year, Mon-Thu 8.45-5.30 & Fri 9-4 (subject to availability). Groups at other times by arrangement.
& ✿
Details not confirmed for 1998

Museum of Army Transport
Flemingate HU17 0NG
☎01482 860445 Fax 01482 872767
The museum tells the story of army transport from horse drawn waggons to the recent Gulf conflict: everything from prototype vehicles to Montgomery's Rolls Royce and the last Blackburn Beverley aircraft. There are also other exhibits to be explored including 'Women at the Wheel' (their role in the war) and an area for children.
Open all year, daily 10-5. (Closed 24-26 Dec).
P ♥ & *(parking next to entrance) toilets for disabled shop* ✿
Details not confirmed for 1998
Cards: ▨ ▧

BRIDLINGTON
Sewerby Hall & Gardens
YO15 1EA
☎01262 673769 (Park) & 677874 (Hall)
Fax 01262 400189
Sewerby Hall and Gardens, set in 50 acres of parkland overlooking Bridlington Bay, dates back to 1715. The Georgian House, with its 19th century Orangery, contains art galleries, archaeological displays and an Amy Johnson Room with a collection of her trophies and mementoes. The grounds include magnificent walled Old English and Rose gardens and host many events throughout the year including medieval jousting, horse pageant, classic cars etc. Activities for all the family include a Children's Zoo and play areas, golf, putting, bowls, plus woodland and clifftop walks. Please ring for further details of special events.
Gardens & zoo open daily all year. Hall open Mar-Apr & Oct-Dec, Sat-Tue 11-4; May-Sep, daily 10-6.
P ♥ ✗ & *toilets for disabled shop*
Details not confirmed for 1998

BURTON AGNES
Burton Agnes Hall
Estate Office YO25 0ND (on A166)
☎01262 490324
Fax 01262 490513
Built in 1598, this is a magnificent Elizabethan house, with furniture, pictures and china amassed by the family owners over four centuries. There is an old gatehouse, walled garden with maze, potager, herbaceous borders, clematis, campanula and geranium collections, jungle garden and giant board games in coloured gardens as well as walks in woodland gardens. The ghost of a young girl is said to haunt the property.
Open Apr-Oct, daily 11-5.
Hall & grounds £4 (ch £2, pen £3.50). Grounds only £2 (ch £1, pen £1.75). Party 30+.
P ♥ & *(scented garden for the blind) toilets for disabled shop garden centre*

Norman Manor House
This is the house that Burton Agnes Hall replaced. It is a rare survivor from Norman times, and though later encased in brick it still has its Norman piers and the groined roof of a lower chamber. An upper room and an old donkey wheel can also be seen.
Open all year.
Free.
✿

HULL
Maister House
160 High St HU1 1NQ
☎01482 324114
The house is a mid-18th-century rebuilding, notable for its splendid stone and wrought-iron staircase, ornate stucco work and finely carved doors. Only the staircase and entrance hall are open.

Open all year, Mon-Fri 10-4 (Closed BH). 80p (incl guide book).
P ✿ ✿ ✿

Maritime Museum
Queen Victoria Square HU1 3DX
☎01482 613902
Fax 01482 613710
Hull's maritime history is illustrated here, with displays on whales and whaling, ships and shipping, and other aspects of this Humber port. There is also a Victorian court room which is used for temporary exhibitions. The restored dock area, with its fine Victorian and Georgian buildings, is well worth exploring too.
Open all year, Mon-Sat 10-5 & Sun 1.30-4.30. (Closed 25-26 Dec, 1 Jan & Good Fri).
Free.
P *(100 yds)* & *shop* ✿

'Streetlife' - Hull Museum of Transport
High St
☎01482 613902
Fax 01482 613710
This purpose built museum uses a 'hands-on' approach to trace 200 years of transport history. With a vehicle collection of national importance, state of the art animatronic displays and stunningly authentic scenarios, you are swept back in time to see Hull's Old Town brought vividly to life. The unique mail coach ride uses the very latest in computer technology to recreate a Victorian journey by four in hand, and other displays recreate the golden age of steam, public transport and the bicycle.
Open all year, Mon-Sat 10-5, Sun 1.30-4.30. (Closed 24-25 Dec & Good Fri).
Free.
P *(0.5m)* ♥ & *toilets for disabled shop*

Wilberforce House
23-25 High St HU1 1NE (follow signs for Old Town)
☎01482 613902
Fax 01482 613710
The early 17th-century Merchants house was the birthplace of William Wilberforce, who went on to become a leading campaigner against slavery. There are Jacobean and Georgian rooms and displays on Wilberforce, the anti-slavery campaign, silver, costume, historic rooms settings, decorative art and dolls. The house also has secluded gardens. There is a special exhibition The A-Z of Costume, with displays of Hull Museum's extensive costume collection. Christmas event - Victorian Christmas. Telephone for details.
Open all year, Mon-Sat 10-5 & Sun 1.30-4.30. (Closed 25-26 Dec, 1 Jan & Good Fri).
£1 (ch under 13 and city residents with pass free)
P *(1.5m)* & *shop* ✿

POCKLINGTON
Burnby Hall Garden & Stewart Collection
The Balk YO4 2QF (off A1079 at turning for Pocklington off B1247)
☎01759 302068
The two lakes in this garden have an outstanding collection of 80 varieties of hardy water lilies, designated a National Collection. The lakes stand within seven acres of beautiful gardens including a lovely walled rose garden, heather beds, a rock garden and a spring and summer bedding area. The museum contains sporting trophies and ethnic material gathered on world-wide travels. Special events for 1998 include: Scottish Country Dancing and band concerts throughout June, July and August, please telephone for further details.
Open 4 April-4 October, daily 10am-6pm. (last admission 5pm)
£2.20 (ch 5-15 80p, pen £1.70). Party 20+.
P ♥ & *(free wheelchair hire) toilets for disabled shop* ✿

SPROATLEY
Burton Constable Hall
Burton Constable HU11 4LN (1.5m N of Sproatley)
☎01964 562400 Fax 01964 563229
This superb Elizabethan house was built in 1570, but much of the interior was remodelled in the 18th century. There are magnificent reception rooms and a Tudor long gallery with a pendant roof: the contents range from pictures and furniture (much of it by Thomas Chippendale) to a unique collection of 18th-century scientific instruments. Outside are 200 acres of parkland landscaped by 'Capability' Brown, with oaks and chestnuts, and a lake with an island. Camping and caravanning sites are available in the park and there is also seasonal fishing.
Open, Hall & grounds Etr Sun-30 Sept, Sat-Thurs. Grounds noon, Hall 1pm. Last admission 4.15pm.
House £4(ch £1.50, pen £3.25).
P ♥ & *toilets for disabled shop* ✿

THORNTON
Thornton Abbey
☎01469 40357
A magnificent 14th-century gatehouse and the ruins of the church and other buildings survive from the Augustinian abbey, founded in 1139. The gate is approached across a dry moat, spanned by a long bridge with arcaded walls and circular towers.
Open all year, Apr-Sep, daily 10-6; Oct-Mar 10-4 or dusk if earlier.
Free.
P & ✿ *(in certain areas)* ✠

YORKSHIRE, NORTH

ALDBOROUGH
Roman Town
(0.75m SE of Boroughbridge, on minor road off B6265 within 1m of junction of A1 & A6055)
☎01423 322768
The pretty present-day village occupies the site of the northernmost civilian Roman town in Britain, with houses, courts, a forum and a temple, surrounded by a 9ft thick, 20ft high wall. All that can be seen today are two mosaic pavements, the position of the wall and excavated objects in the small museum.
Open Apr-Oct, daily 10-6 (closed 1-2pm).
£1.70 (ch 90p, concessions £1.30)
✿ ✠

AYSGARTH
National Park Centre
DL8 3TH
☎01969 663424
A visitor centre for the Yorkshire Dales National Park, with maps, guides, walks and local information. Displays explain the history and natural history of the area.
Open Apr-Oct, daily 10-5. Nov-Mar limited wknd opening.
P *(charged)* ♥ & *shop* ✿
Details not confirmed for 1998
Cards: ▨ ▧

Yorkshire Carriage Museum
Yore Mill DL8 3SR (1.75m E on unclass rd N of A684.Turn rt at Palmer Flatt Hotel, museum 300yds)
☎01969 663399 Fax 01969 663699
A Grade II listed building at Aysgarth Falls built in 1784 which houses a varied collection of Victorian horse drawn vehicles including the 'A Woman of Substance' carriage, a mail coach, a marston hearse, a 'haunted' carriage, a fire engine, etc, all in their original condition. Also an exhibition of one man's collection of handmade scale models of American and traditional English coaches and carriages.
Open Apr-Oct, daily 9.30-7.30, other times 9.30-dusk. Closed 24 Dec-12 Jan.
P *(150 yds) shop garden centre* ✿
Details not confirmed for 1998 ➤

Castle Howard, which was the first building designed by Sir John Vanbrugh, has all the grandeur and nobility of a palace. The dome was the first to be built on a private house in England.

BEDALE
Bedale Hall
DL8 1AA (On A684, 1.5m W of A1 at Leeming Bar)
☎01677 424604 Fax 01677 424604
Housed in a building of 17th-century origin, with Palladian and Georgian extensions, the centre of this fascinating little museum is the Bedale fire engine dated 1742. Old documents, photographs, clothing, toys, craft tools and household utensils give an absorbing picture of the life of ordinary people.
Open Etr-Sep, Mon-Sat 10-4. Oct-Etr, Tue only 10-4. Other times by prior arrangement.
Donation box available.
🅿 ♿ *toilets for disabled shop* ⊗

BENINGBROUGH
Beningbrough Hall
YO6 1DD (off A19, 8m NW of York. Entrance at Newton Lodge.)
☎01904 470666 Fax 01904 470002
Beningbrough was built around 1716, and its structure has hardly been altered since then. It houses 100 pictures from the National Portrait Gallery in London. Perhaps the finest feature of the house is the Great Staircase, built of oak with wide parquetried treads and delicate balusters carved to imitate wrought iron. Ornately carved wood panelling is a feature of several of the rooms, notably the drawing room. The other side of country house life can be seen in the restored Victorian laundry, which has its original stoves, drying racks and other equipment.The gardens include formal areas, a conservatory and a wilderness play area.
Open 4 Apr-1 Nov, Sat-Wed & Good Fri. Also Fris during Jul & Aug. House 11am-5pm. Last admission 4.30pm. Grounds 11am-5.30pm. Last admission 5pm. House, Garden & Exhibition: £5. (ch £2.50) Family ticket £12.50. Garden & Exhibition: £3 (ch £1.50) Family £7.50. Cyclists £1 off any ticket.The house may close for up to 1 hour for wedding ceremonies on Fridays. Garden will remain open.
🅿 ✗ *licensed* ♿ *(access to Victorian laundry, shop & restaurant) toilets for disabled shop* ⊗ ⊗

BRIMHAM
Brimham Rocks
Brimham House, Summerbridge HG3 4DW (off B6265)
☎01423 780688 Fax 01423 781020
A Victorian guidebook describes the rocks as 'a place wrecked with grim and hideous forms defying all description and definition'. The rocks have remained a great attraction, and stand on National Trust open moorland at a height of 950ft. An old shooting lodge in the area is now an information point and shop.

Info centre 28 Mar-1 Nov. June-Sept 11am-5pm daily, Bank Hols and local school hols. Mar-May & Oct-Dec: weekends, BHs and local school hols 11am-5pm-weather permitting. Cars £2. Minibuses £4. Coaches £8. Motorcycles £1.
🅿 ♿ *(specially adapted path) toilets for disabled shop* ⊗

CASTLE BOLTON
Bolton Castle
DL8 4ET (off A684, 6miles W of Leyburn)
☎01969 623981 Fax 01969 623332
Medieval Castle completed in 1399, overlooking Wensleydale. Stronghold of the Scrope family. Mary Queen of Scots, was imprisoned here for 6 months. The Castle was besieged and taken by Parliamentary forces in 1645. Tapestries, tableaux, arms & armour, etc, can be seen. Medieval gardens have been developed. Summer 1998 will see Theatre productions and Living History events. Please ring for details.
Open Mar-Nov.
£3 (ch & pen £2).
🅿 ✗ *shop*
Cards: 🌐 AMEX 🌐 Barclay 🌐 🅂

CASTLE HOWARD
See Malton

CLAPHAM
Yorkshire Dales National Park Centre
LA2 8ED
☎015242 51419
A comprehensive information centre with displays on the local countryside and limestone scenery. A wide range of maps, guides, information leaflets, gifts and souvenirs are stocked and knowledgeable staff are on duty to answer questions. Audio-visual presentation on limestone scenery available.
Open Apr-Oct, daily 10-5.Limited opening Nov-Mar.
🅿 *(charged) (Radar key scheme) shop*
Details not confirmed for 1998
Cards: 🌐 🌐

COXWOLD
Byland Abbey
YO6 4BD (2m S of A170 between Thirsk & Helmsley, near Coxwold village)
☎01347 868614
The abbey was built for the Cistercians and is now a ruin, but enough still stands to show how beautiful it must have been. The ruins date back to the 12th and 13th centuries, and include well-preserved glazed floor tiles. Carved stones and other finds are displayed.
Open Apr-Oct 10-6 (or dusk if earlier), closed 1-2pm.
£1.50 (ch 80p, concessions £1.10).
🅿 ♿ *toilets for disabled* ⊞

DANBY
Moors Centre
Lodge Ln YO21 2NB
☎01287 660654
Fax 01287 660308
The former shooting lodge provides information on the North York Moors National Park, with an exhibition, video and bookshop information desk. There are riverside and woodland grounds, with terraced gardens, a children's play area and a brass-rubbing centre. Special events are held in summer - telephone 01287 660654 to request information.
Open all year, Apr-Oct, daily 10-5; Nov-Mar, Sat & Sun 11-4.
Free.
🅿 ⛟ ♿ *(woodland & garden trails) toilets for disabled shop* ⊗ *(ex in grounds)*

EASBY
Easby Abbey
(1m SE of Richmond off B6271)
Set beside the River Swale, the Premonstratensian Abbey was founded in 1155 and dedicated to St Agatha. Extensive remains of the monks' domestic buildings can be seen.
Open Apr-Oct 10-6 (or dusk if earlier).
£1.50 (ch 80p, concessions £1.10).
🅿 ⊞

ELVINGTON
Yorkshire Air Museum & Allied Air Forces Memorial
Halifax Way YO4 5AU (from York take A1079 (Hull rd) then immediate rt (B1228). Museum is signposted on rt.
☎01904 608595
Fax 01904 608246
The Yorkshire Air Museum is based on a part of the site of a typical World War II bomber base and its aim is to preserve it as a Memorial to the Allied Air Force air and ground crews who served in World War II, and especially those who served in Yorkshire and Humberside. Visitors can see many examples of interesting aircraft, which include one of the last of the RAF's Victor tankers, one of the last of the Lightnings and two Buccaneers. The Museum is 'the home of the Halifax', and one - 'Friday the 13th', a unique example in the country - has been rebuilt here. It is also home to a Mosquito rebuild, the Barnes Wallis Collection, a fine display of the Blackburn Heritage, the 609 (WR) Squadron room and displays of aviation artefacts and ephemera. The Museum recreates the sights, and some of the sounds, of an authentic wartime base.
Open all year, Mon-Fri 10.30-4, Sat & Sun 10.30-5, BH's 10.30-5.
🅿 ⛟ ✗ *licensed* ♿ *toilets for disabled shop*
Details not confirmed for 1998
See advertisement on page 159.

FAIRBURN
RSPB Nature Reserve
2 Springholme, Caudie Hill WF11 9JQ (W of A1, N of Ferrybridge)
☎01767 680551
One-third of the 618-acre RSPB reserve is open water, and over 260 species of birds have been recorded. A visitor centre provides information, and there is an elevated boardwalk, suitable for disabled visitors.
Access to the reserve from the village at all times. Visitor Centre only open Sat, Sun & BHs 10-5. (Closed 25 & 26 Dec). Car park & walkway at centre open daily 9-6 or dusk.
🅿 ♿ *(raised boardwalk for wheelchair) toilets for disabled shop*
Details not confirmed for 1998

GRASSINGTON
National Park Centre
Colvend, Hebden Rd BD23 5LB
☎01756 752774
Fax 01756 752745
The centre is a useful introduction to the Yorkshire Dales National Park. It has a video and a display on 'Wharfedale - Gateway to the Park', and maps, guides and local information are available. There is also a 24-hr public access information service through computer screens and a full tourist information service.
Open Apr-Oct daily, 10-5. Also limited wknds Nov-Mar.
🅿 *(charged)* ♿ *(Radar key scheme) toilets for disabled shop* ⊗
Details not confirmed for 1998
Cards: 🌐 🌐

GUISBOROUGH
Gisborough Priory
(next to parish church)
☎01287 633801
The remains of the east end of the 14th-century church make a dramatic sight here. The priory was founded in the 12th century for Augustinian canons.
Open all year Good Fri-Sep, daily 10-5; Oct-Maundy Thu, Tue-Sun 10-4. Closed 24 Dec-1 Jan.
❄85p (ch 40p, students, pen & UB40 60p)
♿ ⊗ ⊞

HARROGATE
Harlow Carr Botanical Gardens
Crag Lane, Otley Rd HG3 1QB (off B6162,1.5 miles from Harrogate centre)
☎01423 565418
Fax 01423 530663
The gardens were begun in 1950 on a rough site of pasture and woodland. Today there are 68 impressive acres of ornamental and woodland gardens, including the northern trial grounds. There are craft weekends throughout the summer. Courses, demonstrations and practical workshops are held in the Study Centre. Prospectus and full programme of events available on application.
Open all year, Mar-Oct, daily 9.30-6. Nov-Feb, daily 9.30-5 or dusk if earlier.
£3.50 (ch 16 free, pen £2.60).
Party 20+.
🅿 ⛟ ✗ *licensed* ♿ *(electric wheelchairs available, tape recorded tours) toilets for disabled shop garden centre* ⊗
Cards: 🌐 🌐 🅂

The Royal Pump Room Museum
Royal Pde HG1 2RY
☎01423 503340
Fax 01423 840026
The octagonal Pump Room building houses changing exhibitions from the museum's own collections. This part of the building still houses the original sulphur wells, now below modern street level. The wells are enclosed by glass to contain their pungent smell, but the water can be tasted, by those brave enough, at the original spa counter, now the ticket counter.
Open all year, Apr-Oct, Mon-Sat 10-5, Sun 2-5, (Nov-Mar close at 4pm). (Closed 25-26 Dec & 1 Jan).
P *(restricted to 3hrs)* ♿ *toilets for disabled shop* ⊗
Details not confirmed for 1998

HAWES
Dales Countryside Museum Centre
Station Yard DL8 3NT
☎01969 667450
The Dales Countryside Museum contains displays and an extensive collection of bygones and farming implements which explain the changing landscapes and communities of the area. There is a full national park and tourist information service including 24-hr public information terminals, maps, guides, publications and souvenirs.
Open Apr-Oct, daily 10-5. Limited winter opening.
P *(charged)* & *toilets for disabled shop* Details not confirmed for 1998
Cards: 🅰

HELMSLEY
Duncombe Park
YO6 5EB (1m from town centre, off A170)
☎01439 770213 & 771115
Fax 01439 771114
Duncombe Park stands at the heart of a spectacular 30-acre early 18th-century landscape garden which is set in 300 acres of dramatic parkland around the River Rye. The house, originally built in 1713, was gutted by fire in 1879 and rebuilt in 1895. Its principal rooms are a fine example of the type of grand interior popular at the turn of the century. Home of the Duncombes for 300 years, for much of this century the house was a girls' school. In 1985 the present Lord and Lady Feversham decided to make it a family home again and after major restoration, opened the house to the public in 1990. Part of the garden and parkland were designated a 250-acre National Nature Reserve in 1994. Special events include a Country Fair (May), an Antiques Fair (June), Steam Fair (July), Antiques Fair (November). Please telephone for details.
Open: House & Gardens 29 Mar-3 Nov, 11am-6pm (last admission 4.30pm). Apr/Oct: Sun-Thurs; May-Sept: Sun-Fri. Parkland Tearoom & Shop 29 Mar-3 Nov

10.30am-5.30pm.
House & Gardens £5 (ch 10-16, £2.50 &pen £4) Gardens & Parkland £3. (ch £1.50) Parkland only £1.50 (ch 50p)
P ⏸ ✕ *licensed* & *toilets for disabled shop garden centre*

Helmsley Castle
☎01439 770442
The ruined castle dates from the 12th century and later, and stands within enormous earthworks. It was besieged for three months in the Civil War, and destroyed in 1644.
Open all year, Apr-Oct, daily 10-6 (or dusk if earlier); Nov-mid Mar, Wed-Sun 10-4 (or dusk if earlier). Closed 1-2pm all year.
£2.20 (ch £1.10, concessions £1.70).
P *(charged)* ☞ *(in certain areas)* ♿

KIRBY MISPERTON
Flamingo Land Theme Park & Zoo
The Rectory YO17 0UX (off the A169 Malton to Pickering rd, off A64)
☎01653 668287 Fax 01653 668280
If you're looking for a fantastic family day out, you've certainly found it! Set in 375 acres of North Yorkshire countryside. There are rides and attractions for everyone.
Open 5 Apr-end Sept. Weekends and full half term week in Oct.
Prices under review.
P ⏸ ✕ & *(parking) toilets for disabled shop*
Cards: 🅰 💳 💳 🅶

KIRKHAM
Kirkham Priory
(5m SW of Malton on minor road off A64)
☎01653 618768
Set on an entrancing site on the banks of the River Derwent are the ruins of this former house of Augustinian canons. The remains of the finely sculptured 13th-century gatehouse and lavatorium, where the monks washed in leaded troughs, are memorable.
Open Apr-Sep, daily noon-5.
£1.50 (ch 80p, concessions £1.10)
P & ☞ ♿

KNARESBOROUGH
Knaresborough Castle
HG5 8AE
☎01423 503340 Fax 01423 840026
High above the town of Knaresborough, the ruins of this 14th-century castle look down over the gorge of the River Nidd. This imposing fortress was once the hiding place of Thomas Becket's murderers and it also served as a prison for Richard II. Remains include the keep, the sally-port, parts of the curtain wall and the Old Court of Knaresborough, part of which also dates from the 14th century. It now houses a local history museum, and entrance is part of the combined ticket price. A new gallery is devoted to the Civil War in Knaresborough.
Open Etr, May-Sep, daily 10.30-5. Guided tours regulary available.
P & *toilets for disabled* ☞ *(ex grounds)* Details not confirmed for 1998

MALHAM
Yorkshire Dales National Park Centre
BD23 4DA
☎01729 830363
The national park centre has maps, guides and local information together with displays on the remarkable natural history of the area, local community and work of conservation bodies. Audio-visuals are provided for groups and a 24-hour teletext information service is available.
Open Apr-Oct, daily 10-5. Limited winter opening.
P *(charged)* & *(Radar key scheme for toilet) toilets for disabled shop* ☞
Details not confirmed for 1998
Cards: 🅰 💳

MALTON
Castle Howard
YO6 7DA (15m NE of York, off A64)
☎01653 648333 648444 Fax 01653 648462
In its dramatic setting of lakes, fountains and extensive gardens, this 18th-century palace was designed by Sir John Vanbrugh. Principal location for the TV series 'Brideshead Revisited', this was the first major achievement of the architect who later created the lavish Blenheim Palace near Oxford. Castle Howard was begun in 1699 for the 3rd Earl of Carlisle, Charles Howard, whose descendants still call the place 'home'. The striking façade is topped by an 80ft painted and gilded dome. The interior has a 192ft Long Gallery, as well as a Chapel with magnificent stained glass windows by the 19th-century artist, Edward Burne-Jones. Besides the collections of antique furniture, porcelain and sculpture, the Castle contains a number of important paintings, including a portrait of Henry VIII by Holbein and works by Rubens, Reynolds and Gainsborough. The grounds include the domed Temple of the Four Winds by Vanbrugh, and the richly designed family Mausoleum by Hawksmoor. The Rose Garden contains both old-fashioned and modern varieties of roses.
Ray Wood is a 30-acre area with unique collections of rare trees, shrubs, rhododendrons and azaleas. Special events for 1998 include: Rare Plant Fair (20-21 June), Outdoor Concerts (27 June & 22 August), Sealed Knot Society (29-31 August).
Open 1-12 Mar Grounds only. 13 Mar-1 Nov, Grounds & Plant Centre 10, House 11. Last admissions 4.30pm.
£7 (ch £4, pen £6). Party 12+.
P ⏸ ✕ *licensed* & *(chairlift, free adapted transport to house) toilets for disabled shop garden centre* ☞ *(ex guide dogs in house)*
Cards: 🅰 💳 💳 💳 🅶

Eden Camp Modern History Theme Museum
Eden Camp YO17 0SD (junc of A64 & A169)
☎01653 697777 Fax 01653 698243
The story of the peoples' war - the drama, the hardships, the humour -

unfolds in this museum devoted to civilian life in World War II. The displays, covering the blackout, rationing, the Blitz, the Homeguard and others, are housed in a former prisoner-of-war camp built in 1942 for German and Italian soldiers. Voted Yorkshire and Humberside's Visitor Attraction of the Year 1992. Hut 29 depicts the military and political events of 1944, with a special section covering D-Day. Hut 11 will open in 1998, as a children's 'hands-on' educational theme centre.
Open 12 Jan-13 Feb wkdays only; 14 Feb-23 Dec, daily 10-5. Last admission 4pm. Allow at least 3-4hrs for a visit.
£3.50 (ch & pen £2.50) Party 10+.
P ⏸ & *(taped tours, Braille guides) toilets for disabled shop*

Malton Museum
Old Town Hall, Market Place YO17 0LT (leave A64, follow signs for Malton town centre)
☎01653 695136
The extensive Roman settlements in the area are represented and illustrated in this museum, including collections from the Roman fort of Derventio. There are also displays of local prehistoric and medieval finds plus changing exhibitions of local interest.
Open Etr Sat-Oct, Mon-Sat 10-4, Sun 2-4. Parties by arrangement.
£1.50 (ch, pen & students £1) Family ticket(2+2) £4.
P *(adjacent) (pay & display-2hrs)* & *shop* ☞

MIDDLEHAM
Middleham Castle
(2m S of Leyburn on A6108)
☎01969 623899
The town of Middleham (much of which is a conservation area) is dominated by the 12th-century keep which saw its great days during the Wars of the Roses. The seat of the Neville family, the Earls of Warwick, it was the home for a time of the young King Richard III, then Duke of Gloucester, who married the Earl's daughter Anne Neville.
Open all year, Apr-Oct, daily 10-6 (or dusk if earlier); Nov-Mar, Wed-Sun 10-4 (or dusk if earlier). Closed 1-2pm during winter season.
£2.20 (ch £1.10, concessions £1.70).
P & *(ex tower) shop* ♿

MIDDLESBROUGH
Captain Cook Birthplace Museum
Stewart Park, Marton TS7 6AS (3m S on A172 at Stewart Park, Marton)
☎01642 311211 Fax 01642 247038 / 01642 813781
Opened to mark the 250th anniversary of the birth of the voyager in 1728, this museum illustrates the early life of James Cook and his discoveries with temporary exhibitions. Located in spacious and rolling parkland, the site also offers outside attractions for the visitor. A special resource centre is equipped with computers and educational aids. There are Captain Cook Birthday Celebrations in October.
Open all year: Tues-Sun, Summer hrs 10am-5.30pm. Winter hrs 9am-4pm. Last entry 45 mins before closure. Closed Mon except BH, 25-26 Dec & 1 Jan.
£2 (ch & pen £1). Family ticket £5.
P ⏸ & *(lift to all floors, car parking) toilets for disabled shop* ☞

NEWBY HALL & GARDENS
Newby Hall & Gardens
HG4 5AE (4m SE of Ripon & 2m W of A1M, off B6265, between Boroughbridge and Ripon)
☎01423 322583 Fax 01423 324452
This late 17th-century house had its interior and additions designed by Robert Adam, and contains an important collection of classical sculpture and Gobelin tapestries. Twenty-five acres of award-winning gardens include a miniature railway, an adventure garden for children, and a woodland discovery walk. Special events take place throughout the year, including: Spring ➤

Plant Fair (May 3); Rainbow Craft Fair (June 6-7 & Sept 5-6); Historic Vehicle Rally (July 19).

Open Apr-Sep, Tue-Sun & BH's; Gardens 11-5.30; House 12-5. Last admission 5pm (gardens), 4.30pm (house),

❋*House & Garden £5.60, (ch & disabled £3.40, pen £4.70). Gardens only £4 (ch & disabled £2.70, pen £3.50). Party rates and family tickets on application. Under 4's go free.*

🅿️ ♿ *licensed & (wheelchairs available, maps of wheelchair routes) toilets for disabled shop garden centre* ✷

Cards: 🖃 🖃 🖃 🖃

NORTH STAINLEY
Lightwater Valley Theme Park & Shopping Village
HG4 3HT (3m N of Ripon on the A6108)
☎01765 635321 & 635334
Fax 01765 635359

Set in 175 acres of country park and lakeland, Lightwater Valley offers a selection of rides and attractions suitable for all the family. Enjoy the white-knuckle thrills of the world's biggest roller coaster - the Ultimate - as well as the Rat and the Wave, or, for the less adventurous, there are the Ladybird, the steam train, boating lake, and children's visitor farm. Lightwater Village and Factory shopping: 50,000 sq.ft of factory outlets - Buy direct at discounted prices from such companies as British Shoe Corporation, Edinburgh Crystal, Gossard, Warners, Hornsea Pottery etc. Also garden centre and huge Yorkshire Larder Delicatessen, restaurants, bars etc. Please telephone for details of special events.

Theme Park open Etr-Oct, 10-5. Village & Factory Shopping open every day (ex 25 Dec), 10-5.

❋*Village and factory shopping free entry and parking. Prices under review.*

🅿️ ♿ ✕ *licensed & (even pathways, chair lift to restaurant) toilets for disabled shop garden centre* ✷

Cards: 🖃 🖃 🖃 🖃 🖃

NUNNINGTON
Nunnington Hall
YO6 5UY (4.5m SE of Helmsley)
☎01439 748283 Fax 01439 748284

This large 16th- to 17th-century house has panelled rooms and a magnificent staircase. The Carlisle collection of miniature rooms is on display.

Open Apr-1 Nov Wed-Sun except BH Mon in Aug and Tuesdays in Jun, Jul & Aug. 1.30-6pm. (1.30-5.30 Apr & Oct) Also open Good Fri. Last admission 1hr before closing time.

House £4 (ch £2) Family ticket £10. Gardens only £1 (ch free).

🅿️ 🍴 & *toilets for disabled shop* ✷ ❦

ORMESBY
Ormesby Hall
TS7 9AS (3m SE of Middlesborough)
☎01642 324188 Fax 01642 300937

An 18th-century mansion, Ormesby Hall has stables attributed to John Carr of York. Plasterwork, furniture and 18th-century pictures can be seen.

Open 1 Apr-1 Nov; Tues (guided tours, lat tour 3.30pm), Wed, Thurs, Sun 2-5.30pm. BH Mons and Good Friday.

House & Gardens £3.30 (ch £1.60) Family ticket £8. Garden only £2 (ch £1).

🅿️ 🍴 & *toilets for disabled shop* ✷ ❦

OSMOTHERLEY
Mount Grace Priory
DL6 3JG (1m NW)
☎01609 883494

A ruined 14th-century Carthusian priory, next to a 17th-century house. One of the monks's cells has been fully restored to show where the monk lived and worked in solitude, and what life was like in this monastery. There are also extensive remains of the cloister, church and outer court.

Open all year, Apr-Oct, daily 10-6 (or dusk if earlier in Oct). Nov-Mar, Wed-Sun 10-4. Closed 1-2pm during winter season. £2.70 (ch £1.40, concessions £2).

🅿️ & *shop* ✷ ✚ ❦

PARCEVALL HALL GARDENS
Parcevall Hall Gardens Properties Ltd
BD23 6DE (Off B6265 between Grassington and Pateley Bridge)
☎01756 720311

Enjoying a hillside setting east of the main Wharfedale Valley, these beautiful gardens belong to an Elizabethan house which is used as the Bradford Diocesan Retreat House (not open to the public).

Open Good Fri-31 Oct, daily 10-6. Winter visitors by appointment.

£2 (ch 5-12 50p).

🅿️ 🍴

PICKERING
North Yorkshire Moors Railway
Pickering Station YO18 7AJ
☎01751 472508 Fax 01751 476970

Operating through the heart of the North York Moors National Park between Pickering and Grosmont, steam trains cover a distance of 18 miles. Beautiful Newtondale Halt gives walkers easy access to forest and moorland. The locomotive sheds at Grosmont are open to the public. Events throughout the year include Friends of Thomas the Tank Engine, Steam Gala, Santa Specials. Please telephone for details of these and more.

Open 21 March-1 November, daily; Dec, Santa specials and Christmas to New Year running. Further information available from Pickering Station, North Yorkshire.

❋*Prices under review.*

🅿️ *(charged)* 🍴 & *(ramp for trains) toilets for disabled shop*

Cards: 🖃 🖃

Pickering Castle
☎01751 474989

Standing upon its mound high above the town, the 12th-century keep and baileys are all that is left of this favourite royal hunting lodge. There is an exhibition on the castle's history.

Open all year, Apr-Oct, daily 10-6 (or dusk if earlier); Nov-Mar, Wed-Sun 10-4 (or dusk if earlier).Closed 1-2pm all year. Closed 24-26 Dec & 1 Jan. £2.20 (ch £1.10 concessions £1.70).

🅿️ & *(ex motte) shop* ✷ ✚

REDCAR
RNLI Zetland Museum
5 King St TS10 3AH (on corner of King St and The Promenade)
☎01642 485370 & 471813

The museum portrays the lifeboat, maritime, fishing and local history of the area, including its main exhibit 'The Zetland' - the oldest lifeboat in the world dating from 1802. There is also a replica of a fisherman's cottage c1900 and almost 2000 other exhibits. The museum is housed in an early lifeboat station, now a listed building.

Open May-Sep, daily 11-4. Also Etr & 26 Dec. Other times by appointment. Free.

P *(20m)* & *(ground floor accessible only) shop*

RICHMOND
Green Howards Museum
Trinity Church Square, Market Place DL10 4QN
☎01748 822133 Fax 01748 826561

This award-winning museum traces the military history of the Green Howards from the late 17th century onwards. The exhibits include uniforms, weapons, medals and a special Victoria Cross exhibition. Regimental and civic plate is displayed, and there is CD ROM and touch screen video of the First World War Western Front. Audio guide available. Telephone for details of weekend events to commemorate the Malaya Campaign and role of National Servicemen from 1945-63, in conjunction with English Heritage.

Open Feb, Mon-Fri 10-4.30; Mar, Mon-Sat 10-4.30; Apr-Oct, Mon-Sat 9.30-4.30 & Sun 2-4.30; Nov, Mon-Sat 10-4.30.

❋*£2 (ch 5-16 £1).*

P *(in market place)* & *(stairlift for access to all floors) shop* ✷

Richmond Castle
☎ 01748 822493
Built high upon sheer rocks overlooking the River Swale, the castle was begun by Alan Rufus in 1071. It is ruined, but has a splendid 100ft high keep. Two of the towers are left on the massive curtain walls, and also well preserved is Scollard's Hall, which was built in 1080 and may be the oldest domestic building in Britain.
Open all year, Apr-Oct, daily 10-6 (dusk if earlier); Nov-Mar, daily 10-4 (or dusk if earlier, closed 1-2pm). Closed 24-26 Dec & 1 Jan.
£2.20 (ch £1.10, concessions £1.70).
P *(800 yds)* & *shop* ✿ ✚

RIEVAULX
Rievaulx Abbey
YO6 5LB (2.25m W of Helmsley on minor road off B1257)
☎ 01439 798228
The site for this magnificent abbey was given to a band of 12 Cistercian monks in 1131. Building began in about 1132 and most was completed by the end of the 12th century. The abbey was extremely prosperous, and under its third abbot, Aelred (1147-67), there were 140 monks and over 500 lay brothers. During the 15th century parts of the abbey were taken down as numbers fell, and by the time of the Dissolution there were only 22 monks left.
Surrounded by wooded hills, this site in the Rye Valley is one of the most beautiful in England. The remains of the high church and monastic buildings are extensive, and the choir is a notable example of a 13th-century work. The nave, which dates back to 1135, is the earliest large Cistercian nave in Britain.
Open all year, Apr-Jun & Sep-Oct, daily 10-6 (or dusk if earlier) Jul-Aug, 9.30-7; Nov-Mar, daily 10-4 (or dusk if earlier. Closed 1-2pm). Closed 24-26 Dec & 1 Jan.
£2.90 (ch £1.50, concessions £2.20)
P & *shop* ✿ ✚

Rievaulx Terrace & Temples
YO6 5LJ (2m NW of Helmsley on B1257)
☎ 01439 798340
This curved terrace, half a mile long, overlooks the abbey, with views of Ryedale and the Hambleton Hills. It has two mock-Greek temples, one built for hunting parties, the other for quiet contemplation. There are also remarkable frescoes by Borgnis, and an exhibition on English landscape design.
Open April-1 Nov, Apr & Oct daily 10.30-5pm. May-Sept daily 10.30-6pm. Last admission one hour before closing.
£2.80 (ch £1.40). Family £7.
P & *(runaround vehicle available) shop* ✿

RIPLEY
Ripley Castle
HG3 3AY (off A61,Harrogate to Ripon rd)
☎ 01423 770152
Fax 01423 771745
Ripley Castle has been home to the Ingilby family since 1320, and stands in a delightful estate with deer park, lake and walled gardens. Groups and tours are invited to experience centuries of English history through the lives of the Ingilby family. The Castle has a rich history and a fine collection of Royalist armour housed in the 1555 tower. Friendly informative tours bring the passage of time to life. There are also walled gardens, tropical hot houses, woodland walks, pleasure grounds and the National Hyacinth collection in spring.
Open Apr, May & Oct, Sat & Sun, Good Fri & BH 11.30-4.30; Jun & Sep, Tue, Fri, Sat & Sun 11.30-4.30; Jul-Aug, daily 11.30-4.30. Gardens, Mar, Thu-Sun, 11-4; Apr-Oct, daily 11-5; Nov-23 Dec, daily 11-3.30. Parties any day (ex 25 Dec) by arrangement.
P 🍽 & *toilets for disabled shop garden centre* ✿ *(ex guide dogs)*
Details not confirmed for 1998
Cards: 🌑 ⬛ 🔲 ⬛ 🟢

RIPON
Fountains Abbey & Studley Royal
HG4 3DY (4m W off B6265)
☎ 01765 608888 Fax 01765 608889
Founded by Cistercian monks in 1132, Fountains Abbey is the largest monastic ruin in Britain. It was acquired by William Aislabie in 1768, and became the focal point of his landscaped gardens at Studley. These include formal water gardens, ornamental temples, follies and magnificent views. They are bordered by a lake and 400 acres of deer park. Other interesting features include Fountains Hall, built between 1598 and 1611 using the stone from the abbey ruins.
Open all year. Jan-Mar,Oct-Dec 10-5;Apr-Sep 10-7;closed at dusk if earlier. Last admissions 1hr before closing time(ex visitor centre,restaurant & shop in Sep,closes at 5).Closed 24-25Dec,Fri in Nov,Dec,Jan.Estate closes early 10 & 11 July and 8 Aug.
£4.20 (ch £2). Family ticket £10.
P 🍽 ✗ *licensed* & *toilets for disabled shop* ✿

Norton Conyers
HG4 5EQ (from A61, Ripon to Thirsk, left at top of hill just ouside Ripon onto Wath/West Tanfield rd.)
☎ 01765 640333
Fax 01765 601389
This late medieval house with Stuart and Georgian additions has belonged to the Grahams since 1624. The pictures and furniture reflect over 370 years of occupation by the same family. It was visited by James I, Charles I and James II. Another visitor was Charlotte Brontë: a family legend of a mad woman confined in the attics is said to have given her the idea for the mad Mrs Rochester in *Jane Eyre*, and Norton Conyers was an inspiration for Mr Rochester's Thornfield Hall. Family costumes are on display in one of the bedrooms. Please note that ladies are requested not to wear stiletto-heeled shoes. The 18th century walled garden, with its herbaceous borders, small pond and Orangery, is about 100 metres from the house. Garden will be open in aid of the National Gardens Scheme (7 June), and other charity events take place in June/July.
Open - House BH Sun & Mon: Sun 7 June-13 Sept: daily 20-25 July 2pm-5pm. Garden: BH Sun & Mon 12 Apr-13 Sept, 11.30am-5pm: also daily 20-25 July 2pm-5pm.
£2.95 (ch 10-16 £2.50, pen, student, UB40 & disabled £2). Party 20+. Garden entry is free (with donations welcome), although a charge is made at garden chairty openings.
P & *(ramp at entrance) toilets for disabled shop* ✿ *(ex in grounds)*

SALTBURN-BY-THE-SEA
Saltburn Smugglers
Ship Inn TS12 1HF (adjoining Ship Inn, on A174)
☎ 01287 625252
The Saltburn Smugglers re-creates the 18th-century Ship Inn using a series of authentic room settings with sound and lighting effects to tell the story of smuggling on the Cleveland coast. There is a tourist information centre and a souvenir shop.
Open all year, Etr-Sep, daily 10-6; Oct-Etr wknds 10.30-4.
£1.65 (concessions £1.50). Family ticket £4.35. Party.
P *(200 mtrs) (charged)* & *shop* ✿

SCARBOROUGH
Scarborough Castle
YO1 1HY (E of town centre)
☎ 01723 372451
The ruins of Scarborough Castle stand on a narrow headland which was once the site of British and Roman encampments. The curtain wall was probably built several decades before the square keep, which dates from about 1155. The shell of the keep, the 13th-century Barbican and remains of medieval chapels and a house is all that remains of this fine fortress.

Once a stronghold against all-comers, the substantial ruins of Richmond Castle still look daunting as they perch high above the River Swale.

Open all year, Apr-Oct, daily 10-6 (or dusk if earlier); Nov-Mar, Wed-Sun, 10-4 (or dusk if earlier, closed 1-2pm). Closed 24-26 Dec & 1 Jan.
£2.20 (ch £1.10, concession £1.70).
P *(100 yds)* & *(ex in keep)* ✚

SKINNINGROVE
Tom Leonard Mining Museum
Deepdale TS13 4AP (just off A174 between Middlesbrough and Whitby)
☎ 01287 642877
The museum offers visitors an exciting and authentic underground experience on the site of the old Loftus mine, and a chance to see how the stone was drilled, charged with explosives and fired. Exhibits include a collection of original tools, lamps, safety equipment, old photographs and domestic objects, providing a glimpse of mining life both above and below ground.
Open Apr-Oct, daily 1-5 (last admission 3.45pm). Nov-Mar, schools & parties only. Parties by arrangement.
£1.25 (ch 75p). Pre booked parties 12+.
P *shop* ✿

SKIPTON
Skipton Castle
BD23 1AQ
☎ 01756 792442
Fax 01756 796100
Skipton is one of the most complete and well-preserved medieval castles in England. Some of the castle dates from the 1650s when it was rebuilt after being partially damaged following the Civil War. However, the original castle was erected in Norman times, and the gateway with its Norman Arch still exists. The castle became the home of the Clifford family in 1310 and remained so until 1676. Entrance to the castle is through a massive round-towered gateway with the family motto 'Desormais' carved above it. The main buildings inside the walls are surrounded by well-kept lawns and cobblestones. Conduit Court is especially attractive with its ancient yew tree. Illustrated tour sheets are available in English, French, German, Dutch, Italian, Spanish, Japanese or Esperanto. A recent addition is the delightful picnic area with views over Skipton and the woods, situated on the terrace behind the 13th century Chapel of St John the Evangelist, which is now partly restored.
Open all year, daily from 10am (Sun noon). Last admission 6pm (4pm Oct-Feb). (Closed 25 Dec).
£3.80 (inc illustrated tour sheet) (ch under 18 £1.90, under 5 free, over 60 £3.20). Family ticket £10.40. Party 15+.
P *shop*
Cards: 🌑 ⬛ 🔲 ⬛ 🟢

SUTTON-ON-THE-FOREST
Sutton Park
YO6 1DP (on B1363).
☎ 01347 810249 811239
Fax 01347 811251
The early Georgian house contains fine furniture, paintings and porcelain. The grounds have superb, award-winning terraced gardens, a lily pond and a Georgian ice house; walled-in pond garden opened in 1995. There are also delightful woodland walks as well as spaces for caravans.
Open - Gardens Etr-end Sept, daily 11am-5pm. House open Etr Sun & Mon and all BHs Sun & Mon. Private parties any day by appointment.
Gardens only £2 (ch 50p, pen £1.50). House & Gardens (BH) £4 (ch £2.50, pen £3.50)
P 🍽 & *shop* ✿ *(ex gardens)*

WHITBY
Whitby Abbey
(on clifftop E of Whitby town centre)
☎ 01947 603568
Dominating the skyline above the fishing port of Whitby are the ruins of the 13th-century Benedictine abbey. The stone abbey was erected on the site of the wooden abbey of St Hilda, which was built in 657. It was badly damaged by shellfire during World War I.
Open all year, Apr-Sep, daily 10-6; Oct-Mar, daily 10-4 or dusk if earlier. Closed 24-26 Dec & 1 Jan.
✳£1.70 (ch 90p, concessions £1.30).
P *(charged) shop* ✚

Built by the most powerful of the many medieval guilds in York, the Merchant Adventurer's Hall is one of the finest guild halls in Europe.

YORK

The ARC
St Saviourgate YO1 2NN
☎01904 654324 01904 643211
Fax 01904 640029
The ARC is a 'hands-on' experience of archaeology, enjoyed by visitors of all ages. It is housed in the beautifully restored medieval church of St Saviour. Be an archaeologist yourself! Sift through the remains of centuries - bones, shell, pottery and much more. Piece together the lives of our ancestors. Solve the puzzle of how to open a Viking padlock, decipher Viking-age writing or learn to make a Roman shoe. Real archaeologists are on hand to assist you with your discoveries. A range of special events and exhibitions of archaeological interest are held throughout the year.
Open Mon-Fri 10-4, Sat 1-4. (Closed 15 Dec-2 Jan).
✸*£3.50 (concessions £2.75).*
P (50yds) & (induction loop) toilets for disabled shop ✤
Cards: ▬

Borthwick Institute of Historical Research
St Anthony's Hall, Peasholme Green YO1 2PW
☎01904 642315
Originally built in the second half of the 15th century for the Guild of St Anthony, the hall, with its fine timber roof, was later used as an arsenal, a workhouse, a prison and the Bluecoat School from 1705 to 1946. Now part of York University, it houses ecclesiastical archives and exhibitions of documents.
Open all year, Mon-Fri 9.30-1 & 2-5. (Closed Etr & Xmas).
Free.
✤ ▦

City Art Gallery
Exhibition Square YO1 2EW
☎01904 551861
Fax 01904 551866
Six hundred years of painting, from early Italian gold-ground panels to the art of the 20th century. Exceptional in its range and interest, the collection includes works by Parmigianino and Bellotto, Lely, Reynolds, Frith, Boudin, Lowry, Nash, and nudes by Etty. Outstanding collection of studio pottery. Varied and exciting programme of temporary exhibitions and events, gallery shop and facilities for the disabled.
Open all year, Mon-Sat 10-5, Sun 2.30-5, last admission 4.30 (Closed Good Fri, 25-26 Dec & 1 Jan).
P (500mtrs) & (chairlift) toilets for disabled shop ✤
Details not confirmed for 1998

Clifford's Tower
Tower St YO1 1SA
☎01904 646940
Known as Clifford's Tower, after Roger de Clifford who was hung from the castle by chains, York Castle was built in 1086 by William the Conqueror as part of his campaign to subdue the Saxons. He built a large mound, topped with a wooden castle, on the banks of the River Ouse. In 1190 it was burned down when the Jews of York hid in it during the pogrom. Under the reign of King John it was rebuilt in stone and it was completed in 1313. However the castle cracked from top to bottom in 1360, as a result of part of the mound subsiding into the moat. From the end of the 15th century the tower was largely unused. Since 1825 Clifford's Tower has been part of the prison and is now looked after by English Heritage. The wall walk provides one of the best views of York.
Open all year, Apr-Oct, daily 10-6 (or dusk if earlier); Jul & Aug 9.30-7; Nov-mid Mar, daily 10-4 or dusk if earlier. Closed 24-26 Dec & 1 Jan.
£1.70 (ch 90p, concessions £1.30).
Ⓟ ✤ ▦ ♯

Fairfax House
Castlegate YO1 1RN (city centre, close to Jorvik Centre and Cliffords Tower)
☎01904 655543 Fax 01904 652262
An outstanding mid-18th-century house with a richly decorated interior, Fairfax House was acquired by the York Civic Trust in 1983 and restored. Prior to this it had been used as a cinema and a dance hall. The house contains fine examples of Georgian furniture, porcelain, paintings and clocks which form the Terry Collection. This collection was donated by Mr Noel Terry who was the great grandson of Joseph Terry the founder of the York-based confectionery business. There is a special display of a recreated meal dating from 1763 in the dining room and kitchen. The special annual Christmas exhibition, *The Keeping of Christmas*, will be held from 3 December to 6 January. Provisional event: 'Highlights from the Gilbert Collection' - a gold & silver touring exhibition (Sept-Oct). Ring for more details.
Open 20 Feb-5 Jan, Mon-Sat 11-5, (Closed Fri). Sun 1.30-5. Last admission 4.30pm.
£3.50 (ch £1.50, pen & student £3)
P (50yds) (3hr short stay) & (with assistance, phone before visit) shop ✤

Friargate Museum
Lower Friargate YO1 1SL (city centre)
☎01904 658775 Fax 01279 842305
The award-winning Friargate - the most popular family museum in York, and recently featured on Children's ITV - is celebrated for its role in bringing history to life. Over 70 lifesize waxwork figures are exhibited in carefully reconstructed, realistic sets, showing scenes such as Drake and the Armada, the Dukes of York, and the Crown Jewels. There is even a lifelike Yeti or 'Abominable Snowman' for the very brave - sound effects as well! Special drawing and photography facilities are available.
Open Mar-Oct, daily 10-5; Nov-Feb, 10-dusk. (Closed Jan & 25 Dec).
P (0.5m) & (touch tours for the blind) shop
Details not confirmed for 1998

Guildhall
Off Coney St YO1 1QN
☎01904 613161 Fax 01904 552015
The present Hall dates from 1446 but in 1942 an air raid virtually destroyed the building. The present Guildhall was carefully restored as an exact replica and was re-opened in 1960. There is an interesting arch-braced roof decorated with colourful bosses and supported by 12 solid oak pillars.
Although many of the windows in the Guildhall were unglazed until the 18th century, the west window contains stained-glass from 1682, by a York craftsman, and there is also a superb, modern stained glass window by Henry Harvey. This depicts the story of York through the ages. The Inner Chamber adjoining the Hall has two secret doors and a passageway beneath the Guildhall to the river.
Open all year, May-Oct, Mon-Fri 9-5, Sat 10-5, Sun 2-5; Nov-Apr, Mon-Fri 9-5.(Closed Good Fri, Spring BH, 25-26 Dec & 1 Jan).
Free.
P & (electric chair lift/ramps) toilets for disabled ✤ (ex guide dogs) ▦

Jorvik Viking Centre
Coppergate YO1 1NT
☎01904 643211 Fax 01904 627097
Jorvik was the Viking name for York. Between 1976 and 1981 archaeologists made some remarkable discoveries about Jorvik, during a dig in an area known as Coppergate. In 1984 the Viking Centre was opened over the site of the original excavations. The dig shed was a totally new light on the Viking way of life and has revealed many details of tools, clothing, crafts and trade. The Centre displays the archaeological remains - leather, textiles, metal objects and even timber buildings - in a detailed and vivid reconstruction. First there is an audio-visual display to explain exactly who the Vikings were. Then, 'time-cars' carry visitors through a 'time tunnel' from World War II back to Norman times and then to a full-scale reconstruction of 10th-century Coppergate. The busy street scene includes a crowded market, a river wharf with a fully-rigged sailing ship and a family at home. This is all made more authentic by voices speaking in Old Norse and even smells such as cooking, fish, pigsties and rubbish. Finally the tour passes through a reconstruction of Coppergate during the dig of the 1970s. The visit ends in the Skipper Gallery which has a display of some of the 15,000 small objects found during the dig. The Jorvik Festival (February) features longship races, combat re-enactment, crafts displays, torchlit procession and boat burning ceremony. Various special events. Please telephone for details.
Open all year, Apr-Oct daily 9-5.30; Nov-Mar daily 9-3.30. (Closed 25 Dec). Under review.
✸*£4.95 (ch 5-15 £3.50. under 5 free. student/pen £4.60 (proof of status required)) Family £16.*
P (400 yds) (limited to 3 hours) & (time car designed to take a wheelchair) toilets for disabled shop ✤
Cards: ▣ ▬ ⑤

Merchant Adventurers' Hall
Fossgate YO1 2XD
☎01904 654818 Fax 01904 654818
The medieval guild hall of the powerful Merchant Adventurers' Company was built 1357/1361 and is one of the finest in Europe. The Great Hall, where the merchants conducted their business affairs, contains early furniture, one piece dating from the 13th century, paintings, silver, weights and measures, and other objects used by the merchants over the centuries. The building also has an Undercroft where they cared for the poor, a Chapel, and a Jacobean addition for the caretaker.
Open all year, end Mar-early Nov, daily 8.30-5; early Nov-late Mar, Mon-Sat 8.30-3.30. (Closed 10 days Xmas).
£1.90 (ch 7-17 50p, ad over 62 £1.60)
P & toilets for disabled

National Railway Museum
Leeman Rd YO2 4XJ
☎01904 621261
Fax 01904 611112
Your ticket for the National Railway Museum will take you on a spectacular journey through the life and history of railways. A unique collection of engines, trains, paintings and photographs, supported by special exhibitions and interactive displays are a celebration of a revolution that swept the world. Travel back to 1829 and be amazed by the inventive brilliance that made 'Rocket' one of the world's most famous steam locomotives. Experience the golden age of steam travel from our platforms where station sound effects recreate the busy and exciting atmosphere of another era. Queen Victoria's luxurious royal carriage awaits you in all its regal splendour. Come face-to-face with the mighty 'Mallard' - holder of the steam world speed record at 126mph, then speed right up-to-date in front of a life-size section of the Channel Tunnel and mock-up of Eurostar. Many events and exhibitions are planned for 1998, please telephone for details.
Open all year, Mon-Sun 10-6,(Closed 24-26 Dec).
✸*£4.80 (ch 5-16 £2.70, concessions £3.20) Family £13.50. Under 5's free.*
Ⓟ (charged) ♨ ✗ licensed & ("Please Touch" evenings) toilets for disabled shop ✤
Cards: ▣ ▬ ▬ ▨ ⑤

St Williams College
5 College St YO1 2JF (adjacent to York Minster at east end)
☎01904 637134
Fax 01904 654604
St William's College, a 15th-century timber-framed building, housed chantry priests until 1549. It now contains York Minster's Visitor Centre and Conference Centre, shop, restaurant and the medieval rooms are open to view when not being used for functions. Craft Fairs most weekends.

Open all year 10-5 for viewing of medieval rooms subject to private bookings - phone for details. Closed 24-26 Dec & Good Fri.
P ☕ ✗ *licensed shop* ❀
Details not confirmed for 1998

Treasurer's House
Chapter House St YO1 2JD
☎01904 624247 Fax 01904 647372
There has been a house on this site since Roman times and in the basement of this elegant 17th-century building is an exhibition of its history. The house was improved during the 18th century with the addition of a fine staircase. Restored between 1897 and 1930, it was left, with its fine furniture, to the National Trust.
Open 28 Mar-1 Nov, daily except Friday. 10.30-5pm. Last admission 4.30pm.
£3.50 (ch £1.95). Family ticket £8.
P *(400 yds)* ✗ *licensed* ❀ ♿

York Castle Museum
The Eye of York Y01 IRY (city centre,next to Clifford's Tower)
☎01904 653611 Fax 01904 671078
Fascinating exhibits that bring memories to life, imaginatively displayed through reconstructions of period rooms and two indoor streets, complete with cobbles, a Hansom cab and a park. The museum is housed in the city's former prison and is based on an extensive collection of 'bygones' acquired at the beginning of the century. It was one of the first folk museums to display a huge range of everyday objects in an authentic scene. The Victorian street includes a pawnbroker, a tallow candle factory and a haberdasher's. There is even a reconstruction of the original sweet shop of the York chocolate manufacturer, Joseph Terry. An extensive collection of many other items ranging from musical instruments to costumes and a gallery of domestic gadgets from Victorian times to the 1960s (entitled 'Every home should have one') are further attractions to this remarkable museum. The museum also has one of Britain's finest collections of Militaria; this includes a superb example of an Anglo-Saxon helmet - one of only three known. A special exhibition called 'Seeing it Through' explores the life of York citizens during the Second World War. The museum includes the cell where highwayman Dick Turpin was held. Please contact the museum for deatils of exhibition and events.
Open all year, Apr-Oct Mon-Sat 9.30-5.30, Sun 10-5.30; Nov-Mar, Mon-Sat 9.30-4, Sun 10-4. (Closed 25-26 Dec & 1 Jan).
£4.50 (ch, pen, students & UB40 £3.15). Family ticket £13.50. Party 10+.
☕ ♿ *toilets for disabled shop* ❀
Cards: ◪ ▨ ▨ ▨ ▨ ⑤

The York Dungeon
12 Clifford St YO1 1RD
☎01904 632599 Fax 01904 612602
Deep in the heart of historic York, buried beneath it's very paving stones, lies the North's most chillingly famous museum of horror. The York Dungeon brings more than 2,000 years of gruesomely authentic history vividly back to life...and death. As you delve into the darkest chapters of our grim and bloody past, recreated in all its dreadful detail remember - everything you experience really happened... A warning - in the dungeon's dark catacombs it always pays to keep your wits about you. The 'exhibits' have an unnerving habit of coming back to life...
Open all year, daily 10-5.30 (4.30 Oct-Mar).Closed 25 Day.
£4.50 (ch £2.95,students & pen £3.50).
P *(500yds)* ♿ *shop*
Cards: ◪ ▨ ▨ ▨ ▨ ▨ ⑤

York Minster
Deangate YO1 2HG
☎01904 639347
Fax 01904 613049
It is believed that Edwin King of Northumbria built the first church on this site in 627. Since then both Saxons and Normans built cathedrals here, and parts of the latter survive in many places in the present structure. From 1220 to 1472 the present church was built to replace the romanesque one. It is notable for its size - the largest medieval church north of the Alps - and for its wealth of stained glass, most of which is original to the building. Daily worship has been conducted on this site for 13 centuries.
Open daily, Mon-Sat 7-6 (later in summer), Sun after 1pm.
Free admission but following parts charged; Foundations & Treasury £1.80 (ch 70p, pen & students £1.50); Chapter House 70p (ch 30p); Central Tower £2 (ch £1); Crypt 60p (ch 30p).
P *(440yds)* ♿ *(loop system, tactile model, braille guide) toilets for disabled shop* ❀

York Model Railway
Tearoom Square, York Station YO2 2AB (next to York Station)
☎01904 630169
One of the biggest and best model railways in Britain, York Model Railway has two very intricate railway layouts. The larger one is set in town and country landscapes. It comprises hundreds of buildings, about 5500 tiny trees, over 2000 lights and around 2500 people and animals. As many as 14 trains can run in this model at the same time, including the Royal Train, the Orient Express, Inter City 125 and the latest freight and passenger trains. The second model is a much smaller layout and shows a typical German town at night, brightly lit by numerous tiny lights. There are push buttons for children, amid these detailed and accurate scale models, and the Thomas the Tank Engine section will appeal to children of all ages.
Open daily, Mar-Oct 9.30-6, Nov-Feb 10.30-5 (Closed 25-26 Dec).
P *(100 yds)* ♿ *shop*
Details not confirmed for 1998
Cards: ◪ ▨

Yorkshire Museum & Gardens
Museum Gardens YO1 2DR (Park & Ride services operate from 3 sites near A64 and A19)
☎01904 629745 Fax 01904 651221
The winner of a European award, Yorkshire Museum - set in 10 acres of botanical gardens in the heart of the historic city of York - displays some of the finest Roman, Anglo-Saxon, Viking and Medieval treasures ever discovered in Britain. The Middleham jewel, a fine example of English Gothic jewellery, is on display in the Medieval Gallery and, in the Roman Gallery, visitors can see a fine marble head of Constantine the Great, household utensils exhibited in a recreated kitchen and many other artefacts. The Anglo-Saxon Gallery houses the magnificent, delicate silver-gilt Ormside bowl and the skilfully wrought Gilling sword. The Museum also has a fine collection of Rockingham porcelain. Part of York's Roman city walls runs through the Museum Gardens where, amongst a variety of flora and fauna, you can visit a working observatory and the ruins of the medieval St Mary's Abbey with its 14th-century guesthouse - the oldest timber-framed structure in Yorkshire. Special exhibitions this year include Claws - about both big cats and domestic pets (from Apr), and Upright Ape - about the origins of mankind (from late 1998).
Open all year, Apr-Oct, daily 10-5; Nov-Mar, Mon-Sat 10-5, Sun 1-5. Last admission 4.30.
£3.50 (concessions £2.25) Family ticket £10.50.
P *(5 mins walk)* ♿ *(ramps & lift) toilets for disabled shop* ❀
Cards: ◪ ▨ ▨ ▨ ⑤

The York Story
St Mary's, Castlegate YO1 1RN (city centre, near Jorvik Centre)
☎01904 628632
The Heritage Centre is in the predominately 15th-century church of St Mary which has the tallest spire in York, at 152ft. The venue is due to be refurbished as a temporary exhibition centre for major travelling exhibitions. It will reopen to the public in early 1998. Please telephone for details.
Open all year, Mon-Sat 10-5 (Wed 10.30-5), Sun 1-5. (Closed 25-26 Dec & 1 Jan). Subject to closure due to refurbishment.
£1.80 (ch, pen, students & UB40's £1.25). Joint ticket with York Story & York Castle Museum £5. Family ticket £13.50.
P *(1 min walk)* ♿ *shop* ❀

YORKSHIRE, SOUTH

BARNSLEY
Monk Bretton Priory
(1m E of Barnsley town centre, off A633)
☎01226 204089
The priory was an important Cluniac house, founded in 1135. The considerable remains of the gatehouse, church and other buildings can be seen, and include some well-preserved drains.
Open all year, Apr-Sep, daily 10-6; Oct, 10-4; Nov-Mar, Wed-Sun 10-4 or dusk if earlier. (Closed 24-26 Dec & 1 Jan). Free.
☐ ♿ ♯

CONISBROUGH
Conisbrough Castle
DN12 3HH (NE of town centre off A630)
☎01709 863329
The splendid 12th-century keep is the oldest in England and one of the best preserved buildings of the period. It is circular with six buttresses - a unique design - and is surrounded by a curtain wall with solid round towers. The castle features in Sir Walter Scott's *Ivanhoe*.
Open all year, Apr-Sep, Mon-Fri 10-5, Sat & Sun 10-6; Oct-Mar, daily 10-4. Closed 25 Dec & 1 Jan.
£2.50 (ch £1, concessions £1.75).
☐ ♿ ❀ ♯

CUSWORTH
The Museum of South Yorkshire Life
Cusworth H Hall
DN5 7TU
☎01302 782342 Fax 01302 782342
The Museum of South Yorkshire is located in Cusworth Hall, an 18th-century country house set in a landscaped park. It has displays which illustrate the way local people here lived, worked and entertained themselves over the last 200 years.
Open all year, Mon-Fri 10-5, Sat 11-5 & Sun 1-5. (4pm Dec & Jan) (Closed Good Fri, Xmas & 1 Jan). Free.
☐ ♿ *(wheelchair available) toilets for disabled shop* ❀

DONCASTER
Brodsworth Hall
Brodsworth DN5 7XJ (between A635 & A638)
☎01302 722598 Fax 01302 337165
Brodsworth Hall is a remarkable example of a Victorian country house which has survived largely intact. The faded grandeur of the family rooms contrast with the well organised, if spartan, servant's wing. The Victorian gardens are in perfect proportion to the house.
Open Apr-Nov, Tue-Sun & BH's; gardens and tea rooms noon-6, house 1-6 (last admission 5pm); Group visits mornings by appointment. 7 Nov-28 Mar, 11-4, gardens & shops only.
Hall and gardens £4.50 (ch £2.30, concessions £3.40). Gardens only (summer) £2.50 (ch 1.30, concessions £1.90). Gardens only (winter) £1.50 (ch 80p, concessions £1.10)
☐ ☕ ♿ *toilets for disabled shop* ❀ ♯
Cards: ◪ ▨ ▨ ▨ ⑤

Doncaster Museum & Art Gallery
Chequer Rd DN1 2AE (off inner ring road)
☎01302 734293 Fax 01302 735409
The wide-ranging collections include fine and decorative art and sculpture. There are also ceramics, glass, silver, and displays on history, archaeology and natural history. The historical collection of the Kings Own Yorkshire Infantry is housed here, and temporary exhibitions are held. A wide variety of temporary exhibitions are planned for 1998. Please telephone for details.
Open all year, Mon-Sat 10-5, Sun 2-5. (Closed Good Fri, 25-26 Dec & 1 Jan). Free.
☐ ♿ *(lift) toilets for disabled shop* ❀

MALTBY
Roche Abbey
S66 8NW (1.5m S off A634)
☎01709 812739
The walls of the south and north transepts still stand to their full height in this 12th-century Cistercian abbey, providing a dramatic sight for the visitor. There is also a fine gatehouse to the north-west.
Open Apr-Oct, daily 10-6 (dusk if earlier).
£1.50 (ch 80p, concessions £1.10).
☐ ♿ ♯

ROTHERHAM
Museum
Clifton Park, Clifton Ln S65 2AA (situated in Clifton Park. Follow directions to inner ring road)
☎01709 382121 ext 3635
Fax 01709 823631
Housed in a mansion designed by John Carr, the museum is noted for its collection of Rockingham china. Other attractions include the 18th-century rooms, family portraits, the period kitchen, and Victoriana. Regular programme of temporary exhibitions, including 'The Rotherham People's Show' (9 May-30 Aug), 'From Flowers to Fungi - an exhibition of Botanical Art' (12 Sep-1 Nov), 'Photographs of Frank Meadow Sutcliffe', (14 Nov-3 Jan). Please telephone for details.
Open all year, Mon-Thu & Sat 10-5, Sun 2.30-5 (4.30pm Oct-Mar). Closed Xmas & New Year. Free.
☐ ♿ *toilets for disabled shop* ❀

One of the more fearsome exhibits at the Museum of Film, Photography & Television in Bradford

SHEFFIELD

Sheffield was a thriving town, famous for its cutlery, even before Chaucer's time in the 14th century. The site of the Norman castle overlooking the River Don is now occupied by the Castle Market. Industrial prosperity gave the area several dignified Georgian buildings but, unfortunately not a lot remains from before World War II when the city was severely bombed. It is still a prosperous city and its busy modern heart still finds time and space to recall the history of the steel-making which earned the city a worldwide reputation, and to display with pride some of the finest wares produced in its factories over the years.

Bishops House
Meersbrook Park, Norton Lees Ln S8 9BE (2 miles South of Sheffield, on A61 Chesterfield road)
☎0114 255 7701
This 15th-and 16th-century yeoman's house has been restored and opened as a museum of local and social history. Several rooms have been furnished and there are displays of life in Tudor and Stuart times as well as a range of temporary exhibitions. Special educational facilities can be arranged for schools and colleges. Events for 1998 - Plastics - an exhibition examining their history and development in everyday life (Mar-Jul), Armada! - A living history presentation (Jun). Please ring for details.
Open all year, Wed-Sat 10-4.30, Sun 11-4.30; also BH Mon 10-4.30. Some summer closures. (closed 25-29 Dec & 1 Jan). Phone to check opening times.
£1 (ch & pen 50p, UB40's free).
&. shop ✇

City Museum & Mappin Art Gallery
Weston Park S10 2TP (on A57)
☎0114 276 8588
Fax 0114 275 0957
The museum houses exhibits on regional geology, natural history and archaeology, especially from the Peak District. There is a particularly splendid display of cutlery

and Sheffield plate, for which the city is famous, among exhibits on other local industries such as ceramics, clocks, watches and sundials. Educational facilities are available for schools and colleges. The Mappin Art Gallery, housed in a Victorian listed building, organises a programme of temporary exhibitions with emphasis on Contemporary Art and Victorian paintings. Special events: 'Ancient Eygpt: Discovery, Art, and Influence' (til 6 Sep). Series of exhibitions for Photo 98. Major exhibition on Sheffield sculptor George Fullard (9 May-26 Jul), also David Mellor 'Master of Metalwork' (14 Nov-Jan), and there is a new display 'Sheffield - the Ice Age'.
Open all year, Wed-Sat 10-5, Sun 11-5 also BH Mons. (Closed 23 Dec-1 Jan). Please telephone to check opening times.
Free, but charged for special events.
✇ &. (Inductive loop. Handling sessions for pre-booked groups) toilets for disabled shop ✇

Kelham Island Industrial Museum
Alma St S3 8RY (0.5m NW of city centre, take A61 N to West Bar)
☎0114 272 2106
Fax 0114 275 7847
The story of Sheffield, its industry and life. See the mighty River Don Engine 'in steam', the most powerful working steam engine in Europe, reconstructed workshops, working cutler and craftspeople demonstrating traditional 'made in Sheffield' skills - how people lived and worked, a 'living' museum. Displays and an audio visual presentation showing the people and skills that made the City of Sheffield. During the year Kelham Island stages events, displays and temporary exhibitions for the additional interest of visitors, culminating in the annual Christmas Victorian Market. The Museum welcomes families, schools and groups (educational support and classroom available). The Museum can be hired for evening visits and receptions, and a meeting/seminar room is available.
Open Mon-Thu 10-4, Sun 11-4.45.Closed Fri and Sat.
P ✇ &. (wheelchair on request) toilets for disabled shop ✇
Details not confirmed for 1998

YORKSHIRE, WEST

BRADFORD
Bradford, with Leeds and Calderdale, has been associated with wool since medieval times, and the developing techniques of its industry are graphically recreated in the 'living museums'. The city, which became the wool-cloth (worsted) capital of the world in the 19th century, boasts a small cathedral famed for the woolpacks that were hung over the tower to protect it from cannonballs during the Civil War and a magnificent 19th-century Town Hall. Bradford also made railway equipment, cars, trams and motorcycles. The same dynamic spirit that built up the textile industry inspired the establishment in Bradford of the National Museum of Photography, Film and Television and built up Bradford to be a major centre for tourism.

Bolling Hall
Bowling Hall Rd BD4 7LP (1m from city centre off A650)
☎01274 723057
Fax 01274 726220
A classic West Yorkshire manor house, complete with galleried 'housebody' (hall), Bolling Hall dates mainly from the 17th century but has medieval and 18th-century sections. It has panelled rooms, plasterwork in original colours, heraldic glass and a rare Chippendale bed. There is also a 'ghost room'.
Open all year, Wed-Fri 11am-4pm, Sat 10am-5pm, Sun 12pm-5pm. (Closed Mon ex BH, Good Fri, 25 & 26 Dec).
Free.
P &. shop ✇

Bradford Industrial Museum and Horses at Work
Moorside Rd, Eccleshill BD2 3HP (off A658)
☎01274 631756
Fax 01274 636362
Moorside Mills is an original spinning mill, now part of a museum that brings vividly to life the story of the woollen industry in Bradford. The magnificent machinery that once converted raw wool into finest cloth is on display and the mill yard rings with sound of iron on stone as shire horses pull trams, haul buses, or give rides. The mill owner's house beside the mill is also open and gives an idea of domestic life around 1900 and the back-to-back cottages of Gaythorne Row, just across the street, show how the textile workers would have lived from the late 19th century until the 1950s. There are changing exhibitions and daily demonstrations.
Open all year, Tue-Sat 10-5, Sun 12-5. (Closed Mon ex BH)
Free. Charges made for rides.
P ✇ &. (induction loop in lecture theatre) toilets for disabled shop ✇

Cartwright Hall Art Gallery
Lister Park BD9 4NS (1m from city centre on A650)
☎01274 493313
Fax 01274 481045
Built in dramatic Baroque style in 1904, this art gallery has permanent collections of 19th-and 20th-century British art, contemporary prints, and older works by British and European masters, including the 'Brown Boy' by Reynolds.
Open all year Apr-Sep, Tue-Sat 10-5, Sun 1-5. (Closed Mon ex BH, Good Fri, 25 & 26 Dec).
Free.
✇ &. (wheelchair available) toilets for disabled shop ✇

Colour Museum
1 Providence St BD1 2PW (from city centre follow signs B6144(Haworth)then follow brown tourist information signs)
☎01274 390955 Fax 01274 392888
Britain's only Museum of Colour comprises two galleries packed with visitor-operated exhibits demonstrating the effects of light and colour, including optical illusions, and the story of dyeing and textile printing. It even offers the chance to take charge of a modern dye-making factory and to try computer-aided exterior and interior design. There is a programme of special exhibitions and events. Please telephone for details.
Open all year, Tue-Fri 2-5, Sat 10-4. Booked parties Tue-Fri mornings. (Closed Sun, Mon & BH's). Hours may be extended during School Hols, phone for details.
✳£1.50 (concessions £1). Family ticket £3.75.
P (300 yds) &. (lift from street level) toilets for disabled shop ✇
Cards: ▨ ▦

National Museum of Photography, Film & Television
Pictureville BD1 1NQ
☎01274 727488 Fax 01274 394540
The National Museum of Photography, Film and Television portrays the past, present and future of the media using interactive displays and dramatic reconstructions - ride on a magic carpet, become a newsreader for the day or try your hand at vision mixing. Action Replay, the Museum's own theatre company, regularly performs highlights from the galleries. At the heart of the Museum is IMAX, the UK's largest cinema screen, which is over five storeys high. Vast, brilliant images sweep you into another world, exploring the realms of space to the depths of the ocean or indeed any subject big enough to be turned into this extraordinary experience. Pictureville Cinema houses the only public, wide-screen cinerama in the world.
Open all year, Tue-Sun & BH's 10-6. (Closed Mon).
Museum free, IMAX Cinema £3.90 (concessions £2.70).
P (NCP next door) ✇ &. toilets for disabled shop ✇

Transperience
Transperience Way BD12 7HQ
☎01274 690909
At Transperience, the history of transportation is never a dull subject. As you travel on historic vehicles on the Translink system and delve in the story of public transport, you can feel, hear and actually smell what was once considered to be the height of innovation. Test your hand at driving a tram, trolleybus, motorbus or train on the vehicle simulators. There are hi-tech multi-screen productions featuring state-of-the-art lighting and animations, plus an Adventure Park and five exhibition halls to explore. Student parties are welcome and there is an in-house Education Officer.
Open daily Apr-Sep 10.30-5.30; Oct-Mar 10-4.30. Closed 25-26 Dec.
P ✇ ✗ &. (lifts, ramped surfaces) toilets for disabled shop ✇
Details not confirmed for 1998
Cards: ▨ ▦ ▦ ▦ ▧ ▨

BRAMHAM
Bramham Park
LS23 6ND (on A1 4m S of Wetherby)
☎01937 844265 Fax 01937 845923
This fine Queen Anne house was built by Robert Benson and is the home of his descendants. The garden has ornamental ponds, cascades, temples and avenues. International horse trials are held here 11-14 June.
Gardens open Etr, May Day & Spring BH wknds 1.15-5.30; House & gardens 21 Jun-6 Sep, Sun, Tue, Wed & Thu also Aug BH Mon, 1.15-5.30. (Last admission 5pm).
£4 (ch 5 £2, pen £3). Grounds only £2.50(ch 5 £1, pen £2). Party 20+.
P &. toilets for disabled ✇ (ex on lead)

BRIGHOUSE
Smith Art Gallery
Halifax Rd HD6 2EP
☎01484 719222 Fax 01484 719222
Established in 1907 with a fine collection of Victorian art, including works by Atkinson Grimshaw and Marcus Stone, the gallery displays both works from its original founding collection and exhibitions of contemporary art. Lively programme of exhibitions and shows featuring local artists and societies. Please telephone for details.
Open all year, Mon, Tue, Thur & Fri 10-12.30 & 1-6, Sat 10-12.30 & 1-4. (Closed Wed, Sun & BH's).
P (on road) & shop ✹ (ex guide dogs)
Details not confirmed for 1998
Cards: ▨ ▨

GOMERSAL
Red House
Oxford Rd BD19 4JP (on A651)
☎01274 335100 Fax 01274 335105
A delightful period house decorated as the 1830s home of a Yorkshire wool clothier and merchant. The house and family frequently visited by Charlotte Brontë in the 1830s and featured in her novel *Shirley.*
Open all year, Mon-Fri 11-5, Sat-Sun 12-5. Telephone for Xmas opening. (Closed Good Fri & 1 Jan).
Free.
P & (Braille & tape guide available) toilets for disabled shop ✹
Cards: ▨ ▨

HALIFAX
Bankfield Museum
Boothtown Rd, Akroyd Park HX3 6HG
☎01422 354823 & 352334 Fax 01422 349020
Built by Edward Akroyd in the 1860s, this Renaissance-style building is set in parkland on a hill overlooking the town. It has an outstanding collection of costumes and textiles from many periods and parts of the world, including a new gallery featuring East European textiles. There is also a section on toys, and the museum of the Duke of Wellington's Regiment is housed here. Temporary exhibitions are held and there is a lively programme of events, workshops and activities. Please apply for details.
Open all year, Tue-Sat 10-5, Sun 2-5, BH Mon 10-5.(extended closing times at Xmas and New Year, phone for details)
Free.
P & shop ✹
Cards: ▨ ▨ ▨

Calderdale Industrial Museum
Central Works, Square Rd HX1 0QG
☎01422 358087 Fax 01422 349310
Working machines representing 100 years of local industry from textiles to toffee wrapping; steam engines to washing machines. . . with all the sounds and smells to match! There is an under-6's activity area called the Workplays and also a lively programme of events, activities and workshops. Please apply for details.

Open all year, Tue-Sat 10-5, Sun 2-5 (Closed Mon ex BH's, 25-26 Dec & 1 Jan).
✿£1.60 (ch, pen & UB40 80p).
P & (lift) toilets for disabled shop ✹
Cards: ▨ ▨ ▨

Eureka! The Museum for Children
Discovery Rd HX1 2NE (M62 exit 24 follow brown tourist information signs to Halifax centre(A629))
☎01422 330069 Fax 01422 330275
Eureka! is the first 'hands on' museum in Britain designed especially for children up to the age of 12. Wherever you go in Eureka! you can touch, listen and smell, as well as look. There are four main exhibition areas - Me and My Body, Living and Working Together, Invent, Create, Communicate and Things - where visitors can find out how the human body and senses work, investigate the design and uses of everyday objects, role-play in the buildings around the Town Square and explore the world of communications from basic forms through to the hi-tech inventions of today. Outside in the Eureka! Park you can exercise on the Health Trail and enter the Hazard Dome, an audio-visual presentation with special 3-D effects about home safety. A programme of exhibitions, activities, workshops and performances runs throughout the year. 1998 will include: January - April 'Live on Air' a 40 minute workshop where visitors try their hand at putting together a radio programme. May-Aug 'Musical Structures', fascinating and fantastic large scale structures which, when tipped, struck or blown, make wonderful music. Please ring for details of these and other events.
Open all year, daily 10-5 (except 24-26 Dec)
✿£4.95 (ch 3-12 £3.95, under 3 free). Saver ticket £15.75.
P (charged) & (lift,staff trained in sign language,audio guide,workshop) shop ✹
Cards: ▨ ▨ ▨ ▨ ▨ ▨ ▨

Piece Hall
HX1 1RE
☎01422 358087 Fax 01422 349310
The merchants of Halifax built the elegant and unique hall in 1779, as a trading place for pieces of cloth. It has over 300 merchant's rooms around a courtyard, and now houses an industrial museum, art galleries and shops selling antiques, books and other specialities. There is an open market on Friday and Saturday, and a flea market on Thursday. Tourist information centre. Free entertainment most weekends and there is a lively programe of exhibitions, workshops, activities and events throughout the year. Please apply for details. Summer long festival of culture, art, theatre, music etc, ring for details.
Open all year daily 10-5 (Closed 25-26 Dec). Industrial Museum Tue-Sat 10-5, Sun 2-5. Art Gallery Tue-Sun 10-5. Free (ex small admission charge for the Industrial Museum & when special events are held).

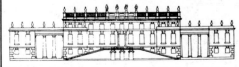

Bramham Park is a fine Queen Anne house, built in the Italianate style by Robert Benson. It stands in a park whose design was modelled on that of the Palace of Versailles.

P (50 yds) ❌ licensed & (lift to all floors) toilets for disabled shop
Cards: ▨ ▨ ▨

Shibden Hall
Lister's Rd HX3 6XG (2km E of Halifax on A58)
☎01422 352246 & 321455 Fax 01422 348440
The house dates back to the early 15th century, and its rooms have been laid out to illustrate life in different periods of its history. The vast 17th-century barn has a fine collection of horse-drawn vehicles and craft workshops such as blacksmiths and saddlers.Four craft weekends featuring over 30 craftworkers demonstrating historic skills, plus a lively programme of craft events, workshops and family activities. Please apply for details. A programme of events relating to crafts or with particular focus on family entertainment is in preparation, please telephone for details.
Open Mar-Nov, Mon-Sat 10-5, Sun 12-5. Closed December to February).
£1.60 (ch 75p,pen 80p) Family £4.50. Party,
P ❌ & shop ✹

HAREWOOD
Harewood House & Bird Garden
LS17 9LQ (junc A61/A659 Leeds/Harrogate Rd)
☎0113 288 6331 Fax 0113 288 6467
The 18th-century home of the Earl and Countess of Harewood contains fine furniture, porcelain and paintings, and its 'Capability' Brown landscaped grounds offer lakeside and woodland walks. The Bird Garden has aviaries for over 150 species. Adventure playground. Numerous special events take place throughout the year including: several exhibitions celebrating the Year of Photography, music concerts including a Jazz Festival (18-19 July) & Last Night of the Proms (6 September); Harewood Classic Car Rally (21 June) and Jaguar Rally (12 July). Also, due to popular demand, the exhibition "The Yorkshire Princess" which celebrates the life of HRH Princess Mary, is to be extended for another season. Telephone for details of these and other events.
Open 17 Mar-25 Oct, daily Bird Garden from 10am, House from 11am. Grounds & Bird Garden open wknds Nov-Dec. 'Freedom ticket'(house, grounds, bird garden, terrace gallery) £6.75 (ch/student £4.75, pen £6.) Family £21. Bird garden, grounds, terrace gallery £5.50 (ch/student £3. pen £4.50) Family £16.75, Group rate15+
P ❌ ❌ licensed & (electric ramp to front door of house) toilets for disabled shop garden centre ✹ (in gardens on lead)
Cards: ▨ ▨ ▨ ▨ ▨ ▨

HAWORTH
Brontë Parsonage Museum
BD22 8DR (on the A6033 leading from A629)
☎01535 642323 Fax 01535 647131
The Brontës were an extraordinary literary family and Haworth Parsonage was their lifelong home. The Rev Patrick Brontë, his wife Maria and their six children came to live at the parsonage in 1820. Maria and Elizabeth, the eldest girls, died here in childhood, not long after their mother. Charlotte, Branwell, Emily and Anne survived, the sisters to write some of the greatest novels in the English language. An intensely close-knit family, the Brontës saw the parsonage as the heart of their world from early childhood to the ends of their brief lives. The Yorkshire moorland setting provided them with inspiration for their writing. The house contains much personal memorabilia, including the furniture Charlotte bought with the proceeds of her literary success, her dress, bonnet and tiny shoes, the Brontë children's earliest literary efforts, their handmade 'little books', Branwell's portraits of local worthies, Emily's writing desk and Anne's books and drawings. The Brontë Society cares for the parsonage, which opened as a museum in 1928.
Open Apr-Sep, daily 10-5; Oct-Mar daily 11-4.30. (Closed 12 Jan-6 Feb & 24-27 Dec).
£3.80 (ch 5-16 £1.20, pen & students £2.80). Family ticket £8.80.
P (charged) & shop ✹

Keighley & Worth Valley Railway & Museum
Keighley, Haworth, Oxenhope & Ingrow West BD22 8NJ
☎01535 645214 & 677777 Fax 01535 647317
The line was built mainly to serve the valley's mills, and goes through the heart of Brontë country. It begins at Keighley (also a BR station), and then climbs up to Haworth, the railway workshops and headquarters. The terminus is at Oxenhope, which has a museum and restoration building. There are approximately 36 steam engines and eight diesels. Events in 1998 include: Thomas the Tank Engine (30-31 May & 6-7 June), Santa (28 Nov & 22 Dec).
All year weekend service, but daily all BH wks & Jul-1st wk Sep.
Full line ticket £5.20 reduced fares for ch & pen. Family ticket £13. Day rover(unlimited travel) £6.50,Family day rover £15. Party rates.
P (charged) ❌ & (wheelchairs can be accommodated in brake car). toilets for disabled shop
Cards: ▨ ▨ ▨

Most of Harewood House dates from the 1770's and the interior is exquisitely designed by Robert Adam, who produced a particularly fine Gallery with a 76ft long ceiling.

HUDDERSFIELD

Automobilia Transport Museum
The Heritage Centre, Leeds Rd HD1 6QA (on A62 Leeds road, 1/3 mile from Huddesfield town centre)
☎01484 559086 Fax 01484 559092
Over 100 vintage and classic vehicles on display and for sale on 2 floors. Museum area exhibits also motorcycles, bicycles, radios, enamel signs, petrol pumps, garage equipment and much more automobilia.
Open all year, Mon-Sat 9-5,Sun 11-4. Groups at other times by arrangement.
£2 (ch 5-15 £1, pen, students & UB40's £1.50). Family ticket £5.
🅿 ♿ ('hands on' for partially sighted) shop ❦

Huddersfield Art Gallery
Princess Alexandra Walk HD1 2SU
☎01484 221964 ext 1962 Fax 01484 221952
The changing displays from the permanent collection include British oil paintings, watercolours, drawings and sculpture from the mid-19th century onwards. Temporary loan art, craft and photography exhibitions are also held throughout the year. Joy Gregory - Cultural Exchange between Europe and the Caribbean (18 Apr-27 Jun), Paintings by John Ross (6 Jun-20 Jul). Phone for details.
Open all year, Mon-Fri 10-5, Sat 10-4. Closed Sun & BH's.
Free.
🅿 ♿ toilets for disabled shop ❦

Tolson Memorial Museum
Ravensknowle Park HD5 8DJ (on A629)
☎01484 223830 Fax 01484 223843
Displays on the development of the cloth industry and a collection of horse-drawn vehicles are shown, together with natural history, archaeology, toys and folk exhibits. There is a full programme of events and temporary exhibitions.
Open all year. Mon-Fri 11-5, Sat & Sun noon-5. (Closed Xmas).
🅿 ♿ toilets for disabled shop ❦
Details not confirmed for 1998

ILKLEY

Manor House Gallery & Museum
Castle Yard, Church St LS29 9DT (behind Ilkley Parish Church, on A65)
☎01943 600066 Fax 01943 817079
The Elizabethan manor house is one of Ilkley's few buildings to pre-date the 19th century. The house was built on the site of a Roman fort and part of the Roman wall can be seen, together with Roman relics and displays on archaeology. Inside there is also a collection of 17th-and 18th-century farmhouse parlour and kitchen furniture, while the art gallery exhibits works by contemporary artists and craftsmen.

Open all year, Wed-Sat 11-5, Sun 1-4. (Closed Good Fri, 25-28 Dec).
Free.
♿ shop ❦

KEIGHLEY

Cliffe Castle Museum & Gallery
Spring Gardens Ln BD20 6LH (NW of town off A629)
☎01535 618230 Fax 01535 610536
French furniture from the Victoria and Albert Museum is displayed, together with collections of local and natural history, ceramics, dolls, geological items and minerals. The grounds of this 19th-century mansion contain a play area and an aviary.
Open all year, Tue-Sat 10-5, Sun 12-5. Also open BH Mon. (Closed Good Fri, 25-28 Dec).
Free.
🅿 ♨ ♿ toilets for disabled shop ❦

East Riddlesden Hall
Bradford Rd BD20 4EA (1m NE of Keighley on south side of Bradford Rd)
☎01535 607075 Fax 01535 691462
This charming 17th-century Yorkshire manor house is typical of its kind, although the plasterwork and oak panelling are contemporary. A small secluded garden is found in the grounds, which also feature one of the largest medieval tithe barns in the north of England.
Open Apr-1 Nov, Sat-Wed & Good Friday, and Thurs in July & Aug. Sat 1-5pm, Sun and weekdays inc BH 12-5pm.last admission 4.30pm. Shop & tearoom open at 12pm.
£3.30 (ch £1.60). Family ticket £8.
🅿 ♨ ♿ shop ❦ 🐾

LEEDS

Armley Mills Industrial Museum
Canal Rd, Armley LS12 2QF (2m W of city centre, off A65)
☎0113 263 7861
Once the world's largest woollen mill, Armley Mills evokes memories of the 18th-century woollen industry, showing the progress of wool from the sheep to knitted clothing. The museum has its own 1930s cinema and illustrates the history of cinema projection, including the first moving pictures taken in Leeds, as well as 1920s silent movies. There are demonstrations of static engines and steam locomotives, a printing gallery and a journey through the working world of textiles and fashion. Telephone for details of exhibitions.
Open all year, Tue-Sat 10-5, Sun 1-5. Last entry 1 hr before closing. (Closed Mon ex BHs.)
£2 (ch 50p pen, students & UB40's £1) Season ticket £10 (concession £5,ch £2.50)
🅿 ♿ (chair-lifts between floors) toilets for disabled shop ❦

City Art Gallery
The Headrow LS1 3AA (city centre, next to town hall and library)
☎0113 247 8248 Fax 0113 244 9689
The City Art Gallery is a purpose-built gallery, originally opened in 1888 but since modified and extended. Home to one of the best collections of 20th century British art outside London, as well as Victorian and late 19th century pictures, an outstanding collection of English watercolours, an exceptional display of modern sculpture and temporary exhibitions focusing on the modern and contemporary. Highlights include works by Holman Hunt, Andre Derain, Stanley Spencer, the Camden Town School, Henry Moore, Barbara Hepworth, Jacob Epstein, Cotman and Turner. Please telephone for details of forthcoming exhibitions.
Open all year, Mon-Sat 10-5, Wed until 8, Sun 1-5.Closed BHs.
Free.
P ♨ ✗ licensed ♿ (restricted access to upper floor) toilets for disabled shop ❦ (ex guide dogs)
Cards: 🚐 🚘 ⑤

City Museum
The Headrow LS1 3AA
☎0113 247 8275
See the world in a day - with something for everyone in this museum, exhibits as diverse as a Bengal tiger, an Egyptian mummy, Roman remains, dinosaurs, fossils and minerals, and costumes and crafts from five continents. Temporary exhibitions.Refurbished galleries covering ethnography, archaeology, and natural history. Events for National Museums Week - including the Heavy Rock Show, when you can bring in you geological samples for identification (16-23 May).
Open Tue-Sat 10-5 (closed Tue following BH).
Free.
P (200 yds away) ♿ (lifts to all floors) toilets for disabled shop ❦
Cards: 🚘

Kirkstall Abbey & Abbey House Museum
Abbey Rd, Kirkstall LS5 3EH (off A65, W of city centre).
☎0113 275 5821
The most complete 12th-century Cistercian Abbey in the country stands on the banks of the River Aire. Opposite Abbey House Museum, once the gatehouse for the 12th century Kirkstall Abbey, the museum now presents a colourful record of Victorian social life. Attractions include the reconstructed cobbled streets with shops and merry-go-round, and the delightful Toy Gallery.
Open all year, Tue-Sat 10-5, Sun 1-5. Open Bank Hol's. Abbey site open dawn-dusk.

£2 (accompanied ch 50p, pen & concessions £1). Season ticket £10 (concessions £5, ch £2.50). Abbey free.
🅿 ♿ toilets for disabled shop ❦
Cards: 🚐 🚘 🚘

Middleton Colliery Railway
Moor Rd, Hunslet LS10 2JQ (junc 45/M1 or follow signs from A61)
☎0113 271 0320 (ansaphone) Fax 01925 831774
This was the first railway authorised by an Act of Parliament (in 1758) and the first to succeed with steam locomotives (in 1812). Steam trains run each weekend in season from Tunstall Road roundabout to Middleton Park. Facilities include a picnic area, nature trail and playgrounds. There is a programme of special events. Please telephone for details.
Moor Road Station open for viewing every wknd. Trains run Apr-early Jan wknds.
🅿 ♿ (ramped access to all areas) shop
Details not confirmed for 1998
Cards: 🚐 🚘

Royal Armouries Museum
Armouries Dr LS10 1LT (off A61 close to Leeds centre, follow brown tourist signs)
☎0113 220 1999 & 0990 106 666 Fax 0113 220 1997
Situated on the canal waterfront in the heart of Leeds, the museum is designed to bring to life the unique and magical history and development of arms and armour. The museum boasts 155,000 square feet, displaying 20,000 items of the national collections. Touch screen computers and live demonstrations add additional dimensions to the five galleries that tell the story of hunting, war, tournament, self defence and the civilisations of Asia. A sixth, the news room, enables visitors to experience the excitement of a live television studio. Outside on the waterfront there is a 3,000 capacity tilt yard for jousting tournaments and the Beating of the Retreat. A craft court will have demonstrations by skilled armourers and the training of hunting dogs and horses. Special events include: Dinosaurs:The Next Generation (til 4 May).
Open daily, summer (May-Aug) 10am-5pm (6pm Aug weekends & school hols), winter (Nov-Feb) 10am-4pm (5pm weekends & school hols) closed Mondays except for pre-booked school & groups.
£7.95 (ch 4-15 £4.95, pen £6.95, students £5.95)
🅿 (charged) ♨ ✗ licensed ♿ toilets for disabled shop ❦
Cards: 🚐 🚘 🚘

Temple Newsam House & Park
LS15 0AE (off A63)
☎0113 264 7321 (House) & 264 5535 (Park) Fax 0113 2602285
Described as 'the Hampton Court of the North' this Tudor and Jacobean mansion boasts extensive collections of decorative arts in their original room settings, including the incomparable Chippendale collection. An extensive programme of renovation is restoring each room to its former glory, using original wall coverings and furniture. Set in 1,200 acres of parkland (landscaped by 'Capability' Brown), the Rare Breeds Centre in the Home Farm delights visitors. The gardens have a magnificent display of rhododendrons, whilst a riot of roses bloom amid vibrant borders in the old walled garden.
Open all year. House: Tue-Sat 10am-5pm, Sun 1-5pm. 1 Nov-28 Dec & Mar Tues-Sat 10am-4pm Sun 12-5pm. Open Bank Hols. Home Farm 10am-4pm(3pm in winter); Gardens 10-dusk; Estate: daily: dawn-dusk. Closed Jan-Feb re-opens 28 Feb.
£2 (concessions £1). Accompanied children 50p. Season ticket £10 (concessions £5, ch £2.50)
🅿 (charged) ♨ ♿ (ramps giving full accesss to parkland) toilets for disabled shop ❦
Cards: 🚐 🚘 🚘

Watch the enormous wheels and cogs of Thwaite Mill's mechanism in action

Tetley's Brewery Wharf
The Waterfront LS1 1QG
☎0113 242 0666
Fax 0113 245 1925
Situated in the heart of Leeds, Tetley's Brewery Wharf introduces visitors to the fascinating history of the English pub. With the aid of actors, visitors will see life in a 14th-century ale-house, through to Elizabethan, Jacobean, Georgian and Victorian hostelries, a 1940s blitzed pub and a futuristic pub. Crafts associated with the history of pubs are demonstrated - from inn sign painting to a cooper making traditional wood barrels. Other attractions include an adventure playground, picnic area, restaurant, and an amphitheatre where a range of events is planned for the holiday season.
Open weekends only until 24 Mar, 25 Mar-Sep open 7 days. Last admission - winter 3.30, summer 4.
🅿 *(charged)* ✖ *licensed* ♿ *(lift & ramps) toilets for disabled shop* ⊗ *(ex guide dogs)*
Details not confirmed for 1998
Cards: 🅰 🔳 🅾 🔳 🔳 Ⓖ

Thackray Medical Museum
Beckett St LS9 7LN (next to St James Hospital)
☎0113 244 4343
Fax 0113 247 0219
Housed in a large Victorian building, next to the famous St James's (Jimmy's) Hospital, the Thackray Medical Museum offers a new and unique hands-on experience to visitors of all ages. A cow from Gloucester, green mould and smelly toilets - all these things have helped transform our lives. Find out how by walking back in time and exploring the sights, sounds and smells of Victorian slum life. Discover how people really lived 150 years ago. Spot the bed bugs...! Will the injured mill girl survive her operation? Feel what its like to be pregnant! Walk through a giant gut and find out why your tummy rumbles. How does your skeleton move and what does the doctor see inside your ear? Explore amazing objects from a surgical chain-saw to Prince Albert's Medicine Chest.
Open all year, Tue-Sun & BH Mons 10-5.30 (Nov-Mar 10-5). Closed Xmas/New Year.
✳£3.95 (ch 4-16 £2.75, pen, students & unemployed £3). Family ticket £10.75. Party 12+.
🅿 🍴 ♿ *(wheelchair loan, induction loop) toilets for disabled shop* ⊗
Cards: 🅰 🔳 🔳 Ⓖ

Thwaite Mills
Thwaite Ln, Stourton LS10 1RP (2m S of city centre, off A61)
☎0113 249 6453
Fax 0113 246 5561
A knowledgeable guide will take you on a fascinating tour of this water-powered mill which sits between the River Aire and the Aire and Calder Navigation. Two great swishing wheels continually drive a mass of cogs and grinding wheels which crushed stone for putty and paint throughout the 19th century. This was the hub of a tiny island community, and the Georgian mill-owner's house has been restored, and houses displays exploring the mill's history. Visitors can watch the story on video before or after the guided tour. Tours start on the hour and last approximately 45 minutes.
Open Tues-Sat 10am-5pm & Sun 1-5pm. 1 Nov-31 Dec and March Tues-Sat 10am-4pm, Sun 12-4pm. Open BH Mon. Closed Jan & Feb.
£2 (ch 50p, £1 concessions). Season ticket £10 (accompanied ch £2.50, concessions £5) Party 15+.
🅿 ♿ *(wheelchair lifts) toilets for disabled shop* ⊗
Cards: 🅰 🔳 🔳

Tropical World
Canal Gardens, Roundhay Park LS8 2ER (3m N of city centre off A58 at Oakwood)
☎0113 266 1850
Adjacent to Canal Gardens is Tropical World, one of the UK's most visited garden attractions. The atmosphere of the tropics is re-created as visitors walk among banana, citrus, pineapple and other exotic trees. A waterfall cascades into a rock-pool at the rate of 1,000 gallons a minute and in other pools terrapins and carp can be found. Elsewhere are many displays of live reptiles and exotic insects. In the Butterfly House more than 30 species can be seen feeding off the plants. There is also a Nocturnal House, a South American Rainforest (containing a wide range of exotic orchids) and a Desert House (with specimens of cacti and succulents gathered from the deserts of the world).
Open daily 10-dusk; special times at Christmas.
£1 (ch 8-16 50p)
🅿 ♿ *shop* ⊗
Cards: 🔳

LOTHERTON HALL
Lotherton Hall
Aberford LS25 3EB (off the A1, 0.75m E of junct with B1217)
☎0113 281 3259
Built in Edwardian times, the former home of the Gascoigne family is now a country house museum. It contains furniture, pictures, silver and ceramics from the Gascoigne collection, and works of art on loan from Leeds galleries. Other attractions include a gallery of Oriental art, a display of British fashion, contemporary crafts and frequent special exhibitions. Outside, the Edwardian garden, bird garden and deer park are delightful places in which to stroll.
Open Tues-Sat 10am-5pm. Sun 1-5pm. Bank Hols. 1 Nov-31 Dec & March Tues-Sat 10am-4pm Sun 12-4pm.
Hall, £2 (ch, pen & students £1, unaccompanied ch 50p). Season ticket £10 (ch £2.50, concessions £5). Party 15+. Free admission to Bird Garden, Gardens & Parkland.
🅿 🍴 ✖ *licensed* ♿ *shop* ⊗ *(ex in park)*

MIDDLESTOWN
National Coal Mining Museum For England
Caphouse Colliery, New Rd WF4 4RH (on A642 between Wakefield & Huddersfield)
☎01924 848806 Fax 01924 840694
A unique opportunity to go 450ft underground down one of Britain's oldest working mine shafts, where models and machinery depict methods and conditions of mining from the early 1800s to the present day. Visitors are strongly advised to wear sensible footwear and warm clothing. Surface displays (both indoor and outdoor), pit ponies, 'paddy' train rides, steam winder, nature trail and adventure playground. Please telephone for details of exhibitions and events
Open all year, daily 10-5. (Closed 24-26 Dec & 1 Jan).
£5.75 (ch £4.25, concessions £4.85).
🅿 🍴 ✖ *licensed* ♿ *(nature trail not accessible) toilets for disabled shop*
Cards: 🅰 🔳 🔳

NOSTELL PRIORY
Nostell Priory
WF4 1QD (6m SE of Wakefield, off A638)
☎01924 863892 Fax 01924 865282
Built by Paine in the middle of the 18th century, the priory has an additional wing built by Adam in 1766. It contains a notable saloon and tapestry room and displays pictures and Chippendale furniture. There is a lake in the grounds. Events being held include the Royal British Legion Rally and a Country Fair.

Open 4 Apr-1 Nov. Apr-Jun, Sept & Oct: Sat & Sun 12pm-5pm. 1 July-3 Sept daily except Friday 12-5. Bank Hols 12-5. Not Good Fri. Last admission 4.30pm. House & Grounds £4 (ch £2). Family ticket £9.50. Grounds only £2.50 (ch £1.50). Family ticket £6.50.
🅿 🍴 ♿ *(lift) toilets for disabled shop* ⊗

OAKWELL HALL
Oakwell Hall
Nutter Ln, Birstall WF17 9LG (6m SE of Bradford)
☎01924 326240 Fax 01924 326249
A moated Elizabethan manor house, furnished as it might have looked in the 1690s. Extensive Country Park with countryside centre. There are period gardens, an equestrian arena and an adventure playground.
Open all year, daily (ex Good Fri, Xmas & New Year).
🅿 🍴 ♿ *(herb garden for the blind) toilets for disabled shop* ⊗
Details not confirmed for 1998

SHIPLEY
Reed Organ & Harmonium Museum
Victoria Hall, Victoria Rd, Saltaire BD18 3LQ
☎01274 585601 after 6pm
Europe's first reed organ museum contains a collection of 70 models. The smallest is no bigger than a family bible and the largest, which belonged to Dr Marmaduke P Conway when he was organist at Ely Cathedral, has three manuals and pedals. If you are a player, you may have the chance to try some of the instruments. There are also harmoniums on display, which have featured on television and radio.
Open Sun-Thu, 11-4. (Closed 2 wks Xmas). £1.50 (ch & pen £1). Family £3.50. Party 10+.
P *(on street)* ♿ *toilets for disabled* ⊗

WAKEFIELD
Wakefield Art Gallery
Wentworth Ter WF1 3QW (N of city centre by Wakefield College and Clayton Hospial
☎01924 305796 Fax 01924 305770
Wakefield was home to two of Britain's greatest modern sculptors - Barbara Hepworth and Henry Moore. The art gallery, which has an important collection of 20th-century paintings and sculptures, has a special room devoted to these two local artists. There are frequent temporary exhibitions of both modern and earlier works covering all aspects of art and crafts. For 1998 these will include 28 Mar-31 May Brigitte Kramer, a photographer from Wakefield's twin Town, Herne in Germany; 13 Jun-19 Jul Michael Steele, sports photography; 1 Aug-13 Sept Henry Moore Own Photographs.
Open all year, Tue-Sat 10.30-4.30, Sun 2-4.30.
Free.
P *(restricted on-street parking) shop* ⊗

WEST BRETTON
Yorkshire Sculpture Park
Bretton Hall WF4 4LG (1 mile from junct 38 on M1)
☎01924 830302 Fax 01924 830044
One of Europe's leading sculpture parks, Yorkshire Sculpture Park has pioneered the siting of sculpture in the open air, organising temporary exhibitions of modern and contemporary sculpture by national and international artists in over 100 acres of beautiful parkland. There are also changing displays from the loan collection by artists including work by Barbara Hepworth, William Tucker, Barry Flanagan, Eduardo Paolozzi, David Nash, Grenville Davey and Sol Le Witt. In the adjacent 96 acre Bretton Country Park, there is a permanent exhibition of monumental bronze sculptures by Henry Moore. Various special exhibitions. Please telephone for details.
Open all year 10-6 (summer) 10-4 (winter). (Closed 25-26 & 31 Dec)
Free. Car parking £1.50.
🅿 *(charged)* 🍴 ♿ *(scooters available for disabled) toilets for disabled shop*

CHANNEL ISLANDS

GUERNSEY

CÂTEL (CASTEL)
Le Friquet Butterfly Centre
GY5 7SS
☎01481 54378 Fax 01481 57104
European and tropical butterflies fly freely in the lush setting of the Butterfly Farm greenhouse, and may be seen hatching from their chrysalids. Other attractions include putting and croquet.
Open Etr-Oct, daily 10-5.
£2 (ch £1.25 & pen £1.50).
🅿 ⏺ ✗ *licensed* & *toilets for disabled shop*
Cards: ◨ ▨

FOREST
German Occupation Museum
GY8 0BG (Behind Forest Church near the airport)
☎01481 38205
The museum has the Channel Islands' largest collection of authentic Occupation items, with tableaux of a kitchen, bunker rooms and a street during the Occupation. Also German fortifications can be visited. Liberation Day 9th May will be celebrated with special events and exhibitions.
Open Apr-Oct 10-5. Nov, Dec, Feb, Mar, Sun, Tues, Thurs 10-4.30. Jan Sundays 10am-12.30pm.
£2.50 (ch £1.25, ch under 5 free).
🅿 ⏺ & *(ramps & handrails)*

ROQUAINE BAY
Fort Grey Shipwreck Museum
GY7 9BY (on coast road at Rocquaine Bay)
☎01481 726518
Fax 01481 715177
The fort is a Martello tower, built as part of the Channel Islands' extensive defences against Napoleon. It is nicknamed the 'cup and saucer' because of its appearance, and houses a museum devoted to wrecks on the treacherous Hanois reefs nearby.

Open Apr-Oct, 10-5.
❄*£2 (students & pen £1). Joint ticket with Castle Cornet & Guernsey Museum £5 (ch £2, students & pen £2.25). Accompanied Children under 12.*
P *(opposite fort) shop* 🐾
Cards: ◨ ▨ ⑤

ST ANDREW
German Military Underground Hospital & Ammunition Store
La Vassalerie GY6 8XR
☎01481 39100
This is the largest structure created during the German Occupation of the Channel Islands, a concrete maze of about 75,000sq ft, which took slave workers three-and-a-half years to complete, at the cost of many lives. The hospital was only used for about six weeks, to care for wounded German soldiers brought over from France after D-Day. The ammunition store, however, which was larger than the hospital, was packed with thousands of tons of ammunition during its nine months of use. Most of the equipment has been removed, but the central heating plant, hospital beds and cooking facilities can still be seen.
Open Jul-Aug, daily 10-noon & 2-4.30; May-Jun & Sep, daily 10-noon & 2-4; Apr & Oct, daily 10am-12pm; Mar & Nov, Sun & Thu 2-3.
£2.50 (ch 60p).
🅿 & *shop*

ST MARTIN
Sausmarez Manor
Sausmarez Rd GY4 6SG
☎01481 35571 Fax 01481 35572
The Manor has been owned by the same family for centuries, a family which has included artists, generals, admirals, privateers, judges, sportsmen, inventors, cartographers, explorers, adventurers and politicians - most of whom have left some mark on the house or its contents. Each room is a happy contrast in style to its neighbour, with collections of Oriental, French and English furniture and an eclectic variety of paintings. The Formal Garden has herbaceous borders in the style of Gertrude Jekyll, while the Woodland Garden, set around two small lakes and a stream, is inter-planted with colourful shrubs, bulbs and wild flowers from the subtropics to give a jungle atmosphere. Of special note are the 300 plus camelias, young tree ferns, banana and palm trees, and fuchsias, which

encourage butterflies, birds and other animal life. In a section of the wood, a 7.25-gauge ride-on railway runs for over a quarter of a mile over embankments and through cuttings, while in the 16th-century Tudor Barn there is a 310sq ft model railway layout, with up to eight trains running continuously through meticulously scaled countryside, towns and villages. Another special layout of the Robust Playmobile Train Set is available for visitors to operate. In the Little Barn, is one of the three largest collections in Britain of dolls' houses dating from 1820 to the present day. There is also a new pitch and putt course with free equipment hire, and a children's farm with friendly animals including piglets, rabbits, guinea pigs and a pony. Special Events include Motor Show 7 Jun, Dolls' Houses from around the world 26/27 Sep.
House open last BH in May-last Thu in Sep, Mon-Thur, 10.30-11.30am & 2-3pm. Also Etr-end of May & Oct, Mon-Thu mornings 10.30-11.30.
House £4 (ch £1). Woodland Garden £1.50(accompanied ch 50p, disabled free). Dolls House Collection £2. Railway layout £1 (ch & pen 80p). Train rides £1 (ch & pen 80p).
🅿 ⏺ & *(free partial access to garden, close parking) shop (Specialises in dolls houses etc)* 🐾

ST PETER PORT
Castle Cornet
(Half mile from St Peter Port town centre at end of harbour breakwater)
☎01481 721657 Fax 01481 715177
Castle Cornet has been used in warfare from the 13th to the 20th centuries, and has an impressive array of defences. During the Civil War it was garrisoned by the Royalist governor of the island, and although most islanders sympathised with Cromwell, it was not until 1651 that this last Royalist stronghold surrendered. In 1940 the castle was taken over by German troops and adapted for modern warfare.
Today it houses the new Maritime Museum, the Spencer collection of uniforms and badges, the Museum of Guernsey's Own 201 Squadron Royal Air Force, the Royal Guernsey Militia Museum, Art Gallery and Armoury. A gun is fired daily at noon on the order of a man who studies the town church clock through a telescope. A new History of Castle Cornet Museum opened in 1997.

Summer Season of Entertainment includes 2 Shakespeare plays outdoors, Gilbert & Sullivan and a re-enactment camp. Telephone for details.
Open Apr-Oct, daily 10-5.
£4.50 (students/pen £2.25). Joint ticket with Fort Grey & Guernsey Museum £6.50 (ch £2, students & pen £3). Prices under review. Accompanied children under 12 & educational groups free
P *(100 yds) (2 hr time zone, 10hr within 200 yards)* ⏺ *shop* 🐾 *(ex guide dogs)*
Cards: ◨ ▨ ⑤

Guernsey Museum & Art Gallery
Candie Gardens GY1 1UG (in Candie Gardens)
☎01481 726518 Fax 01481 715177
The island's first purpose-built museum tells the story of Guernsey and its people. The museum has an audio-visual theatre and an art gallery, and there are special exhibitions throughout the year. It is surrounded by beautiful gardens. There will be a new permanent art gallery for 1998.
Open all year, daily 10-5 (summer), 10-4 (winter)
£2.50 (students/pen £1.25). Joint ticket with Castle Cornet & Fort Grey £5 (ch £2, students & pen £2.25). Accompanied children under 12.
P *(outside museum) (2hr & 5hr)* ⏺ & *toilets for disabled shop* 🐾
Cards: ◨ ▨ ⑤

VALE
The Rousse Tower
Rousse Tower Headland
Of the original fifteen towers built in 1778-9 in prime defensive positions around the coast of Guernsey, twelve still remain. They were designed primarily to prevent the landing of troops on nearby beaches and, on stretches of coastline where more than one tower was erected, were positioned to provide overlapping fields of fire from their light 1-pounder wallpieces. Musket fire could also be directed on invading forces through the loopholes.
Open 9-5.
🅿 🐾
Details not confirmed for 1998

JERSEY

GOREY
Mont Orgueil Castle
JE3 6ET (A3 or coast rd to Gorey)
☎01534 853292 Fax 01534 854303
The castle stands on a rocky headland, on a site which has been fortified since the Iron Age. It is one of the best-preserved examples in Europe of a medieval concentric castle, and dates from the 12th and 13th centuries. A series of tableaux with a commentary tells the history of the building. Information on special events will be advertised locally or can be obtained from the Jersey Museum or Castle.
Open daily throughout the year 9.30-6; Last admission 5pm. Opening times in winter season 10-dusk.
£3.20 (ch 10-16 & pen £2.10, ch 10 free). Passport to all 6 Jersey Museum Service sites £10 (concessions £6.75). Passport savers ticket and group booking discount under review
P *(200 yds) (discs required at harbour) shop* 🐾
Cards: ◨ ▨ ▨ ⑤

GROUVILLE
La Hougue Bie
JE2 7UA (A6 or A7 to Five Oaks then prines Tower rd.)
☎01534 853823 Fax 01534 856472
This Neolithic burial mound stands 40ft high, and covers a stone-built passage grave which is still intact and may be entered. The passage is 50ft long, and is built of huge stones dragged from quarries; the mound is made from earth, rubble and limpet shells. On top of the mound are two medieval chapels, one of which has a replica of the Holy Sepulchre

The echoing chambers and corridors of the German Underground Hospital are an evocative reminder of the Occupation.

Golden Tamarind at Jersey Zoo.

in Jerusalem below. Also on the site is an underground bunker built by the Germans as a communications centre. It is now an Occupation museum. There are also archaeology and geology displays. There is also the de Quetteville estate's Neolithic house.A storyteller will interpret the site and relate the 'Legend of La Hougue Bie' on specific dates throughout the summer. Contact the Jersey Museum for information on special events.
Open 24 Mar-2 Nov daily 10-5.
£3.20 (ch 10-16 & pen £2.10, ch 10 free). Passport for all 6 Jersey Museums Service sites £10 (concessions £6.75). Under 10's free. Passport saver ticket and group bookings under review.
shop
Cards:

ST BRELADE

Jersey Lavender Farm
Rue du Pont Marquet JE3 8DS (on the B25 from St.Aubin's Bay to Redhouses)
01534 42933 Fax 01534 45613
At this lavender farm visitors can see the complete process of production from cultivation through to harvesting and distillation to the bottling, labelling and packaging of the final product. There is also a short video. Visitors can follow walks through the lavender and herb fields and for those interested in plants and gardens there is the National Collection of Lavandula, a fine herb garden, an extensive collection of dwarf and slow-growing conifers in the Pygmy Pinetum and a collection of 63 varieties of bamboo.
Open 19 May-20 Sep, Mon-Sat 10-5.
£2 (ch 14 free)
(wheelchair loan, wide doors, grab rails etc) toilets for disabled shop garden centre
Cards:

ST CLEMENT

Samarès Manor
JE2 6QW (2m E of St.Helier on St.Clements inner rd)
01534 870551 Fax 01534 68949
There are guided tours of the manor, which stands in 14 acres of beautiful gardens. The Japanese Garden occupies an artificial hill, and has a series of waterfalls cascading over Cumberland limestone. One of Britain's largest and most comprehensive herb gardens is here, with a herb and specialist hardy perennial nursery. Other attractions include a craft centre, farm animals and a children's play area. Rose Show (27-28 June).
Open 4 Apr-10 Oct.
**£3.60 (ch 16 £1.75, pen £2.95).*
licensed (toilets for disabled shop garden centre
Cards:

ST HELIER

Elizabeth Castle
(access by causeway or amphibious vehicle)
01534 23971 Fax 01534 610338
The original Elizabethan fortress was extended in the 17th and 18th centuries, and then refortified by the Germans during the Occupation. There are many buildings and defences to explore, a museum of the Jersey militia, a Granite and Gunpowder exhibition of cannon and fortifications in war and peace, and an exhibition of life in the castle. Information on special events will be available from the Jersey Museum or Castle.
Open Mar 24-Nov 2, daily 9.30-6. Last admission 5.
£3.20 (concessions £2.10, ch 10 free). Passport for all 6 Jersey Museum Service sites £10.(concessions £6.75). Passport saver and group discount under review.
P (20 mins on seafront shop
Cards:

Jersey Museum
The Weighbridge JE2 3NF (near bus station on weighbridge)
01534 633300 Fax 01534 633301
The Jersey Museum, winner of the Museum of the Year 1993 Award, is a specially designed purpose-built venue. It houses 'The Story of Jersey', Jersey's art gallery, an exhibition gallery which features a changing programme, a lecture theatre, and an audio-visual theatre. There is a cafe, shop, and plenty of places to rest and relax. Special exhibitions and events throughout 1998 will be advertised locally and information is available from the museum.
Open all year, Mon-Sat 10-5, Sun 1-5. Winter Mon-Sat 10-4, Sun 1-4. Closed 25/26 Dec and 1 Jan.
£3.20 (ch 10 free, concessions £2.10). Passport ticket for all 6 Jersey Museums Service sites £10 (concessions £6.75). Passport saver ticket and group booking discount under review.
P (5 mins walk) (paycard at most public parking) licensed (audio loop, audio guide for partially sighted, car park) toilets for disabled shop
Cards:

Occupation Tapestry Gallery
New North Quay JE2 3WD (alongside Marina, opposite Liberation Square)
01534 811043 Fax 01534 874099
This converted 19th century warehouse adjacent to Liberation Square, houses the acclaimed Occupation Tapestry, and Maritime Museum. The tapestry consists of twelve two-metre panels and tells the story of the occupation of Jersey during World War II. Each of the twelve parishes took responsibility for the stitching of a panel, making it the largest community arts project ever undertaken on the island. There is an audio-visual presentation. The new Maritime Museum combines hands-on exhibits with historic objects and new art and sculpture commissions to celebrate the relationship of islanders and the sea. Visitors can feel the force of a gale, design and float their own ships and experience the pitch and roll of life at sea, as well as learn about the extent of island trade around the world.
Open all year, daily 10-5 (winter closing at 4pm).
£3.20 (pen/student £2.10).Under 10's free. Passport Saver tickets to all 6 Jersey Museum Services sites available. Passport saver ticket and Group booking discount under review.
P (paycards in public car parks) (braille books, audio guide etc) toilets for disabled shop
Cards:

ST LAWRENCE

German Underground Hospital
Les Charrieres Malorey JE3 1FU
01534 863442 Fax 01534 865970
Close to the entrance is a plaque which records that 'Under these conditions men of many nations laboured to construct this hospital. Those who survived will never forget; those who did not will never be forgotten'. On 1 July 1940 the Channel Islands were occupied by the German forces, and this vast complex dug deep into a hillside is the most evocative reminder of the Occupation. Here in the echoing corridors and chambers visitors can experience the hardships endured by the tunnellers. There is a continuous video presentation which, along with a large collection of memorabilia, brings the experience of the Islanders at war to life and a further exhibition records the impressions of the islanders during 1945, the year of liberation.
Open 15 Mar-8 Nov, daily 9.30-5.30 Last admission 4.15
**£4.20 (ch £2.10).*
licensed (ramp to restaurant & lift in Visitor Centre to restaurant) toilets for disabled shop
Cards:

Hamptonne
La Rue de la Patente JE3 1HS (5m from St.Helier on A1, left up A10 and follow signs)
01534 863955 Fax 01534 863935
Here at Hamptonne, Jersey's country life museum, you will find a medieval 17th-century home, furnished in authentic style and surrounded by 19th-century farm buildings. Discover the history of rural Jersey and its people in the exhibition gallery, wander through the meadows and apple orchard and see a working cider press and apple crusher. Guided tours every day. Living history interpretation and daily demonstrations. Special events information is available from the Museum.
Open 24 Mar-2 Nov, daily 10-5. 2 Nov-24 Mar Sat, Sun & Mon 10am-4pm.
£3.20 (ch 10-16 & concessions £2.10). Passport ticket for all 6 Jersey Museums Services sites £10.00(concessions £6.75). Passport saver ticket and group discount under review.
toilets for disabled shop
Cards:

Jersey Flower Centre
Retreat Farm JE3 1GX
01534 865665 Fax 01534 865554
The Jersey Flower Centre is home to the largest mail order floral company in the world. Take a walk around the giant glasshouses measuring 22,000 sq ft and holding 200,000 plants or view the Flamingo Lake, Wildfowl Sanctuary, Koi Carp Reserve, exotic birds and wildflower meadowland. Visitor Centre incorporating shop, restaurant and children's play area. Attractions include: Flamingo Lake, Wildfowl Sanctuary, Koi Carp Reserve, Wildflower Meadowland, Drought Garden and Woodland View.
Open daily April-October 9.30am-5.30pm.
**£3.25 (ch under 12 free, pen £2.75)*
licensed (Wheelchairs available) toilets for disabled shop
Cards:

ST OUEN

Kempt Tower Visitor Centre
Five Mile Rd
01534 483651
The centre has displays on the past, and the wildlife, of St Ouen's Bay, including Les Mielles, which is Jersey's miniature national park. Nature walks are held every Thursday (May to September). Check local press for details.
Open BH's & Apr & Oct, Thu & Sun only 2-5; May-Sep, daily (ex Mon) 2-5.
shop
Details not confirmed for 1998

ST PETER

Jersey Motor Museum
St Peter's Village JE3 7AG (jct off A12 & B41 at St Peters village)
01534 482966
The museum has a fine collection of motor vehicles from the early 1900s. There are also Allied and German military vehicles of World War II, a Jersey Steam Railway section, aero-engines and other items. A pre-war Jersey AA box is shown, with a collection of AA badges of all periods.
Open end Mar-late Oct, daily 10-5. (Last admission 4.40pm).
£2.25 (ch £1.10). Wheelchair users free.
(access doors avoid turnstiles) shop

The Living Legend
Rue de Petit Aleval JE3 7ET
01534 485496 Fax 01534 485855
Pass through the granite archways into the landscaped gardens and the world of the Jersey Experience where Jersey's exciting past is recreated in a three dimensional spectacle. Learn of the

heroes and villains, the folklore and the story of the Island's links with the UK and her struggles with Europe. Other attractions include an adventure playground, street entertainment, the Jersey Craft and Shopping Village, a range of shops and the Jersey Kitchen Restaurant. New in 1997 was the addition of two 18 hole Adventure Golf course, with multi-level holes and novelty features, set in landscaped water gardens.
Open Apr-1 Nov daily 9.30-5.30; Mar & Nov-3 Dec, Sat-Wed 10-5.
✱£4.70 (ch £2.75, pen £4.20).
P ✗ licensed & (wheelchair available) toilets for disabled shop
Cards: 🖸 🖸 🖸 🖸 🖸 🖸 🖸

Le Moulin de Quetivel
St Peters Valley JE3 3EN (on B58 off A11)
☎01534 483193
There has been a water mill on this site since 1309. The present granite-built mill was worked until the end of the 19th century, when it fell into disrepair; during the German Occupation it was reactivated for grinding locally grown corn, but after 1945 a fire destroyed the remaining machinery, roof and internal woodwork. In 1971 the National Trust for Jersey began restoration, and the mill is now producing stoneground flour again.
Open May-mid Oct, Tue-Thu 10-4.
P & shop ✿ 🚷 🐾
Details not confirmed for 1998

St Peter's Bunker Museum
St Peters Village JE3 7AF (at junc of A12 & B41)
☎01534 481048 Fax 01534 481630
German uniforms, motorcycles, weapons, documents, photographs and other items from the 1940-45 Occupation are displayed in a real wartime bunker. It accommodated 36 men and could be sealed in case of attack. One room has been refitted with authentic bunk beds and figures of soldiers. There is also an Occupation photographic exhibition within the museum.
Open 31 Mar-27 Oct, daily 10-5.
P shop ✿
Details not confirmed for 1998

TRINITY
Jersey Zoological Park
Les Augres Manor JE3 5BP
☎01534 864666 Fax 01534 865161
Gerald Durrell's unique sanctuary and breeding centre for many of the world's rarest and most beautiful animals. In the attractive gardens of the 16th-century manor house, visitors can enjoy the family life of a remarkable collection of exotic creatures, some of them so rare that they are only to be found in Jersey Zoo. Here they have all the benefits of modern, spacious enclosures that encourage natural and entertaining behaviour. Major attractions are the magical Aye-Ayes from Madagascar and the world-famous family of Lowland gorillas.
A comprehensive programme of keeper talks, animal displays and activities enhances the visitor experience and the fascinating story of the work of the Trust around the world is portrayed in a superb film in the Princess Royal Pavilion.
Open all year, daily 9.30-6 (dusk in winter). (Closed 25 Dec).
P ✗ licensed & (trail for the blind, auditory loop in pavilion) toilets for disabled shop ✿
Details not confirmed for 1998
Cards: 🖸 🖸 🖸 🖸 🖸

ISLE OF MAN

BALLAUGH
Curraghs Wild Life Park
(on main rd halfway between Kirk Michael & Ramsey)
☎01624 897323 Fax 01624 897327

Developed adjacent to the reserve area of the Ballaugh Curraghs is the wildlife park, which exhibits a large variety of animals and birds in natural settings. Large walk through enclosures let visitors explore the world of wildlife, including local habitats along the Curraghs nature trail. The miniature railway runs on Sundays. Special events: Barbeques (every Wednesday evening commencing mid-June), Wildlife Fairs (August) Please ring for details.
Open Etr-Oct, daily 10-6. Last admission 5.15pm. Oct-Etr, Sat & Sun 10-4.
✱£3.00 (ch £1.75). Party.
P 🖸 & (loan of electric wheelchair) toilets for disabled shop ✿ (ex guide dogs by arrangement)

CASTLETOWN
Castle Rushen
☎01624 648000
Fax 01624 648000
On view to the visitor are the state apartments of this 14th-century stronghold. There is also a Norman keep, flanked by towers from its later rebuilding, with a clock given by Elizabeth I in 1597. The castle is available for private hire.
Open Etr-Sep, daily 10-5.
£3.50 (ch £2) Family £9. Group.
P (100 yds) & shop ✿
Cards: 🖸 🖸

Nautical Museum
☎01624 648000
Fax 01624 648001
The island's colourful relationship with the sea is illustrated here. There is an 18th-century Manx yacht and interesting Cabin Room and Quayle Room. Other areas comprise displays of net-making equipment and sailing ships.
Open Etr-late Sep, daily 10-5.
£2.50 (ch £1.50). Family £6. Group.
P (50 yds) & shop ✿
Cards: 🖸 🖸

Old Grammar School
☎01624 648000
Fax 01624 648001
Built in the 12th century, the Island's first church, St Mary's, has had a significant role in Manx history. The school dates back to 1570 and evokes memories of Victorian school life.
Open Etr-Sep, 10-5
Free.
P & shop ✿
Cards: 🖸 🖸

CREGNEISH
Cregneash Village Folk Museum
(2m from Port Erin/Port St Mary)
☎01624 648000
Fax 01624 648001
A group of traditional Manx cottages with their gardens and walled enclosures. Inside the cottages furniture and the everyday equipment used by typical Manx crofting communities are displayed. A crofter-fisherman's home, a farmstead, a turner's shed, smithy and a weaver's shed are all represented in realistic settings. Spinning demonstrations are given on certain days and sometimes a blacksmith can be seen at work. In the field adjoining the turner's shed, Manx Loghtan sheep can often be viewed; this ancient breed survives in very small numbers. The rams have a tendency to produce four, or even six, horns.
Open Etr-Sep, daily 10-5.
£2.50 (ch £1.50) Family £6. Pre-booked groups.
P 🖸 ✗ & shop ✿ (ex in grounds)
Cards: 🖸 🖸

DOUGLAS
Manx Museum
☎01624 648000 Fax 01624 648000
The 'Story of Man' begins at Manx Museum, where a specially produced film portrayal of Manx history complements the award-winning gallery displays. This showcase of Manx heritage provides the ideal starting-point to a journey of rich discovery embracing

the length and breadth of the island.
Open all year, Mon-Sat 10-5. (Closed Sun, Xmas, New Year, am of Tynwald Day 5 Jul).
Free.
P ✗ licensed & toilets for disabled shop ✿
Cards: 🖸 🖸

LAXEY
Laxey Wheel
☎01624 648000 Fax 01624 648001
Constructed to keep the lead mines free from water, this big wheel, known as the 'Lady Isabella', is an impressive sight at 72.5ft in diameter. It is the largest working wheel in the world.
Open Etr-Sep, daily 10-5.
£2.50 (ch £1.50) Family £6. Group.
P & shop ✿
Cards: 🖸 🖸

PEEL
House of Manannan
(on quayside)
☎01624 648000
Fax 01624 648001
The latest 'Story of Mann' attraction, opened in May 1997. This new £6 million centre is an unforgettable experience with interactive displays, using 'state of the art' technology. A visit to the House of Manannan leaves the visitor in awe of Manx heritage and eager to learn more.
Open daily 10-5. Closed Xmas/New Year.
£5 (ch 5-15 £2.50). Family ticket £12.50. Party.
P & toilets for disabled shop ✿
Cards: 🖸 🖸

Peel Castle
(on Patricks Isle, facing Peel Bay)
☎01624 648000
Fax 01624 648000
The castle was built to protect the cathedral of St German's, perhaps founded by St Patrick, and contains ruins from the 11th century. A phantom black dog, the Moddey Dhoo, is said to have haunted the castle. Sir Walter Scott used the story in *Peveril of the Peak*.
Open Etr-Sep, daily 10-5.
£2.50 (ch £1.50) Family £6. Party.
P shop ✿
Cards: 🖸 🖸

RAMSEY
'The Grove' Rural Life Museum
(on W side of Andreas Road)
☎01624 648000
Fax 01624 648000
For an intimate glimpse into the everyday life of a previous era this Victorian house is well worth a visit. Inside there are many of the original furnishings and personal belongings of the former owners, the Gibb family, displayed among the minutiae of Victorian life, both upstairs and downstairs. The outbuildings house a collection of early agricultural equipment including a horse-driven threshing mill; one of the few to survive in working order. There is also an exhibition on bees and bee-keeping.
Open Etr-Sep, daily 10-5.
£2.50 (ch £1.50). Family £6. Party.
P 🖸 ✗ licensed & shop ✿
Cards: 🖸 🖸

SNAEFELL MOUNTAIN
Murray's Museum
Bungalow Corner (Junction A14 & A18)
☎01624 861719
The TT races are perhaps the best-known feature of the Isle of Man, and not surprisingly the island has a motorcycle museum. Situated at the Bungalow corner on the TT course, this is an historic collection of 150 motorcycles and cycles, plus motoring and motorcycling memorabilia and equipment.
Open 25 May-Sep daily 10-5.
P 🖸 & shop
Details not confirmed for 1998

SCOTLAND

The directory which follows has been divided into three geographical regions. Counties have not been shown against individual locations as recent legislation has created a number of smaller counties which will be unfamiliar to the visitor. The postal authorities have confirmed that it is no longer necessary to include a county name in addresses, provided a post code is shown.

HIGHLANDS & ISLANDS

This region includes the counties of Aberdeen City, Aberdeenshire, Highland, Moray, Orkney, Shetland and Western Isles.

ABERDEEN
Proudly known as the 'Granite City', Aberdeen gets its nickname from its handsome grey granite buildings - many of them speckled with mica which shines like silver in the sunlight. Here, old and new live comfortably together with some steets and houses dating from the 16th century and still more from the 19th when fishing was the city's principal industry. The port has flourished since the end of the 13th century and the city boasts two imposing cathedrals - those of St Andrew and St Machar - as well as an ancient university founded by James IV of Scotland in 1505. The North Sea oil boom of the 1970s and 1980s created new prosperity in the city which became a boom town.

Aberdeen Art Gallery
Schoolhill AB10 1FQ
☎01224 646333
Fax 01224 632133
The gallery's 16th to 20th-century Scottish art includes an outstanding collection of modern paintings. Also here are watercolours, sculpture and decorative arts, and a print room and art library.
Open all year, Mon-Sat 10-5 (8pm Thu) Sun 2-5. (Closed 25 & 26 Dec, 1 & 2 Jan).
P (500 yds) 🚃 & toilets for disabled shop ✿
Details not confirmed for 1998
Cards: 🖸 🖸 🖸 🖸

Aberdeen Maritime Museum
Provost Ross's House, Shiprow AB11 5BY
☎01224 585788
Fax 01224 632133
The museum is in Provost Ross's House, Aberdeen's oldest building (1593). It highlights the city's maritime history, and its oil industry, in dramatic fashion. A National Trust for Scotland visitor centre and shop is open part of the year; at other times the area is used for special maritime exhibitions. Recent new displays and multi-media presentations tell the fascinating story of the North East's long association with the sea.
Open all year, Mon-Sat 10-5 (Closed 25-26 Dec & 1,2 Jan).
P 250yds 🚃 ✗ licensed & toilets for disabled shop ✿
Details not confirmed for 1998
Cards: 🖸 🖸 🖸

Cruickshank Botanic Garden

Aberdeen Maritime Museum explores Scotland's long association with the sea.

University of Aberdeen, St Machar Drive, AB24 3UU (enter by gate in Chanonry, in Old Aberdeen)
☎01224 272704 Fax 01224 272703
Developed at the end of the 19th century, the 11 acres include rock and water gardens, a rose garden, a fine herbaceous border, an arboretum and a patio garden. There are collections of spring bulbs, gentians and alpine plants, and a fine array of trees and shrubs.
Open all year, Mon-Fri 9-4.30; also Sat & Sun, May-Sep 2-5.
Free.
P *(200metres) (residents only in immediate vicinity)* 占 ✺

James Dun's House
61 Schoolhill AB10 1JT
☎01224 646333 Fax 224 632133
This 18th-century house is used as a venue for a frequently changing special exhibitions programme covering photography, fine art, applied art and local history.
Open all year, Mon-Sat, 10-5. (Closed 25-26 Dec,1 & 2 Jan)
P *500yds* ✺
Details not confirmed for 1998

Provost Skene's House
Guestrow, (off Broad St) AB10 1AR
☎01224 641086 Fax 01224 632133
The handsome 16th-century town mansion has notable decorated ceilings and panelling, and is now a museum of local history and social life, with rooms furnished in period style. A visit commences in the orientation room where the fascinating history of the building is explained.
Open all year, Mon-Sat 10-5. (Closed 25 & 26 Dec, 1 & 2 Jan)
P *(200yds)* ⬛ 占 ✺
Details not confirmed for 1998

Satrosphere ("Hands-On" Science & Technology) Centre)
19 Justice Mill Ln AB11 6EQ
☎01224 213232
Fax 01224 211685
Satrosphere, the Discovery Place, is different from many museums or exhibition centres. It is an Interactive Centre where everything is 'hands-on'. Displays aren't locked in glass cases and there are certainly no *Do Not Touch* signs. The emphasis is on doing and finding out, not just looking and standing back. There is a shop with exciting and unusual gifts. Special events include: children's science workshops during the Easter and summer school holidays, and special themes run throughout the year. Please telephone for details.
Open all year, Mon & Wed-Fri 10-4, Sat 10-5, Sun 1.30-5. School holidays Mon-Sat 10-5, Sun 1.30-5. (Closed 25-26 Dec & 1-2 Jan).
£3.90 (ch, students, UB40's & pen £2).
P *(charged)* ⬛ 占 *toilets for disabled shop* ✺

The Tolbooth
Castle St
☎01224 621167
Aberdeen's new museum of Civic history is housed in the city's former Wardhouse which served as a prison for Aberdeenshire. The Tolbooth tells the stories of prisoners incarcerated there and the ingenious ways in which some of them escaped. Also featured is the story of local government from the 14th century, when Ale Tasters held a prominent place on the burgh council, to the civic splendour of the Victorian era, manifested in fine provostal robes.
Open Apr-Sep, Tue-Sat 10-5, Thu 10-8, Sun 2-5.
P *(250yds) (NCP car park)* 占 *(lift to top floor) shop* ✺
Details not confirmed for 1998

ALFORD
Alford Valley Railway
AB33 8AD
☎019755 62326 & 62811
Fax 019755 63182
Narrow-gauge passenger railway in two sections: Alford-Haughton Park and Haughton Park-Murray Park approx one mile each. Steam on peak weekends. Diesel traction. Exhibitions. Special events include: Railway Fayre (18 April), Alford Cavalcade Vintage Steam and Car Event (21 July). Steam operated - 1st Sunday of the month (April-September.)
Open Apr, May & Sep wknds from 1-5, Jun-Aug daily from 1pm (30 min service). Party bookings also available at other times.
£1.50 (ch 80p) return fare.
P 占 *(ramps at station platforms) toilets for disabled*

AVIEMORE
Strathspey Steam Railway
Aviemore Station, Dalfaber Rd PH22 1PY (off B970)
☎01479 810725 Fax 01479 811022
This steam railway covers the five miles from Boat of Garten to Aviemore, where trains can also be boarded. The journey takes about 20 minutes, but allow around an hour for the round trip. Timetables are available from the station and the tourist information centre. Aviemore Railway Station is being refurbished and the steam railway hopes to be running trains from there from the start of the season. Special events for 1998 include: Friends of Thomas the Tank Engine weekends (2-

4 May, 5-6 September), Enthusiasts Day (May 23), Santa trains (13,19 & 20 December).
Open Jun-Sep daily. Diesel service on Sats & selected days 29 Mar-29 Oct, (including every weekend, Wed & Thu between these dates)
£5 Basic return; £12.50 Family return.
P ⬛ 占 *shop*
Cards: 🔲 🔲 🔲

BALLINDALLOCH
The Glenlivet Distillery
AB37 9DB (Off B9008 10m N of Tomintoul)
☎01542 783220 Fax 01542 783218
Discover the home of this world famous 12 year old malt whisky. Enjoy a tour of the distillery, established legally in 1824 by George Smith. The visitor centre not only includes a guided tour of the whisky production facilities but also a chance to see inside the vast bonded warehouses where the spirit matures. The new multimedia exhibition and interactive presentations communicate the unique history, traditions and quality inherent in the Glenlivet 12 Year Old Single Malt Scotch Whisky. There is also a cafe and shop.
Open: mid Mar-end Oct, Mon-Sat 10-4, Sun 12.30-4. Jul & Aug remains open until 6 daily.
£2.50 for over 18's which includes £2 voucher redeemable in distillery shop against the purchase of a 70cl bottle of whisky. This charge covers entry to exhibition, guided tour of Distillery & a free dram of whisky. (ch18 free, under 8's not admitted to production areas)
P ⬛ 占 *toilets for disabled shop* ✺
Cards: 🔲 🔲 🔲 🔲 🔲

BALMACARA
Balmacara (Lochalsh Woodland Garden)
IV40 8DN (3m E of Kyle of Lochalsh, off A87)
☎01599 566325 Fax 01599 566359
The Balmacara estate was bequeathed to The National Trust for Scotland in 1946, and comprises some 5600 acres and seven crofting villages, including Plockton, a conservation area. There are excellent views of Skye, Kintail (the Five Sisters), and Applecross. The area is excellent for walking, both on the estate and on forestry land nearby. A ranger/naturalist service is available on some days. The main visitor attraction is the Lochalsh Woodland Garden. To call Ranger/naturalist (based on Kintail) Tel: Willie Fraser (01599) 511231.
Open all year daily 9-sunset.
Woodland garden £1 (honesty box), (concessions 50p)
P ⬛

BALMORAL
Balmoral Castle Grounds & Exhibition
AB35 5TB (on A93 between Ballater & Braemar)
☎013397 42334 & 42335 Fax 013397 42271
Balmoral is the focal point of what is now known as Royal Deeside, a landscape of woodlands and plantations sweeping up to grouse moors and distant mountains. Queen Victoria and Prince Albert first rented Balmoral Castle in 1848, and Prince Albert bought the property four years later. He commissioned William Smith to build a new castle, which was completed by 1855 and is still the Royal Family's Highland residence. The wooded grounds and gardens can be visited from May to July. Country walks and pony trekking can be enjoyed, and an exhibition of paintings and other works of art can be seen in the castle ballroom, together with a Travel and Carriage exhibition and a wildlife exhibition in the Carriage Room.
Open 10 Apr-30 May Mon-Sat 10-5. 1 Jun-2 Aug Sun-Sat 10-5.
£3.50 (ch under 16 £1. pen £2.50)
P *(150 yds)* ⬛ 占 *(wheelchairs available & free parking enquire at main gate) toilets for disabled shop* ✺ *(ex guide dogs)*
Cards: 🔲 🔲 🔲 🔲 🔲

BANCHORY
Banchory Museum
Bridge St
☎01771 622906 Fax 01771 622884
Newly housed in purpose-built premises, Banchory Museum has displays of Scott Skinner (The 'Strathspey King'), natural history including two stags fighting, royal commemorative china, local silver artefacts among many other exhibits. There will be a new royal commemorative display to celebrate the centenary of Queen Victoria's Diamond Jubilee.
Open Etr-May & Oct, wknds & public holidays 11-1, 2-5; Jun-Sep, daily 10-1, 2-5.
Free.
P *(100yds) (limited)* 占 *(toilet in staff area, ask attendant) toilets for disabled shop* ✺ *(ex guide dogs)*

BANFF
Banff Museum
High St AB45 1AE
☎01771 622906 Fax 01771 622884
Displays of geology and natural history on the ground floor (Natural History display won the Glenfiddich Living Scotland Award in 1989). Upper Gallery houses local history material, Banff silver, arms and armour, and displays relating to James Ferguson (18th century astronomer) and Thomas Edward (19th century Banff naturalist).
Open Jun-Sep, Fri-Wed 2-5.15.
Free.
P *(200yds)* 占 *shop* ✺

Duff House
AB4 3SX (0.5m S, access south of town).
☎01261 818181
Fax 0131 244 3030
The house was designed by William Adam for William Duff, later Earl of Fife. The main block was roofed in 1739, but the planned wings were never built. Although it is incomplete, the house is still considered one of Britain's finest Georgian baroque buildings. There is an exhibition on its history.
Under repair, interior not accessible, can be viewed from outside.
P ✺ ▮
Details not confirmed for 1998

BETTYHILL
Strathnaver Museum
KW14 7SS
☎01641 521418
The museum has displays on the clearances, with a fine collection of Strathnaver Clearances furnishings, domestic and farm implements, and local books. There is also a Clan Mackay room. The museum's setting is a former church, a handsome stone building with a magnificent canopied pulpit dated 1774. The churchyard contains a carved stone known as the Farr Stone, which dates back to the 9th century and is a fine example of Pictish art.
Open Apr-Oct, Mon-Sat 10-1 & 2-5; Nov-Mar restricted opening.
£1.50 (ch 40p, pen £1, students 75p).
P 占 *shop* ✺ *(ex guide dogs)*

BOAT OF GARTEN
RSPB Nature Reserve Abernethy Forest
Forest Lodge PH25 3EF (signposted from B970)
☎01479 831694
Home of the Loch Garten Osprey site this reserve holds one of most important remnants of Scots Pine forest of the Scottish Highlands. Within its 30,760 acres are contained forest bogs, moorland, mountain top, lochs and crofting land. In addition to the regular pair of nesting ospreys, there are breeding colonies of Scottish crossbill, capercaillies, black grouse and many others. Winter visitors include greylag geese and goosanders. Mammals include red squirrel, pine marten, wildcat and both red and roe deer. The ospreys can be viewed through telescopes and there is a live TV link to the nest. There are marked woodland walks. ➤

Crathes Castle is crowned by the square turrets and conical pepper-pot towers typical of a 16th-century Scottish castle.

Reserve open at all times. Osprey Centre daily, end Apr-Aug 10-6.
✽£2 (ch 50p, concessions £1) Family £4.
🅿 shop ✖
Cards: 🔳 🔳 🔳 🔳

BRODIE CASTLE
Brodie Castle
IV36 0TE (4.5m W of Forres, off A96)
☎01309 641371 Fax 01309 641600
The Brodie family were granted land in this area in 1160, and lived in the castle for hundreds of years. It was passed to the National Trust for Scotland by the 25th Chief of the family in 1980. It is a handsome, gabled Scottish castle, and contains numerous treasures acquired over the centuries: fine furniture, porcelain, and an impressive collection of paintings including 17th-century Dutch works, 19th-century English watercolours and French Impressionists. The extensive grounds have a woodland walk, daffodils and a wildlife hide. There is also an adventure playground. Facilities for the disabled include wheelchair loan, a wheelchair carrier giving access to all public rooms on the first floor, purpose-built toilets for wheelchair users, audio tape and information in braille. Special events will be held in the Drawing Room and in the Castle grounds. Please telephone for details of recitals, concerts, open air theatre etc.
Open Apr-30 Sep, Mon-Sat 11-5.30, Sun 1.30-5.30; wknds in Oct, Sat 11-5.30, Sun 1.30-5.30. (last admission 4.30). Grounds open all year, 9.30-sunset. Other times by appointment.
£4.20 (concessions £2.80). Grounds £1. Family ticket £11.20. Party.
🅿 🍴 ♿ (audio tape & information sheet in Braille) toilets for disabled shop ✖ (ex guide dogs) 🏆

BUCKIE
Buckie Drifter
Freuchny Rd AB56 1TT (1m off the A98 between Elgin and Fraserburgh)
☎01542 834646 Fax 01542 835995
The Buckie Drifter is an exciting maritime heritage centre, where you can discover what life was like in the fishing communities of Moray District during the

herring boom years of the 1890s and 1930s. Sign on as a crew member of a steam drifter and find out how to catch herring. Try your hand at packing fish in a barrel. Discover the undersea life of the herring through 'hands-on' displays and find out why conservation is a feature of the fishing industry today. A series of changing displays are a feature of the museum.
Open Apr-Oct, Mon-Sat 10-6, Sun 12-6. Last admission 5pm.
✽£2.50 (ch & pen £1.60). Family ticket £7. Party £2.25. 1998 Prices Under Review.

🅿 ✖ licensed ♿ (car parking, touch display on lower floor & audio guide) toilets for disabled shop ✖ (ex guide dogs)

CARRBRIDGE
Landmark Highland Heritage & Adventure Park
PH23 3AJ (off A9 between Aviemore & Inverness)
☎01479 841613 Fax 01479 841384
The innovative centre has an exhibition on the history of the Highlands and a 3-D show on The Great Wood of Caledon. The Forestry Heritage Park has a 65ft forest viewing tower, a working steam-powered sawmill and various exhibitions and buildings. There are demonstrations of timber sawing, bodging and log hauling by a Clydesdale horse throughout the day. Attractions include the new 3 track Watercoaster, a fun maze, an adventure play area, a craft and book shop, restaurant, and snack bar with picnic area. Please telephone for details and free leaflet.
Open all year, daily, Apr-mid Jul 9.30-6; mid Jul-mid Aug 9.30-8; Sep-Oct 9.30-5.30; Nov-Mar 9.30-5.
Apr £4.95 (ch £3.25); May-Jun £5.30 (ch £3.65); Jul-Oct £5.80 (ch £4); Nov-Mar £3.50 (ch £2.25). Family tickets available.
🅿 ✖ licensed ♿ toilets for disabled shop Cards: 🔳 🔳 🔳 🔳

CAWDOR
Cawdor Castle
IV12 5RD (on B9090 off A96)
☎01667 404615 Fax 01667 404674
Home of the Thanes of Cawdor since the 14th century, the castle has a drawbridge, an ancient tower built round a tree, and a freshwater well inside the house. There are nature trails, a 9-hole golf course and a putting green. Gardens Weekend 6-7 June - guided tours of gardens and Bluebell Walk in Cawdor Big Wood.
Open 1 May-11 Oct, daily 10-5.30. (Last admission 5pm).
£5.20 (ch 5-15 £2.80, pen £4.20). Family ticket £14. Party 20+. Gardens, grounds & nature trails only £2.80.
🅿 🍴 ♿ toilets for disabled shop ✖ (ex guide dogs)

CLAVA CAIRNS
Clava Cairns
(6m E of Inverness)
☎0131 668 8800 Fax 0131 668 8888
On the south bank of the River Nairn, this

group of circular burial cairns is surrounded by three concentric rings of great stones. It dates from around 1600BC, and ranks among Scotland's finest prehistoric monuments.
Open all times.
🅿 ✖ 🍴
Details not confirmed for 1998

CORGARFF
Corgarff Castle
(8m W of Strathdon village)
☎01975 651460
The 16th-century tower was besieged in 1571 and is associated with the Jacobite risings of 1715 and 1745. It later became a military barracks. Its last military use was to control the smuggling of illicit whisky between 1827 and 1831.
Open Apr-Sep, Mon-Sat 9.30-6.30, Sun 2-6.30; Oct-Mar Sat 9.30-4.30, Sun 2-4.30.
🅿 🍴
Details not confirmed for 1998

CRAIGELLACHIE
Speyside Cooperage Visitor Centre
Dufftown Rd AB38 9RS (1m S of Craigellachie on A941)
☎01340 871108
Fax 01340 881303
Award-winning working cooperage with unique visitor centre, where skilled coopers and their apprentices practise their ancient craft of coopering. Each year they repair around 100,000 oak casks which will be used to mature many different whiskies. The 'Acorn to Cask' exhibition traces the history and development of the coopering industry and includes a Victorian cooperage with life-size models which speak in the local dialect. There is a viewing gallery over the bustling workshops and guided tours. All the text has been translated into French, German, Italian, Spanish and Japanese. The gift shop specialises in quality wooden items, many of which are not available anywhere else in Britain. Picnic area and Member of theMalt Whisky Trail.
Open all year except Christmas and New Year, Mon-Fri 9.30-4.30, also Jun-Sep on Sat 9.30-4.30.
✽£2 (ch & pen £1.50). Family ticket £5.75. Party 15+ £1.40. 1998 Prices Under Review.
🅿 ♿ (Special picnic table) toilets for disabled shop ✖ (ex guide dogs)
Cards: 🔳 🔳 🔳 🔳 🔳

The Tapestry Bedroom at Cawdor Castle, ancestral home of the Thanes of Cawdor.

Strategically placed on Loch Ness, the ruins of Urqhart Castle are all that remains of Scotland's largest castle. The castle is an ideal place for Loch Ness Monster spotting.

CRATHES

Crathes Castle & Gardens

AB31 3QJ (On A93, 3m E of Banchory)
☎01330 844525
Fax 01330 844797

This impressive 16th-century castle with magnificent interiors and painted ceilings has royal associations dating from 1323. There is a walled garden of over three acres and a notable collection of unusual plants. Yew hedges date from 1702, and seasonal herbaceous borders are a special feature. Eight gardens, extensive grounds and six nature trails, including one for the disabled, are among the attractions, plus a wayfaring course and children's adventure playground. The grounds are ideal for nature study. There are six trails and a visitor centre with permanent exhibitions. Ring for details of events.
*Open: Castle & Visitor Centre Apr-Oct, daily 11-5.30. Last admission 4.45).
Garden & grounds open all year, daily 9.30-sunset. Admission to castle by timed ticket arrangement. (entry may be delayed on busy days)
Castle, Garden & Grounds £4.80 (ch & concessions £3.20). Grounds £2 (ch £1.30). Family ticket £12.80.*
🅿 ✖ *licensed* ♿ *(tape for visually impaired) toilets for disabled shop* 🐾 *(ex guide dogs)* 🐕

CROMARTY

Hugh Miller's Cottage

Church St IV11 8XA
☎01381 600245

Hugh Miller, a stonemason who became an eminent geologist and writer, was born in the cottage in 1802. It was built by his great-grandfather in around 1698, and now has an exhibition and video on Miller and his work. The cottage garden was redeveloped in 1995, using a colourful range of native plants.
*Open May-Sep, Mon-Sat 11-1 & 2-5, Sun 2-5.
£2 (ch & concessions £1.30). Family ticket £5.30. Party.*
P *(5mins) (disabled is directly outside)* 🐾 *(ex guide dogs)* 🐕

CULLODEN MOOR

Culloden Battlefield

1V1 2ED (5m E of Inverness)
☎01463 790607 Fax 01463 794294

A cairn built in 1881 recalls the last battle fought on mainland Britain, on 16 April 1746, when 'Bonnie' Prince Charles Edward Stuart's army was bloodily routed by the Duke of Cumberland's forces. The battlefield has been restored to its state on the day of the battle. Old Leanach Cottage survived the battle, and now houses Living History enactments during the summer season. The Graves of the Clans and the Well of the Dead can also be seen. There is a visitor centre with a new permanent Jacobite exhibition, audio-visual show, (also in Gaelic, German, French, Italian and Japanese), bookshop and restaurant. There are also guided actor tours of the battlefield in season, please telephone for details.
*Open - site always. Visitor Centre open Feb-Mar & Nov-30 Dec, daily 10-4. (Closed 25 & 26 Dec, shop closed 1-7 Nov); Apr-Oct, daily 9-6; Audio visual show closed 30 mins before Visitor Centre.
Admission to visitor centre & museum (includes audio-visual programme & Old Leanach Cottage) £3 (ch, pen & students £2). Family ticket £8 Party.*
🅿 ✖ ♿ *(wheelchair, induction loop for hard of hearing,raised map). toilets for disabled shop* 🐾 *(ex guide dogs)* 🐕

DRUMNADROCHIT

Official Loch Ness Monster Exhibition

Loch Ness Centre IV3 6TU (on A82)
☎01456 450573 & 450218 Fax 01456 450770

A fascinating computer-controlled, multi-media presentation lasting 40 minutes. Ten themed areas cover the story from the pre-history of Scotland, through the cultural roots of the legend of the monster in Highland folklore, and into the fifty-year controversy which surrounds it. The exhibition was totally renewed in July 1989 and the centre encompasses the Nessie Giftshop, Keepers Cottage Workshop, the House of Heraldry, a kilt-maker, coffee shop and a hotel.
*Open all year; Etr-May 9.30-5.30; Jun-Sep 9.30-6 (9-8.30 Jul & Aug); Winter 10-4. Last admission 1hr before closing.
✱£4.50 (ch £2.50, pen & students £3.50). Family ticket £11.50.*
🅿 🍽 ✖ *licensed* ♿ *(parking) toilets for disabled shop* 🐾 *(ex in grounds)*
Cards: 🆇 ▬ ▬ 🅂

Urquhart Castle

(on A82)
☎01456 450551

The castle was once Scotland's biggest and overlooks Loch Ness. It dates mainly from the 14th century, when it was built on the site of an earlier fort, and was destroyed before the 1715 Jacobite rebellion.
Open all year, Apr-Sep, daily 9.30-6.30; Oct-Mar, Mon-Sat 9.30-4.30, Sun 9.30-4.30. (Closed 25-26 Dec & 1-2 Jan).
🅿 *shop* 🐾 🐕
Details not confirmed for 1998

DUFFTOWN

Balvenie Castle

AB55 4DH
☎01340 820121

The ruined castle was the ancient stronghold of the Comyns, and became a stylish house in the 16th century.
Open Apr-Sep, Mon-Sat 9.30-6.30, Sun 2-6.30.
🅿 ♿ *shop* 🐕
Details not confirmed for 1998

Dufftown Museum

The Tower, The Square AB55 (5 miles S of Craigellachie on A941)
☎01309 673701 Fax 01309 675863

This small museum has displays on the local area, including the ancient religious site of Mortlach with a history from the 6th century to the present day. Other displays show aspects of social history and Dufftown's most famous product - malt whisky.
Open 7 Apr-1 Jun, Mon-Fri 10-4. 2 Jun-Aug, Mon-Sat 10-4.30. 1-28 Sep, Mon-Sat 10-4. 29 Sep-24 Oct, Mon-Fri 10-4. Free.
P *(adjacent)* ♿ *shop* 🐾

Glenfiddich Distillery

AB55 4DH (N of town, off A941)
☎01340 820373 Fax 01340 820805

Set close to Balvenie Castle, the distillery was founded in 1887 by William Grant and has stayed in the hands of the family ever since. Visitors can see the whisky-making process in its various stages, including bottling, and then sample the finished product. A theatre provides an audio-visual show (in six languages) on the history and manufacture of whisky, and there is a Scotch whisky museum.
*Open all year Mon-Fri 9.30-4.30, also Etr-mid Oct Sat 9.30-4.30, Sun 12-4.30. (Closed Xmas & New Year).
✱(Free at the moment, issue of charging currently under review as all other distilleries charge admission)*
🅿 ♿ *(ramp access to production area & warehouse gallery) toilets for disabled shop* 🐾 *(ex guide dogs)*
Cards: 🆇 ▬ ▬ 🅂

DUFFUS

Duffus Castle

(off B9012)
☎0131 668 8800 Fax 0131 668 8888

The remains of the mighty motte-and-bailey castle are surrounded by a moat. Within the eight-acre bailey is a 15th-century hall, and the motte is crowned by a 14th-century tower.
Open at all reasonable times.
🅿 🐾 🐕
Details not confirmed for 1998

DUNBEATH

Laidhay Croft Museum

KW6 6EH (1m N on A9)
☎01593 731244

The museum gives visitors a glimpse of a long-vanished way of life. The main building is a thatched Caithness longhouse, with the dwelling quarters, byre and stable all under one roof. It dates back some 200 years, and is furnished as it might have been 100 years ago. A collection of early farm tools and machinery is also shown. Near the house is a thatched winnowing barn with its roof supported on three 'Highland couples', or crucks.
*Open Etr-mid Oct, daily 10-6.
£1 (ch upto 50p?)*
🅿 🍽 ♿ *toilets for disabled*

ELGIN

Elgin Cathedral

North College St IV30 1EL
☎01343 547171

Founded in 1224, the cathedral was known as the Lantern of the North and the Glory of the Kingdom because of its beauty. In 1390 it was burnt, with most of the town, by the Wolf of Badenoch - Alexander Stewart, Earl of Buchan - who had been excommunicated by the bishop. Although it was rebuilt, it fell into ruin after the Reformation. The ruins are quite substantial, however, and there is still a good deal to admire, including the fine west towers and the octagonal chapter house.
Open all year, Apr-Sep, Mon-Sat 9.30-6.30, Sun 2-6.30; Oct-Mar, Mon-Sat 9.30-4.30, Sun 2-4.30. (Closed Thu pm & Fri in winter; 25-26 Dec & 1-3 Jan).
🅿 *shop* 🐕
Details not confirmed for 1998

Elgin Museum

1 High St IV30 1EQ (opp 'Safeway'. Follow brown signs)
☎01343 543675 Fax 01343 543675

This award-winning museum is internationally famous for its fossil fish and fossil reptiles, and for its Pictish stones. The displays relate to the natural and human history of Moray. Temporary exhibitions have covered such subjects as Doctor Who, Jacobites, Schooldays and Dolphins. Exhibitions for 1998 May include: Embroidery (Apr-May), Africa (Jun) Biodiversity (mid Jul-Oct). Also activities for Museums Week and Geology Week, please telephone for details.
Open Apr-Oct, Mon-Fri 10-5, Sat 11-4, Sun 2-5.

➤

In countryside of heather and peat bog, a beautiful garden has been made at Inverewe where the warm Gulf Stream creates a frost-free zone on this windswept coast.

£1.50 (ch 50p, pen, students & UB40 75p). Family ticket £3.50.
P (50mtrs) & (handrails inside & out. All case displays at sitting level) toilets for disabled shop ✹ (ex guide dogs)

Pluscarden Abbey
IV30 3UA (6m SW on unclass road)
☎01343 890257 Fax 01343 890258
The original monastery was founded by Alexander II in 1230 and then burnt, probably by the Wolf of Badenoch who also destroyed Elgin Cathedral. It was restored in the 14th and 19th centuries, and then reoccupied in 1948 by Benedictines from Prinknash. It is now once more a religious community. Retreat facilities are available for men and women. Guides on duty at weekends and busy periods. Natural beeswax polish and natural apiary remedies now available. All services (with Gregorian chanting) are open to the public. Pluscarden Pentecostal Lectures (2-4 Jun). Inauguration of new organ in July or August, 50th Anniversary celebrations in September. Please ring for details.
Open all year, daily 4.45-8.30.
Free.
P & (induction loop, ramps to shop) toilets for disabled shop

ELPHIN
Highland & Rare Breeds Farm
IV27 4HH (on A835 in Elphin)
☎01854 666204 Fax 01854 666204
There are over thirty six breeds, both ancient and modern, some of which visitors may stroke or feed, also a pets' corner, riverside walk and a theme shop. Guided tours are available by prior arrangement. Sheep-shearing demonstrations are planned for July, and handspinning demonstrations throughout the season.
Open mid May-Sep daily 10-5.
✱£3 (ch £2, students & pen £2.50)
P & (assistance available) toilets for disabled shop ✹
Cards: ⬛ ⬛ ⬛

FETTERCAIRN
Fasque
AB30 1DN (0.5m N on B974)
☎01561 340569 & 340202
Fax 01561 340325
Fasque has been the home of the

Gladstone family since 1829, and W E Gladstone, four times Prime Minister, lived here from 1830 to 1851. There are impressive state rooms and a handsome, sweeping staircase, but more interesting in many ways are the extensive servants' quarters. The life and work of the large household staff is illustrated, and there are also collections of farming machinery and other local items. The spacious park has red deer and Soay sheep.
Open May-Sep, daily 11-5.30. (Last admission 5pm).
P ⬛ & (wheelchairs available) shop ✹
Details not confirmed for 1998

FOCHABERS
Baxters Visitor Centre
IV32 7LD (1m W of Fochabers on A96)
☎01343 820666 Fax 01343 821790
The Baxters food firm started here almost 130 years ago and now sells its products in over 60 countries. Visitors can see the shop where the story began, take a guided tour of the factory, watch an audio-visual display, and visit four shops. See the great hall, audio-visual theatre and cooking theatre.
Open all year, Mon-Fri 10-5.30 Daily.
✱Free. The cooking demonstration theatre will be by appointment & charged for.
P ✗ licensed & (parking facilities) toilets for disabled shop ✹
Cards: ⬛ ⬛ ⬛ ⬛

Fochabers Folk Museum
High St IV32 7EP
☎01343 821204 Fax 01343 821291
This converted church exhibits the largest collection of horse-drawn vehicles in the North of Scotland. There are also displays of the many aspects of village life through the ages, including model engines, clocks, costumes, a village shop and Victorian parlour.
Open all year, daily 9.30-1 & 2-6. Winter closing 5pm.
Free.
P & shop ✹

FORRES
Dallas Dhu Distillery
(1m S of Forres off the Grantown road)
☎01309 676548
A perfectly preserved time capsule of the distiller's art. It was built in 1898 to supply malt whisky for Wright and Greig's 'Roderick Dhu' blend. Visitors are

welcome to wander at will through this fine old Victorian distillery, or to take a guided tour, dram included.
Open all year, Apr-Sep, Mon-Sat 9.30-6.30, Sun 2-6.30. Oct-Mar, Mon-Sat 9.30-4.30, Sun 2-4.30. (Closed Thu pm & Fri in winter, 25 & 26 Dec, 1 & 3 Jan).
P & toilets for disabled shop ✹ ▮
Details not confirmed for 1998

Falconer Museum
Tolbooth St IV36 0PH (on A96)
☎01309 673701 Fax 01309 675863
This museum was founded by bequests made by two brothers, Alexander and Hugh Falconer. Hugh was a distinguished scientist, a friend of Darwin, recipient of many honours and Vice-President of the Royal Society. On display are fossil mammals collected by him, and items relating to his involvement in the antiquity of mankind. Other displays are on local wildlife, geology, archaeology and history. Regular temporary exhibitions are held throughout the year. There is also a display about The Corries folk duo.
Open all year. Jan-Mar Mon-Fri 10-5; Apr-Oct, Mon-Sat 10-5; Nov-Dec, Mon-Fri 10-5.
Free.
P (100yds) & shop ✹ (ex guide dogs)

Suenos' Stone
☎0131 668 8800 Fax 0131 668 8888
The 20ft-high stone was elaborately carved in the 9th or 10th century, with a sculptured cross on one side and groups of warriors on the other. Why it stands here no one knows, but it may commemorate a victory in battle.
Open & accessible at all times.
P ✹ ▮
Details not confirmed for 1998

FORT GEORGE
Fort George
IV1 2TD (11m NE of Inverness)
☎01667 462777
Built following the Battle of Culloden as a Highland fortress for the army of George II, it is one of the outstanding artillery fortifications in Europe and still an active army barracks. Reconstructed barracks of the 18th and 19th centuries, Seafield Collection of Arms, chapel and Regimental Museum of the Queen's Own Highlanders.

Open all year, Apr-Sep, Mon-Sat 9.30-6.30, Sun 2-6.30; Oct-Mar, Mon-Sat 9.30-4.30, Sun 2-4.30. (Closed 25-26 Dec & 1-3 Jan).
P & toilets for disabled shop ✹ ▮
Details not confirmed for 1998

Queen's Own Highlanders
Regimental Museum Collection
IV1 2TD
☎01463 224380 Fax 01463 224380
Fort George (above) has been a military barracks since it was built in 1748-1769, and was the Depot of the Seaforth Highlanders until 1961. The museum of the Queen's Own Highlanders (Seaforth and Camerons) collection is sited in the former Lieutenant Governor's house, where uniforms, medals and pictures are displayed.
Open Apr-Sep, Mon-Sat 10-6, Sun 2-6; Oct-Mar, Mon-Fri 10-4. (Closed Good Fri-Etr Mon, Xmas, New Year & BH).
Free. (Admission charged by Historic Scotland for entry to Fort George).
P & (stair lift to 1st floor, wheelchair on 1st floor) toilets for disabled shop ✹ (ex guide dogs)

FORT WILLIAM
Inverlochy Castle
PH33 6SN (2m NE)
☎0131 668 8800 Fax 0131 668 8888
The castle was begun in the 13th century and added to later. It is noted in Scottish history for the battle fought nearby in 1645, when Montrose defeated the Campbells.
Open Apr-Sep. Key available from keykeeper.
✹ ▮
Details not confirmed for 1998

West Highland Museum
Cameron Square PH33 6AJ
☎01397 702169
Fax 01397 702169
The displays illustrate traditional Highland life and history, with numerous Jacobite relics. One of them is the 'secret portrait' of Bonnie Prince Charlie, which looks like meaningless daubs of paint but reveals a portrait when reflected in a metal cylinder.
Open all year Mon-Sat; May-Oct 10-5, also Jul & Aug Sun 2-5. Nov-Apr 10-4.
£2 (ch 50p, concessions £1.50)
P (100 yds) (charged in Jun-Jul, 2hrs stay)
& (disabled facilities during 1996) toilets for disabled shop ✹ (ex guide dogs)

GAIRLOCH
Gairloch Heritage Museum
Auchtercairn IV21 2BJ
☎01445 712287
A converted farmstead now houses the award-winning museum, which shows the way of life in this typical West Highland parish from early times to the 20th century. There are hands-on activities for children and reconstructions of a croft house room, a school room, a shop, and the inside of a local lighthouse. Restored fishing boats are also shown. Evening demonstrations during July and August, spinning, baking, butter-making and net and creel making. There will be a series of events arranged to celebrate the museum's 21st season. Please ring for details.
Open Apr-mid Oct, Mon-Sat 10-5. end Oct-Mar by arrangement.
£1.50 (ch 50p & pen £1)
P ⬛ ✗ licensed & (toilets for wheelchair visitors 100yds from entrance) shop ✹

GLENCOE
Glencoe & North Lorn Folk Museum
PA39 4HS
Two heather-thatched cottages in the main street of Glencoe now house items connected with the Macdonalds and the Jacobite risings. A variety of local domestic and farming exhibits, dairying and slate-working equipment, costumes and embroidery is also shown.
Open mid May-Sep, Mon-Sat 10-5.30.
£1 (ch 50p).
P & shop

Glencoe Visitor Centre
PA39 4HX (on A82, 17m S of Fort William)

☎01855 811307 Fax 01855 811772

Glencoe has stunning scenery and some of the best climbing (not for the unskilled) and walking country in the Highlands. Its wildlife includes red deer and wildcats, golden eagles and ptarmigan. The A82 Glasgow to Fort William road runs through the glen, so it is also more accessible than some. It is best known, however, as the scene of the massacre of February 1692, when, under Government orders, a party of troops billeted here tried to murder all their Macdonald hosts - men, women and children. The Visitor Centre is at the north end of the glen, close to the scene of the massacre. It has a display on the history of mountaineering in the glen, provides information on walks, and has a video programme telling the story of the 1692 Massacre of Glencoe. Ranger service.
Open; Site all year. Visitor Centre Apr-18 May & Sep-Oct, daily 10-5; 19 May-Aug, daily 9.30-5.30. (last admission 30 mins before closing).
50p (ch & pen 30p). Includes parking.
P 🅿️ ♿ *(induction loop in video programme room) toilets for disabled shop* ⌖ *(ex guide dogs)* ⌖

Highland Mysteryworld
PA39 4HL (on A82, 10m S of Fort William)

☎01855 811660 Fax 01855 821463

Don't miss out on Scotland's new exciting attraction, set in a spectacular location at the foot of dramatic Glencoe. You'll have great fun at Highland Mysteryworld, where the ancient mysteries of the Highlands are energised right before your eyes. Discover the myths, learn the legends and sense the superstitions in a magical world brought to life by actors and the latest animatronics effects. At Highland Mysteryworld you can explore five fabulous indoor attractions. With the Astromyth Theatre, Roots of Rannoch, Clootie Well, Viking Foodship and Mysterymall there is something to suit all ages. Other facilities include: lochside

trails, the Myworld Adventure Playground, supervised Creche and a Leisure Centre with indoor heated pool.
Open mid Mar-end Oct, daily, peak 10-6, off peak 10-4.
£4.95 (concessions £2.95). Family (2 adults & 2 ch) £12.00.
P 🅿️ ✖ *licensed ♿ toilets for disabled shop*
Cards: ▨ ▨ ▨ ▨ ⬚

GLENFINNAN
Glenfinnan Monument
PH37 4LT (on A830, 18.5miles W of Fort William)

☎01397 722250

The monument commemorates Highlanders who fought and died for Bonnie Prince Charlie in 1745. It was built in 1815, and has an awe-inspiring setting at the head of Loch Shiel. There is a visitor centre with information (commentary in four languages) on the Prince's campaign. The Glenfinnan Games will be held on the 15th of August.
Open - Site all year. Visitor Centre, Apr-18 May & 1 Sep-Oct, daily 10-1 & 2-5; 19 May-Aug, daily 10-6.
£1.50 (ch £1). Family ticket £4. Includes parking.
P 🅿️ ♿ *(information centre only) shop* ⌖

GOLSPIE
Dunrobin Castle
KW10 6SF (1m NE on A9)

☎01408 633177 & 633268
Fax 01408 633800

The ancient seat of the Earls and Dukes of Sutherland takes its name from Earl Robin, who built the original square keep in the 13th century. The castle is now a splendid, gleaming, turreted structure, thanks largely to 19th-century rebuilding, and has a beautiful setting overlooking the sea. Paintings (including Canalettos), furniture and family heirlooms are on display inside, and the gardens are on a grand scale to match the house (they were modelled on those at Versailles). A summer house in the grounds is now a museum with a variety of exhibits.
Open Etr-15 Oct, Mon-Sat 10.30-5.30, Sun 12-5.30. Closes 1 hr earlier Etr, May

& Oct. Last admission half hour before closing.
P ♿ *(access by arrangement only) shop* ⌖
Details not confirmed for 1998

HELMSDALE
Timespan
Dunrobin St KW8 6JX

☎01431 821327

The North's most exciting heritage centre features the dramatic story of the Highlands, from Picts and Vikings, to the last burning of a witch and the Highland Clearances through to crofting, fishing and the present day oil fields. Scenes from the past are re-created using life-size sets, sound effects, and an audio-visual programme. There is a riverside garden and gift shop, an art gallery and coffee lounge.
Open Etr-mid Oct, Mon-Sat 9.30-5, Sun 2-5 (6pm Jul-Aug). Last admission one hour before closing.
✲*£3 (ch £1.75 pen & student £2.40). Family ticket £7.85.*
P 🅿️ ♿ *toilets for disabled shop garden centre* ⌖ *(ex guide dogs)*
Cards: ▨ ▨

HUNTLY
Brander Museum
The Square

☎01771 622906 Fax 01771 622884

The museum has local history displays, and also holds changing special exhibitions every year.
Open all year, Tue-Sat 10-12 & 2-4. Free.
P *(25yds)* ♿ *(telephone for details as not yet known) shop* ⌖ *(ex guide dogs)*

Huntly Castle
AB54 5BP

☎01466 793191

The original medieval castle was rebuilt a number of times and destroyed, once by Mary, Queen of Scots. It was rebuilt for the last time in 1602, in palatial style, and is now an impressive ruin, noted for its ornate heraldic decorations. It stands in wooded parkland.
Open all year, Apr-Sep, Mon-Sat 9.30-6.30, Sun 2-6.30; Oct-Mar, Mon-Sat 9.30-

4.30, Sun 2-4.30. (Closed Thu pm & Fri in winter; 25-26 Dec & 1-3 Jan).
P ⚑
Details not confirmed for 1998

INVERNESS
Castle Stuart
Petty Parish IV1 2JH (5m E of Inverness, off A96)

☎01463 790745 Fax 01463 792604

Ancient home of the Earls of Moray and the Stuart family, constructed in 1621 when the Royal House of Stuart had ruled the United Kingdoms of England and Wales, Scotland and Ireland for some twenty years. It is located within the sound of the cannon's roar from High Culloden Moor, where the last attempt to restore the Stuart monarchy ended in defeat. The interior has been restored to its former glory with Jacobean furnishings, armour and historic relics.
Open all year, daily 10-5.
£4 (ch £2, pen & students £3).
P *shop* ⌖
Cards: ▨ ▨

INVERURIE
Carnegie Museum
Town House, The Square

☎01771 622906 Fax 01771 622884

This busy shopping and business centre is ringed by many prehistoric sites; and in more recent times the canal to Aberdeen was started from one of its suburbs. Together with enterprising thematic exhibitions (changed about three times a year), Inverurie's fine museum displays canal relics and items on local history and archaeology.
Open all year, Mon-Tue & Thu-Fri 2-5, Sat 10-1 & 2-4. (closed Wed & Sat) Free.
P *(50 yds) shop* ⌖ *(ex guide dogs)*

KEITH
Strathisla Distillery
Seafield Av AB55 3BS (0ff A96, in town)

☎01542 783044 Fax 01542 783039

At Strathisla Distillery, home and heart of Chivas Regal, we welcome you as our guests. Enjoy our hospitality and the unhurried pace of the self-guided tour of the oldest distillery in the highlands, founded in 1786. Discover the art of the blender before sipping a superb dram in luxurious comfort.
Open Feb-mid Mar, Mon-Fri 9.30-4; mid Mar-end Nov, Mon-Sat 9.30-4, Sun 12.30-4.
£4 including £2 voucher redeemable in the distillery shop against the purchase of 70cl bottle of whisky. (ch18 free, children under 8 are not admitted to production areas, but are welcome in the centre)
P *(access is very limited) shop* ⌖ *(ex guide dogs)*
Cards: ▨ ▨ ▨ ▨ ⬚

KEMNAY
Castle Fraser
AB51 7LD (off A944, 4m N of Dunecht)

☎01330 833463

The massive Z-plan castle was begun about 1575 and completed in 1636. Its architectural embellishments were mainly carried out by two notable families of master masons, Bell and Leiper, and their work helped to make it one of the grandest of the Castles of Mar. An earlier fortified tower house is incorporated in the design. The interior was remodelled in 1838 and decoration and furnishings of that period survive in some of the rooms. A formal garden has been created in the old walled garden. Estate trails and a children's adventure play area have been added. Concerts, recitals, open-air events: contact property for full programme.
Open - Castle Good Fri-Etr Mon, May-Jun & Sep, daily 1.30-5.30; Jul-Aug, daily 11-5.30; wknds in Oct 1.30-5.30 (last admission 4.45). Garden all year, daily 9.30-6; Grounds all year daily 9.30-sunset. Castle, Garden & grounds £4.20 (concessions £2.80). Garden & Grounds £2 (concessions £1.30). Family ticket available.
P 🅿️ ♿ *shop garden centre* ⌖ *(ex guide dogs, certain areas)* ⌖

The Great Hall of Castle Fraser is reached by a winding staircase and from the round tower there are views over the castle's wooded parkland.

KILDRUMMY

Kildrummy Castle
AB3 8RA (10m W of Alford)
☎01975 571331
An important part of Scottish history, at least until it was dismantled in 1717, this fortress was the seat of the Earls of Mar. Now it is a ruined, but splendid, example of a 13th-century castle, with four round towers, hall and chapel all discernible. Some parts of the building, including the Great Gatehouse, are from the 15th and 16th centuries.
Open summer only, Apr-Sep, Mon-Sat 9.30-6.30, Sun 2-6.30.
🅿 & toilets for disabled shop ▌
Details not confirmed for 1998

Kildrummy Castle Gardens
AB33 8RA (on A97)
☎019755 71277 & 71203
With the picturesque ruin as a backdrop, these gardens are not only beautiful but also noted for their botanic interest. An alpine garden in an ancient quarry and a water garden are just two of its features, while the surrounding woods give interesting short walks. There is also a small museum, a video room showing a 15-minute film of the changes in the garden through the seasons, a children's play area and a sales area selling unusual plants.
Open Apr-Oct, daily 10-5.
£2 (children go free)
🅿 🍴 & toilets for disabled shop

KINCRAIG

Highland Wildlife Park
PH21 1NL (on B9152, 7m S of Aviemore)
☎01540 651270 Fax 01540 651236
In this magnificent natural setting get eye-to-eye with Scottish wildlife - past and present! As you drive through the main reserve see awe-inspiring European bison grazing alongside wild horses, red deer and highland cattle plus a wide variety of other species. Then in the walk-round forest, woodland and moorland habitats prepare for close encounters with a whole host of animals such as wolves, capercaillie, arctic foxes, wildcats, pine martens, beavers, otters and owls. Visitor centre with cafeteria, gift shop and exhibition. Free pet kennels at entrance gate. Free guide book. An exciting programme of special events is planned for 1998. As well as regular sheepdog demonstrations there will be themed event days with walks, talks, face-painting, mask-making, quizzes and a whole lot more! There is also the chance to talk to keepers during the carnivore feed times. New for 1998 is the Amazing Wolf Territory complete with raised walkway and viewpoint. Special events are held every weekend Apr-Oct, ring for details.
Open Apr-Oct, daily 10-last entry 4pm, (5pm Jun-Aug). Nov-Mar 10-last entry 2pm weather permitting.
❋£6-£17 per car. Walkers £6 (concessions £3.10).
🅿 🍴 & toilets for disabled shop 🐾
Cards: ◪ 💳

KINGUSSIE

Highland Folk Museum
Duke St PH21 1JG (12m SW of Aviemore off the A9 at Kingussie)
☎01540 661307 Fax 01540 661631
The Museum has a comprehensive highland collection of social history material, displayed in realistic settings and reconstructed buildings. Displays include traditional farming, farm machinery, country crafts, domestic life, costume and furniture.
Open Mar-Oct, Mon-Sat 10-6, Sun 2-6.
£3 (ch & pen £2).
🅿 & toilets for disabled shop 🐾 (ex guide dogs)

Ruthven Barracks
(0.5m SE of Kingussie)
☎0131 668 8800 Fax 0131 668 8888
Despite being blown up by 'Bonnie' Prince Charlie's Highlanders, these infantry barracks are still the best preserved of the four that were built after the Jacobite uprising. The considerable ruins are the remains of a building completed in 1716 on the site of a fortress of the 'Wolf of Badenoch'.
Open at any reasonable time.
🅿 🐾 ▌
Details not confirmed for 1998

KIRKHILL

Moniack Castle (Highland Winery)
IV5 7PQ (7m from Inverness on A862)
☎01463 831283 Fax 01463 831419
A unique Scottish enterprise is undertaken in the former fortress of the Loval chiefs: commercial wine-making is not a usual Scottish industry, but nevertheless a wide range of 'country'-style wines is produced, including elderflower and silver birch; and also mead and sloe gin. A wine bar and bistro are added temptations.
Open all year, Mon-Sat 10-5. (11-4 in winter).
Free.
🅿 🍴 ✕ licensed shop 🐾
Cards: ◪ 💳

LEWIS, ISLE OF

ARNOL

Black House Museum
PA86 9DB
☎01851 710395
A traditional Hebridean dwelling is built without mortar and roofed with thatch on a timber framework. It has a central peat fire in the kitchen, no chimney and a byre under the same roof. The Black House museum is an excellent example and it retains many of its original furnishings.
Open Apr-Sep, Mon-Sat 9.30-6.30; Oct-Mar, Mon-Thu & Sat 9.30-4.30.
🅿 & shop 🐾
Details not confirmed for 1998

CALLANISH

Callanish Standing Stones
PA86 9DY (12m W of Stornoway)
☎0131 668 8800 Fax 0131 668 8888
An avenue of 19 monoliths leads north from a circle of 13 stones with rows of more stones fanning out to south, east and west. Probably constructed between 3000 and 1500BC, this is a unique cruciform of megaliths.
Open & accessible at all times.
🅿
Details not confirmed for 1998

CARLOWAY

Dun Carloway Broch
(1.5m S of Carloway)
☎0131 668 8800 Fax 0131 668 8888
Brochs are late-prehistoric circular stone towers, and their origins are mysterious. One of the best examples can be seen at Dun Carloway, where the tower still stands about 30ft high.
Open at all reasonable times.
🅿 ▌
Details not confirmed for 1998

MARYCULTER

Storybook Glen
AB12 5FT (5m W of Aberdeen on B9077)
☎01224 732941
This is a children's fantasy land, where favourite nursery rhyme and fairytale characters are brought to life. Grown-ups can enjoy the nostalgia and also the 20 acres of Deeside country, full of flowers, plants, trees and waterfalls.
Open Mar-Oct, daily 10-6; Nov-Feb, Sat & Sun only 11-4.
£3.40 (ch £1.70, pen £2.50).
🅿 🍴 ✕ licensed & toilets for disabled shop 🐾

MARYPARK

Glenfarclas Distillery
AB37 9BD (4m W of Aberlour on A95 to Grantown-on-Spey)
☎01807 500245 & 500257 Fax 01807 500234
Home of one of the finest Highland malt whiskies, this distillery provides an interesting exhibition illustrating the whisky's history and production. There is also a shop and visitor centre. A recent addition is a cask-filling store where visitors may watch new whisky being poured into oak casks when filling is in progress. Please telephone for details of International Whisky Festival.
Open all year; Apr-Sep, Mon-Fri 9.30-5, Sat 10-4.(Jun-Sep, also Sun 12.30-4.30); Oct-Mar, Mon-Fri 10-4. Last tour 1hr before closing time. Coaches by arrangement.
❋£2.50 per adult. Prices under review.
🅿 & (only visitor centre is accessible) toilets for disabled shop 🐾 (ex guide dogs in Vis.Centre)
Cards: ◪ 💳 💳 💳 🏧

METHLICK

Haddo House
AB41 0ER (off B999, 4m N of Pitmedden)
☎01651 851440 Fax 01651 851888
Haddo House is renowned for its association with the Haddo Choral Society and is the venue for international concerts which attract top performers from around the world. It is a splendid Palladian-style mansion built in the 1730s to designs by William Adam. Home to the Earls of Aberdeen, the house was refurbished in the 1880s in the 'Adam Revival' style and still retains much of its original flavour. The adjoining country park, run by Aberdeenshire Regional Council, offers a network of enchanting woodland paths and attracts all kinds of wildlife. Hundreds of birds can be seen on the loch and there is an observation hide for visitors. Concerts, plays, recitals etc. Contact property for details.
Open - House Good Fri-Etr Mon & May-Sep, daily 1.30-5.30; wknds in Oct 1.30-5.30 (last admission 45 mins before closing). Garden & country park open all year, daily 9.30-sunset.
£4.20 (ch & pen £2.80). Family ticket £11.20. Party.
🅿 ✕ & (lift to first floor of house & wheelchair) toilets for disabled shop 🐾 (ex in grounds, guide dogs ok) 🐕

MINTLAW

Aberdeenshire Farming Museum
Aden Country Park AB42 5FQ (1m W of Mintlaw on A950)
☎01771 622906 Fax 01771 622884
The award-winning heritage centre is housed in 19th-century farm buildings, once part of the estate which now makes up the Aden Country Park (above). Two centuries of farming history and innovation are illustrated in an exciting exhibition, a pleasant way to take a break from enjoying the surrounding countryside. The story of the Aden estate is also interestingly illustrated. The newly reconstructed farm of Hareshowe shows how a family in the north-east farmed during the 1950s - access by guided tour only.
Open May-Sep, daily 11-4.30; Apr & Oct, wknds only noon-4.30. Last admission 30 mins before closing. Park open all year, daily 7-10.
Free.
🅿 & (garden for partially sighted) toilets for disabled shop 🐾

Aden Country Park
AB42 5FQ (1m W Mintlaw off A950)
☎01771 622857 Fax 01771 622884
The grounds of a former estate provide over 200 acres of beautiful woodland and open farmland for the visitor to explore. A network of footpaths winds through specially developed nature trails and gives a chance of seeing a great variety of plants and other wildlife. The Ranger Service offers a programme of varied events and is available ans is available for bookings by appointment. A new Wildlife Discovery Centre will be opening in 1998, ring for further details or for a programme of events.
Open all year, summer 7-10, winter 7-7.
Free except for some special events
🅿 & (sensory garden, electric chair, parking) toilets for disabled shop 🐾 (ex on lead)

NEWTONMORE

Clan Macpherson House & Museum
Main St PH20 1DE
☎01540 673332
Containing relics and memorials of the clan chiefs and other Macpherson families as well as those of Prince Charles Edward Stuart, this museum also displays the Prince's letters to the Clan Chief of 1745 and one to the Prince from his father the Old Pretender, along with royal warrants and the green banner of the clan. Other interesting historic exhibits include James Macpherson's fiddle, swords, pictures, decorations and medals. Highland games take place on the first Saturday in August.
Open May-Sep, Mon-Sat 10-5.30, Sun 2.30-5.30. Other times by appointment.
🅿 & toilets for disabled shop 🐾
Details not confirmed for 1998

OLD DEER

Deer Abbey
(10m W of Peterhead)
☎0131 668 8800 Fax 0131 668 8888
The remains of the Cistercian Abbey, founded in 1218, include the infirmary, Abbot's House and the southern claustral range. The University Library at Cambridge now houses the famous Book of Deer.
Open at all reasonable times.
🅿 🐾 ▌
Details not confirmed for 1998

ORKNEY

BIRSAY

Earl's Palace
KW15 1PD
☎0131 668 8800 Fax 0131 668 8888
The gaunt remains of the residence of the late-16th-century Earl of Orkney, constructed round a courtyard.
Open all year.
🐾 ▌
Details not confirmed for 1998

DOUNBY

Brough of Birsay
(6m NW)
☎0131 668 8800 Fax 0131 668 8888
This ruined Romanesque church stands next to the remains of a Norse village. The nave, chancel and semicircular apse can be seen along with claustral buildings. Crossings must be made on foot at low-water - there is no boat.
Open at all reasonable times.
▌
Details not confirmed for 1998

Click Mill
(NE of village,off B9057)
☎0131 668 8800
Fax 0131 668 8888
This is an example of the rare Orcadian horizontal watermill, and is in working condition.
Open at all reasonable time.
▌
Details not confirmed for 1998

Skara Brae
(9m W of Kirkwall on A965)
☎01856 841815
Engulfed in drift sand, this remarkable group of well-preserved Stone Age dwellings is the most outstanding survivor of its kind in Britain. Stone furniture and a fireplace can be seen.
Open all year, Apr-Sep, Mon-Sat 9.30-6.30, Sun 2-6.30; Oct-Mar, Mon-Sat 9.30-4.30, Sun 2-4.30. (Closed 25-26 Dec & 1-3 Jan).
🅿 🐾 ▌
Details not confirmed for 1998

FINSTOWN

Maes Howe Chambered Cairn
(9m W of Kirkwall, on A965)
☎01856 761606
The masonry of Britain's finest megalithic tomb is in a remarkable state of preservation. Dating from neolithic times, it contains Viking carvings and runes.
Open all year, Apr-Sep, Mon-Sat 9.30-

6.30, Sun 2-6.30; Oct-Mar, Mon-Sat 9.30-4.30, (ex closed Wed & Thur am), Sun 2-4.30. (Closed 25-26 Dec & 1-3 Jan).

🅿 ♿ *shop* ⊗ 🏮

Details not confirmed for 1998

Stenness Standing Stones

(3m SW off A965)

☎ *0131 668 8800 Fax 0131 668 8888*

Dating back to the second millenium BC, the remains of this stone circle are near the Ring of Brogar - a splendid circle of upright stones surrounded by a ditch.

Open at any reasonable time.

🅿 🏮

Details not confirmed for 1998

HARRAY

Orkney Farm & Folk Museum

KW17 2JR

☎ *01856 771411 & 771268 Fax 01856 874615*

The museum consists of two Orkney farmhouses with outbuildings. Kirbuster (Birsay) has the last surviving example of a 'Firehoose' with its central hearth; Corrigall (Harray) represents an improved farmhouse and steading of the late 1800s. Both display period furnishings, farm implements and native breeds of sheep among their exhibits.

Open Mar-Oct, Mon-Sat 10.30-1 & 2-5, Sun 2-7.

🅿 ♿ *shop* ⊗ *(ex guide dogs)*

Details not confirmed for 1998

KIRKWALL

Bishop's & Earl's Palaces

☎ *01856 875461*

The Bishop's Palace is a hall-house of the 12th century, later much altered, with a round tower built by Bishop Reid in 1541-48. A later addition was made by the notorious Patrick Stewart, Earl of Orkney, who built the adjacent Earl's Palace between 1600 and 1607 in a splendid Renaissance style.

Open Apr-Sep, Mon-Sat 9.30-6.30, Sun 2-6.30.

♿ 🏮

Details not confirmed for 1998

Tankerness House Museum

Broad St KW15 1DH

☎ *01856 873191 Fax 01856 874616*

One of the finest vernacular town houses in Scotland, this 16th-century building now contains a museum of Orkney history, including the islands' fascinating archaeology. Summer exhibition: The Skaill Hoard - A Viking silver hoard found in Orkney in the 19th century. (April-September)

Open all year, Mon-Sat 10.30-12.30 & 1.30-5 (May-Sep Sun 2-5).

P (50yds) ♿ *shop* ⊗ *(ex guide dogs)*

Details not confirmed for 1998

STROMNESS

Orkney Maritime & Natural History Museum

52 Alfred St KW16 3DF

☎ *01856 850025*

The museum focuses on Orkney's broad maritime connections, including fishing, whaling, the Hudson's Bay Company, the German Fleet in Scapa Flow, and the award winning Pilot's House extension. The Natural History Gallery will be closed for restoration. Summer Exhibition (Apr-Sep) 'Voices from the Great War' - Orkney's involvement in World War One.

Open May-Sep, Mon-Sun 10-5; Oct-Apr, Mon-Sat 10.30-12.30 & 1.30-5. (Closed Xmas, New Year & 3 wks Feb-Mar).

£1.50 (ch 35p). Family ticket £3.50.

P (50yds) ♿ *shop* ⊗ *(ex guide dogs)*

Pier Arts Centre

KW16 3AA

☎ *01856 850209 Fax 01856 851462*

The collection is housed in a warehouse standing on its own stone pier. A children's workshop operates during the school summer holidays and there is a constantly changing programme of exhibitions, including Margaret Melvis (4 Apr-9 May), Alan Davie (6 Jun-11 Jul).

Open all year, Tue-Sat 10.30-12.30 & 1.30-5. Free.

P (100 yds) ♿ *shop* ⊗ *(ex guide dogs)*

WESTRAY

Noltland Castle

☎ *0131 668 8800 Fax 0131 668 8888*

Started in the 16th century, this ruined castle was never completed. It has a fine hall, vaulted kitchen and a notable winding staircase.

Open all reasonable times. Application to key keeper.

⊗ 🏮

Details not confirmed for 1998

OYNE

Archaeolink

Berryhill AB52 6QT (1m off A96 on B9002)

☎ *01464 851500 Fax 01464 851544*

An exciting new attraction in rural Aberdeenshire. A stunning audio-visual show together with a Myths and Legends Gallery and a whole range of interpretation techniques will allow the visitor to explore what it was like to live 6000 years ago. In addition there are landscaped walkways, and outdoor activity areas including an Iron Age farm, within the 38 acre park. A full programme of events is planned, including Roman Weekend (25/26 July) - battle re-enactment of Mons Grampius (AD83), Roman games, Celtic combats, crafts, marching drills and chariot display. Also Ancient Craft Fair in the autumn - an opportunity to watch people working at traditional crafts. Please telephone for details.

Open all year, Mar-Oct, Sun-Sat 9.30-5; winter weekdays 11-4, winter weekends 10-4.

£3.90 (ch 5-16, concessions £2.35, ch under 5 free). Family ticket £10. Party 10+.

🅿 ⬛ ✕ *licensed* ♿ *toilets for disabled shop* ⊗ *(ex guide dogs)*

Cards: 🌑 ▭ ▭ ▭ ⑤

PETERCULTER

Drum Castle

AB31 3EY (3m W of 10 m from Aberdeen off A93)

☎ *01330 811204*

The great Square Tower was built in the late 13th century and is one of the three oldest tower houses in Scotland. It has associations with King Robert the Bruce. The handsome mansion was added in 1619. There is a collection of family memorabilia in the Irvine Room. The grounds contain the 100-acre Old Wood of Drum, a natural oak wood. There is also a garden of historic roses, woodland walks, play and picnic areas. For details of recitals and other special events please telephone.

Open Good Fri-Etr Mon & May-Sep, daily 1.30-5.30; wknds in Oct 1.30-5.30. Last admission 4.45. Grounds open all year 9.30-sunset.

£4.20 (ch & pen £2.80). Family ticket £11.20. Party.

🅿 ⬛ ♿ *(wheelchair available) shop* ⊗ *(ex guide dogs)*

PETERHEAD

Arbuthnot Museum & Art Gallery

St Peter St AB42 6QD

☎ *01771 622906 Fax 01771 622884*

Specialising in local exhibits, particularly those relating to the fishing industry, this museum also displays Arctic and whaling specimens and a British coin collection. The regular programme of exhibitions changes approximately every six weeks.

Open all year, Mon, Tue & Thu-Sat 10.30-1.30 & 2.30-5, Wed 10.30-1. (Closed PH). Free.

P (150 yds) *shop* ⊗ *(ex guide dogs)*

PITMEDDEN

Pitmedden Garden

AB41 0PD (1m W of Pitmedden on A920)

☎ *01651 842352 Fax 01651 843188*

The fine late 17th-century 5-acre walled garden has been recreated here, and sundials, pavilions and fountains are dotted among the formal parterres. The Museum of Farming Life has been recently refurbished. There is also a visitor centre, a woodland walk, and a special dog walk.

Open - Garden, Museum of Farming Life & Visitor Centre open May-Sep, daily 10-5.30 last admission 5pm.

Garden, Museum of Farming Life & Visitor Centre £3.70 (ch & concessions £2.50). Family ticket £9.90. Garden & grounds only £1 honesty box. Party.

🅿 ⬛ ♿ *(2 wheelchairs available) toilets for disabled shop* 🍴

Tolquhon Castle

(2m NE off B999)

☎ *01651 851286*

Now roofless, a late 16th-century quadrangular mansion encloses an early 15th-century tower. There is a fine gatehouse and courtyard.

Open all year, Apr-Sep, Mon-Sat 9.30-6, Sun 2-6; Oct-Mar wknds only Sat 9.30-4.30, Sun 2-4.30. (Closed 25-26 Dec & 1-2 Jan).

🅿 ♿ *toilets for disabled* ⊗ 🏮

Details not confirmed for 1998

POOLEWE

Inverewe Garden

IV22 2LG (6m NE of Gairloch, on A832)

☎ *01445 781200 Fax 01445 781497*

The presence of the North Atlantic Drift enables this remarkable garden to grow rare and sub-tropical plants. At its best in early June, but full of beauty from March to October, Inverewe has a backdrop of magnificent mountains and stands to the north of Loch Maree. Fishing available on three lochs. Boat and fishing rod hire available.

Open - Garden all year, Apr-Oct, daily 9.30-9. Nov-14 Mar 9.30-5.30. Visitor Centre Apr-Oct, daily 9.30-5.30. Guided walks 15 Mar-Oct Mon-Fri at 1.30.

£4.80 (concessions £3.20). Family ticket £12.80. Party.

🅿 ✕ *licensed* ♿ *(some paths difficult) toilets for disabled shop* ⊗ *(ex guide dogs)* 🍴

RHYNIE

Leith Hall & Garden

Kennethmont AB54 4NQ (on B9002, 1m W of Kennethmont)

☎ *01464 831216*

Home of the Leith family for over 300 years, the house dates back to 1650, and has a number of Jacobite relics, a major exhibition 'For Crown and Country: the Military Lairds of Leith Hall', and fine examples of needlework. It is surrounded by charming gardens and extensive grounds which contain ponds, trails, a bird hide and unusual semicircular 18th-century stables. Telephone for details of special events such as concerts and recitals.

Open - House Good Fri-Etr Mon & May-Sep, daily 1.30-5.30; wknds in Oct 1.30-5.30. (Last admission 45 mins before closing). Gardens and grounds all year 9.30-sunset.

£4.20 (ch & concessions £2.80). Family ticket £11.20. Gardens & grounds only £2 (ch & concessions £1.30). Party.

🅿 ⬛ ♿ *(parking next to hall, scented garden for the blind) toilets for disabled* ⊗ *(ex guide dogs)* 🍴

ROTHES

Glen Grant Distillery

AB38 7BS (On A941, in Rothes)

☎ *01542 783318 Fax 01542 783304*

Founded in 1840 in a sheltered glen by the two Grant brothers. The distillery produces a light, floral malt whisky which ➤

Details not confirmed for 1998

Skara Brae, the remarkable Stone Age village, was preserved by drifting sand

is 'different by tradition'. Enjoy a tour and discover the secrets of the distillery, including the delightful Victorian garden originally created by Major Grant, recently restored to its former glory, where you can enjoy a dram from Major Grant's Whisky safe. Gift shop, audio-visual presentation and gardens.
Open mid Mar-end Oct, Mon-Sat 10-4, Sun 11.30-4. Jun-end Sept remains open until 5 daily.
£2.50 includes £2 voucher redeemable in the distillery shop against 70cl bottle of whisky. Inclusive charge for garden visit & distillery tour. A free dram is offered to over 18s. (ch18 free, children under 8 not admitted to production areas, but are welcome in centre & garden)
🅿 ♿ *(reception centre & still house) toilets for disabled shop* ⊗
Cards: 🌀 ▭ 🌀

SHETLAND

LERWICK
Clickhimin
ZE1 0QX (1m SW)
☎ 0131 668 8800 Fax 0131 668 8888
The remains of a prehistoric settlement that was fortified at the beginning of the Iron Age with a stone-built fort. The site was occupied for over 1000 years. The remains include a partially demolished broch (round tower) which still stands to a height of 17ft.
Open at all reasonable time.
🔳
Details not confirmed for 1998

Fort Charlotte
ZE1 0JN (overlooking harbour)
☎ 0131 668 8800 Fax 0131 668 8888
An artillery fort, begun in 1665 to protect the Sound of Bressay during the Anglo-Dutch War. The fort was burned by the Dutch in 1673, together with the town of Lerwick. It was repaired in 1781 during the American War of Independence. The fort is pentagonal with high walls and seaward-facing gunports.
Open at all reasonable time.
🔳
Details not confirmed for 1998

Shetland Museum
Lower Hillhead ZE1 0EL
☎ 01595 695057 Fax 01595 696729
The massive brass propeller blade outside the building is from the 17,000-ton liner

Oceanic, wrecked off Foula in 1914. The recently refurbished archaeology gallery covers Neolithic burials and axe-making; Bronze Age houses, Iron Age farming and domestic life. There are Medieval fishing and agriculture displays, and church history. The maritime gallery has also been recently re-designed, and covers line and herring fishing, the merchant marine, and traditional boat models. There are also agricultural and social history displays, including peat-working, corn harvest, local businesses, medals, bootmaking, and Shetland weddings.
Open all year Mon, Wed, Fri 10-7, Tue, Thu, Sat 10-5.
Free.
🅿 ♿ *(lift, wheelchair available) toilets for disabled shop* ⊗ *(ex guide dogs)*

MOUSA ISLAND
Mousa Broch
(Accessible by boat from Sandwick)
☎ 0131 668 8800 Fax 0131 668 8888
This broch is the best-preserved example of an Iron Age drystone tower in Scotland. The tower is nearly complete and rises to a height of 40ft. The outer and inner walls both contain staircases that may be climbed to the parapet.
Open at all reasonable times.
🔳
Details not confirmed for 1998

SCALLOWAY
Scalloway Castle
☎ 0131 668 8800 Fax 0131 668 8888
The ruins of a castle designed on the medieval two-step plan. The castle was actually built in 1600 by Patrick Stewart, Earl of Orkney. When the Earl, who was renowned for his cruelty, was executed in 1615, the castle fell into disuse.
Open at all reasonable time.
🅿
Details not confirmed for 1998

SUMBURGH
Jarlshof Prehistoric Site
(At Sumburgh Head, approx 22m S of Lerwick)
☎ 01950 460112
One of the most remarkable archaeological sites in Europe. There are remains of Bronze Age, Iron Age and Viking settlements as well as a medieval farm. There is also a 16th-century Laird's House, once the home of the Earls Robert and Patrick Stewart, and the basis of 'Jarlshof' in Sir Walter Scott's novel *The Pirate*.

Open Apr-Sep, Mon-Sat 9.30-6.30, Sun 2-6.30.
🅿 ♿ 🔳
Details not confirmed for 1998

SKYE, ISLE OF

ARMADALE
Clan Donald Vistor Centre
IV45 8RS (0.5m from Armadale Pier A851)
☎ 01471 844305 & 844227 Fax 01471 844275
Skye's award-winning Visitor Centre is situated at the south end of the island. Armadale Castle and Gardens were built in 1815 as the home of Lord Macdonald. The sculptured ruins of the castle now house the Museum of the Isles, with an exhibition and slide-show. A library and study centre offer genealogical research and access to historical records. Surrounding the castle are 40 acres of beautiful woodland gardens and nature trails. The Countryside Ranger Service provides a full summer programme of walks, talks and children's afternoons. The converted stables house a restaurant/tearoom and gift shop. Special events for 1998: (16 May) Scottish Harp Competition, (late May - tbc) Garden & Craft Fair (13 Jun) Sheepdog Trials, (19 June) Piping Competition, (30 Jun-4 Jul) Archery Tournament.
Open 24 Mar-8 Nov.Limited winter opening.
❋£3.40 (concessions £2.20). Family ticket £9. Party.
🅿 🍴 ✗ *licensed* ♿ *(wheelchairs available, hearing loop in Audiovisual room) toilets for disabled shop garden centre*
Cards: 🌀 ▭ 🌀 💳

DUNVEGAN
Dunvegan Castle
IV55 8WF
☎ 01470 521206 Fax 01470 521205
This fortress stronghold set on the sea loch of Dunvegan has been the home of the Chief of Macleod for 790 years. On view are books, pictures, arms and treasured relics of the clan. There is a display that traces the history of the family and the clan from their days as Norsemen until the present day. A pedigree Highland Cattle fold is also a major attractions as is the boat trip to the nearby Seal Colony - take your camera as

the boatmen are trained to get close enough to the seals to enable some wonderful photographs to be taken. There is also the opportunity for a cruise of the loch aboard a turbo diesel boat *MacLeod of MacLeod* which seats 35.
Open 20 Mar-31 Oct, Mon-Sat 10-5.30, Sun, castle 1-5.30, gardens 10-5.30. Last admission 5pm. Nov-Mar by appointment only.
🅿 🍴 ✗ *licensed shop* ⊗ *(ex in grounds)*
Details not confirmed for 1998

SPEY BAY
Tugnet Ice House
Tugnet IV32 7PJ (8m E of Elgin on A96, then onto B9104 towards Spey Bay, establishment is 1m further along)
☎ 01309 673701 Fax 01309 675863
The largest ice house in Scotland, built in 1830, now contains exhibitions on the history and techniques of commerical salmon fishing on the River Spey, with an audio-visual programme. There are sections on the geography, wildlife and industries of the Lower Spey area, such as ship-building at nearby Kingston.
Open - unable to confirm 1998 times.
Free.
🅿 ♿ *toilets for disabled shop* ⊗ *(ex guide dogs)*

STONEHAVEN
Dunnottar Castle
AB39 2TL (2m S of Stonehaven on A92)
☎ 01569 762173
A must for anyone who takes Scottish history seriously, this once-impregnable fortress, now a spectacular ruin, was the site of the successful protection of the Scottish Crown Jewels from the might of Cromwell.
Open all year, summer Mon-Sat 9-6, Sun 2-5; winter Mon-Fri 9-sunset. Last entry 30 minutes before closing. Closed Xmas/New Year.
❋£3 (ch 5-15 £1)
🅿 ⊗ *(ex on lead)*

Tolbooth Museum
Old Pier
☎ 01771 622906 Fax 01771 622884
Built in the late 16th centrury as a storehouse for the Earls Marischal at Dunnottar Castle, the building was the Kincardineshire County Tollbooth from 1600. Displays feature local history and fishing.
Open Jun-Sep, Mon & Thu-Sat 10-noon & 2-5; Wed & Sun 2-5.
Free.
P (100yds) ♿ *shop* ⊗ *(ex guide dogs)*

STRATHPEFFER
Highland Museum of Childhood
The Old Station IV14 9DH
☎ 01997 421031
The museum is situated in a renovated Victorian railway station of 1885, along with various craft shops. In early June Victorian days are held. Strathpeffer also has Highland Games in early August. Children's Workshops are run in the school holidays.
Open mid Mar-Oct, daily 10-5, (Sun 2-5) also Jul & Aug evenings 7-9. Other times by arrangement.
£1.50 (ch, pen & students £1). Family ticket (2 adults & 3 children) £3.50.
🅿 🍴 ♿ *shop* ⊗
Cards: 🌀 ▭ 🌀

TOMINTOUL
Tomintoul Museum
The Square AB3 9ET (on A939, 13miles E of Grantown)
☎ 01309 673701 Fax 01309 675863
Situated in one of the highest villages in Britain, the museum features a reconstructed crofter's kitchen and smiddy, with other displays on the local wildlife, the story of Tomintoul, and the local skiing industry.
Open 7 Apr-1 Jun, Mon-Fri 10-4; 2 Jun-Aug, Mon-Sat 10-4.30; 1-28 Sep, Mon-Sat 10am-4pm; 29 Sep-24 Oct Mon-Fri 10-4.
Free.
🅿 ♿ *(handling display for visually impaired) shop* ⊗ *(ex guide dogs)*

In the distance, beyond Sandwick, is Mousa Island on which stands Mousa Broch, the best preserved Iron-Age stone-built tower in Scotland.

Blair Atholl was the last castle in Britain to be besieged. The tower named after the first owner, Cummings, was damaged during a Jacobite siege in 1746.

TORRIDON

Torridon Countryside Centre

The Mains IV22 2EZ (N of A896).
☎01445 791221 Fax 01445 791261
Set amid some of Scotland's finest mountain scenery, (including Laithach - 3,456ft-which has seven peaks, and Beinn Allign -3,232ft-both will be of interest to geologists and naturalists.) the centre offers audio-visual presentations on the local wildlife. At the Mains nearby there are live deer to be seen, and there is also a static display on the life of the red deer.
Open - Countryside Centre May-Sep, Mon-Sat 10-5, Sun 2-5. Estate and Deer Museum daily all year. Audio-visual display & Deer Museum £1.50 (ch & concessions £1). Family ticket £4.
🅿 ♿ toilets for disabled 🦌

TURRIFF

Fyvie Castle

Fyvie AB53 8JS (8m SE of Turriff on A947)
☎01651 891266
This superb castle dating from the 13th century has five towers, each built in a different century by one of the families who lived here. It is now one of the grandest examples of Scottish baronial architecture. The castle contains the finest wheel stair in Scotland, and a 17th-century morning room which, along with other rooms, has been decorated and furnished in lavish Edwardian grandeur. There is an exceptional collection of portraits, with works by Batoni, Raeburn, Romney, Gainsborough, Opie and Hoppner; and arms, armour and 16th-century tapestries can also be seen. Please telephone for details of special events - these include concerts, recitals, and battle re-enactments.
Open Apr-Jun & Sep daily 1.30-5.30. Jul-Aug daily 11-5.30, wknds Oct 1.30-5.30. (last admission 4.45). Grounds open all year, daily 9.30-sunset.
£4.20 (ch & pen £2.80). Family ticket £11.20. Party 20+. Grounds honesty box £1.
🅿 ♿ (small lift, braille sheets) toilets for disabled shop 🐕 (ex guide dogs) 🦌

WESTHILL

Garlogie Mill Power House Museum

Skene (Take Alford road from Aberdeen, at end of Garlogie village turn right into mill grounds)
☎01771 622906
Fax 01771 622884
A restored building housing the power sources for the now-demolished mill. Notable for the presence of the succession of power generating machinery used, in particular the only beam engine of its type left in situ in Scotland.
Open Thu-Mon 12.30-5, May-Sep Free.
🅿 ♿ toilets for disabled shop 🐕 (ex guide dogs)

WICK

Caithness Glass Factory & Visitor Centre

Airport Industrial Estate KW1 5BP (on Northern side of Wick, beside Airport on A99 road to John O'Groats)
☎01955 602286
Fax 01955 605200
All aspects of glassmaking are on view, from the initial processing of the raw materials to the finished article. Visitors can see the jewellery and engraving departments at work and learn about the history of Caithness Glass in the exhibition. There is a factory shop, and a restaurant.
Open all year, Factory shop & Restaurant Mon-Sat 9-5 (Sun, Etr-Dec 11-5). Glassmaking Mon-Fri 9-4.30. Free.
🅿 ✗ licensed ♿ toilets for disabled shop 🐕
Cards: 🔲 🔲 🔲 🔲

Castle of Old Wick

(1m S)
☎0131 668 8800
Fax 0131 668 8888
A ruined four-storey, square tower that is probably of the 12th century. It is also known as Castle Oliphant.
Open except when adjoining rifle range is in use.
🐕 🦌
Details not confirmed for 1998

Wick Heritage Centre

20 Bank Row KW1 5HS
☎01955 605393
Fax 01955 605393
The heritage centre is near the harbour in a complex of eight houses, yards and outbuildings. The centre illustrates local history from Neolithic times to the herring fishing industry. In addition, there is a complete working 19th-century lighthouse, and the famous Johnston collection of photographs. The centre has won five major awards including 'Best of Better Britain 1992'.
Open Jun-Sep, daily 10-5. (Closed Sun).
✳*£2 (ch 50p).*
🅿 ♿ toilets for disabled

CENTRAL SCOTLAND

This region includes the counties of Angus, Argyll & Bute, City of Edinburgh, Clackmannanshire, Dundee City, East Lothian, Falkirk, Fife, Inverclyde, Midlothian, Perth & Kinross, Stirling and West Lothian which reflect the recent national changes.

ABERDOUR

Aberdour Castle

KY3 0SL
☎01383 860519
The earliest surviving part of the castle is the 14th-century keep. There are also later buildings, and the remains of a terraced garden, a bowling green and a fine 16th-century doocot (dovecote).
Open all year, Apr-Sep, Mon-Sat 9.30-6.30, Sun 2-6.30; Oct-Mar, Mon-Sat 9.30-4.30, Sun 2-4.30. (Closed Thu pm, Fri in winter, 25-26 Dec & 1-3 Jan).
🅿 ♿ toilets for disabled shop 🎴
Details not confirmed for 1998

ABERLADY

Myreton Motor Museum

EH32 0PZ (1.5m from A198, 2m from A1)
☎01875 870288
This is a charming and wide-ranging collection, with cars and motorcycles from 1896, cycles from 1863 and commercial vehicles, historic British military vehicles, advertising signs and automobilia.
Open all year, daily 10-6 (summer); 10-5 (winter). (Closed 25 Dec & 1 Jan). £3 (ch 16 £1).
🅿 ♿ shop 🐕 (ex guide dogs)

ALLOA

Alloa Tower

Alloa Park FK10 1PP (on A907)
☎01259 211701
Beautifully restored by the Alloa Tower Building Preservation Trust and Clackmannanshire Council, the tower, completed in 1467, is the only remaining part of the ancestral home of the Earls of Mar. It was splendidly remodelled by the 6th Earl and partially completed before he was sent into exile after the 1715 Jacobite uprising. The structure retains rare medieval features, notably the complete timber roof structure and groin vaulting. A superb loan collection of portraits and chattels of the Erskine family includes paintings by Jameson and Raeburn. Special events include concerts and recitals, please telephone for details.
Open Etr & May-Sep, daily 1.30-5.30. £2.40 (concessions £1.60). Family ticket £6.40. Party.
🅿 ♿ toilets for disabled 🐕 🦌

ALVA

Mill Trail Visitor Centre

Glentana Mill, West Stirling St FK12 5EN (situated on A91 approx 8m E of Stirling)
☎01259 769696 Fax 01259 763100
In the heart of Scotland's woollen mill country, the Centre recounts the history of Scotland's woollen and tweed traditions, and features machines from spinning wheels to large motorised looms of the type in use today. Hear 12 year old Mary describe her working day as a mill girl 150 years ago, and then contrast her story with our modern working woolen mill. Factory bargains and local crafts. Tourist information centre, café.
Open all year, Jan-Jun 10-5; Jul-Sep 9-6; Oct-Dec 10-5. Closed Xmas/New Year. Free.
🅿 ♿ toilets for disabled shop 🐕

ANSTRUTHER

Scottish Fisheries Museum

St Ayles, Harbour Head KY10 3AB
☎01333 310628
A cobbled courtyard at the harbour is the setting for the displays on Scotland's fishing history. Chief attractions are the boats (real and model), and the fisherman's cottage. The museum is housed in a range of 16th- to 19th-century buildings, and has recently extended into an old boatyard alongside.
Open all year, Apr-Oct, Mon-Sat 10-5.30, Sun 11-5; Nov-Mar, Mon-Sat 10-4.30, Sun 2-4.30. (Closed 25-26 Dec & 1-2 Jan). Last admission 45 mins before closing.
£3.50 (concessions £2.50). Family ticket £9.50. Party 12+.
P (20 yds) (charge in summer) 🍴 ♿ (ramps) toilets for disabled shop 🐕 (ex guide dogs)

ARBROATH

Arbroath Abbey

☎01241 878756
The 'Declaration of Arbroath' - declaring Robert the Bruce as king - was signed at the 12th-century abbey on 6 April 1320. The abbot's house is well preserved, and the church remains are also interesting.
Open all year, Apr-Sep, Mon-Sat 9.30-6.30, Sun 2-6.30; Oct-Mar, Mon-Sat 9.30-4.30, Sun 2-4.30. (Closed 25-26 Dec & 1-3 Jan)
🅿 ♿ 🐕 🎴
Details not confirmed for 1998

Arbroath Museum
Signal Tower, Ladyloan DD11 1PU (On A92)
☎01241 875598
Fish and Arbroath Smokies, textiles and engineering feature at this local history museum housed in the 1813 shore station of Stevenson's Bell Rock lighthouse. Other displays include maritime wildlife, school days, and a wash house and parlour with a wailing baby and a cat.
Open all year, Mon-Sat 10-5; Jul-Aug, Sun 2-5.(Closed 25-26 Dec, 1-2 Jan).
🅿 ⅆ *shop* ✤
Details not confirmed for 1998

BALERNO
Malleny Garden
EH14 7AF (off Lanark Rd (A70))
☎0131 449 2283
The delightful gardens are set around a 17th-century house (not open). There is a good selection of shrub roses, a woodland garden, and a group of four clipped yews, the survivors of a group of 12 which were planted in 1603. The National Bonsai Collection for Scotland is also at Malleny.
Open Apr-Oct, daily 9.30-7; Nov-Mar, daily 9.30-4. House not open.
£1 (honesty box)
🅿 ⅆ ✤ *(ex guide dogs)* ✤

BANNOCKBURN
Bannockburn Heritage Centre
Glasgow Rd FK7 0LJ (2m S of Stirling off M80/M9 junc 9)
☎01786 812664
The Heritage Centre stands close to the Borestone site, which by tradition was King Robert the Bruce's command post before the Battle of Bannockburn, June 1314, at which the Scots trounced the English. It was a turning-point in Scottish history, and Bruce is commemorated by a bronze equestrian statue, unveiled in 1964. The site is enclosed by the Rotunda. The centre has an exhibition, 'The Kingdom of the Scots', and an audio-visual display on the battle.
*Open - Rotunda & site always open.
Heritage Centre & Shop; Mar & Nov-23 Dec, daily 11-3; Apr-Oct daily 10-5.30. (Last audio-visual showing half hour before closing)
Admission to Heritage Centre incl. audio-visual presentation £2.40 (ch & concessions £1.60) Party £1.90 (ch/school £1). Family £6.40.*
🅿 ⅆ *(Induction loop for the hard of hearing) toilets for disabled shop (Closed Nov 1-10)* ✤ *(ex site only)* ✤

BARRY
Barry Mill
DD7 7RJ (2m W of Carnoustie)
☎01241 856761
This restored 18th-century mill works on a demonstration basis. Records show that the site has been used for milling since at least the 16th century. Displays highlight the important place the mill held in the community, milling and supplying oats for all the local farms. Waymarked walk and picnic area.
*Open Good Fri-Etr Mon & May-Sep, daily 11-5; wknds in Oct, 11-5.
£2. (concessions £1.30) Family £5.30.
Group. Schhol parties.*
🅿 ⅆ *ramp from car park to mill toilets for disabled (grounds only)* ✤

BIRKHILL
The Birkhill Clay Mine
(via A706 from Linlithgow, A904 from Grangemouth, coaches via A706).
☎01506 825855 Fax 01506 828766
No simulations here, this is a real clay mine deep in the steep wooded Avon Gorge. Experience life underground, and visit the original mill, clay handling buildings and haulage gear. Work is in progress on a car park, picnic area, underground walks and a nature trail.
Open 1 Apr-15 Oct weekends only. 8 Jul-20 Aug daily. Holiday Mon's 17 Apr, 1 & 29 May.
🅿
Details not confirmed for 1998

BLAIR ATHOLL
Atholl Country Collection
The Old School PH18 5SP
☎01796 481232
Artefacts and photographs illustrate local life and trades from 1850 onwards. Displays include a crofter's kitchen, a 'smiddy' (smithy), dress, a byre (with stuffed Highland cow), a gamekeeper's corner, road, rail and postal communications, the church and school. There is a Kiddies' Kist, where everything can be lifted up and examined.
*Open end May-mid Oct 1.30-5, also from 10 Jun-Aug & Sep weekdays.
£2 (ch £1). Prices under review.*
🅿 ⅆ *shop*

Blair Castle
PH18 5TL (7m NW of Pitlochry, off A9)
☎01796 481207 Fax 01796 481487
Traditional Home of the Dukes of Atholl and the Atholl Highlanders, the Duke's unique private army. The castle dates back to the 13th century but was altered in the 18th century and later given a castellated exterior. The oldest part is Cumming's Tower, built in about 1270. There are 32 rooms open to the public, with paintings, Jacobite relics, lace, tapestries, china, arms and armour, and Masonic regalia to be seen. The extensive grounds include a deer park, and visitors may follow nature trails or go pony trekking. A restored 18th-century walled garden opened to visitors in 1997. Numerous events are held throughout the year, including the annual parade of the Duke's Private Army (23 May), Highland Games (24 May), Horse Trials and Three Day Event (27-30 August) and the Glenfiddich Piping Championships (31 Oct-1 Nov).
*Open daily 1 Apr-30 Oct. 10am-6pm. Last admission 5pm.
£5.50 (ch £4 pen £4.50). Family ticket £17. Party rates available.*
🅿 *(charged)* ⅋ ⅆ *licensed* ⅆ *(toilets, but not suitable for severely disabled) shop*
✤ *(ex in grounds)*
Cards: 🅰 💳 💳 🅶

BLAIR DRUMMOND
Blair Drummond Safari & Leisure Park
FK9 4UR (M9 exit 10, 4m along A84 towards Callander)
☎01786 841456 & 841396
Fax 01786 841491
Drive through the wild animal reserves and see at close range the monkeys, zebras, North American bison, antelope, lions, tigers, white rhino and camels. Pets' Farm is home to a wide variety of animals including piglets, llamas, wallabies, rheas, goats and peafowl. Other attractions include the sea lion show, a ride on the boat safari through the waterfowl sanctuary and around Chimpanzee Island, an adventure playground, flying fox cable slide across the lake, giant astraglide, and pedal boats. There is a new den for European brown bears and a new zebra reserve. There are also Zimbabwean elephants, giraffes and ostriches. The pet farm includes penguins, otters, ringtail lemurs, Capuchin monkeys and meerkats. There is a new "Chakula Grill" at the lakeside and activities for children such as Superbounce, continental dodgems and face painting.
*Open Mar 28-Oct 5, daily 10-5.30. Last admission 4.30.
£8 (ch 3-14 & pen £4, ch under 3 free). Party 15+ (paid in advance) £7, (ch & pen £3.50) School groups- Driver & 1 adult free with 10 paying children. Special rates for hospitals, ring for details.*
🅿 ⅋ ✕ *licensed* ⅆ *(special menus & waitress service if booked in advance) toilets for disabled shop* ✤ *(ex guide dogs)*

BO'NESS
Bo'ness & Kinneil Railway
Bo'ness Station, Union St EH51 9AQ (A904 from all directions, signposted)
☎01506 822298 Fax 01506 828233
The nostalgia and romance of steam lives on at the Bo'ness and Kinneil Railway. Historic railway buildings, including the station and train shed, have been relocated from sites all over Scotland. In a purpose built exhibition hall, the Scottish Railway Exhibition tells the story of the development of railways in Scotland, and their impact on the people of Scotland. Take a seven mile trip by steam train to the tranquil country station at Birkhill. The rich geology of the area with its 300 million year old fossils is explained during conducted tours of the caverns of Birkhill Fireclay Mine. Picnic sites and souvenir shop. A new restaurant will open at Bo'ness Station in 1998. Special events throughout the year: (10-13 Apr) Easter Egg Specials, (16-17 May & 8-9 Aug) Thomas the Tank Engine Weekends, (21 Jun) Vintage Vehicle Rally, (5,6 Sept) Diesel Gala Weekend, (28-29 Nov & 5-6, 12-13, 19-20 Dec) Santa Steam Trains.
Open 4 Apr-18 Oct, Sat & Sun; Fri 3 Apr & Mon 13 Apr, 4 May, 25 May, 31 Aug. Daily except Mon 3 Jul-30 Aug. Also school days 3, 4, 10, 11, 17, 18 June. Steam trains depart Bo'ness 11.20, 12.30, 14.00, 15.15, and diesel at 16.30. July & Aug also steam train at 10.30. Return fare £3.90 (ch 5-15 £1.90, concessions (disabled or over 60) £2.60). Family ticket £9.70 Inclusive ticket for return train fare and tour of Birkhill Fireclay Mine £6.30 (ch £3.10, concessions £4.20), Family ticket £15.70.
🅿 ⅆ ✕ ⅆ *(ramps to stn, and adapted carriage) shop*
Cards: 🅰 💳

Kinneil Museum & Roman Fortlet
Duchess Anne Cottages, Kinneil Estate EH51 0PR
☎01506 778530
The museum is in a converted stable block of Kinneil House. The ground floor has displays on the industrial history of Bo'ness, while the upper floor looks at the history and environment of the

Kinneil estate. The remains of the Roman fortlet can be seen nearby. An audio visual theatre shows 2000 years of history.
Open all year, Apr-Sep, Mon-Fri 10-12.30 & 1.30-5, Sat 10-5 & May-Aug, Sun 10-5; Oct-Mar, Sat only 10-5.
Free.
P & shop ✗

BRUAR

Clan Donnachaidh (Robertson) Museum
PH18 5TW (approx 4m N of Blair Atholl, on B8079)
☎01796 483264 Fax 01796 483338
Clan centre for Robertsons, Duncans, Reids and other associated names. Changing displays feature the history of the clan and its people,exhibits include Jacobite relics, maps, silver, tartan and archives. There will be an exhibition to commemorate the 200th Anniversary of the Battle of Camperdown, featuring Admiral Duncan.
Open Apr-Oct Mon-Sat 10-5, Sun 11-5, Jun-Aug closes at 5.30.
P & shop ✗ (ex guide dogs)
Details not confirmed for 1998
Cards: ▨ ▨

BURNTISLAND

Burntisland Edwardian Fair Museum
102 High St
☎01592 412860 Fax 01592 412870
All the fun of the fair at this Scottish Museum of the Year Award Winner. Burntisland Museum has recreated a walk through the sights and sounds of the town's fair in 1910, based on a painting of the scene by local artist Andrew Young. See reconstructed rides, stalls and side shows of the time and view the local history gallery.
Open all year, Mon, Wed, Fri & Sat 10-1 & 2-5; Tue & Thu 10-1 & 2-7pm. Closed public holidays.
P (on street parking) ✗
Details not confirmed for 1998

BUTE, ISLE OF

ROTHESAY

Ardencraig
PA20 9HA (1m off A844, S of Rothesay)
☎01700 504225 Fax 01700 504225
Particular attention has been paid to improving the layout of the garden and introducing rare plants. The greenhouse and walled garden produce plants for floral displays throughout the district. A variety of interesting fish is kept in the ornamental ponds and the aviaries have some interesting birds.
May-Sep.
Free.
P ✐ & ✗ (ex guide dogs)

Bute Museum
Stuart St PA20 0BR
☎01700 502033 (contact) 505067 (museum)
The contents are all from the Isle of Bute, and are housed in two galleries. The natural history room has birds, mammals and seashore items; and the history room has varied collections of recent bygones, such as models of Clyde steamers, photographs of 'old' Rothesay, farming and history items. There is a collection of early Christian crosses, and the prehistoric section has flints and pots from two Neolithic burial cairns. A comprehensive geological survey of the island can be seen, and there is also a children's 'touch table'. Details of nature trails on the island are on sale. A special exhibition of local interest is held during Highland Week, and there is an exhibition of local common wild flowers from spring to autumn. Guided walks of the area take place in the summer months. Walkers meet at the museum. Also during the summer, photographic exhibitions which coincide with local events. Contact 01700 502033 for details.
Open all year, Apr-Sep, Mon-Sat 10.30-

4.30, Sun 2.30-4.30; Oct-Mar, Tue-Sat 2.30-4.30 (Closed Sun & Mon).
✳£1 (ch 30p, pen 60p)
P & (touch table for blind) shop ✗ (ex guide dogs)

Rothesay Castle
☎01700 502691
The focal point of Rothesay is this 13th-century castle. It has lofty curtain walls defended by drum towers and enclosing a circular courtyard.
Open all year, Apr-Sep, Mon-Sat 9.30-6.30, Sun 2-6.30; Oct-Mar, Mon-Sat 9.30-4.30 Sun 2-4.30. (Closed Thu pm & Fri in winter; also 25-26 Dec & 1-3 Jan).
P & ▮
Details not confirmed for 1998

CALLANDER

Rob Roy and Trossachs Visitor Centre
Ancaster Square FK17 8ED (on A84)
☎01877 330342 Fax 01877 330784
The fascinating story of Scotland's most famous outlaw, Rob Roy MacGregor is vividly portrayed through an exciting multi-media theatre and explained in the carefully researched 'Life and Times' exhibition. Also full tourist information centre covering the beautiful Trossachs area, Scottish bookshops and specially themed souvenirs. Evening entertainment, including traditional Scottish music evenings, celidhs and illustrated talks, is arranged 6 nights a week from June to October; telephone for details. School pack available.
Open Jan & Feb, weekdays 10-4.30; Mar-May & Oct-Dec, daily 10-5; Jun & Sep, daily 9.30-6; Jul-Aug, daily 9-6.
£2.50 (ch & pen £2). Family ticket £7.
P & toilets for disabled shop ✗ (ex guide dogs)
Cards: ▨ ▨

CAUSEWAYHEAD

Wallace Monument
FK8 2AD (the Monument may be reached by heading along the A907, Stirling to Alloa Rd)
☎01786 472140 Fax 01786 461322
The 220ft tower was built in 1869, and Sir William Wallace's two-handed sword is preserved inside. Seven battlefields and a fine view towards the Highlands can be seen. Displays include a Hall of Heroes, an audio-visual show on the life of Wallace, the Forth Panorama.
Open Jan-Feb, weekends 10-4; Mar-May, daily 10-5; Jun-Aug, daily 9.30-6.30; Sep, daily 10-6; Oct, daily 10-5; Nov-Dec, daily 10-4. Closed Xmas & 1-2 Jan.
£3 (ch & pen £2, student £2.75).
P ✐ (accessible visitors pavillion at foot of hill) shop ✗
Cards: ▨ ▨ ▨ ▨ ▨

CRICHTON

Crichton Castle
(2.5m SW Pathhead)
☎01875 320017
The castle dates back to the 14th century, but most of what remains today was built over the following 300 years. A notable feature is the 16th-century wing built by the Earl of Bothwell in Italian style, with an arcade below.
Open Apr-Sep, Mon-Sat 9.30-6.30, Sun 2-6.30.
P shop ▮
Details not confirmed for 1998

CRIEFF

Glenturret Distillery
The Hosh PH7 4HA (1.5m NW off A85)
☎01764 656565 Fax 01764 654366
The distillery dates from 1775 and is the oldest in Scotland. It uses the pure water of the Turret Burn to make award-winning whiskies, sold at twelve, fifteen and twenty-one years of age.
Open Mar-Dec, Mon-Sat 9.30-6 (last tour 4.30), Sun 12-6 (last tour 4.30); Jan, Mon-Sat 11.30-4 (last tour 2.30). Sundays from 12 noon. (closed 25/26 Dec, 1/2 Jan)
Guided tours and Audio visual exhibition £3.50 (ch 12-17 £2.30 ch under 12 Free).
P ✗ licensed & toilets for disabled shop ✗
Cards: ▨ ▨ ▨ ▨

Innerpeffray Library
PH7 3RF (4.5m SE on B8062)
☎01764 652819
This is Scotland's oldest free lending library. It was founded in 1691 and is still open every day except Thursdays. It is housed in a late-18th-century building which is interesting in itself, and contains a notable collection of bibles and rare books. Adjacent is St Mary's Chapel, the original site for the library and the Drummond family burial place.
Open all year, Mon-Wed & Fri-Sat 10-12.45 & 2-4.45, Sun 2-4. (Closed Thu).
£2 (ch & pen £1)
P ✐ shop ✗

CULROSS

Culross Palace, Town House & The Study
West Green House KY12 8JH (off A985, 3m E of Kincardine Bridge)
☎01383 880359
Culross is unique - a Royal Burgh that has remained virtually unchanged for 200 years. It dates mostly from the 16th and 17th centuries, when it prospered in the coal and salt trades developed by Sir George Bruce. When business declined in the 1700s, Culross stayed as it was, unable to afford improvements like wider streets. Its present appearance is due to the National Trust for Scotland, which has been gradually restoring the burgh since the 1930s. The aim has been to provide modern living standards without destroying the burgh's character, and the small houses with their red-pantiled roofs are still lived in by local people.
The Trust has a visitor centre and exhibition in the Town House (1626). The house called The Study (1610) is also open for visitors to view the Norwegian painted ceiling in the drawing room. The first building bought by the Trust in Culross was The Palace, home of Sir George Bruce. It has terraced gardens and painted rooms. Many other buildings can be seen from the outside.
Open - Town House & Study; Apr-Sep daily 1.30-5. Oct Sat & Sun only 11-5. (last admission 4). Palace Apr-Sep daily 11-5.
£4.20 (ch & concession £2.80). Family ticket £11.20. Ticket includes Palace.
P ✐ & toilets for disabled shop ✗ (ex guide dogs) ♨

CUPAR

Hill of Tarvit Mansionhouse & Garden
KY15 5PB (2.5m S of Cupar, off A916)
☎01334 653127
The present Mansionhouse was virtually rebuilt in 1906 by Sir Robert Lorimer for Mr F B Sharp to provide a suitable setting for his notable collection which includes French, Chippendale and vernacular furniture, Dutch paintings and pictures by Raeburn, Ramsay and Flemish tapestries, and Chinese porcelain. The restored Edwardian laundry is also open. The formal gardens to the south were also designed by Lorimer to form an appropriate setting for the House. Scotstarvit Tower is nearby. There is a hilltop walk and also a short dog walk in the grounds. Concerts are held regularly throughout the year and there are monthly art exhibitions.
Open Good Fri-Etr Mon & May-Sep, daily 1.30-5.30; wknds in Oct 1.30-5.30 (last admission 4.45). Garden & grounds Apr-Oct daily 9.30-9.30. Nov-Mar daily 9.30-4.30.
House & Garden £3.70 (ch & concessions £2.50). Family ticket £9.90. Garden only, honesty box £1. Party.
P ✐ & toilets for disabled shop ✗ (ex guide dogs) ♨

The Scottish Deer Centre
Bow-of-Fife KY15 4NQ (3 miles West of Cupar on the A91.)
☎01337 810391
Fax 01337 810477
Guided tours take about 30 minutes and allow visitors to meet and stroke deer. Children can help with bottle-feeding young fawns,(at certain times of year) and there are indoor and outdoor adventure play areas. Other features include regular falconry displays, viewing platform and a tree top walkway. Visitors can take time to browse in our courtyard shopping area and relax in the courtyard coffee shop.
Open daily, Etr-Oct 10-6, Nov-Etr 10-5.
£2.95 (ch £1.75, concessions £2). Family ticket £11.50. Party 20+.
P ✗ & (special parking bay, loan of wheelchairs) toilets for disabled shop ✗
Cards: ▨ ▨ ▨ ▨ ▨ ▨

The 13th century castle is the focal point of Rothesay

Spectacular butterflies fly free in the artificial rainforest created at Edinburgh Butterfly World, where tropical insects and plants also flourish.

DALKEITH
Edinburgh Butterfly & Insect World
Dobbies Garden World, Lasswade EH18 1AZ (0.5m S of Edinburgh city bypass at Gilmerton junct)
☎ 0131 663 4932 Fax 0131 654 2548
Richly coloured butterflies from all over the world can be seen flying among exotic rainforest plants, trees and flowers. The tropical pools are filled with giant waterlilies and colourful fish, and are surrounded by lush vegetation. Also displayed are scorpions, leaf cutting ants, beetles, tarantulas and other remarkable creatures. There is a unique honeybee display and daily insect handling sessions.
Open Summer daily 9.30-5.30; winter daily 10-5. Closed 25/26 Dec & 1/2 Jan.
£3.75 (ch 3-15 £2.65, pen & students £2.85). Family ticket £12. Party 10+.
🅿 🍴 ♿ *toilets for disabled shop garden centre ⊗ (ex guide dogs)*
Cards: 🔲 🔲

DIRLETON
Dirleton Castle
EH39 5ER (on A198)
☎ 01620 850330
The oldest part of this romantic castle dates from the 13th century. It was besieged by Edward I in 1298, rebuilt and expanded, and then destroyed in 1650. Now the sandstone ruins have a beautiful mellow quality. Within the castle grounds is a garden established in the 16th century, with ancient yews and hedges around a bowling green.
Open all year, Apr-Sep, Mon-Sat 9.30-6.30, Sun 2-6.30; Oct-Mar, Mon-Sat, 9.30-4.30, Sun 2-4.30. (Closed 25-26 Dec & 1-3 Jan).
🅿 ♿ *shop* ▮
Details not confirmed for 1998

DOLLAR
Castle Campbell
FK14 7PP (10m W of Stirling on A91)
☎ 01259 742408
Traditionally known as the 'Castle of Gloom', the 15th-to 17th-century tower stands in the picturesque Ochil Hills and gives wonderful views. It can be reached by a walk through the magnificent Dollar Glen. Care must be taken in or after rain when the path may be dangerous.
Open Apr-Sep, Mon-Sat 9.30-6.30, Sun 2-6.30; Oct-Mar, Mon-Sat 9.30-4.30, Sun 2-4.30. (Closed Thu pm & Fri in winter, 25-26 Dec & 1-3 Jan).
🅿 *shop* ▮ ☕
Details not confirmed for 1998

DOUNE
Doune Castle
FK16 6EA (8m S of Callander on A84)
☎ 01786 841742
The 14th-century stronghold with its two fine towers has been restored. It stands on the banks of the River Teith, and is associated with Bonnie Prince Charlie and Sir Walter Scott.
Open all year, Apr-Sep, Mon-Sat 9.30-6.30, Sun 2-6.30; Oct-Mar 9.30-4.30, Sun 2-4.30. (Closed Thu pm & Fri in winter; 25-26 Dec & 1-3 Jan).
🅿 *shop* ▮
Details not confirmed for 1998

Doune Motor Museum
The Doune Collection, Carse of Cambus FK16 6HD (8m NW of Stirling on A84)
☎ 01786 841203 Fax 01786 842070
Around 50 cars are displayed, and motoring events are held throughout the season.
Open 1 Apr-30 Nov, daily, 10am-5pm.
✳£3, (ch £2, oap £2.50)
🅿 🍴 ♿ *(ramped areas to museum & cafeteria) toilets for disabled shop ⊗*
Cards: 🔲 🔲 🔲

DUNDEE
Barrack Street Natural History Museum
Barrack St DD1 1PG
☎ 01382 432067 Fax 01382 432070
Displays on Scottish wildlife of the Lowlands and Highlands are shown, including the skeleton of the Great Tay whale. A major gallery for changing art exhibitions explores nature and environmental themes. Head for the Hills, an exhibition on upland areas, habitats and conservation, is on the ground floor. Special events include Wildlife Photographer of the Year exhibition, please ring for details.
Open all year, Mon 11-5, Tue-Sat 10-5. (Closed 25-26 Dec & 1-3 Jan).
Free.
P *(NCP 500 yds) shop ⊗ (ex guide dogs)*

Broughty Castle Museum
Broughty Ferry DD5 2BE (4m E, off A930)
☎ 01382 436916
The 15th-century castle was rebuilt to defend the estuary in the 19th century. It now houses displays on Dundee's whaling history, a major industry for Dundee, which built most of Britain's whaling ships. Other sections display arms and armour, local history and seashore life. There are superb views across the Tay estuary from the observation room.
Open all year, Mon 11-1 & 2-5, Tue-Thu 10-1 & 2-5. (Sun 2-5 Jul-Sep only).
(Closed 25-26 Dec & 1-3 Jan).
Free.
🅿 *shop ⊗ (ex guide dogs)*

Camperdown Country Park
DD2 4TF (A90 to Dundee and turn onto A923 Coupar Angus rd, turn left at 1st rdbt to Camperdown Country Park)
☎ 01382 434296 Fax 01382 433211
The 19th-century mansion of Camperdown House was built for the son of Admiral Lord Duncan, who defeated the Dutch at the Battle of Camperdown in 1797. The house is set in nearly 400 acres of fine parkland with a wide variety of trees, some of them rare. Most notable is the Camperdown elm, a weeping form of wych-elm. The park also offers attractions such as a golf course, a wildlife centre with a collection of native and domestic animals, and an award-winning adventure play area with the Battle of Camperdown as its theme. There is an extensive network of footpaths and forest trails to follow, and the house itself has a restaurant and function area. The Countryside Ranger service is based in the Park, available for environmental projects and interpreting the Park. They also organise various events and walks and have a Ranger Centre in Templeton Woods. There is a playground designed for the disabled and able-bodied. Special events for 1998 - Dundee City of Discovery Flower Show (4,5,6 Sep).
Open all year - park. Wildlife Centre - daily, Apr-Sep 10-3.45, Oct-Mar 10-2.45. Park - free admission. Wildlife centre £1.50 (ch £1.05)
🅿 ♿ *(ramps) toilets for disabled shop ⊗ (ex guide dogs)*

Discovery Point
Discovery Quay DD1 4XA (in Dundee follow signs for Historic Ships)
☎ 01382 201245 Fax 01382 25891
Discovery Point is the home of *RRS Discovery*, Captain Scott's famous Antarctic ship. Within the £6 million complex there are eight exhibition areas. Spectacular lighting, graphics and special effects re-create key moments in the *Discovery* story, including Locked in Ice, a dramatic presentation on three giant screens showing how Scott and his men adapted to their harsh environment, culminating in *Discovery* being blasted free from the crushing pack ice. Also learn what happened to the ship after the expedition, during the First World War and the Russian Revolution, and also her involvement in the first survey of the migration patterns of whales. The ship has been extensively restored below decks.
Open all year, Apr-Oct, Mon-Sat 10-5, Sun 11-5; Nov-27 Mar, last admission 4pm. Closed 25 Dec & 1-2 Jan.
🅿 *(charged)* 🍴 ♿ *(in-house wheelchairs & lifts, parking, ramps onto ship) toilets for disabled shop ⊗*
Details not confirmed for 1998
Cards: 🔲 🔲 🔲

HM Frigate Unicorn
Victoria Dock DD1 3JA
☎ 01382 200900 200893
Fax 01382 200923
The *Unicorn* is the oldest British-built warship afloat, and is Scotland's only example of a wooden warship. Today she makes an apt setting for a fascinating museum of life in the Royal Navy during the days of sail, with guns, models and displays.
Open all year, 25 Mar-31 Oct, daily 10-5; Nov-mid Mar open five days a week. Closed 25 Dec & 1 Jan.
£3 (concessions £2). Party 20+.
🅿 🍴 ♿ *shop ⊗ (no exceptions)*

McManus Galleries
Albert Square DD1 1DA (off A85)
☎ 01382 432020 Fax 01382 432052
A resplendent Victorian building in the city centre is the home of Dundee's main museum. It has collections of silver, ceramics, glass and furniture, and displays on local archaeology, civic and social history, trades and industries. The major art gallery has an important collection of Scottish and Victorian works of art, and touring exhibitions are a regular feature.
Open all year, Mon 11-5, Tue-Sat 10-5. (Closed 25-26 Dec & 1-3 Jan).
Free.
P *(100 yds)* 🍴 ♿ *(wheelchair available & high arm chairs, audio loop) toilets for disabled shop ⊗ (ex guide dogs)*

Mills Observatory
Balgay Park, Glamis Rd DD2 2UB
☎ 01382 435846 Fax 01382 435962
The observatory was built in 1935, and has a Victorian 10in Cooke refracting telescope among its instruments. The gallery has displays on astronomy and space exploration. There is a small planetarium for booked groups only. Open nights during the winter months, children's activities during the summer holidays.
Open all year, Apr-Sep, Tue-Fri 11-5, Sat 2-5; Oct-Mar, Tue-Fri 4-10, Sat 2-5. (Closed 25-26 Dec & 1-3 Jan).
Free.
🅿 *shop ⊗ (ex guide dogs)*

Verdant Works
West Henderson's Wynd DD2 5BT
☎ 01382 225282 Fax 01382 221612
Dating from 1830, this old Jute Mill covers 50,000 square feet around a cobbled courtyard. Restored as a living museum of Dundee and Tayside's textile history, Phase I explains what jute is, where it comes from and why Dundee became the centre of its production. Working machinery illustrates the production process from raw jute to woven cloth. A cinema showing a specially commissioned film explores the relationship between jute and Dundee, and there are also displays and interactive computers. Phase II deals with the uses of jute and its effects on Dundee's social history. Phase III illustrates Dundee and Journalism, particularly comic characterisation, and also Dundee's connections with Jam and Marmalade.
Open Apr-Oct, Mon-Sat 10-5, Sun 11-5. Nov-Mar, last admission 4pm. Closed 25 Dec & 1-2 Jan.
🅿 ♿ *(wheelchairs induction loops) toilets for disabled shop ⊗*
Details not confirmed for 1998
Cards: 🔲 🔲 🔲

DUNFERMLINE

Andrew Carnegie Birthplace Museum

Moodie St KY12 7PL (400yds S from Dunfermline Abbey)

☎ 01383 724302 Fax 01383 729002

The museum tells the story of the humble handloom weaver's son who was born here in 1835, created the biggest steel works in the USA, and then became a philanthropist on a huge scale. The present-day work of the philanthropic Carnegie Trust is also explained. Weaving days will be held on the first Friday of every month (May-Oct); on these days, the restored Jacquard handloom will be worked by a member of the Angus Handloom Weavers. Exhibition on Andrew Carnegie's 'Round the World' trip of 1879.

Open all year, Apr, May, Sep & Oct, Mon-Sat 11-5, Sun 2-5; Jun-Aug, Mon-Sat 10-5, Sun 2-5; Nov-Mar, daily 2-4.

£1.50 (ch 15 free, concessions 75p).

🅿 ♿ *toilets for disabled shop ※ (ex guide dogs)*

Dunfermline Abbey

Pittencrieff Park

☎ 01383 739026

The monastery was a powerful Benedictine house, founded by Queen Margaret in the 11th century. The foundations of her church still lie beneath the nave of a later, more elaborate Norman nave. The site of the choir is occupied by a modern parish church, at the east end of which are the remains of the 13th-century St Margaret's shrine. The grave of King Robert the Bruce is marked by a modern brass in the choir. The monastery guest house became a royal palace, and was the birthplace of Charles I. The ruins of other monastic buildings can be seen.

Open all year, Apr-Sep, Mon-Sat 9.30-6.30, Sun 2-6.30: Oct-Mar, Mon-Sat 9.30-4.30, Sun 2-4.30. (Closed Thu pm & Fri in winter; 25-26 Dec & 1-3 Jan).

🅿 ♿ *shop ※ 🎫*

Details not confirmed for 1998

Dunfermline Heritage Trust

Abbot House, Maygate KY12 7NE

☎ 01383 733266

Fax 01383 624908

This medieval house, now refurbished as a heritage centre for the ancient capital of Scotland, features an award-winning journey through 1000 years of history from the Picts to the present day.

Open daily 10-5. Last entry to upper exhibitions 4.15pm. Closed 25 Dec & 1 Jan.

P (150yds) 💺 ♿ *(parking on site) toilets for disabled shop ※ (ex garden)*

Details not confirmed for 1998

Cards: 🅰 🌌

Dunfermline Museum & Small Gallery

Viewfield Ter KY12 7HY

☎ 01383 313838

Fax 01383 313837

Interesting and varied displays on local history are shown, including domestic articles and damask linen - an important local product. The Small Gallery has changing art and craft exhibitions every month.

Open all year, Mon-Sat 11-5. (Closed Sunday's, Christmas & New Year)

Free.

🅿 *(charged)* ♿ *shop ※ (ex guide dogs)*

Pittencrieff House Museum

Pittencrieff Park KY12 8QH

☎ 01383 722935 & 313838

Fax 01383 313837

The fine 17th-century mansion house stands in a park with lawns, hothouses and gardens. In the house itself there are galleries with displays on the history of the house, park and costume. Temporary art exhibitions are shown in the top gallery. The house and park were given to the town by Andrew Carnegie.

Open May-Oct, daily ex Tue.

Free.

♿ *(ramp) shop ※ (ex guide dogs)*

DUNKELD

The Ell Shop & Little Houses

The Cross PH8 0AN (off A9, 15m N of Perth)

☎ 01350 727460

The National Trust for Scotland owns two rows of 20 houses in Dunkeld, and has brought them up to modern standards without destroying their character. Most were built after the Battle of Dunkeld in 1689. The houses are let, and therefore not open to the public. There is a Trust display and audio-visual show in the tourist information centre.

Open Ell Shop Apr-Sep, Mon-Sat 10-5.30, also Sun Jun-Aug 1.30-5.30; Oct-23 Dec, Mon-Sat 10-4.30. (Closed 1-10 Nov). Exterior of Little Houses can be viewed all year.

Free.

P (300yds) ♿ *toilets for disabled shop ※ (ok in village) 🎫*

EAST FORTUNE

Museum of Flight

East Fortune Airfield, North Berwick EH39 5LF (Signposted from A1 near Haddington)

☎ 01620 880308 or 0131-225 7534 Fax 01620 880355

Aircraft on display include a Supermarine Spitfire MK 16, De Haviland Sea Venom, Hawker Sea Hawk and Comet (4). The museum is set out in a former airship base, and also has a section on Airship R34 which flew from here to New York and back in 1919. There is also an extensive display of rockets and aero-engines. Special Events - Festival of Flight (18/19 Jul).

Open Etr-31 Oct daily, 10.30-5. Nov-Mar weekdays 11-3.

£2 (ch & concessions £1). Family ticket £5.

🅿 💺 ♿ *toilets for disabled shop ※ (ex guide dogs)*

EAST LINTON

Hailes Castle

(1m SW on unclass rd).

☎ 0131 668 8800 Fax 0131 668 8888

The castle was a fortified manor house of the Gourlays and Hepburns. Bothwell brought Mary Queen of Scots here when they were fleeing from Borthwick Castle. The substantial ruins include a 16th-century chapel.

Open at all reasonable times.

※ 🎫

Details not confirmed for 1998

Preston Mill & Phantassie Doocot

EH40 3DS (signposted from A1)

☎ 01620 860426

This is the oldest working water-driven meal mill to survive in Scotland, and was last used commercially in 1957. It has a conical roof and red pantiles. There is an old mill pond with ducks. A short walk leads to Phantassie Doocot (dovecote), built for 500 birds.

Open Good Fri-Easter wknd and May-Sep, Mon-Sat 11-1 & 2-5pm, Sun 1.30-5pm; wknds in Oct, 1.30-4. Last entry 20 mins before closing morning and afternoon.

£2 (ch & concessions £1.30). Family ticket £5.30. Party.

🅿 ♿ *toilets for disabled shop ※ (ex guide dogs) 🎫*

EDINBURGH

Edinburgh has a glorious setting, with unexpected views of the sea and hills wherever you happen to be, and a skyline dominated by the great crag on which the castle stands. From here the medieval Old Town runs down to the Palace of Holyrood House, and through the heart of the Old Town runs the Royal Mile, lined with historic buildings like the Outlook Tower with its camera obscura, the tall tenement of Gladstone's Land, Lady Stair's house and a number of museums, all full of interest. It is also well worth spending time exploring the many 'wynds' and alleys that run down steeply from either side of the Royal Mile. Edinburgh's second main area is the New Town, a place of elegant squares and terraces built for the city's merchants and aristocrats in the late-18th century, seen at its grandest in Charlotte Square. There is a third town as well - the districts of grand Victorian houses - and Edinburgh is also a city of villages, each with their own character. Always fascinating to visit, Edinburgh becomes a riot of theatre and music both on and off the streets during the International Festival and Fringe Festival in August. An especially popular event is the military searchlight tattoo held in front of the castle.

Brass Rubbing Centre

Trinity Apse, Chalmers Close, High St EH1 1SS

☎ 0131 556 4364 Fax 0131 557 3364

Housed in the historic, 15th-century remnant of Trinity Apse, the Centre offers the chance to make your own rubbing from a wide range of replica monumental brasses and Pictish stones. Tuition is available.

Open Jun-Sep, Mon Sat 10-6; Oct-May, Mon-Sat 10-5.

shop ※

Details not confirmed for 1998

Camera Obscura

Castlehill, Royal Mile EH1 2LZ (next to Edinburgh castle).

☎ 0131 226 3709 Fax 0131 225 4239

Step inside this magical 1850s 'cinema' for a unique experience of Edinburgh. As the lights go down a brilliant moving image of the surrounding city appears. The scene changes as a guide operates the camera's system of revolving lenses and mirrors. As the panorama unfolds the guide tells the story of the city's historic past. Also of interest is the Rooftop Terrace, and exhibitions on International Holography, Pinhole Photography and Victorian Edinburgh.

Open all year, daily, Apr-Oct 9.30-6; Nov-Mar 10-5. (Closed 25 Dec). Open later Jul-Aug, phone for details.

Up to June 1998 £3.50 (ch £1.80, students £2.80, pen £2.25) Family £10.50. Jul-Aug 1998 £3.95 (ch £1.95, students £3.15, pen £2.50) Sept 1998 to be advised.

P (300mtrs) *shop ※ (ex guide dogs)*

Cards: 🅰 🌌 🌉 🔢 💳

City Art Centre

2 Market St EH1 1DE

☎ 0131 529 3993 Fax 0131 529 3986

The City Art Centre houses the city's permanent fine art collection and stages a constantly changing programme of temporary exhibitions drawn from all parts of the world. It has six floors of display galleries (linked by an escalator), a shop, cafe and facilities for disabled visitors. Please ring for details of special events.

Open Jun-Sep, Mon-Sat 10-6 (Sun 2-5 during Edinburgh Festival); Oct-May, Mon-Sat 10-5.

P (500yds) 💺 ♿ *(induction loop, lifts) toilets for disabled shop ※ guide dogs*

Details not confirmed for 1998

Cards: 🅰 🌌 🌉 🔢 💳

As night falls over Edinburgh, the Castle on its huge volcanic outcrop is silhouetted against the skyline.

Craigmillar Castle
(2.5m SE)
☎*0131 661 4445*
Mary Queen of Scots retreated to this 14th-century stronghold after the murder of Rizzio, and the plot to murder Darnley, her second husband, was also hatched here. There are 16th-and 17th-century apartments.
Open all year, Apr-Sep, Mon-Sat 9.30-6.30, Sun 2-6.30. Oct-Mar, Mon-Sat 9.30-4.30. Sun 2-4.30. (Closed Thu pm & Fri in winter, 25-26 Dec & 1-3 Jan).
P ♿ *shop*
Details not confirmed for 1998

Edinburgh Castle
☎*0131 225 9846*
This historic stronghold stands on the precipitous crag of Castle Rock. One of the oldest parts is the 11th-century chapel of the saintly Queen Margaret, but most of the present castle evolved later, during its stormy history of seiges and wars, and was altered again in Victorian times. The apartments of Mary Queen of Scots can be seen, including the bedroom where James I of England and VI of Scotland was born. Also on the rock is James IV's 16th-century great hall. The vaults underneath have graffiti by 19th-century French prisoners of war. The Scottish crown and other royal regalia are displayed in the Crown Room, and the spectacular Military Tattoo is held on the Esplanade, built in 1753 - shortly after the castle's last siege in 1745. Also notable is the Scottish National War Memorial, opened in 1927 on the site of the castle's church. A new 'Honours of the Kingdom' exhibition tells the fascinating story and history of the Scottish crown jewels. There is still a military presence in the castle, and some areas cannot be visited.
Open Apr-Sep, daily 9.30-6. Oct-Mar, daily 9.30-5. Last ticket sold 45 mins earlier than closing time. Times may occasionally be altered during the Tattoo or for State and military events.
P *(charged)* ✕ *licensed* ♿ *(free transport to top of Castle Hill lift) toilets for disabled shop*
Details not confirmed for 1998

Edinburgh Zoo
Murrayfield EH12 6TS (3m W of Edinburgh City Centre on A8 towards Glasgow)
☎*0131 334 9171 Fax 0131 316 4050*
Scotland's largest and most exciting wildlife attraction, set in 80 acres of leafy hillside parkland, just ten minutes from the city centre. With over 1,000 animals ranging from the tiniest poison arrow frog to the massive white rhinos, including many threatened species. See the world's largest penguin pool with underwater viewing, famous penguin parade at 2pm March to September (October-weather permitting) and the new Darwin Maze, named after the naturalist Charles Darwin and based on the theme of evolution.
Open all year, Apr-Sep, Mon-Sat 9-6, Sun 9.30-6. Closes 4.30pm Oct-Mar.
**£6 (ch(3-14)£3.20, student £4.40). Family ticket £16.50.*
P *(charged)* ✕ *licensed* ♿ *(wheelchair loan free, 1 helper free - phone in advance) toilets for disabled shop*
Cards:

General Register House
(East end of Princes St) EH1 3YY
☎*0131 535 1314 Fax 0131 535 1360*
The headquarters of the Scottish Record Office and repository for the national archives of Scotland, designed by Robert Adam and founded in 1774. The historical and legal search rooms are available to researchers, and changing exhibitions are held.
Open Mon-Fri 9-4.45. Exhibitions 10-4. (Closed certain PHs & part of Nov).
♿ *toilets for disabled shop*
Details not confirmed for 1998

Georgian House
7 Charlotte Sq EH2 4DR (2mins walk W end of Princes Street)
☎*0131 225 2160 Fax 0131 226 3318*
The house is part of Robert Adam's splendid north side of Charlotte Square, the epitome of Edinburgh New Town architecture. The lower floors of No 7 have been restored in the style of around 1800, when the house was new. It gives a vivid impression of Georgian life, in both the grand public rooms and the servants' areas. Visitors can watch videos on life in the Georgian house, and the New Town.
Open Apr-Oct, Mon-Sat 10-5, Sun 2-5. Last admission 4.30pm.
£4.20 (ch & pen £2.80); (includes audio-visual show). Family ticket £11.20. Party.
P (100 yds) (meters. disabled is directly outside) ♿ *(induction loop for hard of hearing) shop (ex guide dogs)*

The Palace of Holyrood House and the rugged hills of Arthur's Seat make a superb vista from Calton Hill in Edinburgh.

Gladstone's Land
477b Lawnmarket EH1 2NT (5mins walk from Princes Street via Mound)
☎*0131 226 5856*
Built in 1620, this six-storey tenement, once the house of a prosperous Edinburgh merchant, still has its arcaded front - a rare feature now. Visitors can also see unusual tempera paintings on the walls and ceilings. It is furnished as a typical home of a 17th-century merchant, complete with ground-floor shop front and goods of the period.
Open Apr-Oct, Mon-Sat 10-5, Sun 2-5. Last admission 4.30pm.
£3 (ch, pen & students £2). Family ticket £8. Party.
P (440yds meters) (outside for disabled) ♿ *(tours for the blind can be arranged) shop (ex guide dofs)*

Huntly House
142 Canongate EH8 8DD
☎*0131 529 4143*
Fax 0131 557 3346
This is one of the best-preserved 16th-century buildings in the Old Town. It was built in 1570 and later became the headquarters of the Incorporation of Hammermen. It is now the main museum of local history, and has collections of silver, glassware, pottery, other items such as street signs, along with a collection relating to Field Marshal Earl Haig, a World War I general.
Open all year, Mon-Sat, Jun-Sep 10-6, Oct-May 10-5. (During Festival period only, Sun 2-5).
P (100 yds) meters ♿ *shop*
Details not confirmed for 1998

John Knox House
The Netherbow, 43-45 High St EH1 1SR (between The castle and Holyrood House)
☎*0131 556 9579*
Fax 0131 556 7478
John Knox is said to have died in the house, which was built by the goldsmith to Mary, Queen of Scots. Renovation work has revealed the original floor in the Oak Room, and a magnificent painted ceiling. The house is traditionally associated with John Knox the Reformer and contains an exhibition about his life and times.
Open all year, Mon-Sat 10-5. (Closed Xmas). Last admission 30 mins before closure.
**£1.75 (ch 7-15 75p, students & pen £1.25). Party 120+.*
✕ ♿ *(House on 3 levels) toilets for disabled shop (ex guidance dogs)*
Cards:

Lauriston Castle
Cramond Rd South, Davidson's Mains EH4 6AG (NW outskirts of Edinburgh, 1m E of Cramond)
☎*0131 336 2060*
Fax 0131 557 3346
The castle is a late 16th-century tower house with 19th-century additions but is most notable as a classic example of the Edwardian age. It has a beautifully preserved Edwardian interior by one of Edinburgh's leading decorators, and still has the feel of an Edwardian country house. There are spacious, pleasant grounds. Please telephone for details of special events.
Open all year by guided tour only; Apr-Oct, 11-1, 2-5; Nov-Mar, wknds 2-4. (Last tour commences 40 minutes before each closing time). Closed Fri.
P ♿ *shop*
Details not confirmed for 1998

Museum of Childhood
42 High St (Royal Mile) EH1 1TG
☎*0131 529 4142 Fax 0131 558 3103*
One of the first museums of its kind, it was reopened in 1986 after major expansion and reorganisation. It has a wonderful collection of toys, games and other belongings of children through the ages, to delight visitors both old and young. Ring for details of special events.
Open all year, Mon-Sat, Jun-Sep 10-6; Oct-May 10-5. (During Festival period only, Sun 2-5).
P ♿ *(3 floors only) toilets for disabled shop*
Details not confirmed for 1998

National Gallery of Scotland
The Mound EH2 2EL (off Princes Street)
☎*0131 624 6200 Fax 0131 343 3250*
The National Gallery of Scotland occupies a handsome neo-classical building designed by William Playfair. It is home to Scotland's greatest collection of European paintings and sculpture from the Renaissance to Post-Impressionism. It contains notable collections of works by Old Masters, Impressionists and Scottish artists. Among them are the ***Bridgewater Madonna*** by Raphael, Constable's ***Dedham Vale***, and works by Titian, Velazquez, Van Gogh and Gauguin. Drawings, watercolours and original prints by Turner, Goya, Blake and others are shown on request, Monday to Friday 10-12.30 and 2-4.30.
Open all year, Mon-Sat 10-5, Sun 2-5; (Extended opening hours during the Edinburgh Festival period). Winter (Oct-Mar) some rooms may be closed for the odd day. (Closed 25-26 Dec & 1 Jan).
**Free. Admission charged to some major exhibitions.*
P (150yds) ♿ *(ramps & lift) toilets for disabled shop (ex guide dogs)*
Cards:

Nelson Monument
Calton Hill
☎*0131 556 2716 Fax 0131 557 3346*
Designed in 1807 and erected on Calton Hill, the monument dominates the east end of Princes Street. Visitors climbing to the top will enjoy superb views of the city. Every day except Sunday the time ball drops at 1pm as the gun at the castle goes off.
Open all year, Apr-Sep Mon 1-6 Tue-Sat 10-6; Oct-Mar Mon-Sat 10-3.
P *shop*
Details not confirmed for 1998

Newhaven Heritage Museum
24 Pier Place, Newhaven EH6 4LP
☎*0131 551 4165 Fax 0131 557 3346*
The museum tells the story of the village and its people. It looks at fishing, other sea trades, customs and superstitions. There are displays on the development of this tightly-knit community, its leisure activities and choirs. The story is told through reconstructed sets of fisherfolk, objects, photographs, first-hand written and spoken accounts of people's lives. Also features hands-on exhibits, music and video.
Open all year, Mon-Sun 12-5. (closed 25-26 Dec & 1-2 Jan)
Free.
P ♿ *shop (ex guide dogs)*

Palace of Holyroodhouse
EH8 8DX (at east end of Royal Mile)
☎*0131 556 7371 & 0131 556 1096 (info)*
Fax 0131 557 5256
The Palace grew from the guesthouse of the Abbey of the Holyrood, said to have been founded by David I after a miraculous apparition. Mary, Queen of Scots, had her court here from 1561 to 1567, and 'Bonnie' Prince Charlie held levees at the Palace during his occupation of Edinburgh. The Palace is still used by the Royal Family, but can be visited when they are not in residence. Little remains of the original abbey except the ruined 13th-century nave of the church. The oldest part of the palace proper is James V's tower, with Mary's rooms on the second floor. A plaque

marks the spot where Rizzio was murdered. The audience chamber where she debated with John Knox can also be seen. There are fine 17th-century state rooms, and the picture gallery is notable for its series of Scottish monarchs, starting in 330BC with Fergus I. The work was done by Jacob de Wet in 1684-5, many of the likenesses are based on imagination. The grounds are used for royal garden parties in summer.
Open daily. Apr-Oct 9.30-5.15, Nov-Mar 9.30-3.45. Closed 25-26 Dec and when Queen in residence.
£5.30 (ch under 16 £2.60, pen £3.70). Family ticket £13.
🅿 & *(first floor by lift, wheelchair available) toilets for disabled shop* 🐾
Cards: 🖃 ▦ ▦ ◉ ▨ 🅂

Parliament House
Supreme Courts, 2-11 Parliament Square EH1 1RQ (behind St Giles Cathedral)
☎ *0131 225 2595 Fax 0131 240 6755*
Scotland's independent parliament last sat in 1707, in this 17th-century building hidden behind an 1829 façade. It is now the seat of the Supreme Law Courts of Scotland and has been adapted to its changed use, but the Parliament Hall still has its fine old hammerbeam roof. A large stained glass window depicts the inauguration of the Court of Session in 1540.
Open all year, Mon-Fri 10-4.
Free.
P *(400 mtrs)* 🍴 ✗ & *toilets for disabled* 🐾 *(ex guide dogs)*

The People's Story
Canongate Tolbooth, 163 Canongate EH8 8BN
☎ *0131 225 2424 ext 4057*
Fax 0131 557 3346
The museum, housed in the 16th-century tolbooth, tells the story of the ordinary people of Edinburgh from the late 18th century to the present day. Reconstructions include a prison cell, 1930s pub and 1940s kitchen supported by photographs, displays, sounds, smells and a video.
Open Jun-Sep, Mon-Sat 10-6; Oct-May, Mon-Sat 10-5. Also, open Sun during Edinburgh Festival 2-5.
& *(first floor accessible by lift) toilets for disabled shop* 🐾
Details not confirmed for 1998

Royal Botanic Garden
Inverleith Row EH3 5LR (1m N of city centre)
☎ *0131 552 7171 Fax 0131 552 0382*
Discover the wonders of the plant kingdom in Scotland's premier garden. Established in 1670, on an area the size of a tennis court, it now comprises over 70 acres of beautifully landscaped grounds. Spectacular features include the world famous Rock Garden, the new Pringle Chinese Collection, and a magnificent arboretum. The amazing Glasshouse Experience, featuring Britain's tallest Palm House, leads you on a journey of discovery through Asia, Africa, the Mediterranean and the southern hemisphere.
Open all year Nov-Jan, 9.30-4; Feb & Dec 9.30-5; Mar & Sept 9.30-6; Apr-Jun 9.30am-7pm; Jul-Aug 9.30am-8pm. (closed 25 Dec & 1 Jan)
Donations.
🅿 🍴 ✗ *licensed* & *(wheelchairs available at east/west gates) toilets for disabled shop garden centre* 🐾 *(ex guide dogs)*
Cards: 🖃 ▦ ▦ 🅂

Royal Museum of Scotland (Chambers St)
Chambers St EH1 1JF
☎ *0131 225 7534 Fax 0131 220 4819*
This magnificent museum houses extensive international collections covering the Decorative Arts, Natural History, Science, Technology and Working Life, and Geology. A lively programme of special events including temporary exhibitions, films, lectures and concerts takes place throughout the year.
Open all year, Mon-Sat 10-5, Sun 12-5.

(Closed 25-26 Dec & 1-2 Jan).
Free.
🅿 *(charged)* 🍴 & *toilets for disabled shop* 🐾

Royal Observatory Visitor Centre
Blackford Hill EH9 3HJ
☎ *0131 668 8405 Fax 0131 668 8429*
Explore our computer gallery with the latest CD-ROMS about space and astronomy. Enjoy excellent views of Edinburgh from the rooftop. Marvel at one of Scotland's largest telescopes. Play with light, lenses, and prisms. Learn about the history of the Observatory, and its current work in Hawaii and Australia. Public observing on Friday evenings (end October to March, weather permitting) 7.30pm sharp.
Open Mon-Sat 10-5, Sun noon-5.
£2.50 (ch £1.50). Family ticket £5.
🅿 & *(most floors accesible by lift) toilets for disabled shop* 🐾 *(ex guide dogs)*
Cards: 🖃 ▦ ▦

Scotch Whisky Heritage Centre
354 Castlehill EH1 2NE (at the top of the Royal Mile, beside Edinburgh Castle)
☎ *0131 220 0441 Fax 0131 220 6288*
Located at the top of Castle Hill is a fascinating attraction where you can travel through time to discover the history of Scotland's most famous export - whisky! Take a guided tour, meet our ghostly Blender, enjoy the barrel car ride and the sights, sounds and smells which evoke a vivid and memorable picture of the secrets of whisky making and the importance of the Scottish climate. Enter the lives of the Higland crofters distilling whisky for their own consumption and marvel at the technical advances that enable whisky production to be carried on today. An extra bonus is the free dram of Scotch whisky offered to every adult visitor.
Open daily, 10-5.30. (extended in summer). Closed 25 Dec.
P *(.25m)* & *toilets for disabled shop* 🐾 *(ex guide dogs)*
Details not confirmed for 1998
Cards: 🖃 ▦ ▦ ◉ ▨ 🅂

Scottish National Gallery of Modern Art
Belford Rd EH4 3DR (in the West End of Edinburgh)
☎ *0131 624 6200 Fax 0131 343 3250*
This gallery houses Scotland's finest collection of 20th century paintings and graphic art and includes works by Picasso, Matisse, Giacometti, Sickert and Hockney. It also houses an unrivalled collection of 20th century Scottish art, from the Colourists right up to the contemporary scene. It also possesses German Expressionism and French Art within its international collection and one of the most important Dada and Surrealist collections in the world.
Open all year, Mon-Sat 10-5 & Sun 2-5. (Extended opening hours during the Edinburgh Festival). (Closed 25-26 Dec & 1 Jan).
✻*Free. Admission charged to some major exhibitions.*
🅿 🍴 & *(ramps & lift) toilets for disabled shop* 🐾 *(ex guide dogs)*
Cards: 🖃 ▦ ▦ ▨ 🅂

Scottish National Portrait Gallery
1 Queen St EH2 1JD (parallel to Princes Street)
☎ *0131 624 6200 Fax 0131 343 3250*
The collection housed within this striking red Victorian building provides a visual history of Scotland from the 16th century to the present day, told through the portraits of the people who shaped it: royals and rebels, poets and philosophers, heroes and villains. Among the most famous are Mary, Queen of Scots; Ramsay's portrait of David Hume and Raeburn's Sir Walter Scott. The building also houses the National Collection of Photography.
Open all year, daily, Mon-Sat 10-5, Sun 2-5. (Extended opening hours during the Edinburgh Festival. (Closed 25-26 Dec & 1 Jan).

✻*Free. Admission charged to some major exhibitions.*
P *(200yds)* 🍴 & *(ramps & lift) toilets for disabled shop* 🐾
Cards: 🖃 ▦ ▦ ▨ 🅂

Scottish United Services Museum
Edinburgh Castle (in Edinburgh castle)
☎ *0131 225 7534*
Fax 0131 225 3848
The museum is in Edinburgh Castle. Exhibition is 'The Story of the Scottish Soldier'. The museum may close early in 1998 for refurbishment - please telephone to avoid disappointment.
Open all year, Apr-Oct, Mon-Sat 9.30-6, Sun 11-6; Nov-Mar, Mon-Sat 9.30-5, Sun 12.30-5.
Free admission after paying entrance fee to the Castle.
P & *toilets for disabled shop* 🐾

West Register House
Charlotte Square EH2 4ET
☎ *0131 535 1314 Fax 0131 535 1360*
The former church of St George (1811) was designed by Robert Reid in Greco-Roman style and is now the modern record branch of the Scottish Record Office. It houses the exhibition '800 Years of Scottish History', and the Search Room is available to researchers.
Open Mon-Fri 9-4.45. Exhibitions 10-4. (Closed certain PHs & part of Nov).
& *toilets for disabled* 🐾 *for 1998*
Details not confirmed for 1998

The Writers' Museum
Lady Stair's House, Lady Stair's Close, Lawnmarket EH1 2PA
☎ *0131 529 4901*
Fax 0131 557 3346
The Writers' Museum is situated in the historic Lady Stair's House which dates from 1622. It is now a museum housing various objects associated with Robert Burns, Sir Walter Scott and Robert Louis Stevenson. Temporary exhibitions are planned throughout the year.
Open all year, Mon-Sat, Jun-Sep 10-6; Oct-May 10-5. (During Festival period only, Sun 2-5).
shop 🐾
Details not confirmed for 1998

EDZELL
Edzell Castle
(on B966)
☎ *01356 648631*
The 16th-century castle has a remarkable walled garden built in 1604 by Sir David Lindsay. Flower-filled recesses in the walls are alternated with heraldic and symbolic sculptures of a sort not seen elsewhere in Scotland, with niches for birds to nest in above. There are ornamental and border gardens and a garden house.
Open all year, Apr-Sep, Mon-Sat 9.30-6.30, Sun 2-6.30; Oct-Mar, Mon-Sat 9.30-4.30, Sun 2-4.30. (Closed Thu pm & Fri in winter; 25-26 Dec & 1-3 Jan).
🅿 & *toilets for disabled shop garden centre* 🚩
Details not confirmed for 1998

FALKIRK
Callendar House
Callendar Park FK1 1YR (from W M80 junct 4; from E M9 junct 4/5; A803 to Falkirk, follow signs into Callendar Park)
☎ *01324 503770 Fax 01324 503771*
Mary, Queen of Scots, Oliver Cromwell, Bonnie Prince Charlie, noble earls and wealthy merchants all feature in the the history of Callandar House. Today, costumed interpreters describe the early 19th-century life in the well-preserved kitchens and the 900 year history of the house is illustrated in the 'Story of Callendar House' exhibition. The house is set in Callandar Park which offers many leisure attractions including boating, pitch and putt, a play area, and woodland walks. 1997 saw the opening of a major new exhibition area: "William Forbes' Falkirk" with new interpretive areas and interactives. Christmas at Callandar House will include spitroasting goose in the kitchen, traditional tree and carols in main hall, Christmas lunches in the teashop.
Open all year, Mon-Sat 10-5. Apr-Sep Sun 2-5.
£1.80 (ch & pen 90p). Family ticket £4.60.
🅿 🍴 ✗ & *(ramps & lift) toilets for disabled shop* 🐾 *(ex guide dogs)*
Cards: 🖃 ▦ 🅂

Rough Castle
(1m E of Bonnybridge)
☎ *0131 668 8800 Fax 0131 668 8888*
The impressive earthworks of a large Roman fort on the Antonine Wall can be seen here. The buildings have disappeared, but the mounds and terraces are the sites of barracks, granary and bath buildings. Running between them is the military road which once linked all the forts on the wall and is still well defined.
Open any reasonable time.
🅿 🐾 🚩
Details not confirmed for 1998

FALKLAND
Falkland Palace & Garden
KY15 7BU (off A912, 11m N of Kirkaldy)
☎ *01337 857397 Fax 01592 261919*
The hunting palace of the Stuart Kings and Queens, situated below the Lomond Hills. The French Renaissance style of the south range is admired as the best of its kind in Britain. The palace is also noted for the beautiful interiors of the Chapel Royal and the King's Bedchamber, and for the royal tennis court of 1539, the oldest in Britain. The garden has a spectacular delphinium border, and is heavily perfumed in summer. There is a gift shop, and in the Town Hall, an exhibition of the history of the palace and the royal burgh. Recorded sacred music is played hourly in the Chapel. Please telephone for details of concerts, recitals etc.
Open Apr-Oct, Mon-Sat 11-5.30, Sun 1.30-5.30. (last admission to palace 4.30, to garden 5). Town Hall by appointment. Palace & Garden £4.80 (ch £3.20). Family ticket £12.80. Garden only at reduced rates.
🅿 & *shop* 🐾 *(ex guide dogs)* 🍴

Among the notable features of Kellie Castle are the plasterwork and panelling which is painted with romantic landscapes.

GLAMIS

Angus Folk Museum

Kirkwynd Cottages DD8 1RT (off A94, in Glamis)

☎01307 840288

A row of stone-roofed, late 18th-century cottages now houses the splendid Angus Folk Collection of domestic equipment and cottage furniture. Across the wynd, an Angus stone steading houses The Life on the Land Exhibition.

Open Good Fri-Etr Mon & May-Sep, daily 11-5; wknds in Oct 11-5. (Last admission 4.30pm).

£2.40 (concessions £1.60). Family ticket £6.40.

🅿 ♿ *toilets for disabled* 🐾 *(ex guide dogs)* 🐝

Glamis Castle

DD8 1RJ (5m W of Forfar on A94)

☎01307 840393 Fax 01307 840733

The splendid, turreted and battlemented castle is the family home of the Earls of Strathmore, and was the childhood home of HM The Queen Mother. The present castle dates from the 15th century, but there is known to have been a building here for many centuries. One of the oldest parts is known as Duncan's Hall, a reminder of the murder of King Duncan in Shakespeare's *Macbeth* ('All hail, Macbeth! hail to thee, Thane of Glamis!'). Other noteworthy rooms are the chapel with its painted panels, and the drawing room. There are fine collections of china, pictures, tapestries and furniture, and the grounds can also be explored. Various events during the summer, including Strathmore Vehicle Vintage Club Extravaganza, 12 July, Grand Scottish Promenade Outdoor Concert (25 July).

Open 29 Mar-25 Oct 10.30-5.30 (Jul-Aug open from 10am). Last admission 4.45pm. Other times by prior appointment.

Castle & grounds £5.20 (ch £2.70, pen & students £4). Grounds only £2.40 (ch & pen £1.30).

🅿 ✗ *licensed* ♿ *toilets for disabled shop* 🐾 *(ex in grounds)*

GLENGOULANDIE DEER PARK

Glengoulandie Deer Park

PH16 5NL (8m NW of Aberfeldy on B846).

☎01887 830261 Fax 01887 830261

Various native birds and animals are kept in surroundings as similar to their natural environment as possible, and there are herds of red deer and Highland cattle. Pets must not be allowed out of cars.

Open Apr-Oct, 9am-1hr before sunset.

❄️*£1. Cars £4.*

🅿 *shop* 🐾

GOGAR

Suntrap Garden Oatridge College Horticultural Centre

43 Gogarbank EH12 9BY (between A8 & A71 W of city bypass)

☎0131 339 7283 & 01506 854387 Fax 01506 853373

The three-acre garden comprises of many gardens within a single garden, including Italian, Rock, Rose, Peat and Woodland. Details from the Principal, Oatridge Agricultural College, Ecclesmachan, Broxburn, West Lothian, EH52 6NH. Open Day 6 June.

Open all year; Apr-Sep, daily 9.30-4.30; Oct-Mar, Mon-Fri 9.30-4.30. Closed 2 weeks Xmas & New Year.

£1 (accompanied ch and NT members free).

🅿 ♿ *toilets for disabled*

INGLISTON

Scottish Agricultural Museum

EH28 8NB (at East Gate of Royal Highland Showground)

☎0131 333 2674 Fax 0131 333 2674

A fascinating collection illustrating rural Scotland through the ages: the tools and equipment, the workers and their families. Visitors can see the oldest threshing mill in the world, models of the first reaping machines, numerous old photogrphs, interesting folk art and a range of excellent audio-visual presentations. Please telephone for details of the Royal Highland Show.

Open Apr-Sep, daily 10-5; Oct-Mar, Mon-Fri. Closed Xmas & New Year.

❄️*Free except charge for admission to showground in Jun.*

🅿 📺 ♿ *toilets for disabled shop*

INVERESK

Inveresk Lodge Garden

EH21 7TE (A6124 S of Musselburgh)

☎0131 665 1855

This charming terraced garden, set in the historic village of Inveresk, specialises in plants, shrubs and roses suitable for growing on small plots. The 17th-century house makes an elegant backdrop.

Open all year, Mon-Fri 10-4.30, Sat-Sun 2-5 (Closed Sat Oct-Mar).

£1 (honesty box).

🅿 ♿ 🐾 *(ex guide dogs)* 🐝

KELLIE CASTLE & GARDENS

Kellie Castle & Gardens

KY10 2RF (3m NW of Pittenweem on B9171)

☎01333 720271

Fax 01333 720326

The oldest part of this castle dates from about 1360, but it is as a fine example of 16th-and 17th-century domestic architecture that Kellie is renowned.

Inside, the most notable features are the plasterwork and the panelling, which is painted with romantic landscapes, and furniture designed by Sir Robert Lorimer. The castle has a Victorian nursery, an old kitchen, and a Victorian walled garden, where plants and shrubs are grown organically. There are also audio-visual shows. Please telephone for details of concerts, recitals etc.

Open - Castle Good Fri-Etr Mon & May-Sep, daily 1.30-5.30; wknds in Oct 1.30-5.30 (last admission 4.45). Gardens & grounds open all year, Apr-Oct, daily 9.30-sunset.

Castle & gardens £3.70 (ch & concessions £2.50), gardens only £1. Party 20+ .

🅿 📺 ♿ *(Induction loop for the hard of hearing) shop* 🐾 *(ex guide dogs)* 🐝

KILLIECRANKIE

Killiecrankie Visitor Centre

NTS Visitor Centre PH16 5LG (3m N of Pitlochry on B8079)

☎01796 473233

Fax 01796 473233

The visitors' centre at this historic spot features an exhibition illustrating the battle that took place near here in 1689; there are also displays on the natural history of the area and ranger services. The battle site was where the Jacobite army, led by 'Bonnie Dundee' (who was mortally wounded in the attack) routed King William's troops. The wooded gorge is a notable beauty spot admired by Queen Victoria, and there are some splendid walks. Guided ranger walks and actor tours are available in the summer.

Visitor Centre, Exhibition, shop & snack bar Apr-Oct, daily 10-5.30. Site all year daily.

£1 honesty box.

🅿 📺 ♿ *(visitor centre only) toilets for disabled shop* 🐝

KILLIN

Breadalbane Folklore Centre

Falls of Dochart FK21 8XE (on A82, turn right at Crianlarich onto A85 towards Perth/Stirling. Then join A827 to Killin)

☎01567 820254

Fax 01567 820764

Overlooking the beautiful Falls of Dochart, the Centre gives a fascinating insight into the legends of Breadalbane - Scotland's 'high country'. Learn of the magical deeds of St Fillan and hear tales of mystical spirits, ancient prophesies, traditional folklore and clan history. Housed in historic St Fillans Mill which features a restored waterwheel. Tourist Information and gift shop.

Open Feb, wknds 10-4; Mar-May & Oct, daily 10-5; Jun & Sep, daily 9.30-6; Jul-Aug, daily 9.30-6.30. Closed Nov-Jan except 27 Dec-4 Jan.

£1 (ch & pen 0.75p)

🅿 *(30 mtrs)* ♿ *toilets for disabled shop* 🐾 *Cards:* 💳 💳 💳 💳

KINROSS

Kinross House Gardens

KY13 7ET (M90 Edinburgh to Perth, junct 6 to Kinross, and signposted in village)

☎01577 862900

Yew hedges, roses and herbaceous borders are the elegant attractions of these formal gardens. The 17th-century house was built by Sir William Bruce, but is not generally open to the public.

Gardens only open May-Sep, daily 10-7.

£2 (ch 50p).

🅿 ♿ 🐾

Loch Leven Castle

Castle Island (on an Island in Loch Leven accessible by boat from Kinross)

☎0131 668 8800

Fax 0131 668 8888

Mary Queen of Scots was imprisoned here in this five-storey castle in 1567 - she escaped 11 months later and gave the 14th-century castle its special place in history.

Open Apr-Sep, Mon-Sat 9.30-6.30, Sun 2-6.30.

🅿 *shop* 🐾 🚩

Details not confirmed for 1998

RSPB Nature Reserve Vane Farm

By Loch Leven KY13 7LX (on southern shore of Loch Leven, entered off B9097 to Glenrothes, 2m E junct5 M90)

☎01577 862355 Fax 01577 862013

One of the RSPB's most popular reserves in Scotland. Well placed beside Loch Leven, there is a nature trail and hides overlooking the Loch. Noted for its pink-footed geese, the area also attracts whooper swans, greylag geese, long-eared owls and great spotted woodpeckers amongst others. Over 250 species of plants have been recorded and roe deer and fox are regular visitors. Details of special events are available from the Visitors Centre.

Open daily, Apr-Xmas, 10-5; Jan-Mar 10-4.

❄️*£2 (ch 50p, concessions £1) Family £4.*

🅿 📺 ♿ *(ramps into visitor centre) toilets for disabled shop* 🐾 *(ex guide dogs) Cards:* 💳 💳 💳 💳

KIRKCALDY

Kirkcaldy Museum & Art Gallery

War Memorial Gardens KY1 1YG (next to Kirkaldy train stn)

☎01592 412860 Fax 01592 412870

Set in lovely grounds it features a suberb collection of 19th-and 20th-century Scottish paintings, an award-winning permanent local history exhibition and a lively changing exhibition programme. Gallery shop and cafe incorporating Wemyss pottery displays.

Open all year, Mon-Sat 10.30-5, Sun 2-5. (Closed public hols).

Free.

🅿 📺 ♿ *toilets for disabled shop* 🐾 *(ex guide dogs)*

KIRRIEMUIR

Barrie's Birthplace

9 Brechin Rd DD8 4BX (on A90/A926 6m NW of Forfar)

☎01575 572646

The creator of Peter Pan, Sir James Barrie, was born in Kirriemuir in 1860. The upper floors of No 9 Brechin Road are furnished as they may have been when Barrie lived there, and the adjacent house, No 11, houses an exhibition about his literary and theatrical works. The wash-house outside was his first 'theatre' and gave him the idea for Wendy's house in 'Peter Pan'.

Open Good Fri-Etr Mon & May-Sep, Mon-Sat 11-5.30 & Sun 1.30-5.30; wknds in Oct 11-5.30, Sun 1.30-5.30. Last admission 5pm.

£2 (ch & pen £1.30). Family ticket £5.30. Adult party. Child/school party.

🅿 *(100yds)* 📺 ♿ *(stairlift, audio programmes) shop* 🐾 *(ex guide dogs)* 🐝

LINLITHGOW

Blackness Castle

EH49 7AL (4m N)

☎01506 834807

Once this was one of the most important fortresses in Scotland. Used as a state prison during covenanting time and in the late-19th century as a powder magazine, it was one of four castles left fortified by the Articles of Union. Most impressive are the massive 17th-century artillery emplacements.

Open all year, Apr-Sep, Mon-Sat 9.30-6.30, Sun 2-6.30. Oct-Mar, Mon-Sat 9.30-4.30, Sun 2-4.30. (Closed Thu pm & Fri in winter; 25-26 Dec & 1-3 Jan).

🅿 *shop* 🚩

Details not confirmed for 1998

House of The Binns

EH49 7NA (4m E of Linlithgow off A904)

☎01506 834255

An example of changing architectural tastes from 1612 onwards, the House of The Binns reflects the transition from fortified stronghold to spacious mansion. It was once a tall, grey, three-storeyed building with small windows and twin turrets; and after additions, reshaping and refacing it has evolved into a fine U-shaped house, with crenellations and embellished windows. The most outstanding features are the beautiful early 17th-century moulded plaster

include a statue walk and water garden, an avenue of Australian gum trees, a Japanese garden, many rare shrubs, a narrow gauge steam and diesel railway, a weaver's workshop and a silversmith's.
*Open Etr-mid Oct, .daily 10.30-5.30. Gardens all year.
£4.50 (ch £1.50, pen & students £3.50).*
🅿 🍴 ♿ *toilets for disabled shop garden centre (on leads in grounds only)*
Cards: ▭

MUTHILL
Drummond Castle Gardens
PH7 4HZ (2m S of Crieff on A822)
☎01764 681257 681433
Fax 01764 681550
The gardens of Drummond Castle were originally laid out in 1630 by John Drummond, 2nd Earl of Perth. In 1830, the parterre was changed to an Italian style. One of the most interesting features in the garden is the multi-faceted sundial designed by John Mylne, Master Mason to Charles I. The Formal garden is said to be one of the finest in Europe and is the largest of its type in Scotland, and recently featured in the film 'Rob Roy'. Open in aid of Scotland's Garden Scheme first Sunday in August.
*Open - Gardens May-Oct, daily 2-6 (Last admission 5pm). Also Easter for 4 days.
£3 (ch £1.50 & pen £2).*
🅿 ♿ *shop (on leads in grounds)*

NEWTONGRANGE
Scottish Mining Museum
Lady Victoria Colliery EH22 4QN (on A7)
☎0131 663 7519
Fax 0131 654 1618
Based at the historic Lady Victoria colliery, Scotland's National Coal Mining Museum offers entertaining tours led by ex-miners. Visit the pit-head, Scotland's largest steam winding engine, and a full-scale replica of a modern underground coalface. Underground working conditions and life in the mining community are vividly portrayed by an audio-visual show and an award-winning series of life-sized 'talking tableaux'. Visitor centre with giftshop and tearoom.
*Open Mar-Oct, daily 10-4. Last tour 3pm.
£3 (ch & concessions £2). Family ticket £9. Party 20+.*
🅿 🍴 ♿ *toilets for disabled shop ✂ (ex guide dogs)*

NORTH BERWICK
Tantallon Castle
EH39 5PN (3m E on A198)
☎01620 892727
A famous 14th-century stronghold of the Douglases facing towards the lonely Bass Rock from the rocky Firth of Forth shore. Nearby 16th-and 17th-century earthworks.
Open all year, Apr-Sep, Mon-Sat 9.30-6.30, Sun 2-6.30; Oct-Mar, Mon-Sat 9.30-4.30, Sun 2-4.30. (Closed Thu pm & Fri in winter; 25-26 Dec & 1-3 Jan).
🅿 ♿ *shop ✂ 🍴*
Details not confirmed for 1998

The childhood home of J M Barrie, creator of Peter Pan, has been preserved. His father's woodcarving shop is on the ground floor and the living rooms above.

ceilings inside. This is the historic home of the Dalyell family - General Tam Dalyell raised the Royal Scots Greys here in 1681. There are panoramic views over the Firth of Forth from a site in the grounds. Magnificent snowdrops and daffodils in spring.
*Open: House, May-Sep, daily ex Fri, 1.30-5.30 (last admission 5). Parkland, Apr-Oct, daily 9.30-7; Nov-Mar, daily 9.30-4 (last admission 30 mins before closing).
£3.70 (ch & pen £2.50). Family tickets £9.90. Schools £1. Members of the Royal Scots Dragoon Guards, in uniform, admitted free.*
🅿 ♿ *(braille sheets) ✂ (ex guide dogs) 🍴*

Linlithgow Palace
☎01506 842896
The magnificent ruin of a great Royal Palace, set in its own park or 'peel'. All the Stewart kings lived here, and work commissioned by James I, III, IV, and VI can be seen. The great hall and the chapel are particularly fine. James V was born here in 1512 and Mary, Queen of Scots in 1542.
Open all year, Apr-Sep, Mon-Sat 9.30-6.30, Sun 2-6.30; Oct-Mar, Mon-Sat 9.30-4.30, Sun 2-4.30. (Closed 25-26 Dec & 1-3 Jan).
🅿 ♿ *shop ✂ 🍴*
Details not confirmed for 1998

MILNATHORT
Burleigh Castle
KY13 7XZ
☎0131 668 8800 Fax 0131 668 8888
Dating from 1582, this tower house has an enclosed courtyard and roofed angle tower.
Open all year, daily.
✂ 🍴
Details not confirmed for 1998

MONTROSE
House of Dun
DD10 9LQ (on A935, 3m W of Montrose)
☎01674 810264 Fax 01674 810722
A Georgian house, overlooking the Montrose Basin, built in 1730 for David Erskine, Lord Dun, to designs by William Adam, and particularly noted for its exuberant plasterwork. The house was opened to the public in 1989 after extensive restoration, and displays a fine collection of family portraits, fine furniture and porcelain. The courtyard

buildings house a working loom, restaurant and NTS shop. Walled garden and woodland walks. Lady Augusta Kennedy-Erskine, who lived here in the mid-19th century, was the daughter of William IV and the actress Mrs Jordan, the house contains many royal mementoes of this period. Please telephone for details of special events, which may include concerts and recitals.
*Open Good Fri-Etr Mon & May-Sep, daily 1.30-5.30; wknds in Oct 1.30-5.30. (last admission to house 5). Garden & Grounds, all year daily 9.30-sunset.
£3.70 (ch & concessions £2.50). Family ticket £9.90. Party. Grounds only £1.*
🅿 ✕ ♿ *(braille sheets, house wheelchair & stair lift) toilets for disabled shop ✂ (ex guide dogs) 🍴*

Montrose Museum & Art Gallery
Panmure Place DD10 8HE (opposite Montrose Academy)
☎01674 673232 & 875598 (pm)
Extensive local collections cover the history of Montrose from prehistoric times to local government reorganisation, the maritime history of the port, the natural history of Angus, and local art. Exhibits include Pictish stones, Montrose silver and pottery, whaling artefacts and Napoleonic items (including a cast of his death mask); also paintings by local artists and sculpture by William Lamb.
Open all year, Mon-Sat 10-5. Closed 25-26 Dec & 1-2 Jan.
🅿 ♿ *shop ✂*
Details not confirmed for 1998

MULL, ISLE OF

CRAIGNURE
Mull & West Highland Narrow Gauge Railway
Craignure (old pier) Station PA65 6AY
☎01680 812494 (in season) or 01680 300389 Fax 01680 300595
The first passenger railway on a Scottish island opened in 1984. Both steam and diesel trains operate on the ten-and-a-quarter inch gauge line, which runs from Craignure to Torosay Castle. The line is one-and-a-quarter miles long, and there are extensive and dramatic woodland and mountain views. The latest acquistion - a steam locomotive built in Sheffield in

1993 - has been named Victoria because of the help received from the Puffing Billy Railway in Australia, based near Melbourne, Victoria. The engine is based on their 2' 6" gauge engines. A new diesel hydraulic locomotive will be arriving in June or July, and it is hoped to have a birthday party for the locomotive 'Waverley', which will be 50 years old, in May. Please telephone for details.
*Open Easter week to mid Oct.
Return £3.30 (ch £2.20); Single £2.20 (ch £1.40). Family ticket return £8.75, single £6.*
🅿 ♿ *(provision to carry person seated in wheelchair on trains) shop*

Torosay Castle & Gardens
PA65 6AY (1m S of Ferry Terminal at Craignure)
☎01680 812421
Fax 01680 812470
Much of this Victorian castle is open to the public together with its delightful Italian terraced gardens, designed by Lorimer. The Scottish baronial architecture is complemented by the magnificent setting and inside the house there are displays of portraits and wildlife pictures, family scrapbooks and a study of the Antarctic. The Edwardian library and archive rooms particularly capture the flavour of their era. Charms of the garden

NORTH QUEENSFERRY
Deep-Sea World
KY11 1JR
☎01383 411411
Fax 01383 410514
Here visitors have the opportunity to get a diver's eye view of a spectacular underwater universe. A moving walkway travels along the largest underwater transparent viewing tunnel and enables visitors to walk along the sea bed without getting their feet wet. On this marine safari through crystal-clear sea water you can come face-to-face with large sharks, giant rays, crabs and lobsters, and conger eels. New exhibits are introduced regularly. Watch out for the piranhas and seahorses!
Open all year, daily, Apr-Oct 10-6; Jul & Aug 10-6.30pm; Nov-Mar, Mon-Fri 11-5, Sat-Sun 10-6.
£6 (ch 3-15 £3.50), concessions £4.25) Family ticket £16.50
🅿 ♥ ✕ *licensed* & *(ramps) toilets for disabled shop* ⚇ *(ex guide dogs)*
Cards: 🖃 🖃 🖃 ⚇

PENICUIK
Edinburgh Crystal Visitor Centre
Eastfield Industrial Estate EH26 8HB (on A701)
☎01968 675128
Fax 01968 674847
A tour around the factory allows visitors to see the various stages in the art of glassmaking, including glass blowing, the 'lehr', cutting, polishing, engraving and sand etching. An exhibition and video entitled 'Capturing the Light' explains the process further.
Open all year. Factory tours Mon-Fri 9-3.30. Also (Closed 25-27 Dec & 1-2 Jan). Visitor Centre Mon-Sat 9-5, Sun 11-5. Tours £2 (concessions £1). Family ticket £5. Party 15+.
🅿 ♥ & *(ramp to first floor) toilets for disabled shop* ⚇ *(ex guide dogs)*
Cards: 🖃 🖃 🖃 ⚇

PERTH
Black Watch Regimental Museum
Balhousie Castle, Hay St PH1 5HR
☎01738 621281 ext 8530 Fax 01738 643245
The treasures of the 42nd/73rd Highland Regiment from 1739 to the present day are on show in this museum, together with paintings, silver, colours and uniforms.
Open all year, May-Sep, Mon-Sat 10-4.30 (Closed last Sat in Jun); Oct-Apr, Mon-Fri, 10-3.30 (Closed 23 Dec-6 Jan). Other times & Parties 16+ by appointment.
❄*Donations.*
🅿 *shop* ⚇ *(ex guide dogs)*

Branklyn Garden
116 Dundee Rd PH2 7BB (on Dundee Rd, A85)
☎01738 625535
Once described as the finest garden of its size in Britain, Branklyn covers little more than two acres and is noted for its collection of rhododendrons, shrubs and alpines. There are regular conducted tours of the garden, and botanical painting courses are held. The garden attracts botanists from all over the world and there is usually a display in the summerhouse.
Open Mar-Oct, daily 9.30-sunset. £2.40 (ch £1.50). Family ticket £6.40. Party 20+ £1.90 (ch/concessions £1)
🅿 ⚇ *(ex guide dogs)* ♥

Caithness Glass Factory & Visitor Centre
Inveralmond Industrial Est PH1 3TZ (on the Perth Western Bypass, A9, at the Inveralmond Roundabout)
☎01738 637373 Fax 01738 622494
All aspects of paperweight-making can be seen from the viewing gallery at this purpose-built visitors' centre. There is also a paperweight collectors' gallery, a factory shop, restaurant, children's play area and tourist information centre. There is a new upper-level viewing gallery for a 'bird's eye view' of the glassmakers, and an audio-visual theatre.
Open all year, Factory shop & restaurant Mon-Sat 9-5, Sun 10-5 (Nov-Mar, Sun 11-5). Glassmaking Mon-Fri 9-4.30. Free.
🅿 ✕ *licensed* & *(wheelchair available) toilets for disabled shop* ⚇ *(ex guide dogs)*
Cards: 🖃 🖃 🖃 ⚇ ⚇

Huntingtower Castle
PH1 3JL (2m W)
☎01738 627231
Formerly known as Ruthven Castle and famous as the scene of the so-called 'Raid of Ruthven' in 1582, this structure was built in the 15th and 16th centuries and features a painted ceiling.
Open all year, Apr-Sep, Mon-Sat 9.30-6.30, Sun 2-6.30; Oct-Mar, Mon-Sat 9.30-4.30, Sun 2-4.30. (Closed Thu pm & Fri in winter; 25-26 Dec & 1-3 Jan).
🅿 ⚇ ♥
Details not confirmed for 1998

Perth Museum & Art Gallery
78 George St PH1 5LB
☎01738 632488 Fax 01738 443505
This purpose-built museum houses collections of fine and applied art, social and local history, natural history and archaeology. Temporary exhibitions are held throughout the year, including 'The River Tay' - Jan-Dec 1998.
Open all year, Mon-Sat 10-5. (Closed Xmas-New year). Free.
P *(adjacent)* & *shop* ⚇ *(ex guide dogs)*

PITLOCHRY
Edradour Distillery
PH16 5JP (2.5m E on the A924)
☎01796 472095 Fax 01796 472002
It was in 1825 that a group of local farmers founded Edradour, naming it after the bubbling burn that runs through it. It is Scotland's smallest distillery and is virtually unchanged since Victorian times. Visitors can have a dram of whisky while watching an audio-visual in the malt barn and then see the disillers' art practised here as it has been for over 160 years.
Open, early Mar-end Oct, Mon-Sat 9.30-5. Winter months, Mon-Sat 10-4, shop only. Tours by arrangement in winter months. Free.
🅿 & *toilets for disabled shop* ⚇ *(ex guidance dogs)*
Cards: 🖃 🖃 🖃 🖃

Faskally
(1m N on the B8019)
☎01350 727284 Fax 01350 728635
On the shores of Loch Faskally, the mature, mixed woodland incorporates forest walks, a nature trail and picnic area
Open all year-dawn to dusk. Free.
🅿 & *toilets for disabled* ♿

Hydro-Electric Visitor Centre, Dam & Fish Pass
PH16 5BX
☎01796 473152
The hydro-electric visitor centre consists of a souvenir shop; an exhibition showing how electricity is brought from the power station to the customer; access to the turbine viewing gallery and video shows. The salmon ladder viewing chamber allows visitors to see the fish as they travel upstream to their spawning ground. There is also a walkway across the top of the dam.
Open Apr-Oct, daily 10-5.30. £1.80 (ch 80p, concessions £1). Family ticket £3.60.
🅿 & *(monitor viewing of salmon fish pass) toilets for disabled shop* ⚇
Cards: 🖃 🖃 🖃 🖃

PORT OF MENTEITH
Inchmahome Priory
(4m E of Aberfoyle, off A81)
☎01877 385294
Walter Comyn founded this Augustinian house in 1238, and it became famous as the retreat of the infant Mary Queen of Scots in 1543. The ruins of the church and cloisters are situated on an island in the Lake of Monteith.
Open Apr-Sep, weekdays 9.30-6.30, Sun 2-6.30. Ferry subject to cancellation in adverse weather conditions.
🅿 *shop* ♥
Details not confirmed for 1998

PRESTONPANS
Scottish Mining Museum
Prestongrange (on B1348)
☎0131 653 2904 Fax 01620 828201
The oldest documented coal mining site in Britain with 800 years of history, this museum shows a Cornish Beam Engine and on-site evidence of associated industries such as brickmaking and pottery, plus a 16th-century customs port. The 'Cutting the Coal' exhibition, in the Power House, has an underground gallery, a coalface, a reconstruction of a colliery workshop and a wonderful collection of coal-cutting machines and equipment. There is a guided tour of the site. Special Events - weekend events for families and children in July/August, please ring for details. Steam Days - first Sunday of every month plus third Sunday of June, July and August - rides on working colliery locomotives.
Open Apr-Oct, daily 11-4. Last tour 3pm. Free.
🅿 & *toilets for disabled shop* ⚇ *(ex guide dogs)*

QUEEN'S VIEW
Queen's View Visitor Centre
PH16 5NR (7m W of Pitlochry on B8019)
☎01350 727284 Fax 01350 728635
Queen Victoria admired the view on a visit here in 1866, and there is a splendid viewpoint which also has access for the disabled. Forest walks take the visitor to viewpoints, an excavated ring fort and a reconstructed 18th-century farm village. The Visitor Centre has an exhibition describing the history of the area and places to visit.
Open Apr-Oct, daily 10-6. Free.
🅿 *(charged)* ♥ & *toilets for disabled shop*
Cards: 🖃 🖃

ST ANDREWS
British Golf Museum
Bruce Embankment KY16 9AB (opposite Royal & Ancient Golf Club)
☎01334 478880 Fax 01334 473306
What do ballooning, music and archery have to do with the game of golf? A visit to the British Golf Museum will transport you down a pathway of surprising facts and striking feats from 500 years of golf history and provide answers to these and many other questions. Using touch screens, diverse displays and exciting exhibits, the museum traces the history of the game throughout the ages in such a way as to appeal to both golfers and non-golfers alike.
Open all year, Etr-mid Oct daily 9.30-5.30; mid Oct-Etr Thu-Mon 11-3. (closed Tue & Wed).
£3.75 (ch 15 £1.50, pen & students £2.75). Family ticket £9.50. Group 10+
🅿 *(charged)* & *toilets for disabled shop* ⚇

Castle & Visitor Centre
☎01334 477196
This 13th-century stronghold castle was the setting for the murder of Cardinal Beaton in 1546. The new visitor centre incorporates an exciting multi-media exhibition describing the history of the castle and nearby cathedral.
Open all year, Apr-Sep, Mon-Sat 9.30-6.30, Sun 2-6.30; Oct-Mar, Mon-Sat 9.30-4.30, Sun 2-4.30. (Closed 25-26 Dec & 1-3 Jan).
P & *toilets for disabled shop* ⚇ ♥
Details not confirmed for 1998

Cathedral (& Museum)
☎01334 472563
The cathedral was the largest in Scotland, and is now an extensive ruin. The remains date mainly from the 12th

---

THE BLACK WATCH MUSEUM

Balhousie Castle

Perth

Two and a half Centuries of Treasures of the 42nd/73rd Highland Regiments

May to September, Monday to Saturday (including public holidays) 1000-1630 (except last Saturday of June); October to April, Monday to Friday, 1000-1530

ADMISSION FREE

Parties over 10, please phone 0131 3108530 prior to arrival

VISITORS CENTRE AND FISH LADDER

A friendly welcome awaits you at the Hydro-Electric Visitors Centre here at Pitlochry.

Open: April–October

7 days a week 10.00am-5.30pm

For group booking please phone the supervisor

01796 473152

These charming gardens are the perfect setting for the Victorian Torosay Castle

and 13th centuries, and large parts of the precinct walls have survived intact. Close by is St Rule's church, which the cathedral was built to replace. St Rule's probably dates from before the Norman Conquest, and is considered the most interesting Romanesque church in Scotland.
The museum is housed in a 14th-century building and contains an important collection of Celtic and medieval sculpture and artefacts. There is also a fascinating array of later gravestones on display.
Open all year, Apr-Sep, Mon-Sat 9.30-6.30, Sun 2-6.30; Oct-Mar, Mon-Sat 9.30-4.30, Sun 2-4.30. (Closed 25-26 Dec & 1-3 Jan).
P & shop ⊗ ▮
Details not confirmed for 1998

SCONE
Scone Palace
Scone Palace PH2 6BD (2m NE of Perth on A93)
☎01738 552300 Fax 01738 552588
Scottish kings were crowned at Scone until 1651; it was the seat of government in Pictish times; and it was the site of the famous coronation Stone of Destiny, brought there in the 9th century until it was seized by the English in 1296. The castellated edifice of the present palace dates from 1803 but incorporates the 16th-century and earlier buildings. The displays inside include a magnificent collection of porcelain, furniture, ivories, clocks and 16th-century needlework; one of the bed hangings was worked by Mary, Queen of Scots. The grounds include an outstanding pinetum, woodland garden and brilliant displays of rhododendrons and azaleas (at the right time of the year). Although one of the most historic houses in Scotland, its chief attraction lies in its much-loved and 'lived-in' atmosphere - it still remains a family home. Events for 1998 include horse trials, the Scottish game fair (5-6 July), and Farming of Yesteryear. Please telephone for details.
Open 10 Apr-12 Oct, daily 9.30-5.15 (last admission 4.45). Special parties outside normal opening hours & during winter by arrangement.
Palace & Grounds £5.20 (ch £3). Grounds only £2.60 (ch £1.50) Family £15. Party 20+.
P ⊒ ✗ licensed & toilets for disabled shop
Cards: ▬ ▬ ▬

SOUTH QUEENSFERRY
Dalmeny House
EH30 9TQ
☎0131 331 1888 Fax 0131 331 1788
This is the home of the Earl and the Countess of Rosebery, whose family have lived here for over 300 years. The house, however, only dates from 1815 when it was built in Tudor Gothic style. There are vaulted corridors and a splendid Gothic hammerbeamed hall, but the main rooms are in classical style. Dalmeny House has a magnificent situation on the Firth of Forth and there are delightful walks in the wooded grounds and along the shore. Inside, it has fine French furniture, tapestries and porcelain from the Rothschild Mentmore collection. Early Scottish furniture is also shown, with 18th-century portraits, Rosebery racing mementoes and a display of pictures and items associated with Napoleon.
Open July-Aug, Sun 1-5.30, Mon-Tue 12-5.30. Last admission 4.45. Open other times by arrangement for groups.
£3.60 (ch 10-16 £2, pen £3.20, students £2.80). Party 20+.
P ⊒ & toilets for disabled ⊗ (ex guide dogs or in grounds)

Hopetoun House
EH30 9SL (2m W of Forth Road Bridge, off B904)
☎0131 331 2451 Fax 0131 319 1885
One of Scotland's finest stately home was built in 1699 to a design by William Bruce, but between 1721 and 1754 it was enlarged by William and Robert Adam. The magnificent reception rooms have notable paintings by artists such as Gainsborough and Raeburn, and there are also fine examples of furniture and a collection of china. A museum in the stables features an exhibition entitled 'Horse and Man in Lowland Scotland'. The grounds are extensive, and include deer parks with red and fallow deer, and a herd of the rare St Kilda sheep. It is possible to play croquet or pétanque for a fee. Walks along the coast give views of the Forth bridges, which can also be seen from a special viewing platform. Facilities include a nature trail and a free Ranger Service. If prior notice is given special arrangements can be made for blind and disabled visitors. Special events include a Country Fair in July. An annual event organised by Hopetown featuring various entertainment, side shows, music, a craft marquee and other attractions. An ideal family day out, telephone for further details.

Open 28 Mar-28 Sep, daily 10-5.30 (last admission 4.30).
£4.50 (ch £2.50). Grounds £2.50 (ch £1.50).
P ⊒ ✗ licensed & toilets for disabled shop garden centre (on leads)
Cards: ▬ ▬

Inchcolm Abbey
Inchcolm Island (1.5m S of Aberdour Access by ferry Apr-Sep)
☎01383 823332
Situated on a green island on the Firth of Forth, the Augustinian abbey was founded in about 1123 by Alexander I. The well-preserved remains include a fine 13th-century octagonal chapter house and a 13th-century wall painting.
Open Apr-Sep, Mon-Sat 9.30-6.30, Sun 2-6.30.
shop ⊗ ▮
Details not confirmed for 1998

Queensferry Museum
53 High St EH30 9HP
☎0131 331 5545
Fax 0131 557 3346
The museum tells the story of South Queensferry and its people. It looks at the development of the Queensferry Passage, the growth of the former Royal Burgh and the building of the rail and road bridges which span the Forth. There are displays on the life work and pastimes of Queensferry people and a life-size model of the Burry Man, a centuries-old custom. There are changing exhibitions and a new hands-on display on the natural history of the Forth.
Open all year, Mon & Thu-Sat 10-1, 2.15-5 (Sun noon-5)
Free.
P (0.25m) shop ⊗ (ex guide dogs)

STIRLING
Mar's Wark
Broad St FK8 1EE
☎0131 668 8800
Fax 0131 668 8888
Now partly ruined, this Renaissance-style mansion was built in 1570 by the 1st Earl of Mar, Regent of Scotland. With its gatehouse enriched with sculptures, it is one of several fine buildings on the road to Stirling Castle. The Earls of Mar lived there until the 6th Earl fled the country after leading the 1715 Jacobite Rebellion.
Open at all times.
▮
Details not confirmed for 1998

Museum of Argyll & Sutherland Highlanders
☎01786 75165 Fax 01786 446038
Situated in the King's Old Building in Stirling Castle, the museum tells the history of the Regiment from 1794 to the present day. Displays include uniforms, silver, paintings, colours, pipe banners, and commentaries. There is a fine medal collection covering the period from the Battle of Waterloo to the present day. Five permanent exhibits mark the bi-centenary of the Regiment.
Open Etr-Sep, Mon-Sat 10-5.30, Sun 11-5; Oct-Etr, Mon-Sun 10-4.
Entry to museum free but entry fee to castle.
P (castle esplanade) shop ⊗

Old Town Jail
St John St FK8 1EA (follow signs for castle up the hill, jail on left at top of St John's St)
☎01786 450050 Fax 01786 471301
Built in 1847 to replace the old Tolbooth jail, this is an outstanding example of Victorian architecture. A living history performance means the visitor can learn about the daily life of the prisoners and the strict regime practised in the prison. A glass sided lift enables access to the rooftop, where magnificent views of Stirling and the surrounding area can be enjoyed.
Open daily, Apr-29 Sep 9.30-6. Last tour 5. Oct-Mar 9.30-4. Closed Xmas, 3 Sep-Dec & Feb-Mar 9.30-4. Closed Xmas & 1-2 Jan.
❄£2.75 (concessions £2). Family ticket £8.
P & (lift to viewpoint) toilets for disabled shop ⊗
Cards: ▬ ▬ ▬ ▣

Royal Burgh of Stirling Visitor Centre
Castle Esplanade FK8 1EH (next to Stirling Castle)
☎01786 479901 & 462517 Fax 01786 451881
The colourful and definative introduction to Royal Stirling. For centuries, Stirling lay at the centre of Scotland's turbulent history, from the Wars of Independence, through the reign of the Stuart monarchs to a Medieval burgh. Many historic attractions remain and this free multi-lingual audio-visual show recounts the full vibrant history of Stirling from earliest times to the present day.
Open all year, Jan-Mar & Nov-Dec, daily 9.30-5; May-Jun & Sept-Oct, daily 9.30-6; Jul-Aug, daily 9-6.30. Closed Xmas/New Year.
Free.
P & (Induction loop for the hard of hearing) toilets for disabled shop ⊗ ♨

Smith Art Gallery & Museum
Dumbarton Rd FK8 2RQ (junc 10 off M9 follow town centre signs)
☎01786 471917 Fax 01786 449523
This lively, award-winning museum and gallery presents a variety of exhibitions drawing on its own rich collections and works from elsewhere. A range of programmes and events offers the opportunity to see, find out about and join in art, history, craft and design. There is a small shop. Victorian Stirling exhibition for 1998.
Open all year, Tue-Sat 10.30-5, Sun 2-5.
Free.
P ⊒ & (wheelchair lift, induction loop in theatre) toilets for disabled shop ⊗ (ex guide dogs)

Stirling Castle
Upper Castle Hill FK8 1EJ
☎01786 450000
Sitting on top of a 250ft rock, Stirling Castle has a strategic position on the Firth of Forth. As a result it has been the scene of many events in Scotland's history. Much of the castle that remains today is from the 15th and 16th centuries, when it became a favourite royal residence. James II was born at the castle in 1430. Mary Queen of Scots spent some years there, and it was ➤

James IV's childhood home. The old towers were built by James IV, as was the fine great hall. Among its finest features are the splendid Renaissance palace built by James V, and the Chapel Royal, rebuilt by James VI.
Open all year, Apr-Sep, daily 9.30-6; Oct-Mar, daily 9.30-5. Last ticket sold 45 mins prior to closing time.
P *(charged)* X *licensed* & *toilets for disabled shop* ✍ ▌

WEEM
Castle Menzies
PH15 2JD (1.5m from Aberfeldy on B846)
☎ 01887 820982
Restored seat of the Chiefs of Clan Menzies, and a fine example of a 16th-century Z-plan fortified tower house. Involved in the turbulent history of the Highlands it was occupied by various military forces on occasions up to World War II. Prince Charles Edward Stuart stayed here briefly on his way to Culloden in 1746. The whole of the 16th century building can be fully explored. Small clan museum.
Open 1 Apr-17 Oct, wkdays 10.30-5, Sun 2-5. Last entry 4.30pm.
£3 (ch £1.50, pen £2.50).
P ▇ & *toilets for disabled shop* ✍ *(ex guide dogs)*

SOUTHERN LOWLANDS & BORDERS

This region includes the counties of City of Glasgow, Dumfries & Galloway, East Ayrshire, East Dunbartonshire, East Renfrewshire, North Ayrshire, North Lanarkshire, Renfrewshire, Scottish Borders, South Ayrshire, South Lanarkshire, West Dunbartonshire.

ALLOWAY
Burn's Cottage
Burns National Heritage Park KA7 4PY (2m S of Ayr)
☎ 01292 441215
Fax 01292 441750
Thatched cottage built in 1757, now a museum, birthplace of Robert Burns in 1759. The cottage has recently undergone extensive refurbishment and contains an audio-visual presentation. Adjacent museum contains a large number of the poets' songs, poems, letters and personal relics. On display are the original manuscripts of 'Auld Lang Syne' and 'Tam O'Shanter'. Special events are held during Burns Week (18-25 Jan).
Open all year, Apr-Oct 9-6; Nov-Mar 10-4 (Sun 12-4).
£2.50 (ch & pen £1.25) includes entry to Burns Monument & Gardens. Family ticket £6. Combined ticket also available £4.25 (ch £2.50). Prices under review.
P ▇ & *toilets for disabled shop*

Burn's Monument
KA7 4PQ (2m S of Ayr)
☎ 01292 441321
Robert Burns was born in the thatched cottage in 1759, two years after it was built. It is now a museum. The monument was built in 1823 to a fine design by Thomas Hamilton Junior, with sculptures of characters in Burns' poems by a self-taught artist, James Thom.
Open as for **Burns' Cottage**.
P &

Tam O'Shanter Experience
Burns National Heritage Park, Murdoch's Lone KA7 4PQ
☎ 01292 443700
Fax 01292 441750
The newly refurbished centre, opened by the Queen in 1995, gives a potted introduction to the life of Robert Burns, with two audio-visual theatres, one about the life of Robert Burns, the other being an exciting multi-screen 3D presentation of the Tale of Tam O'Shanter with lightening flashes and thunder bellows. There are also tranquil landscaped gardens. Please telephone for details.
Open all year, daily 9-6.
Audio visual theatres £2.50 (ch & pen £1.25). Party. Combined ticket available, £4.25 (ch £2.50).
P ▇ X *licensed* & *toilets for disabled shop* ✍

ARDUAINE
Arduaine Garden
PA34 4XQ (20m S of Oban, on A816)
☎ 01852 200233 Fax 01852 200233
An outstanding 18-acre garden on a promontory bounded by Loch Melfort and the Sound of Jura, climatically favoured by the North Atlantic Drift or Gulf Stream. Nationally noted for rhododendrons and azalea species and other rare trees and shrubs.
Open all year, daily 9.30-sunset.
£2.40 (concessions £1.60). Adult party. Child/school party.
P & *toilets for disabled* ✍ *(ex guide dogs)* ▾

ARDWELL
Ardwell House Gardens
DG9 9LY (10m S of Stranraer, on A716)
☎ 01776 860227
Fax 01776 860288
Country house gardens and grounds with flowering shrubs and woodland walks. Plants for sale. House not open to the public.
Open Mar-Oct, 10-5. Walled garden & greenhouses close at 5pm.
£1.50 (ch & pen 75p).
P *garden centre*

ARRAN, ISLE OF

BRODICK
Brodick Castle, Garden & Country Park
KA27 8HY (Ferry from Ardrossan-Brodick. From N end of Arran-Kintyre frequent in Summer, limited in winter)
☎ 01770 302202
Fax 01770 302312
The site of Brodick Castle has been fortified since Viking times, but the present castle dates from the 13th century, with extensions added in 1652 and 1844. It was a stronghold of the Dukes of Hamilton and more recently became the home of the late Duchess of Montrose. Splendid silver, fine porcelain and paintings acquired by generations of owners can be seen, including many sporting pictures and trophies.
There is a formal garden, dating from the 18th century and restored in Victorian style, but the most impressive part of the grounds is the woodland garden. It was started by the Duchess in 1923, and is world-famous for its rhododendrons and azaleas. A self-guided walk leads to its heart, and there are weekly guided walks in summer. The grounds also have an ice house, a Bavarian summer-house and an adventure playground, ranger service and display centre. Please ring for details of concerts, open-air theatre etc.
Open all year, Garden & Country Park, daily 9.30-sunset. Castle open Good Fri-Oct daily 11.30-5. Last admission 4.30pm.
Castle & Gardens £4.80 (concessions £3.20). Garden only £2.40. Family ticket £12.80. Party.
P X & *(Braille sheets, motorised buggy, wheelchairs & stairlift) toilets for disabled shop* ✍ *(ex guide dogs)* ▾

Isle of Arran Heritage Museum
Rosaburn KA27 8DP (Right at Brodick Pier, approx 1m)
☎ 01770 302636
The setting is an 18th-century croft farm, including a cottage restored to its pre-1920 state and a 'smiddy' where a blacksmith worked until the late 1960s. Displays are wide-ranging - archaeology,

geology, farming, shipping etc, as well as a heritage project carried out in conjunction with a local high school. There are also occasional demonstrations of horseshoeing, sheepshearing, weaving and spinning, a veteran car rally and a golf tournament - please ring for details.
Open Apr-Oct, Mon-Sat 10-5 high season. Apr-Oct, Mon-Sat 11-4 low season and every Sunday.
✲*£2 (ch £1, pen £1.25) Family £5.*
P ▇ & *shop*

AUCHINDRAIN
Auchindrain Township-Open Air Museum
PA32 8XN (5.5m SW of Inverarary)
☎ 01499 500235
Auchindrain is an original West Highland township, or village, of great antiquity, and the only communal tenancy township to have survived on its centuries-old site. The township buildings, which have been restored and preserved, are furnished and equipped to present the visitor with a fascinating glimpse of Highland life in the last century.
Open Apr-Sep, daily 10-5.
£3 (ch £1.50, pen £2.50). Family ticket £8. Prices under review.
P ▇ *shop*

AYR
Maclaurin Art Gallery & Rozelle House
Rozelle Park, Monument Rd KA7 4NQ (on B7024 between Ayr town centre & Burns Cottage)
☎ 01292 445447 & 443708
Fax 01292 442065
Temporary exhibition programme throughout the year featuring British and International artists in addition to local groups and organisations. Permanent collections always on display. Henry Moore bronze sculpture. High quality crafts in exhibitions and on sale.
Open all year, Mon-Sat 10-5, Sun (Apr-Oct only) 2-5. (Closed Xmas & New Year).
P ▇ X & *shop* ✍ *(ex guide dogs)*
Details not confirmed for 1998

This magnificent memorial is to Robbie Burns and was built in 1823 to commemorate Scotland's most famous poet at his birthplace.

BALLOCH
Balloch Castle Country Park
G83 8LX (A82 for Dumbartonshire, Balloch from Glasgow. A811 for Balloch from Stirling.)
☎ 01389 758216 Fax 01389 755721
Set at the southern end of Loch Lomond, the country park encompasses varying habitats with many trails, a walled garden, and lawns for picnics giving wonderful views. Overlooking the lawns is Balloch Castle, built in 1808. Its visitor centre gives an introduction to local history and wildlife. An events programme is available in March. The park is part of a larger regional park which covers an area of 170 square miles. Contact park for details of special events.
Open Visitor Centre, Apr-Oct daily 10-5.45 Country Park 8-dusk.
Free.
P & *(Large area for wheelchairs) toilets for disabled shop*
Cards: ◪ ▦

BARCALDINE
Barcaldine Castle
Ledaig PA37 1SA (9m N of Oban on A828 Oban/Fort William road. Take left turn to Tralee in Benderloch)
☎ 01631 720598 Fax 01631 720598
16th century home of the Campbells of Barcaldine. The last of the seven castles built by Black Duncan to be held in Campbell hands. Associated with the Appin Murder and Glencoe Massacre. Haunted by the Blue Lady - will you meet her? Lived in by the family, who have taken on the arduous task of renovation.
Open May-Sep, daily 11-5.30.
✲*£2.95 (ch £1.50, concessions £2.65)*
P ▇ *shop* ✍

Sea Life Centre
PA37 1SE (10m N of Oban on A828)
☎ 01631 720386 Fax 01631 720529
Set in one of Scotland's most picturesque locations, Oban Sea Life Centre provides dramatic views of native undersea life from stingrays and seals to octopus and catfish. There are daily talks and feeding demonstrations and during the summer young seals can be viewed prior to their release back into the wild.

There is a restaurant, gift shop, children's play park, and nature trail. 'World of the Jellyfish' is a new feature.
Open all year, Feb-Nov, daily 9-6. (Jul-Aug 7pm); Dec & Jan, Sat & Sun only.
❋£5.50 (ch £3.50, pen & students £4.50). Party 10+.
🅿 ✕ licensed ⴲ (assistance available for wheelchairs) toilets for disabled shop ⚥ (ex guide dogs)
Cards: ▨ ▨ ▨ ▨ ▨

BARGANY
See Old Dailly

BEARSDEN
Roman Bath-House
Roman Rd G61 2SG
☎0131 668 8800 Fax 0131 668 8888
Considered to be the best surviving visible Roman building in Scotland, the bath-house was discovered in 1973 during excavations for a construction site. It was originally built for use by the Roman garrison at Bearsden Fort, which is part of the Antonine Wall defences.
Open all reasonable times.
ⴲ ⚥ ▮
Details not confirmed for 1998

BENMORE
Younger Botanic Garden
PA23 8QU (7m N of Dunoon on A815)
☎01369 706261 & 840599 (shop) Fax 01369 706369
Enter the magnificent avenue of Giant Redwoods, planted in 1863, and follow a variety of waymarked trails through this botanical paradise in a highland glen setting. From the formal garden, through the hillside woodlands, make your way to a stunning viewpoint with a spectacular outlook across the garden and the Holy Loch to the Firth of Clyde and beyond. Amongst many highlights are the stately conifers, some of Britain's tallest trees, over 250 varieties of colourful rhododendrons and an extensive magnolia collection. Please telephone for details of special events.
Open Mar-Oct, daily, 9.30-6.
£3 (ch £1, concessions £2.50). Family £7.
🅿 💺 ✕ licensed ⴲ toilets for disabled shop garden centre
Cards: ▨ ▨

BIGGAR
Gladstone Court Museum
ML12 6DT (entrance by 113 High St)
☎01899 221573 & 221050
An old-fashioned village street is portrayed in this museum, which is set out in a century-old coach-house. On display are reconstructed shops, complete with old signs and advertisments; a bank; a telephone exchange; a photographer's booth and other interesting glimpses into the recent past.
Open Etr-Oct, daily 10-12.30 & 2-5, Sun 2-5.
£1.80 (ch 90p, pen £1.30). Family ticket £4.80. Party. Discount for visits to other Biggar museums.
🅿 ⴲ shop ⚥ (ex guide dogs)

Greenhill Covenanters House
Burn Braes ML12 6DT
☎01899 221572
This 17th-century farmhouse was brought, stone by stone, ten miles from Wiston and reconstructed at Biggar. It has relics of the turbulent 'Covenanting' period, when men and women defended the right to worship in Presbyterian style. Audio presentations.
Open Etr-early Oct, daily 2-5.
£1 (ch 60p, pen 70p). Family ticket £2.40. Party. Discount for visitors to other Biggar museums.
🅿 ⴲ shop ⚥ (ex guide dogs)

Moat Park Heritage Centre
ML12 6DT
☎01899 221050 Fax 01899 221569
The centre illustrates the history, archaeology and geology of the Upper Clyde and Tweed valleys with interesting displays. Great Biggar Vintage and Veteran Vehicle Rally (16 Aug).

Open all year, Apr-Oct, daily 10-5, Sun 2-5; Nov-Feb, weekdays during office hours. Other times by prior arrangement.
£2 (ch £1, pen £1.60). Family ticket £5. Party. Discount for visits to other Biggar museums.
🅿 ⴲ (upper floor with assistance on request) toilets for disabled shop ⚥ (ex guide dogs)

BLANTYRE
David Livingstone Centre
165 Station Rd G72 9BT (M74 junc 5 onto A725, to A724, take signs for Blantyre, right at lights, Centre is at foot of hill)
☎01698 823140 Fax 01698 821424
Share the adventurous life of Scotland's greatest explorer, from his childhood in the Blantyre Mills to his explorations in the heart of Africa, all dramatically illustrated in the historic tenement where he was born. New facilities include a jungle garden, art gallery, social history exhibition, children's animated display, African playground and riverside walks. There is also a cafe and themed gift shop. Events are planned throughout the season, contact the centre for details.
Open Mar-Dec, Mon-Sat 10-6, Sun 12.30-6. Last admission 5pm. Other times by arrangement.
❋£2.95 (ch £1.60 concessions £1.95). Family ticket £7.50. Party.
🅿 💺 ⴲ toilets for disabled shop (only guide dogs inside)
Cards: ▨ ▨

BOTHWELL
Bothwell Castle
G71 8BL (approach from Uddingston off B7071)
☎01698 816894
Besieged, captured and 'knocked about' several times in the Scottish-English wars, the castle is a splendid ruin. Archibald the Grim built the curtain wall; later, in 1786, the Duke of Buccleuch carved graffiti - a coronet and initials - beside a basement well.
Open all year, Apr-Sep, Mon-Sat 9.30-6.30, Sun 2-6.30; Oct-Mar, Mon-Sat 9.30-4.30, Sun 2-4.30. (Closed Thu pm & Fri in winter; also 25-26 Dec & 1-3 Jan).
🅿 ⴲ shop ▮
Details not confirmed for 1998

BROUGHTON
Broughton Place
ML12 6HJ (N on A701)
☎01899 830234
The house was designed by Sir Basil Spence in 1938, in the style of a 17th-century Scottish tower house. The drawing room and main hall are open to the public, and have paintings and crafts by living British artists for sale. The gardens are open and give fine views of the Tweeddale Hills. There are also national collections of Thalictrum and Tropaeolum. A full programme of exhibitions is available on request.
Open - Gallery 29 Mar-20 Oct & 15 Nov-20 Dec, daily (ex Wed) 10.30-6. Gallery free; Garden donations.
🅿 ⴲ shop garden centre ⚥ (ex guide dogs)

CAERLAVEROCK
Caerlaverock Castle
Glencaple DG1 4RU (8m SE of Dumfries)
☎01387 770244
This ancient seat of the Maxwell family is a splendid medieval stronghold dating back to the 13th century. It has high walls and round towers, with machicolations added in the 15th century.
Open all year, Apr-Sep, Mon-Sat 9.30-6.30, Sun 2-6.30; Oct-Mar 9.30-4.30, Sun 2-4.30. (Closed 25-26 Dec & 1-3 Jan).
🅿 ⴲ shop ▮
Details not confirmed for 1998

WWT Caerlaverock
Eastpark Farm DG1 4RS (9m SE of Dumfries, signposted from A75)
☎01387 770200 Fax 01387 770200
Enjoy the sights and sounds of some of the most spectacular wildlife in Britain,

---

including the entire Svalbard population of Barnacle Geese which spends the winter on the Solway Firth, making this site one of the most important for wintering wildfowl in the UK, and indeed, an internationally important wetland. Observation facilities include twenty hides, three towers and a heated observatory which offer outstanding views of the huge numbers of wintering wildfowl. Nature trails meander through a wealth of wildflowers and a wide variety of other wildlife can be seen, notably the rare Natterjack Toad and a family of Barn Owls which can be observed via a closed circuit television system. Multiple access visitor facilities, picnic area and refreshments. Special programme of events and activities. Please telephone for details.
Open daily 10-5 (Closed 25 Dec).
❋£3.00 (ch £1.80). Family ticket £7.80. Party 20+.
🅿 ⴲ toilets for disabled shop ⚥
Cards: ▨ ▨ ▨

CARDONESS CASTLE
Cardoness Castle
DG7 2EH (1m SW of Gatehouse of Fleet off A75)
☎01557 814427
A 15th-century stronghold overlooking the Water of Fleet. It was once the home of the McCullochs of Galloway. The architectural details inside the tower are of very high quality.
Open all year, Apr-Sep, Mon-Sat 9.30-6.30, Sun 2-6.30; Oct-Mar, wknds only. Sat 9.30-4.30, Sun 2-4.30 (Closed 25-26 Dec & 1-3 Jan).
🅿 shop ▮
Details not confirmed for 1998

CARNASSARIE CASTLE
Carnassarie Castle
PA31 8RQ (2m N of Kilmartin off A816)
☎0131 668 8800 Fax 0131 668 8888
Built in the 16th-century by John Carswell, first Protestant Bishop of the Isles, the castle was taken and partly destroyed in Argyll's rebellion of 1685. It consists of a tower house and courtyard built on to it.
Open at all reasonable times.
🅿 ⚥ ▮
Details not confirmed for 1998

CASTLE DOUGLAS
Threave Castle
(3m W on A75)
☎01831 168512
Archibald the Grim built this lonely castle in the late 14th century. It stands on an islet in the River Dee, and is four storeys high with round towers guarding the outer wall. Access to the island is by boat.
Open Apr-Sep, Mon-Sat 9.30-6.30, Sun 2-6.30.
🅿 ⚥ ▮
Details not confirmed for 1998

Threave Garden & Estate
DG7 1RX (1m W of Castle Douglas off A75)
☎01556 502575
Fax 01556 502683
The best time to visit is in spring when there is a dazzling display of some 200 varieties of daffodil. The garden has something to see all year round, however, and includes a walled garden and glasshouses. The house is the National Trust for Scotland's School of Practical Gardening. The surrounding estate is renowned for its wildlife, and includes five bird hides and several marked walks.
Open all year. Garden, daily 9.30-sunset. Walled garden and glasshouses daily 9.30-5. Visitor centre, Shop & Exhibition Apr-Oct daily 9.30-5.30. (Last entry 30 minutes before closing).
£4 (ch & concessions £2.70).Family ticket £10.70:
🅿 ✕ licensed ⴲ (wheelchairs available incl. electric wheelchair) toilets for disabled shop garden centre ⚥ (ex guide dogs) ✿

CLARENCEFIELD
Comlongon Castle
DG1 4NA
☎01387 870283
Fax 01387 870266
An exceptionally well-preserved 15th-century Border castle currently being restored. It contains many original features including dungeons, kitchen, great hall, Heraldic devices, and bed chambers with 'privies'. It's set in gardens and woodland with secluded walks, and is haunted by a 16th-century suicide.
Open Mar-Oct, telephone for opening times.
🅿 ⴲ ⚥
Details not confirmed for 1998
Cards: ▨ ▨ ▨ ▨ ▨

COATBRIDGE
Summerlee Heritage Trust
West Canal St ML5 1QD
☎01236 431261
Fax 01236 440429
Summerlee is a major 20-acre museum of social and industrial history centring on the remains of the Summerlee Ironworks which were put into blast in the 1830s. The aim of the Museum is to preserve and interpret the history of the local iron, steel and engineering industries and the communities that depended upon them for a living. The exhibition hall features displays of social and industrial history including working machinery and recreated workshop interiors. Outside, Summerlee operates the only working tram in Scotland, an underground coalmine and reconstructed miners rows with interiors dating from 1840. The gallery shows regularly changing exhibitions. Special events throughout the year include a Spring Fling with children's entertainment, Historic Vehicle Festival, Holiday Activity Week, Steam and Model Fair.Telephone for details.
Open daily 10-5pm. (Closed 25-26 Dec & 1-2 Jan).
Free.
🅿 💺 ⴲ (wheelchair available & staff assistance) toilets for disabled shop ⚥

COLDSTREAM
Hirsel
Douglas & Angus Estates, Estate Office, The Hirsel TD12 4LP (0.5m W on A697)
☎01890 882834 & 882965
Fax 01890 882834
The Hirsel is the seat of the Home family, and its grounds are open all year. The focal point is the Homestead Museum, craft centre and workshops. From there, nature trails lead around the lake, along the Leet Valley and into a wood which is noted for its rhododendrons and azaleas. Tea room, picnic areas. A May Fair (3,4,5 May), and Christmas Craft Fair (8,9 Nov) are planned for 1998.
Garden & Grounds open all year, daylight hours. Museum 10-5. Craft Centre Mon-Fri, 10-5, weekends noon-5.
Free.
🅿 (charged) 💺 ⴲ toilets for disabled shop (ex on lead)

CREETOWN
Creetown Gem Rock Museum
Chain Rd DG8 7HJ (follow signs from A75)
☎01671 820357 & 820554
Fax 01671 820554
Discover a-world famous collection of gems, crystals, minerals and fossils, right in the heart of Galloway. Lovingly assembled by two generations, this is a beautiful and educational experience. Interactive computer displays provide an opportunity to learn more, and audio visual displays explain how minerals are formed.
Open Mar-Etr, daily 10-4; Etr-Sep, daily 9.30-6; Sep-23 Dec, daily 10-4; 25 Dec-7 Jan closed; 8 Jan-Feb, Sat & Sun only 10-4 or by appointment during the week.
£2.75 (ch 5-15 £1.75, pen £2.25). Family ticket £7.25. Party 20+.
🅿 💺 ⴲ toilets for disabled shop ⚥
Cards: ▨ ▨ ▨ ▨ ▨

Built on a clifftop 150 feet above the sea, Culzean Castle is one of Scotland's finest castles with lavishly furnished public rooms and walled and terraced gardens.

CULZEAN CASTLE
Culzean Castle & Country Park
KA19 8LE (4m W of Maybole, off A77)
☎01655 760274 & 760269 Fax 01655 760615

The castle and country park together make one of the most popular days out in Scotland. The great 18th-century castle stands on a clifftop site in spacious grounds and was designed by Robert Adam for David, 10th Earl of Cassillis. It is noted for its oval staircase, circular drawing room and plasterwork. The Eisenhower Room explores the general's link's with Culzean.

Culzean was Scotland's first country park, and covers 563 acres with a wide range of attractions - shoreline, woodland walks, parkland, an adventure playground, and gardens, including a walled garden of 1783. The visitor centre has various facilities and information, and is also the base of the ranger naturalists who provide guided walks and other services. Many events are held each year, both in the castle and park.

Country park open all year, daily 9.30-sunset. Castle & visitor centre open Apr-Oct, 10.30-5.30. Last admission 5pm. Other times by appointment.
Country Park £3.50, concessions £2.40. Castle £4.20 (concessions £2.80). Combined ticket for castle and country park £6.50 (concessions £4.40) Family combined ticket £17. Party20+
🅿 🍴 ✗ *licensed* ♿ *(wheelchairs available, lift in castle) toilets for disabled shop garden centre (ex castle, ex guide dogs)* 🐕

DRUMCOLTRAN TOWER
Drumcoltran Tower
(7m NE of Dalbeattie)
☎0131 668 8800 Fax 0131 668 8888
The 16th-century tower house stands three storeys high and has a simple, functional design.
Open at any reasonable time.
♿ 🔲
Details not confirmed for 1998

DRYBURGH
Dryburgh Abbey
(5m SE of Melrose on B6404)
☎01835 822381
The abbey was one of the Border monasteries founded by David I, and stands in a lovely setting on the River Tweed. The ruins are equally beautiful, and the church has the graves of Sir Walter Scott and Earl Haig.

Open all year, Apr-Sep, weekdays 9.30-6.30, Sun 2-6.30; Oct-Mar weekdays 9.30-4.30, Sun 2-4.30. (Closed 25-26 Dec & 1-3 Jan).
🅿 ♿ *shop* ♿ 🔲
Details not confirmed for 1998

DUMBARTON
Dumbarton Castle
☎01389 732167
The castle is set on the 240ft Dumbarton Rock above the River Clyde, and dominates the town (the capital of the Celtic kingdom of Strathclyde). Most of what can be seen today dates from the 18th and 19th centuries, but there are a few earlier remains, and the rock gives spectacular views.
Open all year, Apr-Sep, Mon-Sat 9.30-6.30, Sun 2-6.30; Oct-Mar, Mon-Sat 9.30-4.30, Sun 2-4.30. (Closed Thu & Fri pm in winter also 25-26 Dec & 1-3 Jan).
🅿 *shop* ♿ 🔲
Details not confirmed for 1998

DUMFRIES
Burns House
Burns St DG1 2PS
☎01387 255297
Fax 01387 265081
It was in this ordinary sandstone house in a backstreet of Dumfries that Robert Burns spent the last three years of his short life; he died here in 1796. It is now a place of pilgrimage for Burns enthusiasts from around the globe. The house retains much of its 18th-century character and contains many fascinating items connected with the poet. There is the chair in which he wrote his last poems, many original letters and manuscripts, and the famous Kilmarnock and Edinburgh editions of his work.
Open all year, Apr-Sep, Mon-Sat 10-5, Sun 2-5; Oct-Mar Tue-Sat 10-1 & 2-5. Free.
P (100 yds) shop

Burns Mausoleum
St Michael's Churchyard
☎01387 255297 Fax 01387 265081
The mausoleum is in the form of a Greek temple, and contains the tombs of Robert Burns, his wife Jean Armour, and their five sons. A sculptured group shows the Muse of Poetry flinging her cloak over Burns at the plough.
Unrestricted access.
Free.
P (100 yds) ♿ (visitors with mobility difficulties tel 01387 255297)

Dumfries Museum & Camera Obscura
The Observatory DG2 7SW
☎01387 253374 Fax 01387 265081
Situated in and around the 18th-century windmill tower, Dumfries Museum is the largest museum in south west Scotland. Its collections were started over 150 years ago and have developed into a vast source of information on the area. Exhibitions trace the history of the people and landscape of Dumfries and Galloway. The Camera Obscura is to be found on the top floor of the windmill tower. It was installed in 1836 when the building was converted into an observatory. On the table-top screen you see a panoramic view of Dumfries and the surrounding countryside. Please telephone for details of special events and exhibitions.
Open all year, Apr-Se Mon-Sat 10-5, Sun, 2-5; Oct-Mar, Tue-Sat 10-1 & 2-5.
Free except Camera Obscura £1.20 (concessions 60p)
🅿 ♿ (camera obscura not accessible, parking available) toilets for disabled shop

Old Bridge House Museum
Mill Rd DG2 7BE
☎01387 256904 Fax 01387 265081
The Old Bridge House was built in 1660, into the fabric of the 15th-century Devorgilla's Bridge; it is the oldest house in Dumfries. A museum of everyday life in the town, it has an early 20th-century dentist's surgery, a Victorian nursery and kitchens of the 1850s and 1900s.
Open Apr-Sep, Mon-Sat 10-5, Sun 2-5. Free.
🅿 ♿ *shop*

Robert Burns Centre
Mill Rd DG2 7BE
☎01387 264808 Fax 01387 265081
This award-winning centre concentrates on the connections between Scotland's national poet, Robert Burns, and the town of Dumfries. The centre is situated

From the lowlands of Scotland to the heart of Africa: The life of David Livingstone, Scotland's most celebrated explorer, is documented in the tenement where he was born in Blantyre.

in the town's 18th-century watermill on the west bank of the River Nith and tells the story of Robert Burns' last years spent in the busy streets and lively atmosphere of Dumfries in the 1790s. In the evening the centre offers top quality feature films in the Film Theatre.
Open all year, Apr-Sep, daily 10-8 (Sun 2-5); Oct-Mar, Tue-Sat 10-1 & 2-5. Free except audio-visual theatre £1.20 (concessions 60p).
🅿 ♨ ♿ *(Induction loop hearing system in auditorium) toilets for disabled shop*

DUNDRENNAN

Dundrennan Abbey
(6.5m SE of Kirkcudbright)
☎01557 500262
The ruined abbey was founded for the Cistercians. The east end of the church and the chapter house are of exceptional architectural quality. Mary Queen of Scots is thought to have spent her last night in Scotland here on 15 May 1568, before seeking shelter in England, where she was imprisoned and eventually executed.
Open summer only, Apr-Sep, Mon-Sat 9.30-6.30, Sun 2-6.30. (Closed Thu pm & Fri).
🅿 ♿ ⚘ 🚩
Details not confirmed for 1998

DUNS

Jim Clark Room
44 Newtown St TD11 3AU
☎01361 883960 Fax 01361 884 104
The Jim Clark Room houses a fascinating collection of trophies, awards, photographs and memorabilia of twice World Motor Racing Champion, and local farmer, Jim Clark. The Room also has a video presentaion and a small shop.
Open Etr-Sep, Mon-Sat 10-1 & 2-4, Sun 2-4; Oct, Mon-Sat 1-4 & Sun 2-4.
✳*£1 (ch & pen 50p, ch under 5 free). 1 ch free with each paying adult.*
P (on street) ♿ (ramps, wheelchair space, large print notices etc) shop ⚘ (ex guide dogs)

Manderston
TD11 3PP (2m E of Duns on the A6105)
☎01361 883450 Fax 01361 882010
This grandest of grand houses gives a fascinating picture of Edwardian life both above and below stairs. It was built for the millionaire racehorse owner Sir James Miller. The architect was told to spare no expense, and so the house boasts features such as the world's only silver staircase, a ballroom painted in Sir James's racing colours, and painted ceilings. The state rooms are magnificent, and the domestic quarters are also quite lavish. Outside buildings include the handsome stable block and marble dairy, and there are fine formal gardens, with a woodland garden and lakeside walks.
Open 14 May-27 Sep, Thu & Sun 2-5.30 (also late Spring & Aug English BH Mons).
Telephone for details.
🅿 ♨ ♿ *shop*

EYEMOUTH

Eyemouth Museum
Auld Kirk, Manse Rd TD14 5JE
☎018907 50678
The museum was opened in 1981 as a memorial to the 129 local fishermen lost in the Great Fishing Disaster of 1881. Its main feature is the 15ft Eyemouth tapestry, which was made for the centenary. There are also displays on local history, and temporary exhibitions.
Open Apr-Jun & Sep, Mon-Sat 10-5, Sun 2-4; Jul-Aug, Mon-Sat 10-6; Sun 11-4; Oct, Mon-Sat 10-12.30 & 1.30-4.30, Closed Sundays.
£1.75 (concessions £1.25). 1 accompanied ch free with each adult. Party.
P (250 yds) (45min on street outside) ♿ shop
Cards: 💳 💳

GALASHIELS

Lochcarron Cashmere & Wool Centre
Waverley Mill, Huddersfield St TD1 3BA
☎01896 752091 & 751100
Fax 01896 758833
The museum brings the town's past to life with photographs and captions. The focal point is a display on the town's important woollen industry, and there are everyday items of the past on show. Guided tours of the mill take about 40 minutes.
Open all year, Mon-Sat 9-5, Sun (Jun-Sep) 12-5. Mill tours Mon-Thu at 10.30, 11.30, 1.30 & 2.30, Fri am only.
✳*Museum free. Mill tour £2 (ch 14 free).*
P ♿ toilets for disabled shop
Cards: 💳 💳 💳 💳 💳 💳

GALSTON

Loudoun Castle Theme Park
KA4 8PE (signposted from A74(M), from A77 and from A71)
☎01563 822296
Fax 01563 822408
Castle ruins, woodland and country walks at Scotland's largest theme park, with roller coasters, go karts, log flume and Britain's largest carousel. Many other attractions.
Open Etr-Oct from 10am.
✳*Height; over 1.25m £7.50, over 0.90m £7, under 0.90m free (pen £4).*
🅿 ♨ ✗ *licensed ♿ toilets for disabled shop ⚘ (ex guide dogs)*
Cards: 💳 💳 💳

GIGHA ISLAND

Achamore Gardens
PA41 7AD
☎01583 505267 or 505254
Fax 01583 505244
The wonderful woodland gardens of rhododendrons and azaleas were created by Sir James Horlick Bt, who bought the little island of Gigha in 1944. Many of the plants were brought in laundry baskets from his former home in Berkshire, and others were added over the following 29 years. Sub-tropical plants flourish in the rich soil and virtually frost-free climate, and there is a walled garden for some of

the finer specimens. There is an hotel on the island where tea, coffee, or meals may be purchased.
Open all year, daily.
£2 (ch £1).
🅿 ♿

GLASGOW

Glasgow was the second city of the British Empire, a 'dear, dirty city' which was a hub of the Industrial Revolution. Now it is clean, and has become a major attraction for visitors, who are discovering its artistic and architectural riches and its inimitable atmosphere. The biggest surprise for newcomers is the amount of open space in the city, which has over 70 richly varied public parks and several public golf courses. Glasgow Green has been open common land for centuries, but the heyday of the park was in the 19th century, when numerous stretches of land were bought and laid out for the public. In the heart of the city is the medieval cathedral, close to Provand's Lordship, Glasgow's oldest house, and to an array of splendid Victorian buildings. At the end of the Victorian era, Charles Rennie Mackintosh led the way in making Glasgow a centre for Art Nouveau; his style is epitomised by the Willow Tea Rooms, which are serving tea once more. Mackintosh's home has been reconstructed in the Hunterian Art Gallery, one of Glasgow's impressive galleries and museums. The most astonishing is the Burrell Collection, but there are many others in easy reach of the city centre.

Botanic Gardens
Queen Margaret Dr, off Great Western Rd G12 0UE
☎0141 334 2422
The gardens were established in 1817 from an older university physick garden, and moved to this site in 1842. There is an outstanding plant collection, but the most remarkable feature is the 23,000 sq ft Kibble Palace, a spectacular glasshouse with soaring tree ferns inside, set off by a number of Victorian sculptures. There are more conventional glasshouses too, showing orchids and other exotica. The grounds are laid out with lawns and beds, including a chronological border and a herb garden. At the northern edge the ground slopes down to the River Kibble, which is crossed by footbridges.
The Kibble Palace open 10-4.45 (4.15 in winter).The main glasshouse open Mon-Sat 1-4.45 (4.15 in winter), Sun 12-4.45 (4.15 in winter). Gardens open daily 7-dusk.
♿ *toilets for disabled ⚘ (ex in grounds)*
Details not confirmed for 1998

Burrell Collection
Pollok Country Park G43 1AT (2m S of city centre)
☎0141 649 7151 Fax 0141 636 0086
John Julius Norwich has said that 'in all history, no municipality has ever received from one of its native sons a gift of such munificence'. The Burrell Collection was amassed over some 80 years by Sir William Burrell, who presented it to Glasgow in 1944. It is now beautifully housed in a specially designed gallery, opened by Her Majesty The Queen on 21 October 1983.
Among the 8000 items in the collection are Ancient Egyptian alabaster; Chinese ceramics, bronzes and jade; Japanese prints; Near Eastern rugs and carpets; Turkish pottery; and European medieval art, including metalwork, sculpture, illuminated manuscripts, ivories, and two of the world's best collections of stained

glass and tapestries. There are also medieval doorways and windows, now set in the walls of mellow sandstone; British silver and needlework; and paintings and sculptures, ranging from the 15th to the early 20th centuries, with work by Cranach, Bellini, Rembrandt, Millet, Degas, Manet, Cezanne and others. Wise visitors come back more than once, partly because there is too much to see at one go, and partly to revisit their favourite treasures.
Open all year, Mon, Wed-Sat 10-5, Sun 11-5. (Closed Tue, 25-26 Dec & 1-2 Jan).
🅿 *(charged)* ✗ *licensed ♿ (wheelchairs available, tape guides for blind) toilets for disabled shop ⚘*
Details not confirmed for 1998

Cathedral
Castle St G4 0QZ
☎0141 552 6891
This is the most complete medieval cathedral surviving on the Scottish mainland. It was founded in the 6th century by St Kentigern, better known as Mungo ('dear one'), Glasgow's patron saint, and dates from the 13th and 14th centuries. The Cathedral was threatened at the time of the Reformation, but the city's trade guilds formed an armed guard to ensure that no damage was done. The choir pews are named after those guilds, and after more modern city organisations which helped with renovation work in the 1950s. The Cathedral is on two levels, and the lower church contains the tomb of St Kentigern, covered by an embroidered cloth. Nearby is the St Kentigern tapestry, presented in the 1970s.
Open all year, Apr-Sep, weekdays 9.30-6.30, Sun 2-6.30; Oct-Mar, weekdays 9.30-4.30, Sun 2-4.30. (Closed 25-26 Dec & 1-3 Jan).
shop ⚘ 🚩
Details not confirmed for 1998

Gallery of Modern Art
Queen St G1 3AZ
☎0141 229 1996 Fax 0141 204 5316
Opened in March 1996, the Gallery of Modern Art is set in a magnificent, refurbished neo-classical building in the heart of the city. It houses Glasgow's collection of post-war art and design over four floors of display space, themed to reflect the natural elements of Fire, Earth, Water and Air. The works on display are of truly international class, with exhibits by world-renowned innovators such as Niki De Saint Phalle, Sebastiao Salgado and Eduard Bersudsky. Scotland's own artists have distinguished themselves in recent years and examples of the work of Peter Howson, John Bellany, Alan Davie, Adrian Wiszniewski and Alison Watt take pride of place. Ring for details of exhibitions.
Open all year, Mon, Wed-Sat 10-5, Sun 11-5. Closed Tuesdays.
P (200yds) ✗ licensed ♿ toilets for disabled shop ⚘
Details not confirmed for 1998
Cards: 💳 💳 💳

Glasgow Art Gallery & Museum
Kelvingrove G3 8AG (1m W of city centre)
☎0141 287 2699 Fax 0141 287 2690
The gallery's extraordinary wealth of pictures includes works by Giorgione and Rembrandt, and is especially strong on the French Impressionists, Post-Impressionists, and Scottish artists from the 17th century to the present day. Other areas show sculpture, porcelain, silver, and a magnificent display of arms and armour. One section is devoted to the 'Glasgow Style', with furniture by Charles Rennie Mackintosh and others. Archaeology, ethnography and natural history are also featured, and special attention is paid to Scottish wildlife. Ring for details of special events.
Open all year, Mon-Sat 10-5, Sun 11-5. (Closed 25-26 Dec & 1-2 Jan).
🅿 ♨ ✗ *licensed ♿ toilets for disabled shop ⚘*
Details not confirmed for 1998

Glasgow Cathedral was founded by St Mungo, now the city's patron saint, in the 6th century. The building dates mainly from the 13th and 14th centuries.

Greenbank Garden

Flenders Rd, Clarkston G76 8RB (off A726 on southern outskirts of the city)
☎0141 639 3281
The spacious walled and woodland gardens are attractively laid out in the grounds of an elegant Georgian house (not open), and are best seen between April and October. The aim is to help local owners of small gardens, and a very wide range of flowers and shrubs is grown to show what is possible. There is also a garden and greenhouse designed for disabled enthusiasts, with special gardening tools. A programme of the many walks and other events is available on request. No dogs in garden, please.
Garden open all year, daily 9.30-sunset. (Closed 25-26 Dec & 1-2 Jan). House open Apr-Oct Sun only 2-4. Shop & Tearoom open Apr-Oct, daily 11-5; Nov-Mar, Sat & Sun 2-4.
£3 (concessions £2). Family ticket £8. Party.
P ♥ & *(wheelchairs available) toilets for disabled shop (& plant sales) ⊛ (ex guide dogs)* ❦

Hunterian Art Gallery

The University of Glasgow G12 8QQ
☎0141 330 5431 Fax 0141 330 3618
The core of the collection is a group of paintings bequeathed in the 18th century by Dr William Hunter, but it has grown a good deal since his time. There are important works by James McNeill Whistler, an ever-growing collection of 19th-and 20th-century Scottish paintings, contemporary British art and sculpture, and a remarkable re-creation of Charles Rennie Mackintosh's home, including the windows and front door. The print collection has some 20,000 items, from Old Masters to modern, and there is a changing programme of print exhibitions.
Open all year. Main gallery Mon-Sat 9.30-5. Mackintosh House Mon-Sat 9.30-12.30 & 1.30-5. Telephone for PH closures.
Free.
P (500 yds) (pay & display) & *(lift, wheelchair available) toilets for disabled shop ⊛ (ex guide dogs)*
Cards: ▣ ▤ ⑤

Hunterian Museum

The University of Glasgow G12 8QQ (2m W of city centre)
☎0141 330 4221 Fax 0141 330 3617
The museum is named after the 18th-century physician, Dr William Hunter, who bequeathed his large and important collections of coins, medals, fossils, geological specimens and archaeological and ethnographic items to the university. Since the museum opened in 1807 there have been many additions, and the emphasis is now on Geology, Archaeology, Coins and Anthropology. The exhibits are shown in the main building of the university, and temporary exhibitions are held. The main exhibitions are Earth....Life - a history of the evolution of our planet and life on it; and Roman Scotland, outpost of an Empire.
Open all year, Mon-Sat 9.30-5. (Closed certain PH's phone for details).
P (100yds) & *(access by lift, prior arrangement) toilets for disabled shop ⊛*
Details not confirmed for 1998

Hutchesons' Hall

158 Ingram St G1 1EJ
☎0141 552 8391 Fax 0141 552 7031
This handsome early 19th-century building was designed by David Hamilton and is now a listed building. There is a visitor centre and a shop. A video about Glasgow's Merchant City is shown daily from March to September. The Hall is available for hire. Please telephone for details of concerts, recitals etc.
Open all year Mon-Sat 10-5. (Closed PH's & 24 Dec-6 Jan). Hall on view subject to functions in progress.)
Free.
P *(on street) (meters)(outside for disabled) & toilets for disabled shop ⊛* ❦

McLellan Galleries

270 Sauchiehall St G2 3EH
☎0141 331 1854 Fax 0141 332 9957
The McLellan Galleries were officially re-opened on 2nd March 1990 by Her Majesty The Queen, on her visit to inaugurate Glasgow as European Cultural Capital 1990. With over 1,200 sq metres of top gallery space, the McLellan Galleries provide Glasgow Museums with the opportunity to bring to Glasgow major exhibitions and establish Glasgow as Britain's second art city, with a popular and international exhibition programme.
Open Mon-Sat 10-5, Sun 11-5 during exhibitions.
P *(500mtrs) & (assistance available) toilets for disabled shop ⊛*
Details not confirmed for 1998
Cards: ▣ ▤ ▬

Museum of Transport

Kelvin Hall, 1 Bunhouse Rd G3 8DP (1.5m W of city centre)
☎0141 287 2628 Fax 0141 305 2692
The first Museum of Transport was an old tram depot, but in 1988 the collections were handsomely rehoused in Kelvin Hall. The new museum is a feast of nostalgia for older Glaswegians and a fascinating look at the past for younger visitors, with Glasgow buses, a reconstruction of a Glasgow side street in the year 1938, and Glasgow trams (last used in 1962, when they made their way around the city in a grand, final procession). There are Scottish-made cars, fire engines, horse-drawn vehicles, cycles, a new display of around 25 historic motorcycles, and a walk-in car showroom with vehicles from the 1930s to the present day. Railways are represented by steam locomotives and a Glasgow subway station; and the already notable collection of ship models has been expanded.
Open all year, Mon, Wed-Sat 10-5, Sun 11-5. (Closed Tue, 25-26 Dec & 1-2 Jan).
P *(charged)* ✗ *licensed & (assistance available) toilets for disabled shop ⊛*
Details not confirmed for 1998

People's Palace

Glasgow Green G40 1AT (1m SE of city centre)
☎0141 554 0223
Fax 0141 550 0892
This museum looks at the work and leisure of the ordinary people of Glasgow, with exhibits ranging from a 2nd-century Roman bowl to mementoes of the Jacobite risings, football games and boxing matches. Glasgow's trades and industries are illustrated with fine products of the city's potteries, textile mills and foundries; and there is an interesting section on Glasgow's tobacco trade and immensely rich 'Tobacco Lords'. There are also numerous banners, posters and other material from Glasgow's days of campaigning for wider voting rights, votes for women and recognition of trade unions. New displays look at the history of work in Glasgow, the city's housing and the political and civic visions which have shaped the city. Beyond the main museum building is the glass-and-iron expanse of the Winter Gardens, a huge conservatory with tropical plants.
Re-opening after refurbishment April 1998, Mon, Wed-Sat 10-5, Sun 11-5. Closed Tue.
P ♥ & *toilets for disabled shop garden centre ⊛*
Details not confirmed for 1998

Pollok House

G43 1AT (2m S of city centre)
☎0141 632 0274 Fax 0141 649 0823
Given to the city at the same time as the land for Pollok Country Park, the house contains the remarkable Stirling Maxwell collection of Spanish paintings, including works by El Greco, Murillo and Goya. Silver, ceramics and furniture collected by the family over the generations are also on display.
Open from Etr-1 Oct, Mon-Sat 10-5, Sun 11-5.
P ♥ & *shop ⊛*
Details not confirmed for 1998

Provand's Lordship

3 Castle St G4 0RB (1m E of city centre)
☎0141 552 8819
The Prebend of Provan (see Provan Hall) used this house as his city residence. It was built in 1471 as a manse for the Cathedral and St Nicholas Hospital, and is the city's oldest house. Mary, Queen of Scots is reputed to have stayed here; in Victorian times it was used as an alehouse; in the early 1900s it was a sweet shop; and the city hangman used to live in a lean-to next door (now demolished). The house has been carefully restored and displays furniture, pictures and stained-glass panels from various periods in the city's history. There is a fine collection of 17th-century Scottish furniture, and the machines which made the sweets in the house's sweetshop days can be seen.
Open all year, Mon, Wed-Sat 10-5, Sun 11-5. (Closed Tue, 25-26 Dec & 1-2 Jan).

P *shop ⊛*
Details not confirmed for 1998

Rouken Glen Park

Giffnock G46 7UG
☎0141 621 3137
Fax 0141 621 3125
Fine walks can be taken along riverside pathways through the deep, wooded glen, and the waterfall at the head of the glen is a noted beauty spot. The park also offers the pleasures of a large walled garden and spreading lawns, a picturesque loch for boating, a large enclosed children's play area (dog free), 'Butterfly Kingdom' and an art gallery.
Open all year, daily.
Free.
P ♥ ✗ *licensed & (Radar key) toilets for disabled garden centre*

St Mungo Religious Life & Art Museum

2 Castle St G4 0RH (1m NE of city centre)
☎0141 553 2557 Fax 0141 552 4744
This unique museum, opened in 1993, explores the universal themes of life and death and the hereafter through beautiful and evocative art objects associated with different religious faiths. Three galleries focus on art, world religions and religion in Scotland. Britain's only authentic Zen garden contributes its own unique sense of peace. Special exhibition: The Veil in Islam-Compares Western perceptions of the Islamic veil with the reality. (August-November)
Open all year, Mon, Wed-Sat, Sun 11-5. Closed Tue, 25- 26 Dec & 1-2 Jan.
P *(charged)* ✗ *licensed & (taped information & lift) toilets for disabled shop ⊛*
Details not confirmed for 1998

Tenement House

145 Buccleuch St, Garnethill G3 6QN (N of Charing Cross)
☎0141 333 0183
This National Trust for Scotland property shows an unsung but once-typical side of Glasgow life: it is a first-floor flat, built in 1892, with a parlour, bedroom, kitchen and bathroom, furnished with the original recess beds, kitchen range, sink, and coal bunker, a rosewood piano and other articles. It was the home of Miss Agnes Toward from 1911 to 1965, and was bought by an actress who carefully preserved its 'time capsule' quality until the Trust acquired and restored it. Today the contents of the flat are interesting for the vivid picture they give of one section of Glasgow society. Two flats on the ground floor provide reception, interpretative and educational facilities.
Open Mar-Oct, daily 2-5. (Last admission 30 mins before closing); weekday morning visits by educational & other groups (not to exceed 15), by advance booking only.
£3 (ch & concession £2). Family ticket £8. Party (not exceeding 15).
P (100yds) *(v.restricted, recommend parking in town (braille guide) ⊛ (ex guide dogs)* ❦

University of Glasgow Visitor Centre

University Av G12 8QQ
☎0141 330 5511
Fax 0141 330 5225
The University of Glasgow's Visitor Centre is a spacious, pleasant attraction with leaflets, publications and video displays explaining how the university works, what courses are available and which university events are open to the public. It forms the starting point for guided tours of the university's historic attractions, including the Hunterian Museum, Memorial Chapel, Bute and Randolph Halls, Professors' Square and Lion and Unicorn Staircase.
Open all year, Mon-Sat 9.30-5. Also May-Sep, Sun 2-5.
Free.
P ♥ & *toilets for disabled shop ⊛*
Cards: ▣ ▤ ⑤

GLENLUCE
Glenluce Abbey
(2m N of village)
☎01581 300541
The abbey was founded for the
Cistercians in 1192 by Roland, Earl of
Galloway. The ruins include a vaulted
chapter house, and stand in a beautiful
setting.
*Open all year, Apr-Sep, Mon-Sat 9.30-
6.30, Sun 2-6.30; Oct-Mar, Sat 9.30-4.30,
Sun 2-4.30. (Closed 25-26 Dec & 1-3
Jan).*
P & shop
Details not confirmed for 1998

GORDON
Mellerstain House
TD3 6LG (5m E of Earlston, on unclass
road)
☎01573 410225
Fax 01573 410636
One of Scotland's finest Georgian
houses, Mellerstain was begun by
William Adam and completed by his son
Robert in the 1770s. It has beautiful
plasterwork, period furniture and
pictures; terraced gardens and a lake.
Special events for 1998 include a vintage
car rally (7 June).
*Open Easter, then May-Sept daily ex Sat.
12.30-5 (Last admission 4.30pm).*
£4.50 (ch £2, pen £3.50). Party 20+.
P & shop (ex guide dogs)

GREAT CUMBRAE ISLAND
Museum of the Cumbraes
Garrison House KA28 0DG (Ferry to
Millport, from Largs Cal-Mac Terminal.
Bus meets each ferry.)
☎01475 530741 (Mon-Fri)
The Garrison House was built in 1745 by
Captain Crawford as a barracks for his
crew of 'The Royal George', a customs
ship. It now houses a small museum
which displays the history and life of the
Cumbraes. Along with artefacts from the
collection, the museum displays a major
exhibition each summer. There is also a
fine collection of local photographs.
Open Jun-Sep, Mon-Sat 11-1 & 1.30-5.
P (front of building) & (ex guide dogs)
Details not confirmed for 1998

GREENOCK
McLean Museum & Art Gallery
15 Kelly St PA16 8JX (close to Greenock
West Railway Station)
☎01475 723741 Fax 01475 731347
James Watt was born in Greenock, and
various exhibits connected with him are
shown. The museum also has an art
collection, and there are displays on
shipping (including river paddle steamers
and cargo vessels), natural history,
Egyptology and ethnography. Temporary
exhibition gallery. Dinosaur exhibition
summer 1998 - 'Dinosaurs Then & Now'.
*Open all year, Mon-Sat 10-5. Closed local
& national PH.*
Free.
P (200mtrs) & toilets for disabled
shop (ex guide dogs)

HAMILTON
Chatelherault
Ferniegair ML3 7UE (2.5km SE of
Hamilton on A72 Hamilton-
Larkhall/Lanark Clyde Valley tourist
route.)
☎01698 426213 Fax 01698 421532
Chatelherault was built by William Adam
for the Duke of Hamilton in the 1730's,
as a hunting lodge, staff accommodation
and kennels. It is set in 500 acres of park
containg areas of outstanding natural
beauty and nature conservation, as well
as physical evidence of land use
including mining, quarrying, Cadzow
Castle, a possible hillfort, and ancient
oak fort and deer park, and a herd
of white Cadzow cattle. There is a
restored lodge, a Visitors Centre,
and function/business facilities
are available.
*Open all year, Mon-Sat 10-5, Sun 12-5.
House closed all day Friday.
Free.*
P & (architect designed for disabled
access) toilets for disabled shop garden
centre (ex grounds, ex guide dogs)

Low Parks Museum
129 Muir St ML3 6BJ
☎01698 283981 Fax 01698 283479
A new complex telling the story of
Hamilton and the Clyde Valley has been
created by linking the former District
Museum and The Cameronians (Scottish
Rifles) Museum. Housed in the oldest
surviving building in the town, dating
from 1696, the museum features a
restored 18th century assembly room
and exhibitions on Hamilton Palace and
The Cameronians. The world-wide
service of the Regiment, from its
foundation in the Covenanting period
through to its disbandment in 1968, is
represented in the display.
Open 10-5 Mon-Sat (ex.Fri), 12-5 Sun.
P & (disabled toilet being built) shop
Details not confirmed for 1998

HAWICK
Drumlanrig's Tower
Tower Knowe TD9 7JL
☎01450 373457 Fax 01450 378526
Drumlanrig's Tower has a fascinating
history, beginning in its earliest years
when the Tower served as a fortified
keep in the 12th century - occupied by
the Black Douglas of Drumlanrig; through
to a more genteel age in the 18th century
when Anne, Duchess of Monmouth and ➤

Charles Rennie Mackintosh was a leading exponent of Art Nouveau in Scotland. The interior of his house has been
reconstructed in the Hunterian Art Gallery.

Buccleuch transformed it into a glittering residence. Later the Tower served as a gracious hotel. Now transformed into a major visitor attraction with historic room setting, costumed figures, dioramas, sownds, smells and audio visual programmes. Many special events throughout the year.
Open peak season 10-7; other times 10-5.
P *(300 yds)* & *toilets for disabled shop* ⚕
Details not confirmed for 1998

HERMITAGE
Hermitage Castle
TD9 0LU (5.5m NE of Newcastleton off A7)
☎01387 376222
A vast, eerie ruin of the 14th and 15th centuries, associated with the de Soulis, the Douglases and Mary Queen of Scots. Much restored in the 19th century.
Apr-Sep, Mon-Sat 9.30-6.30, Sun 2-6.30.
P & 🗡
Details not confirmed for 1998

HUNTERSTON
Hunterston Power Station
KA23 9QJ (off A78, S of Largs)
☎0800 838557
This is a nuclear power station of the advanced gas-cooled reactor (AGR) type. A purpose-built visitor centre contains exhibits, interactive models, videos, and a lecture theatre. Parties of up to 50 are taken on guided tours of the power station and shown a video presentation on the generation of nuclear power.
Open - Visitors' Centre, daily 9.30-4.30 (Closed Xmas & New Year). Tour times 9.45, 11.15, 1.30 & 3.
P & *(trained guides for visually impaired visitors) toilets for disabled shop* ⚕
Details not confirmed for 1998

INNERLEITHEN
Robert Smail's Printing Works
7/9 High St EH44 6HA
☎01896 830206
These buildings contain a Victorian office, a paper store with reconstructed waterwheel, a composing room and a press room. The machinery is in full working order and visitors may view the printer at work and have 'hands-on' experience in typesetting in the composing room.
Open May-Sep Mon-Sat 10-1 & 2-5, Sun 2-5; wknds in Oct: Sat 10-1 & 2-5, Sun only 2-5. (Last tour 45mins before closing morning & afternoon).
£2.40 (ch & concessions £1.60). Family ticket £6.40. Party.
P *(300yds)* & *shop* ⚕ *(ex guide dogs)* 🐾

INVERARAY
Bell Tower of All Saints' Church
The Avenue PA32 8XT
☎01499 302259
The tower was built in the 1920s and stands at 126ft. It has the world's second heaviest ring of ten bells, installed as a Campbell War Memorial in 1931. An exhibition is mounted on campanology inside and there are visiting bell ringers who give recitals, usually once a month. A splendid view rewards those who climb to the roof.
Open mid May-Sep, daily 10-1 & 2-5.
£1.50 (ch & pen 75p).
P *(adjacent to tower)* & *shop* ⚕ *(ex guide dogs)*

Inveraray Castle
PA32 8XE
☎01499 302203 Fax 01499 302421
The third Duke of Argyll (the chief of Clan Campbell) engaged Roger Morris to build the present castle in 1743; in the process the old Burgh of Inveraray was demolished and a new town built nearby. The beautiful interior decoration was commissioned by the 5th Duke from Robert Mylne; the great armoury hall and staterooms are of particular note and the furniture, tapestries and paintings throughout are well worth viewing.
Open Apr to mid Oct. Apr-Jun, Oct & Sep, Mon-Thu & Sat 10-1 & 2-5.45. Sun 1-5.45; Jul & Aug, Mon-Sat 10-5.45, Sun

1-5.45. Last admission 12.30 & 5. £4.50 (ch under 16 £2.50, concessions £3.50) Family ticket £12. School parties. Groups 20+.
P 🍴 & *shop* ⚕ *(ex guide dogs)*

Inveraray Jail
Church Sq PA32 8TX
☎01499 302381 Fax 01499 302195
Enter Inveraray Jail and step back in time. See furnished cells and experience prison sounds and smells. Ask the 'prisoner' how to pick oakum. Turn the heavy handle of an original crank machine, take 40 winks in a hammock or listen to Matron's tales of day-to-day prison life as she keeps one eye on the nursing mother, barefoot thieves and the lunatic in her care. Visit the magnificent 1820 courtroom and hear trials in progress. Imaginative exhibitions including 'Torture, Death and Damnation'.
Open all year, Nov-Mar, daily 10-5 (last admisssion 4); Apr-Oct, daily 9.30-6 (last admission 5pm). (Closed 25 Dec & 1 Jan). Extended hours in summer.
P *(100 yds)* & *(wheelchair ramp at rear) toilets for disabled shop*
Details not confirmed for 1998
Cards: 🂠 💳 🂡

IRVINE
Glasgow Vennel Museum & Burns Heckling Shop
10 Glasgow Vennel KA12 0BD
☎01294 275059
The Glasgow Vennel Museum and Gallery has a reputation for exciting and varied exhibitions, ranging from international artists to local school groups. Behind the museum is the Heckling Shop where Robert Burns, Scotland's most famous poet, spent part of his youth learning the trade of flax dressing. In addition to the audio-visual programme on Burns, there is a reconstruction of his lodgings at No 4 Glasgow Vennel, Irvine.
Open all year - Jun-Sep, Mon-Sat 10-5, Sun 2-5 (Closed Wed); Oct-May, Tue, Thu-Sat 10-5. Closed for lunch 1-2.
P *(residential area)* & ⚕
Details not confirmed for 1998

Scottish Maritime Museum
Harbour St KA12 8QE (Follow AA signs from Irvine)
☎01294 278283 Fax 01294 313211
The museum has displays which reflect all aspects of Scottish maritime history. Vessels can be seen afloat in the harbour and undercover. Experience life in a 1910 shipyard worker's tenement flat. Board the clipper 'The Carrick' can be boarded to view restoration work underway. There is an annual exhibition.
Open Apr-Oct, daily 10-5.
£2 (ch & pen £1). Family ticket £4.
P 🍴 & *toilets for disabled shop* ⚕ *(ex guide dogs)*

JEDBURGH
Jedburgh Abbey
4-5 Abbey Bridgend
☎01835 863925
Standing as the most complete of the Border monasteries, although it has been sacked and rebuilt many times, Jedburgh Abbey has been described as 'the most perfect and beautiful example of the Saxon and early Gothic in Scotland'. It was founded as a priory in the 12th century by David I and remains of some of the domestic buildings have been uncovered during excavations.
Open all year, Apr-Sep, Mon-Sat 9.30-6.30, Sun 2-6.30; Oct-Mar, Mon-Sat 9.30-4.30, Sun 2-4.30. (Closed 25-26 Dec & 1-3 Jan).
P & *(limited access) toilets for disabled shop* ⚕ *(ex guide dogs)*
Details not confirmed for 1998

Mary Queen of Scots House
Queen St TD8 6EW
☎01835 863331 Fax 01450 378526
Mary, Queen of Scots visited Jedburgh in 1566, and had to prolong her stay because of ill-health. This splendid house is now a museum devoted to her

memory and tragic history. An unusual feature of this 16th-century fortified dwelling is the left-handed spiral staircase: the Kers, the owners of the house, were left-handed and the special staircase allowed the men to use their sword hands. The museum presents a thought-provoking interpretation of her tragic life with period rooms, stunning murals and personal items connected to Mary, Queen of Scots.
Open Mar-Nov, daily 10-5 (4.30 Sun).
P *(300 yds)* & *shop* ⚕
Details not confirmed for 1998

KELSO
Floors Castle
TD5 7SF (1m N)
☎01573 223333 Fax 01573 226056
Sir Walter Scott described this fairy-tale castle as 'altogether a kingdom for Oberon and Titania to dwell in'. Today it is the home of the 10th Duke of Roxburghe and its lived-in atmosphere enhances the superb collection of French furniture, tapestries and paintings contained inside. The house was designed by William Adam in 1721 and extended by W H Playfair over a century later; it enjoys a magnificent setting overlooking the River Tweed and the Cheviot Hills beyond. A holly tree in the grounds is said to mark the spot where James II was killed; and an attractive walled garden, garden centre and play area are among the attractions outside. Events include Teddy Bears' Picnic (7 Jun), Massed Pipebands Display (30 Aug).
Open 10 Apr-25 Oct, daily 10-4.30. (last admission 4)
£4.50 (ch 2-15 £2.50, pen £3.75). Family ticket £12. Grounds only £2. Group rates for 20+.
P 🍴 ✕ *licensed* & *(lift) toilets for disabled shop garden centre*
Cards: 🂠 💳 💳 🂡 🂡 🂡

Kelso Abbey
☎0131 668 8800 Fax 0131 668 8888
Founded by David I in 1128 and probably the greatest of the four famous Border abbeys, Kelso became extremely wealthy and acquired extensive lands. In 1545 it served as a fortress when the town was attacked by the Earl of Hertford, but now only fragments of the once-imposing abbey church give any clue to its long history.
Open at any reasonable time.
&
Details not confirmed for 1998

KILBARCHAN
Weaver's Cottage
The Cross PA10 2JG (off A737, 12m SW of Glasgow)
☎01505 705588
Together with a fascinating display of weaving equipment, demonstrations of the craft are given in this delightful museum, Fridays and most weekends. Also displayed in the 18th-century weaver's cottage is a collection of early domestic utensils. Video programme available. There is an attractive traditional cottage garden.
Open Good Fri-Sep, daily, 1.30-5.30; wknds in Oct, 1.30-5.30 (last admission 5).
£2 (ch & concessions £1.30). Family ticket £5.30 Party.
P ⚕ *(ex guide dogs)* 🐾

KILMARNOCK
Dean Castle Country Park
Dean Rd KA3 1XB
☎01563 522702 Fax 01563 572552
This fine castle has a 14th-century fortified keep and 15th-century palace, and is the ancestral home of the Boyd family. The restoration work which has taken place shows the building in almost its original splendour, and inside there is an outstanding collection of medieval arms and armour, musical instruments and tapestries and a display of Burns' manuscripts. The castle is set in a beautiful wooded country park with rivers, gardens, woodlands, adventure

playground, children's corner and aviaries. A full programme of events takes place from Apr-Sep.
Open: Country Park all year, dawn to dusk. Dean Castle daily noon-5. Visitor centre & Tearoom 11-5(summer), 11-4(winter). Rare Breeds centre 1-5(summer), 1-4(winter).
❋*Country park, visitor centre or rare breeds centre free. No charge to castle for E Ayrshire residents. Non-residents charges: £2.50 (ch £1.25 -under 5 free, pen £1.25, disabled free).*
P 🍴 & *(disabled garden, car parks, ramps & level paths) toilets for disabled shop* ⚕ *(ex only guide dogs inside)*
Cards: 🂠 💳 🂡

Dick Institute
Elmbank Ave KA1 3BU
☎01563 26401 Fax 01563 29661
Museum exhibiting geology, natural history, engineering, archaeology and local history. Newly modernised art gallery with an important permanent collection of paintings and touring exhibitions of prints, photography and crafts. Works by contemporary artists often for sale.
Open all year, Gallery: Mon, Tue, Thu & Fri 10-8, Wed & Sat 10-5. Museum: May-Sep, Mon, Tue, Thu & Fri 10-8, Wed & Sat 10-5; Oct-Apr Mon-Sat 10-5.
P & *toilets for disabled shop* ⚕
Details not confirmed for 1998

KILMARTIN
Dunadd Fort
(1m W of Kilmichael Glassary)
☎0131 668 8800
Fax 0131 668 8888
Dunadd was one of the ancient capitals of Dalriada from which the Celtic kingdom of Scotland was formed. Near to this prehistoric hill fort (now little more than an isolated hillock) are carvings of a boar and a footprint; these probably marked the spot where early kings were invested with their royal power.
Open & accessible at all reasonable times.
⚕ 🗡
Details not confirmed for 1998

KILMUN
Argyll Forest Park
Forest Enterprise PA23 8SE (on A880 1m from junc with A815)
☎01369 840666 Fax 01369 840617
The Argyll Forest Park extends over a large area of hill ground and forest, noted for its rugged beauty. Numerous forest walks and picnic sites allow the forest to be explored in detail. The Arboretum walks and the route from the Younger Botanic Gardens to Puck's Glen are of special scenic quality; a series of guided walks and other ranger-led activites within the forest park are planned; also deer watches, and 4X4 safaris; please contact the above address for details.
Open all year.
Free.
P

KILSYTH
Colzium House & Estate
Colzium-Lennox Estate G65 0RZ (on A803)
☎01236 823281 Fax 01236 823281
The old castle was associated with Montrose's victory over the Covenanters in 1645; the museum, courtyard, ice-house and walled garden make interesting viewing and the grounds include a children's zoo and forest walks.
Open - House Etr wknd-Sep wknd, Mon-Fri, 9-5 & Sun, 10-6. (Closed when booked for private functions). Grounds open at all times. Museum open by appointment.
P 🍴 &
Details not confirmed for 1998

KIRKBEAN
Arbigland Gardens
DG2 8BQ (1m SE, adjacent to Paul Jones cottage).
☎01387 880283 Fax 01387 880 344
Extensive woodland, formal and water

Arbigland Gardens

Kirkbean, Dumfries and Galloway
Tel: (0138788) 0283   Fax: (0138788) 0344

John Paul Jones, the US Admiral, worked here with his father who was the gardener in the 1740s.

Woodland, water and formal gardens, leading to a sandy, sheltered bay. Ideal for children.

For opening times and admission charges see gazetteer entry.

---

gardens are set around a delightful sandy bay which is ideal for children. John Paul Jones, the US Admiral, worked in the gardens as a young boy (his father was the gardener here in the 1740s). His birthplace, which can be seen nearby, is now a museum.
Open Gardens May-Sep, Tue-Sun 2-6. Also open BH Mon. House 22 May-31 May.
£2 (ch 50p, pen £1.50).
P & toilets for disabled shop

KIRKCUDBRIGHT
Broughton House & Garden
12 High St DG6 4JX (off A711/A755)
☎01557 330437
An 18th-century house where Edward A Hornel, on of the 'Glasgow Boys' group of artists, lived and worked from 1901-1933. A collection of his work, extensive library of local history, including limited editions of Burns' works, and Japanese-style garden created by Hornel.
Open daily, Apr-Oct 1-5.30. (last admission 4.45pm)
£2.40 (concessions £1.60). Family ticket £6.40. Party.
P (on street) (limited space) 🚫 (ex guide dogs) 🚻

MacLellan's Castle
☎01557 331856
This handsome structure has been a ruin since the mid-18th-century: it was once an imposing castellated mansion, elaborately planned with fine architectural detail. Something of its 16th-century grandeur still remains.
Open summer only, Apr-Sep, Mon-Sat 9.30-6.30, Sun 2-6.30; (Closed 25-26 Dec & 1-3 Jan).
P & 🚫 ▮
Details not confirmed for 1998

Stewartry Museum
Saint Mary St DG6 4AQ (200mtr S of St Cuthbert's Church)
☎01557 331643 Fax 01557 330005
A large and varied collection of archaeological, social history and natural history exhibits relating to the Stewartry district.
Open Mar-Oct, Mon-Sat 11-4 (5pm in May, Jun & Sep; 6pm in Jun-Sep also Sun 2-5); Nov-Feb, Mon-Sat 11-4.
£1.50 (ch free with adult, concessions 75p).
P (outside) & shop 🚫

Tolbooth Art Centre
High St DG6 4JL
☎01557 331556 Fax 01557 330005
The Tolbooth is one of Kirkcudbright's most historic buildings dating from 1629. It was converted into an art centre in 1993, with two main functions. Firstly it provides an interpretive introduction to the Kirkcudbright artists's colony, which flourished in the town from the 1880's, through an audio-visual show and a permanent display of the artists' works. It also provides studio and exhibition space for contemporary local and visiting artists.

There is a programe of exhibitions from March to October and many artists will be working in the studios while exhibiting. Phone for details.
Open Mar & Oct, Mon-Sat 11-4; May-Jun & Sept, Mon-Sat 10-6; Nov-Feb, Mon-Sat 11-4. Open Sun Jun-Sep 2-5.
£1.50 (ch free, concessions 75p)
P (on street parking) 🏆 & (lift) toilets for disabled shop 🚫

KIRKOSWALD
Souter Johnnie's Cottage
Main Rd KA19 8HY (on A77, 4m SW of Maybole)
☎01655 760603
'Souter' means cobbler and the village cobbler who lived in this 18th-century cottage was the inspiration for Burns' character Souter Johnnie, in his ballad *Tam o'Shanter*. The cottage is now a Burns museum and life-size stone figures of the poet's characters can be seen in the restored ale-house in the cottage garden.
Open Good Fri-30 Sept daily 11.30-5; wknds in Oct, 11.30-5. Last admission 4.30
£2 (ch & concessions £1.30). Family ticket £5.30. Party.
P (75yds) & (only one small step into cottage) 🚫 (ex guide dogs) 🚻

LANGBANK
Finlaystone Country Estate
PA14 6TJ (10m W of Glasgow Airport on A8)
☎01475 540285 & 540505
A charming exhibition of Victoriana are displayed in a homely family house with historical connections to John Knox and Robert Burns. The house, though, is only a foil to the considerable natural beauty;

most visitors to Finlaystone are drawn by the formal gardens, walled gardens, woodland walks and adventure playgrounds. Disabled visitors will enjoy the small scented garden. There are purpose-built toilets for wheelchair users in the visitor centre. The 'Dolly Mixture', an exciting international collection of dolls can be found in the Visitor Centre. Celtic Craft Fair - late Aug/early Sept - date to be decided, please telephone for details.
Open all year. Woodland & Gardens daily, 10-5. House, open Sundays Apr-Aug or by appointment.
Garden & Woods £2.40 (ch & pen £1.40); Guided tour of house (Sun only), £1.50 (ch, pen: £1). 'The Dolly Mixture' Doll Museum 50p.
P 🏆 & (lift to second floor pathways for wheelchairs) toilets for disabled shop 🚫 (ex on lead)

LARGS
Kelburn Country Centre
Fairlie KA29 0BE (2m S off A78)
☎01475 568685
Fax 01475 568121
Historic home of the Earls of Glasgow, Kelburn enjoys spectacular views over the Firth of Clyde. Kelburn Castle overlooks beautiful Kelburn Glen with its romantic walks, waterfalls, gorges and gardens. Turn-of-the-century farm buildings have been converted and house a museum, Kelburn Story Cartoon Exhibition, activity workshop, soft play room, tea room, gift shop and information office. Experience Kelburn's newest attraction, The Secret Forest, by exploring its winding paths and discover fantasy follies, including The Maze of the Green Man and The Gingerbread House. There are also adventure playgrounds, a pets' corner, a nature centre, picnic areas and horse riding. For those looking for some real action, there is a Marine Commando assault course.
Open all year, Apr-Oct, daily 10-6; Nov-Mar, 11-5.
P 🏆 ✗ licensed & (Ranger service to assist disabled) toilets for disabled shop
Details not confirmed for 1998
Cards: 🗠 ▭ 🗠

Vikingar
Greenock Rd KA30 8QL
☎01475 689777 Fax 01475 689444
Vikingar! is the amazing multi-media experience that takes you from the first Viking raids in Scotland to their defeat at the Battle of Largs. Located in the beautiful coastal resort of Largs, Vikingar! provides Scotland's most exciting and award-winning all-weather attraction. Additional facilities at Vikingar! include a swimming pool, a 500-seat theatre and cinema, cafe and theatre bar, children's Viking themed soft play area and fitness/health care facilities. Phone for information about forthcoming events.

The Largs Viking festival will be held in the first week of September.
Open all year (closed 25-26 Dec and 1-2 Jan).
✳£3.50 (ch & pen £2.50).
P 🏆 ✗ licensed & toilets for disabled shop 🚫 (ex guide dogs)
Cards: 🗠 ▭ 🗠 🗠

LAUDER
Thirlestane Castle
TD2 6RU (off A68, follow signs on main road approaches)
☎01578 722430 Fax 01578 722761
This fairy-tale castle has been the home of the Maitland family, the Earls of Lauderdale, since the 12th century, and part of the family still live in one of the wings. Some of the most splendid plasterwork ceilings in Britain may be seen in the 17th-century state rooms. The former family nurseries now house a sizeable collection of antique toys and dolls, while in the south wing there are several interesting displays illustrating Border country life. The informal grounds, with their riverside setting and views of nearby grouse moors, include a woodland walk and picnic tables. Please ring for details of special events.
Open 10-17 Apr, May-Jun & Sep, Mon & Wed-Thu & Sun; Jul-Aug, daily (ex Sat) 2-5. July-Aug 12-5pm. (last admission 4.30pm). Grounds open on dates listed above noon-6.
£4. Family ticket £10. Grounds only £1.50. Party £3
P 🏆 shop 🚫 (ex guide dogs)

LOCHAWE
Cruachan Power Station
Dalmally PA33 1AN (A85 18miles East of Oban)
☎01866 822618 Fax 01866 822509
A vast cavern hidden 1km inside Ben Cruachan, which contains a 400,000-kilowatt hydro-electric power station which is driven by water drawn from a high-level reservoir up the mountain. Touch screen information and computer graphics reveal all in the free exhibition. A guided tour takes you inside the mountain and reveals the generators in their underground cavern. There is a cafe and picnic site on the banks of the Loch.
Open Etr-end of Nov, daily 9.30-5 (last tour 4.15). Jul-Aug 9.30-6 (last tour 5.15)
£3 (ch 6-16 £1.50, concessions £2.50)
P 🏆 & toilets for disabled shop 🚫 (ex guide dogs)

LOCHWINNOCH
Lochwinnoch Community Museum
High St PA12 4AB
☎01505 842615 Fax 0141 889 9240
Local agriculture, industry and village life are reflected in the series of changing exhibitions displayed in this enterprising museum. There is an annual art exhibition and occasional special ➤

The perfect symmetry of Inveraray Castle was created in 1743 for the Duke of Argyll.

exhibitions based on the district's varied collections.
Open all year, Mon, Wed & Fri 10-1, 2-5 & 6-8; Tue & Sat 10-1 & 2-5. (Closed public holidays).
🅿 � (ex guide dogs)
Details not confirmed for 1998

RSPB Nature Reserve
Largs Rd PA12 4JF (on A760, Largs road, opposite Lochwinnoch station)
☎ 01505 842663 Fax 01505 843026
An attractive Norwegian timber building in the Lochwinnoch Nature Reserve, incorporating an observation tower offering fine views of the reserve and the surrounding countryside, an RSPB shop, and an exhibition and lecture room with a video system and displays. A nature trail leads from the centre, through deciduous woodland to two observation hides. An attractive second trail, featuring a boardwalk across the marsh, leads from the centre to a third birdwatching hide; all hides have been designed specifically for the convenience of disabled visitors. Guided walks throughout the year. Please telephone for details.
Open all year, daily 10-5. (Closed Xmas & New Year).
❋£2 (ch 50p, concessions £1). Family ticket £4.
🅿 ⅖ (wheelchairs available,access 3 hides) toilets for disabled shop ✗
Cards: ▨ ▨ ▨ ▨

MAYBOLE
Crossraguel Abbey
(2m S)
☎ 01655 883113
The extensive remains of this 13th-century Cluniac monastery are impressive and architecturally important. The monastery was founded by Duncan, Earl of Carrick and the church, claustral buildings, abbot's house and an imposing castellated gatehouse can be seen.
Open Apr-Sep, Mon-Sat 9.30-6.30, Sun 2-6.30. Closed Thurs pm & Fri.
🅿 ⅖ shop ✗ 🏵
Details not confirmed for 1998

MELROSE
Abbotsford House
TD6 9BQ (2m W off A6091)
☎ 01896 752043 Fax 01896 752916
Set on the River Tweed, Sir Walter Scott's romantic mansion remains much the same as it was in his day. Inside there are many mementoes and relics of his remarkable life and also his historical collections, armouries and library, with some 9000 volumes. The mansion was built by Scott between 1811 and 1822, and he lived here until his death ten years after its completion.

Open daily from 3rd Mon in Mar-Oct, Mon-Sat 10-5. Sun in Mar-May & Oct 2-5. Sun Jun-Sep 10-5.
£3.50 (ch £1.80). Party- £2.50, (ch £1.30)
🅿 🖳 ⅖ toilets for disabled shop ✗ (ex guidance dogs)

Harmony Garden
St Mary's Rd TD6 9LJ
☎ 01721 722502 Fax 01721 724700
Set around the early 19th century Harmony Hall (not open to visitor)s, this attractive walled garden has magnificent views of Melrose Abbey and the Eildon Hills. Opening to visitors for the first time in 1998, the garden comprises lawns, herbaceous and mixed borders, vegetable and fruit areas, and a rich display of spring bulbs.
Open Apr-Sep, Mon-Sat 10-5.30, Sun 1.30-5.30.
£1 (honesty box),
🅿 ⅖ ✗ 🏵

Melrose Abbey & Abbey Museum
☎ 01896 822562
The ruin of this Cistercian abbey is probably one of Scotland's finest, and has been given added glamour by its connection with Sir Walter Scott. The abbey was repeatedly wrecked during the Scottish wars of independence, but parts of the nave and choir survive from the 14th century, and include some of the best and most elaborate traceried stonework in Scotland. Most of the ruins belong to a 15th-century reconstruction. The abbey has many interesting features: the heart of Robert the Bruce is buried somewhere within the church; note too the figure of a pig playing the bagpipes, set on the roof. The museum, sited at the entrance to the ruins and housed in the 16th-century Commendator's House, is an interesting addition to this historic ruin.
Open all year, Apr-Sep Mon-Sat 9.30-6.30, Sun 2-6.30; Oct-Mar, Mon-Sat 9.30-4.30, Sun 2-4.30.
🅿 ⅖ shop ✗ 🏵
Details not confirmed for 1998

Priorwood Garden & Dried Flower Shop
TD6 9PX (off A6091)
☎ 01896 822493
This small garden specialises in flowers which are suitable for drying. It is formally designed with herbaceous and everlasting annual borders, and the attractive orchard has a display of 'apples through the ages' including ancient varieties. Visitors can see plants being dried and buy dried flower arrangements in the Priorwood shop.
Open Garden & Shop; Apr-Sep, Mon-Sat

10-5.30, Sun 1.30-5.30; Oct-24 Dec, Mon-Sat 10-4, Sun 1.30-4. Shop in Abbey St only; 9 Jan-Mar, Mon-Sat 12-4; Apr-24 Dec, Mon-Sat 10-5.30, Sun 1.30-5.30. (Closed 31 Oct-7 Nov).
Honesty box £1.
🅿 ⅖ shop 🏵

MINARD
Crarae Gardens
PA32 8YA (10m S of Inveraray on the A83)
☎ 01546 886614 & 886388 Fax 01546 886388
Set in a Highland Glen beside Loch Fyne, these gardens are among Scotland's loveliest. They are noted for their rhododendrons, azaleas, conifers and ornamental shrubs, which include a number of rare species. Abundant new plantings in the lower garden have been funded privately and by the Highlands and Islands Partnership Programme. A further fifty acres of forest garden will be open in the summer, with the support of the Millenium Forest For Scotland and the Highlands and Islands Partnership Programme. This will involve the restoration of 110 plots of Arboretum over a 5 year period.
Open all year, daily, summer 9-6; winter during daylight hours. Visitor centre, Etr-Oct 10-5.
£2.50 (ch £1.50). Family ticket £7.50.
🅿 ⅖ toilets for disabled shop garden centre
Cards: ▨ ▨

MONIAIVE
Maxwelton House Trust
DG3 4DX (A76 from Dumfries to Thornhill, after 2m take B729 to Monavie, 11m along road is Maxwelton House)
☎ 01848 200385
The house dates from the 14th and 15th centuries and was originally the stronghold of the Earls of Glencairn and later, in 1682, the birthplace of Annie Laurie of the famous Scottish ballad. The house was completely restored by the late Hugh C Stenhouse in 1971 and today's attractions include a museum, chapel, gardens, gift shop and tearoom.
Open last Sun in May-Sep, Sun-Fri 11-5. Etr-May by booking only.
£4 (ch 16 £2 & pen £3)
🅿 🖳 ✗ shop

NEW ABBEY
New Abbey Corn Mill
(8m S of Dumfries on A710)
☎ 01387 850260
Built in the late 18th century, this water-driven corn mill is still in working order, and regular demonstrations are held.
Open all year, Apr-Sep, Mon-Sat 9.30-

6.30, Sun 2-6.30; Oct-Mar, weekdays 9.30-4.30, Sun 2-4.30. (Closed Thu pm & Fri in winter; 25-26 Dec & 1-3 Jan).
🅿 (100yds) ✗ 🏵
Details not confirmed for 1998

Sweetheart Abbey
DG2 8BU
☎ 01387 850397
Lady Devorgilla of Galloway founded Balliol College in Oxford in memory of her husband John Balliol; she also founded an abbey in his memory in 1273. When she died in 1289 she was buried in front of the high altar with the heart of her husband resting on her bosom; hence the name 'Sweetheart Abbey'. This monument, inspired by love and loyalty, now stands as one of Scotland's most beautiful ruins. It features an unusual precinct wall of enormous boulders.
Open Apr-Sep Mon-Sat 9.30-6.30, Sun 2-6.30.
🅿 ⅖ (with assistance) toilets for disabled ✗ 🏵
Details not confirmed for 1998

OBAN
Caithness Glass Visitor Centre
The Waterfront, Railway Pier PA34 4LW
☎ 01631 563386 Fax 01631 563386
Well stocked factory shop selling wide range of perfect and slightly imperfect paperweights and glassware. There is also an audio-visual and interpretive exhibition on glassmaking and the story of Caithness Glass.
Open all year, Factory Shop, Audio visual & interpretative exhibition : Mon-Sat 9-5 (open late Jun-Sep). Etr-Nov Sun 11-5. Free.
🅿 (100yds) ⅖ shop ✗

Dunstaffnage Castle
(3m N on peninsula)
☎ 01631 562465
Now ruined, this four-sided stronghold has a gatehouse, two round towers and walls 10ft thick. It was once the prison of Flora MacDonald.
Open Apr-Sep, Mon-Sat 9.30-6.30, Sun 2-6.30.
🅿 shop 🏵
Details not confirmed for 1998

OLD DAILLY
Bargany Gardens
KA26 9PH (4m NE on B734 from Girvan)
☎ 01465 871249 Fax 01465 714191
Woodland walks display snowdrops, daffodils and bluebells in spring, and a fine show of azaleas and rhododendrons is to be seen around the lilypond in May and June. Ornamental trees give autumn colour, and visitors can buy plants from the gardens.
Open Gardens Mar-Oct, daily 7pm (or dusk).
Contribution Box.
🅿 ⅖

PAISLEY
Coats Observatory
49 Oakshaw St West PA1 2DR
☎ 0141 889 2013 Fax 0141 889 9240
Astronomy, meteorology and space flight, along with the history of the building, are the subjects of displays on show in this observatory built in 1883. Recent renovations have installed modern technology, and the observatory has resumed an important role in astronomy and meteorology.
Open all year, Mon, Tue & Thu 2-8, Wed, Fri & Sat 10-5. Oct-Mar Thu 7-9 weather permitting. (Closed Xmas & New Year). Free.
shop ✗

Paisley Museum & Art Galleries
High St PA1 2BA
☎ 0141 889 3151 Fax 0141 889 9240
Pride of place here is given to a world-famous collection of Paisley shawls. Other collections illustrate local industrial and natural history, while the emphasis of the art gallery is on 19th-century Scottish artists and an important studio ceramics collection.

Regular demonstrations are held at New Abbey Corn Mill

Open all year, Mon-Sat 10-5. (Closed PH).
P (200yds) & (parking on site) toilets for
disabled shop (Specialises in Paisley
goods) ✾ (ex guide dogs)
Details not confirmed for 1998

PALNACKIE
Orchardton Tower
(6m SE of Castle Douglas)
☎0131 668 8800 Fax 0131 668 8888
John Cairns built this rare example of a
circular tower in the late 15th century.
Open all reasonable times, on application to
key keeper. (Closed 25-26 Dec & 1-2 Jan).
P✾▮
Details not confirmed for 1998

PEEBLES
Kailzie
EH45 9HT (2.5m SE on B7062)
☎01721 720007 Fax 01721 720007
These extensive grounds with their fine
old trees provide a burnside walk flanked
by bulbs, rhododendrons and azaleas. A
walled garden contains herbaceous,
shrub rose borders, greenhouses and a
small formal rose garden. There is a
waterfowl pond, gift shop an art gallery,
and a childrens' play area. Trips to
Peebles by horse and carriage.
Open 25 Mar-Oct, daily 11-5.30. Grounds
close 5.30pm. Garden open all year.
£2 (ch 50p). Snowdrop day and garden
walks £1.
P✿✗ licensed & (ramps in garden &
gravel paths) toilets for disabled shop

Neidpath Castle
EH45 8NW (1m W on A72)
☎01721 720333 Fax 01721 720333
Successively owned by the families of
Fraser, Hay (Earl of Tweeddale), Douglas
(Earl of March) and Wemyss (Earl of
Wemyss and March), Neidpath Castle
occupies a spectacular position on the
Tweed. The 14th-century stronghold has
been interestingly adapted to 17th-
century living; it contains a rock-hewn
well, a pit prison, a small museum, and a
tartan display, and batiks depicting the
life and times of Mary, Queen of
Scots,and has picturesque views. There
are fine walks and a picnic area. First
weekend in October, a re-enactment of
'Border Reivers'.
Open Thu before Etr-Sep, Mon-Sat 11-5,
Sun 1-5.
£2.50 (ch £1, concessions £2). Family
ticket £6.50. Party 20+.
P (charged) shop

PORT GLASGOW
Newark Castle
☎01475 741858
The one-time house of the Maxwells,
dating from the 15th and 17th centuries.
The courtyard and hall are preserved.
Fine turrets and the remains of painted
ceilings can be seen, and the hall carries
an inscription of 1597.
Open Apr-Sep, Mon-Sat 9.30-6.30, Sun 2-
6.30.
P shop▮
Details not confirmed for 1998

PORT LOGAN
Logan Botanic Garden
DG9 9ND (on B7065)
☎01776 860231 Fax 01776 860333
Take a trip to the south west of Scotland
and experience the southern hemisphere
in Scotland's most exotic garden.
Logan's exeptionally mild climate allows
a colourful array of tender plants to thrive
out-of-doors. Amongst the many
highlights are tree ferns, cabbage palms,
unusual shrubs, climbers and tender
perennials found within the setting of the
walled, water, terrace and woodland
gardens. The Discovery Centre provides
activities and information for all ages and
the soundalive self-guided tours help you
to really make the most of your visit.
Please telephone for details of special
events.
Open Mar-Oct, 9.30-6, daily.
£3 (ch £1, concessions £2.50). Family
ticket £7.
P ✗ licensed & (wheelchairs available for
loan) toilets for disabled shop garden
centre ✾ (ex guide dogs)
Cards: ▨ ▨

RUTHWELL
Ruthwell Cross
(off B724)
☎0131 668 8800 Fax 0131 668 8888
Now in a specially built apse in the parish
church, the carved cross dates from the
7th or 8th centuries. Two faces show
scenes from the Life of Christ; the others
show scroll work, and parts of an ancient
poem in Runic characters. It was broken
up in the 18th century, but pieced
together by a 19th-century minister.
Open all reasonable times. Key from Key
Keeper, Kirkyett Cottage, Ruthwell.
P✾▮
Details not confirmed for 1998

Savings Banks Museum
DG1 4NN (6m W of Annan)
☎01387 870640
Housed in the building where Savings
Banks first began, the museum traces
their growth and development from 1810
up to the present day. Exhibits include
original letters, books and papers. The
museum also traces the life of Dr Henry
Duncan, father of savings banks, and
restorer of the Ruthwell Cross. Multi-
lingual leaflets available.
Open all year, daily (ex Sun & Mon Oct-
Mar), 10-1 & 2-5.
Free.
P & (touch facilities for blind, guide
available) shop✾

SALTCOATS
North Ayrshire Museum
Manse St, Kirkgate KA21 5AA
☎01294 464174 Fax 01294 464234
This museum is housed in an old 18th-
century church. On display is a rich
variety of artefacts from the North
Ayrshire area, including archaeological
and social history material. The museum
also houses a fine collection of Ayrshire

Whitework, a town hall clock and a
recreation of a turn-of-the-century
kitchen. There is a continuing programme
of temporary exhibitions.
Open all year, Mon-Sat (ex Wed) 10-1 &
2-5.
Free.
P (50 yds) & toilets for disabled ✾ (ex
guide dogs)

SANQUHAR
Sanquhar Tolbooth Museum
High St DG4 6BN
☎01659 250186 Fax 01387 265081
This museum focuses on the history of
Upper Nithsdale and is housed in the
town's fine 18th-century tolbooth. It tells
the story of the mines and miners of the
area, its earliest inhabitants, native and
Roman, the history and customs of the
Royal Burgh of Sanquhar and local
traditions. There is an exhibition on the
world famous craft of Sanquhar knitting
and a life-like reconstruction of Sanquhar
jail. An audio-visual show introduces the
visitor to the history and natural beauty of
the surrounding countryside. Special
events include 400th Anniversary of the
Royal Burgh of Sanquhar, events taking
place around the Riding of the Marches
ceremonies, exhibiton about the tradition
and its origins (15-18 Aug).
Open Apr-Sep, Tue-Sat 10-1 & 2-5, Sun 2-
5.
Free.
P shop

SELKIRK
Bowhill House and Country Park
TD7 5ET (3m W of Selkirk off A708)
☎01750 22204
Fax 01750 22204
An outstanding collection of pictures,
including works by Van Dyck, Canaletto,
Reynolds, Gainsborough and Claude
Lorraine, are displayed in this, the Border-
home of the Duke of Buccleuch and
Queensberry KT. In addition to these
there is an equally stunning collection of
porcelain and furniture, much of it made
in the Paris workshop of André Boulle.
Memorabilia and relics of people such as
Queen Victoria and Sir Walter Scott, and
a restored Victorian kitchen add further
interest inside the house. Outside, the
wooded grounds are perfect for walking.
Children will enjoy the adventure
playground and, no doubt, the gift shop.
There is also a theatre and an audio-visual
display. Art courses are held here.
Open, Park: May-Aug 12-5 (ex Fri). House
& park: Jul, daily 1-4.30.
House & grounds £4 (ch under 5 &
wheelchair users free, pen & groups
£3.50). Grounds only £1.
P✿✗ licensed & (guided tours for the
blind) toilets for disabled shop (Jul) ✾ (ex
in park)
Cards: ▨

Halliwells House Museum
Halliwells Close, Market Place TD7 4BC
(off A7 in town centre)
☎01750 20096 Fax 01750 23282

The former role of Selkirk's oldest
surviving dwelling has been recreated in
this enterprising museum. The home and
ironmonger's shop, lovingly restored, can
be seen together with the story of the
town's development and frequent
temporary exhibitions.
Open Apr-Oct, Mon-Sat 10-5 (Jul & Aug
until 6), Sun 2-4.
Free.
P & toilets for disabled shop ✾ (ex guide
dogs)

Sir Walter Scott's Courtroom
Market Place TD7 4BT (on A7 in town
centre)
☎01750 20096 Fax 01750 23282
Built in 1804 as the new sheriff court and
town house for Selkirk, it was here that
the novelist Sir Walter Scott pursued his
work as Sheriff of the County of Selkirk.
Now re-opened as a museum with
displays and audio-visual presentations
about Scott's life, his writing, his
contempraries (James Hogg and Mungo
Park) and his time as sheriff.
Open May-Sep, Sat 10-4, Sun 2-4; Oct,
Mon-Sat 1-4.
£1. (concessions 50p)
P (100mtrs) (time limit-onstreet, none for
car park) ✗ shop ✾ (ex guide dogs)

SMAILHOLM
Smailholm Tower
TD5 7RT (6m W of Kelso on B6937)
☎01573 460365
An outstanding example of a classic
Border tower-house, probably erected in
the 15th century. It is 57ft high and well-
preserved. The tower houses an
exhibition of dolls and a display based on
Sir Walter Scott's book 'Minstrels of the
Border'. It consists of tapestries and
costume figures.
Open Apr-Sep, Mon-Sat 9.30-6.30, Sun 2-
6.30. (Closed in winter).
P✾▮
Details not confirmed for 1998

STOBO
Dawyck Botanic Garden
EH45 9JU (8m SW of Peebles on B712)
☎01721 760254 Fax 01721 760214
Follow the landscaped walks through this
historic arboretum and discover the many
delights of Dawyck. An impressive
collection of mature specimen trees -
some over 40m tall and including the
unique Dawyck Beech-stand, majestically
towering above a variety of flowering
shrubs and herbaceous plants. Explore
Heron Wood and the world's first
Cryptogamic Sanctuary and Reserve to see
'non-flowering' plants. Notable features
include the Swiss Bridge, a fine estate
chapel and stonework/terracing produced
by Italian craftsmen in the 1820's.
Open Mar-Oct, daily 9.30-6.
£3 (ch £1, concessions £2.50). Family
ticket £7.
P ✿ & toilets for disabled shop garden
centre ✾ (ex guide dogs)
Cards: ▨ ▨

DRUMLANRIG CASTLE

Dumfriesshire home of the Duke of Buccleuch and Queensberry KT.

17th century house, with extensive gardens and Country Park. Renowned art collection, including works by Leonardo, Holbein and Rembrandt. French furniture. Bonnie Prince Charlie relics.

Castle shop with quality goods. Tearoom. Bird of Prey Centre. Craft Workshops. Adventure Playground. Visitor Centre.

18 miles north of Dumfries on A76
16 miles from Elvanfoot off M74.

For details:

01848-330248/331682

STRANRAER
Castle Kennedy Gardens
Stair Estates DG9 8BX (5m E on A75)
☎ *01776 702024 Fax 01776 706248*
Situated on a peninsula between two lochs, the gardens around the Old Castle were first laid out in the early 18th century and, after years of neglect, were restored and developed in the 19th. They are noted for their rhododendrons and azaleas (at their best in May and early June) and walled kitchen garden with fine herbaceous borders (best in August and September). The gardens contain many avenues and walks amid some beautiful scenery.
Open Apr-Sep, daily 10-5.
£2 (ch 15 £1, pen £1.50). Party 20+.
P ✋ & *toilets for disabled shop garden centre*
See advertisement on page 195

TARBOLTON
Bachelors' Club
Sandgate St KA5 5RB (on B744, 7.5m NE of Ayr)
☎ *01292 541940*
In this 17th-century thatched house, Robert Burns and his friends formed a debating club in 1780. Burns attended dancing lessons and was initiated into freemasonry here in 1781. The house is furnished in the period.
Open Good Friday to 30 Sept, daily 1.30-5.30; wknds in Oct 1.30-5.30.-last admission 5pm.
£2 (concessions £1.30) Family £5.30.
Schools £1. Adult party £1.60
P *(in village)* & ✿ *(ex guide dogs)* ✖

TAYNUILT
Bonawe Iron Furnace
(0.75m NE off B845)
☎ *01866 822432*
The furnace is a restored charcoal blast-furnace for iron-smelting and making cast-iron. It was established in 1753 and worked until 1876. The most complete furnace and ancillary buildings in Britain, the works exploited the Forest of Lorne to provide charcoal for fuel.
Open Apr-Sep, Mon-Sat 9.30-6.30, Sun 2-6.30.
P & *toilets for disabled shop* ▌
Details not confirmed for 1998

THORNHILL
Drumlanrig Castle
DG3 4AQ (4m N of Thornhill off A76)
☎ *01848 331682 & 330248*
This unusual, pink sandstone castle was built in the late 17th century in Renaissance style. Ringed by rugged hills, the castle was erected on the site of earlier Douglas strongholds and has connections with Robert Bruce and Mary, Queen of Scots. It contains a celebrated collection of paintings by Rembrandt, Da Vinci, Holbein, Murillo and many others. There is also French furniture, as well as silver and relics of Bonnie Prince Charlie. The old stable block has a craft centre with resident craft workers, a gift shop,

tearoom and a visitor's centre. The grounds offer an extensive garden, a birds of prey centre, cycle museum, cycle hire, an adventure woodland play area and woodland walks. Ring for details of special events.
Open early May-late Aug, Castle open seven days a week. Guided tours and restricted route may operate at various times, please verify before visiting. Prices under review.
P ✋ & *(lift for wheelchair users) toilets for disabled shop* ✿ *(ex in park on lead)*
Cards: ▣ ▤ ▨

TONGLAND
Tongland Tour
Tongland Power Station DG6 4LT (on A711 2m N of Kirkcudbright)
☎ *01557 330114*
An area of outstanding natural beauty which is testimony to the harmonious relationship between hydro power and the environment. This tour of part of the Scottish Power Galloway hydro-electricity scheme includes a video presentation and a visit to the dam and the power station. There is a fish ladder at the dam which provides the chance to see salmon returning to their spawning grounds. A free mini bus operates every day at 9.45am from the Tourist Information Centre at Kirkcudbright. Please call for details of admission charges etc 01557 330114.
Open May-Sep, Mon-Sat, and Sundays during August.
Contact tour guides at centre for details of admission charges.
P & *(only Fish Pass is not accessible)*

TRAQUAIR
Traquair House
EH44 6PW (1m S of Innerleithen on B709).
☎ *01896 830323 & 830785*
Fax 01896 830639
This is said to be Scotland's oldest inhabited, and most romantic, house. It dates back to the 12th century and 27 Scottish monarchs have stayed here. William the Lion Heart held court at Traquair, and the house has rich associations with Mary, Queen of Scots and the Jacobite risings. The large Bear Gates were closed in 1745, not to be reopened until the Stuarts should once again ascend the throne.
The house contains a fine collection of historical treasures and a unique 18th-century brewhouse which is licensed to make and sell its own beer. Outside there is a maze, croquet, and the opportunity for woodland walks by the River Tweed. There are also craft workshops and an art gallery. Full programme of Summer Events includes Mini Tattoo (7 Jun), Scottish Beer Festival (23-24 May), Traquair Fair (1-2 Aug), Needlework Weekend (12-13 Sep).
Open 11 Apr-Sep daily, 12.30-5.30 (ex Jun, Jul & Aug 10.30-5.30). Last admission 5pm. Oct, Fri-Sun. Grounds open Apr-Sep, 10.30-5.30.

£4.50 (ch £2.25, pen £3.50) Family £12.Groups 20+ £3.50.
P ✋ ✖ *licensed* & *shop*
Cards: ▣ ▤ ▨
See advertisement on page 191.

UDDINGSTON
Glasgow Zoopark
Calderpark G71 7RZ
☎ *0141 771 1185 Fax 0141 771 2615*
The developing, open-plan zoo has birds, mammals and reptiles housed in spacious new enclosures and buildings. There are many rare animals and the zoo's specialities are cats and reptiles. Other attractions include ample picnic sites, children's farm and seasonal displays.
Open all year, daily 10-5 (or 6pm depending on season).
P ✋ & *(key for toilet at gate) toilets for disabled shop* ✿
Details not confirmed for 1998

WANLOCKHEAD
Museum of Lead Mining
ML12 6UT (on B797 at N end of Mennock Pass).
☎ *01659 74387*
Fax 01659 74481
Wanlockhead, Scotland's highest village, set in the beautiful Lowther Hills, is the home of the Museum of Lead Mining. A guided tour takes the visitor into the underground world of Lochnell Lead Mine. The Visitor Centre houses a collection of rare minerals all found locally. There are 'hands-on' displays, mineral collecting areas and an open-air visitor trail. A one-and-a-half-mile walkway takes the visitor to an 18th-century lead mine, smelt mill and miners' cottages furnished in the styles of 1740 and 1890. An unusual feature is a Miners' Reading Society library, which was founded in 1756 with a multimedia interactive presentation. Gold panning tuition is available at the new Gold Panning Centre - take home any gold you find. Special events planned for 1998 include Gold Panning Championships (May 23/24), Mineral Road Show (5 Jul), Family Fun Day (23 Aug), Scottish Festival (13 Sept) and Hallowe'en (31 Oct). Please telephone for details.
Open Apr-Oct, daily 11-4.30 (last mine tour 4). July-Aug 10-5. Oct-Mar by arrangement.
£3.50 (ch £1.50, concessions £2.50).
Family ticket £8.50.
P ✖ *licensed* & *toilets for disabled shop* ✿ *(ex guide dogs)*
Cards: ▣ ▤ ▨

WHITHORN
Whithorn-Cradle of Christianity
45-47 George St DG8 8NS
☎ *01988 500508*
Fax 01988 500508
The Whithorn Dig, in Galloway, is the site of the first Christian settlement in Scotland - the Candida Casa of St Ninian. Visitors can learn of the discoveries by way of an audio visual show, exhibitions, murals, models and displays of finds. Friendly guides explain the excavation. Museum of Early Christian stones. The Discovery Centre has a 3-D jigsaw to explain the archaeology. Craft and book shop.
Open daily, Apr-Oct 10.30-5.
✻*£2.70 (ch, pen & UB40's £1.50). Family ticket £7.50. Season ticket. Party.*
P *(70 yds)* & *(one short staircase with 'stairmatic') toilets for disabled shop*

Whithorn Priory
☎ *01988 500508*
The first Christian church in Scotland was founded here by St Ninian in 397, but the present ruins date from the 12th century. The ruins are scanty but there is a notable Norman door, the Latinus stone of the 5th century and other early Christian monuments.
Open Apr-Sep, Mon-Sat 9.30-6.30, Sun 2-6.30;
P & ✿ ▌
Details not confirmed for 1998

The directory which follows has been divided into three geographical regions. Counties have not been shown against individual locations as recent legislation has created a number of smaller counties which will be unfamiliar to the visitor. The postal authorities have confirmed that it is no longer necessary to include a county name in addresses, provided a post code is shown.

NORTH WALES

This region includes the counties of Anglesey, Conwy, Denbighshire, Flintshire, Gwynedd and Wrexham.

ANGLESEY, ISLE OF

BEAUMARIS
Beaumaris Castle
LL58 8AP
☎ *01248 810361*
Beaumaris was the last of the great castles built by Edward I around the coast of North Wales, and there is an exhibition on his castles in the Chapel Tower. The building took from 1295 to 1312 to complete and involved a huge workforce: a record for 1296 mentions 400 masons and 2000 labourers, besides 100 carts and wagons and 30 boats carrying stone and seacoal. In the early 1400s it was captured by Owain Glyndwr and then retaken, and in later centuries it was plundered for its lead, timber and stone. Despite this it remains one of the most impressive and complete castles built by Edward I. It has a perfectly symmetrical, concentric plan, with a square inner bailey and curtain walls, round corner towers and D-shaped towers in between. There are also two great gatehouses, but these were never finished. Around it is an outer curtain wall with small towers, and a moat which has been restored. The original defended dock for shipping has also survived.
Open all year, late Oct-late Mar, Mon-Sat 9.30-4, Sun 11-4; late Mar-late Oct daily 9.30-6.30. (Closed 24-26 Dec & 1 Jan).
P & *shop* ✿ ☺
Cards: ▣ ▤
Prices not confirmed.

Beaumaris Gaol & Courthouse
Steeple Ln LL58 8EW
☎ *01248 810921*
Fax 01248 750282
With its treadmill and grim cells, the gaol is a vivid reminder of the tough penalties exacted by 19th-century law. One particularly gruesome feature is the route that condemned prisoners took to the scaffold. The courthouse, built in 1614 and renovated early in the 19th-century, is a unique survival of a Victorian court room.
Open Etr, end May-Sep, daily 10.30-5. Other times by arrangement only.
Gaol £2.75 (ch, pen £1.75). Courthouse £1.50 (ch, pen £1). Combined ticket £3.40 (ch £2.20 & pen £2.20). Family ticket £7.75.
P *(500yds)* & *shop* ✿ *(ex guide dogs)*

Museum of Childhood
1 Castle St LL58 8AP (on A545. Opposite Beaumaris Castle)
☎ *01248 712498*
Fax 01248 716869
Many rare and valuable exhibits are shown in the nine rooms of the museum, which illustrates the life and interests of children and families over 150 years. They include money boxes, dolls, educational toys and games, early clockwork trains, cars and aeroplanes, push toys and cycles. Also shown are things that were used rather than played with by children, such as pottery and

glassware, and pieces of furniture. A gallery shows paintings and prints of children. Winner of the BTA and National Heritage Museum of the Year Awards.
Open daily 10.30-5.30, Sun 12-5. Last admission 4.30, Sun 4. (Closed Nov-2nd wk Mar).
£2.95 (ch £1.65, pen/students £2.25). Family ticket £8.50. Free entry for wheelchairs.
P *(50yds)* & *shop* ❀ *(ex guide dogs)*

BRYNCELLI DDU
Bryn Celli Ddu Burial Chamber
(3m W of Menai Bridge off A4080)
☎ *01222 500200*
Excavated in 1865, and then again in 1925-9, this is a prehistoric circular cairn covering a passage grave with a polygonal chamber.
Open at all times.
Free.
P & ❀ ☺

BRYNSIENCYN
Anglesey Sea Zoo
The Oyster Hatchery LL61 6TQ (follow Lobster signs along A4080 to zoo)
☎ *01248 430411*
Fax 01248 430213
The sea zoo is a unique collection of marine life found around Anglesey and the North Wales coast. The sea creatures are housed in glass-sided and open-topped tanks of all shapes and sizes, which are intended to provide as natural and unrestricted an environment as possible. Another important consideration has been providing cover for visitors. There are also shoaling tanks, a wave tank, tide tank, wreck room and touch pools. A recent addition is an exhibit called 'The Big Fish Forest'. This is a huge kelp forest enclosed by the largest unsupported acrylic panel in Britain.
Open Mar-Oct, daily 10-5; Nov-Feb, daily 11-3. Closed 18-26 Dec, 1-5 Jan.
P ▣ ✗ *licensed* & *(wheelchair available) toilets for disabled shop*
Details not confirmed for 1998
Cards: ▣ ▦ ▦ ▣

HOLYHEAD
RSBP Nature Reserve South Stack
South Stack LL65 3HB (A5 to Holyhead then follow brown tourist signs)
☎ *01407 764973*
High cliffs with caves and offshore stacks, backed by the maritime heathland of Holyhead Mountain, make this an ideal reserve to watch seabirds. Live video pictures of breeding seabirds are shown in the cliff-top information centre during the summer. Choughs, guillemots, razorbills, fulmars and puffins may be seen.
Open: Visitor Centre daily, Apr-mid Sep, 11-5. Reserve open daily at reasonable times.
Free.
P ❀
Cards: ▣ ▦ ▦ ▣

LLANALLGO
Din Llugwy Ancient Village
(1m NW off A5025)
The remains of a 4th-century village can be seen here. There are two circular and seven rectangular buildings, still standing up to head height and encircled by a pentagonal stone wall some 4 to 5ft thick.
Open at all times.
Free.
❀ ☺
Cards: ▣ ▦

PLAS NEWYDD
Plas Newydd
LL61 6DQ (2m S of Llanfairpwll, on A4080)
☎ *01248 714795 Fax 01248 713673*
Built by James Wyatt in the 18th century, this house stands on the Menai Strait in unspoilt surroundings, and enjoys uninterrupted views of the Snowdonia mountain range. Beautiful lawns and parkland surround the house and there is a fine spring garden, summer garden and later massed hydrangeas and autumn colour. Also a woodland walk with access to a marine walk. The Rhododendron Garden is open from April - early June only. An exhibition of Rex Whistler's work is on show with his largest wall painting. Relics of the first Marquess of Anglesey and the Battle of Waterloo are kept here, along with the Ryan collection of military uniforms and headdresses. Special events for 1998 include: Open air theatre, opera, jazz, evening concerts in the Music Room, and family events. Please contact property for details.
Open 1 Apr-1 Nov, Sun-Thurs. House 12-5pm, garden 11am-5.30pm. Last admission 30mins before closing.
£4.20 (ch £2.10). Family (2 adults & 2 ch) £10.50. Pre-booked groups (15+) £3.40. Garden only: Adults £2, Ch.£1. NT Members free.
P ▣ ✗ *licensed* & *(Close parking, wheelchairs, stairclimber) toilets for disabled shop* ❀ ▦

BANGOR
Penrhyn Castle
LL57 4HN (1m E at Bangor, at Llandegai on A5122, just off A55)
☎ *01248 353084 Fax 01248 371281*
The splendid castle with its towers and battlements was commissioned in 1827 as a sumptuous family home. The architect was Thomas Hopper, who was also responsible for the panelling, plasterwork and furniture, still mostly in the 'Norman' style of the mid-19th century. Notable rooms include the great hall, heated by the Roman method of hot air under the floor, the library with its heavily decorated ceiling and great arches, and the dining room, which is covered with neo-Norman decoration. Among the furniture is a slate bed weighing over a ton, and a decorated brass bed made specially for Edward VII at the then huge cost of £600.
The Penrhyn Castle Industrial Railway Museum occupies the stableyard. The

At Penrhyn Castle there is an unusual bed made of slate weighing over a ton.

40-acre grounds include a walled garden, wild garden and attractive woodland. There are wonderful views over Anglesey, Puffin Island, the North Wales coast and Snowdonia. Special events for 1998 include: concerts in the Grand Hall, open air theatre, and family fun days - please ring for details.
Open 25 Mar-1 Nov, daily (ex Tue) Castle 12-5pm. Grounds and stableblock exhibitions 11am-5.30pm (Jul & Aug 10-5.30). Last admission 4.30pm. Last audio tour 4pm.
❋*All inclusive ticket: £4.80 (ch £2.40). Family ticket £12. Party 15+. Grounds & stableblock only £3 (ch £1.50) (NT members free).*
P ✗ & *toilets for disabled shop* ❀ *(ex guide dogs)* ▦

BEDDGELERT
Sygun Copper Mine
LL55 4NE (1m E of Beddgelert on A498)
☎ *01766 510100 Fax 01766 510102*
With the help of an expert guide, and an audio-visual underground tour, visitors can explore the workings of this 19th-century copper mine set deep within the Gwynant Valley where magnificent stalactite and stalagmite formations can be seen. The less energetic can enjoy a continuous audio-visual presentation and a display of artefacts found during excavations.
Open all year, daily 10-6. (last tour 5).
❋*£4.50 (ch £3, pen £3.75). Family ticket £13.50*
P & *toilets for disabled shop*
Cards: ▣ ▦ ▦ ▦ ▣

BERRIEW
Glansevern Hall Gardens
Glansevern SY21 8AH (on A483 between Welshpool and Newtown)
☎ *01686 640200 Fax 01686 640829*
Glansevern Hall was built in the Greek

Revival style for Arthur Davies Owen Esq. He chose a romantically positioned site on the banks of the River Severn with gentle hills rising in the background. Fifteen years ago Neville & Jenny Thomas acquired the property and began to develop the gardens, respecting the plantings and features of the past, and added a vast collection of new and interesting species. Covering some 15 acres, set in wider parkland and on mostly level ground. There are many fine and unusual trees, a lakeside walk, water gardens, rose gardens and a rock garden.
Open 2 May-27 Sep, BH Mon, Fri-Sat 2-6.
£2 (pen £1.50, ch 15 free). Party.
P ▣ & *(most areas accessible) shop garden centre*

BETWS-Y-COED
Conwy Valley Railway Museum
Old Goods Yard LL24 0AL (adjacent to BR station)
☎ *01690 710568 Fax 01690 710132*
The two large museum buildings have displays on both the narrow-and standard-gauge railways of North Wales, including railway stock and other memorabilia. There are working model railway layouts, a steam-hauled miniature railway in the grounds, which cover over four acres, and a 15in-gauge tramway to the woods. The latest addition is the quarter-size steam 'Britannia' loco which is now on display. For children there are also self-drive mini-dodgems, Postman Pat, school bus and Toby Tram.
Open Etr-Oct, daily 10-5.30, then weekends until Mar.
£1 (ch & pen 50p). Family ticket £2.50. Steam train ride 75p. Tram ride 60p.
P ▣ & *(Ramps & Clearances for wheelchairs) toilets for disabled shop (ex in museum)*
Cards: ▣ ▦ ▦

BLAENAU FFESTINIOG
Ffestiniog Pumped Storage Scheme
Ffestiniog Information Centre, Tan-Y-Grisiau LL41 3TP (off A496)
☎01766 830465
Fax 01766 833472
The scheme was the first hydro-electric pumped storage scheme, and was opened by Her Majesty the Queen in 1963. Water is released from an upper dam, through turbines, to generate electricity when needed, and then pumped back up when demand is low. Guided tours are available, and the information centre includes a souvenir shop and cafe.
Open Etr-Oct, Sun-Fri, 10-4.30. Other times by prior arrangement.
✱£2.50 (ch, students & pen £1.25), Family ticket (2 adults, 2 children) £6.50
P ⬛ shop ✺ (ex in grounds)

Gloddfa Ganol Slate Mine
LL41 3NB (1m N on A470)
☎01766 830664
Fax 01766 830527
Visitors can put on safety helmets and go into the extensive underground workings of this slate mine, which is the world's largest. There are special conducted tours by Land Rover for the more adventurous, which explore some of the miles of chambers and tunnels hundreds of feet up in the mountain. The massive machinery used in slate mining is displayed in the mill, and the art of slate splitting is demonstrated. Gloddfa Ganol is an active mine. Today's open-cast blasting operations can be seen from the safety of the Mining Museum, and with the help of video films, exhibitions and demonstrations visitors achieve a valuable insight into the complex nature of the slate industry.
Open Etr-Oct, Mon-Fri, also Sun BH wknds & summer school holidays.
P ⬛ ✗ licensed & shop
Details not confirmed for 1998

Llechwedd Slate Caverns
LL41 3NB (25m from A55 N Wales Expressway S on A470. 10M from A5 junct with A470 Beside A470 from Llandudno)
☎01766 830306 Fax 01766 831260
The Miners' Underground Tramway carries visitors into areas where early conditions have been recreated, while the Deep Mine is reached by an incline railway and has an unusual audio-visual presentation. Free surface attractions include several exhibitions and museums, slate mill and the Victorian village which has Victorian shops, bank, Miners Arms pub, lock-up and working smithy. Our 5 and a half million visitors have included Princess Margaret, the Duchess of Gloucester and Crown Prince Hiro of Japan. 1997 was our Silver Jubilee year.
Open all year, daily from 10am. Last tour 5.15 (Oct-Feb 4.15). (Closed 25-26 Dec & 1 Jan).
Single Tour £6.50 (ch £4.50, pen £6).
P ⬛ ✗ licensed & toilets for disabled shop (also Victorian shops in the Village) ✺ (ex on surface)
Cards: 🅰 ▬▬ ▬▬ 🅢 💳

BODELWYDDAN
Bodelwyddan Castle
LL18 5YA (adjacent to A55, near St Asaph)
☎01745 584060 Fax 01745 584563
Set in rolling parkland against the impressive background of the Clwydian Hills, this imposing Victorian country house has been magnificently restored to its former glory. The lavish interiors reflect various periods and design styles from the 19th century and provide a sumptuous setting for a collection of over 200 portraits on loan from the National Portrait Gallery. It is the finest collection of Victorian portraiture outside London and contains work by William Holman-Hunt, John Singer Sargent and G F Watts. The portraits are complemented by furniture from the Victoria and Albert

Museum and sculptures from the Royal Academy of Arts. A 'hands-on' exhibition of Victorian amusements and inventions features parlour games, puzzles and optical illusions - a veritable extravaganza of Victorian fun and games for all ages. A programme of events and temporary exhibitions takes place throughout the year. Please telephone for details.
Open Apr-Oct, Sat-Thu (every day in Jul-Aug), 10-5 (Castle galleries open at 10.30). Nov-Easter 11-4 (not Mon or Fri).
£4.30 (ch, students & disabled £2.70, pen & UB40's £3.80) Family ticket £13.
P ⬛ & (lift to first floor & Braille Guide) toilets for disabled shop ✺ (ex guide dogs)
Cards: 🅰 ▬▬ ▬▬ 💳

CAERNARFON
Caernarfon Castle
LL55 2AY
☎01286 677617
Edward I began building the castle and extensive town walls in 1283 after defeating Llywelyn ap Gruffyd (the last independant ruler of Wales). Completed in 1328, it has unusual polygonal towers, notably the 10-sided Eagle Tower, and the walls have bands of colour. There is a theory that these features were copied from the walls of Constantinople, to reflect a tradition that Constantine the Great was born nearby, at the Roman fort of Segontium. Caernarfon was the largest of Edward I's castles in Wales, and the Chamberlain Tower has an exhibition on the castles of Edward I. His son and heir was born and presented to the Welsh people here, setting a precedent that was followed in 1969, when Prince Charles was invested as Princes of Wales - there is a 'Prince of Wales' exhibition in the North-East Tower and a display of investiture robes. A wall walkway links the Eagle Tower to the Queen's Tower, which houses the museum of the Royal Welch Fusiliers. The regiment dates back to 1689 and eight Victoria Crosses are on display. There is also a 'Prospect of Caernarfon' exhibition on the ground floor of the Eagle Tower.
Open all year, late Oct-late Mar, Mon-Sat 9.30-4, Sun 11-4; late Mar-late Oct daily 9.30-6.30. (Closed 24-26 Dec & 1 Jan)
✱£3.80 (reductions £2.80). Family ticket £10
P shop ✺ 😊
Cards: 🅰 ▬▬

Segontium Roman Fort & Museum
Llanbeblig Rd LL55 2LN (on A4085 leading to Beddgelert approx 1m from Caernarfon)
☎01286 675625 Fax 01286 678416
Segontium Roman Museum tells the story of the conquest and occupation of Wales by the Romans and displays the finds from the auxiliary fort of Segontium, one of the most famous in Britain. You can combine a visit to the museum with exploration of the site of the Roman Fort, which is in the care of Cadw: Welsh Historic Monuments. The exciting discoveries displayed at the museum vividly portray the daily life of the soldiers stationed in this remote outpost of the Roman Empire.
Open Apr & Oct, Mon-Sat 9.30-5.30, Sun 2-5. May-Sep, Mon-Sat 9.30-6, Sun 2-6. Nov-Feb, Mon-Sat 9.30-4, Sun 2-4. Closed 24-26 Dec & 1 Jan.
£1 (concessions & children 60p).
P ✺

CERRIGYDRUDION
Llyn Brenig Visitor Centre
LL21 9TT (on B4501)
☎01490 420463 Fax 01490 420694
The 1,800-acre estate has a unique archaeological trail and round-the-lake walk of 10 miles (completion certificate available). The Nature Trail can offer glimpses of native trout or crossbills. A hide is available: best viewing is November to March. Disabled anglers are catered for with a specially adapted fishing boat and an annual open day. The centre has a bilingual exhibition on

geology, archaeology, history and natural history.
Open mid Mar-Nov daily 9am-5pm. Free. (ex water sports & fishing).
P (charged) ⬛ & (boats for disabled & fishing open days) toilets for disabled shop ✺ (ex guide dogs)

CHIRK
Chirk Castle
LL14 5AF (8m S of Wrexham, signposted off A483)
☎01691 777701 Fax 01691 774706
Chirk Castle is one of a chain of late-13th-century Marcher castles. Its high walls and drum towers have hardly changed, but the inside shows the varied tastes of 700 years of occupation. One of the least-altered parts is Adam's Tower. Elsewhere, many of the medieval-looking decorations were by Pugin in the 19th century. The elegant stone staircase and delicate plasterwork of the staterooms date from the 18th century when Chirk was transformed in neo-classical style. There is a 17th-century Long Gallery, and the servants' hall has its old list of rules. The equally varied furnishings include fine tapestries. Outside is a formal garden with clipped yew hedges, and a landscaped park with splendid wrought-iron gates by the Davies brothers. Special events for 1998: Open Air concerts and theatre, family fun days, please telephone for details.
Open 1 Apr-27 Sep, daily (ex Mon & Tue) (but open BH Mons); 3 Oct-1 Nov, Sat & Sun only; Castle 12-5, Grounds 11-6. Last admission 4.30pm.
£4.60 (ch £2.30) Family ticket £11.50. Party. Garden only £2.40 (ch £1.20) National Trust members free.
P ✗ licensed & (Stairclimber) toilets for disabled shop ✺ (ex guide dogs) 👜

COED-Y-BRENIN
Coed-y-Brenin Forest Park & Visitor Centre
(Off A470(T) 3m S of Trawsfynydd, 8m N of Dolgellau. Clearly signed from main rd)
☎01341 422289
Fax 01341 423893
Located in the heart of Coed-y-Brenin, the visitor centre provides an excellent introduction to the area with its range of displays and audio-visual programmes. Coed-y-Brenin means King's Forest, and it was named to commemorate the Silver Jubilee of King George V in 1935. There are over 50 miles of waymarked walks, delightful picnic spots and a wildlife conservation hide. Guide leaflets on the surrounding trails are provided by the centre, where visitors can also see a fascinating display on the gold mines which were once worked in this area. Mountain bikes are available for hire at the visitor centre. There are 70 kilometres of waymarked mountain bike trails with some of the best riding in the UK. Guided mountain bike rides and skills workshops will be held along with a 3 day bike stage race around Whitsun Bank Holiday. There is a children's play area, and a new orienteering course. For details of these and more events contact the Visitor Centre.
Open Apr-Oct 10-5. Other dates by prior bookings.
P (charged) ⬛ & toilets for disabled shop
Details not confirmed for 1998

COLWYN BAY
Welsh Mountain Zoo
Old Highway LL28 5UY (off bypass, A55)
☎01492 532938 Fax 01492 530498
The zoo and gardens are set in a 37-acre estate overlooking Colwyn Bay, with magnificent panoramic views of the coast and mountains. The animals are housed in natural settings, interspersed with gardens and woodland. The traditional range of zoo animals can be seen, from lions and elephants to penguins and parrots, and the zoo also attracts a variety of local wildlife. There are falconry displays during the summer months, and Californian sealions can be seen performing tricks at feeding time.

Visit the Chimpanzee World complex, featuring the unique Chimp Encounter, and a South American small monkey breeding centre. There is also a Jungle Adventureland and Tarzan Trail activity area, and a Children's Farm.
Open all year, 9.30-last admission 5pm. (4pm Nov-Feb).
P ⬛ ✗ licensed & (free admission for the blind & wheelchair visitors) toilets for disabled shop ✺
Details not confirmed for 1998

CONWY
Aberconwy House
LL32 8AY (At junction of Castle St & High St)
☎01492 592246 Fax 01492 585153
This house dates from the 14th century; it is the only medieval merchant's house in Conwy to have survived the turbulence, the fire and pillage of this frontier town for nearly six centuries. Furnished rooms and an audio-visual presentation show daily life in the house at different periods in its history.
Open Apr-1 Nov, daily (ex Tues) 10-5. last admission 4.30.
£2 (ch £1). Family ticket £5. Prebooked parties £1.80. NT members free.
P (100yds & 0.5 mile) (public C/P charges) shop ✺ (ex guide dogs) 👜
Cards: 🅰 ▬▬ 💳

Conwy Castle
LL32 8AY (by A55 or B5106)
☎01492 592358
The castle is a magnificent fortress, built from 1283-7 by Edward I. There is an exhibition on castle chapels on the ground floor of the Chapel Tower. The castle forms part of the same defensive system as the extensive town walls, 1400yds long and some 30ft high, which are among the most complete in Europe. They have 21 (originally 22) towers, and sweep up and down hills as they encircle the town. The best view of the castle and walls is from the other side of the river, which is spanned by three bridges designed to complement the scene. The graceful suspension bridge was built by Telford in 1826, the tubular bridge by Stephenson in 1848, and the road bridge was completed in 1958.
Open all year, late Oct-late Mar, Mon-Sat 9.30-4, Sun 11-4; late Mar-late Oct daily 9.30-6.30. (Closed 24-26 Dec & 1 Jan)
✱£3 (reductions £2). Family ticket £8.
P & toilets for disabled shop ✺ 😊
Cards: 🅰 ▬▬

Conwy Suspension Bridge
LL32 8LO (adjacent to Conwy Castle)
☎01492 573282
Designed by Thomas Telford, this was the first bridge to span the river at Conwy, and its opening in 1826 marked the end of the ferrymen's long monopoly. The bridge has recently been restored and the toll house furnished as it would have been a century ago.
Open Apr-1 Nov, daily (ex Tue) 10-5. Open 7 days Jul-Aug. Last admission 30 mins before closing.
£1 (ch 50p)
& ✺ 👜

Smallest House
The Quay LL32 8BB (leave A55 at Conwy signpost, trough town, at bottom of high st for the quay, turn left)
☎01492 593484
The 'Guinness Book of Records' lists this as the smallest house in Britain. Just 6ft wide by 10ft high, it is furnished in the style of a mid-Victorian Welsh cottage.
Open Apr-mid Oct daily 10-6 (10-9.30/10pm in Jul & Aug). In winter by arrangement.
50p (ch under 5 free).
P (100 yds) & shop

CORWEN
Rug Chapel
Rug
☎01490 412025
Rug Chapel was built in 1637 for Colonel William Salusbury, famous Civil War defender of Denbigh Castle. A rare little

The defence of Harlech Castle during the Wars of the Roses inspired the song *Men of Harlech*

altered example of a seventeenth century private chapel, it reflects the Colonel's High Church religious views. Prettily set in a wooded landscape, the chapel's modest exterior gives little hint of the wonders within. Local artists and carvers were given free rein. More soberly a rare wall painting with a skeleton and symbols of mortality reminds the congregation (in Welsh verse) that life is short.
Open May-Sep 10-2 & 3-5. Closed Sun & Mon (ex B/H's).
P & *toilets for disabled shop* ⌚ ☺
Cards: ▨ ▧

CRICCIETH
Criccieth Castle
LL52 0DP (off A497)
☎01766 522227
The castle dates from the 13th century and was taken and destroyed by Owain Glyndwr in 1404. Evidence of a fierce fire can still be seen. The gatehouse leading to the inner ward remains impressive, and parts of the walls are well preserved. Perched on its rocky peninsula, the castle commands superb views over the resort and Tremadog Bay.
Open all year, late Mar-mid Jun, daily 9.30-6.30; mid Jun-Sep, daily 10-6; winter 9.30-4. Closed 24-26 Dec & 1 Jan.
Prices not confirmed.
P *shop* ⌚ ☺
Cards: ▨ ▧

CYMER ABBEY
Cymer Abbey
(2m NW of Dolgellau on A494)
☎01341 422854
The abbey was built for the Cistercians in the 13th century. It was never very large, and does not seem to have been finished. The church is the best-preserved building, with ranges of windows and arcades still to be seen.
Open all year, late Oct-late Mar, Mon-Sat 9.30-4, Sun 2-4; late Mar-late Oct, daily 9.30-6.30. (Closed 24-26 Dec & 1 Jan)
Prices not confirmed.
P & ⌚ ☺
Cards: ▨ ▧

DENBIGH
Denbigh Castle
(via A525, A543 & B5382)
☎01745 813979
The castle was begun by Henry de Lacy in 1282 and has an inspiring and impressive castle gatehouse, with a trio of towers and a superb archway, which is surmounted by a figure believed to be that of Edward I.

Open May-Sep daily 10-5; Oct-Apr 9.30-4. Closed 24-26 Dec & 1 Jan.
Free.
P & *shop* ⌚ ☺

Town Walls & Leicester's Church
Noted for their almost complete circuit, the town walls were started in 1282 at the same time as the castle. The remains include one of the gateways and the unfinished Leicester's Church, built by the Earl of Leicester, favourite of Elizabeth I, who meant it to become the cathedral of the diocese.
Open May-Sep daily 10-5.
Prices not confirmed.
P ⌚
Cards: ▨ ▧

DOLWYDDELAN
Dolwyddelan Castle
LL25 0EJ (on A470 Blaenau Ffestiniog to Betws-y-Coed)
☎01690 750366
The castle is reputed to be the birthplace of Llywelyn the Great. It was captured in 1283 by Edward I, who immediately began strengthening it for his own purposes. A restored keep of around 1200, and a 13th-century curtain wall can be seen. An exhibition on the castles of the Welsh Princes is located in the keep.
Open all year, late Oct-late Mar, Mon-Sat 9.30-4; late Mar-late Oct daily 9.30-6.30. (Closed 24-26 Dec & 1 Jan).
✱£1.70 (reductions £1.20). Family ticket £4.
P ⌚
Cards: ▨ ▧

EWLOE
Ewloe Castle
(NW of village on B5125)
The remains of Ewloe Castle stand in Ewloe Woods. It was a native Welsh castle, and Henry II was defeated nearby in 1157. Part of the Welsh Tower in the upper ward still stands to its original height, and there is a well in the lower ward. Remnants of walls and another tower can also be seen.
Open at all times.
Free.
⌚ ☺

FAIRBOURNE
Fairbourne Railway
Beach Rd LL38 2PZ
☎01341 250362
ax 01341 250240
One of the most unusual of Wales's 'little trains' - it was built in 1890 as a horse-drawn railway to carry building materials

for the seaside resort of Fairbourne. It was later converted to steam, and now runs two-and-a-half miles from Fairbourne to the end of the peninsula and the ferry for Barmouth. Its route passes one of the loveliest beaches in Wales, with views of the beautiful Mawddach Estuary. An enjoyable round trip can be made from Barmouth in summer, crossing the Mawddach by ferry, catching the narrow gauge steam train to Fairbourne and then taking the British Rail train - or walking - across the Mawddach Viaduct. At Gorsaf Newydd terminus visitors can see locomotive sheds and engineering works. A Kite Festival is held on 20/21 June.
Open 5 Apr-29 Sep, times vary according to season and events. Trains may run during Oct half term holiday and Santa trains at Xmas.
✱2nd class return £3.50 (ch £2.15, pen £2.90). 1st class return £4.60 (ch £2.70, pen £3.70).
P ⊒ ✗ *licensed shop*

FLINT
Flint Castle
CH6 5PH
☎01352 733078
The castle was started by Edward I in 1277 and overlooks the River Dee. It is exceptional for its great tower, or Donjon, which is separated by a moat. It may have been the castle's chief residence. Other buildings would have stood in the inner bailey, of which parts of the walls and corner towers remain.
Open at all times.
Free.
P ⌚

GLYN CEIRIOG
Chwarel Wynne Mine & Museum
Wynne Quarry LL20 7DA (on B4500)
☎01691 718343
Chwarel Wynne Mine extends two and a half miles underground and was continuously worked from 1750 to 1928, during which time it produced more than 2000 tons of slate annually. The methods of mining and processing the slate are explained in a half-hour guided tour of the underground workings. The museum illustrates the history of the slate industry in North Wales. On show are tools, photographs and documents relating to mining along with objects relating to life in a slate-quarrying village almost a century ago. Film show. The mine has a beautiful setting in a 12-acre site, and there is a nature trail.

Open Etr-Oct, daily 10-5. Parties welcome at other times by prior appointment.
P ⊒ & *shop*
Details not confirmed for 1998

HARLECH
Harlech Castle
LL46 2YH (from A496)
☎01766 780552
Harlech Castle was built in 1283-81 by Edward I, with a sheer drop to the sea on one side. Owain Glyndwr starved the castle into submission in 1404 and made it his court and campaigning base. Later, the defence of the castle in the Wars of the Roses inspired the song *Men of Harlech*. Today the sea has slipped away, and the castle's great walls and round towers stand above the dunes. The gatehouse is especially impressive, and there are magnificent views of Snowdonia and across Tremadog Bay.
Open all year, late Oct-late Mar, Mon-Sat 9.30-4, Sun 11-4; late Mar-late Oct, daily 9.30-6.30. Closed 24-26 Dec & 1 Jan.
✱£3 (reductions £2). Family ticket £8.
P *(disabled spaces in car park) shop* ⌚ ☺
Cards: ▨ ▧

HOLYWELL
Basingwerk Abbey
Greenfield Valley Heritage Pk, Greenfield
☎01352 714172
The abbey was founded about 1131 by Ranulf de Gernon, earl of Chester. The first stone church dates from the beginning of the thirteenth century, alterations taking place in subsequent years. In the late fifteenth century the abbey was much praised for its hospitality and the great beauty of its setting. The last abbot surrendered the house to the crown in 1536. The Abbey is close to the Heritage Park Visitor Centre and access to the Museum and Farm Complex at Greenfield Valley.
Open all year, 9.30-6.30 daily.
Free.
P ✗ & *(disabled facilities in Heritage Park) toilets for disabled shop* ⌚ ☺

LLANBEDR
Maes Artro Centre
LL45 2PZ (on A496)
☎01341 241467
An old wartime RAF camp has been imaginatively converted to display a varied range of exhibitions and activities. An original air raid shelter has been restored with light and sound effects; the history of RAF Llanbedr is illustrated; and a Spitfire, used in the TV series *A Piece of Cake*, is on show. Rural Heritage Exhibition, a 'Village of Yesteryear', military tanks, RAF Rescue helicopter, a log fort playground and nature trails are all set among the lovely wooded grounds. Large Marine Life Aquarium.
Open mid May-mid Sep, daily 10-5.30.
✱£3.00 (ch & pen £2.50).
P ⊒ & *toilets for disabled shop*
Cards: ▨ ▧

LLANBERIS
Dinorwig Discovery
Oriel Eeyri LL55 4TU (on A4086, Llanberis by-pass)
☎01286 870636 Fax 01286 871331
The tours of the Power Station begin at Dinorwig Discovery. An introductory, multi-media show and electricity gallery are features of the centre, which also boasts the 'Anthony Hopkins Snowdonia' theatre.
Open Mar-Oct, daily, 10-5 peak season, 10.30-3.30 mid-season & 11-3 low season. Booked tours at other times please ring.
P *(charged)* ⊒ & *(vehicle with chair lift available for tour) toilets for disabled shop* ⌚
Details not confirmed for 1998
Cards: ▨ ▨ ▧ ◉

Dolbadarn Castle
LL55 4UD (A4086)
☎01286 870253
Built by Llywelyn the Great in the early 13th century, this Welsh castle overlooks

➤

Llyn Padarn in the Llanberis pass.
Open all year, late Oct-Mar, daily 9.30-4;
Apr-late Oct 9.30-6.30. Closed 24-26 Dec
& 1 Jan.
Prices not confirmed.
🅿 ✍ ♿
Cards: 💳 💳

Llanberis Lake Railway
Padarn Country Park LL55 4TY (off
A4086)
☎ *01286 870549*
Steam locomotives dating from 1889 to
1948 carry passengers on a four-mile
return journey along the shore of Padarn
Lake. The terminal station is adjacent to
the Welsh Slate Museum, within the
Padarn Country Park. The railway was
formerly used to carry slate.
Open Easter-late Oct. Trains run
frequently every day (ex Sat), 11-4.30 in
peak season. Send for free timetable.
£4 (ch £2.50). Family ticket available.
🅿 *(charged)* 🍴 ♿ *(Disabled carriage*
available) toilets for disabled shop ✍
(train & shop)

Snowdon Mountain Railway
LL55 4TY (on A4086, Caernarfon to Capel
Curig road. 7 1/2 miles from Caernarfon)
☎ *01286 870223 Fax 01286 872518*
Britain's only public rack-and-pinion
railway is operated by five vintage steam
and four modern diesel locomotives, and
a three car diesel electric railcar set. The
journey of just over four-and-a-half miles
takes passengers more than 3000ft up to
the summit of Snowdon; breathtaking
views include, on a clear day, the Isle of
Man and the Wicklow Mountains in
Ireland. The railway was opened in 1896.
The round trip to the summit and back
takes 2 1/2 hours including 1/2 hour at
the summit.
Open 15 Mar-1 Nov, daily from 9am
(weather permitting).
❄*Return £14.50 (ch £10.50). Single*
£10.50 (ch £7.50). Family ticket £40.
Party 15+ (except from July 15 to August
31)
🅿 *(charged)* 🍴 ♿ *(some carriages*
suitable for disabled, wheelchair
available) toilets for disabled shop (not at
peak times)
Cards: 💳 💳 💳 💳 💳

Welsh Slate Museum
Gilfach Ddu LL55 4TY (0.25m off A4086.
The Museum is within Padarn Country
Park at Llanberis)
☎ *01286 870630 Fax 01286 871906*
Until its closure in 1969 the Dinorwic
Quarry was one of the largest in Britain,
employing over three thousand men in its
heyday. The workshops, most of the
machinery and plant have been
preserved, including the foundry and the
Dinorwic water wheel. The museum
which was subsequently founded on the
site includes displays and audio-visual
presentations depicting the life here, and
much of the original atmosphere still
prevails. We have a new shop displaying
traditional crafts - many of which were
made here at the museum by our skilled
craftsmen. Also, restored Chief
Engineer's House, foundry, mess room,
smithy. Craft demonstrations, working
waterwheel, video presentation.
Exhibitions for 1998 include; Slate
Segments (Jan-28 Jun), Kyffin Williams'
Slate Sculptures (4 Jul-4 Oct). Grand Re-
Opening of Heritage Lottery
Developments with fireworks etc, July
(ring for details),Bank Holiday Fair (30-31
Aug), and Winter Fair (29-30 Dec).
Open Mar-Sep, daily 9.30-5.30; Oct-Mar,
Mon-Fri only 10-4. Last admission 1 hour
before closing.
£3 (ch, pen, students, UB40s £1.80)
Family ticket £7.
🅿 *(charged)* ♿ *(nearly all accessible) shop*
Cards: 💳 💳 💳 💳 💳

LLANDUDNO JUNCTION
RSPB Nature Reserve
LL31 9XZ (off A55)
☎ *01492 584091*
A newly-opened reserve with a nature
trail and 3 hides for viewing lapwings and

Steam trains have struggled up Snowdon for almost 100 years on a track that climbed 3140ft in just over 4½ miles. It
operates on a rack and pinion system.

shelduck amongst many others. There is
a visitor centre with a viewing area which
overlooks the estuary and Conwy Castle,
and new facilities planned for the future.
Phone for details of events.
Open daily, 10-5 (or sunset if earlier)
Free.
🅿 ♿ *toilets for disabled shop* ✍
Cards: 💳 💳 💳 💳

LLANFIHANGEL-Y-PENNANT
Castell-y-Bere
☎ *01222 500200*
The castle was begun around 1221 by
Prince Llewelyn ap Iorwerth of Gwynedd
to guard the southern flank of his
principality. Typically Welsh in its design
with its D-shaped towers, it was an
ambitious work with finds of highly
decorated stone proclaiming the castle's
quality and Llewelyn's ambition. Although
a little off the beaten track, the castle lies
in a spectacular setting, overshadowed
by the Cader Idris range.
Open all reasonable times.
Free.
✍ ♿

LLANGOLLEN
Doctor Who Exhibition & Model
Railway World
Lower Dee Exhibition Centre LL20 8RX
(from Llangollen Bridge, 500yds along
road towards Wrexham)
☎ *01978 860584 Fax 01978 861928*
The world's largest collection of Doctor
Who items direct from the BBC, original
costumes, models and Hall of Monsters,
also 'Bessie', the Doctor's car. Model
Railway World illustrates the history of
model railways, from the earliest hand
made models of the 1920s up to the
present day, as well as working layouts
of various sizes, and examples of rolling
stock from around the world. For details
of Doctor Who weekends please
telephone 01978 860533.
Open 10-5. Closed 25/26 Dec & 1 Jan.
Doctor Who Experience £4 (ch £2).
Family ticket £10; Model Railway World
£3 (ch £2). Family ticket £7.50; Boat
Museum £1 (ch 50p). Family ticket £2.
Combination ticket to all attractions £7
(ch £4). Family ticket £17.50.
🅿 🍴 ✗ *shop* ✍
Cards: 💳 💳 💳

Horse Drawn Boats and Canal
Exhibition Centre
The Wharf, Wharf Hill LL20 8TA
☎ *01978 860702 & 01691 75322*

Visitors can enjoy horsedrawn boat trips
along the beautiful Vale of Llangollen, as
well as a fascinating museum illustrating
the heyday of canals in Britain. (NB The
museum has been relocated to the
Doctor Who exhibition approx. 200 yards
from the wharf) The imaginative displays
include working and static models,
photographs, murals and slides. There is
also a narrowboat trip which crosses
Pontcysyllte Aqueduct, the largest
navigable aqueduct in the world.
Open Etr-Oct, daily (limited opening in
Oct).
Museum £1 (ch 70p). Horse Drawn Boat
Trip from £3 (ch £2). Narrowboat Trip
£5.50 (ch £4.50).
P *(400 yds)* 🍴 ✗ *licensed* ♿
(alighting/pick-up point available) toilets
for disabled shop ✍ *(ex guide dogs)*
Cards: 💳 💳 💳 💳

Llangollen Station
(At the junction of the A5 & A539)
☎ *01978 860979 Fax 01978 860979*
The restored Great Western Railway
Station is situated in the town centre and
beside the River Dee. Locomotives and
rolling stock are displayed, and passenger
trains run on a fourteen-and-a-half-mile
round trip between Llangollen and
Carrog. A special coach for the disabled
is sometimes available. Events for 1998
will include Transport Extravaganza
weekends in the Spring and Autumn,
Thomas the Tank Engine weekends,
Santa Specials, and special 'Wine and
Dine' trains on Saturday evenings
(summer only) and Sunday lunchtimes.
Please ring for details of events.
Open - Station wknds, Steam hauled
trains Apr-Oct Sun & daily in Jul & Aug,
diesel trains for some off peak services.
Santa specials during Dec.
Station Free, except for special event
days when charge of £1 (ch 50p) this is
deducted from fare if travelling; Return
Fares 1st class £8.60 (ch £4.50) 2nd class
£6.60 (ch £3). Single Fare 1st class £5.90
(ch £3.70) 2nd class £4 (ch £2).
Pensioners one third reduction.
P *(400 yds) (parking only at Carrog stn)*
🍴 ♿ *(special coach for disabled parties*
on some trains) toilets for disabled shop
(at Llangollen only)
Cards: 💳 💳 💳 💳 💳

Plas Newydd
Hill St
☎ *01978 861314*
The 'Ladies of Llangollen', Lady Eleanor

Butler and Sarah Ponsonby, lived here
from 1780 to 1831. The original stained-
glass windows, carved panels, and
domestic miscellany of two lives are
exhibited along with prints, pictures and
letters.
Open Apr-Oct, daily, 10-5.
❄*Adults £2. Children £1. Family £5. Party*
20+.
🅿 ♿ *toilets for disabled* ✍ *(ex guide dogs*
or in grounds)

Valle Crucis Abbey
LL29 8DD (on B5103, off A5 W of
Llangollen)
☎ *01978 860326*
Set in a deep, narrow valley, the abbey
was founded for the Cistercians in 1201
by Madog ap Gruffydd. Substantial
remains of the church can be seen, and
some beautifully carved grave slabs have
been found. There is a small exhibition on
the Cistercian monks and the abbey.
Open all year, Apr-Sep, daily 10-5; Oct-
Mar 9.30-4. (Closed 24-26 Dec & 1 Jan)
Prices not confirmed.
🅿 ♿ *shop* ✍ ♿

LLANGYBI
St Cybi's Well
☎ *01766 810047*
Cybi was a sixth-century Cornish saint,
known as a healer of the sick, and St
Cybi's Well (or Ffynnon Gybi) has been
famous for its curative properties through
the centuries. The corbelled beehive
vaulting inside the roofless stone
structure is unique in Wales.
Open at all times.
Free.
♿ ✍ ♿
Cards: 💳 💳

LLANRWST
Gwydir Uchaf Chapel
(0.5m SW off B5106)
☎ *01492 640578*
Built in the 17th century by Sir John
Wynn of Gwydir Castle, the chapel is
noted for its painted ceiling and
wonderfully varied woodwork.
Open all year, Mon-Fri 8.30-4.
Free.
🅿 ♿ ✍ ♿
Cards: 💳 💳

LLANUWCHLLYN
Bala Lake Railway
The Station LL23 7DD (off the A494 Bala
to Dolgellau road)
☎ *01678 540666 Fax 01678 540666*

Steam locomotives which once worked in the slate quarries of North Wales now haul passenger coaches for four-and-a-half miles from Llanuwchllyn Station along the lake to Bala. The railway has one of the four remaining double-twist lever-locking framed GWR signal boxes, installed in 1896. Some of the coaches are open and some closed, so passengers can enjoy the beautiful views of the lake and mountains in all weathers; the latest corridor coach has facilities for the disabled. Please telephone for details of Special Events, including Children's Fun Weekend (18-19 Jul), and Santa's annual visit to the Railway (5-6 Dec).
Open Easter to 4 Oct, daily (except certain Mon & Fri in Apr, May, Jun and Sept)
£6.00 return. Family ticket £13. Senior Citizens £5
(wheelchairs can be taken on train) shop

LLANYSTUMDWY
Lloyd George Memorial Museum & Highgate Victorian Cottage
LL52 0SH (on A497 between Pwllheli & Criccieth)
01766 522071
Visitors can explore the life and times of David Lloyd George in this museum. His boyhood home is recreated as it would have been when he lived there between 1864 and 1880, along with his Uncle Lloyd's shoemaking workshop. Also Highgate Cottage's Victorian garden. There will also be temporary exhibitions and activities. Please contact Museum for details.
Open Etr, daily 10.30-5; May, Mon-Fri 10.30-5; June, Mon-Sat 10.30-5; Jul-Sep daily 10.30-5; Oct, Mon-Fri, 11-4. Other times by appointment, telephone 01286 679098 or 01766 522071 for details.
£2.50 (ch & pen £1.50). Family ticket £6.00.
(wheelchair access in garden, with assistance) toilets for disabled shop (ex guide dogs)
Cards:

PENARTH FAWR
Penarth Fawr
(3.5m NE of Pwllheli off A497)
01766 810880
The hall, buttery and screen are preserved in this house which was probably built in the 15th century.
Open at all times.
Free.

PENMACHNO
Penmachno Woollen Mill
LL24 0PP (2m off A5, between Llangollen/Betws-Y-Coed)
01690 710545
The 17th-century quarrymen and farmers wore flannel shirts made from cloth woven by local cottage weavers. The cloth was washed and finished in the Pandy (fulling mill). Power looms introduced in the 19th century now weave lightweight tweed and rug cloth. The Story of Wool exhibition explains the process and its history, and there is a mill shop and cafe. In June there is a sheep shearing competition and sheepdog trial sponsored by Penmachno Wollen Mill.
Open daily 10-5.30; Nov-Feb open 10-4.30.
Free.
shop

Ty Mawr
(From A5 3m S of Betws-y-coed take B4406 to Penmachno. House is 2.5m NW of Penmachno by forest road)
01690 760213
Situated in the beautiful and secluded Wybrnant valley, Ty Mawr was the birthplace of Bishop William Morgan (1545-1604), the first translator of the entire Bible into Welsh. The house has been restored to its probable 16th-17th century appearance and includes a display of Welsh Bibles, including William Morgan's Bible of 1588. The Wybrnant Nature Trail, a short walk, covers approximately one mile from the house and back.
Open 2 Apr-Sep, Thu-Sun & BH Mons 12-5; Oct-1 Nov, Thu, Fri & Sun 12-4. Last admission 30 mins before closing.
£2 (ch £1). Family ticket £5. Party.
(ex grounds)

PLAS-YN-RHIW
Plas-yn-Rhiw
LL53 8AB (12m from Pwllheli signposted from B4413 to Aberdaron)
01758 780219
House with gardens and woodlands down to the sea on west shore of Porth Neigwl (Hell's Mouth Bay). This is a small manor house, part medieval, with Tudor and Georgian additions and ornamental gardens with flowering trees and shrubs including sub-tropical specimens, divided by box hedges and grass paths. There is a stream and waterfall, rising behind to the snowdrop wood. 31 July-Open air Shakespeare 'Richard III'.
Open 27 Mar-19 May, Thu-Mon noon-5; mid May-Sep, Wed-Mon noon-5; last admission 1/2 hr before closing.
toilets for disabled shop
Details not confirmed for 1998

PORTHMADOG
Ffestiniog Railway
Harbour Station LL49 9NF (SE end of town, on the A487)
01766 512340 Fax 01766 514576
Narrow gauge steam railway running for 13.5 miles through Snowdonia National Park, between Porthmadog and Blaenau Ffestiniog. Breathtaking views, superb scenery. Buffet service on all trains including licensed bar (in corridor carriages). Comfortable seating, some trains heated, toilet facilities on corridor carriages. A Railway Museum is situated within the harbour station. Special events during 1998 will include Friends of Thomas the Tank Engine Weekends, Vintage Weekend and Santa Specials. Please telephone for details.
Open late Mar-early Nov, daily service and also 26 Dec-1 Jan. Weekend service Nov-Dec (most days). Limited service Feb & Mar. Museum open when trains operating.
Full distance return £12.80 (1 child free with each adult). Other fares available. Museum donations welcomed.
(charged) licensed (Wheelchair ramps recently installed) toilets for disabled shop (closed 24/25 Dec)
Cards:

PORTMEIRION
Portmeirion
LL48 6ET (Off A487 at Minffordd)
01766 770228 Fax 01766 771331
Welsh architect Sir Clough Williams Ellis built his fairy-tale, Italianate village on a rocky, tree-clad peninsula on the shores of Cardigan Bay. The nucleus of the estate is a sumptuous waterfront hotel, rebuilt from the original house and containing a fine 18th-century fireplace and a library moved here from the Great Exhibition of 1851. A bell-tower, castle and lighthouse mingle with a watch-tower, grottoes and cobbled squares among pastel-shaded picturesque cottages let as holiday accommodation. A number of shops sell a variety of goods and the whole village is set in 175 acres of sub-tropical coastal cliff and wooded gardens.
One of the finest wild gardens in Wales is here - the 60-acre Gwyllt Gardens. They include miles of dense woodland paths and are famous for their fine displays of rhododendrons, azaleas, hydrangeas and sub-tropical flora. There is a mile of sandy beach and a playground for children. Toll-paying visitors can see the place where Noel Coward wrote 'Blithe Spirit', and the location for the cult TV series 'The Prisoner'.
Open all year, daily 9.30-5.30.
£3.70 (ch £1.90, pen £3.20). Party 20+.
licensed toilets for disabled shop garden centre
Cards:

RHUDDLAN
Rhuddlan Castle
LL18 5AD
01745 590777
The castle was begun by Edward I in 1277, on a simple 'diamond' plan with round towers linked by sections of 9ft thick curtain wall. The moat was linked to a deep-water canal, allowing Edward's ships to sail from the sea to the castle.
Prices not confirmed.
Open May-Sep, 10-5.
shop

TAL-Y-CAFN
Bodnant Garden
LL28 5RE (8m S of Llandudno & Colwyn Bay on A470)
01492 650460 Fax 01492 650448
Situated above the River Conwy with beautiful views over Snowdonia, these gardens are a delight. They were first laid out in 1875 but in 1900 the 2nd Lord Aberconway started to improve them dramatically. Five terraces in the Italian style were constructed below the house, and between two large, existing cedars he placed a lily pool. On the lowest terrace is a canal pool with an open-air stage at one end and a reconstructed Pin Mill at the other.
Part of the grounds have been made into a beautiful woodland garden in a sheltered valley. This is notable for its rhododendrons and other delicate shrubs. There are also many azaleas, a rock garden, and a laburnum walk. Contact for details of open air theatre.
Open 4 Mar-end Oct, daily 10-5 (last admission half hour before closing)
£4.60 (ch £2.30). Party 20+
(steep in places with many steps not easy for wheelchairs) toilets for disabled shop garden centre (ex harnessed guide dogs)

TREFRIW
Trefriw Woollen Mill
LL27 0NQ (on B5106 in centre of Trefriw)
01492 640462
Fax 01492 640462
Established in 1859, the mill is situated beside the fast-flowing Afon Crafnant, which is used to drive two hydro-electric turbines to power the looms. All the →

Transformed from a large cottage. Plas Newydd was created between 1780 and 1829 into a fantasy of timber, oriel windows and stained glass by the 'Ladies of Llangollen'.

Portmeirion is a fantasy village of colour-washed houses created among the grey slate villages of Gwynedd by the architect Clough Williams-Ellis in the 1920s.

machinery of woollen manufacture can be seen here: blending, carding, spinning, dyeing, warping and weaving. The mill produces traditional Welsh bedspreads and tweeds, and there is a large shop selling its products. In the Weaver's Garden, there are plants traditionally used in the textile industry, mainly for dyeing. Hand-spinning demonstrations.
Mill open Etr-Oct, Mon-Fri 10-5. Weaving demonstrations & turbine house: open all year, Mon-Fri 10-5.
Free (ex school parties which must be pre-booked).
P (35 yds) ☕ & shop (Specialises in woven goods) ✿ (in shop & grounds, not mill)

TYWYN
Talyllyn Railway
Wharf Station LL36 9EY (A493 Machynlleth to Dolgellau for Tywyn station, B4405 for Abergynolwyn)
☎01654 710472 Fax 01654 711755
This is the oldest 27in-gauge railway in the world. It was built in 1865 to run from Tywyn on Cardigan Bay to Abergynolwyn slate mine some seven miles inland. The railway was also the first to be saved by a voluntary preservation society, after the slate quarry closed in 1947. The railway climbs the steep sides of the Fathew Valley and on the way there are stops at Dolgoch Falls or to allow passengers to visit the Nant Gwernol forest. The train takes 2 hours and 30 minutes to cover the round trip. The original 1865 locomotive and coaches which opened the line is still in regular operation together with restored locomotives and coaches from other narrow guage railways. The Rev. Awdry's Peter Sam regularly works the line. All scheduled passenger trains are steam hauled. Special events include Rolt Vehicle Rally (25 May), Victorian Week (2-83 Aug), 'Race the Train' charity competition (15 August). Nearly 1,000 runners follow the track and usually as many as 100 will beat the train. Also a Land rover Rally (30 August), Peter Sam's Birthday (31 Aug). Please phone for details of these and other events.
Open 22 Feb-29 Mar, Sun only; 30 Mar-31 Oct, daily. Xmas holiday sevice 26 Dec-2 Jan. Timetable available.
£8 return ticket (ch accompanied £2). Intermediate fares available.
P (charged) & (prior arrangement useful) toilets for disabled shop
Cards: ▨ ▨ ▨

WREXHAM
Erddig
LL13 0YT (off the A525, 2m S of Wrexham and the A483/A5152 Oswestry road)
☎01978 355314 Fax 01978 313333
Owned by the National Trust, Erddig is a treasure house of furnishings, utensils and tools of a country house since the 1700s. Built in 1680, the house was enlarged and improved during the next half century by a wealthy London lawyer with a passion for gilt and silver furniture. The house still has its original furnishings including a magnificent state bed in Chinese silk.
The house is especially notable for the view it gives of both 'upstairs' and 'downstairs' life. There is a range of restored outbuildings which show the workings of the laundry, the bakehouse - where bread is still baked - and the estate smithy and sawmill.
The gardens are unusual in that they have been very little changed since the 18th century. Special events for 1998 include: Open air Shakespeare, open air opera and jazz, family fun days and Teddy Bears' Picnic. Please ring for details.
Open 21 Mar-2 Oct, Sat-Wed (open Good Friday), house 12-5, garden 11-6 (Jul-Aug gardens 10-6); 3 Oct-1 Nov, Sat-Wed, house 12-4, garden 11-5.
All inclusive tickets inc: Family rooms, below stairs, outbuildings & gardens £5.60 (ch £2.80). Party 15+. Below stairs, outbuildings & garden £3.60 (ch £1.80) Family ticket (2 adults & 2 ch) £9.00. National Trust members free.
P ✗ licensed & toilets for disabled shop ✿ (ex guidance dogs) ▨
Cards: ▨ ▨ ▨ ▨

MID WALES

This region includes the counties of Carmarthenshire, Ceredigion, Pembrokeshire and Powys.

ABERAERON
Llanerchaeron
SA48 8DG (2m E of Aberaeron off A482)
☎01545 570200 Fax 01545 571759
A rare survivor of the core of a Welsh gentry estate. Aquired by The National

Trust in 1994 having received minimal maintenance in recent decades. Parts of the property are open to visitors to see restoration work in progress at this early stage.
Open 2 Apr-4 Oct, Thu-Sun & BH Mons 11-5. Last admission 30 mins before closing. Park open all year dawn to dusk.
£2 (ch £1). Family ticket £5. Party.
P & toilets for disabled ✿ (ex on lead) ▨

ABERCRAF
Dan-Yr-Ogof Showcaves
SA9 1GJ (midway between Swansea & Brecon on A4067)
☎01639 730284 Fax 01639 730293
Winner of twelve major tourism awards, Dan-Yr-Ogof Showcave is the longest in Britain. Cathedral Showcave is the largest single chamber in any British showcave and Bone Cave was home to man 3,000 years ago. There is also a Dinosaur Park, an Iron Age village, museum, craft shop and new Shire Horse Heritage Centre.
Open Apr-Oct, daily from 10am. Please telephone for Oct.
£5.95 (ch £4).
P & toilets for disabled shop
Cards: ▨ ▨ ▨ ▨ ⓢ

ABERGWILI
Carmarthen Museum
SA31 2JG (2m E of Carmarthen, on A40)
☎01267 231691
Fax 01267 223830
Housed in the old palace of the Bishop of St David's and set in seven acres of grounds, the museum offers a wide range of local subjects to explore, from geology and prehistory to butter making and pottery and Welsh furniture and folk art. There are Roman and medieval displays, and temporary exhibitions are held.
Open all year, Mon-Sat 10-4.30. (Closed Xmas-New Year).
Free.
P ☕ & toilets for disabled shop ✿ (ex guide dogs)

ABERYSTWYTH
National Library of Wales
Penglais Hill SY23 3BU (off Penglais Hill, A487 in the Northern portion of Aberystwyth)
☎01970 623816
Fax 01970 615709
The huge library is one of Britain's six copyright libraries, and specialises in Welsh and Celtic literature. It has maps, manuscripts, prints and drawings, as well

as books in all languages. A major permanent exhibition 'A Nation's Heritage' is on view and there is a programme of travelling exhibitions. Please telephone for details.
Open all year, exhibitions, library & reading rooms Mon-Fri 9.30-6, Sat until 5. (Closed BH's & first wk Oct).
Free.
P ☕ & toilets for disabled shop ✿

AMROTH
Colby Woodland Garden
SA67 8PP (1.5 miles inland from Amroth beside Carmarthen Bay, follow brown signs from A471)
☎01834 811885
The tranquillity and seclusion of this sheltered valley combined with the splendour of the woodland garden makes Colby one of the most beautiful National Trust properties in Pembrokeshire. There are many pleasant meadow and woodland walks. From early spring to the end of June the garden is a blaze of colour, from the masses of daffodils to the rich hues of rhododendrons, azaleas and bluebells. Events for 1998 include: Rare Plant Sale (14 June); Family Fun Days (16 Apr, 28 May, 27 Aug); Shakespeare in the Meadow -'Taming of the Shrew' (June ring to confirm date), Alice in Wonderland in the Meadow (August ring to confirm date). End of season plant sale (23 Aug).
Open Apr-Oct, daily 10-5. Walled garden Apr-30 Oct 11-5. Last admission 30 mins before closing.
£2.80 (ch £1.40). Family ticket £7. Pre-booked parties £2.30 (ch £1.15) NT members free.
P ☕ & (Limited due to terrain) toilets for disabled shop ✿ ▨
Cards: ▨ ▨ ▨

BRECON
Brecknock Museum
Captain's Walk LD3 7DW (Near centre of town on junction of The Watton & Glamorgan St.)
☎01874 624121
Fax 01874 611281
A wealth of local history is explored at the museum, which has archaeological and historical exhibits, with sections on folk life, decorative arts and natural history. There is a 19th-century Assize Court and one of the finest collections of Welsh Lovespoons. A full exhibition programme - particularly of work by local artists - is planned for 1998, including Brecknock's Historic Houses Revisited (14 Mar-26 Apr), Jennifer Conway's Country Collection (2 May-7 Jun), Glyn Morgan; Fifty Year's Work (7 Mar-7 Jun), Watercolour Society of Wales (13 Jun-31 Jul), Jazz Festival Exhibition (Aug). Art 2000 - By Mystic Birth, an exhibition for Christmas (Dec-early Jan).
Open all year, Mon-Fri 10-5, Sat 10-1 & 2-5, closed 4 Nov-Feb. (also open Sun Apr-Sep) . Closed Good Fri & 25/26 Dec & 1 Jan.
Free.
P & (limited parking, must be accompanied by able-bodied) toilets for disabled shop ✿ (ex guide dogs)

South Wales Borderers (24th Regiment) Museum Museum
The Barracks, The Watton LD3 7EB (close to town centre, well signed)
☎01874 613310
Fax 01874 613275
This is the museum of the South Wales Borderers and Monmouthshire Regiment, which was raised in 1689 and has been awarded 23 Victoria Crosses. Amongst the collections is the Zulu War Room, devoted to the war and in particular to the events at Rorke's Drift, 1879, when 121 men fought 4500 Zulus.
Open all year, Apr-Sep daily; Oct-Mar, Mon-Fri 9-1 & 2-5. (Closed Xmas & New Year).
£1 (ch 16 50p). Subject to Review.
P (town centre) & (Ramp access from main road) shop ✿ (ex guide dogs)
Cards: ▨ ▨ ▨

CAPEL BANGOR
Rheidol Hydro Electric Power Station & Visitor Centre
Cwm Rheidol SY23 3NF (Off A44 at Capel Bangor)
☎01970 880667 Fax 01970 880670
A guided tour of the power station can be taken. It lies in a secluded valley, and other facilities include a fish farm, forest walks and a lakeside picnic area. There is a visitor centre.
Open Apr-Oct, daily 10-4 for tours of the Power Station & visitor centre.
Free.
🅿 ♿ toilets for disabled

CAREW
Carew Castle & Tidal Mill
SA70 8SL (on A4075, 4m E of Pembroke)
☎01646 651657 & 651782
Fax 01646 651782
This magnificent Norman castle - later an Elizabethan residence - has royal links with Henry Tudor and was the setting for the Great Tournament of 1508. Special events for the year include theatre interpretation, a schools programme, holiday activities and concerts - details available spring 1998. Nearby is the Carew Cross (Cadw), an impressive 13ft Celtic cross dating from the 11th century. Carew is one of only four restored tidal mills in Britain, with records dating back to 1558. The fine four-storey building houses a theatre showing an introductory film, and there are talking points explaining the milling process. A permanent exhibition 'The Story of Milling' - milling through the ages. Events for 1998 include a theatre interpretation and holiday activities. Please telephone for details.
Open Etr-Oct, daily 10-5.
✳£2.50 (ch & pen £1.60).Family ticket £6.50. Single ticket (castle or mill) £1.70 (ch £1.20).
🅿 ♿ (ramps) toilets for disabled shop
Cards: 🔲 🔲 🔲

CARREG CENNEN CASTLE
Carreg Cennen Castle
SA19 6UA (unclassified road from A483 to Trapp village)
☎01558 822291
A steep path leads up to the castle, which is spectacularly sited on a limestone crag. It was first built as a stronghold of the native Welsh and then rebuilt in the late 13th century. Most remarkable among the impressive remains is a mysterious passage, cut into the side of the cliff and lit by loopholes. The farm at the site has a rare breeds centre and a tea room.
Open all year, late Oct-late Mar, daily 9.30-4; late Mar-late Oct daily 9.30-6.30.(9.30-8 Jun-Aug). Closed 24-26 Dec & 1 Jan.
✳£2.20 (reductions £1.70). Family ticket £6.
🅿 ♿ shop
Cards: 🔲 🔲

CILGERRAN
Cilgerran Castle
SA43 2SF (off A484 & A478)
☎01239 615007
Set picturesquely above a gorge of the River Teifi - famed for its coracle fishermen - Cilgerran Castle dates from the 11th to 13th centuries. It decayed gradually after the Civil War, but its great round towers and high walls give a vivid impression of its former strength.
Open all year, late Oct-late Mar, daily 9.30-4; late Mar-late Oct daily 9.30-6.30. Closed 24-26 Dec & 1 Jan.
Prices not confirmed.
♿ shop
Cards: 🔲 🔲

CRYMYCH
Castell Henllys Fort
Pant-Glas, Meline SA41 3UT (Off A487 between Eglwyswrw and Newport Pembrokeshire)
☎01239 891319 Fax 01239 891319
This Iron Age hill fort is set in the beautiful Pembrokeshire Coast National Park. Excavations began in 1981 and three

roundhouses have been reconstructed. A forge, smithy, and looms can be seen, with other attractions such as trails and a herb garden. Special events for 1998 include exhibitions by local Craft Guild during school holidays, story telling days of Celtic Mythology, Iron Age Craft workshops. Please telephone for details.
Open Apr-late Oct, daily 10-5. Last entry 4.30
✳£2.50 Adult (ch & pen £1.60) Family £6.50
🅿 ♿ toilets for disabled shop
Cards: 🔲 🔲

DRE-FACH FELINDRE
Museum of the Welsh Woollen Industry
SA44 5UP (16m W of Carmarthen off the A484, 4m E of Newcastle Emlyn)
☎01559 370929 Fax 01559 371592
The museum is housed in the former Cambrian Mills and has a comprehensive display tracing the evolution of the industry from its beginnings to the present day. Demonstrations of the fleece to fabric process are given on 19th-century textile machinery. Special events: please telephone.
Open all year, Apr-Sep, Mon-Sat 10-5; Oct-Mar, Mon-Fri 10-5. (Closed 24-26 Dec & 1 Jan). Evening visits by prior arrangement.
✳£2.50 (ch £1.50, pen/students/UB40 £1.50). Family ticket £6.50.
🅿 ♿ (Wheelchair access to ground floor & ample seating) toilets for disabled shop garden centre (ex galleries)
Cards: 🔲 🔲 🔲

DRYSLWYN
Dryslwyn Castle
(on B4279)
☎01222 500200
The ruined 13th-century castle was a stronghold of the native Welsh. It stands on a lofty mound, and was important in the struggles between English and Welsh. It is gradually being uncovered by excavation.
Open - entrance by arrangement with Dryslwyn Farm.
Free.
🅿

EGLWYSFACH
RSPB Nature Reserve
Cae'r Berllan SY20 8TA (6m S of Machynlleth on A487 in Eglwys-Fach. Signposted from main road)
☎01654 781265 Fax 01654 781328
Lying at the head of the Dyfi estuary off the A487 Machynlleth to Aberystwyth

road this grazed saltmarsh is bordered by freshwater marsh and some remnant peat bogs. The reserve covers 1043 acres. In the oakwoods are pied flycatchers, redstarts, wood warblers, nut hatches, and both great spotted and lesser spotted woodpeckers. Goldcrests and coal tits prefer the conifers and sedge and grasshopper warblers the marshland. Buzzards, kestrels and sparrowhawks breed in the wood whilst redbreasted mergansers and common sandpipers frequent the river. Peregrines can be seen all year while Merlins and hen harriers hunt over the reserve during the winter. Wigeon and a small flock of Greenland white-fronted geese winter here. Badgers and polecats live here and there are many species of butterfly. Phone for an events leaflet.
Open daily, 9am-9pm (or sunset if earlier). Visitor Centre & shop: Mar-Oct 9-5; Nov-Feb 10-4 (ex Fri)
✳£2 (ch 50p, concessions £1.50) Family £5.
🅿 ♿ shop
Cards: 🔲 🔲 🔲 🔲

FELINWYNT
Felinwynt Rainforest & Butterfly Centre
Rhosmaen SA43 1RT (from A487 Blaenannerch Airfield turning, turn onto B4333. Signposted)
☎01239 810882 Fax 01239 810882
A chance to wander amongst free-flying exotic butterflies accompanied by the recorded wildlife sounds of the Peruvian Amazon. A waterfall, ponds and streams contribute to a humid tropical atmosphere and provide a habitat for fish and native amphibians. See the exhibition of rainforests of Peru and around the world. Free paper and crayons to borrow for children.
Open daily first Sunday May-end of Sep, 10.30-5.
£2.75 (ch 4-14 £1 pen £2.50)
🅿 ♿ shop (ex guide dogs)

GWBERT-ON-SEA
Cardigan Island Coastal Farm Park
SA43 1PR (off Cardigan bypass at Aberystwyth junc, go into Cardigan, right at Gwbert junc, follow rd for 3m)
☎01239 612196
A beautiful farm park located right on the cliff tops opposite Cardigan Island, which is just 200 yards offshore. The island is a Dyfed Wildlife Trust Nature Reserve, and is home to many species of birds. A colony of Atlantic grey seals breed in the

many caves below the park, and can be seen at close quarters for most of the year. Bottle-nosed dolphins can often be seen as they chase the salmon up the nearby Teifi Estuary. Rare choughs nest on the cliffs. The farm park has a variety of friendly farm animals that can be hand-fed, including sheep, goats, llama, ducks, geese, pigs, ponies, rare breed cattle and a donkey! Say 'G'day' to Bruce the wallaby. October is the month that seal pups are born, and can often be seen from the safely-fenced cliffs.
Open all year; 9am-7pm (dusk in winter). Some animals may be removed during the winter due to inclement weather.
✳£1 coin per head through automatic coin-operated turnstile. (ch under 3 free).
🅿 ♿ (very limited access) (dogs must be on leads)

KIDWELLY
Kidwelly Castle
SA17 5BQ (via A484)
☎01554 890104
This is an outstanding example of late-13th-century castle design, with its 'walls within walls' defensive system. There were later additions made to the building, the chapel dating from about 1400. Of particular interest are two vast circular ovens.
Open all year, late Oct-late Mar, Mon-Sat 9.30-4, Sun 11-4; late Mar-late Oct, daily 9.30-6.30. Closed 24-26 Dec & 1 Jan.
✳£2.20 (reductions £1.70). Family ticket £6.
🅿 ♿ toilets for disabled shop
Cards: 🔲 🔲

Kidwelly Industrial Museum
Broadford SA17 4LW (signposted from Kidwelly by-pass)
☎01554 891078
Two of the great industries of Wales are represented in this museum: tinplate and coal mining. The original buildings and machinery of the Kidwelly tinplate works, where tinplate was hand made, are now on display to the public. There is also an exhibition of coal mining with pit-head gear and a winding engine, while the more general history of the area is shown in a separate exhibition.
Open Etr, Jun-Aug, PH wknds, Mon-Fri 10-5, Sat-Sun 2-5. Last admission 4pm (5pm Jul-Aug). Other times by arrangement for parties only.
Free.
🅿 ♿ toilets for disabled shop (ex in grounds)

Perched on the edge of a 330ft limestone cliff, Carreg Cennan Castle is all that a castle should be – even as a ruin.

LAMPHEY
Lamphey Palace
SA71 5NT (off A4139)
☎01646 672224
This ruined 13th-century palace once belonged to the Bishops of St Davids.
Open May-Sep, daily 10-5. Access at other reasonable times.
Free.
🅿 ♿ *toilets for disabled shop* ⚘ 😊

LAUGHARNE
Dylan Thomas' Boat House
Dylans Walk SA33 4SD (14m W of Carmarthen)
☎01994 427420 Fax 01554 747501
Under Milk Wood was written here by Wales's most prolific 20th-century poet and writer. The waterside house, set on the 'heron priested' shore of the Taf estuary, contains much original furniture, family photographs, an art gallery and displays on the life and works of Dylan Thomas. There is an audio-visual presentation available. Nearby is the writing shed where Dylan Thomas actually wrote so many of his well-known poems and short stories.
Open all year, May-Oct, daily 10-5; Nov-Apr, daily 10.30-3.
£2 (ch & pen £1, ch under 7 free). Party 5+
P *(10mins walk)* 🍽 *shop* ⚘ *(ex guide dogs)*
Cards: 💳 💳 💳

Laugharne Castle
King St SA33 4SA
☎01994 427906
Newly opened to the public, picturesque Laugharne Castle stands on a low ridge overlooking the wide Taff Estuary. A medieval fortress converted into an Elizabethan mansion, it suffered a civil war siege and later became the backdrop for elaborate Victorian gardens, now recreated. Laugharne Castle has also inspired two modern writers - Richard Hughes and Dylan Thomas.
Open May-Sep, 10-5 daily.
P *(150 mtrs)* ♿ *toilets for disabled shop* ⚘ 😊
Details not confirmed for 1998
Cards: 💳 💳

LLANDEILO
Dinefwr Park
SA19 6RT (
☎01558 823902 Fax 01558 822036
At the heart of Welsh history for a thousand years, the Park as we know it today took shape in the years after 1775, when the medieval castle, house, gardens, woods and deer park were integrated into one vast and breathtaking landscape. Footpaths through the park lead to the castle, bog wood and beech clumps and have outstanding views of the Towy Valley. Access to Church Woods and Dinefwr Castle is through the landscaped park. Ground floor and basement of Newton House are open. Rare White Park Cattle in Park.
Open 2 Apr-1 Nov, daily (ex Tue & Wed) 11-5. Last admission 30 mins before closing. Park is open during daylight hours in winter.
Free.
🅿 🍽 ♿ *toilets for disabled shop* ⚘ *(ex outer park on lead)* 🐕

LLANELLI
WWT Llanelli
Penclacwydd, Llwynhendy SA14 9SH (3m E of Llanelli, off A484)
☎01554 741087
Fax 01554 741087
A wide variety of wild birds, including Oystercatcher, Redshank, Curlew, Little Egret and occasionally Osprey, can be seen during the right season on the stunning reserve at WWT Llanelli, an internationally important wetland site set in the shadow of a traditional industrial area. The grounds are beautifully landscaped and as visitors walk round, they may well be joined by friendly Hawaiian Geese. Other features include a closed circuit television system transmitting pictures of wild birds on the

reserve, a wetland craft area and a flock of colourful Caribbean Flamingos. Facilities for the disabled include easy access on level paths throughout the grounds, special viewing areas, free wheelchair loan and purpose-built toilets. Special programme of events and activities. Please telephone for details.
Open summer 9.30-5.30, winter 9.30-4.30. Closed 24-25 Dec.
❄*£3.75 (ch £2.25). Family ticket £9.75. Party 10+.*
🅿 ♿ *toilets for disabled shop* ⚘
Cards: 💳 💳 💳 💳 💳

LLANFAIR CAEREINION
Welshpool & Llanfair Light (Steam) Railway
SY21 0SF (beside A458)
☎01938 810441 Fax 01938 810861
The Llanfair Railway is one of the Great Little Trains of Wales - the nearest to England. It offers an 8-mile trip through glorious scenery by narrrow-gauge steam train. The line is home to a collection of engines and coaches from all round the world. Please ring for details fo special events in 1998.
Open Etr-29 Sep, wknds; Etr, May Day BH, Spring BH wk; 18 Jun-11 Jul, Tue-Thu; 15 Jul-6 Sep, daily. Trains from Llanfair at 10.30, 1.30 & 4.15pm; from Welshpool 11.45, 2.45 & 5.15. Extra trains at BHs. 1998 Times to be Finalised.
£7.50 return (ch 5-15 £3.75). Family ticket £17.
🅿 🍽 ♿ *(two coachs adapted for wheelchairs) toilets for disabled shop*
Cards: 💳 💳 💳

LLANSTEFFAN
Llansteffan Castle
(off B4312)
☎01267 241756
The ruins of this 11th-to 13th-century stronghold stand majestically on the west side of the Towy estuary.
Open - access throughout the year.
Free.
⚘ 😊

LLANYCEFN
Penrhos Cottage
SA66 7XT (Near Maenclochog & Llanycefn, N of Haverfordwest.)
☎01437 731328 Fax 01437 731743
Local tradition has it that cottages built overnight on common land could be claimed by the builders, together with the ground a stone's throw away from the door. This thatched cottage is an example, built with help from friends and family; and it remained in the same family from the time it was built until the late 1960s, when the county council bought it. Its character has been maintained, and it gives the visitor an insight into traditional Welsh country life. Various outbuildings complete the picture.
Open mid May-Sep Mon-Fri, by appointment only. Tel: 01437-731328.
❄*£1.50 (ch, pen 75p).*
P *(roadside)* ♿ *shop* ⚘ *(ex in grounds or guide dogs)*

LLAWHADEN
Llawhaden Castle
☎01437 541201
The castle was first built in the 12th century to protect the possessions of the bishops of St David's. The 13th-and 14th-century remains of the bishops' hall, kitchen, bakehouse and other buildings can be seen, all surrounded by a deep moat.
Open at all times. Key keeper arrangement.
Free.
♿ ⚘ 😊

MACHYNLLETH
Celtica
Y Plas, Aberystwyth Rd SY20 8ER (2 minutes walk S of town clock. Car park entrance off Aberystwyth Rd)
☎01654 702702 Fax 01654 703604
Located in a restored mansion house, Celtica is an exciting heritage centre introducing the history and culture of the

Celtic people. The sights and sounds of Celtic life are brought alive in the Celtica exhibition as you go on an unforgettable journey portraying the Celtic spirit of the past, present and future. There is also an interpretive centre dedicated to Welsh and Celtic history, a children's indoor play area, and conference and meeting rooms. Education resources are available and groups are welcome. Storytelling, puppet shows, lectures, music and craft events are planned for 1998. Telephone for further details.
Open daily 10-6 (last admission 4.40). Evening opening for pre-booked groups. Closed 24/25 Dec.
£4.65 (concessions £3.50). Family ticket £12.75.
🅿 🍽 ✖ *licensed* ♿ *(Lift & ramps to public areas; Induction loop) toilets for disabled shop (Celtic theme)* ⚘ *(ex guide dogs)*
Cards: 💳 💳 💳 💳 💳

Centre for Alternative Technology
SY20 9AZ (2.5m N on A487)
☎01654 702400 Fax 01654 702782
The Centre for Alternative Technology is an internationally renowned display centre, promoting practical ideas and information on sustainable technologies. The exhibition includes displays of wind, water and solar power, organic gardens, low-energy dwellings, and a unique water-powered railway which ascends a 200ft cliff from the car park. The Wave Tank and the underground 'Mole-Hole' are particularly popular with children. There is a restaurant and bookshop on site. Educational services and residential courses are available.
Open Mar-Oct; 10-5.30; Nov-Feb; 11-4. Closed 23-26 Dec & 5-23 Jan.
❄*Mar, Apr & Oct £4.95 (ch £2.75, concessions £3.75). Family ticket £13.95. May-Sep £5.50 (ch £2.75, concessions £3.75). Family ticket £14.50. Nov-Feb £3.95 (ch £2.30, concessions £3). Family ticket £10.95.*
🅿 🍽 ♿ *(wheelchair available) toilets for disabled shop* ⚘ *(ex guide dogs)*
Cards: 💳 💳 💳 💳 💳

MONTGOMERY
Montgomery Castle
☎01222 500200
Initially an earth and timber structure guarding an important ford in the river Severn, Montgomery was considered a 'suitable spot for the erection of an impregnable castle' in the 1220s. Even though building and modifications continued until 1251-53, the final conquest of Wales by Edward I meant the castle lost much of its role. In the 16th century, one of the first brick houses in Wales was built within the inner ward and during the Civil War a fierce battle was fought for possession of the castle.
Open all year, any reasonable time.
Free.
♿ ⚘ 😊

NARBERTH
Oakwood Park
Canaston Bridge SA67 8DE (signposted off the A40, between Carmarthen and Haverfordwest at Canaston Bridge. Take A4075 for 2m)
☎01834 891373 891376
Fax 01834 891380
The activities offered here are numerous and include treetops rollercoaster, pirate ship, boating lake, waterfall and bobsleigh rides, miniature trains, go-karts and assault courses and a theatre show. There is a huge undercover Playland as well as an outdoor children's theme park playtown. Plus 'Megafobia', Europe's largest wooden rollercoaster, Vertigo, a 140 foot skycoaster, Snake River Falls, Europe's first watercoaster. Also new are gold panning in Jakestown and new puppet show in Jakestown Music Hall. The smallest rollercoaster in the west for children is found in Playtown, the Kiddiecoaster. See the animals at Cuddle Farm. Late night opening end July-end August, with Caribbean entertainment in the tropical paradise of Coconut Creek, complete with palm trees, six piece steel band, barbeque and Slippy Joe's Beach Bar. Western style food and entertainment is available in the saloon in Jakestown. Please telephone for details.
Open 4 Apr-27 Sept 1998 daily from 10am. Adults & ch over 10 £9.95; ch 3-9yrs £8.95, under 2 free, pen & disabled £7.95. Party 20+. Family ticket £35.95.
🅿 🍽 ✖ *licensed* ♿ *toilets for disabled shop* ⚘ *(ex guide dogs)*
Cards: 💳 💳 💳

NEWPORT
Pentre Ifan Burial Chamber
(3m SE from B4329 or A487)
☎01222 500200
Found to be part of a vanished long barrow when excavated in 1936-37, the remains of this chamber include the capstone, three uprights and a circular forecourt.
Open - access throughout the year.
Free.
⚘ 😊

PEMBROKE
The Museum of the Home
7 Westgate Hill SA71 4LB (Opposite Pembroke Castle)
☎01646 681200
A pleasant domestic setting provides an opportunity to view some of the objects that have been part of everyday life over the past three hundred years.
Open May-Sep, Mon-Thu 11-5, other times by arrangement.
£1.20 (ch & pen 90p).
P *(100 yards) (Public Pay & Display)* ⚘

Pembroke Castle
SA71 4LA (west end of Main St)
☎01646 681510
Fax 01646 622260
This 12th-to 13th-century fortress has an impressive 80ft-high round keep. There is

also a new Interpretative Centre with introductory video and Pembroke Yeomanry exhibition.
Open all year, daily, Apr-Sep 9.30-6; Mar & Oct 10-5; Nov-Feb, 10-4. (Closed 25-26 Dec & 1 Jan).
£2.95 (ch under16 & pen £1.95, ch under5 & wheelchairs free). Family ticket £8.
P (200 yds) ☕ ♿ toilets for disabled shop (must be on leads)
Cards:

PONTERWYD

Llywernog Silver-Lead Mine
Llywernog Mine SY23 3AB (11m E of Aberystwyth on A44)
☎01970 890620 Fax 01545 570823
The Llywernog Silver-Lead Mine is an award-winning family attraction located high up in the beautiful Cambrian Mountains of Mid Wales. Visitors can safely explore tunnels and chambers dating from the 18th century and see veins of silver-lead ore running through the rocks. At surface, the old mine buildings contain exhibitions which tell the colourful story of the 'boom days', and heritage collections of old tools, working water wheels and quaint machinery. Children (and adults) can pan for silver and 'fools gold' and operate simple pumps and equipment. Rocks, mineral specimens and mining souvenirs can be purchased at the shop, together with locally-made silver jewellery.
Open Etr-Oct, daily 10-6 (Oct 5pm). Last admission 1 1/2 hours before closing time. Nov-Dec Tue/Wed/Thurs 11am-dusk.
£4.50 (ch 5-15 £2.85, pen & students £3.85). Family ticket (2 adults, 3 children) £14.
P ☕ ♿ shop
Cards:

PRESTEIGNE

The Judge's Lodging
Broad St LD8 2AD (on B4362)
☎01544 260650/1 Fax 01544 260652
A stunningly restored Victorian town house with integral courtroom, cells and service areas. Visitors step back into the 1870s, accompanied by an 'evesdropping' audiotour of voices from the past, featuring the voice of Robert Hardy. The trappings of the 1870s are all around, from the Judge's chair to his chamberpot! Please contact for details of special events, which will include Living History re-enactment weekends, Servants Evenings, Dinner Parties, Victorian Cookery Classes, etc.
Open daily, Mar-Apr 10-4; May-Oct 10-6. Closed Nov-Feb.
£3.50 (ch & concessions £2.50). Party.
P ♿ (lift, disabled pack for inaccesible items) shop

PUMSAINT

Dolaucothi Gold Mines
SA19 8US
☎01558 650359
Here is an opportunity to spend a day exploring the gold mines and to wear a miner's helmet and lamp while touring the underground workings. The information centre and a walk along the Miners' Way disclose the secrets of 2000 years of gold mining. A unique blend of history and beauty, this is the only place in Britain where the Romans mined gold.
Open Apr-Sep, Sat-Wed 10-5. (Jul-Aug daily 10-5). Guided underground tours: 16 May to 13 Sep.
Property admission, site: £3 (ch £1.50) Family ticket £7.50. NT members free. Guided underground tours £3.50 (ch £1.75) Family ticket £8.50. NT members: £2 (ch £1). All inclusive family ticket £15.
P ☕ shop (on leads, but not on tours)
Cards:

ST DAVID'S

St Davids Bishop's Palace
SA62 6PE (on A487)
☎01437 720517
These extensive and impressive ruins are all that remain of the principal residence of the Bishops of St Davids. The palace shares a quiet valley with the cathedral, which was almost certainly built on the site of a monastery founded in the 6th century by St David. The Bishop's Palace houses an exhibition: 'Lords of the Palace'.
Open all year, late Oct-late Mar, Mon-Sat, 9.30-4, Sun 2-4; late Mar-late Oct, daily 9.30-6.30. Closed 24-26 Dec & 1 Jan.
Prices not confirmed.
P ♿ toilets for disabled shop
Cards:

St David's Cathedral
The Close SA62 6PE
☎01437 720202 Fax 01437 721885
Begun 1181 on the site reputed to be where St David founded a monastic settlement in the 6th century. The present building was altered during the 12th to the 14th centuries and again in the 16th. It also has an extension added in 1993, so the the archictecture is varied. The ceilings oak, painted wood and stone vaulting are of considerable interest. The floor of the nave slopes a metre over its length while the entire length of the cathedral the difference is four metres.
Open all year 8.30-6.
Suggested donation of £2.00.
P (300yds) ☕ ♿ toilets for disabled shop (ex guide dogs)

ST FLORENCE

Manor House Wildlife & Leisure Park
Ivy Tower SA70 8RJ (on B4318)
☎01646 651201 Fax 01646 651201
The park is set in 35 acres of delightful wooded grounds and award-winning gardens. The wildlife includes exotic birds, reptiles and fish. Also here are a pets' corner, a children's playground, amusements and radio-controlled models. Other attractions include a giant astraglide slide, a go-kart track and model railway exhibition. There are falconry displays daily. Daily Events Timetable includes: 11:00 Bottle Feeding, 11:30 Penguin and other Feeding, 12:30 Snake Experience, 2:00 Falconry Displays, 3:00 Snake Experience, 4:00 Bottle Feeding, 5:00 Penguin and Otter Feeding. Ring for details.
Open Etr-Sep, daily 10-6.
**£3.50 (ch £2.50, pen £3, disabled/helpers £2.50) Family ticket (2 adults, 2 children) £11. Party 20+.*
P ☕ ♿ toilets for disabled shop garden centre

SCOLTON

Scolton Manor Museum
SA62 5QL (5m N of Haverfordwest, on B4329)
☎01437 731328 (Mus) & 731457 (Park) Fax 01437 731743
Scolton Manor Museum is situated in Scolton Country Park. The early Victorian mansion and refurbished stables and the large exhibition hall illustrate the history and natural history of Pembrokeshire. There are new displays in the House and Stables, plus an adjacent 'Pembrokeshire Railways' exhibition. Within the mansion are period rooms on three floors. The 60 acres of grounds have fine specimen trees and shrubs and informal areas are managed as a nature reserve. Environmentally friendly Visitor Centre, alternative energy and woodland displays, guided walks, children's play areas, demonstrations and various Country Park events. Please telephone for details.
Open; Museum Apr-Oct, Tue-Sun & BH's 10.30-5.30; Country Park all year ex 25 & 26 Dec, Etr-Sep 10-7, Oct-Etr 10-4.30.
**Museum: £1.50 (ch, pen 75p). Country Park car park £1 all day.*
P (charged) ☕ ♿ (disabled parking area near house) toilets for disabled shop (ex guide dogs & in grounds)

STRATA FLORIDA

Strata Florida Abbey
SY25 6BT (unclassified road from Pontrhydfendigaid, reached from B4340)
☎01974 831261
Little remains of the Cistercian abbey founded in 1164, except the ruined church and cloister. Strata Florida was an important centre of learning in the Middle Ages, and it is believed that the 14th-century poet Dafyd ap Gwilym was buried here.
Open all year, Oct-Mar at all times; Apr-Sep daily 10-5.
Prices not confirmed.
P ♿ shop
Cards:

TALLEY

Talley Abbey
(B4302 from Llandeilo)
☎01558 685444
Only beautiful ruins now remain of this once magnificent abbey, including two pointed archways set in the remains of the north and east walls of the church's central tower. The abbey was founded in 1197 by Rhys ap Gruffudd, and was virtually destroyed in the uprising led by Owain Glyndwr.
Open all year, late Oct-late Mar, Mon-Sat 9.30-4, Sun 2-4; late Mar-late Oct, daily 9.30-6.30. Closed 24-26 Dec & 1 Jan. Key keeper arrangement.
Prices not confirmed.
P
Cards:

TENBY

Tenby Museum & Art Gallery
Castle Hill SA70 7BP (Near the centre of town on Castle Hill)
☎01834 842809 Fax 01834 842809
The museum is situated on Castle Hill. It covers the local heritage from prehistory to the present in galleries devoted to archaeology, geology, maritime history, natural history, militaria and bygones. The art gallery concentrates on local associations with an important collection of works by Augustus and Gwen John. There is a new art gallery featuring temporary exhibitions and a new local history display explores the 'Religious Life on Caldey Island'. Forthcoming exhibition for 1998: 'Portraits by Augustus John' (4 Apr-30 Oct). Special displays to celebrate the museum's 120th anniversary.
Open all year, Etr-Oct, daily 10-5; Nov-Etr, Mon-Fri 10-5.
£1.50 (ch 75p, concessions £1). Family ticket £3.
P (5 mins walk) ♿ shop (ex guide dogs)

Tudor Merchant's House
Quay Hill SA70 7BX
☎01834 842279
Recalling Tenby's history as a thriving and prosperous port, the Tudor Merchant's house is a fine example of gabled 15th-century architecture. There is a good Flemish chimney and on three walls the remains of frescoes can be seen. A small herb garden has been created.
Open 2 Apr-Sep, Mon-Tue, Thu-Sat 10-5, Sun 1-5. 1-31 Dec Mon-Tue, Thu-Fri 10-3, Sun 12-3.
£1.80 (ch 90p). Groups £1.40 (ch 70p). NT members free.
P (500yds) (no coaches nearby) (garden could be accessed) (ex guide or small dogs)

TRETOWER

Tretower Court & Castle
NP8 2RF (3m NW of Crickhowell, off A479)
☎01874 730279
The castle is a substantial ruin of an 11th-century motte and bailey, with a three-storey tower and 9ft-thick walls. Nearby is the Court, a 14th-century fortified manor house which has been altered and extended over the years. The two buildings show the shift from medieval castle to more domestic accommodation over the centuries, and an audio-cassette tour is available.
Open Mar, daily 10-5; Apr-late Oct, daily 10-6.
Prices not confirmed.
P ♿ toilets for disabled shop
Cards:

WELSHPOOL

Powis Castle
SY21 8RF (1m S of Welshpool, signposted off A483)
☎01938 554338 Fax 01938 554336
The world famous Garden, overhung with enormous clipped yew trees, shelters rare and tender plants in colourful herbaceous borders. Laid out under the influence of the Italian and French styles, the Garden retains its original lead statues, an Orangery and an aviary on the terraces. Perched on a rock above the Garden terraces, the medieval castle contains one of the finest collections of paintings and furniture in Wales. It was originally built as a fortress by Welsh princes and was later adapted and enriched by generations of Herberts and Clives. The beautiful collection of treasures from India displayed in the Clive Museum includes textiles armour, bronzes, jade, ivory, and a magnificent tent. Please telephone for details of special events, which include concerts, plays, walks, and craft demonstrations.
Open Castle & museum: 1 Apr-28 Jun and 2 Sep-1 Nov, Wed-Sun 1-5; Jul-Aug Tue-Sun 1-5; Open all Bank Hol's in season. Garden is open same days as castle and museum 11-6. Last admission to all parts is 30 mins before closing.
Castle, Museum & Gardens £7.50, (ch under 17 £3.75) Family ticket £18.75. Group member £6.50. Garden only: £5 (ch £2.50) Family £12.50, Group member £4. NT members & ch under 5 free.
P ✕ licensed ♿ toilets for disabled shop garden centre (ex guide dogs)

SOUTH WALES

This region includes the counties of Blaenau Gwent, Bridgend, Caerphilly, Cardiff, Merthyr Tydfil, Monmouthshire, Neath Port Talbot, Newport, Rhondda Cynon Taff, Swansea, Torfaen and Vale of Glamorgan.

ABERDULAIS

Aberdulais Falls
SA10 8EU (from M4 junct 43, take A465, signposted Vale of Neath)
☎01639 636674
Fax 01639 645069
For over 300 years this famous waterfall has provided the energy to drive the wheels of industry. Nestling amongst the site's historic remains, a unique hydro-electric scheme has been developed to harness this great natural resource. The Turbine House provides visitor access to the top of the falls, with views of the power equipment, fish pass and displays. A special lift has been installed to allow disabled visitors access to roof level with excellent views of the Falls and the new water wheel. Please contact for details of special events for 1998.
Open: March: Sat & Sun 11am-4pm only. 1 Apr-1Nov Mon-Fri 10am-5pm, Sat, Sun & Bank Hols 11am-6pm (last admission 30 mins before closing). Winter openongs: Christmas shop open Nov & Dec, Tues-Sun 10am-4pm.
£2.80 (ch £1.40) Family ticket £7. July/Aug special offer-one child (16 or under) with each adult. Parties 15+. NT members free.
P ☕ ♿ (lift for disabled to view falls) toilets for disabled shop (on leads)

BARRY

Welsh Hawking Centre
Weycock Rd CF62 3AA (on A4226)
☎01446 734687
There are over 200 birds of prey here, including eagles, owls and buzzards as well as hawks and falcons. They can be seen and photographed in the mews and some of the breeding aviaries, and there are flying demonstrations at regular intervals during the day. A variety of ➔

tame, friendly animals, such as donkeys, goats, pigs, lambs, cows and rabbits will delight younger visitors.
Open all year, daily 10.30-5, 1hr before dusk in winter. (Closed 25 Dec).
🅿 🖱 🔥 *shop* ❀
Details not confirmed for 1998
Cards: ◨ ▩

BLAENAVON
Big Pit Mining Museum
NP4 9XP (M4 Exit J26/25, follow signs along A4042 & A4043 to Pontypool & Blaenavon. Signposted off A465)
☎ 01495 790311
Fax 01495 792618
The 'Big Pit' closed as a working mine in 1980, but today visitors can don safety helmets and cap lamps, and descend the 300ft shaft to find out what life was like for generations of miners in South Wales. There is an exhibition in the old pithead baths and a reconstructed miner's cottage can also be seen. Stout shoes and warm clothes are recommended.
Open Mar-Nov, daily 9.30-5, last tour 3.30. Dec-Feb telephone for opening details.
❋*Underground & surface £5.50 (ch £3.75, pen £5.25). Family ticket £16. Surface only £1.75 (ch £1, OAPs £1.50)*
🅿 🖱 🔥 *(underground tours by prior arrangement) toilets for disabled shop (Welsh crafts, books & publications) (not on underground tours)*
Cards: ◨ ▩ ▨

Blaenavon Ironworks
North St
☎ 01495 792615
The Blaenavon Ironworks were a milestone in the history of the Industrial Revolution. Constructed in 1788-99, they were the first purpose-built multi-furnace ironworks in Wales. By 1796, Blaenavon was the second largest ironworks in Wales, eventually closing down in 1904. Visitors can now view much of the work site including the impressive water balance tower and 'Stack Square', a rare survival of ironworkers' housing dating from 1792.
Open May-Sep, Mon-Sat 11-5, Sun 2-5. Prices not confirmed.
🅿 ❀ ♿
Cards: ◨ ▩

BRIDGEND
Newcastle
☎ 01656 659515
The small castle dates back to the 12th century. It is ruined, but a rectangular

tower, a richly carved Norman gateway and massive curtain walls enclosing a polygonal courtyard can still be seen.
Open - accessible throughout the year. Key keeper arrangement.
Free.
🅿 ❀
Cards: ◨ ▩

CAERLEON
Caerleon Fortress Baths, Amphitheatre & Barracks
NP6 1AE (on B4236)
☎ 01663 422518
Caerleon was an important Roman military base, with accommodation for thousands of men. The foundations of barrack lines and parts of the ramparts can be seen, with remains of the cookhouse, latrines and baths. The amphitheatre nearby is one of the best examples in Britain. The Fortress Baths were excavated in the 1970s and represent the most complete example of a Roman legionary bath building in Britain.
Open all year, late Mar-late Oct daily 9.30-6.30; late Oct-late Mar, Mon-Sat 9.30-4, Sun 2-4. (Closed 1 Jan & 24-26 Dec).
Prices not confirmed.
🅿 🔥 *shop* ❀ ♿
Cards: ◨ ▩

Roman Legionary Museum
High St NP6 1AE (Situated 10mins from the M4/Severn Bridge. Take Junction 25 from the M4 onto the B4596)
☎ 01633 423134 Fax 01633 422869
The museum illustrates the history of Roman Caerleon and the daily life of its garrison. On display are arms, armour and equipment, with a collection of engraved gemstones, a labyrinth mosaic and Roman finds from the legionary base at Usk. Please telephone for details of children's holiday activities.
Open all year, 15 Mar-15 Oct, Mon-Sat 10-6, Sun 2-6; 16 Oct-14 Mar, Mon-Sat 10-4.30, Sun 2-4.30. (Closed 25 & 26 Dec).
❋*£2 (ch & concessions £1.20). Joint ticket available with Roman Baths & Amphitheatre £3 (ch £1.80)*
P (100yds) 🔥 *toilets for disabled shop* ❀
(ex guide dogs)
Cards: ◨ ▩ ▨ ▩ ◪

CAERPHILLY
Caerphilly Castle
CF8 1JL (on A469)
☎ 01222 883143
The concentrically planned castle was begun in 1268 by Gilbert de Clare and

completed in 1326. It is the largest in Wales, and has extensive land and water defences. A unique feature is the ruined tower - the victim of subsidence - which manages to out-lean even Pisa! The south dam platform, once a tournament-field, now displays full sized working replica medieval siege-engines, while fascinating exhibitions can be seen.
Open all year, late Mar-late Oct, Mon-Sat 9.30-4, Sun 11-4; late Mar-late Oct, daily 9.30-6.30. Closed 24-26 Dec & 1 Jan.
❋*£2.20 (reduced £1.70). Family ticket £6*
🅿 🔥 *shop* ❀ ♿
Cards: ◨ ▩

Llancaiach Fawr Manor
Gelligaer Rd, Nelson CF46 6ER (M4 Junction 32, A470 to Merthyr Tydfil. then toward Ystrad Mynach A472 follow brown tourist signs)
☎ 01443 412248 Fax 01443 412688
Step back in time to the exciting Civil War period at this fascinating living history museum. The year is 1645 and you are invited into the Manor to meet the servants of 'Colonel' Edward Prichard - from the puritanical to the gossipy. Please telephone for details of special events for 1998.
Open all year, Mon-Fri 10-3.30 (last admission), Sat 12-4.30 (last admission).Sundays 12pm-4pm.
£4.10 (ch £2.75, concessions £2.85). Family ticket £11.95. Sunday Special offer: Tour of the Manor & Sun.lunch. Adults £6, Ch.£4
🅿 🖱 ✕ *licensed* 🔥 *(lift in visitor centre to audio visual show) toilets for disabled shop* ❀ *(ex in grounds)*
Cards: ◨ ▩ ▨

CAERWENT
Caerwent Roman Town
(off A48)
☎ 01222 500200
A complete circuit of the town wall of 'Venta Silurum', together with excavated areas of houses, shops and a temple.
Open - access throughout the year.
Free.
❀ ♿

CALDICOT
Caldicot Castle, Museum & Countryside Park
NP6 4HU (from M4 junct 23 or M48 junct 2. Signposted from both A48 and B4245)
☎ 01291 420241
Fax 01291 435094
Caldicot Castle's well-preserved fortifications were founded by the Normans and fully developed, in royal hands, by the late 14th century. Restored as a family home by a wealthy Victorian, the castle offers the chance to explore medieval walls and towers in a setting of tranquil gardens and wooded Country Park.
Open Mar-Oct, Mon-Fri 10.30-5, Sat & BH 10.30-5, Sun 1.30-5.
£1.50 (ch, pen & student 85p). Party 10+. Pre-booked educational parties - free. Free for residents of Monmouthshire county.
🅿 🖱 🔥 *toilets for disabled shop*
Cards: ▨

CARDIFF
Cardiff - the capital city of Wales - has been a prominent town since Roman times and Cardiff Castle dates back 1,900 years. The castle, having been magnificently refurbished in the 19th century, reflects Cardiff's history as a flourishing industrial city and port. The city's wealth depended on coal mining, iron and steel works and tinplate mills. Today it is a flourishing commerical city with an exciting cultural base. The castle is a stone's throw from one of the finest civic centres in Britain

and from a fine shopping centre with a colourful covered market reputed to have the finest wrought-iron structure since the Crystal Palace. At its heart is a magnificent 2,000-seat concert hall with a worldwide reputation. There are thousands of acres of beautiful parks in the city offering a lovely riverside walk to Llandaff Cathedral as well as several excellent museums illustrating life in Wales.

Cardiff Castle
Castle St CF1 2RB (City Centre)
☎ 01222 878100
Fax 01222 231417
The Norman castle was built on the site of a Roman fort, and Roman walls some 10ft thick can still be seen. There is also a Norman keep and a 13th-century tower. Apartments were started in the 15th century, but the present-day character of the castle comes from its transformation in the 19th century, when the immensely rich 3rd Marquess of Bute employed William Burges to restore and rebuild it. Together they created a romantic fantasy of a medieval castle, decorated with wall paintings, tapestries and colourful carvings of birds, animals, knights and ladies. Also here are the military museums of the Royal Regiment of Wales and Queen's Dragoon Guards.
Open all year, daily (ex Xmas & New Year BH's). Royal Regiment of Wales Museum, Wed pm, Thu-Sat. Queen's Dragoon Guards Museum, Mon-Tue, Wed am, Sat-Sun. Conducted tours Mar & Oct, daily 10-12.30 & 2-4 (Castle closes 5pm). Apr-Sep, daily 10-12.40 & 2-5 (Castle closes 6pm); Nov-Feb daily 10.30-3.15 (Castle closes 4.30pm). Only short tours when functions in progess. Conducted tours all year.
P (200 yds) 🖱 🔥 *toilets for disabled shop* ❀ *(ex in grounds)*
Details not confirmed for 1998

Dyffryn Gardens
St Nicholas CF5 6SU (6m W of city centre off A48)
☎ 01222 593328
Fax 01222 591966
'A Garden for all Seasons', describes Dyffryn, one of Wales' finest landscaped gardens. The beautiful grounds offer an endless variety of colour and form with many small theme gardens, a heather bank, arboretum and glass houses. The 55 acres also include a kitchen garden. Various events are held throughout the year including craft fairs and music and arts festivals. There will also be numerous musical and theatrical presentations. Please telephone for details.
Open all year, 10am-dusk
£3 (ch & pen £2). Family ticket £6.50. Party 20+.
🅿 🖱 ✕ *licensed* 🔥 *(wheelchairs, parking) toilets for disabled shop garden centre*
Cards: ◨ ▩ ▨

Llandaff Cathedral
Llandaff CF5 2YF (A48 off M4)
☎ 01222 564554
A medieval cathedral begun in the 12th century on the site of an early Christian place of worship. The cathedral was severely damaged during the bombing raids on Cardiff during World War II. The interior is dominated by a modernistic post-war 'Christ in Majesty' sculpture by Epstein.
Open all year.
🅿 🖱 ✕ 🔥 *(Wheelchair available) toilets for disabled shop* ❀ *(ex guide dogs)*
Details not confirmed for 1998

Restored and rebuilt in the 19th century, Cardiff Castle is a romantic fantasy of a medieval castle

National Museum Of Wales (Main Building)
Cathays Park CF1 3NP (Situated in Cathays Park in the heart of Cardiff)
☎01222 397951 Fax 01222 373219
The National Museum and Gallery Cardiff is sure to have something to spark your interest. Its unique amongst British museums and galleries in its range of art and science displays.
The Art Galleries provide magnificent settings for works by some of the world's most famous artists, including the Impressionists in the outstanding Davies collection.
'The Evolution of Wales' exhibition takes you on a spectacular 4600 million year journey, tracing the development of Wales and the world from the very beginning of time.
In the 'Natural History of Wales' exhibition you can see birds, animals and plants at the seashore and visit woods in the summer and winter.
There are displays of Bronze Age gold, early Christian monuments, Celtic treasures, silver, coins and medals, ceramics, fossils and minerals, as well as exciting temporary exhibitions. Princes as Patrons (31 Jul-8 Nov), Children's activities in the school holidys, Summer Fun (8-9 Aug), Christmas Event (Dec).
Open all year, Tue-Sun 10-5. (Closed Mon (ex BHs), 24-25 Dec).
❋£3.25 (ch & concessions £2). Family ticket £7.50.
🅿 (charged) ✗ licensed ♿ (wheelchair available) toilets for disabled shop ❀ (ex guide dogs)
Cards: 🖃 🖃 🖃 🖃 🖃

Techniquest
Stuart St CF1 6BW (Junction 33 from M4, Follow A4232 to Cardiff Bay)
☎01222 475475 Fax 01222 482517
Located in the heart of the Cardiff Bay redevelopment area, here you will find science and technology made accessible - and fun - at Britain's leading hands-on discovery science centre, where visitors of all ages can participate in the activities and experiment with the exhibits. See yourself as others see you, instead of the mirror-image you are used to.
Understand how aircraft fly . . . Techniquest makes it easy. Special events take place throughout the year. Great fun for all the family. Please telephone for details of dates.
Open all year (ex Xmas), Mon-Fri 9.30-4.30; Sat-Sun & BH's 10.30-5.
❋£4.50 (ch 5-16 & concessions £2.50). Family ticket £11.50.
🅿 💺 ♿ (lift) toilets for disabled shop ❀ (ex guide dogs)
Cards: 🖃 🖃 🖃 🖃 🖃

CHEPSTOW
Chepstow Castle
NP6 5EZ
☎01291 624065
Built by William FitzOsbern soon after the Norman Conquest, Chepstow is the first recorded Norman stone castle. It was used as a base for advances into Wales, and stands in a strategic spot above the Wye. Not only could it easily be defended, but it also overlooked a harbour. The castle was strengthened in the following centuries, but was not besieged (as far as is known) until the Civil War, when it was twice lost to the Parliamentarians. The remains of the domestic rooms are evidence of past splendour, and the massive gatehouse with its portcullis grooves and ancient gates is still impressive, as are the walls and towers with their variety of slots for arrows and guns. An extension of the castle was the Port Wall, which ran round the town. An exhibition, 'Chepstow - A Castle at War', provides visitors with an insight into the building of the medieval castle and its role in the Civil War.
Open all year, late Oct-late Mar Mon-Sat 9.30-4, Sun 11-4; late Mar-late Oct daily 9.30-6.30. (Closed 24-26 Dec & 1 Jan).
❋£3 (reductions £2) Family ticket £8.
🅿 ♿ shop ❀ ♨
Cards: 🖃 🖃

Chepstow Museum
Gwy House, Bridge St NP6 5EZ (opposite Chepstow Castle car park)
☎01291 625981
Fax 01291 625983
Now set out in a fine 18th-century house, the museum has exhibitions of the history of Chepstow, the lower Wye Valley and the surrounding area. Exhibition themes change regularly. Special facilities, activities and information is available to pre-booked groups in the education resource centre, nearby. Contact the Education Resource Officer at Chepstow Museum for more details. Chepstow Festival Summer Exhibition July - September.
Open Jan-Jun & Oct-Dec, Mon-Sat 11-1 & 2-5, Sun 2-5; Jul-Sep, Mon-Sat 10.30-1 & 2-5.30, Sun 2-5.30.
❋£1 (ch free if accompanied, pen 75p). Party. Pre booked educational groups free.
P (opposite) (Charged parking) ♿ toilets for disabled shop ❀ (ex guide dogs)

CILFREW
Penscynor Wildlife Park
SA10 8LF (Leave M4 at Junction 43 onto A465. Park is 2 1/2 miles N of Neath)
☎01639 642189
Fax 01639 635152
Tropical birds, penguins, meerkats, and parrots are seen here in an attractive setting among trees, streams and ponds, where visitors can also feed rainbow trout or see their tropical relatives, touch or hold the animals in the Zoo Centre, feed llamas and donkeys, and walk in the farmyard. A chair lift goes to the cliff top for the alpine ride (summer only), and there is a children's playground.
Open all year, daily 10-6, dusk in winter. (Closed 25 Dec).
🅿 💺 ♿ toilets for disabled shop ❀
Details not confirmed for 1998

COITY
Coity Castle
CF35 6BG
☎01656 652021
A 12th-to 16th-century stronghold, with a hall, chapel and the remains of a square keep.
Open all year, at all times. Key keeper arrangement.
Free.
P ❀ ♨

CRYNANT
Cefn Coed Colliery Museum
SA10 8SN (1m S on A4109)
☎01639 750556
Fax 01639 750556
The museum is on the site of a former working colliery, and tells the story of mining in the Dulais Valley. A steam-winding engine has been kept and is now operated by electricity, and there is also a simulated underground mining gallery, boilerhouse, compressor house, and exhibition area. Outdoor exhibits include a stationary colliery locomotive. Forest walks and picnic sites nearby. Exhibitions relating to the coal mining industry are held on a regular basis.
Open daily, Apr-Oct 10.30-5; Nov-Mar, groups welcome by prior arrangement.
❋£2.50 (ch & pen £1.25) ch under 5 & registered disabled free. Party 10+.
🅿 💺 ♿ toilets for disabled shop
Cards: 🖃 🖃

CWMBRAN
Greenmeadow Community Farm
Greenforge Way NP44 5AJ (Follow signs for Cwmbran then brown tourist signs (with sheep on) to farm)
☎01633 862202
Fax 01633 489332
Just four miles from the M4, this is one of Wales' leading farm attractions - milking demonstrations, tractor and trailer rides, dragon adventure play area, farm trail, nature trail and lots more. Phone for details of lambing weekends, shearing, country fair and agricultural shows, Halloween and Christmas events.
Open summer 10-6, winter 10-4. Closed 25 Dec.

Adult £3 (ch £2.25) Family (2 adults & 3 children) £10.
Prices not confirmed.
🅿 💺 ✗ licensed ♿ (tractor & trailer rides for wheelchair users) toilets for disabled shop

CWMCARN
Cwmcarn Forest Drive
NP6 (8m N of Newport on A467, Junction 28 off M4)
☎01633 400205
Fax 01633 400135
A seven-mile scenic drive with spectacular views over the Bristol Channel and surrounding countryside. Facilities include barbecues, picnic and play areas, and forest and mountain walks. The area is run by the Forest Enterprise. Special events are being held throughout the year. Please telephone for details.
Open Good Friday-Oct, daily 11-7
🅿 ♿ shop
Details not confirmed for 1998

CYNONVILLE
South Wales Miners Museum
Afan Argoed Country Park SA13 3HL (on A4107 6 miles NE of Port Talbot, leave M4 at Junction 40.)
☎01639 850564 & 850875
The picturesquely placed museum gives a vivid picture of mining life, with coal faces, pit gear and miners' equipment. Guided tours of the museum on request. The country park has forest walks and picnic areas, and a visitor centre.
Open all year daily, Mar-Sep 10.30-6, (5pm rest of year).
🅿 (charged) 💺 ✗ ♿ (mechanical & manual wheel chairs on request) toilets for disabled shop ❀
Details not confirmed for 1998

GROSMONT
Grosmont Castle
(on B4347)
☎01981 240301
Grosmont is one of the 'trilateral' castles of Hubert de Burgh (see also Skenfrith and White Castle). It stands on a mound with a dry moat, and the considerable remains of its 13th-century great hall can be seen. Three towers once guarded the curtain wall, and the western one is well preserved.
Open - access throughout the year.
Free.
♿ ❀ ♨

LLANRHIDIAN
Weobley Castle
SA3 1HB (from B4271 or B4295)
☎01792 390012
A 12th-to 14th-century fortified manor house with an exhibition on the history of Weobley and other historic sites on the Gower peninsula.
Open all year, late Oct-late Mar, Mon-Sat 9.30-4, Sun 2-4; late Mar-late Oct, daily 9.30-6.30. (Closed 24-26 Dec & 1 Jan).
Prices not confirmed.
🅿 ♿ shop ❀
Cards: 🖃 🖃

LLANTHONY
Llanthony Priory
☎01222 500200
In the early 12th century William de Lacey discovered the remains of a hermitage dedicated to St David, built six centuries earlier; by 1108 a church had been consecrated on the site and just over a decade later the priory was complete. Forty years after an uprising in 1135, when the priory was brought to a state of seige, Hugh de Lacey provided the funds for a new church, and it is this that makes the picturesque ruin seen today. Its architectural styles range from Norman to Early English, and the visitor can still make out the west towers, north nave arcade and south transept. The former priest's house is part of a hotel. The priory is reached by narrow roads through lovely scenery.
Open - access throughout the year.
Free.
🅿 ♿ toilets for disabled ❀ ♨

LLANTILIO CROSSENNY
Hen Gwrt
(off B4233)
☎01222 500200
The rectangular enclosure of the former medieval house, still surrounded by a moat.
Open - access throughout the year. Free.
⚠ ♿ ⚒

MARGAM
Margam Park
SA13 2TJ (Junction 38 off M4, follow signs approx. 300yards on A48 towards Pyle)
☎01639 881635 Fax 01639 895897
Margam Park's 850 acres of open parkland and forest are full of natural and historic treasures. The castle and abbey ruins, the waymarked walks, gardens and adventure playground, all go toward a memorable day out for the visitor. Fairytale Land, road train and farm train, a large hedge maze, a fallow deer herd and the Margam Orangery, the largest of its kind in Britain, add to the appeal of this notable beauty spot.
Open all year, Apr-Sep daily 10-6 (last admission 5pm). Oct-Mar, Wed-Sun 10-5 (last admission 3pm).
⚠ 🍴 ✗ *licensed* ♿ *(free wheelchair loan, garden for disabled) toilets for disabled shop*
Details not confirmed for 1998

MERTHYR TYDFIL
Brecon Mountain Railway
Pant Station Dowlais CF48 2UP (2.5m NE to the N of A465)
☎01685 722988 Fax 01685 384854
After eight years of planning and construction, this narrow-gauge railway was opened in 1980. It follows part of an old British Rail route which was closed in 1964 when the iron industry in South Wales fell into decline. The present route starts at Pant Station, three miles north of Merthyr Tydfil, and continues for 3.5 miles through the beautiful scenery of the Brecon Beacons National Park, as far as the two-and-a-half-mile long Taf Fechan reservoir. The train is pulled by a vintage steam locomotive, a delight in itself, and for lovers of vintage locomotives the workshops at Pant Station are well worth a visit. The display includes engines built in Germany and the USA as well as Great Britain, and some have spent their days on railways in far-flung corners of the earth.
Opening times on application to The Brecon Mountain Railway, Pant Station, Merthyr Tydfil.
✽*Fares are under review, please ring for details.*
⚠ 🍴 ♿ *(adapted carriage) toilets for disabled shop*

Cyfarthfa Castle Museum & Art Gallery
Cyfarthfa Park CF47 8RE (off A470,N towards Brecon, follow brown signs.)
☎01685 723112 Fax 01685 722146
The home of the Crawshay family, who took over the Cyfarthfa Ironworks which employed 1,500 men by the turn of the 19th century, is an imposing Gothic mansion. It was built in 1825 and the magnificent gardens, designed at around the same time, still survive today. The state rooms are given over to a museum which not only covers the social and industrial life of the area, but also houses collections of fine and decorative art, natural history items, archaeology and Egyptology.
Apr-Oct: Mon-Sun 10-6 (last admission 5.30). Oct-March: Mon-Sun 10-3.30 (last admission 3)
⚠ 🍴 ♿ *(stair lift & wheelchair available) toilets for disabled shop* ♒ *(ex guide dogs)*
Details not confirmed for 1998

Ynysfach Iron Heritage Centre
Ynysfach Rd CF48 1AG (off main road from Cardiff to Brecon, behind Merthyr College)
☎01685 721858 Fax 01685 721858
This heritage centre once housed the beam-blowing engine of the Ynysfach Iron Works. Exhibitions in the superbly restored building introduce the history of Merthyr Tydfil's once-famed iron industry with an 18-minute audio-visual programme narrated by actor Philip Madoc, full-size models of ironworkers, maps and photographs.
Open Mar-Oct, Mon-Fri 10-5, wknds & BH 2-5. Nov-Feb, Mon-Fri 10-5. (Closed wknds & Xmas).
⚠ 🍴 *shop* ♒
Details not confirmed for 1998

MONMOUTH
Nelson Museum & Local History Centre
New Market Hall, Priory St NP5 3XA (Town centre)
☎01600 713519
The bulk of the Nelson Museum collection was formed by Lady Llangattock who lived near Monmouth. On show are commemorative glass, china, silver, medals, books, models, prints and the prize exhibit: Admiral Nelson's fighting sword. The local history displays deal with Monmouth's past as a fortress market town in the Wye Valley, and include a section on the co-founder of the Rolls Royce company, Charles Stewart Rolls, who was also a pioneer balloonist, aviator and, of course, motorist. Exhibition to commemorate 200th anniversary of the Battle of the Nile, July and August 1998.
Open all year, Mon-Sat 10-1 & 2-5; Sun 2-5. Closed Xmas & New Year.
✽*£1 (pen, students 75p) accompanied ch under 18 free.*
P *(200 yds)* ♿ *shop* ♒ *(ex guide dogs)*
Cards: 💳

NEATH
Neath Abbey
SA10 7DW
☎01639 812387
These ruins were originally a Cistercian abbey founded in 1130 by Richard de Grainville.
Open at all times. Key keeper arrangement.
Free.
⚠ ♿ ♒ ⚒

NEWPORT
Tredegar House & Park
Coedkernew NP1 9YW (2m W, signposted from A48/M4 junc.28)
☎01633 815880 Fax 01633 815895
Tredegar was home to one of the greatest of Welsh families, the Morgans, later Lords Tredegar, for over five centuries, but for years their house has remained relatively unknown. Today it stands out as one of the most magnificent 17th-century houses in Britain. A tour of the interior vividly illustrates what life was like for the Morgans and their servants, giving visitors a fascinating insight into life 'above' and 'below' stairs. The house and gardens are set within a 90-acre landscaped park. Carriage rides, formal gardens, self-guided trails, craft workshops, boating, and an exciting adventure playfarm provide a wide variety of things to do and see.
Open Good Fri-Sep, Wed-Sun & BHs 11.30-4.(Tue during school holidays. Wknds only in Oct. Special Xmas opening). Also open for group visits at other times.
⚠ *(charged)* 🍴 ✗ *licensed* ♿ *(wheelchairs for loan) toilets for disabled shop (ex guide dogs)*
Details not confirmed for 1998
Cards: 💳

OGMORE
Ogmore Castle
☎01656 653435
Standing on the River Ogmore, the west wall of this castle is 40ft high. A hooded fireplace is preserved in the 12th-century, three-storey keep and a dry moat surrounds the inner ward.
Open - access throughout the year. Key keeper arrangement.
Free.
⚠ ♿ ♒ ⚒

OXWICH
Oxwich Castle
SA3 1NG (A4118 from Swansea, 11m SW of Swansea)
☎01792 390359
Beautifully situated on the lovely Gower peninsula, this Tudor mansion is a striking testament in stone to the pride and ambitions of the Mansel dynasty of Welsh gentry. Like many successful Tudor gentlemen, Sir Rice Mansel converted his ancestral home into an up to date mansion, its defences are mainly for show, and the house itself is comparatively modest. His son, however, added a stupendous multi-storey wing, dwarfing his father's house with this E-shaped extravaganza, which houses an exhibition on historical Gower and 'Chieftains and Princes of Wales'. Please telephone for details of special events.
Open May-Sep, 10-5 daily.
✽*£1.70 (concessions £1.20). Family ticket £4*
⚠ ♿ *(Radar key toilet) toilets for disabled* ♒ ⚒
Cards: 💳 💳

PARKMILL
Gower Heritage Centre
Y Felin Ddwr SA3 2EM (Follow signs for South Gower on A4118 W from Swansea. W side of Parkmill village)
☎01792 371206
Fax 01792 371471
This Heritage Centre is based around a 12th century water-powered cornmill. The site also contains a number of craft workshops, a museum and a miller's cottage, all set in attractive countryside in an area of outstanding natural beauty. Special events for 1998 include; Gower Folk Festival (19-21 June), Gower Festival (19 July), Opera Workshops (23 July & 13 August) and Sea Shanty Festival (22 August).
Open daily, Mar-Oct 10-7; Nov-Feb 10-5. Closed 25 Dec.
£2.30 (ch & pen £1.30). Family ticket £6.30. Party.
⚠ 🍴 ♿ *toilets for disabled shop*
Cards: 💳

PENARTH
Cosmeston Lakes Country Park & Medieval Villa ge
Cosmeston Lakes Country Park, Lavernock Rd CF64 5UY (on B4267 between Barry and Penarth)
☎01222 709141 & 701678
Fax 01222 708686
Deserted during the plagues and famines of the 14th century, the original village was rediscovered through archaeological excavations. Now the buildings have been faithfully reconstructed on the excavated remains, within the Cosmeston Lakes Country Park, creating

Cyfarthfa Castle, an imposing Gothic mansion with magnificent gardens, dates back to 1825

GOWER HERITAGE CENTRE
Crafts and Countryside Centre

The Gower Heritage Centre is a restored 14th century corn mill complex which has become a popular and acclaimed tourist attraction situated in the heart of the beautiful Gower Peninsula in the village of Parkmill ★ Working Water Wheel ★ Restored Corn Mill ★ Craft Workshops ★ Rural Heritage Display ★ Picnic Area ★ Disabled Facilities ★ Tea Room ★ Car and Coach parking ★ Children's Play Area ★ Free parking for Three Cliffs Beach ★

Preserving the Past for the Future
GOWER HERITAGE CENTRE, Y FELIN DDŴR, PARKMILL, GOWER
SWANSEA, WEST GLAMORGAN
TEL: (01792) 371206 FAX: (01792) 371471

a living museum of medieval village life. Special events throughout the year, including Living History, with baking, archery, hawking etc, Medieval Court and trial Sessions (24-25 May), Call to Arms 1346 (preparations for the Battle of Crecy) (27-28 Jun). Medieval Battle and Jousting 1316 (Welsh uprising led by Llewellyn Bren) (25-26 Jul), Grand Medieval Fair (30-31 Aug), Civil War Weekend (26-27 Sep), Hallowe'en (31 Oct), Medieval Christmas Celebrations (20 Dec). Please telephone for further details of events.
Open all year, daily 10.30-5 in Summer, 10.30-4 in Winter. Closed 25 Dec. Adult £3, (concessions £2) Family ticket £6.50.
🅿 🍴 ✕ ♿ *toilets for disabled shop*

PENHOW
Penhow Castle
NP6 3AD (on A48 between Newport & Chepstow. Use M4 Junction 24)
☎01633 400800
Fax 01633 400990
This, the oldest inhabited castle in Wales, was originally a small border fortress and was the first British home of the famous Seymour family. The building presents a fascinating picture of castle life through nine centuries, now lovingly restored by the present owner. Visitors explore at their own pace from battlements to kitchens, guided by the acclaimed Walkman Tours. Rooms include the Norman bedchamber, the 15th-century Great Hall with its fine screen and minstrels' gallery, the elegant Charles II dining room with original panelling and the cosy Victorian housekeepers room. There will be Christmas Candlelit Tours from 15 November to 5 January. Other Special Events include 'Young Adventurer' tours, daily throughout Easter and Summer school holidays.
Open Good Fri-end Sep, Wed-Sun & BH 10-5.15 last admission; "Candlelit Tours" by arrangement; Aug open daily; Winter Wed 10-4 & selected Suns 1-4.
£3.35 (ch £2.05). Family ticket (2 adults & 2 children) £8.75. Party 20+
🅿 🍴 (refreshment bar) ♿ (audio-tours for blind) shop ⊗ (ex guide dogs)

RAGLAN
Raglan Castle
NP5 2BT (signposted off A40)
☎01291 690228
This magnificent 15th-century castle is noted for its 'Yellow Tower of Gwent'. It was built by Sir William ap Thomas and slighted during the Civil War, after a long siege. The ruins are still impressive, however, and the castle's history is illustrated in an exhibition situated in the closet tower and two rooms of the gate passage.
Open all year, late Oct-late Mar, Mon-Sat 9.30-4, Sun 11-4; late Mar-late Oct, daily 9.30-6.30. (Closed 24-26 Dec & 1 Jan).

Prices not confirmed.
🅿 ♿ *shop* ⊗
Cards: 🪙 🪙

RHOOSE
Wales Aircraft Museum
Cardiff (Wales) Airport CF6 9BD
☎01446 711141
The museum displays military and civil aircraft of post World War II interest, including the magnificent Vulcan B2 bomber - XM569 as well as undercover exhibitions, models etc.
Open Apr-Sep, daily 10-5; Oct-Mar, wknds.
Prices not confirmed.
🅿 🍴 ♿ *toilets for disabled shop*
Details not confirmed for 1998

ST FAGANS
Museum of Welsh Life
CF5 6XB (4m W of Cardiff, 3m from Junction 33 on the M4, along the A4232)
☎01222 573500
Fax 01222 573490
1998 is the 50th anniversary of The Museum of Welsh Life - a place where you can walk back in time. A stroll around the indoor galleries and one hundred acres of beautiful grounds is guaranteed to give you a fascinating insight into how people in Wales have lived, worked and spent their leisure hours since Celtic times. Its a 'hands-on' place - where you can see people practising the traditional means of earning a living, the animals they kept and even, at special times of the year, the ways in which they celebrated the seasons. Come and experience the best of the past. Events include; Historic Car Rally (18-19 Apr), 300th Anniversary of Battle of St Fagans and May Fair (2-4 May), Midsummer Festival and Concert (21 Jun), Open Air Theatre (1 Aug), Harvest Festival (26/27 Sep), Hallowe'en (31 Oct), 1940's Christmas Celebration (2-6 Dec). Please telephone for details.
Open all year daily, Jul-Sep 10-6, Oct-Jun 10-5. Closed 24-26 Dec.
❄Etr-Oct: £5.25 (ch £2.75, OAP/students/UB40 £3.75) Nov-Etr: £4.25 (ch £2.25, OAPs/students/UB40 £3.25)
🅿 🍴 ✕ *licensed* ♿ *(wheelchairs available on a 'first come-first served' basis) toilets for disabled shop* ⊗ *(ex guide dogs)*
Cards: 🪙 🪙 🪙 🪙

ST HILARY
Old Beaupre Castle
(1m SW, off A48)
☎01446 773034
This ruined manor house was rebuilt during the 16th century. Its most notable features include an Italianate gatehouse and porch. The porch is an unusual three-storeyed structure and displays the Basset arms.
Open - access throughout the year. Key keeper arrangement.
Free.
🅿 ⊗ ☺

SKENFRITH
Skenfrith Castle
☎01222 500200
This 13th-century castle has a round keep set within an imposing towered curtain wall. It was built by Hubert de Burgh as one of three 'trilateral' castles to defend the Welsh Marches.
Open - access throughout the year. Key keeper arrangement.
Free.
🅿 ⊗ ☺ 🐄

SWANSEA
Glynn Vivain Art Gallery
Alexandra Rd
SA1 5DZ
☎01792 655006 & 651738
Fax 01792 651713
The gallery has an outstanding collection of Swansea porcelain and pottery, European and Oriental pottery, and glass including paperweights. There are paintings, drawings and sculptures by British and foreign artists, with the emphasis on Welsh artists. Major exhibition programme all year round (Swansea Festival, September-November); progressive education and community arts services. Gallery shop for cards, books, prints, jewellery and unusual gifts.
Open all year, Tue-Sun & BH Mon 10-5. Closed 25, 26 Dec & 1 Jan.
P (200 yards, NCP) ♿ *also sculpture court toilets for disabled shop* ⊗ *(ex guide dogs, hearing dogs)*
Details not confirmed for 1998
Cards: 🪙 🪙

Swansea Maritime & Industrial Museum
Museum Square, Maritime Quarter
SA1 1SN (M4 junct 42, on main rd into Swansea city centre)
☎01792 650351 & 470371
Fax 01792 654200
This museum complex in the Swansea maritime quarter contains a complete, working woollen mill as well as a selection of floating boats to explore from April to October. These include a tug, lightship and pilot cutter. There are also displays relating to the Port of Swansea, its industries and its environment, transport exhibits, and maritime and agricultural sections. There is a programme of temporary exhibitions.
Open all year, Tue-Sun 10-5.(last admission 4.45pm). Closed Mon except BH Mon, 25, 26 Dec & 1 Jan.
Free.

P (50yds) (charged) 🍴 ♿ *shop* ⊗ *(ex guide dogs)*
Cards: 🪙 🪙 🪙

TINTERN
Tintern Abbey
NP6 6SE (via A466)
☎01291 689251
Standing serenely beside the banks of the River Wye, the ruins of the Cistercian monastery church are still surprisingly intact. The monastery was established in 1131 and it continued to thrive and become increasingly wealthy well into the 15th century. During the Dissolution, the monastery was closed and most of the buildings, other than the church, were completely destroyed. During the 18th century the ruins of Tintern were considered to be one of the essential sites to visit. Many poets and artists came to see the majestic arches, fine doorways and elegant windows, and recorded their experiences in poetry and paintings.
Open all year, late Oct-late Mar, Mon-Sat 9.30-4, Sun 11-4; late Mar-late Oct, daily 9.30-6.30. Closed 24-26 Dec & 1 Jan.
Prices not confirmed.
🅿 ♿ *toilets for disabled shop* ⊗ ☺
Cards: 🪙 🪙

TONGWYNLAIS
Castell Coch
CF4 7YS (A470 to Tongwynlais junction, then B4262 to castle on top of hill)
☎01222 810101
Castell Coch is Welsh for red castle, a good name for this fairy-tale building with its red sandstone walls and conical towers rising out of the wooded hillside. The castle was originally built in the 13th century but fell into ruins, and the present castle is the late-19th-century creation of William Burges and the 3rd Marquis of Bute, who commissioned him to restore it. An exhibition provides an illustrated history of Bute, of Burges and of the building they created. It has three round towers with conical roofs, a drawbridge and portcullis. Inside, the castle is decorated in fantasy style with many murals, giltwork, statues and carvings. The most spectacular room is probably Lady Bute's bedroom, which has a domed ceiling painted on the theme of the Sleeping Beauty.
Open all year, late Oct-late Mar, Mon-Sat 9.30-4, Sun 11-4; late Mar-late Oct, daily 9.30-6.30. Closed 24-26 Dec & 1 Jan. ➤

Historic buildings from all over Wales have been carefully reconstructed at St Fagans to form a living monument to the past.

✿£2.20 (reductions £1.70). Family ticket
£6. Ch under 5 free.
🅿 shop ✿ ⚅
Cards: 🆊 ⚅ ▬

TREHAFOD
Rhondda Heritage Park
Lewis Merthyr, Coed Cae Rd CF37 7NP
(between Pontypridd & Porth, off A470;
follow brown tourist signs from M4)
☎01443 682036 Fax 01443 687420
The Rhondda Heritage Park is a unique
Living History attraction, based at the
Lewis Merthyr Colliery.
Visitors can take the Cage Ride to 'Pit
Bottom' and explore the underground
workings of a 1950's pit on the
subterranean tour 'A Shift In Time'. The
Tour guides, who were miners
themselves, are able to answer visitors'
questions and contribute anecdotes of
life underground. Children will love the
journey back to the surface on the
thrilling ride through the tunnels.
Visitors can also experience the unique
character and culture of the world
famous Rhondda Valleys, as seen
through the eyes of three generations of
a mining family, in the innovative multi-
media presentation 'Black Gold - The
Story of Coal'.
Other facilities include 'Trefor and Bertie's
Energy Zone' - an actioned packed
children's play area, Gallery Restaurant,
exhibition gallery and contemporary
artefacts museum illustrating living
conditions throughout the ages.
Open all year, daily 10-6. Closed Mon
from Oct-Etr. Last admission 4.30pm.
Closed 25 & 26 Dec.
✿£4.95 (ch & concessions £4.25, students
£3.50). Family ticket £16. Party 10+.
🅿 ♥ ✕ ✆ (Wheelchair available,
accessible parking) toilets for disabled
shop ✿ (ex guide dogs)
Cards: 🆊 ⚅ ▬ ▬

USK
Gwent Rural Life Museum
Malt Barn, New Market St NP5 1AU
☎01291 673777
An award-winning collection of farm tools,
machinery, wagons and domestic items.
Open Etr-Oct, daily 10-5 (ex Sat & Sun
am) Last admission 4.30. Winter hours
contact the Museum.
£1.50 (ch 75p, pen £1). Party.
🅿 ✆ (special tape recording of tour for
deaf) shop

WHITE CASTLE
White Castle
NP7 8UD (7m NE of Abergavenny,
unclass road N of B4233)
☎01600 780380
The impressive 12th- to 13th-century
moated stronghold was built by Hubert
de Burgh to defend the Welsh Marches.
Substantial remains of walls, towers and
a gatehouse can be seen. This is the
finest of a trio of castles, the others
being at Skenfrith and Grosmont.
Open all year, Apr-Sep daily 10-6; Oct-
Mar 9.30-4.
✿£1.50 (reductions £1). Family ticket £4.
No charge for admission Oct-Mar.
🅿 ✆ ✿
Cards: 🆊 ▬

NORTHERN IRELAND

BELFAST

BELFAST
**The bustling city of Belfast is
enviably situated within easy
access of the coast and the peaceful
countryside. Within the city, there
are some beautiful parks, including
the famous Botanical Gardens,**

**where there is plenty of interest
throughout the year; winter is an
especially good time to visit the
Tropical Ravine and the Palm
House, the earliest surviving
structure of curvilinear glass and
cast iron in the world. Shoppers are
served by all leading High Street
stores, as well as by more specialist
shops which market the famous
Waterford crystal, Belleek china,
linen, damask, and Donegal tweed.
Eating out can be quite an
adventure, especially in the area
between the City Hall and
Shaftesbury Square, which has
been known as the Golden Mile. In
its length one can dine on Italian,
French, Indian, Mongolian and
Chinese specialities, but do not
forget the traditional Irish dishes -
Ardglass herring, or Guinness with
Strangford oysters, which you can
sample in the congenial
surroundings of The Crown Liquor
Saloon. This Victorian pub dates
from 1849 and is a notable Belfast
landmark, now owned by the
National Trust.**

Belfast Castle
Antrim Rd BT15 5GR (2.5m from city
centre, take Antrim road towards
Glengormley then left into Innisfayle
Park, signed)
☎01232 776925 Fax 01232 370228
This Scottish baronial-style castle with its
great square six-storey tower and
baroque staircase, was built in 1870 by
the 3rd Marquis of Donegall. It was
presented to the city by the Earl of
Shaftesbury in 1934 and was restored in
1980 at a cost of £2.2 million, re-opening
to the public in October 1988. It is used
for all types of functions and is open daily
for morning coffee, lunch, afternoon tea
and dinner. There is a Heritage Centre on
the second floor. The castle stands on
the lower wooded slopes of Cave Hill, an
area popular for walks and picnics. The
climb to the top of the hill will reward you
with far-reaching views. Cavehill Carnival
family fun day - first Sunday in August.
Open all year, daily. Castle open to public
viewing. Food & drink available all day &
evening. (closed only 25 Dec)
Free.
🅿 ♥ ✕ licensed ✆ (lift to all floors,
ramps being installed early '98) toilets for
disabled shop ✿ (ex guide dogs)
Cards: 🆊 ▬ ▬ ▬ ⚅ ▬

Belfast Zoological Gardens
Antrim Rd BT36 7PN (6m N, on A6)
☎01232 776277 Fax 01232 370578
The 50-acre zoo has a dramatic setting on
the face of Cave Hill and enjoys
spectacular views. Attractions include the
award-winning primate house (gorillas
and chimpanzees), penguin enclosure,
free-flight aviary, African enclosure, and
underwater viewing of sealions and
penguins. There is a group of very rare
spectacled bears, also red pandas. Free-
ranging lemurs and other animals can
also be seen.
Open all year (ex 25 Dec), daily Apr-Sep
10-5; Oct-Mar 10-3.30 (Fri 10-2.30)
✿Admission charged (ch under 4, pen &
disabled free). Party. (Prices under review)
🅿 ♥ ✆ (Free admission & reserved
parking) toilets for disabled shop ✿ (ex
guide dogs)
Cards: 🆊 ▬

Botanic Gardens
Stranmillis Rd BT7 1JP
☎01232 324902 Fax 01232 237070
Thirty-eight acres to the south of the city
make up these lovely botanical gardens.
One highlight of the park is the beautiful
glass-domed Victorian Palm House, built
by Richard Turner, the Dublin iron
founder, between 1839-52. This palm
house predates the one in Kew Gardens
and is one of the earliest curved-glass
and iron structures in the world. It has
recently been re-stocked with exotic

plants. Another feature is the Tropical
Ravine - visitors stand on a balcony to get
a wonderful view through a steamy
ravine full of exotic plants.
Open all year, Park daily 8-dusk. Tropical
ravine and palmhouse Mon-Fri 10-12.30
& 1-5 (summer), closes 4.30 (winter);
wknds open 1-5 (summer), 1-4 (winter).
🅿 (street) ✆
Details not confirmed for 1998

Giant's Ring
(0.75m S of Shaws Bridge)
☎01232 235000 Fax 01232 310288
A huge, circular, Bronze-age enclosure
nearly 200ft in diameter similar in style to
Stonehenge, with a stone chambered
grave in the centre and bordered by
banks 20ft wide and 12ft high. Very little
is known for sure about this site, except
that it was used for ritual burial. The
circular enclosure was used as a horseracing circuit in the 18th century, while
the punters stood on the banks.
Open all times.
🅿
Details not confirmed for 1998

Malone House-Barnett Demesne
Upper Malone Rd BT9 5PB
☎01232 681246 Fax 01232 682197
An early 19th-century Georgian mansion
overlooking the River Lagan, beautifully
restored in 1983 after fire gutted the
interior. Owned by Belfast City Council,
the house is now used for trade shows
and functions. There is a restaurant. The
Higgin Art Gallery is also open to visitors.
Open all year, Mon-Sat 9.30-5.30. (Closed
Xmas Day & Boxing Day)
🅿 ✕ licensed ✆ toilets for disabled ✿
Details not confirmed for 1998
Cards: 🆊 ▬ ▬ ⚅

Ulster Museum
Botanic Gardens BT9 5AB (M1/M2 to
Balmoral exit)
☎01232 383000 Fax 01232 383003
The Ulster Museum is both a national
museum and an art gallery. The
collections are Irish and International in
origin and cover antiquities, art, botany
and zoology, geology and local history
(including industrial archaeology). Some
of the permanent displays on show
include The Dinosaur Show; Made in
Belfast; Armada Treasures; The Irish
Flora and Fauna and many more. New
gallery 'Early Ireland - 10000BC-1500 BC'
opened autumn 1996, featuring the Ice
Age to the early Bronze Age. A
programme of temporary exhibitions,
films and Sunday afternoon events is also
available. Educational activities for adult
groups, families and schools. Access to
research collections by appointment.
Telephone for information, ext 3030.
Open all year, Mon-Fri 10-5, Sat 1-5, Sun
2-5. (Closed 12 Jul).
🅿 (100yds on street) (Clearway 0800-
0930 & 1630-1800) ♥ ✆ (all galleries
except one. Loop system, wheelchair
lifts) toilets for disabled shop ✿ (ex guide
dogs)
Details not confirmed for 1998
Cards: 🆊 ▬ ▬

CO ANTRIM

ANTRIM
Antrim Round Tower
(N of town)
☎01232 235000 Fax 01232 310288
Antrim round tower stands among lawns
and trees but it once was surrounded by
monastic buildings. Antrim was an
important early monastery, probably a
6th-century foundation, closely linked
with Bangor.
Open all year.
🅿 ✆
Details not confirmed for 1998

Shane's Castle
BT41 4NE (on A6)
☎01849 463380 & 428216
Fax 01849 468457
The entrance to Shane's Castle is on the

A6 Randalstown Road. Home of the
O'Neills, the first castle was built in the
17th century. Nash redesigned the castle
in the early 19th century, but it was
destroyed by fire before his designs
could be fully realised. Only the fine
conservatory (where camellias are
grown) and the terraces remain of his
work. A second castle was built in the
mid-19th century, but this too was gutted
by fire in the troubles of 1922. Part of the
estate, which stretches from the
outskirts of Antrim along the shores of
Lough Neagh to the village of
Randalstown, is open to the public.
Attractions include - rare breeds, deer
park, nature trail, butterfly area, ancient
graveyard and O'Neill vault. Special
events include the Northern Ireland
Game Fair (27-29 June)
Open Etr-Oct. Please telephone to
confirm details.
🅿 ♥ ✕ ✆ toilets for disabled shop
Details not confirmed for 1998

BALLYCASTLE
Bonamargy Friary
(E of town, at golf course)
☎01232 235000 Fax 01232 310288
Founded by Rory MacQuillan around
1500 and later passed on to the
MacDonnells, Earls of Antrim, there are
still remains of the friary gatehouse,
church and cloister for visitors to see.
Open all year.
🅿 ✆ ✿
Details not confirmed for 1998

BALLYLUMFORD
Ballylumford Dolmen
(on B90 on NW tip of Island Magee)
☎01232 235000 Fax 01232 310288
Incorporated in the front garden of a
house in Ballylumford Road are the
remains of this huge 4-5,000-year-old
single-chamber Neolithic tomb, also
known as the Druid's Altar.
Open all year.
✆
Details not confirmed for 1998

BALLYMENA
Harryville Motte
(N bank of river Braid)
☎01232 235000 Fax 01232 310288
On a ridge to the south of the town, this
Norman fort, with its 40ft-high motte and
rectangular bailey, is one of the finest
examples of Norman earthworks left in
Northern Ireland.
Open all year.
🅿 ✆ ✿
Details not confirmed for 1998

BALLYMONEY
Heritage Farm Park
Leslie Hill BT53 6QL (1m NW of
Ballymoney on MacFin Rd)
☎012656 66803 Fax 012656 66803
An 18th-century estate with a Georgian
house, magnificent period farm buildings,
and fine grounds with paths, lakes and
trees. Among the attractions are an
extensive collection of rare breeds,
poultry, horsedrawn machinery and
carriages, exhibition rooms, a museum,
working forge, walled garden and an
adventure playground. There are horse
and trap rides and pony rides for children.
Deer park. Special events throughout the
year.
Open Jul-Aug Mon-Sat 11-6, Sun 2-6; Jun
Sat-Sun & BH's 2-6; Etr-May & Sep Sun
& BH's 2-6.
£2.50 (ch £1.70). Family ticket £7.50.
🅿 ♥ ✆ (ramps) toilets for disabled shop
garden centre (must be on leads)

BUSHMILLS
Old Bushmills Distillery
BT57 8XH (On the Castlecatt rd)
☎012657 31521 Fax 012657 31339
Old Bushmills was granted its licence in
1608 and is the oldest licenced whiskey
distillery in the world. Enjoy a guided tour
when the age-old art of whiskey making
will be explained as you walk around the
Distillery. After your tour take part in a
comparative tasting and become a
whiskey expert. Relax in the homely

The splendid palm house, designed by Charles Lanyon and constructed in 1840, is a prominent feature of Belfast's lovely Botanical Gardens.

Distillery Kitchen coffee shop or visit two delightful shops.
Open Apr-Oct, Mon-Sat 9.30-5.30, Sun noon-5.30; Nov-Mar, Mon-Fri 6 tours daily, 10, 11, noon, 1.30, 2.30 & 3.30.
£3 (pen & student £2.50, accompanied ch £1.50) Family ticket £8. (2 adults, 2 or more children).
P ⚑ & *toilets for disabled shop* ⚑ *(ex guide dogs)*
Cards: ▨ ▦

CARRICK-A-REDE
Carrick-a-Rede Rope Bridge and Larrybane Visitors Centre
(E of Ballintoy on B15)
☎012657 62178 & 31159
This shaky rope bridge, made of planks of wood and wire and suspended 80ft above the sea, bridges the 60ft gap between cliffs and a small rocky island. The bridge owes its existence to the salmon who regularly make the dash through the chasm and get netted for their efforts, and to the fishermen who need access to the commercial fishery on the south-east side of the island. The bridge has been put across the gap each spring and dismantled every autumn for about the last 300 years. From the Larrybane car park, where there is a National Trust Information Centre, the Trust have made a clifftop path to the bridge and the views are lovely.
Open - Visitor centre Etr-June, 11-6; Jul-Aug, daily 10-6. Bridge open daily 10-6, Jul-Aug 10-8.
Parking, cars £2.50, coaches £6.
P *(charged)* ⚑ & *(information centre) toilets for disabled* ⚑

CARRICKFERGUS
Carrickfergus Castle
(on N shore of Belfast Lough)
☎01960 351273 Fax 01960 365190
Imposingly placed on a rocky headland overlooking Belfast Lough, this is the best preserved and probably the most fought-over Norman castle in Ireland. Built by John de Courcy, Earl of Ulster, after 1180, it served a military purpose for more than eight centuries. Exhibits include a giant model of the castle, a short film, and a banqueting suite. The castle is often used as a venue for medieval banquets and fairs. There is a new visitors' centre, shop and refreshment point.
Open all year, Apr-Sep, weekday 10-6, Sun 2-6; Oct-Mar closes at 4.
P ⚑ & *toilets for disabled shop* ⚑
Details not confirmed for 1998

Town Walls
☎01232 235000
Fax 01232 310288
Lord Deputy Sir Arthur Chichester enclosed Carrickfergus with stone walls from 1611 onwards and more than half

the circuit is still visible, often to its full height of 4 metres to the wall walk.
Visible at all times.
P &
Details not confirmed for 1998

CHURCHTOWN
Cranfield Church
(3.75m SW of Randalstown)
☎01232 235000 Fax 01232 310288
This small medieval church is situated on the shores of Lough Neagh. Beside it is a famous holy well.
Open all year.
P & ⚑
Details not confirmed for 1998

GIANT'S CAUSEWAY
Giant's Causeway Centre
44 Causeway Rd BT57 8SU (2m N of Bushmills on B146)
☎012657 31855
Fax 012657 32537
Only discovered in 1692 and now designated a World Heritage Site, this dramatic rock formation is undoubtedly one of the wonders of the natural world. The Centre provides an exhibition and audio-visual show, and tourist information. There are also craft and souvenir shops, a National Trust tearoom and a restaurant. Ulsterbus provides a minibus service to the stones and there are guided walks, picnic tables and special facilities for the disabled.
Open all year, daily 10-4 (6pm Jun & Sep-Oct; 7pm Jul-Aug).
❋*Audio-visual show (25 min) £1 (ch 50p). Family ticket £2.50. Causeway coaster fare to Grand causeway currently £1 return, 60p single, (oap & ch 50% reduction). All Prices Under Review.*
P *(charged)* ⚑ ✕ & *(mini bus transport with wheelchair hoist, reserved parking) toilets for disabled shop* ⚑ *(ex guide dogs)*
Cards: ▨ ▦ ▩

LARNE
Olderfleet Castle
☎01232 235000
Fax 01232 310288
A 16th-century tower house, the last surviving of three which defended Larne.
Open at all times.
Details not confirmed for 1998

LISBURN
Duneight Motte and Bailey
(2.3m S beside Ravernet River)
☎01232 235000
Fax 01232 310288
Impressive Anglo-Norman earthwork castle with high mound-embanked enclosure, making use of the defences of an earlier pre-Norman fort.
Open all year.
Details not confirmed for 1998

Irish Linen Centre & Lisburn Museum
Market Sq BT28 1AG (signposted both in and outside the town centre)
☎01846 663377 Fax 01846 672624
The Irish Linen Centre at Lisburn Museum tells the story of the Irish linen industry both past and present. The recreation of individual factory scenes brings the past very much to life and a series of imaginative hands-on activities describe the linen manufacturing processes. A highlight of the exhibition is the handloom weaving workshop. The Museum has regularly changing exhibitions of local interest and is developing a permanent exhibition relating to the history of the Lagan Valley. A speciality linen and craft shop sells local pottery and jewellery. There is also a Tourist Information Desk for the local area.
Open all year, Monday-Saturday, 9.30am-5pm.
Adult £2.75 (concessions £1.75). Family ticket £5-7. Party.
P *(200m) (limited for disabled and coaches)* ⚑ & *(lift, induction loop, staff trained in sign language) toilets for disabled shop* ⚑ *(ex guide dogs)*
Cards: ▨ ▦ ▩ ▨ ▩

PORTBALLINTRAE
Dunluce Castle
(off A2)
☎012657 31938 Fax 01232 318288
Extensive and picturesque ruins of a 16th-century castle perched on a rocky crag high above the sea. Stronghold of the MacQuillans and MacDonnells, who significantly altered the original stonebuilt fortress. Randal MacDonnell built a house in the centre of the castle, of which parts of the Great Hall remain, as do the towers and early 17th-century gatehouse. The castle has new displays and there is an audio-visual show. The cave below the ruins provided a secret way into and out of the castle from the sea.
Open all year, Apr-Sep, weekdays 10-7, Sun 2-7; Oct-Mar, Tue-Sat 10-4, Sun 2-4.
P & *toilets for disabled shop* ⚑
Details not confirmed for 1998

TEMPLEPATRICK
Pattersons Spade Mill
751 Antrim Rd BT38 9AP (2m SE on A6)
☎01849 433619
This is the last surviving water-driven spade mill in Ireland. It has been completely restored by the National Trust and is now back in production. For details of events please telephone (01849) 433619.
Open Etr, Apr-May & Sep, wknds 2-6; Jun-Aug, daily (ex Tue) 2-6, also on Bank Hols.
£2.50 (ch £1.25), Family Ticket £6.25. Party £1.75
P & *(ramps wheelchair available) toilets for disabled* ⚑

Templetown Mausoleum
Situated in the graveyard of Castle Upton, this family mausoleum is in the shape of a triumphal arch and was designed by Robert Adam.
Open daily during daylight hours.
Free.
🚌 ⚑

CO ARMAGH

ARMAGH
Armagh County Museum
The Mall BT61 9BE
☎01861 523070 Fax 01861 522631
Housed in an interesting 19th-century schoolhouse, this museum contains an art gallery and library, as well as an interesting collection of local folkcrafts and natural history that excellently illustrate the life and history of the city and county of Armagh. Special events are planned thoughout the year. Telephone for further details.
Open all year, Mon-Fri 10-5, Sat 10-1 & 2-5.
Free.
P & *toilets for disabled shop* ⚑ *(ex guide dogs)*

Armagh Friary
(SE edge of town)
☎01232 235000 Fax 01232 310288
Situated just inside the gates of the former Archbishop's Palace are the remains of the longest friary church in Ireland (163ft). The friary was established in 1263 by Archbishop O'Scanail and destroyed by Shane O'Neill in the middle of the 16th century to prevent it being garrisoned by Elizabethan soldiers.
Open all year.
P &
Details not confirmed for 1998

Armagh Planetarium & Science Centre
College Hill BT61 9DB (on main Armagh-Belfast rd)
☎01861 523689 & 524725
Fax 01861 526187
A trip to Armagh Planetarium is just the start of a journey that takes visitors to the outer limits of the universe. Attractions include: The Star Theatre, a multi-media environment equipped with the latest technology and featuring a virtual reality digital system; The Hall of Astronomy, devoted to 'hands on' explanations of astronomical concepts: The new Eartharium Building, containing exhibits on the environment scale, the seasons and the structure of the earth. Surrounding the Planetarium is the Astropark, a 25-acre 'hands on' park devoted to explaining scale in the universe.
Open all year, Hall of Astronomy Mon-Fri 10-4.45, shows daily at 3. Also open Sat & Sun 1.15-4.45, shows every Sat & Sun 2 & 3. Additional shows during Etr, Xmas & BH's.
£3.75 (ch & pens £2.75). Family ticket £12. Exhibition area £1.
P ⚑ & *(Loop system in theatre) toilets for disabled shop* ⚑ *(ex guide dogs)*
Cards: ▨ ▦ ▩

Navan Centre
Killylea Rd BT60 4LD (2m W on A28)
☎01861 525550 Fax 01861 522323
Navan Fort is one of Europe's most important Celtic sites; the seat of the ancient Kings of Ulster and setting for the legends of the mythical Cuchulainn. The Centre unveils the history and archaeology of the fort and its landscape in a stunning visual interactive display.
Open all year, Apr-Jun & Sep, Mon-Sat 10-6, Sun 11-6; Jul-Aug, Mon-Sat 10-7, Sun 11-7; Oct-Mar, Mon-Fri 10-5, Sat 11-5, Sun noon-5.
£3.95 (ch 16 £2.25, pen, students & UB40's £3). Family ticket £7 (1 adult) & £10 (2 adults) & £9.
P ⚑ & *(loop for hearing aids) toilets for disabled shop* ⚑ *(ex guide dogs)*
Cards: ▨ ▦

Strong nerves are all that are needed to make the crossing of the Carrick-a-Rede Rope Bridge and the views are wonderful – if you can bear to look!

Palace Stables Heritage Centre
The Palace Demesne BT60 4EL
☎01861 529629 Fax 01861 529630
This picturesque Georgian building, set around a cobbled courtyard, has been lovingly restored and now houses a heritage centre where visitors can experience stable life in the 18th century. An exhibition A Day in the Life uses audio-commentary, life-like models and spectacular, colourful murals. Visitors can browse around the Tack Room and the Coachman's House and glimpse the working and living conditions of a coachman. Other attractions include the hayloft, children's play area, Ice House & servants tunnel, education room, audio-visual theatre, craft shop and restaurant. Adventure play area and 'Garden of the Senses', designed for sensory stimulation. Both are situated in the historic woodland surrounding the 18th century palace. Living History - Georgian interpretation by authentic costumed characters. Also an Orienteering Course. Special Events include Living History festivals, Murder Mystery evenings, Christmas Craft Fair, education workshops. Please telephone for details. Antique and Collectors Fair - last Sunday every month.
Open all year, Apr-Aug, Mon-Sat 10-5.30, Sun 1-6; Sep-Mar, Mon-Sat 10-5, Sun 2-5. Last tour 1hr before closing.
£3 (ch 4-16 £1.90, pen £2.40). Family ticket £8.50
🅿️ ✕ ♿ (Ramps & Lift in stables) toilets for disabled shop (courtyard only)
Cards: ▨ ▨

St Patrick's Trian
40 English St BT61 7BA
☎01861 521801 Fax 01861 510180
This exciting complex situated in the centre of Armagh City illustrates the development of Armagh from prehistoric times to the present day, and also reveals Armagh's importance as a world ecclesiastical centre. The development also houses The Land of Lilliput, (which is based on Gulliver's Travels; The Craft Courtyard; Pilgrim's Table Conservatory Restaurant, educational and conference facilities.
Open all year, Mon-Sat 10-6, Sun 2-5; Jul-Aug, Mon-Sat 10-5. Last tour 1hr before closing.
Armagh Story & The Land of Lilliput combined ticket £3.30 (ch £1.75, pen & student £2.45). Family ticket £8.60.
🅿️ (charged) ✕ ♿ (specially designed for disabled) toilets for disabled shop
Cards: ▨ ▨

CAMLOUGH
Killevy Churches
(3m S lower eastern slopes of Slieve Gullion)
☎01232 235000 Fax 01232 235000

The ruins of the two churches (10th-and 13th-century) stand back to back, at the foot of Slieve Gullion sharing a common wall, but with no way through from one to the other. The churches stand on the site of an important nunnery founded by St Monenna in the 5th century. A huge granite slab in the graveyard supposedly marks the founder's grave. A holy well can be reached by climbing the path north of the graveyard. The nunnery was in use until the Dissolution in 1542.
Open all year.
♿
Details not confirmed for 1998

JONESBOROUGH
Kilnasaggart Inscribed Stone
(1.25m S)
☎01232 235000 Fax 01232 310288
A granite pillar stone dating back to 8th century, with numerous crosses and a long Irish inscription carved on it.
Open all year.
P
Details not confirmed for 1998

MOY
Argory
Derrycaw Rd BT71 6NA (4m NE)
☎018687 84753 Fax 018687 89598
Originally the home of the McGeough family, this Regency house is situated on a hillside overlooking the Blackwater River. The Argory is full of period furniture and bric-a-brac. Of particular interest is the house's very unusual acetylene lighting, installed by the family in 1906, the cast-iron stove in the hall and the cabinet barrel organ. Lovely rose garden and walled pleasure gardens. For details of special events telephone 018687 84753.
Open Etr, daily; Apr-May & Sep, wknds & BH; Jun-Aug, daily (ex Tue) 2-6. Open from 1pm on BHs. Last tour 5.15.
🅿️ (charged) ♿ (special parking facilities, wheelchair available) toilets for disabled shop
Details not confirmed for 1998

NEWRY
Moyry Castle
(7.5m S)
☎01232 235000 Fax 01232 310288
This tall, three-storey keep was built by Lord Mountjoy, Queen Elizabeth's deputy, in 1601, its purpose to secure the Gap of the North which was the main route into Ulster.
Open all year
Details not confirmed for 1998

OXFORD ISLAND
Lough Neagh Discovery Centre
Oxford Island National Nature, Reserve BT66 6NJ (signposted from M1, exit 10)
☎01762 322205 Fax 01762 347438
Learn about the history and wildlife of the Lough in relaxed comfort through a series of exciting audio-visual shows, interactive games and exhibition. Then experience the wonders of Oxford Island for yourself: natural history, wildlife, family walks and much more - all in a spectacular setting on the water's edge.
Open all year, Apr-Sep 10-7; Oct Mar 10-5.
✳£3 (ch £1.80, concessions £2.30). Family ticket £6.70.
🅿️ ✕ ♿ (grounds accessible in part, bird watching hides) toilets for disabled shop
Cards: ▨ ▨ ▨

PORTADOWN
Ardress House
Annaghmore BT62 1SQ (7m W on B28)
☎01762 851236 Fax 01762 851236
Plain 17th-century house transformed around 1770 by its visionary, architect owner George Ensor, who added elegant wings and superb Adamesque plasterwork carried out by the Dublin expert, Michael Stapleton. The house has a fine picture gallery on loan from the Earl of Castlestewart. The grounds are beautifully unspoilt and there is a farmyard with livestock and a display of farm implements. Plus children's playground and river walks.
Open Etr, daily; Apr-May & Sep, wknds & BH's; Jun-Aug, daily (ex Tue) 2-6. House, grounds & farmyard £2.30 (ch £1.15). Family ticket £5.75. Party
🅿️ ♿ toilets for disabled shop (ex guide dogs)

TYNAN
Village Cross
☎01232 235000
Fax 01232 310288
A carved High Cross, 11ft tall, which lay broken in two pieces for many years, but was skilfully mended in 1844. The carvings depict Adam, Eve and the serpent entwined around an apple tree.
Open all year
🅿️ ♿
Details not confirmed for 1998

CO DOWN

ARDGLASS
Jordan's Castle
☎01232 235000 Fax 01232 310288
Although Ardglass is an important fishing port today, it was once the busiest seaport in Northern Ireland. Between the 14th and 15th centuries a ring of tower houses and fortified warehouses was built to protect the port. Jordan's Castle, a late-15th-century, four-storey tower house situated in the centre of town, is one of these. Besieged in the early 1600s and held for three years, the castle was bought, repaired and filled with bygones by a Belfast solicitor in the early part of this century.
Open Jul-Aug; Tue-Sat 10-7, Sun 2-7. Other times on request.
Details not confirmed for 1998

BALLYWALTER
Grey Abbey
(on east edge of village)
☎01232 235000
Fax 01232 310288
Founded in 1193 by Affreca, daughter of the King of the Isle of Man, these extensive ruins of a Cistercian abbey, sitting in lovely sheltered parkland, are among the best preserved in Northern Ireland. The chancel, with its tall lancet windows, magnificent west doorway and an effigy tomb - believed to be Affreca's - in the north wall, are particularly interesting.
The abbey was burned down in 1572, and then re-used as a parish church. There are many 17th- and 18th-century memorials to be seen in the church ruins, which occupy a pleasant garden setting. The abbey now has a beautiful medieval herb garden, with over 50 varieties of plants, and a new visitors' centre.

Open Apr-Sep; Tue-Sat 10-7, Sun 2-7.
🅿️ ♿ toilets for disabled
Details not confirmed for 1998

CASTLEWELLAN
Drumena Cashel
(2.25m SW)
☎01232 235000 Fax 01232 310288
There are many stone ring forts in Northern Ireland, but few so well preserved as Drumena. Dating back to early Christian times, the fort is 30m in diameter and has an 11m accessible underground stone-built passage, probably used as a refuge and for storage.
Open all times
P
Details not confirmed for 1998

COMBER
WWT Castle Espie
Ballydrain Rd BT23 6EA (3m S of Comber, 13m SE of Belfast. Signed from the A22 Comber-Killyleagh-Downpatrick road)
☎(01247) 874146 Fax 01247 873857
Located on the shores of Strangford Lough, Castle Espie is home to the largest collection of wildfowl in Ireland. New hides enable visitors to watch the splendour of migratory waders and wildfowl. Beautiful landscaped gardens, a taxidermy collection and fine paintings by wildlife artists can also be seen. Visitors, especially children, are encouraged to feed the birds, many of which are rare and endangered.The Centre is of interest all year round - woodland walks are especially enjoyable in the summer, as are the Downy Duckling Days during July. Thousands of birds migrate to the reserve in winter and Bird Walks are held on the last Thurday of every month. The Centre's effluent is treated in a reed bed filtration system which can be seen on one walk. Downy Duckling Days will be held in July while September sees the Brent Goose Festival. Ring for details.
Open all year; summer, Mon-Sat 10.30-5, Sun 11.30-6; winter Mon-Sat 11.30-4, Sun 11.30-5. (Closed 25 Dec).
🅿️ ✕ ♿ (hides have wheelchair platforms) toilets for disabled shop
Details not confirmed for 1998
Cards: ▨ ▨ ▨ ▨

DONAGHADEE
Ballycopeland Windmill
(1m W, on B172)
☎01247 861413 Fax 01232 310288
The only complete working windmill in Northern Ireland, this tower cornmill was built in the late-18th century. Fully operational until 1914 for the milling of wheat, oats and the making of animal foodstuffs, the mill has intricate wooden machinery. There are additional displays in the Miller's House and drying kiln.
Open all year Apr-Sep, Tue-Sat 10-7, Sun 2-7; Oct-Mar, Sat 10-4, Sun 2-4.
🅿️ shop
Details not confirmed for 1998

DOWNPATRICK
Down County Museum & St Patrick Heritage Centre
The Mall BT30 6AH
☎01396 615218
Fax 01396 615590
The museum occupies the old county gaol built between 1789 and 1796. The Saint Patrick Heritage Centre in the former gatehouse tells the story of Ireland's patron saint. In the recently restored governor's residence are galleries relating to the human and natural history of County Down. The story of the settlement of Ireland from 7000BC to recent times, is told with texts and artefacts ranging from flint arrowheads to Dinky toys. The three-storey cell block has been renovated and some of the 18th-century cells on the ground floor can be seen, together with additional exhibition areas. Special Events: 1798 Conference (12-14 Jun), Midsummer Fun Day (21 Jun), Hallowe'en Party (31 Oct), Festive Fun Night (16 Dec).

Open all year, Jun-Aug, Mon-Fri 11-5, wknds 2-5; rest of year, Tue-Fri 11-5 & Sat 2-5. Also open all BH's.
Free.
P (100yds) ⚑ & (wheelchair available, handling boxes on application) toilets for disabled shop ⌖ (ex guide dogs)

Inch Abbey
(0.75m NW off A7)
☎01232 235000 Fax 01232 310288
Beautiful riverside ruins of a Cistercian abbey founded by John de Courcy around 1180. Of particular note is the tall, pointed, triple east window.
Open Apr-Sep 10-7, Sun 2-7. Oct-Mar free access.
P &
Details not confirmed for 1998

Loughinisland Churches
(4m W)
☎01232 235000
Fax 01232 310288
This remarkable group of three ancient churches stands on an island in the lough, accessible by a causeway. The middle church is the oldest, probably dating back to the 13th century, with a draw-bar hole to secure the door. The large North church was built in the 15th century, possibly to replace the middle church and continued in use until 1720. The smallest and most recent church is the South (MacCartan's) church.
Open all times
P & ⌖
Details not confirmed for 1998

Mound of Down
(on the Quoile Marshes, from Mount Crescent)
☎01232 235000 Fax 01232 310288
A hill fort from the Early Christian period, conquered by Anglo-Norman troops in 1177, who then built an earthwork castle on top. This mound in the marshes, beside the River Quoile, was the first town before the present Downpatrick.
Open all times
P
Details not confirmed for 1998

Struell Wells
(1.5m E)
☎01232 235000 Fax 01232 310288
Pilgrims come to collect the healing waters from these holy drinking and eye wells which are fed by a swift underground stream. Nearby are the ruins of an 18th-century church, and, even more interesting, single-sex bath-houses. The men's bath-house is roofed, has an anteroom and a sunken bath, while the ladies' is smaller and roofless.
Open all times
P ⌖
Details not confirmed for 1998

DROMARA
Legananny Dolmen
(4m S)
☎01232 235000 Fax 01232 310288
Theatrically situated on the slopes of Slieve Croob, this tripod dolmen with its three tall uprights and huge capstone is the most graceful of Northern Ireland's Stone Age monuments. There are views to the Mourne Mountains.
Open at all times
& ⌖
Details not confirmed for 1998

HILLSBOROUGH
Hillsborough Fort
☎01846 683285 Fax 01232 310288
On a site that dates back to early Christian times, the existing fort was built in 1650 by Colonel Arthur Hill to command a view of the road from Dublin to Carrickfergus. The building was ornamented in the 18th century. It is set in a forest park with a lake and pleasant walks.
Open all year; Apr-Sep, Tue-Sat 10-7, Sun 2-7; Oct-Mar, Tue-Fri 10-4, Sat 10-4, Sun 2-4.,
P &
Details not confirmed for 1998

HOLYWOOD
Ulster Folk and Transport Museum
Cultra BT18 0EU (on A2)
☎01232 428428
Fax 01232 428728
Opened in 1964, in the grounds of Cultra Manor, this museum is in two parts. The Folk Museum, which covers a 137-acre site, has a wonderful collection of rural and urban buildings that have been taken from original settings all over Ulster, and reconstructed at the Museum. They include: farmhouses, cottages, watermills, a small town with shops, a school, churches, printer's workshops, bank and terraced houses, which recreate the Ulster landscape of the 1900's. In the rural area there are farm animals native to Ireland and the fields are cultivated using traditional farming methods. The Transport Museum exhibits all forms of transport, including the popular Titanic exhibition and the spectacular Irish Railway Collection. Telephone for details on 24hr-information line 01232 421444
Open all year Apr-Jun & Sep, Mon-Fri 9.30-5, Sat 10.30-6, Sun noon-6; Jul-Aug, Mon-Sat 10.30-6, Sun noon-6; Oct-Mar, Mon-Fri 9.30-4, Sat-Sun 12.30-4.30.
P ⚑ & toilets for disabled shop
Details not confirmed for 1998
Cards: ▨ ▨ ▨

KILKEEL
Greencastle
(4m SW)
☎01232 235000
Fax 01232 310288
Looking very much like an English Norman castle with its massive keep, gatehouse and curtain wall, this 13th-century royal fortress stands on the shores of Carlingford Lough, with fine views of the Mourne Mountains. Greencastle has an eventful military history, it was beseiged and taken by Edward Bruce in 1316, attacked and spoiled by the Irish at least twice later in the 14th century, and maintained as a garrison for Elizabeth in the 1590s.
Open Jul-Aug, Tue-Sat 10-7, Sun 2-7.
P &
Details not confirmed for 1998

KILLINCHY
Sketrick Castle
(3m E on W tip of Sketrick Islands)
☎01232 235000 Fax 01232 310288
A badly ruined tall tower house, probably 15th-century. The ground floor rooms include a boat bay and prison. An underground passage leads from the north-east of the bawn to a freshwater spring.
Open at all times.
P &
Details not confirmed for 1998

NEWCASTLE
Dundrum Castle
(4m N)
☎01232 235000
Fax 01232 310288
This medieval castle, one of the finest in Ireland, was built in 1777 by John De Courcy in a strategic position overlooking Dundrum Bay, a position which offers visitors fine views over the sea and to the Mourne Mountains. The castle was captured by King John in 1210 and was badly damaged by Cromwellian troops in 1652. Still an impressive ruin, it shows a massive round keep with walls 16m high and 2m thick, surrounded by a curtain wall, and a gatehouse which dates from the 13th century.
Open Apr-Sep, Tue-Sat 10-7, Sun 2-7.
P & toilets for disabled
Details not confirmed for 1998

Maghera Church
(2m NNW)
☎01232 235000 Fax 01232 310288
The stump of a round tower, blown down in a storm in the early 18th century, survives from the early monastery, with a ruined 13th-century church nearby.
Open all year.
P &
Details not confirmed for 1998

NEWTOWNARDS
Mount Stewart House, Garden & Temple of the Winds
Greyabbey BT22 2AD (5m SE off A20)
☎012477 88387 & 88487
Fax 012477 88569
On the east shore of Strangford Lough, this 18th-century house was the home of the Stewart family (who later became Marquesses of Londonderry) and the place where Lord Castlereagh, Foreign Secretary from 1812 to 1823, grew up. The house is the work of three architects - James Wyatt in the 1780s and George Dance and probably Vitruvius Morrison in the early 19th century. Much of the house's contents have associations with Castlereagh, and there are interesting paintings, including one by Stubbs, as well as silver and porcelain. Outside, in the lovely, inspired gardens (among the very best of the National Trust's), many rare and subtropical trees thrive, while by the shore of Strangford Lough is the Temple of the Winds, built by James Stewart in 1782 for the first Marquess.
Open House Etr, daily; May-Sep daily (ex Tue); Apr & Oct wknds, 1-6. Temple of The Winds (open dates as house) 2-5. Garden Apr-Sep, daily & Oct, wknds 11-6. House Garden & Temple: £3.50 (ch £1.75). Family ticket £8.75. Garden: £3, (ch £1.50) Family ticket £7.50. Party.
P ⚑ & (4 wheelchairs(2 electric) available) toilets for disabled shop ⌖

Scrabo Tower
Scrabo Country Park, 203A Scrabo Rd BT23 4SJ (1m W)
☎01247 811491 Fax 01247 820695
The 135ft high Scrabo Tower, one of Northern Ireland's best-known landmarks, dominates the landscape of North Down and is also the centre of a country park around the slopes of Scrabo Hill. The Tower provides a fascinating series of interpretative diplays about the surrounding countryside and the viewing platform boasts spectacular views over Strangford Lough and Co Down. The park provides walk through fine beech and hazel woodlands and the unique sandstone quarries display evidence of volcanic activity as well as breeding sites for peregrine falcons.
Open Etr, May-Sep, Sat-Thu 11-6.30. Country park open all year, daily, 11-6.30.
P shop ⌖
Details not confirmed for 1998

PORTAFERRY
Exploris
The Rope Walk, Castle St BT22 1NZ (A20 or A2 or A25 to Strangford Ferry Service)
☎012477 28062 Fax 012477 28396
Exploris is Northern Ireland's only public aquarium. Situated in Portaferry on the shores of Strangford Lough it houses some of Europe's finest displays. The Open Sea Tank holds 250 tonnes of sea water, and the Shoal Ring, where visitors are surrounded by hundreds of shoaling fish, is 6m in diameter. You can take a journey from Strangford Lough through the neck of the Lough - the Narrows, and out into the Irish Sea without any risk of seasickness! The complex includes a park with duck pond, picnic area, children's playground, caravan site, woodland, tennis courts and bowling green. Phone for details of events programme.
Open all year, Mon-Fri 10-6, Sat 11-6, Sun 1-6. (Sep-Feb closing 1 hr earlier).
P ⚑ & (lift available) toilets for disabled shop ⌖
Details not confirmed for 1998
Cards: ▨ ▨ ▨

SAINTFIELD
Rowallane Garden
BT24 7LH (1m S of Saintfield on A7)
☎01238 510131 Fax 01238 511242
Beautiful, exotic, 50-acre gardens started by the Rev John Moore in 1860 and continued by his nephew Hugh Armytage-Moore. The gardens contain exquisite plants from all over the world. Particularly noted for its rhododendrons and azaleas and for the wonderful floral displays in spring and summer, displayed in a natural setting. The gardens have the national collection of large-flowered Hybrid Penstemons. There are monthly demonstrations on The Art of the ➤

Ardress House provides insight into the life-style of the gentleman-farmer during the 17th, 18th and 19th centuries.

The interior of Lismacloskey House – one of the many fascinating buildings reconstructed at the award-winning Ulster Folk and Transport Museum.

Gardener. Midsummer Jazz Evening (20 Jun), Horse Drive (21 Jun), Wood Turning Event (8-9 Aug), Annual Plant Sale (24-25 Oct), Yuletide Market (12-13 Dec).
Open Apr-Oct, Mon-Fri 10.30-6, Sat & Sun 2-6; Nov-Mar, Mon-Fri 10.30-5. Closed 25/26 Dec & 1 Jan
Apr-Oct £2.50 (ch £1.25); Nov-Mar £1.50 (ch 75p).
🅿 💺 ♿ *(parking facilities) toilets for disabled (must be on leads)* 🌂

STRANGFORD
Audley's Castle
(1.5m W by shore of Strangford Lough)
☎ *01232 230560*
Fax 01232 310288
Fifteenth-century tower house on Strangford Lough which offers lovely views from its top floor. The internal fittings are complete.
Open Apr-Sep, daily 10-7.
🅿 ✍
Details not confirmed for 1998

Castle Ward
BT30 7LS (0.5m W of Strangford Village on A25)
☎ *01396 881204*
Fax 01396 881729
The curious diversity of styles in this house is due to the fact that its owner, Bernard Ward, later First Viscount Bangor, and his wife could never agree; so the classical style preferred by the Viscount and the more elaborate Gothic look favoured by his wife were both incorporated in the house. Not altogether surprisingly, the couple separated shortly after the house was completed! The servants' living quarters are separate from the house and are reached by an underground passage. Fully equipped laundry in the courtyard. Small theatre in part of the large barn. Castle Ward is beautifully placed overlooking Strangford Lough. The gardens, complete with a small lake, and a classical summerhouse, are richly planted and especially beautiful in spring.
House open Etr, daily; Apr & Sep-Oct, wknds; May-Aug, daily (ex Thu) 1-6. Estate grounds all year, daily dawn-dusk.
🅿 *(charged)* 💺 ✗ ♿ *(wheelchair*

available, may be driven to house) toilets for disabled shop
Details not confirmed for 1998
Cards: 🅰 💳

Strangford Castle
☎ *01232 235000 Fax 01232 310288*
A three-storey tower house built in the 16th century, overlooking the small double harbour of Strangford.
Visable from outside.
✍
Details not confirmed for 1998

WARRENPOINT
Narrow Water Castle
(1m NW)
☎ *01232 235000*
Fax 01232 310288
Both picturesque and complete in detail, this 16th-century battlemented tower house is surrounded by a wall and juts out into the river estuary which it was originally built to defend.
Open Jul-Aug, Tue-Sat 10-7, Sun 2-7.
🅿
Details not confirmed for 1998

CO FERMANAGH

BELLEEK
Belleek Pottery
3 Main St BT93 3FY
☎ *013656 58501 59300*
Fax 013656 58625
Known worldwide for its fine Parian china, Ireland's oldest and most historic pottery was started in 1857 by the Caldwell family. Meet the craftspeople at work whilst touring the Pottery and marvel at their workmanship. Visit the museum with its exhibits which date back over 100 years, and take a look in the showroom.
Open all year, Mar-Jun, Mon-Fri 9-6, Sat 10-6, Sun 2-6; Jul-Aug, Mon-Fri 9-8, Sat 10-6, Sun 11-8; Sep, Mon-Fri 9-6, Sat 10-6, Sun 2-6; Oct, Mon-Fri 9-5.30, Sat 10-5.30, Sun 2-6; Nov-Feb, Mon-Fri 9-5.30. Guided tours £2.00.

🅿 ✗ ♿ *(wheelchairs can be provided) toilets for disabled shop* ✍ *(small dogs allowed)*
Cards: 🅰 💳 ➖ 🔟 💳 💷

CASTLE ARCHDALE BAY
White Island Church
(in Castle Archdale Bay; ferry from marina)
☎ *01232 235000 Fax 01232 310288*
Lined up on the far wall of a small, roofless 12th-century church are eight uncanny carved-stone figures. Part Christian and part pagan in appearance, their significance has been the subject of great debate. The church ruins sit on an early monastic site.
Open Jul-Aug, Tue-Sat 10-7, Sun 2-7.
🅿 ✍ 🚽
Details not confirmed for 1998

DERRYGONNELLY
Tully Castle
(3m N, on W shore of Lower Lough Erne)
☎ *01232 235000 Fax 01232 310288*
Extensive ruins of a Scottish-style stronghouse with enclosing bawn overlooking Lough Erne. Built by Sir John Hume in the early 1600s, the castle was destroyed, and most of the occupants slaughtered, by the Maguires in the 1641 Rising. There is a replica of a 17th-century garden in the bawn.
Open Apr-Sep Tue-Sat 10-7, Sun 2-7; Oct-Mar 10-4.(2-4 Sun).
🅿 ♿ ✍
Details not confirmed for 1998

ENNISKILLEN
Castle Coole
BT74 (1.5m SE on A4)
☎ *01365 322690 Fax 01365 325665*
One of the finest classical mansions in Northern Ireland, if not in the British Isles. No expense was spared in the building of this mansion for the First Earl of Belmore between 1789 and 1795. James Wyatt was the architect, the lovely plasterwork ceilings were by Joseph Rose, and the chimneypieces the work of Richard Westmacott. Vast amounts of Portland stone were specially imported, together with an Italian expert in stonework, and joiners from England

were brought in to make the shutters and doors. The house is filled with beautiful Regency furniture. Don't miss the sumptuous state bed in scarlet silk. Outside the lawns slope gently towards Lough Coole which is home to a flock of greylag geese.
Open Etr, daily; Apr & Sep, wknds & BH's; May-Aug, daily (ex Thu) 1-6. Last tour 5.15.
£2.80 (ch £1.40). Family ticket £7.00. Estate £2.50 per car. Party £2.50.
🅿 *(charged)* 💺 ♿ *(may be driven to house) toilets for disabled shop* 🌂

Devenish Island
(2m N)
☎ *01232 235000 Fax 01232 310288*
In an attractive setting, two miles downstream from the city centre, this island (once the site of a monastery founded in the 6th century by St Molaise - regarded as one of the 12 apostles of Ireland) has a considerable number of interesting ecclesiastical remains. The ruins of Teampull Mor, with its fine south window, date back to the 13th century, while St Molaise's house - the remains of a tiny but sturdy church (roofless now) - to the 12th century. Facing this little church is a perfect 80ft-tall round tower. Also dating back to the 12th century, this tower is built on five floors accessible by ladders. The ruins of the Augustinian priory of St Marys' has an elaborately carved north chancel door and a pretty 15th-century cross in the graveyard.
Open Apr-Sep, Tue-Sat 10-7, Sun 2-7.
🅿 *shop* ✍
Details not confirmed for 1998

Enniskillen Castle
☎ *01365 322711*
Overlooking Lough Erne, this castle, a three-storey keep surrounded by massive stone-built barracks and with a turreted fairytale 17th-century water gate, now houses two museums and a heritage centre. In the castle keep is a small museum displaying Royal Enniskillen Fusiliers regimental exhibits, while the other rooms contain the Fermanagh County Museum's collection of local antiquities.
Open all year Mon 2-5, Tue-Fri 10-5 (closed 1-2, Oct-Apr), Sat 2-5 May-Aug, Sun 2-5 Jul-Aug, all day BH's.
🅿 ♿ *shop* ✍
Details not confirmed for 1998

Florence Court
BT92 1DB (8m SW via A4 & A32)
☎ *01365 348249 Fax 01365 348873*
Named after the wife of John Cole, the father of the First Earl of Enniskillen, this 18th-century mansion overlooks wild and beautiful scenery towards the Mountains of Cuilcagh. The interior of the house, particularly noted for its flambuoyant rococo plasterwork, was gutted by fire in 1955, but has been meticulously restored. The mansion is situated in beautiful parkland full of fine old trees, including the Florence Court Yew - mother of all Irish yews. There are pleasure grounds with an Ice House, Summer House and Water Powered Sawmill, also a walled garden and fine views.
Open Etr, daily 1-6; Apr & Sep wknds & BH's 1-6; May-Aug, daily (ex Tue) 1-6. £2.80 (ch £1.40). Family ticket £7.00. Estate only £2.00 per car.
🅿 *(charged)* 💺 ♿ *(electric wheelchair available) toilets for disabled shop* 🌂

Marble Arch Caves
Marlbank Scenic Loop BT92 1EW (off A4 Enniskillen-Sligo road)
☎ *01365 348855 Fax 01365 348928*
Magical cave system - one of Europe's finest - under the Mountains of Cuilcagh. Here visitors are given a tour round a wonderland of stalagmites, stalactites, underground rivers and lakes, which starts with a boat trip on the lower lake. The streams which flow down and then disappear into the mountain feed the caves and then emerge at Marble Arch, a huge 30ft detached limestone bridge.

Open late Mar-Sep. From 10 daily.
Admission prices under review.
P **🍴** shop 🐾 (ex guide dogs)
Cards: 🅰 💳 💳 🅾

Monea Castle
(6m NW)
☎01232 235000 Fax 01232 310288
A fine example of a plantation castle still with much of its enclosing bawn wall intact, built around 1618. Of particular interest is the castle's stone corbelling - the Scottish method of giving additional support to turrets.
Open at any reasonable time.
P &
Details not confirmed for 1998

LISNASKEA
Castle Balfour
☎01232 235000 Fax 01232 310288
Dating from 1618 and refortified in 1652, this is a T-plan house with vaulted rooms. Badly burnt in the early 1800s, this house has remained in ruins.
Open at all times.
P &
Details not confirmed for 1998

NEWTOWNBUTLER
Crom Estate
BT92 8AP (3m W)
☎013657 38174 38118 (fax too)
Fax 013657 38174
770 hectares of woodland, parkland and wetland, one of Northern Ireland's most important nature conservation areas. The Visitor Centre on the shore of Upper Lough Erne houses an exhibition, lecture room, tea room and seven holiday cottages. Nature trails are signposted through woodlands to the ruins of the old castle, past the old boat house and picturesque summer house. Day tickets for pike fishing and boat hire available from the Visitor Centre. The Castle is not open to the public. For details of events for 1998 telephone (013657) 38118.
Open Apr-Sep, daily 10-6, noon-6 Sun. parking £3

CO LONDONDERRY

COLERAINE
Hezlett House
Castlerock BT51 4TN (5m W on Coleraine/Downhill coast road)
☎01265 848567
A low, thatched cottage built around 1690 with an interesting cruck truss roof, constructed by using pairs of curved timbers to form arches and infilling around this frame with clay, rubble and other locally available materials.
Open Etr, daily; Apr-Jun & Sep wknds & BH's; Jul-Aug, daily (ex Tue) 12-5. £1.80 (ch 90p). Family ticket £4.50.
P 🐾 (ex in gardens) 🐾

Mount Sandel
(1.25m SSE)
☎01232 230560 Fax 01232 310288
This 200ft oval mound overlooking the River Bann is believed to have been fortified in the Iron Age. Nearby is the earliest known inhabited place in Ireland, where post holes and hearths of wooden dwellings, and flint implements dating back to 6,650BC have been found. The fort was a stronghold of de Courcy in the late 12th century and was refortified for artillery in the 17th century.
Open at all times.
P &
Details not confirmed for 1998

COOKSTOWN
Tullaghoge Fort
(2m S)
☎01232 235000
Fax 01232 310288
This large hilltop earthwork, planted with trees, was once the headquarters of the O'Hagans, Chief Justices of the old kingdom of Tyrone. Between the 12th and 16th centuries the O'Neill Chiefs of Ulster were also crowned here - the King Elect was seated on a stone inauguration chair, new sandals were placed on his feet and he was then anointed and crowned. The last such ceremony was held here in the 1590s; in 1600 the stone throne was destroyed by order of Lord Mountjoy.
Open at all times.
P
Details not confirmed for 1998

Wellbrook Beetling Mill
Corkhill BT80 9RY (4m W in Co Tyrone, 0.5m off A505)
☎016487 51735
This 18th-century water-powered linen mill was used for bleaching and, until 1961, for finishing Irish linen. Beetling was the name given to the final process in linen making, when the material was beaten by 30 or so hammers (beetles) to achieve a smooth and slightly shiny finish. The National Trust acquired the mill and restored it to working order.
Open Etr, daily; Apr-Jun & Sep, wknds & BH's; Jul-Aug, daily (ex Tue) 2-6.
P & shop 🐾
Details not confirmed for 1998

DOWNHILL
Mussenden Temple Bishop's Gate and Black Glen
Mussenden Rd BT51 4RP (1m W of Castlerock off A2)
☎012658 48728
Spectacularly placed on a cliff edge overlooking the Atlantic, this perfect 18th-century rotunda was modelled on the Temple of Vesta at Tivoli. Frederick Hervey, Bishop of Derry and 4th Earl of Bristol, had the temple built as a summer library for his cousin, but sadly she died before its completion, so he studied there himself. The temple, with its magnificent views of the Antrim and Donegal coasts, is only a part of the Earl Bishop's Downhill demesne; visitors entering by the Bishop's Gate can enjoy a beautiful glen walk up to the headland where the temple stands.
Open Temple: Etr, daily, noon-6; Apr-Jun & Sep, weekends & BH's noon-6; Jul-Aug, daily noon-6.
Free.
P & 🐾

DUNGIVEN
Banagher Church
(2m SW)
☎01232 235000
Fax 01232 310288
This church was founded by St Muiredach O'Heney in 1100 and altered in later centuries. Today impressive ruins remain. The nave is the oldest part and the square-headed lintelled west door is particularly impressive. Just outside, the perfect miniature stone house, complete with pitched roof and the sculpted figures of a saint at the doorway, is believed to be the tomb of St Muiredach. The saint was said to have endowed his large family with the power of bringing good luck. All they had to do was to sprinkle whoever or whatever needed luck with sand taken from the base of the saint's tomb.
Open at all times.
P &
Details not confirmed for 1998

Dungiven Priory
(SE of town overlooking River Roe)
☎01232 235000
Fax 01232 310288
Up until the 17th century Dungiven was the stronghold of the O'Cahan chiefs, and the Augustinian priory, of which extensive ruins remain, was founded by the O'Cahans around 1150. The church, which was altered many times in later centuries, contains one of Northern Ireland's finest medieval tombs. It is the tomb of Cooey na Gall O'Cahan who died in 1385. His sculpted effigy, dressed in Irish armour, lies under a stonework canopy. Below are six kilted warriors.
Open - Church at all times, chancel only when caretaker available. Check at house at end of lane.
P &
Details not confirmed for 1998

LIMAVADY
Rough Fort
(1m W off A2)
Early Christian rath.
Open at all times.
Free.
🚻 🐾

LONDONDERRY
City Walls
☎01232 235000
Fax 01232 310288
The finest and most complete city walls to be found in Ireland. The walls, 20-25ft high, are mounted with ancient cannon, and date back to the 17th century. The walled city is a conservation area with many fine buildings. Visitors can walk round the city ramparts - a circuit of one mile.
Open all times.
P (charged) &
Details not confirmed for 1998

Foyle Valley Railway Museum
Foyle Rd BT48 6SQ
☎01504 265234
Fax 01504 377633
A fascinating collection of relics from the four railway companies which served Londonderry are on display here at the Foyle Valley Railway Heritage Centre. Majestic steam locomotives, diesel railcars and all the paraphernalia of a station can be seen, along with the Railway Gallery which tells the story of the people who ran the railways and those who used the trains.
Open all year, Apr-Sep Tue-Sat & PH's 10-5, Sun 2-6; Oct-Mar Tue-Sat 10-5.
P & toilets for disabled shop garden centre 🐾
Details not confirmed for 1998

Tower Museum
Union Hall Place BT48 6LU
☎01504 372411
Fax 377633
The exhibition recounts the history of Londonderry from pre-historic times to the present day using real artifacts, theatrical displays and eleven audio-visual programmes showing the spread of Irish monasticism, the famous Siege of Derry and the road to the partition of Ireland.
Open all year, Sep-Jun Tue-Sat 10-5. Jul-Aug Mon-Sat 10-5, Sun 2-5. Also open all BH Mons.
P (300 yds) & toilets for disabled shop 🐾
Details not confirmed for 1998

MAGHERA
Maghera Church
(E approach to the town)
☎01232 235000 Fax 01232 310288
Important 6th-century monastery founded by St Lurach, later a bishop's see and finally a parish church. This much-altered church has a magnificently decorated 12th-century west door. A cross-carved stone to the west of the church is supposed to be the grave of the founder.
Key from Leisure Centre.
P &
Details not confirmed for 1998

MONEYMORE
Springhill
BT45 7NQ (1m from Moneymore on B18)
☎016487 48210 F
ax 016487 48210
Dating back to the 17th century, this attractive, pleasingly symmetrical manor house was originally the home of the Scottish Conyngham family. Today much of the family furniture, books and bric-a-brac have been retained. Outside, the laundry, stables, brewhouse, and old dovecote make interesting viewing, as does the excellent costume museum. ➤

Easter Eggcentricities (12 Apr), Mid-Ulster Vintage Vehicle Club Rally (6 Jun), Teddy Bears' Picnic (13 Jun).
Open Etr, daily 2-6; Apr & Sep, wknds & BH's 2-6; Jun-Aug, daily (ex Thu) 2-6.
£2.50 (ch £1.25). Family ticket £6.25. Party.£2
P ⬛ & *toilets for disabled shop (must be on leads)* ⅍

CO TYRONE

ARDBOE
Ardboe Cross
(off B73)
☎ 01232 235000
Fax 01232 310288
Situated at Ardboe Point, on the western shore of Lough Neagh, is the best example of a high cross to be found in Northern Ireland. Marking the site of an ancient monastery, the cross has 22 sculpted panels, many recognisably biblical, including Adam and Eve and the Last Judgment. It stands over 18ft high and dates back to the 10th century. It is still the rallying place of the annual Lammas, but praying at the cross and washing in the lake has been replaced by traditional music-making, singing and selling of local produce. The tradition of 'cross reading' or interpreting the pictures on the cross, is an honour passed from generation to generation among the men of the village.
Open at all times.
P &
Details not confirmed for 1998

BALLYGAWLEY
U S Grant Ancestral Homestead & Visitor Centre
Dergenagh, Ballygawley Rd BT70 1TW
(off A4, 3m on Dergenagh road, signposted)
☎ 016625 57133
Fax 01868 767911
Ancestral homestead of Ulysses S Grant, 18th President of the United States of America. The homestead and farmyard have been restored to the style and appearance of a mid-19th-century Irish smallholding. The small cottage consists of two rooms, furnished with replica period pieces, and the farmyard contains examples of agricultural implements used by the 19th-century farmer. The outbuildings house additional displays of agricultural implements. The Visitor Centre houses a shop and a display area with exhibitions on the Ulster Scots Plantation and a new American Civil War exhibition. There is also a small audio-visual theatre with two video screenings. Recently opened is a Wildlife garden, Cycle Hire facility (pre-booking advised) waymarked walking and cycling trails. A variety of events includes Easter Bunny Day, May Madness, Teddy Bears' Picnic, Yankee Doodle day (4 July), Vintage Bygones Display (3 Oct), Hallowe'en Event (31 Oct). Please ring for details of these and other events.
Open Etr-Sep, Mon-Sat 12-5, Sun 2-6. Other times by arrangement. (Closed 25-26 Dec & 1 Jan).
£1 (ch & concessions 50p). Party 10+
P ⬛ & *shop (only guide dogs inside)*

BEAGHMORE
Beaghmore Stone Circles and Alignments
☎ 01232 235000
Fax 01232 310288
Discovered in the 1930s, these impressive, ritualistic stones have been dated back to the early Bronze, and maybe even Neolithic Ages. There are three pairs of stone circles, one single circle, stone rows or alignments and cairns, which range in height from one to four feet. This is an area littered with historic monuments, many discovered by people cutting turf.
Open at all times.
P &
Details not confirmed for 1998

BENBURB
Benburb Castle
☎ 01232 235000
Fax 01232 310288
The castle ruins - three towers and massive walls - are dramatically placed on a cliff-edge 120ft above the River Blackwater. The northwest tower is newly restored and has dizzy cliff-edge views. The castle, built by Sir Richard Wingfield around 1615, is actually situated in the grounds of the Servite Priory. There are attractive walks down to the river.
Castle grounds open at all times. Special arrangements, made in advance, necessary for access to flanker tower.
P &
Details not confirmed for 1998

CASTLECAULFIELD
Castle Caulfield
☎ 01232 235000
Fax 01232 310288
Sir Toby Caulfield, an Oxfordshire knight and ancestor of the Earls of Charlemont, built this manor house in 1619 on the site of an ancient fort. It was badly burnt in 1641, repaired and lived in by the Caulfield/Charlemont family until 1670. It boasts the rare distinction of having had Saint Oliver Plunkett and John Wesley preach in its grounds. Some fragments of the castle are re-used in the fine, large 17th-century parish church.
Open at all times.
P &
Details not confirmed for 1998

NEWTOWNSTEWART
Harry Avery's Castle
(0.75m SW)
☎ 01232 235000
Fax 01232 310288
The hilltop ruins of a Gaelic stone castle, built around the 14th century by one of the O'Neill chiefs, are the remains of the oldest surviving Irish-built castle in the north. Only the great twin towers of the gatehouse are left. A new stairway enables the public to gain access to one of these.
Open at all times.
⅍ 🚗
Details not confirmed for 1998

OMAGH
Ulster American Folk Park
BT78 5QY (5m NW Omagh)
☎ 01662 243292
Fax 01662 242241
An outdoor museum, established in 1976, that traces the history of Ulster's links with America and the emigration of Ulster residents to North America during the 18th and 19th centuries. The 70-acre site is divided into two parts - Old World and New World. The Old World is centred around the restored farmhouse of Thomas Mellon, who emigrated to Pennsylvania in 1818, and later founded the Mellon Bank of Pittsburgh. In the New World are log houses and outbuildings - all are suitably furnished.
There is also the cottage of John Joseph Hughes, who emigrated from Augher in 1817, became first Catholic Archbishop of New York and initiated the building of St Patrick's Cathedral there in 1858. There are also demonstrations of Old and New World crafts, such as horseshoeing and thatching. A modern visitor centre, with exhibitions and audio-visual presentations, provides further information. A special feature is the Emigration Gallery area complete with dockside buildings and emigrant ship. The Centre for Emigration Studies is based here, with a research library and emigration database - please ring for details. A full programme of special events is planned for 1998 and includes: Easter Weekend - Easter Bonnet Parade, Egg Painting Competition; American Independence Day (to be held in July), and the seventh annual Appalachian and Bluegrass Music Festival (to be held on the 4-5 September); Annual Halloween Festival (30-31 October).
Open Etr-Sep, daily 11-6.30, Sun & BH 11.30-7; Oct-Etr Mon-Fri 10.30-5. Last admission 1hr 30mins before closing.
£3.50 (ch & pen £1.70). Family ticket £10.
P ⬛ & *toilets for disabled shop* ⅍ *(ex guide dogs)*
Cards: 🔲 ▭ 🔳 ▭ 🔲

Ulster History Park
Cullion BT79 7SU (7m on B48)
☎ 016626 48188
Fax 016626 48011
The Ulster History Park tells the story of settlement in Ireland with the aid of full-scale models of the houses and monuments built through the ages. These range from a mesolithic encampment (c8000-4000BC); the houses and megalithic tombs of the first farmers (c4000-2200BC); a ring fort, crannog, round tower and Norman motte-and-bailey, and a 17th-century Plantation settlement. Exhibitions and audio-visual presentations expand the theme. There is a cafeteria, shop and picnic facilities.
Open all year, Apr-Sep Mon-Sat 10.30-6.30, Sun 11.30-7, BH's 10.30-7; Oct-Mar Mon-Fri 10.30-5. Last admission 1hr 30mins before closing time.
£3.25 (ch, students, pen & registered disabled £1.95). Family ticket (2 adults, 4 children) £10. Group 15+
P ⬛ & *toilets for disabled shop* ⅍ *(ex guide dogs)*
Cards: 🔲 ▭

STEWARTSTOWN
Mountjoy Castle
Magheralamfield (3m SE, off B161)
☎ 01232 235000 *Fax 01232 310288*
Ruins of an early 17th-century brick and stone fort, with four rectangular towers, overlooking Lough Neagh. The fort was built for Lord Deputy Mountjoy during his campaign against Hugh O'Neill, Earl of Tyrone. It was captured and re-captured by the Irish and English during the 17th century and was also used by the armies of James II and William III.
Open at all times.
P
Details not confirmed for 1998

STRABANE
Gray's Printing Press
49 Main St BT82 8AU
☎ 01504 884094
Strabane was once an important printing and book-publishing centre, the only relic of which is a small shop in Main Street - Gray's Printing Shop. The shop now houses a Printing Museum containing three 19th-century presses, while upstairs the development of printing techniques over sixty years is illustrated. Two young men who served their apprenticeships in Strabane during the 18th century went on to great things: John Dunlap emigrated to Philadelphia, where he founded 'The Pennsylvania Packet' - America's first 'daily'; James Wilson who also emigrated to Philadelphia becoming a printer, newspaper editor and judge whose grandson was President Woodrow Wilson.
Open Apr-Sep, daily (ex Thu, Sun & BH's) 2-5.30. Other times by prior arrangement.
P *(100yds) shop* ⅍ ⅍
Details not confirmed for 1998

This traditional homestead and farmyard, ancestral home of President Ulysses Grant of the United States of America, is furnished in period style.

REPUBLIC OF IRELAND

CO CLARE

BALLYVAUGHAN
Aillwee Cave
☎065 77036 & 77067 Fax 065 77107
An underground network of caves beneath the world famous Burren. Guided tours take you through large caverns, over bridged chasms and alongside thunderous waterfalls. There is a craftshop, a dairy where cheese is made, a speciality food shop, and a tea room.
Open mid-Mar-Nov, 10-5.30 (Jul-Aug 6.30pm).
IR£4 (ch IR£2.50). Family ticket IR£12.
🅿 (charged) 🍴 ✕ licensed ♿ toilets for disabled shop 🐾 (in cave)
Cards: ◪ ▤

BUNRATTY
Bunratty Castle & Folk Park
(8 miles from Limerick city on N18 road to Ennis)
☎061 361511 & 360788
Fax 061 361020
Restored in 1960, this is Ireland's most complete medieval castle. It houses the Lord Gort collection of furniture, objet d'art, and paintings and tapestries dating from before 1650. One-day tours operate in season from Limerick and include a medieval banquet at the castle. Irish village life at the turn of the century is tellingly re-created in the folk park in the grounds, with its typical 19th-century rural and urban dwellings. There are eight farmhouses, a watermill, a blacksmith's forge, and a village street complete with shops and pub.
Open all year, daily 9.30-5.30 (last admission 4.15pm). Folk Park also open Jun-Aug 6.30 (last admission 5.30pm).
IR£4.95 (ch IR£2.50, pen/student IR£3.60). Family ticket IR£11.85.
🅿 🍴 ✕ licensed ♿ toilets for disabled shop
Cards: ◪ ▤ ▦ ◉

LISCANNOR
O'Brien's Tower & Cliffs of Moher
(6m NW of Lahinch)
☎065 81565 & 061 360788 Fax 061 361020
Just north of Liscannor on the coast of West Clare, are the famous Cliffs of Moher, defiantly standing as giant natural ramparts against the aggressive might of the Atlantic Ocean. They rise in places to 700ft, and stretch for almost 5 miles. O'Brien's Tower was built in the early 19th century as a viewing point for Victorian tourists on the highest point. From here you can view the Clare coastline, the Aran Islands and mountains as far apart as Kerry and Connemara. There is a visitor centre with tourist information.
Open daily Mar-Oct, 10-6 (subject to weather conditions). Visitor centre open all year daily 10am-6pm.
IR90p(ch IR60p). Effective from 1 April 1998.
🅿 (charged) 🍴 ♿ toilets for disabled shop
Cards: ◪ ▤ ▦ ◉

QUIN
The Craggaunowen Bronze Age Project
(clearly signed from N18, 10km N from village of Sixmilebridge)
☎061 367178 & 360788 Fax 061 361020
Contains a full-scale reconstruction of a crannog, a Bronze Age lake dwelling. The project includes a reconstructed ring fort and replicas of furniture, tools and utensils. Also on display is the *Brendan*, a replica of the leather boat used by St

Brendan the Navigator in the 6th century. The boat was sailed across the Atlantic Ocean in 1976 and 1977. Ring for details of special events.
Open Apr-Oct daily 10-6 (last admission 5pm). Mid May-mid Aug 9-6.
IR£4 (ch IR£2.70, pen/students IR£3.10). Family ticket IR£10.60
🅿 🍴 ♿ toilets for disabled shop
Cards: ◪ ▤ ▦ ◉

CO CORK

BALLINCOLLIG
The Royal Gunpowder Mills
(on Cork/Killarney road)
☎021 874430 Fax 021 874836
The Royal Gunpowder Mills is an amazing industrial complex on the banks of the River Lee. The mills supplied vast quantities of explosives for the British military forces, throughout the world from 1794 to 1903. Today visitors can experience the sights and sounds of this enormous factory. Personalised tours are provided from 10am to 6pm daily. The highlight of the tour includes a visit to the restored incorporating mill. An audio visual display is also provided.
Open daily, Apr-Sep 10-6. Last tour at 5.15pm.
🅿 🍴 ♿ toilets for disabled shop 🐾
Details not confirmed for 1998

BANTRY
Bantry House
(Main gate at harbour wall)
☎027 50047 Fax 027 50795
A Georgian mansion, surrounded by gardens, with a collection of furniture, tapestries etc by the Second Earl of Bantry. A tea room and craft shop are housed in the wings and there is an exhibition in the stables.
Open Mar-Oct.
🅿 🍴 ♿ shop 🐾 (ex in grounds)
Details not confirmed for 1998
Cards: ◪ ▤ ▦

BLARNEY
Blarney Castle & Rock Close
(5m from Cork on main road towards Limerick)
☎021 385252 & 385669 Fax 021 381518
The site of the famous Blarney Stone, known the world over for the eloquence it is said to impart to those who kiss it. The stone is in the upper tower of the castle, and the visitor, held by his feet, must lean backwards down the inside of the battlements in order to receive the gift of the gab.
Open - Blarney Castle & Rock Close, Jun-Jul Mon-Sat 9-7.30; Aug Mon-Sat 9-7.30; May Mon-Sat 9-7; Sep Mon-Sat 9-6.30; Apr & Oct Mon-Sat 9-sunset; summer Sun 9.30-5.30; winter Sun 9.30-sunset.

Blarney House & Gardens Jun-mid Sep Mon-Sat noon-6.
🅿 ♿ shop 🐾
Details not confirmed for 1998
Cards: ◪ ▤ ▦

CARRIGTWOHILL
Fota Wildlife Park
Fota Estate (Turn for Corby from N25, Cork-Waterford road)
☎021 812678 Fax 021 812744
Situated 10 miles from Cork, on the Cobh road. Established in 1983 with the primary aim of conservation, Fota has more than 70 species of exotic wildlife in open, natural surroundings with no obvious barriers. Giraffes, zebras, ostrich, antelope and other animals enjoy 40 acres of grassland through which visitors can walk on an unfenced road in complete safety. Monkeys swing through mature trees on lake islands, while kangaroos, macaws and lemurs have complete freedom of the park. Only the cheetahs have a conventional fence. Facilities include children's play train, lakeside coffee shop and picnic benches. Also here is an internationally renowned arboretum, with a particularly good selection of trees from China, Japan, New Zealand, Australia, South America and the Himalayas.
Open Apr-Oct, Mon-Sat 10-6, Sun 11-6 (last admission 5); Reduced rates and facilities on weekdays in Oct.
✼*IR£3.70 (ch & pen IR£2.20, students IR£3.30). Family day ticket IR£15.*
🅿 (charged) 🍴 ♿ (Ramps where required) toilets for disabled shop 🐾

CLONAKILTY
West Cork Model Village Railway
Inchydoney Rd (signposted at road junction. Village is at Bay side of Clonakilty)
☎023 33224 Fax 023 34843
The Model Railway village depicts the prominent buildings landmarks and way of life in the six major towns and villages of West Cork, namely Clonakilty, Bandon, Skibbereen, Dunmanway, Kinsale and Bantry. The towns are modelled at the height of activity. Fair days and the hectic day-to-day life of the mills and breweries are depicted. Phase one is currently open and shows a detailed model of Clonakilty. Visitors enter through a lifesize replica of Clonakilty Station as it was in the 1940s. In the centre a series of models, artefacts and displays prepare the visitor for their model village experience. The model town of Bandon was added in 1996, and Kinsale was completed in 1997. Kinsale depicts the life of the fishing town and also includes the model of Charlesfort, one of the largest models in Europe. Ring for details of special events.
Open Feb-17 Mar weekends only 1-5. 17 Mar-Oct, daily Mon-Fri 11-5, Sat/Sun 1-5.

Jul-Aug extended hours 10-6.
IR£3 (ch IR£1, pen & students IR£1.75). Family ticket IR£7.
🅿 🍴 ♿ (tearoom not accessible, shop accessible) toilets for disabled 🐾 (ex guide dogs)

COBH
The Queenstown Story
Cobh Railway Station
☎021 813591 Fax 021 813595
A dramatic multi-media exhibition of the origins, history and legends of Cobh. Explore conditions on board early emigrant vessels, including the dreaded 'coffin ship'. Learn about an 'Irish Wake', the special farewell for emigrating sons and daughters. Experience life aboard a convict ship leaving Cobh for Australia in 1801. Discover Cobh's special connections with the ill-dated Titanic and relive the horror of World War One and the sinking of the Lusitania with the loss of 1,198 lives.
Open all year 10-6. Last admission 5pm.
✼*IR£3.50 (ch12 IR£2, pen & students IR£3). Family ticket IR£10.*
🅿 🍴 ✕ ♿ toilets for disabled shop 🐾
Cards: ◪ ▤ ▦ ◉

CORK
Cork City Gaol
Convent Av, Sundays Well (2km from Patrick St. Cork, off Sunday's Well Rd)
☎021 305022 Fax 021 307230
A superbly restored prison building which housed prisoners in the 19th century, often in very wretched conditions. Furnished cells, lifelike characters, sound effects and amazing exhibits combine to allow visitors to experience day-to-day life for prisoners and gaoler. Inter-active multimedia are incorporated into an audio-visual presentation of the social history of Cork City, which mirrors national history. Suitable for all ages, individual sound tours are available in English, French, Spanish, Italian, Irish and German. A new permanent exhibition - Radio Museum Experience - is located in the restored 1920's broadcasting studio, home to Cork's first radio station, 6CK.
Open Mar-Oct, daily 9.30-6; Nov-Feb, daily 10-4. Last admission 1hr before closing.
IR£3.50 (ch IR£2, pen & student IR£2.50). Family ticket (2adult,3children) IR£9.
🅿 ♿ (customer care policy - individual attention) toilets for disabled shop 🐾 (ex guide dogs)

Cork Public Museum
Fitzgerald Park, Mardyke (N of University College)
☎021 270679 Fax 021 270931
Displays illustrating the history of the city are housed in this museum. The collections cover the economic, social and municipal history from the Mesolithic ➔

The west coast of Clare has some of Ireland's most spectacular scenery, and the cliffs of Moher are undoubtedly the most impressive of all.

period, with emphasis on civic regalia, and the trades and crafts of the 19th and 20th centuries. There are fine collections of Cork Silver and Glass and Youghal Needlepoint Lace.
Open all year, Jun-Aug Mon-Fri 11-1 & 2.15-6, Sun 3-5; Sep-May Mon-Fri 11-1 & 2.15-5, Sun 3-5. (Closed Sat, BH wknds & PH)
Mon-Fri free; Sun, Family IR£1.50 individual IR75p. Students, pen & unwaged free
P *(100 yds) shop* ⚘ *(ex guide dogs)*

GLENGARRIFF
Garinish Island
(1.5km boat trip from Glengarriff)
☎ *(027) 63040*
Fax 027 63149
An Italianate garden, designed by Harold Peto, bathed in the warm waters of the Gulf Stream provides an ideal setting for the collection of tender plants which thrive here. A Martello Tower, Clock Tower, a Grecian Temple overlooking the sea and magnificent pedimented gateways are some of the architectural features of the garden.
Open Jul-Aug, Mon-Sat 9.30-6.30, Sun 11-7; Apr-Jun & Sep, Mon-Sat 10-6.30, Sun 1-7; Mar & Oct, Mon-Sat 10-4.30, Sun 1-5. Last landing 1 hour before closing.
IR£2.50 (ch IR£1 & pen IR£1.75) Family ticket IR£6
⛱ *(minimal due to boat access) toilets for disabled shop (must be on leads)*

MIDLETON
Jameson Heritage Centre
(20m E of Cork towards Waterford.)
☎ *(021) 613594 & 613596*
Fax 021 613642
A tour of the Jameson Heritage Centre consists of a 20 minute audio/visual presentation, then a 35 minute guided tour of the Old Distillery and then back to the Jameson Bar for a whiskey tasting - minerals are available for children. The guided tour and audio-visual aids are available in five languages.
Open daily, Mar-Oct 10-6. Last tour 4. Nov-Feb Mon-Fri, two tours 12 & 3. Sat/Sun, two tours 2 & 4. Closed for Xmas.
IR£3.50 (ch IR£1.50). Family ticket IR£9.50
P ⚏ ⛱ *toilets for disabled shop* ⚘ *(ex guide dogs)*
Cards: ▨ ▥ ▤ ◐

CO DONEGAL

ARDARA
Ardara Heritage Centre
☎ *(075) 41704*
Fax 075 41381
The Heritage Centre offers information about this fabulous region mountain passes, forests, lakes and historical landmarks. It is an area rich in folklore and archeology, as well as a cultural centre for traditional music. Ardara is the heart of Ireland's manufacture of handwoven tweed, hand knitwear and hand loomed woollens and there are many craft and factory shops as well as exhibitions within the Heritage Centre.
Open Apr-Sep, 10-6.
P ⚏ ⛱✗ *toilets for disabled shop* ⚘ *(ex guide dogs)*
Details not confirmed for 1998

BALLYSHANNON
The Water Wheels
Abbey Assaroe (cross Abbey River on Rossnowlagh Rd, next turning left & follow signs)
☎ *072 51580*
Abbey Assaroe was founded by Cistercian Monks from Boyle Abbey in the late 12th century. The Cistercians excelled in water engineering and canalised the river to turn water wheels for mechanical power. The mills were restored in 1989 and there is a coffee shop and auditorium. One waterwheel now powers a generator which supplies

light and heat. The site occupies an unusual position overlooking the Erne Estuary and the Atlantic.
Open Easter week & May-Aug, 10.30-6.30. Other times, Sun 1.30-dusk.
Charge for audio-visual display IR£1
P ⚏ ✗⛱ *toilets for disabled shop garden centre*

BUNCRANA
Guns of Dunree Military Museum
Fort Dunree, Dunree (6m NW, on eastern shore of Lough Swilly)
☎ *077 61817*
Fort Dunree Military Museum is the first and only permanent and professionally-designed military museum in Ireland. It is located a few miles north-west of Buncrana along the Inis Eoghain 100, the motoring circuit of the beautiful Inishowen Peninsula in North Donegal. The museum houses a collection of artefacts and an audio-visual display which vividly illustrates the working of a coastal defence battery extending back of 180 years. There are walks around the complex from which the visitor can enjoy magnificent panoramic views.
Open daily 14 Jun-16 Sep 10.30-6, Sun 1-6.
P ⚏ ⛱ *shop* ⚘
Details not confirmed for 1998

LETTERKENNY
Glebe House & Gallery
Church Hill (signed from Letterkenny)
☎ *074 37071 Fax 074 37072*
The Regency house set in beautiful woodland gardens along the shore of Lough Gartan, was given to the nation, along with his art collection, by the artist Derek Hill. The interior of the house is decorated with original wallpapers and textiles by William Morris. The art collection is extensive with paintings by many leading 20th century artists, Japanese prints including works by Hokusai and Hiroshige and a fabulous collection of Victoriana.
Open Etr & mid May-End Sept 11-6.30. Last tour of house 5.30
IR£2 (ch & student IR£1, pen IR£1.50). Party.
P ⚏ ⛱ *shop* ⚘ *(ex guide dogs)*

LIFFORD
Cavanacor Historic House & Craft Centre
Ballindrait (1.5m from town off Strabane/Letterkenny road)
☎ *(074) 41143 Fax 074 41143*
Built in the early 1600s and commanding a view of the Clonleigh valley and the River Deele, Cavanacor House is the ancestral home of James Knox Polk, 11th President of the USA (1845-1849). King James II dined under the sycamore tree which still stands in front of the house in 1689. There is a display of the history of the house and the surrounding area and over 10 acres of landscaped gardens and an old-fashioned walled garden. The Art Gallery will feature exhibitions of new work by national and international artists. Please ring for details.
Open Etr-Aug, Tue-Sat 12-6, Sun 2-6. Closed Mon ex BH's.
IR£2.50 (ch & pen IR£1.75). Family ticket IR£7.50.
P ⚏ ✗⛱ *shop garden centre (on leads)*

CO DUBLIN

BALBRIGGAN
Ardgillan Castle
(on R127)
☎ *01 8492212 Fax 01 8492786*
A large and elegant country manor house built in 1738, set amid 194 acres of parkland overlooking the sea and coast as far as the Mourne Mountains. There is a permanent exhibition of the 17th century 'Down Survey' maps, various temporary exhibitions. Guided tours of the Castle include ground floor rooms and basement kitchens. Tours of the Gardens during June, July and August begin at 3.30pm every Thursday. Special exhibitions: (12-26 Jun) National Art Exhibition, (1-17 Aug) Craft Potter Society of Ireland Ceramics Exhibition.
Open 20 Dec-31 Jan, Sun 2-4pm (closed 25 Dec); Apr-Sep, Tue-Sun & BH's 11-6; Oct-Mar, Wed-Sun & BH's 11-4.30. IR£2.50 (pen/students IR£1.50). Family ticket IR£6. Party.
P ⚏ ⛱ *toilets for disabled* ⚘

DONABATE
Newbridge House and Traditional Farm
☎ *01 8436534 & 8462184*
Fax 01 8462537
Newbridge House was designed by George Semple and built in 1737 for Charles Cobbe, Archbishop of Dublin. The house contains many splendidly refurbished rooms featuring plasterwork, furniture and paintings. The finest room in the house is the Red Drawing Room, which has a beautiful white marble chimney pice and a rococo plaster ceiling attributed to Richard Williams. Other rooms open on the ground floor include the library, dining room, sculpture gallery and Museum of Curiosities. The latter features many artefacts collected by the Cobbe family on their travels throughout the world. Downstairs you will find the kitchen and the laundry. Special events throughout the year include demonstrations of sheep shearing, weaving, dying, pottery and harness making.
Open Apr-Sep Tue-Fri 10-1 & 2-5, Sat 11-6, Sun & PH 2-6; Oct-Mar Sat-Sun & PH 2-5. Parties at other times by arrangement.
P ⚏ ⛱ *shop* ⚘
Details not confirmed for 1998

DUBLIN
Dublin is a delightful city with many outstanding examples of 18th-century architecture. Birthplace and inspiration of many great authors, its contrasts are apparent everywhere: sweeping avenues and intimate sidestreets, chic shops and smokey pubs, stately museums and colleges, and terraces with faded exteriors emanating character. A good place to begin a tour of this compact city is O'Connell Bridge, leading to the city's main shopping area, O'Connell Street, where the best buys are local products, such as linen and lace, homespun tweeds

Visitors to Blarney Castle must lean backwards and hang upside down to kiss the world famous Blarney Stone for the gift of 'the gab' or eloquence.

and knitwear. City attractions include Parnell Square, one of Dublin's earliest and most attractive squares of handsome brick-faced Georgian houses; Charlemont House, containing the Hugh Lane Municipal Gallery of Modern Art; Nassau Street, with its bookstores; the National Gallery, housing more than 2000 works of art; the National Museum's fascinating collection of Irish treasures; the Civic Museum, and Trinity College Library. Dublin Castle's state apartments have guided tours every half-hour, and the Guinness brewery offers visitors a 30-minute film show, followed by a tasting.

Christ Church Cathedral
Christchurch Place
☎01 6778099 Fax 01 6798991
Founded in 1038, although largely rebuilt since then, it retains its ancient crypt. Many objects of historic interest occupy the interior.
Open 10-5.
P (100yds) ⅍ *shop* ⌘
Details not confirmed for 1998

Drimnagh Castle
Long Mile Rd, Drimnagh
☎01 4502530 Fax 01 4505401
The last surviving medieval castle in Ireland with a flooded moat, Drimnagh dates originally to the 13th century. The Great Hall and Undercroft have been restored to their medieval grandeur, set off by the 17th-century style formal gardens, all of which are open to the public. Continuously inhabited until 1954, it is now populated by a team of crafts men, apprentices and young trainees, restoring the later tower, stables and coach-house with the same meticulous attention to detail as was used for the older parts. Please contact for details of special events, including family fun days etc.
Open Apr-Sep, Wed, wknds & BH's 12-5; Oct-Mar, Sun & BH's 2-5.
IR£1.50 (ch IR50p, pen & students IR£1). Party.
P ☕ ⅍ *(gravel courtyard and garden. steps)* ⌘ *(ex guide dogs)*

Dublin Castle
Dame St
☎(01) 6777129
Fax (01) 6797831
With two towers and a partial wall, this is the city's most outstanding legacy of the Middle Ages. Of interest are the Record Tower, state apartments, Church of the Most Holy Trinity and Heraldic Museum. The inauguration of the President of Ireland and related ceremonies are held in St. Patrick's Hall, an elegant state apartment.
✗ ⅍ *toilets for disabled*
Details not confirmed for 1998

Dublinia
St Michael's Hill, Christ Church
☎01 6794611
Fax 01 6797116
The story of medieval Dublin. Housed in the former Synod Hall beside Christ Church Cathedral and developed by the Medieval Trust, Dublinia recreates the period from the arrival of Strongbow and the Anglo-Normans in 1170 to the closure of the monasteries by Henry VIII in 1540. Using an audio-visual guide, sets, reconstructions, scale model with commentary and an audio-visual presentation, the tale of medieval Dublin unfolds.
Open Apr-Sep 10-5; Oct-Mar, Mon-Sat 11-4, Sun/BH 10-4.30. Closed 24-26 Dec.
IR£3.95 (ch/pen/student/unwaged IR£2.90). Family ticket IR£10. All rates include admission to cathedral.
P (100yds) ☕ ⅍ *(3 floors accessible, but bridge and tower are not) toilets for disabled shop* ⌘ *(ex guide dogs)*
Cards: 🖳 ▦ 🔲

Dublin Writers Museum
18 Parnell Square North
☎01 8722077 Fax 01 8722231
The Dublin Writers Museum and Irish Writers Centre is housed in two restored 18th-century buildings which retain many of their Georgian characteristics, and a modern annexe with lecture rooms and exhibition spaces. Dublin's rich literary heritage can be followed through displays tracing the written tradition in Ireland from the Book of Kells in the 8th century to the present day. Paintings, letters, photographs and artefacts are also on show. An audio tour, in French, Spanish, German, Italian and Japanese is included in the admission price.
Open all year, Mon-Sat 10-5 & Sun & BH 11-6. Jun-Aug, Mon-Fri 10-6pm.
IR£2.95 (ch IR£1.30, concessions IR£2.50). Family ticket IR£8.
P (200 yds) (Metered) ☕ ✗ *licensed shop* ⌘

Guinness Hop Store
St.James's Gate
☎01 4084800 Fax 01 4084965
Established in 1876, the HopStore remained crammed with hopsacks until 1957, when a new hop store came into use. It has now been converted to 'The World of Guinness' which shows the history of the famous brewery through museum exhibits and audio-visual presentations. In 'The Cooperage', there is a comprehensive collection of cooper's tools and oak casks displayed in an authentic brewery setting. There is also a Transport Gallery and a Sample Bar, where you can taste the famous drink. A gallery dedicated to the world-famous Guinness advertising and a coffee-shop are recent additions. Also a souvenir shop, crammed with Guinness branded merchandise of all types.
Open all year, daily (Closed 25-26Dec & Good Fri) Jan-Mar & Oct-Dec, Mon-Sat 9.30-4 (Sun & PH 12-4) Apr-Sep Mon-Sat 9.30-5 (Sun & PH 10.30-4.30)
£4 (ch £1, pen/students £3) Group 20.
P ☕ ⅍ *toilets for disabled shop* ⌘
Cards: 🖳 ▦ 🔲

Howth Castle Rhododendron Gardens
Howth (9m NE of Dublin city centre, via Fairview Clontarf & Sutton)
☎01 8322624 & 8322256
Fax 01 8392405
On the northern boundary of Dublin Bay, the castle is justly famous for its attractive gardens and it is especially lauded for its rhododendron walk. The walk is open all year, but is at its floral best in May and June. There are views north to the Mourne Mountains and to the west of Dublin Bay.
Open all year, daily 8am-dusk. (Closed 25 Dec).
Free.
P ☕ ✗ *licensed* ⅍ *(ramped entrance) toilets for disabled* ⌘ *(ex guide dogs)*
Cards: 🖳 ▦ 🔲

Hugh Lane Municipal Gallery of Modern Art
Charlemont House, Parnell Square
☎01 8741903
Fax 01 8722182
Situated in Charlemont House, one of Dublin's finest Georgian buildings. Established in 1908 the Gallery's collection comprises an extensive range of Irish and International paintings, sculpture, works on paper and stained glass. The founding collection, donated by Sir Hugh Lane and his supporters includes fine examples of Impressionist art, including works by Monet, Rodin and Degas. There is also a collection of English Victorian paintings, and the Gallery holds one of the most extensive collections of 20th century Irish art. The most recent aquisitions reflect the gallery's role as a gallery of modern art, featuring contemporary work by Irish and international artists such as Sean Scully, Niki de Saint Phalle, Joseph Beuys and William Scott. Special events for 1998 include exhibitions by Rita Duffy, Janet

The superb glasshouses at the National Botanic Gardens in Dublin were erected between 1834 and 1869.

Mullarney, and works by graduates of the National College of Art and Design Master of Arts Degree. There are also regular concerts at noon on Sundays throughout the year and public lectures every Sunday, and also public lectures every Sunday. Please contact the Gallery for a Programme of Events.
Open all year, Tue-Thu 9.30-6, Fri-Sat 9.30-5, Sun 11-5. Late night opening Thu until 8, Apr-Aug only. (Closed Mon). (Closed Good Fri & 24-25 Dec).
Free.
P (100 metres) (meter parking) ✗ *licensed* ⅍ *(Ramp & reserved parking) toilets for disabled shop* ⌘ *(ex guide dogs)*

Irish Museum of Modern Art
Royal Hospital Kilmainham, Kilmainham (from City Centre pass Heuston Station, 1st left on St John's Rd)
☎01 6718666
Fax 01 6718695
The museum is housed in the Royal Hospital Kilmainham, a large impressive 17th-century building laid out around an elegant courtyard. It presents a wide-ranging programme of Irish and International 20th-century art from its own collections and through temporary exhibitions, along with talks, seminars and musical events. Exhibitions planned for 1998 include Peter Shelton (5 Mar-14 Jun), Brian Cronin (31 Mar-2 Jun), The Glen Dimplex Artist's Award (8 Apr-5 Jul), Outsiders Art (11 Jun - mid-September, Nissan Art Project (Summer), William Scott (21 Jul-1 Nov), Hughie O'Donoghue (end Oct - mid-Feb), Ilya Kabakov (19 Nov-Apr), Glen Dimplex Artists Award (Apr-June '99), Joseph Beuys (8 May-Jul '99).
Open all year Tue-Sat 10-5.30, Sun & BH's 12-5.30. (Closed 24-26 Dec & 17 Mar)
Free.
P ☕ ⅍ *(wheelchair available) toilets for disabled shop* ⌘

James Joyce Centre
35 North Great George's St
☎01 8788547 Fax 01 8788488
Situated in a beautifully restored 18th century Georgian townhouse, the Centre is dedicated to the promotion of a greater interest in, and understanding of, the life and works of Joyce. There is a well-stocked library open to visitors, exhibition rooms, videos and tapes. Please telephone for details of special events which will be taking place in 1998.
Open all year, Mon-Sat 9.30-5, Sun 12.30-5.
£2.75 (ch 50p, pen & students £2). Party.
P (200 mtrs) ☕ ⅍ *toilets for disabled shop* ⌘
Cards: ▦ 🔲

Kilmainham Gaol
Inchicore Rd
☎01 4535984 Fax 01 4532037
An unparalleled historical resource in the understanding of Ireland's emergence as a modern nation.
Access by guided tour only. Open Apr-Sep, daily 9.30-6 (last tour 4.45); Oct-Mar, Mon-Fri 9.30-5 (last tour 4pm), Sun 10-6 (last tour 4.45pm).
P (on street parking only) ☕ ⅍ *toilets for disabled* ⌘
Details not confirmed for 1998

Marsh's Library
St Patrick's Close
☎01 4543511 Fax 01 4543511
The first public library in Ireland dating from 1701. It was designed by William Robinson and the interior has been unchanged for nearly 300 years. The collection is of approximately 25,000 volumes of 16th, 17th and early 18th centuries books. Marsh's is a superb example of a 17th century scholar's library. Until May 1998: 'Eve Revived' - early printed books relating to women in Marsh's Library.
Open Mon & Wed-Fri, 10-12.45 & 2-5; Sat 10.30-12.45.
P ⌘ ♿
Details not confirmed for 1998

National Botanic Gardens
Glasnevin
☎(01) 8374388 & 8377596 Fax 01 8360080
The National Botanic Gardens, established in 1795 and covering an area of 48 acres, contains fine collections of trees and shrubs, as well as renowned herbaceous borders. Separate areas are devoted to annuals and vegetables, and to native Irish plants, arranged according to habitats. A self-guiding trail, highlighting some interesting hardy Chinese species, has been laid out for the visitor to follow. The glasshouses contain collections of palms, rare cycads, tropical ferns, cacti and alpines. A feature of special interest is the recently restored iron and glass Curvilinear Range (1843-1869) principally designed and built by Richard Turner.
Open all year, summer Mon-Sat 9-6, Sun 11-6; winter Mon-Sat 10-4.30, Sun 11-4.30. (Closed 25 Dec).
P ⅍ *(Wheelchair available) toilets for disabled* ⌘
Details not confirmed for 1998

National Gallery of Ireland
Merrion Square
☎01 6615133 Fax 01 6615372
Founded in 1854 and opened to the public in 1864. In addition to the national collection of Irish art, the Gallery houses the national collection of European Old

➤

Masters from the fourteenth to twentieth centuries. Temporary exhibitions for 1998 include Graphic Art Exhibition (20 May-23 Aug). Please contact for details.
Mon-Sat 10-5.30 (Thu 10-8.30), Sun 2-5. Closed 24-26 Dec.
Free.
P (5 mins walk) (meter parking) 🍽 ✗ licensed 🚻 (braille/audio tours, lifts, ramps, parking bay) toilets for disabled shop 🚭

Natural History Museum
Merrion St
☎ 01 6777444 Fax 01 6766116
The Natural History Museum was recently described by Professor Stephen Jay Gould as one of the world's finest and fullest exhibits in the old and still-stunning cabinet style. Founded by the Royal Dublin Soceiety in 1792, it has occupied its present premises since 1857. It was taken over by the state in 1877. There are extensive zoological exhibitions and geological specimens are also on display. The ground floor is devoted to Irish fauna while the first floor contains examples of all the major animal groups including many rare specimens. The Blaschka glass models of marine animals are world-famous. The museum is also an important research institute.
Open Tue-Sat 10-5, Sun 2-5.
P (parking meters wkdays) 🚻 🚭
Details not confirmed for 1998

Newman House
University College Dublin, 86 St Stephens Green (South side of St.Stephen's Green)
☎ 01 7067422 & 4757255 Fax 01 7067211
Newman House consists of two superb Georgian townhouses which contain some of Ireland's finest 18th-century plasterwork and decoration. As the founding home of University College Dublin in 1854, the house has been associated with many famous literary and historical figures, including James Joyce, Gerard Manley Hopkins, and Cardinal Newman. A major restoration programme, begun in 1989, has restored No 85 to its former Georgian splendour.
Jun-Aug, Tue-Fri 12-5; Sat 2-5; Sun 11-1. At other times tours by prior arrangement only.
IR£2 (concessions IR£1).
P (100 yards) (metres) ✗ licensed shop 🚭

Number Twenty Nine
29 Lower Fitzwilliam St (SE corner of Merrion Sq.)
☎ 01 7026165
Fax 01 6615376
Number Twenty-Nine is an exhibition of the homelife of a middle-class merchant family in late 18th and early 19th century Dublin. It is presented by the Electricity Supply Board and the National Museum of Ireland and one visit will only whet the appetite for more! There are occasional evening events. Young Musicians in the Drawing Room. Wednesdays during February and November. Please ring for reservations.
Open all year, Tue-Sat 10-5, Sun 2-5. (Closed Mon & 2 wks prior to Xmas).
IR£2.50 (ch 16 and under free, pen, students & unemployed IR£1.
P (charged) 🍽 shop 🚭
Cards: 🖃 🖃

Phoenix Park Visitor Centre
Phoenix Park
☎ 01 6770095
Fax 01 8205584
Situated in Phoenix Park the Visitor Centre provides an historical interpretation of the park from 3500BC through a series of attractive displays. Part of the building is devoted to nature and there is a colourful film of Phoenix Park. The castle, probably dating from the early 17th century has been restored to its former glory.
Open daily all year; Jan-mid Mar Sat-Sun 09.30-16.30. mid-end Mar daily 09.30-17.00. Apr-May daily 09.30-17.30. June-

Sept daily 09.30-18.30. October daily 09.30-17.00. Nov-Dec daily 09.30-16.30. Last admission 45 mins before closing.
IR£2 (ch & students IR£1, pen IR£1.50). Family ticket IR£5.
P 🍽 🚻 toilets for disabled shop 🚭 (ex guide dogs)

Royal Zoological Society of Ireland
Phoenix Park (3m from city centre in Phoenix Park)
☎ 01 6771425 Fax 01 6771660
The gardens were founded in 1830 and today exhibit many species of birds and mammals. It takes part in 25 regional and international breeding programmes for endangered species. A major development plan is underway at present and the new reptile house offers a state of the art facility. Recently opened Monkey World incorporates new island homes for the monkeys and environment improvements for the apes. "Fringes from the Arctic" is a new themed area. Also a new City Farm. Most bank holiday weekends feature special promotions. Please ring for details.
Open all year, Mon-Sat 9.30-6, Sun 10.30-6. Gardens close sunset in winter. (Closed 25 & 26 Dec)
IR£5.80 (ch & pen IR£3.10, ch under 3 free). Family ticket IR£15.50-IR£17.80 Party 20+ (phone for details).
P 🍽 ✗ licensed 🚻 (Wheelchairs are available) toilets for disabled shop 🚭
Cards: 🖃 🖃

George Bernard Shaw House
33 Synge St
☎ 01 4750854 & 8722077
Fax 01 8722231
The modest 1840s terrace house where the playwright and Nobel prizewinner George Bernard Shaw was born and spent the first eleven years of his life. It was here he began to gather a store of characters whom he would later recreate in his plays. The house has been fully restored and refurbished in such a way as to recreate the atmosphere and character it must have had when the Shaw family lived there.
Open May Oct, Mon-Sat 10-1 & 2-5, Sun & BH's 11.30-1, 2-6.
P (charged) shop garden centre 🚭 (ex guide dogs)
Details not confirmed for 1998

DUN LAOGHAIRE
James Joyce Tower
Sandycove (1m SE from Dun Laoghaire by coast rd to Sandycove Point or turn off main Dun Laoghaire-Dalkey road)
☎ 01 2809265 & 8722077
Fax 2809265
Built by the British as a defence against a possible invasion by Napoleon, the tower has walls approximately 8ft thick and an original entrance door 13ft above the ground. The tower was once the temporary home of James Joyce, who depicted this setting in the opening scene of *Ulysses*. The structure is now a museum devoted to the author. The annual Bloomsday celebrations will be celebrated on 16 June, and will include readings and performances.
Open Apr-Oct Mon-Sat 10-1 & 2-5, Sun & PHs 2-6; Nov-Mar by arrangement.
P (100 yds) 🚻 shop 🚭 (ex guide dogs)
Details not confirmed for 1998

MALAHIDE
Fry Model Railway
Malahide Castle
☎ 01 8463779 & 8462184
Fax 01 8462537
The Fry Model Railway is a rare collection of '0' gauge trains and trams, depicting the history of Irish rail transport from the first train that ran in 1834. Cyril Fry began to build his model collection in the late 1920s, in the attic of his home. All the models are built to scale, and they are now housed in a purpose-built setting adjacent to Malahide Castle.
Open all year, Apr-Oct, Mon-Thu 10-1 & 2-5, Sat 11-1 & 2-6, Sun & PH 2-6 (also

The World of Guinness at the Hop Store shows the famous brewery through the years.

Jun-Aug Fri 10-1 & 2-5, Jul-Aug Sun & PH's 11.30-1 & 2-6); Oct-Mar Sat-Sun & PH 2-5. Parties at other times by arrangement.
P 🚻 shop 🚭
Details not confirmed for 1998

Malahide Castle
☎ 01 8462184 & 8462516
Fax 01 8462537
One of Ireland's oldest castles, with a late medieval core as the nucleus to the romantic and beautiful structure, in 250 acres of grounds; the contours of the castle have changed very little in 800 years. Tours offer views of Irish period furniture and historical Irish portrait collections. Additional paintings from the National Gallery depict Irish life from the last few centuries.
Open all year, Apr-Oct, Mon-Fri 10-5, Sat 11-6, Sun & PH 11.30-6; Nov-Mar, Mon-Fri 10-5, Sat-Sun & PH 2-5. Closed for tours 12.45-2pm.
P 🍽 ✗ licensed shop 🚭
Details not confirmed for 1998
Cards: 🖃 🖃 🖃 🖃

CO GALWAY

GALWAY
Nora Barnacle House Museum
Bowling Green (close to St Nicholas Collegiate Church)
☎ 091 564743
Just a few steps from Shop Street, by St Nicolas Collegiate Church nestles the smallest museum in Ireland, a perfect setting in which to take you back through the romantic mists of time. This tiny turn-of-century house was the home Nora Barnacle, companion, wife and lifelong inspiration of James Joyce. It was here in 1909, sitting at the kitchen table that Joyce first met his darling's mother. Letters, photographs and other exhibits of the lives of James Joyce & Nora Barnacle make a visit here a unique experience. Bloomsday (16th June) - readings and tour.
Open Mon-Sat 2-5, mid May-mid Sep.
P 100yds shop
Details not confirmed for 1998

Royal Tara China Visitor Centre
Tara Hall, Mervue (off N17 opp Trappers Rest or left off N6 after Ryan's Hotel)
☎ 091 751301 Fax 091 757574
Royal Tara China is the country's leading manufacturer of fine bone china, cold

cast bronze miniature pubs, castles and cottages, and exclusive handpainted pieces. Situated in a magnificent Georgian mansion minutes from Galway's city centre. Take the free tour of the factory and witness the creation of many exquisite pieces, which may be purchased from the factory showrooms. Tours every hour from 9.30 - 3.30. 'Life in Lights' - fundraiser for Galway Hospice every evening in December.
Open all year, 9-6 (8.30am-8pm Jul-Sep, 9am-9pm Dec). Guided factory tours Mon-Fri 9.30-3.30.
Free.
P 🍽 ✗ 🚻 toilets for disabled shop 🚭 (ex guide dogs)
Cards: 🖃 🖃 🖃 🖃

Spanish Arch Civic Museum
☎ 091 567641
In the south-west quarter, the arches date from the days when Spain and Ireland had trading ties. Galway City Museum at the arch is devoted to the city's history. A large map of the city in 1651 can be seen in the museum. Examples of medieval stonework, stone axe heads and scrapers dating from 3,500 years BC, a peat fire, photographs of 19th century traditional dress, memorabilia of Connaught Rangers Regiment etc.
Open all year daily, Mar-Oct 10-5.15. Nov-Feb 2-4 times under review.
✲IR£1. (concessions IR50p).
P (100yds) (parking discs required) 🚻 🚭 (ex guide dogs)

GORT
Thoor Ballylee
(1km off the N18, 1km off the N66)
☎ 091 631436 Fax 091 565201
This tower house is the former home of the poet William Butler Yeats and where he completed most of his literary works. The tower has been restored to appear exactly as it was when he lived there, and houses an Interpretative Centre with audio-visual presentations and displays of his work.
Open Etr-Sep, daily 10-6.
IR£3.00 (ch IR£1, pen & students IR£2.50). Family ticket IR£6. Party.
P 🍽 🚻 (audio-visual presentation) toilets for disabled shop 🚭
Cards: 🖃 🖃

KINVARRA
Dunguaire Castle
☎ 091 37108 & 061 360788 Fax 061 361020

Dunguaire Castle has stood for hundreds of years on the site of the 7th-century stronghold of Guaire, the King of Connaught. The castle bridges 13 centuries of Irish history from the skirmishes, battles and sieges that characterise its colourful past to the literary revival of the early 20th century. Today the restored castle gives an insight into the lifestyle of the people who lived there from 1520 to modern times.
Open May-Oct, daily 9.30-5.30 (last admission 5pm).
IR£2.60 (ch IR£1.50, pen/student IR£1.40). Family ticket IR£6.60.
P *shop* *(ex guide dogs)*
Cards: 🔲 🔳 🔳

ROUNDSTONE
Roundstone Musical Instruments
Craft Centre
☎ 095 35875 Fax 095 35980
Situated in an old Franciscan monastry at Roundstone is the craft workshop of Malachy Kearns who makes Ireland's oldest product - the Bodhrán (Bow-rawn). It is an 18inch one-side drum made from goatskin treated by a traditional process. The drum is played with a tipper or beater while the tone is varied by pressing the back of the skin with the other hand. Visitors can see the drums being made and also decorated with handpainted designs by Anne Kearns. Bodhráns can be purchased and special designs commissioned, seconds are available too, as are smaller drums. See the first Riverdance drums that Malachy made here. Have your photo taken standing on them! Seals and dolphins come up to the monastry walls during the summer. The Irish Government acknowledged Malachy's work by putting him on the 32p postage stamp in autumn 1997. A new museum dealing with the history of the bodhrán opens in spring 1998.
Open all year daily 9-6.
Free.
P 🍴 & *toilets for disabled shop*

CO KERRY

CASTLEISLAND
Crag Cave
(1m N, signposted off N21)
☎ 066 41244 Fax 066 42352
Crag Cave is one of the longest surveyed cave systems in Ireland with a total length of 3.81km (12,510ft). The existence of the cave was known locally for many years but the present show cave was only discovered in 1983 by a Welsh diver Martyn Farr. It is a spectacular world, where pale forests of stalagmites and stalagtites, thousands of years old, throw eerie shadows around vast echoing caverns complemented by dramatic sound and lighting effects. This is an all-weather tourist attraction and a guided tour lasts about 30 minutes.
Open daily, Mar-Nov 10-6 (Jul-Aug until 7pm).
IR£3 (ch IR£1.75, Pen & Students IR£2.50). Family ticket IR£8. Party.
P 🍴 X *licensed* & *(ramp to visitor centre) toilets for disabled shop*
Cards: 🔲 🔳 🔳

DUNQUIN
The Blasket Centre
(10m W of Dingle town, on Slea Head Drive.)
☎ 066 56444 & 56371 Fax 066 56446
In the early part of this century a small group of writers from the remote Blasket Island, just off the coast of County Kerry, achieved world renown. They told their own story in their own language - Irish. The centre describes the lives of the hardy Blasket Islanders before the sad abandonment of the island in 1953. The literary works produced in the 1920s and 30s included masterpieces such as "The Islandman" and "Twenty Years A-Growing" which have been translated from the Gaelic to English, French, German and many other languages. Facilities include a state-of-the-art

exhibition and an audio-visual documentary on the Blasket Heritage, together with a restaurant and bookshop. Research and conference facilities also available.
Open daily, Etr-late Oct 10-6 (7pm Jul-Aug). Open on request all year for groups over 30.
IR£2.50 (ch & student IR£1, pen IR£1.75). Family tcket IR£6.
P 🍴 X *licensed* & *(Reserved parking) toilets for disabled*

KENMARE
Kenmare Heritage Centre
The Square
☎ 064 31633 Fax 064 34506
Kenmare has been designated a Bord Failte Heritage Town under the theme of "A Planned Estate Town". The town grew around the mineworks founded in 1670, planned by Sir William Petty, ancestor of the Lansdownes, local landlords. The Heritage Centre covers the history of Kenmare including famous visitors. The effects of the Famine; the landlords; historical sites; the Nun of Kenmare and a Kenmare lace exhibition. Audio tours are available in three languages.
Open Apr-Sep, Mon-Sat 9.30-5.30 (also Sun Jul-Aug)
IR£2 (ch 12 IR£1, pen & student IR£1.50). Family ticket IR£5.
P *(400mtrs)* & *toilets for disabled shop* *(ex guide dogs)*
Cards: 🔲 🔳

KILLARNEY
Killarney Transport Museum
Scotts Hotel Gardens (centre of town, opposite railway station)
☎ 064 34677 Fax 064 32638
The glorious years of motoring can be re-lived in this unique collection of fascinating Irish veteran, vintage and classic cars, motorcycles, bicycles, carriages and fire engines. Exhibits include the 1907 Silver Stream (reputed to be the rarest car in the world, it was designed and built by an Irishman and he only made one!); a 1904 Germain, and a 1910 Wolseley Siddeley driven by WB Yeats. The museum also has a 1930s garage with the tools, spare parts, oil cans and even a mechanic working on a car. Also, the whole history of cycling is represented; from the pedal-less hobby-horse (1825) up to Stephen Roche's training cycle. For details of special events, which include 'Gordon Bennett' rally (May), 'Classic Tour of Ireland' (May), Classic car tours (all summer), please telephone.
Open Mar-Oct, daily 10-6, Nov-Feb 11-4. Open at other times by appointment IR£2.50 (ch IR£1, students & pen IR£2). Family ticket IR£6. Wheelchair visitors free. Party.
P & *shop*

TRALEE
Blennerville Steam Railway
Ballyard Station, Dingle Rd (follow signs for Dingle on N86/R559)
☎ (066) 28888 Fax 066 27444
The Tralee-Blennerville Steam Railway is part of the famous Tralee & Dingle Light Railway (1891-1953) restored in 1993 from Tralee to Blennerville (3km). Steam trains, powered by T & D Loco No. 5 (1892), operate from Tralee (Ballyard Station) to Blennerville. The carriages, though not original, are fitted out in the traditional style. An on-board commentary is provided. The line was featured in the Great Railway Journeys of the World TV series.
Open daily Apr-Nov.
P & *shop*
Details not confirmed for 1998

Blennerville Windmill Visitor & Craft Centre
Blennerville (1m W, on N86/R559)
☎ (066) 21064 Fax 066 27444
The largest working windmill in Britain and Ireland is the focal point of a major visitor and craft complex. Blennerville was a major port of emigration during the mid-19th century. Visitor facilities include an audio-visual theatre, exhibitions on flour milling and 19th-century emigration,

craftworkshops, craft shop and restaurant. Admission includes the guided tour. On a site adjoining the windmill a reconstruction of the 19th-century Tralee emigrant vessel, the "Jeanie Johnston" (1847-58), is being built in preparation for the 150th anniversary of the Great Irish Famine (1845-48) in 1997/8 when it will sail to North America.
Open daily, Apr-Nov.
P 🍴 X *licensed shop*
Details not confirmed for 1998

Kerry The Kingdom Museum
Ashe Memorial Hall, Denny St
☎ (066) 27777
Fax 066 27444
This is one of Ireland's most visited attractions. The museum tells the story of Kerry (and Ireland) from earliest times. The centre comprises three attractions within the splendidly restored Thomas Ashe Memorial Hall (1923-28): an audio-visual presentation on Kerry's spectacular scenery and historic monuments; the priceless treasures of Kerry origin in the Kerry Museum, which was listed among Europe's top twenty museums in 1994; Geraldine Tralee - a reconstruction of Tralee during the Middle Ages when Tralee was the principal seat of the Anglo-Norman FitzGeralds (Geraldines). Visitors travel by time car through the reconstructed streets and houses of the medieval town. Synchronised sound, lighting and odour effects help to make this an almost life-like experience!
Open daily, Mar-Oct 10-6; Aug 10-7; Nov-Dec 12-5. (Closed 24-26 Dec).
P *(100mtrs)* *(disc parking area)* 🍴 & *(enter through tourist office entrance) toilets for disabled shop garden centre*
Details not confirmed for 1998

VALENTIA ISLAND
The Skellig Experience
(Ring of Kerry road, signed after Cahersiveen town then Valentia bridge or ferry from Renard Point)
☎ 064 31633
Fax 064 34506
The Skellig Rocks are renowned for their scenery, sea bird colonies, lighthouses, Early Christian monastic architecture and rich underwater life. The two Skellig island - Skellig Michael and Small Skellig - stand like fairytale castles in the Atlantic Ocean, rising to 218 metres and their steep cliffs plunging 50 metres below the sea. The Heritage Centre, (on Valentina Island, which is reached from the mainland via a bridge), has an audio visual show running at regular intervals to tell the story of the Skellig Michael monastery. Other information is provided on the seabirds and their habitat, the 161 years of lighthouse service to mariners and the colour and magic of underwater Skellig using graphics models and sound. A personal audio tour is available in three languages.
Open Apr-Jun & Sep 10-7, Jul-Aug 9.30-7.
IR£3 (ch IR£1.50, pen & student IR£2.70). Family ticket IR£7.
P 🍴 & *toilets for disabled shop* *(ex guide dogs)*
Cards: 🔲 🔳 🔳 🔳

CO KILDARE

CELBRIDGE
Castletown House
(13m from Dublin, follow signs to Celbridge from N4)
☎ 01 6288252
Fax 01 6271811
Ireland's largest and finest Palladian country house, begun c1722 for William Conolly, speaker of the Irish House of Commons. Designed by Italian architect, Alessandro Galilei, and also in part by Irish architect Sir Edward Lovett Pearce. The state rooms include the 'Pompeian' Long Gallery with its Venetian chandeliers, the only surviving 18th-century print room in Ireland, the recently

restored green silk drawing room and magnificent staircase hall with Lafranchini plasterwork. There is a fine collection of 18th-century Irish furniture and paintings.
Castletown will be closed until autumn 1998 for restoration work.
P *shop* *(ex guide dogs)*
Details not confirmed for 1998

KILDARE
Japanese Gardens
Irish National Stud, Tully (Off the N7, 1mile outside Kildare town)
☎ 045 521617 522963
Fax 045 522964
One visit - two different worlds! Situated in the grounds of the Irish National Stud, the gardens were established by Lord Wavertree between 1906 and 1910, and symbolise 'The Life of Man' in Japanese-style landscape. Visitors can explore the gardens using self-guide leaflets; guided tours are available for groups booked in advance. Facilities include a picnic area, craft shop, restaurant, garden centre and Lego play area for children. Admission covers the Japanese Gardens and The Irish National Stud. Guided tours of The Stud are available. Also visit the Horse Museum which includes the skeleton of Arkle. See Vintage Crop - winner of the prestigious Melbourne Cup in 1993.
Open 12 Feb-12 Nov, daily 9.30-6, last admission 5pm.
✳*IR£5 (ch 12 IR£2, students & pen IR£3.50). Family ticket IR£12. Prices under review.*
P X *licensed* & *(all parts of stud accessible, only small part of gardens) toilets for disabled shop garden centre* *(ex on lead)*
Cards: 🔲 🔳

CO KILKENNY

KILKENNY
Kilkenny Castle
☎ 056 21450
Fax 056 63488
Situated in a beautiful 50-acre park, the castle dates from 1172. The first stone castle was built 20 years later by William Marshall, Earl of Pembroke. It was home of the very powerful Butler family, Earls and Dukes of Ormonde from 1391 to 1935. In state care since 1969, to date two wings have been restored and opened to the public. Within the next two years the final phase of restoration should be complete. The Kitchen serves as a restaurant from May to September. The Butler Art Gallery, situated in the former servants' rooms, mounts frequently changing exhibitions of contemporary art.
Open all year - Jun-Sep daily 10-7; Apr-May daily 10.30-5; Oct-Mar Tue-Sat 10.30-12.45 & 2-5, Sun 11-12.45 & 2-5. Last tour 45mins before closing. Closed Xmas & Good Fri.
IR£3 (ch, students IR£1.25 & pen IR£2). Family ticket IR£7.50.
P *(charged)* 🍴 & *(ex guide dogs)*

CO LIMERICK

FOYNES
Flying Boat Museum
(on N69, 23m from Limerick City)
☎ 069 65416 Fax 069 65416
The museum recalls the era of the flying boats during the 1930s and early 1940s when Foynes was an important airport for air traffic between the United States and Europe. The flying boats brought in a diverse range of people from celebrities to refugees. Located in the original terminal building, it is the only museum of its kind in the world. There is a comprehensive range of exhibits, graphic illustrations and a 1940s style cinema featuring a 17 minute film - all original footage from the 30s and 40s. It was here that Irish coffee was first invented in 1943 by Chef Joe Sheridan. In 1998 ➤

the Powers Irish Coffee Festival (including the World Irish Coffee Making Championship) will be held August 13-16.
Open daily, 31 Mar-31 Oct 10-6. Last admissions 5.15pm
IRE3 (ch IRE1.50, student IRE2.50). Family ticket IRE8.
P ☕ & *toilets for disabled shop* ✄ *(ex guide dogs)*
Cards: ▣ ▦

HOLYCROSS
Lough Gur Stone Age Centre
Bruff Rd (17 km S of Limerick City, off R512 rd to Kilmallock)
☎ *061 385186 & 061 360788*
Fax 061 361020
Lough Gur introduces visitors to the habitat of Neolithic Man on one of Ireland's most important archaeological sites. Near the lake is an interpretative centre which tells the story of 5000 years of man's presence at Lough Gur. The centre features an audio-visual presentation, models of stone circles, burial chambers and facsimiles of weapons, tools and pottery found in the area. Walking tours covering the archaeological features of the area are conducted at regular intervals.
Open May-Sep, daily 10-6 (last admission 5pm)
IRE2.10 (ch IRE1.20, pen IR1.60). Family ticket IRE5.60).
P ☕ & *shop* ✄ *(ex guide dogs)*
Cards: ▣ ▦ ▦ ▥

KILCORNAN
Celtic Park & Gardens
(N69 Limerick to Tralge rd)
☎ *061 394243*
Fax 353 69 64257
The Celtic Park and Gardens are located on an original Celtic settlement within one of the most important Cromwellian plantations in the south-west of Ireland. The park, its two loughs and its environment are completely unspoilt by modern man. Visitors walking through the park are able to see a church built in 1250, a Mass rock, dolmens, a 6/7th century wooden church, a stone circle, lake dwellings, cooking site and other fascinating sights including one of the finest examples of an early surviving historic ring fort. The surrounding landscape offers meadow, scrubland, cragland and bog with many species of wild flower. The classic-style gardens afford a panoramic view of the surrounding countryside. The gardens contain over 1000 roses, flowering shrubs, a rockery, herbaceous borders, shrubbery, collonades and gravel paths with limestone kerbing in an oasis of quiet and beauty.
Open daily, Mar-Oct 9-7. Last entry 6pm.
P ☕ *shop (on lead)*
Details not confirmed for 1998

LIMERICK
Hunt Museum
The Custom House, Rutland St
☎ *061 312833*
Fax 061 312834
The Hunt Museum is housed at the impressively restored Old Custom House. Three floors of galleries exhibit an internationally renowned collection of 2000 pieces of art and antiquity which was collected by John and Gertrude Hunt and presented to the people of Ireland. It includes statues in stone, bronze and wood, crucifixes, panel paintings , metalwork, jewellry, enamels and ceramics.
There are drawings by Picasso and da Vinci, and a gold cross worn by Mary, Queen of Scots. Irish pieces include the Antrim Cross and the Cashel Bell. There are temporary exhibitions planned throughout 1998.
Open daily Tues-Sat 10-5, Sun 2-5. Closed Mon.
IRE3.90 (ch & students IRE2.50). Family ticket IRE9. Party.
P *(100mtrs) (parking discs for street parking)* ☕ ✗ *licensed* & *toilets for disabled shop* ✄
Cards: ▣ ▦

King John's Castle
Nicholas St
☎ *061 411201 & 360788*
Fax 061 361020
A national monument marked by an imposing twin-towered gatehouse and battle-scarred walls. The 13th-century King John's Castle is an impressive Anglo-Norman fortress where imaginative models and three-dimensional displays demonstrate 800 years of Limerick's and Ireland's history. An audio-visual show depicts the wars, sieges and treaties of its past, and in the courtyard there are copies of ancient war machines.
Open Apr-Oct daily 9.30-5.30 (last admission 4.30); Nov-Apr, Sun 11-4 (last admission 3pm).
IRE3.90 (ch IRE2.20, pen IRE2.85). Family ticket IRE10.10.
P ☕ & *(lifts and ramps) toilets for disabled shop* ✄ *(ex guide dogs)*
Cards: ▣ ▦ ▦ ▥

CO MONAGHAN

INNISKEEN
Patrick Kavanagh Rural & Literary Resource Centre
Candlefort (between Carrickmacross N2 & Dundalk N1)
☎ *042 78560*
Fax 042 78560
Inniskeen, birthplace of Patrick Kavanagh, one of Ireland's foremost 20th-century poets, is a village at the heart of Irish legend and heritage. Examples of early Rock Art and stone circles testify to the ancient history of Inniskeen. The village grew around the ancient monastery of St Daig MacCairill which was founded by 562, and its strong, 10th-century round tower still stands. The rolling hills have inspired poets and scholars, bards and heroes. The Patrick Kavanagh Rural and Literary Resource Centre, housed in the former parish Church, chronicles the ancient history of the region and its role in developing Kavanagh's genius. There are exhibitions and an audio-visual on Kavanagh as well as a research library and Kavanagh country tours, Ireland's only performance tour (booking essential). Please telephone for details of special events.
Open all year, Mon Fri 11-5, wknds & BH's 2-6. (Closed 1 Oct-31 May, closed wknds & BH's 1 Dec-16 Mar)
P ☕ & *toilets for disabled shop*
Details not confirmed for 1998
Cards: ▣ ▦

MONAGHAN
Monaghan County Museum
1-2 Hill St (eanr town centre, opposite Tourist Information office)
☎ *(047) 82928*
Fax 047 71189
This is a modern European and national prize-winning museum of local archaeology, history, arts and crafts. Throughout the year various special exhibitions take place.
Open all year, Tue- Sat 11-1 & 2-5. Free.
P *(near town centre) (restricted on street parking)* & ✄

CO OFFALY

BIRR
Birr Castle Demesne
☎ *0509 20336*
Fax 0509 21583
A large landscaped park with a lake, rivers and waterfalls, containing important plant collections particularly of magnolias, maples, limes and oaks. A catalogue is available of the 2650 listed plants in the collection, some of which are labelled. The demesne is particularly colourful in the spring and autumn, and is

Travel by car through the reconstructed streets of medieval Tralee at the museum of Kerry The Kingdom.

possibly best noted for its formal gardens, containing cloisters or alleys, of hornbeam and the tallest box hedges in the world. The Demesne is also home to the Great Birr Telescope, built in 1844. It has now been restored to its former glory and is open for viewing to the general public.
Open all year -9am-6pm Exhibition open May-Sep daily 2.30-5.30.
P ☕ & *toilets for disabled garden centre*
Details not confirmed for 1998

CO ROSCOMMON

BOYLE
Frybrook House
☎ *079 63513*
Fax 079 62909
Built circa 1750 for Henry Fry, who was to become Chief Magistrate of the area, the house is a rare example of an original and largely unaltered late 18th century town house and garden. The house contains many interesting architectural features, with fine decorative plasterwork and an Adam fireplace in the main drawing room. The 6 acres of grounds are laid out as a miniature landscape park, with views over the Boyle River.
Open Jun-1 Sep, Wed-Sun 2-6. Advisable to check opening dates.
Free.
P &

King House
(in town centre, turn off N4 (Dublin to Sligo road) at Boyle Abbey, house signposted)
☎ *079 63242*
Fax 079 63243
Built by Sir Henry King, MP, around 1730, King House is of unique architectural and historical importance. Home to the king family until 1788, when it became a military barracks and was home to the famous Connaught Rangers Regiment and latterly the national army. Now magnificently restored, it is an award-winning attraction containing several entertaining and informative exhibitions. The stories of the ancient kings of Connact and the Gaelic way of life are explored, as is the King family history from 1603-1987. Further areas focus on the many battles and triumphs of the Connaught Rangers Regiment. There is also an exhibition featuring Georgian architectural and building techniques and the achievments of the restoration programme. Special events include the Boyle Arts Festival, last week July, first week August.
Open 10-6; Etr wknd (Sat-Mon), Apr wknds, May-Sep daily, Oct wknds & BH. Last admission 5pm.
P ☕ ✗ & *(lift to all areas) toilets for disabled shop* ✄
Details not confirmed for 1998

STROKESTOWN
Strokestown Park House Garden & Famine Museum
Strokestown Park
☎ *078 33013*
Fax 078 33712
Strokestown Park is a good example of an early 18th-century gentleman farmer's country estate. Built in Palladian style in the 1730's for Thomas Mahon MP, the house reflects perfectly the confidence of the newly emergent ruling class. The 4 acre pleasure garden has also been restored and is open to the public.The Famine Museum, located in the stable yards commemorates the Great Irish Famine of the 1840s when blight devastated the Irish potato crop, the staple foood of Ireland, and one-quarter of the Irish population - in excess of 2 million people - either died or emigrated. Strokestown was particularly significant in that the landlord, Major Denis Mahon, was assassinated as a result of his

attempts to clear two-thirds of his destitute tenants through eviction and assisted-emigration to North America.
Open daily, Apr-Oct 11-5.30.
✱*House, museum & garden £7.50, house & museum £5.70, house & garden £5.25, museum & garden £5.25, house only/museum only £3, garden only £2.50. Concessions.*
🅿 ✕ *licensed* ♿ *(Access for ramps) toilets for disabled shop*
Cards: 💳 💳

CO TIPPERARY

CAHIR
Swiss Cottage
Kilcommon (1m from town on Ardfinnan road)
☎052 41144
A delightful thatched "cottage orné" built in the early 1800's on the estate of the Earls of Glengall - a design by the famous Regency architect John Nash. The second Sunday of September is Heritage Day.
Open mid Mar-Apr & Oct-Nov, Tue-Sun 10-1 & 2-4.30; May-Sep, daily 10-6. Last admission 30mins before closing. IRE2 (ch & student IRE1, pen IRE1.50). Family ticket IRE5. Party 20+
🅿 ⚘ *(ex guide dog)*

CASHEL
Brú Ború Heritage Centre
☎062 61122
Fax 062 62700
Brú Ború - the palace of Ború - is a national heritage centre at the foot of the Rock of Cashel, a 4th century stone fort. It is a cultural and interpretative village designed around a village green and is home to the study and celebration of native Irish music, song, dance, story telling, theatre and Celtic studies. There is a Folk Theatre where three performances are held daily in the summer and in the evening, banquets evoke the Court of Brian Ború the 11th-century High King of Ireland with songs, poems and sagas. The Teach Ceoil - music house - has a more informal atmosphere for the celebration of Irish music, song and dance. In addition there is a Genealogy Centre.
Open Jan-May & Oct-Dec, Mon-Fri 9.30-5.30; Jun-Sep Tue-Sat 9.30-11, Sun-Mon 9.30-5.30.
Admission to centre free. Night show IRE6.
🅿 *(charged)* ⚘ ✕ *licensed* ♿ *(wheelchair bay in theatre) toilets for disabled shop* ⚘
Cards: 💳 💳 💳 💳

CO WATERFORD

BALLINAMULT
Touraneena Heritage Centre
Touraneena, BALLINAMULT (off R672, 12m from Dungarvan)
☎058 47353
Fax 058 47353
A 300 year old traditional Irish thatched farm, authentically furnished, home of the O'Keefe family for eight generations, featuring a working dairy, blacksmith's forge, vintage farm machinery, gypsy wagon, stable loft and hatchery, depicting Irish rural life in 1890s. The authentic atmosphere is enhanced by staff dressed in costume, live butter-making demonstrations and Irish dancing (jigs and reels) on Sunday afternoons and daily bread and scone baking on a traditional open turf fire. For children there is a pet farm, most animals can be handled and a play area with swings, slides, roundabouts etc.
Open May-Oct, daily 10-7
🅿 ⚘ *shop (on lead)*
Details not confirmed for 1998

LISMORE
Lismore Castle Gardens
☎058 54424 Fax 058 54896
Lismore castle is the Irish home of the Duke of Devonshire. It has been in the Cavendish family since 1748 when the 4th Duke of Devonshire married Lady Charlotte Boyle, the only daughter and heiress of the 4th Earl of Cork. The beautifully situated walled and woodland gardens contain a fine collection of camellias, magnolias and other shrubs and a remarkable Yew Walk. It is said that Spenser wrote part of his *Faerie Queene* in these gardens. The walls and towers at the western boundary of the garden were built in 1626-7 by the first Earl of Cork, they played an important part in the siege of the castle in 1642.
Open 25 Apr-27 Sep, daily 1.45-4.45. IRE2.50 (ch 16 IRE1.50). Party 20+.
🅿

WATERFORD
Waterford Crystal Visitor Centre
(on N25, 1m from city centre)
☎051 73311 Fax 051 78539
These are the largest manufacturers of mouth-blown and hand-cut crystal. There are factory tours everyday to see mastercraftsmen mouth-blow and hand-cut this famous crystal. Visitors can talk to the master engravers and see the crystal being sculptured. In the gallery there is the finest display of Waterford crystal on display and and audio-visual presentation every 20 minutes.
Tours of factory: Mar-Oct, daily 8.30-4.15; Nov-Feb, Mon-Fri 9-4.
🅿 ⚘ ✕ ♿ *(special tours on request) toilets for disabled shop* ⚘
Details not confirmed for 1998
Cards: 💳 💳 💳 💳

CO WEXFORD

FERRYCARRIG
Irish National Heritage Park
(2m from Wexford, on N11)
☎053 20733 Fax 053 20911
Fourteen historical sites set in a magnificent 35-acre mature forest explaining Ireland's history from the Stone and Bronze Ages, through the mighty Celtic period and concluding with the Vikings and Normans. Among the exhibits are a reconstructed Mesolithic camp, a Viking boatyard with 2 full size ships and a Norman motte and bailey. See also our Ancient Breed Animals. There is a multi-language audio-visual presentation on "Ireland Through the Ages." Guided tours are available and there is a celtic-themed restaurant,and Craft shop. Please ring for details of forthcoming special events for 1998.
Open Apr-Oct daily 9.30-6.30. Last admission 5. Allow 1.5 hour for visit. IRE4 (pen & students IRE3.50). Family ticket IRE10.50. Group rates available on request.
🅿 ✕ ♿ *toilets for disabled shop* ⚘ *(ex guide dogs)*
Cards: 💳 💳

NEW ROSS
Dunbrody Abbey Visitors Centre
Dunbrody Abbey, Campile (10 miles from New Ross at the base of the Hook Peninsular)
☎051 88603
The visitor centre is based around the Abbey itself and Dunbrody Castle. There is an intriguing yew hedge maze with 1550 yew trees and a museum. In addition there is a golf pitch and putt course with competions organised twice a month.
Open Apr-Sep 10-6 (7pm Jul-Aug).
✱*IRE1.50 (ch IRE1). Family ticket IRE3. Maze/Golf IRE1.50, (ch IRE1). Family IRE3.*
🅿 ⚘ *shop garden centre (specialising in conifers & shrubs)*

John F Kennedy Arboretum
(12km S of New Ross, off R733)
☎051 388171 Fax 051 388172
The John F Kennedy Arboretum, formally opened in 1968, covers 623 acres across

the hill of Slievecoiltia which overlooks the Kennedy ancestral home at Dunganstown. Six counties can be seen from the viewing point. There are 4,500 types of trees and shrubs representing the temperate regions of the world, and laid out in botanical sequence. There is a lake and 200 forest plots, planted according to their geographic origin. There is a visitor centre and during the season there is pony and trap transport.
Open daily, May-Aug 10-8; Apr & Sep 10-6.30; Oct-Mar 10-5. Last admission 45 mins before closing. (Closed Good Friday & 25 Dec).
IRE2 (ch & student IRE1, pen IRE1.50). Family ticket IRE5. Party 20+. Heritage card (12month) visits all Heritage Service sites. Adult IRE15, OAP IRE10, ch/student IRE6
🅿 ⚘ ♿ *toilets for disabled shop (dogs on leash)*

WEXFORD
The Irish Agricultural Museum
Johnstown Castle Old Farmyard (4m SW, signposted off N25)
☎053 42888 Fax 053 42004 & 42213
This interesting museum has extensive displays on rural transport, farming and the activities of the farmyard and the farmhouse. Large scale replicas of different workshops, including a blacksmith, cooper and basket worker can be seen here. Other attractions include displays on dairying, cycling, and sugar-beet harvesting and a collection of Irish country furniture. The museum is situated in the estate farm buildings which were erected in 1810 and are themselves now of historic interest. There is a new exhibition on lawn maintenance, and for 1998 there will be a major exhibition on the history of the potato in Ireland.
Open all year, Jun-Aug Mon-Fri 9-5 & Sat-Sun 2-5; Apr-May & Sep-14 Nov Mon-Fri 9-12.30 & 1.30-5, Sat-Sun 2-5; 15 Nov-Mar Mon-Fri 9-12.30 & 1.30-5. (Closed 25 Dec-2 Jan). IRE2.00 (ch & students IRE1.25). Parking charge May-Sep.
🅿 *(charged)* ⚘ ♿ *toilets for disabled shop* ⚘ *(ex small dogs)*

Johnstown Castle Gardens
(4m SW)
☎053 42888 Fax 053 42004
The 19th-century mansion is closed to the public but visitors can explore the 50 acres of grounds containing over 200 different varieties of trees and shrubs, ornamental lakes with wildfowl, and walled gardens and hothouses. The ruins of Rathlannon Castle, a medieval tower house can also be seen.
Open all year, daily 9-5.30. (Closed 25 Dec).
🅿 ⚘ ♿ *toilets for disabled shop*
Details not confirmed for 1998

Wexford Wildfowl Reserve
North Slob (take coast road over bridge for 3km, signs show turning at right)
☎053 23129 Fax 053 24785
The reserve is of international importance for Greenland White-fronted Geese (as it has one-third of the world's population), Brent Geese, Bewick's Swans and Wigeon. The reserve is a superb place for birdwatching and there are hides and a tower hide available as well as a visitor centre with an audio-visual display in the reception room. Special items will be arranged during the Wexford Festival (last 2 weeks October). Various other events also - please telephone for details.
Open all year, 15 Apr-Sep 9-6; Oct-14 Apr 10-5.
Free.
🅿 ♿ ⚘ *(ex guide dogs)*

CO WICKLOW

ENNISKERRY
Powerscourt Gardens Exhibition
Powerscourt Estate (just off N11 S of Bray, next to Enniskerry village)
☎01 2046000 Fax 01 2863561

One of the world's great gardens situated 20km south of Dublin in the foothills of the Wicklow Mountains. The gardens were begun by Richard Wingfield in the 1740s and stretch out over 47 acres. It is a sublime blend of formal gardens, sweeping terraces, statuary and ornamental lakes together with secret hollows, rambling walks, walled gardens and over 200 variations of trees and shrubs. Powerscourt House now incorporates an 'innovative shopping experience', Terrace Restaurant, and an exhibition which traces the history of the estate, house, and gardens. It also tells the story of the disastrous fire of 1974 which gutted the house.
Open - Gardens 1 Mar-31 Oct daily 9.30-5.30; Waterfall Mar-Oct daily 9.30-7; 1 Nov-28 Feb daily 10.30-dusk.(Please check winter opening times as they are subject to change)
Gardens & House exhibition: IRE5 (ch IRE3, students IRE4.50) House only IRE1.50 (ch IRE1, students IRE1.30) gardens only IRE3.50 (ch IRE2, students IRE3.20) Waterfall IRE2 (ch IRE1, students IRE1.50) (Winter rates are fairly cheaper)
🅿 *(charged)* ⚘ ✕ *licensed* ♿ *(Lift to first floor, Wheelchair available) toilets for disabled shop garden centre* ⚘ *(ex guide dogs)*
Cards: 💳 💳

KILQUADE
National Gardens Exhibitions Centre
Calumet Nurseries (7m S of Bray - turn off the N11 at Kilpedder)
☎01 2819890 Fax 01 2810359
The centre offers plenty of ideas of the gardener or new home-owner. There are 15 different gardens designed by some of Ireland's leading landscapers and designers, in which there are several water features and a man-made mountain stream. There is a garden centre adjacent to the exhibition. There are lectures during the year and guided tours during summer. Ring for details and a calender of events.
Open Feb-22 Dec, Mon-Sat 10-6, Sun 1-6.
IRE2.50 (ch under 16 Free, pen IRE2). Party IRE2.
🅿 ⚘ ♿ *garden centre* ⚘ *(ex guide dogs)*
Cards: 💳 💳

RATHDRUM
Avondale House & Forest Park
(1.6km S of town. R752 off N11)
☎0404 46111
Fax 0404 46111
It was at Avondale House in 1846 that one of the greatest political leaders of modern Irish history, Charles Stewart Parnell, was born. The house is now a museum to his memory and a major refurbishment programme has restored much of the house to its decor of 1850. Parnell spent much of his time at Avondale until his death in October 1891. Visitors are introduced to Avondale by way of a specially commissioned video which describes the life of Parnell.
House & Park open daily. House: May-Sept 10am-6pm Oct-Apr 11am-5pm. Last admission 1 hour before closing. (House closed Good Friday & Xmas hols, advisable to check times). Grounds open at all times.
House IRE3 (pen IRE2). Family ticket IRE6, extra children £1.50 each. Party. Parking; car IRE2, minibus IRE3, coach IRE5. Prices under review.
🅿 *(charged)* ⚘ ♿ *(Special carpark & one forest trail accessible) shop* ⚘ *(ex guide dogs & on lead)*

Reader's Recommendations

If you have recently enjoyed a day out at a place that you think should be in this book, use this form to tell us more about it. *Please send it to*

Days Out in Britain,
Lifestyle Guides,
Hotel Services Department,
Fanum House,
Basingstoke, RG21 4EA.

If you don't want to cut up your book, please feel free to photocopy the form.

Your name and address

....

....

....

Post Code ....Tel. No...

Name and address of establishment

....

....

....

Post Code ....Tel. No...

Tell us about the place you visited and why you think it
should be in Days Out

....

....

....

....

....

....

....

....

....

....

Reader's Recommendations

If you have recently enjoyed a day out at a place that you think should be in this book, use this form to tell us more about it. *Please send it to*

Days Out in Britain,
Lifestyle Guides,
Hotel Services Department,
Fanum House,
Basingstoke, RG21 4EA.

If you don't want to cut up your book, please feel free to photocopy the form.

Your name and address

....

....

....

Post Code ....Tel. No...

Name and address of establishment

....

....

....

Post Code ....Tel. No...

Tell us about the place you visited and why you think it
should be in Days Out

....

....

....

....

....

....

....

....

....

....

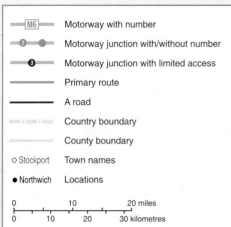

—M6—	Motorway with number
—⊙—●—	Motorway junction with/without number
—❸—	Motorway junction with limited access
———	Primary route
———	A road
⋯⋯	Country boundary
⋯⋯	County boundary
○ Stockport	Town names
● Northwich	Locations

0	10	20 miles
0	10 20	30 kilometres

Any establishment may be located by using the National Grid Reference given beside its Index entry. The grid for Ireland is unique to this map and the Grid References given beside all Irish entries in the Index refer to this map only.

The first number of the Grid Reference refers to the atlas page (eg Map 02). The following two letters (eg ST) refer to the major squares marked by the heavier blue lines on the atlas pages. For a more precise location, each of these grid squares is subdivided by marks along the edge of the map indicating smaller squares (numbered horizontally 0-9 from west to east and 0-9 vertically from south to north). The large square is subdivided by a fainter blue line on grid mark 5 for easier use. The point where two grid 'lines' intersect forms the bottom left-hand corner of the square in which the establishment is located.

For example, if the reference is Map 02 ST97, the place (in this case Chippenham) is to be found on atlas page 2, in major grid square ST, after grid line 9 along from the left, and above grid line 7 up from the bottom.

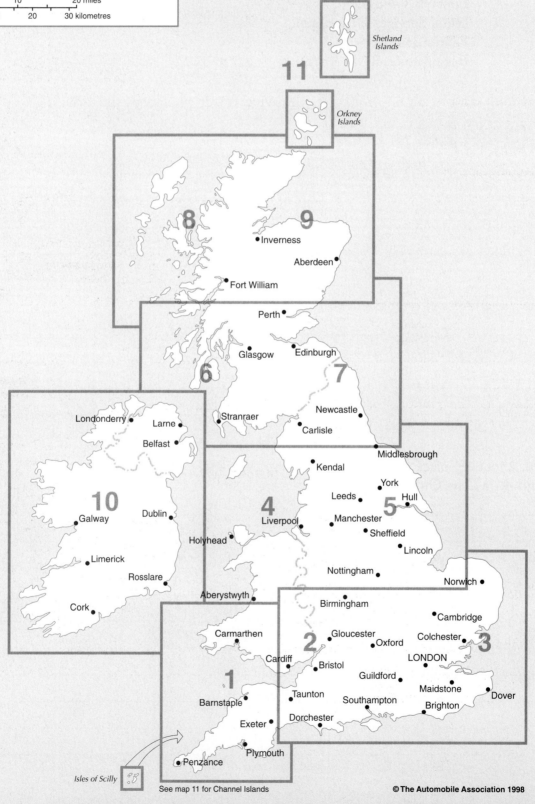

See map 11 for Channel Islands

© The Automobile Association 1998

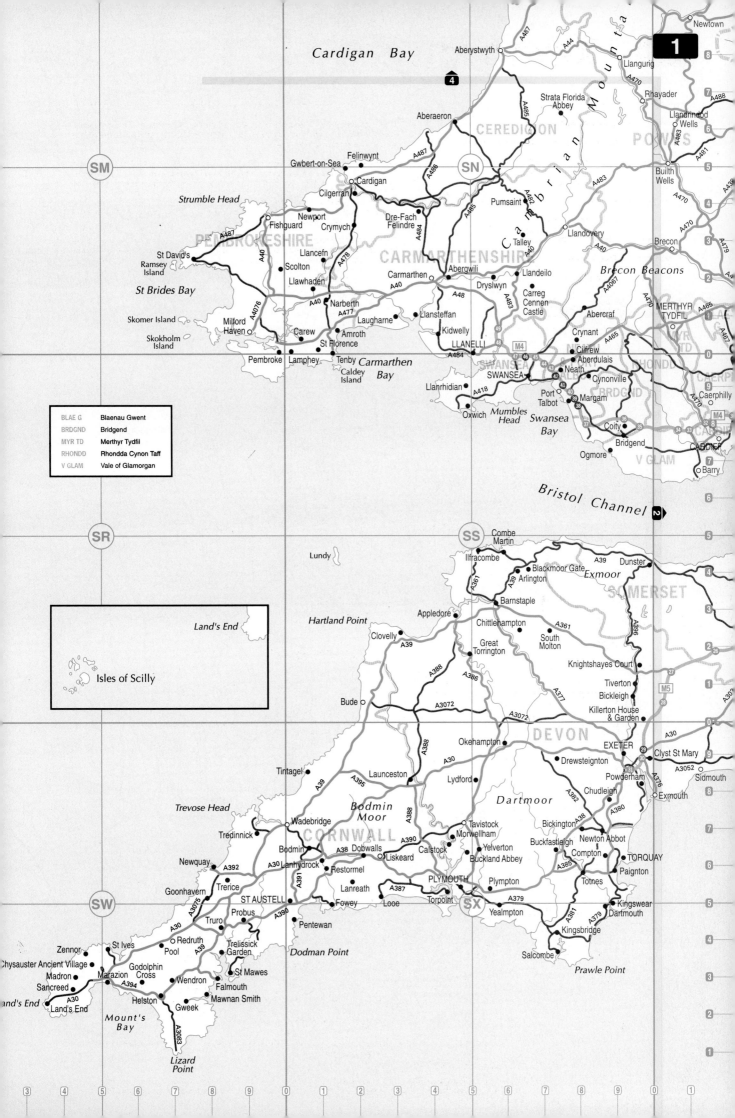

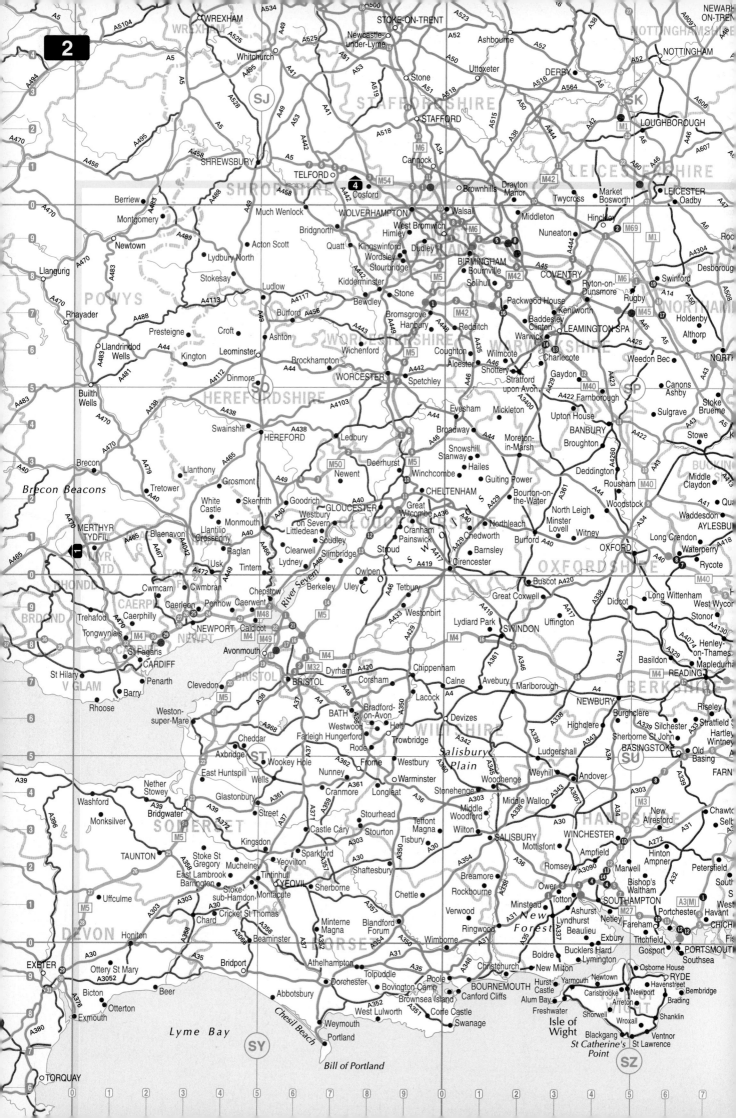

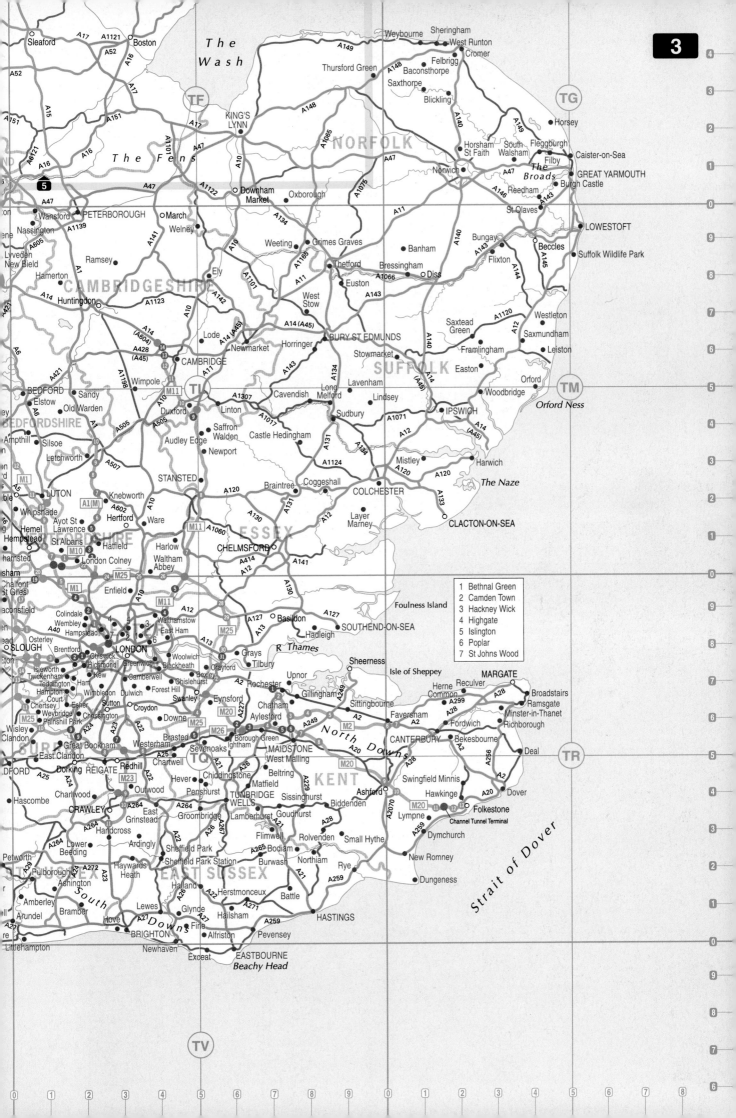

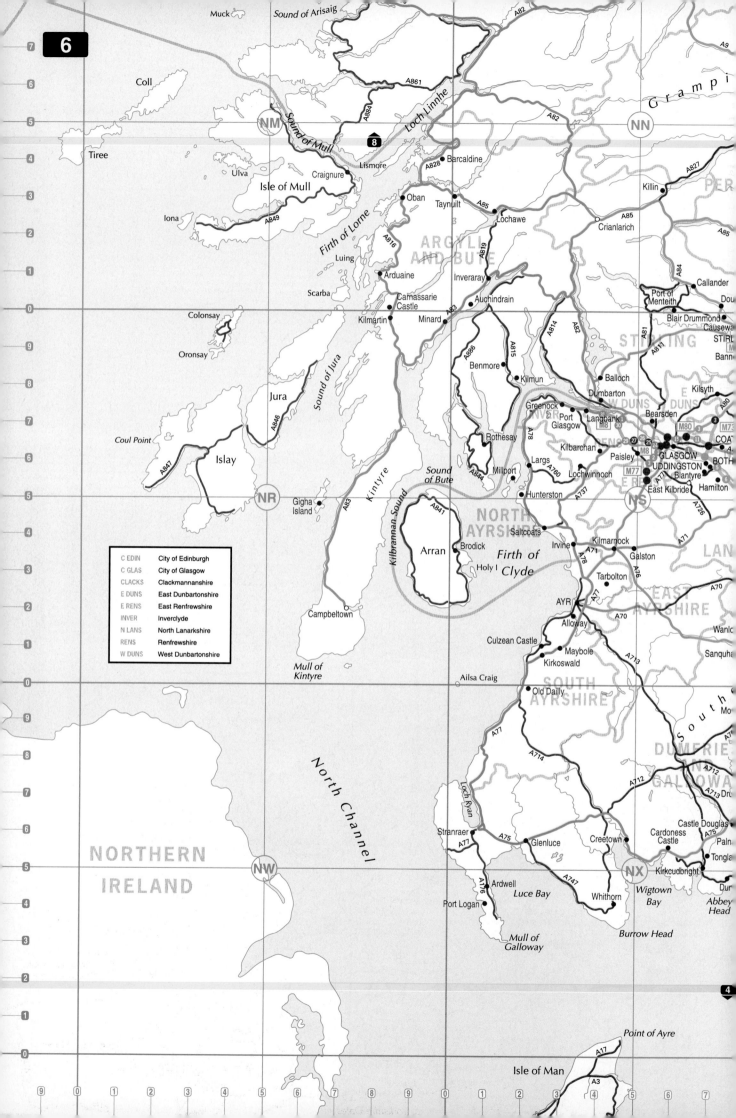

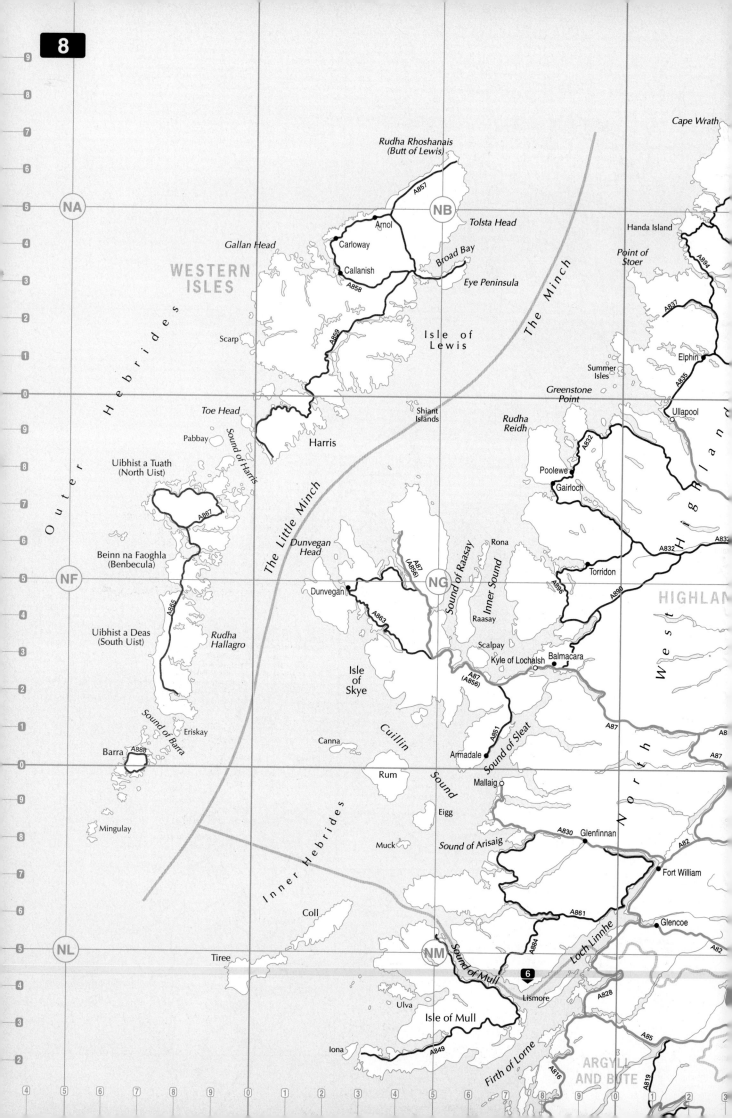

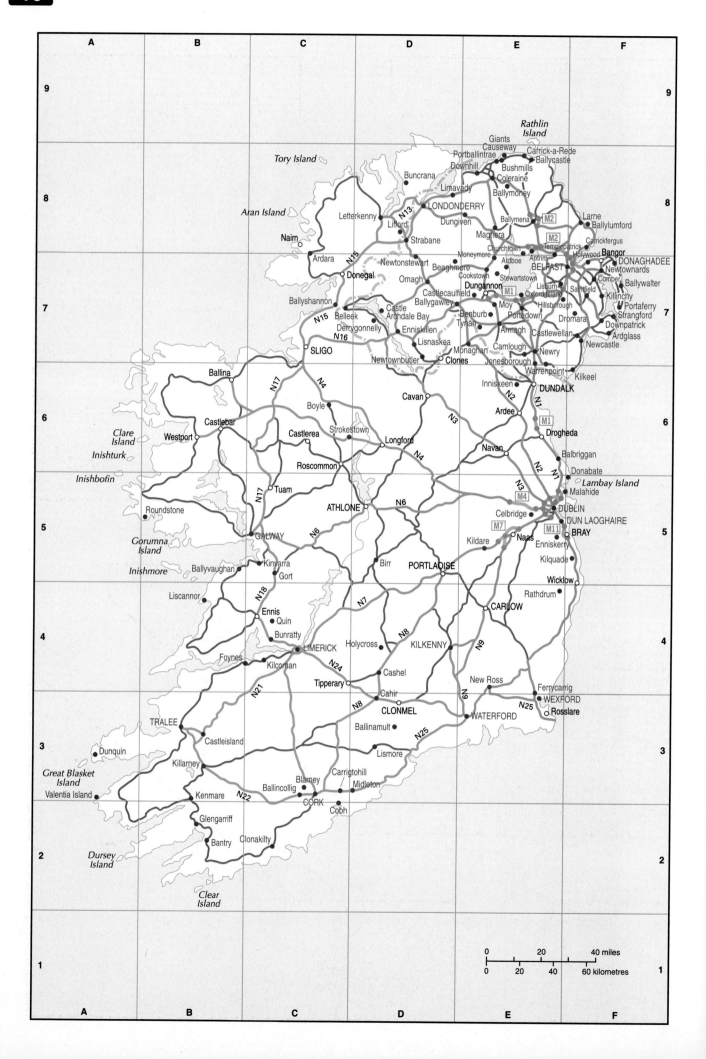

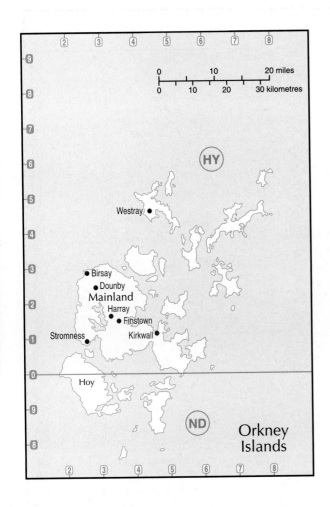

Orkney Islands

HY

Westray •

Birsay •
Dounby •
Mainland
Harray •
• Finstown
Stromness • • Kirkwall

Hoy

ND

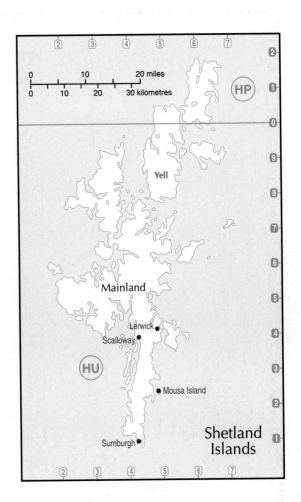

Shetland Islands

HP

Yell

Mainland

Lerwick •
Scalloway •

HU

• Mousa Island

Sumburgh •

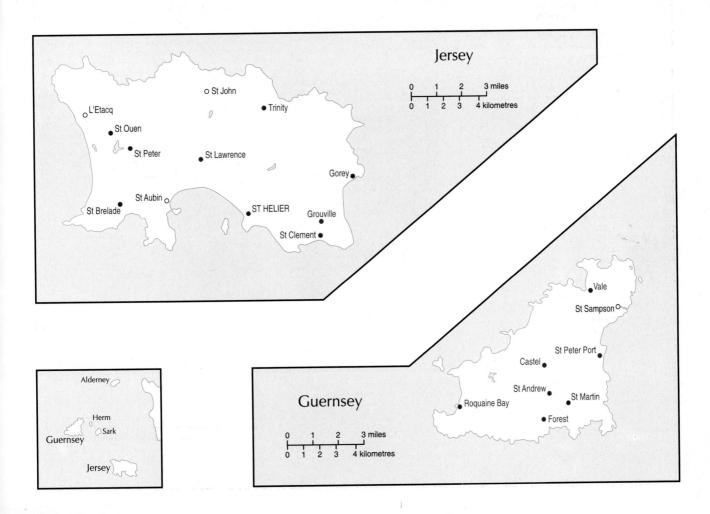

Jersey

○ St John
• Trinity
L'Etacq ○
• St Ouen
• St Peter   • St Lawrence
Gorey •
St Aubin ○
St Brelade •   • ST HELIER
Grouville •
St Clement •

0   1   2   3 miles
0   1   2   3   4 kilometres

Alderney

Herm
Sark
Guernsey

Jersey

Guernsey

0   1   2   3 miles
0   1   2   3   4 kilometres

Vale •
St Sampson ○
St Peter Port •
Castel •
St Andrew •   • St Martin
Roquaine Bay •
• Forest

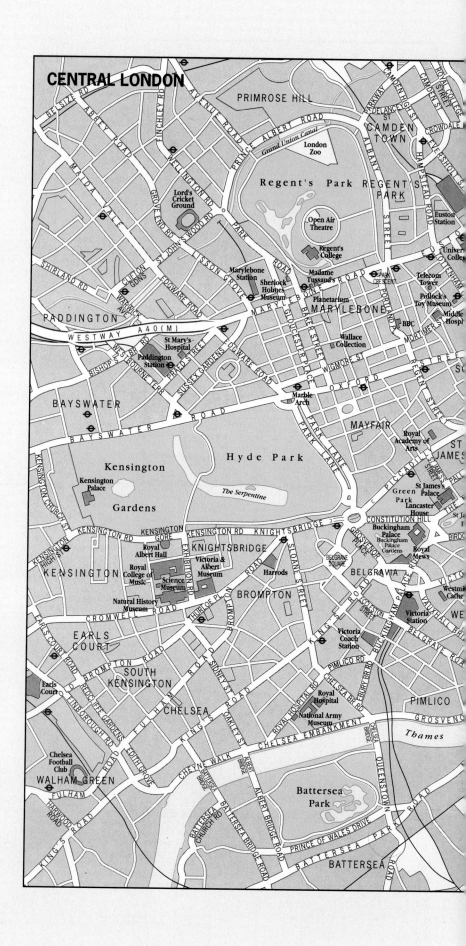

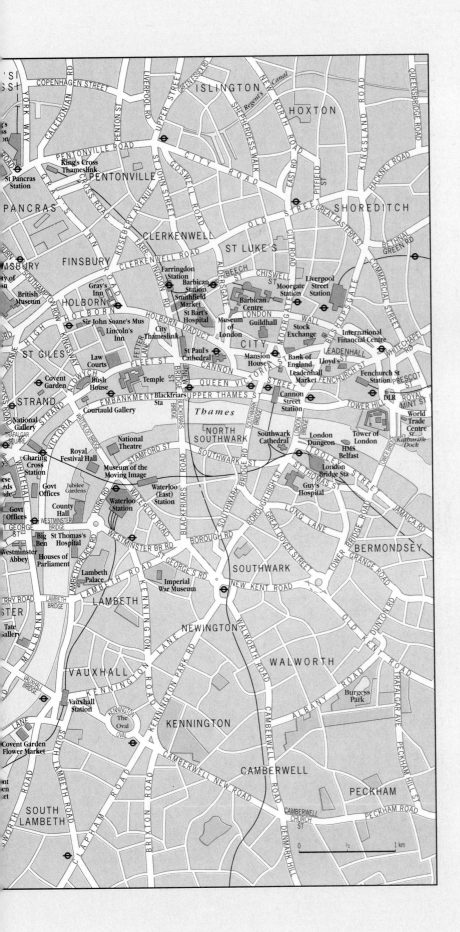

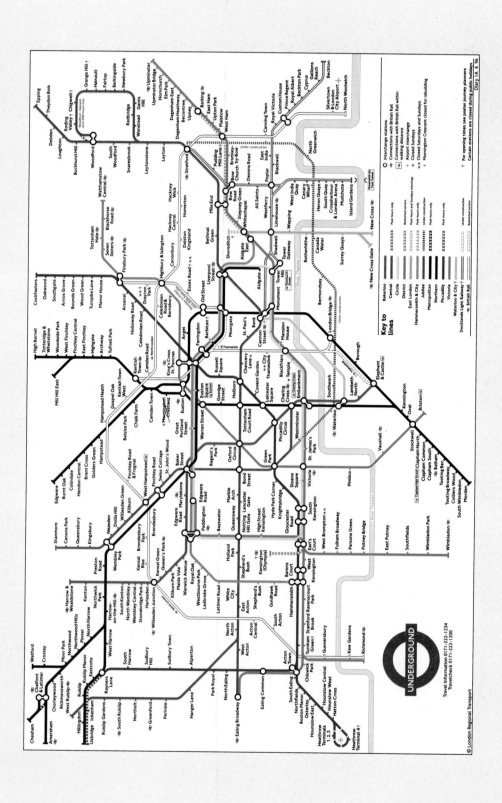

Reader's Recommendations

If you have recently enjoyed a day out at a place that you think should be in this book, use this form to tell us more about it. *Please send it to:*

Great Days Out,
Lifestyle Guides,
Hotel Services Department,
Fanum House,
Basingstoke RG21 2EA.

Your name and address

....

....

....

....

Post Code   Tel No.

Name and address of the establishment

....

....

....

Post Code   Tel No.

Tell us about the place you visited and why you think it should be in Great Days Out.

....

....

....

....

....

....

....

....

....

....

Reader's Recommendations

If you have recently enjoyed a day out at a place that you think should be in this book, use this form to tell us more about it. *Please send it to:*

Great Days Out,
Lifestyle Guides,
Hotel Services Department,
Fanum House,
Basingstoke RG21 2EA.

Your name and address

....

....

....

....

Post Code   Tel No.

Name and address of the establishment

....

....

Post Code   Tel No.

Tell us about the place you visited and why you think it should be in Great Days Out.

....

....

....

....

....

....

....

....

....

Reader's Recommendations

If you have recently enjoyed a day out at a place that you think should be in this book, use this form to tell us more about it. *Please send it to:*

**Great Days Out,
Lifestyle Guides,
Hotel Services Department,
Fanum House,
Basingstoke RG21 2EA.**

Your name and address

....

....

....

Post Code   Tel No.

Name and address of the establishment

....

....

Post Code   Tel No.

Tell us about the place you visited and why you think it should be in Great Days Out.

....

....

....

....

....

....

....

....

....

Index